The Jerusalem Talmud

Second Order: Moʻed

Tractates Šabbat and ʻEruvin

Studia Judaica

Forschungen zur Wissenschaft des Judentums

Begründet von
Ernst Ludwig Ehrlich

Herausgegeben von
Günter Stemberger

Band 68

De Gruyter

The Jerusalem Talmud
תלמוד ירושלמי

Second Order: Moʻed
סדר מועד
Tractates *Šabbat* and *ʿEruvin*
מסכתות שבת ועירובין

Edition, Translation, and Commentary

by

Heinrich W. Guggenheimer

De Gruyter

ISBN 978-3-11-068126-0
e-ISBN (PDF) 978-3-11-028903-9

This volume is text- and page-identical with the hardback published in 2012.

Library of Congress Control Number: 2020943496

Bibliographic information published by the Deutsche Nationalbibliothek
The Deutsche Nationalbibliothek lists this publication in the
Deutsche Nationalbibliografie;
detailed bibliographic data are available on the Internet at http://dnb.dnb.de.

© 2020 Walter de Gruyter GmbH, Berlin/Boston

Printing and binding: CPI books GmbH, Leck

www.degruyter.com

Preface

The present volume is the fourteenth in this series of the Jerusalem Talmud, the first in a four-volume edition, translation, and Commentary of the Second Order of this Talmud. The principles of the edition regarding text, vocalization, and Commentary have ben spelled out in detail in the Introduction to the first volume. The text in this volume is based on the manuscript text of the Yerushalmi edited by J. Sussman for the Academy of the Hebrew Language, Jerusalem 2001. The text essentially represents an outline, to be fleshed out by a teacher's explanation. The translation should mirror this slant; it should not endow the text with literary qualities which the original does not posses. In particular, the translation is not intended to stand separate from the Commentary.

The extensive Commentary is not based on emendations; where there is evidence from manuscripts, quotes by early Medieval authors, or early prints, to correct scribal or corrector's errors, the proposed correction is given in the Notes. As in the preceding volumes, for each paragraph the folio and line numbers of the Krotoschin edition are added. It should be remembered that these numbers may differ from the *editio princeps* by up to three lines. It seems to be important that a translation of the Yerushalmi be accompanied by the text, to enable the reader to compare the interpretation with other translations.

Again, biblical quotations are given with the accents, except for words which differ (usually by *plene* spelling) from the masoretic texts. Since the quotes are part of oral tradition, the deviations in spelling are examples of substandard spelling, rather than changes in the text.

Again, I wish to thank my wife, Dr. Eva Guggenheimer, who acted as critic, style editor, proof reader, and expert on the Latin and Greek vocabulary. Her own notes on some possible Latin and Greek etymologies are identified by (E. G.).

Contents

Introduction to Tractates Šabbat and Eruvin	1
Šabbat Chapter 1, יציאות השבת	7
Chapter 2, במה מדליקין	87
Chapter 3, כירה	125
Chapter 4, במה טומנין	163
Chapter 5, במה בהמה	176
Chapter 6, במה אשה	189
Chapter 7, כלל גדול	229
Chapter 8, המוציא יין	304
Chapter 9, רבי עקיבה	326
Chapter 10, המצניע	356
Chapter 11, הזורק	366
Chapter 12, הבונה	387.
Chapter 13, האורג	404
Chapter 14, שמונה שרצים	416
Chapter 15, אילו קשרים	437
Chapter 16, כל כתבי הקודש	447
Chapter 17, כל הכלים	470
Chapter 18, מפנין	485
Chapter 19, רבי אליעזר	495
Chapter 20, תולין	523
Chapter 21, Mishnah	533
Chapter 22, Mishnah	535
Chapter 23, Mishnah	538
Chapter 24, Mishnah	541
Eruvin Chapter 1, מבוי	545
Chapter 2, עושין פסין	600
Chapter 3, בכל מערבין	619
Chapter 4, מי שהוציאוהו	657
Chapter 5, כיצד מעברין	675

Eruvin Chapter 6, הדר	703
Chapter 7, חלון	734
Chapter 8, כיצד משתתפין	755
Chapter 9, כל גגות	776
Chapter 19, המוצא תפילין	789
Erratum	822

Indices

Sigla	823
Index of Biblical quotations	823
Index of Talmudical quotations	
Babylonian Talmud	825
Jerusalem Talmud	828
Mishnah	829
Tosephta	830
Midrashim	831
Rabbinic Literature	831
Index of Greek, Latin, and Arabic, Words	832
Author Index	834
Subject Index	835

Introduction to Tractates Šabbat and ʿEruvin

While the two Tractates always appear as separate entities, together they form a standard long Tractate of 30 Chapters on the rules of the Sabbath, parallel to the 30 Chapters each of Tractates *Neziqin* on civil law and *Kelim* on ritual impurity. This may explain the absence of Chapters 21-24 of *Šabbat* in the Yerushalmi manuscripts, including the Genizah text; these Chapters were not lost in transmission; they never existed. Therefore it is appropriate to treat the two Tractates as an organic whole. The reason why they appear under separate names can only be surmised. One may conjecture that Tractate *Šabbat* treats those rules which in principle, though certainly not in detail, were accepted by all Jewish sects, whereas ʿ*eruvin* are purely pharisaic-rabbinic institutions.

In the Leiden manuscript and the *editio princeps* of the Yerushalmi, the two Tractates are different from all others in that the Chapters are not subdivided into *Halakhot*. This seems to be a particularity not of the original composition but of the source from which the manuscript was copied, since Genizah fragments have indications of division into *Halakhot*[1]. The spelling in these Tractates is not uniform; e.g., the name Zeʿira appears in all forms, from the pure Galilean זעורה through זעירא, זעירה, to the pure Babylonian זירא.

The list of activities forbidden on the Sabbath (Mishnaiot *Šabbat* 7:2-4) includes, "transporting from one domain to another" as an appendix; it does not mention "leaving one's Sabbath domain" since the latter while sinful is not a capital crime. Tractate *Eruvin* is dedicated almost entirely to instances where these two prohibitions can be attenuated; a great part of Tractate *Šabbat* is devoted to the details of the prohibition of transporting, probably because this is the most intrusive of Sabbath restrictions and because it is non trivial in

---

1. Cf. L. Ginzberg, *Yerushalmi Fragments from the Genizah*, New York 1909, p. 97 l. 9.

this context to distinguish between violations of biblical Sabbath law and those of customary or rabbinic sectarian restriction[2]. The former are characterized as "creating liability" (for a purification sacrifice in case of unintended infraction) while the latter are simply "forbidden." An understanding of the Tractates requires close attention to this semantic distinction.

Tractate *Šabbat* starts by detailing the rules of prohibited transport; liability is created only if one person lifts up the object, transports it in violation of the rules, and then deposits it. If not all three conditions are satisfied, the acts will simply be forbidden. The remainder of the first Chapter is devoted to activities which are restricted Friday afternoon in preparation of the Sabbath.

The second Chapter deals with the rules and the obligation of illuminating the house for the Friday evening meal. Our sources seem to indicate that the Karaite prohibition of light and fire on the Sabbath is just that, a Medieval restriction, not a revival of Sadducee practice. On the other hand, the elevation of the obligation of candle lighting to a formal act with its own benediction cannot be traced back further than Gaonic times[3]. The topic is continued in Chapter Three which spells out the rules of cooking without making fire on the Sabbath while Chapter Four explains how food can be kept warm in a *Kochkiste* for the Sabbath day.

Since the Fourth Commandment prescribes Sabbath rest for all domestic animals, Chapter Five details the distinctions between admissible necessities and prohibited loads on animals led out to pasture. Similarly, Chapter Six explains the difference between admissible human clothing and jewelry and prohibited loads.

The central Chapter Seven contains the rules of liability for Sabbath infractions and the full list of the forbidden 39 categories of work. As mentioned earlier, the last category mentioned is that of transporting between domains differing in status. While such transport always is prohibited, it

---

2. The prohibition of transporting from inside a house to the outside is described as biblical in the Sadducee *Damascus Document*, CD XI 7-8.
3. The Gaonic sources are collected in *Otzar HaGaonim Shabbat* p. 27.

creates liability only for quantities larger than prescribed minima. The list of these minima, which vary from category to category, is started in the second part of the Chapter and continued in the following Chapters Eight, Nine (with an interruption not connected to the laws of the Sabbath in the first part of the Chapter), and Ten. Chapter Eleven treats the connected topic of transport by throwing between domains of differing status.

Chapters Twelve to Fifteen detail the minimal amounts of work which create liability for infractions of the other 38 categories of forbidden work. Chapter Sixteen states which rabbinic rules are waived for transporting and extinguishing in case of combatting or preventing a fire, and interacting with Gentile firemen. Chapters Seventeen, Eighteen, and partially Twenty, return to the topic of transporting, this time the rabbinic prohibition of moving things which it is inappropriate to use on the Sabbath, technically called *muqseh*[4]. Since the entire system of *muqseh* is not biblical, the emphasis there is on what is permitted, not what is forbidden.

Since it is a biblical requirement to perform circumcision on the eighth day of a male baby's life, a baby born on the Sabbath must be circumcised on the Sabbath even though circumcision otherwise would be a Sabbath violation and deadly sin. The extent of the exemption from Sabbath rules is the topic of Chapter Nineteen.

As mentioned earlier, Mishnah Tractates 21-23 have no *halakhah*.

Tractate *Eruvin* has two major topics. The biblical commandment (*Ex.* 16:29) *nobody should leave his place on the Seventh Day* is read to mean that nobody may move outside of his town on the Sabbath. The definition of "town" includes the adjacent open area which in keeping with the definition of Levitic cities (*Num.* 35:5) is taken as a rectangle, oriented strictly NS, EW, whose border is distant 2'000 cubits from the wall (or last house) of the town. The cubit (of 6 hand-breadths divided into 4 thumb-breadths each) used here is one 8'000th of a פָּרְסָה, which should not be identified with the Greek-Persian

---

4. *Muqseh* of unprepared foodstuffs, whose ingestion might violate a biblical prescription (*Ex.* 16:23) is accepted in the *Damascus Document* (CD X 22); *muqseh* of implements and articles of trade may be indicated there (l. 18), other .*muqseh* prohibitions are CD XI 9-11.

παρασάγγης but with the Egyptian σχοῖνος of about 4150 m,[5] resulting in a cubit of ~51.9 cm and a hand-breadth of ~8.6 cm.[6] Under certain conditions one starts measuring not from the last house but only at a distance of $\sqrt{5000}$ cubits from it. In terms of integer cubits and hand-breadths, this number is best approximated from below by $70^2/_3$ (or 70 cubits + 4 hand-breadths.) Since this number is Mishnaic, it also is accepted in the Babli even though $\sqrt{5000} = 50\sqrt{2}$, and $\sqrt{2}$ everywhere in the Babli is taken to be 1.4. The level of mathematical sophistication in Mishnah and Yerushalmi consistently is higher than that of the Babli.

The purely pharisaic-rabbinic institution of *eruv tehumin* permits a person to change his official domicile from his dwelling to a point near the Sabbath boundary of his town by depositing some food at that point on Friday afternoon. Then on the Sabbath he may walk 2'000 cubits from the point in any direction; he may reach points outside his town's Sabbath domain but in theory he only has a circular domain at his disposal, not a rectangular one. In fact the domain will not be circular since every built-up area where the distance from one house to the next is not more than $70^2/_3$ cubits is only counted as 4 cubits. The technical rules for determining the Sabbath boundary of a town are in Chapter 5; those for making *eruv tehumin* form part of Chapters 3 and 8. Chapter 4 details the rules pertaining to people who voluntarily or involuntarily leave their Sabbath domain without *eruv*.

In a house or a fenced-in property[7] of a single owner one may carry without limitation. From the house to the public road one may not carry anything. In a fenced-in multi-party property, carrying is prohibited only rabbinically. Such a property may be turned into common domain by *eruv ḥaṣerot*, effected by depositing in one of the dwellings opening into the domain some food collected from all dwellers using the common property. A dead-end street, while being public property, is not a thoroughfare; for the

---

5. F. Hultsch, *Griechische und römische Metrologie*[2], Berlin 1882.
6. The Babli units of the same name are somewhat different; for volume measures cf. Chapter 8, Note 40. In most situations a "hand-breadth" means the breadth of an individual's hand, up to about 10.5 cm, not a standardized measure. The standard cubit is only used for determining the boundaries of the Sabbath domain.
7. If the property is purely agricultural it may not exceed 5'000 square cubits.

rules of the Sabbath it does not classify as public domain and can be turned into the private sphere of the dwellers in the street by fixing a symbolic gate at the entrance and depositing an *eruv* (in this case called *participation*) in one of the dwellings in the street (Chapters 1,3,7)[8]. Additional topics are the construction of "private domains" for caravans resting for the Sabbath (Chapter 1) and for the care of domestic animals (Chapter 2), the possibility of *eruvin* in multi-party domains inhabited also by Gentiles of Sadducees, the latter opposed to the idea of *eruvin*[9] (Chapter 6), the relationships between two adjacent multi-party domains with separate *eruvin* (Chapter 7) and flat level roofs in a compactly settled urban area (Chapter 9).

The last Chapter 10 as closure of the combined Sabbath Tractates contains sundry rules of the Sabbath, not *Eruvin*, and a discussion of which rabbinical Sabbath rules are waved in the Temple.

The interpretation of both Tractates in translation and commentary is decisively influenced by the treatise of Saul Liebermann, *Hayerushalmi Kiphshuto*, 2nd edition, New York and Jerusalem 1995[10].

---

8. *Eruv tavšilin* belongs to the rules of holidays and is treated in Tractate *Besah*.
9. CD 11:4: "A person may not willingly participate in an *eruv* on the Sabbath". An intermediate position between the Sadducee rejection and the Hillelite Mishnah rules may be that of the House of Shammai, cf. Chapter 3, Note 73.
10. The references to the Tosephta are given for Liebermann's edition (New York 1962) whose numbering in Tractate *Šabbat* differs widely from Zuckermandel's.

יְצִיאוֹת הַשַׁבָּת פרק ראשון

(fol. 32c) **משנה א**: יְצִיאוֹת הַשַׁבָּת שְׁתַּיִם שֶׁהֵן אַרְבַּע בִּפְנִים וּשְׁתַּיִם שֶׁהֵן אַרְבַּע בַּחוּץ. בְּאֵי זֶה צַד. הֶעָנִי עוֹמֵד בַּחוּץ וּבַעַל הַבַּיִת בִּפְנִים. פָּשַׁט הֶעָנִי אֶת יָדוֹ לִפְנִים וְנָתַן לְתוֹךְ יָדוֹ שֶׁל בַּעַל הַבַּיִת אוֹ שֶׁנָּטַל מִתּוֹכָהּ וְהוֹצִיא הֶעָנִי חַיָּיב וּבַעַל הַבַּיִת פָּטוּר.

Mishnah 1: There are two [kinds] of transport on the Sabbath which are four [kinds] inside, and two [kinds] which are four [kinds] outside[1]. How is this? The poor man stands outside and the householder inside. If the poor man stretched out his hand inside and delivered into the householder's hand or took something from it and brought it outside, the poor man is liable but the householder is not liable.

משנה ב: פָּשַׁט בַּעַל הַבַּיִת אֶת יָדוֹ לַחוּץ וְנָתַן לְתוֹךְ יָדוֹ שֶׁל עָנִי אוֹ שֶׁנָּטַל מִתּוֹכָהּ וְהִכְנִיס בַּעַל הַבַּיִת חַיָּיב וְהֶעָנִי פָּטוּר.

Mishnah 2: If the householder stretched out his hand outside and delivered into the poor man's hand or took something from it and brought it inside, the householder is liable but the poor man is not liable.

משנה ג: פָּשַׁט הֶעָנִי אֶת יָדוֹ לִפְנִים וְנָטַל בַּעַל הַבַּיִת מִתּוֹכָהּ אוֹ שֶׁנָּתַן לְתוֹכָהּ וְהוֹצִיא שְׁנֵיהֶן פְּטוּרִין.

Mishnah 3: If the poor man stretched out his hand inside and the householder took from it or gave into it and he then took it out, neither is liable.

משנה ד: פָּשַׁט בַּעַל הַבַּיִת אֶת יָדוֹ לַחוּץ וְנָטַל הֶעָנִי מִתּוֹכָהּ אוֹ שֶׁנָּתַן לְתוֹכָהּ וְהִכְנִיס שְׁנֵיהֶן פְּטוּרִין:

Mishnah 4: If the householder stretched out his hand outside and the poor man took from it or gave into it and he then took it in, neither is liable.

משנה ה: לֹא יֵשֵׁב אָדָם לִפְנֵי הַסַּפָּר סָמוּךְ לַמִּנְחָה עַד שֶׁיִּתְפַּלֵּל. לֹא יִכָּנֵס לֹא לַמֶּרְחָץ וְלֹא לַבּוּרְסְקִי לֹא לוֹכַל וְלֹא לָדִין. אִם הִתְחִילוּ אֵין מַפְסִיקִין. מַפְסִיקִין לִקְרִיַּת שְׁמַע וְאֵין מַפְסִיקִין לִתְפִילָּה:

Mishnah 5: A person should not sit before the barber close to the time of afternoon prayers unless he has prayed[2]. Nor should one enter the bathhouse or the tannery, nor start eating, nor sit in judgment; if they started they should not interrupt. One interrupts for the recitation of the *Shema`* but not for prayer[3].

משנה ו: לֹא יֵצֵא הַחַיָּט בְּמַחֲטוֹ סָמוּךְ לַחֲשֵׁיכָה שֶׁמָּא יִשְׁכַּח וְיֵצֵא. לֹא הַלִּבְלָר בְּקוּלְמוֹסוֹ. וְלֹא יְפַלֶּא אֶת כֵּלָיו וְלֹא יִקְרָא לְאוֹר הַנֵּר. בֶּאֱמֶת הַחַזָּן רוֹאֶה מֵאֵיכָן הַתִּינוֹקוֹת קוֹרִין אֲבָל הוּא לֹא יִקְרָא. כַּיּוֹצֵא בוֹ לֹא יֹאכַל הַזָּב עִם הַזָּבָה מִפְּנֵי הֶרְגֵּל עֲבֵרָה:

Mishnah 6: A tailor should not leave with his needle close to sundown lest he forget and leave[4]; nor the scribe with his pen. He should not check his garments for lice nor read by candlelight[5]. In truth[6] they said that the teacher may look where the children are reading[7] but he may not read himself. Similarly, the male sufferer from gonorrhea should not eat with a female sufferer from flux because of inducement to sin[8].

משנה ז: אֵילּוּ מֵהֲלָכוֹת שֶׁאָמְרוּ בַּעֲלִיַּת חֲנַנְיָה בֶן חִזְקִיָּה בֶן גָּרוֹן כְּשֶׁעָלוּ לְבַקְּרוֹ. נִמְנוּ וְרַבּוּ בֵּית שַׁמַּאי עַל בֵּית הִלֵּל וּשְׁמוֹנָה עָשָׂר דָּבָר גָּזְרוּ בוֹ בַיּוֹם:

Mishnah 7: These[9] are of the practices which were pronounced at the upper floor of Hananiah ben Ḥizqiah ben Garon[10], when they came to visit him. They voted and the House of Shammai had the majority over the House of Hillel; eighteen items they decided on that day[11].

משנה ח: בֵּית שַׁמַּאי אוֹמְרִים אֵין שׁוֹרִין דְּיוֹ סַמְמָנִין וְכַרְשִׁינִין אֶלָּא כְּדֵי שֶׁיִּשּׁוֹרוּ מִבְּעוֹד יוֹם. וּבֵית הִלֵּל מַתִּירִין:

Mishnah 8: The House of Shammai say, one does not soak ink[12], chemicals, or vetch[13], unless they will be soaked when it still is daylight; but the House of Hillel permit it.

משנה ט: בֵּית שַׁמַּאי אוֹמְרִים אֵין נוֹתְנִין אוּנִין שֶׁל פִּשְׁתָּן לְתוֹךְ הַתַּנּוּר אֶלָּא כְּדֵי שֶׁיַּהֲבִילוּ מִבְּעוֹד יוֹם. וְלֹא אֶת הַצֶּמֶר לַיּוֹרָה אֶלָּא כְּדֵי שֶׁיִּקְלוֹט אֶת הָעַיִן. וּבֵית הִלֵּל מַתִּירִין.

Mishnah 9: The House of Shammai say, one does not put bundles of flax into an oven unless they are steamed when it is still daylight[14], nor wool into a vat unless it may absorb the dye, but the House of Hillel permit it.

משנה י: בֵּית שַׁמַּאי אוֹמְרִים אֵין פּוֹרְשִׂין מְצוּדוֹת חַיָּה וְעוֹפוֹת וְדָגִים אֶלָּא כְּדֵי שֶׁיִּצּוֹדוּ מִבְּעוֹד יוֹם. וּבֵית הִלֵּל מַתִּירִין:

Mishnah 10: The House of Shammai say, one does not set traps for wild animals, or birds, or fish unless they may be caught when it is still daylight, but the House of Hillel permit it.

ŠABBAT CHAPTER ONE

משנה יא: בֵּית שַׁמַּאי אוֹמְרִים אֵין מוֹכְרִין לַנָּכְרִי וְאֵין טוֹעֲנִין עִמּוֹ וְאֵין מַגְבִּיהִין עָלָיו אֶלָּא כְּדֵי שֶׁיַּגִּיעַ לְמָקוֹם קָרוֹב. וּבֵית הִלֵּל מַתִּירִין:

Mishnah 11: They House of Shammai say, one does not sell to a Non-Jew, nor put a load on him unless he may reach a nearby destination[15], but the House of Hillel permit it.

משנה יב: בֵּית שַׁמַּאי אוֹמְרִים אֵין נוֹתְנִין עוֹרוֹת לְעַבְּדָן וְלֹא כֵלִים לְכוֹבֵס נָכְרִי אֶלָּא כְּדֵי שֶׁיֵּעָשׂוּ מִבְּעוֹד יוֹם. וּבְכוּלָּן בֵּית הִלֵּל מַתִּירִין עִם הַשָּׁמֶשׁ:

Mishnah 12: The House of Shammai say, one does not give hides to the tannery worker nor clothing to the Non-Jewish washer unless the work may be done when it is still daylight. In all cases, the House of Hillel permit as long as the sun still shines[16].

משנה יג: אָמַר רַבָּן שִׁמְעוֹן בֶּן גַּמְלִיאֵל נוֹהֲגִין הָיוּ בֵּית אַבָּא שֶׁהָיוּ נוֹתְנִין כְּלֵי לָבָן שֶׁלָּהֶן לְכוֹבֵס נָכְרִי שְׁלֹשָׁה יָמִים קֹדֶם לַשַּׁבָּת. וְשָׁוִין אֵילוּ וָאֵילוּ שֶׁטּוֹעֲנִין בְּקוֹרוֹת בֵּית הַבַּד וּבְעִגּוּלֵי הַגַּת:

Mishnah 13: Rabban Simeon ben Gamliel says, my father's house used to give their white garments to a Non-Jewish washer three days before the Sabbath[17]. They both agree that one may load the beam of the olive press and the round stone of the wine press[18].

משנה יד: אֵין צוֹלִין בָּשָׂר בָּצָל וּבֵיצָה אֶלָּא כְּדֵי שֶׁיִּצּוֹלוּ מִבְּעוֹד יוֹם. אֵין נוֹתְנִין אֶת הַפַּת לַתַּנּוּר עִם חֲשֵׁיכָה וְלֹא חֲרָרָה עַל גַּבֵּי גֶחָלִים אֶלָּא כְּדֵי שֶׁיִּקְרְמוּ פָנֶיהָ. רִבִּי אֱלִיעֶזֶר אוֹמֵר כְּדֵי שֶׁיִּקְרוֹם הַתַּחְתּוֹן שֶׁלָּהּ:

Mishnah 14: One does not roast meat, onions, or an egg, unless they be roasted when it still is daylight[19]. One does not put bread dough into the oven when it gets dark nor pita on coals unless they form a crust. Rebbi Eliezer says, unless they form a crust at their bottoms[20].

משנה טו: מְשַׁלְשְׁלִין אֶת הַפֶּסַח בַּתַּנּוּר עִם חֲשֵׁכָה. וּמַחֲזִין אֶת הָאוּר בִּמְדוּרַת בֵּית הַמּוֹקֵד. וּבַגְּבוּלִין כְּדֵי שֶׁיִּצַּת הָאוּר בְּרוּבָּן. רִבִּי יְהוּדָה אוֹמֵר אַף בַּפֶּחָמִין כָּל שֶׁהֵן:

Mishnah 15: One hangs the Passover lamb into the oven when it gets dark[21]. One starts a fire at the fire place in the heating chamber[22], but outside the Temple only if the fire has started burning on most of the logs[23]. Rebbi Jehudah says, on charcoal any amount[24].

1   On the Sabbath it is forbidden to move any load from a private to the public domain (or for a distance of at least 4 cubits in the public domain.) Inside a private domain there are no restrictions unless the article may not be moved at all. While any transport between domains is forbidden, it is a prosecutable offense only if there is a completed action, i. e., one person lifted the item up, transported it, and put it down. This applies both to transport from the private domain to the public one ("inside") and *vice versa* ("outside"). In each case, the transport may be effectuated either by the person inside or the person outside (in which case the person is prosecutable but the person standing in the other domain is not involved) or it may be taken up by one person, taken over while moving by another person who then puts it down. In this case both participants have sinned but are not prosecutable. The possible cases are enumerated in Mishnaiot 1-4. "Liable" and "not liable" refer both to the possibility of prosecution for intentional Sabbath desecration and the obligation of a purification sacrifice in the case of unintentional infraction.

2   This Mishnah is not connected with the laws of the Sabbath in contrast to the following ones for which it is an introduction. The general rule is that once there is an obligation to pray, the obligation should be fulfilled before any profane action is taken, in particular if the intended action may be a lengthy one. The problem with afternoon prayers is that it is possible to pray starting half an hour after noon ("the great *minhah*") but the actual obligation starts only an hour and a quarter before sundown ("the small *minhah*"). The "hours" mentioned here are variable, one-twelfth of the time between sunrise and sundown. From the Halakhah in the Yerushalmi it is clear that only the small *minhah* is taken into account; in the Babli (9b) both times are considered.

3   While there exists a general biblical obligation to pray (*Sifry Deut.* 41 based on *Deut.* 10:12) neither time nor texts are fixed by biblical law. Therefore there is no biblical obligation to pray at any fixed time; all rules are rabbinic even if based on *Dan.* 6:11, a book without standing in *halakhah*. On the other hand, the recitation of the *Shema`* evenings and mornings is a biblical requirement (*Deut.* 6:7,11:19). An ongoing activity one interrupts for biblical but not for rabbinic obligations.

4   Obviously one is permitted to wear clothing on the Sabbath, and in general also jewelry. A person who is not a tailor may wear a jewelry pin on the Sabbath. But a tailor may not wear a pin stuck somewhere on his jacket since this is a tool of his trade rather than ornamentation. Therefore he has to remove all needles and pins stuck in his garment on Friday afternoon.

5   While the use of lights is required on Friday night (as opposed to later Karaite teaching) it is forbidden to move the lights or refill a lamp with fuel on the Sabbath. Therefore one has to refrain from any activity which might induce one to move a light to improve visibility, such as reading.

6   Any rule introduced by "in truth" is unquestioned ancient practice.

7   Since school children are interested in having the light go out so they do not have

to study any more, one does not have to be afraid that they will move the light for better reading.

8   This has nothing to do with the rules of the Sabbath; it is listed here as another example of a rabbinic prohibition instituted to avoid the possible breaking of a biblical law. The male *zav* is the sufferer from gonorrhea (*Lev.* 15:1-15); his impurity is severe, infectious, and needs an elaborate ceremonial for cleansing the healed patient. The female *zavah* suffers from excessive menstruation or other bloody discharges; her impurity similarly is severe, infectious, and needs a (less elaborate) ceremonial for cleansing the healed patient (*Lev.* 15:25-30). Since sexual relations with a menstruating woman are forbidden (*Lev.* 15:24, 18:19), by extension relations with the *zava* also are forbidden. Therefore, situations that might lead to intimacy with a *zavah* have to be avoided.

9   The Yerushalmi version (and Maimonides's text) refers to the preceding Mishnaiot 1-6. The Babli's version ואלו "and the following" refers to the following Mishnaiot.

10   He is famous for having explained away the apparent contradictions between the book of Ezechiel and the Pentateuch; his explanations have not come down to us. "Ben Garon" or "Ben Gurion" seems to have been his family name.

11   These 18 prohibitions which were forced by the House of Shammai on the House of Hillel are only partially the rules explained in the Mishnaiot here; different lists are given in the Talmudim.

12   Blocks of soot or sepia used to make India ink. This and the following rules are based on a fundamental disagreement between the House of Shammai, who hold that a person may not use his vessels for any procedure which he could not do on the Sabbath, and the House of Hillel who allow a person's machines to work for him as long as he does not risk temptation to interfere with their working on the Sabbath.

13   For animal feed.

14   Flax is first soaked in water, then heated in an oven to whiten the fibers. At the start of the heating process the soaked fibers give off steam.

15   Where he can unload. While the Gentile is not obligated to keep the Sabbath, the House of Shammai prohibit the Jew from causing any work that would have been forbidden to himself. The House of Hillel disagree since the Gentile is an intelligent being responsible for his own actions.

16   As long as the Gentile is an independent contractor, the Jew can hand work over to him even in the last seconds before sundown.

17   While they promulgated the rules of the House of Hillel as generally valid, they privately followed the rules of the House of Shammai.

18   The House of Shammai agrees with the House of Hillel that one may fill oil- or wine-press on Friday afternoon, install the pressure mechanism, and let the fluid ooze out during the Sabbath. The reason is that the forbidden work on the Sabbath would be the crushing of olives or grapes, not the flowing out of oil or grape juice. But this crushing is done immediately when pressure is exerted, on Friday.

19   Cooking by human intervention on the

Sabbath is forbidden. Since roasting is a short process which needs constant attention, it cannot be done on the Sabbath.

20 Once the crust has formed, bread quickly bakes by itself and does not need human help. Since the process of baking pita-bread is very short, there is no danger that the baker would stir the coals. Removing the pita from the walls of the oven where they are baked is classified as an art, not work.

21 If the 15th of Nisan is a Sabbath, the Passover sacrifice has to be roasted in the night; overriding the rabbinic Sabbath prohibition. Naturally the roasting process has to begin when it is still Friday; the only leniency is that no minimal time has to elapse between the start of roasting and sundown. Although roasting was specifically prohibited in Mishnah 14 even if no further human intervention was necessary, in this case it is permitted since the Passover lamb is prepared and eaten by a group, not a single cook, and they can be expected to watch one another that no stirring of coals or adding of fuel will occur.

22 The fireplace in the Temple where the priests can warm themselves in cold nights. Again this fire burns in the presence and for the benefit of a group and no desecration of the Sabbath is expected. As a general rule, rabbinic restrictions relating to the Sabbath are not applied in the Temple.

23 Since it would be a Sabbath desecration to intervene to get a fire started (*Ex.* 35:3) one has to be sure that the fire in the fireplace does not need human intervention. This means that all logs must have started burning.

24 He holds that charcoal burns easily; even if only one log started to burn, all of them will burn in due course without human intervention.

(2a line 43) יְצִיאוֹת הַשַּׁבָּת כול׳. מָהוּ שְׁתַּיִם שֶׁהֵן אַרְבַּע. שְׁתַּיִם לְחִיּוּב וּשְׁתַּיִם לִפְטוּר אוֹ אַרְבַּע לְחִיּוּב וְאַרְבַּע לִפְטוּר. נִשְׁמְעִינָה מִן הָדָא. שְׁבוּעוֹת שְׁתַּיִם שֶׁהֵן אַרְבַּע. אָמַר רִבִּי בָא. תַּמָּן כּוּלְּהוֹן לְחִיּוּב. בְּרַם הָכָא חִיּוּב וּפְטוּר אַתְיָנָן מַתְנֵי. הָדָא אֲמָרָה. ד' לְחִיּוּב וְד' לִפְטוּר. אָמַר רִבִּי יוֹסֵי. מַתְנִיתָא אֲמָרָה כֵן. שְׁבוּעוֹת שְׁתַּיִם שֶׁהֵן אַרְבַּע. לֹא לְחִיּוּב. וְדִכְוָותָהּ. יְצִיאוֹת הַשַּׁבָּת שְׁתַּיִם שֶׁהֵן אַרְבַּע לְחִיּוּב. וְהָא תַנֵּי. דַּלְתוֹת הַהֵיכָל שְׁנַיִם שֶׁהֵן אַרְבַּע. אִית לָךְ לְמֵימַר. לֹא לְחִיּוּב וְלֹא לִפְטוּר. נִיתְנֵי. שְׁנַיִם עָשָׂר פָּטוּר. לֹא אַתְיָנָן מִיתְנֵי אֶלָּא פָטוּר שֶׁהוּא כְּנֶגֶד חִיּוּב. אָמַר רִבִּי חִייָא בַּר אַבָּא. מָהוּ הָחֵן פְּטוּר דְּתַנִּינָן הָכָא. מוּתָּר. אָמַר רִבִּי יוֹסֵי. עָנִי וְעָשִׁיר אֶחָד הֵן וּמָנוּ אוֹתָן חֲכָמִים שְׁנַיִם. הַכְנָסָה וְהוֹצָאָה אֶחָד הֵן וּמָנוּ אוֹתָן חֲכָמִים שְׁנַיִם. יְצִיאוֹת הַשַּׁבָּת אֵין הַכְנָסָה בִּכְלָל. הַמּוֹצִיא מֵרְשׁוּת לִרְשׁוּת אֵין הַמַּכְנִיס בִּכְלָל. נִשְׁמְעִינָה מִן הָדָא. דָּמַר רִבִּי יָסָא בְּשֵׁם רִבִּי יוֹחָנָן. הַכְנִיס חֲצִי גְרוֹגֶרֶת וְהוֹצִיא חֲצִי גְרוֹגֶרֶת חַיָּיב. מִנַּיִין שֶׁהוֹצָאָה קְרוּיָה מְלָאכָה. רִבִּי שְׁמוּאֵל בַּר נַחְמָן בְּשֵׁם רִבִּי יוֹנָתָן שָׁמַע לָהּ מִן הָדָא. וַיְצַו מֹשֶׁה וַיַּעֲבִירוּ קוֹל בַּמַּחֲנֶה לֵאמֹר אִישׁ וְאִשָּׁה אַל־יַעֲשׂוּ־עוֹד מְלָאכָה לִתְרוּמַת הַקֹּדֶשׁ וַיִּכָּלֵא הָעָם מֵהָבִיא. נִמְנְעוּ הָעָם מִלְּהוֹצִיא מִבָּתֵּיהֶן וְלִיתֵּן לַגִּזְבָּרִים. רִבִּי חִזְקִיָּה בְּשֵׁם רִבִּי אִלָּא. אֲפִילוּ הַכְנָסָה אַתְּ שָׁמַע מִינָהּ. כְּשֵׁם שֶׁנִּמְנְעוּ הָעָם מִלְּהוֹצִיא מִבָּתֵּיהֶן וְלִיתֵּן לַגִּזְבָּרִין כָּךְ נִמְנְעוּ הַגִּזְבָּרִין מִלְּקַבֵּל מִיָּדָן וּלְהַכְנִיס

לְלִישָׁנָא. רִבִּי חִזְקִיָּה בְּשֵׁם רִבִּי אֲחָא שָׁמַע כּוּלְּהוֹן מִן הָדֵין קִרְייָא. לֹא תוֹצִיאוּ מַשָּׂא מִבָּתֵּיכֶם בְּיוֹם הַשַׁבָּת וְכָל־מְלָאכָה לֹא תַעֲשׂוּ.

3 כולהון | G כולהון | 4 יוסי G | יוסה שבועות G | שבועית 5 תני G | תניין ולא G | אי (או!) | 6 ניתני | G נתני מיתני | G מיתני 7 מהו G | מהוא הכא | G הכה יוסי G | יוסה 8 שנים G | אחד אחד | G שנים 9 הדא G | הדה יסא G | יוסה 10 שהוצאה G| שהוציאה 13 מבתיהן | G מבתיהם לגיזברים | G לגיזברין חזקיה | G אחא 14 שנמנעו G | שנימנעו מבתיהם | G מבתיהן לגיזברין | G לגיזברים נימנעו | G נימנעו 15 כולהון | G כולהן הדין | G הדה קרייא G | קריה

[25]"Export on the Sabbath," etc. What means "two which are four"? Two which are four for liability and two which are four for no liability, or four for liability and four for no liability? Let us hear from the following[26]: "There are two kinds of oaths which are four kinds." Rebbi Abba said, there all are about liability, but here we come to state both liability and no liability[27]. This implies four of liability and four of no liability. Rebbi Yose said, the Mishnah says so, "there are two kinds of oaths which are four kinds," not because of liability? And similarly, "there are two kinds of export on the Sabbath which are four kinds," because there is liability. But was it not stated[28], "the doors of the Temple hall were two which are four?" Can you say, liability and no liability? Should we state twelve cases of no liability[29]? We only come to state cases of no liability which correspond to cases of liability. Rebbi Ḥiyya bar Abba said, what is this "no liability" which we stated here? Permitted[30]! Rebbi Yose said, the poor man and the rich man are one but the Sages counted them as two. Bringing in or taking out are one but the Sages counted them as two[31]. Taking out on the Sabbath does not include bringing in; if one exports from one domain to the other, does this not include the one who imports? Let us hear from the following, as Rebbi Yasa said in the name if Rebbi Joḥanan: Somebody who brings in half the size of a dried fig and takes out half the size of a dried fig is liable[32]. And from where that taking out is called work? Rebbi Samuel bar Naḥman in the name of Rebbi Jonathan[33] understood it from the following[34]: *Moses ordered, they made a public proclamation in the camp as follows, men or women should no longer do work to contribute to the sanctuary.* The people refrained from taking objects out from their houses to give them to the collectors. Rebbi Ḥizqiah[35] in the name of Rebbi Ila: You even understand bringing in from this. Just as the people refrained from taking objects out of their houses to give to the collectors so the collectors did

not accept anything from them to bring into the office. Rebbi Hizqiah in the name of Rebbi Aḥa understood everything from the following[36]: *do not bring out any load from your houses on the Sabbath day, and perform no work.*

25   For this and the following paragraphs there exists a reasonably complete Genizah text (G) edited by L. Ginzberg (שרידי ירושלמי New York 1909 p. 62). A slightly garbled parallel is in *Ševuot* 1:1, explained there in Notes 5-20. The Notes here are restricted to references and short explanations.

26   Mishnah *Ševuot* 1:1.

27   For R. Abba, there is a difference between the Mishnaiot in *Šabbat* and *Ševuot* in that in the case here at least one person involved always is not liable whereas in *Ševuot* only one person is mentioned and all cases are of liability. For R. Yose, the parallel is only that of Mishnaiot 1-2, not 3-4. Each Mishnah describes two cases of liability; these are two covering in all four cases of liability as in *Ševuot* 1:1.

28   Mishnah *Middot* 4:1. The Mishnah is purely descriptive of the construction of Herod's Temple; the notions of liability or no liability are inappropriate.

29   There are four cases in the Mishnah where one party is liable and the other is not involved. Then there are four cases in which both parties are involved but nobody is criminally liable. One might construct another four cases where nobody is liable; e. g., if the poor man reaches into the house, picks something up, which the householder then takes from his hand and deposits outside.

30   Since in Mishnaiot 1-2 only one person acts, it is inappropriate to apply the label "not liable" to the other person. Babli 2b/3a.

31   In G, *Ševuot* 1:1, *editio princeps,* and a quote in RITBA *Ševuot* 1:1: "Taking out or bringing in are two but the Sages counted them as one." As noted later in this paragraph, taking out is called work by Jeremiah (which cannot be used as a legal text but is confirmation of the interpretation of the law) whereas bringing in is only forbidden by the argument that taking out from A to B is bringing in to B from A.

32   Even an intrinsic liability can be prosecuted only if a minimal amount was transported, which for food is determined as the size of a dried fig (Chapters 7-8). Since taking out and bringing in small quantities are to be combined, taking out and bringing in are representatives of one and the same action, *viz.,* transporting.

33   In *Ševuot* 1:1 and the Babli (6b): R. Johanan; quoted without attribution by R. Hananel *Šabbat* 3b; in a number of Medieval sources R. Jonathan.

34   *Ex.* 36:6. Babli 96a.

35   Missing in *Ševuot*. In G, R, Aḥa in the name or R. Ila; in *Sefer Ha`ittim* (ed. Mekize Nirdamim p. 300) R. Aḥa in the name of R. Hiyya. In *Sefer Miswot Gadol #65,* (part 1, fol. 17a in Venice edition) R. Hiyya in the name of R. Aḥa.

36   *Jer.* 17:22.

(2b line 21) רִבִּי יָסָא בְּשֵׁם רִבִּי יוֹחָנָן. הִכְנִיס חֲצִי גְרוֹגֶרֶת וְהוֹצִיא חֲצִי גְרוֹגֶרֶת חַיָּיב. מַה דָּמַר רִבִּי יוֹחָנָן דְּלָא כְרִבִּי יוֹסֵה. דְּתַנֵּי. הוֹצִיא חֲצִי גְרוֹגֶרֶת וְחָזַר וְהוֹצִיא חֲצִי גְרוֹגֶרֶת בְּהֶעֱלֵם אֶחָד חַיָּיב. בִּשְׁנֵי הֶעֱלֵימוֹת פָּטוּר. רִבִּי יוֹסֵי אוֹמֵר. בְּעוֹלָם אֶחָד בִּרְשׁוּת אֶחָד חַיָּיב. בְּעוֹלָם אֶחָד בִּשְׁתֵּי רְשׁוּיוֹת אוֹ בִשְׁנֵי הֶעֱלֵימוֹת בִּרְשׁוּת אֶחָד פָּטוּר. וְקַשְׁיָין. אִילּוּ הוֹצָאָה וְהוֹצָאָה אֵינָן מִצְטָרְפוֹת כְּרִבִּי יוֹסֵה לֹא כָל־שֶׁכֵּן הַכְנָסָה וְהוֹצָאָה. הֲוֵי מַה דָּמַר רִבִּי יוֹחָנָן דְּלָא כְרִבִּי יוֹסֵי.

3 העלימות G עילמות | עילמות G יוסי | יוסה. בעלם | ג בהיעלם   4 העלימות G העלמות | אחד G | ג אחת וקשיין G | וקשייה   5 שכן | ג שכין   יוסי | גG יוסה

אָמַר רִבִּי אִילָא. לֹא סוֹף דָּבָר שְׁנֵי פְתָחִים פְּתוּחִים לִשְׁתֵּי פַלְטִיּוֹת. אֶלָּא אֲפִילוּ פְתוּחִין לְפַלְטִית אַחַת אוֹף רִבִּי יוֹסֵי מוֹדֶה. דְּרִבִּי יוֹסֵי מְדַמֵּי רְשֻׁיּוֹת לְהֶעֱלֵימוֹת לְחִיּוּב. כָּמָּה דְּרִבִּי יוֹסֵי מְדַמֵּי רְשֻׁיּוֹת לְהֶעֱלֵימוֹת לְפָטוּר כָּךְ מְדַמֵּה רְשֻׁיּוֹת לְהֶעֱלֵימוֹת לְחִיּוּב. שֶׁאִם הוֹצִיא כִגְרוֹגֶרֶת בְּפֶתַח זֶה וְכִגְרוֹגֶרֶת בְּפֶתַח זֶה כְּעוֹלָם אֶחָד שֶׁמָּא אֵינוֹ חַיָּיב שְׁתַּיִם.

1 פלטיות G פלטייות   פתוחין | ג פתוחים   2 לפלטיות | גG לפלטיה   לפלטיה G | אוף - G | יוסי | יוסה מודה G | ג מודי   יוסי | גG יוסה   להעלימות | ג להעלמות   כמה | ג הכמה   3 יוסי | יוסה G | יוסה כד G כנו (- כן הוא) | מדמה G | מדמי   מדמה | ג מדמי   להעלימות | ג להעלמות   להעלימות G | ג להעלמות לפטור | גG לחייב. להעלימות G ליעלימות ג להיעלמות לחייב | ג ליפ[טור] ליפטיר   4 הזה | G וכרוגרת | ג וכרוגרת   זה | G הזה   כהעלם | ג בהילעם

אָמַר רִבִּי יוּדָן. רִבִּי יוֹסֵי מְדַמֶּה רְשֻׁיּוֹת לַאֲכִילַת פְּרָסִים. שֶׁאִם אָכַל חֲצִי זַיִת בְּתוֹךְ כְּדֵי אֲכִילַת פְּרָס הַזֶּה וַחֲצִי זַיִת בְּתוֹךְ כְּדֵי אֲכִילַת פְּרָס הַזֶּה שֶׁמָּא אֵינוֹ פָטוּר. אָכַל כַּמָּה זֵיתִים בְּכַמָּה פְרָסִים בְּעוֹלָם אֶחָד אֵינוֹ חַיָּיב אֶלָּא אַחַת.

1 ר' | ג דר'   יוסי | גG יוסה   מדמה | ג מדמי   רשויות | ג רשיות   2 הזה | ג זה   3 בעלם | ג בהיעלם

רַבָּנִין דְּקֵיסָרִין אָֽמְרִין. עַד דְּאַתְּ מְדַמֵּי לָהּ לַחֲלָבִים דַּמִּינָהּ לַשַּׁבָּת. שֶׁאִם אָרַג חוּט אֶחָד בְּתוֹךְ בֶּגֶד הַזֶּה וְחוּט אֶחָד בְּתוֹךְ בֶּגֶד זֶה שֶׁמָּא זֶה שֶׁמָּא אֵינוֹ פָטוּר. אָרַג כַּמָּה חוּטִין בְּכַמָּה בְגָדִים בְּעוֹלָם אֶחָד אֵינוֹ חַיָּיב אֶלָּא אַחַת.

1 רבנין G | רבנן   דאת | ג דו (=דהוא)   דמינה | ג ידמינה   שאם | ג שאילו   2 בתוך בגד | ג בבגד (2)   הזה G ג זה   בגד | - G | בעלם G | ביעלם ג בהיעלם

[37]Rebbi Yasa in the name of Rebbi Joḥanan: If one brought in half a dried fig and took out half a dried fig he is liable[38]. What Rebbi Joḥanan said does not follow Rebbi Yose[39], as it was stated[40]: "If one took out half a dried fig and again took out half a dried fig during one period of oblivion, he is liable; during different periods of oblivion he is not liable. Rebbi Yose said, during one period of oblivion and one domain he is liable, during one period of oblivion and two domains or during two periods of oblivion and one domain he is not liable.[41]" We find this difficult. If two different transports do not combine following Rebbi Yose, *a fortiori* also not bringing in and taking out[42]? Therefore what Rebbi Joḥanan said could not follow Rebbi Yose.

Rebbi Ila said, not only if two doors open to two public roads[43] but even if they open to the same public road will Rebbi Yose agree[44], for Rebbi Yose compares domains to periods of oblivion in matters of liability[45]. Just as Rebbi Yose compares domains to periods of oblivion in absence of liability so Rebbi Yose compares domains to periods of oblivion in matters of liability[46]. For if he took out the volume of a dried fig through this door and the volume of a dried fig through that door in one period of oblivion is he not liable twice[47]?

[48]Rebbi Yudan said, Rebbi Yose compares domains to eating slices[49]. For if one ate the volume of half an olive during the time needed to eat one slice and another volume of half an olive in the time needed to eat another slice, is he not free from liability? If one ate several volumes of olives during several times needed to eat a slice in one period of forgetting, he is liable only once.

[50]The rabbis of Caesarea say, before you compare this to fat, compare it to the rules of Sabbath itself. For if one was weaving one thread on this piece of cloth and weaving one thread on that piece of cloth, is he not free from liability? If he wove several threads on several pieces of cloth in one period of oblivion he is liable only once.

37 For this and the next paragraph there also exists an additional Genizah text (א) also edited by L. Ginzberg, *loc. cit.* p. 64.

38 Here and in the following, "liable" only refers to the obligation to bring a purification sacrifice in case of unintentional infraction of the Sabbath rules. Since an intentional sin cannot be atoned for by a sacrifice (*Num.* 16:30), a sacrifice is possible only if the perpetrator was oblivious either of the fact that the act was forbidden or, in the case of the Sabbath, that the day was a Sabbath. Sins committed during different periods of oblivion require different sacrifices. In addition, the prohibition of work on the Sabbath is not a single prohibition but, as explained in Chapter 7, a set of 39 different prohibitions, each with different minima of forbidden work which trigger the obligation of a sacrifice. Minimal infractions of different prohibitions do not combine to produce the obligation of a sacrifice. On the other hand, infractions which are subsumed under the same prohibition, even if one is clearly biblically prohibited (אַב מְלָאכָה "a master work" such as transporting *from* a private to the public domain) and one which is classified by a logical argument as belonging to the same class (תּוֹלָדָה "a derivative", as transporting *to* the private domain) do combine to create the obligation of a sacrifice.

39 The Tanna, ben Halafta, the greatest

authority of the fourth generation of Tannaim.

40 Babli 80b, *Bava batra* 55b, *Keritut* 17a. The first part is a Tosephta, *ed.* Liebermann 9:11, *ed. princeps* 10:7.

41 Since transporting has three components, lifting in one domain, removing to another, and depositing in the other domain, for R. Yose they cannot be combined unless all three components are the same (within one period of oblivion.)

42 The argument is not convincing since transporting into is a derivative of trans--porting from. R. Yose still could hold that the actions combine to create liability if the domains involved are the same.

43 Greek πλατεῖα (sc., ὁδός) "a wide (road)", equivalent of Hebrew רְחוֹב.

44 Since it is assumed that each private house has only one door to the street, there are two different private domains involved; the transgressions do not combine for R. Yose.

45 Different domains from which transport starts or where transport ends are like different periods of oblivion for which no common purification sacrifice is possible by biblical standards.

46 Clearly the correct text is that of G: "Just as Rebbi Yose compares domains to periods of oblivion in matters of liability so Rebbi Yose compares domains to periods of oblivion in absence of liability." The fact that incomplete actions in two different periods of oblivion do not combine to create the liability (or possibility) of a sacrifice is only a corollary to the statement that all infractions of the same kind committed during the same period of oblivion are atoned for by one single sacrifice.

47 For R. Yose, who negates the possibility of any sacrifice if the amounts each time are insufficient. For the anonymous majority, the situation is the opposite; two transports of insufficient quantities from two domains combine to create liability for a sacrifice but transports of greater quantities from different domains in one period of oblivion are atoned for by a single sacrifice.

48 This paragraph and the next also appear in *Horaiot* 3:3 (Notes 66-72) in a different context. (R. Yose mentioned there is the fifth generation Amora).

49 This refers to sacrifices due for eating forbidden food. Since purification sacrifices are due only for transgressions punishable at least by extirpation (Mishnah *Horaiot* 3:7), the only example of such solid food is forbidden fat. A sacrifice for inadvertent consumption of forbidden fat is due if at least the volume of an average olive was eaten in the time needed to eat a slice of bread. The slice is defined (Tosephta *Nega`im* 7:10) as half a loaf when three loaves are baked from a *kav* of flour (about 35 cl)

50 Cf. *Horaiot* 3:3 Note 70. The rabbis of Caesarea object to comparing the rules of the Sabbath to any other biblical prohibition. Mishnah 13:1 states that weaving is forbidden and the threshold for an action requiring a purification sacrifice is weaving two threads. For the majority, weaving two threads in one oblivion triggers the obligation of a sacrifice, for R. Yose only if the two rows were added to the same piece of cloth.

(2b line 40) רִבִּי יוֹסֵי בְשֵׁם רִבִּי יוֹחָנָן. הַמּוֹצִיא אֵינוֹ חַיָּיב עַד שֶׁיַּנִּיחַ. רִבִּי יַעֲקֹב בַּר אָחָא בְשֵׁם רִבִּי יוֹחָנָן. עַד שֶׁיִּטּוֹל וְעַד שֶׁיַּנִּיחַ. רִבִּי זְעִירָא בָעֵי. עַד שֶׁיִּטּוֹל עַל מְנָת לְהָנִיחַ. נָטַל לֶאֱכוֹל וְנִמְלַךְ לְהָנִיחַ לֹא. הֱוֵי (חַיָּיב) מַה דָּמַר רִבִּי יוֹחָנָן דְּלֹא כְרִבִּי יוֹסֵי. דְּתַנֵּי. הוֹצִיא חֲצִי גְרוֹגֶרֶת וְהִנִּיחָהּ וְחָזַר וְהוֹצִיא חֲצִי גְרוֹגֶרֶת. אִם הִנִּיחָהּ בְּתוֹךְ ד' אַמּוֹת לָרִאשׁוֹנָה חַיָּיב. וְאִם לָאו פָּטוּר. רִבִּי יוֹסֵי אוֹמֵר. אִם הֶעֱבִירוֹ דֶרֶךְ עָלֶיהָ חַיָּיב. וְאִם לָאו פָּטוּר. רִבִּי יוֹסֵי עָבִיד הַמְהַלֵּךְ כִּמְנִיחַ. כְּמָה דְּרִבִּי יוֹסֵי עָבִיד הַמְהַלֵּךְ כִּמְנִיחַ לְחִיּוּב כָּךְ הוּא עָבִיד הַמְהַלֵּךְ כִּמְנִיחַ לִפְטוֹר. כֵּיוָן שֶׁהוֹצִיאָהּ נַעֲשָׂה כְּמוֹ שֶׁהִנִּיחָהּ שָׁם וִיהֵא פָּטוּר. תִּיפְתָּר שֶׁהָיְתָה נְתוּנָה בְּתוֹךְ ד' אַמּוֹת. כְּהָדָא דְּתַנֵּי. וְאִם לָאו פָּטוּר. אָמַר רָבָא בַּר בְּרֵיהּ דְּרַב פַּפִּי. תִּיפְתָּר שֶׁהָיָה הַפֶּתַח רָחָב חָמֵשׁ אַמּוֹת וְהוֹצִיא אַחַת לְכָאן וְאַחַת לְכָאן. וַהֲרֵי לֹא הוֹצִיא אֶת הַשְּׁנִייָה בְּתוֹךְ ד' אַמּוֹת לָרִאשׁוֹנָה.

1 יוסי G | ג יוסה שינוי G שעה שינוח | 2 זעירא G | זעורא ג זעירה | 3 ונמלך | ג ונימלך חייב G | ג -
מה G | מן דמר | ג דא' | 4 והניחה | ג והיניחה הניחה | ג היניחה ד' G | ג ארבע | 5 -
ג אמר יוסי G | ג יוסה (2) | או' | ג - | העבירו G | ג העבירה | עביד G | ג עבד | 6 כמה | ג הכמה דר' | G | ר'
יוסי G | ג יוסה עביד G | ג עבד | לחייב | ג לחיוב עביד | ג עבד | לפטור G | ג לפטור ליפטור | 7 נעשה G | ג יעשה
כמו | G ג כמי ג כמה שהוציאה G | ג שהיניחה ד' אמות G | ג ארבע אמות לפתח כהדא G | ג כדה | 8 רבא G |
ר' בא 9 לכאן G | ג לכן

Rebbi Yose in the name of Rebbi Johanan: The one who takes out is not liable until he put it down[51]. Rebbi Jacob bar Aha in the name of Rebbi Johanan: Unless he take up and put down. Rebbi Ze`ira required, unless he take it up with the intention to put it down[52]. Not if he lifted it to eat and then changed his mind to put it down[53]. What Rebbi Johanan said does not follow Rebbi Yose, as it was stated[54]: "If he took out half the volume of a dried fig and put it down, and then took out another volume of half a dried fig. If he put it[55] down within four cubits of the first piece he is liable, otherwise he is not liable. Rebbi Yose[39] said, if he transported it over it, he is liable, otherwise he is not liable." Rebbi Yose considers the person walking as if he was putting down[56]. Just as Rebbi Yose considers the person walking as if he was putting down for liability so he considers the person walking as if he was putting down for non-liability. When he took it out he is considered having put it down; then he should be free from liability[57]. Explain it if it was put down within four cubits [of the door][58], as it was stated[41], "otherwise he is not liable." Rebbi Abba the son of Rebbi Pappaeus said, explain it if the door was five cubits wide and he brought one out on this side, the other on the other side. Then the second was not taken out within four cubits of the first[59].

51 As explained in Note 1, the Sabbath is desecrated only by a complete action, lifting up, transporting from one domain to another, and depositing. If the last act is

missing, there was no punishable desecration.

The tradent R. Yose is the fifth generation Amora.

52   This is a necessary clarification of the preceding statement. Not only must there be a complete action, but all three parts must be executed with the intent to perform the action. In *Ex.* 35, the prohibition of work on the Sabbath is repeated (vv. 1-3) as part of the commandment to build the Tabernacle (vv. 4-35). In 35:33, the construction of the Tabernacle is described as "thinking work". It is concluded that only "thinking work" is punishable (criminally or by a sacrifice) as desecration of the Sabbath. In the special case of transporting, there is desecration only if the three parts are done with compatible intent, if the lifting up was intended to be followed by a putting down..

53   It is perfectly legitimate to take food to eat in the domain where it was at the start of the Sabbath. If the first stage of a transport was executed in a perfectly permitted way based on a true thought, it never can become the first leg in a criminal transport. While the change of intent and the following action were forbidden and sinful, there can be no criminal or sacrificial liability attached to them. (As statement of R. Johanan himself, Babli 5b, *Eruvin* 20b, *Ketubot* 31a).

54   An anonymous *baraita* following the statement here attributed to R. Yose is Tosephta 9:11(ed. S. Liebermann); the first part Babli 80a.

Since in the public domain one is only permitted to move things by a distance of less than four cubits, things farther away are as in two different domains. If each transport was less that a minimal amount, the actions cannot be combined.

56   Later in the Halakhah and in the Babli (5b, 91b, *Eruvin* 98a, *Ketubot* 31b) this opinion is attributed to Ben Azzai, a generation before R. Yose. It is agreed by everybody that standing still while transporting an object is legally putting it down, not on the ground but on the static person. This is the same as depositing the object on a pillar. R. Yose holds that a slow motion such as walking is the equivalent of standing still for a negligible time at many places. An action which does not result in instant deposition is throwing.

According to R. Yose, if the second object ever was within 4 cubits of the place where the first was deposited, the two actions combine for liability, even if the second was ultimately deposited somewhere else.

57   If the object is considered deposited the moment it was taken out of a private domain by a walking person, then any subsequent motion is a new transport. Since R. Yose (Note 44) only considers combining transports if they originate and terminate in the same domains, the fact that later the second object was transported over the first should be irrelevant.

58   Added from G and ג.

59   For the anonymous Tanna the final place of deposit determines liability; for R. Yose there is no liability if the two paths never were within 4 cubits of one another.

(2c line 8) תַּמָּן תַּנֵּינָן. רִבִּי מֵאִיר אוֹמֵר. אִם הָיְתָה שַׁבָּת וְהוֹצִיאוֹ. אָמְרוּ לוֹ. אֵינוֹ הַשֵּׁם: שֶׁזֶּה חַיָּיב מִשּׁוּם מְהַלֵּךְ וְזֶה חַיָּיב מִשּׁוּם מַנִּיחַ. מַנּוּ אָמְרוּ לוֹ. רִבִּי יוֹסֵי. מְחִלְפָה שִׁיטָתֵיהּ דְּרִבִּי יוֹסֵי. תַּמָּן לָא עָבַד הַמְהַלֵּךְ כְּמַנִּיחַ וָכָה עָבִיד הַמְהַלֵּךְ כְּמַנִּיחַ. אָמַר רִבִּי יוּדָן. תִּיפְתָּר שֶׁהָיָה מוּטָּל עַל הָאַסְקוּפָה מְקֻצָּתוֹ בִּפְנִים וּפִיו לַחוּץ וּפָשַׁט יָדוֹ וּנְטָלָהּ וַאֲכָלָהּ. וַהֲרֵי לֹא הִלֵּךְ.

2 מחלפה G | מחלפת יוסי G | יוסה   3 וכה G | וכן הוא

There[60], we have stated: "Rebbi Meïr says, if it was a Sabbath and he carried it out[61]. They told him, it is not the category[62]." Because this one is liable because of walking and that one is liable because of putting down[63]. Who is "they said to him"? Rebbi Yose[64]! The argument of Rebbi Yose is inverted. There, he does not consider the person walking equal to one who was putting down but here he is considering the person walking equal to one who was putting down[65]! Rebbi Yudan said, explain it that he was laying on the threshold[66] partially inside, his mouth outside, when he stretched out his hand, took it, and ate it. Then he did not walk[67].

60 Mishnah *Keritut* 3:4.

61 As noted before, a purification offering is possible only for transgressions punishable at least by extirpation. The Mishnah gives an example that a single act may trigger the obligation of 4 purification and one reparation offerings. An impure person who eats a piece of well-being offering (*Lev.* 7:20) which is fat (v.25) and more than 2 days old (v. 18) on the Day of Atonement (23:29). For the illicit use of a *sanctum* a reparation sacrifice is due (5:15-16). R. Meïr adds that if the day also was a Sabbath and the person would take the piece in a private domain, carry it out and eat it in the public domain, an additional purification offering is needed.

The text and R. Yudan's explanation make it clear that the Yerushalmi does not read with some Babli sources "carried it out in his mouth."

62 The five sacrifices are due for eating one piece; the Sabbath infraction would be for carrying. S. Liebermann explains אֵינוֹ הַשֵּׁם as "is not simultaneous."

63 Eating may also be done while walking; the Sabbath infraction becomes a liability only when the motion stopped.

64 There is no other reference to the fact that the objection to R. Meïr originates with the Tanna R. Yose.

65 This argument may support Liebermann's interpretation. Since for R. Yose a person walking is considered stopping at every place, the Sabbath infraction and the desecration of the sacrifice are simultaneous.

66 An Accadic word (*askuppum*). The word describes not only the threshold but also the stairs leading from the road to the house. [Also cf. Latin *scapus* "post or newel of a circular staircase; main stile of a door on which it hinges" (E. G.)]

67 If the piece of fat was lying inside the private domain, the Sabbath violation did not involve any movement of his body; the

reference to R. Yose's opinion about transporting on the Sabbath is irrelevant, as is the explanation given in the preceding sentence. The difference in the status of the required sacrifices is as indicated in Note 62.

(2c line 12) אָמַר רִבִּי יַנַּאי. בָּלַע חֲצִי זַיִת והקיעו וְחָזַר וּבְלָעוֹ חַיָּיב. הִכְנִיס חֲצִי גְרוֹגֶרֶת וְחָזַר וְהוֹצִיאָהּ פָּטוּר. מַה בֵינָהּ לְבֵין קַדְמָיְיתָא. תַּמָּן נֶהֱנָה חִיכּוֹ בִכְזַיִת. בְּרַם הָכָא לֹא נִתְעַסֵּק בִּכְגרוֹגֶרֶת שְׁלֵימָה. אָמַר רִבִּי יוֹסֵי. פְּעָמִים שֶׁהוּא מִתְעַסֵּק בִּגְרוֹגֶרֶת שְׁלֵימָה וְהוּא פָטוּר. הֵיךְ עֲבִידָא. הוֹצִיא חֲצִי גְרוֹגֶרֶת וְהִנִּיחָהּ וְחָזַר וְהוֹצִיא חֲצִי גְרוֹגֶרֶת וְלֹא הִסְפִּיק לְהַנִּיחָהּ עַד שֶׁנִּשְׂרְפָה הָרִאשׁוֹנָה. וַהֲרֵי נִתְעַסֵּק בִּגְרוֹגֶרֶת שְׁלֵימָה וְהוּא פָטוּר. בְּגִין מְדַמְיָיתָהּ לַחֲלָבִין וְהוּא עָבַד כֵּן.

4 גרוגרת G | בוגרת   5 בכגרוגרת G | בגרוגרת

Rebbi Yannai said, one who swallowed half the volume of an olive, then threw it up, and again swallowed it, is liable[68]. But one who brought in half the volume of a dried fig and took it out again, is not liable[69]. What is the difference between this and the first one? There his palate enjoyed the volume of an olive, but here he never dealt with a full volume of a fig.

Rebbi Yose said, sometimes a person may be dealing with a full volume of a fig and not be liable. How is this possible? He took out half of the volume of a dried fig[70], put it down, again took out half of the volume of a dried fig, but did not manage to put it down before the first one was burned. He was dealing with a full volume of a fig but is not liable[71]. Because he compared it to forbidden fat he contrived this[72].

68   In the Babli, *Hulin* 103b, statement and supporting argument are by R. Assi (Yasa) in the name of R. Johanan. The food swallowed is supposed to be forbidden fat.

69   This is not the situation discussed in Note 32 where half a fig was brought in and half a fig taken out; in all a whole fig was transported. But here the same half fig was transported twice; neither transport created liability.

70   Here starts a new Genizah leaf (G), also edited by L. Ginzberg, *loc. cit.* p. 65.

71   In the Tosephta 9:11 (ed. Liebermann): "If the first half was eaten before the second came to rest he is not liable, whether in one or in two periods of oblivion." As explained earlier, quantities less than the minimum trigger liability only if they exist together.

The statement is referred to as obvious in the Babli, 80a.

72   This is R. Yose's explanation of R. Yannai's statement. Since for fat a single half olive can create liability, there is good reason to formulate R. Yannai's rule in the way indicated. For the Sabbath, R. Yannai's statement is unnecessary; it is formulated purely as companion piece to the statement about fat.

(2c line 19) אָמַר רִבִּי יוֹחָנָן. הַמּוֹצִיא מֵרְשׁוּת הַיָּחִיד לִרְשׁוּת הָרַבִּים דֶּרֶךְ כַּרְמְלִית חַיָּיב מִן הַמּוֹצִיא לְאַחֲרָיו. מִן הָדָא. הַמִּתְכַּוֵּין לְהוֹצִיא לְפָנָיו וּבָא לוֹ לְאַחֲרָיו פָּטוּר. לְאַחֲרָיו וּבָא לוֹ לְפָנָיו חַיָּיב. וְאֵיפְשָׁר שֶׁלֹּא יֵעָשֶׂה בֵינוֹ לְבֵין הַכּוֹתֶל כַּרְמְלִית. אָמַר רִבִּי יוֹסֵי. תִּיפְתָּר שֶׁהָיוּ פָנָיו הֲפוּכוֹת לַכּוֹתֶל וּמַשּׂוֹאוֹ לְאַחֲרָיו וּבְכָךְ יָצָא מַשּׂאוֹ תְחִילָּה. רִבִּי חִייָה בַּר אַבָּא בְּעָא קוֹמֵי רִבִּי מָנָא. וְזוֹ לֹא דֶרֶךְ הוֹצָאָה הִיא. אָמַר לֵיהּ. שָׁכֵּן כַּתַּפָּייָא אוּמְנַיָּיא עָבְדִין כֵּן. וַיְידָא אָמְרָה דָא. דָּמַר רִבִּי אָחָא רִבִּי מַיְישָׁא בְּשֵׁם רִבִּי יוֹחָנָן. הַמּוֹצִיא אוֹכְלִים וּנְתָנָן עַל הָאַסְקוּפָּה. וְהָא אַסְקוּפָּה לָאו כַּרְמְלִית הִיא. וּבָאִישׁ לְרִבִּי יוֹסֵי דְּלָא אֲמָרָהּ מִן גַּרְמֵיהּ.

2 הדא G | הדה   3 יעשה G | יעשיה   לבין G | לבין עצמו   ברמלית G | לכרמלית   4 ובכך G | וכבר
אבא G | אדא   5 היא G | הוא   כתפייא אומניא G | כַּתַּפָיָה אומנייה   6 אוכלים G | אכלין   והא G | ודא

Rebbi Johanan said, if one exports from a private domain to the public domain through *karmelit*[73], he is liable because of him who carries on his back[74], from the following:[75] "One who intends to carry on his front but it turns out that he carried on his back is not liable. On his back and he carried on his front he is liable.[76]" For it is impossible that between him and the wall should not *karmelit* be created[77]. Rebbi Yose said, explain it that his face was turned to the wall and his load on his back and so[78] his load exited first. Rebbi Hiyya bar Abba[79] asked before Rebbi Mana: But this is not a usual way of carrying out[80]! He told him, professional porters act in this way. But the following implies it, as Rebbi Aha, Rebbi Maisha said in the name of Rebbi Johanan: "If one carries out foodstuffs and puts them on the threshold.[81]" Is the threshold not *karmelit*[82]? Rebbi Yose was sorry that he had not said this himself.

73 *Karmelit* is a part of the public domain not readily accessible to the public (Chapter 13 Note 68). The two main examples are "the sides of a thoroughfare", the part of a street close to the houses if that part is not easy to use because of stairs extending from the houses or if the fronts of the houses do not form a straight line. The other is "valley", a rural access path which is public domain, not a thoroughfare but meant only as a path for farmers working adjacent fields.

Since *karmelit* is not a thoroughfare (defined as road of at least 16 cubits width) it does not qualify as public domain for which transport from a private domain is forbidden. The statement of R. Johanan implies that he cannot consider walking as equivalent of standing still (Note 56) since transporting from a private domain to *karmelit* followed by transport from *karmelit* to public domain, while forbidden on the Sabbath, does not generate liability (Note 81).

(The etymology of the word *karmelit* is unknown. Cf. Accadic *karmiš* "like a ruin".)

74 Because of the argument presented in

the next sentence about the difference of carrying a load in front or back.

75 Mishnah 10:4.

76 If a person carries valuables, he will want to carry them on his front so as to be in control. If then it happens that he carried them on his back, his action does not actualize his intentions; it does not qualify as "thinking work" (Note 52) and does not trigger liability. But if he intended to carry the load on his back but in fact carried it on his front, he is more in control than he intended; such an improvement qualifies as "thinking work".

77 A person standing close to that wall in the public domain in any case creates *karmelit* around himself since he bars the access of others to this place. This is formulated in 10:2 as "nothing movable in the public domain creates *karmelit* except a human."

78 Instead of "and so" G reads "already", which results in a smoother text. The person exited the house backwards.

79 G reads: Ada. This reading is the only one possible since R. Hiyya bar Abba lived several generations before R. Mana II.

80 Work done כְּלְאַחַר יָד "as if with the back of one's hand" is not "thinking work" and does not create liability.

81 Mishnah 10:2. "If one carries out foodstuffs and puts them on the threshold, whether he or somebody else carries them to the street there is no liability since it was not done in one action."

82 If the door is open, the threshold belongs to the house; if it is closed it is part of the public domain.

(2c line 28) רַב הוּנָא בְשֵׁם רַב. הַכֹּל מוֹדִין בְּזוֹרֵק שֶׁהוּא חַיָּב. דְּבָרֵי הַכֹּל הוּא שֶׁאֵין אֲוִיר כַּרְמְלִית כְּמַמָּשָׁה. וּמַה פְּלִיגִין. בְּמוֹצִיא. בֶּן עַזַּאי פּוֹטֵר. וַחֲכָמִים מְחַיְּיבִין. בֶּן עַזַּאי עָבַד הַמְהַלֵּךְ כְּמֵנִיחַ. וְרַבָּנִין לָא עָבְדִי מְהַלֵּךְ כְּמֵנִיחַ. רַב חִסְדָּא שָׁאַל לְרַב הוּנָא. עַל דַּעְתֵּיהּ דְּבֶן עַזַּאי. אֵין אָדָם מִתְחַיֵּיב בְּתוֹךְ אַרְבַּע אַמּוֹת לְעוֹלָם. מִכֵּיוָן שֶׁהוֹצִיאָן נַעֲשָׂה כְּמוֹ שֶׁהִנִּיחָה עַל כָּל־אַמָּה וְאַמָּה וִיהֵא פָטוּר.

1 הוּנָא G | חוּנָא 'אֵין אֲוִיר ברמלית G | לֵית 2 עַזַּאי G | עַזִּי עָבַד G | לָא עָבַד 3 שָׁאַל G | שַׁאוּל חוּנָא G | חוּנָה 4 שֶׁהוֹצִיאָן G | שֶׁהוֹצִיאָה נַעֲשָׂה | נַעֲשָׂה G | יֵעֲשֶׂה שֶׁהִנִּיחָה G | שֶׁהִנִּיחָה

רַב יְהוּדָה בְשֵׁם רַב. הַכֹּל מוֹדִין בְּמוֹצִיא שֶׁהוּא פָטוּר. דְּבָרֵי הַכֹּל הוּא שֶׁהַמְהַלֵּךְ כְּמֵנִיחַ. וּמַה פְּלִיגִין. בְּזוֹרֵק. בֶּן עַזַּאי פּוֹטֵר וַחֲכָמִים מְחַיְּיבִין. בֶּן עַזַּאי עָבַד אֲוִיר כַּרְמְלִית כְּמַמָּשָׁה וְרַבָּנִן לָא עָבְדִי אֲוִיר כַּרְמְלִית כְּמַמָּשָׁה.

1 הוּא G | הִיא שֶׁהַמְהַלֵּךְ, G שֶׁאֵין הַמְהַלֵּךְ 2 עַזַּאי G | עַזִּי אֲוִיר G | אֲוִויר

מַתְנִיתָא מְסַיְּיעָא לְדֵין וּמַתְנִיתָא מְסַיְּיעָא לְדֵין. מַתְנִיתָא מְסַיְּיעָא לְרַב הוּנָא. הָיָה עוֹמֵד בִּרְשׁוּת הָרַבִּים וְזָרַק לְדִיר אוֹ לְסַהַר דֶּרֶךְ כַּרְמְלִית חַיָּב. וְאִם הוֹצִיא פָטוּר. מַתְנִיתָא מְסַיְּיעָא לְרַב יְהוּדָה. הַמּוֹצִיא אוֹכְלִין וּנְתָנָן עַל הָאִסְקוּפָּה בֵּין שֶׁחָזַר וְהוֹצִיאָן בֵּין שֶׁהוֹצִיאָן אַחֵר פָּטוּר. שֶׁלֹּא עָשָׂה מְלַאכְתָּן בְּבַת אַחַת. הָא אִם עָשָׂה מְלַאכְתָּן בְּבַת אַחַת חַיָּב. בֶּן עַזַּאי אוֹמֵר. אֲפִילוּ עָשָׂה מְלַאכְתּוֹ בַת אַחַת פָּטוּר. וְהָא תַנִּינָן. רִבִּי מֵאִיר אוֹמֵר. אִם הָיְתָה שַׁבָּת וְהוֹצִיאוֹ. וְאָמְרוּ לוֹ. אֵינוֹ הַשֵּׁם: שֶׁזֶּה חַיָּב מִשּׁוּם מְהַלֵּךְ וְזֶה חַיָּב מִשּׁוּם מֵנִיחַ. עַל דַּעְתֵּיהּ דְּרַב הוּנָא דְּלֹא כְבֶן

עַזַּאי. עַל דַּעְתֵּיהּ דְּרַב יְהוּדָה דְּלֹא כְבֶן עַזַּאי וּדְלֹא כְרַבָּנָן. אָמַר רִבִּי חִינָנָא. מָנוּ אָמְרוּ לוֹ. חֲכָמִים. שֶׁהֵן בְּשִׁיטַת בֶּן עַזַּאי.

1 מתנית' מסייעא לדין ומתנית' מסייעא לדין G | מתני מסייעה לדן ומתני מסייעה לדן   מסייעא | G מסייעה הונא G | חונה   2 לדיר | G לדר   מסייעא | G מסייעה   3 אוכלין | G אכלין   4 הא אם | G מפני שלא עשה מלאכתו בת אחת הא   בת | G בת   6 הונא | G חונה   עזאי | G עזי   7 עזאי | G עזי   חיננא | G חננה 8 עזאי | G עזי

Rav Huna in the name of Rav: Everybody agrees that for throwing one is liable[83]. It is everybody's opinion that the air space over *karmelit* is not like its essence. Where do they disagree? If one carries out. Ben Azzai declares him not liable but the Sages declare him liable. Ben Azzai makes the person walking as if he was putting down[56] but the Sages do not make the person walking as if he was putting down. Rav Ḥisda asked Rav Huna: In Ben Azzai's opinion nobody ever could become liable for four cubits! Since when he transported something, it is made[84] as if he put it down within every cubit; he should be not liable[85].

Rav Jehudah in the name of Rav: Everybody agrees that for carrying out one is not liable. It is everybody's opinion that walking counts as if one was putting down. Where do they disagree? If one is throwing, for Ben Azzai declares him not liable but the Sages declare him liable. Ben Azzai considers the air space over *karmelit* like its essence[86] but the Sages consider the air space over *karmelit* not like its essence..

A *baraita* supports one and a *baraita* supports the other. A *baraita* supports Rav Huna[87]: [88]If he was standing in the public domain and threw over *karmelit* into a stable or corral, he is liable; but if he carried it he is not liable. A *baraita* supports Rebbi Jehudah: [81]"If one carries out foodstuffs and puts them on the threshold; whether he or another person then carries it out, he is not liable since the work was not performed in one step." Therefore if the work was completed in one step[89] he would be liable. Ben Azzai said, even if be completed the work at one time he would not be liable. But did we not state: "Rebbi Meïr says, if it was Sabbath and he carried it out[61]. They told him, it is not the category[62]." Because this one is liable because of walking and that one is liable because of putting down. In the opinion of Rav Huna one is not following Ben Azzai[90]. In the opinion of Rav Jehudah one follows neither Ban Azzai nor the Sages[91]. Rebbi Ḥinena said, who is :they said to him"? The Sages who follow Ben Azzai.[92]

83 One continues the discussion of transporting from a private to the public domain or vice-versa through a *karmelit* region. In the Babli (6a), it is a statement of R. Johanan.

84 In G: "It is considered as if".

85 This refers to a person carrying in the public domain. It is a desecration of the Sabbath to carry a load nonstop for at least 4 cubits in the public domain. Since for Ben Azzai every step in walking is considered a stop, it is impossible to carry anything nonstop for 4 cubits. The objection is left without any answer in the Leiden ms., G, and the lengthy quote in *Sefer Ha`ittim* (p. 307). But in Tosaphot (5b, s.v. בשלמא) the Yerushalmi is quoted as answering that a person still could become liable by jumping.

86 In this interpretation, which has no parallel in the Talmudim, anything in the airspace over a *karmelit* is considered lying there.

87 It would seem obvious that the names "Huna" and "Jehudah" should be switched.

But the attributions are identical in the Leiden ms., G, and the lengthy quote in *Sefer Ha`ittim* (p. 307).

88 A similar text is in Tosephta 10:1 (ed. Liebermann).

89 As noted before, the work of transporting consists of lifting, moving, and depositing. If this is done from private to public domain, it is a desecration of the Sabbath. But a combination of two actions, both involving *karmelit* and therefore not creating liability, still does not create liability.

90 Since practice follows the opinion of those who "said to him" in Mishnah *Keritut* 3:4, for Rav Huna it is clear that walking is not considered depositing.

91 Since for Rav Jehudah everybody agrees that walking is considered depositing according to everybody, those who "said to him" seem to be nonexistent.

92 The Tanna R. Yose as explained earlier.

(2c line 46) רְבִּי יוֹחָנָן בָּעֵי. הָיָה עוֹמֵד בִּרְשׁוּת הָרַבִּים וְזָרַק וְקִידֵּם וְקָלְטָהּ. מָהוּ. וְלָאו מַתְנִיתָהּ הִיא. קָלְטָהּ אַחֵר קָלְטָהּ כֶּלֶב אוֹ שֶׁנִּשְׂרָפָה. פָּטוּר. רִבִּי שְׁמוּאֵל בְּשֵׁם רִבִּי זְעִירָא. בְּחוֹטֵף כֵּן. הָא אִם קָלַט חַיָּב. מַה בֵּין נָחָה לָאָרֶץ לְנָחָה לְתוֹךְ יָדוֹ. תַּמָּן לָמָּה הוּא חַיָּב. תַּפָּן הוּא זָרַק וְאַחֵר קִיבֵּל. בְּרַם הָכָא הוּא זָרַק הוּא קִיבֵּל. וּתְהֵא פְשִׁיטָא לֵיהּ שֶׁהוּא פָּטוּר. אִילוּ זָרַק בִּימִין וְהוֹצִיא וְקָלַט בִּשְׂמֹאל שֶׁמָּא אֵינוֹ חַיָּב מִן הָדֵין פִּיו. וּפִיו לָאו כְּאַחֵר הוּא. וְכָא שְׂמֹאלוֹ כְּאַחֵר הוּא. אָמַר רִבִּי יוּדָן. פְּשִׁיטָא לֵיהּ לְרִבִּי יוֹחָנָן שֶׁזָּרַק בִּימִין וְקָלַט בִּשְׂמֹאל שֶׁהוּא חַיָּב. וּמַה צְרִיכָא לֵיהּ. בְּזָרַק בִּימִין וְקָלַט בִּימִין. רַבָּנִין דְּקַיְסָרִין. רִבִּי שַׁמִּי בְּשֵׁם רִבִּי אֶחָא. אֲפִילוּ זָרַק בִּימִין וְקָלַט בִּשְׂמֹאל צְרִיכָה לֵיהּ חַיָּב. אִין תֵּימַר פִּיו. וּפִיו כֵּיוָן שֶׁאֲכָלָהּ כְּאַחֵר הוּא. בְּרַם הָכָא יָדוֹ כְּאַחֵר הוּא. רִבִּי מָנָא בָּעֵי. מֵעַתָּה הוֹצִיא כִּגְרוֹגֶרֶת בִּשְׁתֵּי יָדָיו יְהֵא פָּטוּר מִשּׁוּם שְׁנַיִם שֶׁעָשׂוּ

מְלָאכָה אַחַת. אָמַר לֵיהּ רִבִּי חִייָא בַּר אָדָא. וָדָא הִיא בַּעֲשׂוֹתָהּ. וְלֹא כֵן תַּנֵּי. יָחִיד שֶׁעֲשָׂאָהּ חַייָב. שְׁנַיִם שְׁלֹשָׁה שֶׁעֲשׂוּ פְּטוּרִין.

1 ולאו G | ולא 2 שנשרפה G | שנישרפה זעירא G | זעורא 3 הא G | הוא לנחה G | מה ביו נחה 4 קיבל (2nd time) G | קבל ותהא G | ותְהֵי פשיטא G | פשיטה 6 הוא G | היא פשיטא G | פשיטה ליה | G - 7 בזרק G | בשׂורק אחא G | אחה 8 אין G | או 9 הוא G | היא משום G | משם 10 תני G - שעשאה G | שעשה

Rebbi Johanan asked: If he was standing in the public domain, threw, and then caught it, what[93]? Is that not a Mishnah[94], "if another person caught it, a dog caught it, or it was burned, he is not liable"? Rebbi Samuel in the name of Rebbi Ze'ira: So it is if he snatches; therefore if he caught it he is liable[95]. What is the difference between its coming to rest on the ground to coming to rest in his arm? There[96], why is he liable? There he threw and another one received it but here he threw, he received it[97]. Should it be obvious for him that he is not liable? Would he not be liable because of his mouth[98] if he threw with his right hand and received with his left? Is his mouth not like another person? Here, his left hand should be like another person[99]. Rebbi Yudan said, it is obvious to Rebbi Johanan that he is liable if he threw with his right hand and received with his left. What was his problem? If he threw with his right and and received with his right hand[100]. The rabbis of Caesarea, Rebbi Shammai in the name of Rebbi Aha: He[101] is in doubt whether he is liable even if he threw with his right hand and received with his left. If you want to say "his mouth[98]", his mouth is like another person since he ate it; but is here his hand like another person[102]? Rebbi Mana asked, if this be so, then even if he exported the volume of a dried fig in both hands he should be not liable because of one action executed by two persons[103]! Rebbi Hiyya bar Ada said to him, is that *when he did it*[104]? But was it not stated: An individual who acted is liable, two or three who acted are not liable[105].

93 Transporting something in the public domain for a distance of at least 4 cubits is a desecration of the Sabbath. Therefore, throwing something a distance of at least 4 cubits creates liability the moment the thrown object touches the ground. The question is whether there is liability if the thrower himself runs and catches the object in the air, at a distance of at least 4 cubits from where it was thrown. Babli 5a.

94 Mishnah 11:7. The thrower did not intend to throw it to another person or to a dog; the object was intercepted. Therefore, the original intent was not fulfilled; there is no liability. If the object was burned in flight, there is no putting down; the action is

incomplete and there is no liability even if the original intent was that it should be burned in flight.

95 In the question asked by R. Johanan one has to distinguish whether the original intent was that the object should be caught in flight, when there is liability, or whether the object was snatched in flight against the original intent, when there is no liability.

96 In the Mishnah there is liability if the object is a ball thrown from one person to another and the recipient is supposed to catch the ball.

97 The Mishnah does not directly address R. Johanan's problem.

98 This refers to the explanation given earlier by R. Yudan (Note 67) which shows that receiving an object in his mouth is a valid putting down.

99 And the legal situation depends on the original intent.

100 Throwing from one hand to the other is a normal action but throwing with one hand and receiving with the same has to be classified "as if with the back of one's hand" (Note 80) and automatically exclude liability.

101 R. Johanan.

102 Does it make any difference which hand is used since it always is the same person?

103 Therefore it is not possible to distinguish between hands in these matters.

104 *Lev.* 4:27. The verse is emphatic that purification sacrifices are available only for single perpetrators acting in error: *If one person of the people of the land sin in error, if he act in one of the commandments of the Eternal which is a prohibition, and be damaged.*

105 Babli 3a,5a; *Sifra Wayyiqra I Parashah* 7(9).

(2c line 60) אָמַר רִבִּי יוֹחָנָן. הָיָה עוֹמֵד בִּרְשׁוּת הָרַבִּים וְקָלַט גְּשָׁמִים מֵאֲוֵיר מְחִיצוֹת וְהוֹצִיא. חַייָב. רִבִּי בּוּן בַּר חִייָא בְשֵׁם רִבִּי זְעִירָא. בַּחוֹטֵף כֵּן. הָא אִם קָלַט פָּטוּר. מַה בֵין נָתַן לוֹ אַחֵר מַה בֵין נָתְנוּ לוֹ שָׁמַיִם. אַתְיָיא כְרִבִּי. דְּרִבִּי עָבַד אֲוֵיר מְחִיצוֹת כְּמַמָּשָׁהּ.

הָיָה עוֹמֵד בִּפְנִים וְיָדוֹ מְלִיאָה פֵירוֹת פְּשׁוּטָה לַחוּץ וְקִדֵּשׁ עָלָיו הַיּוֹם אָסוּר לְהַחֲזִירָהּ. רִבִּי אָחָא בְשֵׁם רִבִּי בָּא. כְּמָאן דָּמַר. אָסוּר לְהִשְׁתַּמֵּשׁ בַּאֲוֵיר מְחִיצוֹת. אִית תַּנָּיֵי תַנֵי. מוּתָּר. הֲווֹן בָּעֵי מֵימַר. מָאן דָּמַר מוּתָּר. בְּשֶׁיֵּשׁ שָׁם רוֹחַב אַרְבָּעָה. וּמָאן דָּמַר אָסוּר בְּשֶׁאֵין שָׁם רוֹחַב אַרְבָּעָה. אֲמַר רִבִּי יוֹסֵי בֵּירִבִּי בּוּן. בֵּין זֶה וּבֵין זֶה אָסוּר. כְּמָאן דָּמַר. אָסוּר לְהִשְׁתַּמֵּשׁ בַּאֲוֵיר עֲשָׂרָה. מַיי כְדוֹן. מָאן דָּמַר. אָסוּר. לְמַטָּה מֵעֲשָׂרָה. וּמָאן דָּמַר מוּתָּר. לְמַעְלָה מֵעֲשָׂרָה.

1 מאויר G | מאוויר 2 חייא G | חייא 3 אתייא G | אתייה כד' G | כרבי אויר G | אוויר 4 להחזירה G | להחזיר 5 כמאן G | כמן להשתמש G | לישתמש באויר G | באוויר 6 בעיי G | בעה מאן G | מן 7 יוסי G | יוסה אסור G | - כמאן G | כמן להשתמש G | לישתמש 8 מאן G | מן ומאן G | ומן

Rebbi Johanan said, if somebody was standing in the public domain, collected rain from the airspace of walls and carried it out, he is liable. Rebbi Abun bar Hiyya in the name of Rebbi Ze`ira, it is so if he grabbed it, but if he collected it he is not liable[106]. What is the difference between whether another person gave him or if Heaven gave? It follows Rebbi, for Rebbi made the airspace of walls like their substance[107].

If he was standing inside and his hand full of produce was stretched to the outside when the day became holy he is forbidden to take it back[108]. Rebbi Aḥa in the name of Rebbi Abba: following him who said that it is forbidden to use the space below ten [hand-breadths][109]. There are Tannaim who state, it is permitted. They wanted to say, he who says it is permitted if there was four [cubits] of space; but he who says it is forbidden if there was not four [cubits] of space[110]. Rebbi Yose ben Rebbi Abun said, in both cases (it is forbidden)[111] it follows him who said that it is forbidden to use the space below ten [hand-breadths]. What about it? He who says it is forbidden below ten [hand-breadths]; he who says it is permitted, above ten [hand-breadths][112].

106 The statement of R. Joḥanan is made more precise. If somebody opens his hands to collect raindrops, the rain falls into his hand; he does not lift it. Therefore, if he then moves the rain water in his hand, the motion is not complete; he cannot be liable. It must be that he collects the water actively, by wiping it off a wall or a roof. If then he moves away, the motion is complete and he is liable. Babli 5a.

107 This really refers to another situation. If he stands in a room enclosed by 4 walls, for Rebbi anything which enters the airspace of this enclosure is as if it was at rest on the floor. Therefore anything received in his hand is as if taken up from the floor.

108 He was in a private domain, his hand stretched out to the public domain, and remained so at sundown of Friday evening.

Then the situation is as described in Mishnah 2.

109 Since the numerals are masculine they refer to hand-breadths (טְפָחִים). While in theory private domain extends to an unlimited height, the public domain extends only to a height of 10 hand-breadths. Anything higher is מְקוֹם פְּטוּר "exempt space", where unlimited motion and unlimited transfer to private domain is permitted. Therefore the *baraita* must assume that the outstretched hand was within 10 hand-breadths from the ground.

110 A room of less that four-by-four cubits is *karmelit*, not a private domain. Babli 3b.

111 The word, missing in G, must be deleted as a scribal error since it contradicts the statement which follows.

112 Babli 3b.

(2c line 70) מתני׳. הֶעָנִי חַיָּיב וּבַעַל הַבַּיִת פָּטוּר. רַב יְהוּדָה בְּשֵׁם שְׁמוּאֵל. וְהִיא שֶׁתְּהֵא יָדוֹ שֶׁלְעָנִי בְּתוֹךְ עֲשָׂרָה לַקַּרְקַע. אָמַר רִבִּי זְעִירָא. בְּרָחוֹק מִן הַכּוֹתֶל ד׳. אֲבָל אִם אֵינוֹ רָחוֹק מִן הַכּוֹתֶל אַרְבָּעָה כַּרְמְלִית הוּא. רִבִּי לְעָזָר בְּשֵׁם רִבִּי שִׁמְעוֹן כַּרְסָנָה. בְּשֶׁחָיוּ פָנָיו הֲפוּכוֹת לַפְּלַטְיָא. אֲבָל אִם הָיוּ פָנָיו הֲפוּכוֹת לַכּוֹתֶל כַּרְמְלִית הִיא.

2 זעירא G | זעירא   3 הוא G | היא   לעזר G | ליעזר   4 לפלטיא G | לפלטיה אבל G | -

רִבִּי חִסְדָּא בְשֵׁם אַשִׁי. קָנֶה נָעוּץ בִּרְשׁוּת הָרַבִּים גָּבוֹהַּ עֲשָׂרָה טְפָחִים. הַמִּשְׁתַּמֵּשׁ מִתּוֹכוֹ לִרְשׁוּת הָרַבִּים וּמֵרְשׁוּת הָרַבִּים לְתוֹכוֹ חַיָּיב. רַב אָמַר. תַּרְכּוֹס שֶׁהוּא עוֹמֵד בִּרְשׁוּת הָרַבִּים גָּבוֹהַּ עֲשָׂרָה טְפָחִים וְרוֹחַב ד׳. הַמִּשְׁתַּמֵּשׁ מִתּוֹכוֹ לִרְשׁוּת הָרַבִּים וּמֵרְשׁוּת הָרַבִּים לְתוֹכוֹ חַיָּיב. תַּנֵּי רִבִּי הוֹשַׁעְיָה. מְנוֹרָה שֶׁהִיא עוֹמֶדֶת בִּרְשׁוּת הָרַבִּים גָּבוֹהָה עֲשָׂרָה טְפָחִים וּפִירְחָהּ אַרְבָּעָה. הַמִּשְׁתַּמֵּשׁ מִתּוֹכָהּ לִרְשׁוּת הָרַבִּים וּמֵרְשׁוּת הָרַבִּים לְתוֹכָהּ חַיָּיב. אָמַר רִבִּי מָנָא. לֹא סוֹף דָּבָר מְנוֹרָה. אֶלָּא אֲפִילוּ קָנֶה בִּרְשׁוּת הָרַבִּים גָּבוֹהַּ עֲשָׂרָה טְפָחִים וְטַבְלָה נְתוּנָה בְרֹאשׁוֹ. הַמִּשְׁתַּמֵּשׁ מִתּוֹכוֹ לִרְשׁוּת הָרַבִּים וּמֵרְשׁוּת הָרַבִּים לְתוֹכוֹ חַיָּיב.

1 חסדא G | חַסְדָּא   אשי G | אַסִּי   Here ends the Genizah fragment

Mishnah: "The poor man is liable but the householder is not liable." Rav Jehudah in the name of Samuel: Only if the poor man's hand is within ten hand-breadths from the ground[113]. Rebbi Ze'ira said, if he is distant four [hand-breadths] from the wall. But if he is not distant four [hand-breadths] from the wall, it is *karmelit*[73]. Rebbi Eleazar in the name of Rebbi Simeon Karsanah: If his face was turned towards the public road[43]. But if his face was turned towards the wall it is *karmelit*.

Rebbi Hisda in the name of Ashi[113*]: If a stick stuck in the public domain ten hand-breadths high, anybody who uses anything from in it into the public domain or from the public domain into it is liable[114]. Rav said, a leather container[115] which stands in the public domain, ten hand-breadths high and four wide; anybody who uses anything from in it into the public domain or from the public domain into it is liable. Rebbi Hoshaia stated[116]: "A candelabra which stands in the public domain, ten hand-breadths high and its flower four [wide]; anybody who uses anything from in it into the public domain or from the public domain into it is liable." Rebbi Mana said, not only a candelabra but even a stick stuck in the public domain ten hand-breadths high with a tablet[117] fixed to its head, anybody who uses anything from in it into the public domain or from the public domain into it is liable.

113 Since otherwise he transports from a private to an exempt domain which does not create liability, Note 109.

The quote of the Mishnah is from Mishnah 1. But from the discussion it seems that here starts the discussion of Mishnah 2, "the householder is liable but the poor man is not liable," since R. Ze'ira makes a difference whether the poor man receives the item in *karmelit* or not. But R.

Ze'ira must follow R. Johanan that carrying through *karmelit* does not relieve from liability if the object was lifted in a private and deposited in a public domain. But if the householder lifts an object in his house and deposits it in *karmelit*, he is not liable. This also applies if the poor man is standing close to the house with his face to the house; he stands in *karmelit* (S. Liebermann).

113* As shown by G and the quote later in this Chapter (Note 170) one has to read: Rav Hisda in the name of Assi.

114 As explained later in this paragraph, the top of the stick must be at least four-by-four hand-breadths wide. Since the public domain extends only to a height of ten hand-breadths, the airspace is available for the creation of other domains. A surface of less than four-by-four hand-breadths is not usable; but if it has the minimal size it creates a new private domain and all the prohibitions of transport to and from a public domain do apply. If the surface area is less than the required minimum it is exempt space and all transports to and from it do not create liability; cf. Note 170. Babli 5a, 101a, *Eruvin* 33b.

115 In Mishnah *Kelim* 24:5, the sources read תרבוס which the Geonic Commentary explains as درج "box (for money or jewels)"; the translation follows Maimonides who defines it as a leather box (more appropriate for the text of the Mishnah).

116 Tosephta (ed. Liebermann) 10:7.

117 Latin *tabula*. Cf. *Erubin* 3(3) (21a line 30).

(2d line 8) מְנַיִין לְמַעֲלָה מֵי' שֶׁהִיא רְשׁוּת אַחֶרֶת. רִבִּי אַבָּהוּ בְשֵׁם רִבִּי שִׁמְעוֹן בֶּן לָקִישׁ. וְנוֹעַדְתִּי לָךְ שָׁם וְדִבַּרְתִּי אִתְּךָ מֵעַל הַכַּפּוֹרֶת אֲשֶׁר עַל אָרוֹן הָעֵדוּת מִבֵּין שְׁנֵי הַכְּרֻבִים. וְכָתוּב. אַתֶּם רְאִיתֶם כִּי מִן־הַשָּׁמַיִם דִּיבַּרְתִּי עִמָּכֶם: מַה דִּיבּוּר שֶׁנֶּאֱמַר לְהַלָּן רְשׁוּת אַחֶרֶת אַף דִּיבּוּר שֶׁנֶּאֱמַר כָּאן רְשׁוּת אַחֶרֶת. וַאֲרוֹן לֹא תִשְׁעָה טְפָחִים הוּא. דְּבֵית רִבִּי יַנַּאי אָמְרֵי. וְכַפּוֹרֶת טֶפַח. רִבִּי זְעִירָא בָעֵי. מְנַיִין לַכַּפּוֹרֶת שֶׁהִוא טֶפַח. תַּנָא רִבִּי חֲנַנְיָה בַּר שְׁמוּאֵל. כָּל־הַכֵּלִים שֶׁהָיוּ בַּמִּקְדָשׁ נָתְנָה הַתּוֹרָה מִידַּת אוֹרְכּוֹ וְרוֹחְבּוֹ וְנָתְנָה שִׁעוּר קוֹמָתָן. חוּץ מִן הַכַּפּוֹרֶת שֶׁנָּתְנָה הַתּוֹרָה מִידַּת אוֹרְכָּהּ וְרָחְבָּהּ וְלֹא נָתְנָה שִׁעוּר קוֹמָתָהּ. תְּלַמְּדִינָהּ מִכְּלִי קָטוֹן שֶׁבַּמִּקְדָּשׁ. וְעָשִׂיתָ לּוֹ מִסְגֶּרֶת טֹפַח סָבִיב. מַה כָּאן טֶפַח אַף כָּאן טֶפַח. אוֹ אֵינוֹ אֶלָּא וְעָשִׂיתָ זֵר־זָהָב לְמִסְגַּרְתּוֹ סָבִיב: מַה כָּאן כָּל־שֶׁהוּא אַף כָּאן כָּל־שֶׁהוּא. מַאי כְדוֹן. רַב אָחָא בַּר יַעֲקֹב אוֹמֵר. פְּנֵי. וְאֵין פְּנֵי פָּחוֹת מִטֶּפַח.

1 מי' | ס מעשרה   2 אשר על ארון העדות מבין שני הכרובים | ס -   3 דיברתי | ס דברתי   4 אמרי | ס אמרין   5 זעירא | ס זעורה שהוא | ס שהיא תנא | ס תנה בר | ס בן   6 אורכו ורחבו | ס אורבן ורחבן ונתנה שיעור | ס ושיעור   7 תלמדינה | ס ונלמדינה קטון | ס קטן   9 פחות | ס פחותים

רִבִּי יוֹסֵי בָעֵי. אִילּוּ מִגְדָּל הָיָה עוֹמֵד בְּתוֹךְ הַבַּיִת גָּבוֹהַּ כַּמָּה. שֶׁמָּא אֵינוֹ מוּתָּר לְהִשְׁתַּמֵּשׁ מִתּוֹכוֹ לַבַּיִת וּמִן הַבַּיִת לְתוֹכוֹ. אֶלָּא בְּשָׁעָה שֶׁהָיָה מַרְבֵּעַ לָהֶן אֶת הָרוּחוֹת אָנָן קַיָּימִין. נִיחָא כְמָאן דְּאָמַר. בְּאַמַּת שִׁשָּׁה. בְּרַם כְּמָאן דְּאָמַר. בְּאַמַּת חֲמִשָּׁה. וַאֲרוֹן לָאו שִׁבְעָה טְפָחִים וּמֶחֱצָה הוּא. רִבִּי יַעֲקֹב בַּר אָחָא אָמַר. דְּבֵית רִבִּי יַנַּאי וְרִבִּי שִׁמְעוֹן בֶּן יוֹצָדָק. חַד יָלִיף לָהּ מִן אָרוֹן. וְחוֹרָנָה יָלִיף לָהּ מִן הָעֲגָלוֹת. וְלָא יָדְעִין מָאן יָלִיף לָהּ מִן אָרוֹן וּמָאן יָלִיף לָהּ מִן עֲגָלוֹת.

מִסְתַּבְּרָה דְּבֵית רִבִּי יַנַּאי יְלִיפִין לָהּ מִן אָרוֹן. דְּבֵית רִבִּי יַנַּאי אָמְרִין. וְכַפּוֹרֶת טֶפַח. רִבִּי שִׁמְעוֹן בֶּן יוֹצָדָק יְלִיף לָהּ מִן הָעֲגָלוֹת. רִבִּי זְעִירָא בָעֵי. מְנַיִין לַעֲגָלוֹת שֶׁהֵן גְּבוֹהוֹת עֲשָׂרָה. אָמַר רִבִּי יוֹסֵה. וַאֲפִילוּ תֹאמַר גְּבוֹהוֹת עֲשָׂרָה. וְלֹא כֵן תַּנֵּי רִבִּי נְחֶמְיָה. צַב כְּמִין קַמְרֶסְטָא הָיוּ. אִילּוּ חוֹר בִּרְשׁוּת הָרַבִּים גָּבוֹהַּ עֲשָׂרָה וְרָחָב אַרְבָּעָה. שֶׁמָּא אֵינוּ אָסוּר לְהִשְׁתַּמֵּשׁ מִתּוֹכוֹ לִרְשׁוּת הָרַבִּים וּמֵרְשׁוּת הָרַבִּים לְתוֹכוּ. אֶלָּא בְשָׁעָה שֶׁהָיוּ מוֹשִׁיטִין אֶת הַקְּרָשִׁים מַזּוֹ לָזוֹ תִּרוּטוֹת הָיוּ.

1 יוסי | ס יוסה   3 לאו | ס לא   5 ידעין | ס ידעינן יליף | ס דיליף   ארון | ס הארון יליף | ס דיליף עגלות | ס העגלות   6 יליפין | ס ילפין   ארון | ס הארון   אמרין | ס אמרי   וכפורת | ס ארון תשעה וכפורת   ר' | ס ור'   7 זעירא | ס זעורה   8 ר' | ס בשם ר'   קמרסטא | ס קמרסטה

[118]From where that higher than ten [hand-breadths] is a different domain? Rebbi Abbahu in the name of Rebbi Simeon ben Laqish: *There I shall make My Appearance to you, and I shall speak to you from above the cover (which is on the Ark of the Covenant) from between the two Cherubim*[119]. And it is written, *you have seen that from Heaven I spoke to you*[120]. Since speech mentioned there is from another domain, also speech mentioned here is from another domain. But is the Ark not nine hand-breadths[121]? In the House of Rebbi Yannai they said, the cover was one hand-breadth[122]. Rebbi Ze`ira asked, from where that the cover was one hand-breadth? Rebbi Hananiah bar Samuel stated, for all the vessels in the Sanctuary the Torah gave the measure of length and width, and gave the measure of its height. Except for the cover where the Torah gave the measure of length and width, but did not give the measure of its height. Therefore we shall learn it from the smallest vessel in the Sanctuary, *you shall make for it a frame of one hand-breadth all around*[122]. Since there it was one hand-breadth, so also here one hand-breadth. But maybe it is only *make a golden wreath as its frame all around*[122]? Since there it is a minimal size, so here also a minimal size. What about it? Rav Aha bar Jacob said, *face*. There is no *face* less than a hand-breadth[123].

Rebbi Yose asked, if there were a very high chest standing in a house, would it not be permitted to use anything from in it into the house or from the house into it[124]? But we are dealing when it was indicating to them the geographic directions[125]. This is understandable for him who said, a cubit of six [hand-breadths][126]. But for him who said, a cubit of five hand-breadths? Would the Ark not be seven and one half hand-breadths? Rebbi Jacob bar Aha said, the House of Rebbi Yannai and Rebbi Simeon ben Yoṣadaq. One learns it from the Ark, but the other learns it from the wagons[127]. We do not know who learned it from the Ark and who learned in from the wagons. It is reasonable that the House of Rebbi Yannai learned it from the Ark since the House of Rebbi Yannai said, the cover was one hand-breadth[128]. Rebbi Simeon ben Yoṣadaq learns if from the Wagons. Rebbi Ze'ira asked, from where that the Wagons were ten [hand-breadths] high[129]? Rebbi Yose said, and even if you said that they were ten high, did not Rebbi Neḥemiah state that the Freight Wagons were like a cupola[130]? If there was a hole in the public domain ten deep and four wide, would it no be forbidden to use anything from in it into the public domain or from the public domain into it[131]? But when they were transferring the planks from one to the other they were straight[132].

118 A copy of this paragraph, closer to the original, is in *Sukkah* 1:1 (ט) 51d l. 56. The parallel discussion in the Babli is *Sukkah* 5a. Since the entire discussion is Amoraic, one must conclude that for earlier times the limitation of the public domain to 10 hand-breadths from the ground was tradition not subject to verification from biblical sources.

119 *Ex.* 25:6. The words in parentheses are not in the verse and not in ט; they are added to indicate that the argument is about the Ark.

120 *Ex.* 20:22.

121 1.5 cubits (*Ex.* 25:10).

122 In the Babli, *Sukkah* 5b, this is questioned but in the end accepted. The biblical data do not fit the assertion. The cover was square of surface area 3.75(cubit)^2 (*Ex.* 25:17). The hand-breadth and the cubit are not well defined.. If we take a small hand-breadth of 9 cm, cubit 54 cm, then a cover of one hand-breadth height would have a volume of 98.415 (dm)^3. Since the cover was of pure gold, of specific weight about 19, the total weight would have been 1870 kg. But the total weight of gold contributed for the Tabernacle (*Ex.* 38:24) was 29.25 talents or, on a basis of 12.5 g for the sheqel, about 1097 kg, not to speak of the fact that a weight of almost 1.9 tons would have crushed the wooden ark. All these data were well within the knowledge of antiquity. One has to conclude that they imagined the cover to be hollow.

123 This cryptic statement is explained in the Babli (in the name of Rav Aḥa bar Jacob's teacher Rav Huna) as referring to *Lev.* 16:2 where Aaron is warned not to appear *before the face of the cover* except on the day of Atonement. This implies that the cover was not simply a sheet lying over the ark but had a face, a vertical dimension which is not negligible.

124 It is impossible to say that in general a new domain starts at 10 hand-breadths since it is commonly accepted that a private domain remains such to an indeterminate height. The Ark was standing in the private

domain of the Sanctuary; a reference to it seems to be irrelevant.

125 In the desert, the Ark was traveling in front of the people (*Num.* 10:33) while the Sanctuary was carried in the middle (v. 17). At the resting place, the Ark automatically assumed a West-East direction so that the Sanctuary could be placed around it and the tribes camped correctly in the four directions of the compass (*Num.* 2). The Ark had functions outside the Sanctuary; the reference is legitimate.

126 In Mishnaic times, the building cubit was a standard 6, the vessel cubit 5 hand-breadths. If the Ark was built to vessel standards, it cannot be used to define domains. Whether the vessel standard was used in the Temple is a matter of controversy in the Babli, *Menahot* 98a.

127 In *Ex.* 31:12-18 and 35:1-3 the observation of the Sabbath is emphasized in the instructions for the building of the Tabernacle. One concludes that the work forbidden on the Sabbath is exactly work needed in building or transporting the Tabernacle. The wagons mentioned here are the 6 wagons donated by the tribal chiefs for the transport of the Sanctuary (*Num.* 7:3).

128 The reading of ס is preferable: Nine hand-breadths of the Ark and one of the cover.

129 There are no biblical indications about the height of the wagons' platforms above ground.

130 Greek καμάρα, Latin *camara, -ae, f.* (also *camera*) "arched or vaulted roof or ceiling, distinct from an outer roof".

The wagons are called עֶגְלֹת צָב. Now צָב means "turtle"; from this comes the usual translation "covered wagon", using the image of the domed back of the turtle. The expression really is a technical term "freight-wagon", Accadic *subbum, sūbum*.

131 This is a side remark. A hole in the public domain 10 hand-breadths deep and 4 by 4 wide creates a new domain and is considered a private domain from which nothing may be transported to the public domain. This cannot be derived by comparison either to the Ark or to the wagons.

132 Whether the wagons were covered with a convex covering or not is irrelevant since at the moment of loading the planks and the gobelins of the Sanctuary they were uncovered and certainly had flat loading areas. For the meaning of "straight" for תְּרוּטוֹת cf. Mishnah *Middot* 2:5.

(2d line 33) שְׁנֵיהֶן פְּטוּרִין. רִבִּי יַעֲקֹב בַּר אָחָא בְשֵׁם חִזְקִיָּה רַבָּנָן בְּשֵׁם רִבִּי יוֹחָנָן. מִשֵּׁם שְׁנַיִם שֶׁעָשׂוּ מְלָאכָה אַחַת. רַב שָׁאַל לְרִבִּי. נָתַן לוֹ אֶחָד חֲבִילָה עַל כְּתֵיפוֹ וְשָׁכַח וְהוֹצִיאָהּ. בְּמַחְזוֹרָא תִּנְיָינָא. אָמַר לֵיהּ. חַיָּיב. שֶׁאֵינָהּ דּוֹמָה לְאוֹתָהּ. סָבַר רִבִּי. כֵּיוָן שֶׁעָקַר אֶת רַגְלָיו כְּמוֹ שֶׁעָקַר אֶת הַחֵפֶץ. עַל דַּעְתֵּיהּ דְּרִבִּי. הָיָה עוֹמֵד בִּרְשׁוּת הָרַבִּים וְזָרַק וְקִידֵּם וּקְלָטָהּ לִרְשׁוּת הַיָּחִיד מָהוּ. וְלֹא רִבִּי הוּא. דְּרִבִּי עָבַד אֲוֵיר מְחִיצוֹת כְּמַמָּשָׁן. לֹא צוֹרְכָא דְּלֹא הָיָה עוֹמֵד בִּרְשׁוּת הַיָּחִיד וְזָרַק וְקִידֵּם וּקְלָטָהּ לִרְשׁוּת הָרַבִּים מָהוּ. אַשְׁכַּח תַּנֵּי. רִבִּי פּוֹטֵר עַד שָׁעָה שֶׁתָּנוּחַ.

"Neither is liable.[133]" Rebbi Jacob bar Aha in the name of Ḥizqiah, the rabbis in the name of Rebbi Joḥanan: In the category of two people performing one work[104]. Rav asked Rebbi, if another person put a bundle on his back, when he forgot and brought it out[134]? On the occasion of the second repetition[135] he told him, he is liable because it does not compare to this. Rebbi is of the opinion that when he started to walk it is as if he had taken up the object[136]. In the opinion of Rebbi, if he stood in the public domain and threw but ran and caught it[137] in a private domain, what? But is that not Rebbi since Rebbi made the airspace enclosed by walls like its essence[138]? It is only necessary in case he stood in the private domain and threw but ran and and caught it in a public domain, what? It was found stated: Rebbi declares him not liable until the moment it comes to rest[139].

133 Quote from Mishnaiot 3-4, starting the discussion of these.

134 Is this considered an incomplete action since another person lifted and put the load on him (Babli 3a).

135 The Babli (3b) reports that the question was asked when Rebbi was teaching (or editing) another tractate; it was Rebbi's practice not to answer questions which did not concern the subject he was currently concerned with. He gave the answer only when he took up Mishnah Šabbat another time.

136 If the other person had put the load on him while he was walking, there could be no liability since the action was not that of a single person. But if the load was resting on his back, when he then started walking he started moving the object and this makes the action complete.

137 If this is a question different from the one asked earlier, it must mean that "absorbed it" has to mean that his body absorbed the shock of impact of the object, not that he caught it in his hands.

138 Therefore automatically the action is completed and there is liability.

139 Public domain by definition is not enclosed by walls; an object is at rest only at the moment it stopped moving. If the object fell down because it hit his body, there was no putting down and no completed action.

(2d line 41) אָמַר רִבִּי אָבוּן. רִבִּי וּבֶן עַזַּאי וְרִבִּי עֲקִיבָה שְׁלָשְׁתָּן אָמְרוּ דָבָר אֶחָד. רִבִּי עָבַד אֲוֵיר מְחִיצוֹת כְּמַמָּשָׁן. בֶּן עַזַּאי עָבַד אֲוֵיר כַּרְמְלִית כְּמַמָּשָׁהּ. רִבִּי עֲקִיבָה עָבַד אֲוֵיר רְשׁוּת הָרַבִּים כְּמַמָּשָׁהּ.

Rebbi Abun said, Rebbi, Ben Azzai, and Rebbi Aqiba, all three said the same. Rebbi made the airspace enclosed by walls like its essence[138]. Ben Azzai made the airspace enclosed by *karmelit* like its essence[86]. Rebbi Aqiba made the airspace over public domain like its essence[140].

140 For example in Mishnah 11:1 where he declares that a person throwing from one private domain to another over the public domain is liable, a statement opposed by the majority.

(2d line 42) אַרְבַּע רְשׁוּיוֹת לַשַּׁבָּת. רְשׁוּת הַיָּחִיד רְשׁוּת הָרַבִּים וְכַרְמְלִית וּמְבוֹאוֹת שֶׁאֵינָן מְפוּלָּשִׁין. וְאֵי זֶהוּ רְשׁוּת הַיָּחִיד. חָרִיץ שֶׁהוּא עָמוֹק עֲשָׂרָה וְרָחָב אַרְבָּעָה. וְגָדֵר שֶׁהוּא גָבוֹהַּ עֲשָׂרָה וְרָחָב אַרְבָּעָה. זוֹ הִיא רְשׁוּת הַיָּחִיד גְּמוּרָה. וְאֵי זֶהוּ רְשׁוּת הָרַבִּים גְּמוּרָה. אִסְטְרַטְיָיא וּפַלַטְיָא וּמִדְבָּר וּמְבוֹאוֹת הַמְפוּלָּשִׁין. אֵין מוֹצִיאִין מֵרְשׁוּת הַיָּחִיד לִרְשׁוּת הָרַבִּים וְלֹא מַכְנִיסִין מֵרְשׁוּת הָרַבִּים לִרְשׁוּת הַיָּחִיד. וְאִם הוֹצִיא אוֹ הִכְנִיס שׁוֹגֵג חַיָּב חַטָּאת. מֵזִיד חַיָּב כָּרֵת וְנִסְקָל. אֶחָד הַמּוֹצִיא וְאֶחָד הַמַּכְנִיס אֶחָד הַמּוֹשִׁיט וְאֶחָד הַזּוֹרֵק. יָם וּבִקְעָה וְאִיסְטְוָנָא וְאַסְקוּפָּה וְכַרְמְלִית אֵינָן לֹא רְשׁוּת הָרַבִּים וְלֹא רְשׁוּת הַיָּחִיד. וְאֵין נוֹשְׂאִין וְנוֹתְנִין בָּהֶן וְאִם נָשָׂא וְנָתַן בָּהֶן פָּטוּר.

[141]"There are four kinds of domain on the Sabbath: Private domain, public domain, *karmelit*, and dead-end streets[142]. What is private domain? A ditch ten deep and four wide, or a wall ten high and four wide; this is completely private domain. And what is completely public domain? A street[143], a wide road[43], desert, and passages open at both ends[144]. One does not export from a private to a public domain nor import from a public to a private domain. If somebody exported or imported in error he is liable for a purification sacrifice; intentionally he is liable for extirpation or is stoned[145], whether he exports or imports, or lifts or throws. An ocean, or a valley[73], or a platform[146], or a threshold, or *karmelit*[147] are neither public nor private domain; one does not carry there[148] but if one carried he is not liable."

141 Tosephta 1:1, Babli 6a.
142 In the Babli: "Exempt space". This is what one would expect. Dead-end streets can be either public domain or *karmelit*; their particular status is that by an *eruv* they can be transformed into private domains, whereas passages open at both ends in general cannot. These differences belong to Tractate *Eruvin*.
143 Latin *strata (sc. via)*.
144 It is "completely public" because it cannot be turned into a private domain by a symbolic *eruv*.
145 Desecration of the Sabbath is punishable by Heaven's extirpation if there are no witnesses or nor proper warning was given, and by the courts if there are witnesses both for due warning and the act itself.
146 Latin *stibadium, -ii, n.*, Greek στιβάδιον; a semi-circular couch.
147 Or any other kind of *karmelit*.
148 A rabbinic prohibition of carrying further than four cubits because the *karmelit* looks like public domain.

(2d line 54) אָמַר רַב יוֹסֵף. אַף אֲנָן תַּנֵּינָן כּוּלְּהוֹן. יָם. דְּתַנֵּינָן תַּמָּן. הַזּוֹרֵק בַּיָּם אַרְבַּע אַמּוֹת פָּטוּר. לֹא סוֹף דָּבָר אַרְבַּע אַמּוֹת בַּיָּם. אֶלָּא אֲפִילוּ זוֹרֵק בְּכָל־הַיָּם פָּטוּר. שֶׁכָּל־הַיָּם נִקְרָא כַרְמְלִית. בִּקְעָה. דְּתַנֵּינָן. הַבִּקְעָה בִּימוֹת הַחַמָּה רְשׁוּת הַיָּחִיד לַשַּׁבָּת וּרְשׁוּת הָרַבִּים לַטּוּמְאָה. וּבִימוֹת הַגְּשָׁמִים רְשׁוּת (הַיָּחִיד) [הָרַבִּים] לְכָאן וּלְכָאן. אִם אוֹמֵר אַתְּ. רְשׁוּת הַיָּחִיד לְכָאן וּלְכָאן. לֹא תְהֵא טְעוּנָה הַקָּפַת כְּלִי בְהֵמָה. וְתַנֵּינָן. הִקִּיפוּהָ בִּכְלֵי בְהֵמָה מְטַלְטְלִין בְּתוֹכָהּ. אִסְטְוָנָא. דְּתַנֵּינָן. וְכֵן גְּשָׁרִין הַמְפוּלָּשִׁין מְטַלְטְלִין תַּחְתֵּיהֶן בַּשַּׁבָּת. דִּבְרֵי רִבִּי יְהוּדָה. וַחֲכָמִים אוֹסְרִין. אַסְקוּפָה. דְּתַנֵּינָן. הַמּוֹצִיא אוֹכְלִין וּנְתָנָן עַל הָאַסְקוּפָה. בֵּין שֶׁחָזַר וְהוֹצִיאָן בֵּין שֶׁהוֹצִיאָן אַחֵר. פָּטוּר. שֶׁלֹּא עָשָׂה מְלַאכְתּוֹ בְּבַת אֶחָת. הָא אִם עָשָׂה מְלַאכְתּוֹ בְּבַת אֶחָת חַיָּיב. בֶּן עַזַּאי אוֹמֵר. אֲפִילוּ אִם עָשָׂה מְלַאכְתּוֹ בְּבַת אֶחָת פָּטוּר. כַּרְמְלִית. תַּנֵּי רִבִּי חִיָּיא. כַּרְמֵל. רַךְ מָלֵא. אֵינוֹ לֹא לַח וְלֹא יָבֵשׁ אֶלָּא בֵּינוֹנִי. וְהָכָא אֵינָהּ לֹא רְשׁוּת הָרַבִּים וְלֹא רְשׁוּת הַיָּחִיד אֶלָּא כַּרְמְלִית. אֵי זוֹ הִיא כַרְמְלִית. רִבִּי יָסָא בְּשֵׁם רִבִּי יוֹחָנָן. כְּגוֹן חֲנוּתֵיהּ דְּבַר יוּסְטִינֵי. חָצֵר שֶׁלָּרַבִּים וּמְבוֹאוֹת שֶׁאֵינָן מְפוּלָּשִׁין אִם עֵירְבוּ מוּתָּרִין. וְאִם לֹא עֵירְבוּ אֲסוּרִין.

Rav Joseph said, in fact we have stated[149] all of these. The sea as we have stated there[150]: "One who in the sea throws four cubits is not liable." Not only in the sea four cubits, but even if he throws the entire length of the sea he is not liable, for the entire sea is called *karmelit*[151].

A valley[73] as we have stated[152]: "A valley during the dry season is private domain for the Sabbath but public domain for impurity[153]. During the rainy season it is (private) [public][154] domain for both." If you say private domain for both it should not need surrounding by animals' gear, but we have stated[155]: "If they surrounded it by animals' gear one carries in the interior."

A platform, as we have stated[156]: "And similarly one carries under open bridges on the Sabbath, the words of Rebbi Jehudah; but the rabbis forbid.[157]"

A threshold[158], as we have stated: [81]"If one carries out foodstuffs and puts them on the threshold; whether he or another person then carries it out, he is not liable since the work was not performed in one step." Therefore if the work was completed in one step[89] he would be liable. Ben Azzai said, even if he completed the work at one time he would not be liable.

Karmelit. Rebbi Ḥiyya stated: *karmel* "soft full", neither moist nor dry but average[159]. And here it is neither public nor private domain but *karmelit*. What is *karmelit*? Rebbi Yasa in the name of Rebbi Joḥanan, for example the store of Bar Justinus[160]. A multi-party courtyard and dead-end streets: if there is an *eruv* they are permitted, but if no *eruv* was made they are forbidden[161].

149 While the technical term *karmelit* does not appear in the Mishnah, all the examples enumerated in the Tosephta are found in the Mishnah and the rules can be deduced from Mishnaic quotes.

150 Mishnah 11:5.

151 Since nobody can walk in the sea, it cannot be considered public domain.

152 Mishnah *Taharot* 6:4. The "valley" is agricultural domain accessible only by rural paths, not by a paved road. In the dry season, after the grain was cut and before the fields are ploughed for new seeds, the fields are accessible to everybody. Since there is nothing hidden there, it is like public domain for impurity but since it is not easy of access it cannot be considered public domain for the rules of the Sabbath.

153 Where any question of ritual impurity is resolved by presumption of purity, *Sotah* 1:2 Note 88.

154 The word in parentheses is from the text of the scribe here, the reading in the Mishnah, the quote in the Babli (*Šabbat* 6b, *Bava batra* 123b), and alluded to in *Bava batra* 9:8 (Note 87). The text in brackets is that of the first corrector. It was noted by *Qorban Ha`edah* (as emendation of the Venice text since the ms. was not accessible to this author) and supported by convincing arguments by S. Liebermann (תלמודא דקיסרין p. 17 Note 2, הירושלמי כפשוטו p. 15) and J. N. Epstein (*Tarbiz* 5, 1934, p. 264) that the text of the scribe is correct and the correction a corruption. In the rainy season the fields are sown, the grain is growing, and any trespass by unauthorized persons is criminal. There is no doubt that the fields have the status of private domain both for the Sabbath and for cases of doubt about impurity.

155 Mishnah *Eruvin* 1:8.

A caravan which in the dry season uses a "valley" as camping ground for a stay over the Sabbath is required to turn the fields into a guarded place by arranging the (camel or donkey) loads as a symbolic wall (of 10 hand-breadths height). In the interior then one may carry unrestrictedly. This proves that in the dry season the fields are not private domains in the commonly accepted sense; they are *karmelit*.

156 Mishnah *Eruvin* 9:5.

157 It is supposed that the bridges are not simply a roadway on a flat support but that they have side walls extending somewhat under the roadway so that seen from below they delineate the space under the bridge. The Sages forbid to carry for four cubits or more in the informally defined space but they refrain from imposing liability; this proves that the prohibition is purely rabbinical; the space can be neither private nor public domain.

158 This is a repetition of an earlier text as referred to by the Notes.

159 The same etymology of the quadrilitteral כרמל is given in *Sifra Wayyiqra I Parsheta* 13(8), *Pereq* 15(1).

160 In the Babli (7a) the example is given of a stoa, a roofed domain bounded by pillars. Since such a stoa is a pedestrian mall, not accessible to vehicular traffic; if there is an additional obstacle to free circulation it becomes *karmelit*. S. Liebermann conjectured that the store in question was situated in such a stoa.

161 A domain which is not public by biblical standards can be turned into a

private domain by an *eruv*, "mixing" (of domains), by arranging the potential of a common meal for all interested persons. A genuinely public domain cannot be turned into a private domain. Therefore the domains mentioned as candidates for *eruv* cannot be public domains. They also cannot be private domains since then they would need no *eruv*.

(2d line 64) רִבִּי זְעִירָה בְּשֵׁם רַב יְהוּדָה רִבִּי זְעִירָא בְּשֵׁם רַב חִינָנָא בְּשֵׁם רַב חֲנִינָה. סִימְטִיּוֹת שֶׁבֵּין הָעֲמוּדִים נִידוֹנִין כְּכַרְמְלִית. רִבִּי שְׁמוּאֵל בַּר חִייָה בַּר יְהוּדָה בְּשֵׁם רִבִּי חֲנִינָה. פִּירְחֵי הָעֲמוּדִים נִידוֹנִין כְּכַרְמְלִית. לָכֵן צְרִיכָה בְּגָבוֹהִין שְׁלֹשָׁה. חִייָה בְּרֵיהּ דְּרַב. כָּל-הַמְעַכֵּב דְּרִיסָה בִּרְשׁוּת הָרַבִּים נִידוֹנִין כְּכַרְמְלִית. רַבָּנָן דְּקַיְסוֹרִין אֶמְרִין. אֲפִילוּ קוֹצִין אֲפִילוּ זְכוּכִית. לָכֵן צְרִיכָה בְּשֶׁאֵינָן גְּבוֹהִין שְׁלֹשָׁה.

Rebbi Ze`irah in the name of Rav Jehudah; Rebbi Ze`ira in the name of Rav Hinena in the name of Rebbi Hanina[162]: landings[163] between pillars are judged as *karmelit*[164]. Rebbi Samuel bar Hiyya bar Jehudah[165] in the name of Rebbi Hanina: The flowers[166] of the pillars are considered *karmelit*. There it is necessary that they be higher than three [hand-breadths][167]; Hiyya the son of Rav: Anything which hinders access in the public domain is considered *karmelit*. The rabbis of Caesarea say, even thistles, even glass. This is necessary if they are not three [hand-breadths] high[168].

162 It seems that the correct reading is quoted by Rashba (*ad* 7a): "Za`ir bar Hinena in the name of Rebbi Hanina."

163 Even though the reading סמטיות ("paths", Latin *semita, -ae* f.) is confirmed by Rashba, the translation follows an emendation of *Yefe Enaim*, J. N. Epstein (*Tarbiz* 1(2) p. 135), and S. Liebermann, to read מסטיות (with consonantal first *vaw*), the Galilean form of Babylonian אצטבא used in the parallel 7a (as in *Pesahim* 5:8).

164 Since these are obstacles to free circulation; Note 160.

165 In the Yerushalmi this student of R. Hanina's always is quoted with names of father and grandfather; in the Babli (*Bava mesi`a* 72b) he is quoted as R. Samuel bar Hiyya.

166 The spaces under the capital of a Corinthian pillar which are too close to the pillar to be part of a thoroughfare.

167 The sentence can use some re-arrangement: Anything which hinders access in the public domain because it (or its enclosure) is at least three hand-breadths high is considered *karmelit*.

168 While for Hiyya bar Rav the three hand-breadths rule is always needed (Babli 7a), for the rabbis of Caesarea it is suspended if the place cannot be stepped on.

ŠABBAT CHAPTER ONE

(2d line 75) וְאָמַר רִבִּי יוֹסֵה. אִיסְקוּפָּה שֶׁאָמְרוּ רְחָבָה אַרְבָּעָה וְאֵינָהּ גְּבוֹהָה עֲשָׂרָה. אִין תֵּימַר. גְּבוֹהָה עֲשָׂרָה וּרְחָבָה אַרְבָּעָה. רְשׁוּת בִּפְנֵי עַצְמוֹ הוּא. אִין תֵּימַר. גְּבוֹהָה עֲשָׂרָה וְאֵינָהּ רְחָבָה אַרְבָּעָה. הָדָא דָּמַר רַב חִסְדָּא בְשֵׁם אַסִּי. קָנֶה נָעוּץ בִּרְשׁוּת הָרַבִּים גָּבוֹהַּ עֲשָׂרָה טְפָחִים מוּתָּר לְכָאן וּלְכָאן. וּבִלְבַד שֶׁלֹּא יַחֲלִיף. אֶלָּא כֵן אָנָן קַייָמִין. בְּשֶׁאֵינָהּ לֹא רְחָבָה אַרְבָּעָה וְלֹא גְבוֹהָה עֲשָׂרָה.

אִיסְקוּפָּה שֶׁלִּפְנֵי הַפֶּתַח. אֲחֵרִים אוֹמְרִים. כָּל־זְמַן שֶׁהַפֶּתַח פָּתוּחַ כּוּלָּהּ כִּלְפָנִים. נָעוּל כּוּלָּהּ כַּלְחוּץ. מָה אָנָן קַייָמִין. אִם בִּמְקוּרָה אֲפִילוּ נָעוּל כּוּלָּהּ כִּלְפָנִים. אִם בְּשֶׁאֵינָהּ מְקוּרָה אֲפִילוּ פָּתוּחַ כּוּלָּהּ כַּלְחוּץ. אֶלָּא כֵן אָנָן קַייָמִין. בְּשֶׁחֶצְיָיהּ מְקוּרָה וְחֶצְיָיהּ אֵינָהּ מְקוּרָה. מָהוּ נָעוּל כּוּלָּהּ כַּלְחוּץ. מוּתָּר לְהִשְׁתַּמֵּשׁ מִתּוֹכָהּ לַחוּץ וּמִן הַחוּץ לְתוֹכָהּ. בְּשֶׁהָיָה בַּפֶּתַח חוֹר אָסוּר לְהִשְׁתַּמֵּשׁ מִתּוֹכָהּ לַחוֹר וּמִן הַחוֹר לְתוֹכָהּ. רִבִּי נָתָן אוֹמֵר. נָעוּל כּוּלָּהּ כַּלְחוּץ. פָּתוּחַ חֶצְיָיהּ כִּלְפָנִים וְחֶצְיָיהּ כַּלְחוּץ. וְלֹא כֵן סָבְרִינָן מֵימַר. אַסְקוּפָה אַרְבָּעָה מֵאַחַר שֶׁיִּנָּעֵל הַפֶּתַח כּוּלָּהּ כַּלְחוּץ. אַף כְּשֶׁהַפֶּתַח פָּתוּחַ חֶצְיָיהּ כִּלְפָנִים וְחֶצְיָיהּ כַּלְחוּץ.

And Rebbi Yose[169] said: The threshold about which they spoke is four wide but not ten high. If you would say, ten high and four wide, it is a domain by itself[114]. If you would say, ten high but not four wide, that is what Rav Ḥisda said in the name of Assi: If a stick stuck in the public domain ten hand-breadths high, it is permitted both ways on condition that he not exchange[170]. But we must deal with the case that it is neither four wide nor ten high[171].

A threshold in front of the door; others[172] say whenever the door is open it is entirely inside[173], when it is locked it is entirely outside. What are we dealing with? If it is roofed[174] even when it is locked it is entirely inside, if it is not roofed even when it is open it is entirely outside. But we must deal with the case that it is partially roofed[175] and partially not roofed. What does it mean, when it is locked it is entirely outside? It is permitted for use from it to the outside and from the outside to it. If there was a hole in the door it is forbidden for use from it to the hole and from the hole to it. Rebbi Nathan says, when it is locked it is entirely outside; when it is open it is partially inside and partially outside. And that is what we wanted to say; a threshold of four when the door is locked is entirely outside, also when the door is open it is partially inside and partially outside[176].

169 The parallel in *Eruvin* 1(1), Note 162, shows that the name is Yasa, R. Johanan's student, and not the fifth generation R. Yose.

170 This is the necessary complement to the earlier statement by Rav Hisda, Note 114. The prohibition to use exempt space as an intermediate station in transport from private to public domain is in the Babli 8b; Tosephta 1:6.

171 This text contradicts the prior statement that we are dealing with a domain four-by-four wide but not ten high. In addition, a place in the public domain not four-by-four wide and not ten high is public domain and not *karmelit*. One has to read: "four wide but not ten high" as noted by *Qorban Ha`edah*.

172 Babli 6a,9a. Even though in the Mishnah "others" means R. Nathan, here it cannot mean this since R. Nathan dissents.

173 If the threshold is not 10 hand-breadths higher than the public domain. As Rashba explains (*ad* 9a), since the outside platform is flush with the interior of the house there is no need to rabbinically forbid carrying from the house to the platform. Tosephta 1:6.

174 The entrance to the house is covered by a roof fastened to the house and two outside pillars. There is no reason not to consider this part of the house.

175 There are two possible interpretations. One is that one refers to the entrance to a house where the platform in front of the door extends beyond the roof. The other is that one speaks of the entrance to a dead-end street which was made into a private domain by a log lying horizontally over the entrance which is higher than the public road into which it opens. In that case the log, in order to count as a roof, must be four hand-breadths wide.

176 Because only the space under the roof is counted as part of the house.

(3a line 14) מתני' לֹא יֵשֵׁב אָדָם לִפְנֵי הַסַּפָּר כוֹל'. אֲנַן תַּנֵּינָן. סָמוּךְ לַמִּנְחָה. תַּנֵּי רִבִּי חִיָּיה. סָמוּךְ לַחֲשֵׁיכָה. מַתְנִיתִין צְרִיכָה לְמַתְנִיתֵיהּ דְּרִבִּי חִיָּיה. מַתְנִיתֵיהּ דְּרִבִּי חִיָּיה צְרִיכָה לְמַתְנִיתִין. אִילּוּ תַּנָא רִבִּי חִיָּיה וְלָא תַּנִּינָן אֲנַן הֲוֵינָן אֲמָרִין. לֹא אָמַר אֶלָּא חֲשֵׁיכָה. הָא מִנְחָה לֹא. הֲוֵי צוֹרְכָה לְמַתְנִיתִין. אוֹ אִילּוּ תַּנָא רִבִּי חִיָּיה וְלָא תַּנִּינָן אֲנַן הֲוֵינָן אֲמָרִין. כּוּלְּהוֹן דְּתַנִּינָן מִנְחָה. מִנְחָה. וְכוּלְּהוֹן דְּתַנִּינָן חֲשֵׁיכָה. חֲשֵׁיכָה. מִן מַה דְּתַנִּינְתָהּ מִנְחָה וְתַנִּיתָהּ רִבִּי חִיָּיה רוֹבָה חֲשֵׁיכָה. הָדָא אָֽמְרָה. אֲפִילוּ חֲשֵׁיכָה דְּתַנִּינָן דְּבַתְרָהּ מִנְחָה הִיא.

רִבִּי חֲנַנְיָה בֶּן אֲחוֹי דְּרַב הוֹשַׁעְיָה אָמַר. מַתְנִיתִין בְּעַמֵּי הָאָרֶץ. מִן מַה דְּתַנֵּי רִבִּי חִיָּיה בַּחֲבֵירָיו. רַבָּנָן דְּקֵיְסָרִין אָמְרִין. מַתְנִיתִין כְּרִבִּי יְהוּדָה. מִן מַה דְּתַנֵּי רִבִּי חִיָּיה כְּרַבָּנָן.

Mishnah: "A person should not sit before the barber,"[177] etc. We have stated "close to the afternoon prayers." Rebbi Hiyya stated, close to darkness. Our Mishnah needs Rebbi Hiyya's *baraita* and Rebbi Hiyya's *baraita* needs our Mishnah. If Rebbi Hiyya had stated rather than we, we would have said that he means exactly darkness but not the afternoon prayers. Therefore our Mishnah is necessary. But if Rebbi Hiyya had stated rather than we[178], we would have said that everywhere "afternoon prayers" is stated it means afternoon prayers, and everywhere "darkness" is stated it means darkness. Since we stated "afternoon prayers" and Rebbi Hiyya stated "darkness", this implies that "darkness" stated later refers to the time of afternoon prayers[179].

Rebbi Hananiah the son of Rav Hoshaia's brother[180] said, our Mishnah refers to the vulgar, what Rebbi Hiyya stated to fellows[181]. The rabbis of Caesarea say our Mishnah is following Rebbi Jehudah[182], what Rebbi Hiyya stated follows the rabbis.

177 Here starts the discussion of Mishnah 5.

178 Clearly this must read: "If we had stated but R. Hiyya did not." This is Rav Nissim of Kairuan's reading [י.נ. אפשטין, שני] קטעים מספרי רב נסים בר יעקב, קובץ על יד ג (1939).]

179 The times indicated in Mishnah 6 are no different from those in Mishnah 5 even though the terminology is different. In itself, the expression "the time of the afternoon prayers" is ambiguous. It may denote "the great *Minhah*", the time when afternoon prayers first become possible, half an hour after Noontime, or "the small *Minhah*" when prayers become mandatory, one and a quarter hours before sundown. It is clear that the Yerushalmi identifies "*Minhah*" as "the small *Minhah*". The Babli 9b seems to disagree.

180 A student of R. Ze`ira.

181 Cf. Introduction to Tractate *Demay*. The vulgar are persons following rabbinic rules in general; the fellows follow all detailed rules, in particular those of purity and tithing. As S. Liebermann has noted, the anonymous Yerushalmi as a matter of principle considers the Mishnah and R. Hiyya's Tosephta (which is not the Tosephta in our hands) as complementary whereas named authors tend to consider them as competing systems.

182 In Mishnah *Berakhot* 4:1, R. Jehudah states that afternoon prayers are only permitted until "the small *Minhah*" while the rabbis permit it until nightfall.

(3a line 24) לִפְנֵי הַסַּפָּר סָמוּךְ לַמִּנְחָה עַד שֶׁיִתְפַּלֵּל. לֹא יִכָּנֵס לַמֶּרְחָץ. הַתְחָלַת הַסַּפָּר אֵי זוֹ הִיא. מִשֶּׁיַּתְחִיל לְגַלֵחַ. וְהָתָנֵי. יָשַׁב לוֹ לְגַלֵחַ. בָּאוּ וְאָמְרוּ לוֹ. מֵת אָבִיו. הֲרֵי זֶה מַשְׁלִים אֶת רֹאשׁוֹ. אֶחָד הַמְגַלֵחַ וְאֶחָד הַמִּתְגַּלֵחַ. לֹא אֲתִיָּא אֶלָּא מִשֶּׁיִתְעַטֵּף בְּלוֹנְטִית. הַתְחָלַת הַמֶּרְחָץ אֵי זוֹ הִיא. רִבִּי זְרִיקָן בְּשֵׁם רִבִּי חֲנִינָא אָמַר. מִשֶּׁיַּתִּיר חֲגוֹרוֹ. רַב אָמַר. מִשֶּׁיַּתִּיר מִנְעָלוֹ. כְּהָדָא רִבִּי יְהוֹשֻׁעַ בֶּן לֵוִי הֲוָה יָלִיף שָׁמַע פַּרָשָׁתָה מִן בַּר בְּרֵיהּ בְּכָל עֲרוֹבַת שׁוּבָּא. חַד זְמַן אִינְשִׁי. וְעָאַל מִיסְחֵי בְּהָהֵן דֵּימוֹסִין דְּטִיבֶּרְיָא. וַהֲוָה מִיסְתַּמִּיךְ עַל כְּתַפְתֵּיהּ דְּרִבִּי חִייָא בַּר בָּא. אִינְהַר דְּלָא שָׁמַע פַּרְשָׁתֵיהּ מִן בַּר בְּרֵיהּ וְחָזַר וּנְפָק לֵיהּ. מָה הֲוָה. רִבִּי דְּרוֹסִי אָמַר. סָף הֲוָה. רִבִּי לָעֲזָר בֵּירִבִּי יוֹסֵי אוֹמֵר. שָׁלִיחַ מָנוֹי הֲוָה. אָמַר לֵיהּ רִבִּי חִייָא בַּר בָּא. וְלֹא כֵן אַלְפָן רִבִּי. אִם הִתְחִילוּ אֵין מַפְסִיקִין. אָמַר לֵיהּ. חִייָה בְּנִי. קַלָּה הִיא בְּעֵינֶיךָ.

שֶׁכָּל־הַשֹּׁמֵעַ פָּרָשָׁה מִן בֶּן בְּנוֹ כְּאִלּוּ הוּא שׁוֹמְעָהּ מֵהַר סִינַי. וּמַה טַעֲמָא. וְהוֹדַעְתָּם לְבָנֶיךָ וְלִבְנֵי בָנֶיךָ: יוֹם אֲשֶׁר עָמַדְתָּ לִפְנֵי יי אֱלֹהֶיךָ בְּחֹרֵב.

רִבִּי חִזְקִיָּה רִבִּי יִרְמְיָה רִבִּי חִיָּיא בְשֵׁם רִבִּי יוֹחָנָן. אִם יָכוֹל אַתָּה לְשַׁלְשֵׁל אֶת הַשְּׁמוּעָה עַד מֹשֶׁה שַׁלְשְׁלָהּ. וְאִם לָאו. תְּפוֹשׂ אוֹ רִאשׁוֹן אוֹ אַחֲרוֹן אַחֲרוֹן. מַה טַעֲמוֹ. וְהוֹדַעְתָּם לְבָנֶיךָ וְלִבְנֵי בָנֶיךָ יוֹם אֲשֶׁר עָמַדְתָּ. עַד יוֹם אֲשֶׁר עָמַדְתָּ לִפְנֵי יי אֱלֹהֶיךָ בְּחוֹרֵב. גִּידוּל אָמַר. כָּל־הָאוֹמֵר שְׁמוּעָה מִפִּי אוֹמְרָהּ יְהֵא רוֹאֶה בַּעַל הַשְּׁמוּעָה כְּאִלּוּ הוּא עוֹמֵד כְּנֶגְדּוֹ. וּמַה טַעֲמוֹ. אַךְ־בְּצֶלֶם | יִתְהַלֶּךְ־אִישׁ. כָּתוּב רַב־אָדָם יִקְרָא אִישׁ חַסְדּוֹ וְאִישׁ אֱמוּנוֹת מִי יִמְצָא. רַב־אָדָם יִקְרָא אִישׁ חַסְדּוֹ. זֶה שְׁאָר כָּל־אָדָם. וְאִישׁ אֱמוּנִים מִי יִמְצָא. זֶה רִבִּי זְעִירָא. דָּמַר רִבִּי זְעִירָא. לֵית אֲנַן צְרִיכִין חֲשָׁשִׁין לִשְׁמוּעָתֵיהּ דְּרַב שֵׁשֶׁת דְּהוּא גַבְרָא מְפַתְחָא. אָמַר רִבִּי זְעִירָא לְרִבִּי יָסָא. חָכִים רִבִּי לְבַר פְּדָיָה דְאַתְּ אֲמַר שְׁמוּעָתָא מִן שְׁמֵיהּ. אֲמַר לֵיהּ. רִבִּי יוֹחָנָן אֲמָרָן מִשְׁמוֹ. אֲמַר רִבִּי זְעִירָא לְרִבִּי בָּא בַּר זַבְדָּא. חָכִים רִבִּי לְרַב דְּאַתְּ אֲמַר שְׁמוּעָתָא מִן שְׁמֵיהּ. אֲמַר לֵיהּ. רַב אָדָא בַּר אַהֲבָה אֲמָרָן מִשְׁמוֹ.

"Before the barber close to the time of afternoon prayers unless he had prayed. Nor should one enter a bathhouse.[183]" What is the start of hair-dressing? When he starts cutting the hair. But did we not state, if he sat down to have his hair cut and they came and told him that his father had died, he finishes [grooming] his head, whether it was the person grooming or the one being groomed. It is done only when he is wrapped in the shoulder cloth[184].

[185]What is the start of bathing? Rebbi Zeriqan in the name of Rebbi Hanina said, when he opened his belt[184]. Rav said, when he took off his shoe. As the following. Rebbi Joshua ben Levi was used to hear the lesson of his grandson every Friday. Once he forgot and went bathing in the public baths of Tiberias; he was leaning on Rebbi Hiyya bar Abba's shoulder. He remembered that he had not heard his grandson's lesson, turned around and left. When was this? Rebbi Derosai said, he was anointing himself. Rebbi Eleazar ben Rebbi Yose says, he had taken off his clothes. Rebbi Hiyya bar Abba said to him, did our teacher not teach us "if they started they should not interrupt"? He said to him, Hiyya my son, is that unimportant in your eyes? For anyone who hears the lesson from his grandson is as if he heard it from Sinai. What is the reason? *You shall make it known to your sons and grandsons, the day when you stood before the Eternal, your God, at Horeb*[186].

Rebbi Ḥizqiah, Rebbi Jeremiah, Rebbi Ḥiyya in the name of Rebbi Joḥanan: If you can link the tradition back to Moses, link it. Otherwise, take either the very first or the very last [source][187]. Giddul said, anybody who quotes somebody should consider it as if the author of the quote stood before him. What is the reason? *Only in image a man wanders*[188]. It is written, *many a man professes good will, but where will you find one you can trust*[189]? That is Rebbi Ze`ira[190], as Rebbi Ze`ira said, we do not take the traditions of Rav Sheshet into account since he is blind. Rebbi Ze`ira said to Rebbi Yasa, does the Rabbi know Bar Pedaiah that you quote traditions in his name? He said to him, Rebbi Joḥanan quoted them in his name. [191]Rebbi Ze`ira said to Rebbi Abba bar Zavda, does the Rabbi know Rav that you quote traditions in his name? He said to him, Rav Ada bar Ahavah quoted them in his name.

183 Quote from Mishnah 5.
184 Latin *linteum, i*, n. "towel". Babli 9b.
185 This and the following paragraph are copied somewhat defectively in *Qiddušin* 1:7 (Notes 594-605).
186 *Deut.* 4:10. A slightly different interpretation un the name of R. Joshua ben Levi in the Babli, *Qiddušin* 30a.
187 In a lengthy chain of tradition, the list of intermediaries can be abbreviated.
188 *Ps.* 39:7.
189 *Prov.* 20:6.
190 Who is the only one strictly following Giddul in questioning any tradition where the tradent could not possibly have known personally the person whom he is quoting, a requirement in a purely oral tradition. R. Joḥanan permits only to abbreviate the list of intermediaries, not the last one from whom the speaker heard it.
191 Chapter 14, end (15a line 1).

(3a line 50) וְלֹא לַבּוּרְסְקִי. אִיתָא חֲמִי. בְּדֵילִין מִמִּי שֶׁרֵיחוֹ רַע. וְאַתְּ אֲמַר הָכֵין. לָא אַתְיָא דְלָא מִשְׁיתְלַבֵּשׁ בְּגָדֵי אוּמְנָתוֹ.

וְלֹא לֶאֱכוֹל. הַתְחָלַת אֲכִילָה אֵי זוֹ הִיא. רִבִּי אֲחָא רִבִּי בָּא בְשֵׁם ר'. מִשִּׁיטּוֹל יָדָיו. רִבִּי אַחָא אָמַר. לְקִידּוּשׁ אִתְאֲמָרַת. רִבִּי בָּא אָמַר. לִבְרָכָה אִתְאֲמָרַת. רַב נָסַב לְיָדוֹי. רְמַז חִייָה בְרֵיהּ לִמְזוֹנָא. בָּעָא מִיתֶּן לֵיהּ. אֲמַר לֵיהּ. כְּבָר הִתְחַלְנוּ בִּסְעוּדָה.

דְּלְמָא. רִבִּי מְיָישָׁא וְרִבִּי שְׁמוּאֵל בַּר רַב יִצְחָק הֲווֹן יָתְבִין אֲכְלִין בְּחָדָא מִן כְּנִשְׁתָּא עִלַּיְיתָא. אָתָא עוֹנָתֵיהּ דִּצְלוּתָא. קָם לֵיהּ רִבִּי שְׁמוּאֵל בַּר רַב יִצְחָק מִיצַלְיָיא. אֲמַר לֵיהּ רִבִּי מְיָישָׁא. וְלֹא כֵן אַלְפָן רִבִּי. אִם הִתְחִילוּ אֵין מַפְסִיקִין. וְתָנֵי חִזְקִיָּה. כָּל־מִי שֶׁהוּא פָּטוּר מִן הַדָּבָר וְעוֹשֵׂהוּ נִקְרָא הֶדְיוֹט. אֲמַר לֵיהּ. וְהָתַנִּי. חָתָן פָּטוּר. וְהָתַנִּי. חָתָן אִם רוֹצֶה לִקְרוֹת קוֹרֵא. אֲמַר לֵיהּ. יָכִיל אֲנָא פְתִיר לָהּ כְּרַבָּן גַּמְלִיאֵל דְּאָמַר. אֵינִי שׁוֹמֵעַ לָכֶם לְבַטֵּל מִמֶּנִּי מַלְכוּת שָׁמַיִם שָׁעָה אַחַת׃

1 מייש׳ | ב יסא [192] חוון | ב הוו - | ב מן   2 אתא | ב אתת עניתיה | ב עונתה קם | ב וקם ליה | ב לא

4 והתני | ב והא תנינין¹⁹³ לקרות קורא | ב - יכיל | ב ולא דרבן גמליאל היא. היא. אמ' ליה 5 פתיר לה | ב
פתר 6 שעה אחת | ב -

"Nor the tannery.¹⁸³" Come and look, does one not avoid people who stink? And you say so? It comes only when he puts on his work clothes¹⁹⁴.

"Nor start eating. ¹⁸³" What is the start of eating? Rebbi Aha, Rebbi Abba in the name of Rebbi¹⁹⁵: When he washed his hands. Rebbi Aha said, this was said for *Qiddus*¹⁹⁶. Rebbi Abba said, this was said for the benediction¹⁹⁷. Rav had washed his hands when his son Hiyya gave a sign to the waiter, who wanted to serve him. He told him, we already started the meal¹⁹⁸.

¹⁹⁹Clarification²⁰⁰. Rebbi Miasha and Rebbi Samuel bar Rav Isaac were sitting and eating in one of the upper synagogues. There came the time of prayer and Rebbi Samuel bar Rav Isaac got up to pray. Rebbi Misha said to him, Teacher, did you not teach us that once one started one does not interrupt? And Hizqiah stated, every one who is not under an obligation and does it anyway is called uneducated²⁰¹? He said to him, did we not state, "the bridegroom is not liable²⁰²," "the bridegroom if he wants to recite recites²⁰³." He answered him, I can explain this following Rabban Gamliel who said, "I shall not listen to you to lift from me the Kingdom of Heaven for one moment²⁰²."

192 A scribal error as seen from the sequel.
193 The correct version.
194 A reasonable explanation of this paragraph has been given by S. Liebermann. R. Yose (the Amora) states later in the discussion of Mishnah 5 that one interrupts what one is doing for the recitation of the *Šemaʿ* but not for prayer since the recitation does not need concentration and therefore needs only a short moment whereas prayer requires concentration and a longer interruption. The question raised here is that it is forbidden to recite the *Šemaʿ* (or quote any verse) at smelly places (cf. *Berakhot* 3:5). Since tanning of hides produces bad smell, the tanner cannot recite anything unless he remove himself from his place of work and cleanse himself thoroughly, which consumes more time than people usually spend for prayer. Therefore reciting the *Šemaʿ* for a tanner should follow the rules of prayer and he should not be required to interrupt his work. The answer is that he is required to interrupt only if he already has put on his work clothes but not entered the tannery. The fact is noted in the Babli (9b), the question is not asked.

195 For "Rebbi" read "Rav"; according to Liebermann this is the reading of M. Halawa.

196 It seems that this refers to a discussion reported only in the Babli (*Pesahim* 106b) that Rav allows *Qiddus*, the declaration of the Sanctification of the Sabbath, to be

recited either on wine or on bread. The decision what to do has to be made before the washing of the hands.

197 As soon as one has washed his hands he has to start the meal by reciting the benediction over bread (on a weekday).

198 In Mishnah *Berakhot* 8:2 it is stated that the House of Shammai permit mixing the cup for *Qidduš* after one has washed his hands but the House of Hillel require that the cup be mixed before one washes. Since Rav had washed his hands, he would have been able to recite *Qidduš* over wine only if the wine had been mixed and poured before the washing of the hands when the benedictions over wine and *Qidduš* are not counted as interruption between washing and starting the meal (as in the German *minhag*).

199 This paragraph is a copy of one in *Berakhot* 2:9 (Notes 354-360), ב.

200 Greek δήλωμα, ατος, τό.

201 Greek ἰδιώτης, -ου, ὁ.

202 Mishnah *Berakhot* 2:6.

203 Mishnah *Berakhot* 2:9.

(3a line 62) וְלֹא לָדִין. רַב יִרְמְיָה וְרַב יוֹסֵף. חַד אָמַר. מִשֶּׁיֵּשְׁבוּ לָדִין. וְחוֹרָנָא אָמַר. מִשֶּׁיַּשְׁמִיעוּ טַעֲנוֹתֵיהֶן.

"Nor sit in judgment.[183]" Rav Jeremiah and Rav Joseph. One said, when they sat down to judge; the other said, when they start presenting their arguments[204].

204 Babli 10a in somewhat greater detail. S. Liebermann points out that in the Babli the authors are R. Jeremiah and R. Jonah. (The reading "Rav Jeremiah" is a distortion of the Wilna edition.) Since R. Jonah was the companion of R. Yose the Amora it seems that in both Talmudim one has to read R. Jeremiah (the teacher of RR. Yose and Jonah) and not Rav Jeremiah (bar Abba) of the very first generation of Amoraim, and in the Yerushalmi R. Yose.

(3a line 63) אִם הִתְחִילוּ אֵין מַפְסִיקִין. מַפְסִיקִין לִקְרִיַת שְׁמַע וְאֵין מַפְסִיקִין לִתְפִילָה: אָמַר רִבִּי אֲחָא. קְרִיַת שְׁמַע דְּבַר תּוֹרָה וּתְפִילָה אֵינָהּ דְּבַר תּוֹרָה. אָמַר רִבִּי בָּא. קְרִיַת שְׁמַע זְמַנָּהּ קָבוּעַ. תְּפִילָה אֵין זְמַנָּהּ קָבוּעַ. אָמַר רִבִּי יוֹסֵה. קְרִיַת שְׁמַע אֵינָהּ צְרִיכָה כַּוָּנָה וּתְפִילָה צְרִיכָה כַּוָּנָה. אָמַר רִבִּי מָנָא. קַשְׁיְיתָהּ קוֹמֵי רִבִּי יוֹסִי. וַאֲפִילוּ תֵימָא. קְרִיַת שְׁמַע אֵינָהּ צְרִיכָה כַּוָּנָה. שְׁלֹשָׁה פְסוּקִים הָרִאשׁוֹנִים צְרִיכָה כַּוָּנָה. מִן גּוֹ דְּאִינּוּן צְבָחַר הוּא מְכַוֵּין.

2 ותפילה | בב תפילה   3 יוסה | ב יוסי   ותפילה | בב תפילה   4 מנא | ב מני קשייתה | ב קשיתה קומי | ב קומוי תימא[205] | בב תימר   5 - | ב אינן צריכה | בב צריכין צבחר | בב ציבחר הוא | ב - מכוין | ב מיכוין

רִבִּי יוֹחָנָן אָמַר בְּשֵׁם רִבִּי שִׁמְעוֹן בֶּן יוֹחַי. כְּגוֹן אָנוּ שֶׁעוֹסְקִין בְּתַלְמוּד תּוֹרָה אֲפִילוּ לִקְרִיַת שְׁמַע אֵין אָנוּ מַפְסִיקִין. רִבִּי יוֹחָנָן אֲמָרָהּ עַל גַּרְמֵיהּ. כְּגוֹן אָנוּ שֶׁאֵין אָנוּ עוֹסְקִין בְּתַלְמוּד תּוֹרָה אֲפִילוּ לִתְפִילָה אָנוּ מַפְסִיקִין. דֵּין כְּדַעְתֵּיהּ וְדֵין כְּדַעְתֵּיהּ. רִבִּי יוֹחָנָן כְּדַעְתֵּיהּ. דְּרִבִּי יוֹחָנָן אָמַר. הַלְוַואי מִתְפַּלְלִין כָּל־הַיּוֹם. לָמָה. שֶׁאֵין תְּפִילָה מַפְסֶדֶת. רִבִּי שִׁמְעוֹן בֶּן יוֹחַי כְּדַעְתֵּיהּ. דְּרִבִּי

שִׁמְעוֹן בֶּן יוֹחַי אָמַר. אִילּוּ הֲוֵינָא קָאִים עַל טוּרָא דְסִינַי בְּשַׁעְתָּא דְּאִיתְיְהִיבַת אוֹרַיְתָא לְיִשְׂרָאֵל הֲוֵינָא מִתְבַּע קוֹמֵי רַחֲמָנָא דְּאִיתְּבְּרִי לַהֲדֵין נָשָׁא תְּרֵין פּוּמִין. חַד דִּיהֱוֵי לָעֵי בָּאוֹרַיְתָא וְחַד דִּיִתְעֲבֵיד בֵּהּ כָּל־צוּרְכּוֹי. חָזַר וְאָמַר. מָה אִין חַד הוּא לֵית עָלְמָא יָכִיל קָאִים בֵּיהּ מִן דִּילְטוּרְיָא דִילֵיהּ. אִילּוּ הֲווֹן תְּרֵי עַל אַחַת כַּמָּה וְכַמָּה. אָמַר רִבִּי יוֹסֵה קוֹמֵי רִבִּי יִרְמְיָה. אָתְיָיא דְּרִבִּי יוֹחָנָן כְּרִבִּי חֲנַנְיָה בֶּן עֲקִיבָה. דְּתַנֵּי. כּוֹתְבֵי סְפָרִים תְּפִילִּין וּמְזוּזוֹת מַפְסִיקִין לִקְרִיַת שְׁמַע וְאֵין מַפְסִיקִין לִתְפִילָּה. רִבִּי חֲנַנְיָה בֶּן עֲקִיבָה אוֹמֵר. כְּשֵׁם שֶׁמַּפְסִיקִין לִקְרִיַת שְׁמַע כָּךְ מַפְסִיקִין לִתְפִילָּה וְלִתְפִילִּין וְלִשְׁאָר כָּל־מִצְוֹתֵיהֶן שֶׁלַּתּוֹרָה. וְלֹא מוֹדֵי רִבִּי שִׁמְעוֹן בֶּן יוֹחַי שֶׁמַּפְסִיקִין לַעֲשׂוֹת סוּכָה וְלַעֲשׂוֹת לוּלָב. וְלֵית לֵיהּ לְרִבִּי שִׁמְעוֹן בֶּן יוֹחַי. הַלֹּמֵד לַעֲשׂוֹת וְלֹא הַלֹּמֵד שֶׁלֹּא לַעֲשׂוֹת. שֶׁהַלֹּמֵד שֶׁלֹּא לַעֲשׂוֹת נוֹחַ לוֹ אִילּוּ לֹא נִבְרָא. אָמַר רִבִּי יוֹחָנָן. הַלֹּמֵד שֶׁלֹּא לַעֲשׂוֹת נוֹחַ לוֹ אִילּוּ נֶהֶפְכָה שְׁלָיָיתוֹ עַל פָּנָיו וְלֹא יָצָא לָעוֹלָם. טַעֲמֵיהּ דְּרִבִּי שִׁמְעוֹן בֶּן יוֹחַי. זֶה שִׁינּוּן וָזֶה שִׁינּוּן. וְאֵין מְבַטְּלִין שִׁינּוּן מִפְּנֵי שִׁינּוּן. וְהָא תַנֵּינָן. הַקּוֹרֵא מִכָּן וְאֵילָךְ לֹא הִפְסִיד. כְּאָדָם שֶׁהוּא קוֹרֵא בַתּוֹרָה: הָא בְעוֹנָתָהּ חֲבִיבָה הִיא יוֹתֵר מִדִּבְרֵי תוֹרָה. אָמַר רִבִּי יוּדָן. רִבִּי שִׁמְעוֹן בֶּן יוֹחַי עַל יְדֵי שֶׁהָיָה חָדִיד בְּדִבְרֵי תוֹרָה לְפִיכָךְ אֵינָהּ חֲבִיבָה עָלָיו יוֹתֵר מִדִּבְרֵי תוֹרָה. אָמַר רִבִּי בָּא מָרֵי. לֹא תַנִּינָן אֶלָּא. כְּאָדָם שֶׁהוּא קוֹרֵא בַתּוֹרָה: הָא בְעוֹנָתָהּ כְּמִשְׁנָה הִיא. רִבִּי שִׁמְעוֹן בֶּן יוֹחַי כְּדַעְתֵּיהּ. דְּרִבִּי שִׁמְעוֹן בֶּן יוֹחַי אָמַר. הָעוֹסֵק בַּמִּקְרָא מִידָּה שֶׁאֵינָהּ מִידָּה. וְרַבָּנָן עֲבָדִין מִקְרָא כְּמִשְׁנָה.

1 אמ' | ב ב - שעוסקין | ב שאנו עוסקין 2 שאין אנו | ב שאנו עוסקין 3 דין | ב דן ודין | ב ודן 4 הלואי | ב וולואי ב הלווי מתפללין | ב שמתפלל אדם תפילה | ב התפילה 5 הוינא | ב הווינא בשעתא | ב בשעתה דאיתייהיבת | ב דאיתיחיבת אוריתא | ב תורה ב אורייתה 6 מתבע | ב מתבעי ב מתביע קומי | ב קומוי מן קומו דאיתברי | ב דיתברי ב דייתברי להדין | ב - ב להדן לבר נשא | ב ברנשה פומין | ב פמין דיהוי | ב יהוי באוריתא | ב אוריתה 7 דיתעביד | ב דעביד ב דיהוי ביה עביד בה | ב ליה ב ביה צורכוי | ב צורכיה ומר | ב ואמר מה | ב ומה יכיל | ב יכול קאים | ב קאם דילטוריא | ב דליטורייה 8 דיליה | ב דידיה תרי | ב תרין ב תריין וכמה | ב ואחת כמה יוסה | ב יוסי קומי | ב קומוי אתייא | ב אתיא ב אתיה יוחנן | ב יוחנן ב חנניה 9 חנניה בן עקיבה | ב חנינא בן עקיבה ב חנניה בן עקיבה תפילין | ב תפילים 10 מפסיקין | ב מפסיקים חנניה בן עקיבה | ב חנינא בן עקיבה ב חנניה בן עקביה[206] 11 ולתפילין | ב ולתפילים 12 לעשות | ב על מנת לעשות ב לעשות לו ליה לר' | ב ר' ולא | ב לא 13 אילו | ב לו אמ' | ב ואמ' שלא לעשות | ב - 14 אילו | ב שאילו שלייתו | ב שליתו על פניו | ב מלפניו טעמיה | ב לעולם טע' זה | ב זהו וזה | ב וזהו 15 מבטלין | ב מבטל מכאן ואיל | ב מיכן והלך לא הפסיד | ב ולא הספיק[207] 17 היא יותר | ב - ב היא יותר - | ב היא היא 18 חדיד | ב ב תדיר[208] יותר | ב יותר בא | ב אבא 20 העוסק | ב העסק העוסקין ורבנן | ב ורבנין עבדין | ב עבדי

[209]"One interrupts for the recitation of the *Shemaʿ* but not for prayer[183]." Rebbi Aḥa said, the recitation of *Shemaʿ* is a Biblical obligation; prayer is not a Biblical obligation. Rebbi Abba said, the time for the recitation of the *Shemaʿ* is fixed, the time for prayer is not fixed. Rebbi Yose said, the recitation of *Shemaʿ* does not need concentration, prayer needs concentration. Rebbi Mana said: I objected before Rebbi Yose: Even if you say that the recitation of the *Shemaʿ* does not need concentration, the first three verses need concentration. Since there are so few, one will concentrate.

Rebbi Johanan said in the name of Rebbi Simeon ben Yohai: "For example we, who are engaged in the study of Torah, do not interrupt even for the recitation of the *Shema`*." Rebbi Johanan used to say about himself: "For example we, who are not engaged in the study of Torah, do interrupt even for prayer.[210]"

This one follows his own opinion and that one follows his own opinion. Rebbi Johanan follows his own opinion since Rebbi Johanan said, if only a man prayed the entire day. Why? Because prayer is never in vain.

Rebbi Simeon ben Yohai follows his own opinion since Rebbi Simeon ben Yohai said, if I had stood at Mount Sinai at the moment that the Torah was given to Israel, I would have implored the All-Merciful that He should create two mouths for a man; one for him to exert himself in Torah, and the other one for his needs. But he changed and said, with one mouth already the world almost cannot exist because of the denunciations[211]; if there were two how much more would there be?

Rebbi Yose said before Rebbi Jeremiah: The position of Rebbi Johanan is identical with that of Rebbi Hananiah ben Aqiba, as we have stated: "The scribes of Torah scrolls, *Tefillin*, and *Mezuzot*, do interrupt for the recitation of *Shema`* but do not interrupt for prayer. Rebbi Hananiah ben Aqiba[212] said, just as they interrupt for *Shema`*, so they interrupt for prayer, *Tefillin*, and all other commandments of the Torah."

Would not Rebbi Simeon ben Yohai agree that one interrupts to make a *sukkah* or a *lulav*? Does not Rebbi Simeon ben Yohai make the distinction between one who studies to do and one who studies in order not to do? Because he who studies in order not to do would have been better off had he not been born[213]. And did not Rebbi Johanan say, he who studies in order not to do would have been better off if the placenta he was in was twisted around and he never would have entered the world? The reason of Rebbi Simeon ben Yohai is that this one is repeated study and that one is repeated study and one does not push aside one study for the other study. But did we not state[214]: "He who reads after that did not lose, he is like a man reading in the Torah"? Hence, at the right time it is preferred to Torah. Rebbi Yudan said that Rebbi Simeon ben Yohai, since he was enjoying studying Torah, did not prefer

Shema' to the study of Torah. Rebbi Abba Mari said, did we not state: "He is only like a man studying Torah." Hence, at the right time it is like Mishnah. Rebbi Simeon ben Yoḥai follows his own opinion since Rebbi Simeon ben Yoḥai said, he who studies the written Torah does himself good that is not so good. But the rabbis equate the study of the Bible with that of the oral law[215].

205 A Babylonism.
206 This is the correct reading (Babli *Sukkah* 26a).
207 A scribal error.
208 There exists an additional Genizah fragment of *Berakhot* and some quotes of Medieval authors in *Berakhot* reading חדיד, but the reading common to ב ב (and the Rome ms.) seems preferable (against Liebermannn's opinion).
209 There exists a parallel text in *Berakhot* 1:5 (Notes 163-175) available both in the Leiden ms. (ב) and a Genizah text edited by L. Ginzberg (ב) שרידי הירושלמי pp. 4-5.

Where these two sources concur, their text seems preferable.
210 An interesting variant is in ב: "Even though we are engaged in the study of Torah, we do interrupt even for prayer." The version of the text here is adopted by the Babli, 11a.
211 Latin *delator, -oris*, m. "informant".
212 With the parallel sources read "Aqabiah".
213 Babli *Berakhot* 17a; *Lev. r.* 35(6), *Sifra Behuqqotai* Introduction (5).
214 Mishnah *Berakhot* 1:5.
215 Babli *Bava mesi'a* 33a.

(3b line 21) מתני' לא יצא החייט במחטו סמוך לחשיכה שמא ישכח ויצא כול'. תני. לא יצא החייט במחט שבכליו. ולא הלבלר בקולמוס שבאזנו. ולא הצבע בדיגמא שבאזנו. ולא השולחני בדינר שבאזנו. ואם יצא הרי אילו פטורין. דברי רבי מאיר. רבי יהודה אומר. אומן דרך אומנתו חייב. הא שאר כל־אדם יוצאין בכך. מחלפה שיטתיה דרבי מאיר. דתנינן תמן. יצאת חייבת חטאת. דברי רבי מאיר. וכא הוא אמר הכין. רבי מנא אמר לה סתם. רבי אבון בשם רבי יוחנן. תמן דרך הוצאה בנשים. ברם הכא הרי טפילין יוצאין בכך. מחלפין שיטתין דרבנן. דתנינן תמן. וחכמים פוטרין בכובלת ובצלוחית של פילייטון. הא במחט נקובה חייב. הדא היא אומן באומנתו חייב. אמר רבי יוסי בר אבון. תיפתר באשה גדלת.

Mishnah: "A tailor should not leave with his needle close to sundown lest he forget and leave,"[216] etc. It was stated[217]: "A tailor should not leave with a needle in his garment[218], nor a scribe[218a] with the pen behind his ear, nor a dyer with a sample behind his ear[219], nor a money-changer with a denar behind his ear. If one of these left they are not liable, the words of Rebbi Meïr[220]. Rebbi Jehudah says, a craftsman in the ways of his craft is liable[221], therefore everybody else[222] may leave with one of these."

The argument of Rebbi Meïr seems inverted, as we have stated there[223]: "If she left she is liable, the words of Rebbi Meïr," and here he says so? Rebbi Mana said it without attribution, Rebbi Abun in the name of Rebbi Joḥanan: There women usually do it, but here only children leave with this[224]. The argument of the rabbis seems inverted, as we have stated there[223]: "But the Sages declare not liable with a plate of make-up or a flask of perfume[225]." Therefore with a needle with ear she is liable[226]. Is that a craftsman who is liable in the way of his craft[227]? Rebbi Yose ben Abun said, explain it for a woman hairdresser[228].

216 Quote from Mishnah 6. The entire paragraph is repeated in Chapter 6, on Mishnah 3.

217 Tosephta 1:8; Babli 11b.

218 Friday afternoon he should not leave his work place and go into the public domain lest he carry his tool with him once the Sabbath starts.

218a Latin *libellarius, -ii, m.*

219 He carries a sample (Greek δεῖγμα) of his work with him to show potential customers.

220 Since they did not take up the tools of their trade with the intent of carrying them on the Sabbath, there is no complete work even if they fail to remove them and while they sinned they are not liable criminally or for a sacrifice.

221 He holds that a professional takes up his tools for any use he may find for them; therefore for him the work always is complete.

222 A non-professional may leave his house on Friday afternoon with a tool that is not of his trade for even if he did forget to lay it down before sunset he would not be liable.

223 Mishnah 6:3: A woman may not leave (on the Sabbath, from a private domain into the public one) with a needle that has an ear; if she left . . ." A needle with an ear is used for sewing. Since every woman sews, she is a professional and R. Meïr should declare her not liable following his opinion in the Tosephta.

224 Since all women are sewing, the rule of the professional does not apply. But professionals do not carry the tools of their trade on the Sabbath, only their small children play adults with these tools or toy imitations on the Sabbath.

225 Latin *foliatum, -ii, n., scil. unguentum*, unguent or oil made of the leaves of spicenard..

226 As S. Liebermann points out, the text in Chapter 3 reads "with a needle *without* ear she is liable." This must refer to a pin which is not a decoration.

227 Since we follow the rule that in a dispute between R. Meïr and R. Jehudah practice follows R. Jehudah, the Sages here are identical with R. Jehudah in the Tosephta. Since a pin is not a universal tool of women, why should she be liable for carrying a pin under the craftsmen's rule?

228 The verb גָדַל means "to braid". The

hairdresser uses a pin to separate strands of unwashed hair of her clients which cling together. This is a tool of trade.

(3b line 33) מתני׳. וְלֹא יָפְלֶה אֶת כֵּלָיו וְלֹא יִקְרָא לְאוֹר הַנֵּר כול׳. אֲפִילוּ בָחוֹל אָסוּר. שֶׁאֵינוֹ דֶרֶךְ כָּבוֹד. תַּנֵּי. הַמְפַלֶּה אֶת כֵּלָיו נוֹטֵל וְזוֹרֵק וּבִלְבַד שֶׁלֹּא יִמְלוֹל. אַבָּא שָׁאוּל אוֹמֵר. מוֹלֵל וְזוֹרֵק וּבִלְבַד שֶׁלֹּא יַהֲרוֹג. חִזְקִיָּה אָמַר. הַהוֹרֵג כִּינָּה בַשַׁבָּת כְּהוֹרֵג גָּמָל. שְׁמוּאֵל מְקַטֵּעַ יָדֶיהָ וְרִיגְלָהּ וְיָהֵב לָהּ קוֹמֵי מַיִינוּקָה. רִבִּי יוֹסֵי בֵּירִבִּי בּוּן יָהִיב לִי גּוּ צְלוֹחִיתָא. אָמַר רִבִּי שִׁמְעוֹן בֶּן חֲלַפְתָּא. וְלֹא מֵחֲלָזוֹן שָׁמַעְנוּ. וַחֲלָזוֹן יֵשׁ לוֹ גִידִים וַעֲצָמוֹת. וְלֹא כֵן תַּנֵּי. כָּל־דָּבָר שֶׁאֵין לוֹ גִידִים וַעֲצָמוֹת אֵינוֹ חַי יוֹתֵר מְשִׁישָׁה חֳדָשִׁים. דָּמַר רִבִּי יוֹסֵי בֵּירִבִּי בּוּן בְּשֵׁם רַב זְבִיד. אַחַת לְשֶׁבַע שָׁנִים הַקָּדוֹשׁ בָּרוּךְ הוּא מַחֲלִיף אֶת עוֹלָמוֹ. קָמְקָמָה מִיתְעֲבֵיד חוּ רַב פדה. חוּ אפר מִתְעֲבֵיד שר. מִימִיתָא דְרֵישָׁא מִיתְעֲבֵיד עַקְרָב. ודמנייא סממי. תּוֹלַעְתָּא דְסוּסְיָא מִתְעַבְדָא אוֹרְעִי. וּדְתוֹרְתָא דבַרי. צָבוּעַ הַזָּכָר נַעֲשָׂה נְקֵיבָה. עַכְבְּרָא דְטוּרָא מִתְעֲבֵיד חֲזִיר בָּר. שִׁיזְרְתָא דְנוּנָא מִיתְעֲבֵיד נָדָל. וּדְבַר נָשָׁא חִיוִי. אֵימָתַי. בִּזְמַן שֶׁאֵינוֹ כּוֹרֵעַ כָּל־קוֹמָתוֹ עַד הַשִּׁזְרָא.

Mishnah[216] "He should not check his garments for lice nor read by candlelight," etc. Even on weekdays it is forbidden since it is not decent[229]. It was stated[230]: One who checks his garments takes and throws away; only he should not rub[231]. Abba Shaul says, he may rub and throw away, only he should not kill. Ḥizqiah said, one who kills a louse is like one who kills a camel[232]. Samuel broke off its hands and feet and gave if to the children[233]. Rebbi Yose ben Rebbi Abun put it in a flask[234]. Rebbi Simeon ben Ḥalafta said, did we not understand this from the purple snail? Does the purple snail have sinews and bones? But was it not stated: Any which has neither sinews nor bones does not live more than six months[235]? For Rebbi Yose ben Rebbi Abun said in the name of Rav[236] Zevid, the Holy One, praise to Him, turns around His world once in seven years[237]. [238]*Qamqama* turns into *Ḥu-Rav-Padah*. *Har-Efer* turns into *Šer*. The head louse turns into a scorpion and the one of garments into a lizard. A horse worm turns into a wasp, that of cattle into a bee. A male hyena turns into a female, a field rat turns into a wild boar. The spine of a fish turns into a centipede, of a human into a snake. When? If he does not bow down with his entire spine[239].

229 It seems that one should read with the Tosephta (16:22 ed. Liebermann) "On weekdays it is forbidden in public". Opposed in the Babli 12a by Rav Huna.

230 Babli 12a, Tosephta (16:22 ed. Liebermann). In these sources the statements of the anonymous Tanna and Abba Shaul are switched.

231 If he caught a louse, he should throw it away and not kill it by rubbing it between thumb and a finger.

232 Babli 12a, in the name of the Tanna R. Eliezer. Since mammals were slaughtered in the Tabernacle, killing a mammal on the Sabbath certainly is a capital crime. Babli 107b.

233 Since underage children do not have religious obligations, they may kill lice with impunity. The Babli, 12a, reports the same from R. Nahman.

234 To kill the lice after the end of Sabbath.

235 While murder is always forbidden, killing a person who according to medical science does not have 12 months to live is not prosecutable. On the other hand, purple dye was used in creating the priestly vestments and the gobelins of the Tabernacle; therefore killing a purple snail for the production of dye is a capital crime. If a louse does not live a full year, killing it is a capital crime according to the second argument and does not create liability by the first. The two rules appear to be inconsistent. Cf. Babli *Hulin* 58a.

236 Red: Rebbi.

237 While a louse *qua* louse cannot live a full year, it may morph into something which can; therefore killing it is forbidden on the Sabbath.

238 These sentences are difficult to understand. There exists a parallel in the Babli *Bava qamma* 16a where R. Hananel quotes the Yerushalmi *in extenso*:

ר' יוסי ב"ר בון בשם ר' זביד אחת לשבה הקב"ה מחליף עולמו ממוחו דרישא מתעבד עקרב ודמעיא סממה תולעתא דסוסיא מתעבדא עוראי. ודתורתא מתעבדא דברי עכברא דתעבד מתעבד חזיר בר. שיזורתא דנונא מתעבדא נדל. דתניא צבוע זכר לאחר ז' שנים נעשה ערפד לאחר ז' שנים נעשה קימוש. קימוש לאחר ז' שנים נעשה חיה ויש אומרים חוה חוה לאחר ז' שנים נעשה שד שדרתו של אדם לאחר ז' שנים נעשה נחש והני מילי בההוא דלא כרע במודים.

Rebbi Yose ben R. Abun in the name of R. Zevid: the Holy One, praise to Him, turns around His world once in seven years. The marrow in the head becomes a scorpion and that of innards a lizard. A horse worm turns into a wasp, that of cattle into a bee. The spine of a fish turns into a centipede. As is stated, a male hyena after seven years turns into a bat, a bat after seven years turns into a hedgehog, a hedgehog after seven years turns into a wild animal; some say a snake. A snake after seven years turns into a demon. A human's spine after seven years turns into a snake; this refers to one who does not bow down at "we thank".

Since all words in this version are identifiable, it has to be considered as *lectio facilior*. In the original version, קמקמה is unidentified (unlikely قمقام "moth"). Kohut proposes Farsi خمخم "crab". Liebermann reads קמוסא "hedgehog". The three words חו רב פדה should be read as one, חרפדה which is the same as ערפד "bat", חר אפר again is a corruption of the same word. דמנייא seems to be a corruption of the word דמעיא quoted by R. Hananel. Also שר seems a misreading for שד "demon".

The last sentence refers to the penultimate benediction in the *Amidah*, the main prayer, where one is required to bow down while reciting "we are thanking You". This last statement is quoted in many Medieval liturgical tractates, starting with R. Amram Gaon's *Siddur*.

(3b line 47) תַּנֵּי רִבִּי חִיָּיה. אֲבָל מִסְתַּכֵּל הוּא מַה שֶּׁבְּכוֹס וּמַה שֶׁבִּקְעָרָה וְאֵינוֹ חוֹשֵׁשׁ. אִית דְּבָעֵי מֵימַר. שֶׁהוּא לְשָׁעָה. וְאִית דְּבָעֵי מֵימַר. מִפְּנֵי הַנְּקִיּוּת וּמִפְּנֵי הַסַּכָּנָה. מַה נְפִיק מִבֵּינֵיהוֹן. לְקַנֵּב חִיזְרִין. מַה דָּמַר. שֶׁהוּא לְשָׁעָה. אָסוּר. וּמַה דָּמַר. מִפְּנֵי הַנְּקִיּוּת וּמִפְּנֵי הַסַּכָּנָה. מוּתָּר. רַב יִרְמְיָה סָלַק לְגַבֵּי רַבָּסִי. מְזַג לֵיהּ כָּסָא. שָׁרֵי מִסְתַּכֵּל בֵּיהּ. אָמְרָה לֵיהּ בְּנֵי בֵּיתֵיהּ. חֲמִי מַה הוּא עָבִיד. אָמַר לָהּ. דְּהוּא נָהוּג בְּשִׁיטָתֵיהּ דְּרַבּוֹ. דְּתַנֵּי רִבִּי חִיָּיה. מִסְתַּכֵּל הוּא מַה שֶּׁבְּכוֹס וּמַה שֶׁבִּקְעָרָה וְאֵינוֹ חוֹשֵׁשׁ.

Rebbi Ḥiyya stated: But one may investigate what is in the cup or the pot without worry[239]. Some want to say, because it is for a short time[240]; but some want to say because of cleanliness or danger[241]. What is the difference between them? To separate lettuce leaves[242]. For him who says, because it is for a short time, it is forbidden. For him who says, because of cleanliness or danger, it is permitted. Rav Jeremiah[243] visited Rav Assi, who mixed a cup for him. He started inspecting it. His house companion[244] said to him, look what he is doing! He told her, because he follows his teacher's[245] argument, as Rebbi Ḥiyya stated: But one may investigate what is in the cup or the pot without worry.

239 Babli 12b. While the Mishnah forbids investigating one's garments for lice Friday nights, he permits investigating food.
240 A cursory inspection will not lead one to move a candle.
241 To inspect food for worms or other contamination is a biblical obligation which has precedence over rabbinic prohibitions.
242 To prepare lettuce, the leaves have to be washed and/or inspected for worms and snails. This takes time.

243 The Babylonian Rav Jeremiah bar Abba, student and colleague of Rav who was nephew and student of R. Ḥiyya. Babli 12b.
244 Rav Assi's wife.
245 Rav. In the Babli, it was Rav Jeremiah's servant who inspected the cup; in that version רביה has to be translated "his master" with no reason indicated why Rav Jeremiah should follow R. Ḥiyya.

(3b line 54) וְלֹא יִקְרָא לְאוֹר הַנֵּר. שְׁמוּאֵל אֲמַר. לֹא שָׁנוּ אֶלָּא אֶחָד. הָא שְׁנַיִם מֵאַחַר שֶׁיְּכוֹלִין לִמְחוֹת זֶה עַל יְדֵי זֶה מוּתָּר. מַתְנִיתָא דִשְׁמוּאֵל פְּלִיגָא עֲלוֹי. אֶחָד הַנֵּר שֶׁהוּא יָכוֹל לְהַטּוֹתוֹ וְאֶחָד הַנֵּר שֶׁאֵינוֹ יָכוֹל לְהַטּוֹתוֹ. עוּלָא בַּר יִשְׁמָאֵל בְּשֵׁם רִבִּי לְעָזָר. אֲפִילוּ כַּמָּה. עַל דַּעְתֵּיהּ דְּרִבִּי לְעָזָר אֲפִילוּ גָבוֹהַּ כַּמָּה. אֲפִילוּ נָתוּן בְּבַיִת אֶחָד. אֲפִילוּ נָתוּן בִּסְפֵּיקוּלָה.

"Nor read by candlelight"[216]. Samuel said, they stated that only for a single person[246]. Therefore for two, who can hinder one another, it is permitted. Samuel's *baraita*[247] disagrees with him: "Both a light which he can turn as one which he cannot turn." Ulla bar Ismael in the name of Rebbi Eleazar: Even many. In the opinion of Rebbi Eleazar even if it[248] is very high, even if it is in (one)[249] house, even if it is on a look-out[250].

246 A single person may not do anything which might lead him to move a burning light (Note 5), two people who can warn one another if one be tempted to touch the light may read together.
247 Tosephta 1:11. This characterizes the Tosephta as Babylonian.
248 If the burning light is out of reach of the person who is reading.
249 With the Tosephta read אַחֵר "another".
250 Latin *specula, -ae, f.*

(3b line 60) תַּנֵּי. שֶׁמָּא יִשְׁכַּח וְיַטֶּה. אָמַר רִבִּי יִשְׁמָעֵאל. אֲנִי אֶקְרָא וְלֹא אַטֶּה. וְשָׁכַח וְהָיָה קָרוֹב לְהַטּוֹת. וְאָמַר. גְּדוֹלִים הֵן דִּבְרֵי חֲכָמִים שֶׁאָמְרוּ. שֶׁמָּה יִשְׁכַּח וְיַטֶּה. רִבִּי נָתָן אוֹמֵר. הִיטָּה אוֹתוֹ מַמָּשׁ. וְכָתַב עַל פִּנְקְסוֹ וְאָמַר. יִשְׁמָעֵאל בֶּן אֱלִישָׁע הִיטָה הַנֵּר בַּשַּׁבָּת. לִבְשֶׁיִּבָּנֶה הַבַּיִת יְהֵא חַיָּיב חַטָּאת.

תַּמָּן תַּנִּינָן. אַל תַּאֲמֵן בְּעַצְמָךְ עַד יוֹם מוֹתָךְ. מַעֲשֶׂה בְחָסִיד אֶחָד שֶׁהָיָה יוֹשֵׁב וְשׁוֹנֶה. אַל תַּאֲמֵן בְּעַצְמָךְ עַד יוֹם זִקְנוּתָךְ. כְּגוֹן אֲנִי. אֲתַת חֲדָא רוּחָא וּנְסִיתֵיהּ. וּשְׁרֵי תָּהִי בֵיהּ. אֲמָרָה לֵיהּ. לֹא תִצּוּק. רוּחַ אֲנָא. אֲזִיל וְאִישְׁתַּוֵּי לְחַבְרָיךְ.

It was stated, lest he forget and turn[251]. [252]"Rebbi Ismael said, I will read but not turn. He forgot and almost turned. He said, how great are the words of the Sages who said, lest he forget and turn. Rebbi Nathan says, he actually turned and wrote on his writing tablet[252a], Ismael ben Elisha turned the light on the Sabbath. When the Temple will be rebuilt he is liable for a purification sacrifice."

There, we have stated[253]: "Do not believe in yourself up to the day of your death." It happened that a pious man sat and stated, do not believe in yourself up to your old age, as I am. There came a spirit to tempt him, and he started to err after her[254]. She told him, do not feel bad, I am a spirit. Go and be equal to your colleagues[255].

251 Babli 12b. This is the reason why reading by candlelight is forbidden.
252 Tosephta 1:13, Babli 12b.
253 Mishnah *Avot* 2:4.
253a Greek πίναξ, -ακος, ὁ.
254 He asked her for sex.

255 Formulate the Mishnah to read "up to the day of your death."

(3b line) מתני׳. בֶּאֱמֶת הַחַזָּן רוֹאֶה אֵיכָן הַתִּינוֹקוֹת קוֹרִין כול׳. אָמַר רִבִּי לָעֶזָר. כָּל־מָקוֹם שֶׁשָּׁנִינוּ. בֶּאֱמֶת. הֲלָכָה לְמֹשֶׁה מִסִּינַי. מָהוּ מְתַקֵּן. רָאשֵׁי פְרָקִים פְּסוּקִין. תַּנֵּי. רַבָּן שִׁמְעוֹן בֶּן גַּמְלִיאֵל אוֹמֵר. הַתִּינוֹקוֹת מְתַקְּנִין לָהֶן רָאשֵׁי פְּסוּקֵיהֶן לְאוֹר הַנֵּר. מַיי כְדוֹן. אִילֵּין בָעֵיי דְיִטְפֵּי בוּצִינָא. וְאִילֵּין לָא בָעֵיי דְיִטְפֵּי בוּצִינָא.

Mishnah: "In truth they said that the teacher may look where the children are reading." Rebbi Eleazar said that every place where they stated "in truth" it is practice going back to Moses on Mount Sinai[256]. What does he have to put in order? The beginnings of paragraphs [or] verses[257]. It was stated[258]: "Rabban Simeon ben Gamliel said, children prepare the beginnings of verses by candlelight." What about it? These want the light to go out[7], those[259] do not want the light to go out.

256 Chapter 10 (Note 48), *Kilaim* 2:2 Note 36, *Terumot* 2:1 Note 16, *Nazir* 7:3 Note 179 (in Chapter 10 and *Nazir* in the name of R. Eliezer); Babli 92b, *Bava mesi`a* 60a. Since the prohibition to read by candlelight is purely rabbinic, the expression "going back to Moses on Mount Sinai" is an exaggeration. Probably it simply should say "it is practice", i. e., without dissent; this is the formulation of the Babli, 92b.

257 Since one does not teach children new subjects on the Sabbath but one helps them to commit to memory what they did learn during the week, all they have to see are the beginnings of verses to remember the full text.

258 Tosephta 1:12.

259 The adults who are forbidden to read by candlelight.

(3b line 73) מתני׳. כַּיּוֹצֵא בּוֹ לֹא יֹאכַל הַזָּב עִם הַזָּבָה כול׳: תַּנֵּי. רִבִּי שִׁמְעוֹן בֶּן לָעֶזָר אוֹמֵר. רְאֵה עַד אֵיכָן פָּרְצָה טָהֳרָה. שֶׁנֶּאֱמַר כִּי מְעַט בְּי אֲשֶׁר־הָיָה לְךָ לְפָנַי וַיִּפְרוֹץ לָרוֹב. וּבֵית אֲבוֹתֵיהֶם פָּרְצוּ לָרוֹב: שֶׁלֹּא גָזְרוּ לוֹמַר שֶׁלֹּא יֹאכַל טָהוֹר עִם הַטָּמֵא. אֶלָּא אָמְרוּ לֹא יֹאכַל הַזָּב עִם הַזָּבָה. הָא זָב עִם מְצוֹרַעַת מוּתָּר. וְיָשֵׁב מִחוּץ לְאָהֳלוֹ וְלֹא מִחוּץ לְאָהֳלָהּ. מְצוֹרָע עִם זָבָה אָסוּר. מְצוֹרָע עִם מְצוֹרַעַת אָסוּר.

Mishnah[216]: "Similarly, the male sufferer from gonorrhea should not eat with a female sufferer from flux." It was stated[260]: Rebbi Simeon ben Eleazar says, look how far purity did spread, as it is said[261], *for the little which you had expanded mightily;* [262]*and their families expanded mightily*. They did not decide to say, the pure may not eat with the impure[263], but they said, the male sufferer from gonorrhea should not eat with a female sufferer from flux[264]; therefore the male sufferer from gonorrhea with a female sufferer from skin disease is permitted[265]. *He shall dwell outside his tent*[266] but not outside her tent. A male sufferer from skin disease with a female sufferer from flux is forbidden; a male sufferer from skin disease with a female sufferer from skin disease is forbidden[267].

260 Babli 13a, Tosephta 1:14.
261 *Gen.* 30:30.
262 *1Chr.* 4:38. The implication is that in both cases the increase was the reward of exact observation of the rules of purity.
263 From the parallels it is clear that one should not read "the pure may not eat with the impure (m.)" but "the pure may not eat with the impure (f.)", i. e., a husband may not eat with his wife during her menstrual impurity. They did not have to spell this out because people by themselves followed this rule.
264 As an example of the general rule that a male may not eat with a woman with whom he could not sleep.
265 Since a female sufferer from skin disease is not restricted in her sexual activity as will be shown in the next sentence.
266 *Lev.* 14:8. The "tent" is an euphemism for the wife with whom he sleeps, as in *Deut.* 5:27, where Moses reports that he was commanded by God to tell the people "to return to their tents" after the epiphany of Sinai where they had been forbidden intercourse for three days prior (*Ex.* 19:15), except for Moses who was commanded "to stay with Me" (*Deut.* 5:28).

The use of the masculine suffix, *his* tent, is interpreted to exclude the female from restriction of sexual activity. The verse refers to the healed sufferer from skin disease in the process of his purification. There is a dispute whether the prohibition of sexual relations extends to the time of actual sickness. The Babylonian sources [*Keritut* 8b, also *Mo`ed qatan* 7a; *Sifra Mesora` Parashah* 2(11)] are unanimous that the prohibition does not extend. This also seems to be implied by Mishnah *Nega`im* 14:2. But the text here implies that any male sufferer from skin disease is forbidden sexual relations (which in *Sifra* is labelled as opinion of R. Yose ben R. Jehudah.)
267 Since the prohibitions only depend on the status of the male.

(3c line 3) תָּנֵי. בֵּית שַׁמַּי אוֹמְרִים. לֹא יֹאכַל זָב פָּרוּשׁ עִם זָב עַם הָאָרֶץ. וּבֵית הִלֵּל מַתִּירִין. וּמַה טַעֲמֵיהוֹן דְּבֵית הִלֵּל. זֶה זָב וְזֶה זָב. וּמַה טַעֲמְהוֹן דְּבֵית שַׁמַּי. שֶׁהוּא מִתְרַגֵּל עִמּוֹ בִּימֵי טוּמְאָתוֹ הוּא מִתְרַגֵּל עִמּוֹ בִּימֵי טָהֳרָתוֹ. רִבִּי חִייָה רוֹבָה מְפַקֵּד לְרַב. אִין אַתְּ יָכִיל מֵיכוֹל כָּל־שַׁתָּה חוּלִין בְּטָיֳרָה אֱכוֹל. וְאִם לָאו תְּהֵא אָכִיל שִׁבְעָה יוֹמִין מִן שַׁתָּה.

מִיכָּן הָיָה רִבִּי פִּינְחָס בֶּן יָאִיר אוֹמֵר. זְרִיזוּת מְבִיאָה לִידֵי נְקִיּוּת. נְקִיּוּת מְבִיאָה לִידֵי טָהֳרָה. טָהֳרָה מְבִיאָה לִידֵי קְדוּשָׁה. קְדוּשָׁה לִידֵי עֲנָוָה. עֲנָוָה לִידֵי יִרְאַת חֵטְ. יִרְאַת חֵטְ לִידֵי רוּחַ

הַקּוֹדֶשׁ. רוּחַ הַקּוֹדֶשׁ לִידֵי חֲסִידוּת. חֲסִידוּת לִידֵי תְחִיַּת הַמֵּתִים. תְּחִיַּת הַמֵּתִים לִידֵי אֵלִיָּהוּ זָכוּר לַטּוֹב. זְרִיזוּת לִידֵי נְקִיּוּת. וְכִלָּה וְכִפֵּר. נְקִיּוּת לִידֵי טָהֳרָה. וְכִפֶּר עָלֶיהָ הַכֹּהֵן וְטָהֵרָה. טָהֳרָה לִידֵי קְדוּשָׁה. וְטִיהֲרוֹ וְקִידְּשׁוֹ. קְדוּשָׁה לִידֵי עֲנָוָה. כִּי כֹה אָמַר רָם וְנִשָּׂא שֹׁכֵן עַד וְקָדוֹשׁ שְׁמוֹ מָרוֹם וְקָדוֹשׁ אֶשְׁכּוֹן וְאֶת־דַּכָּא וּשְׁפַל־רוּחַ. עֲנָוָה לִידֵי יִרְאַת חֵטְא. דִּכְתִיב עֵקֶב עֲנָוָה יִרְאַת יְיָ. אָמַר רִבִּי יִצְחָק בַּר אֶלְעָזָר. מַה שֶּׁעָשְׂתָה חָכְמָה עֲטָרָה לְרֹאשָׁהּ עָשְׂתָה עֲנָוָה עָקֵב לְסוּלְיָיסָהּ. דִּכְתִיב רֵאשִׁית חָכְמָה | יִרְאַת יְיָ. וּכְתִיב עֵקֶב עֲנָוָה יִרְאַת יְיָ. יִרְאַת חֵטְא לִידֵי רוּחַ הַקּוֹדֶשׁ. דִּכְתִיב אָז תָּבִין יִרְאַת יְיָ וְדַעַת אֱלֹקִים תִּמְצָא· רוּחַ הַקּוֹדֶשׁ לִידֵי חֲסִידוּת. דִּכְתִיב אָז דִּבַּרְתָּ־בְחָזוֹן לַחֲסִידֶיךָ. חֲסִידוּת לִידֵי תְחִיַּת הַמֵּתִים. דִּכְתִיב וְנָתַתִּי רוּחִי בָּכֶם וִחְיִיתֶם. תְּחִיַּת הַמֵּתִים לִידֵי אֵלִיָּהוּ זָכוּר לַטּוֹב. דִּכְתִיב הִנֵּה אָנֹכִי שׁוֹלֵחַ לָכֶם אֵת אֵלִיָּה הַנָּבִיא לִפְנֵי בּוֹא יוֹם יְיָ הַגָּדוֹל וְהַנּוֹרָא וְהֵשִׁיב לֵב־אָבוֹת עַל־בָּנִים וְלֵב בָּנִים עַל־אֲבוֹתָם. תַּנֵּי בְשֵׁם רִבִּי מֵאִיר. כָּל־מִי שֶׁהוּא קָבוּעַ בָּאָרֶץ יִשְׂרָאֵל וְאוֹכֵל חוּלָּיו בְּטָהֳרָה וּמְדַבֵּר בִּלְשׁוֹן הַקֹּדֶשׁ וְקוֹרֵא אֶת שְׁמַע בַּבֹּקֶר וּבָעֶרֶב מוּבְטָח לוֹ שֶׁהוּא מֵחַיֵּי הָעוֹלָם הַבָּא.

It was stated[268]: "The House of Shammai say, a Pharisee sufferer from gonorrhea may not eat with a vulgar[269] sufferer from gonorrhea, but the House of Hillel permit it." What is the reason of the House of Hillel? This one suffers from gonorrhea and that one suffers from gonorrhea[270]. But what is the reason of the House of Shammai? If he gets used to him during the days of his impurity he will remain used to him in the days of his purity[271]. The Elder Rebbi Hiyya commanded Rav[272], if you are able to eat profane food in purity the entire year long, eat it. But if not, eat it seven days per year[273].

[274]"From here did Rebbi Phineas ben Yair say, promptitude brings to cleanliness, cleanliness brings to purity, purity brings to holiness, holiness to meekness, meekness to fear of sin, fear of sin to the Holy Spirit, the Holy Spirit to piety, piety to the Resurrection of the Dead, the Resurrection of the Dead through Elijah, may his remembrance be a blessing."

"Promptitude to cleanliness," *he finishes, and he atones*[275].

"Cleanliness to purity," *the Cohen shall atone for her, then she will be pure*[276].

"Purity to holiness," *he shall purify it and sanctify it*[277].

"Holiness to meekness," *for so says the High and Elevated One, Who thrones eternally, His name is Holy, in sublimity and holiness I dwell, and the suppressed and of meek spirit*[278].

"Meekness to fear of sin," *the consequence of meekness is fear of the Eternal*[279]. Rebbi Isaac bar Eleazar said, what wisdom proclaimed as a crown to its head, meekness made a heel for its sandal[280], for it is written, *the head of wisdom is the fear of the Eternal*[281], but it is written, *the heel of meekness is fear of the Eternal*[279].

"Fear of sin to the Holy Spirit," as it is written, *then you will understand and knowledge of God you will find*[282].

"The Holy Spirit to piety," as it is written, *then You spoke in a vision to Your pious*[283].

"Piety to the Resurrection of the Dead," as it is written, *I shall give My Spirit into you and you will live*[284].

"The Resurrection of the Dead through Elijah, may his remembrance be a blessing," as it is written, *behold I am sending to you Elijah the prophet, before the coming of the great and awesome day of the Eternal, that he turn the fathers' hearts to the sons and the sons' hearts to their fathers*[285].

It was stated in the name of Rebbi Meïr: Anybody permanently in the Land of Israel who eats his profane food in purity, speaks in the holy language, and recites the *Shema`* mornings and evenings is assured to participate in the life of the World to Come[286].

268 Babli 3a, Tosephta 1:15.
269 A vulgar person is one who does not observe the rules of purity outside of the Temple and cannot be trusted to tithe his produce. A Pharisee is a person who observes these obligations with all their rabbinic additions, cf. Introduction to Tractate Demay. It is possible that here the labels "vulgar" and "Pharisee" refer only to the observation of the rules of purity in daily life.
270 Since the sufferer from gonorrhea is severely impure, even if he is Pharisee he cannot eat anything in purity.
271 A pure Pharisee cannot eat with a vulgar person because the latter by his touch will make the food impure.
272 Who came from Babylonia, an impure country, where eating one's food in purity is impossible in principle.
273 The Days of Repentance between New Year's Day and the Day of Atonement [ROSH *Rosh Hashanah,* end, in the name of Raviah (ed. Aptowitzer) vol. 2 p. 208, cf. the earlier sources noted there, Note 6].
274 This *baraita* is the end of the Babylonian Mishnah *Sotah* (quoted in *Avodah zarah* 20b); it is not in the Yerushalmi Mishnah. The entire paragraph appears in a slightly different version (adapted to the Babylonian Mishnah) in the hand of the first corrector in *Šeqalim* 3:4;

the differences will be indicated in the Notes. The *Šeqalim* text, with the Babylonian version, consist- ently has the full form "*a* brings to *b*".

There also exists a Genizah text edited by L. Ginzberg (*op. cit.* Note 25 p. 66ff.) which here is too fragmentary to be of much use.

The different version has the sequence cleanliness purity holiness meekness fear of sin piety Holy Spirit resurrection. In Yerushalmi sources it also is found in *Cant. rabba* 1(9) whereas the version in the text here is in the Munich ms. of the Babli *Avodah zarah* 20b. The *Šeqalim* text is reproduced in *Midrash Prov.* Chap.15[32]. The different implications naturally require different verses.

275 It seems that the correct quote is given in *Šeqalim*: וְכִלָּה מִכַּפֵּר *he finishes to atone* (*Lev.* 16:20). The High Priest, who has to perform all the rites of the day of Atonement unaided, has to be quick because only if he finishes all required ceremonies will there be atonement.

276 *Lev.* 12:8.

277 *Lev.* 16:19.

278 *Is.* 57:15. The verse is explained differently in the Babli, *Megillah* 31a.

279 *Prov.* 22:4. In the first quote, the implied meaning "consequence" is intended, in the second the original meaning "heel".

280 Latin *solea, -ae* f. "sandal".

281 *Ps.* 111:10. The usual meaning is *the beginning of wisdom is . . .*

282 *Prov.* 2:5.

283 *Ps.* 89:20.

284 *Ez.* 37:14.

285 *Mal.* 3:23-24.

286 In *Šeqalim*: ". . . eats his produce in purity, . . ., may be told that . . .".

(3c line 28) מתני׳. אֵילוּ מֵהֲלָכוֹת שֶׁאָמְרוּ בַּעֲלִיַּית חֲנַנְיָה בֶן חִזְקִיָּה בֶן גָּרוֹן כְּשֶׁעָלוּ לְבַקְּרוֹ כול׳. אוֹתוֹ הַיּוֹם הָיָה קָשֶׁה לְיִשְׂרָאֵל כַּיּוֹם שֶׁנַּעֲשָׂה בּוֹ הָעֵגֶל. רְבִּי לִיעֶזֶר אוֹמֵר. בּוֹ בַיּוֹם גָּדְשׁוּ אֶת הַסְּאָה. רְבִּי יְהוֹשֻׁעַ אוֹמֵר. בּוֹ בַיּוֹם מֶחֲקוּ אוֹתָהּ. אָמַר לוֹ רְבִּי לִיעֶזֶר. אֵילוּ הָיְתָה חֲסֵירָה וּמִילְאוּהָ. יָאוּת. לְחָבִית שֶׁהִיא מְלֵיאָה אֱגוֹזִין. כָּל־מַה שֶׁאַתָּה נוֹתֵן לְתוֹכָהּ שׁוּמְשְׁמִין הִיא מַחֲזֶקֶת. אָמַר לוֹ רְבִּי יְהוֹשֻׁעַ. אֵילוּ הָיְתָה מְלֵיאָה וְחִיסְּרוּהָ. יָאוּת. לְחָבִית שֶׁהָיְתָה מְלֵיאָה שֶׁמֶן. כָּל־מַה שֶׁאַתָּה נוֹתֵן לְתוֹכָהּ מַיִם הִיא מְפַזֶּרֶת אֶת הַשֶּׁמֶן.

Mishnah[287]: "These[9] are of the practices which were pronounced at the upper floor of Ḥananiah ben Ḥizqiah ben Garon[10], when they came to visit him," etc. [288]"This day was hard for Israel like the day on which the Golden C alf was made. Rebbi Eliezer said, on that day they filled the bushel to overflow. Rebbi Joshua said, on that day they filled the bushel to the rim. Rebbi Eliezer said to him, if it was deficient and they filled it it would have been reasonable, as with an amphora full of nuts; if you fill it with sesame seeds it will be strengthened[289]. Rebbi Joshua said to him, if it had been full and they diminished it, it would have been reasonable, as with an amphora filled with oil; if you add water to it it dilutes the oil.[290]"

287 Quote from Mishnah 7.
288 Cf. Tosephta 1:16-17, Babli 153b (17a).
289 There is much empty space between the nuts where sesame seeds may fall it. If they settle at the bottom, the amphora becomes more stable. If it had said, מַחֲזֶקֶת אוֹתָם the translation would have been "contains them".
290 They are engaged in a discussion about the principles of Pharisaic Judaism, couched in a dispute whether to compare the legalistic rabbinic framework to a bushel of dry or fluid measure. R. Eliezer, an adherent of the House of Shammai who was a student of the Hillelite Rabban Johanan ben Zakkai, compares biblical commandments to nuts in a barrel and rabbinic additions to small grains which fill the spaces between the nuts and give stability to the amphora. His view of Judaism is static; he views all rabbinic enactments as positive.

By contrast, R. Joshua compares biblical commandments to oil; his view of Judaism is dynamic. He accepts rabbinic enactments only if they do not threaten to cause overflow, in which case biblical commandments may be lost because of rabbinic stringencies. He has a dim view of the ordinances from the House of Hananiah ben Hizqiah ben Garon.

(3c line 36) תַּנָא רִבִּי יְהוֹשֻׁעַ אוֹנְיָיא. תַּלְמִידֵי בֵית שַׁמַּי עָמְדוּ לָהֶן מִלְמַטָּה וְהָיוּ הוֹרְגִין בְּתַלְמִידֵי בֵית הִלֵּל. תַּנֵּי. שִׁשָּׁה מֵהֶן עָלוּ וְהַשְׁאָר עָמְדוּ עֲלֵיהֶן בַּחֲרָבוֹת וּבִרְמָחִין. תַּנֵּי. שְׁמוֹנָה עָשָׂר דָּבָר גָּזְרוּ וּבִשְׁמוֹנָה עֶשְׂרֵה רַבּוּ וּבִשְׁמוֹנָה עֶשְׂרֵה נֶחְלְקוּ. וְאֵילוּ הֵן שֶׁגָּזְרוּ. עַל פִּיתָּן שֶׁלְּגוֹיִם וְעַל גְּבִינָתָן וְעַל שַׁמְנָן וְעַל בְּנוֹתֵיהֶן וְעַל שִׁכְבַת זֶרְעָן וְעַל מֵימֵי רַגְלֵיהֶן וְעַל הִילְכוֹת בַּעַל קֶרִי וְעַל הִילְכוֹת אֶרֶץ הָעַמִּים. תַּמָּן תַּנִּינָן. אֵלּוּ פוֹסְלִין אֶת הַתְּרוּמָה. הָאוֹכֵל אֹכֶל רִאשׁוֹן. וְהָאוֹכֵל אֹכֶל שֵׁינִי. וְהַשּׁוֹתֶה מַשְׁקִין טְמֵאִין. וְהַבָּא רֹאשׁוֹ וְרוּבּוֹ בְּמַיִם שְׁאוּבִין. וְטָהוֹר שֶׁנָּפְלוּ עַל רֹאשׁוֹ וְעַל רוּבּוֹ שְׁלֹשָׁה לוּגִּין מַיִם שְׁאוּבִין. וְהַסֵּפֶר וְהַיָּדַיִם וְהַטְּבוּל יוֹם. וְהָאוֹכָלִים וְהַכֵּלִים שֶׁנִּטְמְאוּ בְמַשְׁקִין:

רַבָּנָן דְּקַיְסָרִין אָמְרֵי. אֵילּוּ שֶׁגָּזְרוּ מִמַּה שֶׁעָרַבּוּ שׁוּבְעָה אִינּוּן. וְאֵילֵּין אִינּוּן חוֹרָנְיָיתָא. מִי שֶׁהֶחֱשִׁיךְ בַּדֶּרֶךְ נוֹתֵן כִּיסוֹ לְנָכְרִי. כַּיּוֹצֵא בוֹ לֹא יֹאכַל הַזָּב עִם הַזָּבָה מִפְּנֵי הֶרְגֵּל עֲבֵרָה: כָּל־הַמִּיטַּלְטְלִין מְבִיאִין טוּמְאָה כְּעוֹבִי הַמַּרְדֵּעַ. כֵּיצַד בּוֹצְרִין בֵּית הַפְּרָס. הַמַּנִּיחַ כֵּלִים תַּחַת הַצִּינּוֹר. עַל שִׁשָּׁה סְפֵיקוֹת שׂוֹרְפִין אֶת הַתְּרוּמָה. אָמַר רִבִּי יוֹסֵי בֵּירִבִּי בּוּן. אַף גִּידּוּלֵי תְרוּמָה. אֵילּוּ הֵן שֶׁגָּזְרוּ. אִילֵּין עֲשָׂרְתֵּי קַדְמָיָיתָא וְהַשְּׁאָר מִן מַה דְּתַנֵּי רִבִּי שִׁמְעוֹן בֶּן יוֹחַי. בּוֹ בַיּוֹם גָּזְרוּ עַל פִּיתָּן וְעַל גְּבִינָתָן וְעַל יֵינָן וְעַל חוּמְצָן וְעַל צִירָן וְעַל מוּרְיָיסָן וְעַל כְּבוּשֵׁיהֶן וְעַל שְׁלוּקֵיהֶן וְעַל מְלוּחֵיהֶן וְעַל הַחִילְקָה וְעַל הַשְּׁחִיקָה וְעַל הַטִּיסָנֵי וְעַל לְשׁוֹנָן וְעַל עֵדוּתָן וְעַל מַתְּנוֹתֵיהֶן וְעַל בְּנֵיהֶן וְעַל בְּנוֹתֵיהֶן וְעַל בְּכוֹרֵיהֶן.

Rebbi Joshua from Ono stated: The students of the House of Shammai were standing downstairs and killing the students of the House of Hillel. It was stated, six of them went up; the rest were standing around them with swords and lances.

It was stated, eighteen things they decided, in eighteen they were a majority and in eighteen they were divided[291]. The following they decided: About Gentiles' bread, and about their cheeses, and about their oil[292], and about their daughters[293], and about their semen, and about their urine[294], and about the rules of a person with an emission[295], and about the rules of the land of Gentiles[296]. There we have stated[297]: "The following make heave unusable. One who eats food impure in the first degree, and one who eats food impure in the second degree[298], and one who drinks impure drinks[299], and one who comes with his head and most of his body in drawn water[300], and a pure person on whose head and most of his body fell three *log* drawn water[301], and a scroll[302], and hands[303], and the *Tevul Yom*[304], and food and vessels which became impure by fluids[299]."

The rabbis of Caesarea said, of those which they decided there were seven of those where they had a majority[305]. The others are the following: A person being on the road when it gets dark gives his wallet to a Non-Jew[306]. Similarly, the male sufferer from gonorrhea should not eat with a female sufferer from flux because of inducement to sin. All movables transmit impurity by the thickness of the yoke[307]. How one harvests grapes on a broken field[308]. One who puts vessels under the pipe[309]. For six doubts one burns heave[310]. Rebbi Yose ben Rebbi Abun said, also the growth of heave[311]. The following they decided: the first ten and the remainder from what Rebbi Simeon ben Yohai stated: On that day they decided about their bread, and their cheeses, and their wine[292], and their vinegar[312], and their fish brine[313], and their *muries*[314], and their preserves, and their parboiled food, and their corned food[315], and on split grain, and on ground food, and on peeled barley[316,317], on their speech[318], and on their testimony[319], and on their gifts[320], on their sons[294], and on their daughters[293], and on their firstlings[321].

291 In this opinion, there were 54 items up for discussion, 18 were unanimously decided, 18 where the House of Shammai had a majority but it was not unanimous and

not accepted by the House of Hillel, and 18 where the discussion was inconclusive. This explains the difficulty both Talmudim have to come up with the list of the 18 decrees which were definitely issued. In the Babli 14b only two groups of 18 are mentioned.

292 The prohibitions, later partially lifted, of Gentile bread, cheese, and olive oil, are discussed in *Avodah zarah* Chapter 2; a copy of some of the discussion is reproduced later in the present Chapter.

293 A Gentile female is treated from birth as permanently impure like a menstruating woman, making sexual relations with her a rabbinic deadly sin. Babli *Avodah zarah* 36b.

294 While biblically a living Gentile cannot be impure and neither are his body fluids, rabbinically his semen and urine are treated as if he were impure as a sufferer from gonorrhea, to avoid homosexual contacts. Babli *Avodah zarah* 36b.

295 The restrictions on religious performances imposed on a person having had sexual relations or an emission of semen before he went to a *miqweh*, as detailed in Tractate *Berakhot* 3:4, Notes 173-200.

296 The land outside the territory of Israel obviously was considered impure already in the times of the prophet Amos (*Am.* 6:17). Who formalized the rules of this impurity is a matter of controversy (Babli 14b). It seems that the new decision was to decree impurity for regions of the Holy Land inhabited by Gentiles (*Hagigah* 3:4, 79b l. 75, Babli 25a).

297 Mishnah *Zavim* 8:12. The Mishnah is also quoted and discussed in the Babli 13b as list of the 18 items.

298 Heave must be eaten in purity (*Num.* 18:11,13). According to biblical standards, only original impurity or at most its first derivative can make food impure. Therefore heave which was touched by a person who ingested food one or two steps removed from original impurity should become impure in the second or third degree and therefore be permitted for the Cohen. By rabbinic usage, heave may become impure in the second degree and invalid in the third.

299 While solid food impure in the k-th degree imparts impurity of the (k+1)st degree on what it touches, by rabbinic practice impure fluid always causes impurity of the first degree in what comes in touch with it. This is a precaution because the body fluids of a sufferer from gonorrhea are carriers of original impurity.

300 This is a purely rabbinic decree instituted so people should not substitute a bathtub for a ritual bath (*miqweh*).

301 This is an appendix to the decree described in the preceding Note. A *log* is slightly more than half a liter.

302 A Torah scroll makes hands which touch it impure in the second degree. This was instituted to hinder people to store food next to the Torah scroll, which would expose the scroll to the danger of being eaten by mice. As a consequence one has to cover one's hand with the *tallit* if for some reason one has to manipulate the parchment with one's hands.

303 Washed hands are pure. They remain pure only as long as one is aware of their washed status. At the moment one's attention is diverted from this, they revert to the status of unwashed hands and automatically are impure in the second degree (even if the person's body remains

pure.) Therefore touching heave with unwashed hands invalidates heave as impure in the third degree. (Cf. Tractate *Yadaim*).

304 By biblical decree, an impure person who purifies himself by immersion in a *miqweh* may consume sanctified food only after the next sundown (*Lev.* 22:7). The biblical text does not specify what the status is of the person between immersion and sundown, when he is called *tevul yom* "immersed during daytime". While he is pure, by rabbinic convention (but following some opinions by biblical decree) he invalidates sanctified food by his touch as if he were impure in the second degree (cf. *Sotah* 5:2 Notes 42,46,47,68.)

305 They disagree with the statement that 36 items were discussed; some decrees were passed by a majority short of unanimity. Cf. Babli 17b.

306 A Jew on the road late on Friday evening may give his valuables to a non-Jew and retrieve them later. While in general it is forbidden to ask a Gentile to do something for a Jew which is forbidden to himself, this is an exception.

307 The standard bar of a yoke has circumference of one hand-breadth, therefore a diameter of 1/π hand-breadth. By biblical decree, a "tent" under which there is a corpse induces original impurity in everything under it if only it is susceptible to impurity. By definition, a "tent" is any cover at least one hand-breadth wide. By rabbinic decree this is extended to round beams of circumference of one hand-breadth. Tosephta 1:18.

308 A "broken field" is a field which contained a grave (of uncertain location) ploughed under, where the entire field might be impure since a bone may have been dislocated by the plough. The problem is to harvest the grapes in purity to make pure wine; Mishnah *Ahilut* 18:1. The House of Hillel have a prescription for this; the House of Shammai disagree and require the grapes to be cut from the vine with a flintstone knife (or some other permanently pure implement) and transported in a basket woven of willow twigs, which is impervious to impurity. It is asserted that practice has to follow the House of Shammai.

309 The waters of a *miqweh* become invalid if they are in a vessel. If one builds a conduit of spring water into the *miqweh* which never had the status of a vessel, this is fine. But if the pipe is supported somewhere by vessels, the House of Shammai declare the *miqweh* invalid in all cases, against a more lenient opinion of the House of Hillel who declare it valid if the vessels were forgotten, not put there intentionally. Tosephta 1:19.

310 Mishnah *Tahorot* 4:5. While in general it is forbidden to burn edible heave which is not certainly impure, there is a list of six cases in which one considers a doubt as equivalent to certitude of impurity.

311 If heave of grain is taken as seed grain, the entire crop has the status of heave even though by biblical rules the new growth would not have been heave. (Babli 17b; Mishnah *Terumot* 9:4 Note 57).

312 Which may have been wine originally. Wine vinegar needs certification of kosher supervision.

313 Which may be from forbidden fish, without fins and scales.

314 Latin *muria, -ae* or *muries, -ei* f. "brine, fish sauce"; cf. *Avodah zarah* 2:4,

Note 241.

315 Anything cooked by Gentiles is rabbinically forbidden under the rules and exceptions detailed in Tractate *Avodah zarah Chapter 2.*

316 Mishnah *Makhshirin* 6:2. Produce may become impure only if it had been "prepared" for it by intentional contact with one of the fluids which may cause impurity (water, wine, olive oil, blood, milk, bee's honey). It is assumed that any grain undergoing some manufacturing process was moistened to facilitate the production; therefore it is treated as certainly susceptible to impurity.

317 טיסָנֵי is Greek πτισάνη, Latin transcription *ptisana. tisana, -ae,* f. peeled barley.

318 This item is not clear. It may mean a prohibition to study Greek or Latin, or it may be identical to the next item, that Gentile testimony is inadmissible in a rabbinic court. The first interpretation is preferable since then the statement of R. Simeon contains exactly 18 items, i. e., it is his list of the 18 items.

319 The only testimony of Gentiles admitted in a rabbinic court is the testimony of a Jew that a Gentile gave certain information without being asked.

320 One should not in general accept gifts from a Gentile; cf. *Avodah zarah* Chapter 1.

321 This also is not clear. It may refer to the rule that a firstling born of an animal partially owned by a Gentile is profane.

(3c line 55) פִּיתָּן. רִבִּי יַעֲקֹב בַּר אָחָא בְּשֵׁם רִבִּי יוֹנָתָן. מֵהֲלָכוֹת שֶׁלְעִימְעוּם הִיא. אָמַר רִבִּי יוֹסֵה. קַשִּׁיָיתָהּ קוֹמֵי רִבִּי יַעֲקֹב בַּר אָחָא. מָהוּ מֵהֲלָכוֹת שֶׁלְעִימְעוּם. כָּךְ אָנוּ אוֹמְרִים. בְּמָקוֹם שֶׁפַּת יִשְׂרָאֵל מְצוּיָה בְּדִין הָיָה שֶׁתְּהֵא פַת גּוֹיִם אֲסוּרָה. וְעִמְעֲמוּ עָלֶיהָ וְהִתִּירוּהָ. אוֹ בְמָקוֹם שֶׁאֵין פַּת יִשְׂרָאֵל מְצוּיָה בְּדִין הָיָה שֶׁתְּהֵא פַת גּוֹיִם מוּתֶּרֶת. וְעִמְעֲמוּ עָלֶיהָ וַאֲסָרוּהָ. אָמַר רִבִּי מָנָא. וְיֵשׁ עִימְעוּם לְאִיסּוּר. וּפַת לָאו תַּבְשִׁילֵי גוֹיִם הוּא. כָּךְ אָנוּ אוֹמְרִים. בְּמָקוֹם שֶׁאֵין תַּבְשִׁילֵי יִשְׂרָאֵל מְצוּיִין בְּדִין הָיָה שֶׁיְּהוּ תַבְשִׁילֵי גוֹיִם מוּתָּרִין. וְעִמְעֲמוּ עָלֶיהָ וַאֲסָרוּם. אֶלָּא כֵינֵי. בְּמָקוֹם שֶׁאֵין פַּת יִשְׂרָאֵל מְצוּיָה בְּדִין הָיָה שֶׁתְּהֵא פַת גּוֹיִם אֲסוּרָה. וְעִמְעֲמוּ עָלֶיהָ וְהִתִּירוּהָ מִפְּנֵי חַיֵּי נֶפֶשׁ. רַבָּנִין דְּקַיְסָרִין בְּשֵׁם רִבִּי יַעֲקֹב בַּר אָחָא. כִּדְבָרֵי מִי שֶׁהוּא מַתִּיר. וּבִלְבַד מִן הַפַּלְטָר. וְלֹא עָבְדִין כֵּן.

[322]**Their bread.** Rebbi Jacob bar Aḥa in the name of Rebbi Jonathan: this is of the practices of obfuscation. Rebbi Yose said, so I asked before Rebbi Jacob bar Aḥa: What means "of the practices of obfuscation? Do we say, at a place where Jewish bread is available it is logical that Gentile bread should be forbidden and they obfuscated about it and permitted it? Or at a place where Jewish bread is not available it would be logical that Gentile bread should be permitted and they obfuscated about it and forbade it? Rebbi Mana said, is there any obfuscation for prohibition? But is bread not like cooking of

Gentiles? Are we saying: At a place where no Jewish cooking is available it would be logical that Gentile cooking should be permitted? But it must be the following: At a place where Jewish bread is not available it would be logical that Gentile bread should be forbidden and they obfuscated about it and permitted it because of the necessities of life. The rabbis of Caesarea in the name of Rabbi Jacob bar Aha: Following the words of him who was permitting, but only from the store; but one does not do this.

(3c line 65) אָמְרוּן קוֹמֵי רִבִּי חִייָה רוֹבָא. תַּנֵּי רִבִּי שִׁמְעוֹן בֶּן יוֹחַי כֵּן. אוֹכֶל תִּשְׁבְּרוּ מֵאִתָּם בַּכֶּסֶף וַאֲכַלְתֶּם וְגַם־מַיִם תִּכְרוּ מֵאִתָּם וגו'. מַה מַיִם לֹא נִשְׁתַּנּוּ מִבְּרִיָּיתָן אַף כָּל־דָּבָר שֶׁלֹּא נִשְׁתַּנָּה מִבְּרִיָּיתוֹ. הֵתִיבוּן. הֲרֵי מוּטְלֻיָּיה וּפַנְקָרִיסִים וְקוּבְּטִיּוֹת וּקְלָיוֹת וְחַמִּין שֶׁלָּהֶן הֲרֵי אֵילוּ מוּתָּרִין. נִיחָא כּוּלְּהוֹן שֶׁהֵן יְכוֹלִין לְהַשְׁרוֹת וְלַחֲזוֹר כְּמוֹ שֶׁהָיוּ. קְלָיוֹת מָה. אָמַר רִבִּי יוֹסֵי בֵּירִבִּי בּוּן בְּשֵׁם רַב. כָּל־אוֹכֶל שֶׁהוּא נֶאֱכָל חַי כְּמוֹת שֶׁהוּא אֵין בּוֹ מִשּׁוּם תַּבְשִׁילֵי גוֹיִם וְיוֹצְאִין בּוֹ מִשּׁוּם עֵירוּבֵי תַבְשִׁילִין. מַה מְקַיֵּים רִבִּי חִייָה רוֹבָא אוֹכֶל תִּשְׁבְּרוּ מֵאִתָּם. בָּאוֹכֶל תִּשְׁבְּרוּ. הֶאֱכַלְתּוֹ שְׁבַרְתּוֹ. שֶׁאִם הָיָה קָשֶׁה עָלֶיךָ כְּאוֹכֶל תְּשַׁבְּרוֹ. וְאִם לָאו. הַקְרַע עָלָיו כֶּסֶף. אָמְרִין. כֵּן הֲוָה רִבִּי יוֹנָתָן עָבַד. כַּד הֲוָה חֲמֵי בַּר נַשׁ רַב עָלֵיל לְקַרְתֵּיהּ הֲוָה מְשַׁלַּח לֵיהּ אִיקְרִין. מַיי אָמַר. דְּאִין אָתָא דַיָּין דְּיִיתַם אוֹ דַיָּין דְּאַרְמְלָא נִישְׁכַּח אַפִּין מְפַיְּיסֵיהּ עֲלוֹי.

They said before the Elder Rabbi Hiyya: Rabbi Simeon ben Yoḥai stated thus: *Food you shall buy from them with money and eat, and also water you may acquire*[323], etc. As water is not changed from its natural state, so anything which was not changed from its natural state. They objected: Are there not their dry beans, פנקריסין and קובטיות, roasted grain, and hot water permitted? One understands all of these because they can be soaked and return to their former state. What about roasted grain? Rabbi Yose ben Rabbi Abun in the name of Rav said: Any food which can be eaten alone raw is not in the category of Gentile cooking but one may use it for *eruv tavšilin*[324]. How does Rabbi Hiyya explain *food you shall buy from them*? You shall buy with food. If you fed him you bought him. If he causes you trouble buy him with food or otherwise ply him with him money. They said, that is what Rabbi Jonathan did. When he saw that a superior came to his town, he sent him an honor gift. What did he say? If a suit involving an orphan or a widow came he would have a way to mollify him.

(3d line 1) גְּבִינָתָן. אָמַר רִבִּי יִרְמְיָה. חֲלֵב הַגּוֹי לָמָּה הוּא אָסוּר. מִשּׁוּם תַּעֲרוֹבֶת בְּהֵמָה טְמֵיאָה. וְתַנֵּי כֵן. עוֹמֵד הוּא יִשְׂרָאֵל בָּעֵדֶר וְהַגּוֹי חוֹלֵב וּמֵבִיא לוֹ וְאֵינוֹ חוֹשֵׁשׁ. רִבִּי בָּא בְּשֵׁם רַב

יְהוּדָה. רִבִּי סִימוֹן בְּשֵׁם רִבִּי יְהוֹשֻׁעַ בֶּן לֵוִי. חֲלָב הַגּוֹי לָמָּה הוּא אָסוּר. מִשּׁוּם גִּילּוּי. וְיַעֲמִיד. אָמַר רִבִּי שְׁמוּאֵל בַּר רַב יִצְחָק. מִפְּנֵי אֶרֶס הַנָּתוּן בֵּין הַנְּקָבִים. וְתַנֵּי כֵן. שְׁלֹשָׁה אֵירָסִין הֵן. אֶחָד צָף וְאֶחָד שׁוֹקֵעַ וְאֶחָד עָשׂוּי כִּשְׂבָכָה וְעוֹמֵד לְמַעֲלָה. בִּימוֹי דְּרִבִּי יִרְמְיָה אִיתְגַּלְיָין גִּיגְיָיתָא דְסֹדְרָה רוֹבָא. אִישְׁתּוֹן קַדְמָאֵי וְלָא מַייתוּן. אֲחֳרָאֵי וּמַייתוּן. אֲנִי אוֹמֵר. אֶרֶס שׁוֹקֵעַ הֲוָה. פָּעֲלַיָּיא הֲווֹ בְּטוּרָא. אִתְגַּלְיַית קוּלְתָּה דְמַיָּא. שָׁתוֹן קַדְמָאֵי וְלָא מַייתוּן. אֲחֳרָאֵי וּמַייתוּן. אֲנִי אוֹמֵר. אֵירֶס שׁוֹקֵעַ הֲוָה.

הַשֶּׁמֶן וְהַחוֹמֶץ הַצִּיר וְהַמּוּרְיֵיס וְהַדְּבָשׁ אֵין בָּהֶן מִשּׁוּם גִּילּוּי. וְרִבִּי שִׁמְעוֹן אוֹסֵר. מוֹדִין חֲכָמִים לְרִבִּי שִׁמְעוֹן כְּשֶׁרָאוּ אוֹתוֹ נוֹקֵר. וְתַנֵּי כֵן. אֲבַטִּיחַ שֶׁנִּיקַּר וְאָכְלוּ מִמֶּנּוּ עֲשָׂרָה בְּנֵי אָדָם וְכֵן יַיִן שֶׁנִּתְגַּלָּה וְשָׁתוּ מִמֶּנּוּ עֲשָׂרָה בְּנֵי אָדָם אָסוּר לוֹכַל וְלִשְׁתּוֹת אַחֲרֵיהֶן. אֲנִי אוֹמֵר. אֵירֶס שׁוֹקֵעַ הָיָה.

Their cheese. Rebbi Jeremiah said, why is a Gentile's milk forbidden? Because of admixture from forbidden animals. It was stated so: "There is nothing to worry if the Jew stands with the herd while the Gentile milks and brings to him." Rebbi Abba in the name of Rav Jehudah, Rebbi Simon in the name of Rebbi Joshua ben Levi: Why is a Gentile's milk forbidden? Because of uncovering. Let him make cheese! Rebbi Samuel ben Rav Isaac said, because of the poison left between the holes. It was stated so: There are three kinds of poison; one swims, one sinks down, and one is similar to a net on top. In the days of Rebbi Jeremiah the barrels of the Great Assembly were uncovered. The first ones drank and did not die. The later ones died. I say that it was sinking poison. Workers were in the field. The water pitcher was uncovered. The first ones drank and did not die. The later ones died. I say that it was sinking poison.

[325]"Uncovering is not a danger for oil and vinegar, brine, and *muries*, and honey, but Rebbi Simeon forbids. The Sages agree with Rebbi Simeon when it was seen pecking." It was stated thus[326]: "If a watermelon was pecked and ten people ate from it or wine was uncovered and ten people drank from it, it is forbidden to eat or drink after them; I say that there was sinking poison."

(3d line 15) שַׁמְנָן. מִי אָסַר אֶת הַשֶּׁמֶן. רַב יְהוּדָה אָמַר. דָּנִיֵּאל אָסַר אֶת הַשֶּׁמֶן. וַיָּשֶׂם דָּנִיֵּאל עַל לִבּוֹ אֲשֶׁר לֹא־יִתְגָּאַל בְּפַת־בַּג הַמֶּלֶךְ וּבְיֵין מִשְׁתָּיו. רִבִּי אָחָא רִבִּי תַּנְחוּם בַּר חִייָה בְּשֵׁם רִבִּי יוֹחָנָן וְאִית דְּאָמְרֵי לָהּ בְּשֵׁם רִבִּי יְהוֹשֻׁעַ בֶּן לֵוִי. שֶׁהָיוּ עוֹלִין עָלָיו לְהַר הַמֶּלֶךְ וְנֶהֱרָגִין עָלָיו.

וּמִי הִתִּירוֹ. רְבִּי וּבֵית דִּינוֹ הִתִּירוּ בַשֶּׁמֶן. בִּשְׁלֹשָׁה מְקוֹמוֹת נִקְרָא רְבִּי יְהוּדָה הַנָּשִׂיא רַבּוֹתֵינוּ. בְּגִיטִּין וּבַשֶּׁמֶן וּבְסַנְדָּל. וְיִקְרְאוּ לוֹ בֵּית דִּין שַׁרְיָיא. שֶׁכָּל־בֵּית דִּין שֶׁהוּא מְבַטֵּל שְׁלֹשָׁה דְבָרִים הוּא נִקְרָא בֵּית דִּין שַׁרְיָיא. אָמַר רְבִּי יוּדָן בֵּירְבִּי יִשְׁמָעֵאל. בֵּית דִּינוֹ חָלוּק עָלָיו בְּגִיטִּין. רְבִּי יוֹחָנָן בָּעֵי. וְלֹא כֵן תַּנִּינָן. שֶׁאֵין בֵּית דִּין יָכוֹל לְבַטֵּל דִּבְרֵי בֵית דִּין חֲבֵרוֹ עַד שֶׁיִּהְיֶה גָדוֹל מִמֶּנּוּ בְחָכְמָה וּבְמִּנְיָין. וְרְבִּי וּבֵית דִּינוֹ מַתִּירִין מַה שֶּׁאָסַר דָּנִיֵּאל וַחֲבוּרָתוֹ. אֶלָּא רְבִּי יוֹחָנָן כְּדַעְתֵּיהּ. דָּמַר רְבִּי יוֹחָנָן בְּשֵׁם רְבִּי לֶעְזָר בֵּירְבִּי צָדוֹק. מְקוּבָּל אֲנִי שֶׁכָּל־ גְּזֵירָה שֶׁבֵּית דִּין גּוֹזְרִין עַל הַצִּיבּוּר וְלֹא קִיבְּלוּ רוֹב הַצִּיבּוּר עֲלֵיהֶן אֵינָהּ גְּזֵירָה. וּבָדְקוּ וּמָצְאוּ גְּזֵירָה שֶׁלְּשֶׁמֶן וְלֹא קִיבְּלוּ רוֹב הַצִּיבּוּר עֲלֵיהֶן.

יִצְחָק בַּר שְׁמוּאֵל בַּר מַרְתָּא נְחַת לִנְצִיבִין. אַשְׁכַּח רְבִּי שְׂמְלַאי הַדְּרוֹמִי יָתִיב וְדָרִישׁ. רְבִּי וּבֵית דִּי הִתִּירוּ בַשֶּׁמֶן. שְׁמוּאֵל קִיבֵּל עֲלוֹי וְאָכַל. רַב לָא אָכַל. אָמַר לֵיהּ שְׁמוּאֵל. אֱכוֹל. דְּלָא כֵן אֲנָא כָּתֵיב עָלָךְ זָקֵן מַמְרֵא. אָמַר לֵיהּ. עַד דַּאֲנָא תַּמָּן אֲנָא יְדַע מָאן עִירְעַר עֲלֵיהּ. רְבִּי שְׂמְלַאי הַדְּרוֹמִי. אָמַר לֵיהּ. מָהוּ מַר לֵיהּ בְּשֵׁם גַּרְמֵיהּ. לֹא בְשֵׁם רְבִּי וּבֵית דִּינוֹ. אַטְרַח עֲלוֹי וְאָכַל.

Their oil. Who forbade the oil? Rav Jehudah said, Daniel forbade it. *Daniel was careful not to defile himself by the king's repast and the wine he drank*[327]. Rebbi Aḥa, Rebbi Tanḥum bar Ḥiyya in the name of Rebbi Joḥanan, but some say it in the name of Rebbi Joshua ben Levi: For it they were climbing up King's Mountain and were killed for it.

And who permitted it? Rebbi and his court permitted it. At three places is Rebbi Jehudah the Prince called "our teachers," in divorce documents, oil, and a sole. They should have called him "a permissive court", for any court which permits three [previously forbidden] things is called "permissive court." Rebbi Yudan ben Rebbi Ismael said, his court disagreed with him about bills of divorce.

Rebbi Joḥanan asked: Did we not state[328], "for no court may invalidate the words of another court unless it be greater in wisdom and numbers"? And Rebbi and his court permit what Daniel and his companions forbade? Rebbi Joḥanan follows his own opinion, for Rebbi Joḥanan said in the name of Rebbi Eleazar ben Rebbi Ṣadoq, I have a tradition that any restrictive edict passed by a court which is not accepted by the majority of the public is not an edict. They checked and found in the matter of the edict about oil and did not find that a majority of the public followed it.

Isaac bar Samuel bar Martha went down to Nisibis. He met Rebbi Simlai the Southerner who sat and expounded: Rebbi and his court permitted the oil. Samuel accepted this and ate. Rav did not eat. Samuel told him, eat! Otherwise I shall declare you a rebellious Elder. He answered him, when I still was there I knew who complained about it, Rebbi Simlai the Southerner. He told him, did he say it in the name of himself? No, in the name of Rebbi Jehudah the Prince. He bothered him and he ate.

323 This and the following paragraphs are from *Avodah zarah* 2:9, partially also from *Ševi`it, Terumot,* and *Ma`aser Šeni;* fully documented with variant readings and explained there in Notes 347-386. The order of the paragraphs is different. One discusses the original list of the 18 decrees.

324 The symbolic common meal of the dwellers at a dead-end street which converts it into a private domain, cf. Note 142.

325 This paragraph is from *Terumot* 8:5, Notes 139-142.

326 Tosephta *Terumot* 7:17, Babli *Avodah zarah* 30b.

327 *Dan.* 1:8.

328 Mishnah Idiut 1:5.

(3d line 35) בְּנוֹתֵיהֶן. אָמַר רִבִּי לְעָזָר. בְּשִׁבְעָה מְקוֹמוֹת כָּתוּב לֹא תִתְחַתֵּן בָּם. אָמַר רִבִּי אַבִּין. לוֹסַר שִׁבְעָה עֲמָמִים. תַּנָּא רִבִּי יְהוֹשֻׁעַ אוֹנְיָיה. לוֹסַר אֶת בֵּיצֵיהֶן. תַּנֵּי רִבִּי יִשְׁמָעֵאל. וְאֵת בֵּת הַיַּעֲנָה. זוֹ בֵיצַת הַנַּעֲמִית.

שִׁכְבַת זַרְעָן. וְלֹא כֵן אָמַר רִבִּי אָחָא רִבִּי חִינָנָא בָשֵׁם רִבִּי יוֹחָנָן. שִׁכְבַת זַרְעוֹ שֶׁלְגּוֹי טְהוֹרָה. שֶׁאֵי אֶיפְשַׁר לְשִׁכְבַת זֶרַע לָצֵאת בְּלֹא מֵימֵי רַגְלַיִם.

וְעַל הִילְכוֹת בַּעַל קֶרִי. רִבִּי בָּא בַר אָחָא בְשֵׁם רִבִּי. שׁוֹנֶה הֲלָכוֹת וְאֵינוֹ שׁוֹנֶה אֲגָדוֹת. תַּנֵּי בְשֵׁם רִבִּי יוֹסֵי. שׁוֹנֶה הֲלָכוֹת רוֹגְלִיּוֹת. וּבִלְבַד שֶׁלֹּא יַצִּיעַ אֶת מִשְׁנָתוֹ. וְאִית דְּבָעֵי מֵימַר. וּבִלְבַד שֶׁלֹּא יַזְכִּיר אֶת הָאַזְכָּרוֹת.

וְעַל הִילְכוֹת אֶרֶץ הָעַמִּים. וְלֹא כֵן אָמַר רִבִּי זְעִירָא בַּר אַבִּינָא בְשֵׁם רַב יִרְמְיָה. יוֹסֵף בֶּן יוֹעֶזֶר אִישׁ צְרֵידָה וְיוֹסֵי בֶּן יוֹחָנָן אִישׁ יְרוּשָׁלַיִם גָּזְרוּ טוּמְאָה עַל אֶרֶץ הָעַמִּים וְעַל כְּלִי זְכוּכִית. רִבִּי יוֹנָה אָמַר. רִבִּי יְהוּדָה בֶּן טַבַּאי. רִבִּי יוֹסֵי אָמַר. רִבִּי יְהוּדָה בֶּן טַבַּאי וְשִׁמְעוֹן בֶּן שֶׁטַח גָּזְרוּ טוּמְאָה עַל כְּלִי מַתָּכוֹת. הִלֵּל וְשַׁמַּי גָּזְרוּ עַל טַהֲרַת הַיָּדַיִם. רִבִּי יוֹסֵי בֵּירִבִּי בּוּן בְּשֵׁם רִבִּי לֵוִי. כָּךְ הָיְתָה הֲלָכָה בְיָדָן וּשְׁכָחוּהָ. וְעָמְדוּ הַשְּׁנַיִם וְהִסְכִּימוּ עַל דַּעַת הָרִאשׁוֹנִים. לְלַמְּדָךְ שֶׁכָּל־דָּבָר שֶׁנּוֹתְנִין בֵּית דִּין נַפְשָׁן עָלָיו סוֹפוֹ לְהִתְקַיֵּים בְּיָדָן כְּמָה שֶׁנֶּאֱמַר לְמֹשֶׁה בְסִינַי. וְאַתְיָא כַּיי דָּמַר רִבִּי מָנָא. כִּי לֹא־דָבָר רֵק הוּא מִכֶּם. וְאִם דָּבָר רֵק הוּא. מִכֶּם. לָמָה הוּא. שֶׁאֵין אַתֶּם יְגֵעִין בּוֹ. כִּי־הוּא חַיֵּיכֶם. אֵימָתַי הוּא חַיֵּיכֶם. בְּשָׁעָה שֶׁאַתֶּם יְגֵעִין בּוֹ.

Their daughters. Rebbi Eleazar said, in seven places it is written *do not intermarry with them*[329]. Rebbi Abun said, to forbid seven peoples[330]. Rebbi Joshua from Ono stated, to forbid their eggs. Rebbi Ismael stated, *and the ostrich's daughter*[331]. This is the ostrich's egg[332].

Their semen. But did not Rebbi Aha, Rebbi Hinena say in the name of Rebbi Johanan, a Gentile's semen is pure for semen cannot be discharged without urine[333].

About the rules of a person with an emission[295]. Rebbi Abba bar Aha in the name of Rebbi. He may study practical rules but not homiletics. It was stated in the name of Rebbi Yose: He may repeat known rules but he may not expound the Mishnah. Some want to say, he may not mention the Divine Name[334].

And about the rules for the land of Gentiles. [335]But did not Rebbi Ze'ira bar Abinna[336] say in the name of Rav Jeremiah: Joseph ben Yoezer from Sereda and Yose ben Johanan from Jerusalem decreed impurity of the land of Gentiles and of glass vessels; Rebbi Jonah said, Rebbi Jehudah ben Tabbai. Rebbi Yose said, Rebbi Jehudah ben Tabbai and Simeon ben Šetah decreed impurity of metal vessels; Hillel and Shammai decreed about purity of hands[337]. Rebbi Yose ben Rebbi Abun in the name of Rebbi Levi: so practice had been in their hands but they forgot it. The secondary [authorities] came and agreed with the intent of the first ones. To teach you that everything for which the Court made a real effort will in the end be confirmed for them as it was said to Moses on Sinai. This comes as Rebbi Mana said, *for it is not an empty matter for you*[338], if it is an empty matter, it is from you since you do not exert yourselves for it. *For it is your life.* When is it your life? Any time you are exerting yourselves for it.

329 The text as quoted is written only once, *Deut.* 7:3, an equivalent text is *Ex.* 34:16. In any case, since the prohibition is biblical, how can it be counted as rabbinic decree? Babli *Avodah zarah* 36b. In the Genizah fragment published by L. Ginzberg (p. 67) one reads בשבועה מקומות "in oath places". S. Liebermann wants to delete "places" and retain the statement "an oath, it is written", i. e., it cannot be a rabbinic prohibition. The text as it appears here is quoted in *Sotah* 1:8 (Note 285)

330 As enumerated in *Deut.* 7:1. The prohibition of all other Gentiles is rabbinic.

331 *Lev.* 11:16.

332 Eggs of impure birds are forbidden like the birds. Babli *Ḥulin* 64b.

333 Since the rules of impurity of genital discharges were given only to the "children of Israel" (*Lev.* 15:2). Any purity imputed to Gentiles must be rabbinic only; Babli *Niddah* 34a.

334 This paragraph is a short quote from *Berakhot* 3:4 (Notes 186-189); Babli *Bera-* *khot* 22a.

335 This paragraph is from *Ketubot* 8:11, explained there in Notes 96-105. Cf. Babli 14b.

336 Read with *Ketubot*: "R. Ze`ira, R. Abuna".

337 They codified popular practice that unwashed hands are always impure in the second degree.

338 *Deut.* 32:42. Quoted in *Sukkah* 4:1.

(3d line 52) שְׁמוּאֵל אָמַר. לֹא שָׁנוּ אֶלָּא בְתוֹךְ י״ח. הָא חוּץ לִי״ח אֲפִילוּ קָטָן מְבַטֵּל. הֲתִיבוּן. הֲרֵי שְׁבִיעִית. הֲרֵי חוּץ לִי״ח דָּבָר. וְרִבִּי יוֹחָנָן מַקְשֵׁי לָהּ. רִבִּי קְרִיסְפְּדָא בְשֵׁם רִבִּי יוֹחָנָן. רַבָּן גַּמְלִיאֵל וּבֵית דִּינוֹ הִתִּירוּ בְאִיסּוּר שְׁנֵי פְרָקִים הָרִאשׁוֹנִים. רִבִּי (יוֹנָתָן) [יוֹחָנָן] בָּעֵי. וְלֹא כֵן תַּנִּינָן. שֶׁאֵין בֵּית דִּין יָכוֹל לְבַטֵּל אֶת דִּבְרֵי בֵית דִּין חֲבֵרוֹ אֶלָּא אִם כֵּן גָּדוֹל מִמֶּנּוּ בַחָכְמָה וּבַמִּנְיָין. אָתָא רַב אָבוּן רַב יְהוּדָה בְשֵׁם שְׁמוּאֵל. לֹא שָׁנוּ אֶלָּא חוּץ לִי״ח. הָא בְתוֹךְ י״ח אֲפִילוּ גָדוֹל אֵינוֹ מְבַטֵּל. מִפְּנֵי שֶׁעָמְדָה לָהֶן בְּנַפְשׁוֹתֵיהֶן. אָמַר רִבִּי מָנָא. לֹא מִסְתַּבְּרָא דְּלָא הוֹאִיל וְהוּא אוֹנֶס בָּטֵל. הֲתִיבוּן. הֲרֵי שֶׁמֶן. הֲרֵי בְתוֹךְ י״ח. וְרִבִּי (יוֹנָתָן) [יוֹחָנָן] מַקְשֵׁי לָהּ. רַב כַּהֲנָא בְּרֵיהּ דְּרִבִּי חִייָה בַּר אַבָּא. רִבִּי אָחָא מַטֵּי בָהּ בְּשֵׁם רִבִּי יוֹחָנָן. שֶׁמֶן בִּיטְלוּ מְבוּטָּל.

נַחְמָן בְּרֵיהּ דְּרִבִּי שְׁמוּאֵל בַּר נַחְמָנִי בְשֵׁם רִבִּי שְׁמוּאֵל בַּר נַחְמָנִי. חָמֵשׁ חַטָּאוֹת מֵיתוֹת רָצוּ בֵית דִּין לְבַטֵּל מְבַטְּלִין. אָמַר רִבִּי חִייָא בַּר אָדָא. הָדָא דְּאַתְּ אָמַר. שֶׁלֹּא יָדְחוּ לְמִיתָה וְיִפְּלוּ לִנְדָבָה. אֲבָל לִיקָרֵב עַל גַּבֵּי הַמִּזְבֵּחַ אֵין חַטָּאת מֵיתָה קְרִיבָה.

Samuel said, they taught this only about the eighteen. Therefore, other than the eighteen even a lesser [court] may abolish[339]. They objected, is there not the Sabbatical year? This is not of the eighteen items, and Rebbi Johanan (said it)[340] and asked about it. Rebbi Krispedai[341] in the name of Rebbi Johanan: Rabban Gamliel and his court abolished the prohibitions of the first two terms[342]. Rebbi (Jonathan) [Johanan][343] asked. Did we not state[328], "for no court may invalidate the words of another court unless it be greater in wisdom and numbers"? There came Rav Abun, Rav Jehudah in the name of Samuel: they taught this only about other [decrees] than the eighteen. Therefore, the eighteen even a greater one cannot abolish, because they fought for it with their lives. Rebbi Mana said, this makes it reasonable that it is not so; since this is a case of force it is invalid[344]. They objected, is there not oil which is of the eighteen? And Rebbi (Jonathan) [Johanan][343] objected! Rav Cahana the son of Rebbi Ḥiyya bar Abba; Rebbi Aḥa bent it in the name of Rebbi Joḥanan: Oil, they abolished what was abolished[345].

Naḥman, the son of Rebbi Samuel bar Naḥmani in the name of Rebbi Samuel bar Naḥmani: The five kinds of purification sacrifices which are left to die, if the Court decides to abolish, they may abolish[346]. Rebbi Ḥiyya bar Ada said, that means that they are not sent to die but are used for voluntary sacrifices. But as far as sacrificing on the altar is concerned, no purification sacrifice destined to die may be sacrificed[347].

339 A court of lesser standing than the one which issued a decree may abolish it as long as it is not of the Eighteen Decrees described earlier.

340 The word was written by the scribe; it was deleted by the corrector. As S. Liebermann has shown, the deletion is unjustified. R. Johanan both formulated a tradition and questioned its validity. The following text is fromŠevi`it 1:1, Notes 6-7.

341 InŠevi`it 1:1, his name is Crispus.

342 Agricultural work is forbidden in the Sabbatical year. In TractateŠevi`it, rabbinic interpretation infers from verses that also the preparation of fields or orchards for the new sowing or planting season, in summer and early fall, is forbidden in the months preceding New Year's day of the Sabbatical. These terms are different for sowing and planting; they are referred to as "the two periods."

However, since the biblical commandment of the Sabbatical is intrinsically connected with that of the Jubilee, it cannot be in force when the Jubilee is not in force, i. e., if not all of Israel dwells on the ancestral land distributed by Joshua. Therefore during the Second Commonwealth the Sabbatical was a rabbinic institution. Rabban Gamliel (of Jabneh, the first Patriarch after the destruction of the Second Temple) decided that in the absence of the Temple the rabbinic institution of the Sabbatical should continue without extensions. While his Court was the highest authority in his time, he could not compete in standing with the Men of the Great Assembly who established the rules for the Second Commonwealth.

343 The text in parentheses is that of the Leiden ms., the [correct] one in brackets is from the Geniza fragment which is legible at this place.

344 The first argument was that the 18 decrees must be inviolate because people were killed for it; R. Mana's argument is that the decrees were imposed by force and therefore are intrinsically invalid.

345 As stated earlier, the decree about Gentile olive oil never was accepted by the people; it never became enforceable law.

346 Mishnah *Temurah* 3:1. A purification sacrifice is an obligation; it cannot be offered voluntarily nor can there be more

than one sacrifice for one obligation. Also it is most holy; its sacred status cannot be abolished. Therefore the calf born to an animal dedicated as purification sacrifice, or a substitute for such an animal, or one whose owner had died, or a dedicated one which became too old to be sacrificed, or one which was lost and found later when it had developed a defect and the owner in the meantime had offered a substitute, are intrinsically holy but forbidden as sacrifices.

The rule, classified in the Babli (*Bekhorot* 16a, *Temurah* 18a) as "tradition", i. e., being part of the original institutions of post-exilic Judaism, possibly older, is treated here as rabbinic interpretation.

347 While biblically the animal cannot become a sacrifice in any form, if it develops a blemish it can be sold as profane and the money used for additional Temple sacrifices.

(3c line 67) מתני'. בֵּית שַׁמַּאי אוֹמְרִים אֵין שׁוֹרִין דְּיוֹ סַמְמָנִין וְכַרְשִׁינִין כול'. וּמָה טַעֲמָהוֹן דְּבֵית שַׁמַּי. שֵׁשֶׁת יָמִים תַּעֲבוֹד וְעָשִׂיתָ כָּל־מְלַאכְתֶּךָ: כָּל־מְלַאכְתֶּךָ. גּוֹמְרָהּ מִבְּעוֹד יוֹם. וּמָה טַעֲמְהוֹן דְּבֵית הִלֵּל. שֵׁשֶׁת יָמִים תֵּעָשֶׂה מַעֲשֶׂיךָ וּבַיּוֹם. מַא מְקַייְמִין בֵּית הִלֵּל טַעֲמוֹן דְּבֵית שַׁמַּי. שֵׁשֶׁת יָמִים תַּעֲבוֹד וְעָשִׂיתָ כָּל־מְלַאכְתֶּךָ: בְּעוֹבְדֵי בְיָדָן. וּמַא מְקַייְמִין בֵּית שַׁמַּי טַעֲמוֹן דְּבֵית הִלֵּל. שֵׁשֶׁת יָמִים תֵּעָשֶׂה מַעֲשֶׂיךָ וּבַיּוֹם. כְּהָדָא דְתַנֵּי. פּוֹתְקִין אַמַּת הַמַּיִם לְגִינָה מֵעֶרֶב שַׁבָּת וְהִיא שׁוֹתָה וְהוֹלֶכֶת בַּשַּׁבָּת. נוֹתְנִין קִילוֹרִית עַל גַּבֵּי הָעַיִן מֵעֶרֶב שַׁבָּת וְהוּא מִתְרַפֵּא וְהוֹלֶכֶת בַּשַּׁבָּת. נוֹתְנִין רְטִייָה עַל גַּבֵּי מַכָּה מֵעֶרֶב שַׁבָּת וְהִיא מִתְרַפֵּא וְהוֹלֶכֶת בַּשַּׁבָּת. נוֹתְנִין מַגְמָר תַּחַת הַכֵּלִים מֵעֶרֶב שַׁבָּת וְהֵן מִתְעַשְּׁנִין וְהוֹלְכִין בַּשַּׁבָּת. נוֹתְנִין גָּפְרִית תַּחַת הַכֵּלִים מֵעֶרֶב שַׁבָּת וְהֵן מִתְגַּפְּרִין וְהוֹלְכִין בַּשַּׁבָּת. אֵין נוֹתְנִין חִטִּים לָרֵחַיִים שֶׁל מַיִם אֶלָּא כְּדֵי שֶׁיִּיטָּחֵנוּ כָּל־צוֹרְכָּן מִבְּעוֹד יוֹם. אָמַר רִבִּי חַגַּיי. מִפְּנֵי שֶׁהֵן מַשְׁמִיעוֹת אֶת הַקּוֹל. אָמַר לֵיהּ רִבִּי יוֹסֵי. יָאוּת סָבַר כְּרִבִּי יְהוּדָה. בְּרַם כְּרַבָּנִין. כְּמָה דְאִינּוּן אָמְרִין תַּמָּן מִשֵּׁם לֹא הוּתְחַל בְּכָל־טִיפָּה וְטִיפָּה. כֵּן אִינּוּן אָמְרִין הָכָא מִשּׁוּם לֹא הוּתְחַל בְּכָל־חִיטָּה וְחִיטָּה. אָמַר רִבִּי יוֹסֵי בֵּירִבִּי בּוּן. מִפְּנֵי שֶׁהוּא שָׁכָח וְתוֹקֵעַ אֶת הַיָּתֵדִי.

Mishnah: "The House of Shammai say, one does not soak ink[12], chemicals, or vetch,"[348] etc. What is the reason of the House of Shammai? *Six days you shall work and do all your deeds*[349]. *All your deeds*, finish them by daylight. What is the reason of the House of Hillel? *Six days you shall work on your works and on [the seventh] day*[350]. How do the House of Hillel explain the reason of the House of Shammai, *six days you shall work and do all your deeds*? When they work with their hands[351]. How do the House of Shammai explain the reason of the House of Hillel, *six days you shall work on your works and on [the seventh] day*? Following what was stated[352], "One opens a water canal leading into a garden on Friday evening and it is continuously watered on the Sabbath. One puts ointment[353] on an eye on Friday evening and it is continuously healing on the Sabbath. One puts a compress on a wound on Friday evening and it is continuously healing on the Sabbath. One puts burning incense under clothing on Friday evening and it is continuously smoked on the Sabbath. One puts sulfur under clothing on Friday evening and it is continuously sulfured on the Sabbath. One may not give wheat into a water mill on Friday evening unless it will be completely ground as long as it is daylight." Rebbi Haggai said, because it is making noise[354]. Rebbi Yose said to him, this is fine if one holds with Rebbi Jehudah. But for the rabbis, just as they say because not every single drop was started, so they say here because not every grain kernel was started[355]. Rebbi Yose ben Rebbi Abun said, because he is apt to forget and will push the peg[356].

348 Quote from Mishnah 9.

349 *Ex.* 20:9. The argument is quoted in Tosephta 1:21, *Mekhilta dR. Simeon ben Yohai* p. 149.

350 *Ex.* 23:12.

351 While work on the Sabbath is forbidden, letting machines work for you on the Sabbath is permitted.

352 Tosephta 1:23, Babli 18a; *Mekhilta dR. Simeon ben Yohai* p. 149. The Tosephta stated rules common to the Houses of Hillel and Shammai even if the reasons for permission or prohibition may be different for the Houses. It is clear from the Tosephta that the House of Shammai forbid soaking ink in water during the Sabbath only because nothing of it is usable when the Sabbath begins, while watering a garden or smoking out lice from a garment is useful even if done only for a short time. The Babli disagrees, 18a (Explanation of S. Liebermann.)

353 Greek κολλύριον, τό.

354 In the Babli 18a this is an argument of the Babylonian Rabba. Since some grain will have been turned into flour, without this argument also the House of Shammai would permit milling flour in a watermill on the Sabbath.

355 This refers to Mishnah 2:4 where R. Jehudah permits feeding a burning light on the Sabbath with oil dripping from a vessel above the fire while the majority forbid it.

356 According to him by biblical law milling on the Sabbath in an automatic mill is permitted according to both Houses; the prohibition is purely rabbinic; both Houses agree that it should be forbidden because the miller will hear when the milling is done and move a peg on his mill, which is a Sabbath desecration.

בֵּית שַׁמַּי אָמְרוּ לְבֵית הִלֵּל דָּבָר אֶחָד וְלֹא יָכְלוּ לְהָשִׁיבָן. בֵּית הִלֵּל אָמְרוּ לְבֵית שַׁמַּי (4a line 9)
דָּבָר אֶחָד וְלֹא יָכְלוּ לְהָשִׁיבָן. אָמְרוּ לָהֶן בֵּית הִלֵּל לְבֵית שַׁמַּי. אֵין אַתֶּם מוֹדִין לָנוּ שֶׁטּוֹעֲנִין
קוֹרַת בֵּית הַבַּד וּבְעִיגּוּלֵי הַגַּת עִם חֲשֵׁיכָה. וְלֹא יָכְלוּ לְהָשִׁיבָן. אָמַר רִבִּי זְעִירָא. אִילּוּלֵא דְלָא
מַעֲלֶה רֵישִׁי בֵּינֵי אַרְיְוָותָא הֲוֵינָא אֲמַר טַעֲמָא. תַּמָּן כְּבָר נֶעֶקְרָה כָּל־טִיפָה וְטִיפָה מִמְּקוֹמָהּ.
הָכָא מָה אִית לָךְ מֵימַר.

בֵּית שַׁמַּי אָמְרוּ לְבֵית הִלֵּל דָּבָר אֶחָד וְלֹא יָכְלוּ לְהָשִׁיבָן. אָמְרוּ בֵּית שַׁמַּי לְבֵית הִלֵּל. אֵין
אַתֶּם מוֹדִין לָנוּ שֶׁאֵין צוֹלִין בָּשָׂר וּבֵיצָה וּבָצָל אֶלָּא כְּדֵי שֶׁיִּצּוֹלוּ כָּל־צוֹרְכָן מִבְּעוֹד יוֹם. וְלֹא יָכְלוּ
לְהָשִׁיבָן. אָמַר רִבִּי זְעִירָא. אִילּוּלֵא דְלָא מַעֲלֶה רֵישִׁי בֵּינֵי אַרְיְוָותָא הֲוֵינָא אֲמַר טַעֲמָא. תַּמָּן
בָּשָׂר וּבָצָל וּבֵיצָה דַּרְכָּן לְהִתְהַפֵּךְ. הָכָא מָה אִית לָךְ מֵימַר. אָמַר רִבִּי יוּדָן. נִצְלוּ כַאֲכִילַת בֶּן
דְּרוֹסַאי. אָסְרוּ דָּבָר שֶׁדַּרְכּוֹ לְהִתְהַפֵּךְ עַד כְּדֵי שֶׁיִּצָּלֶה כָּל־צוֹרְכוֹ מִבְּעוֹד יוֹם. אָמַר רִבִּי מָנָא. לֹא
מִסְתַּבְּרָא דְלָא מוּתָּר. דִּינּוּן יָכְלִין לְמֵימַר לוֹן. הֵיאַךְ אַתֶּם מְשִׁיבִין לָנוּ מִדָּבָר שֶׁדַּרְכּוֹ לִצְלוֹת
כָּל־צוֹרְכוֹ מִבְּעוֹד יוֹם עַל דָּבָר שֶׁאֵין לְהַשְׁרוֹת דַּרְכּוֹ כָּל־צוֹרְכוֹ מִבְּעוֹד יוֹם.

The House of Shammai put a question to the House of Hillel which they could not answer; the House of Hillel put a question to the House of Shammai which they could not answer. [357]"The House of Hillel said to the House of Shammai, do you not agree with us that one may load the beam of the olive press and the round stone of the wine press[18]? They did not find an answer." Rebbi Ze`ira said, if I would not put my head between the lions I could give a reason. There, each drop already was dislocated[358]; here what can you say?

The House of Shammai put a question to the House of Hillel which they could not answer. [359]"The House of Shammai said to the House of Hillel, do you not agree with us that one does not roast meat, or onions, or an egg, unless they be completely roasted when it is still daylight[19]? They did not find an answer." Rebbi Ze`ira said, if I would not put my head between the lions I could give a reason. There, onion, meat, or egg, usually are flipped[360]; here, what can you say? Rebbi Yudan said, if they were roasted like Ben Derosai's food[361]. They forbade something which usually is flipped unless it be completely roasted as long as it is still day. Rebbi Mana said, it is not reasonable that it should be permitted. For they can say to them, how can you respond to us with something which ordinarily is completely roasted when it still is day about something which ordinarily cannot be completely soaked when it still is day[362]?

357 Tosephta 1:21.

358 The essential work was done before the Sabbath started, cf. Note 355.

359 Tosephta 1:20.

360 If one roasts on a hot metal plate one has to continuously flip the meat etc. to avoid it being burned. If one roasts on a spit one has to continuously turn the spit. In both cases, one may not do this by biblical decree.

361 The technical term for very rare food. Technically cooked food is considered cooked before the Sabbath if it was rare by sundown. But this cannot apply to roasted food for people who do not eat their food very rare.

362 R. Mana argues that even for the House of Shammai very rare cooked food is considered completely cooked for the rules of the Sabbath, the only exception being roasted food which requires constant flipping since otherwise the House of Hillel could argue that the objection of the House of Shammai compares apples and oranges.

(4a line 25) מתני'. בֵּית שַׁמַּאי אוֹמְרִים. אֵין נוֹתְנִין אוּנִין שֶׁלְפִּשְׁתָּן בְּתוֹךְ הַתַּנּוּר כול'. מַהוּ מִיתְהַנֵּי. אָמַר רִבִּי אַבָּהוּ. כְּגוֹן אִילֵּין קוּרְיָיאֵי דְּלָא מְקַפְּדִין. רַב יְהוּדָה בְּשֵׁם שְׁמוּאֵל. וְהִיא שֶׁתְּהֵא הַיּוֹרָה עֲקוּרָה. אֲבָל אִם הָיְתָה הַיּוֹרָה קְבוּעָה אֲסוּרָה. מִפְּנֵי שֶׁהוּא מִתְיָירֵא שֶׁמָּא מִתְאַכֵּל צִיבְעוּ וְהוּא מוֹסִיף מוֹי. רִבִּי שְׁמוּאֵל בְּשֵׁם רִבִּי אַבָּהוּ. בֵּית הִלֵּל יָלְפִין מְלֶאכֶת הֶיתֵּר מִמְּלֶאכֶת אִיסּוּר. אִילוּ עָשָׂה כֵן בַּשַּׁבָּת שֶׁמָּא אֵינוֹ אָסוּר. וְדִכְוָוֹתָהּ עָשָׂה כֵן מִבְּעוֹד יוֹם מוּתָּר.

Mishnah: "The House of Shammai say, one does not put bundles of flax into an oven,"[363] etc. What profit does he have? Rebbi Abbahu said, for example these villagers who do not care[364].

Rav Jehudah in the name of Samuel: Only if the vat was taken off. But if the vat was fixed, it is forbidden, since he will be afraid that his dye will have been absorbed and he will add water[365]. Rebbi Samuel in the name of Rebbi Abbahu: The House of Hillel learn permitted work from forbidden work. Would it not be forbidden if he did it on the Sabbath? When he did similarly as long as it is still daytime it is permitted[366].

363 Quote from Mishnah 10. The discussion is only about the second part of the Mishnah, about the dyer and his vat.

364 Which dyer would start dying on Friday afternoon when he knows the he will not have control over the process and cannot guarantee the outcome? If he dyes cloth for a rural population which is not insistent on quality. Then he can use his installation also on the Sabbath and reduce his overhead to undercut the competition.

365 Even the House of Hillel will allow only to keep the cloth in the dye but not to heat it on the Sabbath since that would require periodically adding water which is a deadly sin on the Sabbath.

366 If the vat is taken off the fire before sundown, the House of Hillel have absolutely no restrictions about what may be done Friday afternoons.

(4a line 33) מתני'. בֵּית שַׁמַּאי אוֹמְרִים אֵין פּוֹרְסִין מְצוּדוֹת חַיָּה וְעוֹפוֹת וְדָגִים כול'. מִי מוֹדִיעַ. אִם נִתְקַלְקְלָה הַמְּצוּדָה דָּבָר בָּרִיא שֶׁנִּיצוֹדוּ מִבְּעוֹד יוֹם. וְאִם לֹא נִתְקַלְקְלָה הַמְּצוּדָה דָּבָר בָּרִיא שֶׁלֹּא נִיצוֹדוּ מִבְּעוֹד יוֹם. וַאֲפִילוּ נִתְקַלְקְלָה הַמְּצוּדָה חָשׁ לוֹמַר שֶׁמָּא לֹא נִיצוֹדוּ מִבְּעוֹד יוֹם. אָמַר רְבִּי יוֹסֵי בֵּירְבִּי בּוּן. בְּפוֹרֵשׂ בַּחוֹרְשִׁין. תֵּדַע לָךְ שֶׁהוּא כֵן. דִּתְנָן דָּגִים. וְדָגִים לֹא בְמָקוֹם שֶׁהֵן מְצוּיִין. יָכָא בְמָקוֹם שֶׁחַיָּה וָעוֹף מְצוּיִין.

2 ואם | י אם   3 חש | י וחש   4 יוסי | G יוסה   בפורש G בפורס   דתנן | G דתנינן   5 וכא | G וכה י והכא   שחיה G שחייה   מצויין | G מצויים

רְבִּי חִייָא בְשֵׁם רְבִּי אַתְקִין לְהָל. סָבְרִין מֵימַר. מוּתָּרִין לְמָחָר. רְבִּי חִזְקִיָּה וְרְבִּי עוּזִיאֵל בְּרֵיהּ דְּרְבִּי חוֹנִיָּה דְּבָרַת חַוְורָן. מוּתָּרִין מַמָּשׁ. סָבְרִין מֵימַר. סְפֵיקוֹ הִתִּירוֹ. רְבִּי חֲנַנְיָה וְרְבִּי יוֹנָתָן תְּרֵיהוֹן אֲמְרִין. סְפֵק הָכֵן אָסוּר. וְרְבִּי יוֹחָנָן אָמַר. סְפֵק הָכֵן מוּתָּר.

1 חייא G | י זעורא ר' | י G רב אתקין להל | י - ר' | G -   עוזיאל G | י עוזיאל   2 ספיקו | י ספיקן   3 חנניה | י חנינה 368 ור' | G ר' ספק | G ספיק

רְבִּי חִייָא רוֹבָא וְרְבִּי שִׁמְעוֹן בְּרְבִּי. חַד אָמַר הַגּוֹי צָרִיךְ הָכֵן. וְחָרָנָה אָמַר. אֵין הַגּוֹי צָרִיךְ הָכֵן. וְלָא יָדְעִינָן מָאן אָמַר דָּא וּמָאן אָמַר דָּא. מִן מַה דְּרַב מְעַנֵּי מֵיתֵי קוֹמֵי רְבִּי חִייָא רוֹבָא וְהוּא אָמַר לֵיהּ. הָן הֲוֵיתָא. וְהוּא אָמַר לֵיהּ. שִׁיעֲרָתָהּ הֲוַת עַבְדָא וַהֲוִינָא אָכִיל מִנָּהּ תְּאֵינִין. הֲוֵי דוּ אָמַר. אֵין הַגּוֹי צָרִיךְ הָכֵן.

1 רובא | י רבה   חד | G חדה   2 ידעינן | G י ידעין   מאן | G מן   רובא | G רובה   רבה | G הויתא | י הויתה   עבדא | G עברה   תאינין | י תאינים

חַד תַּלְמִיד מִן סִימָאי אֲזַל לְאַנְטוֹירִיס וְאַייתוֹן לֵיהּ דַּרְמַסְקִינָא וַאֲכַל. חַד תַּלְמִיד מִן דְּרְבִּי יְהוֹשֻׁעַ בֶּן לֵוִי אֲזַל לְתַמָּן וְאַייתֵי לֵיהּ דַּרְמַסְקִינָא וְלֹא אֲכַל. וַאֲתָא וָמַר קוֹמֵי רַבֵּיהּ. אָמַר לֵיהּ. דּוּ נְהִיג כְּשִׁיטָתֵיהּ דְּרְבִּי סִימָאי. דְּרְבִּי סִימָאי אֲמַר. אֵין הַגּוֹי צָרִיךְ הָכֵן. רְבִּי אַבָּהוּ בְשֵׁם רְבִּי יְהוֹשֻׁעַ בֶּן לֵוִי. דַּמְדַּמְנִיּוֹת שֶׁבַּכְּרֶם הֲרֵי אֵילּוּ אֲסוּרוֹת. רַב הוּנָא בְשֵׁם רַב. שָׂצִים שֶׁבַּכְּכָפִים הֲרֵי אֵילּוּ מוּתָּרִין.

1 סימאי G | י דר' סימיי   אנטויריס | י אנטרדס   דרמסקינא | י דורמסקנה   2 ואייתי | י אייתו   דרמסקינא | י דורמסקנה   ואתא ומר | י אתא ואמר ליה | י -   3 נהיג | י נהג   כשיטתיה דר' סימאי | י כשיטת רביה סימאי | י סימיי   4 דמדמיות G דמדמות | G חונה הונא | G י חונה   שצים | י שיצים   שבכפים | י שבככפים   5 אילו G | אלו

[369]Mishnah: "The House of Shammai say, one does set traps for wild animals, or birds, of fish," etc. Who informs? If the trap was sprung, it is certain that they were caught when it still was day. But if the trap was not sprung, it is certain that they were not caught when it still was day. And even if the trap was sprung, in worry one may say that they were not caught when it still was day[370]. Rebbi Yose ben Rebbi Abun said, if it was set in a forest.

You should know that it is so since we have stated "fish". Are fish not there where they are found? Also here at a place where game and birds are found[371].

Rebbi Hiyya in the name of Rebbi instituted that it should not happen[372]. They wanted to say, they are permitted the next day[373]. Rebbi Hizqiah and Rebbi Uziel the son of Rebbi Onias of Barat Hauran: They are really permitted. They wanted to say, its doubt made it permitted. Rebbi Hanina and Rebbi Jonathan both say, if in doubt whether it was prepared it is forbidden[374]. But Rebbi Johanan said, in doubt whether it was prepared it is permitted.

The Elder Rebbi Hiyya and Rebbi Simeon ben Rebbi, one said a Gentile needs preparation, the other said, a Gentile does not need preparation[374]. We did not know who said this and who said that. From that Rav refrained from coming before the Elder Rebbi Hiyya who asked him, where have you been? He told him: a caravan passed by and I ate figs from them[375] this implies that he said, a Gentile does not need preparation.

A student of [Rebbi][376] Simai went to Antipatris[377]; they brought him Morocco-plums[378] and he ate. A student of Rebbi Joshua ben Levi went there; they brought him Morocco-plums and he did not eat. He came and told it to his teacher who said to him, this one follows the argument of Rebbi Simai, as Rebbi Simai said, a Gentile does not need preparation. Rebbi Abbahu in the name of Rebbi Joshua ben Levi: The red grapes in a vineyard are forbidden. Rav Huna in the name of Rav: The hard dates on palm leaves are permitted[379].

367 A Babylonian form.

368 For chronological reasons this is the correct reading.

369 Quote from Mishnah 10. The entire piece is copied from *Beṣah* 3:2 (י); it is a commentary on the Mishnah there. The Genizah text is reasonably complete here (G).

370 Mishnah *Beṣah* 3:2 reads: "One may not take from traps set for game, birds, or fish on the eve of a holiday unless one know that it was caught before the onset of the holiday. It happened that a Gentile brought fish to Rabban Gamliel who said they are permitted but I do not want to accept from him." The question arises how can one know that an animal was trapped unless one go there and take it out before the holiday. Does the first part of the Mishnah have any practical application? The answer is that by observation from afar one may determine

what happened.

The main subject of Tractate *Beṣah* is the requirement, based ostensibly on *Ex.* 16:5, that on the Sabbath and holidays only food prepared beforehand may be consumed. Since cooking on the Sabbath is forbidden, there is no problem regarding Sabbath observation. For the holidays there first is the problem of extending a commandment given for the Sabbath to holidays and second the fact that cooking and other preparation of food is permitted (*Ex.* 13:16). Therefore the application of the requirement of preparation can refer only to the accessibility of raw materials. If an animal is trapped before the onset of the holiday it is prepared in this sense and may be taken and turned into food on the holiday. Another question then is whether the extension of *Ex.* 16:5 to holidays is considered biblical (when cases of doubt have to be resolved restrictively) or rabbinic (when cases of doubt have to be resolved leniently).

371 The rules prescribed are a legal fiction (in the Babli, *Beṣah* 24b, ascribed to the last generation of Tannaïm). They can be relied on only in situations where the probability of correctness is significantly larger than 50%. (Quoted by Tosaphot 17b *s.v.* אלא).

372 In the *editio princeps* and all later editions, the word לְהָל in the Leiden ms. (לְהָל in G) is read as 'לחל, abbreviation of להלכה "as practice". The evidence of G excludes this interpretation. The word is otherwise unknown in the rabbinic, Hebrew or Aramaic, vocabulary. It seems to be the same as Arabic لهلة which in Wehr's Dictionary is described as "used in wishes contrary to what one expects to happen" or in Brelot "(discours) très faible". R. Hiyya reluctantly formulated Rebbi's ruling (or. R. Ze'ira Rav's). The expression is not in *Beṣah*, but there seems to be no reason to delete it from the text.

373 This now refers to the fish brought by a Gentile to Rabban Gamliel. Did he want to say that they can be handled by Jews on the holiday but not eaten on that day or are they as if prepared by a Jew beforehand (Babli *Beṣah* 24a)?

374 As explained earlier, the disagreement is whether the requirement of prior preparation is biblical or rabbinic.

375 The Gentile caravan arriving on the holiday.

376 Reading of G and י.

377 This is generally accepted as explanation of the otherwise unexplained and diverse names reported for the place.

378 According to H. L. Fleischer, New Greek δαμάσκηνος "Damascus plum"; δαμάσκηνα "Damascus plum tree".

379 Grapes which still are hard at harvest time and left to ripen in late autumn do not fall down by themselves; one must assume that they were plucked from the vine on the day they were brought; one may not accept them from a Gentile who brings them on a holiday. But dates in a similar case will fall down, one may assume that they were collected from the ground and may be accepted.

(4a line 54) מתני'. בֵּית שַׁמַּאי אוֹמְרִים. מוֹכְרִין לַנָּכְרִי כוּל׳. אֵי זֶהוּ מָקוֹם קָרוֹב. יָבֹא כַּיֵּי דָמַר שְׁמוּאֵל. כְּגוֹן מֵחוּטְרָא לִנְהַרְדְּעָא. אוֹף הָכָא כֵן. אִית דְּבָעֵי מֵימַר. עַד שֶׁהוּא מַגִּיעַ לְבֵיתוֹ. וְאִית דְּבָעֵי מֵימַר. עַד שֶׁהוּא מַגִּיעַ לְעִירוֹ. רִבִּי עֲקִיבָה אוֹמֵר. כְּדֵי שֶׁיֵּצֵא מִמְּקוֹם הַפֶּתַח וִיקַדֵּשׁ עָלָיו הַיּוֹם. אָמַר רִבִּי יוֹחָנָן. זוֹ דִּבְרֵי רִבִּי יוֹסֵי. וְרִבִּי עֲקִיבָה בָא לְהַכְרִיעַ עַל דִּבְרֵי בֵית הִלֵּל. אֵין נוֹתְנִין לְגוֹי עַל מְנָת לָצֵאת. נָטַל וְיָצָא אֵין אַתְּ זָקוּק לוֹ. אֵין נוֹתְנִין לְכָלֶב עַל מְנָת לָצֵאת. נָטַל וְיָצָא אֵין אַתְּ זָקוּק לוֹ.

Mishnah: "They House of Shammai say, one sells to a Non-Jew,"[380] etc. What means "a nearby destination"? It should be as Samuel said, for example as from Hutra to Nahardea; here it is the same[381]. Some want to say, until he reaches his home. But some want to say, until he reaches his town. Rebbi Aqiba says, that he leaves the place of the door when the day becomes holy around him[382]. Rebbi Johanan said, these are the words of Rebbi Yose: But Rebbi Aqiba comes to determine following the words of the House of Hillel[383]. One does not give to a Gentile on condition that he leave. If he left, you do not have to interfere. One does not give to a dog on condition that he leave. If he left, you do not have to interfere[384].

380 Quote from Mishnah 11.

381 "Nearby" must have a definite legal sense if it is used in the Mishnah. It is not known where Samuel stated his criterion; *Pene Moshe* points to the "lost" Yerushalmi (?) of Chapter 23:4 where the Mishnah uses the same term.

382 Tosephta 1:22.

383 All this is reproduced in the Babli 18b.

Following R. Aqiba, the Gentile must have left the space of 4 cubits around the exit at sundown, "when the day becomes holy." In R. Johanan's interpretation, R. Aqiba determines the exact meaning of the position of the House of Hillel in the Mishnah.

384 These sentences appear as a *baraita* in the Babli, 19a.

(4a line 60) תַּנֵּי. אוּמָנִין גּוֹיִם שֶׁהָיוּ עוֹשִׂין עִם יִשְׂרָאֵל. בְּתוֹךְ בֵּיתוֹ שֶׁלְּיִשְׂרָאֵל אָסוּר וּבְתוֹךְ בָּתֵּיהֶן מוּתָּר. אָמַר רִבִּי שִׁמְעוֹן בֶּן לְעָזָר. בַּמֶּה דְבָרִים אֲמוּרִין. בְּקִיבּוֹלֶת. אֲבָל בְּשָׂכִיר יוֹם אָסוּר. בַּמֶּה דְבָרִים אֲמוּרִין. בְּתָלוּשׁ מִן הַקַּרְקַע. אֲבָל בִּמְחוּבָּר לַקַּרְקַע אָסוּר. בְּעִיר אַחֶרֶת בֵּין כָּךְ וּבֵין כָּךְ מוּתָּר. מָהוּ בֵּין כָּךְ וּבֵין כָּךְ. בֵּין בְּתָלוּשׁ בֵּין בִּמְחוּבָּר. בֵּין בְּשָׂכִיר בֵּין בְּקִיבּוֹלֶת. אָמַר רִבִּי אִילָא. בֵּין בְּתָלוּשׁ בֵּין בִּמְחוּבָּר. וּבִלְבַד בְּקִיבּוֹלֶת. רִבִּי שִׁמְעוֹן בֶּן בַּרְקָנָא בְשֵׁם רִבִּי אָחָא. בְּשַׁבָּת וּבְאָבֵל וּבַעֲבוֹדָה זָרָה הֲלָכָה כְרִבִּי שִׁמְעוֹן בֶּן אֶלְעָזָר.

[385]It was stated: Gentile workmen who were working for an Israel[386], in the Israel's house it is forbidden, in their houses it is permitted. Rebbi Simeon ben Eleazar said, when has this been said? For contract work[387]. But for one hired by the day it is forbidden. When has this been said, when it was cut from the ground, but as long as it is standing on the ground it is forbidden. In another town, in any case it is permitted. What means "in any case"? Whether cut from the ground or standing on the ground; whether a hireling or contract work. Rebbi Illa said, whether separated from the ground or connected to the ground, but only for contract work. Rebbi Simeon ben Barqana[388] in the name of Rebbi Aha: Concerning Sabbath, mourning, and idolatry, practice follows Rebbi Simeon ben Eleazar[389].

385 An almost identical paragraph is in *Avodah Zarah* 1:1 (Notes 53-55), referring to Jewish craftsmen working for Gentile employers on their holidays.

386 On the Sabbath.

387 The craftsman is paid for the completed work, irrespective of the time he needs to compete the job. He is an independent businessman working for himself, not for the Jew.

388 In *Avodah Zarah*: ben Carsana. In the quote by Tosaphot 18a (*s.v.* אין , 17b): ben Cahana.

389 The statement for the Sabbath is here, the one for *Avodah Zarah* is quoted in Note 385. The quote about mourning is a parallel *baraita* in *Semahot* 5:8 detailing the rules under which a craftsman in mourning may work. The statement is accepted as practice in *Halakhot Gedolot* and most medieval halakhic authors.

(4a line 68) אֵין מְשַׁלְּחִין אִיגְרוֹת בְּיַד גּוֹי לֹא בְעֶרֶב שַׁבָּת וְלֹא בַחֲמִישִׁי בַּשַׁבָּת. בֵּית שַׁמַּי אוֹסְרִין אֲפִילוּ בָרְבִיעִי. וּבֵית הִלֵּל מַתִּירִין. אָמְרוּ עָלָיו עַל רבִּי יוֹסֵי הַכֹּהֵן שֶׁלֹּא נִמְצָא כְתָבוֹ בְּיַד גּוֹי מֵעוֹלָם.

אֵין מַפְרִישִׁין לְיָם הַגָּדוֹל לֹא בְעֶרֶב שַׁבָּת וְלֹא בַחֲמִישִׁי בַּשַּׁבָּת. בֵּית שַׁמַּי אוֹסְרִין אֲפִילוּ בָרְבִיעִי. וּבֵית הִלֵּל מַתִּירִין. אִם הָיָה דָּבָר שֶׁלְּסַכָּנָה. כְּגוֹן מָצוֹר לְצִידָן. מוּתָּר.

אֵין מַקִּיפִין עַל עִיר שֶׁלְּגוֹיִם פָּחוּת מִשְּׁלֹשָׁה יָמִים קוֹדֶם לַשַּׁבָּת. הָדָא דְתֵימַר בְּמִלְחֶמֶת הָרְשׁוּת. אֲבָל בְּמִלְחֶמֶת חוֹבָה אֲפִילוּ בַּשַּׁבָּת. שֶׁכֵּן מָצִינוּ שֶׁלֹּא נִכְבְּשָׁה יְרִיחוֹ אֶלָּא בַּשַּׁבָּת. דִּכְתִיב כֹּה תַעֲשֶׂה שֵׁשֶׁת יָמִים: וּכְתִיב וּבַיּוֹם הַשְּׁבִיעִי תָּסוֹבּוּ אֶת־הָעִיר שֶׁבַע פְּעָמִים. וּכְתִיב עַד רִדְתָּהּ. אֲפִילוּ בַשַּׁבָּת.

One sends letters through a Gentile neither on Friday nor on Thursday. The House of Shammai forbid even on Wednesday but the House of Hillel permit[390]. They said about Rebbi Jose[391] the Cohen that his handwriting never was found in the hand of a Gentile.

One embarks on the ocean neither on Friday nor on Thursday. The House of Shammai forbid even on Wednesday but the House of Hillel permit[392]. If it is not dangerous, as from Tyre to Sidon, it is permitted.

One does not lay siege to a Gentile city within three days before the Sabbath. That is in a war of choice[393]. But in a war of obligation even on the Sabbath, for so we find that Jericho was conquered only on a Sabbath, as it is written, *so you shall act for six days*[394], and it is written, *on the Seventh Day you shall circle the city seven times*[395]. And it is written, *until it fell*[396], even on the Sabbath.

---

390 The Babli 19a permits to send letters at any time by government mail or if the Gentile acts as contractor, that he is paid by the piece and not by the time he spends in delivering the mail; then he is a contractor and not an employee of the Jew.

Sefer Hamanhig (*Hilkhot Šabbat* §146) and *Or Zarua* (*Hilkhot Šabbat* §146) argue that the House of Hillel, of whom it is not specified what they permit, must permit to mail a letter even on Friday since if they simply negate the statement of the House of Shammai their position would be identical to that of the anonymous Tanna and should not have been mentioned separately. The same argument holds for the next paragraph.

391 In the Genizah text and several Babli mss.: Joseph.

392 Babli 19a, Tosephta 13:13, *Tanhuma Šelaḥ* 1 (both the Babli version). The reason given by North-African authors is that sea travel always is dangerous and there is a likelihood that the traveller will have to violate the Sabbath. Ashkenazic authors prefer to explain that people embarking shortly befor the Sabbath will be seasick on the Sabbath and unable to enjoy the day. The sentence about short trips which are permitted even on Friday supports the North-African authors.

Sefer Ravan (§60) quotes a reading in the Yerushalmi in the name of his son-in-law R. Joel that the disagreement of the Houses of Hillel and Shammai is about Tuesday, not Wednesday. But in R. Joel's text quoted by his son Ravia (§385) the text is as our Yerushalmi. In *Pesahim* 4:1 (30d l. 32) it is stated that R. Jehudah forbade all travel on the ocean. (He was a student of his father who in turn was a student of R. Eliezer who often followed the teachings of the House of Shammai.) S. Liebermann points out that while not much information can be drawn from the Genizah fragment of which at this point less than a third is legible

in each line, it is clear that a sentence is missing in our Yerushalmi since there the permission to travel from Tyre to Sidon is quoted twice.	395 *Jos.* 6:4. The Seventh Day is interpreted as the Sabbath.
393 Neither the war of Joshua nor a purely defensive war.	396 *Deut.* 20:20. Babli 19a; *Sifry Deut.* #204,203; Tosephta *Eruvin* 3:7. In the last quote, two sources attribute the argument to Shammai and one to Hillel.
394 *Jos.* 6:3.	

4b line 1) מתני׳. אֵין נוֹתְנִין עוֹרוֹת לָעַבְּדָן כול׳. עַד אֵיכָן. יָבֹא כְמָה דָּמַר רִבִּי יוֹחָנָן בְּשֵׁם רִבִּי חוּנְיָא. עַד כְּדֵי הִילוּךְ ד' מִיל. וְכָא נָתַן כֵּלָיו לַכּוֹבֵס נָכְרִי וּבָא וּמְצָאוֹ עוֹבֵד בּוֹ בַשַׁבָּת אָסוּר. אָמַר רִבִּי יוּדָן. וְיֵימַר לֵיהּ דְּלָא יַעֲבִיד. אָמַר רִבִּי יוּדָן אָבוֹי דְרִבִּי מַתַּנְיָיה. הָא דְתֵימַר בְּטוּבַת הֲנָייָה. אֲבָל בַּשָׂכִיר בַּעֲיבִידְתֵּיהּ הוּא עָסִיק.

Mishnah: "One does not give hides to the tannery worker,[397]" etc. How long[398]? It should come like what Rebbi Johanan said in the name of Rebbi Onias[399], the time needed to walk four miles[400]. And here, if he gave his clothing to the Gentile fuller and found him treating them on the Sabbath, it is forbidden[401]. Rebbi Yudan said, he should tell him not to do it. Rebbi Yudan, the father of Rebbi Mattaniah said, that is, for goodwill[402]. But for a fee, he looks after his work.

397 Quote from Mishnah 12.	400 About 1 hour.
398 Since practical rules are given, the question must have been asked for the House of Hillel, what practically means "as long as the sun shines".	401 If the Gentile washed the garments on the Sabbath, the Jew may not wear them.
399 He is R. Onias from Barat Hauran. It is not clear where else R. Johanan in the name of R. Onias gave a similar measure.	402 If the Gentile is not paid, the Jew should tell him not to work for him on the Sabbath. But if he receives a set fee for each piece, he works for himself and is not bound by Jewish rules.

4b line 7) אָמַר רַבָּן שִׁמְעוֹן בֶּן גַּמְלִיאֵל נוֹהֲגִין הָיוּ בֵּית אַבָּא כול׳. לֹא אָמְרוּ אֶלָּא לְבָנִים. הָא צְבוּעִין לֹא. לְפִי דַרְכֵּנוּ לָמַדְנוּ שֶׁהַלְּבָנִים קָשִׁין לְכַבֵּס מִן הַצְּבוּעִין.

וְשָׁוִין כול׳. רִבִּי שְׁמוּאֵל וְרִבִּי יוֹסֵי בֶּן חֲנִינָה. תְּרֵיהוֹן אָמְרִין. כְּבָר נֶעֶקְרָה כָּל־ טִיפָּה וְטִיפָּה מִמְּקוֹמָהּ. רִבִּי אָחָא אָמַר. רִבִּי יוֹסֵי בְּרִבִּי חֲנִינָא בָעֵי. מַהוּ לִיגַּע בַּמּוֹשֵׁךְ. רַבָּנָן דְּקַיְסָרִין אָמְרִין. אִיתְפַּלְגוּן רִבִּי יוֹחָנָן וְרִבִּי יוֹסֵי בַּר חֲנִינָה. רִבִּי יוֹחָנָן אָמַר. אָסוּר. רִבִּי יוֹסֵי בַּר חֲנִינָא אָמַר. מוּתָּר. מַתְנִיתָא פְּלִיגָא עַל רִבִּי יוֹסֵי בַּר חֲנִינָא. וְשָׁוִין שֶׁלֹא יִגַּע בַּמּוֹשֵׁךְ.

"Rabban Simeon ben Gamliel says, in my father's house they used,[403]" etc. They mentioned only white, therefore not colored. Following our routine we infer that white garments are more difficult to wash than colored ones[404].

"They both agree[403]," etc. Rebbi Samuel and Rebbi Yose ben Ḥanina both say, because every single drop was moved from its place[358]. Rebbi Aḥa said, Rebbi Yose ben Rebbi Ḥanina asked, may one touch the flow[405]? The rabbis of Caesarea said, Rebbi Joḥanan and Rebbi Yose bar Ḥanina disagreed; Rebbi Joḥanan said it is forbidden; Rebbi Yose bar Ḥanina said, it is permitted. A *baraita* disagrees with Rebbi Yose bar Ḥanina: They both agree that one may not touch the flow[407].

403 Quote from Mishnah 13.

404 Washing colored clothes requires less care. Babli 19a.

406 While both the Houses of Hillel and Shammai permit starting the process of pressing olives or grapes on Friday evening close to sundown, the question for the House of Hillel is whether the fluid oozing out may be used on the Sabbath or may not be touched as a rabbinic precaution to prevent biblically prohibited use.

407 In the Babli, 19a/b, the full *baraita* quoted shows that this is R. Aqiba's tradition, opposed by R. Ismael and R. Eleazar.

(4b line 15) מתני׳. אֵין צוֹלִין בָּשָׂר בָּצָל וּבֵיצָה אֶלָּא כְּדֵי שֶׁיִּצּוֹלוּ מִבְּעוֹד יוֹם. רִבִּי בּוּן בַּר כָּהֲנָא בְשֵׁם רַבָּנָן. תַּבְשִׁיל שֶׁנִּתְבַּשֵּׁל כָּל־צוּרְכּוֹ מוּתָּר לְשַׁהוֹתוֹ עַל גַּבֵּי כִירָה שֶׁאֵינָהּ קְטוּמָה. רִבִּי זְעִירָא בָּעֵי. בָּשָׂר בָּצָל וּבֵיצָה מִצְטַמֵּק וְרַע לוֹ. וְזֶה מִצְטַמֵּק וְיָפֶה לוֹ וְאַתְּ אָמַר הָכֵין. דִּילְמָא דְלָא אִיתְאֲמָרַת אֶלָּא חַמִּין. אֲתָא רִבִּי שְׁמוּאֵל בָּעֵי רִבִּי זְעִירָא. חַמִּין שֶׁהוּחַמוּ כָּל־צוּרְכָּן אָסוּר לְשַׁהוֹתָן עַל גַּבֵּי כִירָה שֶׁאֵינָהּ קְטוּמָה. רִבִּי בֵּיבַי בְשֵׁם רִבִּי יוֹחָנָן. תַּבְשִׁיל שׁוֹר שֶׁנִּתְבַּשֵּׁל כַּאֲכִילַת בֶּן דְּרוֹסַאי מוּתָּר לְהַחֲזִירוֹ עַל גַּבֵּי כִירָה קְטוּמָה. וַתִייָא כַּיי דָּמַר רִבִּי יַעֲקֹב בַּר אָחָא בְשֵׁם רִבִּי יוֹחָנָן. הַשּׁוֹפֵת אֶת הַקְּדֵירָה עַל גַּבֵּי גֶחָלִים מַתְרִין בּוֹ. לִכְשֶׁיִּתְבַּשֵּׁל כַּאֲכִילַת בֶּן דְּרוֹסַאי אָסוּר. רִבִּי אָחָא רִבִּי תַנְחוּם בַּר חִייָא בְשֵׁם רִבִּי שִׁמְעוֹן בְּרִבִּי. חַמִּין שֶׁהוּחַמוּ כָּל־צוּרְכָּן מוּתָּר לְהַחֲזִירָן עַל גַּבֵּי כִירָה שֶׁאֵינָהּ קְטוּמָה. רִבִּי זְעִירָא בָּעֵי. לִשְׁהוֹת אָסוּר וּלְהַחֲזִיר מוּתָּר. דִּילְמָא דְלָא אִיתְאֲמָרַת אֶלָּא עַל פֶּסַח. אֲתָא רִבִּי אָחָא בְשֵׁם רִבִּי שִׁמְעוֹן בְּרִבִּי. פֶּסַח שֶׁנִּצְלָה כָּל־צוּרְכּוֹ מוּתָּר לְהַחֲזִירוֹ עַל גַּבֵּי כִירָה שֶׁאֵינָהּ קְטוּמָה.

3 מצטמק G | מיצטמיק (2) דילמא G | דלמה דלא G | - 4 איתאמרת G | אתמרת זעירא G | זעורה חמין G | חמים 5 לשהותן G | להשחותן 6 דרוסאי G | דרוסי אחא G | אחה 7 מתרין G | מותרין דרוסאי G | דרוסי 8 אחא G | אחה בר׳ G | בר׳ 9 זעירא G | זעורה 10 - G | פסח אחא G | אחה

Mishnah: "One does not roast meat, onions, or an egg, unless they be roasted when it still is daylight,"[408] etc. Rebbi Bun bar Cahana in the name of the rabbis: A dish which is fully cooked one may leave on a cooking stove which is not covered with ashes[409]. Rebbi Ze'ira asked: Meat, onion, and egg shrink and it is bad for them[410]. This one is shrinking and it is good for it, and you say so? Maybe this was said only for hot water. Rebbi Samuel came, Rebbi Ze'ira asked: It is forbidden to leave hot water which was fully heated on a cooking stove which is not covered with ashes. Rebbi Bevai in the name of Rebbi Johanan: A dish of beef which was cooked as Ben Derosai's food[361] one may return on a cooking stove covered with ashes. This comes like what Rebbi Aha said in the name of Rebbi Johanan: One warns somebody who puts a pot on top of coals. When it will be cooked as Ben Derosai's food it is forbidden.[411] Rebbi Aha, Rebbi Tanhum bar Hiyya in the name of the important Rebbi Simeon: Hot water which was fully heated one may return on a cooking stove which is not covered with ashes[412]. Rebbi Ze'ira asked: To leave on is forbidden but to return is permitted? Maybe it was only said for the Passover sacrifice. There Rebbi Aha in the name of the important Rebbi Simeon: The Passover sacrifice[413] which was fully roasted one may return on a cooking stove which is not covered with ashes.

408 Quote from Mishnah 14.

409 A *kirah* is a portable clay cooking stove, usually with two burners, which is heated with charcoal. If the coals are covered with ashes, one may leave the pot on the fire on the Sabbath since the heat is diminished and the coals will stop to burn. Babli 37b.

410 It is a rule that all food may remain on the stove if continued cooking will detract from its quality; Babli 36b.

411 And the perpetrator will have desecrated the Sabbath.

412 As shown in the sequel, this tradition is impossible and has to be corrected by the last tradent.

413 If Passover falls on a Sabbath and one is required to roast the meat before the Sabbath and to keep it hot until it is eaten after the *seder*. Since it is fully roasted there is no cooking; the only problem is that one might be tempted to tend to the coals, which would be a desecration of the Sabbath. But since the Passover is celebrated in a group, one may assume that the members of the group would prevent anybody from stirring the coals.

(4b line 30) אֵין נוֹתְנִין אֶת הַפַּת לַתַּנּוּר כול'. רִבִּי יַעֲקֹב בַּר אֲחָא בְשֵׁם רִבִּי אַסִּי. זְרִיזוֹת הֵן הַנָּשִׁים בַּפַּת יוֹתֵר מִן הַתַּבְשִׁיל. מַה בֵּין פַּת וּמַה בֵּין תַּבְשִׁיל. תַּבְשִׁיל דַּרְכּוֹ לֶאֱכוֹל רוֹתֵחַ. פַּת אֵין דַּרְכּוֹ לֶאֱכוֹל רוֹתַחַת. תַּמָּן אֲמָרִין. פַּת חַמָּה חַמָּתָהּ בְּצִידָהּ. צִירְעָה צוֹנִין. עַקְרָב חַמִּין. מָאן דְּמִיחֲלַף סַכָּנָה.

מוֹדֶה רִבִּי לְעָזָר בְּלֶחֶם הַפָּנִים שֶׁאֵינָהּ קְרוּיָה לֶחֶם עַד שֶׁיִּקְרְמוּ פָּנֶיהָ בַתַּנּוּר.

"One does not put bread dough into the oven.[408]" Rebbi Jacob bar Aḥa in the name of Rebbi Assi: Women are more careful with bread than with dishes. What is the difference between bread and dish? A dish one usually eats hot, bread one usually does not eat hot[414]. There, they say, hot bread is accompanied by fever. A wasp, cold; a scorpion, hot. He who switches is in danger[415].

Rebbi Eliezer agrees that the shew-bread is not called bread until it develops a crust in the oven[416].

414 Why must a dish be completely cooked before the Sabbath while bread only has to start forming a crust? Since bread is never eaten hot, there is no danger that one would be tempted to stir the coals because of it.

415 This is a piece of Babylonian medicine. Eating hot bread is unhealthy, the sting of a wasp has to be treated by cooling it (Babli *Avodah zarah* 28b), the sting of a scorpion by heat.

416 Even though R. Eliezer holds here that bread is baked if it only developed a crust on one side, he agrees that the shew-bread is not acceptable unless it has a crust on all sides.

(4b line 36) מתני'. מְשַׁלְשְׁלִין אֶת הַפֶּסַח לַתַּנּוּר כול'. תַּמָּן תַּנִּינָן. חֲשֵׁיכָה יָצְאוּ וְצָלוּ אֶת פִּסְחֵיהֶן: וְאַתְּ אָמַר הָכֵין. אָמַר רִבִּי יוֹסֵי. חֲבוּרוֹת זְרִיזוֹת הֵן.

פֶּסַח מַחֲזִירוֹ אַתְּ שָׁלֵם וְאֵין אַתְּ מַחֲזִירוֹ מְחוּתָּךְ. רִבִּי שְׁמוּאֵל בְּשֵׁם רִבִּי זְעִירָא. מִפְּנֵי פְסוּלוֹ. אָמַר רִבִּי יוֹסֵי. לְאוֹכְלוֹ אֵין אַתְּ יָכוֹל. דִּכְתִיב אַל־תֹּאכְלוּ מִמֶּנּוּ נָא. לִצְלוֹתוֹ אֵין אַתְּ יָכוֹל. שֶׁלֹּא יְהֵא כְצוּלָה בַשַּׁבָּת. מִתּוֹךְ שֶׁאַתְּ אוֹמֵר שֶׁהוּא מוּתָּר אַף הוּא אֵינוֹ צוֹלֶה אוֹתוֹ כָּל־צוּרְכּוֹ מִבְּעוֹד יוֹם. מִתּוֹךְ שֶׁאַתְּ אוֹמֵר לוֹ שֶׁהוּא אָסוּר אַף הוּא צוֹלֶה אוֹתוֹ כָּל־צוּרְכּוֹ מִבְּעוֹד יוֹם. רִבִּי לְעָזָר בֵּירִבִּי יוֹסֵי שְׁאִיל. צָלְיוֹ שָׁלֵם וַחֲתָכוֹ מָהוּ מֵיחְזְרִתֵּיהּ וּמַשְׁחַנְתֵּיהּ.

Mishnah: "One hangs the Passover lamb into the oven,[21]" etc. There[417], we have stated: "At nightfall they went out and roasted their Passover sacrifices." And you are saying so[418]? Rebbi Yose said, groups are careful[419].

The Passover sacrifice you return whole, you do not return it carved[420]. Rebbi Samuel in the name of Rebbi Ze`ira: Because of its invalidity[421]. Rebbi Yose said, this is correct. You cannot eat it for it is written[422], *do not eat from it raw*. You cannot roast it for he should not be roasting it on the Sabbath. If you are telling him that he may do it, he will not roast it completely when it still is daylight. Since you tell him that it is prohibited, he will roast it completely when it is still daylight[423]. Rebbi Eleazar ben Rebbi Yose[424] asked, if he roasted it whole and carved it up, may he go back and heat it?

417 Mishnah *Pesahim* 5:10. In contrast to the Mishnah here, this speaks of the case that the 14th of Nisan is a Sabbath; roasting the sacrifice may start only at nightfall, after the end of the Sabbath.

418 From the Mishnah here it seems that roasting may be done on the Sabbath; the Mishnah there excludes it.

419 The reason for the Mishnah here is not because of a biblical prohibition which would be to stir the coals or to add fuel. To avoid the possibility of such violation of the Sabbath one forbids leaving on the fire anything not fully cooked. But for the Passover which is a group celebration, such a fear would be unfounded (Note 21). *Ma`aser šeni* 3:2 Note 36; Babli 20a, *Eruvin* 106a, *Pesahim* 85a.

420 Only the whole animal is a group affair; once individual portions are cut they must follow the rules of common food.

421 This is a new subject. While in general a dish cooked as Ben Derosai's food can be returned and reheated, for the Passover this is forbidden; if the Passover sacrifice is roasted on Friday afternoon it must be well done overall.

422 *Ex.* 12:9.

423 The previous permission (Note 413) to return the Passover sacrifice is given only for the uncut body; once a piece has been cut to check whether it was well done it cannot be returned. This forces one to finish the roasting process before cutting anything.

424 The Tanna, son of R. Yose ben Halafta. His question was answered in the negative by the late Amoraim just quoted.

(4b line 44) רִבִּי זְעִירָא רַב יְהוּדָה בְשֵׁם רַב. אַרְבַּע מְדוּרוֹת בָּל־שֶׁהֵן. מְדוּרַת הַגֶּפֶת מְדוּרַת הַזֶּבֶל מְדוּרַת הַחֵלֶב מְדוּרַת גַּלְעִינִין בָּל־שֶׁהֵן.

רִבִּי בָּא בְשֵׁם רִבִּי חִייָה בַּר אַשִׁי. חוֹתָל שֶׁהוּא מָלֵא גַלְעִינִים בָּל־שֶׁהֵן. רִבִּי בָּא בְשֵׁם רִבִּי חִייָא בַּר אַשִׁי. חוֹתָל שֶׁהוּא מָלֵא גַלְעִינִים. אִם מְכוּנָּסוֹת. בְּרוּבָּן. אִם מְפוּזָּרוֹת. בְּרוֹב בָּל־פְּרִידָה וּפְרִידָה. מַה וּפְלִיג. בָּאן בִּבְרִיאוֹת. וְבָאן בְּתָשׁוּת.

רִבִּי יוֹסֵי בְשֵׁם רַב יִרְמְיָה רִבִּי חֲנַנְיָה מַטֵי בָהּ בְּשֵׁם רַב. חָרִיּוֹת מִלְּמַטָּה וְעֵצִים מִלְמַעֲלָה בֵּיוָן שֶׁעָלָה הָאוֹר בִּנְתַיִים מוּתָּר.

רִבִּי חֶלְבּוֹ בְשֵׁם רַב. קוֹרָה וְרוּבָּהּ בְּרוֹב הֶקֵּיפָהּ. מָהוּ בְּרוֹב הֶקֵּיפָהּ מִמָּקוֹם אַחֵר אוֹ בְרוֹב הֶיקֵּף כּוּלָהּ. אֲשְׁכַּח תַּנֵּי. עַד שֶׁתִּיפָּסֵל מִלַּעֲשׂוֹת מְלָאכָה.

בֵּימֵי מַתְנִיתָא. אַף בְּפֶיחָמִין כָּל־שֶׁהֵן.

Rebbi Ze'ira, Rav Jehudah in the name of Rav: Four pyres are in a minimal amount. A pyre of pressed-out olives, a pyre of manure, a pyre of fat, a pyre of pits are in a minimal amount[425].

Rebbi Abba in the name of Rebbi Hiyya bar Ashi: A willow basket full of pits is in a minimal amount. Rebbi Abba in the name of Rebbi Hiyya bar Ashi: A willow basket full of pits, if they are collection, by their majority; if they are distributed, by the majority of each heap. Do they disagree? Here fat ones, there lean ones[426].

Rebbi Yose in the name of Rav Jeremiah, Rebbi Hananiah bent it in the name of Rav: Cuttings from date palms below and wood on top, when the fire appears between them it is permitted[427].

Rebbi Helbo in the name of Rav Huna: A log and most of it by the majority of its circumference. What means by the majority of its circumference? At one place or at most of its entire surface area? It was found stated: Until it became unfit for work[428].

So is the Mishnah: Also on charcoals any amount[429].

425 These materials can be lit on Friday evening any moment before sundown since if the fire starts anywhere it will quickly spread to all of the fuel

426 The two statements of R. Abba seem to contradict one another. Only kernels containing oil do not need a minimum of burning substance before nightfall.

427 While the Mishnah requires that the fire spread to most of the fuel, if there are two distinct kinds of fuel only one of them has to be aflame in its majority.

428 This means that the Mishnah requires that most of the logs burn before sundown.

429 The plural "charcoals" requires a plural in "any amount".

במה מדליקין פרק שני

(fol. 4b) **משנה א**: בַּמֶּה מַדְלִיקִין וּבַמֶּה אֵין מַדְלִיקִין. אֵין מַדְלִיקִין לֹא בְלֶכֶשׁ וְלֹא בְחוֹסֶן וְלֹא בְכָלָךְ לֹא בִפְתִילַת הָאִידָן וְלֹא בִפְתִילַת הַמִּדְבָּר וְלֹא בִירוֹקָה שֶׁעַל פְּנֵי הַמָּיִם. לֹא בְזֶפֶת וְלֹא בְשַׁעֲוָה לֹא בְשֶׁמֶן קִיק וְלֹא בְשֶׁמֶן שְׂרֵיפָה לֹא בְאַלְיָה וְלֹא בְחֵלֶב. נַחוּם הַמָּדִי אוֹמֵר מַדְלִיקִין בְּחֵלֶב מְבוּשָּׁל. וַחֲכָמִים אוֹמְרִים אֶחָד מְבוּשָּׁל וְאֶחָד שֶׁאֵינוֹ מְבוּשָּׁל אֵין מַדְלִיקִין בּוֹ:

Mishnah 1: With what may one kindle and with what may one not kindle? One kindles neither with bast[1], nor with raw flax, nor with silk noil[2], nor with tow-cotton[3], nor with desert wick[4], nor with green from the surface of water[5]; not with pitch, nor with wax, nor with *qiq* oil[6], nor with oil to be burned[7], nor with fat tail[8], nor with fat[9]. Nahum the Mede says one may kindle with cooked fat[10], but the Sages say whether cooked or uncooked one does not kindle with it.

משנה ב: אֵין מַדְלִיקִין בְּשֶׁמֶן שְׂרֵיפָה בְּיוֹם טוֹב. רִבִּי יִשְׁמָעֵאל אוֹמֵר אֵין מַדְלִיקִין בְּעִטְרָן מִפְּנֵי כְבוֹד הַשַּׁבָּת. וַחֲכָמִים מַתִּירִין בְּכָל הַשְּׁמָנִים שֶׁמֶן שׁוּמְשְׁמִין שֶׁמֶן אֱגוֹזִים שֶׁמֶן צְנוֹנוֹת שֶׁמֶן דָּגִים שֶׁמֶן פַּקּוּעוֹת בְּעִטְרָן וּבְנֵפְט. רִבִּי טַרְפוֹן אוֹמֵר אֵין מַדְלִיקִין אֶלָּא בְשֶׁמֶן זַיִת בִּלְבָד:

Mishnah 2: One does not kindle with oil to be burned on a holiday[7]. Rebbi Ismael says, one does not kindle with *`itran*[11] because of the honor of the Sabbath. But the Sages permit all kinds of oil, sesame oil, nut oil, radish oil[12], fish oil, colocynth oil[13], *`itran*, and naphtha. Rebbi Tarphon says, one kindles only with olive oil.

משנה ג: כָּל־הַיּוֹצֵא מִן הָעֵץ אֵין מַדְלִיקִין בּוֹ אֶלָּא פִשְׁתָּן. וְכָל־הַיּוֹצֵא מִן הָעֵץ אֵינוֹ מְטַמֵּא טוּמְאַת אוֹהָלִים אֶלָּא פִשְׁתָּן. פְּתִילַת הַבֶּגֶד שֶׁקִּיפְּלָהּ וְלֹא הִיבְהֲבָהּ רִבִּי לִיעֶזֶר אוֹמֵר טְמֵאָה וְאֵין מַדְלִיקִין בָּהּ. רִבִּי עֲקִיבָא אוֹמֵר טְהוֹרָה וּמַדְלִיקִין בָּהּ:

Mishnah 3: One does not kindle with any wood product but flax[14]. No wood product may become impure by tent impurity[15] but flax. A wick braided from textile which was threaded but not singed, Rebbi Eliezer says it may become impure[16] and one does not use it to kindle; Rebbi Aqiba says it does not become impure and one may use it to kindle.

משנה ד: לֹא יִקּוֹב אָדָם שְׁפוֹפֶרֶת שֶׁל בֵּיצָה וִימַלְאֶנָּה שֶׁמֶן וְיִתְּנֶנָּה עַל פִּי הַנֵּר בִּשְׁבִיל שֶׁתְּהֵא מְנַטֶּפֶת אֲפִילוּ הִיא שֶׁל חֶרֶס וְרִבִּי יְהוּדָה מַתִּיר. אֲבָל אִם חִבְּרָהּ הַיּוֹצֵר מִתְּחִילָּה מוּתָּר. לֹא יְמַלֵּא אָדָם קְעָרָה שֶׁמֶן וְיִתְּנֶנָּה בְּצַד הַנֵּר וְיִתֵּן רֹאשׁ הַפְּתִילָה בְּתוֹכוֹ בִּשְׁבִיל שֶׁתְּהֵא שׁוֹאֶבֶת. וְרִבִּי יְהוּדָה מַתִּיר:

Mishnah 4: A person may not pierce an eggshell[17], fill it with oil, and put it over a light so it should drip even if it is made from clay; Rebbi Jehudah permits it. But if the potter combined it from the outset it is permitted. A person may not fill a bowl with oil, put it next to a light and dip the end of the wick into it so it should draw; Rebbi Jehudah permits it.

משנה ה: הַמְכַבֶּה אֶת הַנֵּר מִפְּנֵי שֶׁהוּא מִתְיָרֵא מִפְּנֵי גוֹיִם מִפְּנֵי לִסְטִים מִפְּנֵי רוּחַ רָעָה אִם בִּשְׁבִיל הַחוֹלֶה שֶׁיִּישַׁן פָּטוּר. כָּחָס עַל הַנֵּר כָּחָס עַל הַשֶּׁמֶן כָּחָס עַל הַפְּתִילָה חַיָּיב. רִבִּי יוֹסִי פּוֹטֵר בְּכוּלָּן חוּץ מִן הַפְּתִילָה מִפְּנֵי שֶׁהוּא עוֹשָׂהּ פֶּחָם:

Mishnah 5: One who extinguishes a light because he is afraid of Gentiles, of robbers, of evil spirits, or because of a sick person to let him sleep, is not liable[18]. If to save the light, to save the oil, to save the wick, he is liable[19]. Rebbi Yose declares them all not liable except for the wick because he produces charcoal.

משנה ו: עַל שָׁלֹשׁ עֲבֵרוֹת הַנָּשִׁים מֵיתוֹת בִּשְׁעַת לֵידָתָן עַל שֶׁאֵינָן זְהִירוֹת בַּנִּדָּה בַּחַלָּה וּבְהַדְלָקַת הַנֵּר:

Mishnah 6: Because of three sins women die in childbirth, because they are not careful with *niddah*[20], *hallah*[21], and candle lighting[22].

משנה ז: שְׁלֹשָׁה דְבָרִים צָרִיךְ אָדָם לוֹמַר בְּתוֹךְ בֵּיתוֹ עֶרֶב שַׁבָּת עִם חֲשֵׁיכָה. עִשַּׂרְתֶּן עֵירַבְתֶּן הַדְלִיקוּ אֶת הַנֵּר. סָפֵק חֲשֵׁיכָה סָפֵק אֵינוֹ חֲשֵׁיכָה אֵין מְעַשְּׂרִין אֶת הַוַּדַּאי וְאֵין מַטְבִּילִין אֶת הַכֵּלִים וְאֵין מַדְלִיקִין אֶת הַנֵּרוֹת אֲבָל מְעַשְּׂרִין אֶת הַדְּמַאי וּמְעָרְבִין וְטוֹמְנִין אֶת הַחַמִּין:

Mishnah 7: Three things a person has to say in his house Friday afternoon before it gets dark: Did you give tithe[23], did you make an *eruv*[24], kindle the light[25]! If there is a doubt whether it is dark or not dark one does not tithe what is certain[26], nor immerse vessels[27], not kindle lights, but one may tithe what is questionable[28], and make an *eruv*, and store away hot food[29].

---

1   According to the Yerushalmi, bast of a kind of willow, Greek λύγος, ἡ. The Babli, 20b, defines as cedar bast.

2   The Yerushalmi defines both here and in *Kilaim* 9:2 (Note 33) as "imperial אגבין or

"אנבין" ; the Babli 20b agrees that it is some kind of silk worn by exalted personalities.

3   According to the Yerushalmi a wick made of a substance which is imitation wool. According to the Babli, willow bast.

4   According to Rashi's Commentary to the Babli, a wick made of nettle, *ortie*.

5   Dried algae. The list up to here contains materials prohibited as wicks since they do not absorb oil well; if the light starts to flicker one will be impelled to intervene and shake the light to improve its quality; this would be a desecration of the Sabbath by biblical standards. The following list contains fuels which are not well absorbed by any wick and excluded for the same reason.

6   According to one opinion in the Babli (21a), accepted by Maimonides, castor oil. According to the Yerushalmi and the first opinion in the Babli, oil produced from a bird (according to R. Saadia Gaon, the pelican).

7   Olive oil given as heave to a Cohen which became impure and therefore cannot be consumed. The Cohen may use it as fuel. But since it is holy, it is subject to the (rabbinic) rule that *sancta* may not be burned on a day on which defective sacrifices may not be burned, i. e., Sabbath or holiday.

8   A sheep's tail which as a potential sacrifice (*Lev.* 3:9) may not be eaten.

9   Any animal fat which is forbidden for human consumption.

10   Refined lard which may be supposed to burn with a steady flame.

11   According to Rashi, spoiled tar. According to Maimonides, resin. Both Talmudim assert that it smells very badly.

12   Oil extracted from radish seeds.

13   Since the colocynth is a kind of cucumber, here also it must be oil extracted from seeds.

14   Flax is not a tree. The Babli explains that flax is called "wooden flax" in *Jos.* 2:6.

15   The original impurity imparted to anything susceptible of impurity which is under one roof with a corpse. Wooden implements that are not containers cannot become impure. But flax as textile material can become impure.

16   Cloth of the minimal size of a handkerchief [which is defined as (3 finger-widths)[2]] is subject to all kinds of impurity. If the cloth wears out and is shredded to yield thread to make wicks, it is no longer subject to impurity. Once the threads are re-assembled into a wick they become susceptible of impurity once the wick is usable. In R. Aqiba's view, a wick will not burn unless its end has been singed and turned into charcoal; therefore the manufacture of the wick is not complete until it has been singed. Unfinished products do not become impure.

17   An egg-shaped container. If the container is not rigidly connected to the light, one might be tempted to move or remove it.

18   It is supposed that one extinguishes the light because one is afraid of an attack, whether by people or in the case of a mentally ill person who may become violent under the influence of an evil spirit. The "sick person" mentioned in the Mishnah must have a life-threatening sickness. In all these cases there is a danger to life and one is permitted (or required) to extinguish the light. The formulation mentions "not liable"

which usually means "forbidden but not prosecutable" only to obtain a formulation parallel to the statement of R. Yose where the original meaning holds.

19 Since he completed an action according to his wishes. R. Yose holds (with R. Simeon on other occasions) that if the intent was not the action itself but a consequence of it, then in general the action is not prosecutable. In this case, if the intent was to prevent the clay lamp from bursting when the oil was almost used up, extinguishing the flame is not the object of his intent; the action "was not the object of his intent". But if the intent was to preserve the wick, extinguishing the fire will automatically produce a charred tip of the wick which is the essence of producing a usable wick (Note 16) and the action is the object of his intent.

20 All the rules governing her period; in particular informing her husband that she is forbidden to his sexual attentions. He has to depend on the information she gives him.

21 The gift to the Cohen to be given from bread dough; cf. Introduction to Tractate *Hallah*. Here also the husband is dependent on the information given by his wife that he may eat the bread baked by her.

22 Preparing lighting for the Friday evening meal is the duty of the wife (Babli 25b) and should not be delegated to a servant. Since this is an obligation tied to a fixed time it cannot be a biblical commandment as women are not subject to positive commandments tied to fixed times. But in the Halakhah to Mishnah 6 (Note 214) the obligation of the wife to light Sabbath candles is called a (rabbinic) commandment. Cf. Maimonides, *Hilkhot Šabbat* 3:1.

23 New produce grown by Jewish farmers in the Holy Land, once the harvest has been completed, may not be consumed unless heave and tithes were taken. Heave is a small amount and a *sanctum*; one may assume that the farmer took care of it before the produce came to market. But tithe is a full 10% and is essentially a civil obligation for the benefit of Levites; one may not assume that the farmer took care of this obligation. Since food consumed on the Sabbath has to be prepared beforehand (*Ex.* 16:23), it is impossible to take tithe on the Sabbath since this would transform non-edibles into edibles.

24 The symbolic sharing of space, a courtyard or a dead-end street, by several families turning the space into their private domain with regard to the laws of the Sabbath; details are the subject of Tractate *Eruvin*. Sadducees considered pharisaic *eruvim* as Sabbath desecrations.

25 The last action necessary in preparation of the Sabbath. The head of household has to determine that everything is ready for the Sabbath but he does not light himself; this is the obligation of the wife.

26 If there is knowledge that tithe had not been given, the food cannot be made ready for consumption after sundown.

27 Impure vessels which cannot be used in a Cohen's household who eats heave or an Israel's household who eats his profane food in ritual purity cannot be purified by immersion in a *miqweh* during twilight.

28 Produce where there is no certain knowledge, only a suspicion that tithe had not been given, the subject of Tractate *Demay*. Since such produce may be fed to the poor and strangers it cannot be classified

29 Hot food to be kept warm for the Sabbath noon meal in insulating material as explained in Chapter 4.

as "unprepared". Therefore the deficiency may be corrected during twilight hours when any Sabbath restrictions only apply rabbinically.

(4c line 17) בַּמֶּה מַדְלִיקִין וּבַמֶּה אֵין מַדְלִיקִין כול'. לֹא בְלֶכֶשׁ. רִבִּי חִייָא בַּר בָּא אָמַר. לוּגְשָׁא. רִבִּי אָחָא בְשֵׁם רִבִּי לייָא. דָּדִינוֹן. אָמְרִין. הִיא הָדָא הִיא הָדָא.

וְלֹא בְחוֹסֶן. רִבִּי חִינְנָא בְשֵׁם רִבִּי פִּינְחָס. פִּשְׁתָּן שֶׁלֹּא נִנְעָרָה. כְּמָה דְאַתְּ אָמַר וְהָיָה הֶחָסוֹן לִנְעוֹרֶת.

וְלֹא בְכָלָךְ. אנבין קַיְסָרִיי. אָמַר רַבָּן שִׁמְעוֹן בֶּן גַּמְלִיאֵל. חִיזַּרְתִּי עַל כָּל־מַפְרְשֵׁי יַמִּים וְאָמְרוּ לִי. כּוּלְכָּא שְׁמָהּ.

וְלֹא בִפְתִילַת הָאִידָן. עִירָנִיתָא.

וְלֹא בִפְתִילַת הַמִּדְבָּר. כִּשְׁמוּעָהּ.

וְלֹא בִירוֹקָה שֶׁעַל פְּנֵי הַמָּיִם. כִּיתָּן דְּמַיֵּי.

וְלֹא בְזֶפֶת וְלֹא בְשַׁעֲוָה. עַד כָּאן לִפְתִילוֹת. מִיכָּן וָאֵילָךְ לִשְׁמָנִים.

"With what may one kindle and with what may one not kindle? One kindles neither with bast[1]." Rebbi Ḥiyya bar Abba said, λύγος. Rebbi Aha in the name of Rebbi Lia[30], δάδινον[31]. They said, these two are identical[32].

"Nor with raw flax," Rebbi Ḥinena in the name of Rebbi Phineas, flax which was not cleansed, as you say, *the uncleaned flax will be tinder*[33].

"Nor with silk noil[2]," imperial אנבין[34]. Rabban Simeon ben Gamliel said, I asked all seafarers and they told me that it is called *kulka*.

"Nor with tow-cotton[3]," *īrānitā*[35].

"Nor with desert wick[4]," as its meaning[36].

"Nor with green from the surface of water[5];" water flax.

"Also not with pitch, nor with wax[37]," up to here about wicks, from here on about fuels.

30 He is R. La (Ilaï) mentioned at other occasions.

31 δάδινος, -η, -ov, "of pine wood"; δαδινίον "splinter of pine wood", I. Löw's interpretation. Musaphia reads דרינון which he takes to be Greek δρύϊνον "of oak" but Jastrow emends to קדרינון κέδρινον "of cedar" to coincide with the explanation of the Babli. Lieberman accepts Jastrow's emendation on basis of the Geniza fragment edited by Ginzberg (p. 70): ליא. . . דינון. Since the reading דינון clearly is common to the Leiden ms. and the Genizah text, Löw's reading has to be accepted.

32 In any case, one speaks of a wick made of wood bast, from the inside of the bark.

33 *Is.* 1:31. The usual translation is: *the treasure will become tinder.*

34 Cf. in *Kilaim* 9:2 Note 33 the conjecture that it might mean "imperial purple".

35 Diminutive of Aramaic עִירָא, אִירָא "wool".

36 Made from some desert plant.

37 Wax is forbidden as wick, not as fuel. Babli 20b.

(4c line 25) רִבִּי אַבָּהוּ בְשֵׁם רִבִּי יוֹחָנָן. מִפְּנֵי שֶׁהָאוֹר מְמַשֵּׁךְ לַאֲחוֹרָיו וְהוּא שׁוֹכֵחַ וּמוֹצִיא אֶת הַפְּתִילָה. וְעוֹד. שֶׁלֹא הוּצַת הָאוֹר בְּרוֹב הַדֶּלֶק. רִבִּי זְעִירָה בָעֵי. מֵעַתָּה פְּתִילָה צְרִיכָה הַצָּאָתָהּ[38] בְּרוֹב הַדֶּלֶק. אָתָא רִבִּי שְׁמוּאֵל רִבִּי אַבָּהוּ בְשֵׁם רִבִּי יוֹחָנָן. פְּתִילָה צְרִיכָה הוּצָאָתָהּ בְּרוֹב הַדֶּלֶק. הֲתִיבוּן חֲבֵרַייָא. וְהָא קוּרָה. הָא לֹא הוּצַת הָאוֹר בְּרוֹב הַדֶּלֶק. הֵתִיב רִבִּי בָּא בַּר מָמָל. וְהָא שְׁשִׁיתָא. הֲרֵי לֹא הוּצַת הָאוֹר בְּרוֹב הַדֶּלֶק. אָמַר רִבִּי שַׁמַּי. לֹא כֵן אָמַר רִבִּי זְעִירָא רַב יְהוּדָה בְשֵׁם רַב. אַרְבַּע מְדוּרוֹת כָּל־שֶׁהֵן. מְדוּרַת הַגֶּפֶת מְדוּרַת הַזֶּבֶל מְדוּרַת הַחֵלֶב מְדוּרַת גַּלְעִינִין כָּל־שֶׁהֵן. וְעוֹד מִן הָדָא דְרִבִּי תַּחְלִיפָא שָׁאַל לְרַב חִסְדָּא. וְלֹא כֵן אַלְפַן רִבִּי. שַׁבָּת שֶׁחָלָה לִהְיוֹת בַּחֲנוּכָה. שֶׁאָסוּר לִרְאוֹת מַטְבֵּעַ לְאוֹר הַחֲנוּכָה. הֲרֵי אֵינוֹ שׁכֵיחַ וּמוֹצִיא אֶת הַפְּתִילָה. הֱוֵי דְלֵית טַעֲמָא דְלָא מִשּׁוּם שֶׁלֹא הוּצַת הָאוֹר בְּרוֹב הַדֶּלֶק.

Rebbi Abbahu in the name of Rebbi Johanan: Because the fire is [not][39] drawn after it and he forgets and removes the wick; and in addition because the fire was not kindled on most of the fuel[40]. Rebbi Ze'ira asked, does this mean that the kindling of the wick has to reach most of the fuel? There came Rebbi Samuel, Rebbi Abbahu in the name of Rebbi Johanan: the kindling of the wick has to reach most of the fuel. The colleagues objected, is there not wax[41] where the fire does not have to reach most of the fuel? Rebbi Abba bar Mamal objected, is there not a lantern[42] where the fire does not have to reach most of the fuel? Rebbi Shammai said, did not Rebbi Ze'ira, Rav Jehudah say in the name of Rav[43]: Four pyres are in a minimal amount. A pyre of pressed-out olives, a pyre of manure, a pyre of fat, a pyre of pits are in a minimal amount. Also from the following, that Rebbi Tahlifa asked Rav Hisda, did not the rabbi teach us, on a Sabbath which happened during Hanukkah, when it is forbidden to check a coin in the Hanukkah light[44]; there he will not forget and remove the wick. Therefore the reason can only be that the kindling of the wick has to reach most of the fuel.

38 The vocalization follows the ms.	lights is that they are exclusively exhibition objects which cannot be used for any other purpose (Babli 21b; *Soferim* 20:6). On the Sabbath one may not check coins at all; the reference to the Sabbath has to be deleted. It seems that the Yerushalmi holds in contrast to the Babli (21b) that wicks and fuels forbidden for the Sabbath are also forbidden for Hanukkah. Since a Hanukkah light cannot be used for anything but exhibition, if it goes out one does not have to rekindle. Therefore the quality of the wick should not be a decisive factor; the first of R. Johanan's reasons does not apply.
39 Added from the quote in Nahmanides *Milhamot Hashem*, Alfasi Chapter 2; required by the context. The prohibited wicks are those which do not sufficiently draw fuel.	
40 Cf. Chapter 1, Note 428.	
41 Read קירה, Latin *cera* "wax" (S. Lieberman following *Qorban haEdah*).	
42 In Babylonian Aramaic the word is עֲשָׁשִׁית. In a lantern, in contrast to a torch, there is a controlled burn.	
43 Chapter 1, Note 425.	
44 The basic institution of Hanukkah	

(4c line 38) מתני׳. וְלֹא בְשֶׁמֶן קִיק. רִבִּי יוֹסֵה בְשֵׁם רִבִּי לִיָּיא. קִיסּוֹסָא. רִבִּי יוֹנָה רִבִּי זְעִירָה בְשֵׁם רַב יְהוּדָה. עוֹף הוּא וּשְׁמוֹ קִיק. תָּנֵי רִבִּי יִשְׁמָעֵאל. וְאֶת־הַקָּאָת זֶה קִיק.

Mishnah: "Nor with *qīq* oil[6]." Rebbi Yose in the name of Rebbi Lia, κισσός[45]. Rebbi Jonah, Rebbi Ze'ira in the name of Rav Jehudah, it is a bird by the name of *qīq*. Rebbi Ismael stated, *and the qāât*, this is the *qīq*[46].

45 "Ivy".	*Diqduqe Soferim ad loc.* Lev. 11:18, Deut. 14:17.
46 قوق "pelican". Babli *Hulin* 63a, see	

(4c line 40) וְלֹא בְשֶׁמֶן שְׂרֵפָה. אָמַר רַב חִסְדָּא. זֹאת אוֹמֶרֶת שֶׁאָסוּר לְהַצִּית אֶת הָאוּר בִּמְדוּרַת קֳדָשִׁים וְהִיא דְלֵיקָה וְהוֹלֶכֶת בַּשַּׁבָּת. וְהָא תַנִּינָן. וּמְחִיזִין אֶת הָאוּר בִּמְדוּרַת בֵּית הַמּוֹקֵד. וּבַגְּבוּלִין כְּדֵי שֶׁיַּצֵּית הָאוּר בְּרוּבָּן. אָמַר רִבִּי יוֹסֵה. בַּשַּׁבָּת כָּתוּב לֹא־תַעֲשֶׂה כָל־מְלָאכָה. נַעֲשִׂית הִיא מֵאֵילֶיהָ. בְּרַם הָכָא הַתּוֹרָה אָֽמְרָה. אֵין שׂוֹרְפִין אֶת הַקֳּדָשִׁים בְּיוֹם טוֹב. וְאֵין צָרִיךְ לוֹמַר. בַּשַּׁבָּת. מַה חֲמִית לוֹמַר כֵּן. וְלֹא־תוֹתִירוּ מִמֶּנּוּ עַד בּוֹקֶר וְהַנּוֹתָר מִמֶּנּוּ עַד בּוֹקֶר בָּאֵשׁ תִּשְׂרוֹפוּ׃ אַחַד שְׁנֵי בְקָרִים. אַחַד בּוֹקְרוֹ שֶׁלְטֹ״ו וְאַחַד בּוֹקְרוֹ שֶׁלְי״ו. וּכְתִיב וְהַנּוֹתָר מִבְּשַׂר הַזָּבַח בַּיּוֹם הַשְּׁלִישִׁי בָּאֵשׁ יִשָּׂרֵף׃

3 הכא G | הכה 4 לומר G | מימר 5 בוקר G | בקר[47] (2) 6 שלי״ו G | .. שלושה עשר[48]

"Nor with oil to be burned[7]." Rav Hisda said, this implies that it is forbidden to start a fire on a pyre of *sancta* so it should continuously burn on the Sabbath[47]. But have we not stated[48]: "One starts a fire at the fire place in the heating chamber, but outside the Temple only if the fire has started burning on most of the logs." Rebbi Yose said, it is written about the Sabbath, *do not do any work*[49]; it is done automatically. But here the Torah said that one does not burn *sancta* on a holiday, not to speak of the Sabbath. What did you see that you said so? [50]*You shall not leave any leftovers until the morning; what is left over from it until morning you shall burn in fire.* After two mornings, one the morning of the 15th and the other the morning of the 16th. And it is written, *what is left of the well-being sacrifice should be burned on the third day*[51].

47   Since impure heave, which belongs to the class of disabled *sancta,* may not be burned on the Sabbath. Babli 23b, *Menahot* 46b.

48   Mishnah 1:15 (Notes 22,23).

49   *Ex.* 20:10. Here starts a new Genizah leaf, Ginzberg p. 71 (G).

50   *Ex.* 12:10. The mention of two "mornings" implies that different times are implied. Babli 24b, 133a, *Pesahim* 83b, *Temurah* 4b. *Mekhilta dR. Ismael Bo* 6, end, *dR. Simeon benYohai Bo* p.14.

51   *Lev.* 7:17. The sacrifice may be eaten for two days and the intervening night.

(4c line 48) מָהוּ לְהַצִּית אֶת הָאוּר בִּמְדוּרַת חָמֵץ. מָאן דִּילִיף לָהּ מִנּוֹתָר. אָסוּר. וּמָאן דְּלָא יְלִיף לָהּ מִנּוֹתָר. מוּתָּר. רַב אָחָא בְּשֵׁם רַב חִסְדָּא. זֹאת אוֹמֶרֶת שֶׁמּוּתָּר לְהַצִּית אֶת הָאוּר בִּמְדוּרַת קֳדָשִׁים וְהִיא דְלֵיקָה וְהוֹלֶכֶת בַּשַּׁבָּת. וְהָא תַּנִּינָן. אֵין מַדְלִיקִין בְּשֶׁמֶן שְׂרֵיפָה בְּיוֹם טוֹב מִפְּנֵי יוֹם טוֹב שֶׁחָל לִהְיוֹת בְּעֶרֶב שַׁבָּת. מֵעַתָּה אֵין מַדְלִיקִין בְּשֶׁמֶן שְׂרֵיפָה בַּלַּיְלָה עַל שֵׁם שֶׁאֵין שׂוֹרְפִין אֶת הַקֳּדָשִׁים בַּלַּיְלָה. אָמַר רִבִּי יוֹחָנָן. יָרְדוּ לָהּ בְּשִׁיטַת רִבִּי יִשְׁמָעֵאל. כְּמָה דְרִבִּי יִשְׁמָעֵאל אָמַר. תִּינוֹק שֶׁעָיבַר זְמַנּוֹ נִימוֹל בֵּין בַּיּוֹם בֵּין בַּלַּיְלָה. כָּךְ עָבַר זְמַנָּהּ נִשְׂרֶפֶת בֵּין בַּיּוֹם בֵּין בַּלַּיְלָה. וּמָה אִית לָךְ שֶׁמֶן שְׂרֵפָה שֶׁעִיבֵּר זְמַנָּהּ. רִבִּי יוּדָה בַּר פָּזִי. מִכֵּיוָן שֶׁנִּיטְמָאת כְּמִי שֶׁעָבַר זְמַנָּהּ.

1 מהו G | מהוא מאן G | מן מנותר G | מן נותר ומאן G | ומן מנותר G | מן נותר   3 והא G | הא בשמן G | שמן   4 בשמן G | שמן   6 כך עבר G | וכה עיבר

May one light a fire under a pyre of leavened material[52]? For him who infers it from remainder[53], it is forbidden. But for him who does not infer it from remainder, it is permitted. Rav Aha in the name of Rav Hisda: this implies that it is permitted to start a fire on a pyre of *sancta* so it should continuously burn on the Sabbath[54]. But did we not state[55], "one does not kindle with oil to be burned on a holiday," because of a holiday which falls on

Friday[56]. But then one should not light oil to be burned in the night since one does not burn *sancta* in the night[57]! Rebbi Joḥanan said, they followed the argument of Rebbi Ismael[58]. Just as Rebbi Ismael said, a baby whose time has passed can be circumcised either during the day or during the night[59], so when its time has passed the *sanctum* may be burned either during the day or during the night. Where do you have oil to be burned whose time has passed[60]? Rebbi Judah bar Pazi: Since it became impure it is as if its time had passed.

52 There is a biblical obligation to eliminate all leavened matter before Passover (*Ex.* 12:19). The elimination has to be before the time allotted to the slaughtering of the Passover sacrifice (*Ex.* 23:18, 34:25). Therefore the question must be about a large pile of leavened matter which is set on fire at noontime of Passover Eve but which will be completely consumed on the holiday, after nightfall.

53 He is R. Jehudah who insists that leavened matter *must* be eliminated by burning since this is the prescribed manner of disposing of sacrificial meat kept longer than the time allotted to its consumption. *Pesahim* 2:1 28c l. 62, Babli 27b. Since leftover Passover meat may be burned only after the holiday, he also must forbid burning of leavened matter on the holiday.

54 Since R. Jehudah is a minority of one.

55 Mishnah 2:2. Since it says "on the holiday", one could infer that on the Sabbath it is permitted. Then why is "oil to be burned" listed in Mishnah 1?

56 It is true that in biblical law "oil to be burned" may be used for lighting on the Sabbath since the fire would be started on Friday when it is permitted; it only is forbidden rabbinically because on a Friday which is a holiday it would be forbidden.

57 This is a new proof that the reason cannot be that "oil to be burned" must be treated as a *sanctum* since the only *sancta* which may be burned are excess sacrifices of the preceding day whereas invalid *sancta* must be burned during daytime. There is no restriction on the use of "oil to be burned".

58 As reported in the *Mekhiltot* (Note 50).

59 It says (*Lev.* 12:3): *And on the eighth day, the prepuce of his flesh shall be circumcised.* But if the baby was sick or for any other reason could not be circumcised on the eighth day, it may be circumcised at any time afterwards. In Babylonian sources (*Yebamot* 72a/b, *Tosephta Šabbat* 15:9) this opinion is ascribed to R. Eleazar ben R. Simeon, two generations after R.. Ismael.

60 There are no time restrictions for the disposal of "oil to be burned".

(4c line 59) תַּנֵּי רִבִּי יוֹסֵי קוֹמֵי רִבִּי יוֹחָנָן. מְנַיִין לְכָל־הַנִּימוֹלִים שֶׁלֹּא יְהוּ נִימוֹלִים אֶלָּא בַּיּוֹם. תַּלְמוּד לוֹמַר וּבַיּוֹם. אֲמַר לֵיהּ רִבִּי יוֹחָנָן. וְיֵשׁ כָּאן זוֹ. כָּל־מְחוּיָּיבֵי טְבִילוֹת טוֹבְלִין כְּדַרְכָּן בַּיּוֹם חוּץ מִנִּידָּה וְיוֹלֶדֶת שֶׁאֵינָהּ טוֹבֶלֶת אֶלָּא בַּלַּיְלָה. נִידָה שֶׁעָבַר זְמַנָּהּ טוֹבֶלֶת בֵּין בַּיּוֹם בֵּין בַּלַּיְלָה.

דְּרָשָׁהּ רִבִּי חִייָה בַּר אַבָּא לְצוֹרָאֵי. נִדָּה שֶׁעָבַר זְמַנָּהּ טוֹבֶלֶת בֵּין בַּיּוֹם בֵּין בַּלַּיְלָה. תַּמָּן אֲמְרִין. אֲפִילוּ עָבַר זְמַנָּהּ. מִפְּנֵי חֲמוֹתָהּ וּמִפְּנֵי כַלָּתָהּ. אִשָּׁה אַחַת מִשֶּׁלְרַבּוֹתֵינוּ רָאוּ אוֹתָהּ טוֹבֶלֶת כְּדַרְכָּהּ בַּיּוֹם. נֹאמַר. מְעוּבֶרֶת זְמַן הָיְתָה.

Rebbi Yose[61] stated before Rebbi Johanan: From where that all those to be circumcised should only be circumcised during daytime? The verse says, *And on the day*[62]. Rebbi Johanan told him, is that so? All who require immersion immerse themselves normally during daytime except for the woman after her period and one who gave birth who only immerses herself during the night[63]. A woman after her period whose time has passed[64] immerses herself either during the day or during the night. Rebbi Ḥiyya bar Abba preached this to the people of Tyre[65], a woman after her period whose time has passed immerses herself either during the day or during the night. There[66] they say, even one whose time has passed, because of her mother-in-law and her daughter-in-law. They saw a woman of our rabbis[67] immersing herself normally during daytime. We shall say that her time had passed.

61 Read with G (which is very fragmentary at this point): R. Yasa.

62 *Lev.* 12:3. Babli *Yebamot* 72b, *Sifra Tazria' Pereq* 1(1). The argument from the addition "and" is characteristically R. Aqiba's, opposed by R. Ismael.

63 Babli 121a, *Pesaḥim* 90b, *Yoma* 6a, 87a.

64 After the first evening she could have immersed herself after her period; cf.

Niddah 4:1 Note 3. Babli *Niddah* 67b.

65 As practice to be followed.

66 In Babylonia, where the statement was attributed to R. Johanan; *Niddah* 67b. There, the reason is given "because of the discipline of her daughter", that she should learn the rules clearly.

67 The household of R. Jehudah Nesia. The deviation of Galilean from Babylonian practice is confirmed.

(4c line 66) נִדָּה שֶׁנֶּאֶנְסָה וְטָבְלָה. שַׁמַּי בְּשֵׁם רַב. טְהוֹרָה לְבֵיתָהּ וּטְמֵיאָה לְטַהֲרוֹת. רִבִּי לְעָזָר בְּשֵׁם רִבִּי חֲנִינָה. טְמֵיאָה בֵּין לְבֵיתָהּ בֵּין לְטַהֲרוֹת. וּמַאי טַעֲמָא. וְכוּבַּס שֵׁנִית וְטָהֵר. מָה הָרִאשׁוֹנָה לְדַעַת אַף הַשְּׁנִייָה לְדַעַת. וּמִנַּיִין שֶׁהָרִאשׁוֹנָה לְדַעַת. וְצִוָּה הַכֹּהֵן וְכִבְּסוּ. לְדַעַת.

A woman after her period who was immersed by accident, Shammai in the name of Rav: she is pure for her house but impure for purities[68]. Rebbi Eleazar in the name of Rebbi Ḥanina, she is impure both for her house and purities. What is the reason? *It should be washed a second time and will be pure*[69]. Since the first time it was intentionally, also the second time it must be intentionally. And from where that the first time it was intentionally? *The Cohen has to order that they should wash*[70]. Intentionally.

68 She unintentionally fell into water which qualifies as a *miqweh*. In this opinion, an intent to become pure by immersion is needed only to be able to prepare pure food ("purities") whereas to be permitted to her husband ("pure for her house") she only has to be immersed since in the relevant biblical paragraph (*Lev.* 15:19-24) immersion is explicitly required only of people coming in contact with movables on which she sat during her period of impurity. The opposing opinion requires intent for any purification. Babli *Hulin* 31a.

69 *Lev.* 15:59, about impurity of textiles. The remark "a second time" is taken as indication that the second washing has to follow the rules of the first; Babli *Hulin* 31b. A different interpretation in *Sifra Tazria' Pereq* 16(11)

70 *Lev.* 13:54.

(4c line 71) וְכֵן חַמְיָין רַבָּנָן מְקַדְּמִין לְעִיבּוּרָה. רַב נַחְמָן בְּשֵׁם רִבִּי מָנָא. מִצְוָה לְהַקְדִּים כְּדֵי לְזָרֵז בַּמִּצְוֹת.

And so we see that rabbis are early for intercalations. Rav Nahman in the name of Rebbi Mana: It is an obligation to be early, to hasten in commandments[71].

71 This paragraph presents problems. It seems that the beginning sentence should be at the end. Then the meaning is that Rebbi (not Rav) Nahman requires the husband to direct his household to light Sabbath lights, and therefore begin the observance of the Sabbath, somewhat before the time of sundown since in the fulfilling of divine commandments one has to show eagerness. As an example it is noted that the rabbis who form the court which decrees intercalations always arrive early for the deliberations. This is a commentary on the last statement of the last Mishnah in the Chapter.

(4c line 72) בַּת יִשְׂרָאֵל שֶׁבָּאָה לְהַדְלִיק מִכֹּהֶנֶת טוֹבֶלֶת אֶת הַפְּתִילָה בַּשֶּׁמֶן שְׂרֵיפָה וּמַדְלֶקֶת. רִבִּי חוּנָה בְּשֵׁם רִבִּי יַנַּאי. שְׁעַת מִשְׁלַחַת זְאֵבִים הָיִיתָה וְלֹא עָמַד בֵּית דִּין וּבִיטֵּל. כְּמָה דְתֵימַר תַּמָּן לֹא עָמַד בֵּית דִּין וּבִיטֵּל. וְכָא לֹא עָמַד בֵּית דִּין וּבִיטֵּל.

1 שבאה | **ש** שבאת מכהנת | **ש** מן הכהנת בשמן | **שת** שמן   2 ר' | **ש** דבית ר' זאבים | **שת** זאיבים הייתה | **ש** היותה - | **שת** במה דתימר תמן. לא עמד בית דין וביטל וכא | ת אף הכא

[72]"An Israel woman who comes to a priestly woman to get fire dips her wick into oil to burn and lights." Rebbi Huna in the name of the house of Rebbi Yannai: It was a time of wolf packs; there was no court which disestablished. As it was said there, there was no court which disestablished. And here was no court which disestablished.

72 This and the following paragraphs discussing the term "not with oil to be burned" in Mishnah 1 are from *Terumot* 11:7, Notes 141-153. The present paragraph originates in *Ševi'it* 4:2, Notes 38-42. The meaning is that if a rabbinic stringency, such as not permitting occasional use of oil to be burned by lay persons even if it is to the advantage of the Cohen, falls into disuse in a time of emergency, it remains eliminated even after the emergency has passed.

(4c line 75) בִּקְרוֹ שֶׁלְּכֹּהֵן שֶׁהָיָה עוֹבֵר אֵצֶל יִשְׂרָאֵל וְכֵן כֵּלָיו שֶׁלְּכֹהֵן שֶׁהָיָה נֶאֱרָג אֵצֶל יִשְׂרָאֵל הֲרֵי זֶה מַדְלִיק עַל גַּבָּיו שֶׁמֶן שְׂרֵיפָה וְאֵינוֹ חוֹשֵׁשׁ. יִשְׂרָאֵל וְכֹהֵן שֶׁהָיוּ שׁוּתָּפִין בַּחֲנוּת מְמַלֵּא הוּא יִשְׂרָאֵל אֶת הַנֵּר שֶׁמֶן שְׂרֵיפָה וְעוֹלֶה בּוֹ לַעֲלִיָּה וְיוֹרֵד בּוֹ לַחֲנוּת לַעֲשׂוֹת צְרָכָיו שֶׁלְּכֹהֵן אֲבָל לֹא צְרָכָיו שֶׁלְּיִשְׂרָאֵל. כֹּהֵן שֶׁבָּא אֵצֶל יִשְׂרָאֵל לַעֲשׂוֹת עִמּוֹ חֶשְׁבּוֹן וְהִדְלִיק עַל גַּבָּיו שֶׁמֶן שְׂרֵיפָה. אַף עַל פִּי שֶׁעָמַד הַכֹּהֵן וְהָלַךְ לוֹ אֵין מְחַיְּיבִין אוֹתוֹ לְכַבּוֹתוֹ עַד שֶׁיְּכַבֶּה מֵאֵלָיו. רִבִּי חֲנַנְיָה בַּר עַכְבָּרֵי הֲוָה אָזַל וּמְעֲבַד עִיבִידְתֵּיהּ גַּבֵּי רִבִּי חִיָּיה צִיפּוֹרַיָּיא. מִי אָזִיל מֵיזִיל לֵיהּ הֲוָה מַלֵּי בּוֹצִינָא שֶׁמֶן שְׂרֵיפָה. וְלֹא כֵן סָבְרִינָן מֵימַר. לַעֲשׂוֹת צְרָכָיו שֶׁלְּכֹהֵן אֲבָל לֹא צְרָכָיו שֶׁלְּיִשְׂרָאֵל. אָמְרִין. דְּלָא הֲוָה עֲבַד כֵּן לָא הֲוָה אֲתֵי. סָבְרִין מֵימַר. מָטָא בֵּיתֵיהּ מַטְפֵּי לֵיהּ. אָמַר רִבִּי חֲנִינָא. עַל יְדֵי כֵן הֲוָה שָׁהַר וְעַל יְדֵי כֵן הֲוָה קָרֵץ.

[73]"If cattle of a Cohen was passing[74] at an Israel's, or the garment of a Cohen being woven at an Israel's, he lights for this oil to burn without hesitation. If an Israel and a Cohen were partners in a store, the Israel may fill the lamp with oil to burn and go to the upper floor or down into the store in the business of the Cohen, but not the Israel's[75]. If a Cohen came to an Israel to help him with his accounts and he lit oil to burn for him, even after the Cohen left one does not require him to extinguish it before it burns out by itself."[76] Rebbi Hanania from Akhbar worked at R. Hiyya's from Sepphoris. When he left, the latter filled him a lamp full of oil to burn. Were we not of the opinion to say, "to work for a Cohen, but not for an Israel"? They said, if he had not done this for him, he would not have come. They thought, when

he arrived at his house, he had to extinguish it. Rebbi Ḥinena said, by this he awoke, by this he got up early.

73 This paragraph is a composite of two paragraphs in *Terumot* 11:7 (Notes 137-139, 143-145).
74 In *Terumot*: "was fed at the Israel's". In the Tosephta, היה עומד אצל ישראל "was standing at the Israel's." The reading here, עובר, is a misreading of the Tosephta text.
75 Not the Israel's private business. Everything the Israel does in the business is also for the benefit of his partner.
76 Tosephta *Terumot* 10:9.

(4d line 11) אָדָא שַׁמָּשָׁא שָׁאַל לְרִבִּי אִמִּי. בְּגִין דַּאֲנָא צָבַע פְּתִילְתָא מִן חוֹלָא. אֲמַר לֵיהּ. בָּטִיל הוּא עַל גַּב פְּתִילוּת. רִבִּי יוּדָה בֶּן פָּזִי הוֹרֵי לְאִילֵּין דְּבַר נְחֶמְיָה כֵן. רִבִּי אַמִּי נְסַב פְּתִילָא. רִבִּי לִיָּיא לָא נְסִיב פְּתִילָא. וְלָא מוֹדֵי רִבִּי לִיָּיא לְרִבִּי אַמִּי. חֲשַׁשׁ הוּא מְשׁוּם גֶּזֶל. וְכוּפְלָה מְן הָדֵין שַׁמָּשָׁא בְּבֵיתֵיהּ בַּזְבָּזָא בְּהָקְדֵישָׁא.

[77]Ada the nurse asked Rebbi Immi: Since I am dipping wicks at a sick person's? He said to him, it becomes insignificant in the wick. Rebbi Jehudah ben Pazi instructed those of Bar Neḥemiah in this way. Rebbi Immi took a wick, Rebbi Ila did not take a wick[78]. Did Rebbi Ila not agree with Rebbi Immi? Rebbi Ila thought because of robbery because the nurse will spoil the consecrated food[79].

גַּמְלִיאֵל זוּגָא שָׁאַל לְרִבִּי אִיסִי. מַהוּ לְהוֹסִיף לְתוֹכוֹ שֶׁמֶן חוּלִין וּמַדְלִיק. אֲמַר לֵיהּ. לֹא תַנֵּי רִבִּי הוֹשַׁעְיָה אֶלָּא אֵין מְחַייְבִין אוֹתוֹ לְמַצּוֹתוֹ.

Gamliel the twin asked Rebbi Yasa: May one add profane oil and light? He said to him, Rebbi Hoshaia stated only[80] that one is not required to squeeze it out.

אֲמַר רִבִּי אַבָּהוּ. שָׁנָה לִי רִבִּי יוֹנָתָן בֶּן עַכְמַאי. בַּת כֹּהֵן שֶׁהָיְתָה עוֹמֶדֶת עֶרֶב שַׁבָּת עִם חֲשֵׁיכָה וּבְיָדָהּ נֵר שֶׁמֶן שְׂרֵיפָה הֲרֵי זוּ מוֹסֶפֶת לְתוֹכוֹ שֶׁמֶן חוֹל כָּל־שֶׁהוּא וּמַדְלֶקֶת. אֲמַר לֵיהּ רִבִּי זְעֵירָא. וּמַה הֲוָה טִיבֵיהּ. אֲמַר לֵיהּ. אָדָם גָּדוֹל הָיָה וּבָקִי בְּמִשְׁנָתֵינוּ הָיָה וּפִירְשָׁהּ רִבִּי חִייָא דִּכְפַר תְּחֻמִין קוֹמֵי רִבִּי וּמִנְיתֵיהּ חֲכָמִים.

Rebbi Abbahu said, Jonathan ben Akhmai did teach me: The daughter of a Cohen standing on Sabbath eve with a light filled with oil to burn[81], adds some profane oil and lights. Rebbi Ze`ira said, what is the nature of this? He said to him, he was a great personality, well versed in the Mishnah. Rebbi Ḥiyya from Kefar Teḥumin explained this to Rabbi and he appointed him rabbi.

77 Slightly reformulated from *Terumot* 11:7 (Notes 146-153); see the Notes there for the problematic character of the text. S. Lieberman conjectures that the question was not about oil to be burned but that he dipped the wick in heave vinegar to singe it as noted in the discussion of Mishnah 5 (Note 150) and R. Immi permitted it.

78 Dipped in oil to be burned.

79 Robbing the Cohanim of their heave by marginally permitted use.

80 The Tosephta quoted earlier (Note 76).

81 He restricts the prohibition of the Mishnah to the case that pure oil to be burned is used Friday night, not if it is mixed with even a minute quantity of profane oil. The Babli does not mention this.

(4d line 23) וְלֹא בְחֵלֶב. רַב בְּרוֹנָא אָמַר. חֵלֶב מַטִּיף לְתוֹכוֹ שֶׁמֶן כָּל־שֶׁהוּא וּמַדְלִיק. יוֹסֵי בָעֵי. מָה אֲנָן קַיָּימִין. אִם בְּמָחוּי. אֲפִילוּ לֹא נָתַן לְתוֹכוֹ שֶׁמֶן. וְתַנֵּי שְׁמוּאֵל. כָּל־שֶׁמַּתִּיכִין אוֹתוֹ וְאֵינוֹ קָרוּשׁ מָחוּי הוּא. וְאִם בְּשֶׁאֵינוֹ מָחוּי. אֲפִילוּ נָתַן לְתוֹכוֹ שֶׁמֶן. אָתָא רַב חֲנַנְיָה רַב בְּרוֹנָא בְשֵׁם רַב. חֵלֶב מְהוּתָּךְ וְקִירְבֵי דָגִים מַדְלִיקִין בָּהֶן. רִבִּי חִייָה בַּר אַשִׁי עָנִי מֵיתֵי קוֹמֵי רַב. אֲמַר לֵיהּ. הֵן הֲוֵיתָה. אֲמַר לֵיהּ. בְּעָיֵי מְשַׁח דְּזֵית. אֲמַר לֵיהּ. וְלֹא הֲוָה לָךְ קִירְבֵי דָגִים.

1 וּמדליק G | מדליק יוסי בעי | - G | 2 ותני | G ותנה 3 אתא | G אתה רב | ר' G | 4 עני | G ענה 5 ליה | G לה (2) | בעיי | G בעי

אִית תַּנָּיֵי תַנֵּי. מַדְלִיקִין בְּנֶפְט. אִית תַּנָּיֵי תַנֵּי. אֵין מַדְלִיקִין בְּנֶפְט. אָמַר רַב חִסְדָּא. מַה דָמַר. מַדְלִיקִין. בָּהֶן אִיפּוֹמָא. וּמַה דָמַר. אֵין מַדְלִיקִין. בָּהֶן חִיוְרָא דְּהוּא סַכָּנָה.

1 חסדא G | חסדה   2 איכומא G | איבומה   חיורא G | חיוורה

[82]"Nor with fat." Rav Berona said, one mixes some oil with it and kindles[83]. Yose asked, where do we hold? If it was made into a paste, even if he did not mix it with oil, as Samuel stated, any which one turns into a fluid and it does not jell is a paste. But if it was not made into a paste, even if he mixes with oil. There came Rav[84] Hananiah, Rav Berona in the name of Rav: One may kindle with liquefied fat and fish innards. Rebbi Ḥiyya ber Ashi failed to come before Rav. He asked him, where have you been? He answered. I was trying to get olive oil. He asked him, do you not have innards of fish[85]?

Some Tannaim state, one kindles with naphtha; but some Tannaim state, one does not kindle with naphtha. Rav Ḥisda said, he who said one kindles, if it was black; and he who said, one does not kindle, if it was white, because it represents danger[86].

82 For this paragraph there exists a Genizah fragment published by Ginzberg (p. 72), G.

83 Babli 21a, for fat and fish liver.

84 With G, read "Rebbi".
85 In Babylonia where olive oil is not commonly used it is not particularly meritorious to spend time and money on a search for olive oil.
86 Babli 26a where using white (light) naphtha is forbidden even on weekdays because of the danger of an explosion.

(4d line 33) מתני׳. אֵין מַדְלִיקִין בְּשֶׁמֶן שְׂרֵיפָה בְּיוֹם טוֹב כול׳. הָא בְכָל־אִילֵּין קַדְמָאֵי מַדְלִיקִין.

רִבִּי יִשְׁמָעֵאל אוֹמֵר אֵין מַדְלִיקִין בְּעִטְרָן מִפְּנֵי כְבוֹד הַשַּׁבָּת. מַה בֵּין עִיטְרָן מַה בֵּין קִירְבֵי דָגִים. קִירְבֵי דָגִים כָּל־זְמַן שֶׁהֵן דְּלִיקִין אֵין רֵיחָן רַע. כָּבוּ רֵיחָן רַע. עִיטְרָן בֵּין כָּבָה בֵּין דָּלַק רֵיחוֹ רַע. שֶׁלֹּא תֹאמַר. הוֹאִיל וְרֵיחוֹ רַע יְהֵא טָעוּן הַרְחֵק ד׳ אַמּוֹת. לְפוּם כֵּן צָרִיךְ מֵימַר. אֵין מַדְלִיקִין בּוֹ.

1 קירבי | G קרבי   3 לפום | G לפם

וַחֲכָמִים מַתִּירִין בְּכָל הַשְּׁמָנִים. (תְּנֵי.) בְּשֶׁמֶן פְּקוּעוֹת.

1 בשמן פקועות | G בשמן שמשמין בשמן אגו .... פקועות

רִבִּי טַרְפוֹן אוֹמֵר אֵין מַדְלִיקִין אֶלָּא בְשֶׁמֶן זַיִת בִּלְבָד: עָמַד לוֹ רִבִּי יוֹחָנָן בֶּן נוּרִי עַל רַגְלָיו וְאָמַר. מַה יַּעֲשׂוּ אַנְשֵׁי בָבֶל שֶׁאֵין לָהֶן אֶלָּא שֶׁמֶן שׁוּמְשְׁמִין. מַה יַּעֲשׂוּ אַנְשֵׁי מָדַי שֶׁאֵין לָהֶן אֶלָּא שֶׁמֶן אֱגוֹזִים בִּלְבָד. מַה יַּעֲשׂוּ אַנְשֵׁי אַלֶכְּסַנְדְּרִיאָה שֶׁאֵין לָהֶן אֶלָּא שֶׁמֶן צְנוֹנוֹת. מַה יַּעֲשׂוּ אַנְשֵׁי קַפּוֹדְקִיָּא שֶׁאֵין לָהֶן לֹא כָךְ וְלֹא כָךְ (אֶלָּא נֵפְט). אֶלָּא אֵין לְךָ אֶלָּא מַה שֶׁהִתִּירוּ רִאשׁוֹנִים בִּלְבַד.

תַּנֵּי. רִבִּי שִׁמְעוֹן בֶּן אֶלְעָזָר אוֹמֵר. אֵין מַדְלִיקִין צוֹרִי מִפְּנֵי שֶׁהוּא שָׂרָף.

1 אלעזר | G לעזר

"One does not kindle with oil to be burned on a holiday," etc. Therefore one kindles with all those mentioned earlier[87].

"Rebbi Ismael says, one does not kindle with `*iṭran*[11] because of the honor of the Sabbath." What is the difference between `*iṭran* and innards of fish? Innards of fish are not smelling badly as long as they are burning; they are smelling badly when extinguished. `*Iṭran* smells badly whether extinguished or burning[88]. Since it smells badly one should need to distance himself four cubits[89]; therefore it is necessary to say "one does not kindle".

"But the Sages permit all kinds of oil." (State:) colocynth oil[90].

"Rebbi Tarphon says, one kindles only with olive oil." "Rebbi Joḥanan ben Nuri got on his feet and said, if it is so what should the people of Babylonia do who have only sesame oil? What should the people of Media do who have only nut oil? What should the people of Alexandria do who have only radish oil? What should the people of Kappadokia do who have neither one nor the other (but naphtha)⁹¹? But you have only what the earlier ones permitted.⁹²"

It was stated: "Rebbi Simeon ben Eleazar says, one does not kindle with balsamum because it is a resin.⁹³"

87 Babli 24a, Tosephta 2:1.
88 Babli 25b.
89 It should be forbidden to perform any religious duty within four cubits of the source of the bad smell (*Berakhot* 3:5). The disagreeable smell of *'itran* is not of the forbidden kind.
90 The word "state" was crossed out by the corrector; it is not in the *editio princeps*. But as J. N. Epstein has shown (*Tarbiz* 5, pp. 260-261; מבוא לנוסח המשנה p. 951) the

original text is correct and the addition of "colocynth oil" in the Mishnah is a later insert; as a vegetable oil it logically should have been mentioned before fish oil.
91 Deleted by the corrector for no good reason; it is mentioned in the Tosephta and the Babli.
92 Babli 26a, Tosephta 2:3.
93 Babli 25b,26a, Tosephta 2:3. He holds that one uses only oil from seeds, not wood or sap from the stem.

(4d line 47) מתני׳. כָּל־הַיּוֹצֵא מִן הָעֵץ אֵין מַדְלִיקִין בּוֹ אֶלָּא פִשְׁתָּן כול׳. אָמַר רִבִּי שִׁמְעוֹן⁹⁴ בַּר רַב יִצְחָק. כְּתִיב לְהַעֲלוֹת נֵר תָּמִיד. שִׁיעֲרוּ לוֹמַר שֶׁאֵין לְךָ עוֹשֶׂה שַׁלְהֶבֶת אֶלָּא פִשְׁתָּן בִּלְבַד. תַּנֵּי. רִבִּי שִׁמְעוֹן בֶּן אֶלְעָזָר אוֹמֵר. כָּל־הַיּוֹצֵא מִן הָעֵץ אֵין בּוֹ מִשּׁוּם שָׁלֹשׁ עַל שָׁלֹשׁ. מְסַכְּכִים בּוֹ. חוּץ מִן הַפִּשְׁתָּן. אָמַר רִבִּי יוֹסֵי. עָשׂוּ אוֹתוֹ כְּעָבִים הָרַכִּים. דְּתַנִּינַן. הָעָבִים⁹⁵ הָרַכִּים, אֵין בָּהֶם מִשּׁוּם שָׁלֹשׁ עַל שָׁלֹשׁ: אָמַר רִבִּי לְעָזָר. מִן הַמִּשְׁכָּן לָמָדוּ. דִּכְתִיב אֶת הַמִּשְׁכָּן תַּעֲשֶׂה עֶשֶׂר יְרִיעוֹת שֵׁשׁ מָשְׁזָר. וּכְתִיב פַּאֲרֵי פִשְׁתִּים יִהְיוּ עַל־רֹאשָׁם. אַתְּ לָמֵד שֵׁשׁ מִשֵּׁשׁ. וְשֵׁשׁ מִפַּאֲרֵי. וּפַאֲרֵי מִפַּאֲרֵי.

Mishnah⁹⁶. "One does not kindle with any wood product but flax," etc. Rebbi Simeon⁹⁴ bar Rav Isaac said it is written⁹⁷: *to raise permanent light*. They estimated to say that nothing makes a flame like flax⁹⁸. It was stated⁹⁹: "Rebbi Simeon ben Eleazar said, no wood product is subject to the three-by-three rule¹⁶ except flax and one may use it as roofing¹⁰⁰, except flax." Rebbi Yose said, they made it like coarse or soft, as we have stated¹⁰¹: "the coarse and the soft are not subject to the three-by-three rule." Rebbi Eleazar said, they learned it¹⁰² from the Tabernacle as it is written¹⁰³, *the Sanctuary you shall make ten gobelins, twilled byssus*; and it is written¹⁰⁴, *linen turbans* *shall be on their heads.* You learn byssus from byssus, and byssus from turbans, and turbans from turbans[105].

94 Read: R. Samuel ben Rav Isaac.
95 Read: הֶעָבִים.
96 Quote from Mishnah 3.
97 *Ex.* 27:20.
98 The wick in the lamp which was burning through the night had to be of flax.
99 Babli 26a, Tosephta 2:4. According to Rashi this implies that hemp fibers and cloth are impervious to impurity.
100 It is a strict rabbinic rule that the roof of a *sukkah* may not be made with anything susceptible to impurity. Wooden logs as well as stems of plants may be used but not fruits.
101 Mishnah *Kelim* 28:8. Cloth which is either very coarse or very fine cannot be used as handkerchief. Therefore it cannot become impure in the size of (3 fingers)². The minimum size for such fabric to be susceptible to impurity is that of a towel, (3 handbreadths)².

102 The fact that linen textile is called "tent" and therefore brings impurity is implied by the instructions for the building of the Tabernacle.
103 *Ex.* 26.1.
104 *Ez.* 44:16.
105 There is a quote missing for the chain of reasoning. The gobelins which formed the walls of the Tabernacle were partially made of שֵׁש "byssus". The problem is to prove that byssus was made of linen. Since the same word was used in *Ex.* 26.1 and *Ex.* 39:28, speaking of the priestly vestments, *the hat-turbans of byssus*, one may assume that the same turbans and the same materials are mentioned in *Ez.* 44:16, where it is explicitly stated that the priests' turbans are made of linen. Similarly in the Babli *Yoma* 71b; a different derivation in the name of R. Eleazar is in the Babli *Šabbat* 27b/28a.

(4d line 55) רִבִּי אֶלְעָזָר שָׁאַל. מָהוּ לַעֲשׂוֹת אוֹהֶל מֵעוֹר בְּהֵמָה טְמֵיאָה. וְהָכְתִיב וְעוֹרוֹת תְּחָשִׁים. רִבִּי יוּדָה רִבִּי נְחֶמְיָה וְרַבָּנָן. רִבִּי יְהוּדָה אוֹמֵר. טַיְינוֹן. לְשֵׁם צִבְעוֹ נִקְרָא. וְרִבִּי נְחֶמְיָה אָמַר. גלקטינן. וְרַבָּנָן אָמְרִין. מִין חַיָה טְהוֹרָה וּגְדוּלָה בַּמִּדְבָּר. וַתְייָא כַּיי דָּאמַר רִבִּי אֶלְעָזָר בֵּירִבִּי יוֹסֵי רִבִּי אַבָּהוּ בְּשֵׁם רִבִּי שִׁמְעוֹן בֶּן לָקִיש בְּשֵׁם רִבִּי מֵאִיר. כְּמִין חַיָה טְהוֹרָה בָּרָא הַקָּדוֹש בָּרוּךְ הוּא לְמֹשֶׁה בַּמִּדְבָּר. כֵּיוָן שֶׁעָשָׂה בָּה מְלֶאכֶת הַמִּשְׁכָּן נִגְנְזָה. רִבִּי אָבוּן אָמַר. קֶרֶש הָיָה שְׁמוֹ. תַּנֵּי רִבִּי הוֹשַׁעְיָה. דְּחָדָא קֶרֶן. וְתִיטָב לַיי מִשׁוֹר פָּר מַקְרִין וּמַפְרִיס. מִקֶּרֶן כָּתַב רַחֲמָנָא.

Rebbi Eleazar asked, may one make the Tent[106] of leather from an impure animal? But is it not written[107], *and tahaš skins.* [108]Rebbi Jehudah, Rebbi Nehemiah and the rabbis. Rebbi Jehudah says, violet[109]; it was called thus because of its color. Rebbi Nehemiah said, blue[110]. But the rabbis say, a kind of pure animal which grows up in the desert. It comes like what Rebbi

Eleazar ben Rebbi Yose, Rebbi Abbahu[111], Rebbi Simeon ben Laqish in the name of Rebbi Meïr said: [112]The Holy One, praise to Him, created for Moses in the desert a kind of pure animal. After the work of the Tabernacle had been finished it was hidden. Rebbi Abun said, its name was *qereš*. Rebbi Hoshaia stated, a unicorn. *It is preferable to the Eternal over a cattle ox which sprouts a horn and has split hooves*[113]. The All-Merciful wrote[114], it sprouts a horn.

106 Is a tent made of leather from an impure animal a tent in the meaning of *Num.* 19 in which a corpse causes impurity for all persons and vessels inside.

107 *Ex.* 25:5. Since *tahaš* is not mentioned in the lists of pure animals in *Lev.* 11 and *Deut.* 14, one must assume that it was impure. But the Tabernacle is the prime example of a "tent"; if its cover was of leather from an impure animal the question should not arise.

108 A parallel exists in *Eccl. rabba* 1(28).

109 Following Buxtorf, accepted by most moderns, this is Greek ἰάνθινος, -η, -ov, adj., "violet-colored". In *Eccl. r.*, one reads אלטינו.

110 This is identified as Greek γλαύκινος, -η, -ov, adj., "bluish-gray". In *Eccl. r.*, גלטינון.

111 Read: R. Abbahu (the Amora) in the name of R. Eleazar ben R. Yose (the Tanna).

112 The same interpretation in the Babli, 28b.

113 *Ps.* 69:32.

114 The Psalms, as Holy Scriptures, are considered of divine origin.

(4d line 63) תַּמָּן תַּנֵּינַן. כָּל־הַפָּחוּת מִשְּׁלשָׁה עַל שְׁלשָׁה שֶׁהִתְקִינוֹ לָפוּק בּוֹ אֶת הַמֶּרְחָץ וּלְנַעֵר בּוֹ אֶת הַקְּדֵירָה וּלְקַנֵּחַ בּוֹ אֶת הָרֵיחַיִם בֵּין מִן הַמּוּכָן בֵּין שֶׁאֵין מִן הַמּוּכָן טָמֵא. דִּבְרֵי רִבִּי לִיעֶזֶר. רִבִּי יְהוֹשֻׁעַ אוֹמֵר. אַף מַטְלִית חֲדָשָׁה בֵּין מִן הַמּוּכָן בֵּין שֶׁאֵינוֹ מִן הַמּוּכָן טָהוֹר. רִבִּי עֲקִיבָה אוֹמֵר. מִן הַמּוּכָן טָמֵא וְשֶׁאֵינוֹ מִן הַמּוּכָן טָהוֹר׃ מַה בֵּין מִן הַמּוּכָן מַה בֵּין שֶׁאֵינוֹ מִן הַמּוּכָן. בֵּין שְׁכֵינָה לְתוֹךְ הַבַּיִת בֵּין שֶׁהִשְׁלִיכָהּ לְאִישְׁפָּה. וְהָתְנַן. רִבִּי לִיעֶזֶר אוֹמֵר. אַף מַטְלִית חֲדָשָׁה כַּיּוֹצֵא בָהֶן. וְלֵית בַּר נַשׁ אָמַר. אַף אֲפִילוּ אֶלָּא עָדַי מוֹדֵי עַל קַדְמִיתָא. בֵּין שְׁכֵינָה לִטְלוּתָהּ בֵּין שֶׁלֹּא שְׁכֵינָה לִטְלוּתָהּ. הָדָא יַלְפָא מִן הַהִיא וְהַהִיא יַלְפָא מִן הָדָא. הָדָא יַלְפָא מִן הַהִיא. דִּבְרֵי רִבִּי לִיעֶזֶר וְהוּא שֶׁקִּיפְּלָהּ. וְהַהִיא יַלְפָא מִן הָדָא. כְּשֶׁלֹּא שְׁכֵינָהּ לִטְלוּתָהּ. אֲבָל שְׁכֵינָהּ לִטְלוּתָהּ טְמֵיאָה הִיא.

There, we have stated[115]: "A [cloth] less than three by three [fingerwidths] which he took to plug the bath or to pour a pot[116] or to clean a millstone, whether it was prepared or not prepared can become impure[117], the words of Rebbi Eliezer. Rebbi Joshua says, (also a new rag)[118] whether prepared or not prepared, is pure[119]. Rebbi Aqiba says, prepared it may become impure, not prepared it is pure." What is the difference between prepared and not prepared? Whether he made it ready in the house or threw it into the garbage[120]. But did we not state[121]: "Rebbi Eliezer says, also a new rag follows the same rule.[122]" Nobody says "also", "even", unless he agree with the preceding; whether he prepared it to hang it up or did not prepare it to hang it up[123]. This learns from the other and the other learns from this. This learns from the other; the words of Rebbi Eliezer if he folded it[124]. And the other learns from this; if he did not prepare it to hang it up. But if he prepared it to hang it up it may become impure.

115 Mishnah *Kelim* 28:2. Babli 29a.

116 To use it as a potholder.

117 For him the rule that textiles of area less that 9 (fingerwidth)² cannot become impure is an empirical one since such a small piece in general is of no use. If somebody finds a use, the piece becomes a regular piece of textile and is subject to all laws of impurity.

118 Probably the words in parenthesis should be deleted; they are not found in any Mishnah ms. and are copied here from the quote later of Mishnah 27:12.

119 For him the three-finger rule is a permanent rabbinic decree which cannot be changed.

120 A single use does not bring on impurity. If the rag was used once and then thrown away it cannot become impure. But if it is prepared for re-use it becomes valuable and is susceptible to impurity.

121 Mishnah *Kelim* 27:12. תנן is Babylonian spelling.

122 The Mishnah states that an impure piece of (3 fingerwiths)² which was torn loses its impurity only if it is thrown away, with the exception of purple strips which are valuable also in minute sizes and never lose their impurity. R. Eliezer extends the latter rule to unused textiles.

123 For re-use.

124 For the first use; Babli 29b. If it never was intended for use he agrees that it is not susceptible to impurity.

(4d line 74) וּמַה טַעֲמֵיהּ דְּרִבִּי לִיעֶזֶר. נַעֲשָׂה כִּמְטָהֵר כֵּלִים בַּשַּׁבָּת. מִכֵּיוָן שֶׁקִּיפְּלָהּ לֹא טָהֲרָה. שֶׁכֵּן שַׁמָּשִׁים אוּמָנִין רוֹצִין בְּקִיפּוּלָהּ. וְלֹא מִבְּעוֹד יוֹם שֶׁהִיא טְהוּרָה. רִבִּי לְעָזָר בְּשֵׁם רִבִּי הוֹשַׁעְיָה. מִפְּנֵי יוֹם טוֹב שֶׁחָל לִהְיוֹת בְּעֶרֶב שַׁבָּת. וְלֹא מֵאֵלֶיהָ הִיא טְהוּרָה. אָמַר רִבִּי יוֹסֵי בֵּירִבִּי בּוּן. תִּיפְתָּר שֶׁהָיוּ בָהּ שָׁלֹשׁ עַל שָׁלֹשׁ מְצוּמְצָמוֹת.

1 שקיפלה G | שכיפלה   2 אמנין G | אומנים   3 היא G | -   יוסי G | יוסה   4 שלש G | שלוש (2)

רִבִּי אָחָא רִבִּי סִימוֹן בְּשֵׁם רִבִּי שִׁמְעוֹן נְזִירָא. עֲשָׂאָהּ מָזוֹר טְהוּרָה. שָׁרְיָיהּ בַּשֶּׁמֶן לֹא כְמִי שֶׁעֲשָׂאָהּ מָזוֹר. רִבִּי זְעִירָה רִבִּי יַנַּאי רִבִּי יִרְמְיָה בְּשֵׁם רִבִּי יְהוֹשֻׁעַ בֶּן לֵוִי. נְרָאִין דְּבָרִים שֶׁתְּהֵא הֲלָכָה כְּרִבִּי עֲקִיבָה. שֶׁהוּא אוֹמֵר מֵעֵין שְׁנֵיהֶן. וַאֲנָהּ אֶלָּא כְרִבִּי יְהוֹשֻׁעַ מְקוּלֵּי שָׁלֹשׁ עַל שָׁלֹשׁ לֹא סוֹף דָּבָר טְהוֹרָה אֶלָּא אֲפִילוּ טְמֵיאָה. בְּגִין רַב. דְּרַב אָמַר. מַסִּיקִין בְּכֵלִים וְאֵין מַסִּיקִין בְּשִׁבְרֵי כֵלִים.

1 נזירא G | בר נזירה   2 שעשאה G | עשאה ר' ינאי G | רק יוחנן ר' ינייי   3 שלש G | שלוש (2)   4 טמיאה | טמאה G

[125]What is Rebbi Eliezer's reason[126]? He is like one who purifies vessels on the Sabbath[127]. When he threaded it[128], it did not become pure since professional waiters like it threaded. Does it not become pure when it still is daylight? Rebbi Eleazar in the name of Rebbi Hoshaia: because of a holiday which falls on Friday[129]. Does it not become pure automatically? Rebbi Yose ben Rebbi Abun said, explain it if it was exactly three-by-three[130].

Rebbi Aḥa, Rebbi Simon in the name of Rebbi Simeon the *nazir*[131]: If he made it into a bandage it is pure[132]. If one dipped it in oil is it not as if he made a bandage[133]? Rebbi Ze`ira, Rebbi Yannai[134], Rebbi Jeremiah in the name of Rebbi Joshua ben Levi, logically practice should follow Rebbi Aqiba who is similar to both[135], but in fact it follows Rebbi Joshua who is lenient in the matter of three-by-three. Not only pure but even impure, because of Rav, since Rav said one heats with vessels, but one does not heat with pieces of vessels[136].

125 Here starts a new Genizah leaf edited by Ginzberg (p. 73).

126 This refers to the statement of R. Eliezer in the Mishnah who prohibits the use of linen wicks.

127 If the linen was impure and he uses it as wick, the moment it becomes unusable as textile it loses the impurity of textiles. This is the equivalent of repairing defective equipment and is forbidden on the Sabbath.

128 This "threading" is not the "folding" mentioned in the preceding paragraph but the twisting of linen threads to make a wick. Since some people insist on using only twisted wicks, the threads remain usable even if they do not cover an area of (3 fingerwidths)² and do not lose their impurity.

129 It also is forbidden to repair equipment of a holiday; for a similar argument cf. Note 56.

130 Then they lose their impurity the moment a person starts lighting them. One cannot say that the loss of impurity is later an automatic consequence of a prior permitted act of a human. Babli 38b (in the name of the Babylonian Rav Joseph.)

131 In G correctly: R. Simeon the *nazir's* son.

132 Mishnah *Kelim* 28:2. The medication makes the bandage unusable otherwise.

133 Then the wick already is pure and R. Eliezer's reason does not apply.

134 In G one reads "R. Johanan" before the mention of R. Yannai; there is a lacuna preceding this word; it is not clear whether it read "R. Ze`ira in the name of R. Johanan." One has to wonder why R. Jeremiah, the student of R. Ze`ira, reports a different tradition.

135 In Mishnah *Šabbat* 2:3 practice certainly follows R. Aqiba against R. Eliezer. For consistency the practice also should follow R. Aqiba in Mishnah *Kelim* 28:1 where he partially follows R. Eliezer and partially R. Joshua. In general, R. Joshua is an overriding authority.

136 Vessels may become impure but potsherds are pure. Rav permits to use combustible vessels as fuel even though they become pure by losing their qualities as vessels in the fire. He forbids using shards as fuel, which cannot become impure, since they may not be moved on the Sabbath because they are of no use (Chapter 17). There is no connection between susceptibility to impurity and use as wick on the Sabbath. The statement of Rav is quoted in the Babli 28a, 29a, 124b,143a; *Besah* 32a, 33a.

(5a line 9) מתני' לא יקוב אָדָם שְׁפוֹפֶרֶת שֶׁלְבֵיצָה. לָמָה. מִשּׁוּם שֶׁלֹּא הוּתְחַל בְּכָל־טִיפָּה וְטִיפָּה. אוֹ שֶׁמָּה יִשְׁכַּח וִיעָרָה. מַה נָפִיק מִבֵּינֵיהוֹן. הָהֵן זְקוּקָה דִיקלוֹן. אִין תֵּימַר. מִשֵּׁם שֶׁלֹּא הוּתְחַל בְּכָל־טִיפָּה. הֲרֵי לֹא הוּתְחַל בְּכָל־טִיפָּה וְטִיפָּה. אִין תֵּימַר. שֶׁמָּה יִשְׁכַּח וִיעָרָה. הֲרֵי אֵינוֹ שׁוֹכֵחַ וּמְעָרֶה.

4 שוכח G | שכוח

אִם חִיבְּרָהּ הַיּוֹצֵר מִתְּחִילָּה מוּתָּר מִפְּנֵי שֶׁהוּא כְּלִי אֶחָד. שַׁנְיָיא הִיא. שְׁכוּלָּהּ אֶחָד. אֶלָּא אִם חִיבְּרָהּ בְּסִיד אוֹ בְגִיפְסוֹס. יָאוּת. דְּרִבִּי יוּדָה כְדַעְתֵּיהּ. דְּרִבִּי יוּדָה אָמַר. מַשְׁקֶה טוֹפֵחַ חִיבּוּר. תַּנֵּי. פְּתִילָה אַחַת בִּשְׁנֵי כוֹסוֹת בִּשְׁתֵּי קְעָרוֹת בִּשְׁנֵי תַמְחוּיִין אָסוּר. רִבִּי יוּדָה מַתִּיר. רִבִּי חֲנַנְיָה בְשֵׁם רִבִּי פִּינְחָס. רִבִּי יוּדָה כְדַעְתֵּיהּ. דְּרִבִּי יוּדָה אָמַר. מַשְׁקֶה טוֹפֵחַ חִיבּוּר.

1 אלא אם G| אילו אמר   2 בסיד G | ביסיד | או בגיפסס G | ובגיפסוס   3 תמחויין G | תמחויים

"A person may not pierce an eggshell[17]." Why? Because it did not start at each single drop[137], or maybe he might forget and stir? What is the difference between them? This refined [138]דיקלון. If you are saying, because it did not start at each single drop, it did not stop at every single drop; if you say. maybe be might forget and stir, he will not forget and stir.

"If the potter combined it from the outset it is permitted since it is one vessel." There is a difference because all is one, if he combined it by lime or gypsum[139]. Rebbi Jehudah follows his own opinion since Rebbi Jehudah says moist liquid is a connection[140]. It was stated: One wick in two cups, in two pots, in two trays is forbidden; Rebbi Jehudah permits. Rebbi Hananiah in the name of Rebbi Phineas: Rebbi Jehudah follows his own opinion since Rebbi Jehudah says moist liquid is a connection.

137 A condition for leaving things burning on the Sabbath; Chapter 1 Note 355.

138 The identity of this "refined *diklon*" is unknown (as noted by Sokoloff in his

Dictionary of Jewish Palestinian Aramaic) and why one would not be tempted to stir. The conjectures of the commentaries (bast fiber bags, opening of a pitcher) and earlier dictionaries are of no value.

139 Babli 29b, Tosephta 2:6. This is the condition of the majority to allow the light to burn. G has a different text: "*If it had said*, if he combined it by lime or gypsum." This refers to the Mishnah; if the text of the Tosephta had been that of the Mishnah, the question asked in the previous paragraph would have superfluous since the reason for the prohibition cannot be that not every drop was involved.

גִּיפְסוֹס is Greek γύψος "gypsum; cement".

140 In the Babli, *Avodah zarah* 72b, this refers mainly to transfer of impurity. Solid material impure in degree n makes other materials impure in degree $n+1$. There is a discussion about fluids; there are those who assert that fluids do not touch, they combine and everything moistened by impure fluids biblically becomes impure in the same degree as the fluid itself. (Rabbinically it can be stronger impurity; Chapter 1, Note 299). R. Jehudah accepts this statement and extends it to other legal domains, such as the laws of the Sabbath.

(5a line 20) מתני'. הַמְכַבֶּה אֶת הַנֵּר מִפְּנֵי שֶׁהוּא מִתְיָירֵא מִפְּנֵי גוֹיִם כוֹל'. אָמַר רִבִּי שְׁמוּאֵל בַּר רַב יִצְחָק. מִפְּנֵי גוֹיִם שֶׁלְסַכָּנָה. מִפְּנֵי לִיסְטִים שֶׁלְסַכָּנָה. רִבִּי יוֹסֵי בָעֵי. אִי מִפְּנֵי לִיסְטִין שֶׁל סַכָּנָה נִיתְנֵי מוּתָּר. רַבָּנִין דְּקַיְסָרִין בְּשֵׁם רִבִּי יוֹסֵי בֶּן חֲנִינָה. מוּתָּר.

1 אמ' רק | G - 2 מפני | G כיני מתניתה מפני   ליסטין | G לסטיט   3 ניתני | G נתני   רבנין | G רבנן

"One who extinguishes a light because he is afraid of Gentiles,[141]" etc. Rebbi Samuel bar Rav Isaac said, [so is the Mishnah:][142] because dangerous Gentiles, because of dangerous robbers. Rebbi Yose asked, if because of dangerous robbers one should have stated "it is permitted.[143]" The rabbis of Caesarea in the name of Rebbi Yose ben Ḥanina: It is permitted[144].

141 Quote from Mishnah 5.
142 Added from G.
143 If extinguishing the light is needed to save a life, it is not only permitted, it is required. The formulation of the Mishnah, "he is not liable" gives the impression that the action is sinful. This might cause people to hesitate to extinguish the light when it is necessary for survival, a very bad outcome.

144 They reformulated the Mishnah. The Babli, 30a, agrees that in these cases it is permitted; they defend the formulation "not liable" because it also refers to the cases mentioned later in the Mishnah.

(5a line) מַה בֵּין הַמַּצִּיל מִמָּה שֶׁבַּנֵּר מַה בֵּין הַמַּצִּיל מִמָּה שֶׁבַּזַּיִת. רַבָּנִין דְּקַיְסָרִין בְּשֵׁם רִבִּי שִׁילָא דִּינָיה. לֹא דּוֹמֶה הַמַּצִּיל מִגּוּפָהּ שֶׁלְפְּתִילָה לַמַּצִּיל חוּץ מִגּוּפָהּ שֶׁלְפְּתִילָה.

What is the difference between one who saves from what is in the light and one who saves what is in the olive[145]? The rabbis of Caesarea in the name of Rebbi Shila from Naveh: One who saves from the wick itself cannot be compared to one who saves away from the wick itself[146].

145 This is a question about the second part of the Mishnah. Why is the person who extinguishes the light to save oil liable? The person who stores olives to press them later is not liable.

146 The question is not well posed. If one removes oil from a burning lamp one causes the wick to be extinguished earlier; this is an act of extinguishing. But not to press olives is doing nothing. (S. Lieberman prefers to emend בבית "in the house" instead of בזית "in the olive".)

(5c line 25) אָמַר רִבִּי יוֹחָנָן. רִבִּי יוֹסֵי וְרִבִּי שִׁמְעוֹן שְׁנֵיהֶן אָמְרוּ דָּבָר אֶחָד. כְּמָה דְרִבִּי יוֹסֵי אָמַר. עַד שֶׁיְּהֵא לוֹ צוֹרֶךְ בְּגוּפָהּ שֶׁלַּפְּתִילָה. כֵּן רִבִּי שִׁמְעוֹן אוֹמֵר. עַד שֶׁיְּהֵא לוֹ צוֹרֶךְ בְּגוּפָהּ שֶׁלְּדָבָר. מַה אִית לָךְ צוֹרֶךְ בְּגוּפָהּ שֶׁלַּפְּתִילָה. רַבָּנָן דְּקַיְסָרִין רִבִּי לָעְזָר בְּשֵׁם רִבִּי חֲנִינָא. שֶׁכֵּן שַׁמָּשֵׁי אוּמָּנִין מְחָרְכִין לֵיו. וּשְׂעַר רֵאשְׁהוֹן לָא הִתְחָרַךְ. מָהוּ מְחָרְכִין לֵיו. מְפַסְפְּסִין לֵיו.

Rebbi Johanan said, Rebbi Yose and Rebbi Simeon said the same thing. Just as Rebbi Yose said, not unless he needs the body of the wick[147], so Rebbi Simeon says, not unless he needs the body of the thing[148]. How do you need the body of the wick? The rabbis of Caesarea, Rebbi Eleazar in the name of Rebbi Hanina: for so the professional waiters singe in this way, as you say[149], *and the hair on their heads was not singed.* What means "singe in this way"? They singe it[150].

147 In the Mishnah, where he frees from liability all who extinguish the light except the one who does it for the wick.

148 Further on in Mishnah 10:5 R. Simeon frees from liability a person carrying in the public domain if the carrying was not needed for the matter, implying that work on the Sabbath implies criminal liability only if it was needed for the intent. Babli 105b, 107b, 141b, *Sanhedrin* 85a, *Keritut* 20b. In the Yerushalmi later Chap. 13 (14a l. 38), *Beṣah* 1:3 (60b l. 21).

149 *Dan.* 3:27.

150 The biblical root חרך which was no longer understood is explained by the rabbinic Aramaic root פספס which means the same.

Since it would be embarrassing for the waiter if a wick failed to burn when he lights it in front of guests, singeing the wicks before they are needed is professional work done for a purpose. Babli 31b.

(5a line 31) תַּמָּן תַּנִּינָן. כָּל־הַמְקַלְקְלִין פְּטוּרִין חוּץ מִן הַמַּבְעִיר וּמִן הָעוֹשֶׂה חַבּוּרָה. בַּר קַפָּרָא אָמַר. אֲפִילוּ אֵינוֹ צָרִיךְ לְדָם אֲפִילוּ אֵינוֹ צָרִיךְ לָאֵפֶר. מַתְנִיתָא פְלִיגָא עַל רִבִּי יוֹחָנָן. שׁוֹרוֹ שֶׁהִדְלִיק אֶת הַגָּדִישׁ בַּשַׁבָּת חַיָּיב. וְהוּא שֶׁהִדְלִיק אֶת הַגָּדִישׁ בַּשַׁבָּת פָּטוּר. שׁוֹרוֹ שֶׁהִדְלִיק אֶת הַגָּדִישׁ בַּשַׁבָּת חַיָּיב. (לֹא) שֶׁלֹּא לְצוֹרֶךְ. וְהָכָא הוּא שֶׁהִדְלִיק אֶת הַגָּדִישׁ בַּשַׁבָּת פָּטוּר. אֲפִילוּ שֶׁלֹּא לְצוֹרֶךְ. תַּנֵּי. כָּל־הַמִּתְחַיֵּיב בְּנַפְשׁוֹ שׁוֹגֵג מֵבִיא חַטָּאת. אָמַר רִבִּי חֲנַנְיָה בְּרֵיהּ דְּרִבִּי הִילֵּל. מֵאַחַר שֶׁלֹּא לְצוֹרֶךְ הָיָה מִתְחַיֵּיב בְּנַפְשׁוֹ. וְכָאן אֲפִילוּ שֶׁלֹּא לְצוֹרֶךְ יְהֵא פָּטוּר מִן הַתַּשְׁלוּמִין. מִן הָדָא. מַכֵּה בְהֵמָה יְשַׁלְּמֶנָּה וּמַכֵּה אָדָם יוּמָת: מַה מַכֵּה בְהֵמָה לֹא חִלַּקְתָּה בָּהּ בֵּין שׁוֹגֵג לְמֵזִיד לְחַיְּיבוֹ מָמוֹן. אַף מַכֵּה אָדָם לֹא תַחֲלוֹק בֵּין שׁוֹגֵג בֵּין מֵזִיד לְפָטוֹר מָמוֹן.

[151]There, we have stated[152]: "All who destroy are not liable," except the incendiary and one causing an injury. Bar Qappara said, even if he did not need the blood, even if he did not need the ashes[153]. A Mishnah disagrees with Rebbi Johanan: "If his bull set fire to a stack of sheaves on the Sabbath; he is liable, but if he set fire to a stack of sheaves on the Sabbath, he is not liable.[154]" If his bull set fire to a stack of sheaves on the Sabbath; he is liable. Is that not for no purpose? So here if he set fire to a stack of sheaves on the Sabbath, he is not liable, even if it was for no purpose[155]. Rebbi Ḥanania the son of Rebbi Hillel said, since it was for no purpose, did he commit a capital crime? But here even it was for no purpose[156] he should be free from paying restitution, from the following[157]: *The slayer of an animal shall pay for it; the slayer of a human shall die.* Since for the slayer of an animal you did not differentiate between unintentional and intentional to make him liable for money, so for the slayer of a human you cannot differentiate between unintentional and intentional to free him from liability for money[158].

151 The main parallels for the first part of this paragraph are *Eruvin* 10(Note 147) and *Pesaḥim* 6:1(33b l.34), also *Bava qamma* 3:12 (Notes 140-144); cf. Babli *Šabbat* 106a, *Beṣah* 12b, *Yebamot* 16b, *Bava qamma* 34b, *Sanhedrin* 62b.

152 Mishnah 13:3.

153 There is obviously a sentence missing here stating the position of R. Johanan. The sentence is reported in all parallel sources and is quoted by Naḥmanides in his *Novellae* to *Šabbat* 106a (ed. M. Herschler col. 365) as text here: "R. Johanan says, one making a fire only if he needs the ashes, one causing a wound only if he needs the blood."

154 "Liable" and "not liable" here means financial responsibility for damages. The human who sets a fire on the Sabbath does not have to pay since he has committed a capital crime and it is a principle of talmudic law that the possibility of a death penalty bars monetary claims (cf. *Terumot* 7:1 Notes 16 ff.). The payment is excluded even if

there is no possibility of criminal prosecution.

155 The statement of the Mishnah does not mention intent; it excludes payment even if the ashes from the fire are not needed. This indicates that there is potential criminal liability also in this case, disproving R. Johanan's assertion.

156 Nahmanides (*loc. cit.* Note 153) quotes the text as: R. Hanina ben R. Hila said, this is correct. Since if it were for a purpose he would be guilty of a capital crime here even if it was for no purpose he is free from paying restitution.

157 *Lev.* 23:21. Babli *Ketubot* 35a,38a; *Bava qamma* 35a; *Sanhedrin* 74b,84b.

158 The argument based on the Mishnah in *Bava qamma* is disproved; there is no Mishnaic source contradicting R. Johanan.

(5a line 42) וְקַשְׁיָיא עַל דְּבַר קַפָּרָא. הַבְעָרָה לִימְדָה עַל כָּל־הַמְּלָאכוֹת שֶׁבַּתּוֹרָה. כּוּלְהוֹן לְצוֹרֶךְ וְהִיא שֶׁלֹּא לְצוֹרֶךְ. אָמַר רִבִּי יוֹסֵי. אִין יִסְבּוֹר (רִבִּי לְעָזָר) כְּרִבִּי יוֹחָנָן דְּאָמַר. הַבְעָרָה לִימְדָה עַל כָּל־הַמְּלָאכוֹת שֶׁבַּתּוֹרָה. רִבִּי לְעָזָר אָמַר. הַבְעָרָה לִימְדָה עַל עַצְמָהּ. וְלֵית לְרִבִּי לְעָזָר לְאַחַת לְחַיְיבוֹ עַל כָּל־אַחַת וְאַחַת. אַשְׁכַּח תַּנֵּי בְשֵׁם רִבִּי לְעָזָר. הֵנָּה. לְחַיֵּיב עַל כּוּלְהוֹן אַחַת. נִיחָא הַבְעָרָה. חַבּוּרָה. אַב שֶׁלָּהּ לְצוֹרֶךְ וְהִיא שֶׁלֹּא לְצוֹרֶךְ. רִבִּי יוֹסֵי בֵּירִבִּי בּוּן אָמַר. אִיתְפַּלְגוּן רִבִּי לְעָזָר וְרִבִּי יוֹחָנָן. חַד אָמַר. שְׁחִיטָה עִיקָּר וַחֲבוּרָה תוֹלְדָה. וְחוֹרָנָה מַחְלִף.

It is difficult for Bar Qappara. Setting fire taught about all work [mentioned] in the Torah; they are all for a need, itself not for a need[159]? Rebbi Yose said, if (Rebbi Eleazar)[160] would think with Rebbi Johanan who said, setting fire taught about all work [mentioned] in the Torah. Rebbi Eleazar said, setting fire taught about itself[161]. Does Rebbi Eleazar not have *about one*[162] to make him liable for each single one? It was found stated in the name of Rebbi Eleazar, *of these*, to make him liable once for all of them. We understand setting fire. A wound? Its main point[163] for a need, itself not for a need? Rebbi Yose ben Rebbi Abun said, Rebbi Eleazar and Rebbi Johanan disagree. One said, slaughter is the main point and a wound derivative; the other one switches[164].

159 As explained later, the question is asked why setting a fire is singled out in *Ex.* 35:3 as forbidden on the Sabbath since all work is forbidden. One opinion is that it was mentioned to indicate that doing each category of work is a separate offense on the Sabbath. The other opinion is that setting a fire on the Sabbath is no capital crime since no punishment is indicated in Chapter 35. It is clear that Bar Qappara cannot hold the first opinion since he holds that setting a fire is criminal even for no purpose while he must agree that for all (or most) other categories a purpose is needed.

160 The scribe wrote "R. Lazar", the corrector crossed it out because he was of

the opinion that this name is an intrusion here, referring to the Amora R. Eleazar the student and frequent opponent of R. Johanan. But in this paragraph "R. Lazar" means the Tanna R. Eleazar the Qappar, i. e., Bar Qappara. The proof is that later a *baraita* is quoted in his name and also in a disagreement with R. Johanan he is mentioned first, having precedence in time.

161 In the wording of the Babli 70a in the name of the Tanna R. Yose, "setting fire is a separate prohibition". *Yebamot* 6b,33b; *Sanhedrin* 35b,62a; *Keritut* 20b.

162 *Lev. 4:2: A person who sins inadvertently about any of the commandments of the Eternal that should not be done, but he did one of these.* If one stresses the "one" one infers that each single offense requires its own purification sacrifice. If one stresses "these" it follows that one sacrifice atones for multiple infractions. The harmonization of both approaches is a topic for Chapter 7; *Sifra Hovah (Wayyiqra II) Pereq* 1(7).

Nahmanides reads אחרת instead of אחת, "does he not have another (reason)"? The reading of the ms. is preferable.

163 The actions forbidden on the Sabbath are codified in 39 categories. The heading of the category is called its main point, אָב מְלָאכָה "father of action", anything else subsumed under the same category is תּוֹלָדָה "born from it", derivative.

To build the Tabernacle one needed the skins of red goats and of *tahaš*. Therefore slaughter of these animals was part of the building activity and defines a category of work forbidden on the Sabbath.

164 Cf. Chapter 7, Note 422.

(5a line 49) הִבְעִיר וְכִיבָּה בִּנְפִיחָה אַחַת חַיָּב שְׁתַּיִם. אָמַר רִבִּי אֲבָדְיְמִי אָחוֹי דְּרִבִּי יוֹסֵי. הָדָא אָמְרָה. נָפַח בַּכֵּלִים וְשִׁיבְּרָן מְשַׁלֵּם נֶזֶק שָׁלֵם. הַחוֹתָה גְחָלִים מִתַּחַת הַקְּדֵירָה בַּשַׁבָּת חַיָּב. רִבִּי שִׁמְעוֹן בֶּן אֶלְעָזָר בְּשֵׁם רִבִּי לְעָזָר בִּירִבִּי צָדוֹק. חַיָּב שְׁתַּיִם. אַחַת שֶׁכְּבִיבָה אֶת הָעֶלְיוֹנוֹת וְאַחַת שֶׁהִבְעִיר אֶת הַתַּחְתּוֹנוֹת. וְחוֹתֶה גְחָלִים וּמִתְחַמֵּם כְּנֶגְדָּן בַּשַׁבָּת פָּטוּר. רִבִּי יַעֲקֹב בַּר אָחָא אָמַר. בַּמַחֲלוֹקֶת. כְּמַאן דָּמַר אֵינוֹ חַיָּב אֶלָּא אַחַת. בְּרַם כְּמַאן דָּמַר חַיָּב שְׁתַּיִם. חַיָּב. דָּמַר רִבִּי אַבָּהוּ בְּשֵׁם רִבִּי יוֹחָנָן. לֵית כָּאן חַיָּב שְׁתַּיִם אֶלָּא מַעֲלִין עָלָיו כְּאִילוּ חַיָּב שְׁתַּיִם. אָמַר רִבִּי יוּדָן. תַּמָּן אֵינוֹ רוֹצֶה שֶׁיְּבַעֲרוּ וְאֵינוֹ רוֹצֶה שֶׁיְּכַבּוּ. בְּרַם הָכָא רוֹצֶה הוּא שֶׁיְּבַעֲרוּ וְרוֹצֶה שֶׁיְּכַבּוּ.

הִבְעִיר וּבִישֵּׁל. אִית תַּנָּיֵי תַנֵּי. חַיָּב שְׁתַּיִם. אִית תַּנָּיֵי תַנֵּי. חַיָּב אַחַת. מָאן דָּמַר. חַיָּב שְׁתַּיִם. אַחַת מִשּׁוּם מַבְעִיר וְאַחַת מִשּׁוּם מְבַשֵּׁל. וּמָאן דָּמַר. אַחַת. הַיי דָא הִיא. רִבִּי יוּדָה אוֹמֵר. מִשּׁוּם מַבְעִיר. רִבִּי יוֹסֵי אוֹמֵר. מִשּׁוּם מְבַשֵּׁל. וְקַשְׁיָא עַל דְּרִבִּי יוֹסֵי. הַבְעָרָה לִימְדָה עַל כָּל־הַמְּלָאכוֹת שֶׁבַּתּוֹרָה. אֵינוֹ חַיָּב מִשּׁוּם מַבְעִיר אֶלָּא מִשּׁוּם מְבַשֵּׁל.

If one set a fire and extinguished with the same blowing he is liable twice[165]. Rebbi Eudaimon the brother of Rebbi Yose said, this implies that if he blew at vessels and broke them, he pays full damages[166]. He who stirs coals under a pot on the Sabbath is liable. Rebbi Simeon ben Eleazar in the name of Rebbi Simeon ben Rebbi Ṣadoq, he is liable twice, once that he extinguished the upper layer and once that he set fire to the lower layer[167]. But he who stirs coals to warm himself in front of them on the Sabbath is not liable[168]. Rebbi Jacob bar Aḥa said, it is a disagreement; according to him who said that he is liable only once. But according to him who said that he is twice liable he is liable[167]. For Rebbi Abbahu said in the name of Rebbi Joḥanan, he is not twice liable but he is considered as if twice liable[169]. Rebbi Yudan said, there he does not want that they be set on fire and he does not want that they be extinguished[170]. But here he wants that they be set on fire and he wants that they be extinguished.

If one made a fire and cooked, there are Tannaim who state, he is twice liable, and there are Tannaim who state, he is once liable. He who said that he is twice liable, once because of setting a fire and once because of cooking[171]. But he who said once, which one is it? Rebbi Jehudah says, because of setting a fire. Rebbi Yose says, because of cooking. It is difficult for Rebbi Yose; setting fire taught about all work [mentioned] in the Torah; he is not liable because of setting a fire but because of cooking[172]?

165 These are two distinct activities. *Keritut* 20a.

166 Blowing is like acting with one's hands; a human always has to pay full restitution for damages he causes; Mishnah *Bava qamma* 2:10.

167 He cannot hold that one is not liable if the intended result is only a side effect but must extend liability to all cases where the action is intentional. A person who stirs coals wants to increase the efficiency of the heating process; if as a side effect some coals burn less hot it certainly is the unintended side effect of an intentional act. If he nevertheless is held liable for extinguishing, the ruling disputes R. Simeon's position. *Keritut* 20a.

168 Because what he wants is a side effect only and for side effects one does not become liable under the laws of the Sabbath. *Keritut* 20b.

169 Since R. Johanan follows R. Simeon in freeing unintended consequences from legal sanctions he cannot sanction the unintended cooling of coals in the stirring. But this does not mean that it is not morally reprehensible.

170 The one who stirs in order to keep warm is not interested in the combustion process but he who stirs to cook wants to control the process. The two cases are not comparable.

171 This depends on categorizing actions on the Sabbath, whether cooking is subsumed under making a fire or not.

172 There is no problem for the Babli since R. Yose is the author of the opposite opinion, cf. Note 161.

(5c line 59) זָר שֶׁשִּׁימֵשׁ בַּמִּקְדָּשׁ בַּשַּׁבָּת וּבַעַל מוּם שֶׁשִּׁימֵשׁ בְּטוּמְאָה. רִבִּי חִיָּיה רוֹבָה אָמַר. שְׁתַּיִם. בַּר קַפָּרָא אָמַר. אַחַת. מָתִיב בַּר קַפָּרָא לְרִבִּי חִיָּיא רוֹבָא. עֲבוֹדָה שֶׁהַכֹּהֵן מוּתָּר בָּהּ זָר מְחוּיָיב עָלֶיהָ. וּמוֹתִיב לָהּ וְהוּא מְתִיב עָלֶיהָ. וַהֲרֵי קְמִיצָה עַד שֶׁלֹּא נִקְמְצָה אֲסוּרָה לָזֶה וְלָזֶה. מִשֶּׁנִּיקְמְצָה אֲסוּרָה לַזָּרִים וּמוּתֶּרֶת לַכֹּהֲנִים. אָמַר לֵיהּ. שַׁנְיָיא הִיא. דִּכְתִיב וְכָל־זָר לֹא־יֹאכַל קוֹדֶשׁ. וַהֲרֵי מְלִיקָה עַד שֶׁלֹּא נִמְלְקָה אָסוּר לָזֶה וְלָזֶה. מִשֶּׁנִּמְלְקָה אֲסוּרָה לַזָּרִים וּמוּתֶּרֶת לַכֹּהֲנִים. אָמַר לֵיהּ. שַׁנְיָיא הִיא. דִּכְתִיב וְכָל־זָר לֹא־יֹאכַל קוֹדֶשׁ. הֲרֵי טֶבֶל. עַד שֶׁלֹּא נִיתְקַן אָסוּר לָזֶה וְלָזֶה. מִשֶּׁנִּיתְקָן אָסוּר לַזָּרִים וּמוּתָּר לַכֹּהֲנִים. אָמַר לֵיהּ. שַׁנְיָיא הִיא. דִּכְתִיב וְכָל־זָר לֹא־יֹאכַל קוֹדֶשׁ. אָמְרִין. נֵצֵא לַחוּץ וְנִלְמַד. נַפְקוּן וְשָׁמְעוּן. רִבִּי יוֹסֵי אוֹמֵר. שְׁתַּיִם. רִבִּי שִׁמְעוֹן אוֹמֵר. אַחַת. מָאן דָּמַר. אַחַת. מִשּׁוּם זָרוּת. וּמָאן דָּמַר. שְׁתַּיִם. אַחַת מִשּׁוּם זָרוּת. חוֹרָנִייָתָה לָמָּה. מִשּׁוּם שְׁחִיטָה. וַהֲרֵי שְׁחִיטָה בְזָר כְּשֵׁירָה. אֶלָּא מִשּׁוּם הִילּוּךְ זְרִיקָה וְקַבָּלָה. אֵינָהּ אֶלָּא שְׁבוּת. הֲוֵי לֵית טַעֲמָא אֶלָּא מִשּׁוּם אִיכּוּל אֵיבָרִים וּפְדָרִים שֶׁהָיוּ מִתְאַכְּלִין עַל גַּבֵּי הַמִּזְבֵּחַ כָּל־הַלַּיְלָה. עַל דַּעְתֵּיהּ דְּרִבִּי יוּדָה דּוּ אָמַר מִשּׁוּם מַבְעִיר. נִיחָא. עַל דַּעְתֵּיהּ דְּרִבִּי יוֹסֵי דּוּ אָמַר מִשּׁוּם מְבַשֵּׁל. מַה בִּישּׁוּל יֵשׁ כָּאן. מִכֵּיוָן שֶׁהוּא רוֹצֶה בְּאִיכּוּלָן כִּמְבַשֵּׁל הוּא.

[173]An outsider who officiated in the Temple on the Sabbath[174], or a deformed person who officiated in impurity[175], the Elder Rebbi Ḥiyya said, two; bar Qappara said, one. Bar Qappara objected to the Elder Rebbi Ḥiyya: is the outsider liable for any service which is permitted to a Cohen[176]? He[176a] objected and he answered it. Is there not the handful[177]; before the handful was taken it was forbidden for both; after the handful was taken it is forbidden for outsiders and permitted to Cohanim? He said to him, there is a difference, for it is written: *no outsider may eat sanctified food*[178]. Is there not the breaking of the neck[179]; before the neck was broken it was forbidden for both; after the neck was broken it is forbidden for outsiders and permitted to Cohanim? He said to him, there is a difference, for it is written: *no outsider may eat sanctified food*. Is there not the *tevel*[180]; before it was put in order it was forbidden for both; after it was put in order it is forbidden for outsiders and permitted to Cohanim? He said to him, there is a difference, for it is written: *no outsider may eat sanctified food*. They said, let us go outside and learn. They went outside and heard, Rebbi Yose said, two; Rebbi Simeon said, one. He who said one, because of outsider status. He who said two, one because of outsider status; why the other? Because of slaughter[181]. But slaughter by an outsider is valid[182]! But because bringing, sprinkling, and receiving[183]. These are only because of Sabbath rest[184]. Therefore the reason

may be only because of the consumption of limbs and fat which were consumed on the altar during the entire night. In the opinion of Rebbi Jehudah[185] who said because of setting fire it is understandable. In the opinion of Rebbi Yose[185] who said because of cooking, what cooking is here? Since he wants their being consumed it is like cooking.

173 Here starts another Genizah fragment edited by Ginzberg (pp. 74-75) of which very little is readable for this paragraph.

174 He commits a deadly sin by officiating (*Num.* 18:7). In addition, the Temple service on the Sabbath requires many acts, slaughter and burning of sacrifices, which outside the Temple are capital crimes. If the act was unintentional, how many purification sacrifices are due?

175 The deformed Cohen is barred from officiating (*Lev.* 21:16-24). Any impure Cohen is similarly barred (*Lev.* 22:3). Are the disabilities cumulative or is disqualification one and the same? The question is raised but neither discussed nor answered; it is treated in the parallel in the Babli, *Yebamot* 32a.

176 Everybody agrees that as an officiating outsider he is liable for a sacrifice. The question is about the Sabbath. Outside the Temple, the Sabbath prohibitions apply to Cohanim and to everybody else. They are lifted in the Temple precinct by biblical decree. Since there is no verse re-instituting the prohibition for laymen in the Temple precinct one should conclude that violating Sabbath prohibitions in the course of Temple service is not sanctionable irrespective of the person who officiates. This is Bar Qappara's position.

176a S. Lieberman has shown that וּמוֹתָיב should be read as הוּא מוֹתֵיב.

177 We find that prohibitions are to be lifted for Cohanim but not for laymen inside and outside the Temple. A cereal offering is forbidden for all consumption from the moment it was received in a sanctified vessel. The priest has to take a handful from the offering and burn it on the altar; this permits the remainder to be eaten by Cohanim (*Lev.* 6:7-11) but it remains forbidden for all outsiders.

178 *Lev.* 22:10. This is a separate decree independent of Temple or Sabbath.

179 Of sacrifices of birds, *Lev.* 1:15,5:9. In case of a purification offering, the bird has to be eaten by Cohanim and is prohibited to laymen; the live bird is prohibited to everybody.

180 Produce after the harvest of which heave and tithes were not taken. After these were taken the produce becomes profane but heave is reserved to pure Cohanim. This has no connection with Temple service.

181 Of the sacrifices.

182 The office of the Cohen starts only with receiving the victim's blood in a sacred vessel; slaughter of sacrifices, even on the Sabbath, is legitimate for outsiders, mostly Levites. This bolsters Bar Qappara's case. Babli *Yebamot* 33b.

183 The offices of the Cohen after the receiving of the blood. The blood is sprinkled on the wall of the altar.

184 If there are Sabbath violations they are

only of rabbinic prohibitions which as a matter of principle do not apply to the Temple precinct.

185 As explained at the end of the preceding paragraph. This is the reason for the inclusion of this paragraph at this point.

(5b line 7) עַל שָׁלֹשׁ עֲבֵרוֹת הַנָּשִׁים מֵיתוֹת כול׳. אִית תַּנָּיֵי תַנֵּי. יְלָדוֹת. אִית תַּנָּיֵי תַנֵּי יוֹלְדוֹת. מָאן דָּמַר. יְלָדוֹת. תַּנֵּי בְשֵׁם רִבִּי יוּדָה. בַּעֲוֹן הַנְּדָרִים הַבָּנִים מֵתִים. וּמָה טַעֲמָא. לַשָּׁוְא הִכֵּיתִי אֶת־בְּנֵיכֶם. וּמָאן דָּמַר. יוֹלְדוֹת. מִיכָּן שָׁאֵין הַשָּׂטָן מְקַטְרֵג אֶלָּא בִשְׁעַת סַכָּנָה.

2 יודה G | יהודה   3 ומאן G | מן   השטן G | הסטן

"Because of three sins women die in childbirth,[186]" etc. There are Tannaim who state, as children. There are Tannaim who state, in childbirth[187]. He who said as children, it was stated in the name of Rebbi Jehudah: Children die because of the sin of vows[188]. What is the reason? *For the vain I did hit your sons*[189]. But he who said in childbirth, from here that Satan[190] accuses[191] only in times of danger.

186 Quote from Mishnah 6.
187 Babli 32a.
188 Babli 32b, *Ketubot* 72a.
189 *Jer.* 2:30, cf. *Nedarim* 3:2, Note 73.

190 The prosecutor in the Heavenly Court.
191 A Hebrew verb formed from Greek κατηγορέω "accuse". The vocalization בְשַׁעַת is from G.

(5b line 10) רִבִּי פִינְחָס רִבִּי יִרְמְיָה בְשֵׁם רִבִּי חִייָה בַּר בָּא. כְּתִיב וְלִפְנֵי אֶלְעָזָר הַכֹּהֵן יַעֲמֹד וְשָׁאַל לוֹ בְמִשְׁפַּט הָאוּרִים. בְּסֵדֶר הָאוּרִים אֵין כָּתוּב כָּאן אֶלָּא בְּמִשְׁפַּט הָאוּרִים. אֶלָּא מְלַמֵּד. בְּשָׁעָה שֶׁיִשְׂרָאֵל יוֹצְאִין לַמִּלְחָמָה בֵּית דִּין שֶׁלְּמַעְלָה יוֹשְׁבִין עֲלֵיהֶן אִם לְנַצּוֹחַ אִם לְהִינָּצֵחַ. אָמַר רִבִּי חִייָא בַּר בָּא. כְּתִיב כִּי־תֵצֵא מַחֲנֶה עַל־אוֹיְבֶיךָ וְנִשְׁמַרְתָּ מִכֹּל דָּבָר רָע. הָא אִם אֵינוֹ יוֹצֵא אֵינוֹ צָרִיךְ לֵיהּ שְׁמִירָה. אֶלָּא מִיכָּן שָׁאֵין הַשָּׂטָן מְקַטְרֵג אֶלָּא בִשְׁעַת הַסַּכָּנָה.

2 במשפט האורים G | -   4 אויביך G | איביך   5 ליה G | -   השטן G | הסטן   מקטרג G | מקטריג

Rebbi Phineas, Rebbi Jeremiah in the name of Rebbi Hiyya bar Abba: It is written[192], *before Eleazar the priest he shall stand and ask him about the judgment of the illuminati*. It is not written "in the order of the *illuminati*" but "about the judgment of the *illuminati*". This teaches that at the moment when Israel goes to war the Heavenly Court sits because of them, whether to be victorious or to be vanquished. Rebbi Hiyya bar Abba said, it is written[193], *if you camp out against your enemies, guard yourself from every bad thing*. Therefore if he does not go out he does not have to guard himself[194]. But from here that Satan accuses only in times of danger.

אָמַר רִבִּי אֲחָאי בַּר יַעֲקֹב. כְּתִיב וּקְרָאָהוּ אָסוֹן בַּדֶּרֶךְ. הָא בַּבַּיִת לֹא. אֶלָּא מִיכָּן שֶׁאֵין הַשָּׂטָן מְקַטְרֵג אֶלָּא בְּשָׁעַת הַסַּכָּנָה.

1 אחאי G | אחי   2 השטן G | הסטן   הסכנה G | סכנה

Rebbi Aḥai bar Jacob said, it is written[195] *an accident might happen to him on the road*. Therefore not at home. But from here that Satan accuses only in times of danger.

רִבִּי בִּיסְנָא בְּשֵׁם רִבִּי לִיָּיא. כְּתִיב יוֹם־צָרָה וְתוֹכֵחָה וּנְאָצָה הַיּוֹם הַזֶּה. הָא יוֹם אַחֵר לֹא. אֶלָּא מִיכָּן שֶׁאֵין הַשָּׂטָן מְקַטְרֵג אֶלָּא בְּשָׁעַת הַסַּכָּנָה.

1 הזה G | ההוא   הסכנה G | סכנה

[196]Rebbi Bisna in the name of Rebbi Lia: It is written[197], *a day of affliction, and admonition, and insult is this day*. Therefore not another day. But from here that Satan accuses only in times of danger.

רִבִּי אַייבוֹ בַּר נַגּוֹרִי. כָּתוּב בְּהִשָּׁפְטוֹ יֵצֵא רָשָׁע. יֵצֵא צַדִּיק אֵין כָּתוּב כָּאן אֶלָּא בְּהִשָּׁפְטוֹ יֵצֵא רָשָׁע. אֶלָּא מִיכָּן שֶׁאֵין הַשָּׂטָן מְקַטְרֵג אֶלָּא בְּשָׁעַת הַסַּכָּנָה.

1 נגורי G | נגורי   יצא רשע. - G | כאן G | כן   בהשפטו G | בהישפטו   2 השטן G | הסטן   הסכנה G | סכנה

Rebbi Ayvo bar Nagori. It is written[198], *when he will be judged he will be found guilty*. It is not written "he will be justified" but *when he will be judged he will be found guilty*. But from here that Satan accuses only in times of danger.

אָמַר רִבִּי בָּא בַּר בִּינָה. נֶסֶר שֶׁהוּא מָתוּחַ מִגַּג לְגַג אֲפִילוּ רָחָב כַּמָּה אָסוּר לְהַלֵּךְ עָלָיו. לָמָּה. אֶלָּא מִיכָּן שֶׁאֵין הַשָּׂטָן מְקַטְרֵג אֶלָּא בְּשָׁעַת הַסַּכָּנָה.

1 מגג G | מיגג   2 מיכן G | -   השטן G | הסטן

Rebbi Abba bar Bina said, if a plank is extended from one roof to another[199] even if it is rather wide it is forbidden to walk on it. Why? (From here)[200] because Satan accuses only in times of danger.

רַב אָמַר. הַיּוֹשֵׁב בַּבַּיִת מְרוֹעָע עוֹשֶׂה מַלְאַךְ הַמָּוֶת דַּנִיסְטֵיס שֶׁלּוֹ. דִּכְתִיב יַשִּׁיא מָוֶת עָלֵימוֹ. כְּמָה דְּתֵימַר כִּי־תַשֶּׁה בְרֵעֲךָ מַשַּׁאת מְאוּמָה.

1 שלו G | לו   2 דתימ' G | דתמר

Rav said, one who sits in a dilapidated house makes the Angel of Death to his creditor[201], as it is said[202], *he claims death over them*, as you say[203], *if you have any claim against your neighbor*.

אָמַר רִבִּי לֵוִי. בִּשְׁלֹשָׁה מְקוֹמוֹת הַשָּׂטָן מָצוּי לְקַטְרֵג. הַמְהַלֵּךְ בַּדֶּרֶךְ בְּעַצְמוֹ. וְהַיָּשָׁן בְּבַיִת אָפֵל לְעַצְמוֹ. וְהַמְפָרֵשׁ בַּיָּם הַגָּדוֹל. אָמַר רִבִּי יִצְחָק בַּר מַרְיוֹן. אִילּוּלֵי דִכְתִיב כֹּה אָמַר יְיָ הַנּוֹתֵן בַּיָּם דָּרֶךְ. כֵּיוָן שֶׁהָיָה אָדָם יוֹרֵד לְתוֹכוֹ הָיָה מֵת. וְרַבָּנָן אֲמָרֵי. הַנּוֹתֵן בַּיָּם דָּרֶךְ. מִן הָעֲצֶרֶת וְעַד

חָג. וּבְמַיִם עַזִּים נְתִיבָה. מִן הֶחָג וְעַד חֲנוּכָּה. רִבִּי יוֹסֵה בְּרֵיהּ דְּרִבִּי תַּנְחוּם דִּכְפַר אָגִין עוּבְדָּא הָיָה בְּאֵסְיָא. אָתָא בָעֵי מִיפְרוֹשׁ מִן חַגָּא וְעַד חֲנוּכְתָּא. חַמְתֵיהּ חָדָא מַטְרוֹנָה. אָמְרָה לֵיהּ. כְּדוֹן מַפְרְשִׁין. אִיתְחֲמֵי לֵיהּ אֲבוֹי. וְנַס־קְבוּרָה לֹא־הָיְתָה לּוֹ. וְלֹא שָׁמַע לָא לְדִין וְלֹא לְדִין וַאֲזַל בְּיַמָּא. רִבִּי כֹּהֵן אֲחוֹי דְּרִבִּי חִייָה בַּר בָּא הֲוָה פָּרִישׁ. אָתָא בָעֵי מִיפְרוֹשׁ מִן חַגָּא לַחֲנוּכְתָּא. אָמַר לַאֲחוֹי. צְלוֹ עֲלַי. אֲמַר לֵיהּ. אִין. דְּצָלִיתִי עֲלָךְ. אֶלָּא אִין חֲמִיתִינוֹן לְצִיבּוּר מְצַלְיִן לְמִיטְרָא לָא תִתְרָחֵץ עַל צְלוֹתִי. הָא דְּאַתְּ קָטִיר לוּלָבָךְ קְטוֹר רַגְלָךְ.

1 בשלשה G | בשלושה   השטן G | הסטן   בעצמו G | לעצמו   3 אמרי G | אמרין   4 חנוכה G | החנוכה   יוסה G | יושי   5 חגא G | חגה   חנוכתא G | החנוכה   מטרונה G | מטרונא   אמרה G | אמריה   6 לדין G | לדן (2)   7 חייה G | חייא   מיפרוש G | מפרוש חגא G | חגה   חנוכתא G | חנוכתה   6 דצלית G | דצלותי   חמיתינון G | חמיתניין   מצליין G | מצלוי

Rebbi Levi said, at three places the Satan usually accuses: one who is on the road alone, one who sleeps in a dark house alone, and one who sets sail on the ocean. Rebbi Isaac bar Marion said, if it had not been written[204], *so says the Eternal Who makes a path in the Sea*, if a person would set out on it he would die. But the rabbis say, *Who makes a path in the Sea*, from Pentecost to Tabernacles, *and in great waters a trail*, from Tabernacles to Ḥanukkah[205]. Rebbi Yose ben Rebbi Tanḥum from Kefar Agin (a case)[206] was in Essia. He wanted to set sail between Tabernacles and Ḥanukkah. A matron[207] saw him and said to him, now one sets sail? His father appeared to him[208], *but he had no burial*[209]; he listened to neither and travelled by sea. Rebbi Cohen the brother of Rebbi Ḥiyya bar Abba was a sailor. He came to sail between Tabernacles and Ḥanukkah. He said to his brother, pray for me. He answered him yes, I prayed for you, but if you see the public praying for rain[210] do not trust my prayer. Since you bound your *lulav*[211], bind your feet.

194 G: Needs no guard.
195 *Gen.* 42:38.
196 In G (and the *editio princeps* of *ʿEyn Yaʿaqov*) this homily precedes the one of R. Ahai.
197 *2K.* 19:3, *Is.* 37:3.
198 *Ps.* 109:7.
199 The plank is not fastened at both ends.
200 Delete with G.
201 Greek δανειστής, -οῦ, Latin *danista, -ae, m.*, "creditor".

202 *Ps/* 55:16.
203 *Deut.* 24:10.
204 *Is.* 43:16.
205 But the first quarter of the year is off limits for shipping.
206 Erroneous addition by a corrector.
207 Latin *matrona*, the wife of an important personality.
208 In a dream.
209 *Eccl.* 6:3.
210 Since one publicly prays for rain on

the last day of Tabernacles one cannot honestly pray in private for good weather during the winter period.

211 The "four species" taken on Tabernacles (*Num.* 23:40) interpreted as a kind of rain-making equipment.

(5b line 39) מתני׳. עַל שֶׁאֵינָן זְהִירוֹת בַּנִּדָּה וּבַחַלָּה וּבְהַדְלָקַת הַנֵּר: אָדָם הָרִאשׁוֹן דָּמוֹ שֶׁל עוֹלָם. דִּכְתִיב וְאֵד יַעֲלֶה מִן־הָאָרֶץ. וְגָרְמָה לוֹ חַוָּה מִיתָה. לְפִיכָךְ מָסְרוּ מִצְוַת נִדָּה לָאִשָּׁה. וּבַחַלָּה. אָדָם הָרִאשׁוֹן חַלָּה טְהוֹרָה לָעוֹלָם הָיָה. דִּכְתִיב וַיִּיצֶר יְיָ אֱלֹהִים אֶת־הָאָדָם עָפָר מִן־הָאֲדָמָה. וַתְיָיא כַּיי דָּמַר רִבִּי יוֹסֵי בַּר קַצַּרְתָּה. כֵּיוָן שֶׁהָאִשָּׁה מְקַשְׁקֶשֶׁת עִיסָתָהּ בַּמַּיִם הִיא מַגְבָּהַת חַלָּתָהּ. וְגָרְמָה לוֹ חַוָּה מִיתָה. לְפִיכָךְ מָסְרוּ מִצְוַת חַלָּה לָאִשָּׁה. וּבְהַדְלָקַת הַנֵּר: אָדָם הָרִאשׁוֹן נֵרוֹ שֶׁלְעוֹלָם הָיָה. שֶׁנֶּאֱמַר נֵר אֱלֹהִים נִשְׁמַת אָדָם. וְגָרְמָה לוֹ חַוָּה מִיתָה. לְפִיכָךְ מָסְרוּ מִצְוַת הַנֵּר לָאִשָּׁה. תַּנֵּי. רִבִּי יוֹסֵי אוֹמֵר. שְׁלֹשָׁה דִיבְקֵי מִיתָה מִיתָה הֵן וּשְׁלָשְׁתָּן נִמְסְרוּ לָאִשָּׁה. וְאֵילּוּ הֵן. מִצְוַת נִדָּה וּמִצְוַת חַלָּה וּמִצְוַת הַדְלָקָה.

Mishnah. "Because they are not careful with *niddah*[20], and *hallah*[21], and candle lighting[22]." [212]The First Man was the blood of the world, as is written[213], *mist would arise from the land.* Eve caused him death, therefore they handed the commandment of *niddah* to the woman.

"And *hallah*[21]." The First Man was the pure *hallah* of the world, as is written[214], *the Eternal, God, created man, dust from the earth.* This comes as Rebbi Yose ben Qasarta said, when the woman agitates her dough in water she lifts her *hallah*. Eve caused him death, therefore they handed the commandment of *hallah* to the woman.

"And candle lighting[22]." The First Man was the light of the world, as is said[215], *God's light is Adam's soul.* Eve caused him death, therefore they handed the commandment of the light to the woman. [216]It was stated: Rebbi Yose says, there are three clingings of death and all three were handed to woman: These are they, the commandment of *niddah*, the commandment of *hallah*, and the commandment[217] of lighting the light.

212 A related homily in the Babli, 31a/32b.
213 *Gen.* 2:6.
214 *Gen.* 2:7.
215 *Prov.* 20:23.
216 Babli 32a, *Berakhot* 31b. Tosephta 2:10.
217 This homily and the following story of R. Eliezer are the only occurrences where lighting on Sabbath Eve is called a commandment; cf. Note 22.

(5b line 50) מתני'. שְׁלשָׁה דְבָרִים צָרִיךְ אָדָם לוֹמַר בְּתוֹךְ בֵּיתוֹ כול'. תַּנֵּי. רַבָּן שִׁמְעוֹן בֶּן גַּמְלִיאֵל אוֹמֵר. הִילְכוֹת הַקּוֹדֶשׁ וְחַטָּאוֹת וְהֶכְשֵׁירוֹת הֵן הֵן גּוּפֵי הֲלָכוֹת. וּשְׁלָשְׁתָּן נִמְסְרוּ לְעַמֵּי הָאָרֶץ. הִילְכוֹת הַקּוֹדֶשׁ. דְּתַנִּינָן. וְאִם אָמַר. הִפְרַשְׁתִּי לְתוֹכָהּ רְבִיעִית קוֹדֶשׁ. נֶאֱמָן. חַטָּאוֹת. דְּתַנִּינָן. הַכֹּל נֶאֱמָנִים עַל חַטָּאת. הֶכְשֵׁירוֹת. דְּתַנִּינָן. וְעַל כּוּלָּן עַם הָאָרֶץ נֶאֱמָנִין לוֹמַר טְהוֹרִין הֵן. לָא צוּרְכָה דְלָאו. הַדְלִיקוּ אֶת הַנֵּר. עִישַׂרְתֶּן וְעֵירַבְתֶּן הַדְלִיקוּ. אָמַר רִבִּי חִייָא בַּר אַבָּא. מִתּוֹךְ שֶׁאַתָּה מַחְמִיר מֵעָלָיו בְּקַלָּה אַף הוּא מַחְמִיר עַל עַצְמוֹ בַּחֲמוּרָה. אָמַר רִבִּי חַגַּיי. רִבִּי שְׁמוּאֵל בַּר רַב יִצְחָק הֲוָה מְפַקֵּד גּוֹ בֵּיתֵיהּ. עֵירַבְתֶּן הַדְלִיקוּ אֶת הַנֵּר. וְלָמָּה לֹא אָמַר. עִישַׂרְתֶּן. אֶלָּא כָל־מַה דַּהֲוָה אָכִיל. מִן שׁוּקָה הֲוָה אָכִיל.

2 ושלשתן G | ושלושתן 5 ועירבתן הדליקו G |]ועירב[תם חייא בר אבא G | חייה בר אדה 7 הדליקו G הדלקתם עישרתן G | עישרתם

Mishnah: "Three things a person has to say in his house," etc. [218]It was stated: Rabban Simeon ben Gamliel says, the practices of *sancta*, and purifying waters, and preparations for impurity, are of the most important practices and all three have been handed over to the vulgar. The practices of *sancta*, as we have stated[219]: "If he said, I separated into it a quartarius of *sanctum*, he must be believed." Purifying waters, as we have stated[220]: "Everybody is trustworthy about purifying water." Preparations for impurity, as we have stated[221]: "About all these the vulgar is trustworthy to say that they are pure."

It should have been necessary[222]: Kindle the light, did you give tithe, did you make an *eruv*, kindle[223]? Rebbi Hiyya bar Abba[224] said, since you are strict with him for the easier rules he will be strict with himself with the weighty one. Rebbi Haggai said, Rebbi Samuel bar Rav Isaac commanded his house, did you make an *eruv*, did you kindle the light? Why did he not say, did you give tithe? Because all he ate, he ate from the market[225].

218 Babli 32a, Tosephta 2:10.
219 Mishnah *Hagigah* 3:4. A vulgar person is a person who is not careful to keep the laws of purity in his daily life and to be punctilious in observing the laws of tithes (cf. Introduction to Tractate *Demay*, pp. 349-350). The Mishnah states that if a vulgar gives heave from his wine making (which everybody is assumed to do) the Cohen who is a Fellow, punctilious in all these rules, may accept the heave as pure only at grape-pressing time. But if the vulgar tells him that part of the juice is dedicated as libation offering in the Temple, the Cohen may accept it all year long since the vulgar will strictly follow all rules of purity connected with the Temple.
220 Mishnah *Parah* 5:1. Water used for the purification rite with the ashes of the Red Cow (*Num.* 19) must be treated

following very strict rules. Nevertheless any vulgar can be trusted in this matter since the purification rite is needed before a visit to the Temple.

221 Food can become impure only if it is "prepared" for impurity by intentional contact with water (cf. *Demay* 2:3 Note 141, *Terumot* 1:1 Notes 7,9, *Niddah* 2:6 Notes 98-100). Since the vulgar person is impure, if he asserts that something of his is pure it means that it is impervious to impurity.

222 Making a fire on the Sabbath is a biblical Sabbath violation; giving tithe and making an *eruv* at twilight are only rabbinical violations. It should have been necessary to first make sure that no biblical violation occurs; cf. the next paragraph.

223 This last word should be deleted with G.

224 In G: R. Hiyya bar Ada. It is impossible to decide which reading is correct.

225 He was of Babylonian origin and never acquired land in Galilee. Since he bought his food only from trustworthy suppliers he never had to tithe anything (*Demay* 2:2 Note 126).

(5b line 61) מתני׳. סָפֵק חֲשֵׁיכָה סָפֵק אֵינוּ חֲשֵׁיכָה כול׳. מַעֲשֶׂה בְּיַרְבִּי לִיעֶזֶר שֶׁהָיָה גוֹסֵס עֶרֶב שַׁבָּת עִם חֲשֵׁיכָה. וְנִכְנַס הוֹרְקָנוֹס בְּנוֹ לַחֲלוֹץ אֶת תְּפִילָיו. אָמַר לוֹ. בְּנִי. הִינַחְתָּ מִצְוַת הַנֵּר שֶׁהִיא שְׁבוּת וְחַיָּיבִין עָלֶיהָ כָּרֵת. וּבָאתָה לַחֲלוֹץ תְּפִילִין שֶׁאֵינָן אֶלָּא רְשׁוּת וְאֵינָן אֶלָּא מִצְוָה. יָצָא לוֹ וְהָיָה צוֹעֵק וְאָמַר. אוֹי לִי שֶׁנִּטְרְפָה דַעְתּוֹ שֶׁלְאַבָּא. אָמַר לוֹ. דַעְתָּךְ הִיא שֶׁנִּטְרְפָה. דַעְתִּי הִיא לֹא נִטְרְפָה. כֵּיוָן שֶׁרָאוּ תַלְמִידָיו שֶׁהֵשִׁיבוֹ דָבָר שֶׁלְחָכְמָה נִכְנְסוּ אֶצְלוֹ וְהָיוּ שׁוֹאֲלִין אוֹתוֹ. וְהָיָה אוֹמֵר לָהֶן עַל הַטָּמֵא טָמֵא וְעַל הַטָּהוֹר טָהוֹר. וּבָאַחֲרוֹנָה אָמַר טָהוֹר. וְנִסְתַּלְקָה נִשְׁמָתוֹ. אָמְרִין. נִיכָּר רַבִּי שֶׁהוּא טָהוֹר. אָמַר רִבִּי מָנָא. וְעַד כְּדוֹן נִיכָּר. נִכְנַס רִבִּי יְהוֹשֻׁעַ וְחָלַץ אֶת תְּפִילָיו מְנַפְּפוֹ וּמְנַשְׁקוֹ וּבוֹכֶה וְאוֹמֵר. רִבִּי רִבִּי. הוּתָּר הַנֶּדֶר. רִבִּי. רֶכֶב יִשְׂרָאֵל וּפָרָשָׁיו.

2 הינחתה G הנחת | 5 שהשיבו G שהישיבו | שלחכמה G שלחוכמה | 8 ואו׳ G ואמר | הנדר G אס הנדר רבי G רבי רבי

Mishnah: "If there is a doubt whether it is dark or not dark," etc. [226]It happened that Rebbi Eliezer was dying on a Friday when it got dark. His son Hyrcanus entered to remove his phylacteries[227]. He told him, my son, you neglected the commandment of the light which is for the Sabbath and for which one incurs extirpation and you came to remove phylacteries which is only rabbinical and is only a [positive] commandment[228]. He left crying and said, woe to me that my father has lost his mind. He told him, your mind is lost, my mind is not lost. When his students saw that he answered him wisely they entered to him and started asking him. He answered on the impure impure and the pure pure; at the end he said "pure" and his soul vanished. They said, it is clear that our teacher is pure. Rebbi Mana said, it still is clear.

Rebbi Joshua entered, removed his phylacteries, was embracing him, and kissing him, and crying, and said, my teacher, my teacher, the vow has been dissolved[229]; my teacher, *chariot of Israel and its riders*[230].

226 A different version is in the Babli, *Sanhedrin* 68a, and *Avot dR. Natan A*, Chapter 25.

227 Which are worn neither during nighttime nor on the Sabbath.

228 The translation of the technical terms which in the Babli are read as רשות "voluntary act", שבות "rabbinic Sabbath prohibition", and מצוה "commandment" follows S. Lieberman in *Tarbiz* 5 (1934) pp. 97-99.

229 The ban imposed on R. Eliezer for his refusal to accept a majority decision was at variance with his traditions.

230 *2K.* 2:12.

(5b line 73) מתני'. וְאֵין מַטְבִּילִין אֶת הַכֵּלִים. מַתְנִיתָא בְּכֵלִים גְּדוֹלִים. אֲבָל בְּכֵלִים קְטַנִּים מְעָרִים עֲלֵיהֶן וּמַטְבִּילָן. תַּנֵּי רִבִּי הוֹשַׁעְיָה. מְמַלֵּא אָדָם בִּכְלִי טָמֵא מִן הַבּוֹר וּמְעָרִים עָלָיו וּמַטְבִּילוֹ. תַּנֵּי. נָפַל דְּלָיו לְתוֹךְ הַבּוֹר. נָפְלוּ כֵלָיו לְתוֹךְ הַבּוֹר. מְעָרִים עֲלֵיהֶן וּמַטְבִּילָן. תְּרֵין אֲמוֹרִין. חַד אָמַר. בְּכֵלִים שֶׁנִּיטְמְאוּ בְאַב הַטּוּמְאָה. וְחוֹרָנָה אָמַר. בְּכֵלִים שֶׁנִּיטְמְאוּ בְוָלָד הַטּוּמְאָה. וְחוֹרָנָה אָמַר. מָתִיב מָאן דָּמַר בְּאָב הַטּוּמְאָה לְמָאן דָּמַר בּוֹלַד הַטּוּמְאָה. אֲפִילוּ בְחוֹל יְהֵא טָעוּן הָעֲרֵב שֶׁמֶשׁ. אָמַר לֵיהּ. בְּרוֹצֶה לְהִשְׁתַּמֵּשׁ בָּהֶן חוּלִּין בְּטָהֳרָה.

רִבִּי יִרְמְיָה וְרִבִּי זְעִירָה בְּשֵׁם רִבִּי חִיָּיא בַּר אַשִּׁי. אִשָּׁה פִיקַחַת מַדִּיחָה כּוֹס כָּאן קְעָרָה כָּאן תַּמְחוּי כָּאן וְנִמְצֵאת מַרְבֶּצֶת אֶת בֵּיתָהּ בַּשַּׁבָּת.

2 ומטבילן | G ומטבילין אדם | י הוא אדם בכלי | י כלי 3 דליו | י דלייו נפדו כליו | י נפל כליו | ומטבילן | G ומטבילן 4 שניטמאו | G שניטמו (2) בולד | י בולד 5 באב | י בולד בולד | G בולד י באב 6 להשתמש | G י לישתמש 7 זעירה | G זעורה חייא | G חייה פיקחת | G פקחת כאן | G כן (3)

Mishnah: "nor immerse vessels[27]." [231]Our Mishnah is about large vessels but for small vessels one may be cunning about them and immerse them. Rebbi Hoshaia stated, a person may fill an impure vessels from a cistern, be cunning about it[232] and immerse it. It was stated: If his pail fell into a cistern, or his vessels fell into a cistern, he may be cunning about them and immerse them. Two Amoraim, one said, about vessels impure in original impurity[233]; the other said, about vessels impure in derivative impurity. He who said in (original)[234] impurity objected to the one who said in (derivative)[234] impurity, even on a weekday it would require sundown[235]? He answered him, if he wants to use them to eat profane food in purity[236].

Rebbi Jeremiah, Rebbi Ze'ira in the name of Rebbi Ḥiyya bar Ashi. A quick woman will rinse a cup here[237], a pot there, a plate there and end up watering down her house on the Sabbath.

231 A parallel to this paragraph is *Besah* 2:2 (י). Babli *Besah* 18a.
232 The cistern serves as a *miqweh*; the vessel by falling in certainly was completely immersed. But a *miqweh* purifies only with corresponding intent (cf. Note 68); therefore the owner has to be cunning, i. e., remove the vessel from the cistern with the intent that it should be pure.
233 Which is biblical.
234 Clearly one has to switch "original" and "derivative" with the *Besah* text.
235 An impure vessel which becomes pure by immersion in a *miqweh* can be used for sanctified food only after the next sundown (*Lev.* 11:32). For a vessel immersed at twilight this is only after almost 24 hours.
236 The vessel is pure and the food is not sanctified.
237 Washing the dishes after Sabbath meals. The house has a dirt floor and only one story. Babli 95a.

(5c line 8) מתני'. אֲבָל מְעַשְׂרִין אֶת הַדְּמַאי. רִבִּי יוֹסֵה בְּשֵׁם רִבִּי אַבָּהוּ רִבִּי חִזְקִיָּה בְּשֵׁם רִבִּי יוּדָה בַּר פָּזִי. דְּמַיי דְּמִיתְקָן דְּמַאי לֹא תַקָּן.

וּמְעָרְבִין וְטוֹמְנִין אֶת הַחַמִּין: אָמַר רִבִּי חִיָּיא בַּר אֹשִׁי. הָדָא דְתֵימַר בְּעֵירוּבֵי חֲצֵירוֹת. אֲבָל בְּעֵירוּבֵי תְחוּמִין דְּבַר תּוֹרָה הֵן.

1 מתני'. אבל מעשרין את הדמאי. G | דמר אבהו G | אביהא G | דמיתקן G | דמתקן   2   3 וטומנין את החמין G | חייא G | חייה G | הדא דתימר G | הדתמר - G |

Mishnah: "But one may tithe what is questionable[28]." Rebbi Yose in the name of Rebbi Abbahu, Rebbi Hizqiah in the name of Rebbi Jehudah bar Pazi: "maybe it was put in order, maybe it was not put in order.[238]"

"And make an *eruv*, and store away hot food[29]." Rebbi Ḥiyya bar Ashi said, this is about *eruv* of courtyards[24]. But *eruvim* of domains are a matter of biblical law[239].

238 This explains the meaning of the word "demay". The correct text is in *Ma`aser Šeni* 5:9, Note 193.
239 Since adjacent courtyards and dead-end streets are not thoroughfares, there is no biblical prohibition involved in declaring common ground as common private domain. The Sabbath domain belonging to a town is a rectangle oriented North-South and East-West containing the entire town and another 2000 cubits outside town in each of the cardinal directions, inspired by the description of Levitic cities in *Num.* 35:1-8. An *Eruv Tehumin* is a personal action in which a person renounces his right to go outside town in one direction and in compensation may go 4000 cubits in the other direction. If another town would

be reached in this space, that town also becomes part of his Sabbath domain. This action clearly involves public domain by biblical standards (even though the restriction to 2000 cubits may be purely rabbinical) and therefore must be completed before sundown.

כירה שהסיקוה פרק שלישי

(fol. 5c) **משנה א**: כִּירָה שֶׁהֲסִיקוּהָ בְּקַשׁ אוֹ בַגְּבָבָא נוֹתְנִים עָלֶיהָ תַבְשִׁיל. בַּגֶּפֶת וּבְעֵצִים לֹא יִתֵּן עַד שֶׁיִּגְרוֹף אוֹ עַד שֶׁיִּתֵּן אֶת הָאֵפֶר. בֵּית שַׁמַּאי אוֹמְרִין חַמִּין אֲבָל לֹא תַבְשִׁיל. וּבֵית הִלֵּל אוֹמְרִין חַמִּין וְתַבְשִׁיל. בֵּית שַׁמַּאי אוֹמְרִין נוֹטְלִין אֲבָל לֹא מַחֲזִירִין. וּבֵית הִלֵּל אוֹמְרִין אַף מַחֲזִירִין:

Mishnah 1: If a cooking stove[1] was heated with straw or stubbles one may put a dish on it[2], with olive cake[3] or wood he should not put it on unless he emptied or covered it with ashes. The House of Shammai say, hot water but no dish, but the House of Hillel say, hot water and dish. The House of Shammai say one takes away but may not return it but the House of Hillel say one even may return[4].

משנה ב: תַּנּוּר שֶׁהֲסִיקוֹ בְּקַשׁ וּבַגְּבָבָה לֹא יִתֵּן בֵּין מִתּוֹכוֹ בֵּין מֵעַל גַּבָּיו. כֻּפָּח שֶׁהֲסִיקוֹ בְקַשׁ וּבַגְּבָבָא הֲרֵי זֶה כְּכִירַיִם. בַּגֶּפֶת אוֹ בְעֵצִים הֲרֵי הוּא כְתַנּוּר:

Mishnah 2: If an oven[5] was heated with straw or stubbles one may not put anything inside it or on its back. If a single burner[6] was heated with straw or stubbles it is like a cooking stove, with olive cake or wood it is like an oven.

משנה ג: אֵין נוֹתְנִין בֵּיצָה בְּצַד הַמֵּיחַם בִּשְׁבִיל שֶׁתִּתְגַּלְגֵּל וְלֹא יַפְקִיעֶנָּה בְסוּדָרִין וְרִבִּי יוֹסֵי מַתִּיר. וְלֹא יַטְמְנֶנָּה בְחוֹל וּבַאֲבַק דְּרָכִים בִּשְׁבִיל שֶׁתִּיצָּלֶה:

Mishnah 3: One may not put an egg next to the hot water container to make it soft boiled and he may not break it on tissue[7], but Rebbi Yose permits. One should not bury it in dust of roads that it should be roasted[8].

משנה ד: מַעֲשֶׂה שֶׁעָשׂוּ אַנְשֵׁי טִיבֶּרְיָא הֵבִיאוּ סִילוֹן שֶׁל צוֹנִין בְּתוֹךְ אַמָּה שֶׁל חַמִּין. אָמְרוּ לָהֶן חֲכָמִים אִם בַּשַּׁבָּת כְּחַמִּין שֶׁהוּחַמּוּ בַשַּׁבָּת וַאֲסוּרִין בִּרְחִיצָה וּבִשְׁתִיָּיה. וְאִם בְּיוֹם טוֹב כְּחַמִּין שֶׁהוּחַמּוּ בְיוֹם טוֹב וַאֲסוּרִין בִּרְחִיצָה וּמוּתָּרִין בִּשְׁתִיָּיה. מוּלְיָיאר הַגָּרוּף שׁוֹתִין הֵימֶנּוּ בַשַּׁבָּת. אַנְטִיכִי אַף עַל פִּי שֶׁגְּרוּפָה אֵין שׁוֹתִין הֵימֶנָּה:

Mishnah 5: What the people of Tiberias did was to divert a jet of cold water into a canal of hot water. The Sages told them if this is on a Sabbath this is like hot water which was heated on the Sabbath; it is forbidden for washing and drinking. But if it is on a holiday it is like water heated on the holiday; it is forbidden for washing but permitted for drinking. From a cleaned-out cooking vessel⁹ one drinks on the Sabbath; from an Antiochean vessel¹⁰ one does not drink even if it is cleaned out.

משנה ח: הַמֵּיחַם שֶׁפִּינָהוּ לֹא יִתֵּן לְתוֹכוֹ מַיִם צוֹנִין בִּשְׁבִיל שֶׁיֵּחַמּוּ אֲבָל נוֹתֵן הוּא לְתוֹכוֹ וּלְתוֹךְ הַכּוֹס כְּדֵי לְהַפְשִׁירָן. הָאִילְפָּס וְהַקְּדֵירָה שֶׁהֶעֱבִירָן מְרוּתָּחִין לֹא יִתֵּן לְתוֹכָן תַּבְלִין אֲבָל נוֹתֵן הוּא לְתוֹךְ הַקְּעָרָה אוֹ לְתוֹךְ הַתַּמְחוּי. רִבִּי יְהוּדָה אוֹמֵר, לַכֹּל הוּא נוֹתֵן חוּץ מִדָּבָר שֶׁיֵּשׁ בּוֹ חוֹמֶץ וָצִיר:

Mishnah 5: One may not put cold water into a hot water container which was removed¹¹ in order to heat it but one may put into it or into a cup to make it lukewarm. Into a pan¹² or a pot which was taken off the fire boiling one should not give spices¹³ but one may give them into the bowl or into the tray. Rebbi Jehudah says, one may put them in everything except what contains vinegar or fish sauce¹⁴.

משנה ו: אֵין נוֹתְנִין כְּלִי תַּחַת הַנֵּר לְקַבֵּל בּוֹ אֶת הַשֶּׁמֶן וְאִם נְתָנוֹ מִבְּעוֹד יוֹם מוּתָּר. וְאֵין נֵיאוֹתִין מִמֶּנּוּ לְפִי שֶׁאֵינוֹ מִן הַמּוּכָן. מְטַלְטְלִין נֵר חָדָשׁ אֲבָל לֹא יָשָׁן. רִבִּי שִׁמְעוֹן אוֹמֵר כָּל־הַנֵּירוֹת מִיטַּלְטְלִין חוּץ מִן הַנֵּר הַדָּלֵק בַּשַׁבָּת. נוֹתְנִין כְּלִי תַּחַת הַנֵּר לְקַבֵּל נִיצוֹצוֹת וְלֹא יִתֵּן לְתוֹכוֹ מַיִם מִפְּנֵי שֶׁהוּא מְכַבֶּה:

Mishnah 6: One does not put a vessel under the light to catch the oil but when he put it there when it still was daylight it is permitted. One may not use it because it is not prepared¹⁵. One moves a new light but not a used one; Rebbi Simeon says one may move any light except one which was burning on the Sabbath. One may put a vessel under the light to catch the sparks but one may not put water in it since he would extinguish.

1   A portable clay stove with room for two pots; in biblical Hebrew כִּירַיִם (Lev. 11:35); cf. Chapter 1, Note 409.

2   Since these materials burn quickly and do not form charcoal there is no danger that anybody would stir the fuel on the Sabbath when the food was put on the stove on Friday.

3   What remains of the olives after pressing in the oil press.

4   If it was cooked rare before the Sabbath one may even return the pot on the stove after serving since straw and stubbles burn quickly and no long term cooking will ensue nor is there any danger of stirring the embers.

5   A portable clay oven, essentially a truncated cone. The opening at the top causes updraft and a stronger flame.

6   Similar to כִּירָה but with space for only one pot.

7   To make an omelette by the heat of the

sun.

8 Even R. Yose agrees that only quick cooking is permitted by using the heat of the sun, not full scale roasting.

9 Latin *miliarium, -ii,* n. "cooking vessel".

10 It seems that the difference between an Antiochian vessel and a *miliarium* was that the latter had a small container for coals at its bottom but the Antiochian a large one which kept heat for a very long time.

11 It is not clear whether this means that the vessel was removed from the fire or the boiling water removed from the vessel.

12 Greek λοπάς, -άδος, ἡ.

13 Nothing fresh can be put into a cooking pot on the Sabbath. Spices can be put into a serving pot which never was on the fire, since they do not need cooking to be seasoning.

14 These will actually cook the spices when hot even if not on the fire.

15 If edible oil was used as fuel, at the start of the Sabbath it was fuel, not food, and cannot be used as food on the Sabbath (Chapter 2, Note 23).

(5c line 49) כִּירָה שֶׁהִסִּיקוּהָ כול׳. כֵּינֵי מַתְנִיתָא. מְקַיְּימִין עָלֶיהָ תַּבְשִׁיל. מַתְנִיתָא דְּרַבִּי יוּדָה. דְּתַנְיָא. הָיוּ שְׁתֵּי כִירַיִים מַתְאִימוֹת. אַחַת גְּרוּפָה וּקְטוּמָה. וְאַחַת לֹא גְרוּפָה וְלֹא קְטוּמָה. מְקַיְּימִין עַל הַגְּרוּפָה וְעַל הַקְּטוּמָה. מַה מְקַיְּימִין עָלֶיהָ. אֵין מְקַיְּימִין עָלֶיהָ כְּלוּם. וּבֵית הִלֵּל אוֹמְרִין. חַמִּין אֲבָל לֹא תַבְשִׁיל. הֶעֱבִיר אֶת הַמֵּיחָם. הַכֹּל מוֹדִין שֶׁלֹּא יַחֲזִיר. דִּבְרֵי רִבִּי מֵאִיר. רִבִּי יְהוּדָה אוֹמֵר. בֵּית שַׁמַּי אוֹמְרִין. חַמִּין אֲבָל לֹא תַבְשִׁיל. וּבֵית הִלֵּל אוֹמְרִין. חַמִּין וְתַבְשִׁיל. הֶעֱבִיר אֶת הַמֵּיחָם בֵּית שַׁמַּי אוֹמְרִין. לֹא יַחֲזִיר. וּבֵית הִלֵּל אוֹמְרִין. יַחֲזִיר.

2 דתניא G [16 דתני | 3 מקיימין G | מקיימין | 4 כלום G | כולם ובית G | בית 5 ובית G | בית 6 ובית G בית

"If a cooking stove[1] was heated," etc. So is the Mishnah: "one keeps a dish on it.[17]"

The Mishnah is Rebbi Jehudah's, as it was stated[18]: "If there were two coordinated cooking stoves, one emptied or covered with ashes, the other one neither emptied nor covered with ashes, one keeps on the one emptied or covered with ashes. What does one keep on it? The House of Shammai say, one does not keep anything on it. But the House of Hillel say, hot water but no dish. If he removed the hot water pot everybody agrees that he should not return it, the words of Rebbi Meïr. Rebbi Jehudah says, the House of Shammai say, hot water but no dish; but the House of Hillel say, hot water and dish. If he removed the hot water pot, the House of Shammai say he should not return it, but the House of Hillel say, he may return it.[19]"

16 Babylonian spelling.
17 "One may put" in the Mishnah means one may put on the stove on Friday and keep it there on the Sabbath. This is the subject of a lengthy discussion in the Babli (36b-37b).
18 Tosephta 2:13 (ed. Liebermann), 3:3 (ed. Zuckermandel); Babli 37a.
19 This is the text of the anonymous Mishnah even though ordinarily an anonymous Mishnah is presumed to be R. Meïr's.

(5c line 56) רִבִּי חֶלְבּוֹ רַב עָנָן בְּשֵׁם רַב. לֹא שָׁנוּ אֶלָּא עָלֶיהָ. הָא לְתוֹכָהּ לֹא. עַד אֵיכָן. עוּלָא אָמַר. עַד שְׁלֹשָׁה. אָמַר רִבִּי מָנָא. עַד מָקוֹם שֶׁהוּא עוֹשֶׂה חָרִיץ. אָמַר רִבִּי יוֹסֵי בֵּירְבִּי בּוּן. מִפְּנֵי שֶׁהוּא שָׁלִיט בְּמָקוֹם שֶׁהַיָּד שׁוֹלֶטֶת. וַתְיָיא כַּיי דָּמַר רִבִּי זְעִירָה בְּשֵׁם רִבִּי יְהוּדָה. מוּתָּר לְהַפְשִׁיר בְּמָקוֹם שֶׁהַיָּד שׁוֹלֶטֶת. וְאָסוּר לְהַפְשִׁיר בְּמָקוֹם שֶׁאֵין הַיָּד שׁוֹלֶטֶת.

1 עולא | G ר' עולה   2 שלשה | G שלושה עשה[20]

רִבִּי יְהוֹשֻׁעַ בַּר גְּיוּזַרְנָה הֲוָה מְשַׁמֵּשׁ קוֹמֵי רִבִּי זְעִירָה וַהֲוָה מְעַיֵּיל קוֹמוֹי תַּבְשִׁילִין רוֹתְחִין. אָמַר לֵיהּ. הֵיךְ אִיתְעֲבָדָא. אָמַר לֵיהּ. גָּרִיף תִּיפָיָּא וִיהַב בְּגַוָּהּ. אָמַר לֵיהּ. לָא תְהִי עָבִיד כֵּן אֶלָּא גָּרִיף תִּיפָיָא וִיהַב תְּלָתָא כֵּיפִין וְרָמֵי עֲלֵיהוֹן.

רִבִּי אַבָּהוּ חוֹרֵי בְּבוּצְרָה. מְמַלֵּה נַצְרָא רְמַץ וּמֵיתָן תְּלָתָא כֵּיפִין וּמִירְמֵי עֲלֵיהוֹן.

Rebbi Ḥelbo, Rav Anan in the name of Rav: it only said "on top of it." Therefore not into it[21]. How far? Ulla said, up three [hand breadths][22]. Rebbi Mana said, up to where he would make an impression[23]. Rebbi Yose ben Rebbi Abun said, because he has mastery at a place where the hand has mastery[24]. This comes as what Rebbi Ze`ira said in the name of Rebbi[25] Jehudah: It is permitted to make lukewarm at a place where the hand has mastery but it is forbidden at a place where the hand has no mastery[26].

Rebbi Joshua the son of the circumciser was serving Rebbi Ze`ira; he brought him piping hot dishes[27]. He asked him, how was this done? He told him, I cleaned out the stove and put it on top. He told him, you should not do this but clean out the stove, take three stones and cast it on them.

Rebbi Abbahu instructed in Bostra: One fills a vessel[28] with hot ashes, puts on top three stones, and casts on them[29].

20 Here ends the Genizah fragment.
21 On top of the stove, far from the fuel. It is forbidden to leave the food if the pot touches the flame. Babli 37a.
22 Distant from the fire. Numbers in the masculine denote handbreadths.
23 It is forbidden to dislocate the ashes on the coals in the stove, but otherwise there are no limitations.
24 If the pot can be handled with bare hands, without a potholder, there are no restriction on where the pot is put.

The Babli uses the rare biblical word סולדת (*Job* 6:10) "to jump", decreeing that the pot may be returned to the stove only if "the hand does *not* jump", it is not so hot that one needs a potholder. It seems that under the influence of Greek, in the mouth of the Galileans the word *sōletet* sounded to Babylonian ears as *sōledet*.

25 Read with the quote later in the Chapter (Note 148): *Rav. Rashba (Novellae ad* 40b) reads here the full text there.

26 On the Sabbath itself one may use food or drink which are hot but may be touched to warm cold food to lukewarm. In the Babli (40b) Rav Jehudah permits to heat oil even if the hand jumps.

27 On the Sabbath.

28 Greek γάστρα, -τρη, ἡ "belly"-shaped vessel.

29 This is the final decision for practice.

(5c line 65) דָּנִיאֵל בְּרֵיהּ דְּרִבִּי קְטִינָא בְּשֵׁם רִבִּי אַסִּי. שִׁיזְרֵי חָרִיּוֹת כְּגֶפֶת וּכְעֵצִים. הָדָא דְתֵימָר כְּשֶׁהָיוּ לַחִין וְיָבֵשׁוּ. אֲבָל אִם הָיוּ יְבֵישִׁין מִתְּחִילָּתָן כְּקַשׁ וּבִגְבָבָה הֵן.

גְּלָלֵי בְהֵמָה. אִית תַּנָּיֵי תַנֵּי. כְּגֶפֶת וּכְעֵצִים. וְאִית תַּנָּיֵי תַנֵּי. כְּקַשׁ וּבִגְבָבָה. מָאן דָּמַר. כְּגֶפֶת וּכְעֵצִים. בְּדַקָּה. וּמָאן דָּמַר. כְּקַשׁ וּבִגְבָבָה. בְּגַסָּה.

Daniel the son of Rebbi Qaṭina in the name of Rebbi Assi[30]: spines of palm branches are like olive cake and wood. That is, if they had been moist and dried out. But if they were dry from the start[31] they are like straw and stubbles.

Animal droppings. There are Tannaim who state, like olive cake and wood; and there are Tannaim who state, like straw and stubbles. He who says like olive cake and wood, small cattle[32]. And he who says like straw and stubbles, large cattle.

30 Read: Rebbi Daniel the son of Rav Qatina in the name of Rav Assi.

31 If they are dry on the tree.

32 Droppings of sheep and goats are hard, unlike soft cow droppings.

(5c line 71) הַגּוֹרֵף. עַד שֶׁיְּגָרוֹף כָּל־צָרְכּוֹ. מִן מַה דְּתַנֵּי. הַגּוֹרֵף צָרִיךְ לַחֲטֹט בְּיָד. הָדָא אֲמָרָה. עַד שֶׁיְּגָרוֹף כָּל־צוֹרְכּוֹ. וְהַקּוֹטֵם. עַד שֶׁיִּקְטוֹם כָּל־צוֹרְכּוֹ. מִן מַה דְּתַנֵּי. מַלְבָּה עָלֶיהָ נְעוֹרֶת שֶׁלְפִּשְׁתָּן. הָדָא אֲמָרָה. אֲפִילוּ לֹא קִטֵּם כָּל־צוֹרְכּוֹ. וַיֵּי דָּא אֲמְרָה דָא. יוֹם טוֹב שֶׁחָל לִהְיוֹת עֶרֶב שַׁבָּת. אָמַר רִבִּי שִׁיָּין. מַלְבָּה עָלֶיהָ נְעוֹרֶת שֶׁלְפִּשְׁתָּן.

קְטָמָהּ וְנִתְלַבַּת מָהוּ. רִבִּי חִיָּיה רוֹבָא עָלָה לְבֵיתוֹ וְהוֹרֵי. מוּתָּר. בְּעוֹן קוֹמֵי רִבִּי זְעִירָא וְרִבִּי הוֹשַׁעְיָה וְרִבִּי חֲנַנְיָה חֲבֵרֵיהוֹן דְּרַבָּנָן. לִיבָּה. לְשֶׁעָבַר. עָבַד רִבִּי אִמִּי וְאָדְרוֹן חַבְרַיָּא בְּעוֹן מַחֲזִיר עֲלֵיהּ. אָמַר לוֹן רִבִּי חֲנַנְיָה חֲבֵרֵיהוֹן דְּרַבָּנָן. מִן דַּהֲוָה עוֹבְדָא הֲוָה עוֹבְדָא. אָמַר רִבִּי שְׁמוּאֵל בַּר

סִיסְרְטָיי. לְכֵן צְרִיכָה לָבֹה. אָמַר רִבִּי מָנָא. אֲנָא קַשִּׁיתָהּ קוֹמֵי רִבִּי בָּא בְּרֵיהּ דְּרִבִּי פַּפִּי. אֵין תֵּימַר. לְשֶׁעָבַר. אֲפִילוּ לֹא בִישֵּׁל עָלֶיהָ כַּתְּחִילָה.

דְּתַנֵּי. הַמְעַשֵּׂר וְהַמְבַשֵּׁל בַּשַּׁבָּת בְּשׁוֹגֵג יֹאכַל. וּמֵזִיד לֹא יֹאכַל. דִּבְרֵי רִבִּי מֵאִיר. רִבִּי יְהוּדָה אוֹמֵר. שׁוֹגֵג יֹאכַל לְמוֹצָאֵי שַׁבָּת. מֵזִיד לֹא יֹאכַל. רִבִּי יוֹחָנָן הַסַּנְדְּלָר אוֹמֵר. שׁוֹגֵג יֹאכַל לְמוֹצָאֵי שַׁבָּת לַאֲחֵרִים וְלֹא לוֹ. מֵזִיד לֹא לוֹ וְלֹא לַאֲחֵרִים. שְׁמוּאֵל כְּרִבִּי יוֹחָנָן הַסַּנְדְּלָר. רַב כַּד הֲוֵי מוֹרֵי בַחֲבוּרְתֵּיהּ הֲוָה אָמַר כְּרִבִּי מֵאִיר. בָּצִיבּוּרָא הֲוָה מוֹרֵי כְּרִבִּי יוֹחָנָן הַסַּנְדְּלָר. אָמַר רִבִּי שִׁמְעוֹן בַּר כַּרְסָנָה. כְּרִבִּי יִשְׁמָעֵאל בֵּירִבִּי יוֹסֵי דָּרַשׁ לוֹן. דְּתַנֵּי. רִבִּי יִשְׁמָעֵאל בֵּירִבִּי יוֹסֵי אָמַר מִשּׁוּם אָבִיו. כָּל־דָּבָר שֶׁחַיָּיבִין עַל זְדוֹנוֹ כָרֵת וְעַל שִׁגְנָתוֹ חַטָּאת וַעֲשָׂאוֹ בַשַּׁבָּת. בֵּין שׁוֹגֵג בֵּין מֵזִיד אָסוּר בֵּין לוֹ בֵּין לַאֲחֵרִים. וְכָל־דָּבָר שֶׁאֵינָן חַיָּיבִין עַל זְדוֹנוֹ כָרֵת וְעַל שִׁגְנָתוֹ חַטָּאת וַעֲשָׂאוֹ בַשַּׁבָּת. שׁוֹגֵג יֹאכַל לְמוֹצָאֵי שַׁבָּת לַאֲחֵרִים וְלֹא לוֹ. מֵזִיד. לֹא לוֹ וְלֹא לַאֲחֵרִים. בְּעוֹן קוֹמֵי רִבִּי יוֹחָנָן. אַתְּ מַה אָמַר. אָמַר לוֹן. אֲנִי אֵין לִי אֶלָּא מִשְׁנָה. הַמְעַשֵּׂר וְהַמְבַשֵּׁל בַּשַּׁבָּת. שׁוֹגֵג יֹאכַל. מֵזִיד לֹא יֹאכַל. שָׁמַע רַב חִסְדָּא וַאֲמַר. הוּתְּרוּ הַשַּׁבָּתוֹת. רַב חוּנָה בְּשֵׁם רַב וְתַנֵּי רִבִּי חִיָּיא כֵן. בָּרִאשׁוֹנָה הָיוּ אוֹמְרִים. הַשּׁוֹכֵחַ תַּבְשִׁיל עַל גַּבֵּי כִירָה וְקָדְשָׁה עָלָיו אֶת הַשַּׁבָּת. שׁוֹגֵג יֹאכַל. מֵזִיד לֹא יֹאכַל. נֶחְשְׁדוּ לִהְיוֹת מַנִּיחִין מְזִידָיו. וְאוֹמְרִים. שְׁכִיחִין הָיִינוּ. וְאָסְרוּ לָהֶן אֶת הַשּׁוֹכֵחַ. וְהָכָא אָמְרוּ כֵן. אָמַר רִבִּי אִילָא. נֶחְשְׁדוּ לִהְיוֹת מַנִּיחִין וְלֹא נֶחְשְׁדוּ לִהְיוֹת מְבַשְּׁלִין. וְקָנְסוּ בְּמֵזִיד וְלֹא קָנְסוּ בִּמְבַשֵּׁל.

1 דתני { ת תני המעשר והמבשל { ת המבשל בשוגג { ת שוגג ומזיד { ת מזיד   2 שוגג { ת בשוגג מזיד { ת במזיד   ת יאכל { ת יאבל עולמית שוגג { ת בשוגג   3 מזיד { ת במזיד   4 הוה אמ' { ת מורי הוה מורי { ת -   5 כרסנה { ת כרסנא ביר' יוסי { ת בנו של ר' יוחנן בן ברוקה (2) דרש { ת הורי אמ' { ת -   6 משום אביו { ת - שוגג { ת בשוגג   7 מזיד { ת במזיד לאחרים { ת לאחרים לא יאכל שאינן { ת שאין   8 שוגג { ת בשוגג מזיד { ת במזיד   9 אמר { ת את אמר שוגג { ת בשוגג מזיד { ת במזיד   10 רב חונה { ת לא כן אמ' רב הונא חייא { ת חייה   11 חשכיח { ת השוכח כירה { ת כירתו וקדשה עליו את השבת { ת בשבת שוגג { ת בשוגג מזיד { ת במזיד   12 להיות { ת שהיו והכא אמרו כן { ת ואת אמר הכא חכין   13 אילא { ת הילא וקנסו { ת קנסו

One who empties, only if he empties completely, since it was stated: he who empties has to scratch out[33] by hand. This implies that he has to empty completely. If one covers with ashes, does he have to cover completely? Since it was stated: when he kindled flax tow over it[34], this implies even if he did not completely cover it with ashes. When was this said? On a holiday which happens to fall on Friday; Rebbi Ashian said, one kindles flax tow over it.

If he covered it with ashes and it started burning, what? The Elder Rebbi Hiyya went to his house and instructed: it is permitted[35]. They asked before Rebbi Ze`ira, and Rebbi Hoshaia, and Rebbi Hanania the colleagues of the rabbis, "it started burning", in the past. Rebbi Immi passed by; the colleagues were scattered; then they wanted to return to it. Rebbi Hanania the colleague of the rabbis said to them, as the case happened so it happened[36]. Rebbi

Samuel bar Sisartai said, it is questionable for the future[37]. Rebbi Mana said, I objected before Rebbi Abba the son of Rebbi Pappaios: If you say for the past, even if he did not[38] cook on it earlier.

[39]As it was stated[40]: "He who tithes or cooks on the Sabbath, if it was done unintentionally it may be eaten, intentionally it may not be eaten, the words of Rebbi Meïr. Rebbi Jehudah says, unintentionally it may be eaten at the end of the Sabbath, intentionally it may not be eaten. Rebbi Joḥanan the Alexandrian said, unintentionally it may be eaten at the end of the Sabbath by others but not by himself, intentionally neither by him nor by others." Samuel followed Rebbi Joḥanan the Alexandrian. When Rav was instructing his own group he said following Rebbi Meïr; in public he instructed following Rebbi Joḥanan the Alexandrian[41]. Rebbi Simeon bar Karsana said, he explained to us following Rebbi Ismael ben Rebbi Yose, as it was stated[42]: "Rebbi Ismael ben Rebbi Yose[43] said in his father's name, in any case where for an intentional sin one is liable for extirpation and an unintentional sin for a purification offering, if it was committed on the Sabbath unintentionally or intentionally, the result is forbidden both to him and to others. In any case where for an intentional sin one is not liable for extirpation and an unintentional sin no purification offering is due, if it was committed on the Sabbath unintentionally or intentionally, the result unintentional it may be eaten by others after the end of the Sabbath but not by him, intentionally neither by him nor by others." They asked before Rebbi Joḥanan, what do you say? He said, I have only the Mishnah[44]: "He who tithes or cooks on the Sabbath, if in error it may be eaten, if intentionally it may not be eaten." Rav Ḥisda heard this and said, the Sabbaths have been permitted! [45]Rav Huna in the name of Rav, and Rebbi Ḥiyya stated thus: [46]"In earlier times they said, one who forgets some dish on his stove on the Sabbath, unintentionally it may be eaten, intentionally it may not be eaten. People were suspected that they left it intentionally and said, it was forgotten; they forbade it to them when it was forgotten." And here, you say so? Rebbi Ila said, they were suspected to leave it on, they were not suspected to cook. They imposed a fine for forgetting but not for cooking.

132 ŠABBAT CHAPTER THREE

33 The Medieval quotes of this passage (RAN *Šabbat ad* 36b, ed. Mosad Harav Kook col. 126, Ritba *ad* 36b ed. S. Schreiber, Rashba *Šabbat ad* 36b) read לטאט "to sweep out" (with a broom.)

34 In the Babli, 37a, "if he covers it with flax tow" without setting it on fire. The Yerushalmi seems to be of the opinion that this will burn quickly and leave a thin layer of ashes covering the coals.

35 When his wife ("his house") accidentally left something on the stove.

36 It happened that R. Hiyya rules in a case where it was left unintentionally. In R. Hanania's opinion it would be permitted to intentionally leave something on a stove whose coals were incompletely covered.

37 "In the future" means to permit it to do so intentionally in the future; "in the past" means to rules about a question which arises because of what already has happened.

38 Probably this word has to be deleted; it certainly is forbidden to put something on a stove which was lit expressly for Friday night, not for cooking on Friday afternoon.

39 This and the next two paragraphs are from *Terumot* 3:3 (**ת**), Notes 70-88.

40 Tosephta *Šabbat* 2:15, Babli *Ketubot* 34a.

41 Babli *Hulin* 15a.

42 Tosephta *Šabbat* 2:16.

43 In Tosephta, *Terumot* and the quotes in Medieval authors the name is R. Ismael the son of R. Johanan ben Beroqa.

44 Mishnah *Terumot* 2:3.

45 In *Terumot*, this the reason for Rav Hisda's complaint: "for Rav Huna said . . ."

46 Babli 38a.

(5d line 24) חָזְרוּ לוֹמַר. תַּבְשִׁיל שֶׁהוּא מִצְטַמֵּק וְיָפֶה לוֹ אָסוּר. תַּבְשִׁיל שֶׁהוּא מִצְטַמֵּק וְרַע לוֹ מוּתָּר. אֵי זֶהוּ תַּבְשִׁיל שֶׁהוּא מִצְטַמֵּק וְיָפֶה לוֹ. כְּגוֹן אִכְּרוּב וַאֲפוּנִים וּבָשָׂר טָרוּף. אָמַר רִבִּי תַנְחוּם בַּר עִילָאי. אַף רָאשֵׁי לְפָתוֹת וְרָאשֵׁי קֵפָלוֹטוֹת עָשׂוּ אוֹתָן כְּתַבְשִׁיל שֶׁהוּא מִצְטַמֵּק וְיָפֶה לוֹ. בֵּצִים מַה הֵן. רִבִּי יוֹסֵי בְּשֵׁם רִבִּי יִשְׁמָעֵאל בֵּירִבִּי יוֹסֵי. אַבָּא עָלָה לְבֵיתוֹ וּמָצָא שָׁם חַמִּין וְהִתִּיר. בֵּצִים וְאָסַר. רִבִּי שְׁמוּאֵל בַּר נָתָן בְּשֵׁם רִבִּי חָמָא בַר חֲנִינָה. אֲנִי וְאַבָּא עָלִינוּ לְחַמַּת גָּדֵר וְהֵבִיאוּ לְפָנֵינוּ בֵּצִים קְטַנִּים כְּחוּזְרָדִין וְטַעֲמָן יָפֶה כְּפִינְקְרֵיסִין.

1 תבשיל שהוא | ת - 2 כגון אכרוב | ת כרוב ואפונים | ת ואפונין 3 קפלוטות | ת לפתות וראשי קפלוטות 4 בשם | ת בשם ר' ישמעאל. ר' ירמיה ר' חנינה בשם חמין והתיר. בצים ואסר | ת בצים ואסר. חמין והתיר 6 כחוזרדין | ת כחזרדין כפינקריסין | ת בפינקריסין

[47]"They came back to say, a dish which will improve the more it shrinks is forbidden; a dish which will deteriorate the more it shrinks is permitted. What is a dish which improves the more it shrinks? For example cabbage, peas, and chopped meat.[48]" Rebbi Tanhum bar Illa said, they also considered heads of beets and heads of of leeks as dishes which improve the more they shrink. What about eggs? Rebbi Yose in the name of Rebbi Ismael ben Rebbi Yose: My father came home and found hot water and permitted it, eggs and forbade them. Rebbi Samuel bar Natan in the name of Rebbi Hama bar Hanina: I

went with my father to Ḥammat Gader where they brought before us eggs small like crab apples and they tasted delicious like sweetbread[49].

47 The omissions in this text show clearly that the original is in *Terumot*.
48 Tosephta *Šabbat* 2:14 in the name of R. Jehudah. Babli 38a.
49 Greek πάγκρεας, -ατος, τό.

(5d line 32) תַּנֵּי. לֹא תְמַלֵּא אִשָּׁה קְדֵירָה עֲסִיסִיּוֹת וְתוּרְמוֹסִין וְתִתְּנֵם לְתוֹךְ הַתַּנּוּר עֶרֶב שַׁבָּת עִם חֲשֵׁיכָה. וְאִם נָתְנָה מוֹצָאֵי שַׁבָּת אֲסוּרִין בִּכְדֵי שֶׁיֵּיעָשׂוּ. רִבִּי אָחָא אָמַר. בְּמֵזִיד. כְּרִבִּי מֵאִיר. רִבִּי יוֹסֵי אָמַר. בְּשׁוֹגֵג. כְּרִבִּי יוּדָה. אָמַר רִבִּי מָנָא. יָאוּת אָמַר רִבִּי יוֹסֵי רִבִּי. הַנּוֹטֵעַ בַּשַּׁבָּת שׁוֹגֵג יְקַיֵּים. מֵזִיד יַעֲקוֹר. וּבַשְּׁבִיעִית בֵּין שׁוֹגֵג בֵּין מֵזִיד יַעֲקוֹר. רִבִּי יְהוּדָה אוֹמֵר. חִילּוּף הַדְּבָרִים. הַנּוֹטֵעַ בַּשַּׁבָּת בֵּין שׁוֹגֵג בֵּין מֵזִיד יַעֲקוֹר. וּבַשְּׁבִיעִית שׁוֹגֵג יְקַיֵּים וּמֵזִיד יַעֲקוֹר. לָמָּה. מִפְּנֵי שֶׁהֲנָיַית שַׁבָּת עָלָיו. וְכָאן. מִכֵּיוָן שֶׁאַתְּ אוֹמֵר. יַמְתִּין לְמוֹצָאֵי שַׁבָּת כְּדֵי שֶׁיֵּיעָשׂוּ. כְּמִי שֶׁלֹּא נֶהֱנָה מֵחֲמַת שַׁבָּת כְּלוּם. וּמַה טַעֲמוֹן דְּרַבָּנָן. נֶחְשְׁדוּ עַל הַשְּׁבִיעִית וְלֹא נֶחְשְׁדוּ עַל הַשַּׁבָּתוֹת. דָּבָר אַחֵר. מוֹנִין לַשְּׁבִיעִיּוֹת וְאֵין מוֹנִין לַשַּׁבָּתוֹת. הֵיךְ עֲבִידָה. נָטַע פָּחוֹת מִשְּׁלֹשִׁים יוֹם לִפְנֵי שְׁבִיעִית וְנִכְנְסָה שְׁבִיעִית. אִין תֵּימַר. חֲשָׁד. אֵין כָּאן חֲשָׁד. אִין תֵּימַר. מִינְיָין. אֵין כָּאן מִינְיָין. נָטַע פָּחוֹת מִשְּׁלֹשִׁים יוֹם לִפְנֵי שְׁמִינִית וְנִכְנְסָה שְׁמִינִית. אִין תֵּימַר. חֲשָׁד. יֵשׁ כָּאן חֲשָׁד. אִין תֵּימַר. מִינְיָין. יֵשׁ כָּאן מִינְיָין. וַתְיָיא כְּמָאן דְּאָמַר. מִפְּנֵי הַחֲשָׁד. בְּרַם כְּמָאן דְּאָמַר. מִפְּנֵי הַמִּינְיָין. קְנָסוּ בְשׁוֹגֵג מִפְּנֵי הַמֵּזִיד.

1 עסיסיות | ת עסיסיות   2 מוצאי שבת אסורין | ת אסורין למוצאי שבת   שיעשו | ת שייעשו   3 אמ' | ת או' רבי | ת -   בשבת שוגג | ת בשוגג בשבת   4 מזיד | ת במזיד ובשביעית | ת בשביעית שוגג | ת בשוגג   מזיד | ת במזיד   5 הנוטע בשבת בין שוגג בין מזיד יעקור. ובשביעית שוגג יקיים מזיד יעקור | ת בשביעית בשוגג יקיים במזיד יעקור. בשבת בין בשוגג בין במזיד יעקור   למה | ת -   6 שאת | ת שאתה   ימתין | ת המתן   כדי | ת עד כדי   7 דרבנן | ת דרבניין   8 עבידה | ת עבידא   9 שביעית | ת לשביעית   מניין | ת מונין (2)   10 שמינית | ת שביעית   אין תימר. מניין. יש כאן מניין | ת -   11 ותייא | ת ואתיא   החשד | ת מניין   12 המיניין | ת חשד   וקנסו | ת קנסו   בשוגג | ת שוגג   המזיד | ת מזיד

It was stated[50]: "A woman should not fill a pot with '*assisiot*'[51] and lupines and put them into the oven at the start of the Sabbath, at nightfall. If she did, they are forbidden after the end of the Sabbath until the time they could have been done." Rebbi Aḥa said: intentionally, following Rebbi Meïr; Rebbi Yose said: unintentionally, following Rebbi Jehudah. Rebbi Mana said, what my teacher[52] Rebbi Yose said is correct: [53]"He who is planting on the Sabbath, if unintentional, he may keep it, if intentional, he must tear it out. In the Sabbatical year, he must tear it out whether [planting was] unintentional or intentional. Rebbi Jehudah says, it is the other way around. If he was planting on the Sabbath he must tear it out whether it was unintentional or intentional; in the Sabbatical, if unintentional, he may keep it, if intentional, he must tear it out. Why? Because the profit of the Sabbath [is forbidden] to him." And here, since you say that after the end of the Sabbath he has to wait until the time it could have been done, he did not gain anything from the Sabbath. What is the reason of the rabbis? People are suspected about the Sabbatical but not about the Sabbath. Another explanation: One counts Sabbaticals, one does not count Sabbaths. What is this about? If somebody planted less than thirty days before the Sabbatical and now it is the Sabbatical, if it is because of suspicion, there is no suspicion; if it is for counting, it is not counted. Less than thirty days before the eighth year and now it is the eighth year, if it is because of suspicion, there is suspicion; if it is because of counting, there is counting. It follows him who says because of suspicion, but for him who says because of counting they fined the unintentional because of the intentional[54].

50   Tosephta 3:1 (ed. Liebermann), 4:1 (ed. Zuckermandel.) Babli 18b.

51   An undetermined kind of legumes; in the words of the Geonim they exist in the Land of Israel but not in Babylonia. Clearly they need a very long time for cooking similar to lupines. Cf. Arabic عمّ "to be hard". Cf. Latin *siser, -eris*, n. (Greek σίσαρον) "a plant cultivated for its piquant root, perhaps rampion (*campanula rapunculus*) (E. G.).

52   The vocalization is from the ms. It corresponds to the spelling רְבִּי used by Samuel Hannagid in his poem addressed to Rav Nissim and the inscription RABI (soft β) found at Bet-Shearim.

53   Tosephta 2:21. Babli *Gittin* 53b.

54   This last sentence is the opposite of the last sentence in *Terumot*. The latter text seems to be correct since in counting the age of a tree a month more or less is negligible. But one should not plant a tree a month before the Sabbatical, even though this is not forbidden, since the tree's years for ʿorla will be counted from the Sabbatical.

(5d line 48) נָטְלוֹ מִבְּעוֹד יוֹם מַחֲזִירוֹ מִבְּעוֹד יוֹם. נָטְלוֹ מִשֶּׁחֲשֵׁיכָה מַחֲזִירוֹ מִשֶּׁחֲשֵׁיכָה. נָטְלוֹ מִבְּעוֹד יוֹם וְקָדַשׁ עָלָיו הַיּוֹם. רְבִּי סִימוֹן דתרי בְּשֵׁם רְבִּי הוֹשַׁעְיָה. הִנִּיחוֹ בָאָרֶץ אָסוּר לְטַלְטְלוֹ. רְבִּי לָעְזָר בְּשֵׁם רְבִּי הוֹשַׁעְיָה. מְשָׁרֵת הָיִיתִי אֶת רְבִּי חִיָּיה הַגָּדוֹל וְהָיִיתִי מַעֲלֶה לוֹ חַמִּין מִדִּיּוֹטֵי הַתַּחְתּוֹנָה לַדִּיּוֹטֵי הָעֶלְיוֹנָה וּמַחֲזִירָן לַכִּירָה. אָמַר רְבִּי יִרְמְיָה בֵּירְבִּי שִׁמְעוֹן. אֲפִילוּ מִכִּירָה שֶׁהֲבָלָהּ מְמוּעָט לְכִירָה שֶׁהֲבָלָהּ מְרוּבֶּה. אָמַר רְבִּי אַמִּי. זִימְנִין סַגִּין יְתִיבִית קוֹמֵי רְבִּי הוֹשַׁעְיָה וְלֹא שְׁמָעִית מִינֵּיהּ הָדָא מִילְתָא. אָמַר רְבִּי זְרִיקָן לְרְבִּי זְעִירָא. לֹא שָׁמַע מִינֵּהּ מוּתָּר. שָׁמַע מִינָהּ אָסוּר.

תָּלוּי בְּיָתֵד וּנְתָנוֹ עַל גַּבֵּי סַפְסָל. נֹאמַר. אִם הָיָה מְפוּחָם מוּתָּר. וְאִם לָאו אָסוּר. אָמַר רִבִּי יוֹחָנָן בְּרִבִּי מָרִייָה. בְּשֶׁלֹּא הֶעֱבִיר יָדוֹ מִמֶּנּוּ. אֲבָל אִם הֶעֱבִיר יָדוֹ מִמֶּנּוּ אָסוּר.

If he took it when it still was daylight he may return it when it still is daylight. If he took it after dark he may return if after dark[55]. If he took it when it still was daylight and the day became holy for him? Rebbi Simon [bar Thaddeus][56] in the name of Rebbi Hoshaia: If he had put it down on the ground it is forbidden to move it[57]. Rebbi Eleazar in the name of Rebbi Hoshaia: I was serving the Great Rebbi Ḥiyya[58] and I brought him hot water from the lower to the upper apartment[59] and returned it to the stove. Rebbi Jeremiah ben Rebbi Simeon said, even from a stove with little heat to a stove with much heat Rebbi Immi said, many times I was sitting before Rebbi Hoshaia but this I never heard from him. Rebbi Zeriqan said to Rebbi Ze'ira, he did not hear from him that it was permitted; therefore it is forbidden.

If it was hanging from a peg, or it was put on a footstool. Should we say if it was as if on coals[60] it is permitted and if not it is forbidden? Rebbi Joḥanan ben Rebbi Marius said, if he did not remove his hand from it. But if he removed his hand from it it is forbidden[58].

---

55 The pot to a stove either cleaned out or whose embers are covered with ashes.

56 This is the reading of medieval quotes, instead of the unintelligible דתרי of the ms. (RAN on RIF #393; Naḥmanides *Novellae ad* 38a).

57 To return it to the stove; the pot may be used to serve the food.

58 Babli 38b.

59 Greek δίαιτα, ἡ, "dwelling".

60 Still hot.

(5d line 59) מתני'. תַּנּוּר שֶׁהִסִּיקוֹ בַקַשׁ וּבִגְבָבָה כול'. תָּנֵי בַּר קַפָּרָא. אֲפִילוּ לִסְמוֹךְ לוֹ אָסוּר. רִבִּי שַׁמַּי סָמִיךְ לַאֲוִירָה דְתַנּוּרָא. אָמַר לֵיהּ רִבִּי מָנָא. וְהָתַנֵּי בַּר קַפָּרָא. אֲפִילוּ לִסְמוֹךְ לוֹ אָסוּר. רִבִּי מָנָא מֵיקַל לִנְשַׁיָּיא דְשָׁטְחָן בִּגְדֵיהוֹן לַאֲוִירָה דְתַנּוּרָא. רִבִּי יוּדָן בֵּירִבִּי יִשְׁמָעֵאל הוֹרֵי מִדּוֹחַק מִיגְרוֹף תַּנּוּרָא וּמַייתָּן תְּלָתָא כַפִּין וּמִירְמֵי עֲלֵיהוֹן. וּבִלְחוֹד לֹא יָדְעִין מַגִירְמַיִת. אָמַר רִבִּי יוֹסֵי. בְּשַׁבָּת אַתָּה מְהַלֵּךְ אַחַר הֶסֵּיקוֹ. וּבְטוּמְאָה אַתְּ מְהַלֵּךְ אַחַר גִּיפּוּפוֹ.

Mishnah: "If an oven[5] was heated with straw or stubbles," etc. Bar Qappara stated: It is even forbidden to lean against it[61]. Rebbi Shammai leaned against the air space[62] of the oven. Rebbi Mana told him, did not Bar Qapprara state: It is even forbidden to lean against it?

Rebbi Mana cursed women who spread out their dresses over the airspace of the oven[63]. Rebbi Yudan ben Rebbi Ismael with difficulty instructed to clean out the oven, laid there three stones and put on them[64]; only that the neighboring women should not know of this.

Rebbi Yose said, for the Sabbath you go by the heat[65]; for impurity you go after the closure[66].

61   One may not put a pot near the oven so it touches the oven. Babli 38b.

62   Instead of אוירא it is possible to read the ms. as אדירא "threshing floor; heap; hide".

63   To dry them on the Sabbath in the hot updraft generated by the oven.

64   He treated an oven like a stove.

65   Any place with an updraft is treated as an oven; with fire burning without updraft it is a stove, irrespective of its shape.

66   If it has an opening on the bottom as air intake it is an oven; if it is enclosed and only the places for the two pots are open on top it is a stove.

(5d line 67) מתני'. אֵין נוֹתְנִין בֵּיצָה בְּצַד הַמֵּיחַם כול'. תַּפָּן תַּנִּינָן. תַּפּוּחַ שֶׁרְיסְקוֹ וּנְתָנוֹ לְתוֹךְ עִסָּה וְחִימִּיצָהּ הֲרֵי זוּ אֲסוּרָה. תַּנֵּי. רִבִּי יוֹסֵי מַתִּיר. רִבִּי אָחָא רִבִּי אַבָּהוּ בְּשֵׁם רִבִּי יוֹסֵי בַּר חֲנִינָה. מַה פְלִיגִין. בְּמְחַמֵּץ כְּמֵימָיו. אֲבָל הַמְחַמֵּץ בְּגוּפוֹ דִּבְרֵי הַכֹּל מוּתָּר. רִבִּי יוֹסֵי כְּדַעְתֵּיהּ. כְּמָה דוּ אָמַר תַּמָּן. אֵין חִימוּצוֹ בָרוּר. כֵּן הוּא אָמַר הָכָא. אֵין תַּבְשִׁילוֹ תַבְשִׁיל בָּרוּר.

2 מתני' | ח או' מותר בר | תח בן   3 מה פליגין | ח מפליגין דברי הכל | ת -   ר' יוסי כדעתיה | ת -   4 כמה | ח -   דו | ת דר' יוסי   חימוצו | חפ תבשילו תבשיל   ברור | תח חימוץ ברור   תבשילו תבשיל | ח חימוצו חימוץ חימוצו פ חמוצ חמץ

Mishnah: "One may not put an egg next to the hot water container," etc. There[67], we have stated: "If a mashed apple is added to dough which soured, [the dough] is forbidden[68]." [69]It was stated: Rebbi Yose permits it. Rebbi Aha, Rebbi Abbahu in the name of Rebbi Yose ben Ḥanina: They disagree when it becomes sour from the juice [of the apple]. But if it becomes sour from its solid substance it is permitted. Rebbi Yose follows his own opinion. Just as he says there, its souring is not clearly souring, so he says here, its cooking is not clearly cooking[70].

67   Mishnah *Terumot* 10:2.

68   If a heave apple was mixed into profane dough, the mixture is forbidden to lay persons and impure Cohanim.

69   The text also is in *Terumot* 10:2 (ת)

Notes 15-19, *Hallah* 1:1 (ח) Note 21, *Pesaḥim* 2:4 (29b line 22), פ.

70   Apple juice is not a commonly used agent for souring; similarly the sun is not commonly used to fry eggs.

(5d line 72) תַּנָּא. אָמַר רִבִּי יוֹחָנָן בַּר מַרְיָיא. בְּשֶׁלֹּא הֶעֱבִיר יָדוֹ מִמֶּנּוּ. אֲבָל אִם הֶעֱבִיר אָסוּר. פַּגָּה שֶׁטְּמָנָהּ בְּתֶבֶן וַחֲרָרָה שֶׁטְּמָנָהּ בִּגְחָלִים. אִם הָיוּ מִקְצָתָן מְגוּלִּין נִיטָּלִין בַּשַּׁבָּת. וְאִם לָאו אֵין נִיטָּלִין. רִבִּי לְעָזָר בֶּן תַּדַּאי אוֹמֵר. בֵּין כָּךְ וּבֵין כָּךְ תּוֹחֵב בְּשַׁפּוּד וּבְסַכִּין וְנוֹטֵל. אַתְיָיא דְּרִבִּי לְעָזָר בֶּן תַּדַּאי כְּרִבִּי שִׁמְעוֹן. דְּתַנֵּי. לֹא יִגְרַר אָדָם אֶת הַמִּיטָה וְאֶת הַכִּסֵּא וְאֶת הַסַּפְסָל וְאֶת הַקַּתֶּידְרָה מִפְּנֵי שֶׁהוּא עוֹשֶׂה חָרִיץ. וְרִבִּי שִׁמְעוֹן מַתִּיר.

2 בתבן | כ בטבל   3 ניטלין | כ ניטלין בשבת ובסכין | כ או בסכין ונטל | כ ונטלן אתייא | כ אתיא   4 את המיטה ואת הכסא ואת הספסל | כ את הכסא ואת המיטה

רִבִּי בָּא בְשֵׁם רִבִּי חוּנָא רִבִּי חַגַּיי בְשֵׁם רִבִּי זְעִירָא רִבִּי יוֹסֵי בְשֵׁם רִבִּי אִילָא. מוֹדִין חֲכָמִים לְרִבִּי שִׁמְעוֹן בְּכִסֵּא שֶׁרַגְלָיו מְשׁוּקָּעוֹת בַּטִּיט שֶׁמּוּתָּר לְטַלְטְלוֹ. כְּמָא דְאַתְּ אָמַר. מוּתָּר לְטַלְטְלוֹ. וְדִכְוָותָהּ. מוּתָּר לְהַחֲזִירוֹ. אָמַר רִבִּי יוֹסֵי. אַף אֲנָן תַּנֵּינָן. נִיטָּלִין בַּשַּׁבָּת. אָמַר רִבִּי יוֹסֵה בֵּירִבִּי בּוּן. דְּרִבִּי שִׁמְעוֹן הִיא. אָמַר רִבִּי יוֹסֵי. מַתְנִיתָה אָמְרָה כֵן. כָּל־הַכֵּלִים אֵינָן נִגְרָרִין חוּץ מִן הָעֲגָלָה מִפְּנֵי שֶׁהִיא כּוֹבֶשֶׁת:

1 ר' חונא | כ רב חונה חגיי | י חגי זעירה | י זעורה כ זעירא יוסי | י יוסה אילא | כ הילא   2 כמא דאת אמ'. | י - כ וכמה דתימר מותר לטלטלו | י -   3 יוסי | י יוסה אף | כ אוף אמן | כ נן   4 יוסי | כ יוסה

וְהָא תַּנִּינַן. שְׁבִיעִית. שְׁבִיעִית. אִית לָךְ מֵימַר. שְׁבִיעִית כְּרִבִּי שִׁמְעוֹן. דְּפָתַר לָהּ שְׁבִיעִית כְּרִבִּי שִׁמְעוֹן. דְּרִבִּי שִׁמְעוֹן מַתִּיר בִּסְפִיחֵי שְׁבִיעִית. וְאַתְּ אָמַר הָכֵין. אַף עַל גַּב דְּרִבִּי שִׁמְעוֹן מַתִּיר בִּסְפִיחֵי שְׁבִיעִית אִית לֵיהּ מִשּׁוּם שְׁבִיעִית וּמִשּׁוּם קְדוּשַּׁת שְׁבִיעִית. וְתַנִּינָן עַל דְּרִבִּי שִׁמְעוֹן. טְהָרוֹ מִלְּטַמֵּא אֵינוֹ חוֹשֵׁשׁ לֹא מִשּׁוּם שְׁבִיעִית וְלֹא מִשּׁוּם קְדוּשַּׁת שְׁבִיעִית.

1 כר' | כ דר'   דפתר | כ פתר כר' | כ דר'   2 ואת | כ והכא   הכין | כ הכן   3 שביעית ומשום   ותנינן על דר' שמעון. | כ -   4 טהרו מלטמא | כ אוף הכא

It was stated: Rebbi Joḥanan ben Rebbi Marius said, if he did not remove his hand from it. But if he removed it it is forbidden[58].

[71]An unripe fig which he hid in straw or a flat pita which he hid in coals may be taken on the Sabbath if they were partially uncovered, otherwise they may not be taken[72]. Rebbi Eleazar ben Thaddeus said, in any case he can stick in a spit or a knife and take it[73]. This [statement] of Rebbi Eleazar ben Thaddeus follows Rebbi Simeon, as we have stated[74]: "A person may not drag a bed, or a chair, or a footstool[75], or a fauteuil[75a], because he makes a groove, but Rebbi Simeon permits."

[76]Rebbi Abba in the name of Rebbi Ḥuna, Rebbi Ḥaggai in the name of Rebbi Ze'ira, Rebbi Yose in the name of Rebbi Ila: The Sages admit to Rebbi Simeon that a chair whose legs are stuck in mud one is permitted to move on the Sabbath[77]. Since you are saying, it is permitted to move it, similarly it is permitted to return it. Rebbi Yose said, we also have stated[78]: "and they may be removed on the Sabbath." Rebbi Yose ben Rebbi Abun said, this is Rebbi

Simeon's. Rebbi Yose said, a Mishnah says so, "one may not drag any implement except a carriage because it presses[79]."

But we have stated[80]: "The Sabbatical year!" Can you say that "the Sabbatical year" follows Rebbi Simeon[81]? He explains "the Sabbatical year" following Rebbi Simeon since Rebbi Simeon permits the aftergrowth of the Sabbatical year[82], and here you say so? Even though Rebbi Simeon permits aftergrowth of the Sabbatical year, he still holds it subject to the Sabbatical year and the holiness of the Sabbatical year[83]. Also we have stated for Rebbi Simeon who declares it pure so it cannot become impure[84], he worries neither about the Sabbatical year nor about the holiness of the Sabbatical year!

71 This paragraph and most of the next are also in *Kilaim* 1:9 (Notes 167-178). The *baraita* is quoted in Babli *Šabbat* 123a, *Eruvin* 77a.

72 The figs had been covered in straw to hasten the ripening process. By this the owner shows that he does not consider them ready for eating; they are not prepared food for the Sabbath. But if they are partially uncovered they are counted as food. It must be assumed that the coals in which the pita was roasted are now cold; there is no problem of making fire and in moving them.

73 In this case he only moves the food; if the cover (straw or cold coals) is also moved this is incidental and not the goal of his action; it is not forbidden for R. Simeon. But if he would use his hands to take the completely covered food it would have to be his intention to remove the cover first; this is forbidden according to all opinions.

74 In the Babli version (22a, 29b, 46a, *Pesahim* 101a, *Menahot* 41b; Tosephta *Yom Tov* 2:18) only R. Simeon's opinion is quoted.

75 Latin *subsellium*.

75a Greek καθέδρα, ἡ.

76 This paragraph also is in *Besah* 2:9 (61d line 22) (ייי).

77 Since the mud is soft, the groove will disappear by itself; it was not "made".

78 Mishnah *Kilaim* 1:9 referring to turnips and radishes partially hidden.

79 Mishnah *Besah* 2:10. The wheels of the carriage will press the dust down, not move it sideways as would be the case if one drags anything without wheels. The Sages opposing R. Simeon forbid moving the "unprepared" dust even if this was not the intention of the person acting. This Mishnah cannot follow R. Simeon; it contradicts the Mishnah in *Kilaim*.

80 Mishnah *Kilaim* 1:9 declares that harvested produce from the preceding year which was stored in the ground does not become subject to the laws of the Sabbatical.

81 The position of R. Simeon in *Šabbat* is irrelevant for the Sabbatical.

82 This part of the Mishnah still follows R. Simeon but for a different reason. The note "and here you say so?" has to be moved to the end of the next sentence.

83 Even though R. Simeon permits

aftergrowth (except cabbage, Mishnah *Ševi'it* 9:1), spontaneous growth from stray seeds, to be harvested he still requires it to be consumed by humans or animals, not to be used for industrial production.

84 Even though R. Simeon considers last year's produce stored in the earth as produce, not as food, and therefore not susceptible to impurity, it still is last year's produce and may be used for purposes other than food.

(6a line 13) תַּמָּן אָמְרִין. חַמָּה מוּתֶּרֶת. תּוֹלְדַת חַמָּה אֲסוּרָה. רַבָּנָן דְּהָכָא אָמְרִין. בֵּין חַמָּה בֵּין תּוֹלְדַת חַמָּה מוּתֶּרֶת. מַתְנִיתִין פְּלִיגָא עַל רַבָּנִין דְּהָכָא. לֹא יַטְמְנֶנָּה בָּחוֹל וּבַאֲבַק דְּרָכִים בִּשְׁבִיל שֶׁתִּצָּלֶה: שַׁנְיָיא הִיא. שֶׁהוּא עוֹשֶׂה חָרִיץ. אִילוּ אָמַר. בְּקֶמַח. יָאוּת. מַתְנִיתָא פְּלִיגָא עַל רַבָּנִין דְּתַמָּן. דְּתַנֵּי. רַבָּן שִׁמְעוֹן בֶּן גַּמְלִיאֵל אוֹמֵר. מְגַלְגְּלִין בֵּיצִים עַל גַּב גַּג שֶׁלְּסִיד רוֹתֵחַ וְאֵין מְגַלְגְּלִין בֵּיצִים עַל גַּבֵּי עָפָר רוֹתֵחַ. מָה עָבְדִין לָהּ רַבָּנָן דְּתַמָּן. פָּתְרִין לָהּ. חֲלוּקִין עַל רַבָּן שִׁמְעוֹן בֶּן גַּמְלִיאֵל. עַל דַּעְתִּין דְּרַבָּנִין דְּתַמָּן. מַעֲשֶׂה שֶׁעָשׂוּ אַנְשֵׁי טִיבֶּרְיָא. וְעַל דַּעְתִּין דְּרַבָּנִין דְּהָכָא. סָלְקַת מַתְנִיתָא. כְּמַעֲשֶׂה שֶׁעָשׂוּ אַנְשֵׁי טִיבֶּרְיָא.

There[85], they say, the sun is permitted, a derivative of the sun is forbidden[86]. The rabbis here say, both the sun and derivatives of the sun are permitted. Our Mishnah disagrees with the rabbis here: "One should not bury it in dust of roads that it should be roasted." There is a difference, because he makes a groove[87]. If it had said "flour" it would have been correct.[88] A *baraita* disagrees with the rabbis there, as it was stated[89]: "Rabban Simeon ben Gamliel says, one soft-boils eggs on a boiling hot whitewashed roof but one does not soft-boil eggs in boiling hot dust." What do the rabbis there do with this? They explain that they disagree with Rabban Simeon ben Gamliel[90]. In the opinion of the rabbis there, "what the people of Tiberias did.[91]" In the opinion of the rabbis here the Mishnah was finished[92]. "As to what the people of Tiberias did."

85 In Babylonia.
86 One may boil an egg by exposing it to direct sunlight; one may not heat a towel in direct sunlight and then wrap it around an egg outside of direct sunlight.

In the Babli 39a states that the prohibition of derivatives of sunlight is a disagreement between Tannaim but in practice the statement about the rabbis there is confirmed.

87 The prohibition is not against the use of sunlight asa source of heat but the problem of moving dust and creating a permanent depression in the ground.
88 A flat pita could be baked in the sun without creating a groove.
89 Babli 39a; Tosephta 2:22 (ed. Liebermann), 2:12 (ed. Zuckermandel).

90 In the Babli, the Tosephta is explained in parallel to the Mishnah; dust is forbidden not because it was heated in the sum but because it may not be moved.

91 They seem to think that the hot water did not come from the hot springs of Tiberias but was heated in the sun.

92 This translation follows S. Liebermann. Mishnah 4 is separate from Mishnah 3 and treats a different subject, not connected with the problem of cooking by means of the heat of the sun.

(6a line 23) מתני'. מַעֲשֶׂה שֶׁעָשׂוּ אַנְשֵׁי טִיבֶּרְיָא כול'. בָּרִאשׁוֹנָה הָיוּ סוֹתְמִין אֶת הַקָּמִין מֵעֶרֶב שַׁבָּת וְנִכְנָסִין וְרוֹחֲצִין בַּשַּׁבָּת. נֶחְשְׁדוּ לִהְיוֹת מְמַלִּין אוֹתוֹ עֵצִים מֵעֶרֶב שַׁבָּת וְהִיא דְלֵיקָה וְהוֹלֶכֶת בַּשַּׁבָּת. וְאָסְרוּ לָהֶן רְחִיצָה וְהִתִּירוּ לָהֶן זִיעָה. נֶחְשְׁדוּ לִהְיוֹת נִכְנָסִין וְרוֹחֲצִין. וְאוֹמְרִים. מַזִּיעִין הָיִינוּ. וְאָסְרוּ לָהֶן רְחִיצָה וְזִיעָה. הָיוּ שָׁם שְׁתֵּי אַמְבַּטְיוֹת. אַחַת שֶׁלְּמְתוּקִין וְאַחַת שֶׁלַּמְלוּחִין. נֶחְשְׁדוּ לִהְיוֹת מְגַלִּין אֶת הַנְּסָרִין וְרוֹחֲצִין בַּמְּתוּקִין. וְהֵן אוֹמְרִים. בַּמְּלוּחִין רָחַצְנוּ. וְאָסְרוּ לָהֶן אֶת הַכֹּל. כֵּיוָן שֶׁנִּתְגַּדְּרוּ הָיוּ מַתִּירִין לָהֶן וְהוֹלְכִין מַתִּירִין לָהֶן וְהוֹלְכִין עַד שֶׁהִתִּירוּ לָהֶן מֵי מְעָרָה וְחַמֵּי טִיבֶּרְיָא. וְלֹא הִתִּירוּ הֲבָאַת לוּנְטִיוֹת. רִבִּי חֲנִינָה בֶּן עֲקַבְיָה. דְּתַנֵּי. שְׁלֹשָׁה דְּבָרִים הִתִּיר רִבִּי חֲנִינָה בֶּן עֲקַבְיָה. מַתִּיר עֵצָה שֶׁבַּיָּם וְהִתִּיר כְּצוֹצְרָה וְהִתִּיר הֲבָאַת לוּנְטִיוֹת.

Mishnah: "What the people of Tiberias did," etc. [93]Originally they closed the conduit[94] on Friday and they entered[95] and bathed on the Sabbath. They were suspected of filling it with wood on Friday so it would burn continuously on the Sabbath; they forbade them bathing and permitted sweating. They were suspected of coming and bathing but saying "we were sweating." They forbade bathing and sweating to them. If there were there two basins, one of sweet water[96] and one of salt water. They were suspected of uncovering the planks and bathing in sweet water but saying, "we did bathe in salt water;"[97] they forbade them everything. When they were fenced in[98] they continuously permitted them more until they permitted them water in a cave[99] and the hot springs of Tiberias, but they did not permit bringing towels[100]. Who permitted the bringing of linen cloths? Rebbi Ḥanina ben Aqabia, as it was stated[101]: Rebbi Ḥanina ben Aqabia permitted three things. He permitted seaweed[102], he permitted the balcony[103], and he permitted bringing linen cloths.

93 A different version is in the Babli, 40a, as *baraita* in the name of Bar Qappara.

94 Greek καμῖνος, ὁ.

95 The bathhouse.

96 Lukewarm water, result of heating. It seems that "salt water" does not mean sea water but cold water, possibly from Lake Genezareth.

97 Here starts another Genizah fragment edited by Ginsberg (pp. 76-79).

98 The people of Tiberias observed all rabbinic "fences around the law."

99 Where there is no danger that it should have been heated artificially on the Sabbath.
100 Latin *linteum;* linen bath towel.
101 The statement appears three times in the Yerushalmi, here, and *Eruvin* 8 (Note 115), *Sukkah* 1:9 (52c line 32); in the Babli *Eruvin* 87a.
102 In the Babli: עֵצָה "wood branches, splinters". Even though seaweed is naturally wet it is not prepared for impurity (Chapter 1, Note 316) and may be used as insulating material to keep food warm for the Sabbath.
103 If a house is built on a lake shore (or sea shore) and a balcony extends over the water, if the floor of the balcony has an opening through which a pail can be lowered into the water he permits to draw water through the opening on the Sabbath even though there is little likelihood that the water drops drawn were below the balcony at the beginning of the Sabbath.

(6a line 35) תַּמָּן תַּנִּינָן. הָרוֹחֵץ בְּמְעָרָה וּבְמֵי טִיבֶּרְיָא מִסְתַּפֵּג אֲפִילוּ בְעֶשֶׂר לוּנְטִיוֹת וְלֹא יְבִיאֵם בְּיָדוֹ. שְׁמוּאֵל אָמַר. מַה יַּעֲבִיד הָדֵין סְבוּרָה דְלָא יָלִיף וְלָא שִׁימֵּשׁ. וְהָדָא מַתְנִיתָא קוֹדָם עַד שֶׁלֹא הִתִּירוּ הֲבָאַת לוּנְטִיוֹת. רִבִּי יִרְמְיָה וְרִבִּי זְעִירָה רַב יְהוּדָה בְשֵׁם שְׁמוּאֵל. רִבִּי הִתִּיר לוּנְטִיאוֹת. תַּנֵּי. אֵין מִשְׁתַּטְּפִין לֹא בְחַמִּין וְלֹא בַצּוֹנִין. אָמַר רִבִּי יוּדָה בַּר פָּזִי. וְדָא מַתְנִיתָא קוֹדֶם עַד שֶׁלֹא הִתִּירוּ חֲכָמִים חַמֵּי טִיבֶּרְיָא. דְּתָנֵי. הָרוֹחֵץ בְּחַמֵּי טִיבֶּרְיָא הוּא מְזַלֵּף עַל עַצְמוֹ. אֲבָל אֲחֵרִים לֹא יְזַלְּפוּ לוֹ. רִבִּי שִׁמְעוֹן בֶּן מְנַסְיָא אוֹמֵר. אַף הוּא לֹא יְזַלֵּף עַל עַצְמוֹ. מִפְּנֵי שֶׁהוּא מְרַבֶּה אֶת הַהֶבֶל וּמְכַבֵּד אֶת הַקַּרְקַע.

1 וּבְמֵי טִיבְרִיָּא G | אוֹ בְּמֵי טבריה 2 הדין G | הדן סבורא G | סבורה והדא G | והדה מתניתא G | מתניתה 4 לונטיאות G | הבאת לונטיות משתטפין G | מישתטפין ודא מתניתא G | ודה מתניתה 5 עד | - G | חכמ׳ - G | טיברייא G | טבריה בחמי G | במערה בחמי טיברייא G | טבריה 6 מנסא G | מנסייה

רִבִּי אָחָא בַּר יִצְחָק עָאַל מִיסְחֵי עִם בָּא בַּר מָמָל בְּטַרִיס בַּר יְטַסַס. חָמָא חַד בַּר נַשׁ מַזְלִיף עַל גַּרְמֵיהּ. אֲמַר לֵיהּ. כָּזֶה אָסוּר בַּשַּׁבָּת מִפְּנֵי שֶׁהוּא מְרַבֶּה אֶת הַהֶבֶל וּמְכַבֵּד אֶת הַקַּרְקַע. רִבִּי אַבָּהוּ. חוֹרְנֵי מְזַלְּפִין וּנְפַל עֲלוֹי. וְהָא. וְהוּא אָמַר. רִבִּי לְוָנְטִי עָאַל מִיסְחֵי עִם רִבִּי יוֹנָה. חָמָא חַד בַּר נַשׁ מַזְלִיף עַל גַּרְמֵיהּ. אֲמַר לֵיהּ. לֵית אֲנַן צְרִיכִין חָשְׁשִׁין לִיחִידָיָּא.

1 עאל G | על בר יסטסס G | .. כריטה חמא G | חמה מזליף G | מזליף 3 אבהו G | אבהוא ונפל G | ונפיל והא G | וָה חמא G | חמה 4 מזליף G | מזלף ליחידייא G | ליחידיא

רִבִּי יִצְחָק רוֹבָא עָאַל מִיסְחֵי עִם רִבִּי. אֲמַר לֵיהּ. מָהוּ מִיתֵּן צְלוֹחִיתָא גּוֹא עֲגַלְתָּא. אֲמַר לֵיהּ. הָכָא גּוֹ נָטְלָא הִיא נַעֲשֵׂית כִּכְלִי שֵׁנִי.

1 מהו G | מהוא 2 הכא G | הבה

There, we have stated[104]: "If somebody bathes in a cave or in the waters of Tiberias he may dry himself even with ten linen towels[105] but may not bring them in his hand." Samuel said, what should an opinionated person do who never studied and never served[106]? This Mishnah was before they permitted to bring linen towels. Rebbi Jeremiah and Rebbi Ze`ira[107], Rav Jehudah in the name of Samuel: Rebbi permitted linen towels. It was stated: One takes a shower neither with hot water nor with cold water[108]. Rebbi Jehudah bar Pazi said, this *baraita* was before the Sages permitted the hot springs of Tiberias[109], as it was stated: One who bathes in the hot springs of Tiberias may sprinkle on himself, but others may not sprinkle on him. Rebbi Simeon ben Menassia said, he may not even sprinkle on himself since he increases vapor and sweeps the floor.

Rebbi Aḥa bar Isaac went bathing with Abba bar Mamal at the Three Graces[110]. He saw a man sprinkling on himself. He told him, in this way it is forbidden on the Sabbath since he increases vapor and sweeps the floor[111]. Rebbi Abbahu said, others were sprinkling and it fell on him[112]. He answered, but Rebbi Levontin went bathing with Rebbi Jonah[113]. He saw a man sprinkling on himself. He told him, we do not have to be concerned about an isolated opinion[114].

The Elder Rebbi Isaac[115] went bathing with Rebbi. He asked him, may one put a flask in the circle[116]? He told him, put it in the draw-pot[117] and it becomes a secondary vessel.

---

104 Mishnah 22:8.

105 It is forbidden to wring out water from a washcloth on the Sabbath. It also is forbidden to carry a washcloth from one's house to the thermal bath through the public domain. The Mishnah seems to forbid even to bring a washcloth from the anteroom where people undress to the actual bath basin. If one is not afraid the person may actually wring out the water, why may he not bring his washcloth into the room where the bath is?

106 Only a person inexperienced in talmudic discussion could ask such a question; cf. *Peah* 2:6 Notes 116-120.

107 One would have expected "R. Jeremiah, R. Ze`ira, Rav Jehudah in the name" but not student (R. Jeremiah) and teacher (R. Ze`ira) coordinated in the statement.

108 On the Sabbath. Tosephta 3:4 (ed. Liebermann), in the name of R. Meïr; Babli 39b.

109 While one may not heat water on the Sabbath, taking a shower in hot springs is permitted even if sprinkling the hot water on one's body may induce sweating.

110 This is Liebermann's reading, Τρεῖς Χάριτες as a geographic name (?). *Arukh* reads the first word as טירם (s. v. טר) and explains as Latin *thermae*.

111 He decides practice following R. Simeon ben Menassia.

112 He follows the anonymous majority against R. Simeon ben Menassia.

113 The final decision made by an Amora of the last generation.

114 R. Simeon ben Menassia's is an isolated opinion which cannot be followed.

115 In the Babli, R. Isaac bar Eudaimon.

116 If one visits the natural thermal bath on the Sabbath, may one take a flask of oil, and put it in the center near the hot spring's spout to warm it?

117 There will be no problem if one scoops up the hot water in a vessel and then puts the flask of oil into that vessel. "Cooking" in the sense of the laws of the Sabbath occurs only in a primary vessel, one where heat flows from an outside source into it. A secondary vessel is one where heat flows out of it into the cooler surroundings; a secondary vessel never cooks in this sense. Babli 40b.

(6a line 51) רִבִּי יַעֲקֹב בַּר אִידִי בְשֵׁם רִבִּי יְהוֹשֻׁעַ בֶּן לֵוִי. שׁוֹאֲלִין הִילְכוֹת הַמֶּרְחָץ בְּבֵית הַמֶּרְחָץ וְהִילְכוֹת בֵּית הַכִּסֵּא בְּבֵית הַכִּסֵּא. כְּהָדָא רִבִּי שִׁמְעוֹן בֶּן אֶלְעָזָר עָאַל מִיסְחֵי עִם רִבִּי מֵאִיר. אָמַר לֵיהּ. מַהוּ לְקַנֵּחַ. אָמַר לֵיהּ. אָסוּר. מַהוּ לְהָדִיחַ. אָמַר לֵיהּ. אָסוּר. וְלֹא כֵן שְׁמוּאֵל שָׁאֵיל לְרַב. מַהוּ לַעֲנוֹת אָמֵן בְּמָקוֹם מְטוּנָּף. וְהוּא אָמַר. אָסוּר. וְאָסוּר דְּאָמְרִית לָךְ אָסוּר. אַשְׁכַּח תָּנָא תַנֵּי. אֵין שׁוֹאֲלִין הִילְכוֹת הַמֶּרְחָץ בַּמֶּרְחָץ וְהִילְכוֹת הַכִּסֵּא בְּבֵית הַכִּסֵּא.

1 אידי G | אדי   2 והילכות | ע הילכות כהדא G | כהדה עאל | ע לעזר עאל G | ע לעזור אלעזר   3 לקמח | ע שנדיח אסור | G אסיר   להדיח | ע שנקניח ולא כן | G לאכן   4 מהו | G מהוא והוא אמ' | ע אמ' ליה אסור. ואסור | G ע אסיר ואסיר   5 תנא | G | - אין | ע | -G.

[118]Rebbi Jacob bar Idi in the name of Rebbi Joshua ben Levi: One may ask about practice of the bath in the bathhouse and the practice of the toilet in the toilet. As the following: Rebbi Simeon ben Eleazar went bathing with Rebbi Meïr. He asked him, how about drying oneself with a towel? He told him, it is forbidden. How about rinsing? He told him, it is forbidden. But did not Samuel ask Rav, may one say Amen at a dirty place[119]? He told him: it is forbidden and it is forbidden for me to tell you it is forbidden. There was found a Tanna who stated: One does (not)[120] ask about practice of the bath in the bathhouse and the practice of the toilet in the toilet.

118 This paragraph is also in *Avodah Zarah* 3:4, Notes 116-120 (ע). As a matter of principle it is forbidden to talk about holy matters at places where people are naked, as in the bathhouse, or which smell badly, as in an outhouse. The question is whether one may ask for urgently needed answers to questions at such a place. The question arises here because it is reported in the previous paragraph that Rebbi (and in this paragraph R. Meïr) answered a question in the hot springs of Tiberias when naked on the Sabbath.

119 He asked at such a place of bad smell.

120 Of our three sources, two do not have this word; their text is quoted by Nahmanides and his student Rashba in their *Novellae* to Babli 40b. But since the quote comes in support of Rav who forbids, as against prior testimony of Rebbi, R. Meïr, and R. Joshua ben Levi who permit, probably the Leiden text is correct, the word should not be deleted, but practice has to follow Rebbi's group; Babli 40b.

(6a line 57) אִם בְּיוֹם טוֹב כְּחַמִּין שֶׁהוּחַמּוּ בְּיוֹם טוֹב כול'. חַמִּין שֶׁהוּחַמּוּ בְּיוֹם טוֹב וְכֵן חַמִּין שֶׁהוּחַמּוּ מֵעֶרֶב שַׁבָּת לַשַּׁבָּת. רַב וּשְׁמוּאֵל. חַד אָמַר. מַרְחִיץ בָּהֶן פָּנָיו יָדָיו וְרַגְלָיו. וְחָרָנָה אָמַר. מַרְחִיץ בָּהֶן כָּל־גּוּפוֹ אֵיבָרִים אֵיבָרִים. וְלָא יָדְעִין מָאן אָמַר דָּא וּמָאן אָמַר דָּא. מִן מַה דְּתָנֵי שְׁמוּאֵל. מַרְחִיץ בָּהֶן פָּנָיו יָדָיו וְרַגְלָיו. הֲוֵי רַב דּוּ אָמַר. מַרְחִיץ בָּהֶן כָּל־גּוּפוֹ אֵיבָרִים אֵיבָרִים.

1 חמין { י המים 2 בהן | G בהם וחרנה | י וחורנה 3 כל | י - איברים | G איברים אברים (2) מאן | G מו (2) 4 כל | י - איברים | G אברין (2)

חַד פִּילוֹסוֹפְיוֹס שָׁאַל לְבַר קַפָּרָא. אַבְלָט שָׁאַל לְלֵוִי סָרִיסָא. מוּתָּר לִשְׁתּוֹת וְאָסוּר לִרְחוֹץ. אָמַר לֵיהּ. אִם תִּרְאֶה סָרִיס מְחַבֵּק עִם אִשְׁתָּךְ שֶׁמָּא אֵין רַע לָךְ. אָמַר לֵיהּ אִין. וּמָכֵי הוּא לָהּ כְּלוּם. אָמַר לֵיהּ. שֶׁלֹּא תִתְפָּרֵץ. אָמַר לֵיהּ. וְהָכָא שֶׁלֹּא יִתְפָּרְצוּ. כֵּיוָן שֶׁיָּצָא אָמְרוּ לוֹ תַּלְמִידָיו. רַבִּי. לָזֶה דְחִיתָהּ בְּקָנֶה. לָנוּ מָה אַתְּ מֵשִׁיב. אָמַר לוֹ. וַהֲלֹא כְּבָר נֶאֱמַר אַךְ אֲשֶׁר יֵאָכֵל לְכָל־נֶפֶשׁ הוּא לְבַדּוֹ יֵעָשֶׂה לָכֶם:

1 פילוסופיוס | G י פילוסופוס שאל | G שאיל (2) 2 מחבק | G מחביק י מתחבק אין | G אינו 3 לה | י לד תתפרץ | G תיתפרץ 4 לו | י להן The remainder of the paragraph is missing in G.

[121]"If it is on a holiday it is like water heated on the holiday," etc. Hot water heated on a holiday and similarly hot water heated on Friday for the Sabbath, Rav and Samuel, one said, one uses it to wash his face, hands, and feet, while the other said, one uses it to wash his entire[122] body limb by limb. We did not know who said what but since Samuel stated, one uses it to wash his face, hands, and feet, it follows that it was Rav who said, one uses it to wash his entire body limb by limb.

A philosopher asked Bar Qappara; Ablat asked Levi the eunuch[123]: Is it[124] permitted for drinking but forbidden for taking a bath? He told him, if you saw an eunuch embracing your wife, would you not feel badly about it? He said, yes. He asked him, can he squeeze her[125] in any way? He said, that she should not get loose morals. He told him, here also that they should not get loose morals[126]. After he left, his students told him, this one you pushed away with a stick; what do you answer us? He said to (him) [them][127]: Is there not already written[128] *only what is being eaten by everybody, this alone may be made by you.*

121 These paragraphs also are in *Besah* 2:5 (61c line 32) (י). Babli 40a.
122 In *Besah* 2:5, the expression "entire" is missing. Since *Ex.* 12:16 permits to prepare on a holiday what is eaten by everybody, and heating water for bathing is derived from the permission to heat water for consumption, he does not permit the use of a bathtub since the poor do not have bathtubs. Therefore it is necessary to wash each limb separately.
123 If this is not an intended slander then

probably the word is a scribal error for Parisa; cf. *Gittin* 6:7 Note 115.
124 Water heated on the holiday.
125 S. Liebermann thinks that this expression is not obscene but a shortening of מְנַכֶּה "deducts (from her value)".
126 This would imply that the rule is purely rabbinical.
127 The word in brackets is from the text in *Besah*.
128 *Ex.* 12:16.

(6a line 68) מוֹלְיָיר הַגָּרוּף שׁוֹתִין הֵימֶינּוּ בַּשַׁבָּת. הָא אִם אֵינוֹ גָרוּף לֹא. אָמַר רִבִּי שִׁיָין. מִפְּנֵי שֶׁהַגְּחָלִים נוֹגְעוֹת בְּגוּפוֹ. אָמַר רִבִּי חֲנִינָה בְּרֵיהּ דְּרִבִּי הִילֵל. מִפְּנֵי שֶׁהָרוּחַ נִכְנֶסֶת בְּגוּפוֹ וְהַגְּחָלִים בּוֹעֲרוֹת. אָמַר רִבִּי יוֹסִי בֵּירִבִּי בּוּן. מִפְּנֵי שֶׁהוּא עָשׂוּי פְּרָקִים פְּרָקִים וְהוּא מִתְיָירֵא שֶׁמָּא נִתְאַכַּל דִּיבּוּקוֹ וְהוּא מוֹסִיף מַיִם.

1 מולייר G | מוליר   2 הילל G | הלל   3 יוסי G | יוסה מתיירא G | מתירא   4 דיבוקו G | דיבקו

"From a cleaned-out samowar⁹ one drinks on the Sabbath." Therefore not if it was not cleaned out. Rebbi Ashian said, because the coals touch its body¹²⁹. Rebbi Ḥanina the son of Rebbi Hillel said, because the wind enters its body and the coals will burn¹³⁰. Rebbi Yose ben Rebbi Abun said, because it was made in pieces; he is afraid that its glue was weathered away and he adds water¹³¹.

אַנְטִיכִי אַף עַל פִּי שֶׁגְּרוּפָה אֵין שׁוֹתִין מִמֶּנָּה: רִבִּי חֲנַנְיָה רִבִּי יוֹסֵי רִבִּי אָחָא אַבָּא בְּשֵׁם רִבִּי יוֹחָנָן. מִפְּנֵי שֶׁהִיא מִתְחַמֶּמֶת מִכָּתְלֶיהָ. רַבָּנִן דְּקַיְסָרִין רַב הוּנָא בְּשֵׁם רַב. אִם הָיְתָה גְרוּפָה וּפְתוּחָה מוּתָּר.

1 חנניה G | חנניא יוסי G | יסא   2 מכתליה G | מיכתליה דקיסרין G | דקסרין הונא G | חונא

"From an Antiochean vessel¹⁰ one does not drink even if it is cleaned out." Rebbi Ḥananiah, Rebbi Yasa¹³², Rebbi Aḥa Abba in the name of Rebbi Johanan, because it is heated from its walls¹³³. The rabbis of Caesarea, Rav Huna in the name of Rav: If it was cleaned out and open it is permitted¹³⁴.

129 As explained in Note 10, the coals are filled into the double bottom of the vessel.
130 If there are air vents in opposite direction at the bottom, the coals will always burn.
131 Cf. Chapter 1, Note 365.
132 Following G for reasons of chronology.
133 Which makes it a primary vessel (Note 117) in which heating is a biblical prohibition.
134 The Babli disagrees, 41b.

(6a line 76) מתני'. מֵיחַם שֶׁפִּינָהוּ לֹא יִתֵּן לְתוֹכוֹ צוֹנִין כול'. רִבִּי בָּא בַּר בְּרֵיהּ דְּרִבִּי חִייָה בַּר בָּא. רִבִּי חִייָא בְּשֵׁם רִבִּי יוֹחָנָן. לֹא שָׁנוּ אֶלָּא לְתוֹךְ הַכּוֹס. הָא לְתוֹכוֹ לֹא. אָמַר רִבִּי מָנָא.

קַשְׁיִיתָהּ קוֹמֵי רִבִּי בָּא. לֹא תָנֵי רִבִּי יוֹחָנָן עַל סוֹפָא לֹא תָנֵי עַל רֵישָׁא. בִּשְׁבִיל שֶׁיֵּיחַמּוּ. הָא לְהַפְשִׁירָן לֹא. אָתָא רִבִּי בָּא בַּר בַּר כַּהֲנָא רִבִּי חִיָּיא בַּר אַשִׁי בְשֵׁם רִבִּי. אִם לְחַמְּמָן אָסוּר. אִם לְהַפְשִׁירָן מוּתָּר.

1 ר' בא | G רבא בר | G - | 2 חייא | G חייה   3 ר' בא | G ר' בא בריה דר' חייה בר בא   סופה | G סופא
רישא | G רישה שייחמו | G שיחמו   4 אתא | G אתה חייא | G חייה ר' | G רב   אם לחממן | G רב לחוסמן | G לחוסמן

תָּנֵי. נוֹתְנִין חַמִּין לְתוֹךְ צוֹנִין אֲבָל לֹא צוֹנִין לְתוֹךְ חַמִּין. כְּדִבְרֵי בֵית שַׁמַּי. וּבֵית הִלֵּל אוֹמְרִים. בֵּין חַמִּין לְתוֹךְ צוֹנִין בֵּין צוֹנִין לְתוֹךְ חַמִּין מוּתָּר. בַּמֶּה דְבָרִים אֲמוּרִין. בְּכוֹס. אֲבָל בְּאַמְבַּטִי חַמִּין לְתוֹךְ צוֹנִין מוּתָּר וְצוֹנִין לְתוֹךְ חַמִּין אָסוּר. וְרִבִּי שִׁמְעוֹן מַתִּיר. אָתְיָא דְּרַב כְּרִבִּי שִׁמְעוֹן בֶּן מְנַסְיָא וְרִבִּי יוֹחָנָן כְּרִבִּי יוֹחָנָן בֶּן נוּרִי. תָּנֵי. רִבִּי יוֹחָנָן בֶּן נוּרִי אוֹסֵר. מְמַלֵּא הוּא אָדָם חָבִית שֶׁלְּקַמִּים וְנוֹתְנָהּ כְּנֶגֶד הַמְדוּרָה. לֹא בִשְׁבִיל שֶׁתִּיחַם אֶלָּא בִשְׁבִיל שֶׁתָּפִיג צִינָתָהּ. יוֹרְדֵהוּא אָדָם וְטוֹבֵל בְּצוֹנִין וְעוֹלֶה וּמִתְחַמֵּם כְּנֶגֶד הַמְדוּרָה. דִּבְרֵי רִבִּי מֵאִיר. וַחֲכָמִים אוֹסְרִין. יְאוּת אָמַר רִבִּי מֵאִיר. וּמַה טַעֲמוֹן דְּרַבָּנָן.   יֵיבָא כַּיי דָּמַר רִבִּי זְעִירָא בְשֵׁם רַב יְהוּדָה. מוּתָּר לְהַפְשִׁיר בְּמָקוֹם שֶׁהַיָּד שׁוֹלֶטֶת. וְאָסוּר לְהַפְשִׁיר בְּמָקוֹם שֶׁאֵין הַיָּד שׁוֹלֶטֶת. וַאֲפִילוּ בְּמָקוֹם שֶׁאֵין הַיָּד שׁוֹלֶטֶת עַד אֵיכָן. רִבִּי יוּדָה בַּר פָּזִי רִבִּי סִימוֹן בְּשֵׁם רִבִּי יוֹסֵי בֶּן חֲנִינָה. עַד שֶׁיְּהֵא נוֹתֵן יָדוֹ לְתוֹכוֹ וְהִיא נִכְוֵית.

1 תני | G תנו צונין | G צונים   2 צונין | G צונים במה | G במי   3 באמבטי | G בָּאמְבְּטִיס חמין | G חמים
צונין | G צונים ור' שמעון | G ור' שמעון בן מנסיה   5 שתפיג | G שתפוג   9 איכן | מ היכן | מ בר עד |
מ עד כדי   נותן | מ נתון

Mishnah: "One may not put cold water into a hot water container which was removed[11]," etc. Rebbi Abba the (son of the)[135] son of Rebbi Ḥiyya bar Abba, Rebbi Ḥiyya[136] in the name of Rebbi Joḥanan: they stated this only for a cup, therefore not into itself. Rebbi Mana said, I objected before Rebbi Abba [the son of Rebbi Ḥiyya bar Abba][137]: Rebbi Joḥanan could not have stated this on the first part [of the Mishnah] nor on the second part! "In order to heat it", therefore to make it lukewarm is permitted[138]. There came Rebbi Abba bar Cahana, Rebbi Ḥiyya bar Ashi in the name of (Rebbi) [Rav][139]. If to heat it[140], it is forbidden, if to make it lukewarm it is permitted.

It was stated[141]: "One may add hot water to cold but not cold to hot[142], following the words of the House of Shammai. But the House of Hillel say, whether hot to cold or cold to hot it is permitted. When has this been said? Into a cup[143], but into a bathtub[144] hot to cold is permitted but cold to hot is forbidden, and Rebbi Simeon [ben Menassia][145] permits[146]." Rav comes following Rebbi Simeon ben Menassia and Rebbi Joḥanan following Rebbi Joḥanan ben Nuri. It was stated: "Rebbi Joḥanan ben Nuri forbids." [147]"A person may fill an amphora full of water and put it close to the pyre, not that it become hot but to disperse its coldness. A person may immerse himself in cold water, come out and warm himself next to the pyre, the words of Rebbi Meïr, but the Sages forbid." Rebbi Meïr says it correctly; what is the rabbis' reason? ¹⁴⁸It should come as what Rebbi Ze'ira said in the name of Rav Jehudah: It is permitted to make lukewarm at a place where the hand rules²⁴; it is forbidden to make lukewarm at a place where the hand does not rule. ¹⁴⁹Even how far "where the hand does not rule"? Rebbi Jehudah bar Pazi, Rebbi Simon in the name of Rebbi Yose ben Ḥanina: Up to where he puts his hand and it is burned¹⁵⁰.

135 To be deleted with the text of G.
136 He is R. Hiyya bar Abba.
137 To be added with the text of G.
138 R. Johanan must want to say something which is not explicit in the Mishnah. But the second part of the sentence of the Mishnah says explicitly that one may put cold water into the container to make it lukewarm; the only prohibition is to put in there a small amount of cold water which would become really hot (Babli 41a). The same conclusion can be drawn from the first clause in the sentence.
139 The correct version [in brackets] is from G, against the reading of the Leiden ms. Rav Hiyya bar Ashi was Rav's student.
140 In G: "In order to harden it", turning iron into steel by immersing the hot iron into a cold bath. This is an industrial process biblically forbidden on the Sabbath as "hitting with a hammer" (the expression for

"finishing a production process.")
141 Babli 42a.
142 The House of Shammai hold that the matter which is in a vessel always dominates what is added to it; therefore hot water always will heat, which is forbidden, and cold water always will cool, which is permitted.
143 A small quantity which never could heat so much that it could not be touched.
144 Greek ἐμβατή, ἡ "bath".
145 Added from G; necessary by the following text.
146 In the Babylonian sources: "forbids".
147 Babli 40b, Tosephta 3:5 (ed. Liebermann). The position attributed here to R. Meïr there is anonymous.
148 Cf. Notes 25,26.
149 From here on there exists a parallel in *Ma`serot* 1:6 (Notes 160-179) (**פ**).
150 The Babli is more restrictive.

(6b line 18) הַכֹּל מוֹדִין בִּכְלִי שֵׁינִי שֶׁהוּא מוּתָּר. מַה בֵּין כְּלִי רִאשׁוֹן מַה בֵּין כְּלִי שֵׁינִי. אָמַר רִבִּי יוֹסֵי. כָּאן הַיָּד שׁוֹלֶטֶת וְכָאן אֵין הַיָּד שׁוֹלֶטֶת. אָמַר רִבִּי יוֹנָה. כָּאן וְכָאן אֵין הַיָּד שׁוֹלֶטֶת. אֶלָּא עָשׂוּ הַרְחֵק לִכְלִי רִאשׁוֹן וְלֹא עָשׂוּ הַרְחֵק לִכְלִי שֵׁינִי. (מתני׳. הָאִילְפָּס וְהַקְּדֵירָה שֶׁהֶעֱבִירָן מְרוּתָּחִין כול׳.) אָמַר רִבִּי מָנָא. הָהֵן פִּנְכָּא דְאוֹרְזָא מְסַייֵּעַ לְאַבָּא. הָהֵן פִּנְכָּא דִגְרִיסָא מְסַייֵּעַ לְאַבָּא. דְּאַתְּ מְפַנֵּי לֵיהּ מִן אָתַר לָאָתַר. וְעַד כְּדוֹן הוּא רוֹתֵחַ.

2 יוסי | מ יוסי ביר' בון   כאן | G וכאן | G כן | G וכן   text in parentheses not in G, 4-3   4 החן | מ החין
דאורוא | G דאורזה מ דאדיא   דגריסא | G דגריסה מ דגלוסא   5 לאבא | G לאבה   ועד | מ ועוד

Everybody agrees that a secondary vessel[117] is permitted[150]. What is the difference between a primary and a secondary vessel? Rebbi Yose said, here the hand rules, there the hand does not rule[151]. Rebbi Jonah said, in neither case does the hand rule. But they forced distance for a primary vessel[152]; they did not force distance for a secondary vessel. (Mishnah: "Into a pan[12] or a pot which was taken off the fire boiling," etc.)[153] Rebbi Mana said, a pot of rice supports my father, a pot of groats supports my father[154], for you move them from place to place and they still are boiling hot.

150 A secondary vessel is one not being heated. Since it never cooks, all kitchen activities are permitted for food in such a vessel.
151 Babli 40b.
152 Since a primary vessel may cook in a biblically forbidden way, rabbinically activities which do not qualify as cooking by biblical standards also are forbidden. There is no reason to be restrictive for secondary vessels.
153 This sentence, missing in G, should be moved as headlines to the next paragraph.
154 R. Jonah.

(6b line 24) מַהוּ לִיתֵּן תַּבְלִין מִלְּמַטָּה וְלַעֲרוֹת עֲלֵיהֶן מִלְמַעְלָה. רִבִּי יוֹנָה אָמַר. אָסוּר. וְעִירוּיוֹ כִּכְלִי רִאשׁוֹן הוּא. חֵיילֵיהּ דְּרִבִּי יוֹנָה מִן הָדָא. אֶחָד שֶׁבִּישֵּׁל בּוֹ וְאֶחָד שֶׁעֵירָה לְתוֹכוֹ רוֹתֵחַ. אָמַר רִבִּי יוֹסֵי. תַּמָּן כְּלִי חֶרֶס בּוֹלֵעַ. תַּבְלִין אֵינָן מִתְבַּשְּׁלִין. הָתִיב רִבִּי יוֹסֵי בֵּירִבִּי בּוּן. וְהָתַנֵּי אַף בִּכְלֵי נְחוֹשֶׁת כֵּן. אִית לָךְ לְמֵימַר. כְּלִי נְחוֹשֶׁת בּוֹלֵעַ.

1 מלמטה | מ מלמטן מלמעלה | Gמ מלמעלן ועירויו | G וערוי   2 רותח | מ רותח. וכא הוא אמ' הָכֵין   3 יוסי | G יוסה (2)   4 לך | מ -   למימר | Gמ מימר

מַהוּ לַעֲרוֹת מִן הַקִּילּוּחַ. אָמַר רִבִּי חֲנַנְיָה בְּרֵיהּ דְּרִבִּי הִלֵּל. מַחְלוֹקֶת רִבִּי יוֹנָה וְרִבִּי יוֹסֵי. רִבִּי יִצְחָק בַּר גּוּפְתָא בְּעָא קוֹמֵי רִבִּי מָנָא. עָשָׂה כֵן בַּשַּׁבָּת חַיָּיב מִשּׁוּם מְבַשֵּׁל. עָשָׂה כֵן בְּבָשָׂר וְחָלָב חַיָּיב מִשּׁוּם מְבַשֵּׁל. אָמַר לֵיהּ. כַּיי דָמַר רִבִּי זְעִירָא. וְאֵי זֶהוּ חָלוּט בָּרוּר. כָּל שֶׁהָאוּר מְהַלֵּךְ תַּחְתָּיו. וָכָא אֵי זֶהוּ תַבְשִׁיל בָּרוּר. כָּל שֶׁהָאוּר מְהַלֵּךְ תַּחְתָּיו.

2 גופתא | Gמ גופתה   בעא | מ בעי   4 וכא | G וכה   ואי זהו | G איזה הוא מ אי זהו

May one put spices at the bottom and pour on them from above[155]? Rebbi Jonah said, it is forbidden and pouring confers the status of primary vessel. The force of Rebbi Jonah comes from this[156]: "Both vessels used for cooking or into which it was poured boiling." Rebbi Yose said, there a pottery vessel absorbs; spices are not cooked[157]. Rebbi Yose ben Rebbi Abun objected: Did we not state[158], "the same holds for brass vessels." Can one say that brass vessels absorb?

Can one pour in from a stream[159]? Rebbi Ḥanina, the son of Rebbi Hillel, said, the disagreement of Rebbi Jonah and Rebbi Yose. Rebbi Isaac bar Gufta asked before Rebbi Mana: If he did this on the Sabbath, is he guilty because of cooking? If he did this with meat and milk[160], is he guilty because of cooking? He said to him, parallel to what Rebbi Ze`ira said, what is certainly a dumpling[161]? Only if fire burned underneath it. So here also, what is certainly[162] a cooked dish? Only if fire burned underneath it.

155 Since the Mishnah forbids putting spices in a pot not on a fire but still boiling hot.

156 Mishnah *Zevaḥim* 11:7. Lev. 6:21 precribes that pottery vessels after being used to cook a *ḥattat* sacrifice must be broken and metal vessels cleansed and washed. The Mishnah explicitly includes pouring hot water in the biblical definition of "cooking".

157 It is generally agreed that pottery must be broken because it absorbs particles from the sacrifice which on the following day become forbidden. Cf. J. Milgrom, *Leviticus* 1-16, pp. 404-407, New York 1991.

158 *Sifra Saw, Pereq* 7(1). The argument is that Lev. 6:21 reads a passive "a pottery vessel in which something has been cooked", not "in which one cooked". This is taken to mean that one cooks in, not by the vessel. In that case, the vessel is really "secondary vessel" since its walls do not transfer heat to the meat being cooked. The only case one can think of is pouring boiling water into the vessel. Since the argument of R. Yose does not work for metal pots, R. Jonah is justified.

159 If boiling water was poured in a stream coming from a vessel much higher than the receiving one, do we say that the water in the receiving pot certainly is no longer boiling?

160 The prohibition of combining milk and meat together is given three times (*Ex.* 23:19, 34:26, *Deut.* 14:21) with emphasis on cooking.

161 Small pieces of dough cooked in boiling water.

162 Pouring hot water over food on the Sabbath or pouring boiling milk over meat not over the fire are rabbinical prohibitions.

(6b line 34) רִבִּי יוּדָה אוֹמֵר. לַכֹּל הוּא נוֹתֵן. חוּץ מִדָּבָר שֶׁיֶּשׁ בּוֹ חוֹמֶץ וְצִיר: עַל דַּעְתֵּיהּ דְּרִבִּי יוּדָה. מֶלַח בְּצִיר. יַיִן בְּחוֹמֶץ.

2 בציר G‎‏ | מ‎‏ כציר בחומץ G‎‏ | מ‎‏ כחומץ

"Rebbi Jehudah says, one may put them in everything except what contains vinegar or fish sauce[14]." In the opinion of Rebbi Jehudah, salt is like[163] fish sauce and wine[164] like vinegar.

163 The translation follows G and ס.
164 Since the Mishnah here and *Ma`serot* 1:7 show that R. Jehudah holds that fish sauce and wine cure and, therefore, act as if cooking. Cf. Babli 42b.

(6b line 36) אֵין נוֹתְנִין כְּלִי תַּחַת הַנֵּר לְקַבֵּל בּוֹ אֶת הַשֶּׁמֶן. וְאִם נוֹתְנִין מִבְּעוֹד יוֹם מוּתָּר. וְאֵין נֵיאוֹתִין מִמֶּנּוּ לְפִי שֶׁאֵינוֹ מִן הַמוּכָן[165]. רִבִּי חַגַּי בָּעֵי. כָּבָה מִבְּעוֹד יוֹם וְנִתְוַדַּע לוֹ מִשֶּׁחֲשִׁיכָה. חֲבֵרַיָּיא בָּעֵי. כָּבָה בַּשַּׁבָּת זוֹ וְנִתְוַדַּע לוֹ בַּשַּׁבָּת הַבָּאָה. אָמַר רִבִּי יוֹחָנָן. אֵין לָךְ דָּבָר שֶׁהוּא בְעֵינוֹ וְאֵינוֹ בַּהֲכֵנוֹ אֶלָּא דָבָר אֶחָד בִּלְבָד. הָתִיב רִבִּי לְעֶזֶר. הֲרֵי שֶׁמֶן בְּנֵר הֲרֵי בְעֵינוֹ הוּא וְאֵינוֹ בַהֲכֵנוֹ. לְכָךְ נְתָנוֹ מִשָּׁעָה רִאשׁוֹנָה שֶׁיִּכָּלֶה בַנֵּר. הָתִיב רִישׁ לָקִישׁ. הֲרֵי חִטִּין בִּזְרִיעָה בְעֵינָן הֵן וְאֵינוֹ בַהֲכֵנוֹ. לְכָךְ נְתָנוֹ מִשָּׁעָה רִאשׁוֹנָה שֶׁיִּכְּלוּ בַקַּרְקַע. הָתִיבוּן. הֲרֵי בֵיצִים לְאֶפְרוֹחִים הֲרֵי בְעֵינָן הֵן וְאֵינָן בַּהֲכֵנָן. לְכָךְ נְתָנָן מִשָּׁעָה רִאשׁוֹנָה שֶׁיֵּיעָשׂוּ אֶפְרוֹחִין. הָתִיב רִבִּי יִרְמְיָה. הֲרֵי עִיטּוּרֵי סוּכָּה הֲרֵי בְעֵינָן הֵן וְאֵינָן בַּהֲכֵנָן. שַׁנְיָיא הִיא. דְּאָמַר רִבִּי אַבָּמָרִי אֲחוֹי דְּרִבִּי יוֹסֵה. כָּל־שִׁבְעָה הֵן בְּטֵילִין עַל גַּב סוּכָּה. מִיכָּן וָהֵילָךְ בַּהֲכֵנוֹ הֵן. הָתִיב רִבִּי חִינָּנָא. הֲרֵי מוּכִּין שֶׁנִּתְפַּזְּרוּ הֲרֵי בְעֵינָן הֵן וְאֵינָן בַּהֲכֵנָן. הָכָא בְכֵלִים. וּמַה דְּאַתְּ אָמַר תַּמָּן בָּאֲכָלָיו. הָתִיב רִבִּי נָסָא. הֲרֵי מוּקְצֶה שֶׁיָּבַשׁ וְלֹא נָגַע בּוֹ הֲרֵי הוּא בְעֵינוֹ וְאֵינוֹ בַהֲכֵנוֹ. הָכָא בְכֵלִים. וּמַה דְּאַתְּ אָמַר תַּמָּן בָּאֲכָלָיו.

2 חגי G | חגיי   3 חברייא G | חברייה   4 בהכנו G | בהכינו (2)   5 ריש לקיש G | ר' שמעון בן לקיש   6 בהכנו G | בהכינו   נתנו G | נתנן   שיכלה G | שיכלו   7 בהכנן G | בהכינן   שייעשו G | שיעשו   8 בהכנן G | בהכינן   שנייא G | שנייה   דאמ' G | דמר   9 והילך G | והלך   בהכנו G | בהכינו   חיננא G | חננה   שנתפזרו G | שניתפזרו   10 ואינן בהכנן G | ואינו בהכינו   הכא G | הכה   דאת אמר G | דאיתמר   11 באכלין G | באכלים   נסא G | ניסא   12 בהכנו G | בהכינו   הכא G | הכה   באכלין G | באכלים

מתני׳. מְטַלְטְלִין נֵר חָדָשׁ אֲבָל לֹא יָשָׁן כול׳[165]. הָתִיב רִבִּי חִיָּיא בַּר אַדָּא. וְהָא תַנִּינָן. כּוֹפִין סַל לִפְנֵי הָאֶפְרוֹחִין שֶׁיַּעֲלוּ וְשֶׁיֵּרְדוּ. אָמְרִין. הָדָא דְּרִבִּי יוֹחָנָן.

1 חייא בר אדא G | חייה בר אדה   2 הדא G | הדה

"One does not put a vessel under the light to catch the oil but when he put it there when it still was daylight it is permitted. One may not use it because it is not prepared[15]," etc. Rebbi Haggai asked, if it burned out when it still was day but he realized it only after it was dark[166]? The colleagues asked: If it burned out on this Sabbath but he realized it only afterwards on the Sabbath[167]?

Rebbi Johanan said, nothing in its natural form[168] is not prepared except one item. Rebbi Eleazar objected: Is not oil in the lamp in its natural state, nevertheless it is not prepared! It was put there from the start to be used up in the lamp[169]. Rebbi Simeon ben Laqish objected: Is not seed grain in its natural form, nevertheless it is not prepared! It was put there from the start to be used up in the ground. They objected: Are there not eggs used for chicks which are in their natural form, nevertheless they are not prepared! They were put there from the start to become chicks. Rebbi Jeremiah objected: Are there not *Sukkah* decorations which are in their natural form, nevertheless they are not prepared! There is a difference, as Rebbi Abba Mari, Rebbi Yose's brother, said: For the seven days they become insignificant in the *sukkah*. Afterwards they are prepared[170]. Rebbi Hinena objected: Is not lint which was scattered in its natural state, nevertheless it is not prepared! Here about vessels; what we said there about food[171]. Rebbi Nasa objected, are there not figs put out to ferment[172], which dried but he did not touch, in their natural form, nevertheless they are not prepared! [173]Here about vessels; what we said there about food.

(Mishnah: "One moves a new light but not a used one;" etc.) Rebbi Hiyya bar Ada objected: Did we not state[174], "one turns a basket upside down in front of the chicks that they may climb up and down"? They said, this is the one of Rebbi Johanan[173].

165 All quotes from the Mishnah are missing in G.

166 Objectively the light was not burning at nightfall; from this point of view there would be no obstacle to move the lamp for some legitimate purpose on the Sabbath and to use the remainder of the oil even for food. But since in his mind it was off limits at sundown it might be forbidden to him and permitted to everybody else.

167 If the answer to R. Haggai's question would be that it is permitted to him, what if it was burning into the Sabbath and he put a vessel there to catch any drippings from the lamp when it already was burned out. His intention was that the vessel should then be forbidden to be moved on the Sabbath but the objective reality was that nothing happened, and the vessel remains empty. The questions are not answered.

168 Any food which may be eaten as is (therefore not food subject to heave and tithes which had not been taken) is automatically "prepared" in the sense of the Sabbath (Chapter 2, Note 23).

169 While olive or sesame oil can be used either as food or as fuel, once it was actually used as fuel it is no longer food. The same holds for seed grain which actually was used as seed.

170 Since it is generally accepted that decorations belong to a *sukkah*, the decorations even if edible become part of the building. Taking them on holiday or

Sabbath would be equivalent to tearing down a part of the *sukkah*. But after the holiday they are simply fruits hanging on the wall which can be taken at any moment.

171 Lint fibers were used as insulating material to keep food warm for the Sabbath noon lunch. If it was dispersed, it cannot be used for another purpose on this Sabbath. But non-food items never were included in R. Johanan's statement.

172 The technical term for anything which cannot be moved on the Sabbath is מוּקְצָה. The root קיץ means "to cut into pieces," mainly figs for the preparation of fig cakes. The cut-up figs are spread on the roof to ferment in their juice. During the fermentation process they are inedible as such a paradigm for things not ready for use. The question is about fig cakes whose fermentation process was terminated and which are dried and ready as food, but they are out of sight on the roof as *muqseh* and not intended to be food on this Sabbath.

173 As S. Liebermann has pointed out, the text (even though confirmed by G) needs some re-arranging. The quote of the Mishnah clearly is out of place here and belongs to the following paragraph. The answer written down for the question of R. Nasa refers to the question of R. Hiyya bar Ada; the answer given to the latter's question belongs here; the one exception that R. Johanan makes to his rule refers to *muqseh* figs on the roof.

174 Mishnah Šabbat 18:2. The moment the basket becomes part of the chicken coop it cannot be moved on the Sabbath.

(6b line 49) דְּתַנֵּי. כָּל־הַנֵּירוֹת מְטַלְטְלִין חוּץ מִן הַנֵּר הַדָּלֵק בַּשַּׁבָּת. דִּבְרֵי רִבִּי מֵאִיר. רִבִּי יוּדָה אוֹמֵר. נֵר חָדָשׁ מוּתָּר לְטַלְטְלוֹ. וְיָשָׁן אָסוּר לְטַלְטְלוֹ. רִבִּי שִׁמְעוֹן אוֹמֵר. כָּל־הַנֵּרוֹת מִיטַּלְטְלִין חוּץ מִן הַנֵּר הַדָּלֵק בַּשַּׁבָּת. כָּבָה. מוּתָּר לְטַלְטְלוֹ.

2 מיטלטלין | G מטלטלין

רִבִּי יִרְמְיָה וְרִבִּי בָּא תְּרֵיהוֹן בְּשֵׁם רִבִּי יוֹחָנָן. חַד אָמַר. כָּל־הַמְיוּחָד לְאִיסּוּר אָסוּר. דִּבְרֵי רִבִּי מֵאִיר. כָּל־הַמְיוּחָד לְאִיסּוּר אָסוּר. וְחוֹרָנָה אָמַר. כָּל־שֶׁיִּיחֲדוֹ לְאִיסּוּר אָסוּר. וְלָא יְדַעִינָן מָאן אָמַר דָּא וּמָאן אָמַר דָּא. מִן מַה דָּמַר רִבִּי חֲנִינָה. רִבִּי יִרְמְיָה שָׁאַל. הָהֵן לִבְנָה לֹא כִּמְיוּחָד לְאִיסּוּר הוּא. הֱוֵי הוּא דוּ אָמַר. כָּל־הַמְיוּחַד לְאִיסּוּר אָסוּר. מָאן דָּמַר. מְיוּחָד. כָּל־שֶׁכֵּן יִיחֲדוֹ. וּמָאן דָּמַר. יִיחֲדוֹ. הָא מְיוּחַד לֹא.

1 תריהון | G תריהון   2 לאיסור | G לאסור   וחורנה | G וחרנה לאיסור | G לאסור לאיסור | G לאסור ידעינן | G ידעין מאן | G מן ומאן | G ומן   3 חנינה | G חנניה ליבנה | G לבנה לאיסור | G לאסור   4 לאיסור | G לאסור מאן | G מן ומאן | G ומן   ייחדו | G יחדו

מַתְנִיתָא פְּלִיגָא עַל מָאן דָּמַר. כָּל־הַמְיוּחָד לְאִיסּוּר אָסוּר. דְּתַנִּינָן תַּמָּן. מוּכָנָה שָׁלָהּ בִּזְמַן שֶׁהִיא נִשְׁמֶטֶת אֵינָהּ חִיבּוּר לָהּ וְאֵינָהּ נִמְדֶּדֶת עִמָּהּ. וְאֵינָהּ מַצֶּלֶת עִמָּהּ בְּאֹהֶל הַמֵּת. וְאֵין גּוֹרְרִין אוֹתָהּ בַּשַּׁבָּת בִּזְמַן שֶׁיֵּשׁ בְּתוֹכָהּ מָעוֹת. וְתַנֵּי עֲלָהּ. הָיוּ עָלֶיהָ מָעוֹת וְנָפְלוּ. נִגְרֶרֶת. אָמַר רַב שֵׁשֶׁת. דְּרִבִּי שִׁמְעוֹן הִיא. דְּרִבִּי שִׁמְעוֹן אוֹמֵר. כָּבָה מוּתָּר לְטַלְטְלוֹ. אַמְרִין. לָמָּה לֵית אֲנָן פְּתָרִין לָהּ. דִּבְרֵי הַכֹּל הִיא. בְּשׁוּכַח. לֵית אַתְּ יָכִיל. דְּתַנִּינָן תַּמָּן. אִם אֵינָהּ נִשְׁמֶטֶת חִיבּוּר לָהּ.

וְנִמְדֶּדֶת עִמָּהּ. וּמַצֶּלֶת עִמָּהּ בְּאֹהֶל הַמֵּת. וְגוֹרְרִין אוֹתָהּ בַּשַּׁבָּת אַף עַל פִּי שֶׁיֵּשׁ בְּתוֹכָהּ מָעוֹת. אִית מֵימַר הָכָא. דִּבְרֵי הַכֹּל הִיא בְּשׁוֹכֵחַ.

1 מתניתא G | מתניתה פליגא G | פליגה מאן G | מן לאיסור G | לאסור מוכנה G | מֵיכְנָה 2 נמדדת G | נימדדת עמה G | עימה 3 עליה G | בה 5 בשוכח G | בשָׁכֵחַ 6 ונמדדת G | ונימדדת עמה G | עימה באהל G | באוהל 7 אית G | אית לך הכא G | הכה בשוכח G | בָּשָׁכֵיחַ

מַתְנִיתָא פְלִיגָא עַל מָאן דָּמַר. כָּל־הַמְיוּחָד לְאִיסּוּר אָסוּר. דְּתַנִּינָן. הָאֶבֶן שֶׁעַל פִּי הֶחָבִית מַטָּהּ עַל צִדָּהּ וְנוֹפֶלֶת. רַבִּי בָּא בְשֵׁם רִבִּי חִייָא בַר אַשִׁי. פָּתַר לָהּ רַב בְּשׁוֹכֵחַ. וּמָן דְּבַתְרָהּ. הָיְתָה בֵין הֶחָבִיּוֹת מַגְבִּיהָהּ וּמַטָּהּ עַל צִדָּהּ וְהִיא נוֹפֶלֶת. עוֹד הוּא פָּתַר לָהּ רַב בְּשׁוֹכֵחַ.

1 מתניתא G | מתניתה פליגא G | פליגה מאן G | מן לאיסור G | לאסור 2 צדה G | צידה ונופלת G | והיא נופלת ר' חייא G | רב חייה בשוכח G | בשכח

מַתְנִיתָא פְלִיגָא עַל מָאן דָּמַר. כָּל־הַמְיוּחָד לְאִיסּוּר אָסוּר. דְּתַנִּינָן. כּוֹפִין סַל לִפְנֵי הָאֶפְרוֹחִין שֶׁיַּעֲלוּ וְשֶׁיֵּרְדוּ. וְתַנֵּי עֲלָהּ. עָלוּ מֵאֵילֵיהֶן אָסוּר לְטַלְטְלָן. אָמַר רִבִּי בּוּן בַּר חִייָא קוֹמֵי רִבִּי זְעֵירָא. תִּיפְתַּר בְּמָאוּס. אָמַר לֵיהּ. וְהָתַנֵּי רִבִּי הוֹשַׁעְיָה. אֲפִילוּ סָאָה אֲפִילוּ תַּרְקַב. אִית לָךְ מֵימַר. סָאָה וְתַרְקָב מְאוּסִין הֵן

1 מתניתא G | מתניתה פליגא G | פליגה מאן G | מן לאיסור G | לאסור 3 זעירא G | זעורה והתני G | והא תני

As it was stated[175]: "All lights may be moved except the light which was burning on the Sabbath, the words of Rebbi Meïr. Rebbi Jehudah says, it is permitted to move a new light but forbidden to move an old one[176]. Rebbi Simeon says, all lights may be moved except the light which was burning on the Sabbath; if it burned out it is permitted to move it[177]."

Rebbi Jeremiah and Rebbi Abba, both in the name of Rebbi Joḥanan. One said, the words of Rebbi Meïr, anything which is specifically for something prohibited is prohibited[178]. But the other one said, anything which one specified for something prohibited is prohibited. We did not know who said what. Since Rebbi (Ḥanina) [Ḥanania][179] said, Rebbi Jeremiah asked, is this (brick) [lamp][180] not specifically for something forbidden? This implies that he was the one who said, anything which is specifically for something prohibited is prohibited. The one who said specific, so much more if he specified. But he who said if he specified, not if it is specific[181].

A Mishnah disagrees with him who said, anything which is specifically for something prohibited is prohibited, as we have stated there[182]: "Its undercarriage[183], if it can be separated it is not connected to it, will not be measured with it, does not protect in a tent with a corpse; one may not drag it on the Sabbath if it contains coins[184]." And it was stated for this, if there were coins on it but they fell off, it may be dragged[185]. Rav Sheshet said, this is Rebbi Sineon's since Rebbi Simeon said, "if it burned out it is permitted to move it.[186]" They said, why do we not explain it according to everybody, if he forgot[187]. You cannot do this, as we have stated there[182]: "if it cannot be separated it is connected to it, will be measured with it, does protect in a tent with a corpse; one may drag it on the Sabbath even though it contains coins[188]." Can you say about this, it is according to everybody, if he forgot?

A Mishnah disagrees with him who said, anything which is specifically for something prohibited is prohibited, as we have stated[189]: "If there is a stone on top of an amphora he tilts it on its side and it falls down." Rebbi Abba in the name of (Rebbi) [Rav][190] Hiyya bar Ashi: Rav explained this about one who forgot[191]. Also from the sequel, "if it was between amphoras he lifts it, tilts it on its side and it falls down." This also Rav explained about one who forgot.

A Mishnah disagrees with him who said, anything which is specifically for something prohibited is prohibited, as we have stated[174]: "one turns a basket upside down in front of the chicks that they may climb up and down." And it was stated about this, when they climbed on it by themselves it is forbidden to move it[192]. Rebbi Abun bar Ḥiyya said before Rebbi Ze`ira, explain it if it is disgusting[193]. He told him, did not Rebbi Hoshaia state, even a *seah*, even a *three-qab*[194]. Can you say that *seah* and *three-qab* are disgusting?

175 Babli 44a, Tosephta 3:15 (ed. Liebermann).
176 A light which never had been used may be moved on the Sabbath but one which had been used is disgusting; he considers everything disgusting as *muqseh* on the Sabbath.
177 In contrast to R. Meïr he allows a light to be moved after it stopped burning.
178 Any tool which ordinarily is used for work forbidden on the Sabbath may not be moved on that day. The opposite opinion holds that most tools may also be used for permitted activities; a builder's hammer may also be used to split nuts. Only tools or vessels intentionally reserved for forbidden activities are forbidden. This opinion also states that very expensive tools are automatically reserved for their professional use.
179 The reading [of G] has to be preferred to the reading (of the text) since R. Hanina was a first generation Amora, R. Jeremiah a fourth generation one.
180 The translation "brick" reads לבינה

instead of ליבנה. As building material, bricks cannot be moved according to the first opinion; according to the second they might be used as stands for hot pots on a table. The translation of the text of G, לִכְנָה, follows S. Liebermannn (both in *Tarbiz* 5, p. 99 and in *Hayerushalmi Kiphshuto*) who identified the word as Greek λύχνος "lamp". R. Jeremiah asks why R. Meïr permits to move a lamp which was not lit for the Sabbath since it is a tool specifically built for a forbidden activity.

181 In the first opinion, even a tool not specifically used for a forbidden activity becomes forbidden to be moved if it is selected for a forbidden activity; in the second opinion everything depends on use and nothing on general usage.

182 Mishnah *Kelim* 18:2.

183 Greek μηχανή, ἡ, "mechanical device". The object is a שִׁדָה which the Geonic Commentary to *Kelim* defines as "a kind of wooden box made to transport women" (cf. Arabic سَدَّة "bench, seat"). The μηχανή is the contraption where the wheels are attached. If this is permanently fixed to the box it is an appendix to the box and follows its rules; if the box may be lifted it is a tool by itself.

Wooden tools or vessels are impervious to impurity if either they are flat, not enclosing any volume, or are so large that they cannot be lifted empty or full. The latter is determined as a volume of 40 *seah* (a Roman *culeus*) 20 amphoras or 512 liter. For the House of Shammai, the volume enclosed has to be 40 *seah*, but for the House of Hillel the volume of the entire vessel is measured. If the undercarriage can be disconnected it can become impure even if the passenger compartment cannot, its volume is not added to the volume of the compartment according to the House of Hillel, and if it is under one roof with a corpse it is not considered a separate entity but part of the "tent".

184 Since coins are tools of trade forbidden on the Sabbath they cannot be moved; if the undercarriage was the receptacle of coins at nightfall it cannot be moved either.

185 For the second opinion the undercarriage becomes forbidden only if it was consciously selected as container of the coins; but according to the first opinion it should stay forbidden even if the coins fall off.

186 There is no contradiction to R. Meïr from a Mishnah which is R. Simon's. Babli 44b

187 Since there was no conscious selection as vessel for the coins it does not fall under any of R. Meïr's categories. But everybody agrees that coins may not be moved; therefore a container with coins cannot be moved.

188 If the undercarriage is a permanent part of the carriage, the coins become insignificant; the carriage is not the container of the coins. But for R. Meïr one must assume that he prohibits moving the entire carriage with the coins.

189 Mishnah 21:2. If not specifically chosen for forbidden work, all vessels and tools may be moved on the Sabbath. But a stone is no vessel or tool. If the amphora or its contents are needed on the Sabbath, the amphora may be tilted, the stone itself may not be moved by action directed only at the stone.

190 The reading of [G] is correct. It is confirmed by Chapter 18 where a shortened version of this paragraph and a totally identical version of the next are reproduced (Note 51).

191 It is not a tool used for forbidden purposes and there was no selection. Babli 125b.

192 Babli 43a. The question really is directed against the opinion that vessels or tools become *muqseh* only if specifically selected for forbidden purposes. Here the selection is not made by the farmer but by his chicks. A different approach in the Babli, 43a.

193 Following R. Jehudah, cf. Note 176.

194 Half a *seah*, about 6.4 liter.

(6c line 5) רִבִּי יִרְמְיָה בְשֵׁם רַב. הֲלָכָה כְרִבִּי מֵאִיר. שְׁמוּאֵל אָמַר. הֲלָכָה כְרִבִּי יְהוּדָה. רִבִּי יְהוֹשֻׁעַ בֶּן לֵוִי אָמַר. הֲלָכָה כְרִבִּי שִׁמְעוֹן. בְּעוֹן קוֹמֵי רִבִּי יוֹחָנָן. אַתְּ מַה אַתְּ אָמַר. אָמַר לוֹן. אֵין לִי אֶלָּא מִשְׁנָה. כָּל־הַנֵּרוֹת מִיטַלְטְלִין חוּץ מִן הַנֵּר הַדָּלֵק בַּשַּׁבָּת. רִבִּי שִׁמְעוֹן בֶּן לָקִישׁ הוֹרֵי בְאַטַרְבּוּלִיס. מְנוֹרָה קְטַנָּה מוּתֶּרֶת לְטַלְטְלָהּ. רִבִּי חֶלְבּוֹ וְרִבִּי אַבָּהוּ. קוֹמֵי רִבִּי חֶלְבּוֹ לֹא מַעֲבָרִין. קוֹמֵי רִבִּי אַבָּהוּ מַעֲבָרִין. רִבִּי יָסָא סָלַק גַּבֵּי רִבִּי תַנְחוּם בַּר חִייָא. בָּעָה מִיעֲבָרְתֵּיהּ קוֹמוֹי. אֲמַר לֵיהּ. בְּפָנֵינוּ. רִבִּי יוֹסֵה גַלִילַייָא סָלַק קוֹמֵי יוֹסֵי בֶן חֲנִינָה. בָּעָה מִיעֲבָרְתֵּיהּ. אֲמַר לֵיהּ. מָאן שָׁרָא לָךְ. אַשְׁכָּחַת רַב וְרִבִּי יוֹחָנָן אִילֵין דְּאָסְרִין חֲדָא. רִבִּי יְהוֹשֻׁעַ בֶּן לֵוִי וְרִבִּי שִׁמְעוֹן בֶּן לָקִישׁ אִילֵין דְּשָׁרְיָיה חֲדָא. רִבִּי לֵעָזָר בַּר חֲנִינָה. מַעֲשֶׂה הָיָה וְטִילְטְלוּ פּוֹמֵט מִתַּחַת הַנֵּר בַּשַּׁבָּת. מָה אֲנָן קַייָמִין. אִין כְּרִבִּי מֵאִיר. אֲפִילוּ פוֹמֵט יְהֵא אָסוּר. אִין כְּרִבִּי שִׁמְעוֹן. אֲפִילוּ נֵר יְהֵא מוּתָּר. אֶלָּא כֵן אֲנָן קַייָמִין כְּרִבִּי יוּדָה. דְּרִבִּי יוּדָה דוּ אָמַר. נֵר מָאוּס. פּוֹמֵט אֵינוֹ מָאוּס.

Rebbi[195] Jeremiah in the name of Rav: Practice follows Rebbi Meïr. Samuel said, practice follows Rebbi Jehudah. Rebbi Joshua ben Levi said, practice follows Rebbi Simeon[196]. They asked before Rebbi Johanan, you, what are you saying? He told them, I only have the Mishnah: "One may move any light except one which was burning on the Sabbath.[197]" Rebbi Simeon ben Laqish instructed in al-Tarabulus[198], it is permitted to move a small light. Rebbi Helbo and Rebbi Abbahu. Before Rebbi Helbo they did not take away[199], before Rebbi Abbahu they took away. Rebbi Yasa visited Rebbi Tanhum bar Hiyya. He wanted to remove it before him. He told him, before us? Rebbi Yose the Galilean[200] came before Yose ben Hanina; he wanted to take it away. he told him, who permitted you? It is found Rav and Rebbi Johanan, who forbid, are one. Rebbi Joshua ben Levi and Rebbi Simeon ben Laqish, who permit, are one. Rebbi Eleazar bar Hanina: It happened and they moved a metal lamp[201] instead of a pottery light on the Sabbath. Where do we hold? If following Rebbi Meïr, even the metal lamp should be forbidden. If following Rebbi Simeon, even a pottery light should be permitted. But we are following Rebbi Jehudah since Rebbi Jehudah is the one who said, a pottery light is disgusting, a metal light is not disgusting[202].

195 He is the first generation Babylonian Rav Jeremiah bar Abba, student and colleague of Rav.
196 The attributions are different in the Babli 45b, 156b. R. Simeon recognizes almost no categories of *muqseh*.
197 This is R. Simeon's Mishnah but R. Joḥanan is read as endorsing R. Meïr.
198 Tripolis in Lebanon. In the Babli 45b the story is placed at Sidon.
199 Removing a burned-out light on the Sabbath, following R. Simeon.
200 The Amora, not the early Tanna.
201 Rashi's definition in the Babli 44a.
202 Since pottery absorbs oil, a used pottery lamp cannot be cleaned. But a metal lamp can be thoroughly cleaned and made shiny.

(6c line 28) תַּנֵּי. נֵר שֶׁהוּא מוּנָח עַל גַּבֵּי טַבְלָה. מְסַלֵּק אֶת הַטַּבְלָה וְהַנֵּר נוֹפֵל. אָמַר רִבִּי יוֹחָנָן. קָרוֹב הוּא זֶה לָבוֹא לִידֵי חִיוּב חַטָּאת. לְפָנָיו מִשּׁוּם מַבְעִיר. לְאַחֲרָיו מִשּׁוּם מְכַבֶּה. שְׁמוּאֵל בַּר אַבָּא קוֹמֵי רִבִּי יָסָא. בְּכָבָה. אָמַר לֵיהּ. תָּנוּחַ דַּעְתָּךְ. מָה אֲנָן קַיָּימִין. אִין כְּרִבִּי מֵאִיר. אֲפִילוּ טַבְלָה תְהֵא אֲסוּרָה. אִין כְּרִבִּי שִׁמְעוֹן. אֲפִילוּ נֵר יְהֵא מוּתָּר. אֶלָּא כָאן כְּרִבִּי יוּדָה. דְּרִבִּי יוּדָה אָמַר. נֵר מָאוּס. טַבְלָה אֵינָהּ מָאוּסָה.

תַּנֵּי. אִם הִתְנָה עָלָיו יְהֵא מוּתָּר. מָה אֲנָן קַיָּימִין. אִין כְּרִבִּי מֵאִיר. אֲפִילוּ הִתְנָה עָלָיו אָסוּר. אִין כְּרִבִּי שִׁמְעוֹן. אֲפִילוּ לֹא הִתְנָה עָלָיו יְהֵא מוּתָּר. אֶלָּא כֵן אֲנָן קַיָּימִין כְּרִבִּי יוּדָה. דְּרִבִּי יוּדָה אָמַר. נֵר מָאוּס. טַבְלָה אֵינָהּ מָאוּסָה. מָה חֲמִית מֵימַר. כְּרִבִּי יוּדָה אֲנָן קַיָּימִין. דְּתַנֵּי. נֵר שֶׁהוּא מוּנָח אֲחוֹרֵי הַדֶּלֶת פּוֹתֵחַ וְנוֹעֵל בַּשַּׁבָּת וּבִלְבַד שֶׁלֹּא יִתְכַּוֵּון לֹא לְכַבּוֹת וְלֹא לְהַעֲבִיר. רַב וּשְׁמוּאֵל פְּתָרִין לָהּ בְּשׁוֹכֵחַ וּמְקַלְּלִין מָאן דַּעֲבַד כֵּן. יַכְרֵת יְיָ לָאִישׁ אֲשֶׁר יַעֲשֶׂנָּה עֵר וְעוֹנֶה.

מָאן אִית. כָּל־הַמְיֻחַד לְאִיסּוּר אָסוּר. לֹא רִבִּי מֵאִיר. הֲוֵי. מָאן תַּנָּא. אִם הִתְנָה עָלָיו יְהֵא מוּתָּר. רִבִּי שִׁמְעוֹן. אֲבָל כּוֹב וּקְעָרָה וַעֲשָׁשִׁית אַף עַל פִּי שֶׁכָּבוּ אָסוּר לִיגַּע בָּהֶן. רִבִּי טָבִי בְּשֵׁם רַב חִסְדָּא. אֲפִילוּ כְּרִבִּי שִׁמְעוֹן דּוּ אָמַר תַּמָּן מוּתָּר. מוֹדֵי הוּא הָכָא שֶׁהוּא אָסוּר. שֶׁאִם אוֹמֵר אַתְּ לוֹ שֶׁהוּא מוּתָּר. אַף הוּא מְכַבֶּה אוֹתָן וּמִשְׁתַּמֵּשׁ בָּהוֹן.

אָמַר רִבִּי מָנָא. בְּקַדְמִיתָא הֲוֵינָן סָבְרִין מֵימַר. מָה פְלִיגִין בְּאוֹתוֹ שֶׁכָּבָה. בְּשֶׁגֵּרְרוּ הָעַכְבָּרִים אֶת הַפְּתִילָה. בָּאֲפוּצָה. וַאֲפִילוּ תֵימָא בְּשֶׁלֹּא גֵרְרוּ הָעַכְבָּרִים אֶת הַפְּתִילָה. וַאֲפִילוּ תֵימָא שֶׁלֹּא בָאֲפוּצָה. בְּשֶׁיֵּשׁ בְּתוֹכוֹ שֶׁמֶן.

It was stated: If a light was lying on a table he takes away the table and the light falls down[203]. Rebbi Joḥanan said, this one is close to be liable for a purification sacrifice; forwards for setting a fire, backwards for extinguishing[204]. Samuel bar Abba before Rebbi Yasa: when it was extinguished. He told him, may your mind be at rest[205]. Where do we hold? If following Rebbi Meïr, even the table should be forbidden[206]. If following Rebbi Simeon, even the light should be permitted[207]. But here following Rebbi Jehudah, since Rebbi Jehudah says, a pottery light is disgusting, a table is not disgusting.

It was stated: If he stipulated about it[208] it shall be permitted. Where do we hold? If following Rebbi Meïr, even if he stipulated it should be forbidden. If following Rebbi Simeon, even if he did not stipulate it should be permitted. But here we hold following Rebbi Jehudah, since Rebbi Jehudah says, a pottery light is disgusting, a table is not disgusting. From where did you understand to say, we are holding with Rebbi Jehudah? As it was stated: If a light was lying behind a door one opens and closes on the Sabbath if only he not intend either to extinguish or to make it burn. Rav and Samuel explain it about one who forgot but cursed one who would do this[209]; *May the Eternal extirpate the man who does this, awake and answering*[210].

Who has "anything which is specifically for something prohibited is prohibited[178]", not Rebbi Meïr? Therefore, the one who stated "if he stipulated about it it shall be permitted" was Rebbi Simeon. But a cup, or a bowl[211], or a lantern[212], even after they were extinguished it is forbidden to touch them. Rebbi Tabi in the name of Rav Hisda: Even Rebbi Simeon who there says it is permitted here he agrees that it is forbidden, for if you tell him that it is permitted he will extinguish them and use them.

Rebbi Mana said, earlier we were of the opinion to say, where do they disagree[213]? When it was extinguished, if the rats had dragged the wick away[214], when it was compressed[215]. But you may even say[216] if the rats had not dragged the wick away, when it was not compressed, if it contained oil[217].

203 Babli 120b.

204 He is violating a biblical Sabbath commandment. If he tilts the table forward the oil will swamp the wick and the light will burn more brightly; if he tilts backward there will be less oil for the wick and it will burn less bright. The argument presupposes a text like the one quoted in the Babli: "If a light was lying on a table he shakes the table and the light falls down; if it was extinguished it was extinguished." If the light is extinguished on the dirt floor (no danger of setting the house on fire) this is not his action but what happens during the tilting is his intended action.

205 This is an abbreviated version of a

talmudic saying, "may your mind be at rest for you put mine at rest." He accepted the explanation (which would be impossible for the Babli's version.) Nahmanides (*Novellae ad* 120a) quoted by RAN (Commentary to Alfasi #454) prefers the Yerushalmi version to the Babli's.

206 Since the light was burning there at nightfall, the table is its necessary base and forbidden with the light.

207 Since he permits the light to be moved after it burned out, so much more the table.

208 To move the table after the light stopped burning.

209 In the Babli, 120b, the rule is positively accepted by Rav Jehudah, the student of Rav and Samuel; the curse is attributed to Abbaye two generations later.

210 *Mal.* 2:12.

211 Which have been filled with oil and used as lights.

212 Which if empty could be used as a glass bowl. Babli 44a.

213 About the table under a burning light.

214 There was no functioning light anymore, it was not an object specified for prohibited work.

215 If the neck of the lamp is so narrow that the wick is compressed by it then the lamp itself is the base for the light, the table is the base not for the light but the lamp, and is not forbidden to be moved.

216 תימא is Babylonian (Accadic) Aramaic, not Yerushalmi.

217 If the light went out when some edible oil was left, the light can be moved for the food.

(6c line 39) תַּמָּן תַּנִּינָן. נוֹטֵל אָדָם אֶת בְּנוֹ וְהָאֶבֶן בְּיָדוֹ וְכַלְכָּלָה וְהָאֶבֶן בְּתוֹכָהּ. וְתַנֵּי דְּבֵית רִבִּי הָאֶבֶן וְהָאוֹכְלִין בְּתוֹכָהּ. לֹא הֲוִינָן אָמְרִין כְּלוּם. שֶׁהֲרֵי רִבִּי רוֹמָנוֹס הוֹצִיא מַחְתָּה מִשַּׁלְבֵית רִבִּי מְלֵיאָה גְחָלִים בַּשַּׁבָּת. אִית לָךְ מֵימַר. גַּבֵּי גְחָלִים אֲפוּצוֹת הֵן אֶלָּא בִּשְׁבִישׁ לְתוֹכוֹ שָׁמָן. אָמַר רִבִּי אַבָּהוּ. קַיָּימַתֵּיהּ קַרְטֵיס שֶׁל בּוֹסֶם הָיָה בָהּ.

רִבִּי בָא בַּר חִיָּיה בְּשֵׁם רִבִּי יוֹחָנָן. תַּרְכּוּס אָסוּר לְטַלְטְלוֹ. הוֹרֵי רִבִּי אַמִּי. מוּתָּר. רִבִּי יִרְמְיָה חֲמִי לוֹן מְטַלְטְלִין לֵיהּ גּוֹ סַדְרָא רוֹבָא וְלֹא הֲוָה מַמְחֵה בְּיָדָן. דְּבֵית רִבִּי יַנַּאי אָמְרִין. עַד ג' כְּכַסָּא. מִיכָּן וָאֵילַךְ כְּסוּלָם. אָמַר רִבִּי יוֹסֵה בֵּירִבִּי בּוּן. מָאן דְּשָׁרֵי כְּרִבִּי שִׁמְעוֹן. דְּתַנֵּי. לֹא יָגוּר אָדָם אֶת הַמִּיטָה וְאֶת הַכִּסֵּא וְאֶת הַסַּפְסָל וְאֶת הַקָּתֶדְרָה. מִפְּנֵי שֶׁהוּא עוֹשֶׂה חָרִיץ. וְרִבִּי שִׁמְעוֹן מַתִּיר. רִבִּי בָא בְּשֵׁם רִבִּי חוּנָא רִבִּי חַגַּי בְּשֵׁם רִבִּי זְעִירָא רִבִּי יוֹסֵי בְּשֵׁם רִבִּי אִילָא. מוֹדִין חֲכָמִים לְרִבִּי שִׁמְעוֹן בְּכִסֵּא שֶׁרַגְלָיו מְשׁוּקָעוֹת בַּטִּיט שֶׁמּוּתָּר לְטַלְטְלוֹ. כְּמָא דְתֵימַר מוּתָּר לְטַלְטְלוֹ. וְדִכְוָותָהּ מוּתָּר לְהַחֲזִירוֹ. אָמַר רִבִּי יוֹסֵי. אַף אֲנָן נַמִּי תַּנִּינָן. נִיטָּלִין בַּשַּׁבָּת. אָמַר רִבִּי יוֹסֵה בֵּירִבִּי בּוּן. דְּרִבִּי שִׁמְעוֹן הִיא. מַתְנִיתָהּ אָמְרָה כֵן. כָּל־הַכֵּלִים אֵינָן נִגְרָרִין חוּץ מִן הָעֲגָלָה מִפְּנֵי שֶׁהִיא כוֹבֶשֶׁת׃

רִבִּי חוּנָא בְּשֵׁם רִבִּי. לְעִנְיַין שַׁבָּת אִתְאֲמָרַת. חִזְקִיָּה בְּשֵׁם דְּבֵית רִבִּי יַנַּאי. לְעִנְיַין חֲזָקוֹת אִיתְאֲמָרַת. רִבִּי יוֹסֵי מְשׁוּם דְּבֵית רִבִּי יַנַּאי. לְעִנְיַין טוּמְאָה אִתְאֲמָרַת. רִבִּי אָחָא בַּר חִינָּנָא רִבִּי יָסָא בְּשֵׁם רִבִּי יוֹחָנָן. מְנוֹרָה קְטַנָּה מוּתָּר לְטַלְטְלָהּ. וְלֹא כְלִי הוּא. וְלֹא כָל־מַה שֶׁבַּבַּיִת מִן

הַמּוּכָן הוּא. אָמַר רִבִּי יוֹסֵי בֵּירִבִּי בּוּן. תִּפְתַּר שֶׁלְּקָחָהּ עִמּוֹ לִסְחוֹרָה. אוֹ שֶׁבָּאת עֶרֶב שַׁבָּת עִם חֲשֵׁיכָה. וְלֹא שְׁמַעַת מִינָהּ כְּלוּם.

There, we have stated[218]: "A man may carry his son with a stone in his hand, or a basket with a stone in it.[219]" The House of Rebbi stated, food and stone in it, we do not say anything[220], for Rebbi Romanos brought out a pan from Rebbi's house full of coals on the Sabbath. Could you say that coals are pressed? But it must have oil left in it[221]. Rebbi Abbahu said, I confirmed it, cuts of fragrances were on it[222].

Rebbi Abba bat Hiyya in the name of Rebbi Johanan, it is forbidden to move a *tarkos*[223]. Rebbi Immi instructed: it is permitted. Rebbi Jeremiah saw them moving it at the great assembly and did not object to them[224]. In the House of Rebbi Yannai they said, up to three it is a chair, more than this a ladder[225]. Rebbi Yose ben Rebbi Abun said, he who permits follows Rebbi Simeon, as it was stated: "A person may not drag a bed, or a chair, or a footstool, or a fauteuil[75], because he makes a groove, but Rebbi Simeon permits." [76]Rebbi Abba in the name of Rebbi Huna, Rebbi Haggai in the name of Rebbi Ze`ira, Rebbi Yose in the name of Rebbi Ila: The Sages admit to Rebbi Simeon that a chair whose legs are stuck in mud one is permitted to move on the Sabbath[77]. Since you are saying, it is permitted to move it, similarly it is permitted to return it. Rebbi Yose said, we also have stated[78]: "and they may be removed on the Sabbath." Rebbi Yose ben Rebbi Abun said, , it is Rebbi Simeon's. Rebbi Yose ben Rebbi Abun said, a Mishnah says so, "one may not drag any vessel except a carriage because it presses[79]."

Rebbi Huna in the name of Rebbi: It[227] was said relating to the Sabbath. Hizqiah in the name of the House of Rebbi Yannai, it was said relating to presumptions[228]. Rebbi Yose in the name of the House of Rebbi Yannai, it was said relating to impurity[229]. Rebbi Aha bar Hinnena, Rebbi Yasa in the name of Rebbi Johanan[230], it is permitted to move a small light. Is it not a vessel? Is not everything in the house prepared? Rebbi Yose ben Rebbi Abun said, explain it that he took it with him as merchandise[231], or it arrived Friday evening at nightfall, and you cannot infer anything.

218 Mishnah 21:1.
219 It is possible to carry *muqseh* items with other things which may be moved on the Sabbath.

220 The previous statement has to be qualified. While a basket may be moved, a basket containing only a stone becomes a base for a forbidden object and cannot be moved. There must be items in the basket which legitimately may be moved.

221 In the case of a lamp discussed in the preceding paragraph, the first explanation would not cover R. Romanos's action; it must be the second explanation which is operative.

222 In this respect, fragrances are as good as food items.

223 Cf. Chapter 1, Note 115. At this place, Kohut proposes to read תרונס, Greek θρόνος "chair". From the following it follows that one speaks of a chair to which one ascends in steps. {Also cf. Greek θρᾶνος, ὁ "bench, wooden beam" (E. G.).}

224 He did not want to decide between R. Joḥanan and R. Immi.

225 Later it will be discussed where the difference between chair and ladder is relevant.

227 The difference between chair and ladder. A chair is a vessel, a ladder part of the house.

228 A presumption of ownership by undisturbed possession during three years; cf. *Bava Qamma* 7:4 Note 49.

229 A chair becomes impure if a person with gonorrhea or similar discharges exerts pressure (even indirect) on it, without direct contact. A ladder is just a tool.

230 S. Liebermann notes that a sentence seems to be missing here since the following statement is that of R. Simeon ben Laqish, earlier opposed by R. Joḥanan (at least in the interpretation of the compilers of the Yerushalmi, cf. Note 198).

231 Then it is to be used for an activity forbidden on the Sabbath and not prepared.

6c line 62) הָכָא אַתְּ אָמַר. אֵין נוֹתְנִין כְּלִי תַּחַת הַנֵּר. לְקַבֵּל נִיצוֹצוֹת. וְלֹא יִתֵּן לְתוֹכוֹ מַיִם מִפְּנֵי שֶׁהוּא מְכַבֶּה: וְהָכָא אַתְּ אָמַר. נוֹתְנִין כְּלִי תַּחַת הַנֵּר. כָּאן שֶׁיֵּשׁ לוֹ צוֹרֶךְ בַּשֶּׁמֶן. וְכָאן אֵין לוֹ צוֹרֶךְ בַּנִּיצוֹצוֹת.

וְלֹא יִתֵּן לְתוֹכוֹ מַיִם מִפְּנֵי שֶׁהוּא מְכַבֶּה: רַבִּי שְׁמוּאֵל בְּשֵׁם רִבִּי זְעִירָא. דְּרִבִּי יוֹסֵי הִיא. דְּאָמַר רִבִּי יוֹסֵי. הֲוֵינָן סָבְרִין מֵימַר. מָה פְּלִיגִין רִבִּי מֵאִיר וְרַבָּנָן. בְּשֶׁעָשָׂה מְחִיצָה שֶׁלְּכֵלִים. אֲבָל עָשָׂה מְחִיצָה שֶׁל מַיִם לֹא. מִן מַה דָּמַר רִבִּי שְׁמוּאֵל בְּשֵׁם רִבִּי זְעִירָא. דְּרִבִּי יוֹסֵי הִיא. הָדָא אָמְרָה. אֲפִילוּ עָשָׂה מְחִיצָה שֶׁלְּמַיִם הִיא הַמַּחֲלוֹקֶת.

1 זעירא | **16** זירא   יוסי | **16** יוסה   2 דאמ' | **16** אמ'   יוסי | **16** יוסה   הוינן סברין | **16** הוה סברינן   ר' מאיר | **16** מימר ר' יוסה   3 מן מה | **16** ממה

Here you say, "one does not put a vessel under the light," to catch sparks? "But one may not put water in it since he would extinguish." And there you say, "one may put a vessel under the light"? Here he needs the oil but there he does not need the sparks[232].

[233]"But one may not put water in it since he would extinguish." Rebbi Samuel in the name of Rebbi Ze`ira: This is Rebbi Yose's. We were of the

opinion to say, where disagree (Rebbi Meïr) [what Rebbi Yose says]²³⁴ and the rabbis? When he made a barrier of vessels. But not if he made a barrier of water. Since Rebbi Samuel said in the name of Rebbi Ze`ira: This is Rebbi Yose's, it implies that there is disagreement even if he made a barrier of water.

232 Why does the Mishnah first state "one does not put a vessel," and then "one may put a vessel"? It is forbidden only if the result would be usable material.

233 This paragraph is copied in Chapter **16** since it refers to Mishnah 16:6.

234 The correct version [in brackets] is from **16**. In the Mishnah, R. Yose forbids in the case of a fire making a wall out of new pottery vessels filled with water since these will certainly burst and extinguish the fire. He forbids indirect causation of a biblically prohibited action whereas the rabbis permit it in cases of great need. Babli 47b.

במה טומנין פרק רביעי

(fol. 6c) **משנה א**: בַּמֶּה טוֹמְנִין וּבַמֶּה אֵין טוֹמְנִין. אֵין טוֹמְנִין לֹא בַגֶּפֶת וְלֹא בַזֶּבֶל וְלֹא בְמֶלַח וְלֹא בְסִיד וְלֹא בַחוֹל בֵּין לַחִין בֵּין יְבֵשִׁין. לֹא בַתֶּבֶן וְלֹא בַמּוֹכִין וְלֹא בָאוֹגִין וְלֹא בָעֲשָׂבִין בִּזְמַן שֶׁהֵן לַחִין. אֲבָל טוֹמְנִין בָּהֶן כְּשֶׁהֵן יְבֵשִׁין. טוֹמְנִין בַּכְּסוּת וּבַפֵּירוֹת וּבְכַנְפֵי יוֹנָה וּבִנְעוֹרֶת שֶׁל פִּשְׁתָּן וּבִנְסוֹרֶת שֶׁל חָרָשִׁין דַּקָּה. רַבִּי יְהוּדָה אוֹסֵר בַּדַּקָּה וּמַתִּיר בַּגַּסָּה:

Mishnah 1: In what does one store away and in what may one not store away[1]? One does not store away in olive cake[2], nor in manure, nor in salt, nor in lime, nor in sand, whether moist or dry. Not in straw, nor in fibers, nor in grape pits, nor in grasses when they are moist[3] but one may store away in them when dry. One may store away in garments, and produce, and pigeon wings[4], and flax residue, and in fine sawdust. Rebbi Jehudah forbids if it is fine and permits coarse.

משנה ב: טוֹמְנִין בַּשְּׁלָחִין וּמְטַלְטְלִין אוֹתָן בְּגִיזֵּי צֶמֶר וְאֵין מְטַלְטְלִין אוֹתָן. כֵּיצַד עוֹשֶׂה נוֹעֵר אֶת הַכִּסּוּי וְהֵן נוֹפְלוֹת. רַבִּי אֶלְעָזָר בֶּן עֲזַרְיָה אוֹמֵר קוּפָה מַטָּהּ עַל צִידָּהּ וְנוֹטֵל שֶׁמָּא יִטּוֹל וְאֵינוֹ יָכוֹל לְהַחֲזִיר. וַחֲכָמִים אוֹמְרִים נוֹטֵל וּמַחֲזִיר. אִם לֹא כִיסָּהוּ מִבְּעוֹד יוֹם לֹא יְכַסֶּנּוּ מִשֶּׁתֶּחְשַׁךְ. כִּיסָּהוּ וְנִתְגַּלָּה מוּתָּר לְכַסּוֹתוֹ. מְמַלֵּא אֶת הַקִּיתוֹן וְנוֹתֵן לְתַחַת הַכַּר אוֹ תַחַת הַכֶּסֶת:

Mishnah 2: One may store away in raw hides[5], which one may move, and in wool flakes[6], which one may not move. What does one do? He shakes the cover and they fall off. Rebbi Eleazar ben Azariah says, a box he tilts on its side and takes out, lest he take it out and be unable to return it[7]. But the Sages say, he takes and returns. If he did not cover it when it still was daylight he may not cover it when it is dark. If he covered it and it became uncovered, he is permitted to cover it. One may fill a pitcher[8] and put it under the pillow or under the quilt.

1 To keep food warm for the Sabbath meal one prepares a big box which is padded with insulating material in which the hot pots will be embedded. In German this used to be called "Kochkiste." The insulating material may not be anything which in a fermentation process will produce heat.

2 Chapter 3, Note 3.

3 And produce heat in rotting.

4 Down.

5 Untanned fresh hides which in general

are not used nevertheless qualify as implements for the rules of the Sabbath.

6   Unprocessed wool freshly shorn. This is considered raw material, not textile, for the rules of the Sabbath.

7   If in taking out the pot the hollow where it fitted in was filled by the insulating material, there is a rabbinic prohibition of re-excavating the hollow since it would look as if he started hiding the pot only on the Sabbath. The Sages do not dispute this argument; they hold that an experienced housewife will see to it that the pot may be returned if necessary.

8   There is no restriction on making cold water lukewarm.

(6d line 2) בַּמֶּה טוֹמְנִין וּבַמֶּה אֵין טוֹמְנִין כול׳. לְפִי שֶׁהַדְּבָרִים הַלָּלוּ רוֹתְחִין וּמַרְתִּיחִין וְהוּא נוֹטְלָן וְהֵן תַּשִּׁים לְתוֹךְ יָדוֹ וּמַחֲזִירָן וְהֵן מוֹסִיפִין רְתִיחָה. לְפִיכָךְ אָסְרוּ לִטְמוֹן בָּהֶן. וּכְרִבִּי לְעָזָר בֶּן עֲזַרְיָה. דְּרִבִּי לְעָזָר בֶּן עֲזַרְיָה אָמַר. קוּפָה מַטָּהּ עַל צִידָּהּ וְנוֹטֵל. וּכְרַבָּנָן דְּתַמָּן. דְּנוּ אָמְרִין. אִם הָיְתָה יוֹרָה מוּתָּר. תַּמָּן תַּנִּינָן. סָפֵק חֲשֵׁיכָה סָפֵק לֹא חֲשֵׁיכָה. מִפְּנֵי שֶׁלֹא חֲשֵׁיכָה. הָא אִם חֲשֵׁיכָה אָסוּר לִטְמוֹן בָּהֶן. תַּמָּן אָמְרִין. מִפְּנֵי בִיטוּל בֵּית הַמִּדְרָשׁ. אָמַר רִבִּי בָּא. מִפְּנֵי הַחֲשָׁד. שֶׁאִם אוֹמֵר אַתְּ לוֹ שֶׁהוּא מוּתָּר אַף הוּא אֵינוֹ עוֹשֶׂה כָּל־צוֹרְכּוֹ מִבְּעוֹד יוֹם. מִתּוֹךְ שֶׁאַתְּ אוֹמֵר לוֹ שֶׁהוּא אָסוּר אַף הוּא עוֹשֶׂה אוֹתוֹ כָּל־צוֹרְכּוֹ מִבְּעוֹד יוֹם. מַה נָּפַק מִן בֵּינֵיהוֹן. לִטְמוֹן שֶׁלֶג וְצוֹנִין. עַל דַּעְתֵּיהּ דְּרִבִּי בָּא מוּתָּר. עַל דַּעְתּוֹן דְּרַבָּנָן דְּתַמָּן אָסוּר. אָסְרוּ טְמִינָה מִפְּנֵי כִירָה. אָסְרוּ כִירָה מִפְּנֵי טְמִינָה. אָסְרוּ כִירָה שֶׁהַגַּחֲלָה מְמוּעָט מִפְּנֵי כִירָה שֶׁהַגַּחֲלָה מְרוּבָּה. אָסְרוּ תַבְשִׁיל שֶׁנִּתְבַּשֵּׁל כָּל־צוֹרְכּוֹ מִפְּנֵי תַבְשִׁיל שֶׁלֹּא נִתְבַּשֵּׁל כָּל־צוֹרְכּוֹ. אָסְרוּ חַמִּין מִפְּנֵי תַבְשִׁיל שֶׁנִּתְבַּשֵּׁל כָּל־צוֹרְכּוֹ. חָזְרוּ וְהִתִּירוּ חַמִּין.

"In what does one store away and in what may one not store away[1]," etc. Because these things are hot and produce heat; if he takes away and they cool in his hand he returns them and they add heat; therefore they forbade to store away in them following Rebbi Eleazar ben Azariah, for Rebbi Eleazar ben Azariah said, "a box he tilts on its side and takes out." But according to the rabbis there? For they say, if it was a vat it is permitted[9]. And there[10] we have stated "if there be doubt whether it is dark or not dark." Because it was not dark; therefore if it is dark it is forbidden to store away in them. There, they are saying, because of the neglect of the house of study[11]; Rebbi Abba said, because of the suspicion[12]. For if you tell him that he is permitted he will not finish it completely when it still is daylight. Because you tell him that he is forbidden he will finish it completely when it still is daylight. What is the difference between them? To hide away snow and cold water. In Rabbi Abba's opinion it is permitted[8], in the opinion of the rabbis there it is prohibited[13]. They forbade hiding away because of the cooking stove; they forbade the cooking stove because of hiding away[14]. They forbade a cooking stove which creates little heat because of a cooking stove which creates much heat. They forbade a completely cooked dish[15] because of an incompletely cooked dish. They forbade hot water because of a completely cooked dish. They turned around and permitted hot water.

9 It is not clear what they permitted. It seems that they permitted any material if the vessel was large enough that even if it was stored away in a heat-producing medium it woyld not come to a boil.

10 Chapter 2 Mishnah 6.

11 There is a problem why there should be any restrictions for storing away hot food since it was established earlier (Chapter 1, Note 361) that food cooked rare is considered completely cooked and, if left on the stove, will not lead to violation of any biblical commandment. While the rules about continued use of a cooking stove fall under the general rabbinic principles of building a "fence around the law", the rules about storing away seem to be "fences around fences" which are frowned upon. One has to seek other reasons for these rules. The Babylonian rabbis think one tries to force people to finish all household chores before sundown so all can come to the synagogue and hear the sermon; cf. *Sotah* 1:4 Notes 185-191.

12 This is R. Abba's general explanation for "fences around fences", cf. Chapter 5 (7b line 53), Chapter 6 (8a line 65).

13 Since it is an activity in the kitchen. In the Babli 51a it is a matter in dispute between Samuel and Rav.

14 In either case one may not use heat producing materials. This argument disputes the prior assertion that it is because of problems with returning the pot into insulating material which is *muqseh*.

15 For which the rules of stowing away are as strict as those for Ben Derosai's food.

(6d line 33) תַּנֵּי. אֵין טוֹמְנִין בְּרֶמֶץ. אָמַר רִבִּי זְעִירָא. הָדָא אָמְרָה. אֶפֶר שֶׁצָּנַן מוּתָּר לִטְמוֹן בּוֹ. כְּהָדָא בְרַתֵּיהּ דְּרִבִּי יַנַּאי הֲוַת מְשַׁמְּשָׁה קוֹמוֹי אֲבוֹי וַהֲוַת מַעֲלָה קוֹמוֹי תַבְשִׁילִין רוֹתְחִין. אָמַר לָהּ. הֵיךְ אִיתְעֲבִידָא. אָמְרָה לֵיהּ. בְּמָרָא וְגִיפְתָּא. אָמַר לָהּ. לָא תְהִי עָבְדָה כֵן אֶלָּא בְמָרָה גּוֹ קוּפְתָה וִיהָבָה קוּפְתָה עַל גִּיפְתָּא. אָמַר רִבִּי זְעִירָא. בְּהָדָא רִבִּי חֲנִינָה פְלִיג. דָּרַשׁ רִבִּי אָחָא בְשֵׁם רִבִּי חֲנִינָה. הַגֶּפֶת מִלְּמַטָּן וְתֶבֶן מִיכָּן וּמִיכָּן אָסוּר. וּמוֹדֵי בָהּ רִבִּי יַנַּאי.

אַבִּין בָּעֵי. בְּלְקָן מָה הֵן. נִישְׁמַעִינָהּ מִן הָדָא. טוֹמְנִין בַּכְּסוּת וּבַפֵּירוֹת וּבְכַנְפֵי יוֹנָה. רִבִּי יוֹסֶה בֶּן פָּזִי בְשֵׁם רִבִּי יוֹסֵי בַּר חֲנִינָה. הָדָא דְתֵימַר בְּשֶׁלֹּא רָבַת רַקְבּוּבִיתָן. אֲבָל אִם רָבַת רַקְבּוּבִיתָן אָסוּר לִטְמוֹן בָּהֶן.

It was stated: One does not store away in hot ashes[16]. Rebbi Ze`ira said, this implies that it is permitted to store away in cold ashes. As the following: Rebbi Yannai's daughter was serving her father and brought him hot dishes.

He asked her, how was this made? She told him, (with a spade and) [it was hidden in]¹⁷ olive cake. He said to her, you should not do this, but (with a spade) [hide it]¹⁷ in a box and put the box on the olive cake¹⁸. Rebbi Ze'ira said, Rebbi Ḥanina disagrees with this. Rebbi Aḥa preached in the name of Rebbi Ḥanina: Olive cake at the bottom and straw on both sides is forbidden, and Rebbi Yannai agrees¹⁹.

Abbin asked: It he mixed them, what²⁰? Let us hear from the following: "One may store away in garments, and produce, and pigeon wings." Rebbi Yose²¹ ben Pazi in the name of Rebbi Yose bar Ḥanina: This means, if they are not much rotten. But if they are much rotten it is forbidden to store away in them²².

16 Babli 34b.
17 The translation in parenthesis, which does not make much sense, follows the ms. text במרא, במרה. The text in brackets follows the emendation of M. de Lonzano, Azulai, *Qorban heEdah,* and Liebermann: כמרא, כמרה.
18 Differently Babli 47b.
19 As long as the olive cake is inside the box it is forbidden according to everybody.
20 If permitted and prohibited materials were mixed.
21 This appears again later in the Chapter (Note 33) where the name is correctly given, R. Jehudah ben Pazi.
22 Since organic decay everywhere produces heat.

(6d line 43) וְלֹא בָחוֹל. תַּמָּן תַּנִּינָן. מַטִּילִין אוֹתוֹ לַחוֹל בִּשְׁבִיל שֶׁיַּמְתִּיו. הָהֵן חָלָא מִירְתַּח רִתְחָא וּמֵיצֵן צוֹנְנָא. הָהֵן תֶּבֶן בַּעַל פִּקָּדוֹן הוּא. בַּמָּה דְאַתְּ יָהִיב לֵהּ הוּא יָהִיב לָךְ.

כָּל־דָּבָר שֶׁמַּרְחִיקִין אוֹתוֹ מִן הַכּוֹתֶל אָסוּר לְטָמוֹן בּוֹ. אָמַר רִבִּי יוֹסֵי. מִן מַה דְּתַנִּינָן. תֶּבֶן טוֹמְנִין בּוֹ. הָדָא אָמְרָה. אֵין מַרְחִיקִין אוֹתוֹ מִן הַכּוֹתֶל. הֲתִיב רִבִּי חַגַּיי. וְהָתַנֵּי. וְהַמַּשְׁפִּיר בֵּית לַחֲבֵירוֹ לֹא יַעֲשֶׂנּוּ אוֹצָר שֶׁל תְּבוּאָה. לֹא מִפְּנֵי הַמּוֹץ. אָמַר רִבִּי חֲנַנְיָה. מִפְּנֵי הָעַכְבָּרִים. אָמַר רִבִּי פִּינְחָס בֵּירִבִּי חֲנִינָה. אִם מִפְּנֵי הָעַכְבָּרִים נִיתְנֵי אֲפִילוּ אוֹצָר שֶׁלְּכָל־דָּבָר. הֲוֵי יָאוּת קַשִׁי לְרִבִּי חַגַּיי. אוֹתִיב רִבִּי שַׁמַּיי. הֲרֵי סְלָעִים מַרְחִיק אוֹתוֹ מִן הַכּוֹתֶל. מֵעַתָּה אָסוּר לְטָמוֹן בָּהֶן. אָמַר רִבִּי יוֹסֵי. לֹא שֶׁהַסְּלָעִים מַרְתִּיחִין אֶלָּא שֶׁהֵן עוֹשִׂין חֲלוּדָה וְהֵן מַלְקִין אַרְעִיתוֹ שֶׁלְּכוּתָל. וְהָא תַנֵּי. אֵין טוֹמְנִין בִּסְלָעִים. תִּיפְתָּר בִּסְלָעִים שֶׁלְּכֶסֶף. אִית תַּנֵּיי תַּנֵּי. טוֹמְנִין בִּסְלָעִים. וְאִית תַּנֵּיי תַּנֵּי. אֵין טוֹמְנִין. אָמַר רַב חִסְדָּא. מָאן דָּמַר. טוֹמְנִין. בְּשֶׁלְּזָהָב שֶׁלִּנְחוֹשֶׁת. וּמָאן דָּמַר. אֵין טוֹמְנִין. בִּסְלָעִים שֶׁלְּכֶסֶף.

"Not in sand." There, we have stated:[23] "One puts it on sand in order to wait." This sand heats the hot and cools the cold[24]. Straw is like the holder of a deposit; what you give it it gives to you.

It is forbidden to store away in anything which one has to distance from a wall[25]. Rebbi Yose said, since we have stated that one may store away in straw, it follows that one need not distance it from a wall. Rebbi Haggai objected: Was it not stated, one who rents o house from his neighbor may not use it as storage for produce? Why? Not because of the chaff? Rebbi Hanania said, because of the rats. Rebbi Phineas ben Rebbi Hanina said, if it were because of the rats then even a storage for anything. Rebbi Shammai objected, does one not distance rocks from the wall? Then rocks are forbidden to hide away in. Rebbi Yose said, it is not that rocks produce heat but they become rusty and destroy the bottom of the wall[26]. But was it not stated: One does not store away in stones. Explain it for silver ore. There are Tannaim who state, one does store in rocks, and there are Tannaim who state, one does not store. Rav Hisda said, he who says "one stores", with gold or brass ore; he who says "one does not store", with silver ore[27].

23 Mishnah 23:5, detailing what may be done for the corpse of a person who dies on the Sabbath. The statement implies that sand is a coolant; then why is is forbidden for stowing away?

24 In the Babli, *Bava Batra* 19a, this is said of rocks.

25 Mishnah *Bava Batra* 2:1. Any chemically active material cannot be stored close to a wall shared with another owner.

26 *Bava Batra* 2:1, Note 12.

27 Quoted Tosaphot *Bava Batra* 17a *s.v.* סלעים.

(6d line 47) לֹא סוֹף דָּבָר לַחִין. אֲפִילוּ יְבֵשִׁין שֶׁנִּתְלַחְלְחוּ. מָן אִילֵּין מוּכִּין. וּמוּכִּין לֹא כִיבֵשִׁין שֶׁנִּתְלַחְלְחוּ הֵן. רִבִּי יוֹחָנָן בַּר שִׁילָא. הָדָא אָמְרָה. הָהֵן דִּכְמַר אַיידָה צָרִיךְ מַחְסַרְתֵּיהּ צִיבְחַר דְּהוּא אָתֵי מֵיסַב וְהִיא שְׁפְכָה וּמְרְתָּחָה. תַּמָּן תַּנִּינָן. כֶּן בְּגֶפֶת חֲדָשָׁה. אֲבָל בִּישָׁנָה טָהוֹר. וְאֵי זוֹ הִיא חֲדָשָׁה וְאֵי זוֹ הִיא יְשָׁנָה. רִבִּי יוֹסֵי בֵּירִבִּי בּוּן בְּשֵׁם רִבִּי יוֹחָנָן. חֲדָשָׁה בְּתוֹךְ י"ב חוֹדֶשׁ. יְשָׁנָה לְאַחַר י"ב חוֹדֶשׁ.

Not only if they are wet[28] but even if they were dry and became wet, as these fibers; are these not like dry which became wet[29]? Rebbi Johanan bar Shila: This implies that one who hides a cauldron[30] must let it be missing a little lest he take it up and it spills and heats.

There, we stated³¹: "The same holds for new olive cake but old one is pure." What is new and what is old? Rebbi Yose ben Rebbi Abun in the name of Rebbi Johanan: New within 12 months, old after 12 months³².

28 All the materials which are permitted as insulating material if dry.
29 Babli 49a.
30 The translation reads אִיֽירָה (Syriac אִירָא). (אַיְידִי) "because of" is Babylonian Aramaic).
31 Mishnah *Kelim* 9:5. The Mishnah states that while the cake itself is not food, any fluid which oozes from it is olive oil subject to all rules of impurity, but dry olive cake is no longer food and impervious to impurity. By analogy, it is permitted to use dry olive cake to store away hot food on the Sabbath.
32 Cf. *Avodah zarah* 2:5 Note 268, Babli *Avodah zarah* 34a.

(6d line 64) טוֹמְנִין בַּכְּסוּת וּבַפֵּרוֹת וּבְכַנְפֵי יוֹנָה.   רִבִּי יוּדָה בַּר פָּזִי בְשֵׁם רִבִּי יִרְמְיָה בַּר חֲנִינָה. הָדָא דְתֵימַר בִּשֶּׁלֹא רָבַת רַקָבוּבִיתָן. אֲבָל רָבַת רַקָבוּבִיתָן אָסוּר לִטְמוֹן בָּהֶן. וּבִנְעוֹרֶת שֶׁל פִּשְׁתָּן וּבִנְסוֹרֶת שֶׁל חָרָשִׁין. אָנַן תַּנִּינָן. נְסוֹרֶת. תַּנֵּי דְבֵית רִבִּי. נְעוֹרֶת. הָדָא אָמְרָה. הִיא הָדָא הִיא הָדָא.

"One may store away in garments, and produce, and pigeon wings⁴." Rebbi Jehudah ben Pazi in the name of Rebbi Jeremiah bar Hanina³³: This means, if they are not much rotten. But if they are much rotten it is forbidden to store away in them²².

"And in flax residue, and in sawdust." We have stated נְסוֹרֶת. In the House of Rebbi they stated נְעוֹרֶת. This implies that both are the same³⁴.

33 An otherwise unknown author. The reading is suspect; cf. Note 21 (R. Yose ben Hanina).
34 This is true for practical use but the roots are נסר "to saw" and נער "to shake off". The Babli disagrees, 49a.

(6d line 67) טוֹמְנִין בַּשְּׁלָחִין וּמְטַלְטְלִין אוֹתָן. רִבִּי יוּדָה בֶּן פָּזִי בְשֵׁם רִבִּי יוֹנָתָן. הָדָא דְתֵימַר בִּנְתוּנִין אֵצֶל בַּעַל הַבַּיִת. אֲבָל בִּנְתוּנִין בָּאַפּוֹתֵיקֵי לֹא בְדָא. בְּגִיזֵּי צֶמֶר וְאֵין מְטַלְטְלִין אוֹתָן. רִבִּי יוּדָה וְרִבִּי יוֹחָנָן. הָדָא דְתֵימַר בִּנְתוּנִין בָּאַפּוֹתֵיקֵי. אֲבָל בִּנְתוּנִין אֵצֶל בַּעַל הַבַּיִת לֹא בְדָא.

"One may store away in raw hides⁵, which one may move." Rebbi Jehudah ben Pazi in the name of Rebbi Jonathan: This you are saying if they are kept in the household. But if they are kept in storage³⁵ this does not apply. "And in wool flakes⁶, which one may not move." Rebbi Judah and Rebbi

Johanan[36]: This you are saying if they are kept in storage. But if they are kept in the household this does not apply[37].

35 Greek ἀποθήκη, ἡ.
36 It seems that one should read: R. Jehudah ben Pazi in the name of R. Jonathan.

37 In all cases raw materials used in the household may be moved and used on the Sabbath; those held in separate storage rooms are *muqseh*. Cf. Babli 49a,50a.

(6d line 71) רַב יִרְמְיָה בְשֵׁם רַב. פּוֹרְשִׂין מַחֲצֶלֶת עַל גַּבֵּי שַׁיָּיפוֹת שֶׁלְּלְבֵינִים בַּשַּׁבָּת.
1 שייפות | י שיפוף

אָמַר רִבִּי שִׁמְעוֹן בְּרִבִּי. אֲנִי לֹא שָׁמַעְתִּי מֵאַבָּא. אֲחוֹתִי אָמְרָה לִי מִשְּׁמוֹ. בֵּיצָה שֶׁנּוֹלְדָה בְיוֹם טוֹב סוֹמְכִין לָהּ כָּלִי בִּשְׁבִיל שֶׁלֹּא תִתְגַּלְגֵּל. אֲבָל אֵין כּוֹפִין עָלֶיהָ אֶת הַכָּלִי. וּשְׁמוּאֵל אָמַר. כּוֹפִין עָלֶיהָ כֶּלִי. אָמַר רִבִּי מָנָא. וּבִלְבַד שֶׁלֹּא יְהֵא הַכָּלִי נוֹגֵעַ בְּגוּפָהּ שֶׁלְּבֵיצָה.
1 בר׳ | 13 ביר׳ ינאי   2 את הכלי | 13 כלי ושמואל | 13 שמואל   3 כופין | 13 אף כופין הכלי | כלי

תַּנֵּי רִבִּי הוֹשַׁעְיָה. נָחִיל שֶׁלְּדְבוֹרִין פּוֹרְסִין עָלֶיהָ סָדִין בַּחַמָּה מִפְּנֵי הַחַמָּה וּבַגְּשָׁמִים מִפְּנֵי הַגְּשָׁמִים. מַה כְרַב. כִּשְׁמוּאֵל. כָּאן מִלְמַטָּן כָּאן מִלְמַעְלָן.
1 שלדבורים | י שלדבורים   2 מלמטן | י מלמטן | י מלמעלן   מלמעלן | י מלמטן

רִבִּי בִּיסְנָא בְשֵׁם רִבִּי יוֹסֵי בַּר חֲנִינָה. חֲפֵי לְסוֹטוֹת אָסוּר לְטַלְטְלוֹ. מְצַדְתָּא הֲוָה פְרִיסָן וְהָדֵין מִשְׁטַרְפָן גּוֹ שִׁמְשָׁא. אֲתוֹן וְשָׁאֲלוּ לְרַב. מָהוּ מְטַלְטְלָתָן. אֲמַר לוֹן. חַשְׁבוֹן עֲלֵיהוֹן מִתְנִינָן תְּחוֹתֵי רֵשִׁיכוֹן וְשָׁרֵי לְכוֹן מְטַלְטָלָתָן.
1 יוסי | י יוסה הוא | י הוויין פריסן | י פריסין   2 והדין | י והויין משטרפן | י משתרפן   י שאלו | י שאלון מטלטלתן | י מטלטלתון חשבון | י אסור ליגע בהון. חשבין עליהון |ו עליהון   3 מתנינן | י מיתנניין רשיכון | י ראשיכון   מטלטלתן | י מטלטלתון

[38]Rav Jeremiah in the name of Rav: One spreads a mat over rows of bricks on the Sabbath[39].

Rebbi Simeon ben Rebbi [Yannai][40] said: I did not hear from my father; my sister told me in his name. For an egg which was laid on a holiday one props it up against a vessel so it should not roll off. But one does not cover it with a vessel[41]. But Samuel says, one may cover it with a vessel. Rebbi Mana said, only if the vessel not touch the body of the egg[42].

Rebbi Hoshaia stated: One may spread a sheet over a swarm of bees[43] in the summer because of the sun, in the rainy season because of the rain. Is this following Rav? Following Samuel? Here on top, there below[44].

Rebbi Bisna in the name of Rebbi Yose bar Ḥanina: It is forbidden to move the weaver's beam weaving fine cloth[45]. The hunters were spreading [traps] and these were damaged by the sun. They came to ask Rav, may one move them?. He told them, [it is forbidden to touch them.]⁴⁰ Intend to put them under your heads and it is permitted for you to move them⁴⁶.

38 The origin of these paragraphs is Halakhah *Besah* 5:1 (י). Not only is the subject of *muqseh* the main topic of this Tractate but also the somewhat difficult Aramaic of the last sentence is copied correctly in *Besah* but defectively here. The second paragraph also is copied later in Chapter 13 (**13**).

39 Even though the bricks are there as building materials one may turn them into seats if needed since they are not moved. In the Babli's theory, *muqseh* items may not be moved, but they may be touched. It does not seem that this is the Yerushalmi's attitude, as expressed by Rav in the question of the hunters. Nevertheless here the bricks are not touched; people sit on the mat. Babli 43a, *Besah* 36a. In the reading of the Babli this is a Tannaitic statement and the bricks are not there for a future building project but are leftovers from a finished one.

40 Added from the two parallel sources.

41 He holds that a vessel may be moved only for something that itself may be moved. Since the egg was not laid before the holiday it is not prepared and may not be moved.

42 Samuel holds that a vessel may be moved for any legitimate purpose. Babli 42b. R. Mana requires that the vessel be moved in a way which certainly avoids moving the egg.

43 The real reason naturally is to catch the bees when they are swarming on a Sabbath or holiday. If it can be done in a way which also protects the bees it may be done; Babli 43a.

44 Since Rav permits to cover the bricks he also will permit to cover the bees. But since Samuel prohibits touching the egg he might forbid here since the cloth necessarily will touch bees. Samuel also will agree here since the swarm is hanging on the branch of a tree, not lying on the ground and supported by it as in the case of the egg.

45 The translation is tentative. In Chapter 6 appears לסוטה as Aramaic translation of Hebrew רְדִיד, a fancy outer garment of women. The identification of פחי as "weaver's beam" follows a suggestion of Kohut (*Arukh completum s.v.* 2 פחה), accepted by Liebermann, that this is Arabic حقّ.

46 If the traps are actually used as a support for the head they may be moved even though at nightfall this intended use is only in the owner's mind, answering a question remaining undecided in Chapter Three (Note 178 ff.).

(7a line 5) רִבִּי זְעִירָא בְשֵׁם רִבִּי יִרְמְיָה. רָאשֵׁי כְלוֹנְסִיּוֹת שֶׁחִישֵׁב עֲלֵיהֶן מֵאִיתְּמַל מוּתָּר לְטַלְטְלָן. רִבִּי יוֹנָה וְרִבִּי יוֹסֵי סַלְקוּן לְסִדְרָא דְּבַר עוּלָּא דַּהֲנָה רְבָעָה תַּמָּן וַהֲוָה תַּמָּן רָאשֵׁי כְלוֹנְסִיּוֹת. אֲתוּן וּשְׁאָלוּן לֵיהּ. מָהוּ לְטַלְטְלָן. אֲמַר לוֹן. אִם חָשַׁבְתָּם עֲלֵיהֶן מֵאִיתְּמַל מוּתָּר מוּתָּר לְטַלְטְלָן. וְאִם לָאו אֵין אַתֶּם מוּתָּרִים לְטַלְטְלָן.

תַּנֵּי רִבִּי חֲלַפְתָּא בַּר שָׁאוּל. מוּכִּין שֶׁחָשַׁב עֲלֵיהֶן מֵאֶתְמוֹל מוּתָּר לְטַלְטְלָן. תַּנֵּי רִבִּי יוֹסֵי בֶּן שָׁאוּל. צֶבֶר שֶׁל קוֹרוֹת שֶׁחִישֵּׁב עֲלֵיהֶן מֵאֶתְמוֹל מוּתָּר לְטַלְטְלָן. רִבִּי יוֹסֵי רִבִּי חֲנִינָה בְשֵׁם רִבִּי יִשְׁמָעֵאל בֵּירִבִּי יוֹסֵי. רִבִּי יַעֲקֹב בַּר אָחָא רִבִּי יַעֲקֹב בַּר אִידִי רִבִּי חֲנִינָה בְשֵׁם רִבִּי יִשְׁמָעֵאל בֵּירִבִּי יוֹסֵי. אַבָּא שַׁלְחָא הֲוָה וַהֲוָה אָמַר לָנוּ. קַשְׁרוּ לָכֶם רָאשֵׁי גִיזִיּוֹת וְאַתֶּם מוּתָּרִין לְטַלְטְלָן לְמָחָר. חִזְקִיָּה אָמַר. אֲפִילוּ מַלּוּ. רַב אָמַר. חֲרָיוֹת שֶׁגִּידְּעָן לִשְׁכִיבָה אֵינָן צְרִיכוֹת קִישּׁוּר. לָאֹהָלִין צְרִיכוֹת קִישּׁוּר. רַב אַבָּא בַּר חָנָה אָמַר. בֵּין לִשְׁכִיבָה בֵּין לָאוֹהָלִין צְרִיכוֹת קִישּׁוּר. אָמַר רִבִּי חִזְקִיָּה. וְלָא דָמִי קִישּׁוּרֵיהּ דְּרַב בָּאוֹהָלִין לְקִישּׁוּרֵיהּ דְּרַב אַבָּא בַּר חָנָה בַּכֵּלִים. קִישּׁוּרֵיהּ דְּרַב בָּאוֹהָלִין. עַד שֶׁיְּקַשֵּׁר אֶת כָּל־הַקּוֹצִין. קִישּׁוּרֵיהּ דְּרַב אַבָּא בַּר חָנָה בַּכֵּלִים. עַד שֶׁיִּהְיֶה עֲלֵיהֶן תּוֹאַר כְּלִי. אִם אוֹמֵר אָתְּ. עַד שֶׁיְּקַשֵּׁר אֶת הַקּוֹצִין. אֵין מַעֲשֶׂה גָּדוֹל מִזֶּה.

Rebbi Zeʾira in the name of Rebbi Jeremiah[47]: log[48] heads about which he had thought the day before may be moved. Rebbi Jonah and Rebbi Yose went up to the *seder*[49] of Bar Ulla. There was a festive meal there and there were heads of logs there. They came and asked him, may one move them? He told them, if you had intention about them from yesterday it is permitted to move them[50], otherwise you are not permitted to move them.

Rebbi Ḥalaphta ben Shaul stated: Fibers[51] about which he thought the day before he is permitted to move. Rebbi Yose ben Shaul stated: A group of beams about which he thought the day before he is permitted to move. Rebbi Yose, Rebbi Ḥanina in the name of Rebbi Ismael ben Rebbi Yose. Rebbi Jacob bar Aḥa, Rebbi Jacob bar Idi, Rebbi Ḥanina in the name of Rebbi Ismael ben Rebbi Yose. My father was a worker in raw hides. He told us, make a knot of the heads of shearings[52] and you will be permitted to move them tomorrow. Ḥizqiah said, even if one made a tie[53]. Rav said, palm branches which one cut to lie on them do not need to be tied, for tents they have to be tied[54]. Rav Abba bar Ḥana said, both for lying down and for tents it needs tying. Rebbi Ḥizqiah said, the tying of Rav for tents is not the same as the tying of Rav Abba bar Ḥana for vessels. The tying of Rav for tents, only if he ties down all thorns. The tying of Rav Abba bar Ḥana for vessels, if only the appellation of "vessel" applies. If you would say, only if he ties down all thorns, there would be no greater production than this[55].

47 This must be either R. Zeʾira in the name of Rav Jeremiah or Rebbi Jeremiah in the name of Rebbi Zeʾira.

48 Greek κᾶλον, τό, "wooden".

49 The house of study. The only feasts held at such a place were religious

celebrations. R. Jonah and R. Yose must still have been minor members of the rabbinate. (J. N. Epstein in *Tarbiz* 6, 1934, p. 236).

50 If the logs obstructed the enlargement of the area reserved for the attendees at the conference, they could be removed on the Sabbath, when there were many more listeners, if this was the intention from Friday.

51 These are raw materials for manufacturing (even if they are used only to fill pillows). To permit moving them on the Sabbath one has to have the intention to use them for a purpose other than manufacturing.

52 Even though these will be removed in the tanning process which will turn the hides into leather; if some activity was undertaken to indicate that in the meantime the hides will be used to sit on they may be moved on the Sabbath.

53 It does not have to be a real knot, difficult to open; it may be a loose tie.

54 Obviously one cannot make a tent from palm branches on the Sabbath. If one cut down the branches for some use in building, e. g., to patch a roof, they become an implement which may be moved on the Sabbath only if they actually are turned into something on which one can sit without hurting oneself. In the Babli, 125b, the text is tannaitic and the question is about palm branches which were cut as fire wood and now one wants to use them as mats whether they need to be tied or not.

55 Since this is a complete implement, there is no special leniency in permitting it to be moved. Since the rules of *muqseh* are rabbinical, one does not expect to have to follow very strict standards.

(7a line 22) רִבִּי יַעֲקֹב בַּר אִידֵי בְּשֵׁם רִבִּי יוֹחָנָן. לְעוֹלָם אַל יִמְנַע אָדָם עַצְמוֹ מִקֵּילֵךְ לְבֵית הַמִּדְרָשׁ. שֶׁהֲרֵי כַּמָּה פְעָמִים נִשְׁאֲלָה הֲלָכָה זוֹ בְיַבְנֶה. עֲרֵיבַת הַיַּרְדֵּן לָמָּה הִיא טְמֵאָה. וְלֹא אָמַר אָדָם דָּבָר. עַד שֶׁבָּא רִבִּי חֲנִינָא בֶּן אַנְטִיגְנָס וּדְרָשָׁהּ בְּעִירוֹ. עֲרֵיבַת הַיַּרְדֵּן לָמָּה הִיא טְמֵאָה. מִפְּנֵי שֶׁמְּמַלִּין אוֹתָהּ פֵּירוֹת וּמוֹלִיכִין אוֹתָהּ מִן הַיָּם לַיַּבָּשָׁה וּמִן הַיַּבָּשָׁה לַיָּם. וְעוֹד דָּבָר אַחֵר דָּרַשׁ. חָרָיוֹת שֶׁגְּדָעָן בֵּין לִשְׁכִיבָה בֵּין לָאוֹהָלִין צְרִיכוֹת קִישּׁוּר. הֲתִיבוּן. הֲרֵי נָדִירַיָּא דְאַשְׁקְלוֹן. אָמַר רִבִּי יִצְחָק בַּר לְעֶזֶר. שַׁנְיָיא הִיא. שֶׁמְּקַצָּתָן בַּיָּם וּמִקְצָתָן בַּיַּבָּשָׁה.

[56]Rebbi Jacob bar Idi in the name of Rebbi Johanan: A man never should refrain from going to the House of Study; since in Jabneh this question was asked many times, why is a Jordan skiff impure[57]? Nobody answered anything until Rebbi Hanina ben Antigonos came and explained it in his city: Why is a Jordan skiff impure? Because one fills it with produce and transports it from dry land to the sea and from the sea to dry land[58]. In addition he explained that palm branches which one cut both for lying down and for tents need tying[59]. They objected, are there not the infrequent ones[60]

of Askalon? Rebbi Isaac ben Eleazar said, there is a difference since part of them are in the sea and part of them on dry land[61].

56 A parallel is in *Eccl. rabba ad* 1:15, with a different name tradition: R. Jacob bar Aha in the name of R. Johanan, R. Hanina bar Aqabia, R. Eleazar ben Yose. Still other names are given in the Babli, 83b.

57 A small boat made of clay. A clay container holding less than 40 *seah* may become impure, but a ship of any kind is impervious to impurity (Mishnah 9:2). Why should this particular kind of boat be subject to impurity?

58 Since the skiff is so small that it can be put on a carriage and transported on land without being unloaded it follows the rules of land-based vessels.

59 This is tannaitic support for Rav Abba bar Hana.

60 In *Eccl. r.,* יורדי אשקלון "those who go down to Askalon." The translation takes נָדִיר in the usual sense, "infrequent, rare event". The meaning seems to be that this kind of skiff is not appropriate for the ocean and is only rarely seen at Askalon.

61 While vessels of this kind may be used either as containers on land or small boats on water, at Askalon they are either one or the other. Since there the clay boats are never used as containers on land, they are impervious to impurity.

(7a line 30) אֲתִייָא דְרִבִּי בָּא בַּר חָנָא כְּרִבִּי חֲנִינָא. דָּמַר רִבִּי חֲנִינָא. עוֹלִין הָיִינוּ עִם רִבִּי לְחַמַּת גָּדֵר וְהָיָה אוֹמֵר לָנוּ. בַּחֲרוּ לָכֶם חֲלָקֵי אֲבָנִים וְאַתֶּם מוּתָּרִין לְטַלְטְלָן לְמָחָר. רִבִּי זְעִירָא אָמַר. עַד שֶׁיְּקַרְדֵּם. חֲבֶרַיָּיא אָמְרִי. עַד שֶׁיְּשַׁפְשֵׁף. צִיפּוֹרָאֵי אָמְרִין. עַד שֶׁיַּחְשׁוֹב. רִבִּי יוֹחָנָן אָמַר. עַד שֶׁיְּהֵא עֲלֵיהֶן תּוֹאַר כָּלִי. אַשְׁכָּחַת אָמַר רַב חָנָא בַּר אַבָּא וְרִבִּי יוֹחָנָן וְרִבִּי יוֹנָתָן חָדָא. רַב וְרִבִּי זְעִירָא וְרִבִּי יִשְׁמָעֵאל בֵּירִבִּי יוֹסֵי חָדָא. צִיפּוֹרָאֵי וְרִבִּי יוֹסֵי בֶּן שָׁאוּל וְרִבִּי חֲלַפְתָּא בֶּן שָׁאוּל חָדָא. חֲבֶרַיָּיא לֵית לְהוֹן זוּג.

The statement of Rebbi Abba bar Hana follows Rebbi Hanina, as Rebbi Hanina said[62], we were ascending with Rebbi to the Hot Springs of Gadara when he said to us, choose yourselves smooth stones; then you are permitted to move them tomorrow. Rebbi Ze'ira said, only if he chiseled. The colleagues say, only if he polished. The Sepphoreans say, only if he intends. Rebbi Johanan said, only if it falls under the designation of implement. You might say that Rav Hana bar Abba[63], and Rebbi Johanan, and Rebbi Jonathan[64] are one [opinion]. Rav, and Rebbi Ze'ira, and Rebbi Ismael ben Rebbi Yose are one [opinion]. The Sepphoreans, and Rebbi Yose ben Shaul, and Rebbi Halaphta ben Shaul are one [opinion]. The collegues have no pairing[65].

62 Babli 125b.
63 Read: Rav Abba bar Hana.
64 R. Jonathan is not mentioned in the preceding discussion but in the Babli, 83b, he is quoted in the place of R. Jacob bar Idi here. Therefore the opinion of R. Jonathan is the one attributed in the preceding paragraph to R. Hanina ben Antigonos. The other references are to the paragraph before the last.
65 Greek ζυγόν, τό, also ζεῦγος, -εος, τό.

(7a line 37) נְטָלוֹ מִבְּעוֹד יוֹם מַחֲזִירוֹ מִבְּעוֹד יוֹם. נְטָלוֹ מִשֶּׁחֲשֵׁיכָה מַחֲזִירוֹ מִשֶּׁחֲשֵׁיכָה. נְטָלוֹ מִבְּעוֹד יוֹם וְקָדַשׁ עָלָיו הַיּוֹם. רִבִּי בָּא בְשֵׁם רַב יְהוּדָה. אִם נִתְקַלְקְלָה הַגּוּמָא אֲסוּרָה. וּמִכִּירָה לִכְירָה מוּתָּר. מִן הַהוּא דָּמַר רִבִּי לִיעֶזֶר בְּשֵׁם רִבִּי יְהוֹשֻׁעַ. מְשָׁרֵת הָיִיתִי אֶת רִבִּי חִייָא הַגָּדוֹל וְהָיִיתִי מַעֲלֶה לוֹ חַמִּין מִדְּיַיטֵי הַתַּחְתּוֹנָה לַדְּיַיטֵי הָעֶלְיוֹנָה וּמַחֲזִירָן לַכִּירָה. וָמַר רִבִּי יִרְמְיָה בֶּרִבִּי שִׁמְעוֹן. אֲפִילוּ מִכִּירָה שֶׁהֲבָלָהּ מְמוּעָט לַכִּירָה שֶׁהֲבָלָהּ מְרוּבֶּה מוּתָּר.

מִכִּירָה לִטְמִינָה אָסוּר. מִטְּמִינָה לִכְירָה אָסוּר. מִטְּמִינָה לִטְמִינָה צְרִיכָה.

נִתְגַּלֶּה מִבְּעוֹד יוֹם מְכַסֵּהוּ מִבְּעוֹד יוֹם. נִתְגַּלֶּה מִשֶּׁחֲשֵׁיכָה מְכַסֵּהוּ מִשֶּׁחֲשֵׁיכָה. נִתְגַּלֶּה מִבְּעוֹד יוֹם וְקָדַשׁ עָלָיו הַיּוֹם. תַּנֵּי. אֵין טוֹמְנִין חַמִּין מִשֶּׁחֲשֵׁיכָה אֲבָל מוֹסִיפִין עֲלֵיהֶן כְּסוּת וְכֵלִים. כַּמָּה יְהֵא עֲלֵיהֶן וִיהֵא מוּתָּר לְכַסּוֹתָם. רִבִּי זְרִיקָן בְּשֵׁם רִבִּי חֲנִינָה. אֲפִילוּ מַפָּה. אָמַר רִבִּי זְעִירָא. וּבִלְבַד דָּבָר שֶׁהוּא מוֹעִיל. אָמַר רִבִּי חִינָּנָא. כָּל־הַדְּבָרִים מוֹעִילִין. אָמַר רִבִּי מַתַּנְיָה. וְיֵאוּת. אִילוּ מָאן דְּנָסַב מַרְטוּט וִיהַב לָהּ עַל רִישֵׁיהּ בִּשְׁעַת צִינָּתָה דִּלְמָא לָא כְבִישׁ צִינָּתָה.

כָּשֵׁם שֶׁאֵין טוֹמְנִין חַמִּין מִשֶּׁחֲשֵׁיכָה כָּךְ אֵין טוֹמְנִין לֹא שֶׁלֶג וְלֹא צוֹנִין. וְרִבִּי מַתִּיר. הָתִיב שְׁמוּאֵל בַּר אַבָּא עַל הָדָא קַדְמִייְתָא. וְהָא תַנִּי. מְמַלֵּא הוּא אָדָם אֶת הַקִּיתוֹן שֶׁלְּמַיִם וְנוֹתֵן תַּחַת הַכַּר אוֹ תַחַת הַכֶּסֶת. אֶלָּא כְרָבִי. דְּרִבִּי מַתִּיר. כָּאן לְשָׁעָה כָּאן לִשְׁהוֹת.

[66]If he took it when it still was daylight he may return it when it still is daylight. If he took it after dark he may return it after dark. If he took it when it still was daylight and the day became holy for him? Rebbi Abba in the name of Rav Jehudah: If the groove was unusable it is forbidden[67], but from stove to stove it is permitted, from what Rebbi Eliezer said in the name of Rebbi Joshua[68]: I was serving the Great Rebbi Ḥiyya and I brought him hot water from the lower to the upper apartment and returned it to the stove. Rebbi Jeremiah ben Rebbi Simeon said, even from a stove with little heat to a stove with much heat.

From a stove to storing away is forbidden. From storing away to a stove is forbidden. From storing away to storing away is problematic[69].

If it was uncovered[70] when it still was daylight he may cover it when it still is daylight. If it was uncovered after dark he may cover if after dark. If it was uncovered when it still was daylight and the day became holy for him? It was stated[71]: One does not store hot water away after dark but one may add over it garments and vessels. How much must be on them that it be permitted to cover them? Rebbi Zeriqan in the name of Rebbi Ḥanina: Even a handkerchief. Rebbi Ze`ira said, but only something of use. Rebbi Ḥinena said, everything is useful. Rebbi Mattaniah said, this is correct. If somebody would take a rag and put it on his head in the cold, would this not conquer the cold?

Just as one may not store away hot water after nightfall, so one may not store away snow or cold water, but Rebbi permits[70]. Samuel bar Abba objected to this first one; did we not state: "A person may fill a water pitcher[8] and put it under the pillow or under the quilt." But following Rebbi since Rebbi permits. Here for the moment, there to leave it[72].

66 This paragraph, except the sentence of R. Abba in the name of Rav Jehudah, is from Chapter 3, Notes 55-59.

67 If the place where the pot had been now is filled with the insulating material; cf. Note 7.

68 These names are quite impossible; RR. Eliezer and Joshua were first generation Tannaim while R. Hiyya belongs to the generation of transition from Tannaim to Amoraim. The names as given in Chapter 3 have to be accepted.

69 The problem remains unresolved; it remains unresolved in the Babli, 38b.

70 The food stored away.

71 Babli 51a.

72 The statement that after nightfall one may not store away cold water seems to directly contradict the last sentence in the Mishnah, cf. Notes 8,13. The Mishnah refers only to short term storage.

במה בהמה יוצאה פרק חמישי

(fol. 7a) **משנה א**: בַּמֶּה בְּהֵמָה יוֹצְאָה וּבַמָּה אֵינָהּ יוֹצֵאת. יוֹצֵא הַגָּמָל בָּאיפְסָר וְהַנָּקָה בְחָטָם וְהַלִּיבְדְּקֵס בַּפְּרוּמְבִּיָּא וְהַסּוּס בַּשֵּׁיר וְכָל בַּעֲלֵי הַשֵּׁיר יוֹצְאִין בַּשֵּׁיר וְנִמְשָׁכִין בַּשֵּׁיר וּמַזִּין עֲלֵיהֶן וְטוֹבְלִין בִּמְקוֹמָן:

Mishnah 1: With what may an animal go out and with what may it not go out[1]? A camel may go out with a bridle, and a female camel with a nose ring, and a Lybian donkey with a bridle[2], and a horse with a chain, and all that have a chain may go out with the chain and may be drawn with the chain which may be sprinkled upon and immersed in place[3].

משנה ב: חֲמוֹר יוֹצֵא בַּמַּרְדַּעַת בִּזְמַן שֶׁהִיא קְשׁוּרָה לוֹ. הַזְּכָרִים יוֹצְאִין לְבוּבִין. רְחֵילוֹת יוֹצְאוֹת שְׁחוּזוֹת כְּבוּלוֹת וּכְבוּנוֹת וְהָעִזִּים צְרוּרוֹת. רִבִּי יוֹסֵי אוֹסֵר בְּכוּלָּן חוּץ מִן הָרְחֵלִים הַכְּבוּנוֹת. רִבִּי יְהוּדָה אוֹמֵר עִזִּים יוֹצְאִין צְרוּרוֹת לְיַבֵּשׁ אֲבָל לֹא לְחָלָב:

Mishnah 2: A donkey may go out with its saddle cloth[4] if it is tied to it. Rams may go out protected on their bellies[5]; female sheep may go out with their tail bound high, or bound low[6], or wrapped[7], and goats tied[8]. Rebbi Yose prohibits all these except wrapped female sheep. Rebbi Jehudah says goats may go out tied to dry but not for milk[9].

משנה ג: וּבַמָּה אֵינָהּ יוֹצֵאת. לֹא יֵצֵא גָמָל בַּמְּטוּטֶלֶת לֹא עָקוּד וְלֹא רָגוּל וְכֵן שְׁאָר כָּל־הַבְּהֵמוֹת. לֹא יִקְשׁוֹר גְּמַלִּים זֶה בָזֶה וְיִמְשׁוֹךְ. אֲבָל מַכְנִיס חֲבָלִים לְתוֹךְ יָדוֹ וְיִמְשׁוֹךְ וּבִלְבַד שֶׁלֹּא יִכְרוֹךְ:

Mishnah 3: With what may [an animal] not go out? The camel may not go out with its pad, nor bound on one foot, nor bound on two feet, and so all other animals. One may not tie camels one to the other and draw, but he may take the ropes into his hand and draw on condition that he not wrap up[10].

משנה ד: אֵין חֲמוֹר יוֹצֵא בַּמַּרְדַּעַת בִּזְמַן שֶׁאֵינָהּ קְשׁוּרָה לוֹ וְלֹא בְזוֹג אַף עַל פִּי שֶׁהוּא פָקוּק וְלֹא בְסוּלָם שֶׁבְּצַוָּארוֹ וְלֹא בִרְצוּעָה שֶׁבְּרַגְלוֹ. אֵין הַתַּרְנְגוֹלִין יוֹצְאִין בְּחוּטִין וְלֹא בִרְצוּעוֹת שֶׁבְּרַגְלֵיהֶן. וְאֵין הַזְּכָרִים יוֹצְאִין בַּעֲגָלָה שֶׁתַּחַת הָאַלְיָה שֶׁלָּהֶן וְאֵין הָרְחֵלִים יוֹצְאוֹת חֲנוּנוֹת וְאֵין הָעֵגֶל יוֹצֵא בַּגִּימוֹן וְלֹא פָרָה בְעוֹר הַקּוּפָד וְלֹא בִרְצוּעָה שֶׁבֵּין קַרְנֶיהָ. פָּרָתוֹ שֶׁל רִבִּי אֶלְעָזָר בֶּן עֲזַרְיָה הָיְתָה יוֹצְאָה בִּרְצוּעָה שֶׁבֵּין קַרְנֶיהָ שֶׁלֹּא בִרְצוֹן חֲכָמִים:

ŠABBAT CHAPTER FIVE 177

Mishnah 4: A donkey may not go out with its saddle cloth if it is not bound to it, nor with a bell even if it is plugged, nor with a ladder on its neck[11], nor with a strip on its foot. Chicken may no go out with threads or strips on their feet[12]. Rams may not go out with a carriage under their tails[13] nor female sheep with *yahnun*[14], nor a calf with *gimun*[15], nor a cow with hedgehog hide[16], nor with a strip between her horns. Rebbi Eleazar ben Azariah's cow went out with a strip between her horns against the will of the Sages.

1   Since the Sabbath paragraph in the Ten Commandments prescribes rest for animals, one may not let one's animals go into the public domain carrying anything which may be considered a load.

2   Greek φορβειά, ἡ, "mouthband".

3   If the chain became impure the entire animal may be immersed in water and the chain with it; this is counted as immersion in a *miqweh*. If the impurity is that of a corpse, the water with the ashes of the Red Cow may be sprinkled on the chain while it is on the horse.

4   If the donkey is used as a beast of burden, it is covered with cloth before the load is put on. This cloth is protecting the donkey's hide; it is not considered a load if it was tied down before the start of the Sabbath.

5   Against attacks by predators.

6   The tail is bound on their backs to have males mounting them; the tails are bound between their feet to prevent males mounting them.

7   Sheep producing high quality wool may be wrapped in a protective sheath.

8   Female goats may be given brassieres either to protect their udders from the sharp rocks on which they are climbing or to prevent them from nursing their young.

9   He admits protective brassieres since they are necessities of their bodies. He forbids the second reason given in the preceding Note.

10   One may not tie camels to one another because it looks as if he would go on a trip; one person may collect the ropes of many camels together in one hand and lead them out; he may not twist the ropes together to act as one rope.

11   This is not a ladder to stand on but a contraption looking like a miniature ladder put on top of a wound dressing on the donkey's skin with which the dressing is tied down.

12   The strips are signs of ownership. They are for the benefit of the owner, not the chicken.

13   If the tails get very long and heavy, some miniature carriage may be tied to them to protect the tail from injury.

14   Some aromatic tree whose identity is not determined, which was used as medicine against intestinal worms.

15   Various interpretations of this word are given in the Halakhah.

16   Bound near the udder to prevent the calf from suckling.

(7b line 9) בַּמֶּה בְּהֵמָה יוֹצְאָה וּבַמֶּה אֵינָהּ יוֹצְאָה כול׳. תָּנֵי רִבִּי יִשְׁמָעֵאל בֵּירִבִּי יוֹסֵי מִשּׁוּם אָבִיו. אַרְבַּע בְּהֵמוֹת נִמְשָׁכוֹת בָּאיפְסָר וְאֵילוּ הֵן. הַסּוּס וְהַפֶּרֶד הַגָּמָל וְהַחֲמוֹר. אָמַר רִבִּי חִזְקִיָּה. וְסִימָנָא וְכֵן תִּהְיֶה מַגֵּפַת הַסּוּס הַפֶּרֶד הַגָּמָל וְהַחֲמוֹר. רַב אָמַר. הֲלָכָה כְרִבִּי יִשְׁמָעֵאל בֵּירִבִּי יוֹסֵי.

"With what may an animal go out and with what may it not go out," etc. [17]"Rebbi Ismael ben Rebbi Yose stated in his father's name: Four kinds of animals are drawn by the bridle[17a]: the horse, and the mule, the camel, and the donkey." Rebbi Hizqiah said, and its sign, *so will be the plague of the horse, the mule, the camel, and the donkey*[17b]. Rav said, practice follows Rebbi Ismael ben Rebbi Yose[18].

17 Babli 51b,52a. Tosephta 4:1 (ed. Liebermann).
17a Farsi افسار.
17b *Zech.* 14:15.
18 All these animals may be led out on the Sabbath by their bridle.

(7b line 13) לִיבְדְּקָס. אִית תַּנָּיֵי תַנֵּי. לְגָדְקָס. מָאן דָּמַר לִיבְדְקָס. עַל שֵׁם לוּבִים וְכוּשִׁים בְּמִצְעָדָיו. מָאן דָּמַר לְגָדְקָס. אַמְבַּטִּיס. מָהוּ אַמְבַּטִּיס. חֲמוֹר סָלָק.
1 לגדקס | כ ניברקוס   דמר | כ דאמ׳ | - | כ דאמ׳   לגדקס | כ ניברקוס   אמבטס | כ אבהטס (2)   2 דמר | כ דאמ׳   כ שם ליבוי

רִבִּי יוֹנָה אָמַר. רַב הוֹשַׁעְיָה בָעֵי. גֵּרִים הַבָּאִים מִלּוּבֵּי מָהוּ לְהַמְתִּין לָהֶן שְׁלֹשָׁה דוֹרוֹת. אָמַר רִבִּי יוֹנָה בֶּן צְרוּיָה. מִן מָה דָּנָן חָמֵיי פּוּלָא מִצְרִיָּא כְּדוֹן רְטִיב צָוְוחִין אִינּוּן לֵיהּ לוּבִּי. כַּדּוּ נָגִיב אִינּוּן צָוְוחִין לֵיהּ פּוּל מִצְרִי. הָדָא אָמְרָה. גֵּר מִלּוּבֵּי צָרִיךְ לְהַמְתִּין לוֹ ג׳ דוֹרוֹת. הָדָא אָמְרָה. הוּא לוּבִּי הוּא מִצְרִי. רִבִּי יִצְחָק בַּר נַחְמָן בְּשֵׁם רִבִּי אוֹשַׁעְיָה. הֲלָכָה כְּדִבְרֵי הַתַּלְמִיד. דִּבְרֵי חֲכָמִים. כָּל־מִין פְּרָדוֹת אֶחָד.
1 אמ׳ | כ -   מלובי | כ מליבוי   2 בן צרוייה | כ בוצרייה   דנן | כ דאנן חמיי | כ חמי   מצרייא | כ מצריי   כדון | כ כד   כדון | כ כד   3 ג׳ | כ שלשה   4 הוא לובי הוא מצרי | כ היא לוב היא מצרים   אושעיה | כ הושעיה

[19]"A Libyan donkey." Some Tannaim state: "Not a *lgdqs*.[20]" He who says *libdyqos* because of "Libyans and Nubians in His train.[21]" He who says *lgdqs*, ἀμβάτης[22]. What is ἀμβάτης? A donkey stallion.

Rebbi Jonah said, Rav Hoshaia asked: Do proselytes from Libya have to wait three generations[23]? Rebbi Jonah (Ben Seruya) [from Bostra][24] said, from what we see that they call a green Egyptian bean Libyan[25] but a dry one Egyptian, that means a proselyte from Libya has to wait three generations; it means that Libyan is identical with Egyptian. Rebbi Isaac bar Naḥman in the name of Rebbi Hoshaiah: Practice follows the student[26]. The words of the Sages are that all kinds of mules are one[27].

19 The origin of this text is in *Kilaim* 8:4, Notes 62-71. The text here is a copy even though it has a better transcription of the Greek since the last sentence refers tio Mishnah *Kilaim* 8:4 and makes no sense here. A very detailed study of the first six sentences here and in *Kilaim* was done by J. N. Epstein, מבוא לנוסח המשנה[2], Jerusalem 1964, pp. 97-99, where all variant readings of the names here, in *Kilaim*, and *Gen. rabba* (*ad* 49:11) are collected and commented on. The vocalization of ליבדקס is from the Kaufmann ms. of the Mishnah.

20 An unexplained word that was unknown even to the rabbis of the Yerushalmi. *Libdyqos* is adj. Λιβυστικός, -ή, -όν, "Libyan".

21 *Dan.* 11:43.

22 A poetic word, usually ἀναβάτης, -ου, ὁ, "stallion". J. N. Epstein points out that because of the nasal pronunciation of *m* in Galilean speech, an *m* can easily be inserted or disappear, so that ἀμβάτης and ἀναβάτης are really one and the same.

23 *Deut.* 23:8-9 prescribes that an Egyptian proselyte and his direct offspring may not marry anyone born to Jewish parents. {The discussion is purely theoretical since one holds that the political upheavals already from the time of Sanherib did displace all peoples originally mentioned in the Pentateuch, Mishnah *Yadayim* 4:4; cf. *Šulhan 'Arukh Even Ha'ezer* 4:10.}

24 The name is correct in *Kilaim* [in brackets], incorrect here (in parentheses).

25 A bean is لوبيا *lubia* in Arabic and Farsi; according to N. Brüll, the name is originally Coptic.

26 This sentence refers to Mishnah *Kilaim* 8:4 and does not belong here.

27 For the rules of *Kilaim* it does not matter whether father or mother are horse or donkey; they all may be mated together. Babli Hulin 79a.

רִבִּי שְׁמוּאֵל בְּשֵׁם רִבִּי זְעִירָא. כָּמָה דְתֵימַר לְעִנְיָין אִיסּוּר. וְכֵן כָּל־שְׁאָר הַבְּהֵמָה. לְעִנְיָין הֵיתֵר וְכֵן.

Rebbi Samuel in the name of Rebbi Ze`ira: As one says in matters of prohibition "and so all other animals", in matters of permission it is the same[28].

28 Just as in Mishnah 3 the camel is only an example, so also in Mishnaiot 1 and 2 the species of animals are only examples. In any case anything necessary to guard the animals to prevent them from getting lost is not a load and not forbidden on the Sabbath.

(7b line 28) הַסּוּס בַּשֵּׁיר. וְלֹא כֵן תַּנֵּי. כָּל־תַּכְשִׁיטֵי אָדָם טְמֵאִין וְתַכְשִׁיטֵי בְהֵמָה טְהוֹרִין. תִּיפְתָּר בַּעֲשׂוּיִין לְהַנּוֹתָן. וְאֵינוֹ עוֹשֶׂה חָרֵץ. אֶלָּא כְרִבִּי שִׁמְעוֹן. דְּתַנֵּי. לֹא יְגָרֵר אָדָם אֶת הַמִּיטָה וְאֶת הַכִּסֵא וְאֶת הַסַּפְסָל וְאֶת הַקַּתֶידְרָה מִפְּנֵי שֶׁהוּא עוֹשֶׂה חָרֵץ. וְרִבִּי שִׁמְעוֹן מַתִּיר. אָמַר רִבִּי חִינְנָא. כְּהָדָא דְתַנֵּי. דֶּלֶת גּוֹרֶרֶת מַחֲצֶלֶת גּוֹרֶרֶת קִינְקִילוֹן גּוֹרֵר פּוֹתֵחַ וְנוֹעֵל בַּשַּׁבָּת. וְאֵין צָרִיךְ לוֹמַר בְּיוֹם טוֹב. וְתַנֵּי כֵן. מַחֲצֶלֶת שֶׁהִיא קְשׁוּרָה וּתְלוּיָה בְּעַמּוּד פּוֹתֵחַ וְנוֹעֵל בַּשַּׁבָּת. וְאֵין צָרִיךְ לוֹמַר בְּיוֹם טוֹב.

וּמַזִּין עֲלֵיהֶן וְטוֹבְלִין בִּמְקוֹמָן: תַּמָּן תַּנִּינָן. וְלֹא תִטְבֹּל בָּהֶן עַד שֶׁתְּרַפֵּם. וְכָא הוּא אָמַר הָכֵין. אָמַר רִבִּי מָנָא. כָּאן בְּרָפִים. כָּאן בָּאֲפוּצִים.

"And the horse with a chain." But did we not state, all human decorations are impure but decorations of animals are pure[29]? Explain it if they are made to lead them[30]. But then does it not make a groove? But following Rebbi Simeon, as it was stated:[31] "A person may not drag a bed, or a chair, or a footstool[5], or a fauteuil, because he makes a groove, but Rebbi Simeon permits." Rebbi Hinena said, like the following as it was stated[32]: "a hinged door, a hinged mat, hinged lattice gates[33], one may open and lock on the Sabbath, and it is not necessary to say on a holiday." It also was stated[34]: "If a mat was tied to and hanging from a pillar, one may open and lock on the Sabbath, and it is not necessary to say on a holiday."

"Which may be sprinkled upon and immersed in place[3]." There, we have stated[35]: "She may not immerse herself wearing them unless she relaxes them." And here he says so? Rebbi Mana said, here if they are loose, there if they are tight[36].

29 If all decorations of animals are impervious to impurity, how could a chain around a horse's neck ever need immersion?
30 Read להנותן as להנחותן, as gutturals were no longer articulated in Galilean speech (S. Liebermann). The chain is an implement, not a decoration. But then it must have slack and might be drawn on the ground, making a groove.
31 Chapter 3 Note 74 and the sources quoted there.
32 Tosephta *Eruvin* 8:12 (ed. Liebermann), *Yom Tov* 2:19 (as continuation of R. Simeon's Tosephta); *Eruvin* Babli 101a, Yerushalmi Chapter 10, Note 119. The Tosephta need not necessarily be only R. Simeon's teaching since the impression made by the fixed doors on the dirt floor is only a temporary effect.
33 Greek κιγκλίς, -ίδος, ἡ, mostly in plural κιγκλίδες, "lattice gates"; Latin *cancellus, -i,* n. "lattice barrier, grating, grille", cf. *Avodah zarah* Chapter 2 Note 219.
34 *Eruvin* Chapter 10, Note 119,

Tosephta 8:11 (ed. Liebermann).
35 Mishnah 6:1, speaking of ribbons in women's hair. Since purification requires immersion of one's "entire body" in water (*Lev.* 15:16), an immersion is invalid if not the entire surface of the object or subject to be purified is wetted.

36 If the chain is there to lead the horse it cannot be tight. The living horse cannot be impure; it also is not an obstacle to purification. Babli 52b.

(line 7b) מתני׳. חֲמוֹר יוֹצֵא בְּמַרְדַּעַת כול׳. שְׁמוּאֵל אָמַר. בִּקְשׁוּרָה לוֹ מֵעֶרֶב שַׁבָּת. חָנִין מְגוּפְתִּיָּיה אֲמַר קוֹמֵי שְׁמוּאֵל. רַב חִייָא בַּר אַשִׁי לָא נְהִיג כֵּן. אֲמַר לֵיהּ. נְהִיג רַב בִּקְלַסְטִירִין. דְּתַנֵּי. זְכָרִים יוֹצְאִין בִּקְלַסְטִירִין. הֵתִיב רִבִּי אַחָא בַּר פָּפָא קוֹמֵי רִבִּי זְעִירָא. וְהָא תַנֵּי. חֶבֶל שֶׁהוּא קָשׁוּר בַּפָּרָה קוֹשְׁרִין אוֹתוֹ בָּאֵבוּס. בָּאֵבוּס קוֹשְׁרִין אוֹתוֹ בַּפָּרָה. נִיחָא בַּפָּרָה קוֹשְׁרִין אוֹתוֹ בָּאֵבוּס. בָּאֵבוּס קוֹשְׁרִין אוֹתוֹ בַּפָּרָה. וְלֹא נִמְצָא מִשְׁתַּמֵּשׁ בְּצִדְדֵי בְהֵמָה בַּשַּׁבָּת. אֲמַר רִבָּה. תִּיפְתָּר בִּקְשָׁרִין שֶׁאֵינָן שֶׁלְּקַייָמָא. אֲמַר רִבִּי יוֹסֵי. שַׁנְיָיא הִיא צְדָדֵי בְהֵמָה בֵּין קֶשֶׁר שֶׁהוּא שֶׁלְּקַייָמָא בֵּין קֶשֶׁר שֶׁאֵינוֹ שֶׁלְּקַייָמָא. אֲמַר רִבִּי שַׁמַּי. תִּיפְתָּר כְּרִבִּי שִׁמְעוֹן בֶּן אֶלְעָזָר. דְּתַנֵּי. רִבִּי שִׁמְעוֹן בֶּן אֶלְעָזָר אוֹמֵר. מוּתָּר לְהִשְׁתַּמֵּשׁ עַל צְדָדֵי בְהֵמָה בַּשַּׁבָּת. הִיא צְדָדֵי בְהֵמָה הִיא צְדָדֵי אִילָן. אֲמַר רִבִּי מָנָא. קִייַמְתִּיהּ בִּמְסַפֵּק חֶבֶל עַל חֶבֶל.

Mishnah. "A donkey may go out with its saddle cloth," etc. Samuel said, if it was tied to it from before the Sabbath. Ḥanin from Gophtia said before Samuel, Rav Ḥiyya bar Ashi does not act like this. He told him, Rav uses *kleisterin*, as it was stated: rams go out with *kleisterin*[37]. Rebbi Aḥa bar Papa objected before Rebbi Ze`ira: But was it not stated[38]: a rope tied to a cow may be tied to the feeding trough, the feeding trough may be tied to a cow. One understands a cow's may be tied to the feeding trough. May from the feeding trough be tied to a cow? Would he not use the animal's sides on the Sabbath[39]? Rebbi Abba said, explain it for knots which are not permanent[40]. Rebbi Yose said, is there a difference for sides of an animal whether the knot is permanent or not permanent? Rebbi Shammai said, explain it following Rebbi Simeon ben Eleazar, as it was stated, Rebbi Simeon ben Eleazar said, it is permitted to use the sides of an animal on the Sabbath[41]. There is no difference between sides of an animal and sides of a tree[42]. Rebbi Mana said, I confirmed it if he connects rope to rope[43].

37 It is not clear what this means. One possibility is κλεῖστρον, τό = κλεῖθρον "bar, boom, fence". Rosh who quotes the paragraph *in extenso* (Chapter 5 No. 2) reads טרסקל which is a feeding basket bound to the animal's head. Such a feeding basket is

appropriate for cattle used for agricultural work; it is inappropriate for rams. Also since rams are not dangerous, except maybe for competing rams, there seems to be no reason why rams should be muzzled. The only explanation for a lock for rams would be a contraption which would prevent the ram to mount ewes except under control of the owner. This is accepted in Mishnah 2.
38   Babli 113a.
39   Since it is biblically forbidden to ride animals on the Sabbath it is rabbinically forbidden to lean on animals. In harnessing an animal it is difficult to avoid leaning on it.
40   This is difficult to understand. Since making a permanent knot is a biblical violation of the Sabbath (Mishnah 7:2) it is clear that all tying of ropes on the Sabbath must be loops that are easily undone.
41   As anonymous opinion Babli 154b.
42   Since biblically it is forbidden to cut a branch from a tree, rabbinically it is forbidden to climb it on the Sabbath.
43   If the cow is lead to or from the feeding trough, it is not touched at all but a rope attached to the trough is tied or untied to the rope around the cow's neck.

(7b line 44) זְכָרִים יוֹצְאִין לְבוּבִין. שֶׁהוּא נוֹתֵן עוֹר מְבוּרְסִינָיו כְּנֶגֶד לִיבּוֹ וְהוּא מַתְרִיס כְּנֶגֶד חַיָה.

רְחֵילִים יוֹצְאוֹת שְׁחוּזוֹת. אִית תַּנָּיֵי תַנֵּי. שְׁחוּזוֹת. וְאִית תַּנָּיֵי תַנֵּי. שׁוּזוֹת. מָאן דָּמַר שׁוּזוֹת. מִתְעַדָּן. כְּמָה דְתֵימַר. שָׁיִת זוֹנָה וּנְצוּרַת לֵב: מָאן דָּמַר שְׁחוּזוֹת. כְּמָה דְתֵימַר. אֵין מַשְׁחִיזִין אֶת הַסַּכִּין. כְּבוּנוֹת לְמֵילָת. כְּבוּלוֹת שֶׁלֹּא יַעֲלֶה עֲלֵיהֶן הַזָּכָר. רִבִּי אָבוּן בְּשֵׁם רִבִּי חִייָא. וַיִּקְרָא לָהּ אֶרֶץ כָּבוּל. אֶרֶץ שֶׁאֵינָהּ עוֹשָׂה פֵירוֹת.

רִבִּי יְהוּדָה אוֹמֵר עִזִּים יוֹצְאוֹת צְרוּרוֹת לְיַבֵּשׁ אֲבָל לֹא לֶחָלָב: תַּנֵּי. רִבִּי יְהוּדָה בֶּן בְּתִירָה אוֹמֵר. בֵּין לְיַבֵּשׁ בֵּין לֶחָלָב אָסוּר. יָאוּת אָמַר רִבִּי יְהוּדָה בֶּן בְּתִירָה. וּמָה טַעֲמוֹן דְּרַבָּנָן. רִבִּי יוֹסֵי בֵּירְבִּי בָּא בְשֵׁם רַב יְהוּדָה. רִבִּי יוֹחָנָן מַטֵּי בָהּ בְּשֵׁם רַב. הֲלָכָה כְדִבְרֵי מִי שֶׁהוּא אוֹמֵר. בֵּין לְיַבֵּשׁ בֵּין לֶחָלָב אָסוּר מִשּׁוּם מִי מִיפִיס.

"Rams may go out protected on their bellies⁵;" one puts *bursinin*⁴⁴ leather near its heart which is shielding against wild animals.

"Female sheep may go out with their tail bound high," some Tannaim state שְׁחוּזוֹת but some Tannaim state שׁוּזוֹת. He who says שׁוּזוֹת in finery, as you are saying *dressed as prostitute with hidden thoughts*⁴⁵. He who says שְׁחוּזוֹת as you are saying, "one does not sharpen the knife." Wrapped⁷, because of fine wool. Bound low⁶, that no ram may mount her. Rebbi Abun in the name of Rebbi Hiyya: *He called it tied-down land*⁴⁶, land which produces no fruit.

"Rebbi Jehudah says goats may go out tied to dry but not for milk⁹." It was stated: Rebbi Jehudah ben Bathyra says, whether to dry or for milk is forbidden. Rebbi Jehudah ben Bathyra says it correctly; but what is the rabbi's reasoning? Rebbi Yose ben Rebbi Abba in the name of Rav Jehudah; Rebbi Joḥanan bends it in the name of Rav: Practice follows him who said, whether to dry or for milk is forbidden, for who dissolves⁴⁷?

44 According to Salomon Adani, a kind of animal. Others see here "tanned leather" from βυρσεύω "tanning". Greek βυρσίνη, ἡ "leather thong" (E. G.).
45 *Prov.* 7:10. שׁיוּוֹת is a form of שְׁחוּזוֹת, cf. Note 30.

46 *IK.* 9:13. Babli 54a.
47 Since there are no outer signs why the ewe was tied, everybody could say it was not for milk. In the Babli 54a this decision is attributed to Rav Jehudah in the name of Samuel.

(7b line 56) מתני'. וּבַמָּה אֵינָהּ יוֹצְאָה. לֹא יֵצֵא גָמָל בַּמְטוּטֶלֶת. כְּהָדָא כֵּיפָה דְהִיא מַשְׁוְיָא גְבִינְתָא. עֲקוּד. בְּיָדוֹ אַחַת. רָגוּל. בִּשְׁתֵּי רַגְלָיו.

לֹא יִקְשׁוֹר גְּמַלִּים זֶה בָזֶה וְיִמְשׁוֹךְ. אָמַר רִבִּי בָּא. מִפְּנֵי הַחֲשָׁד. שֶׁלֹא יְהוּ אוֹמְרִים. אִישׁ פְּלוֹנִי יָצָא לַעֲשׂוֹת מְלַאכְתּוֹ בַּשַּׁבָּת. אַסִּי אָמַר. לְכִלְאַיִם נִצְרְכָה. רַב יְהוּדָה בְשֵׁם שְׁמוּאֵל אָמַר. מִיָּדוֹ אָסוּר וּמִצַּוָּאר בְּהֵמָה מוּתָּר. שֶׁאֵין לִבְהֵמָה כָּרוּךְ אֶל צַוָּאר בְּהֵמָה אָסוּר. מְשׁוּלְשָׁל מִצַּוָּאר בְּהֵמָה מוּתָּר. רַב הוּנָא וְרַב יְהוּדָה תְּרֵיהוֹן בְּשֵׁם שְׁמוּאֵל. חַד אָמַר. מִיָּדוֹ אָסוּר וּמִצַּוָּאר בְּהֵמָה מוּתָּר. וְחוֹרָנָה מַחֲלִף. מָאן דָּמַר. מִיָּדוֹ אָסוּר. מִשּׁוּם מַשּׂוֹי בַּשַּׁבָּת. וּמִצַּוָּאר בְּהֵמָה מוּתָּר. שֶׁאֵין לִבְהֵמָה מַשּׂוֹי בַּשַּׁבָּת. וּמָאן דָּמַר מִיָּדוֹ מוּתָּר. מִפְּנֵי שֶׁאֵיפְשָׁר. וּמִצַּוָּאר בְּהֵמָה אָסוּר. שֶׁהוּא מְצַוֶּה עַל שְׁבִיתַת בְּהֶמְתּוֹ כָּמוֹהוּ. שֶׁנֶּאֱמַר לְמַעַן יָנוּחַ שׁוֹרְךָ וַחֲמוֹרֶךָ כָּמוֹךָ.

תַּנֵּי. טָפַח מִיָּדוֹ לְצַוָּאר בְּהֵמָה אָסוּר. אָמַר רִבִּי זְעִירָא. מִיָּדוֹ אָסוּר וּמִצַּוָּאר בְּהֵמָה אָסוּר. טָפַח מִיָּדוֹ לְצַוָּאר בְּהֵמָה אָסוּר. וְאֵי זוֹ הִיא שֶׁהוּא מוּתָּר. אָמַר רִבִּי יוֹחָנָן בַּר מַרְיָיא. מָאן דַּעֲבִיד טַבָאוּת נְגִיד לָהּ בְּהָדֵין סוּסְיָא סַרְקַיָּיא.

Mishnah: "With what may [an animal] not go out? The camel may not go out with its pad." Like the curved padding with which one equalizes a hump back⁴⁸. עֲקוּד at one front leg. רָגוּל at both hind legs⁴⁹.

"One may not tie camels one to the other and draw." Rebbi Abba said, because of the suspicion, that they should not say this man goes out to do his job on the Sabbath. Assi said, it was necessary for *kilaim*⁵⁰. Rav Jehudah in the name of Samuel ⁵¹(said, from his hand it is forbidden but from the neck of the animal it is permitted, for if it is not for the animal) wound around the animal's neck it is forbidden⁵², hanging from the animal's neck it is permitted. Rav Huna and Rav Jehudah, both in the name of Samuel. One said, from his hand is forbidden but from the animal's neck it is permitted. The other one inverts. He who says from his hand is forbidden, because of a load on the Sabbath[53]. But from the animal's neck it is permitted, because for the animal it is not a load on the Sabbath. And he who says from his hand is permitted, because it is impossible[54], but from the animal's neck it is forbidden[52], because he is responsible for the rest of his animal as for his own, as it is said, *that your ox and your donkey rest*"[55] *"like you"*[56].

It was stated: A hand-breadth from his hand to the animal's neck is forbidden[57]. Rebbi Ze`ira said, from his hand is forbidden and from his animal's neck is forbidden! A hand-breadth from his hand to the animal's neck is forbidden, what is it that is permitted? Rebbi Joḥanan ben Marius said, one who wants to do it right should lead it like a Saracen horse[58].

48   It seems that human hunchbacks wore some padding to make the hump less visible.

49   Babli 54a.

50   This refers to the rule that in leading a group of camels or horses one should not twist the ropes together but keep them separate in his hand. This is to avoid problems if one rope was of linen and another of wool. Babli 54a

51   The text in parentheses is a duplicate of the following one and is out of place here; it should be disregarded.

52   In this opinion, the rope coiled around the animal's neck is a load forbidden on the Sabbath.

53   Since the animal may be led against its will the rope is a load.

54   It may be necessary to lead the animal to water or to pasture for the animal's benefit and this may be impossible without having control over the animals by the ropes.

55   *Ex.* 23:12.

56   *Deut.* 5:14.

57   Babli 54a. The animal must be led tightly.

58   It is not known what this means.

(7b line 70) מתני'. אֵין חֲמוֹר יוֹצֵא בַּמַּרְדַּעַת כול'. אֲבָל מְטַיֵּיל הוּא בָהּ בֶּחָצֵר. רִבִּי שְׁמוּאֵל בְּשֵׁם רִבִּי זְעִירָא. אַף לְעִנְיָין אִיכּוּף כֵּן. תַּנֵּי. יוֹצֵא הוּא הַחֲמוֹר בְּאִיכּוּף שֶׁלּוֹ בִּשְׁבִיל לְחַמְּמוֹ. אֲבָל לֹא יְקַשּׁוֹר אֶת הַמַּסְרוֹכֵי וְלֹא יַשְׁפִּיל אֶת הָרְצוּעָה שֶׁתַּחַת זְנָבוֹ. רִבִּי יִרְמְיָה בְּעָא קוֹמֵי רִבִּי זְעִירָא. מָנָן אִילֵּין מִילַיָּיא. דְּתַנִּינָן. הִלְכוֹת שַׁבָּת כַּהֲרָרִים הַתְּלוּיִין בְּשַׂעֲרָה. וְאִתְּ אָמַר הָכֵין. וִיתִיבִינֵיהּ. מַה בֵּין סוּלָם לְקִישּׁוּשׁוֹת. סוּלָם יֵשׁ בּוֹ מַמָּשׁ. קִישׁוּשִׁיּוֹת אֵין בָּהֶן מַמָּשׁ. אָמַר רִבִּי חֲנִינָה. וִיתִיבִינֵיהּ. מַה בֵּין קִישּׁוּשׁוֹת לְקָמֵיעַ מוּמְחֶה. דְּתַנֵּי. אָסוּר לִבְהֵמָה לָצֵאת בְּקָמֵיעַ מוּמְחֶה. אָמַר רִבִּי אָבְדִּימֵי. וִיתִיבִינֵיהּ. מַה בֵּין קִישּׁוּשׁוֹת לְאָגֶד שֶׁעַל גַּבֵּי הַמַּכָּה. אִית תַּנָּיֵי תַּנֵּי. אֵין יוֹצְאִין בְּקִישּׁוּשׁוֹת. אִית תַּנָּיֵי תַּנֵּי. יוֹצְאִין. אָמַר רִבִּי חִיָּיא בַּר אָדָא. תַּנָּיָיו אִינּוּן. מָה דָמַר.

יוֹצְאִין בִּקְישׁוּשׁוֹת. יוֹצְאִין בְּאֶגֶד שֶׁעַל גַּבֵּי הַמַּכָּה. וּמָאן דָּמַר. אֵין יוֹצְאִין בִּקְישׁוּשׁוֹת. אֵין יוֹצְאִין בְּאֶגֶד שֶׁעַל גַּבֵּי הַמַּכָּה.

Mishnah: "A donkey may not go out with its saddle cloth," etc. It was stated, "but it may walk around with it in the courtyard[59]." Rebbi Samuel in the name of Rebbi Ze'ira: The same applies to the saddle. It was stated:[60] "a donkey may go out with its saddle to get warm but one may not tie the load belt and not lower the strap under its tail." Rebbi Jeremiah asked before Rebbi Ze'ira: From where these things? As we have stated[61]: "The practices of Sabbath . . . are like mountains hanging on a hair," and you are saying so? He could have objected, what is the difference between a ladder and a package of straw[62]? A ladder is substantial[63], a package of straw is not substantial. Rebbi Ḥanina said, he could have objected, what is the difference between a package of straw and an expert amulet? As we have stated[64], "it is forbidden that an animal go out with an expert amulet." Rebbi Eudaimon said, he could have objected, what is the difference between a package of straw and a wound dressing? There are Tannaim who state, they may not go out with a package of straw; there are Tannaim who state, they may go out. Rebbi Ḥiyya bar Ada said, this is a tannaitic[65] difference. For him who said, they may go out with a package of straw; they may go out with a wound dressing. But for him who said, they may not go out with a package of straw; they may not go out with a wound dressing.

---

59 Babli 53a; Tosephta 4:5 (ed. Liebermann).

60 Babli 53a; in dispute in Tosephta 4:2 (ed. Liebermann). The saddle must have been tied before the Sabbath.

61 Mishnah *Hagigah* 1:8. This belongs to R. Ze'ira's answer; what is forbidden and what permitted is a matter of tradition.

62 Babli 53a; Tosephta 4:5 (ed. Liebermann): "It may go out with a wound dressing and with bundles of straw tied around a broken bone."

63 And therefore is a load.

64 Tosephta 4:5 (ed. Liebermann). An expert amulet is one which already helped to heal three times. A human is permitted to wear such an amulet at all times on the Sabbath.

65 While the earlier reference was to professional Tannaim in amoraic academies, it is now asserted that this is really a dispute dating from tannaitic times even though this is not recorded in our other sources. The question of R. Eudaimon is rejected. While some authorities permit bundles of straw and others prohibit wound dressing, each one will be consistent in his rulings.

(7c line 7) אֵין הַזְּכָרִים יוֹצְאִין בַּעֲגָלָה שֶׁתַּחַת הָאַלְיָה שֶׁלָּהֶן. מִפְּנֵי שֶׁהוּא עוֹשֶׂה חָרֶץ.
אֵין הָרְחֵלִים יוֹצְאוֹת חֲנוּנוֹת. רַב יְהוּדָה אָמַר. כִּיפָּה שֶׁלְּצֶמֶר. רִבִּי יָסָא בְּשֵׁם רִבִּי חָמָא בַּר חֲנִינָה. עִיקָּר הוּא וּשְׁמוֹ יַחֲנוּנָה. רִבִּי זְעִירָא בָּעָא קוֹמֵי רִבִּי יוֹסֵי. לֵית הָדָא אֲמָרָה שֶׁאָסוּר לִבְהֵמָה לָצֵאת בְּקָמִיעַ מוּמְחֶה. אָמַר לֵיהּ. אִין בַּבְלַיָּיא דְקַמְתָּהּ עֲלֵיהּ.

אֵין הָעֵגֶל יוֹצֵא בַגִּימוֹן. רַב הוּנָא אָמַר. בַּר נִירָא. רַב חִסְדָּא אָמַר. פִּינַקְסָה. אַבָּא בַּר רַב הוּנָא אָמַר. שַׁרְתּוּעָה. אִית תַּנָּיֵי תַנֵּי. גִּימוֹן. אִית תַּנָּיֵי תַנֵּי. גִּימוֹל. מָאן דָּמַר. גִּימוֹן. הֲלָכוֹף כְּאַגְמֹן רֹאשׁוֹ. מָאן דָּמַר. גִּימוֹל. וַתַּעֲלֵהוּ עִמָּהּ כַּאֲשֶׁר גְּמָלַתְהוּ. מָאן דָּמַר גִּימוֹן מְסַיֵּיעַ לְרַב חִסְדָּא. מָאן דָּמַר גִּימוֹל מְסַיֵּיעַ לְאַבָּא בַּר רַב הוּנָא וּלְרַב הוּנָא.

וְלֹא הַפָּרָה בְּעוֹר הַקּוּפָּד. שֶׁהוּא נוֹתֵן עוֹר קוּפָּד בֵּין דַּדֶּיהָ בִּשְׁבִיל שֶׁלֹּא תֵינִיק אֶת בְּנָהּ.

"Rams may not go out with a carriage under their tails[13]." Because it makes a groove.

"Nor female sheep with *yaḥnun*[14]." Rav Jehudah says, a woolen cap. Rebbi Yasa in the name of Rebbi Hama bar Ḥanina: It is a root named *yaḥnunâ*. Rebbi Ze`ira asked before Rebbi Yose[66]: Does this not imply that it is forbidden to let an animal go out with an expert amulet[67]? He told him, yes, Babylonian, you understood it.

"Nor a calf with *gimun*[15]." Rav Huna said, a small yoke. Rav Ḥisda said, a wooden tablet[68]. Abba bar Rav Huna said, a spit. Some Tannaim state *gimun*. Some Tannaim state *gimul*. He who said *gimun*, *to bend his head like a reed*[69]. He who said *gimul*, *she brought him up with her after she had weaned him*[70]. He who said *gimun* supports Rav Ḥisda[71]. He who said *gimul* supports Abba bar Rav Huna and Rav Huna[72].

"Nor a cow with hedgehog hide[16]," because one puts hedgehog hide between her udder so she cannot nurse her young.

66 Read: Yasa.
67 Since the root is not ingested, it hangs there as a charm.
68 Greek πίναξ, -ακος, ὁ. Both a tablet and a spit would be hung around the calf's neck to wean it.
69 *Is.* 58:5.
70 *IS.* 1:24.
71 The scribe originally wrote "Huna"; the corrector crossed it out. The original text is correct since the reed bends; bending is the result of a small yoke on the calf's neck.
72 Read: Ḥisda, who also derives the word from the root גמל "weaning".

(7c line 19) פָּרָתוֹ שֶׁל רַבִּי אֶלְעָזָר בֶּן עֲזַרְיָה הָיְתָה יוֹצְאָה בִרְצוּעָה שֶׁבֵּין קַרְנֶיהָ שֶׁלֹּא בִרְצוֹן חֲכָמִים: רִבִּי בָּא וְרִבִּי שְׁמוּאֵל תְּרֵיהוֹן אֱמַרִין. דִּבְרֵי חֲכָמִים. אֲפִילוּ לְהֵימָשֵׁךְ בּוֹ אָסוּר. רִבִּי בָּא בְשֵׁם שְׁמוּאֵל. אִם הָיְתָה קַרְנָהּ קְדוּחָה מוּתָּר. אָמַר רִבִּי יוֹסֵי. קַשְׁיִיתָהּ קוֹמֵי רִבִּי בָּא וָמַר. לֹא תַנִּינָן אֶלָּא הַנָּקָה בַּחֲטָם. רִבִּי זְעִירָה בְשֵׁם שְׁמוּאֵל. שׁוֹר שֶׁעִיסּוּקוֹ רַע יוֹצֵא בַּפְּרוּמְבִּיָּא שֶׁלּוֹ. וְרַבּוֹתֵינוּ שֶׁבַּגּוֹלָה נָהֲגוּ כֵן. רִבִּי לִייָא רַב יְהוּדָה בְּשֵׁם שִׁמְעוֹן בַּר חִייָא. כֶּלֶב יוֹצֵא בַּסּוּגָר שֶׁלּוֹ. אִם לְחַכּוֹת בּוֹ אָסוּר. אִם בִּשְׁבִיל שֶׁלֹּא לֶאֱכוֹל אַפְסָרוֹ מוּתָּר.

2 ור' | י רב שמואל | י ושמואל להימשך | י להמשיך   3 יוסי | י יוסה ומר | י ואמ'   4 זעירה | י זעורה שעיסוקו | י שעיסקו   5 ר' לייא רב יהודה בשם שמעון בר חייא | י ר' אילא ר' יהודה בשם ר' שמעון ביר' חייה   6 לחכות | י להכות

"Rebbi Eleazar ben Azariah's cow went out with a strip between her horns against the will of the Sages." [73]Rebbi Abba: Both (and Rebbi) [Rav and] Samuel are saying, the words of the Sages are that even pulling her with them is forbidden. Rebbi Abba in the name of Samuel: If its horns were drilling it is permitted[74]. Rebbi Yose said, I pointed out the difficulty before Rebbi Abba and he said, we only stated: "the female camel with a nose ring.[75]" Rebbi Ze`ira in the name of Samuel: A badly behaved ox goes out with his bridle; our teachers in the Diaspora do this. Rebbi Illa, Rav Jehudah in the name of [Rebbi] Simeon ben [Rebbi] Ḥiyya: A dog goes out with his muzzle[76]. If to (expect) [punish] him it is forbidden, if so he should not eat his bridle it is permitted.

73 This paragraph and the next are also in *Beṣah* 2:8 (י). While the origin probably is in *Šabbat*, the copy here is rather careless. When there is a difference between the texts, the one from *Beṣah* [in brackets] has to be preferred over the text here (in parentheses).

74 If the horns are dangerously sharp and the strips are not a decoration but a necessary precaution they do not have to be removed.

75 Anything which is only for control of the animal must be of the kind mentioned in the Mishnah; the only other permitted loads are those to protect the lives of humans and animals. Babli 52a.

76 Babli 51b.

(7c line 26) גְּנִיבָא אֲמַר. הֲלָכָה הָיָה מְלַמֵּד וּבָא. כְּהָדָא דִתְנָן. שֶׁלֹּא בִרְצוֹן חֲכָמִים. תַּנֵּי רִבִּי יוּדָה בַּר פָּזִי רַב דְּלָיָה. אֲמְרוּ לוֹ. אוֹ עֲמוֹד מִבֵּינוֹתֵינוּ אוֹ הַעֲבֶר רְצוּעָה מִבֵּין קַרְנֶיהָ. אָמַר רִבִּי יוֹסֵי בֵּירִבִּי בּוּן. שֶׁהָיָה מַתְרִיס כְּנֶגְדָּן. אָמַר רִבִּי חֲנַנְיָה. פַּעַם אַחַת יָצְאַת וְהִשְׁחִירוּ שִׁנָּיו מִן הַצּוֹמוֹת. אָמַר רִבִּי אִידִי דְחוּטְרַיָּה. אִשְׁתּוֹ הָיִית. וּמִנַּיִין שֶׁאִשְׁתּוֹ קְרוּיָה עֶגְלָה. לוּלֵא חֲרַשְׁתֶּם

בְּעֶגְלָתִי לֹא מְצָאתֶם חִידָתִי: תַּמָּן אֲמָרִין. שְׁכִינָתוֹ הָיְתָה. וְיֵשׁ אָדָם נֶעֱנָשׁ עַל שְׁכֵינָתוֹ. אָמַר רִבִּי קִירִיס דְּיִדְמָא. לְלַמְּדָךְ שֶׁכָּל־מִי שֶׁהוּא סָפֵיקָא בְיָדוֹ לִמְחוֹת וְאֵינוֹ מַמְחֶה קַלְקָלָתוֹ תְּלוּיָה בּוֹ.

1 גניבא | י גניבה - | י ר' יונה בוצרייא בעי. אם הלכה היה מלמד ובא | כהדא דתנן | י הדא הוא דתנינן   2 רב |
י דבר העבר | י העביר   3 - | י ומן התענית   4 דחוטריה | י דחוטרא   6 דידמא | י דאירמא   ספיקא | י
ספיקה   קלקלתו | י קלקלה

Ganiva said, he was continuing teaching as ruling. [Rebbi Jonah from Bostra asked, if he was continuing teaching as ruling,] is that what we were stating: "against the will of the Sages"[77]? Rebbi Jehudah bar Pazi (Rav) [following Bar] Delaya[78] stated, they told him, either remove yourself from between us or remove the strip from between its horns. Rebbi Yose ben Rebbi Abun said, he was shielding himself against them[79]. Rebbi Hananiah said, it went out once and his teeth became black from the fasts [and mortification]. Rebbi Idi from (his staff) [Hotra] said, it was his wife[80]. And from where that his wife is called "calf"? *Had you not ploughed with my calf you would not have solved my riddle.*[81] There[82], they are saying, it was his neighbor. Is anybody punished for his neighbor's behavior? Rebbi Qiris from (Didyma) [Irma][83]: To teach you that if anybody has the possibility to protest and he does not protest, the damage is attached to him.

77   A theoretical disagreement is an everyday occurrence; as long as the teacher does not advocate acting against the received majority opinion he should be commended, not rebuked.

78   Bar Delaya was an early Tanna; the reading from *Beṣah* has to be accepted.

79   He actively indicated that the majority opinion was wrong.

80   This explains why "his cow" is mentioned in the singular when he was very rich and the owner of large herds.

81   *Jud.* 14:18.

82   In Babylonia; Bavli 54b.

83   Irma possibly is Urmia in Armenia.

במה אשה יוצאה פרק ששי

(fol. 7c) **משנה א**: בַּמָּה אִשָּׁה יוֹצְאָה וּבַמָּה אֵינָהּ יוֹצְאָה. לֹא תֵצֵא אִשָּׁה לֹא בְחוּטֵי צֶמֶר וְלֹא בְחוּטֵי פִּשְׁתָּן וְלֹא בִרְצוּעוֹת שֶׁבְּרֹאשָׁהּ וְלֹא תִטְבּוֹל בָּהֶן עַד שֶׁתְּרַפֵּם. לֹא בַטּוֹטֶפֶת וְלֹא בְסַנְבּוּטִין בִּזְמָן שֶׁאֵינָן תְּפוּרִין וְלֹא בְכָבוּל לִרְשׁוּת הָרַבִּים. וְלֹא בְעִיר שֶׁל זָהָב וְלֹא בְקַטְלָה וְלֹא בִנְזָמִים וְלֹא בְטַבַּעַת שֶׁאֵין עָלֶיהָ חוֹתָם וְלֹא בְמַחַט שֶׁאֵינָהּ נְקוּבָה וְאִם יָצָאת אֵינָהּ חַיֶּבֶת חַטָּאת:

Mishnah 1: With what may a woman go out and with what may she not go out? A woman may go out neither with woolen or linen threads nor with ribbons on her head[1] and she may not immerse herself wearing them unless she relaxes them[2]. To the public domain[3] not with a frontlet nor with a head-dress hanging down the cheeks as long as they are not sewn[4], nor an under-cap[5]. Also not with a city of gold[6], nor with a chain, nor with nose rings, nor with a ring without a seal, nor with a pin[7]. If she went out she is not liable for a purification offering[8].

משנה ב: לֹא יֵצֵא הָאִישׁ בְּסַנְדָּל מְסוּמָּר וְלֹא בַיָּחִיד בִּזְמַן שֶׁאֵין בְּרַגְלוֹ מַכָּה וְלֹא בִתְפִלָּה וְלֹא בְקַמִּיעַ בִּזְמַן שֶׁאֵינוֹ מִן הַמּוּמְחֶה וְלֹא בַשִּׁרְיוֹן וְלֹא בַקַּסְדָּא וְלֹא בְמַגָּפַיִם וְאִם יָצָא אֵינוֹ חַיָּב חַטָּאת:

Mishnah 2: A man may not go out with a nailed shoe[9], nor with a single one if he does not have a wound on his foot, nor with a phylactery[10] nor with a amulet not written by an expert[11], nor with armor, nor with a helmet, nor with soldier's boots[12]. If he went out he is not liable for a purification offering[8].

משנה ג: לֹא תֵצֵא אִשָּׁה בְמַחַט נְקוּבָה וְלֹא בְטַבַּעַת שֶׁיֵּשׁ עָלֶיהָ חוֹתָם וְלֹא בְכוּכְלְיָיר וְלֹא בְכוֹבֶלֶת וְלֹא בִצְלוֹחִית שֶׁל פִּיַּלְטוֹן וְאִם יָצָאת חַיֶּיבֶת חַטָּאת דִּבְרֵי רִבִּי מֵאִיר. וַחֲכָמִים פּוֹטְרִין בַּכּוֹבֶלֶת וּבִצְלוֹחִית שֶׁל פִּילְיָיטוֹן:

Mishnah 3: A woman may not go out with a needle that has an ear[13], nor with a signet ring[14], nor with a snail-shaped headdress[15], nor with a perfume bouquet[16], nor with a perfume[17] flask; if she went out she is liable for a purification offering, the words of Rebbi Meïr. But the Sages declare her not liable for a perfume bouquet or a perfume flask[18].

משנה ד: לֹא יֵצֵא הָאִישׁ לֹא בְסַיִף וְלֹא בְקֶשֶׁת וְלֹא בִתְרִיס וְלֹא בָאַלָּה וְלֹא בְרוֹמַח וְאִם יָצָא חַיָּב חַטָּאת. רַבִּי לִיעֶזֶר אוֹמֵר תַּכְשִׁיטִין הֵן לוֹ. וַחֲכָמִים אוֹמְרִים אֵינָן לוֹ אֶלָּא גְנַאי שֶׁנֶּאֱמַר וְכִתְּתוּ חַרְבוֹתָם לְאִתִּים וַחֲנִיתוֹתֵיהֶם לְמַזְמֵרוֹת. בִּירִית טְהוֹרָה וְיוֹצְאִין בָּהּ בַּשַּׁבָּת. כְּבָלִים טְמֵאִין וְאֵין יוֹצְאִין בָּהֶן בַּשַּׁבָּת:

Mishnah 4: A man may go out neither with a sword, nor with a bow, nor with a shield, nor with a bludgeon, nor with a spear, and if he went out he is liable for a purification offering. Rebbi Eliezer says, these are adornments for him, but the Sages say, they only are shameful for him, as it is said[19], *they will forge their swords into ploughs and their lances into vintner's knives*. A garter is pure and one may go out with in on the Sabbath[20]. Ropes are impure and one may not go out with them on the Sabbath[21].

משנה ה: יוֹצְאָה אִשָּׁה בְחוּטֵי שֵׂעָר בֵּין מִשֶּׁלָּהּ בֵּין מִשֶּׁל חֲבֶרְתָּהּ בֵּין מִשֶּׁל בְּהֵמָה וּבְטוֹטֶפֶת וּבְסַנְבּוּטִין בִּזְמַן שֶׁהֵן תְּפוּרִין וּבְכָבוּל וּבְפֵיאָה נָכְרִית בֶּחָצֵר וּבְמוֹךְ שֶׁבְּאָזְנָהּ וּבְמוֹךְ שֶׁבְּסַנְדָּלָהּ וּבְמוֹךְ שֶׁהִתְקִינָה לְנִידָּתָהּ. בַּפִּלְפֵּל וּבְגַרְגִּר מֶלַח וּבְכָל דָּבָר שֶׁתִּתֵּן לְתוֹךְ פִּיהָ וּבִלְבַד שֶׁלֹּא תִתֵּן בַּתְּחִילָּה בַּשַּׁבָּת. וְאִם נָפַל לֹא תַחֲזִיר. שֵׁן תּוֹתֶבֶת וְשֵׁן שֶׁל זָהָב רַבִּי מַתִּיר. וַחֲכָמִים אוֹסְרִין:

Mishnah 5: A woman may go out with hair threads, whether her own or another woman's or an animal's[1], with a frontlet with a head-dress hanging down the cheeks if they are sewn[4]; with an under-cap and another's braid into the courtyard[3] with cotton wool in her ear, or cotton wool in her shoes, or cotton wool which she prepared for her period[22]. With pepper or a grain of salt or any other thing she may put into her mouth[23] on condition that she not start on the Sabbath[24], and if it fell out she may not return it. A replacement tooth and a gilt tooth Rebbi permits but the Sages prohibit[25].

משנה ו: יוֹצְאִין בְּסֶלַע שֶׁעַל הַצִּינִית. הַבָּנוֹת יוֹצְאוֹת בְּחוּטִין אֲפִילּוּ בְקִיסְמִים שֶׁבְּאָזְנֵיהֶן. עַרְבִיּוֹת יוֹצְאוֹת רְעוּלוֹת וּמָדִיּוֹת פְּרוּפוֹת וְכָל אָדָם אֶלָּא שֶׁדִּבְּרוּ חֲכָמִים בַּהֹוֶה:

Mishnah 6: One goes out with a tetradrachma on a arthritic foot[26]. Girls go out with threads and even chips in their ears[27]. Arab women go out veiled and Median women pinned[28], and also everybody, but the Sages spoke about what is[29].

משנה ז: פּוֹרֶפֶת עַל הָאֶבֶן וְעַל הָאֱגוֹז וְעַל הַמַּטְבֵּעַ וּבִלְבַד שֶׁלֹּא תִפְרוֹף בַּתְּחִלָּה בַּשַּׁבָּת:

Mishnah 7: She ties down with a stone, or a walnut, or a coin on condition that she not start tying down on the Sabbath[28].

משנה ח: הַקִּטֵּעַ יוֹצֵא בְקַב שֶׁלּוֹ דִּבְרֵי רִבִּי יוֹסֵי וְרִבִּי מֵאִיר אוֹסֵר. אִם יֵשׁ לוֹ בֵית קִיבּוּל כְּתִיתִין טָמֵא. סָמוֹכוֹת שֶׁלּוֹ טְמֵאִין מִדְרָס וְיוֹצְאִין בָּהֶן בַּשַּׁבָּת. וְנִכְנָסִין בָּהֶן לָעֲזָרָה. כְּסֵא וְסָמוֹכוֹת שֶׁלּוֹ טְמֵאִין מִדְרָס וְאֵין יוֹצְאִין בָּהֶן בַּשַּׁבָּת וְאֵין נִכְנָסִין בָּהֶן לָעֲזָרָה. אֲנַקְטְמִין טְהוֹרִין וְאֵין יוֹצְאִין בָּהֶן:

Mishnah 8: The amputee goes out with his prosthesis, the words of Rebbi Yose, but Rebbi Meïr prohibits[30]. If it has an extensive reception area it is impure[31]. His stilts are impure by stepping on[32], one goes out with them on the Sabbath, and one may enter the Temple Court with them[33]. A wheelchair and its supports are impure by stepping on[31], one may not go out with them on the Sabbath, and one may not enter the Temple Court with them[34]. Donkey figures[35] are pure but one may not go out with them.

משנה ט: הַבָּנִים יוֹצְאִין בִּקְשָׁרִים וּבְנֵי מְלָכִים בַּזּוֹגִין וְכָל אָדָם אֶלָּא שֶׁדִּיבְּרוּ חֲכָמִים בַּהוֹוֶה:

Mishnah 9: Boys go out with knots[36] and princes with bells, and so may everybody, but the Sages spoke about what is.

משנה י: יוֹצְאִין בְּבֵיצַת הַחַרְגּוֹל וּבְשֵׁן שֶׁל שׁוּעָל וּבְמַסְמֵר הַצָּלוּב מִשּׁוּם רְפוּאָה דִּבְרֵי רִבִּי יוֹסֵי. וְרִבִּי מֵאִיר אוֹסֵר בַּחוֹל מִשּׁוּם דַּרְכֵי הָאֱמוֹרִי:

Mishnah 10: One may go out with a locust's egg and a fox's tooth and a nail of a crucified person because of healing, the words of Rebbi Yose[37]. But Rebbi Meïr forbids on weekdays because of ways of the Emorite[38].

1   A person may wear clothing but no load in public on the Sabbath. Rabbinically anything which a person is apt to remove from himself to show it to another is considered a load and forbidden. Ribbons in the hair are cheap, easily taken off, and exchanged, and therefore forbidden in contrast to additional human hair which is expensive, complicated to insert, and not exchanged which is permitted (Mishnah 5).

2   If she needs immersion for any reason; Chapter 5 Note 35. This has nothing to do with the rules of the Sabbath.

3   These restrictions only apply to a public domain where carrying is biblically prohibited. They do not apply to carrying in a courtyard common to many dwellings even if this courtyard was not transformed into private domain by an *eruv*.

4   A frontlet is a gold or silver band reaching from ear to ear. One presupposes here that one speaks of a married woman who will not appear in public without her hair being covered by a scarf or a bonnet. If

the band is sewn to the bonnet it cannot be removed in public and therefore may be worn outside on the Sabbath (Mishnah 5).

5 A cap under her bonnet which can be removed without difficulty.

6 A circular diadem depicting a city wall.

7 All these are jewelry and as such part of women's dress; there is a rabbinic injunction against wearing them since they are easily taken off and exchanged.

8 The prohibition is purely rabbinic; it cannot trigger biblical consequences.

9 A work shoe.

10 These are not worn on the Sabbath.

11 The amulet cannot qualify as medical necessity.

12 These are not Sabbath dresses if the person is not on duty.

13 A sewing needle is a tool not a piece of jewelry.

14 A signet ring is a business tool.

15 The word in the Mishnah seems to be Latin *coclear, cochlear, -aris, n.* derivative of *coclea, cochlea, -ae, f.* "snail, spiral", cf. Greek κόχλος, ὁ "shell fish with spiral shell, land snail". Since the term is not discussed in the Halakhah and the Mishnah is from a source other than the body of the Leiden ms., the evidence of parallel Mishnah and Babli mss. make it possible to read כּוֹלְיָאר Latin *collare, -is, n.* "necklace".

16 In the Halakhah the reading is כּוֹכֶלֶת "a plate of *kohl*" needed for eye shade.

17 Latin *foliatum* (*sc. unguentum*), cf. Chapter 1, Note 225.

18 They hold that these items are intimately personal and will never be shown to or exchanged with other women.

19 *Is..* 2:4.

20 The garter is used to hold the stocking; it is an implement for the use of the stocking, not for the use by the human, and therefore not subject to impurity. It is a necessary accessory and may be worn everywhere on the Sabbath.

21 Ropes or chains from ankle to ankle to make girls walk in small steps, disapproved of by Isaias. These are used by humans, therefore they are subject to impurity, and are no garments.

22 All these are personal items which will not be taken off in public.

23 Medical necessities against mouth odor.

24 The treatment cannot start on the Sabbath.

25 The Sages forbid anything which can easily be removed from the jaw.

26 This is the definition of the Halakhah, Note 201.

27 After they got their earlobes pierced before they get earrings.

28 To make sure that the veil stays in place they tie weights, such as pebbles or walnuts, into both ends of the veil and wear them on their backs.

29 The rules are generally valid but are formulated for Arab and Persian women who by local custom are completely covered up.

30 In the Babli and the independent Mishnah mss., the roles of rabbis Meïr and Yose are interchanged.

31 It is supposed that the prosthesis be made of wood. Wooden implements are subject to impurity only if they enclose a volume. If the place where the amputee put the stump of his leg is hollowed out, the

entire implement becomes subject to impurity.

32 Impurities emanating from a human body transmit impurity by their weight even without contact; this is called "Impurity by stepping on"; cf. *Avodah zarah* Chapter 3, Note 179.

33 Since it is a personal appurtenance it will not be exchanged and may be used on the Sabbath.

One may enter the Temple area only barefoot. While the prosthesis serves as a kind of shoe, it is not counted as such for the rules of the Temple.

34 These are implements not custom-made for one person, inadmissible for the Sabbath and the Temple precinct.

35 The Halakhah defines this as ὄνος κατ' ὤμου "donkey on shoulder". According to Rashi a mask; following Rabbenu Hananel a prosthesis for a lost arm.

36 One ties branches of madder to their clothes as good luck charms.

37 In the Babli and the independent Mishnah mss. R. Meïr permits and the Sages forbid.

38 These are instruments of magic and not rational medicine; forbidden as outgrowths of paganism.

(7d line 3) בַּמֶּה אִשָּׁה יוֹצְאָה כול׳. רַב נַחְמָן בַּר יַעֲקֹב אָמַר. עַל יְדֵי שֶׁהִיא מַתֶּרֶתָן שֶׁהֵן חָצִין בְּנִידָּתָהּ וְהִיא שְׁכִיחָה וּמְהַלֶּכֶת בָּהֶן אַרְבַּע אַמּוֹת. אָמַר רִבִּי מָנָא. בְּקַדְמִייָתָא הֲוֵינָן אֲמְרִין. עַל יְדֵי שֶׁהִיא מַתֶּרֶת אֶת הַתָּפוּר. וְלֹא הֲוֵינָן אֲמְרִין כְּלוּם. תַּנֵּי רִבִּי הוֹשַׁעְיָה. חוֹתָל שֶׁל תְּמָרִים קוֹרֵעַ וּמַתִּיר וּבִלְבַד שֶׁלֹּא יִקְשׁוֹר. תַּמָּן תַּנִּינָן. אֵלּוּ חוֹצְצִין בָּאָדָם. חוּטֵי צֶמֶר וְחוּטֵי פִשְׁתָּן וְהָרְצוּעוֹת שֶׁבְּרָאשֵׁי הַבָּנוֹת. שְׁמוּאֵל אָמַר. לֵית כָּאן שֵׁלְשִׁיעַר. עַל דַּעְתֵּיהּ דְּרִבִּי יְהוּדָה אֶלָּא שֶׁלְּצֶמֶר. הָא שֶׁלְּשִׁיעַר דִּבְרֵי הַכֹּל אֵין חוֹצְצִין. רִבִּי בָּא בְשֵׁם רַב יְהוּדָה רִבִּי זְעוּרָא בְשֵׁם רַבָּנִין. הָיְתָה גֵימָא אַחַת. חוֹצֶצֶת. שְׁתַּיִם סָפֵק. שָׁלֹשׁ אֵינָן חוֹצְצוֹת.

רִבִּי זְעוּרָא בָעֵי. קָשַׁר נֵימָא לַחֲבֵירְתָהּ. אַחַת הִיא. אַחַת לִשְׁתַּיִם שְׁתַּיִם הֵן. לִשָׁלֹשׁ שָׁלֹשׁ הֵן. רַב יְהוּדָה אָמַר. זוֹ שֶׁהִיא יוֹרֶדֶת לִטְבּוֹל לְנִידָּתָהּ קוֹשֶׁרֶת שְׂעָרָהּ כִּזְנַב הַסּוּס. לְעוּבְרָה וְסָמִיךְ עֲלוֹי.

"With what may a woman go out," etc. Rav Naḥman bar Jacob said, because she loosens them because they separate for her period and she forgets and walks with them for four cubits[39]. Rebbi Mana said, earlier we were saying because she opens what is sewn[40] but we were not saying anything, as Rebbi Hoshaia stated, a basket of palm leaves for dates one may tear and open but only one may not tie[41]. There, we have stated[42]: "The following separate on a human: threads of wool or of linen and the ribbons on the head of girls." Samuel said, there is no hair here; in the opinion of Rebbi Jehudah, but only wool[43]. Therefore hair does not separate in the opinion of everybody. Rebbi

Abba in the name of Rav Jehudah; Rebbi Ze'ira in the name of the rabbis: One hair separates, two are in doubt, three do not separate[44].

Rebbi Ze'ira asked: If one tied one hair to another, is it one? One to two are they two? To three are they three[45]? Rav Jehudah said, One who goes to immerse herself after her period ties her hair as a pony tail[46]. To act on it[46a] and trust me.

39 A woman may not go out on the Sabbath with ribbons in her hair because if it happens that she has to immerse herself after her period she cannot do this unless she loosen or remove the ribbons since the immersion is valid only if *all* of her body is in the water. Then she might carry them in her hand in the public domain for a distance of four cubits and commit a Sabbath violation by biblical standards.

40 Before he heard the correct explanation by Rav Nahman (in the Babli 57a "bar Isaac") he thought the reason for the Sabbath prohibition and for the mention of immersion in the Mishnah was that the threads or ribbons were tied tightly on her head and she would have to untie a knot which might be a biblical prohibition.

41 A basket of palm leaves in which hard dates are kept to ripen. Since the basket was tied or sewn closed with the intention that it should be opened once the dates are edible the knot cannot be intended to be permanent. Therefore opening the knot is not biblically prohibited. In analogy, re-moving the threads or ribbons from a woman's head is not biblically prohibited; R. Mana's first explanation is invalid. The *baraita* is quoted in the Babli 146a.

42 Mishnah *Miqwaot* 9:1 (Babli 57a).

43 This refers to a statement of the Mishnah which is not quoted: "R. Jehudah said, [threads] of wool or hair do not separate because the water penetrates them" and therefore *all* her body is touched by the water even if a woman wears such threads. The Mishnah implies that the anonymous majority disagrees. Samuel asserts that they disagree only about wool.

44 If one hair is tied in a knot the water cannot penetrate the knot and the immersion is invalid. If two hairs are tied together the situation is unresolved. If three hairs are tied together in one knot, the knot cannot be tight and the water is able to enter.

45 The answer obviously is "yes".

46 If the hair is loosely tied in a pony tail the water can cover all the hair and the hair does not cover shoulders or back.

46a Read לעובדה for לעוברה.

(7d line 16) כָּהֲנָא שָׁאַל לְרַב. מָהוּ מֵיפַק בְּאִילֵּין תִּיפַּיָּיא. אֲמַר לוֹן. כֵּן אָמְרִין. אָסוּר לוֹ לְאָדָם לָצֵאת בְּהֶמְיָינֵי. רַב הוּנָא הוֹרִי לְאִיתְּתֵיהּ דְּרֵישׁ גָּלוּתָא מֵיתַּן לִיבְרָהּ דִּדְהָבָא עַל קַפִּילִיטָהּ. רִבִּי יוֹחָנָן הוֹרִי לְאִילֵּין דְּבֵית כּוֹן תְּמִינָא טַלְיָיהּ דְּמַרְגָּלִיתָא עַל פַּרְגּוּזְתָּא. אֲמַר רִבִּי אִילָא. כָּל־הַמְחוּבָּר לִכְסוּת הֲרֵי הוּא כִּכְסוּת. וְתַנִּינָן. יוֹצֵא הוּא בְזוּגִין שֶׁבִּכְסוּתוֹ וְאֵינוֹ יוֹצֵא בְזוּגִין

שֶׁבְּצַוָּארוֹ. אִית תַּנָּיֵי תַּנֵּי. בֵּין אִילּוּ בֵּין אִילּוּ מְקַבְּלִין טוּמְאָה. וְאִית תַּנָּיֵי תַנֵּי. בֵּין אִילּוּ בֵּין אִילּוּ אֵין מְקַבְּלִין טוּמְאָה. מָאן דָּמַר. בֵּין אִילּוּ בֵּין אִילּוּ מְקַבְּלִין טוּמְאָה. בְּשֶׁעָשָׂה לָהֶן אֱמְבּוֹלִי. וּמָאן דָּמַר. בֵּין אִילּוּ בֵּין אִילּוּ אֵין מְקַבְּלִין טוּמְאָה. בְּשֶׁלֹּא עָשָׂה לָהֶן אֱמְבּוֹלִי. וַאֲפִילּוּ עָשָׂה לָהֶן אֱמְבּוֹלִי יְהוּ טְהוֹרִין. וְלֹא כֵן אָמַר רִבִּי אַבָּהוּ שִׁמְעוֹן בַּר אַבָּא בְשֵׁם רִבִּי יוֹחָנָן. בְּזוֹגִין שֶׁבַּעֲרִיסָה. תְּרֵין אֲמוֹרִין. חַד אָמַר. מוֹלִיךְ וּמֵבִיא וּבִלְבַד שֶׁלֹּא יַשְׁמִיעַ אֶת הַקּוֹל. וְחָרָנָה אָמַר. אִם הִשְׁמִיעַ אֶת הַקּוֹל אָסוּר. וְאִם לָאו מוּתָּר. תַּמָּן. אִם אֵינָן עֲשׂוּיִין לְהַשְׁמִיעַ אֶת הַקּוֹל בַּשַּׁבָּת עֲשׂוּיִין הֵן לְהַשְׁמִיעַ אֶת הַקּוֹל בַּחוֹל. בְּרַם הָכָא. אִם אֵין עֲשׂוּיִין לְהַשְׁמִיעַ הַקּוֹל לֹא בַחוֹל וְלֹא בַשַּׁבָּת מִפְּנֵי מֶה עָשָׂה לָהֶן אֱמְבּוֹלִי.

Cahana asked Rav, may one go out with twisted chains? He told them, does one say, it is forbidden for a man to go out with his belt[47]? Rav Huna instructed the wife of the Head of the Diaspora to put golden felt on the wig[48]. Rebbi Joḥanan instructed these of the House of Con to put a patch with pearls[49] on the jacket. Rebbi Ila said, anything connected to a garment is like the garment[50]. And we have stated, one may go out with bells on his garment but one may not go out with bells around his neck. There are Tannaim who state that in both cases they are subject to impurity, and there are Tannaim who state that in both cases they are not subject to impurity[51]. He who said, in both cases they are subject to impurity, if he made clappers for them, but he who said, in both cases they are not subject to impurity, if he did not make clappers for them. Even if he did make clappers for them they should be pure! Did not Rebbi Abbahu, Simeon bar Abba say in the name of Rebbi Joḥanan: Bells on a crib. Two Amoraim. One said he can move it[52] to and fro, only he should make no sound. But the other said, if he made a sound it is forbidden, otherwise it is permitted. There, although they are not made for sound on the Sabbath they are made for sound on weekdays; but here if they are not made for sound either on the Sabbath or weekdays, why did he make clappers for them[53]?

47 Babli 57a; there permission is given to wear hollow twisted chains.

48 The translation is tentative. With the quote in *Arukh* (לבד 3) one reads ליבדא "felt" instead of ליברה [which might be Latin *libra* "pound" (of 12 oz., 345 g)]. קפיליטה is read as Latin *capillitium, -ii, n.* "the hair" (collective).

49 Latin *margarita, -ae,* f. "pearl".

50 And unquestionably may be worn in public on the Sabbath.

51 Babli 58a, Tosephta 5:7 (ed. Liebermann). If the bells are an intrinsic part of the garment they may become impure as

garments. If they are jewelry, they may become impure as such. If they are neither garment nor jewelry they may become impure only as implements; without clappers they are not implements.

52   The crib may be rocked on the Sabbath only if the bells do not jingle. This would show that bells may have clappers and nevertheless are not designed to make a sound, which would make them non-implements and therefore impervious to impurity.

53   Bells with clappers worn as chains always are subject to impurity. In the Babli 58b they are declared always subject to impurity, even without clappers.

(7d line 32) לֹא בְטוֹטֶפֶת. רִבִּי בּוּן בַּר חִייָה. קוּבְּטִירָה. דָּבָר שֶׁהוּא נוֹתֵן בִּמְקוֹם הַטּוֹטֶפֶת. וְלֹא בְסַנְבּוּטִין. צוֹבְעִין תּוֹתְבָן. לֹא בַכְּבוּל. תַּנֵּי. רִבִּי שִׁמְעוֹן בֶּן אֶלְעָזָר מַתִּיר. רִבִּי אָחָא בְשֵׁם כָּהֲנָא. אַתְיָא דְרִבִּי שִׁמְעוֹן בֶּן אֶלְעָזָר כְּרִבִּי. כְּמָה דְרִבִּי אָמַר. דָּבָר שֶׁהוּא טָמוּן מוּתָּר. כֵּן רִבִּי שִׁמְעוֹן בֶּן אֶלְעָזָר אָמַר. דָּבָר שֶׁהוּא טָמוּן מוּתָּר.

טַכְשִׁיטִין לָמָּה הֵן אֲסוּרִין. אָמַר רִבִּי בָּא. עַל יְדֵי שֶׁהַנָּשִׁים שַׁחְצָנִיּוֹת וְהִיא מַתִּירָתָן לְהַרְאוֹתָן לַחֲבֵירָתָהּ וְהִיא שְׁכֵיחָה וּמְהַלֶּכֶת בָּהֶן אַרְבַּע אַמּוֹת.

"Not with a frontlet." Rebbi Abun bar Hiyya, a Coptic[54] one; something which one puts at the place of a frontlet. "Not with a head-dress hanging down the cheeks," colored ones tucked in[55]. "Nor an under-cap," a cap[56]. It was stated: Rebbi Simeon ben Eleazar permits[57]. Rebbi Aha in the name of Cahana: This of Rebbi Simeon ben Eleazar comes out like Rebbi's. Just as Rebbi said hidden things are permitted[58], so Rebbi Simeon ben Eleazar said, hidden things are permitted.

Why is jewelry forbidden? Rebbi Abba said, because women are vain: she takes them off to show to her friend, forgets, and walks with them four cubits[59].

54   According to H. L. Fleischer, قبطرية. It has to be Egyptian production, not necessarily jewelry, but possibly fine linen as long as it is used as frontlet.

55   Not sewn to the bonnet.

56   Accadic *šukūnu* "cap".

57   Babli 57b.

58   Later in Mishnah 5 where a woman may take out things in her mouth without restriction on the Sabbath. Babli 65a.

59   In the public domain on the Sabbath.

(7d line 39) תַּנֵּי רִבִּי חֲלַפְתָּא בֶּן שָׁאוּל. תַּכְשִׁיטִין אָסוּר לְשַׁלְחָן. אָמַר רִבִּי מִינָא. לֹא אָמְרוּ אֶלָּא לְשַׁלְחָן. הָא לְלָבְשָׁן מוּתָּר. תַּנֵּי. מְטַלְטְלִין אֶת הַשּׁוֹפָר לְהַשְׁקוֹת בּוֹ אֶת הַתִּינוֹק. וְאֶת הַפִּינְקָס וְאֶת הַקַּרְקָשׁ וְאֶת הַמַּרְאָה לְכַסּוֹת בָּהֶן אֶת הַכֵּלִים. אָמַר רִבִּי בּוּן. מַתְנִיתָא אָמְרָה כֵן

שֶׁאָסוּר לְלוּבְשָׁן. דְּתַנִּינָן. כָּל־שֶׁנֵּיאוֹתִין בּוֹ בְּיוֹם טוֹב מְשַׁלְחִין אוֹתוֹ: אִם אוֹמֵר אַתְּ שֶׁמּוּתָּר לְלוּבְשָׁן יְהֵא מוּתָּר לְשַׁלְּחָן. וּמַה הָדָא דְתַנֵּי. מְטַלְטְלִין אֶת הַשּׁוֹפָר לְהַשְׁקוֹת בּוֹ אֶת הַתִּינוֹק. וְאֶת הַקַּרְקָשׁ וְאֶת הַמַּרְאָה לְכַסּוֹת בָּהֶן אֶת הַכֵּלִים. בְּשֶׁיֵּשׁ עֲלֵיהֶן תּוֹאַר כֵּלִי. עַד כָּדוֹן תַּכְשִׁיטִין שֶׁלְּזָהָב. וַאֲפִילוּ תַּכְשִׁיטִין שֶׁלְּכָסֶף. אָמְרִין בְּשֵׁם רִבִּי יִרְמְיָה. אָסוּר. אָמְרִין בְּשֵׁם רִבִּי יִרְמְיָה. מוּתָּר. אָמַר רִבִּי חִזְקִיָּה. אֲנָא יָדַע רֵישָׁא וְסֵיפָא. טַלְיָין דַּקִּיקִין הֲוִיִן מִתְרַבְּיָין בְּדָרְתֵיהּ דְּרִבִּי יִרְמְיָה. אֲתָא וְשָׁאַל לְרִבִּי זְעִירָא. אָמַר לֵיהּ. לָא תֵיסוֹר וְלָא תִישָׁרֵי.

<small>1 תני | י תנה מינא | י מנא   2 ללבשן | י ללובשן ואת | י את   3 ואת | י את (2)   בון | י אבון כן | י - 5 ומה | י מהו ואת | את הפינקס את   6 ואת | י את בהן | י -   עליהן | י עליהם   7 תכשיטין | י בטכשיטין אמרין | י ואמרין   8 רישא וסיפא | י ראשה וסופא הויין | י הוון   9 ושאל | י שאל זעירא | י זעורה תיסור | י תאסור</small>

[60]Rebbi Ḥalaphta ben Shaul stated: It is forbidden to send jewelry. Rebbi Mana[61] said, they said only to send, therefore to wear it is permitted. It was stated: One may move the *shofar*[62] to let a child drink, the writing tablet, and the bell, and the mirror, to cover vessels. Rebbi Abun said, a Mishnah says that it is forbidden to wear it, as we have stated[63]: "Anything which one may use on the holiday one may send." If you say that it is permitted to wear it should be permitted to send. And what is that which was stated: One may move the *shofar* to let a child drink, [the writing tablet,][61] and the bell, and the mirror, to cover vessels? If they are called implements[64]. So far gold jewelry. Also even silver jewelry? They said in the name of Rebbi Jeremiah forbidden, [and] they said in the name of Rebbi Jeremiah permitted. Rebbi Ḥizqiah said, I know the beginning and the end. Small girls were growing up in Rebbi Jeremiah's dwelling. He went and asked Rebbi Ze`ira, who told him: do not forbid and do not permit[65].

60   This does not refer to the Sabbath but to a holiday; it is from *Beṣah* 1:12 (י). It is quoted here as introduction to the next paragraph. On a holiday one may carry in the public domain, therefore one also may send a gift to a friend. But the rules of *muqṣeh* still apply and the only implements that may be moved are those which may be used on the holiday.

61   Following the text in *Beṣah*.

62   The ram's horn. As a musical instrument it cannot be used on a holiday other than New Year's Day. Since writing is forbidden on the holiday, a writing tablet cannot be used. The mirror will be discussed in the next paragraph. This Tosephta (13:16 ed. Liebermann) applies to the Sabbath as well as to holidays since one speaks of moving in a private domain (Babli 35b/36a).

63   Mishnah *Beṣah* 1:11.

64   They must have permitted use. For example, the *shofar* must have been use on a preceding weekday as bottle for a toddler;

the other things mentioned must have been used as covers.

65 Since in principle silver jewelry is forbidden to wear on a holiday as much as gold jewelry, he cannot permit. But since the girls would not listen to him if he would forbid, he should not prohibit. Since this is a rabbinic prohibition only, it is better that people should be ignorant of the prohibition than violate it knowingly.

(7d line 51) אֵין רוֹאִין בַּמַּרְאָה בַשַּׁבָּת. אִם הָיְתָה קְבוּעָה בַּכּוֹתֶל. רִבִּי מַתִּיר. וַחֲכָמִים אוֹסְרִין. רִבִּי אָחָא בְשֵׁם רִבִּי בָא. טַעֲמֵיהּ דְּהָדֵין דְּאָסַר. פְּעָמִים שֶׁהִיא רוֹאָה נֵימָא אַחַת לְבָנָה וְהִיא תוֹלְשָׁתָהּ וְהִיא בָאָה לִידֵי חִיּוּב חַטָּאת. וְהָאִישׁ אֲפִילוּ בַחוֹל אָסוּר. שֶׁאֵינוֹ דֶרֶךְ כָּבוֹד. שְׁלֹשָׁה דְבָרִים הִתִּירוּ לְבֵית רִבִּי. שֶׁיְּהוּ רוֹאִין בַּמַּרְאָה. וְשֶׁיְּהוּ מְסַפְּרִין קוֹמֵי. וְשֶׁיְּהוּ מְלַמְּדִין אֶת בְּנֵיהֶן יווָנִית. שֶׁהָיוּ זְקוּקִין לַמַּלְכוּת. רִבִּי אַבָּהוּ בְשֵׁם רִבִּי יוֹחָנָן. מוּתָּר אָדָם לְלַמֵּד אֶת בִּתּוֹ יְווָנִית. מִפְּנֵי שֶׁהוּא תַכְשִׁיט לָהּ. שָׁמַע שִׁמְעוֹן בַּר בָּא וְאָמַר. בְּגִין דְּרִבִּי אַבָּהוּ בָעֵי מַלְפָה בְּנָתֵיהּ יְווָנִית הוּא תָלֵי לָהּ בְּרִבִּי יוֹחָנָן. שָׁמַע רִבִּי אַבָּהוּ וְאָמַר. יָבֹא עָלַי אִם לֹא שְׁמַעְתִּיהָ מִן רִבִּי יוֹחָנָן.

One may not look into a mirror on the Sabbath. If it was fixed on a wall, Rebbi permits and the Sages prohibit. Rebbi Aha in the name of Rebbi Abba: The reason of him who forbids that occasionally she will see a white hair[66] and tear it out which brings her to the obligation of a purification sacrifice[67]. But for a man it is forbidden also on weekdays because it is not honorable.

[68]Three things they permitted the House of Rebbi, that they might look into a mirror, that they got a haircut with a lock[69], and that they taught their children Greek[70], because they were in need of Roman government connections.

[71]Rebbi Abbahu in the name of Rebbi Johanan: A person may teach Greek to his daughter because it is an ornament for her. Simeon bar Abba heard that and said, because he wants to teach his daughters he attaches it to Rebbi Johanan. Rebbi Abbahu heard this and said, it should come over me if I did not hear this from Rebbi Johanan.

66 Greek νῆμα, -ατος, τό, "thread, hair".
67 For violating the biblical commandment of Sabbath rest. Babli 149a; Tosaphot *Avodah zarah* 29a *s.v.* המסתפר.
68 This paragraph also is in *Avodah zarah* 2:2, Notes 143-144.
69 Greek κόμη, ἡ.

70 Not simply the Greek language which every trader had to master but Greek education, literature, and philosophy, which are intrinsically pagan. Babli *Sotah* 49b.
71 This paragraph also is in *Peah* 1:1 Notes 94-97, *Sotah* 9:16 Note 260.

(7d line 61) תַּנֵי. אֵין יוֹצְאִין בְּאִיסְטְמָא. שְׁלֹשָׁה דְבָרִים נֶאֶמְרוּ בְּאִיסְטְמָא. אֵין בָּהּ מִשּׁוּם כִּלְאַיִם. וְאֵינָהּ מְטַמְּאָה בִנְגָעִים. וְאֵין יוֹצְאִין בָּהּ בַּשַּׁבָּת. רִבִּי שִׁמְעוֹן בֶּן אֶלְעָזָר אוֹמֵר. אַף אֵין בָּהּ מִשּׁוּם עֲטָרָה לַכַּלּוֹת.

It was stated: One may not go out with a head-band[72]. [73]"Three things were said about a head-band: It is not subject to *kilaim*[74], it cannot become impure by skin-disease[75], and one may not go out with it on the Sabbath. Rebbi Simeon ben Eleazar said, also it is not subject to brides' crowns[76]."

72 Greek στέμμα, -ατος, τό "wreath, garland, chaplet". A felt band around the head cover. If the band is removed the head still is covered. Therefore there is the possibility that the woman will remove it in the public domain. A head-band which when removed will expose hair may be worn on the Sabbath since a married woman will never remove it in the public domain. (According to Rashi, a woman who wears her hair tied in a knot over her neck which is not covered by her head-cover covers the knot by an איסטמא.)

73 Babli 57b, Tosephta 4:7.

74 Felt is not woven; only woven textiles are subject to the prohibition of combining wool and linen.

75 The impurity by skin disease is restricted to leather or woven materials (*Lev.* 13:57-58).

76 Which are forbidden as a sign of mourning for the destruction of the Temple (Mishnah *Sotah* 9:16.

(7d line 64) וְלֹא בְעִיר שֶׁלְּזָהָב. רַב יְהוּדָה אָמַר. כְּגוֹן יְרוּשָׁלַיִם דְּדַהֲבָא. רַבָּנִין דְּקַיְסָרִין אָמְרִין. פרוש טוק טקלין. מַעֲשֶׂה בְרִבִּי עֲקִיבָה שֶׁעָשָׂה לְאִשְׁתּוֹ עִיר שֶׁלְּזָהָב. חַמְתֵּיהּ אִיתְּתֵיהּ דְּרַבָּן גַּמְלִיאֵל וְקַנְיַית בָּהּ. אֲתַת וְאָמְרַת קוֹמֵי בַעֲלָהּ. אֲמַר לָהּ. הָכֵין הֲוֵית עָבְדָת לִי כְּמָה דַהֲוַת עָבְדָה לֵיהּ. דַּהֲוַת מְזַבְּנָה מְקַלִיעֲתָא דְרֵישַׁהּ וִיהָבָה לֵיהּ וְהוּא לָעֵי בְאוֹרָיְיתָא. תַּמָּן תַּנֵּינָן. שְׁנַיִם מִשּׁוּם רִבִּי אֱלִיעֶזֶר. יוֹצְאָה אִשָּׁה בְעִיר שֶׁלְּזָהָב וּמַפְרִיחֵי יוֹנִים פְּסוּלִין מִן הָעֵדוּת. תַּנֵי. רִבִּי מֵאִיר מְחַיֵּיב. בֵּין רִבִּי מֵאִיר לְרַבָּנָן נִיחָא. רִבִּי מֵאִיר מְחַיֵּיב וַחֲכָמִים פּוֹטְרִין. בֵּין רִבִּי אֱלִיעֶזֶר לְרַבָּנָן נִיחָא. רִבִּי אֱלִיעֶזֶר מַתִּיר וַחֲכָמִים אוֹסְרִין. בֵּין רִבִּי מֵאִיר לְרִבִּי אֱלִיעֶזֶר קַשְׁיָא. רִבִּי מֵאִיר מְחַיֵּיב וְרִבִּי אֱלִיעֶזֶר מַתִּיר.

"Nor with a city of gold[6]." Rav Jehudah said, for example a Jerusalem of gold[77] The rabbis of Caesarea said, פרוש טוק טקלין[78]. [79]It happened that Rebbi Aqiba made a city of gold for his wife. Rabban Gamliel's wife saw her and became jealous. She came and mentioned it before her husband. He told her, if you had done for me what she did for him, for she sold the braids of her head, gave him, and he studied Torah.

There, we have stated:[80] "Two in the name of Rebbi Eliezer. A woman may go out with a city of gold and participants in pigeon contests are disqualified for testimony." It was stated, Rebbi Meïr declares liable. Between Rebbi Meïr and the rabbis it is understandable, Rebbi Meïr declares liable and the Sages declare not liable[81]. Between Rebbi Eliezer and the rabbis it is understandable, Rebbi Eliezer permits and the Sages prohibit. Between Rebbi Meïr and Rebbi Eliezer it is difficult, Rebbi Meïr declares liable and Rebbi Eliezer permits[82].

77 Babli 59a/b.
78 The *Arukh* reads פרוסטקלין, פרוסטוקטולין, *Or zarua'* 2, 84(4) reads פרוסטוק טקלין. S. Liebermann conjectures that the word is misspelled for כרוסוטפלין and reads χρυσοστέφανος "golden crown". In the first part of the word one might recognize Latin *frons, -dis, f.* "green bough, foliage", poetic "garland of leaves, leafy chaplet", cf. Note 72 (E. G.).
79 The story also is in *Sotah* 9:16 (Notes 256-258), there Babli 49b, here 86a. In the *Sotah* text, *Or zarua'*, and as alternative reading here, "she sold her braided hair".
80 Mishnah *Idiut* 2:7.
81 But rabbinically prohibited.
82 R. Eliezer permits what R. Meïr declares of biblical Sabbath violation. One would have expected a proof from the later R. Meïr, discussed at length in the Babli 59b, 138a.

(7d line 74) רִבִּי אִינְיָינֵי בַּר סוֹסַיי אָמַר מִשּׁוּם רִבִּי לִיעֶזֶר. כָּל־מָקוֹם שֶׁאָמְרוּ. לֹא תֵצֵא. וְאִם יָצָתָה חַיֶּיבֶת חַטָּאת. אֲסוּרָה לָצֵאת בּוֹ בֶחָצֵר. כָּל־מָקוֹם שֶׁאָמְרוּ. לֹא תֵצֵא. וְאִם יָצָתָה אֵינָהּ חַיֶּיבֶת חַטָּאת. מוּתֶּרֶת לָצֵאת בּוֹ בֶחָצֵר. רִבִּי בָּא בַּר כֹּהֵן בָּשֵׁם רַב שֵׁשֶׁת. מַתְנִיתִין אָמְרָה כֵן. וּבַבָּבוּל וּבְפֵיאָה נָכְרִית בֶּחָצֵר. רִבִּי לֵייא בְשֵׁם רִבִּי שִׁמְעוֹן בַּר חִיָּיא. אֲפִילוּ בְמָקוֹם שֶׁאָמְרוּ. לֹא תֵצֵא. וְאִם יָצְאָת אֵינָהּ חַיֶּיבֶת חַטָּאת. אֲסוּרָה לָצֵאת בּוֹ לֶחָצֵר. וְהָאִישׁ עַל יְדֵי שֶׁאֵינוֹ שָׁחוּץ מוּתָּר. נִישְׁמָעִינָהּ מִן הָדָא. רַבָּן גַּמְלִיאֵל בְּרִבִּי יָרַד לְטַייֵל בְּתוֹךְ חֲצֵירוֹ בַּשַּׁבָּת וּמַפְתֵּחַ שֶׁלְּזָהָב בְּיָדוֹ. וְגָעֲרוּ בוֹ חֲבֵירָיו מִשֵּׁם תַּכְשִׁיט. הָדָא אָמְרָה. הֶעָשׂוּי לְשֵׁם תַּכְשִׁיט אָסוּר. הָדָא אָמְרָה. עָשׂוּי לְכָךְ וּלְכָךְ. הָדָא אָמְרָה. אֶחָד הָאִישׁ וְאֶחָד הָאִשָּׁה. הָדָא אָמְרָה. אֲפִילוּ בְמָקוֹם שֶׁאָמְרוּ. לֹא תֵצֵא. וְאִם יָצָתָה אֵינָהּ חַיֶּיבֶת חַטָּאת. אֲסוּרָה לָצֵאת בּוֹ בֶחָצֵר.

Rebbi Iniani bar Sosai said in the name of Rebbi Eliezer[83]: Everywhere they said she may not go out and when she did go out she is obligated for a purification sacrifice she is prohibited to go out with it to the courtyard. Everywhere they said she may not go out and when she went out she is not obligated for a purification sacrifice she is permitted to go out with it to the courtyard. Rebbi Abba bar Cohen in the name of Rav Sheshet, a Mishnah said so: "with an under-cap and another's braid into the courtyard[3,84]." Rebbi Lia in the name of Rebbi Simeon bar Ḥiyya[85]: Even when they said she may not go out but if she went out she is not obligated for a purification sacrifice, she is prohibited to go out with it to the courtyard. Is a man permitted because he is not vain? Let us hear from the following: Rabban Gamliel ben Rebbi went walking in his courtyard on the Sabbath with a golden key in his hand[86]. His colleagues scolded him because of jewelry. This implies that if something is made as jewelry it is forbidden. This implies also if it has a dual purpose. This implies both man and woman. This implies that even when they said she may not go out but if she went out she is not obligated for a purification sacrifice, she is prohibited to go out with it to the courtyard.

83 In the Babli 64b: R. Inani ben Sasson in the name of R. Ismael.

84 The Babli explains that these items are rabbinically permitted only because a woman should be attractive to her husband. In the discussion here the courtyard is a multi-family place not made into common space by an *eruv*.

85 In the Babli 64b a statement of Rav.

86 In cannot be really "in his hand" since clearly this would be carrying. The golden key must have hung on a chain around his neck. Even though it was golden it was a real key to open the door to his house.

According to most Medieval authors men and women today are not vain and do not take off their jewelry to show to others.

(8a line 10) מִפְּנֵי מַה גָּזְרוּ עַל סַנְדָּל מְסוּמָּר. יֵשׁ אוֹמְרִים. שֶׁהָיוּ רוֹאוֹת אֶת רֹאשׁוֹ וּמַפִּילוֹת. יֵשׁ אוֹמְרִים. שֶׁהָיוּ שׁוֹמְעוֹת קוֹלוֹ וּמַפִּילוֹת. וְיֵשׁ אוֹמְרִים. שֶׁהָיוּ נִדְחָקִין זֶה בָזֶה וְהוֹרְגִין זֶה אֶת זֶה. מַה נָּפִיק מִבֵּינֵיהוֹן. הדוסטא. מָאן דָּמַר. שֶׁהָיוּ רוֹאוֹת אֶת רֹאשׁוֹ וּמַפִּילוֹת. מוּתָּר. וּמָאן דָּמַר. שֶׁהָיוּ שׁוֹמְעוֹת קוֹלוֹ וּמַפִּילוֹת אוֹ שֶׁהָיוּ נִדְחָקִין זֶה בָזֶה וְהוֹרְגִין זֶה אֶת זֶה. אָסוּר. וְלֹא בִשְׁעַת הַשְּׁמָד גָּזְרוּ. מִכֵּיוָן שֶׁעָבַר הַשְּׁמָד יְהֵא מוּתָּר. לֹא עָמַד בֵּית דִּין וּבִיטֵּל. מֵעַתָּה אֲפִילוּ בַחוֹל. לָאו אוֹרְחֵיהּ דְּבַר נָשָׁא מִיהֱוֵי לֵיהּ תְּרֵין סַנְדָּלִין. חַד לַחוֹלָא וְחַד לְשׁוֹבַתָא. תַּנֵּי. טָלָה עָלָיו מַטְלֵית מִקַּלְמָטָן מוּתָּר. רבי יודן בֵּירַבִּי יִשְׁמָעֵאל הֲוַת רַגְלֵיהּ שְׁחֶקָה וְעָבְדוּן לֵיהּ כֵּן.

[87]Why did they decree about a nailed shoe? Some say, because they saw the tips and had miscarriages. But some say, they heard its sound and had miscarriages. And some say, they were stampeding and killing one another. What is the difference between them? [88]הדוסטא. Accordig to him who said, because they saw the tips and had miscarriages, it is permitted. But according

to him who said, they heard its sound and had miscarriages or they were stampeding and killing one another, it is forbidden. But did they not decree this in an emergency? When the emergency passed it should have been permitted. There never rose a court which undid it. Then even on a weekday! People do not usually have two pairs of shoes, one for weekdays and one for the Sabbath[89]. It was stated[90]: If one put a patch under it it is permitted. Rebbi Yudan bar Ismael's feet were scratched and they did this for him.

87 Similarly Babli 60a. It seems that originally nailed shoes were military equipment only and seeing men wearing nailed shoes was equivalent with seeing enemy soldiers bent on killing or raping women, or, in the case of the stampede, people hiding in a cave acting on a false rumor of an enemy attack. It is unknown when historically this emergency situation has to be placed, whether in Seleucid or Roman times.

88 The word is unexplained. The best conjecture is by H. L. Fleischer to read הרוסטא and explain it as Persian روستایى "rural", in this case "rural boots".

89 Therefore prohibition on the Sabbath implies prohibition on weekdays. The Babli, referring to more affluent Babylonian society, explains that the accident which caused the original prohibition happened on a Sabbath.

90 Babli 60b.

(8a line 20) כַּמָּה מַסְמְרִין יְהוּ בוֹ. רִבִּי יוֹחָנָן אָמַר. חֲמִשָּׁה. כַּחֲמִשָּׁה סִפְרֵי תוֹרָה. רִבִּי חֲנִינָא אָמַר. שִׁבְעָה. וּכְיָמַיךְ דָּבְאֶךָ: נְהִיגִין רַבָּנִין כָּהֲדָא דְרִבִּי חֲנִינָא. דָּרַשׁ רִבִּי אָחָא בְּשֵׁם רִבִּי חֲנִינָא. תִּשְׁעָה. רִבִּי הָיָה נוֹתֵן שְׁלֹשָׁה עָשָׂר בָּזֶה וְאֶחָד עָשָׂר בָּזֶה. כְּמִנְיָין מִשְׁמָרוֹת. וּכְמִשְׁמָרוֹת נְטוּעִים. מַה מִּשְׁמָרוֹת כ״ד אַף מסמרים כ״ד. רִבִּי יוֹסֵי בֶּן חֲנִינָא אָמַר. כְּלִיבִית אֵינָהּ עוֹלָה לְחֶשְׁבּוֹן מַסְמֵרִים. רִבִּי זְעִירָא שָׁאַל לְרִבִּי בָּא בַּר זַבְדָּא. מָהוּ לִיתְּנָם עַל גַּבֵּי סַנְדָּל אֶחָד. אֲמַר לֵיהּ. שָׁרֵי. מָהוּ לִיתְּנָם עַל גַּבֵּי מִנְעָל אֶחָד. אֲמַר לֵיהּ. שָׁרֵי. אֵין מְגָרְדִין מִנְעָלִים וְסַנְדָּלִים אֲבָל סָכִין וּמַדִּיחִין אוֹתָן. רִבִּי קְרִיסְפָּייָא בְּשֵׁם רִבִּי יוֹחָנָן. תַּלְמִידוֹי דְּרִבִּי חִייָה רוֹבָא אָמְרִין. הָרִאשׁוֹנִים הָיוּ אוֹמְרִין. מְגָרְדִין. וְהַשְּׁנִיִּים הָיוּ אוֹמְרִין. אֵין מְגָרְדִין. וְאַתְּשַׁלַת לְרִבִּי וָמַר. אֵין מְגָרְדִין. אֲמַר רִבִּי זְעִירָא. הָא אֲזִילָא חֲדָא מִן תַּלְמִידוֹי דְּרִבִּי חִייָא רוֹבָא. דְּרַבָּנָן דְּקַיְסָרִין בְּשֵׁם רִבִּי יוֹסֵי בֶּן חֲנִינָה. כְּדִבְרֵי מִי שֶׁהוּא אוֹמֵר. מְגָרְדִין. אָמַר רִבִּי חִייָה בַּר אַשִׁי. נְהִיגִין הֲוֵינָן יָתְבִין קוֹמֵי רִבִּי מַשְׁחִין וּמַשּׁוּגִין. אֲבָל לֹא מְגָרְדִין. אֵין סָכִין מִנְעָלִין וְסַנְדָּלִין. לֹא יָסוּךְ אָדָם אֶת רַגְלוֹ וְהִיא בְתוֹךְ הַמִּנְעָל וְאֶת רַגְלוֹ וְהִיא בְתוֹךְ הַסַּנְדָּל. אֲבָל סָךְ הוּא אֶת רַגְלוֹ וְנוֹתְנָהּ בְּתוֹךְ הַמִּנְעָל וְאֶת רַגְלוֹ וְנוֹתְנָהּ לְתוֹךְ הַסַּנְדָּל. סָךְ שֶׁמֶן וּמִתְעַגֵּל עַל גַּבֵּי קָטוּבָּלִייָא חֲדָשָׁה וְאֵינוֹ חוֹשֵׁשׁ. לֹא יִתְּנֶנָּה עַל גַּבֵּי טַבְלָה שֶׁלְּשַׁיִישׁ וּמִתְעַגֵּל עָלֶיהָ. רַבָּן שִׁמְעוֹן בֶּן גַּמְלִיאֵל מַתִּיר.

אֵין לובְשִׁין מִנְעָלִיו וְסַנְדָּלִיו חֲדָשִׁים אֶלָּא אִם כֵּן לְבֵשָׁן וְהָלַךְ בָּהֶן מִבְּעוֹד יוֹם. כַּמָּה יְהֵא בְהִילוּכָו. בְּנֵי בְרַתֵּיהּ דְּבַר קַפָּרָא אָמְרִין. מִבֵּית רַבָּהּ דְּבַר קַפָּרָא עַד בֵּית רַבִּיהּ דְּרִבִּי הוֹשַׁע. צִיפּוֹרָאֵי אָמְרִין. מִן כְּנִישְׁתָּא דְבַבְלָאֵי עַד דַּרְתָהּ דְּרִבִּי חָמָא בַּר חֲנִינָה. טִיבֶּרָאֵי אָמְרִין. מִן סִידְרָא רוּבָא עַד חָנוּתֵי דְּרִבִּי הוֹשַׁעְיָה.

[91]How many nails should it have? Rebbi Johanan said five, corresponding to the five books of the Torah. Rebbi Ḥanina said seven, *corresponding to your days are your steps*[92]. The rabbis are used to follow Rebbi Ḥanina. Rebbi Aha explained following Rebbi Ḥanina: nine. Rebbi put thirteen on one [shoe] and eleven on the other, for the number of watches. *And like planted nails*[93], since the watches are 24, so the nails 24. Rebbi Yose ben Ḥanina said, a crooked nail is not counted with the nails[94]. Rebbi Ze`ira asked Rebbi Abba bar Zavda: may one put all of them on one sandal? He told him, it is permitted. May one put all of them on one boot? He told him, it is permitted. One does not scrape[95] old boots or sandals but one may oil them or dip them in water. Rebbi Crispus in the name of Rebbi Johanan: The students of the Elder Rebbi Hiyya say that those of first rank said, one may scrape, those of second rank said, one may not scrape. Rebbi was asked and said, one does not scrape. Rebbi Ze`ira said, here goes one of the students of the Elder Rebbi Ḥiyya[96]. The rabbis of Caesarea in the name of Rebbi Yose ben Ḥanina follow him who said he scrapes but only with the back of a knife. Rebbi Ḥiyya bar Ashi said, we used to sit before Rebbi[97] and were oiling and rinsing, but not scraping. [98]Nobody should anoint his foot in a boot or his foot in a sandal but he may oil his foot and step into his boot or oil his foot and step into his sandal. One may oil himself and roll on a new tarpaulin without worry. One should not put it on a marble slab to roll himself in it, but Rabban Gamliel permits it.

One does not wear new boots and sandals except if he wore and walked in them during daytime[99]. How far should he walk? The sons of Bar Qappara's daughter said, from the House of Study of Bar Qappara[100] to the House of Rebbi Hoshea's teacher. The Sepphoreans say, from the Babylonian synagogue to Rebbi Ḥama bar Ḥanina's house. The Tiberians say, from the Academy to Rebbi Hoshaia's store.

91 A somewhat shortened and rearranged   copy of this text is in *Sanhedrin* 10:1 Notes

103-112. Babli *Šabbat* 60b. It is forbidden to wear nail-studded work-boots on the Sabbath. But it is permitted to wear shoes decorated with nails. There are different traditions about the number of nails which will constitute a decoration.

92 *Deut.* 33:24.

93 *Eccl.* 12:11. This is a pun equating מַשְׂמְרוֹת "nails" and מִשְׁמָרוֹת "watches" following Galilean pronunciation which did not differentiate between שׂ and שׁ. The *watches* are the 24 clans of priests (*1Chr.* 24), each of which was serving in the Temple for one week. Rebbi would not put 12 nails on each shoe since even numbers are considered unlucky.

94 In the Babli 60b, the equivalent of כילבית is כלבוס.

95 It is forbidden to scrape off dirt from one's shoes on the Sabbath (except in an unprofessional way, with the blunt back of a knife); Babli 141b.

96 Rebbi certainly is of the authorities of first rank.

97 This is a Babylonian story; with the *Sanhedrin* text one has to red "Rav".

98 The remainder of this paragraph originally is from *Ševi`it* 8:8, Notes 119-124. Olive oil produced in the Sabbatical year has to be used for the personal needs of man or animal; it is permitted to use it to daub one's body but not to prepare leather or leather products. These rules are transferred here to the Sabbath. Babli 141b.

99 On Friday.

100 In the village of Dabbara (Golan) where the lintel of Bar Qappara's House of Study was excavated.

(8a line 43) סַנְדָּל שֶׁנִּפְסְקוּ אָזְנָיו שֶׁנִּפְסְקוּ חַבְטָיו שֶׁנִּפְסְקוּ תַּרְסִיּוֹתָיו אוֹ שֶׁפִּירְשָׁה רוֹב אַחַת מִכַּפָּיו טָהוֹר. נִפְסְקָה אַחַת מֵאָזְנָיו אַחַת מֵחַבְטָיו אַחַת מִתַּרְסִיּוֹתָיו אוֹ שֶׁפִּירְשׁוּ רוֹב מִכַּפָּיו טָמֵא. רִבִּי יְהוּדָה אוֹמֵר. הַפְּנִימִית טְמֵאָה וְהַחִיצוֹנָה טְהוֹרָה. רִבִּי יַעֲקֹב בַּר אָחָא רִבִּי טְבָלַיי חָנִין בַּר בָּא בְשֵׁם רַב. הֲלָכָה כְּרִבִּי יְהוּדָה לְעִנְיָין שַׁבָּת.

1 שנפסקו | א נפסקו (2) רוב | א -   2 מכפיו | א כפוי (2)   3 או' | א אמ' טמאה | א טמיאה   4 יהודה | א יודה

רִבִּי שְׁמוּאֵל בַּר רַב יִצְחָק הֲוָה לֵיהּ עוֹבָדָא. שָׁלַח לְרִבִּי יַעֲקֹב בַּר אָחָא גַּבֵּי רִבִּי חִייָא בַּר בָּא. אָמַר לֵיהּ. כְּשֵׁם שֶׁהֵן חֲלוּקִין בַּשַּׁבָּת כָּךְ הֵן חֲלוּקִין בַּטּוּמְאָה. וְהוֹרֵי לֵיהּ כְּרַבָּנָן. רִבִּי שְׁמוּאֵל בַּר רַב יִצְחָק בָּעֵי. וְשָׁמַע מֵימַר הֲלָכָה כְּרִבִּי יְהוּדָה וְהוּא מוֹרֵי לֵיהּ כְּרַבָּנָן.

1 שלח | א שלח שאל חייא | א חייה   2 חלוקין | א חולקין בשבת | א בטומאה חלוקין | א חולקין בטומאה | א בשבת   3 הלכה | א אין הלכה יהודה | א יודה והוא מורי | א ומורי כרבנון | א כרבנן

רִבִּי אָחָא בַּר יִצְחָק הֲוָה לֵיהּ עוֹבָדָא. שָׁלַח לְרִבִּי זְעֵירָא. רִבִּי זְעֵירָא שָׁאַל לְרִבִּי אִימִּי. אָמַר לוֹ. כְּדִבְרֵי מִי שֶׁהוּא מְטַמֵּא אָסוּר לָצֵאת בּוֹ. כְּדִבְרֵי מִי שֶׁהוּא מְטַהֵר מוּתָּר לָצֵאת בּוֹ. וְלֹא אַפִּיק גַּבֵּי כְּלוּם.

1 שלח | א שלח שאל זעירא | א זעירה (2) שאל | א -   2 לו | א ליה כדברי | א אם כדברי אסור | א מותר כדברי | א ואם כדברי מותר | א אסור   3 אפיק | א אפק גבי | א גבה

[101]"A sandal whose holes, edges, or loops[102] are torn or one of whose soles fell off is pure. If one of its holes, edges, or loops is torn or most of its soles fell of it is impure. Rebbi Jehudah says, on the inside it is impure, on the outside it is pure."[103] Rebbi Jacob bar Aha, Rebbi Tevele, Hanin bar Abba in the name of Rav: Practice follows Rebbi Jehuda as far as the Sabbath is concerned[104]. A case came before Rebbi Samuel bar Rav Isaac. He sent Rebbi Jacob bar Aha to ask Rebbi Hiyya bar Abba. He said to him, just as they disagree about the Sabbath so they disagree about impurity, and instructed him following the rabbis[105]. Rebbi Samuel bar Rav Isaac asked himself: One heard saying, practice follows Rebbi Jehuda, and he instructed him following the rabbis? A case came before Rebbi Aha bar Isaac. He sent to ask Rebbi Ze'ira and Rebbi Ze'ira asked Rebbi Immi. The latter said to him: Following the words of him who declares impure, it is permitted to go out on it on the Sabbath. Following the words of him who declares pure, it is forbidden to go out on it on the Sabbath. He did not get anything out of him[106].

101 This paragraph and the next are also in *Yebamot* 12:2 (Notes 62-80, א).

102 Explanation of *Arukh*, Arabic שראך "loop, net".

103 Tosephta *Kelim Baba Batra* 4:5; Babli *Šabbat* 112a.

Ritual impurity biblically is restricted to Jewish persons, food, vessels and tools, and a leprous house. If a vessel or tool was damaged beyond repair, it becomes ritually pure. As usual, *impure* means "a possible candidate for impurity" and *pure* "unable to become impure." Rebbi Jehudah holds that people will repair even serious damage to their shoes if it can be done so as not to be noticed in public. The rabbis hold that even in such cases, people will not repair severely damaged shoes.

R. Jehudah holds that a person will repair sandals when the repair is not immediately visible from the outside. Therefore, if a strap or hole for the shoelaces is torn at the instep, towards the other foot, the shoe remains usable. The majority holds that one torn strap or a partially torn sole can always be repaired.

104 The same statement in Babli, *Šabbat* 112b.

105 R. Hiyya bar Abba, following his teacher R. Johanan (in a first version). The Babli holds that this tradition of R. Johanan is not trustworthy. It is possible that the Yerushalmi agrees since R. Johanan is not mentioned here, but only his students and later Amoraim.

106 He refused to decide between Rav and the Galilean rabbis. Note that all persons mentioned here are Babylonians; those with the title "Rebbi" are immigrants to Galilee.

(8a line 55) תָּנֵי. אֲבָל מְטַיֵּיל הוּא בָּהֶן עַד שֶׁהוּא מַגִּיעַ עַד פֶּתַח חֲצֵירוֹ. רִבִּי אָחָא וְרִבִּי זְעִירָא הֲווֹן מְטַיְילִין בְּאִיסְטְרָטִין. אִיפְסִיק סַנְדְּלֵיהּ דְּרִבִּי אָחָא. מִן דְּמָטוּן לְפוּלֵי אָמַר לֵיהּ. זֶהוּ פֶּתַח חֲצֵירָךְ. רִבִּי אָחָא כָּרֵיךְ סִבְנַיָּה עֲלֵיהוֹן. רִבִּי אַבָּהוּ כָּרוּךְ אֲגִיד מִלְבְנִיקִי. סָבַר רִבִּי אַבָּהוּ. אֲגוּד מִלְבְנִיקִי מִן הַמּוּכָן הוּא. רִבִּי יוֹנָה טָלְקִיהּ דַּחֲלִיטְרָה וִיקָר אוּף צִיבְחַר הֲוָה סִידְרָה יְקִיר. רִבִּי אֶלְעָזָר מְטַלֵּק לֵיהּ. רִבִּי יִרְמְיָה בָּעֵי קוֹמֵי רִבִּי זְעִירָא. מָהוּ לְהַחֲלִיף. אֲמַר לֵיהּ. שָׁרֵי. אֲפִילוּ כֵן אֲמַר לֵיהּ. פּוּק חֲמֵי חַד סִיב וּסְמוֹךְ עֲלוֹי. נְפַק וְאַשְׁכַּח לְרִבִּי בָּא בַּר מָמָל וּשְׁאַל לֵיהּ וּשְׁרָא. אֲמַר רִבִּי יוֹסֵי. מַתְנִיתִין אֲמָרָה שֶׁהוּא מִין מַלְבּוּשׁ. דְּתַנִּינָן. אוֹ בְשֶׁלִּשְׂמֹאל בַּיָּמִין חֲלִיצָתָהּ כְּשֵׁרָה. הָדָא דְתֵימַר לָאוֹרֶךְ. אֲבָל לְרוֹחַב צָרִיךְ שֶׁיְּהֵא חוֹפֶה אֶת רוֹב הָרֶגֶל.

1 בהן | א בו | א עד פתח | א לפתח   2 באיסטרטין | א באיסרטון איפסיק | א אפיק לפולי | א פילי ליה | א ליה ר' זעירא זהו | א ההן   3 כריך סבניה עליהון | א כרך סבנה כרוך אגיד | א כרך אגוד   4 טלקיה | א טלקא לחנואה אוף | א אף סידרא יקיר | א סדדה יקר ר' | א שלר'   5 מטלק ליה | א מסלק לה בעי | א בעא   6 סיב | א סב לר' | אר'   7 מין | א מן   8 כשרה | א כשירה לאורך | א לרוחב לרוחב | א לאורך

It was stated: But he may walk on it until he reaches the entrance of his courtyard[107]. Rebbi Aḥa and Rebbi Ze'ira were walking on the highway[108]. The sandal of Rebbi Aḥa was torn. When they came to the city gate[109], Rebbi Ze'ira told him, that is the entrance of your courtyard[110]. Rebbi Aḥa wound a fiber around. Rebbi Abbahu wound a bundle of Jew's mallow[111]. Rebbi Abbahu was of the opinion that a bundle of Jew's mallow is ready to be used[112]. Rebbi Jonah threw them away before the fried food [store][113]. That is little honor. The honor of Rebbi Eleazar obliged him to take it off[114]. Rebbi Jeremiah asked before Rebbi Ze'ira: May one switch[115]? He said to him, it is permitted. Nevertheless, he told him: go and look for an Elder and rely on him. He went out and found Rebbi Abba bar Mamal, asked him, and he permitted. Rebbi Yose said, the Mishnah said that this is a kind of clothing[116]: "Or with a left [foot sandal] on the right [foot], the *ḥalîsah* is valid." That means, in (length). But in (width) it must cover most of the foot[117].

107 Even if a sandal is torn and no longer is a piece of clothing that may be moved on the Sabbath, one may walk on it until one reaches one's courtyard where it can be left and picked up after the Sabbath. Babli 112a/b.

108 Latin *strata* (sc. *via*).

109 Greek πύλη.

110 As a rabbi, you must be more strict than people in general.

111 Reading with I. Löw מלכניקי, Arabic ملوخا *corchorus olitorius*, a kitchen vegetable, relative of jute. He derives the name from Greek μολόχη, ἡ "mallow". In the Babli, Sabbath 112a, R. Abbahu told R. Jeremiah to use textile fiber to lightly bind around a torn sandal.

112 As raw textile fiber, its use on the Sabbath would be forbidden. But as kitchen

herb it is food and permitted to be used on the Sabbath.

113 The passage is difficult to understand; in the parallel in *Yebamot* the word [store] is added. Since the store is supposed to be closed on the Sabbath, it just indicates that R. Jonah took off his sandals far from his home when a shoelace broke on the Sabbath.

For the translation of חליטר cf. *Ševi'it* Chapter 7, Note 84. It is not necessary to translate טלק "to throw away" (documented from the Targumim); most of the meanings of Arabic طلق will be acceptable, such as "to take off, let go, loosen."

114 Immediately when a shoelace broke.

115 May one switch left and right sandal on the Sabbath if an outside eye was broken to hide the defect from sight?

116 Mishnah *Yebamot* 12:2 proves that sandal switching is practiced also on weekdays; therefore, it is permitted on the Sabbath since the switched sandals are legitimate pieces of clothing. *Ḥaliṣah* is the ceremony which releases the widow of a childless man from the obligation to marry the levir.

117 This has nothing to do with the prior discussion; it shows what is meant in the Mishnah which states that sandals with torn soles are acceptable to be worn on the Sabbath. With the text in *Yebamot* one has to switch the places of "length" and "width".

(8a line 65) וְלֹא בְיָחִיד. אָמַר רִבִּי אַבָּא. מִפְּנֵי הַחֲשָׁד. שֶׁלֹּא יֹאמְרוּ. אִישׁ פְּלוֹנִי נִפְסַק סַנְדָּלוֹ וּתְלָאוֹ בֵּית שִׁיחְיוּ.

בִּזְמַן שֶׁאֵין בְּרַגְלוֹ מַכָּה. הָא אִם יֵשׁ בְּרַגְלוֹ מַכָּה הוּא נוֹתֵן. עַל אֵי זֶה מֵהֶן הוּא נוֹתֵן. שְׁמוּאֵל אָמַר. עַל אוֹתָהּ שֶׁאֵין בָּהּ מַכָּה הוּא נוֹתֵן. אִם אוֹמֵר אַתְּ. עַל אוֹתָהּ שֶׁיֵּשׁ בָּהּ מַכָּה הוּא נוֹתֵן. מָאן צָיָיר לֵיהּ דְּלָא יִתֵּן עַל חוֹרְתֵיהּ. רִבִּי יוֹחָנָן אָמַר. עַל אוֹתָהּ שֶׁיֵּשׁ בָּהּ מַכָּה הוּא נוֹתֵן. שִׁמְעוֹן בַּר בָּא הֲוָה מְשַׁמֵּשׁ קוֹמֵי רִבִּי יוֹחָנָן וַהֲוָה מוֹשִׁיט לֵיהּ סַנְדְּלֵיהּ כְּחָדָא דְּתַנֵּי בְּדֶרֶךְ הָאָרֶץ. כְּשֶׁהוּא נוֹעֵל נוֹעֵל שֶׁלְיָמִין וְאַחַר כָּךְ נוֹעֵל שֶׁלִּשְׂמֹאל. וּכְשֶׁהוּא חוֹלֵץ חוֹלֵץ שֶׁלִּשְׂמֹאל וְאַחַר כָּךְ חוֹלֵץ שֶׁלְיָמִין. אָמַר לֵיהּ רִבִּי יוֹחָנָן. בַּבְלַיָּיא. לֹא תַעֲבַד כֵּן. שֶׁהָרִאשׁוֹנִים לֹא הָיוּ עוֹשִׂין כֵּן. אֶלָּא כְּשֶׁהוּא נוֹעֵל נוֹעֵל שֶׁלִּשְׂמֹאל וְאַחַר כָּךְ נוֹעֵל שֶׁלְיָמִין. שֶׁלֹּא תְהֵא מַרְאִית שֶׁלְיָמִין פְּגוּמָה. הָדָא אָמְרָה. עַל אוֹתָהּ שֶׁיֵּשׁ בָּהּ מַכָּה הוּא נוֹתֵן. אָמַר לֵיהּ. אֵין בַּבְלַיָּיא דְּקָמְתֵּיהּ עֲלֵיהּ.

"Nor with a single one." Rebbi Abba said, because of the suspicion. That they should not say Mr. X's sandal was torn and and he put it under his arm pit[118].

"If he does not have a wound on his foot." [119]Therefore if he has a wound on his foot he may wear one. On which foot does he wear it? Samuel said, he wears it on the one which has no wound. If you would say that he wears it on the one which has the wound, how does he tie it that he could not put it on the other[120]? Rebbi Joḥanan said, he wears it on the one which has the wound. Simeon bar Abba served Rebbi Joḥanan; he brought him his sandals as it was stated in *Derekh Ereṣ*[121]: When he puts them on, he puts the right foot one on first and after this the left foot one, when he removes them he removes the left foot one and after this the right foot one. Rebbi Joḥanan said to him, Babylonian, you should not act in this way for the earlier generations did not do this. But when he puts them on, he puts the left foot one on first and after this the right foot one, that the right side one should not look deficient. This implies that he wears it on the one which has the wound[122]. He told him, yes, Babylonian, you got it.

118 And carry it in the public domain.

119 The entire argument, partially attributed to other authors, is reformulated in the Babli, 61a.

120 If the wound dressing is hidden in the shoe, nobody would see that the person wears only one shoe because of a wound.

121 Chapter 10.

122 The argument presented by Simeon bar Abba. If one wears a right side shoe alone only if there is a wound, the wound must be on the right hand side. This proves R. Joḥanan's statement.

(8b line 1) יוֹצְאִין בִּתְפִילִּין עֶרֶב שַׁבָּת עִם חֲשֵׁיכָה. וְאֵין יוֹצְאִין בְּסַנְדָּל מְסוּמָּר עֶרֶב שַׁבָּת עִם חֲשֵׁיכָה. מַה בֵּין זֶה לָזֶה. זֶה דַּרְפּוֹ לַחֲלוֹץ. וְזֶה אֵין דַּרְפּוֹ לַחֲלוֹץ.

One may go out on Friday towards nightfall with phylacteries, but one may not go out on Friday towards nightfall with nailed shoes. What is the difference between them? These one usually takes off, those one does not usually take off[123].

123 Neither phylacteries nor nailed shoes may be worn in the public domain on the Sabbath. As the Babli 12a explains, there is a duty to be aware of phylacteries when one wears them; therefore one will be aware of the duty to remove them. But nailed shoes may be worn without remembering that one is wearing them; there is nothing at nightfall to remind the wearer of his duty to remove them.

(8b line 3) אֵי זֶהוּ קָמֵיעַ מוּמְחֶה. כָּל־שֶׁרִיפָּה בּוֹ וְשָׁנָה וְשִׁילֵּשׁ. רִבִּי אַבָּהוּ בְּשֵׁם רִבִּי יוֹחָנָן. נֶאֱמָן הָרוֹפֵא לוֹמַר. קָמֵיעַ זֶה מוּמְחֶה רִיפִּיתִי בּוֹ וְשָׁנִיתִי וְשִׁילַּשְׁתִּי. רִבִּי שְׁמוּאֵל בְּשֵׁם רִבִּי זְעִירָא. רִיפָּא לְאָדָם אֶחָד נֶאֱמָן לְאָדָם אֶחָד. לִשְׁנַיִם נֶאֱמָן לִשְׁנַיִם. לִשְׁלֹשָׁה נֶאֱמָן לְכָל־אָדָם.

יוֹצְאִין בְּקַמֵּיעַ מוּמְחֶה בֵּין בִּכְתָב בֵּין בָּעֲשָׂבִים. וּבִלְבַד שֶׁלֹּא יִתְּנֶנּוּ לֹא בְשִׁיר וְלֹא בְטַבַּעַת. בָּעוּן קוֹמֵי רִבִּי יוֹנָתָן. מָהוּ מִיתְּנִיתֵיהּ בְּהֲהֵן סִילוֹנָה. אָמַר לֵיהּ. וּבִלְבַד שֶׁלֹּא יִתְּנֶנּוּ לֹא בְשִׁיר וְלֹא בְטַבַּעַת. בָּעוּן קוֹמֵי רִבִּי יוֹנָתָן. מָהוּ מַפִּיק בְּהַהוּא מוֹמְיָיקָה. אָמַר לוֹן. מִשֵּׁם תַּכְשִׁיט. אִי מִשֵּׁם תַּכְשִׁיט הֲוָה לוֹ וְדָנִיֵּאל לוֹסַר. וְהַמְנִיכָא דִי־דַהֲבָא עַל־צַוָּארֵיהּ. אִי מִשּׁוּם מַשְּׂאוֹי בַּשַּׁבָּת. נֵימָא. כָּל־הַמְחוּבָּר לִכְסוּת הֲרֵי הוּא כִּכְסוּת.

"What is an expert amulet? Any with which one healed, and repeated, and did it a third time."[124] Rebbi Abbahu in the name of Rebbi Johanan: A healer can be trusted when he says, with this expert amulet I healed, and repeated, and did it a third time. Rebbi Samuel in the name of Rebbi Ze`ira: If he healed one person he is trustworthy for one person, for two persons he is trustworthy for two persons, for three persons he is trustworthy for everybody.

"One may go out with an expert amulet whether written or based on herbs, on condition that it be put neither in a chain nor in a ring."[125] They asked before Rebbi Jonathan, may it be put in a tube? He answered him, "on condition that it be put neither in a chain nor in a ring." They asked before Rebbi Jonathan, may one go out with a necklace? He said, because of jewelry. If because of jewelry, Daniel should have prohibited, *and a golden necklace around his neck*[126]. If[127] because of a load on the Sabbath, we may say[128] that anything connected to a garment is like a garment.

124 Babli 61a, Tosephta 4:9.
125 As Babli and Tosephta explain, since chain and ring are forbidden, people would not realize that one wears them for a legitimate purpose.
126 *Dan.* 5:7. Since Daniel accepted the golden chain he must have worn it also on the Sabbath.
127 Babylonian spelling; the Yerushalmi form would have been אין.
128 Babylonian spelling; the Yerushalmi form would have been נימר.

(8b line 13) רִבִּי יוֹסֵי בֵּירִבִּי בּוּן בְּשֵׁם רִבִּי יוֹסֵי. מַכָּה שֶׁנִּתְרַפְּאָת נוֹתְנִין עָלֶיהָ רְטִיָּיה. שֶׁאֵינָהּ אֶלָּא כְּמַשְׁמֶרָה. רִבִּי אָבוּן בְּשֵׁם רַבָּנִין דְּתַמָּן. נוֹתְנִין עַל גַּבֵּי מַכָּה בַשַּׁבָּת. שֶׁאֵינָהּ אֶלָּא כְּמַשְׁמֶרָה. אָמַר רִבִּי תַּנְחוּמָא. חוּץ מֵעֲלֵי גְפָנִים שֶׁהֵן לִרְפוּאָה.

אָמַר רִבִּי חוּנָה. הָדָא פוּאָה עִקָּר טַב סַגִּין טַב הוּא. כַּד דְּאִית לֵיהּ חֲמִשָּׁה קְטִרִין. שִׁבְעָה קְטִרִין. תִּשְׁעָה קְטִרִין טָבָא סַגִּין. וּבִלְחוּד דְּלָא יִתֵּן מָיי.

אֵין קוֹרִין פָּסוּק עַל גַּבֵּי מַכָּה בַשַּׁבָּת. וְהָדֵין דְּקָרֵי עַל יַבְרוּחָה אָסוּר. בּוֹא וּקְרֵי אֶת הַזֶּה עַל בְּנִי שֶׁהוּא מִתְבַּעֵת. תֵּן עָלָיו סֵפֶר תֵּן עָלָיו תְּפִילִּין בִּשְׁבִיל שֶׁיִּישָׁן. אָסוּר. וְהָא תַנֵּי. וְהָא תַנֵּי. אוֹמְרִים הָיוּ

שִׁיר פְּגוּעִין בִּירוּשָׁלֵַם. אָמַר רִבִּי יוּדָן. כָּאן מִשֶּׁנִּפְגַּע כָּאן עַד שֶׁלֹּא נִפְגַע. וְאֵי זֶהוּ שִׁיר פְּגוּעִין. יי מָה־רַבּוּ צָרָי וְכָל־הַמִּזְמוֹר. יוֹשֵׁב בְּסֵתֶר עֶלְיוֹן עַד כִּי־אַתָּה יְיָ מַחְסִי עֶלְיוֹן שַׂמְתָּ מְעוֹנֶךָ:

1 יוסי | ז יסא   2 אבון | ז בון   על | ז רטייה על   4 חונה | ז הונא   סגין | ז היא סגין   טב הוא | ז - קטרין | ז
או   5 קטרין | ז או קטרין | ז או קטרין | ז קיטרין   טבא סגין. ובלחוד | ז ובלבד   מיי | ז מוי   6 והדין | ז והוהן   דקרי | ז
דקרא   יברוחה | ז יברוחא   וקרי | ז וקרא   את הזה | ז פסוק זה 7 בני | ז בנו   תן עליו | ז או   והא תני | ז והתני
8 פגועין | ז שלפגעים   משנפגע - עד שלא נפגע | ז עד שלא נפגע - משנפגע   פגועין | ז שלפגעים   יי | ז -   9
עליון שמת מעונך - |

Rebbi Yose ben Rebbi Abun in the name of Rebbi Yose: One may put a dressing on a healed wound since it is only protective. Rebbi Abun in the name of the rabbis there: One may put it on a wound on the Sabbath since it is only protective. Rebbi Tanhuma said, except vine leaves which only are for healing[129].

Rebbi Huna said, madder is a good root, the more the better. If it has five knots or seven knots, the best has nine knots, only if it does not ooze fluid[130].

One does not recite a verse over a wound on the Sabbath; the one which one recites about mandrakes[131] is forbidden. Come and recite this verse for my son who is afraid, put on him a scroll[132], put on him phylacteries, so he will go to sleep, is forbidden. But did we not state, they used to recite the Song of the Afflicted in Jerusalem? Rebbi Yudan said, one means after he was hurt, the other before he was hurt[133]. What is the Song of the Afflicted? *Eternal, how many are my oppressors,* and the entire Psalm[134]. *Sitting in the shelter of the Most High* up to: *Truly, You, Eternal, are my refuge, the Most High you put as your help*[133].

129 The paragraph is repeated in *Eruvin* Chapter 10, Note 137, ז.

Compounding medicines on the Sabbath is biblically forbidden (except in case of a life-threatening disease.) Other healing actions are rabbinically forbidden, but purely protective action is not.

130 The Babli 66b is more explicit. It refers to the statement to Mishnah 9, that boys may go out with knots, plants knotted as necklaces. Three madder knots protect, 5 heal, and 7 protect against witchcraft.

131 Mandrakes are mentioned in *Gen.* 30:14-16, *Cant.* 7:14.

132 A Torah scroll. It is forbidden to use *sancta* as charms.

133 Reciting verses as prophylactics is permitted. Babli 61a.

134 *Psalm* 3.

135 *Psalm* 91:1-9.

(8b line 24) תַּנֵי. לֹא יֵצֵא הַחַיָּיט בְּמַחֲטוֹ שֶׁבְּבִכְלָיו. וְלֹא הַלַּבְלָר בְּקוֹלְמוֹס שֶׁבְּאָזְנוֹ. וְהַצַּבָּע בְּדוּגְמָא שֶׁבְּאָזְנוֹ. וְלֹא הַשּׁוּלְחָנִי בְּדֵינָר שֶׁבְּאָזְנוֹ. וְאִם יָצְאוּ הֲרֵי אֵילוּ פְּטוּרִין. דִּבְרֵי רִבִּי מֵאִיר. וַחֲכָמִים אוֹמְרִים. אוּמָּן בְּאוּמְנוּתוֹ חַיָּיב. הָא שְׁאָר כָּל־הָאָדָם יוֹצְאִין בְּכָךְ. מַחְלְפָה שִׁיטָתֵיהּ דְּרִבִּי מֵאִיר. דְּתַנִּינָן תַּמָּן. וְאִם יָצְאָת חַיֶּיבֶת חַטָּאת. דִּבְרֵי רִבִּי מֵאִיר. וְהָכָא הוּא אָמַר הָכֵין. רִבִּי מָנָא אָמַר לָהּ סְתָם. רִבִּי אָבוּן בְּשֵׁם רִבִּי יוֹחָנָן. תַּמָּן דֶּרֶךְ הוֹצָאָה בַּנָּשִׁים. בְּרַם הָכָא טְפֵילִין יוֹצְאִין בְּכָךְ. מַחְלְפָה שִׁיטָתוֹן דְּרַבָּנִין. וַחֲכָמִים פּוֹטְרִין בַּכּוֹבֶלֶת וּבִצְלוֹחִית שֶׁל פִּילְיָיטוֹן: הָא בְמַחַט שֶׁאֵינָהּ נְקוּבָה חַיָּיב. וְדָא הִיא אוּמָּן בְּאוּמְנוּתוֹ חַיָּיב. אָמַר רִבִּי אָבוּן. תִּיפְתָּר בְּאִשָּׁה גִידֶלֶת.

[136] It was stated: "A tailor should not leave with a needle in his garment, nor a scribe with the pen behind his ear, nor a dyer with a sample behind his ear, nor a money-changer with a denar behind his ear. If any of these left they are not liable, the words of Rebbi Meïr. But the Sages say, a craftsman in the ways of his craft is liable, therefore everybody else may leave with one of these."

The argument of Rebbi Meïr seems inverted, as we have stated there: "If she left she is liable, the words of Rebbi Meïr," and here he says so? Rebbi Mana said it without attribution, Rebbi Abun in the name of Rebbi Johanan: There women usually do it, but here only children leave with this. The argument of the rabbis seems inverted, as we have stated there: "But the Sages declare not liable with a plate of make-up or a flask of perfume." Therefore with a needle without ear one is liable. Is that a craftsman who is liable in the way of his craft? Rebbi Abun said, explain it for a woman hairdresser.

136 This is repeated from Chapter 1, Notes 216-228.

(8b line 34) רִבִּי אָחָא בְּשֵׁם רִבִּי אַבָּא בַּר רַב נַחְמָן. דְּרִבִּי נְחֶמְיָה זוֹ הִיא. דְּתַנִּינָן תַּמָּן. טַבַּעַת שֶׁלְּמַתֶּכֶת וְחוֹתָם שֶׁלָּהּ שֶׁל אַלְמוֹג טְמֵאָה. טַבַּעַת שֶׁלְּאַלְמוֹג וְחוֹתָמָהּ שֶׁלְּמַתֶּכֶת טְהוֹר. תַּנֵי. רִבִּי נְחֶמְיָה מַחֲלִיף. וְכֵן הָיָה רִבִּי נְחֶמְיָה אוֹמֵר. בְּטַבַּעַת אַחַר חוֹתָמָהּ. בְּסוּלָּם אַחַר שְׁלִיבָיו. בְּקוֹלָב אַחַר מַעֲמִידָיו. וְנָעוּל אַחַר סִמְנַיְירָיו. אָמַר רִבִּי אִילָא. תִּיפְתָּר דִּבְרֵי הַכֹּל בְּשֶׁהוֹצִיאָהּ לַחְתּוֹם בָּהּ. רִבִּי שְׁמוּאֵל בְּשֵׁם רִבִּי זְעִירָא. הָיְתָה עֲשׂוּיָה לְכָךְ וּלְכָךְ. הוֹצִיאָהּ לַחְתּוֹם בָּהּ חַיָּיב. הוֹצִיאָהּ לְשֵׁם תַּכְשִׁיט פָּטוּר אַף עַל הַחִתּוּם. שֶׁאַף הַחוֹתָם טְפֵילָה לְתַכְשִׁיט.

1 ר׳ אבא G | אבה   2 שלמתכת G | של מתכות   טבעת G | של מתכת   ...טהור G | -   4 בקולב G | בקלוב   מעמידיו G | מעמדיו   ונעול G | וב[נעול]   אילא G | אלא

[137] Rebbi Aḥa in the name of Rebbi Abba bar Rav Naḥman, it is Rebbi Nehemiah's, as we have stated there[138]: "A metal ring with a coral seal is

impure; a coral ring with a metal seal is pure." It was stated about this[139]: "Rebbi Nehemiah switches. And so did Rebbi Nehemiah say, for a ring after its seal[140], for a ladder after its steps, for a קוֹלָב[141] after what fixes it, for a (lock) [yoke][142] after its strips." Rebbi Ila said, explain it according to everybody if she took it out in order to seal with it[143]. Rebbi Samuel in the name of Rebbi Ze'ira: if it was made for dual purpose, if she brought it out in order to seal one is liable[144], if she brought it out as jewelry one is not liable even for the seal for also the seal becomes an accessory of jewelry.

137 Here starts a new Genizah page (G, Ginzberg pp. 80-83).

138 Mishnah *Kelim* 13:6. A metal implement is subject to impurity, a stone one is not. According to the Mishnah, the quantity of material determines the status. If more than 50% of the ring is either metal or coral stone, it is considered as totally metal or stone.

139 Tosephta *Kelim Bava Meṣia`* 3:13, Babli 50b.

140 If the ring exists for its seal, the material of the part used to make the impression is determining; the remainder, even if much larger, is accessory and not determining the status for impurity. The same holds for a ladder which exists only for its steps.

141 According to Rabbenu Hananel (Commentary to *Šabbat* 59b) Arabic قلب "woman's bracelet". Too many words are derived from the root قلب to allow an exact determination; one finds قليب "amulet", قالب "form (for casting)", قلب "axe", and some others. {Cf. also Greek ἐγκόλαψις, -εως, *f.* "engraving" (E. G.).}

142 The word in brackets should be read here. It is indicated in G and found in the parallel texts, Babli, the Tosephta, and *Sifra Behuqqotai Pereq* 3(6). The strips, in the parallel texts סמלונין, also סמיינים, are either wooden or metal bars connecting the yoke to the harness (Rashi), or straps connecting the yoke to the plough (Rabbenu Hananel) or padding under the wood of the yoke to protect the cow's neck (Ravad, Commentary to *Sifra*.)

143 Then the ring is a business tool, not a piece of jewelry, and not included in the general permission to wear clothing.

144 By biblical standards.

(8b line 42) כָּתוּב וַחֲמוּשִׁים עָלוּ בְנֵי־יִשְׂרָאֵל מֵאֶרֶץ מִצְרָיִם: מְלַמֵּד שֶׁהָיוּ מְזוּיָּנִין בַּחֲמִשָּׁה עָשָׂר מִינֵי זַיִין. וְאֵי זוֹ הִיא הָאֵלָה. מִן מַה דְּתַנֵּי רִבִּי יַעֲקֹב בַּר סוֹסַי רִבִּי יוֹסֵה. מֵאֵימָתַי תּוֹרְמִין אֶת הַגּוֹרֶן. מִשֶּׁתִּיעָקֵר הָאֵלָה. הָדָא אֲמָרָה. כָּמִין דְּייקָרָן. וּמַה טַעֲמֵיהּ דְּרִבִּי אֶלְעָזָר. חֲגוֹר חַרְבְּךָ עַל־יָרֵךְ גִּבּוֹר הוֹדְךָ וַהֲדָרֶךָ: מַה טַעֲמוֹן דְּרַבָּנָן. וְכִתְּתוּ חַרְבוֹתָם לְאִתִּים. לְאִטִּין. וַחֲנִיתוֹתֵיהֶם לְמַזְמֵרוֹת. לְמִגְזַיִּין.

1 מזויינים G | מזויינין עשר G | - 2 דתני G | דתנה 4 לאטין G | לְאַטִּיָן

רִבִּי חִיָּיא בְשֵׁם רִבִּי יוֹחָנָן. בִּירִית. כָּל־שֶׁהִיא יְחִידִית. כְּבָלִים. כָּל־שֶׁהַשַּׁלְשֶׁלֶת בֵּנְתַיִם. רִבִּי
יְהוּדָה אוֹמֵר. בִּירִית זוֹ עִצְעָדָה. דָּמַר רַב יְהוּדָה. וַנַּקְרֵ֤ב אֶת־קָרְבַּ֨ן יְי֙ אִישׁ֙ אֲשֶׁ֣ר מָצָ֣א כְלִֽי־זָהָ֗ב
אֶצְעָדָ֤ה וְצָמִיד֙ טַבַּ֣עַת עָגִ֣יל וְכוּמָ֔ז לְכַפֵּ֥ר עַל־נַפְשֹׁתֵ֖ינוּ לִפְנֵ֥י יְיֽ. אֶצְעָדָה זוֹ כַּדוּפְסָלָה. צָמִיד
שַׁרְיָיא. כָּמָה דְאַתְּ אָמַר. וְהַצְּמִידִים עַל־יָדֶיהָ. טַבַּעַת עִזְקַיָּיא. עָגִיל קְדָשִׁיָּיא. כָּמָה דְתֵימַר
וַעֲגִילִים עַל־אָזְנֶךְ. וְכוּמָז. יֵשׁ אוֹמְרִין. זֶה טַפּוֹס שֶׁלָּרָחָם. וְיֵשׁ אוֹמְרִין. זֶה טַפּוֹס שֶׁלְדַּדִּים.

2 רב | G ר' יוחנן רב קרבן | G קורבן   3 נפשותינו | G נפש כדופסלה | G פרופסילה   4 עיזקייא | G
עייזקיה קדשייא | G קודשיה דתימ' | G דתמר

It is written[145]: *Armed did the Children of Israel leave the Land of Egypt.*
This teaches that they were armed with (fifteen) [five][146] kinds of arms. And
what is an אָלָה? Since Rebbi Jacob bar Sosai, Rebbi Yose, stated[147]: "When
does he start to give heave from his threshing floor? When he removes the
אָלָה." This means two-pronged fork[148]. What is Rebbi Eleazar's reason?
Gird your sword on your hip, o hero, your splendor and your glory[149]. What is
the rabbis' reason? *They will forge their swords into ploughs*[19], into
ploughs[150], *and their lances into vintner's knives*, into pruning knives[150].

Rebbi Ḥiyya in the name of Rebbi Johanan: בִּירִית is any single one, כְּבָלִים
any ones connected by a chain[151]. (Rebbi)[152] Jehudah says, בִּירִית is a
step-chain, as Rav Jehudah said, *we are offering a sacrifice to the Eternal,
everybody what he found of gold items*, אֶצְעָדָה וְצָמִיד טַבַּעַת עָגִיל וְכוּמָז, *to atone
for our persons before the Eternal*[153]. אֶצְעָדָה is an anklet[154], צָמִיד are
bracelets, as you are saying, *and the bracelets on her arms*[155]. טַבַּעַת rings.
עָגִיל earrings, as you are saying, *earrings on your ears*[156]. וְכוּמָז some are
saying this is the form of a womb, but some are saying the form of breasts[157].

145 *Ex.* 13:18.
146 With G one has to read "five", not 15 as in the Leiden text. This is a pun on the expression חֲמֻשִׁים "armed" (or حمس "energetic") read as خمس "five". Cf. *Mekhilta dR. Simeon ben Yohai*, ed. Epstein-Melamed, p. 45.
147 Tosephta *Terumot* 3:11, *Ma`serot* 1:6 Notes 132-135.
148 Greek δίκρανον, τό "pitchfork".
149 *Ps.* 45:4.
150 The names of the tools are translated into current usage.
151 Cf. Notes 20,21.
152 As the sequel shows one has to read "Rav". G is lacunary at this place.
153 *Num.* 31:50.
154 With G one has to read Greek ποδοψέλλιον τό "anklet".
155 *Gen.* 27:47.
156 *Ez.* 16:12.
157 Babli 64a. טפוס is Greek τύπος, ὁ,

"carved figure, image".

(8b line 54) כָּתוּב בַּיּוֹם הַהוּא יָסִיר יי אֶת תִּפְאֶרֶת הָעֲכָסִים. קוֹרְדִיקַיָּא. כְּמָה דְּתֵימַר וּבְרַגְלֵיהֶם תְּעַכַּסְנָה: הַשְּׁבִיסִים שלטוניה. כְּמָה דְאַתְּ אָמַר. שָׁבִיס שֶׁלְסְבָכָה. הַסַּהֲרֹנִים עונקייא. כְּמָה דְאַתְּ אָמַר וַיִּקַּח אֶת־הַסַּהֲרֹנִים אֲשֶׁר בְּצַוְארֵי גְמַלֵּיהֶם: הַנְּטִיפוֹת שָׁלְמֵינִי. הַשֵּׁירוֹת שִׁירְאִין. חֲרָעֲלוֹת בְּלַנִידַיָּיא. הַפְּאֵרִים כְּלִילַיָּא. כְּמָה דְאַתְּ אָמַר וּפְאֵרְכֶם עַל־רָאשֵׁכֶם. הַצְּעָדוֹת פְּרוּפָסְלָה. הַקִּשֻּׁרִים קַרְקִישַׁיָּא. וּבָתֵּי הַנֶּפֶשׁ. תִּירְגֵּם עֲקִילָס אסטו מוכריאה. דָּבָר שֶׁנִּיתָּן עַל בַּת הַנֶּפֶשׁ. וְהַלְּחָשִׁים קַדְשַׁיָּא. דָּבָר שֶׁהוּא נִיתַּן עַל בֵּית הַלְּחִישָׁה. הַטַּבָּעוֹת עִזְקְיָא. נִיזְמֵי הָאַף דָּבָר שֶׁהוּא נָתוּן עַל הַחוֹטֶם. הַמַּחֲלָצוֹת פִּירְזוּמַטָא. הַמַּעֲטָפוֹת קוֹלְכִין וּמְעַפְרָן. הַמִּטְפָּחוֹת סַבְּנִיָן רִבְרְבָן. וְהַחֲרִיטִין זַנָּרִין מְצַיְירִין וְאוֹלוֹסְרִיקָא מְצַיְירִין. כְּמָה דְּתֵימַר וַיִּקַּח מִיָּדָם וַיָּצַר אֹתוֹ בַּחֶרֶט. הַגִּלְיוֹנִים גִּלְגַּלַיָּא. הַסְּדִינִים סָדִינַיָּא. הַצְּנִיפוֹת אוֹלָרַיָּיא כְּמָה דְּתֵימַר וְאֹמַר יָשִׂימוּ . . . הַצָּנִיף הַטָּהוֹר עַל־רֹאשׁוֹ. וּכְתִיב וְהָיְיתָ עֲטֶרֶת תִּפְאֶרֶת בְּיַד־יי וּצְנִיף מְלוּכָה בְּכַף־אֱלֹהָיִךְ: הָרְדִידִים לְסוּטָה. כְּמָה דְתֵימַר נָשְׂאוּ אֶת־רְדִידִי מֵעָלַי שֹׁמְרֵי הַחֹמוֹת:

1 קורדיקייא G | קורדקיה במה דתימ' G | במדתמר   2 וברגליחם G | וברגליהן דאת אמ' G | דתמר   3 עונקייא G | מינוקיה   4 שיראין G | שיריה חרעלות G | והרעלות בלנידייא G | בלנידייה כלליא G | כלליה   5 הצעדות G | Gעדות קרקישיא G | קרקשייה תירג' G | תרגם   6 שניתן G | שהוא ניתן בת G | בית קדשיא G | קודשייה עיזקיא G | עזקיה   7 על G | על גב פירזומטא G | פריזומטא קולכין G | קולבין   8 סבניין G | סובניון וחחריטין G | וחחריטים מצויירין G | מציירון ואולוסריקא G | ואוליסיריקא דתימ' G | דתמר   9 גלגלייא G | גלגלייה הצניפות G | הצנופות אולרייא G | אולרייה דתימ' G | דתמר   11 אלהייך G | אקיד

It is written[158], *on that day the Eternal will remove the splendor of the anklets,* bark shoes[159], as you are saying, *with their feet they skid*[160]. *The head bands,* שלטוניה[161], as you are saying "the head-band of the hair net.[162]" *The half-moons,* necklaces[163], as you are saying, *he took the half-moons from the necks of their camels*[164]. *The pendants,* Solomonic jewelry[165]. *Chains,* chains[166]. *Veils,* silken[167]. *Head bands,* diadems, as you are saying, *your head bands on your heads*[168]. *Foot chains,* ποδοψέλλα[154]. *Tyings,* bells. *Belly wraps,* Aquila translated אסטו מוכריאה[169], something which is put on the place of breathing. *And incantations,* precious stones[170] put on the larynx. *Rings,* rings[166]. *Nose rings,* something put on the nose. *Overcoats,* περιζόματα[171]. *Wrappings,* tunics[172] and tunics[173]. *The shawls,* large fine tissues[174]. *Handbags,* decorated belts[175] and decorated pure silk tissues[176]. As you are saying, *he took from their hands and tied it in tissue*[177]. *The head covers,* head covers[166]. *The sheets,* the sheets[166]. *The turbans,* אוֹלָרַיָּא[178], as you are saying, *he said, put . . . the pure turban on his head*[179]. *And the veils*, fine cloth[180], as you are saying, *they took away my veil, the watchmen on the walls*[181].

158 *Is.* 3:18-24. This paragraph simply explains the difficult words in the text, without connection to the rules of the Sabbath.
159 Latin *corticeus, a, um*, "of bark, cork".
160 *Is.* 3:16.
161 The word is unexplained; *Arukh* reads שרטיא. Cf. the late Greek σαταρίς, σαταρνίς, -ιδος, ἡ "woman's headdress" (E. G.).
162 Mishnah *Negaim* 11:11. The Mishnah explains that anything which may become impure by the impurity of a corpse may become impure by skin disease. As explained in Mishnah *Kelim* 28:10, the שְׁבִיס is a decoration of a hair net which covers the front from ear to ear.
163 With G read Greek μανιάκης, -ου, ὁ, "necklace" worn by Persians and Gauls. The word in the Leiden ms. is unexplained.
164 *Jud.* 8:21.
165 The translation is very tentative. The dictionaries propose to read Greek σταλαγμία "ear pendant" assuming the γ was elided.

166 The Aramaic equivalent of the Hebrew word of the verse.
167 For בלנידייא reading Latin *lanicium, -ii, n.*, "wool, silk, cotton" (E. G.).
168 *Ez.* 24:23.
169 The word is unexplained. Cf. Greek στόμιον, τό, "opening, bridle, female ornament for the neck" (E. G.).
170 Arabic قديس "precious stone".
171 Greek "body wrap".
172 Read קולבין for Greek κολόβιον "tunic".
173 The same as before in Aramaic.
174 Greek σάβανον "fine tissue".
175 Greek ζωνάριον "belt".
176 Greek τό ὁλοσερικόν "pure silk tissue".
177 *Ex.* 32:4.
178 The meaning of this word is unknown. Cf. Latin *velarium, -ii, n.* "cover" or *velamen, -nis, n.*, "veil, cover".
179 *Zech.* 3:5.
180 Cf. Chapter 4, Note 45.
181 *Cant.* 5:7.

(8b line 70) אֲנָן כר' אימִּי אָמַר קוֹמֵי רִבִּי יְהוּדָה מְנַשִּׁיָּא בַּר מְנַשֶּׁה יִרְמְיָה. וּבִלְבַד שֶׁלֹּא תֵצֵא לֹא יַלְדָּה בִשְׁלוּזְקִינָה וְלֹא זְקֵינָה בְשַׁלְיַלְדָּה. וְהָתַנִּינָן. הַבָּנוֹת יוֹצְאוֹת בְּחוּטִין. רִבִּי בָּא בְשֵׁם רַב יְהוּדָה. אֲפִילוּ כָרוּךְ עַל צַוָּארָהּ. רִבִּי שְׁמוּאֵל בְּשֵׁם רִבִּי זְעִירָא. תַּמָּן אֲפִילוּ שְׁאֵינָהּ יְכוֹלָה לְהָבִיא חוֹטְמָהּ לְשַׂעֲרָהּ יוֹצְאָה הִיא. בְּרַם הָכָא לֹא תֵצֵא לֹא יַלְדָּה בְשַׁלְזְקֵינָה וְלֹא זְקֵינָה בְשַׁלְיַלְדָּה.

1 אנן כר' אימי G | חנן בר אמי ר' | G רב מנשייא G | בש' מנשייה מנשה G | - 2 והתנינן G | והא תנינן 3 זעירא G | זעירה אפילו G | אף על פי 4 חוטמה G | חוט דומה

Hanan bar Immi said before (Rebbi) [Rav][182] Jehudah [in the name of] Menashia bar (Menashe)[183] Jeremiah: But only that a young girl should not go out with an old woman's nor an old woman with a young girl's[184]. But did we not state: "Girls go out with threads"[185]? Rebbi Abba in the name of Rav Jehudah, even wound around her neck. Rebbi Samuel in the name of Rebbi Ze`ira, there even if she cannot bring (her nose) [a thread similar][186] to her hair she may leave with it[187]. But here, a young girl should not go out with an old woman's nor an old woman with a young girl's.

182 From the sequel it is clear that one has to read "Rav" with G and not "Rebbi" with the Leiden ms.

183 Delete with G.

184 This refers to Mishnah 5. Women may go out with bought braids in their hair but only if the color of the added hair reasonably well matches her own hair so she will not be embarrassed and tempted to remove the added hair in the public domain.

185 Mishnah 6. Rav Jehudah explains that the threads are not necessarily in the hair.

186 With G one has to read the text in brackets.

187 Threads which clearly are not hair may be in any color; they are not intended to look like hair. But imitation hair must look like the real thing.

(8b line 75) אָמַר רִבִּי אַבָּהוּ. כָּל־שֶׁהוּא תּוֹשֵׁב בְּשֵׂיעָר נִקְרָא פֵּיאָה. רִבִּי יַנַּאי זְעֵירָא נְפַל עוֹדְדֵיהּ דְּאוּדְנֵיהּ. בְּעָא מִיחְזַרְתֵּיהּ בְּשַׁבָּתָא. וְנָעֲרוּ בוֹ חֲבֵירָיו מִשּׁוּם תַּכְשִׁיט. רִבִּי יַנַּאי סָבַר מֵימַר. שֶׁמֶן הוּא שֶׁהוּא מְרַפֵּא. וַחֲכָמִים סָבְרִין מֵימַר. מוֹךְ הוּא שֶׁהוּא מְרַפֵּא. וְלֹא כֵן אָמַר רַב יְהוּדָה בְשֵׁם רַב זְעֵירָא. הַחוֹשֵׁשׁ אָזְנוֹ נוֹתֵן שֶׁמֶן עַל גַּבֵּי רֹאשׁוֹ וְלוֹחֵשׁ. וּבִלְבַד שֶׁלֹּא יִתֵּן לֹא בָיָד וְלֹא בִכְלִי. רִבִּי יַנַּאי סָבַר מֵימַר. הֲלָכָה כְרִבִּי יוֹסֵי. וַחֲבֵירוֹי סָבְרִין מֵימַר. אֵין הֲלָכָה כְרִבִּי יוֹסֵי. וְלֹא כֵן אָמַר רִבִּי בָּא בַּר כַּהֲנָא בַר חִייָא בַר אַשִּׁי בְשֵׁם רַב. הֲלָכָה כְרִבִּי יוֹסֵי. רִבִּי יַנַּאי סָבַר מֵימַר. אָדָם לֹא עָשׂוּ אוֹתוֹ כְקַרְקַע. וַחֲבֵירוֹי סָבְרִין מֵימַר. אָדָם כְּקַרְקַע הוּא. וְלֹא כֵן אָמַר רִבִּי זְעֵירָה. עָשָׂה לוֹ רַב חִייָה בַּר אַשִּׁי בֵּית יָד לַמּוֹךְ שֶׁבְּאָזְנוֹ. סָבְרִין מֵימַר. אָדָם כְּקַרְקַע הוּא. וְכֵינִי. אֶלָּא כֵינִי. רִבִּי יַנַּאי סָבַר מֵימַר. אֵין שְׁכִיחַ וּמְהַלֵּךְ בָּהֶן אַרְבַּע אַמּוֹת. וַחֲבֵירוֹי סָבְרִין מֵימַר. שְׁכִיחַ הוּא וּמְהַלֵּךְ בָּהֶן אַרְבַּע אַמּוֹת.

1 אבהו | G אבוהא שהוא | G שהיא נקרא | G ניקרא זעירא | G זעירה עודדיה | G עודה 2 בשבתא | G בשובת. 3 שהוא | G - | רב | G רבי 5 יוסי | G יוסה | the remainder is not legible

Rebbi Abbahu said, anything which sits in the hair is called "wig."[188] The younger Rebbi Yannai[189] had cotton wool in his ear which fell out. He wanted to return it on the Sabbath. His companions rebuked him; was it because of jewelry[190]? Was Rebbi Yannai of the opinion that oil is the healing agent[191], whereas the Sages were of the opinion that the cotton wool was the healing agent? But did not (Rav) [Rebbi] Jehudah say in the name of Rav Ze`ira, a person with earache puts oil on his head and whispers on condition that he use neither hand nor vessel[192]? Was Rebbi Yannai of the opinion that practice follows Rebbi Yose[193] whereas his companions were of the opinion that practice does not follow Rebbi Yose? Buy did not Rebbi Abba bar Cahana, Rav Hiyya bar Ashi say in the name of Rav, practice follows Rebbi Yose? Was Rebbi Yannai of the opinion that they did not consider humans like soil[194] whereas his companions were of the opinion that they made humans like soil? But did not Rebbi Ze'ira say that Rav Hiyya bar Ashi made himself a handle for the cotton wool in his ear[195]? Could they hold that a human is treated like soil? Is this so? But it must be the following: Rebbi Yannai was of the opinion that he would not forget and carry it four cubits in the public domain[196] and his companions were of the opinion that one would forget and carry it four cubits in the public domain.

188 Which is permitted as part of dress.

189 A fourth generation Galilean Amora to be distinguished from the major first generation authority R. Yannai whom practice has to follow.

190 Since a plug of cotton wool obviously is no jewelry the question can only be whether the prohibition to return the plug is analogous to the prohibition of wearing jewelry which can easily be removed.

191 Since he had soaked the plug in oil on Friday and not added anything on the Sabbath there could be no prohibition of medical procedures involved here.

192 In the parallel sources, *Ma`aser Šeni* 2:1 Note 38 and later Chapter 14 (on Mishnah 14:3) the name is Simeon bar Abba in the name of R. Hanina. If the names here are correct one has to read with G "R. Jehudah", the late Galilean Amora, not "Rav Jehudah", the early Babylonian one.

One describes a medical procedure where rubbing with oil is accompanied by whispered recitation of charms. This is approved only in emergency situations.

193 Who says in Mishnah 17:8 that all covers of vessels unconditionally and covers of patches of soil if they have handles may be moved on the Sabbath.

194 Then the question remains how R. Yose treats patches which cover parts of a human body. Are they like covers of vessels or covers of patches of soil?

195 The he could move it on the Sabbath according to all possible interpretations of R. Yose's statement.

196 This essentially being the reason for the prohibition of easily removed jewelry; the first opinion is vindicated.

(8c line 12) אָמַר רִבִּי מָנָא. שְׁמָעֵת טַעַם מִן רִבִּי שְׁמוּאֵל בְּשֵׁם רִבִּי זְעִירָא. וְלָא אֲנָא יָדַע מַה שָׁמְעֵת. מַיי כְדוֹן. אָמַר רִבִּי יוֹסֵי. מִסְתַּבְּרָא בְּשֵׁן שֶׁלְּזָהָב שֶׁעֲמָדָה לָהּ בְּיוֹקֶר לֹא תֵצֵא. דִּי נָפְלָה

וּמְחַזְרָה לֵיהּ. שֵׁן תּוֹתֶבֶת מָה אִית לָךְ. עוֹד הִיא מְבָהֲתָהּ מֵימוֹר לְנַגָּרָא. עֲבֵד לִי חוֹרִי. הִיא נָפְלָה וּמְחַזְרָה לֵיהּ.

1 זעירא G | זעורה   2 לה G | ליה   3 לנגרא G | לנגרה עבד G | עבוד   4 ליה G | לה

רִבִּי יָסָה וְרִבִּי אִמִּי. חַד חֲשַׁשׁ שִׁינֵּיהּ וְהוֹרֵי לֵיהּ חַבְרֵיהּ. חַד חֲשַׁשׁ אוּדְנֵיהּ וְהוֹרֵי לֵיהּ חַבְרֵיהּ. וְלָא יָדְעִין מָה אָמַר דָּא וּמָה אָמַר דָּא. מִן מַה דְּרִבִּי יָסָה שָׁאַל לְאַסְיָינֵיהּ דְּרִבִּי יַעֲקֹב בַּר אָחָא מָה עֲבִידָה שִׁינֵּיהּ דְּרִבִּי יַעֲקֹב בַּר אָחָא חֲבֵירֵינוּ. מִן מַה דְּלָא אָמַר רִבִּי יָסָה לֹא בָטִילָה מִן יוֹמוֹי. הֲוֵי הוּא דְהוֹרֵי לְשִׁינָּא.

רִבִּי יַנַּאי פָּתַר לָהּ בְּפִילְפֵּל וּבְגַרְגֵּר מֶלַח. וַחֲבֵרוֹי פָּתְרִין לֵיהּ עַל כּוּלְהֹן.

1 יסה G | יסא חשש G | חש אודניה G | אדניה   2 מה G | מן ומה G | ומן אחא G | אחה   3 שיניה G | שינה דר' G | כר' אחא G | אחה חבירינו G | חברינו   4 הוא דהורי G | דדהורי   5 בפילפל G | בפלפל

Rebbi Mana said, I heard the reason from Rebbi Samuel in the name of Rebbi Ze'ira but I do not remember what I heard. What about it[197]? Rebbi Yose said, it is understandable that with a golden tooth which was expensive she should not go out, for if she lost it she would put it back[198]. But what can you say about a replacement tooth? Still she would be embarrassed to tell the carpenter, make me another one. If she lost it she would put it back.

Rebbi Yasa and Rebbi Immi. One had a toothache and his colleague instructed him; the other one had an earache and his colleague instructed him. We do not know who said what. Since Rebbi Yasa asked Rebbi Jacob bar Aḥa's doctor, how feels Rebbi Jacob bar Aḥa's tooth, and since Rebbi Yasa never said an unnecessary word[199], it was he who instructed about the tooth.

Rebbi Yannai explains it about peppers or a grain of salt; his companions explain it about everything[200].

197 Why do the Sages prohibit to go out with a removable artificial tooth (Mishnah 5)?

198 In the meantime it would be in her hand, which might happen in the public domain.

199 Reading מלה בטלה "unnecessary word" for לא בטלה "not unnecessary".

As S. Liebermann points out in the name of R. A. I. Kook, since R. Yasa asked the doctor (on a Sabbath) not how is R. Jacob bar Aḥa doing but how is R. Jacob bar Aḥa's tooth doing and he never used a superfluous word, it follows that he permitted treating a toothache on the Sabbath.

200 They explain the Mishnah which prohibits returning to the mouth anything which one was chewing. The younger R. Yannai must read this strictly, only things from the mouth cannot be returned but an earplug perhaps. His companions must hold that nothing in nose, ear, and throat or other human cavities may be returned.

(8c line 22) יוֹצְאִין בְּסֶלַע שֶׁעַל הַצִּינִית. פּוֹדַגְרָה. רִבִּי אָחָא בְּשֵׁם רִבִּי בָּא בַּר מָמָל. אֲפִילוּ טַס. וְהָא תַנִּינָן. הַבָּנוֹת יוֹצְאוֹת בְּחוּטִין. רִבִּי בָּא בְּשֵׁם רַב יְהוּדָה. אֲפִילוּ כָּרוּךְ עַל צַוָּארָהּ. אַבָּא בַּר בָּא מְפַקֵּד לִשְׁמוּאֵל בְּרֵיהּ. לֹא תְקַבֵּל עֲלָךְ מַתְנִיתָא אֶלָּא. אֲבָל לֹא בְקִיסְמִין שֶׁבְּאָזְנֵיהֶן. כֵּינִי מַתְנִיתָא. עַרְבִיּוֹת יוֹצְאוֹת רְעוּלוֹת מָדִיּוֹת פְּרוּפוֹת.

2 אבא G | אבה   4 רעולות G | רעלות

"One goes out with a tetradrachma on a *sinnit*;" ποδάγρα, gout. Rebbi Aḥa in the name of Rebbi Abba bar Mamal, even a metal plate[201].

But did we not state[202], "girls go out with threads"? Rebbi Abba in the name of Rav Jehudah, even wound around her neck[185]. Abba bar Abba[203] commanded to his son Samuel, do not accept this Mishnah, but "not with chips in their ears[27,204]."

So is the Mishnah[205]: "Arab women go out veiled; Median women pinned[28]."

201 Any support for a foot with gout is acceptable. The Babli disagrees, 65a.

202 This should be deleted; the sentence should start with the quote of the Mishnah. The expression "but did we not state" is copied from earlier, Note 185, where it was appropriate.

203 In the Babli he always is called "father of Samuel". The name implies that he was a posthumous child.

204 Since wooden chips in the ears are not jewelry, they qualify as load, not as garment. In the Babli, 85a, it is reported that Samuel's father did not let his daughters go out with threads in their hair.

205 There is no "and"; Median women do not go out veiled.

(8c line 26) תַּנֵּי. רַבָּן שִׁמְעוֹן בֶּן גַּמְלִיאֵל אוֹמֵר. לֹא שָׁנוּ אֶלָּא מַטְבֵּעַ וָאֶבֶן. הָא בֶאֱגוֹז מוּתָּר. מִפְּנֵי שֶׁהוּא מִיטַּלְטֵל. אָמַר רַב אָדָא בַּר אַהֲבָה. אַתְיָא דְּרַבָּן שִׁמְעוֹן בֶּן גַּמְלִיאֵל כְּרִבִּי מֵאִיר. כְּמָה דְרִבִּי מֵאִיר אָמַר. דָּבָר שֶׁהוּא מִיטַּלְטֵל מוּתָּר. כֵּן רַבָּן שִׁמְעוֹן בֶּן גַּמְלִיאֵל אוֹמֵר. דָּבָר שֶׁהוּא מִיטַּלְטֵל מוּתָּר.

1 מטבע G מטביע   2 דרבן | G דרבנן מאיר | G -   3 מאיר | G -

It was stated: Rabban Simeon ben Gamliel says, they stated only coin and stone. Therefore with a nut it is permitted, because it may be moved[206]. Rav Ada bar Ahava said, It results that Rabban Simeon ben Gamliel parallels Rebbi Meïr. Just as Rebbi Meïr said[207], what may be moved is permitted, so Rabban Simeon ben Gamliel said, what may be moved is permitted.

206 This refers to Mishnah 7, that Median women may use a stone or a coin to tie down their head cover only if they already used them for this purpose during the week, so that stone or coin become part of their garment and do not become forbidden to be moved at the start of the Sabbath. Even though a nut is mentioned with stone and coin in the Mishnah, one is permitted to use a new nut on the Sabbath since as food it may freely be moved. As *Or zarua`* §64[20] notes it seems that the Babli 65b makes a distinction in that a stone may be designated (but not yet used) as part of the garment and then used the first time on the Sabbath whereas a coin must have been used before the start of the Sabbath.

207 It is not too clear which statement of Rebbi Meïr is referred to; possibly the authorship of Tosephta 4:13, that anything moveable on the Sabbath may be used to tie down a head cover, is attributed to him. In G, "Meïr" is missing but it cannot be said that the father, Rabban Simeon, decided parallel to the teaching of his son, Rebbi.

(8c line 30) שְׁמוּאֵל אָמַר. יוֹצְאִין בּוֹ מִשּׁוּם סַנְדָּל וְנִכְנָסִין בּוֹ לָעֲזָרָה. רֶבִּי יַנַּאי מַקְשֶׁה. יוֹצְאִין בּוֹ מִשּׁוּם סַנְדָּל. וְהוּא סַנְדָּל. נִכְנָסִין בּוֹ לָעֲזָרָה. וְאֵינוֹ סַנְדָּל. אָמַר רֶבִּי בעא. עַד דִּי הֲוַת מַקְשֶׁה לָהּ עַל דִּשְׁמוּאֵל קַשְׁיָיתָהּ עַל דְּמַתְנִיתִין. סָמוֹכוֹת שֶׁלּוֹ טְמֵאִין מִדְרָס. יוֹצְאִין בָּהֶן בַּשַּׁבָּת וְנִכְנָסִין בָּהֶן לָעֲזָרָה. אָמַר רֶבִּי מָנָא. אֱמוֹר סוֹפָהּ דְּלֵית הִיא פְלִיגָא עַל דִּשְׁמוּאֵל. כְּסָא סָמוֹכוֹת שֶׁלּוֹ טְמֵאִין מִדְרָס. אֵין יוֹצְאִין בָּהֶן בַּשַּׁבָּת וְאֵין נִכְנָסִין בָּהֶן לָעֲזָרָה. אֲנַקְטְמִין טְהוֹרִין וְיוֹצְאִין בָּהֶן׃ מָהוּ אֲנַקְטְמִין טְהוֹרִין. אָמַר רֶבִּי אַבָּהוּ. הוֹנוֹס קַטְמִין חַמְרָא דְּיָדָהּ.

2 בעה | G מנא   3 ויוצאין | G יוצאין   4 פליגא | G פליגה   5 טהורין | G טהורים

Samuel said, one goes out with them[208] because they are like a sandal, and one may enter the Temple Court with them[33]. Rebbi Yannai asked, one goes out with them because they are like sandals, and one may enter the Temple Court with them, because they are not sandals? Rebbi (asked) [Mana][209] said, instead of asking about Samuel he should have asked about the Mishnah, "its supports are impure by stepping on, one may go out with them on the Sabbath, and one may not enter the Temple Court with them.[210]" Rebbi Mana said, say does its last part not disagree with Samuel[211]? "Its supports are impure by stepping on[31], one may not go out with them on the Sabbath, and one may not enter the Temple Court with them[34]. Donkey figures are pure and one may go out with them." What are pure donkey figures? Rebbi Abbahu said, ὄνος κατ᾿ ὦμον, arm's donkey[35,212].

208 The amputee's crutches and protheses as mentioned in Mishnah 8.

209 The correct reading [in brackets] is in G.

210 Why does R. Yannai not point out that the first part of the Mishnah seems to be self-contradictory?
211 If supports which are not fitted exactly for one person may not be used in the public domain on the Sabbath they cannot be considered the equivalent of sandals. The Mishnah is consistent as explained in the commentary to it but Samuel's explanation is not.
212 Differently in the Babli 66b.

(8c line 38) הַבָּנִים יוֹצְאִין בִּקְשָׁרִין. בְּקִשְׁרֵי פוּאָה. וּבְנֵי מְלָכִים בַּזּוּגִין. רִבִּי זְעִירָא אָמַר. בַּזּוּגִין שֶׁבְּצַוָּארוֹ. מָהוּ וְכָל אָדָם. בֵּין קְטַנֵּי עֲנִיִּים בֵּין קְטַנֵּי עֲשִׁירִים. רִבִּי אִילָא אָמַר. בַּזּוּגִין שֶׁבִּכְסוּתוֹ. מָהוּ וְכָל אָדָם. בֵּין גְּדוֹלִים בֵּין קְטַנִּים. מַתְנִיתָה פְלִיגָא עַל רִבִּי זְעִירָא. יוֹצֵא הוּא אָדָם בַּזּוּגִין שֶׁבִּכְסוּתוֹ. וְאֵינוּ יוֹצֵא בַּזּוּגִין שֶׁבְּצַוָּארוֹ. אֶלָּא כָּאן בִּגְדוֹלִים כָּאן בִּקְטַנִּים.

1 בקשרי G | בקישׁ[נרי] 2 מהו | G מהוא 3 מהו | G מהוא פליגא G פליגה 4 כאן | G כן

"Boys go out with knots[36]," knots of madder. "And princes with bells." Rebbi Ze`ira said, with bells around their necks. What means "and so may everybody"? Whether children of the poor or children of the rich. Rebbi Ila said, with bells on his clothing. What means "and so may everybody"? Whether adult or child. A *baraita*[213] disagrees with Rebbi Ze`ira: A person may go out with bells on his clothing but he may not go out with bells around his neck. But here about adults and there about the young[214].

213 Similarly Tosephta 5:7; cf. Note 50.
214 Adults may wear bells and children bundles of madder. The Babli 67a permits only woven images of bells.

(8c line 43) יוֹצְאִין בְּבֵיצַת הַחַרְגּוֹל. טַב לְאוּדְנָא. וּבְשֵׁן שֶׁלְּשׁוּעָל. טַב לְשֵׁינָה. וּבְמַסְמֵר הַצָּלוּב טַב לְעַבְּבִיתָא.

1 לאודנא G | לאדנה 2 לעכביתא G | [לעכ]ביתה

אִית תַּנָּיֵי תַנֵי וּמַחֲלִיף. רִבִּי חֲנַנְיָה בְשֵׁם רִבִּי יוֹחָנָן כְּמַתְנִיתָן. רִבִּי שְׁמוּאֵל רִבִּי אַבָּהוּ בְשֵׁם רִבִּי יוֹחָנָן. כָּל־שֶׁהוּא מְרַפֵּא אֵין בּוֹ מִשׁוּם דַּרְכֵי הָאֱמוֹרִי. דַּרְגֵי דְרַגִיבַת. מִשּׁוּם דַּרְכֵי הָאֱמוֹרִי. רִבִּי יְהוּדָה אָמַר. רִבִּי יְהוּדָה אָמַר. מִשּׁוּם דָּגוֹן עֲבוֹדָה זָרָה. וְרֹאשׁ דָּגוֹן וּשְׁתֵּי כַפּוֹת יָדָיו. דּוֹנוּ דֵנִי. מִשֵּׁם דַּרְכֵי הָאֱמוֹרִי. רִבִּי יְהוּדָה אוֹמֵר. מִשֵּׁם דָּן עֲבוֹדָה זָרָה. וְאָמְרוּ חֵי אֱלֹהֶיךָ דָּן. לָאו לָאו. מִשּׁוּם דַּרְכֵי הָאֱמוֹרִי. רִבִּי יְהוּדָה אוֹמֵר. מִשֵּׁם עֲבוֹדָה זָרָה. וַיֹּאמְרוּ לָאֵל סוּר מִמֶּנּוּ וְדַעַת דְּרָכֶיךָ לֹא חָפָצְנוּ׃

1 ומחליף G | ומחלף אבהו | G אבהוא 2 דרגי דרגיבת G דגנת דרגנת משום | G משם 3 דונו דני | G דני דנוי 5 משם | G משם לאו

There are Tannaim who switch[215]. Rebbi Hananiah in the name of Rebbi Johanan as our Mishnah[216]. Rebbi Samuel, Rebbi Abbahu in the name of Rebbi Johanan, anything which heals is not forbidden because of ways of the Emorite[217]. [218]"דרגי דרגיבת because of ways of the Emorite; Rebbi Jehudah says because of the idol Dagon, *and Dagon's head and his two hands*[219]. דונו דני because of ways of the Emorite; Rebbi Jehudah says because of the idol Dan, *they say, by the life of your god Dan*[220]. No no[221], because of ways of the Emorite; Rebbi Jehudah says because idolatry, *they say no God, turn away from us, we have no desire to know Your ways*[222]."

215 In Mishnah 10 they exchange the names of RR. Yose and Meïr. The Mishnah in the majority of the Babli sources has R. Meïr instead of R. Yose and the Sages instead of R. Meïr, cf. *Diqduqe Soferim Šabbat* p. 73 Note ב. This is important for practice since R. Yose is the dominant authority.

216 He confirms the attributions in our Mishnah text.

217 Babli 67a, *Ḥulin* 77b.

218 Babli 67a/b. Tosephta 7:2,3,10. The identification of the formulas of incantation must be tentative; in no case is it clear in which language they are formulated. We follow the discussion of S. Lieberman in *Tosefta ki-Fshutah Šabbat* pp. 92,93,96.

There seems to be no good explanation of the term דרגי דרגיבת of the Leiden ms. But the remark of R. Jehudah suggests athat in the version of G דגנת דרגנת one should read דגנת דגנת "make grain, make grain" as a charm when sowing grain.

It is conjectured that the expression דונו דני is Greek and refers to the magical practice of binding somebody by spells (either that he cannot move, e. g. *Sanhedrin* 7:19 Notes 371-375, or becomes impotent, Notes 377-381) or one could read δέννω [τὸν] δεῖνα "I am binding X".

219 *1S.* 8:4.

220 *Am.* 8:14.

221 Following M. Herschler one should read with two Tosephta mss. לא לא. In a situation which could represent an unlucky omen one should not say *no, no* as to counteract. (The Babli, *Pesahim* 111 a, recommends reciting an appropriate propitious verse.) In the quote from *Job* one has to read לָאֵל as אֶל לֹא "no god", cf. *Nedarim* 1:4 Note 157 where לא = לחולין = חולין.

222 *Job* 22:14.

(8c line 51) תַּנֵּי רִבִּי חִייָא. עָמַד עֶצֶם בִּגְרוֹנוֹ נוֹתֵן מֵאוֹתוֹ הַמִּין עַל רֹאשׁוֹ וְאֵין בּוֹ מִשּׁוּם דַּרְכֵי הָאֱמוֹרִי. תַּנֵּי רִבִּי לִיעֶזֶר בֶּן יַעֲקֹב. לֹא תְנַחֲשׁוּ וְלֹא תְעוֹנֵנוּ׃ אַף עַל פִּי שֶׁאֵין נַחַשׁ יֵשׁ סִימָן. וּבִלְבַד לְאַחַר שְׁלֹשָׁה סִימָנָיו. כְּגוֹן וַאֲנִי | בְּבֹאִי מִפַּדָּן מֵתָה עָלַי רָחֵל. יוֹסֵף אֵינֶנּוּ וְשִׁמְעוֹן אֵינֶנּוּ וְאֶת־בִּנְיָמִן תִּקָּחוּ וגו'.

ŠABBAT CHAPTER SIX 223

1 חייא G חייה | 2 ליעזר G אליעזר שאין נחש G נָחָשׁ | 4 וגו' G ע"ה כלנה

Rebbi Hiyya stated: If a bone was stuck in his throat he puts of the same kind on top of his head and this is not of ways of the Emorite[223]. Rebbi Eliezer ben Jacob stated: *you shall neither divine nor use incantations*[224]. Even through there is no divining there are signs, but only after three portents[225]; for example *when I came from Padan, Rachel died on me*[226]; *Joseph is no more, Simeon is no more, and you want to take Benjamin*[227], etc

223 Babli 67a. The Babli adds an incantation to be recited.
224 *Lev.* 19:26.
225 If something happened to a person three times he may assume that he is prone to this kind of accident, as Jacob feared for Benjamin's life because he already had lost a wife and two sons.
226 *Gen.* 48:7.
227 *Gen.* 42:36.

(8c line 55) אָמַר רִבִּי אֶלְעָזָר. הוֹלְכִין אַחַר שְׁמִיעַת בַּת קוֹל. מַה טַּעַם. וְאָזְנֶיךָ תִּשְׁמַעְנָה דָבָר מֵאַחֲרֶיךָ לֵאמֹר זֶה הַדֶּרֶךְ לְכוּ בוֹ. רִבִּי לְעָזָר עָאל לְפוֹנִיָיה. אָתָא אַבְטִיוֹנָא וַאֲקוֹמֵיהּ מֵאַחוֹרֵיהּ וְיָתַב לֵיהּ. אָמַר. הָכֵין כָּל־עַמָּא לָא אַקִים לְבַר נָשׁ אֶלָּא לִי. לֵית אֶפְשָׁר דַּאֲנָא נָפִיק מִכָּא עַד דְּנֵידַע מַה הֲוֵי בְּסוֹפֵיהּ. וַהֲוָה תַמָּן חִיוִי. שָׁרֵי נָפִיק וְיָהֵב לֵיהּ עַד דּוֹ תַמָּן אֲחַת דְּרִיבוֹי. וְקָרָא עָלָיו וְאַתֶּן אָדָם תַּחְתֶּיךָ וגו'.

1 אלעזר G לעזר | 2 בו | G בה כי תאמינו וכי תשמאילו אתא G אתה ואקומי G ואקימי | 3 מאחוריה | G - G לֵיהּ | G לה הכן | G הכין כל | G מן כל דאנא | G דנה | 4 מכא G מיכה והוה | G והווה חיוי | G חווָרי נפיק | G נפק רו תמן | G דיתמנן | 5 - | ואתן אדום תחתיך

חַד תַּלְמִיד מִן דְּבַר קַפָּרָא הֲוָה נָפִיק מְקְטוֹעַ כִּיסָין. חַמְתֵּיהּ חַד קַיָּיט חִיוְיָא פְּרֵי בַתְרֵיהּ. אָמַר לֵיהּ. חִיוְיָא פְּרֵי בַתְרָךְ. שַׁבְקֵיהּ וַאֲזַל לֵיהּ בַּתְרֵיהּ. וְקָרָא עֲלוֹי וְאַתֶּן אָדָם תַּחְתֶּיךָ.

1 קפראx G קפרה נפיק | G נפק | 2 ליה | G ליה רבי רבי

גַּרְמָנָיָא עַבְדֵּיהּ דְּרִבִּי יוּדָה נְשִׂיָּיא נְפַק. בָּעֵי מִילַוְויֵהּ לְרִבִּי אִילָא. אָתָא כֶּלֶב שׁוֹטֶה בָּעֵי אִיתְגַּרְיָיא בֵּיהּ בְּרִבִּי אִילָא. גָּעַר בֵּיהּ גַּרְמָנִי. שַׁבְקֵיהּ וַאֲזַל לֵיהּ בַּתְרֵיהּ. וְקָרָא עֲלוֹי וְאַתֶּן אָדָם תַּחְתֶּיךָ.

בַּר קַפָּרָא הֲוָה אִיעֲלַל לְהָדָא קִרְיָיא. מִי עָלַל נְכָשׁ בְּאֶצְבְּעוֹ. עָאל וּשְׁמַע קָלֵיהּ דְּטַלְיָיא קָרֵי. אִם־בְּגַפּוֹ יָבֹא בְּגַפּוֹ יֵצֵא. אָמַר. דּוּמָה שֶׁלֹּא עָלַת בְּיָדִי אֶלָּא הַטָּחָה זוֹ בִּלְבָד. וְכֵן הֲוָות לֵיהּ.

רִבִּי יוֹחָנָן וְרִבִּי שִׁמְעוֹן בֶּן לָקִישׁ הֲווּ מִתְחַמְּדִין מֵיחֱמֵי אַפּוֹי דִּשְׁמוּאֵל. אָמְרִין. נֵלֵךְ אַחַר שְׁמִיעַת בַּת קוֹל. עָבְרוּן קוֹמֵי סִידְרָא. שַׁמְעוֹן קָלֵיהּ דְּטַלְיָיא וּשְׁמוּאֵל מֵת. וְסַיְימוּן. וְכֵן הֲוָות לֵיהּ.

רִבִּי יוֹנָה וְרִבִּי יוֹסֵה סָלְקוֹן מְבַקְרָא לְרִבִּי אָחָא דַהֲוָה תָשִׁישׁ. אָמְרִין. נֵלֵךְ אַחַר שְׁמִיעַת בַּת
קוֹל. שָׁמְעוּן קָלֵיהּ דְּאִיתְּתָא אֶמְרָה לַחֲבֵירָתָהּ. אִיטְפֵּי בּוֹצִינָא. אֶמְרָה לָא יִתְטְפֵי וְלָא מִיטְפֵּי
בּוֹצִינֵיהוֹן דְּיִשְׂרָאֵל.

Rebbi Eleazar said, one follows what one hears from a disembodied voice[228]. What is the reason? *Your ears will hear something from behind you saying, this is the way you should follow*[229] etc. Rebbi Eleazar went to relieve himself. There came a Roman official[230] and removed him (from behind him)[231] and sat down. He said, here nobody removed anybody ever but me. It is impossible that I should leave from here until I know what happened to him. There was a snake there which started coming out and gave him as long as he was there that his intestines descended. He recited about him, *I shall give a man in your stead, etc.*[232], [I shall give an Edomite in your stead.][233]

One of bar Qappara's students went out to cut wood chips. A fig cutter saw that a snake was running after him. He said to him [Rebbi, Rebbi,][232] a snake is running after you. It left him and ran after the latter. He recited about him, *I shall give a man in your stead*[234].

Germania the slave of Rebbi Jehudah Nesia went out and wanted to accompany Rebbi Ila. There came a rabid dog which wanted to attack Rebbi Ila. The German shouted at him, he left him and pursued the other. He recited about him, *I shall give a man in your stead.*

Bar Qappara went to this town; when he entered he injured his finger. He went and heard a child's voice, reciting *if he came alone he shall leave alone*[235]. He said, it seems that only this plastering is going to happen to me. And so it was.

Rebbi Johanan and Rebbi Simeon ben Laqish desired to meet Samuel. They said, let us go after what is heard. They passed by a school and heard a child's voice, *and Samuel died*[235]. They noted it and so it had happened.

Rebbi Jonah and Rebbi Yose went up[236] to visit Rebbi Aha who was weak. They said, let us go after what is heard. They heard a woman's voice saying, the light is extinguished. She answered her, Israel's light is not extinguished and will not be extinguished.

228 Here it does not mean a Heavenly voice but one whose origin is unknown to the hearer. Babli *Megillah* 32a in the name of R. Johanan.
229 *Is.* 30:21.
230 Greek εὔθυνος, ὁ, "corrector, judge, publiv examiner".
231 Not in G and superfluous.
232 *Is.* 43:4.
233 Addition of G which here becomes illegible.
234 Addition of G. The basis of the pun equating אָדָם and אֱדוֹם is the popular name "Edom" given to the Roman government.
235 *Ex.* 21:3.
236 From low-situated Tiberias to mountain top Sepphoris.

(8c line 74) רִבִּי יוֹחָנָן הֲוָה עָבַר בַּשׁוּקָא. חָמָא חַד מְזַבֵּן מִן אִילֵּין מְלטוֹמָה. אָמַר לֵיהּ. מִן אִילֵּין אַתְּ חַי. אָמַר לֵיהּ. אִין. שָׁבְקֵיהּ וַאֲזַל לֵיהּ. בָּתַר שָׁעָה עָבַר גַּבֵּיהּ. אָמַר לֵיהּ. רִבִּי. צְלִי עֲלוַוי. דְּמִן הָהִיא שַׁעְתָּא לָא זַבְנִית כְּלוּם. וְאָמַר לֵיהּ. שְׁנִי אַתְרָךְ. פְּעָמִים שֶׁשִּׁינּוּי הַשֵּׁם גּוֹרֵם. פְּעָמִים שֶׁשִּׁינּוּי הַמָּקוֹם גּוֹרֵם.

תְּרֵין תַּלְמִידִין מִן דְּרִבִּי חֲנִינָה הֲווֹן נָפְקִין מִקְטוֹעַ כִּיסִין. חַמְתּוֹן חָדָא אִיסְטרוֹלוֹגוֹס. אִילֵּין תְּרֵין מִי נָפְקִין וְלָא חָזְרִין. מִי נָפְקִין פְּגַע בָּהֶן חַד סָב. אָמַר לוֹן. זְכוּן עִמִּי. דְּאִית לִי תְלָתָא יוֹמִין דְּלָא טָעֲמִית כְּלוּם. וַהֲוָה עִמּוֹן חַד עִיגּוּל. קָצוֹן פַּלְגָּא וִיהָבִינֵיהּ לֵיהּ. אֲכַל וּצְלִי עֲלֵיהוֹן. אָמַר לוֹן. תִּתְקַיֵּים לְכוֹן נַפְשֵׁיכוֹן בְּהָדֵין יוֹמָא. הֵיךְ דְּקיָּמְתּוֹן לִי נַפְשִׁי בְּהָדֵין יוֹמָא. נַפְקוּן בִּשְׁלוֹם וְחָזְרוּן בְּשָׁלוֹם. וַהֲווּ תַמָּן בְּנֵי אֵינַשׁ דְּשָׁמְעוֹן קָלֵיהּ. אֲמָרִין לֵיהּ. וְלֹא כֵן אֲמַרְתְּ. אִילֵּין תְּרֵין מִי נָפְקִין וְלָא חָזְרִין. אֲמַר. אִי דְּהָכָא גַּבְרָא שָׁקָר דְּאִיסְטרוֹלוֹגִיָּיא דִּידֵיהּ שָׁקָרִין. אֲפִילוּ כֵן אָזְלוֹן וּפְשַׁפְשׁוֹן וְאַשְׁכְּחוֹן חֲכִינָה פַּלְגָּא מוּבְלָא וּפַלְגָּא בְּהָדָא מוּבְלָא. אָמְרוּ. מַה טִיבוּ עֲבַדְתּוּן יוֹמָא דֵין. וְתָנִיין לֵיהּ עוּבְדָא. אָמַר. וּמַה הַהוּא גַבְרָא יָכִיל עָבִיד. דֶּאֱלָהֲהוֹן דִּי יְהוּדָאי מִתְפַּיֵּיס כְּפַלְגוּת עִיגוּל.

7 מובלא G ‖ מובלה (2) 8 יכיל עביד G ‖ יכל עבד דאלההון G ‖ ואלההין מתפיים G ‖ מיתפייס 9 עיגול G ‖ עגיל

Rebbi Johanan was passing by the market. He saw one of those who sell honey cake[237]. He asked him, from this you make a living? He answered, yes. He left him and went away. After an hour he passed by him. He asked him, rabbi, pray for me since from that moment I did not sell anything. He told him, change your place. Sometimes a change of name works, sometimes a change of place works[238].

Two students of Rebbi Ḥanina went out to chop wood. An astrologer[239] saw them, these two if they go out will not return. When they went out they met an old man who told them, acquire merit by me; for three days I did not eat anything. They had a loaf with them, cut off half of it and gave it to him.

He ate and prayed for them; he said to them, may your life be preserved today as you did preserve my life today. They went out in peace and returned in peace. There were people there who had heard his[240] voice and told him, did you not say, these two if they go out will not return? He said, if it is so, this man is a liar and his astrology consists of lies. [241]Nevertheless they went and investigated and found a viper half in this load and half in the other load[242]. They asked, what good deed did you do today? They told him[243] the facts. He said, what can this man do if the Jew's God is propitiated by half a loaf!

237 Greek μελίτωμα, -ατος, τό.
238 Causes a change of luck.
239 Greek ἀστρολόγος, ὁ.
240 The astrologer's.
241 Here starts a new Genizah fragment edited by L. Ginzberg in גנזי שכטר *Genizah Studies in Memory of Doctor Solomon*

Schechter vol. I, New York 1928, pp. 436 ff. (G).
242 Of the wood chips carried by the students.
243 The astrologer, who in the next sentence refers to himself as "this man"..

(8d line 14) רִבִּי חוּנָה מִשְׁתָּעֵי הָדֵין אִיסְטְרוֹלוֹגוֹס. חַד גִּיּוּר הֲוָה עוֹבָדָא. חַד זְמַן בָּעֵי מֵיפוּק. אָמַר. כְּדוֹן נָפְקִין. חָזַר וָמַר. כְּלוּם אִידְבָּקֵת בְּהָדָא אוּמְתָא קַדִּישְׁתָּא לָא לְמִפְרוֹשׁ מִן אִילֵּין מִילַיָּא. נֵיפוּק עַל שְׁמֵיהּ דְּבָרְיָין. קָרִיב לְמַכְסָה וְהַב לֵהּ חַמְרָא וְאָכְלָה. מָאן גְּרַם לֵיהּ דְּיִפּוֹל. בְּגִין דְּהִרְהֵר. מָאן גְּרַם לֵיהּ דְּאִשְׁתֵּיזִיב. בְּגִין דְּאִיתְרְחַץ עַל בָּרְיֵיהּ.

1 הדין G | הדן בעי G | אתה בעי מיפוק G | מפוק 2 אומתא G |]אומ[תה קדישתא G קדישתה 3 מילייא G | מיליוה והב G | יהב לה G | ליה חמרא G | חמרה ואכלה G | ואפילה מאן G | מן דיפול G דיפיל 4 בגין G | ביגין מאן G | מן דאשתיזיב G | דישתֵיזֵיב

[244]Rebbi Huna told the following happening. A convert was an astrologer[245]. Once he wanted to go on a trip. He said, does one go now[246]? He changed his mind and said, did I not cling to this holy people to separate myself from these things? I shall go in the name of our Creator. He came close to the toll gate when his donkey kicked and (ate it) [threw him off][247]. What caused him to fall? Because he thought of it[248]. Why was he saved? Because he trusted in his Creator.

244 A copy of this story is in *Orhot Hayim* 3 p, 620 and from there in other Medieval sources, e. g. *Responsa attributed to Nahmanides* #283. While this text is copied from a source close to the Leiden ms., it exhibits some signs of editing and cannot be considered a direct witness to the text.
245 *Orhot Hayim* adds that he was a dealer in veils.
246 The day was astrologically an unlucky

time to start a business trip.
247 The text in parentheses (from the Leiden ms.) is clearly a scribal error writing כ for פ in the text of G [in brackets]. *Orhot Hayim* adds that the donkey ran off to the next town (where it was found by its owner) clearly without paying the tolls.
248 Of astrology.

(8d line 14) אָמַר רִבִּי לֵוִי. כָּל־הַמְנַחֵשׁ סוֹפוֹ לָבוֹא עָלָיו. וּמַה טַעַם. כִּי לֹא־נַחַשׁ בְּיַעֲקֹב. כִּי לוּ נַחַשׁ. אָמַר רִבִּי אָחָא בַּר זְעִירָא. כָּל־מִי שֶׁאֵינוֹ מְנַחֵשׁ מְחִיצָתוֹ לִפְנִים כְּמַלְאֲכֵי הַשָּׁרֵת. וּמַה טַעַם. כָּעֵת יֵאָמֵר לְיַעֲקֹב וּלְיִשְׂרָאֵל מַה־פָּעַל אֵל· אָמַר רִבִּי חֲנִינָא בְּרֵיהּ דְּרִבִּי אַבָּהוּ· כִּבְחֶצְיֵי יָמָיו שֶׁל עוֹלָם הָיָה אוֹתוֹ רָשָׁע עוֹמֵד. מַה טַעֲמֵיהּ. כָּעֵת יֵאָמֵר לְיַעֲקֹב וּלְיִשְׂרָאֵל מַה־פָּעַל אֵל· אָמַר רִבִּי יִרְמְיָה בֶּן אֶלְעָזָר. עֲתִידָה בַּת קוֹל מְפוֹצֶצֶת בְּאָהֳלֵי צַדִּיקִים וְאוֹמֶרֶת. כָּל־מִי שֶׁפָּעַל עִם אֵל יָבוֹא וְיִטּוֹל שְׂכָרוֹ. רִבִּי בֶּרֶכְיָה בְּשֵׁם רִבִּי אַבָּא בַּר כַּהֲנָא. עָתִיד הַקָּדוֹשׁ בָּרוּךְ הוּא לַעֲשׂוֹת מְחִיצָתָן שֶׁלַּצַּדִּיקִים לִפְנִים מִמְּחִיצָתָן שֶׁלַּמַּלְאֲכֵי הַשָּׁרֵת. וּמַלְאֲכֵי הַשָּׁרֵת שׁוֹאֲלִין אוֹתָן וְאוֹמְרִים לָהֶן. מַה־פָּעַל אֵל· מַה הוֹרָה לָכֶם הַקָּדוֹשׁ בָּרוּךְ הוּא. אָמַר רִבִּי לֵוִי בַּר חַיּוּתָא. וְלֹא כְּבָר עָשָׂה כֵן בָּעוֹלָם הַזֶּה. הַהוּא דִכְתִיב עֲנֵה נְבוּכַדְנֶצַּר וְאָמַר הָא־אֲנָה חָזֵי גּוּבְרִין אַרְבְּעָה שְׁרַיִן מַהְלְכִין בְּגוֹא־נוּרָא וַחֲבָל לָא־אִיתַי בְּהוֹן. וּמַה תַּלְמוּד לוֹמַר וַחֲבָל לָא־אִיתַי בְּהוֹן. אֶלָּא מְלַמֵּד שֶׁהָיוּ סָרִיסִים וְנִתְרַפּוּ. וְרֵיחַיהּ דִּי קַדְמִיתָה אֵין כָּתוּב כָּאן. אֶלָּא וְרֵיחַיהּ דִּי רְבִיעָאָה. הֵן הָיוּ מְכַבְּשִׁין לְפָנָיו אֶת הָאוֹר. דָּמֵי לְבַר־אֱלָהִין· אָמַר רְאוּבֵן. בְּאוֹתָהּ שָׁעָה יָרַד מַלְאָךְ וּסְטָרוֹ לְהַהוּא רְשִׁיעָא עַל פִּיו. אָמַר לֵיהּ. תַּקֵּן מִילָּךְ. וּבַר אִית לֵיהּ. חָזַר וְאָמַר. בְּרִיךְ אֱלָהֲהוֹן דִּי־שַׁדְרַךְ מֵישַׁךְ וַעֲבֵד נְגוֹ. דִּי שָׁלַח בְּרֵיהּ לֵית כְּתִיב כָּאן. אֶלָּא דִּי־שְׁלַח מַלְאֲכֵהּ וְשֵׁיזִב לְעַבְדּוֹהִי דִּי הִתְרְחִצוּ עֲלוֹהִי.

2 אחא G | אחבה G | אחיא זעירא G | זעורה כמלאכי G | כממלאכי 3 חנינא G | חנינה אבהו G | אבהוא 7 השרת G | שרת 8 הורה G | הודה חיותא G | חייתה 9 ההוא G | הדא ענה G | עני ארבעה G | ארבע 11 סריסין G | שריסין ונתרפו G | וניתרפו אין G | לית כאן G | כן רביעא G | רביעייה 12 האור G | האוד ראובן G | ר' ראובן 13 ליה G | ליה רשיעא 14 ושיזיב G | ושיזב

Rebbi Levi said, in the end it will come over anybody engaged in divination[249]. What is the reason? *For there is no divination in Jacob*[250]; for divination is his. Rebbi Aha bar Ze'ira said, the place[251] of anybody not divining will be like that of the Angels of Service. What is the reason? *At that time it will be said to Israel what God wrought.* Rebbi Ḥanina the son of Rebbi Abbahu said, this evildoer lived halfway through the existence of the world[252]. What is the reason? *At that time it will be said to Israel what God wrought.* Rebbi Jeremiah ben Eleazar said, in the future a disembodied voice will explode in the tents of the Just and say, everybody who worked with God should come and take his reward. Rebbi Berekhiah in the name of Rebbi Abba bar Cahana: In the future the Holy One, praise to Him, will make place for the Just inside the place of the Angels of Service; the Angels of Service will ask them and say to them, *what did God do?* What did the Holy One, praise to Him, teach you? Rebbi Levi bar Hayta said, did He not already do this in this world? That is what is written[253], *Nebuchadnezzar started and said, but I am seeing four free men walking in the fire and no blemish is on them.* Why does the verse say, *and no blemish is on them*? This teaches that they were eunuchs but were healed. It is not written "and the looks of the first", but *and the looks of the fourth*; they were suppressing the fire before him. *Is similar to a son of gods.* [Rebbi][254] Reuben said, at that moment an angel descended, hit that evildoer on his mouth, and told him, correct your words; does He have a son? He continued and said, [255]*praised be the God of Shadrak, Meshak, and Abed-Nego*; it does not say "Who sent His son" but *Who sent His angel and rescued His servants who trusted in Him.*

249 His bad omens will hurt him.
250 *Num.* 23:22. Reading לא as לו.
251 Imagining the Future World as a palace in which God resides; the Just will be His courtiers as the Angels are imagined to be. G reads: the place of anybody not divining will be *inside* that of Angels of Service; a higher status. Since this statement is attributed later to R. Berekhiah, at this place the reading of the Leiden ms. has to be preferred.
252 The time elapsed from the creation of Adam to Bileam is equal to the time to elapse between Bileam and the coming of the Messiah. The present author has noted in the Introduction to his edition of *Seder Olam* (Northvale NJ 1998) that the Yerushalmi does not know this Babylonian compilation. We do not know the details of Galilean biblical chronology. According to *Seder Olam*, Bileam's speech is to be dated 2485 A. M.; this would predict the end of this world at 4970 A. M. or 1210 C. E. In Maimonides's interpretation of this passage in his *Epistle to Yemen* the reference is not to the coming of the Messiah but to restoration of prophecy to Israel.
253 *Dan.* 3:25.
254 Added from G.
255 *Dan.* 3:28.

כלל גדול פרק שביעי

משנה א: כְּלָל גָּדוֹל אָמְרוּ בַשַּׁבָּת. כָּל־הַשּׁוֹכֵחַ עִיקַּר שַׁבָּת וְעָשָׂה מְלָאכוֹת הַרְבֵּה בְּשַׁבָּתוֹת הַרְבֵּה אֵינוֹ חַיָּב אֶלָּא חַטָּאת אַחַת. וְהַיּוֹדֵעַ עִיקַּר שַׁבָּת וְעָשָׂה מְלָאכוֹת הַרְבֵּה בְּשַׁבָּתוֹת הַרְבֵּה חַיָּב עַל כָּל־שַׁבָּת וְשַׁבָּת. וְהַיּוֹדֵעַ שֶׁהוּא שַׁבָּת וְעָשָׂה מְלָאכוֹת הַרְבֵּה בְּשַׁבָּתוֹת הַרְבֵּה חַיָּב עַל כָּל־מְלָאכָה וּמְלָאכָה. הָעוֹשֶׂה מְלָאכוֹת הַרְבֵּה מֵעֵין מְלָאכָה אַחַת אֵינוֹ חַיָּב אֶלָּא חַטָּאת אֶחָת:

Mishnah 1: A comprehensive principle they said about the Sabbath. Anybody who is oblivious of the principle of the Sabbath[1] and performed many works on many Sabbaths is obligated for one purification sacrifice only. But one who knows the principle of the Sabbath and performed many works on many Sabbaths[2] is obligated for every single Sabbath; and one who knows that it is the Sabbath and performed many works on many Sabbaths is obligated for every single work. One who performs many works similar to one work[3] is obligated only for one purification sacrifice.

משנה ב: אֲבוֹת מְלָאכוֹת אַרְבָּעִים חָסֵר אַחַת. הַחוֹרֵשׁ הַזּוֹרֵעַ הַקּוֹצֵר הַמְעַמֵּר הַדָּשׁ וְהַזּוֹרֶה הַבּוֹרֵר וְהַטּוֹחֵן וְהַמְרַקֵּד הַלָּשׁ וְהָאוֹפֶה. הַגּוֹזֵז אֶת הַצֶּמֶר הַמְלַבְּנוֹ הַמְנַפְּסוֹ הַצּוֹבְעוֹ הַטּוֹוֵהוּ הַמֵּסֵךְ וְהָעוֹשֶׂה שְׁנֵי בָתֵּי נִירִין הָאוֹרֵג שְׁנֵי חוּטִין הַבּוֹצֵעַ שְׁנֵי חוּטִין הַקּוֹשֵׁר וְהַמַּתִּיר. וְהַתּוֹפֵר שְׁתֵּי תְפִירוֹת הַקּוֹרֵעַ עַל מְנָת לִתְפּוֹר שְׁתֵּי תְפִירוֹת.

Mishnah 2: There are 39 categories of work. He who ploughs, who sows, who harvests, who binds into sheaves, who threshes, and who winnows, who selects, who grinds, and who sifts, who makes dough, and who bakes[4]. He who shears wool, who bleaches it, who cards it, who dyes it, who spins it, who prepares the loom, who ties two threads as warp, who weaves two rows, who hits two threads, who ties, and who unties. Also who sews two stitches, who tears in order to sew two stitches.

משנה ג: הַצָּד צְבִי הַשּׁוֹחֲטוֹ וְהַמַּפְשִׁיטוֹ הַמּוֹלְחוֹ וְהַמְעַבְּדוֹ הַמְחַתְּכוֹ הַכּוֹתֵב שְׁתֵּי אוֹתִיּוֹת וְהַמּוֹחֵק עַל מְנָת לִכְתּוֹב שְׁתֵּי אוֹתִיּוֹת.

Mishnah 3: He who catches a deer, who slaughters it, who skins it, who salts it, who rubs it clean[5], who tans it, who cuts it, who writes two letters, and who erases in order to write two letters[6].

משנה ד: הַבּוֹנֶה וְהַסּוֹתֵר הַמְכַבֶּה וְהַמַּבְעִיר וְהַמַּכֶּה בַפַּטִּישׁ וְהַמּוֹצִיא מֵרְשׁוּת לִרְשׁוּת הֲרֵי אֵילוּ אֲבוֹת מְלָאכוֹת אַרְבָּעִים חָסֵר אַחַת:

Mishnah 4: He who builds, and who tears down, who extinguishes fire, and who lights fire, and who hits with a hammer[7], and who transports from one domain to another[8]; these are the 39 categories of work.

משנה ה: וְעוֹד כְּלָל אַחֵר אָמְרוּ כָּל־הַכָּשֵׁר לְהַצְנִיעַ וּמַצְנִיעִין כָּמוֹהוּ וְהוֹצִיאוֹ בַשַּׁבָּת חַיָּב עָלָיו חַטָּאת וְכָל־שֶׁאֵינוֹ כָשֵׁר לְהַצְנִיעַ וְאֵין מַצְנִיעִין כָּמוֹהוּ וְהוֹצִיאוֹ בַשַּׁבָּת אֵינוֹ חַיָּב אֶלָּא הַמַּצְנִיעוֹ:

Mishnah 5: They said another principle. Anything which can be preserved and one preserves its kind if he took it out on the Sabbath he is obligated for a purification sacrifice because of it[9], but for anything which cannot be preserved and one does not preserve its kind, if he took it out on the Sabbath only the one who preserves is obligated.

משנה ו: הַמּוֹצִיא תֶבֶן כִּמְלוֹא פִי פָרָה. עֵצָה כִּמְלוֹא פִי גָמָל. עָמִיר כִּמְלוֹא פִי טָלֶה. עֲשָׂבִים כִּמְלוֹא פִי גְדִי. עֲלֵי שׁוּם וַעֲלֵי בְצָלִים לַחִין כַּגְּרוֹגֶרֶת. יְבֵשִׁים כִּמְלוֹא פִי גְדִי וְאֵינָן מִצְטָרְפִין זֶה עִם זֶה מִפְּנֵי שֶׁלֹּא שָׁווּ בְשִׁעוּרֵיהֶן. הַמּוֹצִיא אוֹכָלִין כַּגְּרוֹגֶרֶת מִצְטָרְפִין זֶה עִם זֶה מִפְּנֵי שֶׁשָּׁווּ בְשִׁעוּרֵיהֶן חוּץ מִקְּלִפֵּיהֶן וְגַלְעִינֵיהֶן וְעוּקְצֵיהֶן וְסוּבָּן וּמוּרְסָן. רַבִּי יְהוּדָה אוֹמֵר חוּץ מִקְּלִפֵּי עֲדָשִׁים הַמִּתְבַּשְּׁלוֹת עִמָּהֶן:

Mishnah 6: One who brings out straw filling the mouth of a cow, wood shavings filling the mouth of a camel, grain[10] filling the mouth of a sheep, grasses filling the mouth of a goat. Moist garlic leaves and onion leaves the volume of a dried fig[11], if dry filling the mouth of a goat; they are not combined since their measures are not identical. One who brings out foodstuffs in the volume of a dried fig; they are combined since their measures are the same except for their shells, and their pits, and their stalks, and their grit, and their bran. Rebbi Jehudah says except for pods of lentils which are cooked with them.

1   A Jew who never has heard of the laws of the Sabbath. The rule is formulated in terms of oblivion because all laws of purification sacrifices require an element of oblivion.

2   In error.

3   Actions which are classified under the same category of the official 39 prohibitions of the Sabbath.

4   As noted earlier, since the Sabbath prohibition is repeated at the start of the rules of building the Tabernacle, *Ex.* 35:1-3,

one concludes that the prohibited actions are those needed for building the Tabernacle and the Service performed in it. The first series (11 categories) describes actions needed to prepare cereal offerings and the shew-bread. The second series (13 categories) catalogues the making of the priestly garments.

5   To remove both hair outside and remainders of flesh inside to prepare for the tanning process which turns hide into leather.

6   This series of 9 categories describes both sacrifices and the production of writing material which in pre-Mishnaic times was mostly leather.

7   A name for the formal end of any production process.

8   This is mentioned last because in most cases it is a weak prohibition since "public domain" into which one may not transport by biblical standards is exists mostly outside a built-up area.

9   One starts to detail the rules of the category mentioned last. The biblical prohibition is restricted to valuables. However, if a person considers valuable what for others is not, the item becomes biblically forbidden to him for transport.

10 Cut grain with stalks and hulls.

11 Palestinian dried figs of which the large ones would only qualify as medium sized in other countries (Mishnah *Kelim* 17:7).

(8d line 70) כְּלָל גָּדוֹל אָמְרוּ בַשַּׁבָּת כול'. מָהוּ גָדוֹל. אָמַר רִבִּי יוֹסֵה בֵּירִבִּי בּוּן. שֶׁהוּא גָדוֹל מִכְּלָל שְׁבִיעִית. שֶׁהַשַּׁבָּת חָלָה עַל הַכֹּל וּשְׁבִיעִית אֵינָהּ חָלָה אֶלָּא עַל עֲבוֹדַת הָאָרֶץ בִּלְבָד. תַּמָּן תַּנִּינָן. כְּלָל גָּדוֹל אָמְרוּ בַּשְּׁבִיעִית. מָהוּ כְּלָל גָּדוֹל. אָמַר רִבִּי יוֹסֵה בֵּירִבִּי בּוּן. שֶׁהוּא גָדוֹל מִכְּלָל מַעְשְׂרוֹת. שֶׁהַשְּׁבִיעִית חָלָה בֵּין עַל אוֹכְלֵי אָדָם בֵּין עַל אוֹכְלֵי בְהֵמָה. וּמַעְשְׂרוֹת אֵינָן חָלִין אֶלָּא עַל אוֹכְלֵי אָדָם בִּלְבָד. תַּנֵּי בַּר קַפָּרָא. כְּלָל גָּדוֹל אָמְרוּ בְמַעְשְׂרוֹת. מָהוּ כְּלָל גָּדוֹל. אָמַר רִבִּי יוֹסֵה בֵּירִבִּי בּוּן. שֶׁהוּא גָדוֹל מִכְּלָל פֵּיאָה. שֶׁהַמַּעְשְׂרוֹת חָלִין בֵּין עַל דָּבָר שֶׁמַּכְנִיסוֹ לְקִיּוּם וּבֵין עַל דָּבָר שֶׁאֵין מַכְנִיסוֹ לְקִיּוּם. וּפֵיאָה אֵינָהּ חָלָה אֶלָּא עַל דָּבָר שֶׁמַּכְנִיסוֹ לְקִיּוּם. וְאִית דְּבָעֵי מֵימַר. מָהוּ גָדוֹל. מִיכָּן שֶׁיֵּשׁ לְמַטָּה מִמֶּנּוּ.

1 כול' | G - | G | מהו | G מהוא | G מכלל | 2 מכלל | G מיכלל הכל | G כל | 3 מהו כלל גדול | G מהוא גדול | בון | G בין | 5 קפרא | G קפרה | מהו כלל גדול | G מהוא גדול | G שמכנסו | 6 שמכנסו | G שמיכנסו

"A comprehensive principle they said about the Sabbath," etc. What means "comprehensive"? Rebbi Yose ben Rebbi Abun said, because it is more comprehensive than the principle of the Sabbatical year, since the Sabbath falls on everything but the Sabbatical year[12] falls on agricultural work in the Land only. There we have stated[13]: "A comprehensive principle they said about the Sabbatical year." What means "a comprehensive principle"? Rebbi Yose ben Rebbi Abun said, because it is more comprehensive than tithes, for the Sabbatical year falls on human food and animal feed but tithes apply to human food only[14]. Bar Qappara stated: a comprehensive principle they said about tithes[15]. What means "a comprehensive principle"? Rebbi Yose ben Rebbi Abun said, because it is more comprehensive than *peah*. for tithes apply both to food that is stored and to food which is not stored, but *peah* applies only to food used as stored staple[16]. Some want to say, what means "comprehensive"? From here that there are derivatives[17].

12 Sabbath prohibitions refer to all kinds of work everywhere; Sabbatical prohibitions refer only to agricultural work in the Land of Israel.

13 Mishnah *Ševi`it* 7:1.

14 Mishnah *Ma`serot* 1:1: "anything that is food, is guarded, and grows from the earth, is subject to tithes." Babli 68a. G everywhere reads not מַכְנִיסוֹ "what one stores" but מִיכָּנְסוֹ "what he had stored" making the obligation of tithes dependent on the action of the individual.

15 Our Mishnah *Ma`serot* 1:1 which is stated as "a principle" is "a comprehensive principle" for bar Qappara. Babli 68a.

16 Mishnah *Peah* 1:4: "They established a principle for *peah*: Everything that is food, is treated as private property, grows from the earth, is harvested at one time, and is stored, is subject to *peah*." *Peah* is the corner of the field which is reserved for the poor and may not be taken by the farmer.

17 There are categories and sub-categories as for the Sabbath. This is the preferred explanation of the Babli, 68a.

(9a line 6) אֲנָן תַּנִּינָן. כָּל־הַשׁוֹכֵחַ עִיקָר שַׁבָּת. תַּנֵּי דְּבֵית רִבִּי. כָּל־שֶׁאֵינוֹ יוֹדֵעַ עִיקַר שַׁבָּת. רִבִּי לְעָזָר כְּמַתְנִיתָן. רִבִּי יוֹחָנָן כְּהָדָא דְתַנֵּי דְּבֵית רִבִּי. הָא רִבִּי לִיעֶזֶר אָמַר. כָּל־הַשׁוֹכֵחַ עִיקַר שַׁבָּת. הָא אִם אֵינוֹ יוֹדֵעַ כָּל־עִיקָר פָּטוּר. מִן מַה דְּרַב תַּנֵּי מַתְנִיתָן וּפָתַר לָהּ. אֵי זֶהוּ שֶׁאֵינוֹ יוֹדֵעַ עִיקַר שַׁבָּת. קָטָן שֶׁנִּשְׁבָּה בֵּין הַגּוֹיִם. הָדָא אָמְרָה. הִיא הָדָא הִיא הָדָא. הָא אָמַר רִבִּי יוֹחָנָן. כָּל־שֶׁאֵין יוֹדֵעַ עִיקַר שַׁבָּת. הָא אֵינוֹ יוֹדֵעַ וְשָׁכַח חַייָב. מִן מַה דָּמַר רִבִּי שְׁמוּאֵל רִבִּי אָבָהוּ בְּשֵׁם רִבִּי יוֹסֵה בֶּן חֲנִינָא. כָּל־הָדָא הִלְכָתָא כְּרִבִּי לְעָזָר. בְּרַם כְּרַבָּנָן אֵינוֹ חַייָב אֶלָּא אַחַת. הָדָא אָמְרָה. הִיא הָדָא הִיא הָדָא. בָּעוּן קוֹמֵי בְּרֵיהּ דְּרִבִּי יָסָא. אַתְּ מַה שָׁמַעְתָּ מִן אָבוּךְ מִן דְּרִבִּי יוֹסֵי. אָמַר. כְּרִבִּי יוֹחָנָן. אָמַר לוֹן רִבִּי חִזְקִיָּה. לֹא אָמַר כֵּן. אֶלָּא רִבִּי סִימוֹן בַּר זְבְדָּא הֲוָה פָּשַׁט עִם בְּרֵיהּ דְּרִבִּי יוֹסֵה. וּשְׁמַע מִינָּהּ כְּהָדָא דְּרִבִּי לִיעֶזֶר.

1 השוכח G | השכיח 2 כהדא G | כהדה דתני G | דתני השוכח G | השכיח 3 אי זהו G | איזה הוא 4 שנשבה G | שנישבה הדא G | הדה (2) אמ' ר' יוחנן G | ר' יוחנן א' 5 שאין G | שאינו אינו G | אם היה אבהו G | אבהוא 6 חנינא G | חנינה הדא G | הדה הלכתא G | הלכתה כר' ליעזר G | דר' אליעזר הדא | G הדה 7 הדא G | הדה (2) יוסי G | יוסא זבדא G | זבד הוה הווה G | הוה 8 ליעזר G | לעזר

We have stated: "Anybody who is oblivious of the principle of the Sabbath." They stated in the House of Rebbi: Anybody ignorant of the principles of the Sabbath[18]. Rebbi Eleazar follows our Mishnah. Rebbi Johanan follows what was stated in the House of Rebbi. But Rebbi Eliezer said, "anybody who is oblivious of the principle of the Sabbath.[19]" Therefore if he does not know anything of the principles of the Sabbath is he not liable? Since Rav stated our Mishnah and explained it: who is the one who does not know anything of the principles of the Sabbath? A child who was taken prisoner among the Gentiles[20]. This implies that both versions are the same[21]. As Rebbi Johanan said, anybody ignorant of the principles of the Sabbath. Therefore (if he does not) [if he did][22] know and forgot he is liable. Since what Rebbi Samuel, Rebbi Abbahu said in the name of Rebbi Yose ben Hanina: This entire Halakhah follows Rebbi Eliezer, but following the rabbis he is liable only once[23]. This implies that both versions are the same. They asked before Rebbi Yasa's son: What did you hear from your father about Rebbi Yose[24]? He said, following Rebbi Johanan. Rebbi Hizqiah told them, he did not say so. But Rebbi Simon bar Zavda was simply with Rebbi Yose's son and heard from him following Rebbi Eliezer[25].

18 The only other place in which this formulation appears in our sources is *Sifra Hovah (Wayyiqra II) Pereq* 1(7).

19 In Mishnah *Keritut* 3:10 (quoted later in the Chapter, Note 48) he states that one who performs many works of the same category on many Sabbaths in one oblivion is liable for separate sacrifices for each occasion; opposed by R. Aqiba. This refers to the second case trated in Mishnah 1.

20 He never heard of a Sabbath prohibition.

21 There is no material difference between the Mishnah text and the formulation of the House of Rebbi.

22 The text in [brackets] from G is clearly the correct one, not the one in (parentheses) from the Leiden ms.

23 As will be stated in the next paragraph, all actions in one episode of oblivion trigger only one obligation of sacrifice.

24 R. Yose ben Hanina.

25 The formulation in the Mishnah is not practice.

(9a line 17) מְנָן אִילֵּין מִילַּיָּא. וְעָשָׂה אַחַת. וְעָשָׂה הֵנָּה. וְעָשָׂה מֵהֵנָּה: וְעָשָׂה אַחַת. לְחַיֵּיב עַל כָּל־אַחַת וְאַחַת. הֵנָּה. לְחַיֵּיב עַל כּוּלְּהוֹן אַחַת. מֵהֵנָּה: לְחַיֵּיב עַל הַתּוֹלָדוֹת. אוֹ נֵימַר. בַּעֲבוֹדָה זָרָה הַכָּתוּב מְדַבֵּר. תַּנֵּי רִבִּי זַכַּיי קוֹמֵי רִבִּי יוֹחָנָן. זִיבַּח קִיטֵּר וְנִיסֵּךְ בְּהֶעְלֵם אֶחָד חַיָּיב עַל כָּל־אַחַת וְאַחַת. אָמַר לֵיהּ רִבִּי יוֹחָנָן. בַּבְלַיָּיא. עָבַרְתְּ בְּיָדָךְ תְּלָתָא נְהָרִין וְאִיתָבְּרַתְּ. אֵינוֹ חַיָּיב אֶלָּא אַחַת. עַד לָא יַתְבְּרִינֵּיהּ בְּיָדֵיהּ יֵשׁ כָּאן אַחַת אֵין כָּאן הֵנָּה. מִן דְּתַבְרָהּ בְּיָדָיו יֵשׁ כָּאן הֵנָּה אֵין כָּאן אַחַת. וַיְהִי כֵן בַּעֲבוֹדָה זָרָה. בַּעֲבוֹדָתָהּ כַּעֲבוֹדַת הַגָּבוֹהַּ בְּהִשְׁתַּחֲוָיָה. בַּעֲבוֹדָתָהּ לְחַיֵּיב עַל כָּל־אַחַת וְאַחַת. בַּעֲבוֹדַת הַגָּבוֹהַּ לְחַיֵּיב עַל כּוּלְּהוֹן אַחַת. בְּהִשְׁתַּחֲוָיָה לְחַיֵּיב עַל מִקְצָתָהּ. רִבִּי בּוּן בַּר חִייָא בְּשֵׁם רִבִּי שְׁמוּאֵל בַּר רַב יִצְחָק. כְּתִיב אִם הַכֹּהֵן הַמָּשִׁיחַ יֶחֱטָא לְאַשְׁמַת הָעָם

וְהֵבִיא פָר. מִצְוֹת שֶׁהַמָּשִׁיחַ מֵבִיא עֲלֵיהֶן פָּר. יָצְאַת עֲבוֹדָה זָרָה שֶׁאֵינוֹ מֵבִיא עָלֶיהָ פָר אֶלָּא שְׂעִירָה בִלְבָד. הֲתִיבוּן. הֲרֵי חֲלָבִים וַעֲרָיוֹת הֲרֵי הַמָּשִׁיחַ מֵבִיא עָלֶיהָ פָר. לָא אֲתֵינָן מַתְנֵי אֶלָּא דְבָרִים שֶׁיֵּשׁ לָהֶן תּוֹלְדוֹת. חֲלָבִים אֵין לָהֶן תּוֹלְדוֹת. עֲרָיוֹת עָשָׂה בָהֶן אֶת הַמְעָרֶה כְגוֹמֵר. חֲבֵרַיָּיא אָמְרִין. שַׁבָּת הִיא לַיי. לְחַיֵּיב עַל כָּל־שַׁבָּת וְשַׁבָּת. אָמַר רִבִּי אִילָא. כְּתִיב כָּל־הָעוֹשֶׂה בוֹ מְלָאכָה יוּמָת: לֹא הָעוֹשֶׂה בוֹ וּבַחֲבֵירוֹ. אַתְּ אָמַר. אֵין הַשַּׁבָּתוֹת מִצְטָרְפוֹת. חוֹלְקוֹת. אָמַר רִבִּי יוֹסֵי בֶּן רִבִּי בּוּן. כְּשֵׁם שֶׁאֵינָן מִצְטָרְפוֹת כָּךְ אֵין חוֹלְקוֹת.

1 מנן אילין G | מטאלין G | 2 לחייב G | לחייך text of G missing for the next 9 lines 11 חברייא G | חברייה 13 בו ובחברו G | וחברי 14 יוסי G | יוסה בון G | בין שאינן G | שאיו אין G | אינם

From where these things? *He did one, and did these, and did of these. He did one*, to obligate for each one separately; *and did these,* to obligate for all of them together[26]. *Of these*, to obligate for derivatives[27]. Or should we say that the verse refers to idolatry? Rebbi Zakkai stated before Rebbi Johanan: if one sacrificed, and burned incense, and poured a libation in one forgetting he is liable for each one separately. Rebbi Johanan said, Babylonian! You crossed by hand three rivers and were broken[28]; he is liable only once[29]. Before it was broken in his hand there was *one* but no *these*; after it was broken in his hand there was *these* but no *one*[30]. But it could be idolatry worshipped by the rules of worship of Heaven as by prostration. In its own worship to obligate for each one separately. By the rules of worship of Heaven to obligate one for all of them[31]. Like prostration to obligate for partial action[32]. Rebbi Abun bar Hiyya in the name of Rebbi Samuel bar Rav Isaac. It is written[33], *if the anointed priest should sin to damage the people . . . he has to bring a bull*. This excludes idolatry for which he does not bring a bull but only a she-goat[34]. They objected, are there not fat and sexual taboos for which the Anointed brings a bull? We come only to state things that have derivatives. Fat has no derivatives[35]. For sexual taboos He made one who touched equal to one who had full intercourse[36]. The colleagues say, *a Sabbath it is for the Eternal*, to obligate for each single Sabbath[37]. Rebbi Ila said, it is written[38]: *Anybody doing work on it shall by put to death,* not one who does on it and another. You are saying, the Sabbaths do not combine. Do they separate[39]? Rebbi Yose ben Rebbi Abun[40] said, just as they do not combine they do not separate.

26 Lev. 4:2 reads: *If a person should sin inadvertently against any of the prohibitions of the Eternal and did one of these.* The complicated structure of this verse is analyzed in detail in *Sifra Hova (Wayyiqra II) Parshata* 1, *Pereq* 1. The analysis of the Yerushalmi is attributed in the Babli 103b to R. Yose ben Hanina, mentioned at the end of the preceding Paragraph. Echoes of the discussion in *Sifra* are in the Babli 70a.

The questions raised about the verse are twofold. If it had simply said *and did one*, we would have inferred that every single infraction needs a separate sacrifice. If it had said *and did these*, all infractions committed in one state of inadvertence would be covered by one sacrifice. The mention of *one* in parallel with *these* creates a seeming contradiction. In addition, in each case the prefix מ "of" in standard rabbinic interpretation is read as "not all". Then what does it mean that a single prohibition is partially violated?

27 The last question is easily answered for the Sabbath. Later in the Chapter the forbidden actions on the Sabbath are described by 39 categories. The particular actions labelling the categories are called אָב מְלָאכָה "primary actions"; any other action subsumed under the same category is a תּוֹלְדָה "derivative". All actions subsumed under the same category are considered identical in some abstract sense even if they actually are very different; e. g. plucking feathers from a bird is forbidden as a derivative of shearing. Any one of the actions subsumed under one category triggers the liability for a sacrifice; it is not necessary that all actions carrying the same label be acted on. On the other hand, most actions trigger liability only if a certain minimum of work was done, as will be detailed in the following Chapters; an action which is too insignificant remains forbidden but does not trigger liability for a sacrifice.

28 The expression is difficult to understand since one does not cross rivers (in this case Tigris, Euphrates, and Jordan) by hand but by boat. Since the expression is confirmed later in the Chapter and in *Nazir* 6:1, it cannot be emended. It seems that Rav (not Rebbi) Zakkai swam crossing the rivers on his way to Palestine.

29 *Sanhedrin* Chapter 7:11 Note 256. Worshipping strange deities in the way prescribed for Jewish worship in all its forms is one and the same offense. But worshipping strange deities in their own characteristic ways is a separate offense for each deity.

30 Since the question was raised whether *Lev.* 4:2 could be interpreted to refer only to idolatry the answer seems to be in the negative, since for R. Zakkai there are only single offenses (*one*) and no general category (*these*) whereas for R. Johanan the situation is the inverse, in contrast to the Sabbath when liability for a sacrifice can be triggered either by a single action (*one*) or by a multiplicity of different actions all falling under the same category (*these*).

31 Since in the Second Commandment prostration is mentioned before worship of strange deities it clearly is a separate offense. Cf. *Sanhedrin* 7:11 Notes 252 ff.

32 It is punishable even if not executed in the full manner prescribed for the Temple, lying down flat with outstretched arms and legs.

33 *Lev.* 4:3.

34 *Horaiot* Mishnah 2:8.

35 Fat is forbidden if it is from an animal whose kind is acceptable as a sacrifice and which is of the kind exactly prescribed in *Lev.* to be burned on the altar. There are no extensions or derivatives.

36 Forbidden sexual relations are exactly those described in *Lev.* 18. In addition in *Lev.* 20:18 the sex act is defined at touching of sexual organs; the only actions triggering the liability for a sacrifice are explicitly spelled out in the verses; there are no categories nor derivatives. Cf. *Sanhedrin* 7:5 (Notes 72-85).

37 *Lev.* 23:3. Since the attempt to derive the rules of the Mishnah from *Lev.* 4:2 ran into difficulties, they propose a direct interpretation of verses referring to the Sabbath only.

38 *Ex.* 35:2. The Sabbath is mentioned in the singular.

39 That Sabbaths do not combine means that if somebody did less than a punishable amount of work on one Sabbath and again less than a punishable amount the next Sab-bath they do not add up to the liability for a sacrifice even if the actions were committed in the same period of oblivion of the rules of the Sabbath. In this the rules of the Sabbath parallel the rules of forbidden fat. Eating forbidden fat triggers the liability for a sacrifice only if a minimum was eaten within the time of a meal (defined as time needed to eat half a loaf of bread, *Horaiot* 3:3 Note 66). Less than minimum amounts eaten at different times do not trigger liability. On the other hand, once liability was triggered within one period of oblivion, it automatically covers all other offenses of the same kind during the same period of oblivion. The question is now asked whether if an inadvertent desecration of the Sabbath triggered the obligation of a sacrifice and the perpetrator did not become aware of his offense before committing the same also on another Sabbath, he is liable for only one or for several sacrifices?

40 Since the father is known in the Babli as Rabin, the reading of G, ביר, seems better than the reading everywhere in the Leiden ms., בון.

(9a line 35) גָּדוֹל שֶׁנִּשְׁבָּה בֵּין הַגּוֹיִם. רַב וּשְׁמוּאֵל. חַד אָמַר. מוֹנֶה שִׁשָּׁה וְעוֹשֶׂה שַׁבָּת. וְחָרְנָה אָמַר. עוֹשֶׂה שַׁבָּת וּמוֹנֶה שִׁשָּׁה. רִבִּי יִצְחָק בַּר אֶלְעָזָר בְּשֵׁם רַב נַחְמָן בַּר יַעֲקֹב. מוֹנֶה שִׁשָּׁה וְעוֹשֶׂה שַׁבָּת. חֲמִשָּׁה וְעוֹשֶׂה שַׁבָּת. אַרְבָּעָה וְעוֹשֶׂה שַׁבָּת. שְׁלֹשָׁה וְעוֹשֶׂה שַׁבָּת. אֶחָד וְעוֹשֶׂה שַׁבָּת. אָמַר רִבִּי מָנָא. אִין אִישְׁתַּבַּאי בִּתְלָתָא הוּא עָבַד בְּשׁוּבְתָּא. רַב הוּנָא חֵילֵיהּ. לִתְרֵין מַחְזִירִין הוּא עָבַד שׁוּבְתָּא וְאֵין לֹא לְתַמּוּהּ. וְיחוּשׁ לְכָל־הַיָּמִים. כְּהָדָא. קִידֵשׁ אִשָּׁה בְעָילָם. רִבִּי יַעֲקֹב בַּר אָחָא. אִתְפַּלְּגוּן רִבִּי יוֹחָנָן וְרִבִּי שִׁמְעוֹן בֶּן לָקִישׁ. רִבִּי יוֹחָנָן אָמַר. חוֹשֵׁשׁ לְכָל־הַנָּשִׁים. רֵישׁ לָקִישׁ אָמַר. אֵינוֹ חוֹשֵׁשׁ לְכָל־הַנָּשִׁים. תַּמָּן יֵשׁ לוֹ תַקָּנָה. יָכוֹל הוּא לִישָּׂא גִיוֹרֶת. יָכוֹל הוּא לִישָּׂא מְשׁוּחְרֶרֶת. הָכָא מָה אִית לָךְ. תַּמָּן אָמְרִין. חוֹשֵׁשׁ לְכָל־הַיָּמִים וְעוֹשֶׂה כְּדֵי קִיּוּם הַנֶּפֶשׁ.

1 שנישנה G | שנשבת 2 בר אלעזר G | ביר׳ לעזר 4 אין G | או אישתבאי G | אשתבי בשובתא G | שובתיה רב הוה חיליה G | חולין 5 שובתא G | שובתה לתמוה G | תמניה ויחוש G | ויחיש 6 אחא G |

אחה 7 ריש | G [ר' שמעון ב[ן 8 הכא | G הכה

An adult who was taken captive among Gentiles. Rav and Samuel, one said, he counts six and keeps the Sabbath, but the other said, he keeps the Sabbath and counts six[41]. Rebbi Isaac ben Eleazar in the name of Rav Nahman bar Jacob: he counts six and keeps the Sabbath, five and keeps the Sabbath, four and keeps the Sabbath, three and keeps the Sabbath, two and keeps the Sabbath, one and keeps the Sabbath[42]. Rebbi Mana said, if he was abducted on Tuesday he makes the Sabbath (great was his power) [profane][43]. At the second period he makes the Sabbath (if not to wonder) [only the eighth][44]. Therefore he should worry about all days, as by the following: If he preliminarily married a woman in Elam[45]. Rebbi Jacob bar Aha: Rebbi Johanan and Rebbi Simeon ben Laqish. Rebbi Johanan says, he worries about all women. Rebbi Simeon ben Laqish said, he does not worry about all women. There he has a fix, he may marry a convert, he may marry a freedwoman[46]. Here what do you have? There, they are saying, he worries about all days and works for the necessities of life[47].

41 He is now living in a society which knows no weeks. From the moment in which he realizes that he has lost track of the days of the week in one opinion he presumes that this day be Sunday and keeps his week or he presumes that it is Sabbath and continues from there. Babli 69b, the dispute is between a student and the son of Rav.

42 Then he is presumed to keep some Sabbath correctly.

43 In this and the next sentence the Leiden text (in parentheses) is incomprehensible; the Genizah text [in brackets] makes approximate sense. Rebbi Mana sets out to prove that R. Nahman's scheme does not work.

44 It is true that if he realizes his problem on Sunday then he correctly keeps the next Sabbath. If he realizes it on Monday, then he keeps the second Sabbath. But if it is Tuesday then it does not work. All the presumed Sabbaths of Rav Nahman are on workdays. If we presume that Rav Nahman's scheme is periodic, that he pauses after 6,5,4,3,2,1,6,5,4,3,2,1,6,... days then his Sabbath will only be correct in the second period, in fact the seventh of his Sabbaths in the eighth try. In the following scheme the days of the week are numbered (Sabbath = 7) and Rav Nahman's Sabbaths are given in ***bold face***:

3 4 5 6 *7* || 1 2 3 4 5 6 *7* ||
1 2 3 4 5 6 7 || 1 2 *3* 4 5 6 7 ||
1 2 3 *4* 5 6 7 || 1 2 3 4 *5* 6 7 ||

The correct observation of the Sabbath first occurs in the second circuit, the eighth try, as spelled out in the text.

45 Liebermann correctly conjectures that "in Elam" is an error for בָּעוֹלָם "in the

world". He appointed an agent to get him a wife; the agent performed the preliminary marriage to him but he knows neither her identity nor her location. He has to presume that any woman he meets is either his wife or a close relative of hers.

46 Who was recently converted or freed.

47 Babli 69b. *Or zarua` Šabbat* § 15.

(9a line 46) תַּמָּן תַּנִּינָן. אָמַר רִבִּי עֲקִיבָה שָׁאַלְתִּי אֶת רִבִּי אֱלִיעֶזֶר הָעוֹשֶׂה מְלָאכוֹת הַרְבֵּה בְּשַׁבָּתוֹת הַרְבֵּה מֵעֵין מְלָאכָה אַחַת בְּעֶלֶם אֶחָד מָהוּ. חַיָּיב אַחַת עַל כּוּלָּן אוֹ אַחַת עַל כָּל־ אַחַת וְאַחַת. אָמַר לוֹ. חַיָּיב עַל כָּל אַחַת וְאַחַת מִקַּל וָחוֹמֶר. וּמָה אִם הַנִּידָה שֶׁאֵין בָּהּ תּוֹצָאוֹת הַרְבֵּה וְחַטָּאוֹת הַרְבֵּה חַיָּיב עַל כָּל אַחַת וְאַחַת. שַׁבָּת שֶׁיֵּשׁ בָּהּ תּוֹצָאוֹת הַרְבֵּה וְחַטָּאוֹת הַרְבֵּה אֵינוֹ דִין שֶׁיְּהֵא חַיָּיב עַל כָּל אַחַת וְאַחַת. אָמַרְתִּי לוֹ. לֹא. אִם אָמַרְתָּ בַּנִּדָּה שֶׁיֵּשׁ בָּהּ שְׁתֵּי אַזְהָרוֹת. שֶׁהוּא מוּזְהָר עַל הַנִּידָה וְהַנִּידָה מוּזְהֶרֶת עָלָיו. תֹּאמַר בַּשַּׁבָּת שֶׁאֵין בָּהּ אֶלָּא אַזְהָרָה אַחַת. אָמַר לִי הַבָּא עַל הַקְּטַנּוֹת יוֹכִיחַ. שֶׁאֵין בָּהֶן אֶלָּא אַזְהָרָה אַחַת וְחַיָּיב עַל כָּל אַחַת וְאַחַת. אָמַרְתִּי לוֹ. לֹא. אִם אָמַרְתְּ בַּבָּא עַל הַקְּטַנּוֹת שֶׁאַף עַל פִּי שֶׁאֵין בָּהֶן עַכְשָׁיו יֵשׁ בָּהֶן לְאַחַר זְמָן. תֹּאמַר בַּשַּׁבָּת שֶׁאֵין בָּהּ אֶלָּא אֶחָד. לֹא עַכְשָׁיו וְלֹא לְאַחַר זְמָן. אָמַר לִי הַבָּא עַל הַבְּהֵמָה יוֹכִיחַ. אָמַרְתִּי לוֹ. בְּהֵמָה כְשַׁבָּת:

2 מהו G | מהוא   כולן G | כולם   5 אמרת G | נא[מרתה שהוא G שאינו (!)   6 תאמר G | תאמרה   7 בהן G | בהם   8 אמרת G | אמרתה בהן G | בהם   (2) 9 אלא אחד | G -

There, we have stated[48]: "Rebbi Aqiba said, I asked Rebbi Eliezer: If somebody performs many works on many Sabbaths all of the same category in one period of oblivion, what[49]? Is he liable once for all of them or for each single one separately? He told him, he is liable for each occurrence separately by an argument *de minore ad majus*. Since for the menstruating woman, which does not entail many ramifications nor many purification sacrifices,[50] he is liable for each single occurrence[51], for the Sabbath which has many ramifications[52] and many purification sacrifices[53] it is only logical that he be liable for each single occurrence. I told him, no. If you mention the menstruating woman where there are two warnings, for he is warned about a menstruating woman and the menstruating woman is warned about him[54], what can you say about the Sabbath where there is only one warning[55]? He said to me, one who has intercourse with an underage girl shall prove it, where there is only one warning,[56] but he is liable for each single occurrence. I told him, no. If you mention the underage girl who even though there is no warning now there will be one in the future[57], what can you say about the Sabbath where there is only one [warning] whether now or in the future. He told me, one having intercourse with an animal shall prove it. I said to him, the animal is like the Sabbath[58].

48 Mishnah *Keritut* 3:10.

49 As the discussion of this Mishnah will point out, it is not stated whether the oblivion refers to the fact that it is the Sabbath, or that this kind of work is forbidden, or both. Therefore the answer cannot be given by quoting the second part of Mishnah 1 in this Chapter.

50 There is only one prohibition and for one sex act one cannot become liable for more than one sacrifice.

51 In Mishnah *Keritut* 3:7, a statement of Rabban Gamliel and R. Joshua. A person having 5 wives slept with each of them when she was impure in one period of oblivion is liable for 5 sacrifices.

52 There are categories and derivatives requiring one and the same sacrifice.

53 There are different categories, each one requiring a separate sacrifice.

54 The prohibition for the male is spelled out in *Lev.* 18:19. The prohibition for the female is implied by the fact that punishment for an infraction is equal for male and female, *Lev.* 20:18. There can be no punishment unless there is a prohibition.

55 Since the Sabbath is not a person, only the human is prohibited from violating the Sabbath.

56 Since an underage person cannot be criminally liable, warnings do not apply to her. The intercourse prohibited with an underage girl is one which either is incestuous or adulterous.

57 An underage girl is a female; prohibitions apply to adult females.

58 It remains unresolved how many sacrifices are due from a man having intercourse with several animals while he is oblivious of the prohibition of bestiality.

(9a line 59) רִבִּי זְעִירָא בְשֵׁם רַב חִסְדָּא רִבִּי אִילָא בְשֵׁם רִבִּי שִׁמְעוֹן בֶּן לָקִישׁ. תְּרֵיהוֹן אָמְרִין. בִּזְדוֹן שַׁבָּת וּבְשִׁגְגַת מְלָאכוֹת שָׁאֲלוֹ. בְּדָה תַנִּינָן. מְלָאכוֹת הַרְבֵּה. לֹא עַל הַשַּׁבָּתוֹת הוּא מִתְחַיֵּיב. רָבָא בְשֵׁם רַב חִסְדָּא אָמַר. בְּשִׁגְגַת שַׁבָּת וּבִזְדוֹן מְלָאכוֹת שָׁאֲלוֹ. בְּדָה תַנִּינָן. שַׁבָּתוֹת הַרְבֵּה. לֹא עַל הַמְּלָאכוֹת מִתְחַיֵּיב. הָא רִבִּי זְעִירָא בְשֵׁם רַב חִסְדָּא אָמַר רִבִּי אִילָא וְרִבִּי שִׁמְעוֹן בֶּן לָקִישׁ. תְּרֵיהוֹן אָמְרִין. בִּזְדוֹן שַׁבָּת וּבְשִׁגְגַת מְלָאכוֹת שָׁאֲלוֹ. הוֹדִי לֵיהּ וְהוּא לֹא הוֹדִי. מִן מָה דָמַר רִבִּי שְׁמוּאֵל רִבִּי אַבָּהוּ בְשֵׁם רִבִּי יוֹסֵי בֵּירִבִּי חֲנִינָה. כָּל־הָדָא הִילְכְתָא כְּרִבִּי לִיעֶזֶר. בְּרַם כְּרַבָּנָן אֵינוֹ חַיָּיב אֶלָּא אַחַת. הָדָא אָמְרָה דְלֹא הוֹדִי לֵיהּ. הֲוֵי רִבִּי בָּא בְשֵׁם רַב חִסְדָּא. אִם בְּשִׁגְגַת שַׁבָּת וּבִזְדוֹן מְלָאכוֹת שָׁאֲלוֹ. הוֹדִי לֵיהּ לֹא הוֹרִי לֵיהּ. אָמַר רִבִּי זְעִירָא קוֹמֵי רִבִּי יָסָא. מַתְנִיתָן אָמְרָה דְלֹא הוֹדִי לֵיהּ. דְּתַנֵּי. יוֹדֵעַ אֲנִי שֶׁהִיא שַׁבָּת. וְיוֹדֵעַ אֲנִי שֶׁהִיא מְלָאכָה. אֲבָל אֵינִי יוֹדֵעַ אִם מְלָאכָה הִיא זוֹ שֶׁחַיָּיבִין עָלֶיהָ כָרֵת. אִם מֵעִנְיָין אֲבוֹת מְלָאכוֹת עָשָׂה. חַיָּיב עַל כָּל־מְלָאכָה וּמְלָאכָה. אִם מֵעִנְיָין מְלָאכָה אַחַת עָשָׂה. חַיָּיב עַל כָּל־הָעֱלֵם וְהָעֱלֵם. מִפְּנֵי שֶׁהֵן הֶעֱלֵימוֹת הַרְבֵּה. אֲבָל אִם הָיָה הָעֱלֵם אֶחָד אֵינוֹ חַיָּיב אֶלָּא אַחַת. מִן מָה דְלָא מָתִיב לֵיהּ. הָדָא אָמְרָה דְלָא הוֹדִי לֵיהּ.

1 זעירא G | זעורא אילא G | אלא G | 3 רבא G | ר' בא בדא G | בזה G | 4 זעירא G | זעורא אמ' | G - 5
ליה G | לה והוא G | מה G | - 6 אבהו G | אבהוא הדא G | הדה הילכתא G | הלכתה ליעוד G | אלעזר
7 הווי G | הא 8 יסא G | יוסה 9 שהיא G | שהוא וידע G | וידע[ו]

Rebbi Ze'ira in the name of Rav Ḥisda, Rebbi Ila in the name of Rebbi Simeon ben Laqish. Both of them say, he asked him about intent regarding the Sabbath but error regarding the work[59]. About this we have stated "many works". He is not liable because of Sabbaths. Rebbi Abba in the name of Rav Ḥisda said, he asked him about error regarding the Sabbath but intent regarding the work[60]. About this we have stated "many Sabbaths". He is not liable because of the works.

Now Rebbi Ze'ira in the name of Rav Ḥisda, Rebbi Ila in the name of Rebbi Simeon ben Laqish. Both of them say, he asked him about intent regarding the Sabbath but error about the work. Did he concede to him or did he not concede to him[61]? Since what Rebbi Samuel, Rebbi Abbahu said in the name of Rebbi Yose ben Ḥanina: This entire Halakhah follows Rebbi Eliezer, but following the rabbis he is liable only once[23]. This implies that he[62] did not concede to him.

(It was) [Now][63] Rebbi Abba in the name of Rav Ḥisda said, he asked him about error regarding the Sabbath but intent about the work. Did he concede to him or did he not (instruct) [concede to][64] him? Rebbi Ze'ira said before Rebbi Yasa, a *baraita* implies that he did not concede to him, as it was stated[65], "'I know that it is the Sabbath, I know that this is work. But I do not know that this is work for which one becomes liable to extirpation[66].' If he did work of several categories he is liable for every single work[67]. If he did work of one category only, he is liable for every episode of oblivion if there were many oblivions, but if all was one oblivion he is liable only once." Since he did not quote this as an objection it implies that he did not concede to him[68].

59 He knows that it is the Sabbath but he does not know that work is forbidden on the Sabbath. Since purification offerings only are possible for inadvertent sins, he becomes liable by doing the work if later he learns that the work was forbidden.

60 He knows all the laws of the Sabbath but forgot that the day was a Sabbath. If he does work he becomes liable once for each Sabbath spent in oblivion even if he does work of many categories.

61 Did R. Aqiba convince R. Eliezer or

vice versa?

62 Since the rabbis follow R. Aqiba, R. Eliezer cannot have conceded.

63 The text of G [in brackets] seems better than the Leiden text (in parentheses).

64 At all occurrences the scribe first wrote חורי and then corrected to הודי except on this one occasion. Therefore also here the text of G [in brackets] is the correct one.

65 *Sifra Hova (Wayyiqra II) Pereq* 1(7).

66 Purification sacrifices are possible only for inadvertent infractions punishable either by extirpation or by death.

67 Every single category of work which he did.

68 Since R. Aqiba did not point out to R. Eliezer that the Tanna of the *baraita* disagrees with him, he must have known that the latter disagrees. (In *Sifra* the entire theory is attributed to R. Yose of the school of R. Aqiba, two generations after R. Eliezer). G ends here.

(9a line 76) הָא רִבִּי זְעִירָא בְשֵׁם רַב חִסְדָּא רִבִּי אִילָא בְשֵׁם רִבִּי שִׁמְעוֹן בֶּן לָקִישׁ. תְּרֵיהוֹן אָמְרִין. בִּזְדוֹן שַׁבָּת וּבְשִׁגְגַת מְלָאכוֹת. וּשְׁאָלוּ. הָא בְשִׁגְגַת שַׁבָּת וּבִזְדוֹן מְלָאכוֹת אַף רִבִּי אֱלִיעֶזֶר יוֹדִי לְרִבִּי עֲקִיבָה שֶׁאֵינוֹ חַיָּיב אֶלָּא אַחַת. וִיתִיבִינֵיהּ רִבִּי עֲקִיבָה. הֲרֵי מֵזִיד בַּשַּׁבָּת וְשׁוֹגֵג בִּמְלָאכוֹת. הֲרֵי יֵשׁ בָּהּ תּוֹצָאוֹת הַרְבֵּה וְחַטָּאוֹת הַרְבֵּה. וְאַתְּ מוֹרֵי לֵיהּ שֶׁאֵינוֹ חַיָּיב אֶלָּא אַחַת. מִן מַה דְלָא מְתִיב לָהּ. הָדָא אָמְרָה. הִיא הָדָא הִיא הָדָא.

הָא רִבִּי בָא בְשֵׁם רַב חִסְדָּא אָמַר. בְּשִׁגְגַת שַׁבָּת וּבִזְדוֹן מְלָאכוֹת. וּשְׁאָלוּ. הָדָה בִּזְדוֹן שַׁבָּת וּבְשִׁגְגַת מְלָאכוֹת אַף רִבִּי עֲקִיבָה יוֹדֵי לְרִבִּי אֱלִיעֶזֶר שֶׁהוּא חַיָּיב עַל כָּל־אַחַת וָאַחַת. וִיתִיבִינֵיהּ רִבִּי אֱלִיעֶזֶר. הֲרֵי שׁוֹגֵג בַּשַּׁבָּת מֵזִיד בִּמְלָאכוֹת. הֲרֵי אֵין בָּהּ תּוֹצָאוֹת הַרְבֵּה וְחַטָּאוֹת הַרְבֵּה. וְאַתְּ מוֹדִי לִי שֶׁהוּא חַיָּיב עַל כָּל־אַחַת וָאַחַת. מִן מַה דְלָא מְתִיב לֵיהּ. הָדָא אָמְרָה. הִיא הָדָא הִיא הָדָא.

הָא רִבִּי בָא בְשֵׁם רַב חִסְדָּא אָמַר. בְּשִׁגְגַת שַׁבָּת וּבִזְדוֹן מְלָאכוֹת שְׁאָלוּ. וְלֹא מִשּׁוּם שִׁגְגַת שַׁבָּת אַתְּ תּוֹפְסוֹ. רִבִּי חִזְקִיָּה בְשֵׁם רִבִּי בָא. שְׁתַּיִם שָׁאָלוּ. מֵזִיד בַּשַּׁבָּת וְשׁוֹגֵג בִּמְלָאכוֹת. שֶׁיְּהֵא חַיָּיב עַל כָּל־אַחַת וָאַחַת. שׁוֹגֵג בַּשַּׁבָּת וּמֵזִיד בִּמְלָאכוֹת מָהוּ לַעֲשׂוֹת אֶת הַתּוֹלָדוֹת כָּעִיקָּר. אָמַר רִבִּי יַעֲקֹב בַּר דַּסַּיי. וְתַנֵּי דְבֵית רִבִּי כֵן. הָעוֹשֶׂה מְלָאכוֹת הַרְבֵּה בְּשַׁבָּתוֹת הַרְבֵּה מֵעֵין מְלָאכָה אַחַת בְּהֶעְלֵם אַחַת מָהוּ. חַיָּיב אַחַת אוֹ כוּפֵל עַל כָּל־אַחַת וָאַחַת. מְלָאכוֹת הַרְבֵּה מֵעֵין מְלָאכָה אַחַת. הָדָא הִיא מֵזִיד בַּשַּׁבָּת וְשׁוֹגֵג בִּמְלָאכוֹת. שַׁבָּתוֹת הַרְבֵּה מֵעֵין מְלָאכָה אַחַת הָדָא הִיא שׁוֹגֵג בַּשַּׁבָּת וּמֵזִיד בִּמְלָאכוֹת.

הָא רִבִּי זְעִירָא בְשֵׁם רַב חִסְדָּא וְרִבִּי אִילָא בְשֵׁם רִבִּי שִׁמְעוֹן בֶּן לָקִישׁ. תְּרֵיהוֹן אָמְרִין. בִּזְדוֹן שַׁבָּת וּבְשִׁגְגַת מְלָאכוֹת שְׁאָלוּ. וְיֵשׁ אָדָם מִתְחַיֵּיב עַל הַזָּדוֹן. אַתְּ נוֹתֵן שִׁגְגַת מְלָאכוֹת עַל זְדוֹן שַׁבָּת. וְדִכְוָותָהּ. שׁוֹגֵג בַּשַּׁבָּת וּמֵזִיד בִּמְלָאכָה. אַתְּ נוֹתֵן שִׁגְגַת שַׁבָּת עַל זְדוֹן מְלָאכוֹת לְחַיֵּיב עַל כָּל־אַחַת וָאַחַת. וְלֵית לְרִבִּי אֱלִיעֶזֶר לְאַחַת. לְחַיֵּיב עַל כָּל־אַחַת וָאַחַת. אַשְׁכַּח תַּנֵּי בְשֵׁם רִבִּי אֱלִיעֶזֶר. גָּדוֹל שֶׁנִּשְׁבָּה לְבֵין הַגּוֹיִם חַיָּיב עַל כָּל־אַחַת וָאַחַת.

Now Rebbi Ze'ira in the name of Rav Hisda, Rebbi Ila in the name of Rebbi Simeon ben Laqish, both of them say, he asked him about intent regarding the Sabbath but error regarding the work[59]. Therefore, in the case of error regarding the Sabbath but intent about the work even Rebbi Eliezer should agree with Rebbi Aqiba that he is liable only once[69]. But then Rebbi Aqiba should have objected, is there not the case of intent regarding the Sabbath but error about the work[70], where there are many ramifications or many purification sacrifices and you are instructing that he is liable only once! Since he did not object in this way it implies that one case is like the other case[71].

Now Rebbi Abba in the name of Rav Hisda said, he asked him about error regarding the Sabbath but intent regarding the work. Therefore about intent regarding the Sabbath but error regarding the work even Rebbi Aqiba will agree with Rebbi Eliezer that he is liable for every single one[72]. Then Rebbi Eliezer should have objected to him, is there not error regarding the Sabbath but intent regarding the works[73] where there are not many ramifications and many purification sacrifices and you are agreeing with me that he is liable for every single one. Since he did not object in this way it implies that one case is like the other case[74].

Now Rebbi Abba in the name of Rav Hisda said, he asked him about error regarding the Sabbath but intent regarding the work. Do you not catch him because of the error regarding the Sabbath[75]? Rebbi Hizqiah in the name of Rebbi Abba: He asked him two questions. About intent regarding the Sabbath but error regarding the work that he be liable for every single one. In case of error regarding the Sabbath but intent regarding works does one treat the derivatives like that main item[76]? Rebbi Jacob ben Dasai said, and in the House of Rebbi it was stated so: "If somebody performs many works on many Sabbaths all of the same category in one period of oblivion, what? Is he liable once for all of them or once for each single one?" Many works of the same category, this describes intent regarding the Sabbath but error regarding the work. Many Sabbaths all of the same category, this describes error regarding the Sabbath but intent regarding the work[77].

Now Rebbi Ze'ira in the name of Rav Hisda, Rebbi Ila in the name of Rebbi Simeon ben Laqish, both of them say, he asked him about intent regarding the Sabbath but error regarding works. Can anybody become liable intentionally[78]? You superimpose the error regarding works over the intent regarding the Sabbath[79]. Similarly, in case of error regarding the Sabbath but intent regarding the work you superimpose the error regarding the Sabbath over the intent regarding works to hold him liable for each single occurrence. Does Rebbi Eliezer not accept *one*, to obligate for each one separately[26,80]? It was found stated in the name of Rebbi Eliezer: An adult who was abducted among Gentiles[41] is liable for each single one[81].

69 Since a purification offering is possible only for error and the error was about one thing only, *viz.*, that he did not realize that it was Sabbath, there should be only one liability.

70 Clearly here one has to read: error regarding the Sabbath and intent regarding work. This was the scribe's text; the error is the corrector's.

71 In every case does R. Eliezer require a separate sacrifice for each infraction of the Sabbath. The difference between the two versions in the name of Rav Hisda is purely semantic; they agree in fact.

72 Since the question was about works which all belong to the same category, R. Eliezer must hold that the knowledge of which day of the week it is separates one Sabbath from the next; if the person did not know that a certain kind of work is forbidden, each Sabbath creates a new and separate infraction and therefore liability.

73 Read: Intent regarding the Sabbath and error regarding work; corrector's error.

74 One arrives at the same conclusion as before.

75 This is the same question as before, Note 69, as introduction to the opinion of R. Hizqiah in the name of R. Abba. Babli *Keritut* 16a.

76 This introduces a new question. We agree that R. Eliezer holds that each Sabbath is a new entity whose desecration triggers liability. Does he agree that on one Sabbath all infractions of the same category cause only one liability or do actions which are different, even though classified in the same category, trigger different liabilities? Then more than 39 liabilities could be created on one Sabbath, against the Mishnah here and in *Keritut*.

77 This subsumes both opinions attributed to Rav Hisda.

78 Intentional sins can never be atoned by a sacrifice.

79 Even though he knows that it is the Sabbath and he intentionally does the work, if he does not know that this particular action is forbidden, it is an unintentional sin and creates liability for a sacrifice.

80 Probably the reference to *these*, etc., is missing since the quote of part of the *baraita* from *Sifra* is intended to refer to all its parts.

81 For each single Sabbath.

(9b 27) מַה בֵּין מֵזִיד בַּשַּׁבָּת וְשׁוֹגֵג בִּמְלָאכוֹת. מַה בֵּין שׁוֹגֵג בַּשַּׁבָּת וּמֵזִיד בִּמְלָאכוֹת. אָמַר רִבִּי יוֹסֵה. וְלָמָּה מֵזִיד בַּשַּׁבָּת וְשׁוֹגֵג בִּמְלָאכוֹת חַיָּיב עַל כָּל־אַחַת וָאֶחָת. שֶׁאִם אוֹמֵר אַתְּ לוֹ. מְלָאכָה הִיא זוֹ. הוּא פּוֹרֵשׁ מִמֶּנָּה וְעוֹשֶׂה מְלָאכוֹת אֲחֵרוֹת. וְלָמָּה שׁוֹגֵג בַּשַּׁבָּת וּמֵזִיד בִּמְלָאכוֹת אֵינוֹ חַיָּיב אֶלָּא אַחַת. שֶׁאִם אוֹמֵר אַתְּ לוֹ. שַׁבָּת הוּא זוֹ. מִיָּד הוּא פּוֹרֵשׁ. שָׁגַג בָּזֶה וּבָזֶה. רַב הַמְנוּנָא אָמַר. אֵינוֹ חַיָּיב אֶלָּא אַחַת. אָמַר לֵיהּ רִבִּי זְעִירָא. וְלָאו כָּל־שֶׁכֵּן הוּא. אִילוּ מֵזִיד בַּשַּׁבָּת וְשׁוֹגֵג בִּמְלָאכוֹת אֵינוֹ חַיָּיב עַל כָּל־אַחַת וָאֶחָת. מִפְּנֵי שֶׁנִּתּוֹסַף לוֹ שִׁגְנַת מְלָאכוֹת שַׁבָּת אוֹבֵד שִׁגְנַת מְלָאכוֹת.

What is the difference between intentional regarding the Sabbath and in error about works or in error regarding the Sabbath and intentional about works[82]? Rebbi Yose said, why intentional regarding the Sabbath and in error about works makes him liable for each single one? For if you tell him that this is [forbidden] work, he stops doing it and does other works. Why in error regarding the Sabbath and intentional about works makes him liable only once? For if you tell him that it is a Sabbath, he stops immediately. What if he is in error in both respects? Rav Hamnuna said, he is liable only once. Rebbi Ze`ira said to him, is that not a case *a fortiori*? If he is intentional regarding the Sabbath and in error about works, is he not liable for each single one? Because there was added for him the error regarding work on the Sabbath; the error about works is lost[83]?

82 This now refers to Mishnah 1 in this Chapter, as R. Yose explains. In the Babli 70a the same explanation is given in the name of Rav Nahman.

83 Babli 70b disagrees since the final decision by Ravina follows Rav Hamnuna here (*Sanhedrin* 62a, *Ševuot* 19a,26a, *Keritut* 3b).

(9b line 35) רִבִּי יִרְמְיָה בְּעָא קוֹמֵי רִבִּי זְעִירָא. קָצַר חֲצִי גְרוֹגֶרֶת בַּשַּׁבָּת זוֹ בְּזָדוֹן שַׁבָּת וּבְשִׁגְנַת מְלָאכוֹת. וַחֲצִי גְרוֹגֶרֶת שַׁבָּת זוֹ בְשִׁגְנַת שַׁבָּת וּבְזָדוֹן מְלָאכוֹת. שְׁגָגוֹת שֶׁבּוֹ מַה שֶׁיִּצְטָרְפוּ. אֵיפְשָׁר לוֹמַר. שַׁבָּתוֹת מְחַלָּקוֹת שֶׁבָּתוֹת מִצְטָרְפוֹת. הֲרֵי תַמְחוּיִין חוֹלְקִין וְתַמְחוּיִין מִצְטָרְפִין. אָמַר לֵיהּ. אֵינִי יוֹדֵעַ טַעַם תַּמְחוּי. וְלֹא מַתְנִיתָא הִיא. כָּתַב אוֹת אַחַת בַּחוֹל וְאוֹת אַחַת בַּשַּׁבָּת. רִבִּי אֱלִיעֶזֶר מְחַיֵּיב חַטָּאת. וְרִבִּי יְהוֹשֻׁעַ פּוֹטֵר. אָמַר רִבִּי עֲזַרְיָה קוֹמֵי רִבִּי מָנָא. תִּיפְתָּר בְּזָדוֹן. אָמַר לֵיהּ. וְלֹא כָּל־שֶׁכֵּן הוּא. מַה אִם הַזָּדוֹן שֶׁאֵינוֹ חוֹלֵק אֵינוֹ מַצְטָרֵף. שְׁגָגָה שֶׁהִיא חוֹלֶקֶת לֹא כָּל־שֶׁכֵּן שֶׁלֹּא תִצְטָרֵף.

אָמַר רִבִּי חֲנַנְיָה. לֹא אָמַר כֵּן אֶלָּא. קָצַר חֲצִי גְרוֹגֶרֶת בַּשַּׁחֲרִית בְּזָדוֹן שַׁבָּת וּבְשִׁגְגַת מְלָאכוֹת. וַחֲצִי גְרוֹגֶרֶת בֵּין הָעַרְבַּיִם בְּשִׁגְגַת שַׁבָּת וּבִזְדוֹן מְלָאכוֹת. שְׁגָגוֹת שֶׁבּוֹ וּשְׁגָגוֹת שֶׁבּוֹ מָהוּ שֶׁיִּצְטָרְפוּ. אָמַר רִבִּי מָנָא. אַף עַל גַּב דְּלָא אָמַר רִבִּי יוֹסֵה דָא מִילְתָא אָמַר דִּכְוָותֵיהּ. אָכַל חֲצִי זַיִת בִּדְיעַת הַקּוֹדֶשׁ וּבְהֶעְלֵם טוּמְאָה. וַחֲצִי זַיִת בְּעָלֶם הַקּוֹדֶשׁ וּבִידִיעַת הַטּוּמְאָה. הֶעְלֵם שֶׁבּוֹ וְהֶעְלֵם שֶׁבּוֹ מָהוּ שֶׁיִּצְטָרְפוּ.

Rebbi Jeremiah asked before Rebbi Ze'ira: If one harvested half the volume of a dried fig on this Sabbath, intentional regarding the Sabbath and in error regarding the work, and half the volume of a dried fig on another Sabbath, in error regarding the Sabbath and intentional regarding the work; do the errors combine[84]? Is it possible to say Sabbaths divide, Sabbaths combine[85]? Do not trays divide and trays combine[86]? He answered, I do not know the reason for the tray. Is this not a *baraita*? If he wrote one letter on a weekday and one letter on the Sabbath, Rebbi Eliezer declares him liable for a purification sacrifice but Rebbi Joshua declares him not liable[87]. Rebbi Azariah said before Rebbi Mana, explain it by intent. He said to him, is this not an argument *a fortiori*? Since intent neither divides nor combines[88], error which does not divide *a fortiori* does not combine.

Rebbi Ḥanania said, this is not what he said but he harvested half the volume of a dried fig in the morning, intentional regarding the Sabbath and in error regarding the work, and half the volume of a dried fig in the evening, in error regarding the Sabbath and intentional regarding the work; do the errors combine[89]? Rebbi Mana said, even though Rebbi Yose did not address this, he said something similar. If one ate half the volume of an olive being aware of the Sanctuary but oblivious of impurity and half the volume of an olive being oblivious of the Sanctuary but aware of impurity; do the oblivions combine[90]?

84 Since in all he harvested an amount which creates liability. In this version, there are two reasons which invite a negative answer; the actions happened on different days, and the circumstances of the errors are different.

85 The second sentence in Mishnah 1 clearly states that for a person who knows the principle of Sabbath rest, even if he is not aware of the day, separate Sabbaths require separate sacrifices. Therefore the fact that the actions happened on different days should be enough to answer the question in the negative.

86 This argument, also mentioned in the Babli 71a, refers to Mishnah *Keritut* 3:9

where R. Joshua holds that somebody who illegally eats from the meat of one sacrifice prepared in five different dishes is liable for a separate purification sacrifice for every dish of which he ate the volume of an olive. On the other hand, if of two separate dishes he illegally ate half the volume of an olive each, he is liable for one sacrifice. This is a case where dishes both combine for liability and divide liabilities.

87   A later Mishnah will declare that writing on the Sabbath creates liability if one writes two letters. For R. Joshua writing one letter on the Sabbath never creates liability. For R. Eliezer the reason that two letters create liability is that they may form words. For him a letter which forms a word when added to a preexisting letter is word-forming and creates liability (Chapter 13, Note 000).

88   Since intentional sin cannot be atoned for by a sacrifice it is irrelevant for creation of liabilities.

89   This version, where all action happens on one and the same day, is reported in the Babli 71a, where also it is reported that R. Ze`ira holds that since the rules for purification sacrifices are different in both cases they cannot combine.

90   *Ševuot* 2:1 Note 51.

(9b line 49) נִיחָא שַׁבָּת שֶׁבָּאוּ לָהּ יְמֵי הַחוֹל בֵּינְתַיִּים. גַּבֵּי נִידָּה מָה אִית לָךְ. רִישׁ לָקִישׁ אָמַר. תֵּיפְתַּר בְּנַדָּה קְטַנָּה שֶׁבָּאוּ לָהּ יְמֵי הֶפְסֵק טַהֲרָה בֵּינְתַיִּים. רִבִּי אֶלְעָזָר בֵּירִבִּי שִׁמְעוֹן אוֹמֵר. כָּךְ שְׁאָלוֹ. בָּא עַל נִדָּה אַחַת חָמֵשׁ בְּעִילוֹת בְּעֶלֶם אֶחָד מָהוּ. חַיָּיב אַחַת עַל כּוּלָם אוֹ עַל כָּל־אַחַת וְאַחַת. אָמַר לֵיהּ. חַיָּיב עַל כָּל־אַחַת וְאַחַת. וְקַשְׁיָא. אִילּוּ קָצַר וְקָצַר בְּעֶלֶם אֶחָד. כְּלוּם הוּא חַיָּיב עַל כּוּלָם אֶלָּא אַחַת. רִבִּי אֲחָא בְשֵׁם רִבִּי חֲנִינָא. כֵּן. רִבִּי מָנָא מַקְשֵׁי לָהּ. וְלֹא כֵן אָמַר רִבִּי שְׁמוּאֵל רִבִּי אָבָהוּ בְשֵׁם רִבִּי יֹסֵא בֶן חֲנִינָא. כָּל־הָדָא הִילְכְתָא כְּרִבִּי אֱלִיעֶזֶר. בְּרַם כְּרַבָּנָן אֵינוּ חַיָּיב אֶלָּא אַחַת. אַף הָכָא לֹא יְהֵא חַיָּיב אֶלָּא אַחַת. אָמַר רִבִּי יֹסֵה. קַיָּימְתִּיהּ כַּיי דָּמַר רִבִּי אֲחָא בְשֵׁם רִבִּי חֲנִינָא. לֵית כֵּן. קָרְבָּנוֹ דְּקַיְיסָרִין בְּשֵׁם רִבִּי נִיסָא. כָּל־הָדָא הִילְכְתָא דְּרִבִּי אֱלִיעֶזֶר הוּא. וְכָל־דְּיִפּוּק מִינָהּ הֲלָכָה כּוּלָּהּ כְּרִבִּי אֱלִיעֶזֶר.

One understands Sabbath since weekdays come in the meantime. What may you say about the menstruating woman[91]? Rebbi Simeon ben Laqish said, explain it about an underage menstruating woman where days of purity came in the meantime[92]. Rebbi Eleazar ben Rebbi Simeon says, so did he ask him: If he came to one menstruating woman five times in one period of oblivion, what? Is he liable once for all of them or for each single one? He answered him, he is liable for each single one. Rebbi Aḥa in the name of Rebbi Yose ben Ḥanina, it is [not] so[93]. Rebbi Mana asked the following: Did not Rebbi Samuel, Rebbi Abbahu say in the name of Rebbi Yose ben Ḥanina: This entire Halakhah follows Rebbi Eliezer, but following the rabbis he is liable only once[23]? Then here also[94] he should be liable only once.

Rebbi Yose said, I confirmed this following what Rebbi Aḥa said in the name of Rebbi Yose ben Ḥanina, it is not so[95]. Like the rabbis of Caesarea in the name of Rebbi Nisa: This entire Halakhah follows Rebbi Eliezer, and all that is derived from it as all practice follows Rebbi Eliezer[25].

91 This refers back to the Mishnah in *Ketubot*, in particular the last argument between R. Aqiba and R. Eliezer where R. Eliezer asserts that even with underage girls every forbidden sex act creates a new liability. It is agreed that every single Sabbath creates new liabilities since the weekdays in between create awareness of days that are not Sabbaths. Similarly one may argue that having sex with the same woman in different menstrual periods creates separate liabilities since while the male may be oblivious continuously, the woman certainly knows the differences between the periods and she is bound by the law as he is. But an underage girl is not obligated by any law; therefore intercourse with her during different periods in one period of oblivion should create only a single liability.

92 Since we assert that a person who knows about the laws of the Sabbath but does not know which days are Sabbaths is liable separately for each Sabbath on which he worked, we also should assert that a man who knows the laws of *niddah* even if he does not know when his wife is impure is separately liable for intercourse in different periods which are separated by lengthy intervals of purity. Babli *Keritut* 17a.

93 As the text (Note 95) shows later, the text in brackets has to be added. One cannot translate "Rebbi Aḥa (4th generation) in the name of R. Yose ben Ḥanina (2nd) said, so did R. Mana (5th) ask". R. Aḥa asserts that we do not accept R. Eleazar ben R. Simeon's statement.

94 In the case of the man married to an underage girl each period creates only one liability.

95 Cf. Note 93.

(9b line 60) אֲבוֹת מְלָאכוֹת אַרְבָּעִים חָסֵר אַחַת. מִנַּיִין לַאֲבוֹת מְלָאכוֹת מִן הַתּוֹרָה. רִבִּי שְׁמוּאֵל בַּר נַחְמָן בְּשֵׁם רִבִּי יוֹנָתָן. כְּנֶגֶד אַרְבָּעִים חָסֵר אַחַת מְלָאכָה שֶׁכָּתוּב בַּתּוֹרָה. בְּעוֹן קוֹמֵי רִבִּי אָחָא. כָּל־הֵן דִּכְתִיב מְלָאכוֹת. שְׁתַיִם. אָמַר רִבִּי שִׁיָין. אַשְׁגָּרַת עֵייְנֵהּ דְּרִבִּי אָחָא בְּכָל־אוֹרְיָיתָא וְלָא אַשְׁכַּח כְּתִיב דָּא מִילְתָא. בְּעָיָא דָא מִילְתָא. וַיָּבֹא הַבַּיְתָה לַעֲשׂוֹת מְלַאכְתּוֹ מִנְהוֹן. וַיְכַל אֱלֹהִים בַּיּוֹם הַשְּׁבִיעִי מְלַאכְתּוֹ אֲשֶׁר עָשָׂה מִנְהוֹן. תַּנָּא רִבִּי שִׁמְעוֹן בֶּן יוֹחַי. שֵׁשֶׁת יָמִים תֹּאכַל מַצּוֹת וּבַיּוֹם הַשְּׁבִיעִי עֲצֶרֶת לַיי אֱלֹהֶיךָ לֹא תַעֲשֶׂה מְלָאכָה׃ הֲרֵי זֶה בָּא לְהַשְׁלִים אַרְבָּעִים חָסֵר אַחַת מְלָאכוֹת שֶׁכְּתוּבוֹת בַּתּוֹרָה.

רִבִּי יוֹסֵי בֵּירִבִּי בּוּן בְּשֵׁם רִבִּי שְׁמוּאֵל בַּר נַחְמָנִי. כְּנֶגֶד אַרְבָּעִים חָסֵר אַחַת פַּעַם שֶׁכָּתוּב בַּמִּשְׁכָּן עֲבוֹדָה וּמְלָאכָה.

אָמַר רִבִּי יוֹסֵי בֶּן חֲנִינָא. זֶה הַדָּבָר אֵין כָּתוּב כָּאן. אֶלָּא אֵלֶּה הַדְּבָרִים. דָּבָר דִּבְרֵי דְּבָרִים. מִכָּן לָאָבוֹת וּלְתוֹלָדוֹת. רִבִּי חֲנִינָא דְּצִיפּוֹרִין בְּשֵׁם רִבִּי אַבָּהוּ. אל"ף חַד. למ"ד תַּלְתִּין. ה"א חֲמִשָּׁה. דָּבָר חַד. דְּבָרִים תְּרֵי. מִיכָּן לְאַרְבָּעִים חָסֵר אַחַת מְלָאכוֹת שֶׁכְּתוּבוֹת בַּתּוֹרָה. רַבָּנִן דְּקַיסָרִין אָמְרִין. מִן אַתְרֵהּ לָא חָסְרָה כְלוּם. א' חַד. ל' תַּלְתִּין. ח' תְּמָנְיָא. לֹא מִתְמַנְעִין רַבָּנִן דָּרְשִׁין בֵּין ה"א לחי"ת.

"The categories of work are 39." From where that the categories[96] of work are from the Torah? Rebbi Samuel bar Nahman in the name of Rebbi Jonathan: Corresponding to the thirty-nine occurrences of מלאכה in the Torah[97]. They asked before Rebbi Aha, everywhere where מלאכות is written it should count for two! Rebbi Ashian said, Rebbi Aha checked by eye the entire Torah and did not find this word written[98]. The following is necessary: *He came into the house to do his work*[99] is with them. *God completed on the Seventh Day His work which He did*[100], is with them. Rebbi Simeon ben Yohai stated: *Six days you shall eat unleavened bread and on the seventh day you should not do work*[101] comes to complete the 39 "works" written in the Torah.

Rebbi Yose ben Rebbi Abun in the name of Rebbi Samuel bar Nahmani: Corresponding to the 39 times "service" and "work" is written about the Tabernacle[102].

Rebbi Yose ben Hanina said, it does not say "this is the word" but *these are the words.*[103] "Word", "words," "words". From here about categories and derivatives[104]. Rebbi Hanina of Sepphoris in the name of Rebbi Abbahu. *Alef* is one, *Lamed* is 30, *He* is five, "word" is one, "words" are two[105]. From here the 39 "works" written in the Torah. The rabbis of Caesarea say, at its place nothing is missing, א is one, ל 30, ח 8. The rabbis never hesitate to identify ה and [106]ח.

96 A hint that exactly 39 categories of work should be forbidden on the Sabbath (i. e., that a maximum of 39 sacrifices would be required for unintentional violations of the Sabbath rest.)

97 The count works out if one counts all occurrences of מְלָאכָה together with its suffixed forms מְלַאכְתּוֹ, etc., but omitting all construct states מְלֶאכֶת.

98 The plural מְלָאכוֹת is not found in the Pentateuch. Therefore each occurrence of the word counts as one.

99 Gen. 39:11. It must be counted even though the word is in suffixed form and

does not refer to the Sabbath .
100 *Gen.* 2:2.
101 *Deut.* 16:8, the last occurrence of the word in the Torah.
102 In *Ex.* and *Num.* Here again for the word עֲבוֹדָה the base form and the suffixed forms are counted, but the construct state עֲבוֹדַת is not.
103 *Ex.* 35:1, the introductory paragraph which indicates that the Sabbath prohibitions may not be violated in building the Tabernacle, and which therefore forms the basis of the list of the 39 categories from an analysis of the activities needed to build the Tabernacle and to serve in it.
104 The plural indicates that each category stands for many different actions, Babli 70a,

97b. (In the Appendix to *Yalqut Šimony* published by L. Ginzberg in שרידי הירושלמי p. 316 the reading is מכאן לאבות מלאכות "from here for categories", the plural only indicates that there are different categories of work on the Sabbath.)
105 The *gematria* (numerical value if each letter is used as a numeral in the Alexandrian system) of אלה is 36; one has somehow to find another 3 to reach the traditional number of 39.
106 Cf. *Peah* 7:6 Note 113, *Ma`aser Šeni* 5:3, *Sotah* 8:4 Note 179. In all other occurrences of substitution of ח for ה one obtains a word which makes sense; this cannot be said here (Babli *Berakhot* 32a).

(9b line 76) רִבִּי יוֹחָנָן וְרִבִּי שִׁמְעוֹן בֶּן לָקִישׁ עָבְדִין הֲוֵיי בְּהָדָא פִּירְקָא תְּלַת שְׁנִין וּפְלוּג. אַפְּקוֹן מִינֵּיהּ אַרְבָּעִין חָסֵר אַחַת תּוֹלָדוֹת עַל כָּל־חֲדָא וְחָדָא. מַאן דְּאַשְׁכְּחוֹן מִיסְמוֹךְ סַמְכִין. הָא דְלָא אַשְׁכְּחוֹן מִיסְמוֹךְ עַבְדּוּנֵיהּ מִשּׁוּם מַכֶּה בְפַטִּישׁ.
בְּנוֹי דְרִבִּי חִייָא רוֹבָא עָבְדָן הֲוֵיי בְהָדֵין פִּירְקָא שִׁיתָּא יַרְחִין. אַפְּקוֹן מִינֵּיהּ שִׁית מִילִּין עַל כָּל־חֲדָא וְחָדָא. בְּנוֹי דְרִבִּי חִייָא רוֹבָא הֲוֵיי בְשִׁיטַּת אֲבוּהוֹן. דְּתַנֵּי רִבִּי חִייָא. הַקּוֹצֵר הַבּוֹצֵר הַמּוֹסֵק הַגּוֹדֵד הַתּוֹלֵשׁ הָאוֹרֶה כּוּלְהוֹן מִשּׁוּם קוֹצֵר. אָמַר רִבִּי סִידוֹר. יְהוּדָה בְּרִבִּי עָבְדִין הֲוֵיי בְּמַכְשִׁירִין שִׁיתָּא יַרְחִין. בְּסוֹפָא אֲתָא חַד תַּלְמִיד מִן דְּרִבִּי סִימַאי וּשְׁאִיל לֵיהּ וְלָא אַגִּיבֵיהּ. אָמַר. נִיכָּר הוּא זֶה שֶׁלֹּא עָבַר עַל פִּיתְחָהּ שֶׁלַּתּוֹרָה.

Rebbi Johanan and Rebbi Simeon ben Laqish worked on this Chapter for three and one half years[107]. They produced 39 derivatives for each single one. Where they found a way to include it they included it[108]. Where they did not find a way to include it they classified it as "who hits with a hammer."[7,109]

The sons of the Elder Rebbi Ḥiyya worked on this Chapter for six months. They produced six derivatives for each single one. The sons of the Elder Rebbi Ḥiyya follow the method of their father, as Rebbi Hiyya stated[110]: "One who cuts grain, harvests grapes, harvests olives, cuts tree branches, tears out, plucks fruits, are all [liable] because of harvesting.[111]" Rebbi Sidor[112] said, Jehudah the son of the rabbi[113] studied *Makhširin* for six months. In the end there came a student of Rebbi Simai and asked him, but he could not answer. He[114] said, it is recognizable that this one never passed by the gate of the Torah.

107 They made a list of all actions traditionally forbidden on the Sabbath.

108 Where they could they classified them according to the official categories.

109 A catch-all category for actions difficult to categorize. It is clear that the list of prohibited actions must have preceded the classification.

110 Quoted again later in the discussion of Mishnah 2, after Note 267. The Babylonian version of this *baraita* is in the Babli 73b, Tosephta 9:17.

111 These are six actions classified under the same category. "Tearing out" refers among other things to tearing out hairs.

112 His name seems to have been Isidor; changed to avoid the mention of pagan deities.

113 The Elder R. Hiyya. *Makhširin* is a rather short Mishnah Tractate of only 6 Chapters accompanied by Tosephta of 3 Chapters.

114 R. Simai's student. The important one of R. Hiyya's twins was Hizqiah, not Jehudah.

(9c line 10) אַרְבָּעִים אָבוֹת מְלָאכוֹת חָסֵר אַחַת. לֵיְדָה מִילָה. שֶׁאִם עֲשָׂאָן כּוּלָם בְּעֶלֶם אֶחָד אֵינוֹ חַיָּב אֶלָּא אַחַת.

"The categories of work are 39." For which purpose? For if he did all of them in one oblivion he is liable only once[115].

115 This statement contradicts Mishnah 1 and the quote in the Babli (69a) as well as a quote from the Yerushalmi (not in our text) by R. Salomon Adani; it has to be changed into "is liable for each single one."

(9c line 11) תַּנָּא רִבִּי זַכַּאי קוֹמֵי רִבִּי יוֹחָנָן. זִיבַּח קִיטֵּר וְנִיסֵּךְ בְּעֶלֶם אֶחָד חַיָּב עַל כָּל־אַחַת וְאַחַת. אֲמַר לֵיהּ רִבִּי יוֹחָנָן. בַּבְלַיָּיא. עֲבַרְתְּ בְּיָדָךְ תְּלָתָא נְהָרִין וְאִיתָבַּרְתְּ. אֵינוֹ חַיָּיב אֶלָּא אַחַת. עַד לָא יַתְבְּרִינֵּיהּ בְּיָדֵיהּ יֵשׁ כָּאן אַחַת וְאֵין כָּאן הֲנָה. מִן דְּתַבְרָהּ בְּיָדֵיהּ יֵשׁ כָּאן הֲנָה וְאֵין כָּאן אַחַת. רִבִּי בָּא בַּר מָמָל בְּעָא קוֹמֵי דְּרִבִּי זְעִירָא. וִיהֵא חַיָּיב עַל כָּל־אַחַת וְאַחַת. כַּמָּה דְתֵימַר גַּבֵּי שַׁבָּת. לֹא־תַעֲשֶׂה כָּל־מְלָאכָה כְּלָל. לֹא־תְבַעֲרוּ אֵשׁ בְּכֹל מֹשְׁבוֹתֵיכֶם. פְּרָט. הֲלֹא הַבְעָרָה בִּכְלָל הָיְיתָה וְיָצְאת מִן הַכְּלָל לְלַמֵּד. לוֹמַר. מַה הַבְעָרָה מְיוּחֶדֶת מַעֲשֶׂה יְחִידִי וְחִיָּיבִין עָלֶיהָ בִּפְנֵי עַצְמָהּ. אַף כָּל־מַעֲשֶׂה וּמַעֲשֶׂה שֶׁיֵּשׁ בּוֹ לְחַיֵּב עָלָיו בִּפְנֵי עַצְמוֹ. אַף הָכָא. לֹא תַעֲבְדֵם כְּלָל. לֹא־תִשְׁתַּחֲוֶה לָהֶם פְּרָט. וַהֲלֹא הִשְׁתַּחֲוָיָה בִּכְלָל הָיְתָה וְלָמָּה יָצְאת מִן הַכְּלָל. לְלַמֵּד. מַה הִשְׁתַּחֲוָיָה מְיוּחֶדֶת מַעֲשֶׂה יְחִידִי וְחִיָּיבִין עָלֶיהָ בִּפְנֵי עַצְמָהּ. אַף כָּל־מַעֲשֶׂה וּמַעֲשֶׂה שֶׁיֵּשׁ בּוֹ לְחַיֵּב עָלָיו בִּפְנֵי עַצְמוֹ. אֲמַר לֵיהּ. בַּשַּׁבָּת כְּלָל בְּמָקוֹם אֶחָד וּפְרָט בְּמָקוֹם אַחֵר. וּבַעֲבוֹדָה זָרָה

כְּלָל שֶׁהוּא בְצַד הַפְּרָט. אָמַר לֵיהּ. וְהָכְתִיב לֹא תִשְׁתַּחֲוֶה לְאֵל אַחֵר זֹבֵחַ לָאֱלֹקִים יָחֳרָם. הֲרֵי כְּלָל בְּמָקוֹם אֶחָד וּפְרָט בְּמָקוֹם אֶחָר. אָמַר לֵיהּ. כֵּיוָן שֶׁאַתְּ לוֹמֵד מִצִּדּוֹ. אֲפִילוּ כְּלָל בְּמָקוֹם אֶחָד [אִי] אַתְּ לָמֵד. חַבְרַיָּיא אָמְרִין. לֹא שַׁנְיָיא. בֵּין שֶׁכְּלָל בְּמָקוֹם אֶחָד וּפְרָט בְּמָקוֹם אַחֵר. בֵּין שֶׁכְּלָל וּפְרָט בְּמָקוֹם אֶחָד. כְּלָל וּפְרָט הוּא. בַּשַּׁבָּת כְּלָל וְאַחַר כָּךְ פְּרָט. בַּעֲבוֹדָה זָרָה פְּרָט וְאַחַר כָּךְ כְּלָל. רִבִּי יוֹסֵי אָמַר. לֹא שַׁנְיָיא. בֵּין שֶׁכְּלָל וְאַחַר כָּךְ פְּרָט. בֵּין שֶׁפְּרָט וְאַחַר כָּךְ כְּלָל. בֵּין שֶׁכְּלָל וּפְרָט וּכְלָל. כְּלָל וּפְרָט הוּא. בַּשַּׁבָּת כְּלָל בַּעֲבוֹדָתָהּ וּפְרָט בַּעֲבוֹדָתָהּ. בַּעֲבוֹדָה זָרָה כְּלָל בַּעֲבוֹדָתָהּ וּפְרָט בִּמְלָאכוֹת הַגָּבוֹהַּ.

[116]Rebbi Zakkai stated before Rebbi Johanan: If somebody sacrificed, burned incense, and poured a libation in one forgetting, he is guilty for each action separately. Rebbi Johanan told him, Babylonian! You crossed three rivers with your hands and were broken. He is guilty only once! {Before he broke it in his hand there is "one" but not "those"; after he broke it in his hand there are "those" but not "one".} Rebbi Abba bar Mamal asked before Rebbi Ze'ira: Should he[117] not be guilty for each action separately? As you say for the Sabbath: *Do not perform any work*[118], principle. *Do not light fire in any of your dwelling places*[119], a detail. Was not lighting fire subsumed under the principle, but it is mentioned separately from this principle! Since lighting fire is special in that it is the work of a single individual and one would be guilty for it alone, so everything for which one alone is guilty[120]. Also here: *Do not worship them*[121], a principle. *Do not prostrate yourself*[121], a detail. Was not prostrating itself included in the principle and why was it mentioned separately? To infer, to tell you that prostrating oneself is special in that it is the action of a single individual and one would be guilty for it alone, so everything for which one alone is guilty[120]. He answered: For the Sabbath, He mentioned the principle at one place and the details at another place. For idol worship, the principle is found close to the detail[122]. He retorted: Is it not written: *Do not prostrate yourself before another power*[123]? *He who sacrifices to Elohim shall be banned*[124]. He mentioned the principle at one place and the details at another place! He said, since you do [not][125] infer anything from it close up, you cannot infer anything from afar[126]. The colleagues say, it makes no difference; whether He gave the principle at one place and the detail at another, or gave principle and detail at the same place,

it is a matter of principle and detail. For the Sabbath, He first gave the principle and then the detail. For idolatry, He gave the detail and only later the principle[127]. Rebbi Yose said, it makes no difference whether He first gave the principle and then the detail or He gave the detail and only later the principle, or He gave principle, detail, and principle; it is a matter of principle and detail. For the Sabbath, He gave a general prohibition of work, followed by details; for idolatry, He gave the general principle regarding its worship but detailed the works of Heaven[128].

116 This paragraph and the next are also in *Nazir* 6:1 but the origin is here as will be seen in the commentary. The introductory statement is from earlier in the Chapter, Notes 28-30. The text in braces was copied from there and has no place here.

117 The idol worshipper.

118 *Ex.* 20:8.

119 *Ex.* 35:3.

120 A forbidden action on the Sabbath which is executed only by the common effort of several people is not prosecutable. This is an application of the 9th hermeneutical principle of R. Ismael: Any detail which was subsumed under a principle but is mentioned separately in order to instruct, was not mentioned for itself but to explain the entire principle [*Sifra* Introduction 2; *Pereq* 1(1)]. In the text this is called "principle and detail", which in the technical language of the Babli refers to the completely different rule No. 5 [*Sifra* Introduction (1,7)]. In *Mekhilta dR. Ismael* p. 347 the argument is attributed to R. Jonathan (who in the Babli 70a appears as R. Nathan.)

Whether there is a connection between rules 5 and 9 is left open in the Babli, *Baba qamma* 85a, decided in the negative in

Menahot 55b. Menaḥem Cahana, in an exhaustive study of the problem (קווים להתפתחות של מידת כלל ופרט בתקופת התנאים p. 173-216 in: Studies in Talmudic and Midrashic Literature in Memory of Tirzah Lifshitz) holds that the original tannaitic theory knew only of two principles, one which corresponded to the later (Babli, *Sifra*, *Sifry*) rules entitled "principle and detail", "detail and principle", "principle and detail and principle"; the other one referring to all rules which in Babylonian formulation start with "any detail which was subsumed under a principle". His arguments support the thesis of the present commentary that *Mekhilta*, *Sifra*, *Sifry* (and Tosephta) in our hands are essentially Babylonian editions. (A different interpretation of the verses is in the Babli 70a).

121 *Ex.* 20:4.

122 In the same sentence. Cf. Babli *Pesahim* 6b, *Bava qamma* 85a, *Menahot* 55b, *Niddah* 33a.

123 *Ex.* 34:14.

124 *Ex.* 22:19. For this argument the reference to *Elohim* is taken to apply to idols. The masoretic vocalization applying a definite article must refer to God in His

function as Judge, God as Creator, Ruler of the physical world, to Whom propitiatory sacrifices are forbidden; sacrifices are legitimate only if offered to YHWH, God the Merciful and Dispenser of Grace. This is the interpretation adopted at the end of the paragraph. In all of *Lev.* and *Num.*, there is never any mention of a sacrifice to Elohim.

125 Added from the text in *Nazir*, needed for an understanding of the text.

126 Since 34:14 does not teach anything not contained in Ex. 20:5.

127 If *prostrating* had been mentioned after *worshipping*, the 5th hermeneutical principle would imply that the two notions are identical in intent. As the verse stands, it cannot be interpreted as "principle and detail", therefore the 9th principle does not apply to idolatry since the detail does not follow after the principle.

128 The prohibition refers to performing for idolatry any ceremony commanded for the worship of Heaven. The case of R. Zakkai really has no connection with the argument about the status of the mention of prostrating oneself in the Second Commandment.

(9c line 33) אָמַר רִבִּי מָנָא. הַבְעָרָה שֶׁלֹּא לְצוֹרֶךְ יָצָאת. הִשְׁתַּחֲוָיָה לְצוֹרֶךְ יָצָאת. לְצוֹרֶךְ יָצָאת. לְלַמֵּד עַל עַצְמָהּ. שֶׁאֵינָה מַעֲשֶׂה. אַתְיָא כְּהָהִיא דְּתַנֵּי חִזְקִיָּה. זֹבֵחַ לָאֱלֹקִים יָחֳרָם. יָצָתָה זְבִיחָה לְלַמֵּד עַל הַכֹּל. הִשְׁתַּחֲוָיָה לְלַמֵּד עַל עַצְמָהּ. שֶׁאֵינָהּ מַעֲשֶׂה. אוֹ חִלַּף. דָּבָר שֶׁהוּא מַעֲשֶׂה מְלַמֵּד. וְדָבָר שֶׁאֵינוֹ מַעֲשֶׂה אֵינוֹ מְלַמֵּד. דָּמַר רִבִּי יִרְמְיָה. הַבְעָרָה לְצוֹרֶךְ יָצָאת. לְלַמֵּד עַל בָּתֵּי דִינִין שֶׁלֹּא יְהוּ דָנִין בַּשַּׁבָּת. וּמַה טַעֲמָא. נֶאֱמַר כָּאן בְּכָל מוֹשְׁבוֹתֵיכֶם. וְנֶאֱמַר לְהַלָּן וְהָיוּ אֵלֶּה לָכֶם לְחֻקַּת מִשְׁפָּט לְדֹרֹתֵיכֶם בְּכָל מוֹשְׁבוֹתֵיכֶם: מַה מוֹשְׁבוֹתֵיכֶם שֶׁנֶּאֱמַר לְהַלָּן בְּבָתֵּי דִינִין הַכָּתוּב מְדַבֵּר. אַף מוֹשְׁבוֹתֵיכֶם שֶׁנֶּאֱמַר כָּאן בְּבָתֵּי דִינִין הַכָּתוּב מְדַבֵּר. אָמַר רִבִּי שְׁמוּאֵל בַּר אַבְדּוּמָא. מִכֵּיוָן דְּתֵימַר. לְצוֹרֶךְ יָצָאת. כְּמִי שֶׁיָּצָא שֶׁלֹּא לְצוֹרֶךְ. וְדָבָר שֶׁיָּצָא שֶׁלֹּא לְצוֹרֶךְ מְלַמֵּד.

Rebbi Mana said, lighting fire was mentioned unnecessarily[129]; prostrating oneself was mentioned by necessity to explain about itself since it is not work[130]. This follows what Hizqiah stated: *He who sacrifices to powers shall be banned*[124]. Sacrificing was mentioned separately to teach about everything[131], prostrating oneself to explain about itself since it is not work. Rebbi Jeremiah said, lighting fire was mentioned by necessity, to teach that courts should not sit on the Sabbath[132]. What is the reason? It says here, *in all your settlements,* and it says there, *these . . should be rules of law for your generations, in all your settlements*[133]. Since "settlements" mentioned there refers to courts, "settlements" referred to here also refers to courts. Rebbi Samuel bar Eudaimon said, even if you say that it was mentioned separately necessarily is as if it was mentioned separately not by necessity,[134] and any item mentioned separately unnecessarily instructs[135].

129 Since the prohibition of making fire is implied in the Fourth Commandment in any reasonable interpretation. Therefore, making fire is a detail which can be used to characterize all work forbidden on the Sabbath.

130 Nothing is changed or produced by prostrating oneself; it is not obvious that it should be forbidden under any circumstances.

131 Since punishment for sacrificing is spelled out separately, any punishment for an act of idolatry must be given separately by the 9th rule, supporting R. Zakkai against R. Johanan.

132 In the Babli, *Yebamot* 6b, this is a Tannaitic statement from the school of R. Ismael, appended to an argument also quoted in *Mekhilta dR. Ismael, Wayyaqhel*.

133 *Num*. 35:29.

134 Since the argument is based on *Num*. 35:29, not on Ex. 22:19, the latter verse can be used in an application of the 9th rule.

135 It is axiomatic that the Torah contains no unnecessary statements. If an item is singled out and there is no apparent reason for this one has to conclude that anything to be inferred about this particular item applies to all similar cases.

(9c line 43) הָדָא אָמְרָה. דָּבָר אֶחָד שֶׁיָּצָא לְצוֹרֶךְ אֵינוֹ חוֹלֵק. וְשֶׁלֹּא לְצוֹרֶךְ חוֹלֵק. שְׁנֵי דְבָרִים שֶׁיָּצְאוּ מִן הַכְּלָל מָהוּ שֶׁיַּחֲלוֹקוּ. נִשְׁמָעִינַהּ מִן הָדָא. מִנַּיִין הַמַּעֲלֶה מִבְּשַׂר חַטָּאת וּמִבְּשַׂר אָשָׁם וּמִבְּשַׂר קָדְשֵׁי הַקֳּדָשִׁים וּמִבְּשַׂר קֳדָשִׁים קַלִּים וּמוֹתַר הָעוֹמֶר וּשְׁתֵּי הַלֶּחֶם וְלֶחֶם הַפָּנִים וּשְׁיָרֵי מְנָחוֹת וּמִן הַשְּׂאוֹר וּמִן הַדְּבַשׁ עוֹבֵר בְּלֹא תַעֲשֶׂה. תַּלְמוּד לוֹמַר כִּי כָל־שְׂאוֹר וְכָל־דְּבַשׁ לֹא־תַקְטִירוּ מִמֶּנּוּ אִשֶּׁה לַיי. הָא כָּל־שֵׁשׁ מִמֶּנּוּ לְאִישִּׁים הֲרֵי הוּא בְּבַל תַּקְטִירוּ.

רִבִּי אֶלְעָזָר שָׁאַל לְרִבִּי יוֹחָנָן. וְיָצְאוּ שְׁתֵּי הַלֶּחֶם וִילַמְּדוּ עַל הַקֳּדָשִׁים לַכֶּבֶשׁ. אָמַר לֵיהּ. כְּהָדָא דְתַנֵּי. הַמִּזְבֵּחַ. אֵין לִי אֶלָּא הַמִּזְבֵּחַ. וּמִנַּיִין לְרַבּוֹת אֶת הַכֶּבֶשׁ. תַּלְמוּד לוֹמַר וְאֶל־הַמִּזְבֵּחַ לֹא־יַעֲלֶה. יָכוֹל לַעֲבוֹדָה וְשֶׁלֹּא לַעֲבוֹדָה. תַּלְמוּד לוֹמַר לְרֵיחַ נִיחוֹחַ. לֹא אָמַרְתִּי אֶלָּא לַעֲבוֹדָה. אָמַר לֵיהּ. אוֹתָם מִיעוּט. אִילּוּ חַיָּיבִין עֲלֵיהֶן לַכֶּבֶשׁ. וְאֵין שְׁאָר כָּל־הַקֳּדָשִׁים חַיָּיבִין עֲלֵיהֶן לַכֶּבֶשׁ. מִפְּנֵי שֶׁכָּתוּב אוֹתָם. הָא אֵינוֹ כָתוּב אוֹתָם מְלַמְּדִין. הָדָא אָמְרָה. שְׁנֵי דְבָרִים שֶׁיָּצְאוּ מִן הַכְּלָל אֵינָם חוֹלְקִין. אָמַר רִבִּי חֲנַנְיָה בְּרֵיהּ דְּרִבִּי הִלֵּל. לַחֲלוּק אֵינָן חוֹלְקִין. הָא לְלַמֵּד מְלַמְּדִין.

רִבִּי יוֹסֵי בֵּירִבִּי בּוּן לֹא אָמַר כֵּן. אֶלָּא רִבִּי אֶלְעָזָר שָׁאַל לְרִבִּי יוֹחָנָן. וְיָצְאוּ שְׁתֵּי הַלֶּחֶם וִילַמְּדוּ עַל כָּל־הַקֳּדָשִׁים לַכֶּבֶשׁ. אָמַר לֵיהּ. אוֹתָם מִיעוּט. אִילּוּ חַיָּיבִין עֲלֵיהֶן לַכֶּבֶשׁ. וְאֵין שְׁאָר כָּל־הַקֳּדָשִׁים חַיָּיבִין עֲלֵיהֶן לַכֶּבֶשׁ. הָדָא אָמְרָה. דָּבָר אֶחָד שֶׁיָּצָא מִן הַכְּלָל לְצוֹרֶךְ אֵינוֹ חוֹלֵק. וְשֶׁלֹּא לְצוֹרֶךְ חוֹלֵק. וּשְׁנֵי דְבָרִים שֶׁיָּצְאוּ מִן הַכְּלָל אֵינָם חוֹלְקִין. וּכְרִבִּי יִשְׁמָעֵאל חוֹלְקִין. דְּאָמַר רִבִּי בּוּן בַּר חִיָּיה. דִּבְרֵי רִבִּי יִשְׁמָעֵאל. שְׁנֵי דְבָרִים שֶׁיָּצְאוּ מִן הַכְּלָל חוֹלְקִין. דְּתַנֵּי רִבִּי יִשְׁמָעֵאל. לֹא תְנַחֲשׁוּ וְלֹא תְעוֹנֵנוּ. וַהֲלֹא הַנִּיחוּשׁ וְהָעִינּוּן בִּכְלָל הָיוּ. וְיָצְאוּ מִן הַכְּלָל לְחִילּוּק.

This implies that one item which was mentioned separately by necessity does not divide[136]. If it was mentioned not by necessity it divides[137]. If two items were mentioned separately, do they divide? Let us hear from the following: From where that he transgresses a prohibition whoever brings to the altar meat of a purification offering[138], or meat of a reparation offering, or meat of most holy offerings[139], or meat from simply holy offerings[140], or the remainder of the `Omer[141] or the Two Breads[142], or the Shew Bread[143], or remainders of cereal offerings[144], or leaven[145], or date honey[146]? The verse says[147], *for any leaven or any date honey you may not turn into smoke as a fire gift to the Eternal.* Therefore anything that had been given to the fire is under "do not turn into smoke"[148].

Rebbi Eleazar asked Rebbi Johanan. Should not the Two Breads, being mentioned separately, teach about all *sancta* on the ramp[149]? He told him, it follows what was stated, *the altar*[150]; this means not only the altar, from where to include the ramp? The verse says[150], *on the altar they shall not be lifted*. I could think neither as an act of worship nor as act of worship. The verse says[150], *as aroma smell*, I was saying this only as an act of worship[151]. (He retorted,)[152] *them* is a restriction[153]. For these one is liable on the ramp, for all other *sancta* one is not liable on the ramp. Because it is written *them*. If *them* had not been written, it would instruct[154]. That means, two items which were mentioned separately do (not)[155] separate[156]. Rebbi Hananiah the son of Rebbi Hillel said, they do not separate, therefore they instruct[157].

Rebbi Yose ben Rebbi Abun does not say so but Rebbi Eleazar asked Rebbi Johanan, should not the Two Breads, being mentioned separately, teach about all *sancta* on the ramp[149]? He said to him, *them* is a restriction. For these one is liable on the ramp, for all other *sancta* one is not liable on the ramp[158]. This implies that a single item which is mentioned separately necessarily does not divide, but unnecessarily it divides[135]. Two items which are mentioned separately do not divide but according to Rebbi Ismael they do divide, as Rebbi Abun bar Hiyya said, the words of Rebbi Ismael are that two items which are mentioned separately divide[159]. As Rebbi Ismael stated, *you shall neither divine nor cast spells*[160]. Were not divining and spellbinding included in the general class[161]? The were mentioned separately to be treated differently from the general case[162].

136 Since we found a reason why the item was mentioned one cannot infer that it is established as a separate rule.

137 It is a general hermeneutical rule (No. 4) that two parallel items are just that, two separate items, and no additional inferences or comparisons are possible. If both are prohibitions, infractions generate separate liabilities.

138 For purification and reparation offerings, blood is sprinkled on the altar and fat is burned. The meat must be eaten by the priests; it cannot be sacrificed.

139 Most holy offerings are elevation offerings which are completely burned, purification and reparation offerings already mentioned, and the public well-being offering accompanying the Two Leavened Breads on Pentecost which introduce the season of the wheat harvest. Only the last item can be meant here, where the meat also must be eaten by the priests.

140 The family sacrifices, of which only blood and fat are given to the altar, *Lev.* Chapter 3.

141 The barley offering on the Festival of Unleavened Bread, of which a handful is burnt on the altar and the remainder must be eaten by the priests. *Lev.* 23:10.

142 The Two Breads to be brought on Pentecost, to be eaten by the priests with the meat of the public well-being offering (Note 139). *Lev.* 23:17.

143 Of which the incense is burned on the altar; the bread itself has to be eaten by the priests, *Lev.* 24:5-9.

144 To be eaten by the priests after a handful was burned on the altar, *Lev.* Chapter 2.

145 This again refers to the Two Breads, the only leavened offering.

146 Which as an offering of first fruits is consumed by the priest after being presented to the altar but not brought onto the altar. *Deut.* 26:2.

147 *Lev.* 2:12.

148 If any part or appendix had to be given to the fire on the altar, there is a prohibition to put any of the remainder on the altar.

149 The ramp on which the priest ascends to the altar since it is forbidden to build steps to the altar (*Ex.* 20:22). The ramp was physically separated from the altar.

150 *Lev.* 2:12: *As an offering of first fruits you may offer <u>them</u> to the Eternal but on the alter they shall not ascend for pleasant scent.*

151 Since the ramp is inclined, stepping on the ramp in the course of a service would be "ascend for pleasant scent" and is forbidden. But depositing the first fruits on the ramp while the priest remains standing on the floor of the Temple court until he takes them to be consumed is not covered by the prohibition. *Sifra Saw Pereq* 1(11).

152 An addition from the corrector; this has to be deleted since the next paragraph shows that the speaker still is R. Johanan; the following is a continuation of the *baraita* quoted.

153 Anything other than leaven and date honey is not covered by the verse.

154 Then leaven and date honey would just be examples of items to be consumed by the priests.

155 A correction by the scribe himself but in error as shown by the next paragraph.

156 To prohibit burning on the altar what must be consumed by priests or laity it would have been enough to give one example. Since two were given, it implies that bringing to the altar is a separate sin for each of them (and equally all others).

157 Since they are mentioned in one verse they are not two independent items; previous argument is not applicable. Since it is a single item it permits inference for all *sancta*.

158 But on the altar one is liable at least in violation of a positive commandment. Babli *Menahot* 37b/38a.

159 From here on and the next paragraphs there is a parallel (but not an exact copy) in *Sanhedrin* 7:5 Notes 72-125.

One of R. Ismael's hermeneutical principles is that "a detail which was singled out from a general category was singled out not for itself but as an example for the entire category." R. Abun bar Hiyya states that according to R. Ismael this holds only for a single detail, not for two or more.

160 *Lev.* 19:26. Divination is an attempt to predict the future by magical means; spellbinding is practical witchcraft. Both are particular examples in the prohibition of witchcraft (*Ex.* 22:17), but no penalty is indicated.

161 To use witchcraft is a capital crime (Mishnah *Sanhedrin* 7:5); in the absence of witnesses there is an automatic Divine verdict of extirpation. But the special cases of divination and spellbinding only trigger a verdict of extirpation; they are not cases for the human court. This illustrates R. Ismael's principle. In *Sifra Qedošim Pereq* 6(2), R. Ismael and R. Aqiba identify divination and spellbinding as examples of make-believe witchcraft which according to Mishnah *Sanhedrin* 7:19 is not punishable by the human court. Automatically, these are separate examples of sins which require a purification sacrifice if done without criminal intent. A person who unintentionally acts as sorcerer, diviner, and spellbinder has to bring three sacrifices.

(9c line 65) כְּלָל בְּהִיכָּרֵת וּפְרָט בְּהִיכָּרֵת. מִילְתֵיהּ דְּרִבִּי יוֹחָנָן אֲמָרָה. כְּלָל וּפְרָט הוּא. דָּמַר רִבִּי אַבָּהוּ בְשֵׁם רִבִּי יוֹחָנָן. כִּי כָל־אֲשֶׁר יַעֲשֶׂה מִכֹּל הַתּוֹעֵבוֹת הָאֵלֶּה וְנִכְרְתוּ. אֲחוֹתוֹ בִּכְלָל הָיְתָה וְיָצֵאת מִן הַכְּלָל לְחִילוּק עַל הַכְּלָל. הֲתִיב רִבִּי אֶלְעָזָר. וְהָכְתִיב וְעֶרְוַת אֲחוֹת אִמְּךָ וַאֲחוֹת אָבִיךָ לֹא תְגַלֵּה כִּי אֶת־שְׁאֵירוֹ הֶעֱרָה. אָמַר לֵיהּ. לְצוֹרֶךְ יָצֵאת לִידוֹן בְּעֶרְיָהּ. אָמַר לֵיהּ. וְהָכְתִיב וְאִישׁ אֲשֶׁר־יִשְׁכַּב אֶת־אִשָּׁה דָוָה וְגִילָּה אֶת־עֶרְוָתָהּ אֶת־מְקוֹרָהּ הֶעֱרָה. אָמַר לֵיהּ. לְצוֹרֶךְ יָצֵאת לִידוֹן בָּהּ אֶת הַמְעָרָה כְגוֹמֵר. שֶׁלֹּא תֹאמַר. הוֹאִיל וְאֵין חַיָּיבִין עָלֶיהָ אֶלָּא מִשֵּׁם טוּמְאָה לֹא נַעֲשָׂה בוֹ אֶת הַמְעָרָה כְגוֹמֵר. לְפוּם כֵּן צָרַךְ מֵימַר. חַיָּיב עַל כָּל־אַחַת וְאַחַת. אָמַר לֵיהּ. וְהָכְתִיב וְאִישׁ אֲשֶׁר יִשְׁכַּב אֶת־דֹּדָתוֹ עֶרְוַת דֹּדוֹ גִלָּה. אָמַר לֵיהּ. לְצוֹרֶךְ יָצֵאת לִידוֹן בַּעֲרִירִי. וְהָכְתִיב וְאִישׁ אֲשֶׁר יִקַּח אֶת־אֵשֶׁת אָחִיו נִדָּה הִוא. אָמַר לֵיהּ. לְצוֹרֶךְ יָצֵאת לִידוֹן בַּעֲרִירִי. דָּמַר רִבִּי יוּדָן. כָּל־הָהֵן דִּכְתִיב עֲרִירִים יִהְיוּ הַוְיָין בְּלֹא בָנִים. עֲרִירִים יָמוּתוּ קוֹבְרִין אֶת בְּנֵיהֶן.

In general by extirpation, the separate case by extirpation[2]; the word of Rebbi Johanan implies that it is "general case and detail[162]", as Rebbi Abbahu said in the name of Rebbi Johanan, *since anybody who would perform any of these abominations, they will be extirpated*[163]. Was not his sister included in the general class[164] and was mentioned separately of the general class to divide from the general class. Rebbi Eleazar objected, is it not written[165], *the nakedness of your mother's sister and your father's sister you shall not uncover, for he would touch his relative*? He told him, this was mentioned separately for a reason, to judge by "touching"[166]. He said to him, is it not written[167], *a man who would lie with an unwell woman, uncover her nakedness and touch her source*? He told him, this was mentioned separately for a reason, to judge the one "touching" as finishing. That you should not say, since he is liable for her [already][168] for impurity we should not consider for him "touching" as finishing. Therefore it was necessary to mention (that he is liable for each single one.)[169] He said to him, is it not written[170], *a man who would sleep with his aunt, his uncle's nakedness he uncovered*? He told him, this was mentioned separately to judge by childlessness. But is it not written[171], *a man who would marry his brother's wife, she is separated*? He told him, this was mentioned separately to judge by childlessness, as Rebbi Yudan[172] said, where it is written *childless they shall be*[171], they will be without children, *childless they shall die*[170], they bury their children.

162 Hermeneutical principle #5 on R. Ismael's list states that a general expression followed by particulars only refers to the particulars. If both general expression and details declare the same., one has to find a reason why the details have to be mentioned separately.

163 *Lev.* 18:29. This verse decrees a general verdict of extirpation on any violation of sexual taboos spelled out in *Lev.* 18, whether or not they are criminally punishable.

164 The sister is forbidden in *Lev.* 18:9 but in the chapter about penalties, *Lev.* 20:17, the punishment is reserved for Heaven.

165 *Lev.* 20:19. The wording might be slightly misleading.

166 *Lev.* 20:19 makes two statements: The punishment is reserved for Heaven and the sin is committed the moment the genitals of the parties touch, without any penetration. Mishnah *Yebamot* 6:2 extends the equivalence of touching and penetration to all sexual offenses.

167 *Lev.* 20:18. The implications are the same as for v. 19.

168 The word was deleted by the corrector but it is necessary for the understanding of

the text. Since in *Lev.* 15 it is stated that simple touching (not sexual "touching") a *niddah* causes impurity and is forbidden to the male, her prohibition differs materially from the other sexual taboos.

169 This seems to be extraneous to the discussion. However, since the statement is also found in the Genizah text of *Sanhedrin*, it seems to be original and explains that *Lev.* 18:29 decrees separate extirpation and, therefore, separate sacrifices for unintentional sin, for each separate category of incest.

170 *Lev.* 20:20.

171 *Lev.* 20:21.

172 The Amora. His counterpart in the Babli is the third generation Amora Rabba (Rav Abba bar Nahmani). The Babli (*Yebamot* 55a) applies both statements to both verses.

(9d line 2) אָמַר רִבִּי יוֹסֵה. דּוֹדָתוֹ לְצוֹרֶךְ יָצְאַת. לְמָעֵט אֵת אֵשֶׁת אָחִיו מֵאִמּוֹ. נֶאֱמַר כָּאן דּוֹדָתוֹ. וְנֶאֱמַר לְהַלָּן אוֹ־דוֹדוֹ אוֹ בֶן־דוֹדוֹ יִגְאָלֶנּוּ. מַה דּוֹדוֹ שֶׁנֶּאֱמַר לְהַלָּן בַּאֲחִי אָבִיו מֵאָבִיו הַכָּתוּב מְדַבֵּר. אַף דּוֹדָתוֹ שֶׁנֶּאֱמָרָה לְהַלּוֹן בְּאָחוֹת אָבִיו מֵאָבִיו הַכָּתוּב מְדַבֵּר. אַף אֵשֶׁת אָחִיו לְמֵידָה מִדּוֹדָתוֹ. מַה דּוֹדָתוֹ שֶׁנֶּאֱמָרָה לְהַלָּן בְּאָחוֹת אָבִיו מֵאָבִיו הַכָּתוּב מְדַבֵּר. אַף אֵשֶׁת אָחִיו שֶׁנֶּאֱמָרָה כָּאן בְּאֵשֶׁת אָחִיו מֵאָבִיו הַכָּתוּב מְדַבֵּר. עַד כְּדוֹן כְּרִבִּי עֲקִיבָה. כְּרִבִּי יִשְׁמָעֵאל. דְּתַנֵּי רִבִּי יִשְׁמָעֵאל. נֶאֱמַר כָּאן אֵשֶׁת אָחִיו. וְנֶאֱמַר לְהַלָּן וְאִישׁ אֲשֶׁר יִקַּח אֶת־אֵשֶׁת אָחִיו נִדָּה הִוא. מַה נִדָּה יֵשׁ לָהּ הֶיתֵּר לְאַחַר אִיסּוּרָהּ. אַף אֵשֶׁת אָחִיו מֵאָבִיו יֵשׁ לָהּ הֶיתֵּר לְאַחַר אִיסּוּרָהּ. יָצְאַת אֵשֶׁת אָחִיו מֵאִמּוֹ שֶׁאֵין לָהּ הֶיתֵּר לְאַחַר אִיסּוּרָהּ.

Rebbi Yose said, it was necessary that *his aunt* be mentioned separately, to exclude his maternal brother's wife[174]. It is said here *his aunt*, and it is said there[175], *either his uncle or his uncle's son shall free him*. Since by *his uncle* mentioned there, the verse understands his father's paternal brother, also by *his aunt* mentioned here, the verse speaks of his father's paternal sister[176]. Also *his brother's wife*[177] can be inferred from *his aunt*. Since by *his aunt* mentioned there, the verse speaks of his father's paternal brother's wife, also by *his brother's wife* mentioned here, the verse speaks of his paternal brother's wife. So far following Rebbi Aqiba. Following Rebbi Ismael? As Rebbi Ismael stated: It is said here *his brother's wife* and it is said there[178], *a man who would take his brother's wife, she is niddah*[179]. Since a menstruating woman will be permitted after being forbidden, also his paternal brother's wife may be permitted after being forbidden.[180] This excludes his maternal brother's wife, who cannot be permitted after being forbidden[181].

174 From punishment by loss of children (rejected in the Babli, *Yebamot* 55a).

175 *Lev.* 25:49. Since the subject of the entire Chapter is inheritance, it is

understood that only the male line is addressed.

176 In *Sanhedrin*: His paternal uncle's wife. This is more appropriate for the argument here since his father's or mother's sisters are forbidden by *Lev.* 18:12,13 and the prohibition is unproblematic.

177 Who is forbidden in *Lev.* 18:16.

178 *Lev.* 20:21, the penalty clause referring to the prohibition formulated in *Lev.* 18:16.

179 In biblical Hebrew, the meaning of the root נדד is the same as Arabic ناد "to separate, to disperse". This applies both to the menstruating woman (*Lev.* 18:19), to whom relations with her husband are forbidden, and to the person excommunicated (מְנֻדֶּה) who is separated from the community. In rabbinic Hebrew, the word נדה is used exclusively for the menstruating woman; this is the reference made here, even though the argument is equally valid for the excommunicated person. (Babli *Yebamot* 54b.)

180 The menstruating woman *is* permitted after her purification; the brother's wife *may be* permitted, viz., if the brother dies childless. In the latter case, "brother" means paternal brother (*Yebamot* 1:1, Note 45).

181 But for whom no punishment is spelled out.

(9d line 12) הָא רִבִּי יִשְׁמָעֵאל מַקְשֵׁי לָהּ. מְנָן תֵּיתֵי לֵיהּ. רִבִּי אַבָּהוּ רִבִּי אֶלְעָזָר בְּשֵׁם רִבִּי הוֹשַׁעְיָה. שְׁנֵי לָאוִין וְכָרֵת אֶחָד. לָאוִין חוֹלְקִין כְּרִיתוּת. וּמָה טַעֲמָא. עַל־בְּשַׂר אָדָם לֹא יִיסָךְ וּבְמַתְכֻּנְתּוֹ לֹא תַעֲשׂוּ כָּמוֹהוּ. וְכָתוּב אִישׁ אֲשֶׁר יִרְקַח כָּמוֹהוּ וַאֲשֶׁר יִתֵּן מִמֶּנּוּ עַל־זָר וְנִכְרַת מֵעַמָּיו: הֲרֵי יֵשׁ כָּאן שְׁנֵי לָאוִין וְכָרֵת אַחַת. לָאוִין חוֹלְקִין כְּרִיתוּת. מָה עָבַד לָהּ רִבִּי יוֹחָנָן. בַּאֲנָשִׁים הַכָּתוּב מְדַבֵּר. וּבָאַת אֲחוֹתוֹ לְלַמֵּד עַל־כָּל הַנָּשִׁים. וְלֵית לֵיהּ לְרִבִּי אֱלִיעֶזֶר כֵּן. אִית לֵיהּ לֹא תִקְרְבוּ. אֶחָד הָאִישׁ וְאֶחָד הָאִשָּׁה. וּמָה עָבַד לֵיהּ רִבִּי יוֹחָנָן. פָּתַר לָהּ וְאֵינוֹ מְחֻוָּר. וְעוֹד מִן הָדָא. שְׁמוּאֵל בַּר אַבָּא בְעָא קוֹמֵי רִבִּי זְעִירָא. וְיֵצְאוּ שְׁלָמִים וְיַחַלוּקוּ לָאוִין עַל כָּל־הַקֳּדָשִׁים לְטֻמְאָה. אָמַר לֵיהּ. לְצוֹרֶךְ יָצְאוּ. לְמַעֵט אֶת קָדְשֵׁי בֶדֶק הַבַּיִת לִמְעִילָה. שֶׁלֹּא יְהוּ חַיָּיבִין עֲלֵיהֶן מִשּׁוּם פִּיגּוּל וְנוֹתָר וְטָמֵא. וְלֹא מַתְנִיתָא הִיא. קָדְשֵׁי מִזְבֵּחַ מִצְטָרְפִין זֶה עִם זֶה לִמְעִילָה. לְחַיֵּיב עֲלֵיהֶן מִשּׁוּם פִּגּוּל וְנוֹתָר וְטָמֵא. מַה שֶּׁאֵין כֵּן בְּקָדְשֵׁי בֶדֶק הַבַּיִת. אָמַר לֵיהּ. מִכֵּיוָן שֶׁאֵין מִצְטָרְפִין חוֹלְקִין. אָמַר רִבִּי חֲנִינָא. וְכֵינִי. וְיַחְלוּקוּ וְלֹא יִצְטָרְפוּ.

But Rebbi Ismael himself had a problem: from where does one prove it[182]? Rebbi Abbahu, Rebbi Eleazar in the name of Rebbi Hoshaia: Two prohibitions and one extirpation, the prohibitions split the extirpation[183]. What is the reason? [184]*It should not be used to be rubbed on anybody's skin and in its proportions you shall not imitate it*, and it is written, *a person who would compound similarly, or who would put it on a stranger, will be extirpated from his people*, that is two prohibitions and one extirpation. The prohibitions split the extirpation[185]. How does Rebbi Johanan treat this? The verse speaks about males. His sister is mentioned to teach about all females[186]. Does Rebbi

Eleazar not accept this? He has it from *do not come near*[187], equally male or female. How does Rebbi Johanan treat this? He explains it but it is not clear[188], so also from the following: Samuel bar Abba asked before Rebbi Ze'ira, should not well-being sacrifices, being treated separately, split all *sancta* regarding impurity[189]? He told him, it was necessary that they be treated separately, to eliminate *sancta* dedicated for the upkeep of the Temple regarding larceny[190], lest one be liable for them because of mushiness[191], leftovers[192], and impurity. But is that not a Mishnah? "All *sancta* destined for the altar combine with one another with respect to liability for mushiness, leftovers, and impurity[193]," in contrast to *sancta* destined for the upkeep of the Temple[194]. Since they do not combine, they do split[195]. Rebbi Hanina[196] said, so it is. They split but do not combine[197].

182 This refers to the paragraph before the last, where R. Johanan explained that the sister had a special role in the list of incest prohibitions, to deduce that from the different levels of punishment the blanket decree of extirpation really represents separate decrees for each kind of infraction. In *Sanhedrin*, the name here is Johanan. But Ismael may be the correct attribution, since according to one opinion in the Babli, *Zebahim* 107b, this is R. Ismael's position. S. Liebermann prefers to read "Eleazar" since the supporting argument is quoted in the latter's name.

183 This answers the question. It is rather frequent to find verses containing multiple prohibitions covered by one mention of extirpation where the context makes it clear that each single infraction triggers extirpation.

184 *Ex.* 30:32,33 regarding the holy oil. Only v. 33 is discussed.

185 A person who inadvertently compounds aromatic oil in the same composition as holy oil and uses it on people has to bring two sacrifices. Babli, *Makkot* 14b.

186 While in the punishments listed in *Lev.* 20 both sexes are mentioned, the prohibition in Chapter 18 are all formulated for the male, except that the mention of extirpation is formulated (18:29) for "all persons". Since the punishment for marrying one's sister is extirpation (20:17) for both partners, it proves that the "persons" mentioned in 18:29 are both male and female.

187 *Lev.* 18:6, the verse introducing incest prohibitions. While the verse starts איש איש it is agreed that the meaning is not "every man" but "every person".

188 Since איש איש really means "every man" it needs a supporting argument.

מחוור is Babylonian spelling of Galilean מחובר "logically connected"; in the ms. it is a corrector's change.

189 Impurity of well-being sacrifices, the only ones available to lay people, is treated at length in *Lev.* 7:11-27. Impurity of

sacrifices available to priests is treated in *Lev.* 22:1-16. One should assume that a priest who inadvertently eats a combination of impure well-being and other sacrifices has to bring separate purification sacrifices; but this is not the case.

190 While misuse of all kinds of *sancta* is larceny, it is punishable only if the monetary value of the misuse is at least one *peruṭah*. Misuse of one half *peruṭah*'s worth of Temple donations and one half *peruṭah*'s worth of sacrifices is not punishable.

191 Sacrificing with the intent of eating of the sacrificial meat out of its time and place.

192 Eating of sacrificial meat after its allotted time.

193 This shows that well-being and other sacrifices are equal in the hand of the Cohen, Mishnah *Meʿilah* 4:1. The categories of mushiness, leftovers, and impurity do not apply to monetary gifts to the Temple. Anything donated to the Temple which is not a sacrifice or a Temple vessel is sold by the Temple treasurer and thereby reverts to fully profane status.

195 Somebody committing simultaneous larceny involving gifts to the Temple and sacrifices has to atone separately for the two offenses.

196 The *Genizah* text in *Sanhedrin* reads Hinena, preferable for chronological reasons.

197 R. Hanina's statement is an assertion that the rules *are* different for well-being and other sacrifices. This would agree with the Babli, *Meʿilah* 15a, that in fact well-being and purification offerings do not combine; the contrary statement of the Mishnah is classified as a rabbinic stringency.

(9d line 26) כְּלָל בַּעֲשֵׂה וּפְרָט בְּלֹא תַעֲשֶׂה. מִילְתֵיהּ דְּרִבִּי אֶלְעָזָר אָמְרָה. כְּלָל וּפְרָט הוּא. דְּאָמַר רִבִּי אֶלְעָזָר. לוֹקִין עַל יְדֵי חֲרִישָׁה בַּשְּׁבִיעִית. רִבִּי יוֹחָנָן אָמַר. אֵין לוֹקִין עַל יְדֵי חֲרִישָׁה בַּשְּׁבִיעִית. וּמַה טַעֲמָא דְּרִבִּי אֶלְעָזָר. וְשָׁבְתָה הָאָרֶץ שַׁבָּת לַיי כְּלָל. שָׂדְךָ לֹא תִזְרָע וְכַרְמְךָ לֹא תִזְמֹר פְּרָט. הַזֶּרַע וְהַזָּמִיר אַף הֵן בִּכְלָל הָיוּ. וְלָמָּה יָצְאוּ. לְהַקִּישׁ אֲלֵיהֶן. לוֹמַר לָךְ. מַה הַזֶּרַע וְהַזָּמִיר מְיוּחָדִין שֶׁהֵן עֲבוֹדָה בָּאָרֶץ וּבְאִילָן. אַף אֵין לִי אֶלָּא דָבָר שֶׁהוּא עֲבוֹדָה בָּאָרֶץ וּבְאִילָן. מָה עֲבַד לָהּ רִבִּי יוֹחָנָן. שְׁנֵי דְבָרִים הֵן. וּשְׁנֵי דְבָרִים שֶׁיָּצְאוּ מִן הַכְּלָל אֵינָן חוֹלְקִין. וְלֵית לְרִבִּי אֶלְעָזָר חוֹלְקִין. אִית לֵיהּ. לַחֲלוֹק אֵינָן חוֹלְקִין. הָא לְלַמֵּד מְלַמְּדִין. וְלֵית לְרִבִּי יוֹחָנָן מְלַמְּדִין. שַׁנְיָיא הִיא. שֶׁכְּלָל בַּעֲשֵׂה וּפְרָט בְּלֹא תַעֲשֶׂה. וְאֵין עֲשֵׂה מְלַמֵּד עַל לֹא תַעֲשֶׂה. וְאֵין לֹא תַעֲשֶׂה מְלַמֵּד עַל עֲשֵׂה. אָמַר רִבִּי אֶלְעָזָר. וַעֲשֵׂה מְלַמֵּד עַל לֹא תַעֲשֶׂה. וְאֵין לֹא תַעֲשֶׂה מְלַמֵּד עַל עֲשֵׂה. עַל דַּעְתֵּיהּ דְּרִבִּי יוֹחָנָן נִיחָא. מוּתָּר לַחְפּוֹר בָּהּ בּוֹרוֹת שִׁיחִין וּמְעָרוֹת. עַל דַּעְתֵּיהּ דְּרִבִּי אֶלְעָזָר. מַהוּ לַחְפּוֹר בָּהּ בּוֹרוֹת שִׁיחִין וּמְעָרוֹת. כְּשֵׁם שֶׁאֵין מְלַמְּדִין לְעִנְיָין אִיסּוּר. כֵּן לְעִנְיָין הֵיתֵר לֹא יְלַמְּדוּ. אָמַר רִבִּי בָּא קַרְטִגִינָאָה. טַעֲמָא דְּרִבִּי יוֹחָנָן. שֵׁשׁ שָׁנִים תִּזְרָע. וְלֹא בַשְּׁבִיעִית. שֵׁשׁ שָׁנִים תִּזְמֹר כַּרְמֶךָ. וְלֹא בַשְּׁבִיעִית. כְּלָל. לֹא תַעֲשֶׂה שֶׁהוּא בָא מִכֹּחַ עֲשֵׂה הוּא עוֹבֵר בַּעֲשֵׂה. רִבִּי יוֹסֵה אוֹמֵר. אֲפִילוּ עֲשֵׂה אֵין בּוֹ. רִבִּי יִרְמְיָה אוֹמֵר. עוֹבֵר בַּעֲשֵׂה. וְלֵיידָא מִילָּה כְּתִיב מָלֵא וְשָׁבְתָה הָאָרֶץ שַׁבָּת לַיי. לְעִנְיָין לֹא תַעֲשֶׂה שֶׁבּוֹ.

יָכוֹל יְהוּ לוֹקִין עַל הַתּוֹסֶפֶת. רִבִּי יוֹחָנָן פָּתַר מַתְנִיתָא. יָכוֹל יְהוּ לוֹקִין עַל יְדֵי חֲרִישָׁה בַּשְּׁבִיעִית. רִבִּי אֶלְעָזָר פָּתַר לָהּ מַתְנִיתָא יָכוֹל יְהוּ לוֹקִין עַל אִיסּוּר שְׁנֵי פְּרָקִים הָרִאשׁוֹנִים. אִית תַּנָּיֵי תַנֵּי. שֵׁשׁ שָׁנִים תִּזְרַע שָׂדֶךָ וְשֵׁשׁ שָׁנִים תִּזְמוֹר כַּרְמֶךָ. וְאִית תַּנָּיֵי תַנֵּי. שָׂדְךָ לֹא תִזְרָע וְכַרְמְךָ לֹא תִזְמוֹר. מָאן דָּמַר שֵׁשׁ שָׁנִים תִּזְרַע שָׂדֶךָ וְשֵׁשׁ שָׁנִים תִּזְמוֹר כַּרְמֶךָ מְסַייֵעַ לְרִבִּי יוֹחָנָן. וּמָאן דָּמַר שָׂדְךָ לֹא תִזְרָע וְכַרְמְךָ לֹא תִזְמוֹר מְסַייֵעַ לְרִבִּי אֶלְעָזָר.

מַתְנִיתָא פְּלִיגָא לְרִבִּי אֶלְעָזָר. הִשָּׁמֶר. בְּלֹא תַעֲשֶׂה. פֶּן. בְּלֹא תַעֲשֶׂה. וְכָתוּב שָׁם תַּעֲלֶה עוֹלוֹתֶיךָ וְשָׁם תַּעֲשֶׂה. שָׁם תַּעֲלֶה זוֹ הָעֲלִייָה. וְשָׁם תַּעֲשֶׂה זוֹ שְׁחִיטָה וּזְרִיקָה. מַה הָעֲלִייָה שֶׁהִיא בַעֲשֵׂה הֲרֵי הוּא בְלֹא תַעֲשֶׂה. אַף שְׁחִיטָה וּזְרִיקָה שֶׁהֵן בַּעֲשֵׂה יְהוּ בְלֹא תַעֲשֶׂה. בְּגִין דִּכְתִיב שָׁם תַּעֲלֶה וְשָׁם תַּעֲשֶׂה. הָא אִילּוּלֵא הֲוָה כָתוּב שָׁם תַּעֲלֶה וְשָׁם תַּעֲשֶׂה אֵין עֲשֵׂה מְלַמֵּד עַל לֹא תַעֲשֶׂה וְאֵין לֹא תַעֲשֶׂה מְלַמֵּד עַל עֲשֵׂה. מָה עֲבַד לָהּ רִבִּי יוֹחָנָן. שֶׁלֹּא תֹאמַר כְּמָה דְתֵימַר גַּבֵּי שַׁבָּת. חָפַר חָרַץ נָעַץ אֵינוֹ חַייָב אֶלָּא אַחַת. וְדִכְוָותָהּ. שָׁחַט וְזָרַק וְהֶעֱלָה אֵינוֹ חַייָב אֶלָּא אַחַת. לְפוּם כָּךְ צָרַךְ מֵימַר. חַייָב עַל־כָּל־אַחַת וְאַחַת.

If He stated a general principle as a positive commandment but the detail as a prohibition, the word of Rebbi Eleazar is that this is a general principle followed by a detail[198]. [199]Rebbi Eleazar said, one whips for ploughing in the Sabbatical year. Rebbi Johanan said, one does not whip for ploughing in the Sabbatical year. What is Rebbi Eleazar's reason? *The Land shall keep a Sabbath for the Eternal*[200], a general principle. *Your field you shall not sow, your vineyard you shall not prune*[201], detail. Sowing and pruning were included in the general case; why were they mentioned separately? To include with them; since sowing and pruning are particular in that they perform work on the soil or on a tree, I have only what is work on the soil or on a tree. How does Rebbi Johanan treat this? They are two different things, and two different details for one general principle do divide. In Rebbi Eleazar's opinion do they not divide[202]? He holds that because they do not divide, they are for making inferences. In Rebbi Johanan's opinion, are they not for making inferences? There is a difference here because He stated a general principle as a positive commandment but the detail as prohibitions. No positive commandment allows inferences for a prohibition and no prohibition allows inferences for a positive commandment. Rebbi Eleazar said, a positive commandment allows inferences for a prohibition but no prohibition allows inferences for a positive commandment. In Rebbi Johanan's opinion it is obvious that one may dig cisterns, ditches, and caves during it[202*]. In Rebbi Eleazar's opinion, may one dig cisterns, ditches, and caves during it[202*]? Just as one cannot make inferences for prohibitions, so one should not be able to make inferences for permissions[203]. Rebbi Abba from Carthage said, Rebbi Johanan's reason is *six years you shall sow*, not in the Sabbatical; *and six years you shall prune your vineyard*[204], not in the Sabbatical at all. Any prohibition inferred from a positive commandment is a positive commandment; one violates a positive commandment[205]. Rebbi Yose said, there is not even a positive commandment[206]. Rebbi Jeremiah said, one violates a positive commandment. Why is it written that *the Land shall keep a Sabbath for the Eternal*[200]? That is for the prohibition implied by it[207].

I could think that they should be giving lashes for the addition[208]. Rebbi Johanan explains the *baraita*: I could think that one gives lashes for ploughing during the Sabbatical year, but Rebbi Eleazar explains the *baraita*: I could think that one gives lashes for the first two terms[209]. Some Tannaïm state: *Six years you shall sow your field, and six years you shall prune your vineyard*; but some Tannaïm state: *Your field you shall not sow*, etc. He who says *six years* supports Rebbi Johanan; he who says *your field you shall not sow* supports Rebbi Eleazar[210].

A *baraita* disagrees with Rebbi Eleazar: [211]*Beware of*, a prohibition. *Lest*, a prohibition[212]. And it is written[213]: *There, you shall offer your elevation offerings and there you shall make*. *There, you shall offer*, that is the offering; *and there you shall make*, that is slaughtering and sprinkling. Just as offering is a positive commandment and a prohibition[214], so slaughtering and sprinkling which are positive commandments should be covered by a prohibition. Because it is written *there you shall offer, and there you shall make*. Therefore, if *there you shall offer, and there you shall make* were not written, no positive commandment would allow inferences for a prohibition and no prohibition would allow inferences for a positive commandment[215]. How does Rebbi Johanan handle this? That you should not say as you say referring to the Sabbath: If one dug a hole, made a ditch, or dug to put in a pole, he is guilty only of one offense[216]. Similarly, if he slaughtered and offered, he should be guilty only of one offense; therefore, it was necessary to say, he is liable for every single action[217].

198 If a pentateuchal verse partially is an exhortation to action and partially a prohibition, it nevertheless forms a logical unit.

199 From here to the end of the discussion there exists a parallel in *Kilaim* 8:1, Notes 20-36 (Babli *Mo`ed qatan* 3a). The punishment for violating a biblical prohibition for which no penalty is specified is by flogging. The problem is that ploughing is not specifically mentioned in *Lev.* 25.

200 *Lev.* 25:2.

201 *Lev.* 25:4.

202 To require separate atonement if performed inadvertently.

202* During the Sabbatical year.

203 For R. Johanan, if ploughing is not sanctionable, digging for other than agricultural purposes certainly is permitted. But for R. Eleazar digging is work on the soil (in the language of his argument) but not in the field (as forbidden in the verse.)

204 *Lev.* 25:3.

205 As such it is not sanctionable; cf. *Sanhedrin* 5:3, Note 73.

206 He takes R. Eleazar literally at his word. If *Lev.* 25:3-4 represents a general principle followed by a detail (even if the principle is a positive commandment and the detail a prohibition) then by R. Ismael's rule כְּלָל וּפְרָט אֵין בִּכְלָל אֶלָּא מַה שֶׁבִּפְרָט "general principle followed by detail: the general principle only applies to the detail", nothing not mentioned in the verse is prohibited.

Since R. Yose was R. Jeremiah's student, he should be mentioned after his teacher (which he is both in *Sanhedrin* and *Kilaim*.)

207 This refers to R. Yose's opinion, that sowing and pruning are forbidden in the Sabbatical but these and all other agricultural work are violations of the positive commandment to give rest to the Land.

208 The prohibition of agricultural work after the harvest of the preceding year, different for work on the soil or on trees. This has nothing to do with the rules of the Sabbath or with general principles of hermeneutics; it is from *Kilaim* 8:1, Notes 26-28.

209 Rabbinic prohibitions to prepare fields or prune trees after harvest in the year before the Sabbatical. The time tables are different for different kinds of work; Mishnah *Ševi`it* 1:1,2:1.

210 As explained in the preceding paragraph.

211 *Sifry* 70. Babli, *Zebahim* 106a.

212 This is a principle accepted in both Talmudim. A verse stating "beware of" or "lest" does not need an explicit "do not" in order to be classified as a prohibition.

213 *Deut.* 12:13-14: <u>Beware, and do not offer your elevation sacrifices at any place you see. Only at the place which the Eternal will choose . . . there you shall offer your elevation sacrifices and there you shall do everything which I am commanding you.</u> This is a general prohibition followed by two specific positive commandments. The two verses are parallel, not logically consecutive as R. Eleazar would require.

214 A positive commandment to be performed at the Chosen Place and a prohibition everywhere else.

215 As maintained by R. Johanan.

216 The activities quoted here are all derivatives of ploughing (Babli 73b).

217 In the Babli, *Zebahim* 107b, according to one opinion this is R. Ismael's position.

(9d line 60) כָּל־הֵן דְּתַנִּינָן אָבוֹת יֵשׁ לָהֶן תּוֹלָדוֹת. תַּמָּן תַּנִּינָן. אַרְבַּע אָבוֹת נְזִיקִין. הַשּׁוֹר. זֶה הַקֶּרֶן. נְגִיחָה וּדְחִיפָה אָב. תַּנֵּי רִבִּי חִיָּיה. נָשַׁךְ רָבַץ בָּעַט תּוֹלָדוֹת לַקֶּרֶן. תַּמָּן תַּנִּינָן. אֲבוֹת הַטּוּמְאָה הַשֶּׁרֶץ וְשִׁכְבַת זֶרַע. תּוֹלְדוֹת הַשֶּׁרֶץ אֵי זֶהוּ. רִבִּי יוּדָה בְּשֵׁם רִבִּי נָחוּם. מַדָּפוֹת. מָהוּ מַדָּפוֹת. מַגָּעוֹת. אַב הַטּוּמְאָה מְטַמֵּא אֶת הַכֹּל. וּלְוַד הַטּוּמְאָה אֵינוֹ מְטַמֵּא אֶלָּא אוֹכְלִין וּמַשְׁקִין וּכְלֵי חֶרֶשׂ. אוֹכְלִין וּמַשְׁקִין וּכְלֵי אֵינָן נַעֲשִׂין אַב הַטּוּמְאָה לְטַמֵּא. זִיבָה. וְהָכָא תַּנִּינָן. אֲבוֹת מְלָאכוֹת אַרְבָּעִים חָסֵר אַחַת. חֲרִישָׁה אָב. תַּנֵּי רִבִּי חִיָּיה. חָפַר חָרַץ נָעַץ תּוֹלְדוֹת לַחֲרִישָׁה.

Anywhere one stated categories there are derivatives. There, we have stated[218]: "There are four categories of damages. The ox", this is the horn. Goring and pushing are main categories. Rebbi Hiyya stated: If it bit, lay down, kicked, these are derivatives of the horn. There, we have stated[219]: "The categories of impurity, the crawling animal and semen." What are derivatives of crawling animals? Rebbi Jehudah in the name of Rebbi Nahum: pushings. What are pushings? Touching[220]. The main category of impurity makes everything impure, derivative impurity transmits impurity only to food and drink, or clay vessels[221]. Food and drink and [clay][222] vessels cannot become main categories of impurity to transmit impurity[223]. Gonorrhea. And here, we have stated: "The categories of work are 39." Ploughing is a category. Rebbi Hiyya stated: If one dug a hole, made a ditch, or dug to put in a pole, these are derivatives of ploughing[216].

218 Mishnah *Bava qamma* 1:1.

219 Mishnah *Kelim* 1:1.

220 Both in *Šabbat* and *Bava qamma* categories are labels of sets of derivatives. But in *Kelim*, treating of impurity, derivative impurity is less infectuous than original impurity, and there are successive states of derivative impurity. The nature of אָב in impurity really is not comparable to the nature of אָב in the other two cases.

221 This is not an exhaustive list and does not take into account that different implements may be subject to impurities in different degrees depending on the kind of original impurity in question. In general, metal vessels may become impure by touch from derivative impurities but not clay vessels (Mishnah *Zavim* 5:1); all food and drinks may become impure by derivative impurities of the first degree. Babli *Bava qamma* 2b.

222 Missing in the text but indicated by the construct state of the word כְּלִי.

223 This statement requires that מַשְׁקִין be translated as "drinks". The same word may also mean "fluids", but human body fluids may be sources of original impurity and the water used for the ashes of the Red Cow may become the source of original impurity.

(9d line 68) כָּל־אֲבוֹת מְלָאכוֹת מִן הַמִּשְׁכָּן לָמָדוּ. מַה חֲרִישָׁה הָיְתָה בַּמִּשְׁכָּן. שֶׁהָיוּ חוֹרְשִׁין לִיטַּע סַמְמָנִין. כַּמָּה יַחֲרוֹשׁ וִיהֵא חַיָּיב. רִבִּי מַתַּנְיָה אָמַר. כְּדֵי לִיטַּע כְּרִישָׁה. רִבִּי אֲחָא בַּר רַב. כְּדֵי לִיטַּע זְכרוּתָהּ שֶׁל חִיטָה. תַּמָּן תַּנֵּינָן. זֶרַע קִשּׁוּאִין שְׁנַיִם חַיָּיב. זֶרַע דִילוּעִים שְׁנָיִם. זֶרַע פּוֹל מִצְרִי שְׁנַיִם. תַּנֵּי. חִטִּים מָדִיּוֹת שְׁתַּיִם. רִבִּי שְׁמוּאֵל בְּשֵׁם רִבִּי זְעִירָא. חִיטִּין עַל יְדֵי שֶׁהֵן חֲבִיבוֹת עָשׂוּ אוֹתָן כִּשְׁאָר זִירְעוֹנֵי גִינָה שֶׁאֵינָן נֶאֱכָלִין. וְכָל־דָּבָר שֶׁהוּא לַהֲנָיַית קַרְקַע חַיָּיב מִשּׁוּם חוֹרֵשׁ. הַחוֹפֵר. הֶחָוֹרֵץ. הַנּוֹעֵץ. הַמְדַיֵּיר. הַמְעַדֵּר. הַמְזַבֵּל. הַמְכַבֵּד. הַמְרַבֵּץ. הַמְפַעְפֵּעַ גּוּשִׁים. הַמַּבְרֶה בֶחֳרָשִׁים. הַמַּצִּית אֶת הָאוּר בַּחֲרִישַׁת קָנִים וּבְאגַם תְּמָרִים. וּכְרִבִּי זְעִירָא אַמַּת הַמַּיִם שֶׁהִיא מַכְשֶׁרֶת צְדָדֶיהָ לִזְרִיעָה. הַמְסַקֵּל. הַבּוֹנֶה מַדְרֵיגוּת. הַמְמַלֵּא אֶת הַנְּקָעִים שֶׁתַּחַת הַזֵּיתִים. וְהָעוֹשֶׂה עוּגִיּוֹת לַגְּפָנִים. וְכָל־דָּבָר שֶׁהוּא לַהֲנָיַית קַרְקַע חַיָּיב מִשּׁוּם חוֹרֵשׁ.

All categories of work they learned from the Tabernacle[4]. What kind of ploughing was in the Tabernacle? They ploughed to plant dyestuff[224]. How much does one have to plough to become liable? Rebbi Mattaniah said, enough to plant a leek. Rebbi Aha bar Rav said, enough to plant a wheat sprout. There[225], we have stated: "Two green melon[226] seeds make liable, two squash seeds, two Egyptian bean seeds." It was stated, two Median wheat kernels. Rebbi Samuel in the name of Rebbi Ze'ira: Since wheat was so much appreciated they treated it like garden vegetables that are not eaten[225]. For everything which improves the soil one is liable[227] because of ploughing: One who digs[228], who cuts[229], who inserts[230], who deposits dung[231], who hoes, who fertilizes, who sweeps[232], who sprinkles[232], who splits blocks[233], who clears forests, who sets fire to reed thickets[234] or palm swamps, and following Rebbi Ze'ira a water canal prepares its banks for sowing[235], who removes stones[236], who builds terraces[237], who fills the rifts under olive trees, and who makes depressions for vines[238], and for anything which improves the soil one is liable because of ploughing.

224 To dye threads used to weave the gobelins of the Tabernacle and the priest's garments.

225 Mishnah 9:7. The Mishnah details minimal amounts which create liability if carried from private to public domain. Even though in general food requires a minimal amount of the volume of a dried fig, seeds of garden vegetables create liability in smaller amounts. Palestinian dried figs are rather small (Mishnah *Kelim* 17:7).

226 This is Maimonides's determination, cf. *Kilaim* 1:2 Note 38. In modern Hebrew the word means "zucchini".

227 According to the Babli, 103a, the liability is triggered by the most minute amount of work, contradicting the opinions in the Yerushalmi earlier in this paragraph.

228 A cistern or other storage facility.
229 A ditch (for irrigation or drainage).
230 A spike or log in the ground, for making a fence.
231 Leads his animal onto the property so they should fertilize it by their droppings.
232 A dirt floor. As *Or zarua' Šabbat* §55 notes, this disagrees with the Babli which restricts the category of ploughing to land which may be used for agriculture.
233 A block of earth which must be broken up before it can be sown.
234 Also for clearing for agriculture.
235 Since the banks are watered automatically. Babli *Mo'ed qatan* 2b in the name of Rabba (Abba bar Nahmani, contemporary of R. Ze'ira).
236 To turn barren land into an agriculturally usable area.
237 On hill slopes.
238 For watering the individual vines.

(10a line 4) רִבִּי חִיָּיה בְּשֵׁם רִבִּי יוֹחָנָן. הַמְבַשֵּׁל נְבֵילָה בְּיוֹם טוֹב אֵינוֹ לוֹקֶה. שֶׁהוּתַּר מִכְּלַל בִּישׁוּל בְּיוֹם טוֹב. רִבִּי שִׁמְעוֹן בֶּן לָקִישׁ אָמַר. לוֹקֶה. שֶׁלֹּא הוּתַּר מִכְּלָל בִּישׁוּל אֶלָּא לַאֲכִילָה בִּלְבָד. הֵתִיב רִבִּי בָּא בַּר מָמָל עַל דְּרִבִּי יוֹחָנָן. מֵעַתָּה הַחוֹרֵשׁ בְּיוֹם טוֹב אֵינוֹ לוֹקֶה. שֶׁהוּתַּר מִכְּלַל חֲרִישָׁה בְּיוֹם טוֹב. רִבִּי יוֹסֵה בְּשֵׁם רִבִּי אִילָא. לֹא הוּתְרָה חֲרִישָׁה כְּדַרְכָּהּ. רִבִּי שַׁמַּי אָמַר קוֹמֵי רִבִּי יֹסֵה רִבִּי אָחָא בְּשֵׁם רִבִּי אִילָא. דְּרִבִּי שִׁמְעוֹן הִיא. דְּרִבִּי שִׁמְעוֹן אָמַר. עַד שֶׁיְּהֵא לוֹ צוֹרֶךְ בְּגוּפוֹ שֶׁלַּדָּבָר. קָם רִבִּי יֹסֵה עִם רִבִּי אָחָא. אָמַר לֵיהּ. אַתְּ אֲמַרְתְּ דָּא מִילְתָא. וְלֹא כֵן אָמַר רִבִּי יוֹחָנָן. דִּבְרֵי רִבִּי מֵאִיר. עֶשְׂרִים וְאַרְבָּעָה דְבָרִים מְקוּלֵּי בֵית שַׁמַּי וּמְחוּמְרֵי בֵית הִלֵּל. וְזֶה חַד מֵהֶם. נֵימַר כְּ"ג. אֶלָּא רִבִּי מֵאִיר וְרִבִּי שִׁמְעוֹן שְׁנֵיהֶן אָמְרוּ דָּבָר אֶחָד. וְלָכֵן סַבְרִינוּ מֵימַר. רִבִּי יוֹסֵי וְרִבִּי שִׁמְעוֹן שְׁנֵיהֶן אָמְרוּ דָּבָר אֶחָד. נֵימַר. רִבִּי מֵאִיר וְרִבִּי יוֹסֵי וְרִבִּי שִׁמְעוֹן שְׁלָשְׁתָּן אָמְרוּ דָּבָר אֶחָד. אֶלָּא מֵילִין דְּצְרִיכִין לְרַבָּנָן פְּשִׁיטִין לְכוֹן. פְּשִׁיטִין לְרַבָּנָן. קָצַר לְצוֹרֶךְ עֲשָׂבִים חַייָב מִשּׁוּם קוֹצֵר וְאֵינוֹ חַייָב מִשּׁוּם מְיַיפֶּה אֶת הַקַּרְקַע. לֹא צוֹרְכָה דְּלֹא קָצַר לְיָיפוֹת אֶת הַקַּרְקַע. מַהוּ שֶׁיְּהֵא חַייָב מִשּׁוּם קוֹצֵר וּמִשּׁוּם מְיַיפֶּה אֶת הַקַּרְקַע. וַאֲפִילוּ תֵימַר דְּרִבִּי שִׁמְעוֹן הוּא. בְּרַם כְּרַבָּנָן מִכָּל־מָקוֹם הֲרֵי תָרַשׁ. מִכָּל־מָקוֹם הֲרֵי קָצַר. אָמַר רִבִּי מָנָא. מִילֵּיהוֹן דְּרַבָּנָן מְסַייְעִין לְרִבִּי יוֹסֵי. דָּמַר רִבִּי חִיָּיה בְּשֵׁם רִבִּי יוֹחָנָן. דָּג שֶׁסְּחָטוֹ. אִם לְגוּפוֹ הֲרֵי זֶה פָטוּר. אִם לְהוֹצִיא צִיר חַייָב. וַאֲפִילוּ תֵימַר דְּרִבִּי שִׁמְעוֹן הִיא דָמַר. בְּרַם כְּרַבָּנָן מִכָּל־מָקוֹם הֲרֵי סָחַט. מִכָּל־מָקוֹם הֲרֵי הוֹצִיא צִיר.

5 יסה | י יוסה   6 יוסה | י יוסי   את אמרת | י אתה אמרתה   דא | י הדא   ולא | י לא   8 חד | י אחד נימר כ"ג | י נאמר עשרים ושלשה ולכן | י לא כן   9 יוסי | י יוסה (2)   10 שלשתן | י שלשתם דצריכין | י דצריכן פשיטין | י פשיטן (2)   לרבנן | י לרבנן צריכן לכון   11 משום | י משום שהוא דלא | י דילא   12 משום | י משום שהוא   13 הוא | י היא   מכל | י ומכל   14 מסייעין | י מסייען   יוסי | י יוסי רבי   דמר | י דאמ' הרי זה | י -   15 חייב | י הרי זה חייב   דמר | י -   16 מכל | י ומכל

[239]Rebbi Hiyya in the name of Rebbi Johanan: He who cooks carcass meat on a holiday is not flogged, because the category of cooking is permitted on a holiday[240]. Rebbi Simeon ben Laqish said, he is flogged, for the category of cooking is permitted only for food[241]. Rebbi Abba bar Mamal objected to this

[statement] by Rebbi Johanan. Then one who ploughs on a holiday should not be flogged since actions of the category of ploughing are permitted on a holiday[242]. Rebbi Yose in the name of Rebbi Ila: ordinary ploughing was not permitted[243]. Rebbi Shammai said before Rebbi Yose: Rebbi Aha in the name of Rebbi Ila, this[244] is Rebbi Simeon's, for Rebbi Simeon said, only if he needs the essence of the matter[245]. Rebbi Yose met Rebbi Aha. He said to him, did you say this? But did not Rebbi Johanan say, the words of Rebbi Meïr are that in 24 matters the House of Shammai are lenient and the House of Hillel restrictive, and this is one of them. Should we say 23[246]? But Rebbi Meïr and Rebbi Simeon both said the same[247]. But were we not of the opinion that Rebbi Yose and Rebbi Simeon both said the same[248]? Should we say, Rebbi Meïr, Rebbi Yose, and Rebbi Simeon all three said the same[249]? But matters which are problematic for the rabbis are obvious for you; are those which are obvious for the rabbis [problematic for you][250]? If one harvested for grasses[251] he is liable for harvesting but is not liable for improving the soil. There is only the problem if he harvested in order to improve the soil. Is he liable for harvesting and for improving the soil? Even if you say it follows Rebbi Simeon, but for the rabbis in any case he ploughed, in any case he harvested[252]. Rebbi Mana said, the words of the rabbis support Rebbi Yose, for Rebbi Hiyya said in the name of Rebbi Johanan, if one compressed a fish[253], if for its body he is not liable, but if to produce fish sauce he is liable. Even if you say that he said this following Rebbi Simeon, but for the rabbis in any case he compressed, in any case he produced fish sauce[254].

239 This paragraph also is in *Besah* 1:3; its main subject are the rules of the holiday. However, since Mishnah *Megillah* 1:8 states that the only difference between the rules for Sabbath and for holidays is that preparation of food is permitted on holidays, the discussion is relevant also for the rules of the Sabbath.

240 It is presumed that carcass meat, which is forbidden as human food, is not prepared as animal feed. For R. Johanan (Babli *Besah* 12b) since making fire and cooking is permitted for preparing food on the holiday (*Ex.* 12:16) it is permitted for any purpose.

241 He disputes that cooking be permitted for anything that is not food.

242 This refers to Mishnah *Besah* 1:2. Since preparation of food is permitted on a holiday, it is permitted to slaughter for food. If a bird or a wild animal is slaughtered, its blood has to be covered by dust (*Lev.* 18:13). If no dust is available, the House of

Shammai permit to take a prong and dig up some dust; the House of Hillel hold that in this case one should not slaughter but they agree that if one slaughtered one may take a prong and dig. Digging is a derivative of ploughing as noted in the preceding paragraph.

243 Since no spade is authorized, the work is not professional and, since the intent is not to prepare the soil for agriculture, the prohibition is rabbinical; the Houses of Shammai and Hillel do not disagree about the interpretation of a biblical commandment.

244 Both the Houses of Shammai and of Hillel do permit to use a spade; they must hold that the intent determines liability.

245 There is liability only if the prohibited action is the object of his intent, not a by-product. Cf. Chapter 2, Note 19.

246 Since in this interpretation both Houses agree that the digging does not create liability and the biblical commandment to cover the blood overrides the rabbinic "fence around the law".

247 Mishnah *Besah* 1:2 is anonymous and therefore presumed to be R. Meïr's. If it implies the position of R. Simeon then both must agree in this matter. The opponent of R. Simeon in this matter is Rebbi Jehudah, student of his father R. Ilai, who was a student of the Shammaite R. Eliezer. It is intrinsically unlikely that the House of Shammai should accept what later was formulated by R. Simeon.

248 Chapter 2, Note 19. Babli 31b.

249 Then we should hold that this is their (direct or indirect) teacher R. Aqiba's position and it is difficult to fathom who would disagree; but we see that this opinion is not generally accepted in tannaitic sources.

250 The words in brackets are added from the text in *Besah*. "Everybody else questions whether R. Meïr agrees with R. Simeon while you assert this. Then you will have to question what in the sequel is stated as the rabbi's opinion." S. Liebermann refers to this sentence the remark of *Or zarua῾ Šabbat* 55, that he suspects this Yerushalmi paragraph to contain a scribal error.

251 He was weeding and using the uprooted weeds as fodder. This is forbidden on a holiday as it is forbidden on the Sabbath, but since there is a question of multiple liabilities the reference is to the Sabbath.

252 In the Babli, these rabbis are identified with R. Jehudah.

253 A pickled herring which may be eaten cold on the Sabbath. Babli 145a.

254 This is all one liability; since he compressed the fish he produced fish sauce and is liable. The Babli holds that R. Simeon agrees that in this case there is liability; technically this is called פְּסִיק רֵישָׁא "cut off the head". The image is that of a murderer who claims that he never intended to kill his victim, only to cut off his head. Since death is an automatic consequence of cutting off the head, he is guilty of murder. Similarly in the Babli, R. Simeon agrees that an automatic consequence of an intended action is included in the intended action; the Yerushalmi disagrees (and, therefore, does not declare that R. Simeon defines practice.)

(10a line 24) כָּל־דָּבָר שֶׁהָיָה מַבְחִיל אֶת הַפֵּירִי חַיָּב מִשּׁוּם זוֹרֵעַ. הַנּוֹטֵעַ. הַמַּבְרִיךְ. הַמַּרְכִּיב. הַמְקַרְסֵם. הַמְזָרֵד. הַמְפַסֵּל. הַמְזַהֵם. הַמְפָרֵק. הַמְאַבֵּק. הַמְעַשֵּׁן. הַמְתַלֵּעַ. הַקּוֹטֵם. הַסָּךְ. וְהַמַּשְׁקֶה. וְהַמְנַקֵּב. וְהָעוֹשֶׂה בָתִּים. וְכָל־דָּבָר שֶׁהוּא לְהַבְחִיל אֶת הַפֵּירִי חַיָּב מִשּׁוּם זוֹרֵעַ.

זְעוּרָא רַב חִייָה בַּר אַשִׁי בְשֵׁם כָּהֲנָא. הַנּוֹטֵעַ בַּשַּׁבָּת חַיָּב מִשּׁוּם זוֹרֵעַ. רִבִּי זְעוּרָא אָמַר. הַזּוֹמֵר כְּנוֹטֵעַ. נָטַע וְזָמַר בַּשַּׁבָּת. עַל דַּעְתֵּיהּ דְּכָהֲנָא חַיָּב שְׁתַּיִם. עַל דַּעְתֵּיהּ דְּרִבִּי זְעוּרָא אֵינוֹ חַיָּב אֶלָּא אַחַת. כְּלוּם אָמַר רִבִּי זְעוּרָא לֹא הַזּוֹמֵר כְּנוֹטֵעַ. וְלָמָּה הַנּוֹטֵעַ כְּזוֹמֵר. הַכֹּל הָיָה בִכְלַל זְרִיעָה. וְיָצְאָה זְמִירָה לְהַחֲמִיר עַל עַצְמָהּ. מִפְּנֵי שֶׁיָּצָאת זְמִירָה לְהַחֲמִיר עַל עַצְמָהּ אַתְּ פּוֹטְרוֹ מִשֵּׁם זוֹרֵעַ. הֱוֵי. לֹא שַׁנְיָיא. נָטַע וְזָמַר בַּשַּׁבָּת בֵּין עַל דַּעְתֵּיהּ דְּרַב כָּהֲנָא בֵּין עַל דַּעְתֵּיהּ דְּרִבִּי זְעִירָא. חַיָּב שְׁתַּיִם.

1 זעורא | כ ר' זעירא נ ר' זעירה חייה | כ חייא   זעירא | כ זעירא נ זעורה   2 הזומר | נ זומר   זעורא | כ זעירא נ זעורה   3 זעירא | נ זעורה   לא | כנ אלא   הזומר | נ זומר   ולמה | כ שמא נ דילמא   הנוטע | נ נוטע   4 ויצאה | כ יצאת נ ויצאת   5 רב כהנא | כנ דכהנא   6 זעירא | נ זעורה

For any activity which quickens a fruit to ripen one is liable because of sowing. One who plants, who sinks[255], who grafts, who prunes, who trains[256], who removes dead branches, who dirties[257], who removes leaves, who dusts[258], who smokes[259], who removes worms, who sprinkles with ashes[258], who oils, who waters, who drills holes[260], who makes houses[261], and for anything which quickens a fruit to ripen one is liable because of sowing.

[262][Rebbi][263] Ze`ira, Rav Hiyya bar Ashi in the name of Cahana[264]: He who is planting on the Sabbath is guilty because of sowing. Rebbi Ze`ira said, he who prunes is like one who plants. If he planted and pruned on the Sabbath, according to Cahana he is guilty on two counts[265], according to Rebbi Ze`ira only on one count. Did not Rebbi Ze`ira say the pruner is like the planter, did he say perhaps the planter is like the pruner[266]? All was included in the category of sowing; pruning was singled out for particular stringency[267]. Because pruning was singled out for particular stringency you want to exempt it because of sowing? This means, there is no difference. If he planted and pruned on the Sabbath, according to both Cahana and Rebbi Ze`ira he is guilty on two counts.

255 He takes a branch of a vine, bends it down into a ditch, covers the ditch with earth, and lets it come out again. Then the branch will grow roots in the earth and one has a new vine.

256 He binds the branches to an espalier.
257 In modern terms, applying pesticide (Mishnah *Ševi`it* 2:4).
258 This also is a way to combat insect infestations.

259 Either to smoke out worms and insects or to protect against cold spells.

260 Punctures unripe sycamore figs to let them ripen for human consumption.

261 No convincing explanation is available for this expression.

262 This paragraph is also on *Kilaim* 8:1 (Notes 32-36, כ) and *Sanhedrin* 7:5 (Note 125, נ).

263 Added from the parallel sources.

264 Since Hiyya bar Ashi was among the older students of Rav, Cahana mentioned here must be an older Sage (Cahana I) who already was a recognized authority when Rav returned from Galilee to Babylonia.

265 In the interpretation of the Babli, 73b, and *Mo`ed qatan* 2b, this refers to the case where he prunes with the intent of using the cut branches as wood; then he is simultaneously harvesting and sowing.

266 Pruning is a subcategory of sowing concerning the Sabbath just as planting is, but planting is not like pruning for the Sabbatical year since planting belongs to sowing and pruning was mentioned separately in the verse, *Lev.* 25:3.

267 Following the argument made for the Sabbath, it would not have been necessary to have pruning singled out in the laws of the Sabbatical. Since it is obvious that for the Sabbatical, pruning is a separate offense, pruning can be a subcategory of sowing for the Sabbath only as a stringency, not a leniency.

(10a line 34) וְהַקּוֹצֵר. תַּנֵּי רִבִּי חִיָּיא. הַקּוֹצֵר. הַבּוֹצֵר. הַמּוֹסֵק. הַגּוֹדֵד. הַתּוֹלֵשׁ. וְהָאוֹרֶה. כּוּלְּהוֹן מִשּׁוּם קוֹצֵר. הָהֵן דְּגָזַז סְפוֹג גּוּמֵי קוֹרוֹלִין. חַיָּיב מִשּׁוּם קוֹצֵר וּמִשּׁוּם נוֹטֵעַ. הָהֵן דְּגָזַז כּוּסְבָּר כָּרָתִין כַּרְפָּס גַּרְגֵּר טְרִיקְסִימוֹן בְּשׁוּמִין נַעֲנַע חַיָּיב מִשּׁוּם קוֹצֵר וּמִשּׁוּם זוֹרֵעַ. רִבִּי יוֹסֵי בֵּירִבִּי בּוּן בְּשֵׁם רִבִּי שִׁמְעוֹן בֶּן לָקִישׁ. הַנּוֹתֵן עָצִיץ נָקוּב עַל גַּבֵּי עָצִיץ נָקוּב חַיָּיב עָלָיו מִשּׁוּם קוֹצֵר וּמִשּׁוּם זוֹרֵעַ. רִבִּי יוֹסֵי בֵּירִבִּי בּוּן בְּשֵׁם רִבִּי שִׁמְעוֹן בֶּן לָקִישׁ. הַקּוֹצֵץ קוֹרַת שִׁקְמָה חַיָּיב עָלֶיהָ מִשֵּׁם שָׁלֹשׁ. אָמַר רִבִּי יוֹסֵי בֵּירִבִּי בּוּן. וְלָא פְּלִיגִין. הַקּוֹצְצָהּ חַיָּיב מִשּׁוּם קוֹצֵר וּמִשּׁוּם זוֹרֵעַ. הַמּוֹחִקָהּ חַיָּיב מִשּׁוּם מַכֶּה בְפַטִּישׁ. רַבָּנָן דְּקַיְסָרִין אָמְרִין. הָהֵן דְּצַיֵּיד כַּוְורָא וְכָל־דָּבָר שֶׁאַתָּה מַבְדִּילוֹ מֵחִיּוּתוֹ חַיָּיב מִשּׁוּם קוֹצֵר.

"And who harvests." Rebbi Ḥiyya stated[110]: "One who cuts grain, harvests grapes, harvests olives, cuts tree branches, tears out, plucks fruits, are all because of harvesting.[111]" One who cuts sponge[265], papyrus, or corals[266] is liable for harvesting and planting[267]. One who cuts coriander, leeks, celery, rocket[268], endives[269], sesame[270], mint, is liable for harvesting and sowing[271]. Rebbi Yose ben Rebbi Abun in the name of Rebbi Simeon ben Laqish, one who puts a flowerpot with a hole on a flowerpot with a hole is liable for harvesting and sowing[272]. Rebbi Yose ben Rebbi Abun in the name of Rebbi Simeon ben Laqish, one who cuts down the stem of a sycamore is liable three for it[273]. Rebbi Yose ben Rebbi Abun said, they[274] do not disagree. One who cuts it is liable for harvesting and for sowing. One who planes²⁷⁵ it is liable for hitting with a hammer⁷. The rabbis of Caesarea say, one who catches a fish or anything by which he separates it from the environment it needs to live is liable because of harvesting²⁷⁶.

265 Greek σπόγγος, ὁ.

266 Greek κοράλλιον, τό.

267 Since they will regrow, cutting some off makes room for new growth. For these species, planting is the appropriate word.

268 Accadic *gergirū, eruca sativa.*

269 Greek τρώξιμος, -ον, "edible"; τά τρώξιμα "vegetables eaten raw", in rabbinic sources traditionally used for endives.

270 With the quote in *Arukh*, reading כשומין.

271 For garden vegetables, "sowing" is the appropriate word. The reason is the same as in the preceding case, Note 267.

272 If something grows in a flowerpot with a hole in the bottom through which the soil absorbs moisture, removing the pot from the soil amounts to harvesting. Putting it down again, even on an empty flowerpot with a hole in the bottom, enables moisture to be absorbed again and amounts to sowing.

273 Sycamores grow again when cut down. Therefore cutting on the Sabbath is both harvesting and planting. The third offense is not connected with the cutting; Note 275.

274 The two statements in the name of R. Simeon ben Laqish are consistent with one another.

275 This turns a tree into building material.

276 The action which qualifies as harvesting is removing the fish from the water. This applies also to fish already caught but kept in water.

(10a line 44) וְהַמְעַמֵּר. רִבִּי שְׁמוּאֵל בַּר סָסַרְטַאי בָּעֵי. תּוֹלְדוֹת הָעֵימוּר אֵי זוֹ הִיא. רִבִּי יוֹסֵי. שְׁמָעִית מִן דְּרִבִּי שִׁמְעוֹן בְּשֵׁם רִבִּי אָחָא. וְלֵית אֲנָא יָדַע מַה שְׁמָעֵת. מַיֵּי כְדוֹן. הָהֵן דְּכָתֵית אוֹרֶז שְׂעָרִין חֲלִיקָה חַיָּיב מִשּׁוּם דָּשׁ. הָהֵן דְּשָׁטַח צָלִין צִימּוּקִין מְסוּסְלָה בּוּקְלָטָה חַיָּיב מִשּׁוּם מְעַמֵּר. כָּל־שֶׁהוּא נוֹגֵעַ בָּאוֹכָל חַיָּיב מִשּׁוּם מְעַמֵּר. בַּקְּלִיפָּה מִשֵּׁם דָּשׁ.

"He who binds into sheaves." Rebbi Samuel bar Sosartai asked, what are the derivatives of binding into sheaves? Rebbi Yose: I heard the reason following Rebbi Simeon²⁷⁷ from Rebbi Aha, but I do not remember what I heard. What about it? One who pounds²⁷⁸ rice²⁷⁹, barley, groats²⁸⁰, is liable because of threshing. He who spreads out *ṣeli* figs²⁸¹, raisins, ²⁸²מסוסלה, *bucellata*²⁸³, is liable because of binding into sheaves. For anything involving food one is liable because of binding into sheaves, involving shells because of threshing²⁸⁴.

277 R. Simeon ben Laqish who earlier was reported to have established derivatives for all categories mentioned in the Mishnah.
278 To separate the grain from the shell.
279 Greel ὄρυζα, ἡ.
280 Latin *alica, -ae*.
281 He is spreading out fruit or food to dry. The translation of צלין as "figs for drying" is tentative, cf. *Peah* 7:4 Note 86.
282 This word is totally unexplained. Brüll in his review of Levy's Dictionary proposes to read מטוטלה "bunch (of berries)", but the word should denote a definite kind of fruit (or meat?) put out to dry in the sun.
283 A kind of bread consisting only of crust; cf. *Hallah* 1:6 Note 182. Italian *buccella* "bread crust".
284 For consistency, probably one should read the sentence about threshing after the one about binding into sheaves.

(10a line 49) הָדָא אִיתָּתָא כַּד מְעָרְבָא בְחִיטַיָּא. מִשֵּׁם מְרַקְּדָה. כַּד מַפְרְכַיָּא בְרָאשַׁיָּא. מִשֵּׁם דָּשָׁה. כַּד מַתְבְּרָא בְּצְדָדַיָּא. מִשֵּׁם בּוֹרֶרֶת. כַּד מְסַפְּיָא. מִשֵּׁם טוֹחֶנֶת. כַּד מְנַפְּיָא. מִשֵּׁם זוֹרָה. גָּמְרָה מְלַאכְתָּהּ. מִשֵּׁם מַכָּה בְפַטִּישׁ.

הָהֵן כִּיתָנַיָּא בְקוֹפָנָה. מִשֵּׁם דָּשׁ. בְּמַעֲרוֹבָה. בְּאַפְסְטִיתָא. מִשֵּׁם זוֹרָה. בְּכַף. מִשּׁוּם בּוֹרֵר. כַּד מְפַלֵּג. מִשֵּׁם מְנַפֵּס. כַּד מְתַלֵּשׁ. מִשֵּׁם מְחַתֵּךְ. גָּמַר מְלַאכְתּוֹ. מִשֵּׁם מַכָּה בְפַטִּישׁ.

הָהֵן דְּשָׁחַק תּוּמָא. כַּד מְפָרֵךְ בְּרֵישַׁיָּא. מִשּׁוּם דָּשׁ. כַּד מַבְחַר בְּקְלוּפִיָּיתָה. מִשּׁוּם בּוֹרֵר. כַּד שָׁחִיק בְּמַדּוּכְתָּה. מִשּׁוּם טוֹחֵן. כַּד יְהִיב מַשְׁקִין. מִשּׁוּם לָשׁ. גָּמַר מְלַאכְתּוֹ. מִשּׁוּם מַכָּה בְפַטִּישׁ.

הָהֵן סִיקוֹרָה. כַּד מְכַחֵד בִּגְרִירָה בְקְלוּפִיָּיתֵיהּ. מִשּׁוּם בּוֹרֵר. כַּד מְכַתֵּת בְּמַרְגְּזַיֵּיהּ. מִשּׁוּם דָּשׁ. כַּד שָׁחִיק בְּמַדּוּכְתֵּיהּ. מִשּׁוּם טוֹחֵן. כַּד יְהִיב מַשְׁקִין. מִשּׁוּם לָשׁ. כַּד מְשַׁקֵּעַ בְּאַנְטְרִין. מִשּׁוּם בּוֹנֶה. כַּד מְקַטֵּעַ בְּגוּמָא. מִשֵּׁם מְחַתֵּךְ. גָּמַר מְלַאכְתּוֹ. מִשֵּׁם מַכָּה בְפַטִּישׁ.

A woman if she mixes wheat[285], because she is sifting; if she breaks the tips[286], because she is threshing; if she breaks the sides[287], because she is selecting; if she hits, because she is grinding; if she sifts, because she is winnowing; if she completes her work, because she is hitting with a hammer[288].

This linen weaver with a mallet[289] because of threshing; with a roller because of grinding; with a winnowing shovel[290] because of winnowing; with a spoon because of selecting; if he splits because of using a hatchet; if he tears out[291] because of cutting; if he completes his work, because he is hitting with a hammer.

ŠABBAT CHAPTER SEVEN   275

One who is grinding garlic, if he breaks the tips, because he is threshing; if he takes the outer leaves, because he is selecting; if he pounds in a mortar, because he is grinding; if it produces liquid, because of making dough; if he completes his work, because he is hitting with a hammer.

This sausage maker[292], if he selects[293] shavings for casings, because of selecting; if he hacks with a coarse file, because of threshing, if he pounds in a mortar, because he is grinding; if it produces liquid, because of making dough; if he fills a hollow[294], because of building; if he cuts off bast, because of cutting; if he completes his work, because he is hitting with a hammer.

285 If she mixes different qualities of wheat grain and then shakes the mixture to distribute the different kinds evenly, the bran will fall off by the shaking. For each kind of work one investigates the maximum number of liabilities created.
286 Of whole grains. The outer shells will fall off; this is threshing.
287 She takes the grain out of the peel.
288 In contrast to the Babli, the Yerushalmi admits a liability for "hitting with a hammer" for completing professional work even for the preparation of food.
289 Greek κόπανον, τό "pestle".
290 Reading מערוכה for מערובה "mixer".
291 Cutting linen thread, not plucking flax plants.
292 The word appears only here and in *Besah* 4:4. The translation follows Meïri in his Commentary to Babli *Besah* 32a, accepted by S. Liebermann.
293 Reading מבחר for מכחד.
294 Latin *antrum, -i,* "cavity".

(10a line 61) רִבִּי חִייָה בְשֵׁם רִבִּי יוֹחָנָן. דָּגִים שֶׁסְחָטָן. אִם לְגוּפָן פָּטוּר. אִם לְהוֹצִיא צִיר חַיָּיב. רַבָּא אָמַר. כְּבָשִׁים שֶׁסְחָטָן. אִם לְגוּפָן מוּתָּר. וְאִם לְמֵימֵיהֶן אָסוּר. שְׁלָקוֹת בֵּין לְגוּפָן בֵּין לְמֵימֵיהֶן אָסוּר. שְׁמוּאֵל אָמַר. אֶחָד כְּבָשִׁים וְאֶחָד שְׁלָקוֹת בֵּין לְגוּפָן בֵּין לְמֵימֵיהֶן אָסוּר. אָמַר רִבִּי חִזְקִיָּה. הָדָא דְּרַב פְּלִיגָא עַל דְּרִבִּי יוֹחָנָן. אָמַר לֵיהּ רִבִּי מָנָא. לָמָּה. דְּהָהֵן אָמַר אָסוּר וּמוּתָּר. דְּהָהֵן אָמַר חַיָּיב וּפָטוּר.

Rebbi Hiyya in the name of Rebbi Johanan, if one compressed fish[253], if for their body he is not liable, but to produce fish sauce he is liable. Rav[295] said, if one compressed pickles[296], if for their body it is permitted, for their fluid it is forbidden[297]. Preserves[298] both for their body or their fluid is forbidden[299]. Samuel said, both for pickles and for preserves, both for their body or their fluid it is forbidden. Rebbi Hizqiah said, the statement of Rav disagrees with Rebbi Johanan. Rebbi Mana asked him, why? Because one said forbidden and permitted but the other said liable and not liable[300].

295 As the sequel shows, one has to read רב for רבא.
296 Vegetables or fruits preserved in vinegar without cooking.
297 The prohibition is rabbinical only since the fluid absorbed by the pickle it from the outside. Pressing an orange on the Sabbath is a biblical infraction creating liability but squeezing a pickle is not.
298 Preserved by cooking for an extended time.
299 In the Babli 145a: "permitted".
300 R. Johanan notes that compressing fish for their body is rabbinically prohibited but creates no biblical liability while for its fluid it would be a biblical infraction, but Rav states that compressing pickles for their body is permitted, for their fluid does not create biblical liability.

(10a line 67) אָמַר רִבִּי בָּא בַּר מָמָל. בָּצָל שֶׁרִיסְקוֹ. אִם לִיתֵּן טַעַם אָסוּר. אִם לְהוֹצִיא שׂוּרְפּוֹ מוּתָּר. רִבִּי זְעוּרָא בְשֵׁם רַב הוּנָא. צְנוֹן טוֹמְנוֹ בַמֶּלַח. וּבִלְבַד שֶׁלֹּא יְשַׁהֶא. רִבִּי זְעִירָא בְשֵׁם רַב הוּנָא. כֵּילָיו מִבֵּית הָאוּמָּן לוֹבְשָׁן. וְאִם יִתְקָרֵעַ יִתְקָרֵעַ. רִבִּי זְעִירָא בְשֵׁם רַב הוּנָא. נִסְתַּבְּכוּ בְגָדָיו בְּקוֹצִים הֲרֵי זֶה מְפַשְׁרָן בְּמָקוֹם צִינְעָה וּבִלְבַד שֶׁלֹּא יִקְרַע. אָמַר רִבִּי זְעִירָא בְשֵׁם רַב הוּנָא. נָטַל טִיט עַל בְּגָדָיו הֲרֵי זֶה מְמָרְחוֹ בְיָדוֹ אַחַת. וּבִלְבַד שֶׁלֹּא יְכַסְכֵּס. רִבִּי זְעִירָא בְשֵׁם רַב הוּנָא. הָהֵן נִנְעָה. בְּחָדָא שָׁרֵי וּבִתְלַת אָסוּר. וּבְתַרְתֵּי צְרִיכָא. הָהֵן דְּסָחִי. רַב הוּנָא וְרַב יְהוּדָה. חַד אָמַר הָכֵין שָׁרֵי וְהָכֵין אָסוּר. וְחָרָנָה אָמַר. בֵּין הָכֵין וּבֵין הָכֵין אָסוּר. רִבִּי אַבָּא בַּר זְמִינָא עָאַל מִיסְחֵי עִם רִבִּי זְעִירָא. וְלָא שָׁבְקֵיהּ עָבַד דְּלָא הָכֵין וּדְלָא הָכֵין.

Rebbi Abba bar Mamal said, if one crushed an onion, if it was to give taste it is forbidden, if to reduce its sharpness it is permitted[301]. Rebbi Ze'ira in the name of Rav Huna: One may hide a radish in salt on condition not to leave it there[302]. Rebbi Ze'ira in the name of Rav Huna: [If there came][303] his clothes from the tailor he may wear them; if they tore[304] they tore. Rebbi Ze'ira in the name of Rav Huna: If his garments were entangled with thorns he straightens them out in a guarded place on condition that he not tear[304]. Rebbi Ze'ira said in the name of Rav Huna: If (he took) mortar [fell][305] on his garments he may rub it off with one hand, on condition that he not grind down. Rebbi Ze'ira in the name of Rav Huna: mint, one is permitted, three is forbidden, two is questionable[306]. One who bathes, Rav Huna and Rav Jehudah. One said, so it is permitted and so it is forbidden[307]. But the other one said, so and so it is forbidden. Rebbi Abba bar Zamina went bathing with Rebbi Ze'ira; he did not let him do either one or the other.

301 In the first case he creates on the Sabbath a kind of spice that did not exist before; this is rabbinically forbidden. In the second case where he takes already existing food and improves it, it is a permissible way.
302 It cannot stay until after the Sabbath since one may not prepare from the Sabbath for a weekday. Cf. Babli 108b.
303 The addition is from the quote of the sentence in *Meïri ad* 73b.
304 Tosephta *Eruvin* 8:10 (Zuckermandel 11:11). He should not publicly be seen fixing his garments.
305 Reading נטל for נפל.
306 In the interpretation of S. Liebermann, crushing one mint plant is permitted, three already is professional work and forbidden. It probably does not mean that 1, 3, 2 people are involved in the work (cf. Babli 113a).
307 It is not spelled out what kind of washing is permitted and what is forbidden on the Sabbath since R. Ze'ira, whom we follow, only permits dunking oneself in the water but nothing else.

1) נָפְלוּ מַיִם עַל בְּגָדָיו. רַב הוּנָא וְרַב יִרְמִיָה. חַד אָמַר מְנַעֲרָהּ שָׁרֵי. וּמְמַחְקָהּ אָסוּר. וְחוֹרָנָה מַחְלִף. (10b line

רִבִּי בָּא בַּר חִייָא בַּר אַשִׁי. זֶה שֶׁרוֹקֵק מַבְלִיעוֹ בִּכְסוּתוֹ וְאֵינוֹ חוֹשֵׁשׁ. רִבִּי בָּא בְשֵׁם רִבִּי חִייָא בַּר אַשִׁי. אִתְפַּלְגוּן רִבִּי חִייָה רוֹבָא וְרִבִּי שִׁמְעוֹן בְּרִבִּי. חַד אָמַר. רוֹקֵק וְשָׁף. וְחוֹרָנָה אָמַר. אֵינוֹ רוֹקֵק וְשָׁף. מַה פְּלִיגִין. בְּשֶׁאֵין שָׁם פְּסֵיפָס. אֲבָל יֵשׁ שָׁם פְּסֵיפָס רוֹקֵק וְשָׁף. רָקַק וְהִפְרִיחָתוֹ הָרוּחַ חַייָב מִשּׁוּם זוֹרֶה. וְכָל־דָּבָר שֶׁהוּא מְחוּסַּר לָרוּחַ חַייָב מִשּׁוּם זוֹרֶה.

If water fell on his garments. Rav Huna and Rav Jeremiah. One said, to shake it off is permitted, to rub it off is forbidden; but the other one switches[308].

Rebbi Abba (bar)[309] Hiyya bar Ashi, one who spits absorbs it in his garment and does not worry[310]. Rebbi Abba in the name of Rebbi Hiyya bar Ashi, the Elder Rebbi Hiyya and Rebbi Simeon ben Rebbi disagreed. One said, one spits and crushes; the other said, one does not spit and crush. Where do they differ? If it is not on a mosaic floor[311]. But if there is a mosaic floor he spits and crushes. If he spat and the wind carried it away he is liable because of winnowing; and for anything which is diminished by the wind[312] one is liable because of winnowing.

308 The problem is that it may wash the garment; cf. Babli 147a line 1 ff.
309 Read: R. Abba in the name of R. Hiyya bar Ashi, as in the next sentence.
310 He puts his shoe on the spittle and crushes it. This is a problem on a dirt floor. Babli 121b.
311 Greek ψῆφος, ἡ, "pebble, mosaic stone", meaning a stone floor.
312 Since he wanted to spit, it is intentional. If then the wind carries it farther than 4 cubits in the public domain, he is liable. Similarly in other cases where he intentionally initiated the action. Babli *Bava qamma* 60a, *Bava batra* 26a.

(10b line 7) וְהַבּוֹרֵר. אָמַר רִבִּי יוּדָן. יֵשׁ שֶׁהוּא בּוֹרֵר צְרוֹרוֹת כָּל־הַיּוֹם וְאֵינוֹ מִתְחַיֵּיב. יֵשׁ שֶׁהוּא נוֹטֵל כִּגְרוֹגֶרֶת וּמִיָּד מִתְחַיֵּיב. הֵיךְ עֲבִידָה. הָיָה יוֹשֵׁב עַל גַּבֵּי כְרִי וּבָרַר צְרוֹרוֹת כָּל־הַיּוֹם אֵינוֹ מִתְחַיֵּיב. נָטַל לְתוֹךְ יָדוֹ כִּגְרוֹגֶרֶת וּבֵירַר חַיָּב.

"And who selects." Rebbi Yudan said, one picks out pebbles the entire day and does not incur liability, and one takes the volume of a dried fig and immediately incurs liability. How is this? If he was sitting on top of a heap of grain and picks out pebbles the entire day, he does not incur liability[313]; if he took in his hand the volume of a dried fig and picked out he is liable.

313 Since by sitting on top he cannot reach the lower parts of the heap, there will remain pebbles in the grain; the grain will not qualify as pebble-free and command a higher price on the market. Since in the Mishnah "selecting" was mentioned in preparation to milling, and grain with pebbles cannot be milled, his action does not qualify as "selecting" in the sense of the Mishnah. But taking a small quantity in his hand allows him to clear out all stones; this is "selecting" and biblically forbidden on the Sabbath. Babli 74a.

(10b line 11) רִבִּי יוֹנָה בָעֵי. עָשָׂה כֵן בַּשַּׁבָּת. עַל דַּעְתֵּיהּ דְּבֵית שַׁמַּי מָהוּ שֶׁיְּהֵא חַיָּב. אָמַר לֵיהּ רִבִּי יוֹסֵי. וְלָמָּה לֹא. אִילּוּ עָשָׂה כֵן בַּשַּׁבָּת עַל דְּבֵית הִלֵּל שָׁמָּא אֵינוֹ חַיָּב. וְהָכָא חַיָּב. אָמַר רִבִּי מָנָא. יָאוּת אָמַר רִבִּי יוֹנָה אַבָה. לֹא אַתְיָא אֶלָּא עַל דְּבֵית שַׁמַּי. לָמָּה. שֶׁהוּתַּר מִכְּלָל בְּרֵירָה בְּיוֹם טוֹב. לֹא הוּתַּר מִכְּלָל בְּרֵירָה בַּשַּׁבָּת.

1 דעתיה | י - 3 אבה | י אבא שהותר | י הותר

[314]Rebbi Jonah asked, if he did this on the Sabbath, in the opinion of the House of Shammai would he be liable? Rebbi Yose said to him, why not? If he did it on the Sabbath would he not be liable according to the House of Hillel? And here he is liable. Rebbi Mana said, my father Rebbi Jonah said it correctly. It is a problem only for the House of Shammai. Why? Because the

category of selecting was permitted on the holiday, nothing of the category of selecting was permitted on the Sabbath[315].

314 This and the following paragraphs are from *Beṣah* 1:10 (י) and refer to Mishnah *Beṣah* 1:9: "The House of Shammai say, he who selects legumes on a holiday selects the food and eats. But the House of Hillel say, he selects normally, on his chest, or from a basket, or from a pot, but not on a table, nor with a sieve. Rabban Gamliel says, also he puts them in water and scoops off." The House of Shammai permit only to pick out the edible parts and eat them directly. The House of Hillel hold that separating the beans from the chaff belongs to the activities permitted as preparation of food and in principle permit any kind of selection; they only require that it should not be done in a weekday fashion. They certainly will agree that the restrictions are purely rabbinical.

315 The objection of R. Yose is pointless. There is no problem for the House of Hillel since they hold that selecting as a category is permitted on the holiday but forbidden on the Sabbath. But we do not know whether the House of Shammai hold the same and are rabbinically restrictive on the holiday more than the House of Hillel or whether they hold that selecting does not belong to the preparation of food but to preliminaries to preparation which are not exempted on the holiday and for which, therefore, the rules are identical on Sabbath and holiday. Since in his days, in the middle of the Fourth Century, the House of Shammai had disappeared for 250 years, no answer can be given.

(10b line 15) בֵּירֵר אוֹכְלִים מִתּוֹךְ אוֹכְלִים. חִזְקִיָּה אָמַר. חַיָּב. רִבִּי יוֹחָנָן אָמַר. פָּטוּר. מַתְנִיתָה פְלִיגָה עַל חִזְקִיָּה. בּוֹרֵר וְאוֹכֵל בּוֹרֵר וּמַנִּיחַ עַל הַשּׁוּלְחָן. רִבִּי בּוּן בַּר חִיָּיה בְשֵׁם רִבִּי שְׁמוּאֵל בַּר רַב יִצְחָק. תִּיפְתָּר שֶׁהָיוּ אוֹרְחִין אוֹכְלִין רִאשׁוֹנָה וְרִאשׁוֹנָה. וְהָתַנֵּי. וּבִלְבַד שֶׁלֹּא יָבוֹר אֶת כָּל־אוֹתוֹ הַמִּין. אִם עָשָׂה כֵן בַּשַּׁבָּת חַיָּב. עַל דַּעְתֵּיהּ דְּחִזְקִיָּה. שֶׁכֵּן הַבּוֹרֵר כְּדַרְכּוֹ בַּשַּׁבָּת חַיָּב. עַל דַּעְתֵּיהּ דְּרִבִּי יוֹחָנָן. שֶׁכֵּן הַבּוֹרֵר כְּדַרְכּוֹ בְּמָקוֹם אֶחָד חַיָּב. עַל דַּעְתֵּיהּ דְּחִזְקִיָּה. אֲפִילוּ עִיגּוּלִין מִן גַּוָּא עִיגּוּלִין. אֲפִילוּ רִימּוֹנִים מִן גַּוָּא רִימּוֹנִים. אוֹ כֵינִי. אֲפִילוּ בְּנֵי נָשׁ מִן גּוֹ בְּנֵי נָשׁ. מַאי כְדוֹן. כָּל־עַמָּא מוֹדֵיי לְהָדָא דְרִבִּי אִימִּי. דְּרִבִּי אִימִּי הֲוָה לֵיהּ אוֹרְחִין. אַפִּיק קוֹמֵיהוֹן תּוּרְמוֹסִין וּפְסִילָיִין. אָמַר לוֹן. הָבוֹן דַּעְתְּכוֹן דַּאֲתוֹן מֵיכוֹל קִינְסָיָא בְּסוֹפָא.

1 בירר G | ברר   אוכלים G | אכלים (2)   ר' | יור'   2 פליגה | פליגא דאמ' | G - בורר G | ובורר   בון | G בין   חייה G | חייא   3 שמואל G | שמעיאל   תיפתר G | תפתר   שהיו G | בשהיו   והתני | והא תני   5 כדרכו G | (י) -   אחד G | אחר   6 גוא G | גו   אפי' | ואפי'   רימונין G | רימונים   גוא G | גו   או | G אין   7 מיי | י מאי   להדא G | להיא   דר' | G דאמ' ר'   אימי G | אמי   (2) 8 תורמוסין G | תורמסין   ופסילייו | G ופסיליה   ופסיליה | G הבון   יבון | י יהבון   קינסייא G | קינדסיה י קינרסיה   בסופא G | בסופה

[316]If one selected food out of food, Ḥizqiah said, one is liable; Rebbi Joḥanan said, one is not liable[317]. A *baraita* disagrees with Ḥizqiah: He selects and eats, he selects and puts on the table[318]. Rebbi Abun bar Ḥiyya in

the name of Rebbi Samuel bar Rav Isaac: explain it if guests were eating what was served. But was it not stated: On condition that he did not select all of its kind? In the opinion of Ḥizqiah, because one who selects (normally)[319] on the Sabbath is liable. In the opinion of Rebbi Joḥanan, because one who selects normally at (one) [another][320] place is liable. In the opinion of Ḥizqiah, even rings among rings[321], even pomegranates among pomegranates. Or is it so, even people among people[322]? How is this? Everybody agrees with that of Rebbi Immi. For Rebbi Immi had guests; he brought before them lupines[323] and beans[324]. He told them, be careful to eat (the wood-chips)(the sticks) [the artichokes][325] at the end.

316 Here starts a new Genizah fragment (G) edited by L. Ginzberg, p. 84.

The paragraph has a parallel in the Babli, 74a/b.

317 It is somewhat difficult to understand Hizqiah's position. What is biblically forbidden on the Sabbath is removing chaff from food, not food from chaff (except, as mentioned later in this paragraph, if the entire batch was cleaned, when there is no difference what was taken from where.) Biblically Hizqiah would have to forbid to remove the food one does not want to eat from the food one wants to eat; the other way would only be rabbinically forbidden.

318 For immediate consumption. There is no difference whether one puts food in his own mouth or in others'.

319 To be deleted with the other two sources.

320 The text in brackets (following the other two sources) is the correct one. The "other place" is the Sabbath; the origin of this paragraph also is in *Beṣah*. Liability on the Sabbath can always be avoided by doing things in a decidedly unprofessional way; the mention of doing things "normally" is appropriate here.

321 String figs from a heap of string figs.

322 Then it would be forbidden on the Sabbath to call people to read the Torah unless they had been selected beforehand. This we never heard.

323 Greek θέρμος, ὁ.

324 Greek φάσηλος, ὁ.

325 The first alternative is the conjectured meaning of the word in the Leiden text in *Šabbat*, the second word that of the Leiden text in *Beṣah*, the probably correct choice is the third, from the Genizah text, Greek κινάρα. If this reading is accepted, following S. Liebermann, then the statement is that on a holiday it is permitted to select anything for immediate consumption, even if there are no remainders, and eat a different dessert at the end.

(10b line 25) תַּנֵּי. אֵין בּוֹרְרִין לֹא טוֹחֲנִין וְלֹא מַרְקִידִין. הַבּוֹרֵר הַטּוֹחֵן הַמַּרְקִיד בַּשַּׁבָּת נִסְקָל. בְּיוֹם טוֹב סוֹפֵג אֶת הָאַרְבָּעִים. וְהָא תַּנִּינָן. בּוֹרֵר כְּדַרְכּוֹ בְּחֵיקוֹ בְּקָנוֹן וּבְתַמְחוּי. אָמַר רִבִּי

חֲנִינָא עֲנְתּוֹנָיָיא. דְּרַבָּן גַּמְלִיאֵל הִיא. דְּרַבָּן גַּמְלִיאֵל אוֹמֵר אַף מֵדִיחַ וְשׁוֹלֶה׃ וְהָא תַנִּינָן. שֶׁלְבֵית רַבָּן גַּמְלִיאֵל הָיוּ שׁוֹחֲקִין אֶת הַפִּילְפְּלִין בָּרֵחַיִם שֶׁלָּהֶן. מוּתָּר לִטְחוֹן וְאָסוּר לָבוֹר. רִבִּי יוֹסֵה בְשֵׁם רִבִּי אִילָא. לֹא הוּתְרָה טְחִינָה כָדַרְכָּהּ. וּמְנַיִין שֶׁאֵין בּוֹרְרִין וְלֹא טוֹחֲנִין וְלֹא מַרְקִידִין. רִבִּי יוֹסֵי בְשֵׁם רִבִּי שִׁמְעוֹן בֶּן לָקִישׁ. כָּל־מְלָאכָה לֹא־יֵעָשֶׂה בָהֶם עַד וּשְׁמַרְתֶּם אֶת־הַמַּצּוֹת. תַּנֵּי רִבִּי יוֹסֵי בָעֵי. כְּלוּם לְמֵדוּ לְתַבְשִׁיל אֶלָּא מִיכָּן. רִבִּי יוֹסֵה לֹא אָמַר כֵּן. אֶלָּא רִבִּי יוֹסֵה בְשֵׁם רִבִּי שִׁמְעוֹן בֶּן לָקִישׁ. אַךְ אֲשֶׁר יֵאָכֵל לְכָל־נֶפֶשׁ הוּא לְבַדּוֹ יֵעָשֶׂה לָכֶם׃ עַד וּשְׁמַרְתֶּם אֶת־הַמַּצּוֹת. תַּנֵּי חִזְקִיָּה וּפְלִיג. אַךְ הוּא לְבַדּוֹ הֲרֵי אֵילוּ מִיעוּטִין. שֶׁלֹּא לִקְצוֹר וְלֹא לִטְחוֹן וְלֹא לְהַרְקִיד בְּיוֹם טוֹב.

1 לא G | י ולא הטוחן G | והטוחן המרקיד G | והמרקיד 2 ביום G | וביום את הארבעים G | ארבעים והא תנינן | י והתנינן 3 חנינא G | חנינא ענתונייא ענתיה י ענתנייה G | ענתייה י ענתנייה או' | י אמ' והא תנינן G | והא תני 4 את G | י - הפילפלין G | פלפלין י פילפלין מותר | י ומותר ואסור G | אסור ר' | G י א"ר 5 בשם ר' אילא G | ביר' בון ומניין | G ומנין י מניין 6 יוסי | G יוסי י אחא תני | G י - 7 יוסי G | יוסה יוסה | G יוסי 9 לקצור י יקצור לטחון | י יטחון להרקיד | י ירקיד

It was stated: One does neither select, nor grind, nor sift. He who selects, or grinds, or sifts, on the Sabbath is stoned. On a holiday he absorbs the 40[326]. But did we not state[327]: "he selects normally, on his chest, or from a pot"? Rebbi Ḥanina from Antonia said, this is Rabban Gamliel's, for "Rabban Gamliel says, also he puts them in water and scoops off." And (did we not state) [was it not stated][328], in the household of Rabban Gamliel they were grinding pepper in their mills[314]? It is permitted to grind but forbidden to select. Rebbi Yose (in the name of Rebbi Ila) [ben Rebbi Abun][328]: Grinding as a category was not permitted[329]. And from where that one may neither select, nor grind, nor sift? Rebbi (Yose) [Aḥa][328] in the name of Rebbi Simeon ben Laqish: *No work shall be done on them* up to *and you shall guard the unleavened bread*[330]. (It was stated.)[331] Rebbi Yose asked, but did one not infer cooking only from there? Rebbi Yose did not say so, but Rebbi Yose in the name of Rebbi Simeon ben Laqish: *Only what can be eaten by every person this alone may be made by you,* up to *and you shall guard the unleavened bread*[332]. Ḥizqiah stated in disagreement[333]: *only, every, person,* are diminutions, not to select, nor to grind, nor to sift on a holiday.

326 The 39 lashes which are the standard punishment for breaking biblical prohibitions for which no other biblical punishment is specified. The Babli disagrees and declares these activities only rabbinically prohibited on a holiday, cf. Tosaphot 95a, *s. v.* והרודה.

While preparing food is biblically permitted on a holiday as shown later in the paragraph, there is a dispute between the anonymous majority and R. Jehudah whether this includes preparations which could have been made the day before without impairing the quality of the food, which the majority prohibits and R. Jehudah and Rabban Gamliel permit. It is stated here that for the majority the prohibition is biblical, at least concerning preparations for baking.

327 Mishnah *Besah* 1:9. This is the version of the Mishnah always quoted in Halakhot.

328 The text in parentheses from the Leiden ms. is inferior to that of the other two sources in brackets.

329 Rabban Gamliel will agree that milling flour is biblically forbidden on a holiday; he will hold that grinding pepper in a peppermill is not professionally grinding and not something which may be done the day before without impairing the quality of the spice.

330 *Ex.* 12:16-17. The text omitted by the quote "up to" permits preparation of food on a holiday, as quoted later in the paragraph.

331 This has to be deleted with the other two sources.

332 There is nothing missing between the two quotes, so that the note "up to" seems to be superfluous. The meaning is explained in Tosaphot *Besah* 3a s.v. גזרה (at the end): vv. 16,17 form a unit: *what can be eaten by every person this alone may be made by you, and you shall guard the unleavened bread.* Any preparation of *mazzah* which requires guarding against possible leavening is permitted on the holiday, anything preceding this, i. e., mixing flour with water to make dough, is forbidden.

333 Against the Mishnah where the House of Hillel permit selecting. G ends here.

(10b line 37) רִבִּי זְעִירָא רַב חִיָּיה בַּר אַשִׁי בְשֵׁם שְׁמוּאֵל. הַמְשַׁמֵּר חַיָּיב מִשּׁוּם בּוֹרֵר. אָמַר רִבִּי זְעִירָא. לֹא מִסְתַּבְּרָא דְּלֹא מִשּׁוּם מְרַקֵּד. רִבִּי יוֹנָה וְרִבִּי יוֹסֵה תְּרֵיהוֹן אָמְרִין. בְּקַדְמִיתָא הֲוִינָן אָמְרִין. יָאוּת אָמַר רִבִּי זְעִירָא. וּמָה הַמְרַקֵּד קֶמַח מִלְּמַטָּן וְסוֹלֶת מִלְמַעְלָן. אַף הַמְשַׁמֵּר יַיִן מִלְמַטָּן וּשְׁמָרִים מִלְמַעְלָן. וְלֹא הֲוִינַן אָמְרִין כְּלוּם. לָמָּה. שֶׁהוּתַר מִכְּלַל בְּרֵירָה הוּתַר מִכְּלַל שִׁימוּר. הוּתַר מִכְּלַל בְּרֵירָה בּוֹרֵר כְּדַרְכּוֹ בְּחֵיקוֹ וּבְתַמְחוּי. וְהוּתַר מִכְּלַל שִׁימוּר אֲבָל נוֹתְנִין לַתְּלוּיָה בְּיוֹם טוֹב: וְלֹא הוּתַר מִכְּלַל הַרְקָדָה. דָּמַר רִבִּי חֲנִינָא בֶּן יָקָה בְשֵׁם רַב יְהוּדָה. אֵין שׁוֹנִין אֶת הַקֶּמַח אֲבָל מַרְקִידִין לַאֲחוֹרֵי הַנָּפָה. אִין תֵּימַר מִשּׁוּם מְרַקֵּד הוּא. יְהֵא אָסוּר. אָמַר רִבִּי יוֹסֵה בֵּירִבִּי בּוּן. וּדְלֹא כְּרִבִּי יוּדָה. דְּתַנֵּי בְשֵׁם רִבִּי יוּדָה. אֲבָל בְּמַכְשִׁירֵי אוֹכֶל נֶפֶשׁ הִתִּירוּ. בְּעָיָא דָא מִילְּתָא. מַהוּ לְשַׁנּוֹת אֶת הַקֶּמַח לַאֲחוֹרֵי הַנָּפָה כְּרַבָּנָן.

1 זעירא E20 | זעירה י זעורה   שמואל | י רב   2 זעירא | י רב   [זעיר]ה י זעורה   מסתברא E | מיסתברא   דלא | E20 אלא י די לא   מרקד | E20 מרקיד   ר' יונה ור' יוסה | 20 ר' יוסי ור' יונה   3 זעירא | E זעירה י זעורה   ומה | E20 מה   מלמטון | 20 למטן   מלמעלון | 20 למעלן   4 מלמטון | 20 למטן   וסולת | E וסלת   מלמעלון | 20 למעלן   שהותר | י הותר   הותר | י הותר   5 והותר | GE20 י והותר   הותר | E20   הותר | E20   בורר | E בורר   ובורר   הותר מכלל   שימור נותנין לתלויה ביו"ט | E - | אבל | 20 - 6   חנינא | GE20 חנינא   בר יקה | 20 ברוקה   7 הנפה | G הנפק[334]   מרקד | GE20 מרקיד   8 יוסה | י יוסי   ודלא | E דלא י די לא   בשם | י משם   יודה | G יהודה   אבל | GE20 אף במכשירי E מכשירי   9 בעייא GE | י בעייה   דא | י הדא   מילתא | E מילתא G מילתה מלתא   מהו E | מהוא

[335]Rebbi Ze'ira, Rav Hiyya bar Ashi in the name of Samuel: One who filters is liable because of selecting. Rebbi Ze'ira said, it is more reasonable that it should be because of sifting. Rebbi Jonah and Rebbi Yose both said, at the start we were saying that Rebbi Ze'ira said it correctly, since as in sifting the flour is below and the farina[336] on top, so in filtering wine the wine as at the bottom and the yeast on top; but we were not saying anything. Why? Because the category of selecting was permitted, the category of filtering was permitted[337]. The category of selecting was permitted[327]: "he selects normally, on his chest, or from a pot". Also the category of filtering was permitted, "on a holiday one puts into one which was hanging[338]". But the category of sifting was not permitted. As Rebbi Hanina ben Yaqe said in the name of Rav Jehudah, One does not re-sift the flour but one may pass it through the back of the sieve[339]. If you say it is because of sifting, it[340] should be forbidden. Rebbi Yose ben Rebbi Abun said, it does not follow Rebbi Jehudah, for it was stated in the name of Rebbi Jehudah, (in truth) [also][341] preparations for making food they permitted[342]. There is a question about the following: following the rabbis, may one re-sift the flour through the back of the sieve?

334 A scribal error.

335 This text also appears in Chapter 20 (17c line 35, noted 20; the Genizah text of Chapter 20 edited by J. N. Epstein is noted E). The parallel in the Babli is in 138a where the argument of R. Ze'ira is quoted in his name but the introductory statement is in the name of Rav Cahana. In *Beṣah*, the original author is Rav, not Samuel. This may be a *lectio facilior* since Rav Hiyya bar Ashi was a companion of Rav; but if Rav Cahana is Cahana, the stepson of Rav, it would represent a Babylonian tradition.

336 The coarser pieces.

337 On a holiday, as shown later from Mishnaiot.

Here starts a new Genizah leaf (Ginzberg, p. 85).

338 Mishnah *Šabbat* 20:1. According to the anonymous majority on a holiday one may not put a filter on top of a barrel because this is an activity not covered by the general permission to prepare food, but if the filter already was in place one may filter wine on a holiday.

339 This sentence, while it is at this place in all sources, does not belong here but at the very end of the paragraph where it answers to a question raised there. If flour had been sifted before but the housewife wants to sift it again on the holiday before using if for baking, she may turn the sieve upside down and use it with the sieve instead of being concave downwards being convex upwards. This is unprofessional and therefore not biblically forbidden even

according to the opinion stated in the preceding paragraph that all preparations preceding making dough are forbidden on the holiday. Cf. Babli *Beṣah* 29b.

340 Filtering.

341 The text in parentheses is from the Leiden ms.; that of the other sources is in brackets. Both are possible.

342 Tosephta *Megillah* 1:7.

(10b line 48) וְהַטּוֹחֵן. הָהֵן דְּשָׁחַק מֶלַח חֲסַף פִּילְפְּלִין חַיָּיב מִשּׁוּם טוֹחֵן. הָהֵן דִּחֲשַׁר גִּיר גִּבְסִין מוֹץ חוֹל עָפָר חַיָּיב מִשּׁוּם מְרַקֵּד. הָהֵן דְּגָבַל גִּיר גִּבְסִין עָפָר קִילוֹרִין מָלוּגְמָא סַמְמָנִין חַיָּיב מִשּׁוּם לָשׁ. הַלָּשׁ וְהַמְקַטֵּף וְהָעוֹרֵךְ כּוּלְּהוֹן מִשּׁוּם לָשׁ. רִבִּי בָּא בַּר מָמָל בָּעֵי. תַּמָּן אַתְּ אָמַר. וְחַיָּיב עַל לִישָׁתָהּ וְעַל עֲרִיכָתָהּ וְעַל אֲפִייָתָהּ׃ וְהָכָא אַתְּ אָמַר הָכֵין. אֶלָּא תַמָּן יֵשׁ לוֹ לַחֲלוֹק. חַיָּיב עַל כָּל־אַחַת וְאַחַת. בְּרַם הָכָא אֵינוֹ חַיָּיב אֶלָּא אַחַת. אַתְּ חֲמֵי אֲפִייָה תוֹלֶדֶת לְבִישׁוּל וְאַתְּ אָמַר הָכֵין. אֶלָּא בְגִין דְּתַנִּינָן סֵדֶר עִישָׂה תְּנִינָתָהּ עִמָּהֶן.

1 פילפלין חייב משום G | פלפלין חיב משם 2 גבסין G | גפסין מרקד G | מרקיד קילורין G | קרולין 3 הלש G | דלש 4 וחייב G | חייב G | אפייתה G | אפייתה והכא G | והכה 5 הכא G | הכה את G | אתה

"And who grinds." He who pulverizes salt, clay shards, peppers, is liable because of grinding. He who cuts into little pieces chalk, gypsum[343], chaff, sand, dirt, is liable because of sifting. He who kneads chalk, gypsum, dust, eye-salve[344], plaster[345], drugs, is liable because of making dough. One who makes dough, or kneads dough, or forms dough, all are because of making dough. Rebbi Abba bar Mamal asked, there[346] you say, "and he is liable for making its dough, and for its forming, and for its baking," and here you are saying so? But there he has to divide for he is liable for each single one, but here[347] he is liable only once. You see that baking is a derivative of cooking, and you are saying so? But it was stated here since we are stating the order of the dough[348].

343 Greek γύψος, ἡ.

344 Greek κολλύριον, τό.

345 Greek μάλαγμα, -ατος, τό.

346 Mishnah *Menahot* 5:2. The shew bread has to be unleavened. Violating this rule at any stage of the preparation of the bread is a separate biblical violation for each stage.

347 For the rules of the Sabbath, kneading the dough and forming it into the required shape count only as one liability.

348 In Mishnah 2, one would have expected "cooking" to be listed as the name of the category; for it is the more widely applicable notion, and baking as derivative. But since the Mishnah is organized in describing the making of the shew-bread (Note 4) the category of cooking is labelled "baking". Babli 74b.

(10b line 56) הָהֵן דְּאָזִין גִיר קַרְדִין מָשִׁיחַ כִּילוֹס שָׁרֵי זִיפוּת שָׁרֵי מוֹסְרִין. רִבִּי אַבָּהוּ בְשֵׁם רִבִּי יוֹסֵה בַּר חֲנִינָה. הַמַּתִּיךְ אֲבָר חַיָּיב מִשּׁוּם מְבַשֵּׁל. הַצוֹלֶה וְהַמְטַגֵּן הַשּׁוֹלֵק וְהַמְעַשֵּׁן כּוּלּוֹ מִשּׁוּם מְבַשֵּׁל. בִּישֵּׁל בְּחַמֵּי טִיבֶּרְיָא מָהוּ. חִזְקִיָּה אָמַר. אָסוּר. רִבִּי יוֹחָנָן אָמַר. מוּתָּר. אָמַר רִבִּי מָנָא. אֲזָלִית לְקֵיסָרִין וּשְׁמָעִית רִבִּי זְרִיקָן בְּשֵׁם חִזְקִיָּה. לְחִזְקִיָּה צְרִיכָה לֵיהּ פֶּסַח שֶׁנִּתְבַּשֵּׁל בְּחַמֵּי טִיבֶּרְיָא מָהוּ. תְּרֵין אֲמוֹרִין. חַד אָמַר. אָסוּר. וְחָרָנָה אָמַר. מוּתָּר. מָאן דָּמַר. אָסוּר. אַל־תֹּאכְלוּ מִמֶּנּוּ נָא וּבָשֵׁל מְבֻשָּׁל בַּמָּיִם. וּמָאן דָּמַר. מוּתָּר. כִּי אִם־צְלִי־אֵשׁ רֹאשׁוֹ עַל־כְּרָעָיו וְעַל־קִרְבּוֹ:

1 כילוס G | בולוס אבהו G | אבהוא 2 בר G | בן 3 טיבריא G | טבריה מהו G | מהוא 4 ושמעית | ושמעת G [349]

He who burns potter's[350] clay, softens glass[351], melts pitch, melts מוסרין[352]. Rebbi Abbahu in the name of Rebbi Yose bar Ḥanina: One who melts down lead is liable because of cooking[353]. One who roasts, or who fries, who preserves by cooking, or by smoking, all these because of cooking. If somebody cooked in the hot springs of Tiberias, what[354]? Ḥizqiah said, it is forbidden; Rebbi Joḥanan said, it is permitted. Rebbi Mana said, I went to Caesarea and heard Rebbi Zeriqan in the name of Ḥizqiah; for Ḥizqiah it was a problem: what if the Passover sacrifice was cooked in the hot springs of Tiberias[355]? Two Amoraim, one said, it is forbidden; the other said, it is permitted. He who said, it is forbidden, *do not eat from it raw, nor cooked in water*[356]. But he who said, it is permitted, *but only roasted in fire, its head with its feet and its innards*[357].

349 From here to fol. 10c line 19, G is extremely fragmentary.
350 Reading קדר "potter" for unexplained קרד.
351 Following G, reading Greek βῶλος, ἡ, "lump, clod".
352 This word is unexplained. In other contexts, מוסר is "one who delivers; informant". Cf. Greek μίσυ, -υος and -εως, τό, "copper ore from Cyprus" (E. G.).
353 Babli 106a, *Yebamot* 6b.
354 Cooking in hot springs may be forbidden rabbinically; it cannot cause liability. Babli 40b.
355 The question is quite difficult since the Passover must be slaughtered in the Temple and roasted and eaten nearby. The question is really if the Passover was treated by what biblically is not cooking before being roasted, whether this invalidates the sacrifice.
356 *Ex.* 12:9. The first part of the verse invalidates the sacrifice heated by hot water.
357 The second part of the verse validates it if the formal preparation was roasting over an open fire.

(10b line 64) כָּל-אִילֵּין שִׁיעוּרַיָּא. אִם לְאוֹכְלִין. כִּגְרוֹגֶרֶת. אִם לִבְהֵמָה. כִּמְלוֹא פִי גְדִי. אִם לְבַשֵּׁל. כְּדֵי לְבַשֵּׁל בֵּיצָה קַלָּה. [ ] אִם לֶאֱרוֹג. כִּמְלוֹא רוֹחַב הַסִּיט כָּפוּל. אִם לִטְווֹת. כִּמְלוֹא רוֹחַב הַסִּיט כָּפוּל.

All these measures[358], if for food, in the volume of a dried fig, if for an animal, the mouthful of a kid goat, if to cook, to cook a quick egg[359], [ ][360], if to weave, the length of a double *siṭ*[361], if to spin, the width of a double *siṭ*.

358 The general principle underlying the minimal amounts which create liability as explained in the later Mishnaiot of this Chapter and the following Chapters.
359 A chicken egg.
360 In the Leiden ms. there is no lacuna here, but in G one reads . . . . . . לתבל ביצ. This supports the reading in *Or zarua'* Šabbat §62: אִם לְתַבֵּל כְּדֵי לְתַבֵּל בֵּיצָה קַלָּה "if to spice, enough to spice a quick egg".
361 Both Mishnah 7:2 and 13:1 state that liability is created if one weaves two threads. The minimal length of a thread is defined here as a double *siṭ*, but in Mishnah 13:4 as one *siṭ* (a hand-breadth, the width of four thumbs). The text here cannot be changed since "double" is clearly visible in G and is quoted in *Or zarua'*.

(10b line 66) הַגּוֹזֵז אֶת הַצֶּמֶר. גָּזַז סְתָם מָהוּ. נִשְׁמְעִינָהּ מִן הָדָא. הוֹצִיא דְיוֹ. אִם בְּקוֹלְמוֹס. כְּדֵי לִכְתּוֹב שְׁתֵּי אוֹתִיּוֹת. אִם לְהַגִּיהַּ. כְּדֵי לְהַגּוֹת אוֹת אַחַת. תַּמָּן תַּנִּינָן. הַשּׁוֹחֵט אֶת הַבְּכוֹר עוֹשֶׂה מָקוֹם לְקוֹפִיץ מִכָּן וּמִכָּן וְתוֹלֵשׁ הַשֵּׂיעָר. וּבִלְבַד שֶׁלֹּא יְזִיזֶנּוּ מִמְּקוֹמוֹ. וְכֵן הַתּוֹלֵשׁ אֶת הַשֵּׂיעָר לִרְאוֹת מָקוֹם מוּם: רִבִּי אִילָא בְּשֵׁם רִבִּי שִׁמְעוֹן בֶּן לָקִישׁ. הַתּוֹלֵשׁ מִן הַקֳּדָשִׁים פָּטוּר. אָמַר רִבִּי יַעֲקֹב בַּר אָחָא. רֵישׁ לָקִישׁ כְּדַעְתֵּיהּ. דְּאִיתְפַּלְגוּן. הַתּוֹלֵשׁ בַּקֳּדָשִׁים. רִבִּי יוֹחָנָן אָמַר. חַיָּיב. רִבִּי שִׁמְעוֹן בֶּן לָקִישׁ אָמַר פָּטוּר. רִבִּי יִרְמְיָה בָּעֵי. מַחְלָפָה שִׁיטָתֵיהּ דְּרִבִּי שִׁמְעוֹן בֶּן לָקִישׁ. דְּאִיתְפַּלְגוּן. הַתּוֹלֵשׁ כְּנַף בָּעוֹף. הַמּוֹרְטוֹ וְהַקּוֹטְמָהּ. חַיָּיב מִשֵּׁם שָׁלֹשׁ. אָמַר רִבִּי יוֹסֵי בֵּירִבִּי בּוּן. וְלָא פְלִיגִין. הַתּוֹלֵשׁ חַיָּיב מִשּׁוּם גּוֹזֵז. הַמּוֹרְטוֹ חַיָּיב מִשּׁוּם מוֹחֵק. הַקּוֹטְמָהּ חַיָּיב מִשּׁוּם מַכֶּה בְפַטִּישׁ. וְלָא דָמְיָיא. עוֹף שֶׁאֵין לוֹ גִיזָה. תְּלִישָׁתָהּ הִיא גִיזָתָהּ. בְּרַם הָכָא אֵינוֹ חַיָּיב עַד שֶׁיִּגְּזֶז. תֵּדַע לָךְ שֶׁהוּא כֵן. דְּתַנֵּי. תָּלַשׁ מִן הַמֵּיתָה חַיָּב. תְּלִישָׁתָהּ זוֹ הִיא גִיזָתָהּ.

"He who shears wool." If he shore without specification,[361] what? Let us hear from the following: If one brought out ink, if it was in a reed[362], in order to write two letters, if to correct, enough to correct one letter[363]. There, we have stated[364]: "He who slaughters the firstling makes space for the dagger on both sides and tears out the hair, but he should not move it from its place. Similarly, he who tears out hair to see a defect[365]." Rebbi Ila in the name of Rebbi Simeon ben Laqish: One who tears out hair from a dedicated animal is not liable[366]. Rebbi Jacob bar Aḥa said, Rebbi Simeon ben Laqish follows his own opinion, as they disagreed: If one tears out hair from a dedicated animal, Rebbi Joḥanan said, he is liable[367]; Rebbi Simeon ben Laqish said, he is not liable. Rebbi Jeremiah asked, is not Rebbi Simeon ben Laqish's reasoning inverted? Since they disagreed[368]. "One who tears out a wing of a bird, who plucks it, and who cuts it is liable under three [categories].[369]" Rebbi Yose ben Rebbi Abun said, they[370] do not disagree. He who tears out is liable because of shearing; he who plucks out is liable because of wiping clean; he who cuts it is liable because of hitting with a hammer. But it cannot be compared; for a bird which has no shearing, tearing out is its shearing[371]. But here[372] he is not liable unless he sheared. You should know that this is so since it was stated: If he tore from a dead animal he is liable since tearing is its shearing.

361 Since for making textiles it was established that any activity creates liability only if it is enough for a thread of two hand-widths, the question is raised if the shearing was done for no particular purpose. What is the minimum which creates liability?

362 Greek κάλαμος, -ου, m., Latin calamus,- i, m.

363 Writing on the Sabbath creates liability if it may make sense, which means that a word may be formed, or at least two letters. But in correcting, changing a single letter may change the meaning of a word. Therefore if the specific intent was for correcting, the general rule (Mishnah 3) is superseded by a more restrictive one. Similarly here, specific intent in shearing may reduce the amount which creates liability; the absence of specific intent cannot reduce it.

364 Mishnah *Bekhorot* 3:3. Slaughter of a wooly animal cannot be made through thick wool since the fleece might deflect or damage the knife, which would make the slaughter invalid and the animal into carcass meat. Therefore it is necessary to clear some area for the slaughter. It is biblically forbidden to shear a firstling (*Deut*. 15:19). The Mishnah states that tearing out hairs from the animal's fleece is not shearing.

365 Which would make the firstling secular property of the Cohen, (*Deut*. 15:20).

366 As the Sabbath is concerned, this is unprofessional and therefore does not create liability while still being forbidden.

367 As illegitimate use of dedicated property.

368 The previously recorded disagreement with R. Johanan has to be reconciled with the generally accepted Tosephta which follows.

369 Tosephta 9:20.

370 The two opinions of R. Simeon ben Laqish, that tearing out hairs from a four-legged animal does not create liability but tearing out feathers from a bird does.

371 Babli *Bekhorot* 25a.   372 In the case of the four-legged animal.

(10c line 4) הַמְלַבְּנוֹ הָהֵן דִּמְנַפֵּר עָא לְמָנִין נְחַבָלִין אֲלִיקָה. הָדָא אִיתָּתָא דְּשָׁרְקָה אַפָּהּ דְּשָׁרְקָה מַעֲזָלָהּ. הָהֵן חַיָּיטָא דִּיהַב חוּטָא גּוֹ פּוּמֵיהּ. רַב כֹּהֵן בְּשֵׁם רַבָּנִין דְּקַיְסָרִין. הַמְּיַיְנְטוֹן חַיָּיב מִשּׁוּם מְלַבֵּן.

הַמְנַפְּסוֹ. הָהֵן דְּנַפִּיס הוּצִין גּוֹמָא חַיָּיב מִשּׁוּם מְנַפֵּס.

הַצּוֹבְעוֹ. מַה צְּבִיעָה הָיְתָה בַּמִּשְׁכָּן. שֶׁהָיוּ מְשַׁרְבְּטִין בַּבְּהֵמָה בְּעוֹרוֹת אֵלִים מְאָדָּמִים. אָמַר רִבִּי יוֹסֵי. הָדָא אָמְרָה. הָעוֹשֶׂה חַבּוּרָה וְנִצְרַר בָּהּ דַם חַיָּיב. הַמְאַדֵּם אוֹדֶם בַּשָּׂפָה חַיָּיב. הַמּוֹצִיא דָם חַיָּיב מִשּׁוּם נְטִילַת נְשָׁמָה שֶׁבְּאוֹתוֹ הַמָּקוֹם. הַצָּר צוּרָה. הָרִאשׁוֹן חַיָּיב מִשּׁוּם כּוֹתֵב וְהַשֵּׁנִי חַיָּיב מִשּׁוּם צוֹבֵעַ. חִיסֵּר בָּהּ אֵבֶר וּבָא אַחֵר וּגְמָרָהּ חַיָּיב מִשּׁוּם מַכֶּה בַפַּטִּישׁ. וְהַסּוֹחֵט וְהַמְכַבֵּס מְלָאכָה אַחַת הִיא. תַּנֵּי. רִבִּי יִשְׁמָעֵאל בְּנוֹ שֶׁלְּרִבִּי יוֹחָנָן בֶּן בְּרוֹקָה אוֹמֵר. הַצַּבָּעִים שֶׁבִּירוּשָׁלַיִם הָיוּ עוֹשִׂין סְחִיטָה מְלָאכָה בִּפְנֵי עַצְמָהּ. עַל דַּעְתֵּיהּ דְּרִבִּי יִשְׁמָעֵאל בְּנוֹ שֶׁלְּרִבִּי יוֹחָנָן בֶּן בְּרוֹקָה אַרְבָּעִים מְלָאכוֹת אִינּוּן. וְנִיתְנֵי. לֹא אָתֵינָן מִיתְנֵי אֶלָּא מִילִין דְּכָל־עַמָּא מוֹדַיי בָּהֶן.

"Who bleaches it." He who impregnates wood for vessels and ropes for a windlass[373]. This woman who painted her face red[374] and painted her spindle red[375]. This tailor who took a thread into his mouth[376]. Rav Cohen in the name of the rabbis of Caesarea: Asbestos[377] is liable because of bleaching.

"Who cards it." He who cards date palm fiber, papyrus, is liable because of carding[378].

"Who dyes it." What kind of dying was in the Tabernacle? They were clobbering an animal for red skins of rams[379]. Rebbi Yose said, this implies that he is liable who causes a wound which results in echymosis[380]. He who colors his lips red is liable[374]. He who causes bleeding, because of taking away life force at that place[381]. He who makes a shape, the first one is liable because of writing and the second one because of dying[382]. If he left out a limb and another came and finished it, he is liable because of hitting with a hammer[7]. Wringing and washing are the same category of work. It was stated: Rebbi Ismael the son of Rebbi Johanan ben Beroqa says, the dyers in Jerusalem made wringing a separate category of work. In the opinion of Rebbi Ismael the son of Rebbi Johanan ben Beroqa, there are 40 categories of work[383]. Should we state this? We come to state only items to which everybody agrees.

373 For נחבלין אליקה in G one reads חבלין אל יקה. The translation, which is tentative, is based on Liebermann's emendation to read וחבלין לאליקה reading the last word as Greek ἕλικα, accusative of ἕλιξ (identified by Jastrow).
374 In the Babli 95a this is characterized as R. Eliezer's opinion and is not practice since it is only temporary painting.
375 As advertisement that she was available for prostitution. In all these cases, the statement that she is liable for painting is missing. The full text is quoted by some Medieval authors, e. g. *Roqeah Šabbat* 68 (but he reads, "she paints her coat red").
376 The commentaries explain that he does this to bleach the thread.
377 Greek ἀμίαντος, -ον, "pure" (adj.); ὁ ἀμίαντος λίθος, Latin *amiantus* "asbestos".

There is bleaching and dying for mineral material.
378 Even though these are not textiles. Date palm fiber is *lifa* in Arabic.
379 *Ex.* 25:5, 26:14.
380 If the blue spot stays blue more than 24 hours.
381 *Lev.* 17:11. This does not refer to slaughter which is mentioned separately in Mishnah 3, but to a non-lethal wound. Babli 75a/b.
382 Assuming that the first person draws an outline and the second fills it with color. The Babli 75b notes that if the object is decoration of the vessel, he also is liable because of "hitting with a hammer".
383 Since it is not listed separately in the Mishnah.

(10c line 18) הָהֵן דַּעֲבַד חֲבָלִין. הָהֵן דַּעֲבַד מִמְזוֹר חַיָּיב מִשּׁוּם טוֹוֶה. הָהֵן דַּעֲבַד קוּנְטְרָן נָפָן מַחֲצְלָן חַיָּיב מִשּׁוּם מֵיסִיךְ. הָדָא אִיתְּתָא כַּד מִשְׁתִּיָּיא בְּקוּבָיָה. מִשּׁוּם מֵיסָכַת. כַּד יָהֲבָה קַדְמָה. מִשּׁוּם עוֹשָׂה בָתִּין. כַּד מְקִימָה לוֹן. מִשּׁוּם בּוֹנָה. כַּד מְחַיָּיא. מִשּׁוּם אוֹרֶגֶת. כַּד מְקַטְּעָא בְּנֵימַיָּיא. מִשּׁוּם מְחַתֶּכֶת. כַּד גָּמְרָה מְלַאכְתָּהּ. מִשּׁוּם מַכָּה בְפַטִּישׁ. הָהֵן דַּעֲבַד קוּפִּין. כַּד צָפַר. מִשּׁוּם מֵיסִיךְ. כַּד מְחַיֵּיט. כַּד מְחַיָּיא. מִשּׁוּם תּוֹפֵר. כַּף. מִשּׁוּם בּוֹנֶה. כַּד מְקַטֵּעַ. מִשּׁוּם מְחַתֵּךְ. גָּמַר מְלַאכְתּוֹ. מִשּׁוּם מַכָּה בְפַטִּישׁ. הָהֵן דַּעֲבַד מַלִּין עַרְסוֹנָן. לְאוֹרֵךְ. מִשּׁוּם מֵיסִיךְ. לְרוֹחַב. מִשּׁוּם אוֹרֵג. קַנְקְלָטוֹן. מִשּׁוּם עוֹשֶׂה בָתִּים. כַּד מְקַטֵּעַ. מִשּׁוּם מְחַתֵּךְ. גָּמַר מְלַאכְתּוֹ. מִשּׁוּם מַכָּה בְפַטִּישׁ. שְׁנֵי נִירִין בְּחָף אֶחָד וּשְׁנֵי חָפִין בְּנִיר אֶחָד.

5 משום G | משום (all occurrences) מחייט G | מסריט כף. משום G | כך מחתך G | מחתיך 6 מלין G |
מלין לאורך משם מיסיך לרוחב משם אורג כף משם ... כד ... מלאכתו משם מכה בפטיש ההן דעבד   מסיך |
מיסיך G   נירין G | נירים 8

One who makes ropes. The one who twines them is liable because of spinning[384]. One who makes basket work of reeds[385], sieves, bast mats, is liable because of weaving. A woman when she prepares the loom, because of preparing. When she fastens the web,[386] because of tying threads. When she erects [the loom], because of building. When she hits[387], because of weaving.

When she cuts the threads, because of cutting. When she finishes her work, because of hitting with a hammer.

One who makes boxes, when he starts, because of preparing. When he tailors[388], because of sewing. When he bends, because of building. When he cuts, because of cutting. When he finishes his work, because of hitting with a hammer.

One who makes bed-sheets[389], lengthwise because of preparing, crosswise because of weaving. Grating, because of tying threads. When he cuts, because of cutting. When he finishes his work, because of hitting with a hammer.

There are two warp threads per peg and two pegs for each warp thread[390].

384 The Babli 95a rules that braiding women's hair is building.

385 The translation follows Levy; it is tentative.

386 The word in the text is unexplained. The translation follows R. Hananel who in his Commentary to 75a reads קירומה, which is interpreted as Greek καίρωμα, -ατος, τό. This is derived from καίρος, ὁ, "row of thrums in the loom, to which the threads of the warp are attached" and the corresponding verb καιρόω "make fast these threads"; καίρωμα therefoe means "web so fastened".

387 She pushes down the threads of the woof; this is the essence of weaving.

388 This is the only occurrence of חייט used as a verb. G reads "acting as cutter", cf. شرط "to cut, to tear".

389 A conjectured meaning of מלין ערסוון "contents of beds". *Or zarua' Šabbat* 64 reads an unexplained ערסמו. G treats מלין and ערסוון as two different objects and has for both of them the full list of operations. J. Sussman reads in G not מלין (Ginzberg's reading, unidentified as an object) but סליו "baskets".

390 The pegs are on top and bottom of the loom, holding the threads of the warp.

(10c line 28) הָאוֹרֵג שְׁנֵי חוּטִין וְהַפּוֹצֵעַ שְׁנֵי חוּטִין הַקּוֹשֵׁר וְהַמַּתִּיר. מַה קְשִׁירָה הָיְתָה בַּמִּשְׁכָּן. שֶׁהָיוּ קוֹשְׁרִין אֶת הַמֵּיתָרִים. וְלֹא לְשָׁעָה הָיְתָה. אָמַר רִבִּי יוֹסֵה. מִכֵּיוָן שֶׁהָיוּ חוֹנִין וְנוֹסְעִין עַל פִּי הַדִּיבֵּר כְּמִי שֶׁהוּא לְשָׁעָה. אָמַר רִבִּי יוֹסֵי. מִכֵּיוָן שֶׁהִבְטִיחָן הַקָּדוֹשׁ בָּרוּךְ הוּא שֶׁהוּא מַכְנִיסָן לָאָרֶץ כְּמִי שֶׁהִיא לְשָׁעָה. אָמַר רִבִּי פִינְחָס. מִתּוֹפְרֵי יְרִיעוֹת לָמְדוּ. נִפְסַק. הָיָה קוֹשְׁרוֹ. חָזַר וְנִפְסַק. לַעֲשׂוֹתָן קְשָׁרִים קְשָׁרִים אֵי אֶפְשָׁר. אֶלָּא חוֹזֵר וּמַתִּיר אֶת הָרִאשׁוֹן. אָמַר רִבִּי חִזְקִיָּה. הָהֵן חַיָּיטָא אוּמָנָא מְבַלֵּעַ תְּרֵין רָאשִׁיָּה. וְהַיְיְדָא אָמְרָה דָא. דְּאָמַר רִבִּי יוֹסֵי בֵּירִבִּי חֲנִינָא. מֵאוֹרְגֵי יְרִיעוֹת לָמְדוּ. מַה טַעַם. אוֹרֶךְ הַיְרִיעָה הָאֶחָת. כְּדֵי שֶׁתְּהֵא כּוּלָּהּ אַחַת. נִפְסַק הָיָה

קוֹשְׁרוֹ. מִכֵּיוָן שֶׁהָיָה מַגִּיעַ לָאָרִיג הֲוָה שָׁרִי לֵיהּ וּמְעַל לֵיהּ. רִבִּי תַנְחוּמָא בְּשֵׁם רַב חוּנָה. אֲפִילוּ עֶרֶב שֶׁבָּהּ לֹא הָיָה בּוֹ לֹא קֶשֶׁר וְלֹא תיימת.

1 הפוצע | G הבוצע[391] | G - | [392]נדר | G יוסה[392] | G יוסי בי"ר | 2 המיתרים | G המיתרין | G יוסה | 15 חונין ונוסעין | 15 נוסעין וחונין 3 שהוא | 15שהיא לשעה | 15 לעולם יוסי | 15G יוסה בי"ר בון מכיוין | G מכיוין | 4 לשעה | G לעולם 5 לעשותן | G ולע[שותו קשרים | G - | אי איפשר | G איפשר | [393]ראשייה | G רשייה 15 רישיה והיידא | G וידא דאמ' | G דמר יוסי בר חנינא | G יוסה בן חנינה 7 נפסק | G ניפסק 8 ומעל | 15G | ומעיל תנחומא | 15G תנחומה רב | G ר'

"He who weaves two rows, who hits two threads, who ties, and who unties." [394]What tying was in the Tabernacle? They were tying down the ropes[395]. But was this not temporarily[396]? Rebbi Yose says, because they were camping and travelling by the Word[397], was it like temporarily? Rebbi Yose [ben Rebbi Abun][398] said, since the Holy One, praise to Him, has promised them that he will bring them into the Land, it is as if it were (temporary) [permanent][399]. Rebbi Phineas said, they learned it from the gobelin sewers. If [a thread] broke, he was tying it. If it broke again, it was impossible to make many knots but he would untie the first one[400]. Rebbi Ḥizqiah said, an expert tailor merges the two heads[401]. And where was this said? As Rebbi Yose ben Rebbi Ḥanina said, they learned it from the weavers of the gobelins. What is the reason? *The length of one gobelin*[402], that it should be an entity[403]. If [a thread] broke, he was tying it. When he came to the weave, he untied it and brought it in. Rebbi Tanḥuma in the name of (Rav) [Rebbi][404] Huna: Even on its warp there was neither knot nor connection[405].

391 Spelling of the Mishnah in the Yerushalmi and other sources; cf. *Diqduqe Soferim Sabath* p. עה Note פ.

392 Correctly missing in the Leiden ms.

393 The spelling of G is the correct Yerushalmi spelling of "impossible"; the text of the Leiden ms. is a cross between this and the Babli אי אפשר.

394 This paragraph and the next are also in Chapter 15, on Mishnah 15:1 (15).

395 Needed to tie the gobelins which formed the lowest part of the roof to the posts. Mentioned *Ex.* 35:18. Babli 74b.

396 Tying a knot or untying is a Sabbath violation if the knot is intended to be permanent. Since the ropes had to be untied when the Tabernacle was transported, tying and untying could not be Sabbath violations.

397 By Divine order. Since tying and untying was not a decision humans could make; it could as well be considered permanent. In 15 this is a declarative sentence; it is the equivalent of being permanent. Babli *Eruvin* 55b.

398 From G and 15, confirmed by *Or zarua` Šabbat* 67.

399 The text in (parentheses) is that of the corrector of the Leiden ms. and the scribe in

15, the one in [brackets] is of the original scribe here, the corrector in 15, and G. Since the Tabernacle was finally fixed at Shilo, there the ties were permanent. The other argument notes that while the times of disassembly of the Tabernacle were not predictable, the fact of future disassembly was a certainty; these ties were not permanent.

400 Therefore both tying and untying happened during the construction of the Tabernacle and are correctly mentioned in the list of Sabbath prohibitions.

401 The previous argument is not convincing. An expert in invisible mending can connect the threads without a knot being noticeable.

402 *Ex.* 26:2. To form a single unit, a gobelin could not have a broken thread even temporarily.

403 For reasons of chronology, the [reading] of G is to be preferred over that of the (Leiden ms.) here and in Chapter 15.

404 For the purposes of the construction of the Sanctuary everything had to be perfect; no broken threads to be repaired. The only possible explanation remains the first one.

(10c line 39) תַּנֵּי רִבִּי הוֹשַׁעְיָה. חוֹתָל שֶׁלִתְּמָרִים וּפְטִילַיָּיא שֶׁלִתְּמָרִים קוֹרֵעַ וּמַתִּיר. וּבִלְבַד שֶׁלֹּא יְקַשֵּׁר.

1 הושעיה | 15 הושעיא ופטילייא | G ופטיליה

וְאֵין זוֹ הַתָּרָה. נַעֲשָׂה כְשׁוֹבֵר אֶת הֶחָבִית לוֹכַל מִמֶּנָּה גְרוֹגָרוֹת. אָזְנַיִים שֶׁל דִּיסִיקְיָא קוֹשֵׁר וּמַתִּיר. נַעֲשָׂה כְּפוֹתֵחַ וְנוֹעֵל בַּשַּׁבָּת.

1 גרוגרות | G גרוגרת

רִבִּי חֲנִינָה אָמַר. עַד יְחוֹת כָּל־סִיטְרָה. אָמַר רִבִּי יַנַּאי. אָמְרוּ לוֹ לְרִבִּי חֲנִינָא. צֵא וּקְרָא. וְהָא תַּנִּינָן. עָשָׂה שְׁנֵי רָאשִׁיהָ לְצַד אֶחָד. מֵעַתָּה עַד יְסוֹק וִיחוֹת וְיסוֹק. וְהָתַנִּינָן. רִבִּי יְהוּדָה אוֹמֵר עַד שֶׁיְּשַׁלֵּשׁ. מֵעַתָּה עַד יְחוֹת וִיסוֹג וִיחוֹת. אֶלָּא הָכֵן וְהָכֵן. חוּט שֶׁהִשְׁחִילוֹ בְּמַחַט. אֲפִילוּ קָשׁוּר מִיכָּן וּמִיכָּן אֵינוֹ חִיבּוּר. תְּפָרוֹ לַבֶּגֶד. הַחוּט חִיבּוּר לַבֶּגֶד וְאֵינוֹ חִיבּוּר לַמַּחַט. רִבִּי יוֹנָה וְרִבִּי יוֹסֵה תְּרֵיהוֹן אָמְרֵי. בְּקָשׁוּר מִיכָּן וּמִיכָּן. מִילֵיהוֹן דְּרַבָּנָן פְּלִיגִין. דְּאָמַר רִבִּי בָּא רַב יִרְמְיָה בְשֵׁם רַב. הַמְמַתֵּחַ צְדָדָיו בַּשַּׁבָּת חַיָּיב מִשּׁוּם תּוֹפֵר. נֶאֱמַר. מִשּׁוּם תּוֹפֵר וּמִשּׁוּם קוֹשֵׁר.

1 ינייי | כ יניי חנינא | כ חנינה 2 והא תנינן | כ והתנינן יסוק | כ - והא תנינן | כ והתני 3 שישלש | G שישליש יחות | G דיחות הכן והכן | כ הכין והכין שהשחילו | G שהשאילו[405] במחט | כ למחט 4 תפרו | כ - 5 אמרי | G אמרין רב | כ ר' 6 הממתח | כ הממתיח נאמר | כ ויימר משום | G משום[406]

קְרִיעָה בִּבְגָדִים וְחִיתּוּךְ בְּעוֹרוֹת. קְרִיעָה בִּבְגָדִים בָּאֶמְצַע. וְחִיתּוּךְ בְּעוֹרוֹת מִן הַצַּד. וְאִית דִּמְחַלְּפִין. קְרִיעָה בְּעוֹרוֹת וְחִיתּוּךְ בִּבְגָדִים. קְרִיעָה בְּעוֹרוֹת בְּאִילֵּין רְכִיכַיָּיא. וְחִיתּוּךְ בִּבְגָדִים. בְּאִילֵּין לִיבְדַיָּיא.

Rebbi Hoshaia stated, a basket of palm leaves for dates or a plate[407] of palm leaves one may tear and open, only one may not tie[408]. Is this not untying? It is like one who breaks an amphora to eat dried figs[409]. The handles of a double sack[410] one may tie and untie. It is as if one opened or locked on the Sabbath.

[411]Rebbi Ḥanina said, not until it comes down an entire side[412]. Rebbi Yannai said, say to Rebbi Ḥanina, get out and read! Did we not state[413], "if the two ends appear on the same side"? That means, only if it goes up and down and up. And did we not state, "Rebbi Jehudah says, only if there are three needle stitches"? That means that [the thread] goes down, and up, and down. But so and so[414]. A thread drawn through by means of a needle, even if it has a knot on each side, is no connection for cloth. The thread is a connection for cloth but not for the needle[415]. Rebbi Jonah and Rebbi Yose both say, only if it is knotted on both sides. The words of the rabbis disagree since Rebbi Abba, Rav Jeremiah said in the name of Rav: He who straightens out the sides on the Sabbath[416] is liable because of sewing. He should have said, because of sewing and tying knots.

Tearing applies to textiles and cutting to hides[417]. Tearing in the middle and cutting from the sides. There are some who switch, tearing of hides and cutting of textiles. Tearing of hides, those soft ones, and cutting of textiles, felt.

405 A scribal error.
406 Here ends G.
407 Greek πάτελλα, ἡ.
408 Chapter 6, Note 41. Here ends the parallel in Chapter 15.
409 It is permitted in Mishnah 22:3 to break a sealed amphora to reach the food contained in it, on condition that one not intend to make a vessel out of the shards.
410 Greek δισάκκιον, τό.
411 This paragraph is from *Kilaim* 9:7 (Notes 162-167,כ); its topic is *kilaim*, the prohibition to wear linen and wool together, in particular the problem how many stitches it needs to connect linen and woolen cloth to constitute a violation of the prohibition. Only at the end is a connection made with the laws of the Sabbath.
412 For him woolen and linen cloths create *kilaim* only if a full seam was sown. This contradicts the Mishnah quoted next.
413 Mishnah *Kilaim* 9:10.
414 Either one follows the rabbis or R. Jehudah; in no case does one need more than three stitches.
415 If one stitch has been made and now the needle is sticking in the cloth, this does not count since the needle will eventually be removed. In order to create *kilaim*, the thread alone must cross the cloth three times, for two stitches.
416 According to Maimonides (*Šabbat* 10:9), it is the regular procedure in sewing a garment that when a seam is sewn the two sides are stretched to be equal before the thread is knotted. Babli 95a.
417 In Mishnah 2, cutting cloth to prepare for sewing is forbidden as "tearing". In Mishnah 3, cutting hides is forbidden as a

different category. What is the rationale behind this double count, and does "tearing" only apply to textiles and cutting to hides and leather?

(10c line 53) ג. הַצָּד חֲלָזוֹן וּפְצָעוֹ. אִית תַּנָּיֵי תַנֵּי. חַיָּיב שְׁתַּיִם. אִית תַּנָּיֵי תַנֵּי. אֵינוּ חַיָּיב אֶלָּא אַחַת. מָאן דְּאָמַר. שְׁתַּיִם. אַחַת מִשּׁוּם צָד. וְאַחַת מִשּׁוּם נְטִילַת נְשָׁמָה. וּמָאן דְּאָמַר. אַחַת. הַיְיְדָא הִיא מִשּׁוּם נְטִילַת נְשָׁמָה. וְלֵית לֵיהּ צֵידָה. וְאַתְיָא כַהִיא דְּאָמַר רִבִּי אֶלְעָזָר בֵּירִבִּי יוֹסֵה רִבִּי אַבָּהוּ וְרִבִּי שִׁמְעוֹן בֶּן לָקִישׁ בְּשֵׁם רִבִּי מֵאִיר. מִין חַיָּה טְהוֹרָה בָּרָא הַקָּדוֹשׁ בָּרוּךְ הוּא לְמֹשֶׁה בַּמִּדְבָּר. כֵּיוָן שֶׁעָשָׂה בָהּ מְלֶאכֶת הַמִּשְׁכָּן נִגְנְזָה. רִבִּי אָבוּן אָמַר. קֶרֶשׁ הָיָה שְׁמָהּ. תַּנֵּי רִבִּי הוֹשַׁעְיָה. דְּחָדָא קֶרֶן. וְתִיטַב לַייָ מִשּׁוֹר פָּר מַקְרִן וּמַפְרִיס׃ מַקְרֶן כָּתוּב.

3[418]. One who catches a purple snail and crushes it. There are Tannaïm who state that he is liable twice. There are Tannaïm who state that he is liable only once. He who says twice, one because of catching and one because of depriving of life. But he who says once, this is because of depriving of life. Does he not have catching[419]? [420]It comes like what Rebbi Eleazar ben Rebbi Yose, Rebbi Abbahu, Rebbi Simeon ben Laqish in the name of Rebbi Meïr said: The Holy One, praise to Him, created for Moses in the desert a kind of pure animal. After the work of the Tabernacle had been finished it was hidden. Rebbi Abun said, its name was *qereš*. Rebbi Hoshaia stated, a unicorn. *It is preferable to the Eternal to a cattle ox which sprouts a horn and has split hooves*[421]. It is written, it sprouts *a* horn.

418 Here starts discussion of Mishnah 3. Babli 75a.

419 The scribe wrote: Does he not have catching? He does not have catching! The second sentence was unnecessarily deleted by the corrector. The only animal hides used for the construction of the Tabernacle were those of rams, which are domesticated and do not need to be caught, and the *tahaš*, whose nature is in doubt. It is not quite clear what is being proved here. Either the emphasis on the *tahaš* being a pure animal implies that only catching wild pure animals is a violation, or, since the *tahaš* was a temporary phenomenon, it does not imply anything for later generations and no catching of wild animals is a Sabbath violation.

420 The following is from Chapter 2, Notes 111-114.

421 *Ps.* 69:32.

(10c line 60) הַשּׁוֹחֲטוֹ. רִבִּי שִׁמְעוֹן בֶּן לָקִישׁ אָמַר. לֵית כָּאן שְׁחִיטָה. שְׁחִיטָה תּוֹלֶדֶת חֲבוּרָה הִיא. וְלָמָּה לֹא תְנִינָתָהּ עִמָּהוֹן. אֶלָּא בְגִין דְּתַנִּינַן סֵדֶר סְעוּדָה תְנִינָתָהּ עִמָּהוֹן.

הַמְעַבְּדוֹ. מָה עִיבּוּד הָיָה בַּמִּשְׁכָּן. שֶׁהָיוּ מְשַׁרְטְטִין בָּעוֹרוֹת. מַה מְשַׁרְטְטִין לוֹן. מְסַרְגְּלִין לוֹן. וְאַתְיָא כַהִיא דְּאָמַר רִבִּי שְׁמוּאֵל בְּשֵׁם רִבִּי אַבָּהוּ. מוּתָּר לַעֲשׂוֹת אֹהָלִים מֵעוֹר בְּהֵמָה טְמֵאָה.

"Who slaughters it." Rebbi Simeon ben Laqish said, there is no slaughter here; slaughter is a derivative of wounding. And why was it (not)[422] stated with it? Only because we stated the proceedings of a meal it was stated with it.

"Who tans it." What tanning was for the Tabernacle? They were drafting on them. What were they drafting on them? They were drawing lines with a ruler[423]. [424]It follows that what Rebbi Samuel said in the name of Rebbi Abbahu, it is permitted to make tents from the hide of an impure animal.

422 It seems that this word should be deleted; it is not in the quote of the sentence in *Or zarua`* (II §72).

423 Since the hides were used as roofing, there is no indication that they had been shaved off and were tanned. The answer is that in order to be cut to size, they had to be tanned so that at least in the interior lines could be drawn to guide the cutter.

424 It seems that this sentence is misplaced here and belongs to the preceding discussion of the *tahaš*, considering the unicorn as a non-kosher animal and stating that nevertheless the Tent of Meeting was covered by its hides.

(10c line 66) הַמְמַחֲקוֹ. מַה מְחִיקָה הָיְתָה בַּמִּשְׁכָּן. זְעֵיר בַּר חִינְנָא בְּשֵׁם רִבִּי חֲנִינָא. שֶׁהָיוּ שָׁפִין אֶת הָעוֹר עַל גַּבֵּי הָעַמּוּד. חָשַׁף אֶת הָעוֹר עַל גַּבֵּי הָעַמּוּד חַיָּיב. מִשּׁוּם מָה הוּא חַיָּיב. רִבִּי יוֹסֵה בְּשֵׁם רִבִּי יְהוּדָה בֶּן לֵוִי רִבִּי אָחָא בְּשֵׁם רִבִּי יְהוּדָה בֶּן לֵוִי. מִשּׁוּם מְמַחֵק. הָדָא דְּאַתְּ אָמַר בְּחָדָשׁ. אֲבָל בְּיָשָׁן מַחֲלוֹקַת רִבִּי לִיעֶזֶר וַחֲכָמִים. דְּאִיתְפַּלְגוּן. הַמְכַבֵּד. הַמְרַבֵּץ. הַמְנַגֵּב. הַמְמַחֵץ. הַחוֹלֵב וְהָרוֹדֶה חַלּוֹת דְּבָשׁ. חַיָּיב חַטָּאת. דִּבְרֵי רִבִּי אֱלִיעֶזֶר. וַחֲכָמִים אוֹמְרִים. מִשּׁוּם שְׁבוּת. אָמַר רִבִּי יוֹסֵי בֵּירִבִּי בּוּן. וְלֹא פְּלִיגִין. הַמְכַבֵּד הַמְרַבֵּץ חַיָּיב מִשּׁוּם דָּשׁ. הַמְנַגֵּב וְהַמְמַחֵץ חַיָּיב מִשּׁוּם לָשׁ. הַחוֹלֵב וְהָרוֹדֶה חַלּוֹת דְּבָשׁ חַיָּיב מִשּׁוּם קוֹצֵר. הַסּוֹחֵט זֵיתִים מֵאָבֵיהֶן חַיָּיב מִשּׁוּם קוֹצֵר. לְמִי נִצְרְכָה. לְרִבִּי אֱלִיעֶזֶר.

רִבִּי חִייָה בְּשֵׁם רִבִּי יוֹחָנָן. הַגּוֹרֵד רָאשֵׁי כְּלוֹנְסָאוֹת חַיָּיב מִשּׁוּם מְחַתֵּךְ. הַמְמָרֵחַ אֶת הָאִיסְפְּלָנִית חַיָּיב מִשּׁוּם מְמַחֵק.

"Who rubs it clean[5]." What kind of erasure was in the tabernacle? Ze`ir bar Hinena in the name of Rebbi Hanina: They were rubbing the hide[425] on a pillar. One who rubbed hide clear on a pillar is liable. For what is he liable? Rebbi Yose in the name of Rebbi Jehudah ben Levi, Rebbi Aha in the name of

Rebbi Jehudah ben Levi, because of rubbing clean. That is, if it is new. But if it be old[426], it is the disagreement between Rebbi Eliezer and the Sages. Since they disagreed[427]: "One who sweeps, who sprinkles[428], who makes cheese[429], who makes butter[430], who milks, and who takes down honeycombs, is liable for a purification sacrifice. But the Sages say, it is because of Sabbath rest[431]." Rebbi Yose ben Rebbi Abun said, they do not disagree. He who sweeps, who sprinkles, is liable because of threshing. He who makes cheese, who makes butter, is liable because of kneading. He who milks, and who takes down honeycombs, is liable because of harvesting. He who squeezes budding olives is liable because of harvesting. Who needs this? Rebbi Eliezer[432]. He who files off heads of poles is liable because of cutting[433]. He who applies salve on a wet bandage[434] is liable because of rubbing clean.

425 The hides used to makes the covers of the Tabernacles, to clean them from all remainders of flesh clinging to the insides.
426 And rubbing will not change the nature of anything.
427 Tosephta 9:13, Babli 95a.
428 He sweeps or sprinkles water on a dirt floor. For R. Eliezer it is forbidden since he might fill in uneven spots in the floor. For the Sages representing R. Simeon this would be an unintended consequence which never creates liability.

429 According to a Geonic commentary quoted in *Arukh*, "who makes hard cheese."
430 Definition of *Arukh*. Rashi: He makes soft cheese and lets it separate from the whey.
431 Rabbinic restrictions.
432 Since these have no oil, they are squeezed to make them edible as fruit which is permitted for R. Simeon.
433 Babli 75b.
434 Latin *splenium, -ii, n.*.

(10d line 1) מָחַק אוֹת אַחַת גְּדוֹלָה וְיֵשׁ בִּמְקוֹמָהּ כְּדֵי לִכְתּוֹב שְׁתֵּי אוֹתִיּוֹת חַיָּיב. כָּתַב אוֹת אַחַת גְּדוֹלָה אַף עַל פִּי שֶׁיֵּשׁ בִּמְקוֹמָהּ כְּדֵי לִכְתּוֹב שְׁתֵּי אוֹתִיּוֹת פָּטוּר. רִבִּי מְנַחֵם בֵּירִבִּי יוֹסֵי אוֹמֵר. יֵשׁ זֶה חוֹמֶר בְּמוֹחֵק מִכּוֹתֵב. שֶׁהַמּוֹחֵק עַל מְנָת לְתַקֵּן הַיָּיב. וְהַכּוֹתֵב עַל מְנָת לְקַלְקֵל פָּטוּר. יֵשׁ שֶׁהוּא כּוֹתֵב נְקוּדָה אַחַת וְחַיָּיב עָלֶיהָ מִשּׁוּם כּוֹתֵב וּמִשּׁוּם מוֹחֵק. יֵשׁ שֶׁהוּא מוֹחֵק נְקוּדָה אַחַת וְחַיָּיב עָלֶיהָ מִשּׁוּם כּוֹתֵב וּמִשּׁוּם מוֹחֵק. הֵיךְ עֲבִידָא. הָיָה דָּלֶ"ת וַעֲשָׂאוֹ רֵישׁ. רֵישׁ וַעֲשָׂאוֹ דָּלֶ"ת. חַיָּיב מִשּׁוּם כּוֹתֵב וּמִשּׁוּם מוֹחֵק.

"If one erased a big letter where there is space to write in its stead two letters, he is liable. If he wrote one large letter even though there is space to write in its stead two letters, he is not liable. Rebbi Menaḥem ben Rabbi Yose says, this is more serious about him who erases than about him who writes that he who erases in order to correct is liable but he who writes in order to spoil is not liable.[435,436"] It may happen that one writes a single dot and is liable for it because of writing and because of erasing; it may happen that one erases a single dot and is liable for it because of writing and because of erasing. How is this? If it was a ד and he makes it ר, ר and he makes it ד; he is liable because of writing and because of erasing[437].

435 Babli 75b, Tosephta 11:9-10.
436 In general, any action to spoil does not create liability. In this particular case, if a single letter was erased so that there is no longer a recognizable lexeme it is spoiling. But correcting a single letter so that what was not a word now is one creates liability.

437 If both the words with ד or with ר make sense. Babli 104b. (The original text of the Leiden ms. reads: "one writes a single dot *on top*", "one erases a single dot *on top*"; the words "on top" were erased by the corrector, but they are quoted in *Or zarua`* II §77, *Roqeaḥ* 86.)

(10c line 9) ד. מַה בִּנְיָן הָיָה בַּמִּקְדָּשׁ. שֶׁהָיוּ נוֹתְנִין קְרָשִׁים עַל גַּבֵּי אֲדָנִים. וְלֹא לְשָׁעָה הָיְיתָה. אָמַר רִבִּי יוֹסֵה. אָמַר רִבִּי יוֹסֵה. מִכֵּיוָן שֶׁהָיוּ חוֹנִים וְנוֹסְעִים עַל פִּי הַדִּיבֵּר כְּמִי שֶׁהִיא לְעוֹלָם. אָמַר רִבִּי יוֹסֵי בֵּירִבִּי בּוּן. מִכֵּיוָן שֶׁהִבְטִיחָן הַקָּדוֹשׁ בָּרוּךְ הוּא שֶׁהוּא מַכְנִיסָן לָאָרֶץ כְּמִי שֶׁהוּא לְעוֹלָם. הָדָא אָמְרָה. בִּנְיָין לְשָׁעָה בִּנְיָין. הָדָא אָמְרָה. אֲפִילוּ מִן הַצַּד. הָדָא אָמְרָה. אֲפִילוּ נָתוּן עַל גַּבֵּי דָבָר אַחֵר. בִּנְיָין עַל גַּבֵּי כֵלִים בִּנְיָין. אֲדָנִים כְּקַרְקַע הֵן.

4. What building was at the Sanctuary? They were putting the planks on top of the bases[437]. But was this not temporary[396]? Rebbi Yose says, because they were camping and travelling by the Word[397], it was as though permanent. Rebbi Yose ben Rebbi Abun said, since the Holy One, praise to Him, has promised them that He will bring them into the Land, it is as if it were permanent. This implies, a temporary building is a building. This implies, even from the side[438]. This implies even if was put on top of something else. Does it imply that building on implements is building[439]? The bases are like soil[440].

437 As described in *Ex.* 26:15-30.
438 Since the planks were simply put into the bases without either mortar or screws, putting them up was not professional work.

"From the side" is a general expression for "nonprofessional".
439 This would forbid even putting a pot on top of another pot to keep food warm.

440 The planks are never put into the bases unless the latter are firmly stuck in the ground; it is as if the walls of the tabernacle were set into the soil.

(10d line 15) תַּנֵּי. אֶחָד מֵבִיא אֶת הָאֶבֶן וְאֶחָד מֵבִיא אֶת הַטִּיט. הַמֵּבִיא אֶת הַטִּיט חַיָּיב. רִבִּי יוֹסֵה אוֹמֵר. שְׁנֵיהֶן חַיָּיבִין. סָבַר רִבִּי יוֹסֵה. אֶבֶן בְּלֹא טִיט בִּנְיָין. הַכֹּל מוֹדִין שְׁאִים נָתַן אֶת הַטִּיט תְּחִילָּה וְאַחַר כָּךְ נָתַן אֶת הָאֶבֶן שֶׁהוּא חַיָּיב. הַבַּנַּאי שֶׁיֵּישֵׁב אֶת הָאֶבֶן בְּרֹאשׁ הַדִּימוֹס חַיָּיב. לְמִי נִצְרְכָה. לְרַבָּנָן. וְהָתֵן דַּעֲבַד דַּפִּין וְהָתֵן דַּעֲבַד סַפִּינִין. חַיָּיב מִשּׁוּם בּוֹנֶה.

It was stated[441]: "If one brings the stone and another one the mortar, he who brings the mortar is liable. Rebbi Yose says, both are liable." Rebbi Yose is of the opinion that stone without mortar is building[442]. Everybody agrees that if one put up mortar first and someone then brought stone that he is liable. "The builder who set the stone on top of the row[443] is liable.[444]" For whom is this needed? For the rabbis[445]. One who put up planks and one who put up adobe walls is liable because of building[446].

441 Tosephta 11:1, Babli 102b, with different attributions.
442 A common Roman building method.
443 Latin *domus, -us, f.*, Greek δόμος.
444 Continuation on the Tosephta. The fact that it needs a skilled craftsman to exactly adjust the stone even if no mortar is used makes it forbidden Sabbath work.
445 Who in general require mortar as a sign of building activity, but not in this case.
445 Even though no stone is used.

(10d line 21) וְהַסוֹתֵר. וּבִלְבַד לְצוֹרֶךְ. רִבִּי חָמָא בַּר עוּקְבָא בְּשֵׁם רִבִּי שִׁמְעוֹן בֶּן לָקִישׁ. הַגּוֹדֵל כְּלֵי צוּרָה חַיָּיב מִשּׁוּם בּוֹנֶה. רִבִּי אִילָא בְּשֵׁם רִבִּי שִׁמְעוֹן בֶּן לָקִישׁ. הַנּוֹפֵחַ כְּלֵי זְכוּכִית חַיָּיב מִשּׁוּם בּוֹנֶה. רַבָּנָן דְּקֵיסָרִין בְּשֵׁם רִבִּי שִׁמְעוֹן בֶּן לָקִישׁ. יֵשׁ דְּבָרִים קְרוֹבִים וּרְחוֹקִים. וְיֵשׁ דְּבָרִים רְחוֹקִים וּקְרוֹבִים. הַגּוֹדֵל כְּלֵי צוּרָה. וְהַנּוֹפֵחַ כְּלֵי זְכוּכִית. וְהָעוֹשֶׂה כְלִי בִדְפוּס. כּוּלְּהוֹן מִשּׁוּם בּוֹנֶה. הַבּוֹרֵר וְהַמְשַׁמֵּר וְהַמְרַקֵּד כּוּלְּהוֹן מִשּׁוּם מַעֲבִיר פְּסוֹלֶת. כָּל־אֶחָד וְאֶחָד חִיּוּבוֹ בִּפְנֵי עַצְמוֹ. וְלָמָּה לֹא תַנִּינָן הוֹשַׁטָה עִמָּהוֹן. רִבִּי סִימוֹן בְּשֵׁם רִבִּי יְהוֹשֻׁעַ בֶּן לֵוִי. מִפְּנֵי מַחֲלוֹקֶת רִבִּי עֲקִיבָה וַחֲכָמִים. רִבִּי חִזְקִיָּה רִבִּי יוּדָה בֶּן לֵוִי רִבִּי יְהוֹשֻׁעַ בֶּן לֵוִי בְּשֵׁם רִבִּי. יֶתֶר עֲלֵיהֶן הוֹשַׁטָה. וְלָמָּה לֹא תַנִּינָתָהּ עִמָּהוֹן. כָּל־הַמְּלָאכוֹת בְּאַחַת. וְזוֹ בִשְׁתַּיִם. כָּל־הַמְּלָאכוֹת יֵשׁ לָהֶן תּוֹלָדוֹת. וְזוֹ אֵין לָהּ תּוֹלֶדֶת.

"And who tears down," but only for a need[446]. Rebbi Ḥama bar Uqba in the name of Rebbi Simeon ben Laqish: he who braids a palm-leaf basket is liable because of building[447]. Rebbi Ila in the name of Rebbi Simeon ben Laqish: he who blows a glass vessel is liable because of building. The rabbis of Caesarea in the name of Rebbi Simeon ben Laqish: There are things which are close but far away; and there are things which are far away but close[448]. He who braids a palm-leaf basket, and he who blows a glass vessel, and he who makes a vessel in a form[449], all are because of building. He who selects, who filters[450], and who sifts, all because of removing waste. Each of them is separately liable[451]. And why was handing over not stated with them[452]? Rebbi Simon in the name of Rebbi Joshua ben Levi: Because of the disagreement of Rebbi Aqiba and the Sages[453]. Rebbi Ḥizqiah, Rebbi Jehudah ben Levi, Rebbi Joshua ben Levi in the name of Rebbi: In addition, there is handing over. And why was it not stated with them? All categories of work involve one, and this one two[454]. All categories of work have derivatives, but this has no derivative.

446 As the Mishnah stated, tearing down only creates liability if it is for the purpose of building anew.

447 The rule that there is no building *with* vessels does not mean that there is no building *of* vessels. The Babli 75b has a completely different understanding of R. Simeon ben Laqish's statement: "He who decorates a vessel or blows a glass vessel is liable because of "hitting with a hammer.""

448 There are very diverse activities which are classified under the same category for the Sabbath, and there are distinct categories which may be represented by the same abstract definition, as explained in the sequel.

449 Greek τύπος, ὁ. The vessel is cast.

450 R. David Fraenckel points out that "filtering" should be replaced by "winnowing" since filtering was reduced to either selecting or sifting (Note 325). But selecting, winnowing, and sifting are three similar activities but listed as three different categories ("close but far away") whereas the very different activities in fabricating vessels mentioned in the preceding sentence are all classified under the same heading ("far away but close").

451 Since they are separately listed in the Mishnah.

452 Why were the transactions described in Mishnaiot 1:1-2 not mentioned in the list of forbidden actions?

453 In Mishnah 11:1, one who throws from one private domain over a public domain into another private domain, R. Aqiba declares liable but the Sages do not. There is no universally accepted definition of "handing from one domain to another."

454 Since the numerals are in the feminine, they refer to domains, not to persons, as noted by R. David Fraenckel.

(10d line 32) ה'. רִבִּי חוּנָה בְּשֵׁם רִבִּי אֶלְעָזָר. לַעֲבוֹדָה זָרָה אִיתְאָמָרַת. רִבִּי יוֹחָנָן אָמַר. לְאִיסּוּרֵי הֲנָיָיה אִיתְאָמָרַת. רַב חִסְדָּא אָמַר. לַשִּׁיעוּרִין אִיתְאָמָרַת. אִית תַּנָּיֵי תַּנֵי. חַיָּיב חַטָּאת.

אִית תַּנָּיֵי תַנֵּי. כָּל־שֶׁהוּא. מָאן דְּאָמַר. חַייָב חַטָּאת. מְסַייֵעַ לְרַב חִסְדָּא. מָאן דְּאָמַר. כָּל־שֶׁהוּא. מְסַייֵעַ לְרִבִּי אֶלְעָזָר וּלְרִבִּי יוֹחָנָן. רַבָּנָן דְּקֵיסָרִין בְּשֵׁם רִבִּי יוֹסֵי בַּר חֲנִינָה. כְּגוֹן הַמּוֹךְ שֶׁהִתְקִינָה לְנִידָּתָהּ.

5. Rebbi Huna in the name of Rebbi Eleazar: This[455] has been said for idol worship. Rebbi Johanan said, this has been said for things forbidden for usufruct[456]. Rav Hisda said, this has been said for minimal quantities[457]. There are Tannaim who state, he is liable for a purification sacrifice. There are Tannaim who state, a minimal amount[458]. He who said he is liable for a purification sacrifice supports Rav Hisda. He who said a minimal amount supports Rebbi Eleazar and Rebbi Johanan. The rabbis of Caesarea in the name of Rebbi Yose bar Hanina: For example, the wad which she prepared for her menstrual period[461].

455 The statement in Mishnah 5 that "anything which cannot be preserved and one does not preserve its kind, if he took it out on the Sabbath only the one who preserves is obligated." What is anything which cannot be preserved?

456 While idols and their appurtenances also are forbidden for usufruct, the reasoning which would apply the Mishnah to idols applies to anything forbidden for usufruct.

457 In his opinion, anything less than the amounts stated in the following Mishnaiot is not enough to be preserved; the Mishnah does not refer to any particular set of things.

458 Anybody who preserves something which generally is discarded makes it important for himself. Therefore for such a person the minimal amounts stated before do not apply but he is liable for taking out even the most minute amount as long as he preserves this amount by itself. This argument is possible only for R. Eleazar and R. Johanan and conforms to R. Simeon's position in Mishnah 8:1.

459 Which people generally discard. Babli 75b.

(10d line 37) ו. רִבִּי יוֹנָה רִבִּי יוֹסֵי גָלִילְיָא בְּשֵׁם רִבִּי יוֹסֵי בֶּן חֲנִינָה. חָמוֹר מַשְׁלִים לַקַּל. אֵין הַקַּל מַשְׁלִים לֶחָמוֹר. עֲשָׂבִים מַשְׁלִימִין לַתֶּבֶן. אֵין הַתֶּבֶן מַשְׁלִים לַעֲשָׂבִים. תַּמָּן תַּנִּינָן. הַבֶּגֶד וְהַשַּׂק. הַשַּׂק וְהָעוֹר. הָעוֹר וְהַמַּפָּץ. מִצְטָרְפִין זֶה עִם זֶה. רִבִּי שִׁמְעוֹן אוֹמֵר. מִפְּנֵי שֶׁהֵן רְאוּיִין לְטָמֵא מוֹשָׁב: רִבִּי יִרְמְיָה בָּעֵי. נִיחָא יִצְטָרְפוּ לְמוֹשָׁב שֶׁכֵּן שָׁוֵו לְמוֹשָׁב בְּטָפַח. בְּהֶיסֵּק מְנַיִין. אָמַר רִבִּי עֶזְרָא קוֹמֵי רִבִּי מָנָא. שֶׁכֵּן שָׁוֵו בְּהֶסֵּק. אָמַר לֵיהּ. אֲנָן בָּעֵיי הוֹצָאָה וְאַתְּ אָמַר הֶיסֵּק. אָמַר רִבִּי לְעָזָר בַּר יוֹסֵי קוֹמֵי רִבִּי יוֹסֵי. שֶׁכֵּן שָׁוֵו בְּהֶיסֵּק. אָמַר לֵיהּ. נִיתְנֵי. בְּהוֹצָאַת כּוֹס קָטָן. אָמַר רִבִּי חֲנַנְיָה. קוּפְדָּה מַשְׁלִים לִפִיסְתָּהּ. פִּיסְתָּהּ לֹא מַשְׁלְמָה לְקוּפְדָּה. עֲשָׂבִים מַשְׁלִימִין לַתֶּבֶן. אֵין הַתֶּבֶן מַשְׁלִים לַעֲשָׂבִים. תַּנֵּי רִבִּי הוֹשַׁעְיָה. הוֹצִיא תֶבֶן לְפָרָה כִּמְלֹא פִי פָרָה. הוֹצִיא

תֶּבֶן לְגֶדִי כִּמְלֹא פִּי גְדִי חַיָּיב. רִבִּי אִילָא אָמַר. רִבִּי יוֹחָנָן בָּעֵי. מֵעַתָּה הוֹצִיא אוֹכְלִין לַחוֹלֶה כִּמְלֹא פִּי חוֹלֶה יְהֵא חַיָּיב. מוֹדֶה רִבִּי הוֹשַׁעְיָה. שֶׁאִם הוֹצִיא תֶּבֶן לְפָרָה כִּמְלֹא פִּי גְדִי שֶׁהוּא פָּטוּר. דְּלֹא תֵיסְבּוֹר. כְּמָה דְּאִית לֵיהּ לְחוּמְרָא אִית לֵיהּ לְקוּלָּא. רִבִּי בּוּן בְּרִבִּי חִייָה בָּעֵי. הַגַּע עַצְמָךְ שֶׁאֵין בַּתַּבְשִׁיל כִּגְרוֹגֶרֶת. וְכִגְרוֹגֶרֶת מְבַטֵּל גְּרוֹגֶרֶת.

זְעֵיר בַּר חִינְנָא בְּשֵׁם רִבִּי חֲנִינָא. הָדָא דְאַתְּ אָמַר. בָּאֲדוּמּוֹת. אֲבָל בִּשְׁחוֹרוֹת פּוֹרְשׁוֹת הֵן.

Rebbi Jonah, Rebbi Yose the Galilean in the name of Rebbi Yose ben Hanina: The more restrictive completes the less restrictive but the less restrictive does not complete the more restrictive[460]. Grasses complete straw; straw does not complete grasses. There we have stated[461]: "Cloth and sackcloth, sackcloth and leather, leather and bast matting combine with one another. Rebbi Simeon says, because they are apt to become impure as seats." Rebbi Jeremiah asked, one understands that they combine for seats since as seats they equally are by a hand-width. From where in היסק[462]? Rebbi Ezra said before Rebbi Mana, because they are equal in היסק. He told him, we are asking about taking out and you are saying היסק[463]? Rebbi Eleazar bar Yose said before Rebbi Yose, because they are equal in היסק. He said to him, should we state, taking out a small cup[464]? Rebbi Hanania said, meat completes bone pieces, bone pieces does not complete meat[465]; grasses complete straw, straw does not complete grasses. Rebbi Hoshaia stated: If one took out straw for a cow filling the mouth of a cow, took out straw for a goat filling the mouth of a goat, he is liable[466]. Rebbi Ila said that Rebbi Johanan asked, if one took out food for a sick person filling the mouth of a sick person, should he be liable[467]? Rebbi Hoshaia agrees that if he took out straw for a cow filling the mouth of a goat that he is not liable; for you should not think that just as he has it for restriction he also has it for leniency[468]. Rebbi Abun bar Hiyya asked, think of it if the dish was not the volume of a dried fig. Does the volume of a dried fig cancel the volume of a dried fig[469]?

Ze'ir bar Hinena in the name of Rebbi Hanina: This is what you are saying for red ones. But black ones are separated[470].

---

460 In Mishnah 6, related items have different minimal amounts which trigger liability. Any material which has a smaller threshold is added to one which has a larger one to be counted with it but not vice versa. If a person carries grasses and straw together, the entire load follows the rules of straw since the latter requires the volume of

a cow's mouth whereas the former already is a load by the volume of a goat's mouth which is smaller. Babli 76a.

461 Mishnah *Me`ilah* 4:6. Mishnah 3 had stated that materials whose minimal sizes for impurity are different do not combine for impurity. Mishnah 6 states an exception, *viz.*, that materials that may be used to make chairs or beds do combine; similarly to what was stated for the rules of the Sabbath combination material follows the rules of the material which requires a larger minimal amount.

Cloth becomes impure in general if it is at least (3 thumb-widths)² wide, but indirectly if a person who is a source of impurity sits on it (מִדְרָס) only by (3 hand-widths)². The minimal size of a piece of sack-cloth for impurity is (4 hand-widths)², for leather it is (5 hand-widths)², and for bast mats (6 hand-widths)². According to R. Simeon any of these materials if made specifically as a seat becomes impure in the size of (1 hand-width)²; for him the problem does not arise since he accepts impurity of combined material only for מִדְרָס.

462 The expression הֶסֶק is essentially unexplained. At its first occurrence it was inserted by the corrector who wrote this word instead of the scribe's שוחק "pulverizing"; at the other occurrences it is the scribe's. Liebermann conjectures that one should read שַׁבָּת "the Sabbath". This would make sense the first time but not in the following sentences. The related form הַסָּקָה "heating" (in the Yerushalmi, *Pesahim* 3:4 חסיקה; as verb later in Mishnah 12:1 לְהַסִּיק "to heat") is derived from Aramaic סוק "to ascend, climb"; it means "to make rise (the flames)" and clearly is inappropriate here. Very tentatively I am proposing to translate הֶסֶק as "load" from Accadic asāqu, ašāqu "to load, distribute" Arabic وسقة "load".

463 This seems to be excluded by the Mishnah, which indicates varying loads.

464 The meaning of this sentence is totally obscure.

465 The minimum allowed for bone (Mishnah 8:6) is larger than that for meat. It would be possible to translate פיסתה as "slice of bread" but since both meat and bread are human food their minimum is the volume of a dried fig and therefore they combine.

466 Even though it is questionable whether goats eat straw; Babli 76a (in the name of R. Simeon ben Laqish).

467 If the sick person is unable to eat the full volume of a dried fig. The amounts quoted in the Mishnah are fixed quantities.

468 As the text stands it is a triviality and the reference to leniency is unexplained. The parallel in the Babli states that a cow's mouthful of straw even if taken for a camel creates liability, a goat's mouthful does not. But the Babli should not be used to interpret the Yerushalmi in the absence of supporting evidence.

469 This seems to refer to onion- and garlic leaves, where the volume of a dried fig is much too large when these are used as spices. Since onion and garlic leaves give taste in small quantities, their minimal amounts should be much smaller than indicated in the Mishnah. The Mishnah can refer only to onion or garlic as main dish.

470 This refers to R. Jehudah's statement about lentils cooked in their pods. His statement is acceptable only for fresh lentils, not for dry ones whose pods have become indigestible.

המוציא יין פרק שמיני

משנה א: הַמּוֹצִיא יַיִן כְּדֵי מְזִיגַת הַכּוֹס. חָלָב כְּדֵי גְמִיעָה. דְּבַשׁ כְּדֵי לִתֵּן עַל הַכָּתִית. שֶׁמֶן כְּדֵי לָסוּךְ אֵבָר קָטָן. מַיִם כְּדֵי לָשׁוּף אֶת הַקִּילוֹרִית. וּשְׁאָר כָּל-הַמַּשְׁקִין בִּרְבִיעִית. וְכָל-הַשּׁוֹפְכִין בִּרְבִיעִית. רַבִּי שִׁמְעוֹן אוֹמֵר כּוּלָּן בִּרְבִיעִית לֹא נֶאֶמְרוּ כָּל-הַשִּׁעוּרִין הָאֵילוּ אֶלָּא לְמַצְנִיעֵיהֶן:

Mishnah 1: One who brings out wine to mix a cup[1], milk for a sip, honey to put on a sore spot, oil to anoint a small limb[2], water to mix eye salve[3], and all other fluids by a *quartarius*, and all waste water by a *quartarius*. Rebbi Simeon says, all are by a *quartarius*; these measures were said only for those who store them[4].

משנה ב: הַמּוֹצִיא חֶבֶל כְּדֵי לַעֲשׂוֹת אֹזֶן לְקוּפָּה. גֶּמִי כְּדֵי לַעֲשׂוֹת תְּלַאי לְנָפָה וְלִכְבָרָה. רַבִּי יְהוּדָה אוֹמֵר כְּדֵי לַעֲשׂוֹת מִמֶּנּוּ מִידַת מִנְעָל לַקָּטָן. נְיָיר כְּדֵי לִכְתּוֹב עָלָיו קֶשֶׁר מוֹכְסִין. הַמּוֹצִיא קֶשֶׁר מוֹכְסִין חַיָּב. נְיָיר מָחוּק כְּדֵי לִכְרוֹךְ עַל פִּי צְלוֹחִית קְטַנָּה שֶׁל פַּלְיָיטוֹן:

Mishnah 2: One who brings out rope to make a handle for a box, bast to make a hanger of a small or large sieve, Rebbi Jehudah says to make from it an instrument to measure a shoe for a child[5]. Paper to write on it a toll collector's receipt[6]; and anybody who carries out a toll collector's receipt is liable. Erased paper to tie over the the opening of a small perfume[7] flask.

משנה ג: עוֹר כְּדֵי לַעֲשׂוֹת קָמִיעַ. דּוּכְסוּסְטוּס כְּדֵי לִכְתּוֹב עָלָיו מְזוּזָה. קְלָף כְּדֵי לִכְתּוֹב עָלָיו פָּרָשָׁה קְטַנָּה שֶׁל תְּפִלִּין שֶׁהִוא שְׁמַע יִשְׂרָאֵל. דְּיוֹ כְּדֵי לִכְתּוֹב עָלָיו שְׁתֵּי אוֹתִיּוֹת. כְּחוֹל כְּדֵי לִכְחוֹל עַיִן אַחַת. זֶפֶת וְגָפְרִית כְּדֵי לַעֲשׂוֹת נֶקֶב. שַׁעֲוָה כְּדֵי לִיתֵּן עַל פִּי נֶקֶב קָטָן:

Mishnah 3: Leather to make an amulet, split leather[8] to write a *mezuzzah* on, parchment[9] to write on it the smallest paragraph of phylacteries, which is *Shema` Israel*[10], ink sufficient to write two letters with, *kohl* to apply to one eye[11], asphalt and sulphur to fix a hole, wax to close a small hole.

משנה ד: דֶּבֶק כְּדֵי לִתֵּן בְּרֹאשׁ הַשַּׁבְשֶׁבֶת. חַרְסִית כְּדֵי לַעֲשׂוֹת פִּי כּוּר שֶׁל צוֹרְפֵי זָהָב. רַבִּי יְהוּדָה אוֹמֵר כְּדֵי לַעֲשׂוֹת פִּטְפּוּט. סוּבִּין כְּדֵי לִתֵּן עַל פִּי כּוּר שֶׁל צוֹרְפֵי זָהָב. סִיד כְּדֵי לָסוּד קְטַנָּה שֶׁבַּבָּנוֹת רַבִּי יְהוּדָה אוֹמֵר כְּדֵי לַעֲשׂוֹת כִּלְכּוּל. רַבִּי נְחֶמְיָה אוֹמֵר כְּדֵי לַעֲשׂוֹת אַנְדִּיפִי:

Mishnah 4: Glue to put on top of the snare[12], clay soil to make an opening for a goldsmith's oven, Rebbi Jehudah says, to make a stand[13]. Bran to put on the opening of a goldsmith's oven. Lime to apply to a little girl[14], Rebbi Jehudah says, to treat a temple, Rebbi Nehemiah says, to prepare make-up[15].

משנה ח: אֲדָמָה כְּחוֹתָם הַמַּרְצוּפִים דִּבְרֵי רבִּי עֲקִיבָה וַחֲכָמִים אוֹמְרִים כְּחוֹתָם הָאִיגְּרוֹת. זֶבֶל וְחוֹל דַּק כְּדֵי לְזַבֵּל קֶלַח שֶׁל כְּרוּב דִּבְרֵי רבִּי עֲקִיבָה וַחֲכָמִים אוֹמְרִים כְּדֵי לְזַבֵּל כְּרֵישָׁה. חוֹל הַגַּס כְּדֵי לִיתֵּן עַל מְלֹא כַף סִיד. קָנֶה כְּדֵי לַעֲשׂוֹת קוּלְמוֹס. אִם הָיָה עָבָה אוֹ מְרוּסָּם כְּדֵי לְבַשֵּׁל בֵּיצָה קַלָּה שֶׁבַּבֵּיצִים טְרוּפָה וּנְתוּנָה בָּאִילְפָּס:

Mishnah 5: Earth[16] for a seal of merchandise, the words of Rebbi Aqiba, but the Sages say, for seals of letters. Manure and sand to fertilize one cabbage stalk, the words of Rebbi Aqiba, but the Sages say, to fertilize a stalk of leek. Coarse sand to add to a handful of lime, reed to make writing pen. If it was wide or splintered, to cook a most easily cooked egg[17], scrambled in a pan[18].

משנה ו: עֶצֶם כְּדֵי לַעֲשׂוֹת תַּרְוָד רבִּי יְהוּדָה אוֹמֵר כְּדֵי לַעֲשׂוֹת חָף. זְכוּכִית כְּדֵי לִגְרוֹד בָּהּ רֹאשׁ הַכַּרְכָּד. צְרוֹר אֶבֶן כְּדֵי לִזְרוֹק בָּעוֹף רבִּי אֱלִיעֶזֶר בֶּן יַעֲקֹב אוֹמֵר כְּדֵי לִזְרוֹק בַּבְּהֵמָה:

Mishnah 6: Bone to fill a spoon[19]; Rebbi Jehudah says to make a tooth of a key. Glass to scrape the head of the weaver's beam[20]. A pebble to throw at a bird[21]; Rebbi Eliezer ben Jacob says, to throw at an animal.

משנה ז: חֶרֶס כְּדֵי לִיתֵּן בֵּין פַּצִּים לַחֲבֵרוֹ דִּבְרֵי רבִּי יְהוּדָה. רבִּי מֵאִיר אוֹמֵר כְּדֵי לַחְתּוֹת בּוֹ אֶת הָאוּר. רבִּי יוֹסֵי אוֹמֵר כְּדֵי לְקַבֵּל רְבִיעִית. אָמַר רבִּי מֵאִיר אַף עַל פִּי שֶׁאֵין רְאָיָה לַדָּבָר זֵכֶר לַדָּבָר לֹא יִמָּצֵא בִּמְכִתָּתוֹ חֶרֶשׂ לַחְתּוֹת אֵשׁ מִיָּקוּד. אָמַר לוֹ רבִּי יוֹסֵי מִשָּׁם רְאָיָה לַחְשׂוֹף מַיִם מִגֶּבֶא:

Mishnah 7: A potsherd to put between one half-brick and another, the words of Rebbi Jehudah. Rebbi Meïr says, to carry fire with it. Rebbi Yose says, to fill it with a *quartarius*. Rebbi Meïr said, even though it is no proof, it is a hint: [22]*that in its splinters no shard be found to catch fire from the blaze.* Rebbi Yose told him, from there is proof, *to draw water from the pit.*

---

1   As explained in the Halakhah, the normal size of a cup is an Italic *quartarius*, 0.133 l or 4.5 US fl. oz. Wine was never drunk unmixed; the standard is one part of wine for three parts of water. This makes the volume of wine needed for one cup

0.0331 l or 1¹/₈ fl. oz.

2 A small limb of a newborn baby.

3 Chapter 7, Note 344.

4 He holds that people do not store a volume less than a *quartarius* of any fluid; therefore smaller amounts create liability only for persons who would store smaller amounts. Cf. Chapter 7, Note 458.

5 I. e., the length of a child's foot.

6 In the interpretation of the Babli (78b) the confirmation of paid tolls uses a code of two Capital Greek letters.

7 Latin *foliatum, -i* (*scil. unguentum*) "perfume made from leaves of aromatic plants".

8 Greek δίσχιστος, "the thinner, inner part of split leather, in contrast to the thicker outer part קלף" (I. Löw).

9 This is the modern meaning (at least since Geonic times) of the word. Originally it denoted leather made of hide of which the hairy side was peeled off (קולף).

10 *Deut.* 6:4-9.

11 As make-up.

12 To catch birds.

13 A base for a stove or similar appliance.

14 As a depilatory or a beauty treatment to prepare her for the marriage market.

15 Maimonides explains either to curl the hairs of the temple (R. Jehudah) or a lock on the forehead (R. Nehemiah). The definition of כִּלְכּוּל is confirmed by the Babli and Geonic sources.

16 Maimonides: "Sticky red loam used for sealing goods to be transported."

17 A chicken egg.

18 Greek λοπάς, -άδος, ἡ "flat dish".

19 A unit of volume for medical prescriptions.

20 Greek κερκίς, -ίδος, ἡ "weaver's shuttle; peg; pin; measuring rod".

21 To scare it away.

22 *Is.* 30:14.

(11a line 19) הַמוֹצִיא יַיִן כְּדֵי מְזִיגַת הַכּוֹס כול׳. רִבִּי זְעוּרָא שָׁאַל לְרִבִּי יוֹשִׁיָּה. כַּמָּה שִׁיעוּרָן שֶׁלְכּוֹסוֹת. אָמַר לֵיהּ. נִלְמוֹד סָתוּם מִן הַמְפוֹרָשׁ. דְּתַנֵּי רִבִּי חִייָה. אַרְבָּעָה כּוֹסוֹת שֶׁאָמְרוּ יֶשְׁנָן רְבִיעִית יַיִן בָּאִיטַלְקִי.

1 זעורא | פ זעורה ש**18** זעירא   שאל | ש שאיל   יאשיה | פ יושיה ש יאשיהו   כמה | פ**18** כמה הוא ש כמה הא   שיעורו שלכוסות | **18** שיעור הכוסות   2 שאמרו | **18** שלפסח   3 באיטלקי | ש האיטלקי **18** איטלקי

²³"One who brings out wine to mix a cup," etc. Rebbi Ze'ira asked Rebbi Joshiah, what is the measure of cups? He told him, let us infer the hidden from the explicit since Rebbi Hiyya stated, the Four Cups which they said add up to an Italic *quartarius* of wine²⁴.

23 The origin of this text is in *Pesahim* 10:1 (37c l. 14,פ) and for the later parts *Šeqalim* 3:2 (47b l. 54,ע). This paragraph also is copied later in Chapter 18 (16c l. 15, **18**) The *Šeqalim* text was added by a corrector from a different source; readings of this text are given only for the first paragraph since while the texts here and in *Šeqalim* clearly derive from a common source, the actual texts are not copies of one another.

The question is about the minimal

amount of wine one is obligated to drink at the Passover *Seder* where four cups are prescribed (cf. the author's *The Scholar's Haggadah*, Northvale 1995, pp. 185-190.)
24 Since the total volume of wine in 4 cups is one *quartarius,* for a single cup one needs $^1/_4$ *quartarius* of wine and $^3/_4$ *quartarii* of water. Similarly Babli 76b, *Pesahim* 108b.

(11a line) תַּמָּן תַּנִּינָן. מְפַנִּין אַרְבַּע וְחָמֵשׁ קוּפוֹת. רִבִּי זְעוּרָא שָׁאַל לְרִבִּי יוֹשִׁיָה. כַּמָּה שִׁיעוּרָהּ שֶׁלְקוּפָּה. אָמַר לֵיהּ. נִלְמוֹד סָתוּם מִן הַמְפוֹרָשׁ. דְּתַנִּינָן תַּמָּן. בְּשָׁלשׁ קוּפוֹת שֶׁל שָׁלשׁ שָׁלשׁ סְאִין תּוֹרְמִין אֶת הַלִּשְׁכָּה.

1 זעורא | פ זעורה 18ש זעירא   יאשיה | פ יושיה ש אושיא   כמה | פ 18ס כמה היא 18ש כמה הוא   שיעורה | 18
שיעור   2 שלקופה | ש של שלש קופות 18 הקופות

There, we have stated[25]: "One removes four or five baskets." Rebbi Ze`ira asked Rebbi Joshiah, what is the measure of baskets? He told him, let us infer the hidden from the explicit since we have stated there[26]: "The contributions for the Temple were removed in three baskets of three *seah*[27] each."

25 Mishnah 18:1. If one needs space in his storage area to accommodate visitors or students he may make space even if it involves considerable effort.
26 Mishnah *Šeqalim* 3:2. The Temple tax, half a *šeqel* of silver coin, was collected in a separate room. Three times a year three baskets full of silver coins were removed from there to pay for the public service in the Temple.
27 One *seah* is 24 *log* (of 4 *quartarii* each) or 12.8 l; a Roman *urna.*

(11a line 25) רִבִּי יוֹסֵה בֵּרְבִּי בּוּן בְּשֵׁם רִבִּי יוֹחָנָן. דְּרִבִּי יְהוּדָה הִיא. דְּתַנֵּי. מַיִם כְּדֵי גְמִיָּיה. רִבִּי יוּדָה אוֹמֵר. כְּדֵי מְזִינַת הַכּוֹס. יַיִן כְּדֵי גְמִיָּיה. רִבִּי יוּדָה אוֹמֵר. כְּדֵי מְזִינַת הַכּוֹס. מָזוּג בְּכַמָּה. נִשְׁמְעִינָהּ מִן הָדָא. מַיִם כְּדֵי גְמִיָּיה. רִבִּי יְהוּדָה אוֹמֵר. כְּדֵי מְזִינַת הַכּוֹס. יַיִן כְּדֵי גְמִיָּיה. רִבִּי יְהוּדָה אוֹמֵר. כְּדֵי מְזִינַת הַכּוֹס. הָדָא אָמְרָה. מָזוּג. אֲפִילוּ בְּכַמָּה כּוֹסוֹת. כַּמָּה הוּא שִׁיעוּרָן שֶׁלְכוֹסוֹת. רִבִּי אָבוּן אָמַר. טִיטְרַטִין וּרְבִיעַ.

1 יוסה | פ יוסי   ביר' בון | ש בר ביבון   יהודה | פ יודא   2 הכוס | פ (הכוס) המוזג   יין . . . הכוס | פ - 3
גמייה | ש גמיע'   יהודה' | פ יודה   גמייה | ש גמיע'   4 יהודה | פ יודה הדא . . . כוסות | פ - אפילו בכמה
כוסות | ש כדי מזיגת הכוס   5 אבון | פ מנא   טיטרטין | פ טיטרטון ש טוטרטין

Rebbi Yose ben Rebbi Abun said, it[28] is Rebbi Jehudah's. As it was stated[29] "Water, a gulp[30]; Rebbi Jehudah says, for mixing a cup. Wine, a gulp; Rebbi Jehudah says, for mixing a cup."

[31]Mixed by how much? Let us hear from the following: "Water. a gulp; Rebbi Jehudah says, for mixing a cup. Wine. a gulp; Rebbi Jehudah says, for

mixing a cup." This implies even many cups[32]. What is the measure of cups? Rebbi Abun said, τέταρτον is a quarter[33].

28 The Mishnah which determines the minimum amount of wine which creates liability for wine as the quantity needed to mix a cup, and water to mix eye salve.

29 Probably a misquote from a *baraita* similar to Tosephta 8:10 which among other items states "One who brings out wine for a gulp, Rebbi Jehudah says to mix a cup. Water for a gulp, Rebbi Jehudah says to mix eye salve." In both instances the anonymous Mishnah proclaims what the Tosephta states as R. Jehudah's opinion.

30 Half a *quartarius* (cf. Eva and H. Guggenheimer, תרטימר בשר, *Sinai* 81 (1971), p. 191; *Sanhedrin* Chapter 8, Note 15), twice the amount permitted by R. Jehudah.

31 This paragraph also has a parallel in *Šeqalim*, in somewhat different formulation and attributed not to R. Yose ben R. Abun but to R. Yose ben Vivianus.

32 This does not make sense. The correct text seems to be from *Šeqalim*: "mixed for a cup". Since the *baraita* also noted that wine creates liability in the amount of a gulp it implies that the reference is not to unmixed wine, which was not considered a drink of civilized people, but mixed wine. Therefore both for water and for wine the amount is a quarter of a *quartarius*.

33 S. Liebermann has shown that because ה no longer was pronounced in Galilee, וּרְבִיעַ has to be read as הוא רביע. The basic measure is a *quartarius*, a quarter of a *log* (*sextarius*).

(11a line 31) מַהוּ לִשְׁתּוֹתָן בְּכֶרֶךְ אֶחָד. מִן מַה דְּאָמַר רִבִּי יוֹחָנָן בְּהַלֵּל. אִם שָׁמְעָהּ בְּבֵית הַכְּנֶסֶת יָצָא. הָדָא אָמְרָה. אֲפִילוּ שְׁתִּיָין בְּכֶרֶךְ אֶחָד יָצָא. מַהוּ לִשְׁתּוֹתָן מְפוּסָקִין. כְּלוּם אָמְרוּ שֶׁיִּשְׁתֶּה לֹא שֶׁיִּשְׁתַּכֵּר. אִם הוּא שׁוֹתֶה אוֹתָן מְפוּסָקִין אַף הוּא אֵינוֹ מִשְׁתַּכֵּר. מַהוּ לָצֵאת בְּיַיִן שֶׁלִּשְׁבִיעִית. תַּנֵּי רִבִּי הוֹשַׁעְיָה. יוֹצְאִין בְּיַיִן שֶׁלִּשְׁבִיעִית. מַהוּ לָצֵאת בְּקוֹנְדִּיטוֹן. מִן מַה דְּתַנֵּי בַּר קַפָּרָא. קוֹנְדִּיטוֹן כְּיַיִן. הָדָא אָמְרָה. יוֹצְאִין בְּקוֹנְדִּיטוֹן. מַהוּ לָצֵאת מְזוּגִין. מִן מַה דְּתַנֵּי רִבִּי חִיָּיא. אַרְבָּעָה כּוֹסוֹת שֶׁאָמְרוּ יוֹצְאִין בָּהֶן בֵּין חַיִּין בֵּין מְזוּגִין. וְהוּא שֶׁיְּהֵא בָּהֶן טַעַם וּמַרְאֶה יַיִן. אָמַר רִבִּי יִרְמְיָה. מִצְוָה לָצֵאת בְּיַיִן אָדוֹם. מַה טַעַם. אַל־תֵּרֶא יַיִן כִּי יִתְאַדָּם. תַּנֵּי. מְבוּשָּׁל כְּדֵי תַבֵּל. מַהוּ לָצֵאת בְּיַיִן מְבוּשָּׁל. רִבִּי יוֹנָה אָמַר. יוֹצְאִין בְּיַיִן מְבוּשָּׁל. רִבִּי יוֹנָה כְּדַעְתֵּיהּ. דְּרִבִּי יוֹנָה שְׁתֵי אַרְבַּעְתֵּי כָסוֹי דְּלֵילֵי פִסְחָא וְחָזִק רֵישֵׁיהּ עַד עֲצַרְתָּא.

1 בהלל | פ הלל   שמעה | פ שמעו   3 אף הוא | פ -   5 לצאת | פ לצאת בהן   7 מה טע' | פ שנאמר   9 חזק | פ חזיק

May one drink them[34] together? Since Rebbi Johanan said about *Hallel*, if he heard it in the synagogue he has fulfilled his obligation[35], this implies that if he drank them together he fulfilled his obligation. May one drink them with interruptions[36]? They said that he should drink, not that he should get drunk.

If he drinks them with interruptions, would he not become drunk? May one fulfill his obligation with Sabbatical wine[37]? Rebbi Hoshaia stated, one may fulfill his obligation with Sabbatical wine. May one fulfill his obligation with spiced wine[38]? Since Bar Qappara stated, spiced wine is like wine, which implies that one may fulfill his obligation with spiced wine. May one fulfill his obligation with mixed wine[39]? Since Rebbi Hiyya stated: the Four Cups which they prescribed, one may fulfill his obligation either with unmixed or mixed, on condition that it have the taste and looks of wine. Rebbi Jeremiah said, it is meritorious to fulfill one's obligation with red wine. What is the reason? *Do not see wine when it shows its red color*[40]. It was stated, cooked for spice[41]. May one fulfill his obligation with cooked wine[42]? Rebbi Jonah said, one may fulfill his obligation with cooked wine. Rebbi Jonah follows his own opinion, since Rebbi Jonah drank his four cups in the Passover night and had a headache until Pentecost[43].

34 The Four Cups of wine prescribed in the *Seder* night. Normally the first cup is for *Qiddush*, the benediction welcoming the holiday, the second cup comes after recitation of the story of the Exodus from Egypt, the third cup after the meal, and the fourth after finishing the recitation of *Hallel*, Ps. 113-118.

35 In a congregation where men are illiterate and cannot present to their families the text preceding the second and fourth cups, the reader in the synagogue may read for them the Psalms of *Hallel*; then they go home and drink the Four Cups and so have minimally fulfilled their obligations.

36 It is noted elsewhere (cf. Note 30) that the civilized way of drinking a standard cup of one *quartarius* is in two gulps. Assuming normal gulps of wine it follows that a person who drinks his cup in many gulps has a cup much larger than a *quartarius*. This is frowned upon.

37 It is difficult to understand why Sabbatical wine should be forbidden for the *Seder*. One possible explanation is that since Sabbatical produce is for *your domestic animals and the wild animals on the fields* (*Lev.* 25:7), there is an obligation to immediately consume all Sabbatical produce once nothing is left for the wild animals on the fields. If this occurs before Passover one has a problem. But except in a year of draught and famine this will not happen early in Spring.

38 Latin *conditus, -a, -um,* "spiced, preserved".

39 Diluted with water more than in the ratio of 1:3. Babli *Pesahim* 108b.

40 *Prov.* 23:31. While the verse is a warning against alcoholism, it shows that wine is supposed to be red.

41 Cooked wine was not usually used as a drink but as an ingredient for cooking.

42 Where all alcohol has evaporated.

43 If he drank four cups of alcoholic wine; he permitted non-alcoholic wine for sufferers of the same condition, and as a corollary for everybody.

(11a line 43) רִבִּי יוּדָה בֵּירִבִּי אִילְעָאי שָׁתֵי אַרְבַּעְתֵּי כַסּוֹי דְּלֵילֵי פִסְחָא וְחָזֵק רֵישֵׁיהּ עַד חַגָּא. חַמְתֵּיהּ חָדָא מַטְרוֹנָה אַפּוֹי נְהִירִין. אָמְרָה לֵיהּ. סַבָּא סָבָא. חָדָא מִן תְּלַת מִילִין אִית בָּךְ. אוֹ שָׁתֵיי חֲמַר אַתְּ. אוֹ מַלְוֵה בְרִבִּית אַתְּ. אוֹ מְגַדֵּל חֲזִירִין אַתְּ. אָמַר לָהּ. תִּיפַּח רוּחָהּ דְּהַהִיא אִיתָּתָא. חָדָא מִן תְּלָת מִילַיָּיא לֵית בִּי. אֶלָּא אוּלְפָּנִי שְׁכִיחַ לִי. דִּכְתִיב חָכְמַת אָדָם תָּאִיר פָּנָיו.
1 וחזק | פ וחזיק   3 חזירין | פ חזירים דהחיא | פ דהיא   4 תלת | פ אילין תלתי

רִבִּי אַבָּהוּ נְחַת לְטִיבֶּרְיָא. חֲמוֹנֵיהּ תַּלְמִידוֹי דְּרִבִּי יוֹחָנָן אַפּוֹי נְהִירִין. אָמְרוֹן קוֹמֵי רִבִּי יוֹחָנָן. אַשְׁכַּח רִבִּי אַבָּהוּ סִימָה. אָמַר לוֹן. לָמָּה. אָמְרִין לֵיהּ. אַפּוֹי נְהִירִין. אָמַר לוֹן. דִּילְמָא אוֹרָיְיתָא חַדְתָּא שְׁמַעְתָּהּ. סְלִיק לְגַבֵּיהּ. אָמַר לֵיהּ. מַאי אוֹרָיְיתָא חַדְתָּא שְׁמַעְתְּ. אָמַר לֵיהּ. תּוֹסֶפְתָּא עַתִּיקְתָּא. וּקְרָא עֲלוֹי. חָכְמַת אָדָם תָּאִיר פָּנָיו.
1 נחת | פ אתא   2 סימה | פ סימא   3 שמעתה | פ שמע סליק | פ סלק מאי | פ מה אוריתא | פ אורייא

[44]Rebbi Jehudah bar Ilai drank his four cups in the Passover night and had a headache until Tabernacles. A lady[45] saw that his face was shiny. She said to him, old man, old man, one of three things applies to you. Either you are drunk from wine, or you are lending on interest, or you are raising pigs. He answered her, this woman's spirit shall be blown away, not one of these three things applies to me, but my learning is ever present with me, as it is written[46], *a man's wisdom illuminates his face*.

Rebbi Abbahu descended to Tiberias. The students of Rebbi Johanan saw that his face was shiny. They said before Rebbi Johanan, Rebbi Abbahu found a treasure. He asked them, why? They told him, his face is shiny. He said to them, maybe he understood a new teaching. He came to visit him. He asked him, what new teaching did you hear? He said, an old Tosephta. He recited about him, *a man's wisdom illuminates his face*.

44 Babli *Berakhot* 55a; different *Nedarim* 49b.
45 Latin *matrona, -ae*.
46 *Eccl.* 8:1.

(11a line 53) אָמַר רִבִּי חֲנִינָה. לוּגָא דְּאוֹרָיְיתָא תּוֹמַנְתָּא עַתִּיקְתָּא דְּמוּרְיָיסָא דְּצִיפֳּרִין. אָמַר רִבִּי יוֹנָה. חֲכִים אֲנָא לָהּ. דְּבֵית רִבִּי יַנַּאי הֲווֹן מְכִילִין בָּהּ דְּבָשׁ. תַּנֵּי. חֲצִי שְׁמִינִית טְבֶּרְיָינִית הַיְשָׁנָה. אָמַר רִבִּי יוֹחָנָן. הָדָא דִידָן הֲוַות. וְלָמָּה לֹא אָמַר. עַתִּיקְתָא. בְּגִין דַּהֲוָוָת בְּיוֹמוֹי. אִית דְּאָמְרִין. דַּהֲוָוָת זְעֵירָא וְרָבַת וּזְעָרַת. וְלֹא זְעֶרֶת כַּמָּה דַּהֲוָוָת. כַּמָּה הוּא שִׁיעוּרוֹ שֶׁלְּכוֹס. רִבִּי יוֹסֵה בְּשֵׁם רִבִּי יוּדָה בַּר פָּזִי רִבִּי יוֹסֵי בֵּירִבִּי בּוּן בְּשֵׁם שְׁמוּאֵל. אֶצְבָּעַיִם עַל אֶצְבָּעַיִם עַל רוּם אֶצְבַּע וּמֶחֱצָה

וּשְׁלִישׁ אֶצְבַּע. תַּנֵּי. יָבֵשׁ כְּזַיִת. דִּבְרֵי רִבִּי נָתָן. רַבָּנָן דְּקַיְסָרִין בְּשֵׁם רִבִּי יוֹסֵה בֵּירִבִּי בּוּן בְּשֵׁם רִבִּי יוֹחָנָן. אָתְיָא דְּרִבִּי נָתָן כְּרִבִּי שִׁמְעוֹן. כְּמָה דְּרִבִּי שִׁמְעוֹן אוֹמֵר. בָּרְבִיעִית. כֵּן רִבִּי נָתָן אוֹמֵר. בָּרְבִיעִית. לִכְשֶׁיִּקְרָשׁ יְהֵא בוֹ כְּזַיִת.

3 הישנה | פ ישנה אית | פ ואית   5 אצבעים | פ עצבעיים   6 יוסה | פ יוסי

Rebbi Ḥanina said, the *log* of the Torah is the old Sepphorean eighth[47] of fish sauce. Rebbi Jonah said, I know it. In the House of Rebbi Yannai they were measuring honey with it. It was stated, half of the old Tiberian eighth. Rebbi Johanan said, this one we used. Why did he not say, the old one? Because it was in his days. Some are saying, it was small, then was enlarged, and diminished, but it was not made small as before. What is the measure of a cup? Rebbi Yose in the name of Rebbi Jehudah bar Pazi, Rebbi Yose ben Rebbi Abun in the name of Samuel: Two fingers by two fingers high a finger and a half and a third of a finger[48]. It was stated[49], dried like the volume of an olive, the words of Rebbi Nathan. The rabbis of Caesarea in the name of Rebbi Yose ben Rebbi Abun in the name of Rebbi Johanan: Rebbi Nathan follows Rebbi Simeon. Just as Rebbi Simeon says, a *quartarius*, so Rebbi Nathan says, a *quartarius*, when it jells it will have the volume of an olive[50].

47 The unit of which this was an eighth is a third of a *seah*, half a *modius* of 16 *sextarii* (לוּגִּים). These are local measures not recorded in classical literature.

48 This value of $2 \times 2 \times 1^{5}/_{6} = 7^{1}/_{3}$ cubic digits compares to a Babylonian value of 10.8 cubic digits (Babli *Pesaḥim* 109a). A cubit is 24 digits. Various cubits were in use; therefore it is difficult to define this volume in modern terms. The variability of the cubit is mirrored in the Greek world by the many values given for the *stadion*, which varies from 148 m for the (Egyptian) *itinerant stadion* to the Greek sacramental 184 m. Based on the itinerant stadion and 1 mile = 7.5 stadia = 2000 cubits, one would obtain 91 cm³ for the cup.

In *Terumot* 10:7 (Note 80), a *log* is defined as (volume corresponding to a weight of) 200 denar. If volume of water is intended, this would make a cup of 155 cm³. In *Terumot* 5:3, the *log* is defined as the volume of 4 eggs, the *modius* (16 *log*) as 96 eggs (in the Babli, *Eruvin* 83a, 217 eggs, which, however, refers not to the Roman but the Syrian *modius*, twice the volume of the Roman). For the standard *modius* of 8.536 l, this gives the volume of a cup as the standard *quartarius* of 133 cm³ (Note 1).

49 Tosephta 8:10, Babli 77a.

50 Babli 77a. The *Pesaḥim* text ends here.

(11a line 63) רִבִּי סִימוֹן בְּשֵׁם רִבִּי יְהוֹשֻׁעַ בֶּן לֵוִי. מַעֲשֶׂה בְּפִרְדָּה שֶׁלְּבֵית רִבִּי שֶׁמֵּתָה. וְטִהֲרוּ דָּמָהּ מִשּׁוּם נְבֵילָה. רִבִּי אֶלְעָזָר שָׁאַל לְרִבִּי סִימוֹן. עַד כַּמָּה. וְלֹא אַגִּיבֵיהּ. שָׁאַל לְרִבִּי יְהוֹשֻׁעַ בֶּן לֵוִי וְאָמַר לֵיהּ. עַד רְבִיעִית טָהוֹר. יוֹתֵר מִכָּן טָמֵא. וּבָאַשׁ לְרִבִּי אֶלְעָזָר. דְּלָא חָזַר לֵיהּ רִבִּי סִימוֹן שְׁמוּעָתָא. רַב בֵּיבַי הֲוָה יְתִיב מַתְנִי הָדֵין עוֹבְדָא. אָמַר לֵיהּ רִבִּי יִצְחָק בַּר כַּהֲנָא. עַד רְבִיעִית טָהוֹר. יוֹתֵר מִיכָּן טָמֵא. וּבְעִיט בֵּיהּ. אָמַר לֵיהּ רִבִּי זְרִיקָן. בְּגִין דְּשָׁאַל לָךְ אַתְּ בְּעַט בֵּיהּ. אָמַר לֵיהּ. הָא דְלָא הֲוַת דַעְתִּי עֲלַי. כְּדָמַר רִבִּי חָנִין. וְהָיוּ חַיֶּיךָ תְּלוּיִם לְךָ מִנֶּגֶד. זֶה הַלּוֹקֵחַ חִטִּים לַשָּׁנָה. וּפָחַדְתָּ לַיְלָה וְיוֹמָם. זֶה הַלּוֹקֵחַ מִן הַסִּידְקִי. וְלֹא תַאֲמִין בְּחַיֶּיךָ. זֶה הַלּוֹקֵחַ מִן הַפַּלְטָר. וַאֲנָא סָמוּךְ לְפַלְטִירָא. מַיי כְּדוֹן. הֵעִיד רִבִּי יְהוֹשֻׁעַ בֶּן בְּתֵירָא עַל דַּם נְבֵילוֹת שֶׁהוּא טָהוֹר. מָהוּ טָהוֹר. טָהוֹר מִלְּהַכְשִׁיר. הָא לְטַמּוֹת מְטַמֵּא. תַּמָּן תַּנִּינָן. דַּם הַשֶּׁרֶץ בִּבְשָׂרוֹ מְטַמֵּא וְאֵינוֹ מַכְשִׁיר. וְאֵין לָנוּ כַּיּוֹצֵא בוֹ. וְאֵין לָנוּ כַּיּוֹצֵא בוֹ כְּשִׁיעוּר טוּמְאָתוֹ. אֲבָל דָּמוֹ מְטַמֵּא כִּבְשָׂרוֹ. אָמַר רַב יוֹסֵף. מַאן דָּמַר. טָמֵא. כְּרִבִּי יְהוּדָה. טָהוֹר. כְּרִבִּי יְהוֹשֻׁעַ בֶּן בְּתֵירָה. אָמַר לֵיהּ רַב אֲבוּדּוּמָה נְחִיתָה. וְיָאוּת רִבִּי יְהוּדָה מוֹרְיָינָא דִּנְשִׂיָּיה הֲוָה.

Rebbi Simon in the name of Rebbi Joshua ben Levi: It happened that a mule of Rebbi's household died and they declared its blood pure regarding the carcass[51]. Rebbi Eleazar asked Rebbi Simon, how much? He did not answer him. He asked Rebbi Joshua ben Levi who told him, it is pure up to a *quartarius*. More than that is impure[52]. Rebbi Eleazar felt badly that Rebbi Simon had not repeated the tradition to him. Rav Bevai was sitting stating this occurrence. Rebbi Isaac bar Cahana asked him, it is pure up to a *quartarius*; more than that impure? He was unfriendly to him. Rebbi Zeriqan asked him, because he asked you, you were unfriendly to him? He answered him, because my mind was not clear, as Rebbi Ḥanin said, [53]*your life will hang far from you*, that is one who buys a year's supply of wheat, *you will be fearful night and day*, that is one who buys from the Saracen[54], *and you will not believe in your survival*, that is one who buys from the retail store[55], and I am dependent on retail stores. What about it? "Rebbi Joshua ben Bathyra testified about blood of carcasses that it is pure.[56]" What means pure? It is pure in that it does not prepare[57], but for impurity it makes impure. There, we have stated[58] "The blood of a crawling animal (in) [is like][59] its flesh, it makes impure but does not prepare. Nothing else is like this." Nothing else is like this in the amount needed for its impurity[60]. But its blood makes impure like its flesh. Rav Joseph said, he who says "impure" follows Rebbi Jehudah[61]; he who says "pure" follows Rebbi Joshua ben Bathyra. Rav Eudaimon the emigrant told him, this is correct; Rebbi Jehudah was the instructor of the Patriarch[62].

51 A different version of the entire paragraph is in the Babli *Menahot* 103b/104a. It will be explained later what the problem is.

52 A carcass of a non-kosher animal is the source of original impurity, *Lev.* 11:24-28. The question can only refer to blood separate from the carcass. The statement of R. Joshua ben Levi seems to contradict the previous statement. Carcass flesh is the source of impurity only in pieces of at least one olive size. It was stated in the previous paragraph that fluids which congeal form solid material in the size of an olive only if the original volume was at least one *quartarius*. Therefore for impurity carcass blood is not treated differently from flesh.

53 *Deut.* 28:66.

54 Following I. Löw, reading סירקי for סידקי.

55 The explanations of this word vary from πρατήρ (Buxtorf), πωλητήρ (Krauss) "seller", to *panetarius* (Kohut).

56 Mishnah *Idiut* 8:1.

57 Agricultural produce cannot become impure until it is "prepared" for impurity by contact with water (*Lev.* 11:38) or fluids which traditionally are compared with water: human body fluids, grape juice or wine, olive oil, and date honey; cf. *Demay* 2:3, Note 143. It now is asserted that the blood of non-kosher animals cannot be compared with human blood and is inactive in preparing for impurity. This was decided when Rebbi's mule died.

58 Mishnah *Makhširin* 6:5.

59 With all Mishnah mss. and the parallel in *Šeqalim* read כִּבְשָׂרוֹ.

60 Carcasses of the animals (mostly reptiles) enumerated in *Lev.* 11:29-30 generate impurity already in parts in the volume of a lentil.

61 He states in Mishnah *Idiut* 4:1 that the House of Shammai declare all blood of carcasses which is separate from the flesh as impervious to impurity while the House of Hillel declare it impure in amounts larger than a *quartarius*. In his interpretation, R. Joshua ben Bathyra follows the House of Shammai in R. Jehudah's interpretation. For the latter, all blood of Rebbi's mule separate from the body was declared pure.

62 We stay with our first interpretation, that the mule's blood was only declared not to prepare agricultural produce for impurity but that otherwise it follows the rules of impurity of carcass flesh. R. Jehudah cannot have been the kashrut supervisor of Rebbi's court, it must have been that of his father, Rabban Simeon ben Gamliel; but the tradition of his rulings was continued.

(11b line 3) תָּנֵי. דָּם כְּדֵי לִכְחוֹל עַיִן אֶחָת. רִבִּי יוֹסֵי בֵּירְבִּי בּוּן בְּשֵׁם רִבִּי יוֹחָנָן. בְּדַם עֲטַלֵּף שָׁנוּ.

It was stated[63]: "Blood enough to smear on one eye." Rebbi Yose ben Rebbi Abun in the name of Rebbi Johanan: They stated this for a bat's blood.

63 Babli 75a, Tosephta 8:10. In both these sources, it is clear that in general blood follows the rules of other fluids, with quantities smaller than a *quartarius* not creating liability. The only exception is blood used for medical purposes; this is important in itself in any quantity which commonly is used for medical treatment. One has to read the text here in the same sense; for R. Johanan only bat's blood was used in ophtalmology.

(11b line 5) חָלָב. הָדָא דְאַתְּ אָמַר. בַּחֲלַב בְּהֵמָה טְהוֹרָה. אֲבָל בַּחֲלַב בְּהֵמָה טְמֵאָה כְּדֵי לִכְחוֹל עַיִן אַחַת.

"Milk." This you are saying about milk of a pure animal. But milk of an impure animal, enough to smear on one eye[64].

דְּבַשׁ. הָדָא דְאַתְּ אָמַר. בָּהֵין עָתִיקֵי. בְּרַם בָּהֵן דִּידָן לְבַשֵּׁל בֵּיצָה קַלָּה.

"Honey." This you are saying about an old one. But current one enough to boil an easy egg[65].

שֶׁמֶן כְּדֵי לָסוּךְ אֵבֶר קָטָן. וּבִלְבַד אֵבֶר קָטָן שֶׁל קָטָן בֶּן יוֹמוֹ.

"Oil to anoint a small limb," but only a small limb of a newborn[66].

מַיִם כְּדֵי לָשׁוּף בָּהֶם אֶת הַקִּילוֹרִית. אָמַר רִבִּי לְעָזָר. הָדָא דְאַתְּ אָמַר. בְּאִילֵּין מַיָּא דְטַלָּא. בְּרַם בְּאִילֵּין דִּידָן כְּדֵי לְהַדִּיחַ פְּנֵי מְדוֹכָה.

"Water to mix eye salve." Rebbi Eleazar said, this you are saying about dew. But fresh [water] enough to moisten the face of the mortar[67].

וּשְׁאָר כָּל־הַמַּשְׁקִין בִּרְבִיעִית וְכָל־ הַשּׁוֹפָכִין בִּרְבִיעִית. רִבִּי בָּא בְשֵׁם רַב חִסְדָּא. בְּמַפְנֶּה מִבַּיִת לְבַיִת הִיא מַתְנִיתָא.

"And all other fluids by a *quartarius*, and all waste water by a *quartarius*." Rebbi Abba in the name of Rav Hisda: The Mishnah speaks of one who moves from house to house[68].

רִבִּי שִׁמְעוֹן אוֹמֵר כּוּלָּן בִּרְבִיעִית. מְשִׁיבִין חֲכָמִים לְרִבִּי שִׁמְעוֹן. אִיפְשַׁר לוֹמַר. דְּבַשׁ בִּרְבִיעִין. וְחוֹמֶץ בִּרְבִיעִין. וְהוּא מְתִיב לוֹן. כְּמָה דְאִית לְכוֹן. כָּל־הָאוֹכְלִין מִצְטָרְפִין בִּכְכוֹתֶבֶת. כֵּן אוֹף אֲנָן אִית לָן. כָּל־הַמַּשְׁקִין מִצְטָרְפִין בִּרְבִיעִית.

"Rebbi Simeon says, all are by a *quartarius*." The Sages answer Rebbi Simeon: It is impossible to say honey by a *quartarius*, vinegar by a *quartarius*. But he answered them, just as you hold that all solid food combines for the volume of a dried date, so we hold that all drinks combine for a *quartarius*[69].

לֹא נֶאֶמְרוּ כָּל־הַשִּׁיעוּרִין הָאֵילוּ אֶלָּא לְמַצְנִיעֵיהֶן: אָמַר רִבִּי מָנָא. לְמַצְנִיעֵיהֶן כָּל־שֶׁהֵן. וְתַנֵּי כֵן עַל דְּרִבִּי שִׁמְעוֹן. לֹא נֶאֶמְרוּ כָּל־הַשִּׁיעוּרִין הָאֵילוּ אֶלָּא לְמוֹצִיאֵיהֶן. הָא לְמַצְנִיעֵיהֶן כָּל־שֶׁהֵן. וְתַנֵּי כֵן עַל דְּרַבָּנָן. לֹא נֶאֶמְרוּ כָּל־הַשִּׁיעוּרִין הָאֵילוּ אֶלָּא לְמַצְנִיעֵיהֶן: הָא לְמוֹצִיאָן בִּרְבִיעִית.

"These measures were said only for those who store them[4]." Rebbi Mana said, For those who store them in the most minute amount[70]. And we have stated so against Rebbi Simeon: These measures were said only for those who throw them out. Therefore for those who store them in the most minute amount. And we have stated against the rabbis: These measures were said only for those who store them. Therefore for those who throw them out by a *quartarius*.

64 The quantity described by the Mishnah, "milk for a sip", must refer to kosher milk. Non kosher-milk can be used for external medical purposes.

65 Honey used primarily for medical purposes must be honey spoiled as human food.

Apicius (*Apicii decem libri qui dicuntur de re coquinaria*, ed. M. E. Milham, Leipzig 1969, last recipe in book VII) describes cooking an egg using honey. Unfortunately this author never gives quantities.

66 Babli 67b, Tosephta 8:9.

67 Water clean enough to be used medically goes by medical use; all others by the minimum amount used for other purposes. Different Babli 68a.

68 He will use waste water to clean the new house. But real waste water which is poured out because it smells badly goes by any amount that is thrown out on purpose.

69 Honey and vinegar are used in much smaller quantities; a *quartarius* seems to be much too large a measure. But as explained at the end of Chapter 7, materials with different minimal amounts do not combine for liability if taken out together, while for R. Simeon all drinks combine together and this may result in liability where there is none for the rabbis.

Since in Chapter 7 the amount for solid food was given as the volume of a dried fig, and all Medieval quotes of this sentence formulate "all solid food combines for the volume of a dried fig", it seems that the mention of "date" here is a scribal error and should be replaced by "fig."

70 Babli 68a.

(11b line 20) ב'. הַמּוֹצִיא חֶבֶל כְּדֵי לַעֲשׂוֹת אֹזֶן לְקוּפָּה כול'. הָדָא דְאַתְּ אָמַר בָּהֵין רַכִּיכָה. בְּרַם בָּהֵן קַשְׁיָיה כְּדֵי לְבַשֵּׁל בֵּיצָה קַלָּה.

"One who brings out rope to make a handle for a box," etc. This you are saying about soft ones but for hard ones enough to boil an easy egg[71].

גְּמִי כְּדֵי לַעֲשׂוֹת תְּלוֹי לְנָפָה וְלִכְבָרָה. הֲדָא דְאַתְּ אָמַר בָּהֵן גּוּיָיא. בְּרַם בָּהֵן בַּרְיָיא כְּדֵי לַעֲשׂוֹת שְׁנֵי בָתִּים לְנָפָה וְלִכְבָרָה. תַּנֵּי. הוּצִין כְּדֵי לַעֲשׂוֹת אוֹזֶן לִקְפִיפָה מִצְרִית. הֲדָא דְאַתְּ אָמַר בְּאִילֵּין רַכִּיכַיָּא. בְּרַם בָּאִילֵּין קַשְׁיָּיה כְּדֵי לַעֲשׂוֹת צְפוֹרָא. הוֹצִיא כְלִי נְצָרִים חַיָּב. תּוֹרֵי דָקֶל שְׁנַיִם. זְמוֹרוֹת לִנְטִיעָה שְׁתַּיִם. אִם לִבְהֵמָה כִּמְלוֹא פִי גְדִי. אִם לְעֵצִים כְּשִׁיעוּר הָעֵצִים. הוֹצִיא שְׁנֵי נִימִין מִזְּנַב הַסּוּס מִזְּנַב הַפָּרָה חַיָּב. שֶׁכֵּן מַתְקִינִין אוֹתָן לַנִּשְׁבִּין. זִיפֵּי חֲזִיר. אִית תַּנֵּי תַּנֵי. שְׁתַּיִם. אִית תַּנֵּי תַנֵי. אַחַת. מָאן דְּאָמַר. שְׁתַּיִם. בָּאִילֵּין רַכִּיכָתָא. מָאן דְּאָמַר. אַחַת. בָּאִילֵּין קַשְׁיָּיתָא. גַּלְעִינִין לִנְטִיעָה שְׁתַּיִם. אִם לִבְהֵמָה כִּמְלוֹא פִי חֲזִיר. כַּמָּה הוּא מְלֹא פִיו. אַחַת. אֲחֵרִים אוֹמְרִים. חֶשְׁבּוֹן חָמֵשׁ. הוֹצִיא סִיאָה אֵזוֹב וְקוֹרְנִית. אִם לָאוֹכְלִין כִּגְרוֹגֶרֶת. אִם לִבְהֵמָה כִּמְלוֹא פִי גְדִי. אִם לְעֵצִים כְּשִׁיעוּר הָעֵצִים. אִם לְהַזָּיָה כְּשִׁיעוּר הַזָּיָה.

"Bast to make a hanger for a small or large sieve." This you are saying about the inner part. But for the outer parts to make two loops[72] for a small or large sieve. It was stated[73]: "Palm fiber to make a handle for an Egyptian basket." This you are saying for soft ones, but for hard ones to make a border[74]. If one took out a willow container he is liable[75]. Palm leaves two. Vine shoots, for planting two, as animal feed a goat's mouthful, as wood according to the measure of wood[76]. One who brings out two hairs from a horse's tail or a cow's tail is liable because one uses them to make snares[77]. Bristles from pig, there are Tannaim who state, two, and there are Tannaim who state, one[78]. He who says two, of soft ones, but he who says one, of hard ones. Kernels, for planting, two, as animal feed a pig's mouthful[79]. What is its mouthful? One. Others say, the number five[80]. If one took out calamint, hyssop, or thyme[81], if as human food, in the volume of a dried fig, if an animal feed a goat's mouthful, as wood according to the measure of wood[76], if for sprinkling according to the measure of sprinkling[82].

71 If it is used as fuel.
72 If the bast is used to crochet.
73 Babli 68b, Tosephta 8:9.
74 Of a basket.
75 Cf. Tosephta 9:4. A complete vessel always induces liability even if it is miniaturized.
76 Fuel to boil a chicken egg.
77 Babli 90b, Tosephta 9:1.
78 Babli 90b, Tosephta 9:2. According to the Tosephta, R. Simeon states "one"; this is the only opinion quoted in the Babli.
79 Babli 90b.
80 If it were four or less, a number would have been given rather than an indefinite "mouthful".

81 Tosephta 8:31. The determination of the plant names follows Maimonides.
82 In the ceremony purifying from the impurity of the dead (*Num.* 19), two stalks of hyssop are used.

(11b line 34) רִבִּי יְהוּדָה אוֹמֵר כְּדֵי לַעֲשׂוֹת מִמֶּנּוּ מִידַת מִנְעָל לַקָּטָן. וּבִלְבַד קָטָן שֶׁהוּא יוֹדֵעַ לִנְעוֹל.

"Rebbi Jehudah says to make from it an instrument to measure a shoe for a child[5]." But only a child who knows how to tie[83].

הַמּוֹצִיא קֶשֶׁר מוֹכְסִין. תַּנֵּי. הוֹצִיא קֶשֶׁר מוֹכְסִין. עַד שֶׁלֹּא הֶרְאָהוּ לְמוֹכָס חַייָב. מִשֶּׁהֶרְאָהוּ לְמוֹכָס פָּטוּר. רִבִּי יְהוּדָה אוֹמֵר. אַף מִשֶּׁהֶרְאָהוּ לְמוֹכָס חַייָב. שֶׁהוּא רָאוּי לְהַרְאוֹתוֹ לְמוֹכָס אַחֵר. הוֹצִיא שְׁטַר חוֹב. עַד שֶׁלֹּא הֶרְאָהוּ לְבַעַל חוֹב חַייָב. מִשֶּׁהֶרְאָהוּ לְבַעַל חוֹב פָּטוּר. רִבִּי יְהוּדָה אוֹמֵר. אַף מִשֶּׁהֶרְאָהוּ לְבַעַל חוֹב חַייָב. שֶׁהוּא רָאוּי לְהַרְאוֹתוֹ לְבַעַל חוֹב אַחֵר.

"Anybody who carries out a toll collector's receipt is liable." It was stated[84]: "If one carries out a toll collector's receipt, before he showed it to the toll collector he is liable, after he showed it to the toll collector he is not liable. Rebbi Jehudah says, even after he showed it to the toll collector he is liable since he may show it to another toll collector[85]." If one carries out a document of indebtedness, before he showed it to the debtor he is liable, after he showed it to the debtor he is not liable. Rebbi Jehudah says, even after he showed it to the debtor he is liable since he may show it to another debtor[86].

נְייָר מָחוּק. תַּנֵּי. אִם יֵשׁ בּוֹ חָלָק כְּדֵי לִכְתּוֹב שְׁתֵּי אוֹתִיּוֹת חַייָב.

Erased paper It was stated: If it had empty space to write two letters on it he is liable[87].

83 But not a child who needs help with putting on his shoes.
84 Babli 78b, Tosephta 8:11.
85 According to the Babli, to a supervisor of the toll collector who issued the receipt.
86 Tosephta 8:12, Babli 78a. In the Babli the argument of R. Jehudah is more plausible: As long as the debt is not liquidated, even if the debtor has acknowledged the debt and promised to pay, the document is still needed. Once the debt is liquidated, the document either must be cut into pieces or invalidated in other ways; then its status is not that of a document but of erased paper.
87 Even if the paper is not enough to tie over a perfume flask. Babli 78b.

(11b line 42) ג'. עוֹר כְּדֵי לַעֲשׂוֹת קָמִיעַ כול'. אִית תַּנָּיֵי תַנֵּי. כְּדֵי לִיתֵּן עַל הַקָּמִיעַ. מָאן דְּאָמַר. כְּדֵי לַעֲשׂוֹת קָמִיעַ. בָּהֵין רַכִּיכָה. וּמָאן דְּאָמַר. כְּדֵי לִיתֵּן עַל הַקָּמִיעַ. בָּהֵין קַשְׁיָיא.

3. "Leather to make an amulet," etc. There are Tannaim who state, to cover the amulet. He who says to make an amulet, if it is soft[88]. But he who says to cover the amulet, if it is hard.

קְלָף כְּדֵי לִכְתּוֹב עָלָיו פָּרָשָׁה קְטַנָּה שֶׁבַּתְּפִלִּין שֶׁהִיא שְׁמַע יִשְׂרָאֵל. הָדָא דְאַתְּ אָמַר. בְּקוֹלֵף פְּנֵי הָעוֹר. בְּרַם בָּהֵין דּוּכְסוֹסְטוֹן. כְּדֵי לִכְתּוֹב עָלָיו שְׁתֵּי פָרָשִׁיּוֹת שֶׁבִּמְזוּזָה.

"Parchment to write on it the smallest paragraph of phylacteries, which is *Shema` Israel*[10]," that is, if he peels off the outer layer[9]. But split leather[8] to write both paragraphs of a *mezuzzah* on it[89].

דְּיוֹ. הוֹצִיא דְיוֹ. אִם בְּקוֹלְמוֹס. כְּדֵי לִכְתּוֹב שְׁתֵּי אוֹתִיּוֹת. אִם בְּכֵלִי צָרִיךְ יוֹתֵר. תַּמָּן תַּנֵּינָן. כַּמָּה יְהֵא בַמַּיִם וְיִהְיֶה בָהֶם כְּדֵי הַזָּייָה. רִבִּי יִרְמְיָה בָעֵי. לֹא מִסְתַּבְּרָא. אִם בִּכְלִי צָרִיךְ יְתֵיר.

"Ink." If one carried out ink in a reed pen, sufficient to write two letters. If it was in a vessel it needs more[90]. There, we have stated[91]: "How much water is needed for one sprinkling? Rebbi Jeremiah asked, would it not be reasonable that in a vessel it would need more?

כּוֹחַל כְּדֵי לִכְחוֹל עַיִן אַחַת. אָמַר רִבִּי בּוּן בַּר חִייָה. שֶׁכֵּן אִשָּׁה כּוֹחֶלֶת אַחַת מֵעֵינֶיהָ וְיוֹצֵא לַשּׁוּק. אָמַר רִבִּי אָבוּן. אֲפִילוּ זוֹנָה שֶׁבַּזּוֹנוֹת אֵינָהּ עוֹשָׂה כֵן. אֶלָּא שֶׁכֵּן אִשָּׁה חוֹשֶׁשֶׁת אַחַת מֵעֵינֶיהָ וְכוֹחֶלֶת חֲבֵירָתָהּ וְיוֹצֵא לַשּׁוּק. אָמַר רִבִּי מָנָא. מַה תַּנָּא. חוֹשֶׁשֶׁת. שֶׁכֵּן אִשָּׁה כּוֹחֶלֶת אַחַת מֵעֵינֶיהָ וּמְטַמֶּנֶת חֲבֵירָתָהּ וְיוֹצֵא לַשּׁוּק. לִבַּבְתִּינִי בְּאַחַת מֵעֵינָיִךְ. רַבָּנָן דְּקַיְסָרִין בְּשֵׁם רִבִּי בּוּן בַּר חִייָה. שֶׁכֵּן אִשָּׁה סוּמָא בְּאַחַת מֵעֵינֶיהָ וְכוֹחֶלֶת חֲבֵירָתָהּ וְיוֹצֵא לַשּׁוּק.

"Kohl to apply to one eye[11]." Rebbi Abun bar Ḥiyya said, because a woman would paint one eye with kohl and appear in public. Rebbi Abun said, even the most dissolute whore would not do this. But a woman one of whose eyes hurts paints the other with kohl and appears in public. Rebbi Mana said, did we state that she hurts? But a woman would paint one eye with kohl, cover the other, and appear in public[92]. *You captured my heart with one of your eyes*[93]. The rabbis of Caesarea in the name of Rebbi Abun bar Ḥiyya: Because a woman who is blind in one eye paints the other with kohl and appears in public.

זֶפֶת וְגָפְרִית כְּדֵי לַעֲשׂוֹת נֶקֶב. רִבִּי יוֹסֵי בַּר חֲנִינָא אָמַר. בִּמְזַנֵּיק שָׁנוּ.

"Asphalt and sulphur to fix a hole." Rebbi Yose bar Ḥanina said, they stated this about a gusher[94].

שַׁעֲוָה כְּדֵי לִיתֵּן עַל פִּי נֶקֶב קָטָן. תַּנֵּי רִבִּי חִייָה. כְּדֵי לִיתֵּן עַל פִּי סֶדֶק קָטָן.

"Wax to close a small hole." Rebbi Ḥiyya stated: To close a small crevice[95].

88 This can be used as writing material.	92 The other eye being covered by the veil. In the Babli 80a this is noted as praiseworthy behavior.
89 Babli 79b.	
90 Since to fill the pen one needs more of the ink. The Babli disagrees, 80a.	93 *Cant.* 4:9.
	94 Emergency repairs of an amphora.
91 Mishnah *Parah* 12:5. The minimum amount is what is needed to dip the heads of two stalks of hyssop. In a vessel this might require a larger amount. Cf. Note 82.	95 The Babli 80a quotes this for asphalt and sulphur.

(11b line 58) ד. מָהוּ חַרְסִית. חִוְורָה. שְׁמוּאֵל אָמַר. עָפָר כְּדֵי לְכַסּוֹת בּוֹ דַּם צִפּוֹר קְטַנָּה. תַּנֵּי שְׁמוּאֵל. עָפָר וָאֵפֶר כְּדֵי לְכַסּוֹת בּוֹ דַּם צִפּוֹר קְטַנָּה.

תַּנֵּי. חֶרֶשׂ כָּל־שֶׁהוּ גֶּמִי כָּל־שֶׁהוּ מוּתָּר לְטַלְטְלָן בְּתוֹךְ הַבַּיִת. רִבִּי זְעוּרָא בְּשֵׁם שְׁמוּאֵל. וּבִלְבַד מִן הַמּוּכָן. וְתַנֵּי כֵן. מְגוּפַת חָבִית וְחַרְסֶיהָ מוּתָּר לְטַלְטְלָן בְּתוֹךְ הַבַּיִת. הִשְׁלִיכָן לָאַשְׁפָּה אָסוּר לִיגַּע בָּהֶן.

4. What is clay soil? The gray kind. Samuel says, dust in order to cover the blood of a small bird. Samuel stated: Dust and ashes in order to cover the blood of a small bird[96].

It was stated: Potsherds of any size, bast of any size may be moved in the house. Rebbi Ze'ira in the name of Samuel: on condition that it be prepared[97]. It also was stated as follows[98]: The cover of an amphora and its potsherds may be moved in the house. If he threw them in the garbage it is forbidden to move them.

אָמַר רִבִּי. נְרָאִין דִּבְרֵי רִבִּי יְהוּדָה בְּעָשׂוּי כְּבֵיצָה. וְדִבְרֵי רִבִּי נְחֶמְיָה בְּחָבוּט.

"Rebbi said, the words of Rebbi Jehudah are reasonable if it is egg-shaped; those of Rebbi Neḥemiah if it is beaten.[99]"

96 *Lev.* 17:13. The expression "small bird" means "smaller than a pigeon" and is an indirect confirmation of the Italian Jewish tradition of eating certain birds of song. Tosephta 8:19, in the name of R. Ismael ben R. Johanan ben Beroqa.	97 As S. Liebermann has pointed out, the expressions "in the house" and "being prepared" are synonyms (Chapter 2, Note 120). Potsherds are not useless broken pieces of a vessel but have many uses; therefore automatically they are useful

implements and may be moved without restriction. The opposite of "in the house" is not "outside" but "in the garbage". As soon as something has been thrown away as garbage it ceases to be an implement and cannot be moved again.

98 Cf. Tosephta 14:2.

99 Tosephta 8:20. If the lime is solid it may be used as a stick; if soft it must be prepared as cosmetic.

(11b line 64) ה. קָנֶה כְּדֵי לַעֲשׂוֹת קוּלְמוֹס כּוּל׳. רִבִּי חִייָה בְּשֵׁם רִבִּי יוֹחָנָן. וְהוּא שֶׁיְּהֵא מַגִּיעַ לְקִישְׁרֵי אֶצְבְּעוֹתָיו. רִבִּי זְעוּרָה בָּעֵי. נִיחָא עַד הָכָא. דִּלְמָא עַד הָכָא.. תַּמָּן תַּנִּינָן. מַכְתֵּב שֶׁנִּטַּל הַכּוֹתֵב טָמֵא מִפְּנֵי הַמּוֹחֵק. נִטַּל הַמּוֹחֵק טָמֵא מִפְּנֵי הַכּוֹתֵב. רִבִּי זְעוּרָה בָּעֵי. נִיחָא עַד הָכָא. דִּלְמָא עַד הָכָא.. אָמַר רִבִּי יוֹסֵי. כָּל־בֵּיצָה דַּתְנִינָן בְּכֵלִים כְּבֵיצָה מַמָּשׁ. בַּשַּׁבָּת בִּגְרוֹגֶרֶת מִכְּבֵיצָה.

5. "Reed to make a writing pen," etc. Rebbi Ḥiyya in the name of Rebbi Joḥanan: But at least that it reaches to the finger joints[100]. Rebbi Ze'ira asked, one understands up to here. Maybe up to here[101]? There, we have stated[102]: "A pen of which the writing tip was broken off is impure because of the eraser. If the eraser was broken off it is impure because of the writing tip." Rebbi Ze'ira asked, one understand up to here. Maybe up to here[103]? Rebbi Yose said, any "egg" which was stated in *Kelim* means the actual volume of an egg. In *Šabbat* in the volume of a dried fig, of an egg[104].

100 Babli 90b as a tannaitic statement; Tosephta 8:21.

101 The same question is asked in the Babli, which joints are meant? The roots of the fingers or the middle joint? The question is not answered there either.

102 Mishnah *Kelim* 13:2. Any vessel may become impure. When it is broken, it lost its impurity. The Mishnah states that impurity is eliminated only if it is completely unusable, not if a multi-purpose instrument has lost one of its uses. The slate pen is used to write on a wax-covered wooden tablet; its wide back is used to erase the writing and prepare the tablet for new writing.

103 Here also the minimal size of a pen remains undefined as it was for the reed pen.

104 In Mishnah *Kelim* 17:6 it is stated that "volume of an egg" mentioned in the Mishnah means volume of an average sized egg. It is now stated that the volume of "an easily cooked egg" means that of a small chicken egg, the volume of a dried Palestinian fig. Babli 80b.

(11b line 70) ו. עֶצֶם כְּדֵי לַעֲשׂוֹת תָּרְוֺד. רִבִּי יְהוּדָה אוֹמֵר. כְּדֵי לַעֲשׂוֹת חָף. מַהוּ חָף. סַרְגִּיד. תַּמָּן תַּנִּינָן. נִיטְּלוּ חָפָיו. טָמֵא מִפְּנֵי נְקָבִים. נִסְתַּתְּמוּ נְקָבִים. טָמֵא מִפְּנֵי חָפִים. מְחַלְּפָה שִׁיטָתֵיהּ דְּרִבִּי יְהוּדָה. תַּמָּן הוּא עָבַד חָף כְּלוּט וְהָכָא הוּא עָבַד חָף סַרְגִּיד.

6. "Bone to fill a spoonful[19]; Rebbi Jehudah says to make a tooth of a key." What is חָף? A key[105]. There, we have stated:[106] "If the teeth were taken, it is impure because of the holes. If the holes were covered, it is impure because of the teeth." It seems that Rebbi Jehudah's argument is inverted. There he calls חָף a protrusion[107] and here he calls it a key.

זְכוּכִית כְּדֵי לִגְרוֹד בָּהּ רֹאשׁ הַכַּרְכָּד. תַּמָּן תַּנֵּי. וְשֶׁלִּזְכוּכִית לָצוּק בְּתוֹכָהּ שֶׁמֶן׃ וְהָכָא אַתְּ אָמַר הָכֵן. רִבִּי אָחָא רִבִּי מַיִישָׁא רִבִּי כֹהֵן בְּשֵׁם רַבָּנָן דְּקַיְסָרִין. כָּאן בְּעָבָה. כָּאן בְּחַדָּה. אִית דְּבָעֵי מֵימַר. כָּאן בִּמְטַלְטֵל. כָּאן בְּמוֹצִיא.

2 ר' כהן | 17 - דקיסרין | 17 דקיסרי   אית | 17 ואית

"Glass to scrape the head of the weaver's beam[20]." There it was stated[108], "of glass to pour oil into it." And here, you are saying so? Rebbi Aha, Rebbi Maisha, Rebbi Cohen in the name of the rabbis of Caesarea: Here if it is thick, there if it is sharp[109]. Some want to say, here about moving, there about bringing out[110].

105 It seems that the root is شرج "to lock".
106 Mishnah *Kelim* 14:8. The argument is the same as explained in Note 102.
107 Reading בלוט for כלוט. The question really is not about R. Jehudah but about the interpretation given here to his statement. Therefore no answer is needed.
108 Mishnah 17:5. The remainder of the paragraph is repeated in Chapter 17 (17).
109 A blunt piece of thick glass obviously is of no use in scraping a beam. Different things may have different rules.
110 The two Mishnaiot cannot be compared although both are about glass. Here one discusses the minimum quantities which create liability in transport from one domain to another. There one discusses applications of the principle that all vessels may freely be moved within a private domain. As long as a sliver of glass may serve as some kind of vessel, it may be moved without special preparation.

(11c line 2) צְרוֹר אֶבֶן כְּדֵי לִזְרוֹק בָּעוֹף. שִׁמְעוֹן בַּר בָּא בְשֵׁם רִבִּי יוֹחָנָן. כְּדֵי שֶׁיִּזְרוֹק לַאֲחוֹרֵי הָעוֹף וְיַרְגִּישׁ. וְדִכְוָותָהּ. כְּדֵי שֶׁיִּזְרוֹק לַאֲחוֹרֵי הָעוֹף וְיַרְגִּישׁ.

תַּנֵּי. צְרוֹר מְקוּרְזָל כְּזַיִת וּכְאֱגוֹז וּכְבֵיצָה נוֹטְלוֹ וּמְקַנֵּחַ בּוֹ אֶת רַגְלָיו. רִבִּי יִשְׁמָעֵאל בְּרִבִּי יוֹסֵה אָמַר מִשּׁוּם אָבִיו. עַד מְלֹא הַיָּד. רַב יְהוּדָה אָמַר. בַּיְיתוֹס בֶּן זוֹנִין הָיָה יוֹשֵׁב וְשׁוֹנֶה לִפְנֵי רִבִּי. אָמַר. כָּךְ אָנוּ אוֹמְרִים. צָרִיךְ שֶׁיְּהֵא יוֹשֵׁב וּמִשְׁקַל בְּיָד. אָמַר לֵיהּ. הַכֹּל מוּתָּר חוּץ מִן הֶעָשׂוּי כַּחֲפִיסָה. רִבִּי אִילָא בְשֵׁם רִבִּי יַנַּאי. יֵשְׁנוֹ כִּמְלוֹא רֶגֶל מְדוֹכָה קְטַנָּה שֶׁלִּבְשָׂם. אָמַר רִבִּי יוֹסֵה. לֹא אָמְרוּ אֶלָּא שֶׁלִּבְשָׂם. הָא שֶׁלִּבְשָׂמִים לֹא. רִבִּי אִילָא בְשֵׁם רִבִּי שִׁמְעוֹן בֶּן לָקִישׁ. צְרוֹר שֶׁעָלוּ בּוֹ עֲשָׂבִים נוֹטְלוֹ וּמְקַנֵּחַ בּוֹ אֶת רַגְלָיו. וְהַתּוֹלֵשׁ מִמֶּנּוּ בַשַּׁבָּת חַיָּב חַטָּאת. תַּנֵּי רִבִּי

חִיָּיא. חֶרֶס כָּל־שֶׁהוּא אָסוּר לְקַנֵּחַ בּוֹ. אָמַר רִבִּי יוֹסֵי בֵּירְבִּי בּוּן. לֹא סוֹף דָּבָר חֶרֶס אֶלָּא אֲפִילוּ אָזְנֵי חָבִיּוֹת. וְכָל־דָּבָר הַנִּכְנַס לָאוֹר וְיָצָא. רִבִּי יוֹסֵי בֶּן יוֹסֵי אָמַר. צְרוֹר שֶׁקִּינַּח בּוֹ חֲבֵירוֹ וּמַיִם שֶׁאֵין בָּהֶן אַרְבָּעִים סְאָה אָסוּר לְקַנֵּחַ בָּהֶן. רִבִּי חֲנַנְיָה בְשֵׁם רִבִּי מָנָא. מַיִם שֶׁלִּיקְלֵק בָּהֶן הַכֶּלֶב אָסוּר לְקַנֵּחַ בָּהֶן. וְתַנֵּי כֵן. אֵין מְקַנְּחִין לֹא בְפִי הַכֶּלֶב. וְלֹא בִפְנֵי כֶלֶב. וְלֹא בְמַיִם שֶׁלִּקְלֵק בָּהֶן הַכֶּלֶב. וְלֹא בְמַיִם שֶׁאֵין בָּהֶן אַרְבָּעִים סְאָה. וְהָהֵן דִּמְשַׁאֲג גּוֹ בִּיבָנִי וְהָהֵן דִּמְשַׁאֲג אַמְבַּטִּיתָהּ רַע לִטַּבָּעוֹת. רִבִּי יוֹסֵי בֵּירְבִּי בּוּן בְשֵׁם רַב חוּנָה. חֲמִשָּׁה דְבָרִים נֶאֶמְרוּ בְּקַלָּמִית שֶׁלְקָנֶה. אֵין שׁוֹחֲטִים בּוֹ. וְאֵין מוֹחֲלִין בּוֹ. וְאֵין מְחַצְּצִין בָּהּ אֶת הַשִּׁינַּיִם. וְאֵין מְחַתְּחִין בּוֹ אֶת הַבָּשָׂר עַל גַּבֵּי הַשּׁוּלְחָן. וְאֵין מְקַנְּחִין בּוֹ. מִפְּנֵי שְׁרוּחַ רָעָה שׁוֹרָה עָלֶיהָ.

"A pebble to throw at a bird[21]." Simeon bar Abba in the name of Rebbi Johanan: That he throw it after a bird and it would notice it[111]. And similarly, that he throw it after an animal and it would notice it.

It was stated[112]: "A smooth[113] stone the size of an olive, or a walnut, or an egg, he may take and cleanse his feet with it. Rebbi Ismael ben Rebbi Yose said in his father's name: up to a full hand." Rav Jehudah said, Boetius ben Zenon was sitting and repeating before Rebbi; he said, so we are saying, it is necessary that he sit down and take it in his hand. He told him, everything is permitted except what is formed like a small sack. Rebbi Ila in the name of Rebbi Yannai: it may be like the base of a small mortar of a spice dealer. Rebbi Yose said, they only said, of a spice. But not of spices[114]. Rebbi Ila in the name of Rebbi Simeon ben Laqish[115]: A pebble on which grasses grew he may take and cleanse his feet with it. But if he plucks off from it on the Sabbath he is liable for a purification sacrifice. Rebbi Hiyya stated: It is forbidden to cleanse oneself with any potsherd[116]. Rebbi Yose ben Rebbi Abun said, not only potsherds but even handles of amphoras[117], and anything which was brought into the fire and came out again[118]. Rebbi Yose ben Yose said, a pebble which had been used by another person and water in a volume of less than 40 *se'ah* one may not use to cleanse himself[119]. Rebbi Hanania in the name of Rebbi Mana: It is forbidden to cleanse himself with water which a dog licked. And it was stated so: One cleans himself neither with a dog's mouth, nor in presence of a dog, nor with water which the dog had licked off, nor with water in a volume of less than 40 *se'ah*. And if somebody washes in the bath house or washes in a bathtub, it is bad for hemorrhoids.

Rebbi Yose ben Rebbi Abun in the name of Rav Huna: [120]Five things were said about a reed blade: One does not use it to slaughter, nor to circumcise, nor to clean teeth with it, nor does one use it to cut meat on the table, nor does one cleanse himself, because an evil spirit resides on it.

111 The Babli 81a explains this as a pebble of at least 10 denar, 32 g.
112 Babli 81a, Tosephta 13:17. Even though a stone is not a vessel and may not be moved on the Sabbath, for hygienic purposes it is permitted. "To cleanse himself" here means to use as toilet paper. For the different stages of cleansing one may use up to three stones of varying sizes.
113 Explanation of Rashi, in Romance *becudes*.
114 Only a really small mortar whose base fits into the palm of a hand.
115 Babli 81b. Removing the grasses is harvesting. Using the stone to cleanse himself is permitted since no rabbinic prohibitions may interfere with hygienic necessities or, in the language of the Babli, "the honor of people."
116 Since it has a rough surface it may not be used even on a weekday.
117 The Babli 82a disagrees since these in general are smooth.
118 According to the Babli, *Hulin* 16b, anything fired will have a rough surface and there is danger it may lead to hemorrhoids.
119 It seems, unless the water was poured out and any reuse would be impossible.
120 Babli *Hulin* 16b, as tannaitic text. The blades are sharp and may be used for cutting but in general are serrated, which disqualifies them for slaughter and as surgical instruments. While one may cleanse himself with leaves, one may not use any which might cause a lesion which opens the way for pathogenic "evil spirits".

(11c line 24) חֶרֶשׂ (כָּל־שֶׁהוּא) כְּדֵי לִיתֵּן בֵּין פַּצִּים כול׳. רִבִּי יוֹחָנָן אָמַר. מְקַדְּשִׁין בּוֹ. רִבִּי שִׁמְעוֹן בֶּן לָקִישׁ אָמָר. אֵין מְקַדְּשִׁין בּוֹ. רִבִּי לְעָזָר שָׁאַל. עַל דַּעְתֵּיהּ דְּרִבִּי שִׁמְעוֹן בֶּן לָקִישׁ. לָמָּה אֵין מְקַדְּשִׁין בּוֹ. מִפְּנֵי שֶׁאֵינוֹ מְקַבֵּל טוּמְאָה. הֲרֵי כְלֵי גְלָלִים וּכְלֵי אֲבָנִים וּכְלֵי אֲדָמָה הֲרֵי אֵינָן מְקַבְּלִין טוּמְאָה וּמְקַדְּשִׁין בָּהֶן. אֶלָּא מִשּׁוּם שֶׁאֵינוֹ מְקַבֵּל רְבִיעִית. וְלֹא מוֹדֶה רִבִּי שִׁמְעוֹן בֶּן לָקִישׁ בִּכְלִי חֶרֶשׂ קָטָן שָׁלֵם כָּל־שֶׁהוּא שֶׁמְּקַדְּשִׁין בּוֹ. הֲוֵי לֵית טַעֲמֵיהּ אֶלָּא מִשּׁוּם שֶׁאֵין עָלָיו תּוֹאַר כָּלִי. וְקַשְׁיָא עַל דְּרִבִּי יוֹחָנָן. לִפְסוֹל אֶת הַגְּוִיָּיה אֵינוֹ פוֹסֵל. וּלְקַדֵּשׁ מְקַדְּשִׁין בּוֹ. אֶלָּא כְרִבִּי יוֹסֵה. דְּרִבִּי יוֹסֵה אָמַר. אַף שֶׁלְּחֶרֶשׂ כָּל־שֶׁהוּא. כְּלוּם אָמַר רִבִּי יוֹסֵי לֹא בְשָׁלֵם. דִּילְמָא בְשָׁבוּר אָמֵן קַיָּימִין. תַּנֵּי רִבִּי חִייָה מְסַיֵּיעַ לְרִבִּי יוֹחָנָן. תַּנֵּי רִבִּי שִׁמְעוֹן בֶּן יוֹחַי מְסַיֵּיעַ לְרִבִּי שִׁמְעוֹן בֶּן לָקִישׁ.

7. "A potsherd (of any size) to put between one half brick,"[121] etc. Rebbi Johanan said, one may use it to sanctify; Rebbi Simeon ben Laqish says, one may not use it to sanctify. Rebbi Eleazar asked, in Rebbi Simeon ben Laqish's opinion, why may one not use it to sanctify? Because it is impervious to impurity[122]. But are not vessels made of cow dung, stone vessels, earthen vessels impervious to impurity and one may use them to sanctify[123]! But because it does not contain a *quartarius*[124]. But does not Rebbi Simeon ben Laqish agree that one may sanctify using an arbitrarily small complete clay vessel? It is that the only reason is that it does not have the appellation "vessel"[125]. Then it is difficult for Rebbi Johanan. It is not enough to disqualify the body[126] but one may use it to sanctify? But this follows Rebbi Yose, for "Rebbi Yose said, also the most minute amount of clay vessel[127]." Did not Rebbi Yose say this only for a complete one, and do we not deal here with a broken one? What Rebbi Hiyya stated[128] supports Rebbi Johanan; what Rebbi Simeon ben Yohai[129] stated supports Rebbi Simeon ben Laqish.

121 The scribe wrote "a potsherd of any size"; the corrector then changed it into a quote of Mishnah 7. As S. Liebermann points out, the original text is correct and the paragraph starts not with a quote of Mishnah 7 but of a *baraita* close to Tosephta *Kelim Bava qamma* 7:17: "Potsherds which may contain even a minimal amount one used to fill, to sanctify, to sprinkle from it ...". The subject is the ceremony of cleansing from the impurity of the dead (*Num.* 19) which requires that some of the ashes of the Red Cow be in "flowing water drawn into a vessel" (19:17). In this context, "to sanctify" means to put the ashes into the water. From this moment on the slightest inattention will disqualify water and ashes from the ceremony. The paragraph fits in here since both for the rules of the Sabbath and the rules of impurity there is the problem of defining exactly what is called a "vessel".

122 By definition, a vessel is a product of manufacture. Materials in their original state always are impervious to impurity (unless they are derived from animals). A first tentative opinion is that "vessel" is only a manufactured product susceptible to impurity.

123 Mishnah *Parah* 5:5.

124 Which everywhere is the minimum of a substantial volume of fluid.

125 Which is required by the verse and, therefore, cannot be dispensed with.

126 Mishnah *Me`ilah* 4:5 states that ingesting a *quartarius* of impure fluid disqualifies a body from any activity requiring purity. It is difficult to see why this should be relevant to the topic at hand. S. Liebermann, following *No`am Yerushalaim* of R. Joshua Eizik of Slonim, suggests to change "body" into "*miqweh*". The argument for this is that a *miqweh* may not be filled with water drawn by a vessel; in this context a "clay vessel" is defined by Mishnah *Miqwa'ot* 4:3 as one which may contain a minimum volume of one *quartarius*.

127 In Mishnah *Miqwa'ot* 4:3 he states that a clay vessel of *any* size is a "vessel"; the criterion of one *quartarius* applies only to potsherds.

128 Tosephta *Kelim Bava qamma* 7:17.

129 This *baraita* has not come down to us.

רבי עקיבה פרק תשיעי

משנה א: אָמַר רִבִּי עֲקִיבָה מִנַּיִן לַעֲבוֹדָה זָרָה שֶׁהִיא מְטַמְּאָה בְמַשָּׂא כַּנִּדָּה שֶׁנֶּאֱמַר תִּזְרֵם כְּמוֹ דָוָה צֵא תֹּאמַר לוֹ. מַה הַנִּדָּה מְטַמְּאָה בְמַשָּׂא אַף עֲבוֹדָה זָרָה מְטַמְּאָה בְמַשָּׂא:

Mishnah 1: Rebbi Aqiba says, from where that idolatry makes impure by load like a menstruating woman? For it is said[1], *you shall throw it away like feeling miserable; you will call it excrement*. Since the menstruating makes impure by load[2], idolatry also makes impure by load[3].

משנה ב: מִנַּיִן לַסְּפִינָה שֶׁהִיא טְהוֹרָה שֶׁנֶּאֱמַר דֶּרֶךְ אֳנִיָּה בְלֶב יָם. מִנַּיִן לַעֲרוּגָה שֶׁהִיא שִׁשָּׁה עַל שִׁשָּׁה טְפָחִים זוֹרְעִין בְּתוֹכָהּ חֲמִשָּׁה זֵרְעוֹנִים אַרְבַּע בְּאַרְבַּע רוּחוֹת עֲרוּגָה וְאַחַת בָּאֶמְצַע שֶׁנֶּאֱמַר כִּי כָאָרֶץ תּוֹצִיא צִמְחָהּ וּכְגַנָּה זֵרוּעֶיהָ תַצְמִיחַ. זַרְעָהּ תַצְמִיחַ לֹא נֶאֱמַר אֶלָּא זֵרוּעֶיהָ תַצְמִיחַ:

Mishnah 2: From where that a ship is pure[4]? For it is said[5], *the way of a ship in the heart of the Sea*. From where that a garden bed that is six by six hand-breadths one may sow with five kinds of seeds, four at its four sides and one in the middle[6]? For it is said[7], *for like the earth it will bring out its plants and like a garden it will cause it to grow its sown seeds*.

משנה ג: מִנַּיִן לְפוֹלֶטֶת שִׁכְבַת זֶרַע בַּיּוֹם הַשְּׁלִישִׁי שֶׁהִיא טְמֵאָה שֶׁנֶּאֱמַר הֱיוּ נְכוֹנִים לִשְׁלֹשֶׁת יָמִים אַל תִּגְּשׁוּ אֶל אִשָּׁה. מִנַּיִן שֶׁמַּרְחִיצִין אֶת הַקָּטָן בַּיּוֹם הַשְּׁלִישִׁי שֶׁחָל לִהְיוֹת בַּשַּׁבָּת שֶׁנֶּאֱמַר וַיְהִי בַיּוֹם הַשְּׁלִישִׁי בִּהְיוֹתָם כֹּאֲבִים. מִנַּיִן שֶׁקּוֹשְׁרִים לָשׁוֹן שֶׁל זְהוֹרִית בְּרֹאשׁ שָׂעִיר הַמִּשְׁתַּלֵּחַ. שֶׁנֶּאֱמַר אִם יִהְיוּ חֲטָאֵיכֶם כַּשָּׁנִים כַּשֶּׁלֶג יַלְבִּינוּ וגו':

Mishnah 3: From where that one[8] who loses semen on the third day is impure? For it is said[9], *be prepared for three days, do not touch a woman*. From where that one washes[10] a baby on the third day if it falls on a Sabbath? For it is said[11], *it was on the third day when they hurt*. From where that one ties a crimson band to the head of the scapegoat[12]? For it is said[13], *if your sins were like scarlet they will be snow white*, etc.

משנה ד: מִנַּיִן לְסִיכָה שֶׁהִיא כַשְּׁתִיָּה בְּיוֹם הַכִּפּוּרִים. אַף עַל פִּי שֶׁאֵין רְאָיָה לַדָּבָר זֵכֶר לַדָּבָר, שֶׁנֶּאֱמַר וַתָּבוֹא כַמַּיִם בְּקִרְבּוֹ וְכַשֶּׁמֶן בְּעַצְמוֹתָיו:

Mishnah 4: From where that anointing is like drinking on the Day of Atonement[14]? Even though it is no proof, there is a hint, as it is said[15], *it came like water into him and like oil in his bones.*

משנה ה: הַמּוֹצִיא עֵצִים כְּדֵי לְבַשֵּׁל בֵּיצָה קַלָּה. תַּבְלִין כְּדֵי לְתַבֵּל בֵּיצָה קַלָּה וּמִצְטָרְפִין זֶה עִם זֶה. קְלִיפֵי אֱגוֹזִים קְלִיפֵי רִמּוֹנִים אִסְטִיס וּפוּאָה כְּדֵי לִצְבּוֹעַ בָּהֶן בֶּגֶד קָטָן כִּשְׂבָכָה. מֵי רַגְלַיִם נֶתֶר וּבוֹרִית קִימוֹנְיָא וְאַשְׁלָג, כְּדֵי לְכַבֵּס בָּהֶן בֶּגֶד קָטָן כִּשְׂבָכָה. רַבִּי יְהוּדָה אוֹמֵר כְּדֵי לְהַעֲבִיר עַל הַכֶּתֶם:

Mishnah 5: One who brings out wood to cook an easily cooked egg, spices to spice an easily cooked egg, and these combine one with the other[16]. Shells of walnuts, skins of pomegranates, isatis, and madder to dye a small tissue like a hair net[17]. Soda, and soap, Cimolian earth[18], and potash, to wash a small tissue like a hair net; Rebbi Jehudah says, to use on a stain[19].

משנה ו: פִּלְפֶּלֶת כָּל־שֶׁהוּא. וְעִטְרָן כָּל־שֶׁהוּא מִינֵי בְשָׂמִים וּמִינֵי מַתָּכוֹת כָּל־שֶׁהֵן. מֵעֲפַר הַמִּזְבֵּחַ מֵאַבְנֵי הַמִּזְבֵּחַ מִמֶּקֶק סְפָרִים מִמֶּקֶק מִטְפְּחוֹתֵיהֶם כָּל־שֶׁהֵן מִפְּנֵי שֶׁמַּצְנִיעִין אוֹתָן לְגוֹנְזָן. רַבִּי יְהוּדָה אוֹמֵר אַף הַמּוֹצִיא מִמְּשַׁמְּשֵׁי עֲבוֹדָה זָרָה כָּל־שֶׁהוּא שֶׁנֶּאֱמַר וְלֹא יִדְבַּק בְּיָדְךָ מְאוּמָה מִן הַחֵרֶם:

Mishnah 6: Pepper[20] in any amount, 'itran[21] in any amount, spices and metals[22] in any amount. Of the altar's dust, of the altar's stones, of rot of scrolls, of rot of their bindings the most minute amount since one collects them to hide them away[23]. Rebbi Jehudah says, also one who takes out the most minute amount of appurtenances of idol worship, as it is said[24], *nothing of the ban shall cling to your hand.*

משנה ז: הַמּוֹצִיא קוּפַת הָרוֹכְלִין אַף עַל פִּי שֶׁיֵּשׁ בָּהּ מִינִין הַרְבֵּה אֵינוֹ חַיָּב אֶלָּא חַטָּאת אֶחָת. זֵרְעוֹנֵי גִנָּה פָּחוֹת מִכַּגְּרוֹגֶרֶת. רַבִּי יְהוּדָה בֶּן בְּתֵירָא אוֹמֵר חֲמִשָּׁה. זֶרַע קִשּׁוּאִין שְׁנַיִם. זֶרַע דְּלוּעִין שְׁנַיִם זֶרַע פּוֹל מִצְרִי שְׁנַיִם. חָגָב חַי כָּל־שֶׁהוּא. מֵת כַּגְּרוֹגֶרֶת. צִפֹּרֶת כְּרָמִים בֵּין חַיָּה בֵּין מֵתָה כָּל־שֶׁהוּא מִפְּנֵי שֶׁמַּצְנִיעִין אוֹתָהּ לִרְפוּאָה. רַבִּי יְהוּדָה אוֹמֵר אַף הַמּוֹצִיא חָגָב חַי טָמֵא כָּל־שֶׁהוּא מִפְּנֵי שֶׁמַּצְנִיעִין אוֹתוֹ לַקָּטָן לִשְׂחֹק בּוֹ:

Mishnah 7: One who takes out a peddler's bag, even though it contains many kinds, is liable only for one purification sacrifice[25]. Garden seeds less than the volume of a dried fig; Rebbi Jehudah ben Bathyra said, five. Green melon[26] seeds two, squash seeds two, Egyptian bean seeds two. A live locust in any amount, dead in the volume of a dried fig. A vineyard bird[27] either live

328 ŠABBAT CHAPTER NINE

or dead in any amount since one keeps it as medicine. Rebbi Jehudah says, also one who brings out a dead locust[28] in the most minute amount since one keeps it as a toy for children.

1   *Is.* 30:22.

2   In *Lev.* 15:20-21 it is stated that anything the menstruating woman lies on becomes an original source of impurity. This means that if a woman in her period lies on top of ten mattresses and somebody touches the lowest one, which the woman never touched, he becomes impure as if he had touched the woman herself.

3   For R. Aqiba anybody who carries an idol becomes impure even if he never touched the idol.

4   While a ship is a vessel, it is not subject to the impurity of vessels. This not only applies to large vessels which are not subject to impurity if they are so large that they cannot be moved by a single human empty or loaded but even small boats if they are never used on land.

5   *Prov.* 30:19.

6   The problem is that of *kilaim*, the prohibition to grow different kinds of produce on the same field. Different kinds if grown on parallel fields must be separated by an uncultivated strip, but such fields may touch one another at a single point. The minimum size of a plot that can be planted with several kinds is a 6-by-6 hand-breadths plot, cf. Mishnah *Kilaim* 3:1 Notes 1-2; the configuration envisaged by the Mishnah is shown there in fig. 3-1. It is suggested that one divide the plot into 36 squares of one hand-breadth edge length each. Along the four edges, the corner squares are left fallow. Then on each edge, a rectangle, 4 long and 1 wide, can be planted. These 4 rectangles may be planted with 4 different kinds since they meet only at a pair of vertical angles. Together, they contain 16 of the 1-by-1 squares. The interior edges of the rectangles enclose a 4-by-4 square. In this square, a square can be planted in the shape of a diamond, having its vertices at the midpoints of the inner edges of the rectangles. This is permitted as ראש תור. The diagonals of the diamond have length 4; it covers exactly half of the internal square of 16 square hand-breadths. Hence, the entire cultivated area is 8 + 16 = 24 hand-breadths square. [If instead we assume that the fallow squares at the corners have edge length a, then the total cultivated area, in square handbreadths, is

$$f(a) = 4a(6 - 2a) + 0.5(6 - 2a)^2.$$

A simple computation then shows that the maximum is attained for $a = 1$, $f(1) = 24$. One third of the total area must lie fallow.]

7   *Is.* 61:11.

8   Human semen is impure (*Lev.* 15:16-17 and sexual intercourse makes impure, v. 18. Semen which no longer can fertilize is not impure. The question is how long after intercourse must one suspect that semen released by the female still produces impurity? The answer which is given here states that semen may stay alive inside the woman's body for three days.

9   *Ex.* 19:15.

10 A male baby on the third day after

circumcision with warm water, heated for the purpose even on the Sabbath, because it is a medical necessity. The entire series of deductions from Scripture is introduced here because of this rule of the Sabbath.

11 Gen. 34:25.
12 Mishnah *Yoma* 4:2 requires that a crimson band be tied to the horns of the goat sent to the cliff.
13 *Is*. 1:18.
14 The biblical commandment on the Day of Atomement is "to deprive oneself". It is understood that this includes fasting. Not anointing here is declared a derivative of the commandment not to drink.
15 *Ps*. 109:18.
16 Even though it was stated at the end of Chapter Seven that matters which are under different minimal amounts for the Sabbath are not combined and the volume of firewood needed to cook an egg certainly is much larger than the volume of spices used for the egg, the rule "enough to cook an easily cooked egg" is the same in both cases and this is sufficient to declare the rules identical.

17 Crochet work or knitted hair covers have little material and need little dye.
18 Κιμωλία (γῆ), ἡ, a white clay like fuller's earth, used in baths and medicine. The Halakhah presumes different readings for some of the substances mentioned here.
19 Enough to eliminate a blood stain from a woman's period to allow the garment to be purified in a *miqweh*.
20 Rashi holds that פִּלְפֶּלֶת are green peppers in contrast to פִּלְפֵּל which is black pepper.
21 Probably pine sap.
22 Metal bars.
23 Because of their intrinsic sanctity, once they become damaged and no longer usable they must be buried. Since they never can be discarded, even a minuscule amount is valuable.
24 *Deut*. 13:18.
25 Since it is a single act.
26 Cf. *Kilaim* 1:2, Note 38. In modern Hebrew the word means "zucchini".
27 A kind of locust; according to *Sifra Šemini Pereq* 5(9), permitted as food.
28 A locust forbidden as food.

(11c line 75) כָּתוּב תּוֹעֵבָה בְּנִידָה. וְכָתוּב תּוֹעֵבָה בַּעֲבוֹדָה זָרָה וְכָתוּב תּוֹעֵבָה בִּשְׁרָצִים. כָּתוּב תּוֹעֵבָה בְּנִידָה. כִּי כָּל־אֲשֶׁר יַעֲשֶׂה מִכֹּל הַתּוֹעֵבוֹת הָאֵלֶּה וגו'. תּוֹעֵבָה בַּעֲבוֹדָה זָרָה. וְלֹא־תָבִיא תוֹעֵבָה אֶל־בֵּיתֶךָ וגו'. תּוֹעֵבָה בִּשְׁרָצִים. לֹא תֹאכַל כָּל־תּוֹעֵבָה. אֲבָל אֵין אֲנִי יוֹדֵעַ לְאֵי זֶה מֵהֶן הוּקְשָׁה. רִבִּי עֲקִיבָה אוֹמֵר. לְתוֹעֵבָה שֶׁבְּנִידָה הוּקְשָׁה. מַה הַנִּידָה מְטַמֵּא בְמַשָּׂא. אַף עֲבוֹדָה זָרָה מְטַמֵּא בְמַשָּׂא׃ אוֹ מַה הַנִּידָה מְטַמָּא בְאֶבֶן מְסַמָּא. אַף עֲבוֹדָה זָרָה מְטַמָּא עַל גַּבֵּי אֶבֶן מְסַמָּא. רִבִּי זְרִיקָן בְּשֵׁם רַב יְהוּדָה וְאִית דְּאָמְרִין בְּשֵׁם רַב חִסְדָּא. מוֹדֶה רִבִּי עֲקִיבָה לַחֲכָמִים שֶׁאֵין עֲבוֹדָה זָרָה מְטַמֵּא עַל גַּבֵּי אֶבֶן מְסַמָּא. וְרַבָּנָן אָמְרִי. לְתוֹעֵבָה שֶׁבִּשְׁרָצִים הוּקְשָׁה. מַה הַשֶּׁרֶץ מְטַמֵּא בְהֵיסֵט אַף עֲבוֹדָה זָרָה מְטַמֵּא בְהֵיסֵט. אוֹ מַה הַשֶּׁרֶץ מְטַמֵּא בְכַעֲדָשָׁה. אַף עֲבוֹדָה זָרָה מְטַמֵּא בְכַעֲדָשָׁה. רִבִּי זְעוּרָה רִבִּי יִצְחָק בַּר נַחְמָן בְּשֵׁם רִבִּי לְעָזֶר רִבִּי אַבָּהוּ בְּשֵׁם רִבִּי יוֹחָנָן. וַיִּצָּמְדוּ לְבַעַל פְּעוֹר וַיֹּאכְלוּ זִבְחֵי מֵתִים׃ מַה הַמֵּת מְטַמֵּא בִכְזַיִת אַף עֲבוֹדָה זָרָה

מְטַמָּא בִּכְזַיִת. אוֹ מַה הַמֵּת עַד שֶׁיַּכְנִיס רֹאשׁ אֶצְבָּעוֹ. אַף עֲבוֹדָה זָרָה עַד שֶׁיַּכְנִיס רֹאשׁ אֶצְבָּעוֹ. נְתִיצָה נְתִיצָה מִבֵּית הַמְנוּגָּע. מַה בֵּית הַמְנוּגָּע עַד שֶׁיַּכְנִיס רֹאשׁוֹ וְרוּבּוֹ. אַף עֲבוֹדָה זָרָה עַד שֶׁיַּכְנִיס רֹאשׁוֹ וְרוּבּוֹ. אָמַר רִבִּי חֲנַנְיָה. זֹאת אוֹמֶרֶת שֶׁאֵין טוּמְאַת עֲבוֹדָה זָרָה מְחוּוֶרֶת. דְּלֹא כֵן מַקִּישָׁהּ לַקַּלִּים וְאֵינָהּ מַקִּישָׁהּ לַחֲמוּרִין. אָמַר רִבִּי מָנָא. מְחוּוֶרֶת הִיא. וְלָמָּה הוּא מַקִּישָׁהּ לְמֵת לְשָׁרֶץ. לְלַמֵּד מֵהֶם לַקַּלִּים שֶׁבָּהּ. הָדָא דְאַתְּ אָמַר בַּעֲבוֹדָה זָרָה שְׁבוּרָה. אֲבָל בִּשְׁלֵימָה אֲפִילוּ כָּל־שֶׁהוּא. דְּאָמַר רִבִּי חוּנָה רִבִּי חָמָא בַּר גּוֹרְיוֹן בְּשֵׁם רַב. הַבַּעַל רֹאשׁ גְּוִיָּיה הָיָה וּכְאָפוּן הָיָה. וַיָּשִׂימוּ לָהֶם בַּעַל בְּרִית לֵאלֹהִים:

[29]There is written *abomination* about the menstruating woman, and there is written *abomination* about idolatry, and there is written *abomination* about vermin. There is written *abomination* about the menstruating woman, *for anybody who would commit any of these abominations*[30], etc. *Abomination* about idolatry, *and do not bring any abomination into your house*[31], etc. *Abomination* about vermin, *do not eat any abomination*[32]. But I do not know to which of them it was compared. Rebbi Aqiba says, it was compared to *abomination* regarding the menstruating woman. As the menstruating woman imparts impurity by load, also idolatry imparts impurity by load². Or since the menstruating woman imparts impurity through a cover stone[33], does idolatry impart impurity through a cover stone? Rebbi Zeriqan in the name of Rav Jehudah, but some say in the name of Rav Hisda: Rebbi Aqiba agrees with the Sages that idolatry does not impart impurity through a cover stone. But the rabbis say it was compared to *abominations* of vermin. As vermin imparts impurity by motion[34], so also idolatry imparts impurity by motion. Or as vermin in the size of a lentil imparts impurity[35] does idolatry in the size of a lentil also impart impurity? Rebbi Ze'ira, Rebbi Isaac bar Nahman in the name of Rebbi Eleazar, Rebbi Abbahu in the name of Rebbi Johanan: *They were yoked to Baal Peor and ate sacrifices to the dead*[36]. As the dead in the volume of an olive impart impurity so idolatry in the volume of an olive imparts impurity. Or since a corpse imparts impurity once a person puts his finger tips in[37], could I think that idolatry imparts once a person puts his finger tips in? *Tearing down, tearing down* from the leprous house[38]. Since in a leprous house when he entered with his head and most of his body[39], so idolatry when he entered with his head and most of his body. Rebbi Hanania said, this means that the impurity of idolatry is not consistent[40]. For

otherwise, why does one compare if for the facile [impurity] and does not compare for the strict? Rebbi Mana said, it is consistent. Why was it compared to a corpse and to vermin? To inform in both cases about the facile [impurity] attached to it[41]. This is for a broken idol. But a whole one even in the most minute size[42], as Rebbi Huna, Rebbi Hama bar Gorion said in the name of Rav: Baal was the penis gland in the form of a bean: *They selected the Baal of circumcision as god*[43].

29 This and the the following paragraph also are Halakhah 3:8 in *Avodah zara*, where the differences in spelling are noted. Evidence points to *Šabbat* as the primary source. Much of the argument is found in Babli *Šabbat* 82b-83b.

30 *Lev.* 18:29. The verse refers to all prohibitions of a sexual nature.

31 *Deut.* 7:26. This verse refers uniquely to idols and idolatry.

32 *Deut.* 14:2. The verse refers to all food prohibitions.

33 Stone is impervious to impurity. In general, anything not susceptible to impurity cannot transmit impurity. The one and only exception is impurity caused by genital discharges where impurity by load (Note 2) applies to anything under the affected person and even a stone plate covering a mattress will not shield the mattress from impurity if a person afflicted by a genital discharge sits on the stone. Babli *Niddah* 69b.

34 Here one has a serious discrepancy between the technical terminology of the Babli and the Yerushalmi. In the Babli impurity by motion is a form of impurity by load: If a person suffering from a genital discharge moves something indirectly or is moved with it, he imparts impurity. In the Yerushalmi this is consistently designated by its Mishnaic name, מִדְרָס, "stepping on." This kind of impurity emphatically does not exist for vermin, or anything other than genital discharges. Therefore היסט the "motion" mentioned here must be that of a person's hand touching an impure object. Transfer of impurity by touch is the only one mentioned for the eight kinds of impure vermin.

35 Mishnah *Ahilut* 1:8. This minimum size for generation of impurity does not apply to complete limbs.

36 *Ps.* 106:28.

37 This refers to "tent" impurity (*Ševuot* 2:1 Note 34) which is created by *any* part of a person's body being under the same roof as a corpse, even if it is only a finger tip.

38 A house afflicted with recurrent "leprosy" must be torn down (*Lev.* 14:45). Pagan altars must be torn down (*Deut.* 12:3). By the nature of the topics, the verb נתץ is used in the singular in the first case, in the plural in the second. Therefore this is a comparison (הקש), not an "equal cut" (גזירה שוה); the laws will be similar, not exactly identical.

39 Based on *Lev.* 14:46, which decrees impurity for anybody coming *into* the house, *Sifra Mesora` Pereq* 5(4), Mishnah *Nega`im*

13:8.
40 Neither R. Aqiba nor the rabbis are consistent in their comparisons.
41 The impurity of idols and idolatry should follow the rules common for impurities generated either by dead vermin or by bodily discharges. This argument is known in the Babli tradition as הַצַּד הַשָׁוֶה "the equal part;" cf. H. Guggenheimer, *Logical Problems in Jewish Tradition*, in: "Confrontations with Judaism", ed. Ph.

Longworth, London 1966, p. 185.
42 This is consistent with the impurity of animals as food, where a complete creature always is biblically forbidden irrespective of size (cf. *Nazir* 6:1 Note 64).
43 *Jud.* 8:33. Instead of "Baal of Covenant" one reads "Baal of circumcision" referring to the place of circumcision. This identifies the Semitic Baal with the Greek and Roman Priapus.

(11d line 21) מַה טַעֲמֵיהּ דְּרִבִּי עֲקִיבָה. תַּעֵב תְּתַעֲבֶנּוּ. כְּנִידָּה. מַה טַעֲמוֹן דְּרַבָּנִין. שַׁקֵּץ תְּשַׁקְּצֶנּוּ. כִּשְׁרָצִים. מַה מְקַיְּימִין רַבָּנָן טַעֲמֵיהּ דְּרִבִּי עֲקִיבָה. תַּעֵב תְּתַעֲבֶנּוּ. צָאֵיהוּ נַבְּלֵיהוּ. מַה מְקַיֵּים רִבִּי עֲקִיבָה טַעֲמוֹן דְּרַבָּנָן. שַׁקֵּץ תְּשַׁקְּצֶנּוּ. שִׁקְצֵיהוּ נַבְּלֵיהוּ. מִנַּיִן לְרַבָּנָן נַבְּלֵיהוּ. רִבִּי שְׁמוּאֵל רִבִּי אַבָּהוּ בְּשֵׁם רִבִּי אֶלְעָזָר. צֵא תֹּאמַר לוֹ. צוֹאָה תֹּאמַר לוֹ. צָאֵיהוּ נַבְּלֵיהוּ. אֵת שֶׁקּוֹרִין אוֹתוֹ פְּנֵי מֶלֶךְ קוֹרִין אוֹתוֹ פְּנֵי כָלֶב. עֵין כּוֹס עֵין קוֹץ. גַּדְיָה גָלְיָיה. רִבִּי תַּנְחוּמָא בְשֵׁם רַב חוּנָא. הָעַי אֲשֶׁר עִם־בֵּית אָוֶן מִקֶּדֶם לְבֵית־אֵל. מִקֶּדֶם הָיוּ קוֹרִין אוֹתוֹ בֵּיתְאֵל וְעַכְשָׁיו קוֹרִין אוֹתוֹ בֵּית אָוֶן. תַּנֵּי בְשֵׁם רִבִּי אֶלְעָזָר. לֹא רָצָה לְהִיקָּרוֹת עֹמְדָה. קוֹרִין אוֹתָהּ עֲמִידָה. דְּאָמַר רִבִּי אַבָּא בַּר כַּהֲנָא. תַּמָּן צַוְוחִין לְפָעֲלָה טָבָא עִמְדָה. וּצְוָוחִין לִרְחוֹץ שַׁלְמֵימֵי רַגְלַיִם עֲמִידָה. מַה מְקַיֵּים רִבִּי עֲקִיבָה צֵא תֹּאמַר לוֹ. רִבִּי יוֹסֵי בֵּירִבִּי בּוּן רַב חוּנָא בְשֵׁם רַב יוֹסֵף. מִיכָּן שֶׁאֵין אוֹמְרִים לְאָדָם צֵא עַד שֶׁיִּכָּנֵס רֹאשׁוֹ וְרוּבּוֹ.

What is Rebbi Aqiba's reason? *You should treat it as an abomination*[44], like a menstruating woman. What is the rabbis' reason? *You should detest it*, like vermin. How do the rabbis uphold Rebbi Aqiba's reason, *you should treat it as abomination*? Treat it as excrement, make it vile[45]. How does Rebbi Aqiba uphold the rabbis' reason, *you should treat it as abomination*? Call it feces, treat it as excrement, make it vile. From where "make it vile" for the rabbis? Rebbi Samuel, Rebbi Abbahu in the name of Rebbi Eleazar: *you shall call it excrement*; treat it as excrement, make it vile What is called King's Face is called Dog's Face. Spring of the Cup Spring of the Thorn. The Place of Fortune Place of Undress[46]. Rebbi Tanḥuma in the name of Rav Huna: *The Ai which is near Bet-Awen East of Bethel*[47]. Earlier it was called Bethel but now one calls it Bet-Awen[48]. It was stated in the name of Rebbi Eleazar: If one does not want to call it 'Omda one calls it 'Amida[49] since

Rebbi Abba bar Cahana said, there one calls a good deed *'omda*[50] but the flow of urine *'amida*[51]. How does Rebbi Aqiba interpret *you shall call it excrement*? Rebbi Yose ben Rebbi Abin, Rav Huna in the name of Rav Joseph[52]: from here that one does not tell anybody to leave unless he entered with his head and most of his body.

44 *Deut.* 7:26.
45 Babli 46a, *Mekhilta dR. Ismael Mišpatim* 20 (p. 332 ed. Horovitz-Rabin).
46 All these places and most of their idolatrous or obscene meanings are unknown. A similar list is as Tannaitic text in the Babli 46a, Tosephta 6:4. [Perhaps כוס should be read as كس "behind", in particular as part of the female anatomy (E. G.)]
47 *Jos.* 7:2.
48 It seems that the translator of the LXX read the verse in the way of the Talmud and eliminated the mention of Bet-Awen, "the House of Iniquity", as a gloss, as accepted by the moderns. (However, E. Täubler in a marginal Note to his copy of M. Noth's *Das Buch Josua*, Tübingen 1938, identifies Bet-Awen as the old name of "The Ai (ruin)"; cf. Arabic اون "calm, tranquillity".)
49 *Yalqut Jos. ad* 7:2; *Gen. rabba* 39(24), on *Gen.* 12:8.
50 Syriac עמד.
51 Greek ἀμίς, -ίδος, ἡ, "chamber pot" (identified by Musaphia.)
52 Since Rav Joseph lived two generations after Rav Huna, one has to read with the text in *Avodah zarah*: Rebbi Huna.

(11d line 39) אִית מַתְנִיתָא אָמְרָה. עֲבוֹדָה זָרָה כְּנִידָּה וּמְשַׁמְּשֶׁיהָ כְּנִידָה. וְאִית מַתְנִיתָא אָמְרָה. עֲבוֹדָה זָרָה כְּנִידָה וּמְשַׁמְּשֶׁיהָ כְּשֶׁרֶץ. מָאן דְּאָמַר. עֲבוֹדָה זָרָה כְּנִידָה וּמְשַׁמְּשֶׁיהָ כְּנִידָה. נִיחָא. וּמָאן דְּאָמַר. עֲבוֹדָה זָרָה כְּנִידָה וּמְשַׁמְּשֶׁיהָ כְּשֶׁרֶץ. כָּל־עַצְמוֹ אֵין כָּתוּב נִידָה אֶלָא בִמְשַׁמְּשִׁין. וְטִמֵּאתָם אֶת־צִיפּוּי אֱלִילֵי כַסְפֶּךָ וְאֶת־אֲפֻדַּת מַסֵּכַת זְהָבֶךָ. תִּיפְתָּר בַּחֲקוּקִין עַל גּוּפָהּ. רִבִּי יַעֲקֹב דִּכְפַר חָנָן אָמַר. תִּפְתָּר בִּמְשַׁתְּחֲוֶה לָאֵפוֹד עַצְמוֹ. כְּעִנְיָן שֶׁנֶּאֱמַר וַיַּעַשׂ אוֹתוֹ גִדְעוֹן לְאֵפוֹד. מַתְנִיתִין כְּמָאן דְּאָמַר. עֲבוֹדָה זָרָה כְּנִידָה וּמְשַׁמְּשֶׁיהָ כְּנִידָה. וְהָתַנֵּינָן. אֲבָנָיו וְעֵצָיו וַעֲפָרוֹ מְטַמְאִין כַּשֶּׁרֶץ. תִּיפְתָּר שֶׁהִשְׁתַּחֲוֶה לַבַּיִת וְאַחַר כָּךְ בְּנָייוֹ. וְהָא תַּנֵּינָן. שְׁלֹשָׁה בָתִּים הֵן. תִּיפְתָּר שֶׁהִשְׁתַּחֲוֶה לַבַּיִת וְאַחַר כָּךְ חִידְּשׁוֹ. דְּאָמַר רִבִּי זְעוּרָא רַב חוּנָא בְשֵׁם רַב. הַמִּשְׁתַּחֲוֶה לַבַּיִת אֲסָרוֹ. רִבִּי זְעוּרָה רִבִּי אַבָּהוּ בְשֵׁם רִבִּי יוֹחָנָן. הַמַּקְדִּישׁ אֶת הַבַּיִת מוֹעֲלִין בּוֹ. אָמַר רִבִּי זְעוּרָה. הֲוֵוי בָהּ רַבָּנָן פְּלוּגָא. מָאן דְּאָמַר. אֲסָרוֹ. מוֹעֲלִין בּוֹ. מָאן דְּאָמַר. לֹא אֲסָרוֹ. אֵין מוֹעֲלִין בּוֹ. הָתִיב רִבִּי חַגַי קוֹמֵי רִבִּי יוֹסֵה. מַתְנִיתָא פְלִיגָא עַל רַב. הַשּׁוּקֶת שֶׁבַּסֶּלַע אֵין מְמַלִּין בָּהּ. מִפְּנֵי שֶׁחֲקָקָהּ וְאַחַר כָּךְ חִיבְּרָהּ. הָא אִם חִיבְּרָהּ וְאַחַר כָּךְ חֲקָקָהּ לֹא. וְהָהֵן בַּיִת כְּמִי שֶׁחֲקָקוֹ וְאַחַר כָּךְ חִיבְּרוֹ הוּא. מָה עֲבַד לָהּ רַב. פָּתַר לָהּ. סִיתוּתָן שֶׁלַּאֲבָנִים הִיא גָמַר מְלַאכְתָּן. וְלֵית הָדָא פְלִיגֵי עַל רִבִּי יוֹחָנָן. דְּרִבִּי יוֹחָנָן אָמַר. עֲבוֹדָה זָרָה שֶׁנִּשְׁתַּבְּרָה אֲסוּרָה. לֹא כֵן סָבְרִינֵן מֵימַר. אִם בְּשֶׁאֵינוֹ עָתִיד לְהַחֲזִירָן לִכְלָיוֹ. דִּבְרֵי הַכֹּל מוּתָּר. וְהָא תַּנֵּינָן. שָׁלֹשׁ אֲבָנִים הֵן.

תִּיפְתָּר שֶׁהִשְׁתַּחֲוָה לְכָל־אֶבֶן וָאֶבֶן וְאַחַר כָּךְ בְּנָיָיהּ. וַאֲפִילוּ עַל רַבִּי שִׁמְעוֹן בֶּן לָקִישׁ לֵית הִיא פְלִיגָא. דְּרַבִּי שִׁמְעוֹן בֶּן לָקִישׁ אָמַר. עֲבוֹדָה זָרָה שֶׁנִּשְׁתַּבְּרָה מוּתֶּרֶת. לֹא כֵן סָבְרִינָן מֵימַר. אִם בְּעָתִיד לְהַחֲזִירָן לְכֵלָיו. דִּבְרֵי הַכֹּל אָסוּר. וְאָמַר רַבִּי יוּדָן אֲבוֹי דְּרַבִּי מַתַּנְיָה. אִם הָיוּ מוּנָחִין בִּמְקוֹמָן לֹא כְמִי שֶׁהוּא עָתִיד לְהַחֲזִירָן לְכֵלָיו הֵן. וְאִילּוּ בִּמְקוֹמָן הֵן. רִבִּי בָּא בְשֵׁם רַב. הַמִּשְׁתַּחֲוֶה לַבַּיִת אֲסָרוֹ. לָאִילָן לֹא אֲסָרוֹ. וְהָא תַּנִּינָן. שָׁלֹשׁ אֲשֵׁירוֹת הֵן. תִּיפְתָּר שֶׁנִּשְׁתַּחֲוָה לַזְּמוֹרָה וְאַחַר כָּךְ נְטָעָהּ.

לֵוִי אָמַר. מִשְׁתַּחֲוֶה לַבַּיִת אֲסָרוֹ. לַמְעָרָה לֹא אֲסָרוֹ. מַה בֵּין בַּיִת וּמַה בֵּין מְעָרָה. אָמַר רַבִּי חֲנַנְיָה בְּרֵיהּ דְּרַבִּי הִלֵּל. בַּיִת הָיָה לוֹ שְׁעַת תְּלִישָׁה. מְעָרָה לֹא הָיָה לָהּ שְׁעַת תְּלִישָׁה.

There exists a *baraita* which says, idols are like a menstruating woman and its appurtenances are like a menstruating woman. Also there exists a *baraita* which says, idols are like a menstruating woman and its appurtenances are like crawling animals[53]. The one who says, idols are like a menstruating woman and its appurtenances are like a menstruating woman, is understandable. But concerning the one who says, idols are like a menstruating woman and its appurtenances are like crawling animals, is it not called "unwell" only for its appurtenances[54]? *You will defile the coating of your silver gods and the clothing of your molten gold.* Explain it if they were engraved on its body. Rebbi Jacob of Kefar Ḥanan said, explain it if one worships the *ephod* itself[55], similar to what is written, *Gideon turned it into an ephod*[56]. Our Mishnah follows him who said, idols are like a menstruating woman and its appurtenances are like a menstruating woman. But did we not state: "its stones, its wood, and its dust make impure like a crawling animal[57]"? Explain it if he worshipped the house itself and then built it up. But did we not state "there are three houses"[58]? Explain it if he worshipped the house itself and then renovated it, as Rebbi Abba, Rab Huna said in the name of Rav: One who worships a house makes it forbidden[59]. Rebbi Ze`ira, Rebbi Abbahu in the name of Rebbi Joḥanan: If somebody dedicates a house one does commit larceny with it. Rebbi Ze`ira said, about this the rabbis disagree. For him who says that he forbade it one may commit larceny with it, but for him who says that he does not forbid it, one does not commit larceny with it[60]? Rebbi Ḥaggai objected before Rebbi Yose, does not a Mishnah disagree with Rav? "A trough in a rock: one does not fill from it.[61]" Because he excavated it and after that combined it[62]. Then not if he fixed it and after that excavated it[63]. Is this house not as if he excavated it and after that combined it? What does Rav do with it? He explains that the hewing of stones is the completion of work on them[64]. Does this not disagree with Rebbi Johanan, since Rebbi Johanan said, an idol which was broken is forbidden. And so we are thinking to say if in the future he cannot restore it in its entirety it is permitted according to everybody[65]. But did we not state, "there are three kinds of stones"[66]? Explain it that he worshipped every single stone and then builds with them[67]. Even with Rebbi Simeon ben Laqish this does not disagree, as Rebbi Simeon ben Laqish said, an idol which was broken is permitted[68]. And so we are thinking to say if in the future he can restore it in its entirety it is forbidden according to everybody, and Rebbi Yudan, the father of Rebbi Mattaniah, said, if they remain in their place is this not as if in the future he can restore it in its entirety? And these remain at their place. Rebbi Abba in the name of Rav, one who worships a house makes it forbidden[59], a tree he does not make forbidden. But did we not state, "there are three kinds of *Ashera*[69]"? Explain it that he worshipped a vine and then planted it.

Levi said, one who worships a house makes it forbidden[59], a cave he does not make forbidden[70]. What is [the difference] between a house and a cave? Rebbi Hanania the son of Rebbi Hillel said, a house was separated at some time; a cave never was separated.

53 The first opinion is the teaching of R. Aqiba in the Mishnah, the second is ascribed to R. Aqiba in the Babli, *Šabbat* 83a.

54 The full text of *Is.* 30:22, which is the base of R. Aqiba's argument, reads: *You will defile the cover of your silver statues and the clothing of your golden casts; you shall throw it away like feeling miserable, you shall call it excrement.* Therefore the reference of "feeling miserable", which is the description of a female period, refers to appurtenances only. The second version of the position of R. Aqiba seems untenable.

55 The statue and its ornamental vestments were two separate objects of worship. Either explanation is possible.

56 *Jud.* 8:27.

57 Mishnah *Avodah zarah* 3:8. Since this sentence in the Mishnah precedes the statement of R. Aqiba who imposes the impurity of *niddah* also on the stones which form the shell of the house of worship but are not the object of worship.

58 Mishnah *Avodah zarah* 3:9. Only a house originally built as a temple is permanently forbidden; all others can be cleansed by removing the idol and all installations and ornamentations made for it.

How could one decree severe impurity which can be easily eliminated?

59 Rav answers that even a house not built for worship becomes permanently forbidden as if it had been built as a pagan temple, if itself was worshipped. Babli 47b, *Me`ilah* 20a.

60 One compares the rules concerning a pagan temple with those of a house dedicated to the Temple (*Lev.* 27:14-15). Improper use of dedicated things is larceny which must be expiated by a sacrifice and payment of a fine, (*Lev.* 5:14-16). Just as real estate cannot become forbidden by idolatry, larceny by improper use of dedicated objects does not apply to real estate. If a house is considered real estate, it cannot become forbidden by worship, and its improper use while in the possession of the Temple cannot trigger a fine for larceny. If it is not considered real estate since the building materials were movables before being used, but it can become forbidden and improper use can trigger the fine.

61 Mishnah *Parah* 5:7. The ashes of the Red Cow, used to purify a person from the impurity of the dead, must be strewn on *flowing water in a vessel* (*Num.* 19:17). A vessel is movable; therefore a trough hewn into the rock is not a vessel. The water flowing from the source into the trough becomes standing water. Therefore it may be used neither (1) to fill a vessel for the ashes, nor (2) to put some ashes in the water, "to sanctify it", nor (3) to sprinkle the water on impure persons to purify them.

In addition, a corpse in a "tent" makes everything in the tent impure including the contents of vessels whose cover is not tightly fastened (*Num.* 19:15). Since the trough is not a vessel, if it is under one roof with a corpse it only needs to be covered but the cover does not have to be fastened.

A *miqweh* (ritual bath) has to contain 40 *seah* of water. It becomes invalid if 3 *log* ($^1/_8$ *seah*) of water from a vessel is poured into it before it has reached the level of 40 *seah*. If the trough is not a vessel, its water cannot invalidate the *miqweh*. On the other hand, if the trough was a vessel before it was fastened in the rock, it can be used for the ashes of the red cow, and its water will disqualify the *miqweh*.

Since a house was not a vessel before being connected to the ground, it should be considered real estate and not be subject to prohibition because of worship.

62 A vessel which is permanently fixed to the ground remains a vessel and can become forbidden.

63 A piece of loose rock which was cemented to the ground and then a trough was hewn from it does not become a vessel . Then why should a house become forbidden by being worshipped since it becomes a house only after being connected to the ground?

64 It is true that a finished house not built as a temple cannot become forbidden. But if the finished stones for a stone building were worshipped before being cemented in the house they already are forbidden and do not become permitted by use as building blocks.

65 The statement of R. Simeon ben Laqish and the opposing statement of R. Johanan only refer to situations where it is not clear whether the idol can be restored or not.

66 Mishnah *Avodah zarah* 3:10.

67 Then each individual stone remains forbidden; there is no contradiction to the

Mishnah.
68 Babli *Me`ilah* 20a.
69 This refers to a holy tree which is worshipped as *Ashera* (Mishnah *Avodah zarah* 3:11) but no idol is found buried under it. Then as connected to the ground it should not be part of the real estate and not be forbidden. It becomes permanently forbidden only if it was planted as a holy shoot.
70 Even if the cave was excavated for purposes of idol worship it does not lose its character as real estate.

(11d line 65) ב'. וְלֹא מִן הַיָּם לָמַדְתָּ. מַה יָּם טָהוֹר. אַף הַסְּפִינָה טְהוֹרָה. וְלֹא מִן הַשַּׂק לָמַדְתָּ. מַה הַשַּׂק מְשַׁמֵּשׁ בַּיָּם וּמְשַׁמֵּשׁ בַּיַּבָּשָׁה. סְפִינָה מְשַׁמֶּשֶׁת בַּיָּם וְאֵינָהּ מְשַׁמֶּשֶׁת בַּיַּבָּשָׁה. רַבָּנִן דְּקַיְסָרִין אֱמְרֵי. זוֹ סְפִינָה שֶׁלְּחֶרֶס. מַה הַשַּׂק אֵינוֹ מְלַמֵּד עַל כָּל־הָאָמוּר בַּפָּרָשָׁה. יָצָא כְלֵי חֶרֶשׂ שֶׁאֵינוֹ כָתוּב בַּפָּרָשָׁה שֶׁיְּלַמֵּד עָלָיו הַשַּׂק.

2[71]. Did you have to learn from the sea[72], just as the sea is pure so also the ship is pure? Did you not learn this from the sack[73]? The sack may be used both on sea and on dry land; a ship can be used on sea but cannot be used on dry land[74]. The rabbis of Caesarea say, this is about a clay vessel. Since the sack teaches only about what is written in the paragraph[75], this excludes clay vessels which are not mentioned in the paragraph so that the sack could have taught about it.

71 Here starts the discussion of Mishnah 2. Babli 83b.
72 It is very irregular to derive halakhic principles from the Hagiographs since the only admitted source is the Pentateuch.
73 The basic verse is *Lev.* 11:32 where impurity of implements is introduced. These are described as *wooden vessels, or textiles, or leather, or a sack, or anything used in work*. This is read to mean that containers are subject to impurity only if they can be handled like a sack; i. e., transported by a human both empty and filled. Usually a ship is too large to be handled in this way.
74 This is a first argument to deny that a comparison with a sack is possible in this case.
75 Clay vessels are not mentioned in *Lev.* 11:32; the rules for these must be derived from other sources which, however, do not lend themselves to interpretation based on size.

(11d line 70) זֵירוּעֶיהָ. מִיעוּט זֵירוּעֶיהָ שְׁנַיִם. אָמַר רִבִּי שְׁמוּאֵל בַּר סִיסַרְטָא. מִשְּׁנַיִם אַתְּ לָמֵד אַרְבָּעָה. מַה שְּׁנַיִם אַתְּ נוֹתֵן בַּתְּחִילָּה שָׁשָׂה וּמֵיצֵר וְהוֹלֵךְ. אַף אַרְבָּעָה אַתְּ נוֹתֵן בַּתְּחִילָּה שִׁשָּׁה וּמֵיצֵר וְהוֹלֵךְ. אֵיפְשָׁר שֶׁלֹּא יְהֵא שָׁם נֶקֶב אֶחָד פָּנוּי לִיטַּע בּוֹ אֶת הָאֶמְצָעִי. אָמַר רִבִּי יוֹנָה. עֲבוֹדָה פּוֹגַעַת בַּעֲבוֹדָה. וְאֵין מִין פּוֹגֵעַ בַּחֲבֵירוֹ לְחוֹבְשׁוֹ. רִבִּי יְהוֹשֻׁעַ בֶּן לֵוִי אָמַר. זַרְעָהּ זְרָעֶיהָ

זֵירוּעֶיהָ. וּכְרַבִּי יְהוּדָה. דְּרַבִּי יְהוּדָה אוֹמֵר. שִׁשָּׁה. זֶרַע זַרְעָהּ זַרְעֶיהָ זֵירוּעֶיהָ. רִבִּי חַגַּי אָמַר. זַרְעֶיהָ חֲמִשָׁה. כָּל־הָהֵן דַּאֲנָא מַשְׁכַּח וָו אֲנָא מְחִיק לֵהּ. אִישְׁתְּאֶלֶת לְרִבִּי חוּנָה סַפְרָא דְסִדְרָא וַאֲמַר. זֵירוּעֶיהָ מָלֵא. רִבִּי יוֹחָנָן בְּשֵׁם רִבִּי יַנַּאי. כּוּלְּהוֹן חוּץ לְשִׁשָּׁה. אִם כּוּלְּהוֹן חוּץ לְשִׁשָּׁה נִיתְנֵי. תִּשְׁעָה. אָמַר רִבִּי תַנְחוּם בָּצְרָיָה. וְכֵינִי. בַּעֲרוּגָה שֶׁבָּעֲרוּגוֹת הִיא מַתְנִיתָא.

1 זירועיה | כ זרעיה זירועיה | כ זרעים   3 איפשר | כ אי איפשר האמצעי | כ האמצעית   4 פוגע | כ פוגעת אמ' | כ - זרעה | כ זריעיה   5 יהודה | כ יודה (2) או' | כ אמ' זירועיה | כ (זרעה) חגי | כ חגי   6 וו | כ לה וי לה | כ ליה ר' חונה | כ רב הונא דסדרא | כ דסידרא   7 מלא | כ מליא ינאי | כ יניי - | כולהון בתוך ששה כינא בשם ר' שמעון בן לקיש.   8 בוצריה | כ בוצרייא וכיני | כ וכן היא

[76]*Its sown seeds*: the minimum of seeds are two[77]. Rebbi Samuel bar Sisarta said, from two you infer four. Just as for two you start at the beginning of six and reduce continuously, so for four you start at the beginning of six and reduce continuously. It is impossible[78] that there should not be a free space to plant in the middle[79]. Rebbi Jonah said, working space joins working space but a kind does not meet another kind to jail it[80]. Rebbi Joshua ben Levi: *Its seed, its seeds, its sown seeds*[81]. That follows Rebbi Jehudah, since Rebbi Jehudah said six, *seed, its seed, its seeds, its sown seeds*. Rebbi Haggai said, זרעיה has five letters; everywhere I find ו I delete it[82]. This was asked of Rebbi Huna, the scribe of the assembly, and he said, זירועיה is written plene[83]. Rebbi Johanan in the name of Rebbi Yannai: [84][All inside of six[85]. Cahana in the name of Rebbi Simeon ben Laqish:] All at the outside of six[86]. Then we should state "nine!" Rebbi Tanhum from Bostra said, that is true. But our Mishnah speaks of a garden bed in the middle of garden beds[87].

76 The origin of this paragraph is in *Kilaim* 3:1 (Notes 6-18,כ). In the copy here, an essential sentence was omitted by the scribe. On the other hand, the spelling here is somewhat more careful than in *Kilaim*.

77 It does not say, *it will make to germinate its seedling* but *its seedlings*. The verse uses a plural for the seedlings in a garden(interpreted as one garden bed); this proves only that it is possible to sow more than one kind.

78 The correct Yerushalmi form for "impossible"; the form אי אפשר in כ is Babylonian.

79 The argument as explained by R. Simson: At the end of the paragraph, it is stated that one deals with a vegetable bed surrounded by other vegetable beds. The rules of "jailing" (*Kilaim* 2:8 Note 120) prohibit to grow one kind of produce on a field surrounded by four fields on which other kinds are grown and therefore require that at the corners squares of one hand-breadth each must be empty. In order to grow two kinds of plants, one may sow two strips, each 4 hand-breadths long, along parallel edges, each one 2.25 hand-breadths wide, so that the required separation of 1.5

hand-breadths be observed in the middle. But then the argument may be used also for the other two edges. This means that one sows four triangular patches; each one has a base of 4 hand-breadths on an edge of the garden bed, with base angles of 45°. These triangles must be separated by strips 1.5 hand-breadths wide. This means that at the edges, we must leave a square of edge length a empty, whose diagonal is $1.5 = a2^{½}$. Hence, $a = 1.061$; the bases of the triangle can only be 3.878 hand-breadths. In that case, the distance of the third vertex of the triangle from its base is equal to half the base on the edge, or 1.939 hand-breadths. The distance from the center is $a = 1.061 < 1.5$. In order to plant a single seed in the middle, it is therefore necessary to cut off the triangles at distance 1.5 from center and edge, creating four congruent trapezoids. The height of a trapezoid is $h=1.5$, its base $2b=3.878$. By similar triangles, the length t of its top is given by $2b/b = t/(b-h)$ or $t = 0.878$. That makes it possible to plant a single fifth kind in a small space in the middle. The total area planted amounts to four times the area of the trapezoids, 15.044 square hand-breadths, plus the area of the small space in the middle.

80   Each separate kind needs a working space around it, given by the strip of width 1.5 hand-breadths, but the same strip does serve two different kinds without problem. Also, the rules of "jailing" only apply to fields, not to garden beds.

81   Here starts a new approach, *viz.*, that the verse itself implies more than 2 kinds. The word זרוע appears only twice in the Bible, *Is.* 61:11 and in a description of grain (*Lev.* 11:37): *seeds of seedlings that may be sown.* In contrast to modern dictionaries which take זרוע as a word different from זרע, the authors here take it as expansion of זרע "seed." The root is expanded three times, by taking the plural, adding a possessive suffix, and adding the letter ו. Each change is taken as a plural, hence three plurals are added for a total of six units.

82   R. Haggai assumes that originally all Hebrew spelling was what is called defective. Hence, any ו or י that is neither part of the root nor required by grammatical rules is considered an addition by later scribes and therefore is disregarded. That eliminates the ו but leaves the י which is required as sign of plural. One ends up with five letters, following the anonymous opinion in Mishnah *Kilaim* 3:1.

83   The spelling זירועיה in the text is certainly wrong since the expression of *sere* by י is standard only in Mishnaic and later texts, not in Biblical ones. Hence, the *plene* writing refers to the masoretic spelling of the word; one has six letters, supporting Rebbi Jehudah.

84   Added from כ, needed by the context.

85   All seeds are sown in the interior of the bed, away from the corners.

86   The corners at the boundary, which are at the outside, are sown. Then one may sow four 1-by-1 corner patches, four 1-by-1 patches at the center of each edge, and a center diamond, for a total of nine patches.

87   Since the rules of "jailing" apply to garden beds as a whole, not to smaller patches, the corners cannot be sown. This is the opinion of Samuel in the Babli (*Šabbat* 86b). Otherwise, it really is possible to sow

9 kinds, as the Babli puts it (*Šabbat* 86a), in the case of a garden bed planted on land otherwise dry, with no other beds nearby. Rav in the Babli still admits only five kinds even on dry land.

(12a line 5) ג'. אָמַר רִבִּי יוֹחָנָן. מִסִּינַי לָמְדוּ. יָרַד מֹשֶׁה בַּשְּׁלִישִׁי בַּשַּׁבָּת. אָמַר לָהֶן. הֱיוּ נְכוֹנִים לִשְׁלֹשֶׁת יָמִים אַל־תִּגְּשׁוּ אֶל־אִשָּׁה: כָּל־מִי שֶׁפֵּירֵשׁ בַּשְּׁלִישִׁי. יֵשׁ כָּאן (שְׁלִישִׁי) לֵיל רְבִיעִי וּרְבִיעִי לֵיל חֲמִישִׁי וַחֲמִישִׁי. בַּשִּׁישִׁי פֵּלְטָה בַּלַּיְלָה טְמֵאָה בַּיּוֹם טְהוֹרָה. כָּל־מִי שֶׁפֵּירֵשׁ בָּרְבִיעִי. יֵשׁ כָּאן רְבִיעִי לֵיל חֲמִישִׁי וַחֲמִישִׁי. בַּשִּׁישִׁי פֵּלְטָה בַּלַּיְלָה טְמֵאָה בַּיּוֹם טְהוֹרָה. אָמַר רִבִּי יוֹחָנָן. זוֹ בְסִינַי. אֲבָל לְאַדוֹרוֹת אוֹ בְאַרְבַּע אוֹ בְשֵׁשׁ. רִבִּי עֲקִיבָה אוֹמֵר. לְעוֹלָם הֵן חָמֵשׁ. וְכֵן לַדּוֹרוֹת.

3. [88]Rebbi Joḥanan said, they learned from Sinai[89]. Moses came down on the third day of the week[90] and told them, *be prepared for three days, do not approach a woman*[91]. For any one who separated on the third day, there is (the third)[92], the night of the fourth, and the fourth, the night of the fifth, and the fifth. On the sixth, if she ejected in the night she was impure, during the day pure[93]. For any one who separated on the fourth day, there is the fourth, the night of the fifth, and the fifth. On the sixth, if she ejected in the night she was impure, during the day pure[94]. Rebbi Joḥanan said, this was on Sinai. But for future generations either four or six[95]; Rebbi Aqiba says, forever there are five, also for future generations.

88 Here starts discussion of Mishnah 3, although the reference is not to the statement of R. Aqiba in that Mishnah but to Mishnah *Miqwaot* 8:3, quoted in the next paragraph, to which the present is an introduction.

89 The rules of impurity of semen lost by a woman days after intercourse are derived from *Ex.* 19.

90 Tuesday. In this interpretation there were three days of preparation and the revelation on Sinai took place on the Sabbath. If one deletes "of the week", the reference is to the day of the Month.

91 *Ex.* 19:15.

92 This word was written by the scribe, then (wrongly) deleted by the corrector, and therefore missing in the printed editions.

93 The times elapsed in the matter of women's purity are always counted in "terms" of 12 hours each. If a woman had sex in the night from Monday to Tuesday, then six terms have elapsed by Friday, and she can purify herself in a *miqweh* without problems.

94 In this case, four terms have elapsed, as stated as possibility by R. Ismael in Mishnah *Miqwaot* 8:3.

95 Mishnah *Miqwaot* 8:3.

(12a line 11) תַּמָּן תַּנִּינָן. הַפּוֹלֶטֶת שִׁכְבַת זֶרַע בַּיּוֹם הַשְּׁלִישִׁי טְהוֹרָה. דִּבְרֵי רִבִּי אֶלְעָזָר בֶּן עֲזַרְיָה. רִבִּי יִשְׁמָעֵאל אוֹמֵר. פְּעָמִים שֶׁהֵן אַרְבַּע עוֹנוֹת. פְּעָמִים שֶׁהֵן חָמֵשׁ. פְּעָמִים שֶׁהֵן שֵׁשׁ. רִבִּי עֲקִיבָה אוֹמֵר. לְעוֹלָם הֵן חָמֵשׁ: אִם יָצָאת מִקְצָת עוֹנָה הָרִאשׁוֹנָה מַשְׁלִימִין לָהּ מִקְצָת עוֹנָה שִׁשִּׁית. הָא רִבִּי יִשְׁמָעֵאל עָבַד יוֹם עוֹנָה וְלַיְלָה עוֹנָה. וְרִבִּי עֲקִיבָה עָבַד יוֹם עוֹנָה וְלַיְלָה עוֹנָה. מַה בֵּינֵיהוֹן. עוֹנוֹת שְׁלֵימוֹת בֵּינֵיהוֹן. רִבִּי יִשְׁמָעֵאל עָבַד מִקְצָת עוֹנָה כְכוּלָּהּ. וְרִבִּי עֲקִיבָה לָא עָבַד מִקְצָת עוֹנָה כְכוּלָּהּ. וְתַנֵּי כֵן עַל דְּרִבִּי עֲקִיבָה. לְפִיכָךְ אִם נִכְנְסָה מִקְצָת עוֹנָה רִאשׁוֹנָה מַשְׁלִימִין לָהּ מִקְצָת עוֹנָה שִׁשִּׁית. תַּנֵּי. רִבִּי אֶלְעָזָר בֶּן עֲזַרְיָה אוֹמֵר. יוֹם וְלַיְלָה עוֹנָה. וּמִקְצָת עוֹנָה כְכוּלָּהּ. וְתַנֵּי כֵן עַל דְּרִבִּי אֶלְעָזָר בֶּן עֲזַרְיָה. פְּעָמִים יֵשׁ שָׁם יוֹם וְכָל־שֶׁהוּא וְהִיא טְהוֹרָה. שְׁנֵי יָמִים וְחָסֵר כָּל־שֶׁהוּא וְהִיא טְמֵיאָה. יוֹם וְכָל־שֶׁהוּא וְהִיא טְהוֹרָה הֵיךְ עֲבִידָא. שִׁימְּשָׁה אֶת בֵּיתָהּ עֶרֶב שַׁבָּת קוֹדֶם לִשְׁקִיעַת הַחַמָּה וּפָלְטָה בְּמוֹצָאֵי שַׁבָּת לְאַחַר שְׁקִיעַת הַחַמָּה. הֲרֵי יֵשׁ כָּאן יוֹם וְכָל־שֶׁהוּא וְהִיא טְהוֹרָה. שְׁנֵי יָמִים וְחָסֵר כָּל־שֶׁהוּא וְהִיא טְמֵיאָה הֵיךְ עֲבִידָא. שִׁימְּשָׁה אֶת בֵּיתָהּ עֶרֶב שַׁבָּת לְאַחַר שְׁקִיעַת הַחַמָּה וּפָלְטָה בְּאֶחָד בַּשַּׁבָּת קוֹדֶם לִשְׁקִיעַת הַחַמָּה. הֲרֵי יֵשׁ כָּאן שְׁנֵי יָמִים וְחָסֵר כָּל־שֶׁהוּא וְהִיא טְמֵיאָה. אָמַר רִבִּי יוֹחָנָן. מִדִּבְרֵי כוּלָּם. טְבוּלֵי יוֹם קִיבְּלוּ יִשְׂרָאֵל אֶת הַתּוֹרָה. הָדָא דְאַתְּ אָמַר בַּנָּשִׁים. אֲבָל בָּאֲנָשִׁים כְּבַר טְהֲרוּ. מַה טַעַם. וְקִדַּשְׁתָּם הַיּוֹם וּמָחָר וְכִבְּסוּ שִׂמְלוֹתָם: אָמַר רִבִּי יוֹחָנָן. זוֹ דִּבְרֵי רִבִּי אֶלְעָזָר בֶּן עֲזַרְיָה וְרִבִּי יִשְׁמָעֵאל וְרִבִּי עֲקִיבָה. אֲבָל דִּבְרֵי חֲכָמִים. עַד שְׁלֹשָׁה יָמִים. מִיכָּן וְהֵילַךְ הִיא נִסְרַחַת. וְאַתְיָא כְהָהִיא דְּאָמַר רִבִּי זְעוּרָא בְשֵׁם רִבִּי יוֹחָנָן. זֹאת תּוֹרַת הַזָּב וַאֲשֶׁר תֵּצֵא מִמֶּנּוּ שִׁכְבַת־זֶרַע. מַה תּוֹרַת הַזָּב עַד שְׁלֹשָׁה יָמִים. אַף תּוֹרַת שִׁכְבַת זֶרַע עַד שְׁלֹשָׁה יָמִים.

There[96], we have stated: "One who loses semen[8] on the third day is pure, the words of Rebbi Eleazar ben Azariah[97]. Rebbi Ismael says, sometimes they are four terms, sometimes they are five, sometimes they are six[98]. Rebbi Aqiba says, always they are five[99]. If part of the first term had elapsed, one completes it by the sixth term[100]." Therefore Rebbi Ismael makes the day one term and the night one term; Rebbi Aqiba makes the day one term and the night one term. In what do they differ? They differ in complete terms. Rebbi Ismael treats part of a term like the whole, but Rebbi Aqiba does not treat part of a term like the whole. It was stated so about Rebbi Aqiba: "Therefore if part of the first term had elapsed, one completes it by the sixth term"[101]. It was stated: Rebbi Eleazar ben Azariah says, day and night each are a term, and part of a term is like the whole. It was stated so about Rebbi Eleazar ben Azariah: Sometimes after slightly more than a day she is pure; sometimes after slightly less than two days she is impure. How does it happen that after slightly more than a day she is pure? She had intercourse Friday afternoon before sundown and lost Saturday night after nightfall; there is slightly more than a day she is pure[102]. How does it happen that after slightly less than two days she is impure? She had intercourse Friday night after sundown and lost Sunday night before nightfall; there is slightly less than two days she is impure[103]. Rebbi Johanan said, from the words of all of them, Israel received the Torah as immersed on the same day[104]. That is, the women; but the men already were purified. What is the reason? *Sanctify them today and tomorrow and let them wash their garments*[105]. Rebbi Johanan said, these are the words of Rebbi Eleazar ben Azariah, and Rebbi Ismael, and Rebbi Aqiba. But the word of the Sages is, up to three days; after that it decayed. This parallels what Rebbi Ze`ira said in the name of Rebbi Johanan: *This are the instructions for the sufferer from gonorrhea and from whom semen is ejaculated*[106]. Since the instructions of the sufferer from gonorrhea are based on three days[107], also the instructions for semen are up to three days[108].

96   Mishnah *Miqwaot* 8:3.

97   As explained later in the Halakhah, he strictly goes by the count of days, not measuring the time elapsed.

98   He essentially accepts R. Eleazar ben Azariah's interpretation; only he quantifies it in "terms". A term is either a night, from sundown to sunrise, or a day, from sunrise to sundown. Six terms are required if the woman had intercourse at sundown or sunrise, when it is not clear whether ejaculation occurred before or after the start of a new term.

99   In fact he always requires 60 hours elapsed after ejaculation.

100   This sentence is not in the Mishnah mss., but since it also is quoted in the Babli 86a as appendix to this Mishnah and clarifies the statement of R. Aqiba, it should be considered part of the Mishnah.

101   In order to complete the 60 hrs. required by R. Aqiba. The computation of R. Ismael is the same as that of R. Eleazar ben Azariah explained in the sequel.

102   For R. Eleazar ben Azariah the day of intercourse is day 1; she is pure if she loses some semen on day 3. The day starts at sundown. Let ε be a small fraction. If she had intercourse ε hours before sundown and then lost semen the next evening ε hours after sundown it already is the third day and she is pure after $24+2\varepsilon$ hours.

103   If she had intercourse ε hours after sundown then the next $24 - \varepsilon$ still are day 1; if she loses semen ε hours before the end of day 2 she still is impure even though $48 - 2\varepsilon$ hrs. have elapsed.

104   Babli 86b. For profane matters, a person either is pure or impure. But for *sancta*, the purification occurs in two stages. Impurity is removed by immersion in a *miqweh* but purity is acquired only at sundown (*Lev.* 22:6-7). In the meantime, the *tevul yom* person does not contaminate

anything by his touch but is not permitted any sanctified food (cf. *Berakhot* 1:1 Note 3).

105 *Ex.* 19:10. A man may immerse himself immediately after intercourse and become completely pure after the next sundown.

106 *Lev.* 15:32.

107 A sufferer from gonorrhea is impure, but he becomes severely impure requiring purification in flowing water only if he had three emissions within a three-day period (Mishnah *Zavim* 1:1).

108 Babli 86b. While the day of intercourse is counted as day 1, the woman does not become impure by losing semen only on day 4. The derivation of these laws from Sinai is rejected since before the theophany at Sinai the people were not obligated to follow the rules promulgated there.

Here starts a Genizah fragment edited by L. Ginzberg (p. 87-88), G.

(12a line 36) אֲנָן תַּנִּינָן. מַרְחִיצִין אֶת הַקָּטָן. מַרְחִיצִין אֶת הַמִּילָה. רִבִּי אַבָּהוּ בְּשֵׁם רִבִּי יוֹחָנָן. הֲלָכָה כְּמִי שֶׁהוּא אוֹמֵר. מַרְחִיצִין אֶת הַקָּטָן. אָמַר רִבִּי יוֹסֵי. עַל כּוֹרְחָךְ אַתְּ אוֹמֵר. מַרְחִיצִין אֶת הַקָּטָן. תַּנֵּי שְׁמוּאֵל. לְעוֹלָם אֵין מוֹנְעִין לֹא שֶׁמֶן וְלֹא חַמִּין מֵעַל גַּבֵּי מַכָּה בַּשַּׁבָּת. אָמַר רִבִּי יוֹסֵי. כָּל־שָׁעָה הָיָה רִבִּי זְעִירָא רִבִּי אוֹמֵר לִי. תְּנֵי מַתְנִיתָךְ. וְלֹא עוֹד אֶלָּא שֶׁמְּזַלְּפִין חַמִּים עַל גַּבֵּי מַכָּה בַּשַּׁבָּת. אִם אוֹמֵר שֶׁמַּרְחִיצִין אֶת הַמִּילָה. מַה בֵּין מַכָּתוֹ שֶׁלְּגָדוֹל לְמַכָּתוֹ שֶׁלְּקָטָן.

1 רב | **19** ר' G רבי אבהו | G אבהוא   2 יוסה | G יוסי את | G אתה   3 ולא חמין | G לא חמים   4 יוסה | **19** יוסי זעירא | G זעירא רבי | **19** ר' בא G ר' אומ' | G**19** אמר לי. תני | G ליתני

[109]We have stated: "One washes the baby." It was stated in the House of (Rav) [Rebbi][110]: "One washes the circumcision."[111] Rebbi Abbahu in the name of Rebbi Johanan: Practice follows him who says, "one washes the baby"[112]. Rebbi Yose said, you are forced to say, one washes the baby. [113]Samuel stated, one never witholds either oil or warm water from a wound on the Sabbath. Rebbi Yose said, my teacher Rebbi Ze'ira always was saying to me, state in your Mishnah, not only this but one sprinkles warm water on a wound on the Sabbath. If you are saying, "one washes the circumcision", what is the difference between an adult and a baby?

109 This paragraph and the next really are not about Mishnah 9:3 but Mishnah 19:3, which is quoted in the first sentence. The text there was omitted by the scribe and added by the corrector, whose text (**19**) seems to be a copy of the text here, only slightly careless at the end. In addition to G, there also is a slightly enlarged version in *Gen. rabba* 80(8), on *Gen.* 43:25.

110 The text in (parentheses) is from the ms., the one in [brackets] from G and **19** seems to be the correct one; cf. Tosephta

15:4.
111 But not the entire body of a newly circumcised baby.
112 Babli 134b.

113 All this is R. Yose's argument that in Mishnah 19:3 one must state "the baby" since for "the circumcision" the statement would be superfluous.

(12a line 43) רִבִּי אַבָּהוּ בְשֵׁם רִבִּי אֶלְעָזָר. הֲלָכָה כְרִבִּי אֶלְעָזָר בֶּן עֲזַרְיָה. רִבִּי אַבִּין בְשֵׁם רִבִּי אַבָּהוּ. טַעֲמָא דְּרִבִּי אֶלְעָזָר בֶּן עֲזַרְיָה. וַיְהִי בַיּוֹם הַשְּׁלִישִׁי בִּהְיוֹתָם כּוֹאֲבִים. בִּהְיוֹתוֹ כּוֹאֵב אֵין כָּתוּב כָּאן. אֶלָּא בִּהְיוֹתָם כּוֹאֲבִים. בְּשָׁעָה שֶׁכָּל־אֵיבָרֵיהֶם כּוֹאֲבִים עֲלֵיהֶם. רִבִּי יַעֲקֹב בַּר אֲחָא אָמַר. רִבִּי אֶלְעָזָר וְרִבִּי יוֹחָנָן מְפַקְדִין לְחַיָּיתָא. כָּל־שִׁיקוּיִין דְּאַתּוּן עָבְדִין בְּחוֹלָא עֲבָדִין בְּשׁוּבְתָא. לָכֵן צְרִיכָה. אֲפִילוּ בַיּוֹם הַשְּׁלִישִׁי שֶׁחָל לִהְיוֹת בַּשַּׁבָּת. שְׁמוּאֵל אָמַר. מִפְּנֵי הַסַּכָּנָה. רִבִּי יוֹסֵה בָעֵי. אִם מִפְּנֵי הַסַּכָּנָה מְחַמִּין לוֹ חַמִּין. רִבִּי יוֹסֵי בֵּירִבִּי בּוּן בְשֵׁם רַבָּנָן תַּמָּן. מְחַמִּין לוֹ חַמִּין בַּשַּׁבָּת. וְתַנֵּי כֵן. מְחַמֵּם הוּא אָדָם לוּנְטִית וְנוֹתְנָה עַל גַּבֵּי מַכָּה בַּשַּׁבָּת. לֹא יִטּוֹל אָדָם עֲרִיבָה מְלֵיאָה חַמִּין וְיִתְּנֶינָה עַל גַּבֵּי מֵעָיו בַּשַּׁבָּת. רִבִּי יְהוֹשֻׁעַ בֶּן לֵוִי אָמַר. לֵית כָּאן אֶלָּא מוּתָּר.

1 אבין | 19 בון G אבון   2 בהייתו | G בהיותם   3 בשעה | 19 מלמד עליהם | 19 עליהן   4 לחיתא G לחייתה שיקויין | 19 שקויין דאתון עבדין | 19 דעבדין בחולא | 19 לחולה עבדין | 19 -   5 בשבתא | 19 בשבתא אפי' | 19 עבדין אפי'   6 ר' יוסה בעי. אם מפני הסכנה יוסי | G יוסה רבנן | 19 רבניו תמן | 19 דתמן   7 מחמם | 19 מחמין G מחמים לונטית | 19 אלונטית מכה | 19 מעיים   8 ויתנינה G19 ויתננה מעיו | 19 מעיים

Rebbi Abbahu in the name of Rebbi Eleazar. Practice follows Rebbi Eleazar ben Azariah[114]. Rebbi Abbin in the name of Rebbi Abbahu, the reason of Rebbi Eleazar ben Azariah: *it was on the third day when they hurt*[11]. It does not say, "when it hurt", but *when they hurt*, at a time when all their limbs hurt them. Rebbi Jacob bar Aḥa said, Rebbi Eleazar and Rebbi Joḥanan ordered for the women having newborns, that all treatments which you give on a weekday should be given on the Sabbath. This is necessary for the case that the third day falls on a Sabbath. Samuel said, because of the danger. Rebbi Yose asked, if it is because of the danger one heats hot water for him[115]! Rebbi Yose ben Rebbi Abun in the name of the rabbis there: One heats hot water for him. And it was stated thus: A person heats a linen cloth and puts it on (a wound) (his belly)[116] on the Sabbath[117]. A person may not take a bottle full of hot water and put it on his belly on the Sabbath. Rebbi Joshua ben Levi said, on the contrary it is permitted.[118]

114 Who states in Mishnah 19:3 that on the third day after circumcision the boy is considered in mortal danger and therefore everything necessary for his care must be done on the Sabbath. Babli 134b.
115 If there is danger one has to do

everything necessary; there seems to be no need to single out heating water.

116 The first version is that of the ms. and *Gen. r.*; G has a lacuna at this place. The second version is that of **19** and the Babli (40b).

117 Tosephta 3:7.

118 Babli 40b.

(12a line 54) בָּרִאשׁוֹנָה הָיוּ קוֹשְׁרִין אוֹתוֹ בַּחֲלוֹנוֹתֵיהֶם. וְיֵשׁ מֵהֶן שֶׁהָיָה מַלְבִּין וְיֵשׁ מֵהֶם שֶׁהָיָה מַאֲדִים. וְהָיוּ מִתְבַּיְישִׁין אֵילוּ מֵאֵילוּ. חָזְרוּ לִהְיוֹת קוֹשְׁרִים אוֹתוֹ בְּפִתְחוֹ שֶׁלְהֵיכָל. וְיֵשׁ שָׁנִים שֶׁהָיָה מַלְבִּין וְיֵשׁ שָׁנִים שֶׁהָיָה מַאֲדִים. חָזְרוּ וְקָשְׁרוּ אוֹתוֹ בַּסֶּלַע.

2 אילו מאילו | ו אלו מאלו

כְּתִיב לְכוּ־נָא וְנִוָּכְחָה יֹאמַר יי' וגו'. תַּנֵּי. רִבִּי אֱלִיעֶזֶר אוֹמֵר. אִם־יִהְיוּ חֲטָאֵיכֶם כַּשָּׁנִים וגו'. כַּשָּׁנִים שֶׁבֵּין שָׁמַיִם לָאָרֶץ. כַּשֶּׁלֶג יַלְבִּינוּ. יָתֵר מִיכֵּן כַּצֶּמֶר יִהְיוּ· רִבִּי יְהוֹשֻׁעַ אוֹמֵר. אִם־יִהְיוּ חֲטָאֵיכֶם כַּשָּׁנִים· כִּשְׁנֵי אָבוֹת. כַּשֶּׁלֶג יַלְבִּינוּ. יָתֵר מִיכֵּן כַּצֶּמֶר יִהְיוּ· אָמַר רִבִּי יוּדָן בַּר פָּזִי. אִם־יִהְיוּ חֲטָאֵיכֶם כַּשָּׁנִים כַּשֶּׁלֶג יַלְבִּינוּ. בָּרִאשׁוֹן. וְאִם יַאְדִּימוּ כַתּוֹלָע כַּצֶּמֶר יִהְיוּ· בַּשֵּׁינִי. וְרַבָּנָן אָמְרֵי. אִם יְהִיוּ חַטָּאָיו שֶׁלְאָדָם כְּפִי שָׁנָיו. כַּשֶּׁלֶג יַלְבִּינוּ. יָתֵר מִיכֵּן כַּצֶּמֶר יִהְיוּ· אָמַר רִבִּי יוּדָן עַנְתּוֹדְרַיָּיא. בְּשָׁעָה שֶׁעֲווֹנוֹת קַלִּין כַּשֶּׁלֶג יַלְבִּינוּ. בְּשָׁעָה שֶׁהֵן כְּבֵדִין כַּצֶּמֶר יִהְיוּ·

1 ונוחכה | ונווחכה אליעזר | ו אלעזר וגו' | ו -   3 אבות | ו אבות הראשונים יתר ניכן | ו ואם יאדימו כתולע ילבינו. יתר מיכן | ו -   4 כשנים | ו כשני ואם | ו אם   5 ורבנן | ו ורבניו | אם יהיו חטאיו | ו נזמן שעוונותיו כשלג ידון | ו יודא   The remainder is missing.

[119]Originally they were tying it to their windows; some of them were turning white and some turning red; these were ashamed in front of the others. They changed and tied it to the door of the Sanctuary. Some years it was turning white, in others turning red. They changed and tied it to the rock.

It is written[13], *let us go and argue, says the Eternal,* etc. It was stated, Rebbi Eliezer said, *If your sins were like years*[120], etc., like the years from Heaven to Earth[121], *they will be snow white*; more than that, *they shall be like wool*. Rebbi Joshua said, *if your sins were like years*, like the years of the patriarchs, *they will be snow white*; more than that, *they shall be like wool*. Rebbi Yudan bar Pazi said, *If your sins were like years they will be snow white*, the first time, *if they were like purple they shall be like wool*, the second time. But the rabbis said, If the sins of a person are like his years, *they will be snow white*; more than that, *they shall be like wool*. Rebbi Yudan Antordiyya said, at a time when a person's sins are light, *they will be snow white*; at a time when they are serious, *they shall be like wool*.

119 This is the discussion of the last part of Mishnah 3, the crimson band which was tied to the head of the scapegoat, or, as noted in Mishnah *Yoma* 6:6, half of which was tied to

the cliff from which the scapegoat was pushed down. The first paragraph is a *baraita* also reproduced in the Babli, *Yoma* 67a, *Roš Haššanah* 31b. Both paragraphs are copied (the second incompletely) in *Yoma* 6:5 (1).

120 The plural שָׁנִים is derived from שָׁנָה "year", not from שָׁנִי "scarlet". For the other occurrence in *Prov.* 31:21, *Midrash Mishle* (ed. S. Buber, p. 110, Note ל) reads the word as שְׁנַיִם "two, double". The only rabbinic source which recognizes שָׁנִים as "scarlet" is in *Midrash Mishle* (*loc. cit.* p. 112).

121 The numbers given by RR. Eliezer and R. Joshua are identical, 500. Cf. *Berakhot* 1:1, Note 83.

(12a line 65) ד. מְנַיִין לְסִיכָה כול׳. בַּשַּׁבָּת בֵּין סִיכָה שֶׁהִיא שֶׁלְתַּעֲנוּג בֵּין סִיכָה שֶׁאֵינָהּ שֶׁלְתַּעֲנוּג מוּתָּר. בְּיוֹם הַכִּיפּוּרִים בֵּין סִיכָה שֶׁהִיא שֶׁלְתַּעֲנוּג בֵּין סִיכָה שֶׁאֵינָהּ שֶׁלְתַּעֲנוּג אָסוּר. בְּתִשְׁעָה בְּאָב וּבְתַעֲנִית צִיבּוּר סִיכָה שֶׁהִיא שֶׁלְתַּעֲנוּג אָסוּר. שֶׁאֵינָהּ שֶׁלְתַּעֲנוּג מוּתָּר.

תַּנֵּי. שָׁווֹת סִיכָה לִשְׁתִייָה לְאִיסּוּר וּלְתַשְׁלוּמִים אֲבָל לֹא לְעוֹנֶשׁ. בְּיוֹם הַכִּיפּוּרִים לְאִיסּוּר אֲבָל לֹא לְעוֹנֶשׁ. וְהָא תַנֵּי. וְלֹא יְחַלְּלוּ. לְהָבִיא אֶת הַסָּךְ וְאֶת הַשּׁוֹתֶה. אָמַר רִבִּי יוֹחָנָן. לֵית כָּאן סָךְ. אָמַר רִבִּי אַבָּא מָרִי. אִם אוֹמֵר אַתְּ. לֵית כָּאן סָךְ. לֵית כָּאן שׁוֹתֶה. דְּלֹא כֵן דָּבָר שֶׁהוּא בָא מִשְׁנֵי לָוִין מִצְטָרֵף. מְנַיִּין שֶׁהוּא מְחוּוָּר בַּעֲשֵׂה. רִבִּי אֶלְעָזָר בְּשֵׁם רִבִּי סִימַאי. לֹא נָתַתִּי מִמֶּנּוּ לְמֵת. מָה אֲנָן קַיָּימִין. אִם לְהָבִיא לוֹ אָרוֹן וְתַכְרִיכִין. לַחַי אָסוּר לֹא כָל־שֶׁכֵּן לְמֵת. אֵי זֶה דָבָר שֶׁהוּא מוּתָּר לַחַי וְאָסוּר לַמֵּת. הֱוֵי אוֹמֵר. זֶה סִיכָה.

1 תני | ד והא תני   2 להביא | ד לרבות   3 אבא מרי | ד אבמרי   אם או' את | ג ואין ד אין   דלא כן | ג ד דלכן   4 אלעזר | ג ד לעזר   אנן | ג ד נן   5 אי זה | G לאיזה ג ד אי זהו

[122] 4. "From where that anointing," etc. On the Sabbath both anointing for pleasure and anointing not for pleasure are permitted. On the Day of Atonement, both anointing for pleasure and anointing not for pleasure are forbidden. On the Ninth of Av and public fasts[123], anointing for pleasure is forbidden but anointing not for pleasure are permitted.

It was stated: Anointing is equal to drinking regarding prohibition and reparation but not punishment[124]. On the day of Atonement regarding prohibition but not punishment[125]. But was it not stated, *they shall not desecrate*[126], to include him who anoints or drinks? Rebbi Johanan said, there is no "anoints" there. Rebbi Abba Mari said, if there is no "anoints" there is no "drinks". For if it were not so, do matters combine which come from two different prohibitions[127]? From where that there is a clear commandment[128]? Rebbi Eleazar in the name of Rebbi Simai: *I did not give from it to the dead*[129]. Where do we hold? If not to bring a casket or shrouds for him, this is forbidden for the living, therefore certainly for the dead. What is permitted for the living but prohibited for the dead?[130] I am saying that this is anointing[131].

122 This refers to the last part of Mishnah 4. The matter is only marginally related to the rules of the Sabbath; the full text is preserved in *Ma`aser Šeni* 2:1 (Notes 28-35, ג) and *Ta`anit* 1:6 (ז). The Genizah text starts again at the end of the paragraph.

123 Fasts in a winter of draught, whose rules are modeled on those for the Ninth of Av.

124 Referring to illegal use of heave and dedicated food by non-Cohanim and its replacement by 5/4 of the value taken.

125 The only biblical prohibitions on the Day of Atonement are eating, drinking, and working. The other two, anointing and sexual relations, are rabbinic and not subject to biblical punishment.

126 *Lev.* 22:15. The verse refers to the non-Cohen who "eats" holy food in error. Babli *Niddah* 32a.

127 If the verse in *Lev.* is needed to subsume drinking under eating, it is incomprehensible that for inadvertently eating and drinking together on the Day of Atonement one should be responsible only for one sacrifice since in that case, one infringes on two separate biblical prohibitions and should be liable for two separate sacrifices. Similarly, if one illegitimately ate and drank heave one should be liable for two separate fifths. Since in both cases the Mishnah treats eating and drinking together, the verse cannot express a separate status for drinking; the addition of anointing and drinking is rabbinic interpretation but not biblical law and there is no reason to exclude anointing.

128 While illegitimate use of heave oil for anointing is prohibited, it is mentioned in the framework of the farmer's declaration in the Temple, which is a positive commandment. Overstepping the prohibition of anointing when it is forbidden legally is overstepping a positive commandment not under the scope of biblical penal law.

129 *Deut.* 26:14.

130 Cf. *Sifry Deut.* 302.

131 Only consuming Second Tithe is permitted.

(2 line 12b) ה'. וְקַשְׁיָא. כָּמוֹן וּמֶלַח מִצְטָרְפִין. רִבִּי אִילָא בְשֵׁם רִבִּי אֶלְעָזָר. בְּמִינֵי מְתִיקָה שָׁנוּ.

תַּמָּן תַּנִּינָן. שִׁיעוּר הַמְלַבֵּן הַמְנַפֵּץ וְהַצּוֹבֵעַ וְהַטּוֹוֶה. וְהָכָא אַתְּ אָמַר הָכֵין. תַּמָּן בְּצוֹבֵעַ. בְּרַם הָכָא בְּמוֹצִיא לְצְבּוּעַ.

1 את אמר הכין | G איתמר הכן

נֶתֶר. נִטְרוֹן. בִּירִית. בִּירִיתָה. קִימוֹן. קַלְיָא. אֲשָׁלְג. רִבִּי יוֹסֵי בֵּירִבִּי בּוּן אָמַר. אצרוות רוח.

5. This is difficult. May cumin and salt combine[132]? Rebbi Ila in the name of Rebbi Eleazar: they taught this about sweeteners.

There, we have stated:[133] "The measure for one who bleaches, who beats flax, or who dyes, or who spins," and here you are saying so? The one who dyes, here one who brings out to dye[134].

נֶתֶר is νίτρον. בִּירִיתָה is בִּירִית. קימון is *kali*. אֶשְׁלָג, Rebbi Yose ben Rebbi Abun said, אצרות רוח.[135]

132 The Mishnah stated that all kinds of spices combine for the amount needed to cook a small egg. But for salt and cumin very different quantities are needed; this makes the statement indefinite. Babli 89b/90a.

133 Mishnah 13:4.

134 The amount noted in Mishnah 9:5 is much smaller than than given in Mishnah 13:4. The activities in question are not comparable.

135 The technical terms for cleaning materials are explained. νίτρον is soda, *kali* is the plant, saltwort, or its ashes. בִּירִיתָה must be a plant used in the manufacture of soap; the identity of אצרות רוח (if the word is spelled correctly) is everybody's guess. In the Babli 90a, for בִּירִיתָה one reads כבריתא "sulfur"; this identification is rejected there and replaced by "aloe". It seems that here also the materials are of vegetal origin.

(12b line 6) ו'. תַּנֵּי. אַף רֵיחַ רַע כָּל־שֶׁהוּא. אָמַר רִבִּי אִילָא. אַף רִבִּי שִׁמְעוֹן מוֹדֶה בָהּ. מוֹדֵי רִבִּי שִׁמְעוֹן בְּאִיסּוּרֵי הֲנָיָיה.

1 מודה | מודי G 2 הנייה | הניה G

6. [136]It was stated: Also bad smell in any amount. Rebbi Ila said, also Rebbi Simeon agrees to this. Rebbi Simeon agrees in cases of prohibitions of usufruct.

136 The entire text is repeated in Chapter 10, to Mishnah 6. The first assertion also is in the Babli, 90a. If R. Simeon agrees in case of prohibitions of usufruct, the question remains why the statement in Mishnah 6 about idolatry was formulated as a minority opinion of R. Jehudah. On the other hand, since items prohibited for usufruct never can be transported for a legitimate purpose, if R. Simeon would not agree then there would be a general permission to move such items.

(12b line 7) ז. וְקַשְׁיָא. אִילוּ הוֹצִיא וְהוֹצִיא בְּהֶעֱלֵם אֶחָד כְּלוּם הוּא חַיָּיב אֶלָּא אֶחָד. לְמִי נִצְרְכָה. לְרִבִּי אֱלִיעֶזֶר. שֶׁלֹּא תֹאמַר. מִינִים הַרְבָּה יֵיעָשׂוּ בְּהֶעֱלֵימוֹת הַרְבָּה וִיהֵא חַיָּיב עַל כָּל־אַחַת וְאַחַת. לְפוּם כֵּן צָרָךְ מֵימַר. אֵינוֹ חַיָּיב אֶלָּא אַחַת.

1 אחד G | אחת

זֵרעוֹנֵי גִינָה פָּחוֹת מִכַּגְרוֹגֶרֶת. רִבִּי יְהוּדָה בֶּן בְּתֵירָא אוֹמֵר. חֲמִשָּׁה. מָה טַעֲמָא דְרִבִּי יְהוּדָה בֶּן בְּתֵירָא. שֶׁכֵּן דֶּרֶךְ לְהִיזָּרַע בָּעֲרוּגָה.

2 דרך להיזרע G | דרכן ליזרע

זֶרַע קִישּׁוּאִין שְׁנַיִם. זֶרַע דִּילוּעִין שְׁנַיִם. זֶרַע פּוֹל מִצְרִי שְׁנַיִם. תַּנֵּי. חִיטִּים מָדִיּוֹת שְׁתַּיִם. רִבִּי שְׁמוּאֵל בְּשֵׁם רִבִּי זְעִירָא. חִיטִּין עַל יְדֵי שֶׁהֵן חֲבִיבוֹת עָשׂוּ אוֹתָן כִּשְׁאָר זֵרְעוֹנֵי גִינָה שֶׁאֵינָן נֶאֱכָלִין.

2 כשאר G | בשארי

חָגָב חַי כָּל־שֶׁהוּא. מֵת כַּגְרוֹגֶרֶת. הָדָא דְאַתְּ אָמַר. בְּטָהוֹר. אֲבָל בְּטָמֵא כִּמְלוֹא פִי הַכֶּלֶב.

1 הדא דאת אמר G | הדתמר

צִפּוֹרֶת כְּרָמִים בֵּין חַיָּה בֵּין מֵתָה כָּל־שֶׁהִיא. שֶׁמַּצְנִיעִין אוֹתָהּ לִירְפוּאָה. אָמַר רִבִּי אָחָא. שֶׁכֵּן אִשָּׁה סְטִיפָה מוֹשַׁחַת מִמֶּנָּה וְהִיא מִתְרַפָּא. תַּמָּן אָמְרִין. מָאן דְּבָעֵי נִיפְרוֹשׁ מִן דֶּרֶךְ הָאָרֶץ אֲכִיל פֶּלְגָּא וּשְׁבִיק פֶּלְגָּא. שְׁלְשְׂמֹאל אָסוּר וְשֶׁלְיָמִין מוּתָּר. אָבַד כָּל־שֶׁהוּא חָסֵר כָּל־שֶׁהוּא אֵין לוֹ תְקָנָה עוֹלָמִית. כֵּיצַד הוּא עוֹשֶׂה. אָמַר רִבִּי יוֹסֵי בֵּירִבִּי בּוּן. יְהַב לָהּ גּוֹ צְלוֹחִית דְּבַשׁ.

רִבִּי יְהוּדָה אוֹמֵר אַף הַמּוֹצִיא חָגָב חַי טָמֵא כָּל־שֶׁהוּא. הָא טָהוֹר בֵּין חַי בֵּין מֵת כַּגְרוֹגֶרֶת. רִבִּי יְהוּדָה כְדַעְתֵּיהּ. דְּרִבִּי יְהוּדָה אוֹמֵר. אוֹכְלִין טְהוֹרִין אֵין מְשַׁחֲקִין בָּהֶן. וְהָא כְתִיב הִתְשַׂחֶק־בּוֹ כַּצִּפּוֹר. לֹא הֵיתֶר מִן כְּלָל אִיסּוּר הוּא. וְהָא כְתִיב כַּצִּפּוֹר. אָמַר רִבִּי מַתַּנְיָה. מִכֵּיוָן שֶׁהִיא מְחוּסֶּרֶת שְׁחִיטָה כִּטְמֵיאָה הִיא.

7. It is difficult. If he continues to bring out in one forgetting, is he not liable only once[137]? For whom is it necessary? For Rebbi Eliezer[138]. That you should not say, many kinds should be treated like as many forgettings and he would be liable for each single one. Therefore it was necessary to say that he is liable only once.

"Garden seeds less than the volume of a dried fig; Rebbi Jehudah ben Bathyra said, five." What is Rebbi Jehudah ben Bathyra's reason? Because this is what one usually sows in a garden bed.

"Green melon[26] seeds two, squash seeds two, Egyptian bean seeds two." It was stated: Median wheat two[139]. Rebbi Samuel in the name of Rebbi Ze'ira: Because wheat was so much in esteem they treated it like garden vegetables which are not eaten.

"A live locust in the most minute amount, dead in the volume of a dried fig.." That means, if it is pure[140]. But if it is impure, a dog's mouthful.

"A vineyard bird[27] either live or dead in any amount since one keeps it as medicine." Rebbi Aḥa said, for a woman with rough skin rubs in with it and she is healed. There, they said, a person who wants to renounce sexual activity eats half of it and keeps half of it. The left hand part is forbidden, the right hand part is permitted. If anything was lost or missing he has no recourse ever[141]. What should he do? Rebbi Yose ben Rebbi Abun said, he preserves it[142] in a honey flask.

"Rebbi Jehudah says, also one who brings out a dead locust[28] in the most minute amount." Therefore pure in the amount of a dried fig whether alive or dead[143]. Rebbi Jehudah follows his own opinion since Rebbi Jehudah says one does not play with pure food. But is there not written[144], *would you play with him as with a bird?* Is it not permitted out of a prohibition[145]? But is it not written, *as with a bird*[146]*?* Rebbi Mattaniah said, since it is lacking slaughter it is as if impure[147].

137 This refers to the statement in Mishnah 7 that taking out a pedlar's box creates only one liability. Since only one item was taken out, even if it contains many kinds, it is difficult to see why the statement is needed.

138 Who in Mishnah *Keritut* 3:10 states that repeated identical acts in one period of oblivion may trigger many liabilities. Cf. Chapter 7, Note 48 ff.

139 Chapter 7, Note 225. The paragraph also is copied in Chapter 12, Note 55 (**13**).

140 Permitted as food, *Lev.* 11:22.

141 He can never regain his potency.

142 He has to preserve the other part permanently. Probably eating this other part would restore his potency. Babylonian medical instructions are not of the rational kind.

143 He disagrees with the anonymous statement earlier in the Mishnah.

144 *Job* 40:29, speaking of the Behemoth.

145 It is indeterminate whether the Behemoth is pure or impure.

146 There is an opinion that צפור in general means an edible bird, cf. *Nazir* 1:1, Note 29.

147 Any animal or bird is forbidden as food unless it is known that it was slaughtered correctly (Babli *Hulin* 9a).

המצניע פרק עשירי

(fol. 12b) **משנה א**: הַמַּצְנִיעַ לְזֶרַע לְדוּגְמָא וְלִרְפוּאָה הוֹצִיאוֹ בַשַּׁבָּת חַיָּב עָלָיו בְּכָל־שֶׁהוּא. וְכָל־אָדָם אֵין חַיָּבִין עָלָיו אֶלָּא כְשִׁעוּרוֹ. חָזַר וְהִכְנִיסוֹ אֵינוֹ חַיָּב עָלָיו אֶלָּא כְשִׁעוּרוֹ:

Mishnah 1: One who stores as seeds, as sample, or as medicine, if he takes out on the Sabbath he is liable for it in the most minute amount; but every other person is liable only for its quantity[1]. If he brought it back he is liable only for its quantity[2].

משנה ב: הַמּוֹצִיא אוֹכְלִין וּנְתָנוֹ עַל הָאַסְקוּפָה בֵּין שֶׁחָזַר וְהוֹצִיאָם בֵּין שֶׁהוֹצִיאָם אַחֵר פָּטוּר מִפְּנֵי שֶׁלֹּא עָשָׂה מְלַאכְתּוֹ בְּבַת אַחַת. קוּפָּה שֶׁהִיא מְלֵיאָה פֵּירוֹת וּנְתוּנָה עַל הָאַסְקוּפָּה הַחִיצוֹנָה אַף עַל פִּי שֶׁרוֹב הַפֵּירוֹת מִבַּחוּץ פָּטוּר עַד שֶׁיּוֹצִיא אֶת כָּל הַקּוּפָּה:

Mishnah 2: He who takes out foodstuffs and puts them on the threshold[3], whether afterwards either he or another person took it out, is not liable since he did not complete his action in one piece. If a basket full of produce was put on the outer threshold, even if most of the produce is outside one is not liable until one take out the entire basket[4].

משנה ג: הַמּוֹצִיא בֵּין בִּימִינוֹ בֵּין בִּשְׂמֹאלוֹ בְּתוֹךְ חֵיקוֹ אוֹ עַל כְּתֵיפוֹ חַיָּב שֶׁכֵּן מַשָּׂא בְּנֵי קְהָת. לְאַחַר יָדוֹ בְּרַגְלוֹ וּבְפִיו בְּמַרְפְּקוֹ בְּאָזְנוֹ וּבִשְׂעָרוֹ וּבַאֲפוּנְדָּתוֹ וּפִיהָ לְמַטָּה בֵּין אֲפוּנְדָּתוֹ לַחֲלוּקוֹ וּבִשְׂפַת חֲלוּקוֹ בְּמִנְעָלוֹ וּבְסַנְדָּלוֹ פָּטוּר שֶׁלֹּא הוֹצִיא כְּדֶרֶךְ הַמּוֹצִיאִין:

Mishnah 3: One who takes out either with his right hand, or with his left hand, or in his bosom, or on his shoulder, is liable since this was the carrying of the Kehatites[5]. On the back of his hand, on his foot, in his mouth, on his elbow, in his ear, or in his hair, or in his money belt[6] whose opening is downward[7], between his belt and his garment, or in the seam of his garment, in his shoe, or in his sandal, he is not liable since he did not take out in the way of takers-out.

משנה ד: הַמִּתְכַּוֵּין לְהוֹצִיא לְפָנָיו וּבָא לוֹ לְאַחֲרָיו פָּטוּר. לְאַחֲרָיו וּבָא לוֹ לְפָנָיו חַיָּב. בֶּאֱמֶת הָאִשָּׁה הַחוֹגֶרֶת בַּסִּינָר בֵּין מִלְּפָנֶיהָ וּבֵין מִלְּאַחֲרֶיהָ חַיֶּבֶת שֶׁכֵּן רָאוּי לִהְיוֹת חוֹזֵר. רִבִּי יְהוּדָה אוֹמֵר אַף בִּמְקַבְּלֵי פִּיטְקִין כֵּן:

Mishnah 4: One who intends to carry on his front but it turns out that he carried on his back is not liable[8]. On his back and he carried on his front he is liable. In truth[9] a woman who ties to her *sinar*[10] whether in front or back is liable since it is apt to move. Rebbi Jehudah says, the same holds for messengers[11].

משנה ה: הַמּוֹצִיא אוֹכָלִין פָּחוֹת מִכַּשִּׁעוּר בַּכְּלִי פָּטוּר אַף עַל הַכְּלִי שֶׁהַכְּלִי טְפֵילָה לוֹ. אֶת הַחַי בַּמִּטָּה פָּטוּר אַף עַל הַמִּטָּה שֶׁהַמִּטָּה טְפֵילָה לוֹ. אֶת הַמֵּת בַּמִּטָּה חַיָּב וְכֵן כַּזַּיִת מִן הַמֵּת וְכַזַּיִת מִן הַנְּבֵילָה וְכָעֲדָשָׁה מִן הַשֶּׁרֶץ חַיָּבִין. וְרִבִּי שִׁמְעוֹן פּוֹטֵר:

Mishnah 5: He who takes out foodstuffs less than a measure in a vessel is not liable even for the vessel since the vessel is an accessory to it, for a living person on a bier he is not liable[12] even for the bier since the vessel is an accessory to him. For a dead person on a bier he is liable, and so for the volume of an olive from a dead person, or the volume of an olive from a carcass, or of a lentil from a crawling animal[13] one is liable, but Rebbi Simeon declares not liable[14].

משנה ו: הַמּוֹצִיא כִכָּר בִּרְשׁוּת הָרַבִּים חַיָּב. הוֹצִיאוּהוּ שְׁנַיִם פְּטוּרִין. לֹא יָכוֹל אֶחָד לְהוֹצִיאוֹ וְהוֹצִיאוּהוּ שְׁנַיִם חַיָּבִין. וְרִבִּי שִׁמְעוֹן פּוֹטֵר.

Mishnah 6: He who takes out a loaf into the public domain is liable. If two together took it out they are not liable[15]. If one alone is unable to take it out and two took it out they are liable, but Rebbi Simeon declares them not liable.

משנה ז: הַנּוֹטֵל צִפָּרְנָיו זוֹ בָזוֹ אוֹ בְשִׁינָּיו וְכֵן שְׂעָרוֹ וְכֵן שְׂפָמוֹ וְכֵן זְקָנוֹ וְכֵן הַגּוֹדֶלֶת וְכֵן הַכּוֹחֶלֶת וְכֵן הַפּוֹקֶסֶת רִבִּי אֱלִיעֶזֶר מְחַיֵּיב חַטָּאת. וַחֲכָמִים אוֹמְרִין מִשּׁוּם שְׁבוּת. הַתּוֹלֵשׁ מֵעָצִיץ נָקוּב חַיָּב וְשֶׁאֵינוֹ נָקוּב פָּטוּר. וְרִבִּי שִׁמְעוֹן פּוֹטֵר בָּזֶה וּבָזֶה:

Mishnah 7: He who takes off his fingernails one with the other or with his teeth, and similarly his hair, or his mustache, or his beard, and similarly the woman who braids, or who puts on *kohl*, or puts on make-up, Rebbi Eliezer declares liable for a purification sacrifice but the Sages say because of Sabbath rest[16]. One who plucks from a flower pot with a hole is liable[17], with no hole is not liable, but Rebbi Simeon declares not liable in either case[18].

1   The preceding Mishnaiot spell out minimal amounts for different categories of objects. The underlying idea is that smaller amounts are of no value. If somebody takes

out a smaller amount for a specific purpose, he shows that for him it is valuable and, therefore, the general rules do not apply to him.

2   Since the objects were not used for the intended purposes, he now is no different from the general population.

3   Cf. Chapter 1, Note 66.

4   Since the threshold is not outside, there is no completed action by depositing the basket on the threshold, cf. Chapter 1, Note 1. Even if part of the basket is outside, since only the entire basket is moved and not its contents separately, the exact place of the contents is irrelevant, cf. Mishnah 9:7.

5   They were carrying the sacred contents of the Tent of Meeting on their shoulders or in their hands; *Num.* 7:9.

6   Latin *funda, -ae, f.*

7   In this case it cannot serve as a wallet since the money would fall out of the belt. This is a case of unprofessional use which, while prohibited, does not create liability.

8   Explained in Chapter 1, Note 75.

9   Every rule introduced by "in truth" is unquestioned practice.

10   Cf. *Sotah* 1:2, Note 115. According to Rashi, leather underpants; according to Maimonides a sash covering front and back. In modern Hebrew "apron", following Maimonides.

11   פטק is Latin *pittacium*, Greek πιττά-κιον "note delivered from one government office to another; ticket, label, patch."

12   A living being, not only a human, "carries himself"; carrying a live person always is an act performed by two persons, the carrier and the carried and, therefore, creates no liability.

13   I. e., the minimum volume which creates impurity.

14   As work not needed for its own purpose.

15   Cf. Chapter 1, Note 1. R. Simeon holds that even in the latter case there can be no liability attached to work done by several people in common by biblical decree; see in the Halakhah on Mishnah 5.

16   "Sabbath rest" always means "rabbinic prohibition".

Rashi on the Mishnah quotes two interpretations of פוקסת: "putting on make-up" (Yerushalmi), "combing the hair" (Babli). The latter meaning may be connected to Arabic فقس "to draw somebody by the hair."

17   Because it is connected to the ground by the hole at the bottom, plucking from the flower pot is harvesting. If there is no hole at the bottom, plucking is harvesting only rabbinically, not creating liability.

18   If the root of the plant reaches the hole, even R. Simeon agrees that plucking from the flower pot is harvesting.

(12b line 67) הַמַּצְנִיעַ לְזֶרַע כּוֹל׳. רִבִּי יִרְמְיָה אָמַר. רִבִּי יוֹסֵי בֵּירִבִּי חֲנִינָה בָּעֵי. מַתְנִיתָא דְרִבִּי יְהוּדָה. דְּרִבִּי יְהוּדָה אָמַר. אוּמָּן בָּאוּמָּנְתוֹ חַיָּיב. אָתָא רִבִּי יוּדָה בַּר פָּזִי בְשֵׁם רִבִּי יוֹסֵי בֵּירִבִּי חֲנִינָה. דְּרִבִּי יְהוּדָה הִיא. אָמַר רִבִּי יוֹסֵי בֵּירִבִּי חֲנִינָה. לֹא אַתְיָא אֶלָּא לְדִיגְמָא. שֶׁכְּבָר נִתְפָּרֵס הַלּוֹקֵחַ. אֲבָל לְזֶרַע וְלִרְפוּאָה אֲפִילוּ כָּל־שֶׁהוּא חַיָּיב. הַצְנִיעוֹ זֶה וְהוֹצִיאוֹ זֶה פָּטוּר. רִבִּי שִׁמְעוֹן בֶּן אֶלְעָזָר מְחַיֵּיב. מָה אֲנָן קַיָּימִין. אִם בְּשֶׁהוֹצִיאוֹ מִדַּעַת הַשֵּׁינִי. דִּבְרֵי הַכֹּל פָּטוּר. אִם

בְּשֶׁהוֹצִיאוֹ מִדַּעַת הָרִאשׁוֹן. דִּבְרֵי הַכֹּל חַיָּב. אֶלָּא כֵן אֲנָן קַיָּימִין. בִּסְתָם. וְרַבָּנָן אֱמָרֵי. חֲזָקָה. מִדַּעַת הַשֵּׁינִי הוֹצִיאוֹ. רִבִּי שִׁמְעוֹן בֶּן אֶלְעָזָר אוֹמֵר. חֲזָקָה. מִדַּעַת הָרִאשׁוֹן הוֹצִיאוֹ.

"One who stores as seeds," etc. Rebbi Jeremiah said, Rebbi Yose ben Rebbi Hanina asked, is the Mishnah Rebbi Jehudah's[19]? For Rebbi Jehudah said, a craftsman in the ways of his craft is liable[20]. Rebbi Judah bar Pazi came in the name of Rebbi Yose ben Rebbi Hanina: It is Rebbi Jehudah's. Rebbi Yose ben Rebbi Hanina said, this comes only for the sample[21], because the buyer already was satisfied[22]. But as to seeds and medicines even for the most minute amount he is liable. If one stored it and another took it out, he is not liable; Rebbi Simeon ben Eleazar declares him liable[23]. Where do we hold? If he took it out on the second's initiative, everybody agrees that he is not liable; if he took it out on the first's initiative, everybody agrees that he is liable[24]. But we must hold when it was not explained. The rabbis say, it is a common presumption[25] that he took it out on the second's initiative; Rebbi Simeon ben Eleazar says that it is a common presumption that he took it out on the first's initiative.

19 Since the Mishnah is anonymous and therefore practice, this decides that regarding the Sabbath one follows Rebbi Jehudah.

20 Chapter 1, Note 221.

21 Greek δεῖγμα, -ατος, τό, Latin *digma*.

22 R. Meïr, who disagrees with R. Jehudah about the special rule for craftsmen, will nevertheless agree that medicines, which are taken in minute amounts, and seeds, of which every single one counts, make the professional liable in any amount. Their only difference regarding the Mishnah is a sample after it has been shown to the client and is no longer needed, where R. Jehudah declares it the seller's tool but R. Meïr treats it as regular property.

23 Babli 91a in another formulation.

24 In the Babli this seems to be only R. Simeon ben Eleazar's opinion since he formulates: "Anything which is not usually stored, but somebody stored it for his use, and a second person came and took it out, the second becomes liable by the first's intention."

25 This is one of the many meanings of חֲזָקָה: A common presumption to be used in the absence of information to arrive at a judgment. Cf. *Ketubot* 5:5, Note 100.

(12c line 1) ב'. חִזְקִיָּה אָמַר. בְּקוּפָּה שֶׁלְּקִישׁוּאִים וְשֶׁלְּדִילוּעִין הִיא מַתְנִיתָא. שֶׁמִּקְצָת הָאוֹכֶל מִבִּפְנִים וּמִקְצָתוֹ מִבַּחוּץ. אֲבָל בְּקוּפָּה שֶׁהִיא מְלֵיאָה פֵּירוֹת כֵּיוָן שֶׁהוֹצִיא מִמֶּנָּה כִּגְרוֹגֶרֶת חַיָּיב.

אָמְרִין. מִילְתֵהּ דְּרִבִּי יוֹחָנָן פְּלִיגָא. דְּאָמַר רִבִּי חִייָא בְשֵׁם רִבִּי יוֹחָנָן. סָרוּד שֶׁמִּקְצָתוֹ מִבִּפְנִים וּמִקְצָתוֹ מִבַּחוּץ. נָטַל מִיכָּן וְנָתַן לְכָאן פָּטוּר. אִם עֲקָרוֹ. עַד שֶׁיַּעֲקוֹר כּוּלּוֹ כָּאַחַת.

2. Hizqiah said, the Mishnah is about a basket full of green melon and squash, where part of the food is inside and part outside[26]. But a basket full of grain, when he took out in the volume of a dried fig he is liable. They said, Rebbi Johanan's statement disagrees, as Rebbi Hiyya said in the name of Rebbi Johanan: A crocheted cloth[27] part of which was inside and part outside, if he took from one side and put it down on the other he is not liable. If he lifted it, only if he lifted it entirely at the same time.

26 Discussion of the second part of Mishnah 2. He does not hold that the basket has the same status as its contents but only if all produce in the basket are both inside and outside the private domain is there no liability. Babli 92b.

27 Which was used by bakers. In the Babli, *loc. cit.*, R. Johanan is quoted directly that the Mishnah holds even for a basket full of mustard seeds.

(12c line 6) אָמַר רִבִּי מָנָא קוֹמֵי רִבִּי יוֹסֵה. תִּיפְתָּר בְּפָרוּץ. אָמַר לֵיהּ. וְהָא תַּנֵּינָן. קוּפָּה. אִית לָךְ מֵימַר. קוּפָּה פְרוּצָה. מַאי כְדוֹן. אֵין לָךְ מִיטַּלְטֵל בִּרְשׁוּת הָרַבִּים וְנַעֲשָׂה כַרְמְלִית אֶלָּא אָדָם בִּלְבָד. חִזְקִיָּה אָמַר. הוֹצִיא חֲבִילָה מֵרְשׁוּת הַיָּחִיד לִרְשׁוּת הָרַבִּים. עַד שֶׁלֹּא הִנִּיחָהּ בִּרְשׁוּת הָרַבִּים הָיָה רֹאשָׁהּ לְמַעֲלָה מֵעֲשָׂרָה. הוֹאִיל וְאֵין כּוּלָּהּ נִיחָה בִּרְשׁוּת הָרַבִּים פָּטוּר. אָמַר רִבִּי שְׁמוּאֵל בַּר רַב יִצְחָק. הוֹצִיא קוֹרָה מֵרְשׁוּת הַיָּחִיד לִרְשׁוּת הָרַבִּים. עַד שֶׁלֹּא הִנִּיחָהּ בִּרְשׁוּת הָרַבִּים נִכְנַס רֹאשָׁהּ לִרְשׁוּת הַיָּחִיד אֲחֶרֶת. הוֹאִיל וְאֵין כּוּלָּהּ נִיחָה בִּרְשׁוּת הָרַבִּים פָּטוּר. אָמַר רִבִּי יוֹחָנָן. אֶבֶן שֶׁהִיא נְתוּנָה בִּרְשׁוּת הָרַבִּים גְּבוֹהָּ עֲשָׂרָה וּרְחָבָה אַרְבָּעָה הַמִּשְׁתַּמֵּשׁ מְתוּכָהּ לִרְשׁוּת הָרַבִּים וּמֵרְשׁוּת הָרַבִּים לְתוֹכָהּ חַייָב. שְׁמוּאֵל אָמַר. קוּפָּה שֶׁהִיא מְלֵיאָה פֵּירוֹת וּנְתוּנָה בִּרְשׁוּת הָרַבִּים גְּבוֹהָה עֲשָׂרָה וּרְחָבָה אַרְבָּעָה הַמִּשְׁתַּמֵּשׁ מְתוּכָה לִרְשׁוּת הָרַבִּים אוֹ מֵרְשׁוּת הָרַבִּים לְתוֹכָהּ פָּטוּר. מַה פְּלִיג. כָּאן כְּשֶׁהָפְכָהּ עַל צִידָּהּ. וְכָאן בְּשֶׁלֹּא הָפְכָהּ עַל צִידָּהּ. רִבִּי בּוּן בַּר חִייָה בָּעֵי. עָקַר אֶבֶן בִּרְשׁוּת הָרַבִּים גְּבוֹהָּ עֲשָׂרָה וּרְחָבָה אַרְבָּעָה מָה אַתְּ עָבֵד לָהּ. כְּמִשְׁתַּמֵּשׁ מְתוּכָה לִרְשׁוּת הָרַבִּים וּמֵרְשׁוּת הָרַבִּים לְתוֹכָהּ וּמֵרְשׁוּת הָרַבִּים לִרְשׁוּת הָרַבִּים אֲחֶרֶת. רַבָּנָן דְּקַיְסָרִין אָמְרִין. רִבִּי יוֹחָנָן בָּעֵי. נָתַן חֲמִשָּׁה עַל גַּבֵּי חֲמִשָּׁה מָה אַתְּ עָבֵד לוֹן. כְּמִשְׁתַּמֵּשׁ מֵרְשׁוּת הָרַבִּים לְכַרְמְלִית. מִכַּרְמְלִית לִרְשׁוּת הַיָּחִיד. מֵרְשׁוּת הַיָּחִיד לִרְשׁוּת הַיָּחִיד אֲחֶרֶת.

1 תיפתר | A תפתר   2 מיטלטל | A מטלטל   הרבים | A הרבים פטור   3 חזקיה | A ר' חזקיה   4 כולה ניחה | A כל הנייחה   6 נכנס | A הכניס   כולה ניחה | A כל הנייחה   7 גבוה | A גבוהה   10 כאן | A וכן   14 מכרמלית | A ומכ[רמלית]

[28]Rebbi Mana said before Rebbi Yose: Explain it if it was broken open[29]. He said to him, but did we not state 'a basket"; can you say, a basket broken open? What about this? Nothing is moved in the public domain and becomes *karmelit* except a human[30].

Hizqiah[31] said, if he took out a bundle from a private to the public domain and before he put it down already its head was higher than ten [hand-breadths], since it does not completely rest in the public domain he is not liable[32]. Rebbi Samuel ben Rav Isaac said, if he took out a beam from a private to the public domain and before he put it down already its head was in another private domain[33], since it does not completely rest in the public domain he is not liable. Rebbi Johanan said, if a stone is in the public domain, ten [hand-breadths] high and four [hand-breadths] wide[34], anybody who moves from it to the public domain or from the public domain to it is liable. Samuel said, a basket full of produce put into the public domain, ten [hand-breadths] high and four [hand-breadths] wide, anybody who moves from it to the public domain or from the public domain to it is not liable. Do they disagree? Here, if it was turned on its side[35], there if it was not turned on its side. Rebbi Abun bar Hiyya asked, if one moved a stone in the public domain, ten [hand-breadths] high and four [hand-breadths] wide, how do you treat it? As one who moves from it to the public domain or from the public domain to it, or from the public domain to a different public domain? The rabbis of Caesarea said that Rebbi Johanan asked: If one piles five [hand-breadths] on top of five, how do you treat it? As one who moves from a private domain to *karmelit*, from *karmelit* to a private domain, from a private domain to another private domain[36]?

28 Here starts a Genizah fragment edited and commented on by S. Abramson (*Kobez al Yad* 8(18) 1975, pp. 1-14, A). The text is a continuation of the preceding paragraph.

29 Hizqiah's statement does not contradict the Mishnah if we assume that the container was torn open and it is possible to take produce from the public domain directly from the bottom of the basket without lifting over the rim. The objection is that then the vessel no longer is called "a basket".

30 For the notion of *karmelit*, see Chapter 1, Note 73. The transport from a public domain to *karmelit* followed from one from the *karmelit* to the public domain does not create liability. If the basket could be considered *karmelit*, Hizqiah's statement

would be impossible. But since *karmelit* is a notion applicable only to real estate not readily accessible or to a human's hand, Hizqiah's restrictive interpretation of the Mishnah cannot be disproved.

31 A reads "R. Hizqiah". But since his statement is followed by quotes from early Amoraim, the text of the Leiden ms. is preferable.

32 Cf. Chapter 1, Note 109. The air space over public domain is "exempt space" from which motion to and from private or public domains is not restricted.

33 Even though it is a matter of dispute whether carrying from one private domain to another creates liability, it is clear that the beam was not deposited completely in the public domain and, therefore, no complete action was performed. Chapter 1, Note 1.

34 The top of the stone becomes a private domain; it is not part of the exempt space over the public domain. Babli 99b,8a.

35 In Samuel's case, the basket is turned on its side; one may take things out without taking them over the rim of the basket. The fact that one of the sides of the basket is higher than 10 hand-breadths becomes irrelevant in this case.

35 The questions are not answered; it seems that these cases never occurred in practice.

(12c line 26) ג'. רִבִּי יוֹסֵי בָּעֵי. מֵעַתָּה הוֹצִיא בִגְרוֹגֶרֶת עַל כְּתֵיפוֹ חַיָּיב. וְהֵן מַשָּׂא בְנֵי קְהָת. וְכָתוּב וּפְקֻדַּת אֶלְעָזָר | בֶּן־אַהֲרֹן הַכֹּהֵן שֶׁמֶן הַמָּאוֹר וּקְטֹרֶת הַסַּמִּים וּמִנְחַת הַתָּמִיד וְשֶׁמֶן הַמִּשְׁחָה. שֶׁמֶן הַמָּאוֹר בִּימִינוֹ. וּקְטֹרֶת הַסַּמִּים בִּשְׂמֹאלוֹ. וּמִנְחַת הַתָּמִיד שֶׁל יוֹם תְּלוּיָה בִזְרוֹעוֹ. שֶׁמֶן הַמִּשְׁחָה אֵיכָן הָיָה נָתוּן. רִבִּי אָבוּן בְּשֵׁם רִבִּי אֶלְעָזָר. כְּמִין צְלוֹחִית קְטַנָּה הָיָה לוֹ בְּאַפוּנְדָתוֹ. אִין תֹּאמַר שֶׁהָיָה קָטָן. אָמַר רִבִּי יְהוֹשֻׁעַ בֶּן לֵוִי. כְּתוּב וּנְשִׂיאֵי נְשִׂיאֵי הַלֵּוִי אֶלְעָזָר בֶּן־אַהֲרֹן הַכֹּהֵן. דּוּךְ דּוּכָנִים הָיָה. רִבִּי יְהוּדָה בִּירִבִּי אָמַר. מַרְכָּל הָיָה. תַּנֵּי רִבִּי חִיָּיה. וְלָמָּה נִקְרָא שְׁמוֹ מַרְכָּל. שֶׁהָיָה מַר עַל הַכֹּל. אֶלָּא שֶׁאֵין גְּדוּלָה בְּפַלְטִין שֶׁלְּמֶלֶךְ. אָמַר רִבִּי לֵוִי. כְּתִיב וְלָבַשׁ הַכֹּהֵן מִדּוֹ בַד . . . וְהֵרִים אֶת־הַדֶּשֶׁן. אֶלָּא שֶׁאֵין גְּדוּלָה בְּפַלְטִין שֶׁלְּמֶלֶךְ.

1 ג׳. - A | יוֹסִי A | יוֹסֵה 2 וּבַת׳ A | כתוב

Rebbi Yose asked: This implies that if somebody took out the volume of a dried fig on his shoulder, he is liable. Is that the carrying of the Kehatites[36]? But it is written[37], *the office of Eleazar, Aaron's son, the priest: The oil for illumination, the spice incense, the permanent flour offering*[38], *and the anointing oil*. The oil for illumination in his right hand, the spice incense in his left hand, the permanent flour offering of that day hanging on his arm. Where was the anointing oil? Rebbi Abun in the name of Rebbi Eleazar: a small flask he had on his money belt. If you say that he was unimportant, Rebbi Joshua ben Levi said, it is written[39]: *The prince of the princes of the Levites, Eleazar, Aaron's son*. A duke[40] of dukes he was. The great Rebbi

Jehudah said, he was the executive officer. "And why was his title *Markol*? Because he had the say about everything.[41]" Only there is no greatness in the king's palace. Rebbi Levi said, it is written[42], *the priest shall dress in linen garment . . . and remove the ashes*, only there is no greatness in the king's palace.

36 They carried great and important things; it seems impossible to conclude that anything small as a dried fig should have been carried with the Tabernacle.

37 *Num.* 4:16. Since there it is not reported that the other Kehatites would carry his charges, it follows that he himself had to carry everything during their wanderings in the desert. Cf. Rashi 92a on the Mishnah.

38 The daily offering brought by the High Priest, *Lev.* 6:12-16.

39 *Num.* 3:32.

40 Latin *dux, ducis, m.* As in English, the Hebrew form is derived from the root, not the nominative.

41 "Having a say about everything." Tosephta *Šeqalim* 2:15.

42 *Lev.* 6:3.

(12c line 37) ד'. תַּמָּן תַּנִּינָן. רִבִּי שִׁמְעוֹן הַשְּׁזוּרִי וְרִבִּי שִׁמְעוֹן אוֹמְרִים. לֹא נֶחְלְקוּ עַל דָּבָר שְׁהוּא מִשֵּׁם אֶחָד שְׁהוּא חַייָב. עַל מַה נֶחְלָקוּ. עַל דָּבָר שְׁהוּא מִשֵּׁם שְׁנֵי שֵׁמוֹת. שֶׁרִבִּי אֱלִיעֶזֶר מְחַייֵב חַטָּאת וְרִבִּי יְהוֹשֻׁעַ פּוֹטֵר. רִבִּי אִילָא בְשֵׁם רִבִּי אֶלְעָזָר. כְּמָאן דְּאָמַר. בִּשְׁנֵי שֵׁמוֹת נֶחְלָקוּ. בְּרַם כְּמָאן דְּאָמַר. בְּשֵׁם אֶחָד נֶחְלָקוּ. וְכָאן שְׁנֵי שֵׁמוֹת הֵן וְהוּא פָטוּר. לְאַחֲרָיו וּבָא לוֹ לְפָנָיו חַייָב. כְּמָאן דְּאָמַר. בְּשֵׁם אֶחָד נֶחְלָקוּ. בְּרַם כְּמָאן דְּאָמַר. בִּשְׁנֵי שֵׁמוֹת. וְכָאן בְּשֵׁם אֶחָד הוּא וְהוּא חַייָב. רִבִּי אִילָא בְשֵׁם רִבִּי אֶלְעָזָר. תַּנָּיֵי אִינּוּן. מָאן דְּאָמַר תַּמָּן. חַייָב. אוֹף הָכָא. חַייָב. מָאן דְּאָמַר תַּמָּן. פָּטוּר. אוֹף הָכָא. פָּטוּר.

4. There, we have stated[43]: "Rebbi Simeon from Shezur and Rebbi Simeon say, they did not disagree about anything which falls under the same appellation that he is liable. Where did they disagree? About something which is because of two appellations, where Rebbi Eliezer holds him liable for a purification sacrifice but Rebbi Joshua holds him not liable." Rebbi Ila in the name of Rebbi Eleazar: Following him who said that they disagreed about two appellations, but not following him who said that they disagreed about one appellation. Here there are two appellations and he is not liable[44]. "On his back and he carried on his front he is liable;" following him who said that they disagreed about one appellation. But following him who said two appellations? Here it is one appellation and he is liable[45]. Rebbi Ila in the

name of Rebbi Eleazar: it is a case of Tannaim⁴⁶. He who says there "liable", also here "liable"; he who says there "not liable", also here "not liable".

43 Mishnah *Keritut* 4:3. A purification offering is possible only for the awareness that an inadvertent sin punishable with extirpation has been committed. In the interpretation of R. Simeon fron Shezur and R. Simeon (ben Yohai), for R. Eliezer, the awareness of a sin generates the liability, for R. Joshua only the awareness of the exact circumstances of the transgression causes liability, even if the category of the sin is not in doubt.

44 R. Eleazar rejects the interpretation of Mishnah 4 that a person who intended to carry something in front but in fact carried it on his back did not execute his intention whereas one who intended to carry something on his back but in fact carried it in front did better than intended. Then the question arises why in one case is there liability but not in the other. If we say that carrying in front or back are two different appellations within the one category of "taking out", then we should expect R. Eliezer to declare liability in both cases and R. Joshua no liability in either case. Therefore the Mishnah follows R. Eliezer in its first statement, R. Joshua in the second. Since both statements are anonymous, one would expect consistency. The text has to be read as follows:

Following him who said that they disagreed about two appellations, it is clear that R. Eliezer declares liable but not R. Joshua. *But not following him who said that they disagreed about one appellation*. Since the distinction is made only by two authors it is clear that there is an assumption that there is an opposing opinion which holds that R. Joshua frees from liability in any case where there is a doubt even if it is only in the way an intention was executed. *Here there are two appellations and he is not liable* according to both interpretations of R. Joshua (whose opinion is followed in general against R. Eliezer.)

45 Here one reads: *"On his back and he carried on his front he is liable;" following him who said that they disagreed about one appellation* there is a problem to explain this following R. Joshua. *But following him who said two appellations* it is obvious that this Mishnah cannot follow R. Joshua. *Here it is one appellation and he is liable*, according to everybody in the interpretation of RR. Simeon from Shezur and R. Simeon.

46 It is possible to read the entire Mishnah as following R. Joshua as required by our practice, but the second statement follows RR. Simeon from Shezur and R. Simeon in their interpretation of R. Joshua's position and the first statement follows their opponents.

(12c line 46) בֶּאֱמֶת. אָמַר רִבִּי אֱלִיעֶזֶר. כָּל־מָקוֹם שֶׁשָּׁנוּ בֶּאֱמֶת הֲלָכָה לְמשֶׁה מִסִּינַי.

"In truth." Rebbi Eliezer said, any place where "in truth" was stated it is practice going back to Moses on Sinai⁴⁸.

48   Babli 92b. In the two other quotes of this statement, *Kilaim* 2:2 Note 36, *Terumot* 2:1 Note 16, the tradent is R. Eleazar.

(12c line 47) ה'. בַּעֲשׂוֹתָהּ. הַיָּחִיד שֶׁעֲשָׂאָהּ חַיָּיב. שְׁנַיִם שְׁלֹשָׁה שֶׁעֲשׂוּ פְטוּרִין. רִבִּי יֹושֻׁעַ דְּרוֹמַיָּא אָמַר קוֹמֵי רִבִּי יָסָא בְּשֵׁם רִבִּי אֲחָא. קָנֵי גִירְדִּי. רִבִּי פוֹטֵר. רִבִּי אֶלְעָזָר בֵּירִבִּי שִׁמְעוֹן מְחַיֵּיב. אָמַר לוֹ רִבִּי. כָּךְ שְׁמַעְתִּי מֵאָבִיךְ. אָמַר לוֹ. שִׁימַּשְׁתִּי אֶת אַבָּא עוֹמְדוֹת מַה שֶּׁלֹּא שִׁימַּשְׁתּוֹ יְשִׁיבוּת. וְרִבִּי תַלְמִידוֹ דְּרִבִּי שִׁמְעוֹן בַּר יוֹחַי דַּהֲוֵי. לֹא תַלְמִידוֹ דְּרִבִּי יַעֲקֹב בַּר קוֹדְשַׁי הֲוָה. אֶלָּא כָּךְ אָמַר לֵיהּ. שִׁימַּשְׁתִּי אֶת אַבָּא עוֹמְדוֹת מַה שֶׁלֹּא שִׁימַּשְׁתָּ אֶת רַבָּךְ יְשִׁיבוּת. כְּשֶׁהָיָה רִבִּי אֶלְעָזָר בֵּירִבִּי שִׁמְעוֹן נִכְנָס לְבֵית הַוַּעַד הָיוּ פָנָיו שֶׁלְּרִבִּי מַקְדִּירוֹת. אָמַר לֵיהּ אֲבוֹי. וְיָאוּת. זֶה אֲרִי בֶן אֲרִי. אֲבָל אַתָּה אֲרִי בֶן שׁוּעָל. מִן דְּמַךְ רִבִּי אֶלְעָזָר שָׁלַח רִבִּי תְּבַע בְּאִיתְּתֵיהּ. אֲמָרָה לֵיהּ. כְּלִי שֶׁנִּשְׁתַּמֵּשׁ בּוֹ קוֹדֶשׁ יִשְׁתַּמֵּשׁ בּוֹ חֹל.

1 היחיד A ‏| יחיד יושוע A | יושע   2 דרומיא A | דרומייה   יסא A | יוסה   קני A | קנה - | A הל'   3 אמ'
לו A | אמ' לו ר' אלעזר ביר' שמעון   אבא A | אבה   4 בר יוחי A | בן יוחאי   דהוי A | הוי   קודשי A | קורשיי
5 כך A | כן   אבא A | אבה   כשהיה A | וכשהיה   6 ליה A | לו   7 אתה A | את ר' אלעזר A -

5. *When she was doing it*[49]. The individual who did it is liable; two or three who were doing it are not liable. Rebbi Joshua the Southerner said before Rebbi (Yasa) [Yose][50] in the name of Rebbi Aha: A weaver's beam, Rebbi declares not liable, but Rebbi Eleazar ben Rebbi Simeon said, he is liable[51]. Rebbi said to him, so I heard from your father. He answered him, I served my father standing more than you served him sitting. But was Rebbi the student of Rebbi Simeon (bar) [ben] Yohai[52]? Was he not the student of Rebbi Jacob bar (Qodshai) [Qorshai][53]? But so he must have said to him, He answered him, I served my father standing more than you served your teacher sitting. When Rebbi Eleazar ben Rebbi Simeon came to the house of assembly, Rebbi's face darkened[54]. His father told him, it is correct so, for he is a lion son of a lion, but you are a lion son of a jackal[55]. When (Rebbi Eleazar) [he][56] died, Rebbi sent to ask his wife in marriage. She said to him, a vessel which was used in holiness should be used in a profane way?

49   *Lev.* 4:27, establishing the qualifications for a purification offering. The feminine refers to נֶפֶשׁ "a person". The singular both of verb and suffix shows that the verse refers to a single person and a single action. Babli 93a; cf. *Horaiot* 1:1 Note 8, *Sifra Hova (Wayyiqra II) Parashah* 7(4,9).

The paragraph refers to Mishnah 6 which frees from liability two or more people engaged in transporting on the Sabbath.

50   Since R. Joshua the Southerner was a contemporary of R. Yose, two generations

after R. Yasa, the reading of A in [brackets] has to be accepted.

51   Cf. Babli 93b, where this tradition is rejected at the end. The weaver's beam usually is operated by a single person; what is the situation if it was carried into the public domain by two people? It can be carried by one person; by the criterion of Mishnah 5 there should be no liability. But since the beam is large, it is inconvenient to be carried by one person; there is an argument to be made that there is liability.

The spelling of A is correct in normative grammar.

52   In the Leiden ms., this sentence is a corrector's addition. The spelling "bar Yoḥai" is a clear Babylonism; the reading of A in [brackets] is preferable.

53   Probably the reading of the ms. in (parentheses) is preferable. In *Pesaḥim* 10:1 (37b line l. 62) the scribe first wrote קורשיי but then corrected it to קודשיי. In the Babli, *Horaiot* 13b, the early prints and the Munich ms. read קדש (cf. *Diqduqe Soferim, Abodah sarah* etc. *Horaiot* p. כג, Note ﬠ.)

R. Eleazar ben R. Simeon indicates that from the incidental remarks of his father he learned more than Rebbi did in his formal studies.

54   Because R. Eleazar ben R. Simeon always tried to prove him wrong.

55   Babli *Bava mesia`* 84b.

56   The reading of A in [brackets] is preferable.

(12c line 57) ו'. אָמַר רִבִּי שְׁמוּאֵל בַּר רַב יִצְחָק. הָדָא דְאַתְּ אָמַר בִּצְרִיכִין לְכָלֵיהָן. כְּגוֹן אִילֵּין תּוּתַיָּיא. אֲבָל אִם אֵינָן צְרִיכִין לְכָלֵיהָן חַיָּיב אַף עַל הַכְּלִי.

1 ו'. A | מתני'. הדא דאת אמר A | הנ[ד]תמר   2 תותייא A | תותיה   לכלייין A | ול]כיליים כגון אילין תוילנה

6. Rebbi Samuel ben Rav Isaac said, what you are saying is about when the vessel is needed, as for mulberries. But if they do not need their vessel he is liable also for the vessel[57].

57   This refers to Mishnah 5, showing that the Halakhah reads Mishnah 6 before Mishnah 5, as in the Babli. The vessel is secondary to the food only if it is necessary. If the fruits are so large that the vessel is not needed, the vessel no longer is an accessory.

The Babli (93b bottom) has a different take on the problem. The word which illustrates the second alternative in A is unexplained; the editor of A reports that the reading is uncertain.

(12c line 59) אֶת הַחַי בַּמִּיטָה פָּטוּר אַף עַל הַמִּיטָה. דְּחַיָּיא טָעִין גַּרְמֵיהּ. אֶת הַמֵּת בַּמִּיטָה חַיָּיב. דִּבְרֵי הַכֹּל. לֹא כֵן תַּנֵּי. אַף רֵיחַ רַע כָּל־שֶׁהוּא. אָמַר רִבִּי אִילָא. אַף רִבִּי שִׁמְעוֹן מוֹדֶה בָהּ. וּמוֹדֵי רִבִּי שִׁמְעוֹן בְּאִיסּוּרֵי הֲנָייָה. אָמַר רִבִּי יוּדָן. תִּיפְּתָר בְּמֵת גּוֹי וְשֶׁאֵין בּוֹ רֵיחַ רַע וְהוֹצִיאוֹ לְכַלְבּוֹ. תַּנֵּי. חֲצִי זַיִת מִן הַמֵּת וַחֲצִי זַיִת מִן הַנְּבֵילָה וּפָחוּת מִכַּעֲדָשָׁה מִן הַשֶּׁרֶץ חַיָּיב. וְרִבִּי

שִׁמְעוֹן פּוֹטֵר. מַה טַעֲמֵיהּ דְּרִבִּי שִׁמְעוֹן. כְּבָר נִתְמָעֲטָה הַטּוּמְאָה. מַה טַעֲמוֹן דְּרַבָּנָן. בָּהֲהִיא דְּרִבִּי יוּדָן. תִּיפְתָּר בְּמֵת גּוֹי וְשֶׁאֵין בּוֹ רֵיחַ רָע וְהוֹצִיאוֹ לְכַלְבּוֹ.

2 מודה A | מודי   3 תיפתר A | תפתר   4 ופחות מכעדשה A | וכעדשה   5 טעמון A | טעמוהון

"A living person on a bier is not liable[12] even for the bier," for the living carries himself[58]. "A dead person on a bier is liable," the opinion of everybody[59]? Was it not stated, also bad smell in the most minute amount? Rebbi Ila said, also Rebbi Simeon agrees to this. Rebbi Simeon also agrees in cases of prohibitions of usufruct[60]. Rebbi Yudan said, explain it if the corpse is a Gentile's without bad smell and he takes it out for his dog[61]. It was stated: For half the volume of an olive of a corpse and half the volume of an olive of a carcass and less than the volume of a lentil of a crawling animal one is liable, but Rebbi Simeon declares not liable. What is Rebbi Simeon's reason? The impurity already is eliminated[62]. What is the rabbis' reason? Following Rebbi Yudan explain it if the corpse is a Gentile's without bad smell and he takes it out for his dog[61].

58 Babli 94a, 141b; *Eruvin* 103a; *Yoma* 66b.

59 The questioner refers the remark at the end of Mishnah 5, "R. Simeon declares not liable" to the entire statement.

60 Chapter 9, Note 136. How can R. Simeon require the volume of an olive of a corpse since it smells badly and is forbidden for usufruct?

61 Gentile corpses are not forbidden for usufruct. Therefore neither of R. Simeon's exceptions applies.

62 Therefore he does not agree that the volumes may be combined since the minimum amount for a corpse is the volume of an olive but for carcass meat or crawling animal it is a dog's mouthful.

The reading of A, "the volume of a lentil", seems to be a scribal error. Cf. Babli 94b.

(12c line 67) ז'. רִבִּי אַבָּהוּ בְשֵׁם רִבִּי יוֹסֵי בֵּירִבִּי חֲנִינָה. מַה פְלִיגִין. בְּשֶׁנְּטָלָן הוּא. אֲבָל אִם נְטָלָן אַחַר מָאוּסִין הֵן. דִּבְרֵי חֲכָמִים. רִבִּי אָחָא רִבִּי נָחוּם בְּשֵׁם רַב. לְעוֹלָם אֵינוֹ חַיָּיב עַד שֶׁיִּטְּלֶנּוּ בְקַרְסְטָל. רִבִּי אַבָּהוּ בְשֵׁם רִבִּי יוֹסֵי בֶּן חֲנִינָה. הַגּוֹדֶלֶת חַיֶּיבֶת מִשּׁוּם בּוֹנָה. וְאָתְיָא כַּהֲהִיא דְּאָמַר רִבִּי יוֹחָנָן בְּשֵׁם רִבִּי בְּנָיָה. בְּאַתְרִין צְוָוחִין לַקַּלְעִיתָא בַּנְייָיתָא. אָמַר רִבִּי זְעוּרָא. לֹא מִסְתַּבְּרָא דְלָא מִשּׁוּם אֲרִיג. מַחְלְפָא שִׁיטָתֵיהּ דְּרִבִּי זְעוּרָא. דְּתַמָּן אָמַר רִבִּי זְעוּרָא רִבִּי חִייָה בְשֵׁם רִבִּי יוֹחָנָן. הַקּוֹלֵעַ שָׁלֹשׁ נִימִין בָּאָדָם חַיָּיב מִשּׁוּם אֲרִיג. אָמַר רִבִּי זְעוּרָא. לֹא טְווִי וַאֲרִיג הוּא. וְהָכָא הוּא אָמַר הָכֵין. כָּאן בִּמְרוּבָּה וְכָאן בִּמְמוּעָט. הָדָא דְאַתְּ אָמַר בָּאָדָם. אֲבָל בִּבְהֵמָה טָהוֹר. כְּהָדָא דְתַנֵּי. הָעוֹשֶׂה פַסִּיקְיָא לִילְבָּב לִישַׁפֵּר לְהַדִּיק בָּהּ אֶת הַפַּרְצוּפִין לִתְלוֹתָהּ

בְּצַוָּאר בְּהֵמָה. טָהוֹר. הָדָא דְאַתְּ אָמַר. בִּפְשׁוּטִין. אֲבָל בִּמְקוּפָּלִין בֵּין בָּאָדָם בֵּין בִּבְהֵמָה טָמֵא. הַכּוֹחֶלֶת חַיֶּיבֶת מִשּׁוּם כּוֹתֶבֶת. הַפּוֹסֶקֶת חַיֶּיבֶת מִשּׁוּם צוֹבַעַת.

1 ז. A מתני' | אבהו A אבהוא יוסי A יוסה ביר' | A בן | 2 חכמים A חכמין אחא A אחה | 3 בקרסטל A | [בק]לסטר אבהו A אבהוא יוסי A יוסה | 7 הדא דאת אמר A הן]דתמר | 8 להדיק A ולהדיק

7.[63] Rebbi Abbahu in the name of Rebbi Yose ben Rebbi Ḥanina: Where do they differ? If he himself took them but if another took them they are disgusting[64]. The words of the Sages, Rebbi Aḥa, Rebbi Naḥum in the name of Rav, he is never liable unless he take them with a grooming knife[65].

Rebbi Abbahu in the name of Rebbi Yose ben Rebbi Ḥanina: The one who braids is liable because of building[66]. This follows what Rebbi Joḥanan said in the name of Rebbi Banaya: At our place they call builder one who is plaiting[67]. Rebbi Ze`ira said, would it not be reasonable that it should be because of weaving? The argument of Rebbi Ze`ira is inverted, for there said Rebbi Ze`ira, Rebbi Ḥiyya in the name of Rebbi Joḥanan, one who plaits three hairs of a human is liable because of weaving; Rebbi Ze`ira said, is it not spinning rather than weaving? And here he says so! There if they are few, here for many[68]. That is what you say about a human, but for an animal it is pure, as it was stated: One who makes a belt[69] under the heart, to beautify, or to fasten the bags[70], to hang it around an animal's neck, is pure[71]. That is, for simple ones. But if the are folded, whether for human or for animal they are impure[72]. The one who applies kohl is liable because of writing;[73] the one who puts on make-up is liable because of dyeing[66].

63   Discussion of Mishnah 7. In A simply a note: (new) Mishnah.
64   Since it is unprofessional to trim somebody else's fingernail with his fingers, even R. Eliezer must agree that there is no liability created. Babli 94b.
65   Greek κνηστήρ, -ῆρος, ὁ. S. Liebermann, *Tosefta kiFshutah Šabbat* p. 137, Note 31, supported by the reading of A. In the Babli, the word appears as גנוסטר. In contrast to the Yerushalmi which requires a professional tool, the Babli declares liability for the use of any tool, 94b.
66   Babli 94b/95a.
67   *Berakhot* 61a, explaining *Gen.* 2:22, not that God built up the rib, but that He braided the side (the female side of the human created as Siamese twin, *Gen.* 1:27.)
68   Plaiting a few hairs is like spinning, braiding a full head of hair is like weaving.
69   Latin *fascia, -ae, f.*.
70   Latin *marsupium, -ii, n.*.
71   This has nothing to do with the rules of the Sabbath. It is a side remark that only

vessels and implements for human use are susceptible to impurity, not anything manufactured for exclusive use as decoration of animals. Cf. Tosephta *Kelim Bava batra* 4:14.

72 The moment anything can be used as a container it is usable for a human and therefore subject to impurity even if used for animals.

73 Since circling the eye with *kohl* amounts to writing the letter ס or the paleo-Hebrew ʿ*ayin*, o.

(12d line 6) יִצְחָק בַּר אוֹרְיוֹן אָמַר. מַה פְּלִיגִין. בְּשֶׁלֹּא תָלַשׁ כְּנֶגֶד הַנֶּקֶב. אֲבָל אִם תָּלַשׁ כְּנֶגֶד הַנֶּקֶב אַף רִבִּי שִׁמְעוֹן מוֹדֶה. רִבִּי יִרְמְיָה בָּעֵי. הָיָה כולּוֹ בָאָרֶץ וְנֶקֶב חוּץ לָאָרֶץ. אַשְׁכְּחַת אֲמַר. מַה דְצְרִיכָא לְרִבִּי יִרְמְיָה פְּשִׁיטָה לְיִצְחָק בַּר אוֹרְיוֹן. אִילֵּין אִינּוּן. וְהָא אִית לָךְ חוֹרָנִיָין. עָצִיץ נָקוּב מְקַדֵּשׁ בַּכֶּרֶם וְשֶׁאֵינוֹ נָקוּב אֵינוֹ מְקַדֵּשׁ בַּכֶּרֶם. עָצִיץ נָקוּב אֵינוֹ מַכְשִׁיר אֶת הַזְּרָעִים וְשֶׁאֵינוֹ נָקוּב מַכְשִׁיר אֶת הַזְּרָעִים. הַתּוֹלֵשׁ מֵעָצִיץ נָקוּב חַיָיב וּמִשֶּׁאֵינוֹ נָקוּב פָּטוּר. רִבִּי יוֹסֵה אָמַר לָהּ סְתָם. רִבִּי חֲנַנְיָה מָטֵי בָהּ בְּשֵׁם רִבִּי שְׁמוּאֵל בַּר רַב יִצְחָק. הַתּוֹרָה רִיבָּת בְּטָהֳרַת זְרָעִים. מַה טַעַם. וְכִי יִפֹּל מִנִּבְלָתָם עַל־כָּל־זֶרַע זֵרוּעַ אֲשֶׁר יִזָּרֵעַ וגו׳.

Isaac bar Orion said, where do they disagree[74]? If he did not pluck it off over the hole. But if he plucked it off over the hole also Rebbi Simeon will agree. Rebbi Jeremiah asked: If everything was in the Land but the hole outside the Land[75]? It turns out that you may say what was questionable for Rebbi Jeremiah was obvious for Isaac bar Orion. These are it[76]. But there are others! "A flower pot with a hole sanctifies in a vineyard, one without a hole does not sanctify[77]." "A flower pot with a hole cannot prepare plants, one without a hole prepares.[78]" "He who plucks from a flower pot with a hole is liable, from one without a hole he is not liable.[17]" Rebbi Yose referred to it as anonymous statement, Rebbi Hanania quoted it in the name of Rebbi Samuel bar Rav Isaac[79]: The Torah extended the purity of growing plants[80]: *If any of their cadavers falls on any sown seed apt to be sown*, etc.

74 The disagreement between the rabbis and Rebbi Simeon about harvesting from flower pots on the Sabbath; cf. Notes 17,18. The main part of the paragraph is from *Kilaim* 7:6, Notes 80-83.

75 This has nothing to do with the rules of the Sabbath but with agricultural laws, such as heave, tithes, and the Sabbatical year, which are intrinsically restricted to growth of the Holy Land. If the rabbis consider a flower pot agricultural land, what is the status of such a pot standing in the Land but drawing its moisture from outside the Land? For Isaac bar Orion obviously the pot belongs to the outside.

76 This is a shortened reference to the text in *Kilaim* which has become unintelligible. The text referred to reads in

full: It was stated: "the only difference between a flower pot without a hole and one with a hole regards preparation for impurity." That is for Rebbi Simeon, but for the rabbis there are others. (Babli 95a/b,)

77 A part of Mishnah *Kilaim* 7:8 in the independent Mishnah mss., not in the Mishnah of the Yerushalmi. Growth of produce other than vines in a vineyard makes everything forbidden for usufruct; *Deut.* 22:9.

78 Mishnah *Uqesin* 2:10. Food can become impure only after the harvest and only after having been wetted, cf. *Demay* Chapter 2, Note 141. A plant in a pot with hole is a plant in the earth and nothing can make it prepared for impurity at this stage. A plant in a pot without hole is already harvested since it can be plucked on the Sabbath without fear of prosecution; if it is watered, it becomes subject to possible impurity.

79 In another quote of this sentence, in *Ma`serot* 5:2 (Note 46): Rebbi La.

80 *Lev.* 11:37. This explains why R. Simeon agrees with the rabbis that a flower pot with hole is immune from impurity and is not comparable to a pot with hole: The verse insists that anything sown in any way acceptable in agriculture is pure. The main point of the argument is lost in the quote here (which again shows that its origin is in *Kilaim*). The "etc." hides the final statement of the verse: *it is pure*. The quote of the verse also is truncated in the Babli, 95b.

הזורק פרק אחד עשר

(fol. 12d) **משנה א**: הַזּוֹרֵק מֵרְשׁוּת הַיָּחִיד לִרְשׁוּת הָרַבִּים אוֹ מֵרְשׁוּת הָרַבִּים לִרְשׁוּת הַיָּחִיד חַיָּב. מֵרְשׁוּת הַיָּחִיד לִרְשׁוּת הַיָּחִיד וּרְשׁוּת הָרַבִּים בָּאֶמְצַע רִבִּי עֲקִיבָה מְחַיֵּיב וַחֲכָמִים פּוֹטְרִין:

Mishnah 1: If one throws from a private domain to the public domain or from the public domain to a private domain or from a private domain to another private domain when a public domain is between them, Rebbi Aqiba declares him liable[1] but the Sages declare him not liable[2].

משנה ב: כֵּיצַד שְׁנֵי גְזוּזְטְרָאוֹת זוֹ כְּנֶגֶד זוֹ בִּרְשׁוּת הָרַבִּים הַמּוֹשִׁיט וְהַזּוֹרֵק מִזּוֹ לָזוֹ פָּטוּר. הָיוּ שְׁנֵיהֶן בִּדְיוֹטֵי אַחַת הַמּוֹשִׁיט חַיָּב וְהַזּוֹרֵק פָּטוּר שֶׁכָּךְ הָיְתָה עֲבוֹדַת הַלְוִיִּם.

Mishnah 2: How is this? Two balconies[3] one vis-a-vis the other in the public domain: one who hands over or throws from one to the other is not liable[4]. If they both were on the same floor[5], the one who hands over is liable but the one who throws is not liable, for this[6] was the service of the Levites.

משנה ג: שְׁתֵּי עֲגָלוֹת זוֹ אַחַר זוֹ בִּרְשׁוּת הָרַבִּים מוֹשִׁיטִין אֶת הַקְּרָשִׁין מִזּוֹ לָזוֹ אֲבָל לֹא זוֹרְקִין. חוּלְיַת הַבּוֹר וְהַסֶּלַע שֶׁהֵן גְּבוֹהִין עֲשָׂרָה וּרְחָבִין אַרְבָּעָה הַנּוֹטֵל מֵהֶן וְהַנּוֹתֵן עַל גַּבָּן חַיָּב פָּחוֹת מִיכֵּן פָּטוּר:

Mishnah 3: Two carts, one parallel to the other in the public domain: they[7] used to hand over from one to the other but did not throw. The enclosure of a cistern or a rock[8] high ten [hand-breadths] and wide[9] four [hand-breadths]: one who takes from them or puts on them is liable, less than this he is not liable[10].

משנה ד: הַזּוֹרֵק אַרְבַּע אַמּוֹת בַּכּוֹתֶל לְמַעְלָה מֵעֲשָׂרָה טְפָחִים כְּזוֹרֵק בָּאֲוִיר לְמַטָּה מֵעֲשָׂרָה טְפָחִים כְּזוֹרֵק בָּאָרֶץ וְהַזּוֹרֵק בָּאָרֶץ אַרְבַּע אַמּוֹת חַיָּב. זָרַק לְתוֹךְ אַרְבַּע אַמּוֹת וְנִתְגַּלְגֵּל חוּץ לְאַרְבַּע אַמּוֹת פָּטוּר. חוּץ לְאַרְבַּע אַמּוֹת וְנִתְגַּלְגֵּל לְתוֹךְ אַרְבַּע אַמּוֹת חַיָּב:

Mishnah 4: One who throws four cubits to a wall higher than ten hand-breadths[11] is like one who throws in the air, lower than ten hand-breadths is like one who throws on the ground[12] and one who throws four cubits on the ground is liable. One who threw less than four cubits and it rolled further than four cubits is not liable[13]; one who threw more than four cubits and it rolled back within four cubits is liable[14].

משנה ה: הַזּוֹרֵק בַּיָּם אַרְבַּע אַמּוֹת פָּטוּר. אִם הָיָה רְקַק מַיִם וּרְשׁוּת הָרַבִּים מְהַלֶּכֶת בּוֹ הַזּוֹרֵק בְּתוֹכוֹ אַרְבַּע אַמּוֹת חַיָּב. וְכַמָּה הוּא רְקַק מַיִם פָּחוֹת מֵעֲשָׂרָה טְפָחִים. רְקַק מַיִם וּרְשׁוּת הָרַבִּים מְהַלֶּכֶת בּוֹ הַזּוֹרֵק בְּתוֹכוֹ אַרְבַּע אַמּוֹת חַיָּב:

Mishnah 5: One who throws four cubits in the ocean is not liable[15]. If there was a shallow spot in the water and a public thoroughfare passed through it, one who throws four cubits into it is liable[16]. What is a shallow spot in the water? Less than ten hand-breadths. Shallow water[17] and a public thoroughfare passed through it: one who throws four cubits in it is liable.

משנה ו: הַזּוֹרֵק מִן הַיָּם לַיַּבָּשָׁה וּמִן הַיַּבָּשָׁה לַיָּם וּמִן הַיָּם לַסְּפִינָה וּמִן הַסְּפִינָה לַיָּם וּמִן הַסְּפִינָה לַחֲבֵירְתָּהּ פָּטוּר. סְפִינוֹת קְשׁוּרוֹת זוֹ בָזוֹ מְטַלְטְלִין מִזּוֹ לָזוֹ אִם אֵינָן קְשׁוּרוֹת אַף עַל פִּי שֶׁמּוּקָּפוֹת אֵין מְטַלְטְלִין מִזּוֹ לָזוֹ:

Mishnah 6: He who throws from the sea to dry land, or from dry land to the sea, of from the sea to a ship, or from a ship to the sea[18], or from one ship to another[19] is not liable. If ships are tied to one another one carries from one to the other; if they are not tied to one another, even though they be surrounded[20], one does not carry from one to the other[21].

משנה ז: הַזּוֹרֵק וְנִזְכַּר עַד שֶׁלֹּא תֵצֵא מִיָּדוֹ קְלָטָהּ אַחֵר קְלָטָהּ כֶּלֶב אוֹ שֶׁנִּשְׂרְפָה פָּטוּר. זָרַק לַעֲשׂוֹת חַבּוּרָה בֵּין בְּאָדָם בֵּין בִּבְהֵמָה וְנִזְכַּר עַד שֶׁלֹּא נַעֲשֵׂית חַבּוּרָה פָּטוּר. זֶה הַכְּלָל כָּל־חַיָּבֵי חַטָּאוֹת אֵינָן חַיָּבִין עַד שֶׁתְּהֵא תְחִילָּתָן וְסוֹפָן שְׁגָגָה. תְּחִילָּתָן שְׁגָגָה וְסוֹפָן זָדוֹן תְּחִילָּתָן זָדוֹן וְסוֹפָן שְׁגָגָה פְּטוּרִין עַד שֶׁתְּהֵא תְחִילָּתָן וְסוֹפָן שְׁגָגָה:

Mishnah 7: One who throws and remembers before it leaves his hand, if another person caught it, or a dog caught it, or it was burned, he is not liable[22]. If one threw with the intention of causing an injury whether on a human or an animal and he remembered before it caused an injury, he is not liable[23]. This is the principle: All who are liable for a purification sacrifice are liable only if beginning and end were in error. If the beginning was unintentional but the end criminal or the beginning criminal and the end unintentional they are not liable unless beginning and end be unintentional.

1   Under certain conditions as discussed in the Halakhah.

2   Since motion requires start and finish, they consider it a Sabbath violation only if either one of start or finish was in a private and the other in the public domain or both in the public domain at a distance greater than 4 cubits.

3   Greek ἐξώστρα, ἡ "balcony, bridge between two towers (military)", also Latin

exostra. These are at least ten hand-breadths high and four-by-four hand-breadths wide on top, to constitute separate private domains.

4   Since a situation like this never occurred in the service of the Tabernacle. The Merarites had four carts (*Num.* 7:8) to carry the planks which formed the walls of the Tabernacle. When the latter was disassembled the carts were lined up on both of its sides and loaded there; therefore it could happen that a plank was transferred from a cart to one parallel to it (as mentioned in the next Mishnah) but never from a cart to one parallel to it when they were separated by the public domain. The loading docks of the carts were more than ten hand-breadths high and four-by-four hand-breadths wide; this qualifies them as private domains. Since the Tabernacle was disassembled during decamping and the curtains surrounding the Tabernacle removed, the area in which the carts were standing reverted to the status of public domain. (Explanation of Maimonides.)

5   Greek δίαιτα, ἡ. Separate balconies on the same floor, extending over the public domain. If one hands over from one to the other one imitates the Merarites in the desert, which is counted as a Sabbath violation. But since the planks of the Tabernacles never were thrown, throwing from one balcony to an other cannot be sanctioned.

6   Handing over, not throwing.

7   The Merarites (Note 4).

8   Surrounded by public domain.

9   In two directions so that the surface area of the enclosure or the top of the rock is at least 16 (hand-breadths)^2.

10   If the height is less than ten hand-breadths the place is *karmelit*; if the surface area is insufficient the place is either *karmelit* or exempt space (Chapter 1, Note 109), depending on the height.

11   And the object thrown sticks to the wall in exempt space, higher than ten hand-breadths.

12   Since anything within ten hand-breadths of the ground in the public domain is in the public domain.

13   If it touched the ground at a distance of less than 4 cubits the throw is completed; if afterwards it rolls on the ground, even though it is because of the impetus given by the thrower, this is not part of the throwing action as far as the laws of the Sabbath are concerned.

14   As Rashi points out, this statement is necessary only for the case that the object reached farther than 4 cubits but was blown back before it touched the ground. If it touched the ground farther than 4 cubits the statement is a direct consequence of the preceding one as seen from Note 13.

15   Since the sea is *karmelit* (Chapter 1, Note 151).

16   A ford used by travellers on a public road is part of the road and public domain.

17   Not in the ocean. This statement seems to describe the original practice; the statement about a ford in the ocean is a consequence.

18   Following the rules of *karmelit*.

19   Even though each ship is a separate private domain, the domains are separated by *karmelit*, not public domain. Therefore even Rebbi Aqiba must agree that no Sabbath violation can occur in this case.

20   By a fence or other ships.

21 This prohibition is rabbinic. If the ships are not tied together one has to worry that they might become separated by more than 4 cubits of *karmelit* sea. Even though carrying in or through *karmelit* cannot be sanctioned it still is rabbinically forbidden.

22 The liability is for a purification sacrifice. Since such a sacrifice cannot be offered as a voluntary gift, all preconditions for it must be strictly satisfied. The first condition is that a prosecutable offense must have been committed; in this case that lifting, transporting, and depositing must be done by the same person (Chapter 1, Note 1). In the cases described in this sentence, the last condition is not satisfied. "It was burned" means burned in flight.

23 A purification sacrifice is possible only for inadvertent offenses. If during the course of the action the subject became aware of the criminality of his deed, there can be no purification sacrifice.

(12d line 57) הַזּוֹרֵק מֵרְשׁוּת הַיָּחִיד כול'. זְרִיקָה תּוֹלֶדֶת הוֹצָאָה הִיא.

"If one throws from a private domain," etc. Throwing is a derivative of transporting[24].

24 This sentence is the answer to the obvious question, why is a Chapter devoted to throwing when throwing was not listed among the 39 categories of forbidden work? Babli 96b.

(12d line 58) וְלֹא שַׁנְיָיא בֵּין עַל דַּעְתֵּיהּ בֵּין עַל דַּעְתְּהוֹן דְּרַבָּנָן. וְהוּא שֶׁנָּחָה מֵרְשׁוּת הָרַבִּים לִרְשׁוּת הַיָּחִיד. עַל דַּעְתֵּיהּ דְּרִבִּי. אֲפִילוּ לֹא נָחָה. עַל דַּעְתְּהוֹן דְּרַבָּנָן. וְהוּא שֶׁנָּחָה. דְּאָמַר רִבִּי בָּא בַּר חוּנָה בְּשֵׁם רַב. לֹא חִייֵב רִבִּי אֶלָּא עַל יְדֵי רְשׁוּת הַיָּחִיד מְקוּרָה. מִילְתֵיהּ דְּרִבִּי יוֹחָנָן אֲמָרָה. אֲפִילוּ אֵינָהּ מְקוּרָה. דָּאָמַר רִבִּי אִימִי בְּשֵׁם רִבִּי יוֹחָנָן. וְהוּא שֶׁתֶּרֶד לָאֲוֵיר מְחִיצוֹת. רִבִּי אִימִי בָּעָא קוֹמֵי רִבִּי יוֹחָנָן. מַתְנִיתָא דְרִבִּי. דְּרִבִּי עָבַד אֲוֵיר מְחִיצוֹת כְּמַמָּשָׁן. אָמַר לֵיהּ. דִּבְרֵי הַכֹּל הִיא. הָכָא בְגִיטִּין. וִיתִיבִינֵיהּ. רִבִּי אוֹמֵר. מְקוּרָה. וְאַתְּ אֲמָרַת. אֵינָהּ מְקוּרָה. מַה בֵּין גִּיטִּין מַה בֵּין שַׁבָּת. אָמַר רִבִּי אִילָא. בְּשַׁבָּת כָּתוּב לֹא־תַעֲשֶׂה כָל־מְלָאכָה. וְנַעֲשִׂית הִיא מֵאֵילֶיהָ. בְּרַם הָכָא הַתּוֹרָה אָמְרָה וְנָתַן בְּיָדָהּ. בִּרְשׁוּתָהּ.

4 דאמר | ט - אימי | ט אמי ט שתרד | ט שירד 5 כממשן | ט כממשו 6 בגיטין | ט דגיטין 7 מה | ט ומה אילא | ט אבא כל | ט - 8 ונעשית | ט נעשית התורה אמרה | ט -

Is there no difference, whether according to his[25] opinion or that of the rabbis, only if it came to rest from a public domain into a private domain? In Rebbi's opinion, even if it did not come to rest[26]; in the rabbis' opinion, only if it came to rest. For Rebbi Abba bar Ḥuna said in the name of Rav: Rebbi declared liable only for a private domain which was roofed[27]. The word of Rebbi Johanan implies, even if it was not roofed, [28]for Rebbi Immi said in the name of Rebbi Joḥanan: Only if it descended to within the partitions[29]. Rebbi Immi asked before Rebbi Joḥanan: Does the Mishnah follow Rebbi, since Rebbi considers partitions as solidly filled up[27]? He said to him, it is everybody's opinion[30]. Could one not object that Rebbi said, if it is roofed? And you say, it is not roofed?[31] What is the difference between bills of divorce and the Sabbath? Rebbi Ila said, about the Sabbath it is written: *You shall not do any work*[32]; it may make itself automatically[34]. But here *he shall deliver into her hand*[34], into her domain.

25 As follows from the sequel, the question is about interpreting R. Aqiba's position, where there is a dispute between Rebbi (referred to as "he") and the majority of the rabbis of his generation.

26 Since the airspace over a private domain belongs to that domain up to an indeterminate height, Rebbi considers the entry of an object into this airspace as valid delivery; the rabbis read the statement that "a person's courtyard acquires for him" to refer only to the soil, not to the airspace over it. The disagreement essentially refers to matters of civil law; its applicability to the laws of the Sabbath is questioned later in the paragraph. (*Šabbat* 1 Note 107, Babli 4a, 5a, *Gittin* 79a).

In the Babli (4b) it is stated that one who threw from a public domain to another over a private domain is not liable for the Sages but twice liable for Rebbi. Since the Yerushalmi does not quote this statement, it cannot be presupposed here.

27 Babli 4a/5b. An object is delivered into a courtyard only if it comes to rest on the ground. But delivery to a house is effected the moment the object is in the house since even the air in the house is considered soil. For this rule, "house" is any covered place even if it has no walls.

28 From here on the text is copied from *Gittin* 8:3 (ט, Notes 54-57). The topic of divorce at the end is referred to as "here".

29 This refers to the last sentence in Mishnah *Gittin* 8:3. If the husband throws the bill of divorce from his roof to her courtyard, it is possible to say that the bill was delivered the moment it cleared the roof only if the walls of the wife's courtyard are higher than the husband's roof. Otherwise it would be legally delivered only if the bill fell below the level of the courtyard walls. (The same argument is quoted in Samuel's name in the Babli, *Gittin* 79a.)

30 The Babli agrees, *Gittin* 79a, that the delivery of bills of divorce is governed by the rules of property rights, not those of the Sabbath.

31 For the rules of the Sabbath.

32 *Ex.* 20:10.

33 As long as it was not intended that the object should come to rest by the force of the thrower (but it was moved along by some mechanical contraption not directly controlled by the thrower), no violation of the Sabbath occurred. But for delivery of a bill of divorce, it is the fact of delivery rather than its mode which counts.

34 Deut. 24:1.

(12d lin 68) שְׁמוּאֵל אָמַר. לֹא שָׁנוּ אֶלָּא לְמַטָּה מֵעֲשָׂרָה. הָא לְמַעְלָה מֵעֲשָׂרָה אָסוּר. מִילְתֵיהּ דְּרִבִּי אֶלְעָזָר אֳמְרָה. אֲפִילוּ לְמַעְלָה מֵעֲשָׂרָה מוּתָּר. דְּאָמַר רִבִּי אִילָא בְשֵׁם רִבִּי אֶלְעָזָר. מֵעֲגָלוֹת לָמַד רִבִּי עֲקִיבָה. וַעֲגָלוֹת לֹא לְמַעְלָה מֵעֲשָׂרָה אִינִין. אִית תַּנָּיֵי תַנֵּי. כֵּיצַד. אִית דְּלָא תַנֵּי. כֵּיצַד. עַל דַּעְתֵּיהּ דְּרִבִּי אֶלְעָזָר אִית כָּאן כֵּיצַד. עַל דַּעְתֵּיהּ דִּשְׁמוּאֵל לֵית כָּאן כֵּיצַד.

Samuel said, they taught this[35] only about lower than ten [hand-breadths]. Therefore higher than ten [hand-breadths] it is forbidden[36]. The statement of Rebbi Eleazar implied that even higher than ten [hand-breadths] it is permitted[37]. For Rebbi Ila said in the name of Rebbi Eleazar, Rebbi Aqiba learned from the carts[4,38]; and were the carts not higher than ten [hand-breadths][39]? Some Tannaim state "how is this"[40]; some do not state "how is this". In Rebbi Eleazar's opinion there is "how is this", in Samuels's opinion there is no "how is this".

35 The disagreement between R. Aqiba and the Sages about one who throws from one private domain to another over a public domain. In his opinion, R. Aqiba declares him liable because he holds that anything within 10 hand-breadths off the soil is as if it was resting; if the object passed within 10 hand-breadths off the soil it is as if it was exported from a private to the public domain and biblically forbidden.

36 Since it says "forbidden" but not "liable", the prohibition is purely rabbinic, not biblical.

37 Rashba (*Novellae ad 97a*) reads: "The statement of Rebbi Eleazar implied even higher than ten [hand-breadths]," meaning that the dispute between the Sages and R. Aqiba is not dependent on the height on which the object passes over the public domain. He does not read "it is permitted". But his (and a similar remark by Ritba *ad 97a*) cannot be taken as witness to the text since he is dependent on his teacher Nahmanides (*Novellae Sabbath*, ed. M. Herschler, col. 337-338) who does not read "it is permitted" in the quote from the Yerushalmi. But since he finds it necessary in an appendix to his Commentary to justify his not reading the clause it is clear that he amended the text. It follows that the medieval authors confirm the text as given in the ms. This does not mean that Nahmanides's emendation as adopted by Rashba not be justified; it is required by the text which follows.

38 In the Babli (92a, 97a) R. Eleazar derives the prohibition of carrying in the public domain from the work of the Kehatites who carried the contents of the Tabernacles on their shoulders (*Num.* 7:9).

39 Cf. Chapter 1, Notes 127-129.

40 In the first version, which is the text of our Mishnah, Mishnah 2 is a direct continuation of Mishnah 1 and an explanation of the

last sentence in that Mishnah. In the second version the two Mishnaiot are not directly connected.

(12d line 73) רִבִּי יִצְחָק בֵּירִבִּי אֶלְעָזָר שָׁאַל. זָרַק מֵרְשׁוּת הַיָּחִיד לִרְשׁוּת הָרַבִּים וְנִזְכַּר עַד שֶׁהוּא בִּרְשׁוּת הָרַבִּים. עַל דַּעְתֵּיהּ דְּרִבִּי עֲקִיבָה יֵעָשֶׂה כְּמִי שֶׁנָּחָה בִּרְשׁוּת הָרַבִּים וְיְהֵא חַיָּיב שְׁתַּיִם. אָמַר רִבִּי חוּנָה. לֹא חִיֵּיב רִבִּי עֲקִיבָה אֶלָּא עַל יְדֵי רְשׁוּת הַיָּחִיד הַשְּׁנִייָה.

רִבִּי אַבָּהוּ אוֹמֵר בְּשֵׁם רִבִּי אֶלְעָזָר בְּשֵׁם רִבִּי יוֹחָנָן. הָיָה עוֹמֵד בִּרְשׁוּת הָרַבִּים וְזָרַק לְמַעְלָה מֵעֲשָׂרָה. רוֹאִין שֶׁאִם תִּפּוֹל אִם נָחָה בְתוֹךְ אַרְבַּע אַמּוֹת פָּטוּר. וְאִם לָאו חַיָּיב. וְהִתַנֵּי שְׁמוּאֵל. מֵרְשׁוּת הָרַבִּים לִרְשׁוּת הָרַבִּים וּרְשׁוּת הַיָּחִיד בָּאֶמְצַע רוֹאִין שֶׁאִם תִּפּוֹל נָחָה בְתוֹךְ אַרְבַּע אַמּוֹת פָּטוּר. וְאִם לָאו חַיָּיב. תַּמָּן אַתְּ אָמַר. אֵין רְשׁוּת הָרַבִּים מִצְטָרֶפֶת. וְהָכָא אַתְּ אָמַר. רְשׁוּת הָרַבִּים מִצְטָרֶפֶת. אָמַר רִבִּי חוּנָה. תַּמָּן שֶׁאִם תִּפּוֹל קַרְקַע שֶׁתַּחְתֶּיהָ רְשׁוּת הַיָּחִיד. בְּרַם הָכָא שֶׁאִם תִּפּוֹל קַרְקַע שֶׁתַּחְתֶּיהָ רְשׁוּת הָרַבִּים.

Rebbi Isaac ben Rebbi Eleazar asked: If one threw from a private domain to the public domain and remembered when it was over the public domain, in Rebbi Aqiba's opinion it should be considered as if it rested in the public domain and he should be liable twice[41]. Rebbi Huna said, Rebbi Aqiba made him liable only by means of the second private domain[42].

Rebbi Abbahu says in the name of Rebbi Eleazar in the name of Rebbi Johanan: If one was standing in the public domain and threw higher than ten [hand-breadths]. One sees that if it fell down it would come to rest within four cubits he will not be liable, otherwise he will be liable[43]. But did not Samuel state: From public domain to public domain with a private domain in the middle, one sees that if it fell it would come to rest within four cubits he will not be liable, otherwise he will be liable[44]. There, you are saying that public domain is not joining, but here you are saying that public domain is joining[45]? Rebbi Huna said, there where if it falls down the ground under it is private domain but here where if it falls down the ground under it is public domain[46].

41 The statement is elliptic since in Mishnah 7 it is stated that if one throws in oblivion of the Sabbath rules and recognizes his error while the object is in flight there cane be no liability for a purification sacrifice. Therefore one has to assume that there was only a fleeting consciousness of the Sabbath prohibition followed by another period of oblivion. Then for R. Aqiba the moment of recognition should be counted both as rest for a first and start for a second throw and there should be liability for two

sacrifices. (Cf. Babli 4b where Rav Jehudah holds that R. Aqiba in the interpretation of Rebbi declares that there are two liabilities incurred by throwing from public domain to public domain over a private domain.)

42 Since anything can happen as long as the object did not come to rest (as described in Mishnah 7), there can be no liability created before this time.

43 Even though it passed through exempt space.

44 The combined distance travelled over the second public domain must be more than 4 cubits.

45 Why travelling over private domain requires 4 cubits on the other side, with what happened on the other side being disregarded, while travelling through exempt space is no different from travelling over public domain?

46 In the first case, if the object fell down in the private domain there would be no liability since the intention was to throw into the public domain while in the second case there is liability from the moment the projection of the trajectory onto the ground extends to over four cubits.

(13a line 8) תָּנֵי בְשֵׁם רִבִּי יוּדָה. זָרַק אַרְבַּע אַמּוֹת בִּרְשׁוּת הָרַבִּים חַיָּיב. רִבִּי יוּדָה עָבַד אַרְבַּע אַמּוֹת בִּרְשׁוּת הָרַבִּים מְלָאכָה בִּפְנֵי עַצְמָהּ. עַל דַּעְתֵּיהּ דְּרִבִּי יוּדָה אַרְבָּעִים מְלָאכוֹת אִינּוּן. וְנִיתְנִין. לָא אֲתִינָן מַתְנֵי אֶלָּא מִילִין דְּכָל־עַמָּא מוֹדֵי בְהוֹן. רִבִּי זְעִירָא רִבִּי יֹאשִׁיָּה בְשֵׁם רִבִּי יוֹחָנָן. מִתּוֹפְרֵי יְרִיעוֹת לָמַד רִבִּי יְהוּדָה. שֶׁהָיוּ תוֹפְרֵי הַיְרִיעוֹת מְזָרְקִין אֶת הַמְּחָטִין אֵילוּ לָאֵילוּ. וְלָאו כַּרְמְלִית הִיא. אָמַר רִבִּי חִינָּנָא. מִן הַצַּד הָיוּ מְזָרְקִין.

It was stated in the name of Rebbi Jehudah: One who threw four cubits in the public domain is liable[47]. Rebbi Jehudah considers four cubits in the public domain a separate category of work[48]. In Rebbi Jehudah's opinion there are 40 categories of work: should we not state this? We come to state only things about which everybody agrees.

Rebbi Ze'ira, Rebbi Joshia in the name of Rebbi Johanan: Rebbi Jehudah learned this from those who were sewing the gobelins, for those sewing the gobelins were throwing the needles one to another[49]. Is that not *karmelit*[50]? Rebbi Ḥinena said, they were throwing sideways[51].

47 He denies that throwing is a derivative of transporting (Note 24). Babli 97b.

48 If he transported from a domain to another by throwing he is twice liable, Babli 97b.

49 Babli 96b., *Ex.* 26:1-6. R. Jehudah must hold that throwing within 10 handbreadths from the soil is transporting in the public domain.

50 Since the camp was organized as a private domain only after the Tabernacle was in service (*Num.* 2:1), in the period of construction of the Tabernacle they were dwelling in the desert; the space between the

tents was *karmelit*. If the argument is correct then carrying in *karmelit* should be biblically prohibited and causing liability. This contradicts practice (Chapter 1, Note 73).

51 They threw outside of the tents in the public domain. The Babli 96b rejects the entire argument as impossible.

(13a line 15) ב'. רַב אָמַר. לֵית כָּאן פָּטוּר אֶלָּא מוּתָּר. עַל דַּעְתֵּיהּ דְּרַב. לְמַעֲלָה מֵעֲשָׂרָה מוּתָּר. עַל דַּעְתֵּיהּ דִּשְׁמוּאֵל. לְמַעֲלָה מֵעֲשָׂרָה אָסוּר. רִבִּי אִילָא בְשֵׁם רִבִּי שִׁמְעוֹן בֶּן לָקִישׁ. וְהוּא שֶׁתְּהֵא רְשׁוּת הָרַבִּים מַקֶּפְתּוֹ מִכָּל־צַד. רִבִּי יַעֲקֹב בַּר אָחָא בְשֵׁם רִבִּי יוֹחָנָן. אֲפִילוּ מֵרוּחַ אַחַת. מִן אִילֵּין עֲגָלוֹת. וַעֲגָלוֹת לָאו לְמַעֲלָה מֵעֲשָׂרָה אִינּוּן. רִבִּי אָחָא בְשֵׁם רִבִּי מַיישָׁא. בִּלְבָד עַל יְדֵי שְׁנַיִם. בְּכָל־אָתָר אַתְּ אָמַר. שְׁנַיִם שֶׁעֲשָׂאוּ פְטוּרִין. וְהָכָא אַתְּ אָמַר. שְׁנַיִם שֶׁעֲשָׂאוּ חַייָבִין. שַׁנְייָא הִיא. שֶׁכֵּן הָיְתָה עֲבוֹדַת הַלְוִיִּם בְּאֹהֶל מוֹעֵד. מַה הָיְתָה עֲבוֹדַת הַלְוִיִּם בְּאֹהֶל מוֹעֵד. שְׁתֵּי עֲגָלוֹת זוֹ אַחַר זוֹ בִּרְשׁוּת הָרַבִּים מוֹשִׁיטִין אֶת הַקְּרָשִׁים מִזּוֹ לְזוֹ אֲבָל לֹא זוֹרְקִין. תַּנֵּי בַּר קַפָּרָא. שֶׁלֹּא לִנְהוֹג בַּקְּרָשִׁים בְּזָיוֹן.

2[51]. Rav said, here[52] there is no "not liable" but "permitted". In Rav's opinion, higher than ten [hand-breadths] is permitted. In Samuel's opinion, higher than ten [hand-breadths] is forbidden[53]. Rebbi Ila in the name of Rebbi Simeon ben Laqish: on condition that the public domain surround it from all sides[54]. Rebbi Jacob bar Aḥa in the name of Rebbi Joḥanan, even from one side. From these carts. Were the carts not higher than ten [hand-breadths][39]? Rebbi Aḥa in the name of Rebbi Maisha: only by two persons[55]. Everywhere you are saying, two persons acting together are not liable[56], but here you are saying, two persons acting together are liable. There is a difference, because this was the office of the Levites in the Tent of Meeting. What was the office of the Levites in the Tent of Meeting? Two carts one parallel to the other in the public domain. They were handing the planks from one to the other but not throwing[57]. Bar Qappara stated, not to treat the planks[58] with contempt.

51 Here starts the discussion of Mishnaiot 2 and 3. These are considered as one Mishnah, following the independent Mishnah mss. but not the Mishnah in the Yerushalmi *editio princeps*.

52 The first sentence in the Mishnah. For him reaching or throwing over a public domain through exempt space is both biblically and rabbinically permitted.

53 Rabbinically. This is consistent with his opinion that Mishnah 2 is not a continuation of Mishnah 1.

54 The remark about the Levites' carts should be read before this sentence (S. Lieberrmann), cf. Babli 99a. Since when camp was broken the carts were standing in the public domain, the difference between below and above ten hand-breadths

biblically refers only to the situation of private domain surrounded on all sides by public domain. The opinion of R. Joḥanan can be valid only rabbinically.

55 Handing over an object from one private domain to another over public domain is biblically a Sabbath violation only if giver and recipient are two different persons, not if executed by one person alone.

56 Chapter 1, Notes 1,105; Chapter 10, 12c l. 47. Babli 3a.

57 Therefore throwing over the public domain never is a biblical violation in the interpretation of the Sages.

58 In all medieval quotes of this sentence enumerated by Ratner and Liebermann one reads קדשים "*sancta*" for קרשים "planks".

(13a line 25) אָמַר רִבִּי יוֹחָנָן. הָעוֹמֵד וְהֶחָלָל מִצְטָרְפִין (לַעֲשָׂרָה) בָּאַרְבָּעָה. וְהוּא שֶׁיְּהֵא הָעוֹמֵד רָבָה עַל הֶחָלָל. רִבִּי זְעוּרָא בָעֵי. עַד שֶׁיְּהֵא עוֹמֵד שֶׁכָּאן וְעוֹמֵד שֶׁכָּאן רָבָה. אָמַר רִבִּי יוֹסֵה. פְּשִׁיטָא לְרִבִּי זְעוּרָא שֶׁאֵין עוֹמֵד מִצַּד אֶחָד מִצְטָרֵף. פְּשִׁיטָא לֵיהּ שֶׁאֵין עוֹמֵד מִצַּד אֶחָד רָבָה. לֹא צוֹרְכָה דְלֹא אֲפִילוּ עוֹמֵד הַשֵּׁינִי.

1 בארבעה | ז לארבעה   2 זעורא | ז זעירא   3 לר' זעורא | ז ליה לר' זעירא עומד | ז העומד אחד | ז האחד שאין | ז שיהא עומד | ז העומד   4 צורכה | ז צריכה השיני | ז השני

[59]Rebbi Joḥanan said, what is standing and the hollow combine together (to ten)[60] to four, but only if what is standing is more than the hollow[61]. Rebbi Ze`ira asked, only if what is standing on each side is more? Rebbi Yose said, it is obvious for Rebbi Ze`ira that what is standing on one side only does not combine; it is obvious for him that (not)[62] one side must be more. He only questions even the second standing part[63].

59 This paragraph also is *Eruvin* 8 (Note 57, ז). The statement of R. Joḥanan also is quoted there in Chapter 1, Notes 178, 255, Chapter 7, Mote 44. Cf. Babli 99a.

60 This was written by the scribe both here and in the parallel and deleted both times. It is not written in the other quotes of R. Joḥanan. As explained in the next Note, one should follow S. Liebermann in treating the deletion as unnecessary.

61 This now refers to the second part of Mishnah 3 where it is stated that an elevated surface in the public domain, ten hand-breadths high and four-by-four wide, constitutes a separate private domain. It is now stated that it is not necessary that the entire surface be solid material; if one has two walls standing close together, not only may one add the surface areas of the two tops to satisfy the requirement of 16 (hand-breadths)^2, but one even may add the space between the two walls to the count. In the first formulation it only is required that the total solid surface area be larger than the hollow space added. This is the Babli's formulation of similar cases in *Eruvin*.

In this case it would seem that there be no occasion to mention "ten" since a wall cannot be built partially suspended without support. But the wall may be built partially solid and partially on thin pillars; this is the case considered frequently in *Eruvin* (e. g. Mishnah 1:9) and *Sukkah* (e. g. Mishnah 1:9). Therefore it is reasonable that the full text be quoted for the full statement but only the relevant statement about surface area when height is not considered a problem. Cf. Babli *Eruvin* 16a. The Yerushalmi clearly requires the solid part to be larger than the hollow.

62 Delete with the *Eruvin* text; the text here is a scribal error induced by the parallel preceding sentence.

63 First, and this easily is read into R. Johanan's statement, one really requires two walls with a hollow in between, not one almost sufficient wall to which one adds the hollow bordered by a virtual second side. In addition he requires that the surface area of the hollow be smaller than at least one of the solid surfaces. The only question is whether both bounding surfaces must be larger than the hollow part. In the latter case, the surface area of the hollow part must be strictly smaller than one-third of the total surface area.

(13a line 29) חוּלְיַת הַבּוֹר וְהַסֶּלַע שֶׁהֵן גְּבוֹהִין עֲשָׂרָה וּרְחָבִין אַרְבָּעָה. מָה אֲנַן קַיָּימִין. אִם בְּגָבְהָן עֲשָׂרָה (וּרְחָבָּן אַרְבָּעָה) רְשׁוּת בִּפְנֵי עַצְמָהּ הִיא. גְּבוֹהִין עֲשָׂרָה) וְאֵינָן רְחָבִין אַרְבָּעָה. הָדָא הִיא דְאָמַר רַב חִסְדָּא בְשֵׁם אִיסִי. קָנֶה נָעוּץ בִּרְשׁוּת הָרַבִּים גָּבוֹהַּ עֲשָׂרָה טְפָחִים מוּתָּר לְכָאן וּמוּתָּר לְכָאן בִּלְבַד שֶׁלֹּא יַחֲלִיף. אֶלָּא כֵן אֲנַן קַיָּימִין. בְּשֶׁאֵינָן לֹא רְחָבִים אַרְבָּעָה וְלֹא גְבוֹהִין עֲשָׂרָה. לֹא כֵן אָמַר חִייָה בְרֵיהּ דְּרַב. כָּל־הַמְעַכֵּב בִּרְשׁוּת הָרַבִּים נִקְרָא כַרְמְלִית. אָמַר רִבִּי יוּדָן. מַה דְּאָמַר חִייָה בְרֵיהּ דְּרַב. בָּאֶמְצַע. אֲבָל מִן הַצַּד רְשׁוּת הָרַבִּים מְבַטְלְתַהּ.

"The enclosure of a cistern or a rock[8] high ten [hand-breadths] and wide[9] four [hand-breadths]." Where do we hold[64]? If ten high (and four wide, it is a domain by itself. Ten high)[65] but not four wide, that is what Rav Ḥisda said in the name of Issi: If a stick stuck in the public domain ten hand-breadths high, it is permitted both ways; on condition that he not exchange[66]. But we must deal with the case that it is neither four wide nor ten high. But did not Ḥiyya, the son of Rav, say, anything which hinders access in the public domain is called *karmelit*[67]? Rebbi Yudan said, what Ḥiyya, the son of Rav, said refers to the middle[68], but on the side the public domain invalidates it[68].

64 This does not refer to the sentence quoted but to its sequel: "less than this he is not liable." The question is whether this means "less than 10 *or* less than 4" or "less than 10 *and* less than 4".

65 The text in parentheses was added by the corrector. As S. Liebermann has pointed out, this text is irrelevant for the topic here, it is a copy from Chapter 1, Notes 170-171.

66 Therefore the Mishnah should have said "permitted" instead of "not liable" which implies "prohibited but not prosecutable".

67 Again the Mishnah should have

mentioned "permitted".
68 Obviously one has to switch the places of "middle" and "on the side", Chapter 1

Note 73. A bump in the middle of the public domain is not *karmelit,* but remains part of the domain. Cf. Babli *Eruvin* 94a.

(13a line 38) אָמַר רִבִּי יוֹחָנָן. לֵית כָּאן פָּטוּר אֶלָּא מוּתָּר. תַּמָּן תַּנִּינָן. הַמֵּפִיס מוּרְסָא בַּשַּׁבָּת. אִם לַעֲשׂוֹת לָהּ פֶּה חַיָּב. אִם לְהוֹצִיא מִמֶּנָּה הַלֵּיחָה פָּטוּר. אָמַר רִבִּי יוֹחָנָן. לֵית כָּאן פָּטוּר אֶלָּא מוּתָּר. תַּמָּן תַּנִּינָן. הַצָּד נָחָשׁ בַּשַּׁבָּת. אִם בְּמִתְעַסֵּק שֶׁלֹּא יִשְׁכֶנּוּ פָּטוּר. אִם לִרְפוּאָה חַיָּב. אָמַר רִבִּי יוֹחָנָן. לֵית כָּאן פָּטוּר אֶלָּא מוּתָּר. וְעַל לַפָּסִין עִירוֹנִיּוֹת [אֲרוֹנִיּוֹת] שֶׁהֵן טְהוֹרוֹת בְּאֹהֶל הַמֵּת וּטְמֵאוֹת בְּמַשָּׂא הַזָּב. אָמַר רִבִּי זְעוּרָא. וְיֵאוּת. אִם לְצוֹרֶךְ. הָדָא דְּתַנִּינָן. אִם לִרְפוּאָה חַיָּב. הֱוֵי. לֵית כָּאן פָּטוּר אֶלָּא מוּתָּר.

Rebbi Johanan said, there is here no "not liable" but "permitted[69]." There[70], we have stated: "He who opens a boil on the Sabbath, if to make an opening he is liable, if to remove fluid he is not liable.[71]" Rebbi Johanan said, there is here no "not liable" but "permitted." There, we have stated: "One who catches a snake on the Sabbath, if he is active that it should not bite him he is not liable, if for medicine he is liable.[72]" Rebbi Johanan said, there is here no "not liable" but "permitted." There, we have stated: "About rural dishes[73] that they are pure in a tent with a corpse but impure if carried by a sufferer from gonorrhea.[74]" Rebbi Ze'ira said, this is correct. If for a need, that is what we have stated, "if for medicine he is liable." This implies that there is here no "not liable" but "permitted.[75]"

69 In the preceding discussion it was established that the Mishnah refers to a wall lower than ten and narrower than four hand-breadths which therefore is part of the public domain and the access to it is not restricted. The statements attributed here to R. Johanan are credited to Samuel in the Babli, 3a.
70 All the Mishnaiot quoted in the paragraph are from *Idiut* 2:5. The Mishnah lists three items about which R. Ismael said neither "permitted" nor "forbidden" and R. Matthew ben Harash explained that each one has an aspect which is permitted and one which is forbidden.
71 One who opens a boil on the Sabbath makes a wound, which is biblically forbidden. But if it is to remove the pus, the intent is not to make a wound, and following RR. Yose and Simeon there is no biblical prohibition (Chapter 2, Note 19). R. Johanan adds that in this case there is no rabbinic prohibition either.
72 If there is a danger to life it is imperative that the snake be either caught or killed. There is no guilt involved in catching the snake; the expression "not liable" only is used as opposite of "liable"

applicable if the snake is caught for the production of medicines.

73 Greek λοπάς, -άδος, ἡ "dish, frying pan".

The spelling עִירוֹנִיּוֹת is found only here; in the other quote of the Mishnah in the Yeruishalmi, Beṣah 4:3, and in the Mishnah mss. the spelling is as indicated here by the scribe himself in the margin אֲרוֹנִיּוֹת; in Babli Beṣah 32a חרניות "Hauran type vessels". It may not be derived from Mishnaic Hebrew עִיר "village" but Greek ἀρουραῖος, -α. -ov, "from the country, rustic" (E.G.).

74 Here the terms "not liable" and "liable" are not applicable; in a certain sense "permitted" (pure) and "forbidden" (impure) which were referred to in the introductory statement of the Mishnah are applicable. According to Rashi, Beṣah 32a, rural dishes are totally flat earthenware; according to Maimonides such a dish is formed as hollow ovaloid and after firing is sawed apart to produce two dishes. As long as it is not sawed apart it cannot become impure by the impurity of the dead which is inactive on tightly closed vessels or those which enclose no volume (Num. 19:15). Nevertheless it may become impure by being moved by a person whose impurity is caused by his own body.

75 This argument is extremely elliptic. The example of the snake shows that it is impossible to read "not liable" in the Mishnah in its usual sense, "forbidden but not prosecutable", as noted before. Also, in the last sentence, about rural dishes, "liable" and "not liable" are inapplicable. Therefore, also in the first case about the boil, where we have no corroborating evidence that opening it to remove the fluid is not forbidden rabbinically, by analogy one has to agree with R. Joḥanan that the act is permitted.

(13a line 45) ג'. מַתְנִיתִין בְּשֶׁאֵין שָׁם חוֹר. אֲבָל אִם יֵשׁ שָׁם חוֹר מַחְלוֹקֶת רִבִּי מֵאִיר וַחֲכָמִים. עַל דַּעְתֵּיהּ דְּרִבִּי מֵאִיר. בֵּין שֶׁיֵּשׁ בּוֹ אַרְבָּעָה עַל אַרְבָּעָה בֵּין שֶׁאֵין בּוֹ אַרְבָּעָה עַל אַרְבָּעָה אַתְּ רוֹאֶה אֶת הַכּוֹתֶל כְּנָמוּם. עַל דַּעְתּוֹן דְּרַבָּנָן. אִם יֵשׁ בּוֹ אַרְבָּעָה עַל אַרְבָּעָה אַתְּ רוֹאֶה אֶת הַכּוֹתֶל כְּנָמוּם. וְאִם לָאו אֵין אַתְּ רוֹאֶה אֶת הַכּוֹתֶל כְּנָמוּם אֶלָּא כְסָתוּם. רַב חִסְדָּא אָמַר. בְּמוֹדֵד לוּכְסוֹן. וְאֵין סוֹפָהּ לֵירֵד. רִבִּי חִייָה בְשֵׁם רִבִּי יוֹחָנָן. תִּיפְתָּר שֶׁהָיְתָה דְבִילָה שְׁמֵינָה וְהִיא נִיטוֹחָה. רִבִּי חַגַּי בָּעָא קוֹמֵי רִבִּי יוֹסֵה. לֵית הָדָא אָמְרָה שִׁיפּוּעַ מַדְרֵיגָה כְּלִמְטָן. אָמַר לֵיהּ. תַּמָּן זְרָעִים נֶהֱנִין מִן הַמַּדְרֵיגָה. בְּרַם הָכָא דֶּרֶךְ בְּנֵי אָדָם לִהְיוֹת שָׁפִין בָּהּ וְהִיא נוֹפֶלֶת. אִילּוּ אָמַר. כְּשֶׁהָיָה שָׁם חוֹר וְהִיא נֶהֱנִית מִן הַחוֹר כְּשֵׁם שֶׁהַזְּרָעִים נֶהֱנִין מִן הַמַּדְרֵיגָה. יָאוּת. רִבִּי יוֹסֵה רִבִּי אַבָּהוּ בְשֵׁם רִבִּי יוֹחָנָן. בְּשֶׁהָיָה הַמָּקוֹם מוּנְדָּרָן. כְּהָדָא דְתַנִּינָן. זָרַק חוּץ לְאַרְבַּע אַמּוֹת וְנִתְגַּלְגֵּל חוּץ לְאַרְבַּע אַמּוֹת חַייָב: אָתָא רִבִּי חִזְקִיָּה רִבִּי אַבָּהוּ בְשֵׁם רִבִּי יוֹחָנָן. וְהִיא שֶׁנָּחָה.

5 לוכסון | כ לכסן   חייה | כ חייא   6 בעא | כ בעי יוסה | כ יוסי מדריגה | כ המדריגה זרעים | כ זרעין   8 כשהיה | כ בשהיה נהנית | כ נהנה שהזרעים | כ נהנה שהזרעין

3.⁷⁶ Our Mishnah applies if there is no hole there, but if there is a hole, there is the disagreement between Rebbi Meïr and the rabbis. In the opinion of Rebbi Meïr, whether it is four by four or it is not four by four one considers the wall as carved out⁷⁷. In the rabbis' opinion, if it is four by four one considers the wall as carved out, otherwise one does not consider the wall as carved out but as closed. ⁷⁸Rav Hisda said, if it extends⁷⁹ slanting⁸⁰. But will it not finally descend? Rebbi Hiyya in the name of Rebbi Johanan, explain it that it was a soft fig cake and it stuck⁸¹. Rebbi Haggai asked before Rebbi Yose, does this not imply that the declivity of a terrace belongs to the level below⁸²? He said to him, there the vegetables profit from the terrace but here people rub it and it falls down. If it would say, if there is a hole [in the wall] and it profits from the hole just as vegetables profit from the terrace, you would be justified.

Rebbi Yose, Rebbi Abbahu in the name of Rebbi Johanan: If the place was inclined, as we have stated, "one who threw more than four cubits and it rolled beyond⁸³ four cubits is liable." There came Rebbi Hizqiah, Rebbi Abbahu in the name of Rebbi Johanan, only if it came to rest⁸⁴.

76 Here begins discussion of Mishnah 4.

77 The Mishnah implies that one may throw an object against a wall and it stays there. This is possible in two cases. Either the wall has a cavity where the object may come to rest or the object is sticky and clings at least temporarily to a vertical wall. The first alternative is discussed first.

R. Meïr does not consider a hole which is a defect in the wall but one built into the wall as a window, where the wind may enter the house, which presents a narrow slit to the outside but is wide inside. If the width at the other end of the wall is 4 hand-breadths, he completes the trapezoidal shape of the base of the opening to a rectangle to which the rules of private domain do apply. The rabbis reject theoretical extensions of domains. Cf. Tosephta 10:9 (ed. Liebermann).

78 From here on to the end of this paragraph the text is from *Kilaim* 6:2, Notes 32-34, כ.

79 Taking מדד not as Biblical Hebrew "to measure", but from Arabic مدّ. مدد "to extend, to rise". R. Hisda's problem is that nothing can stop on a vertical wall. The same answer is given by R. Hisda's student and son-in-law Rava in Babli *Šabbat* 5b, the material there being sheets of paper or parchment. Since the word is spelled identically both times, the likelihood of a scribal error is very small; the emendation of מדד to מורד proposed by the classical commentators and accepted by the editor of the ms. should be rejected.

80 Greek λοξός, -ή, -όν, *adj.*, "slanting, crosswise".
81 The same answer is given by R. Joḥanan himself in Babli *Šabbat* 7b, 100 a.
82 R. Ḥaggai refers to Mishnah *Kilaim* 6:2 where different crops on terraces one on top of the other are permitted only if the step between terraces is at least 10 handbreadths. He assumes that the reason one insists on a separation of 10 hand·breadths is the same for the rules of the Sabbath and of *kilaim*. In that case, the Mishnah in *Kilaim* seems to extend the reach of any "bottom" upwards to 10 hand- breadths. He is answered that plants may grow on a slanted wall but anything sticking to the lower part of any wall bordering the public domain will be rubbed off; the fig cake cannot be considered to be at rest at such a place. The Babli (*Sabbat* 100a) disagrees with R. Yose and points out that even if a Tannaitic statement such as suggested by him did exist, it would not prove anything since R. Meïr [here and Yerushalmi *Eruvin* 10 (Note 122); Babli *Šabbat* 7b, 100a, *Eruvin* 11b, 33b, 101b, Yoma 11b] considers any depression a separate domain excluded from exempt space.
83 This obviously is a misquote.
84 There is no liability unless the object came to rest since it might either roll back into 4 cubits from its starting point or end up in *karmelit*. Babli 100a.

(13a line 59) ד'. לֹא סוֹף דָּבָר אַרְבַּע אַמּוֹת בַּיָּם. אֶלָּא אֲפִילוּ זָרַק בְּכָל־הַיָּם פָּטוּר. שֶׁכָּל־הַיָּם נִקְרָא כַּרְמְלִית.

וְלָמָּה תְּנִינָתָהּ תְּרֵין זִימְנִין. רִבִּי חֲנַנְיָה בְשֵׁם רִבִּי פִּינְחָס. בְּשֶׁהָיוּ שְׁנֵי רְקָקִים. אֶחָד הָרַבִּים מְהַלְּכִין בּוֹ וְאֶחָד אֵין הָרַבִּים מְהַלְּכִין בּוֹ אֶלָּא כְשֶׁהֵן נִדְחָקִין. שֶׁלֹּא תֹאמַר. הוֹאִיל וְאֵין הָרַבִּים מְהַלְּכִין בּוֹ אֶלָּא כְשֶׁהֵן נִדְחָקִין אֵינוֹ רְשׁוּת הָרַבִּים אֶלָּא רְשׁוּת הַיָּחִיד. לְפוּם כָּךְ צָרַךְ מֵימַר. רְשׁוּת הָרַבִּים הוּא.

4[85]. Not only four cubits in the sea, but even if he threw across the entire sea he is not liable, since any sea is called *karmelit*.

And why was it stated twice[86]? Rebbi Ḥananiah in the name of Rebbi Phineas, if there were two shallows, one which was used as a thoroughfare and one used by the public only in case of emergency. That you should not say, since the public are using it only in case of emergency it is not public domain but private domain[87], therefore it was necessary to say that it is public domain.

85 Here starts discussion of Mishnah 5.
86 Where is the need for the wordiness of the Mishnah and the repetitous treatment of shallows? A different answer, referring to river fords, in the Babli 100b.
87 Clearly this should be "*karmelit*".

(13a line 65) ה'. אַבָּא בַּר רַב חוּנָא אָמַר. בִּקְשׁוּרוֹת בְּגֶמִי. רִבִּי יוֹסֵי בֵּירִבִּי בּוּן אָמַר. וְהֵן שֶׁעֵירִיבוּ. רִבִּי חִיָּיה רִבִּי אִימִּי תְּרֵיהוֹן בְּשֵׁם רִבִּי לֶעְזָר. חַד אָמַר. בְּשֶׁאֵין בֵּינֵיהֶן רוֹחַב אַרְבַּע. וְחוֹרָנָה אָמַר. אֲפִילוּ יֵשׁ בֵּינֵיהֶן רוֹחַב אַרְבַּע. וְלָא יָדְעִין מָאן אֲמַר דָּא וּמָאן אֲמַר דָּא. מִן מַה דְאָמַר רִבִּי יוֹסֵה רִבִּי יַעֲקֹב בַּר זַבְדִּי רִבִּי חִיָּיה בְּשֵׁם רִבִּי אֶלְעָזָר. אֲפִילוּ אֵינָן גְּבוֹהוֹת עֲשָׂרָה. הֱוֵי דוּ אָמַר. בְּשֶׁאֵין בֵּינֵיהֶן רוֹחַב אַרְבָּעָה.

הֲווֹן בָּעֵי מֵימַר. מָאן דְּאָמַר. בְּשֶׁאֵין בֵּינֵיהֶן רוֹחַב אַרְבָּעָה אֲפִילוּ אֵינָן גְּבוֹהוֹת עֲשָׂרָה. מָאן דְּאָמַר. גְּבוֹהוֹת עֲשָׂרָה אֲפִילוּ יֵשׁ בֵּינֵיהֶן רוֹחַב אַרְבַּע. אָמַר רִבִּי חֲנַנְיָה בְּרֵיהּ דְּרִבִּי הִילֵּל. וְהוּא שֶׁיְּהֵא כָל־אֲוֵיר כַּרְמְלִית בְּתוֹךְ עֲשָׂרָה.

5[88]. Abba bar Rav Huna said, it they are tied together with bast[89]. Rebbi Yose ben Rebbi Abun said, only if they made an *eruv*[90]. Rebbi Ḥiyya, Rebbi Immi, both in the name of Rebbi Eleazar. One said, if the distance between them is less than four[91]; but the other said, even if the distance between them is four[91]. We did not know who said what. Since Rebbi Yose, Rebbi Jacob bar Zavdi, Rebbi Ḥiyya said in the name of Rebbi Eleazar, even if they are not ten [hand-breadths] high, it is he who said, if the distance between them is less than four [hand-breadths][92].

They wanted to say, he who said, if the distance between them is less than four [hand-breadths], even if they are not ten [hand-breadths] high. He who said, if they are ten [hand-breadths] high, even if the distance between them is four[93]. Rebbi Ḥananiah the son of Rebbi Hillel said, only if the airspace of *karmelit* be within ten [hand-breadths][94].

88 Here starts discussion of Mishnah 6, starting with the second sentence.
89 Even if the tie-up of flimsy material. Babli 100b, statement of Rav Huna.
90 A symbolic mixing of food from both ships, following the rules of *eruv* applying if different dwellers share an apartment building or a courtyard common to several single family houses, as explained in Tractate *Eruvin*. Ships tied together are considered the equivalent of apartments occupied by different people in the same house.
91 While the numerals here are in the feminine and represent cubits, they should be read in the masculine and represent handbreadths.
92 Since no space less than four hand-breadths wide can define a separate domain, the two ships form one private domain. If the distance is at least four hand-breadths, they are separated by *karmelit*.
93 If the decks of the ships are not ten hand-breadths above the surface of the water, one may move objects from one to the other only if they form a single domain as explained in the preceding Note. If the decks are higher than 10 hand-breadths, any

traffic between the ships would be through exempt space since *karmelit* as derivative of the public domain also extends only up to 10 hand-breadths above the ground.

94 The remainder is exempt space.

(13a line 75) סְפִינָה שֶׁבַּיָּם גְּבוֹהָה עֲשָׂרָה טְפָחִים אֵין מְטַלְטְלִין לַיָּם וְלֹא מִן הַיָּם לְתוֹכָהּ. רִבִּי יְהוּדָה אוֹמֵר. אִם הָיְתָה עֲמוּקָה מִן הַמַּיִם עֲשָׂרָה טְפָחִים וְאֵינָהּ גְּבוֹהָה מִן הַמַּיִם עֲשָׂרָה טְפָחִים מְטַלְטְלִין מִתּוֹכָהּ לַיָּם. אֲבָל לֹא מִן הַיָּם לְתוֹכָהּ. רִבִּי אַבָּהוּ אָמַר. רִבִּי יוֹחָנָן בָּעֵי. וְלָמָּה מִתּוֹכָהּ לַיָּם מוּתָּר. מִפְּנֵי שֶׁאֵינָהּ גְּבוֹהָה עֲשָׂרָה. אֵין כֵּינִי. אֲפִילוּ מִן הַיָּם לְתוֹכָהּ. וְלָמָּה מִן הַיָּם לְתוֹכָהּ אָסוּר. מִפְּנֵי שֶׁהִיא עֲמוּקָה עֲשָׂרָה. אֵין כֵּינִי. אֲפִילוּ מִתּוֹכָהּ לַיָּם. אָמַר רִבִּי אָבוּן. וְלָמָּה מִתּוֹכָהּ לַיָּם מוּתָּר. מִפְּנֵי סַכָּנָה.

סֶלַע שֶׁבַּיָּם גָּבוֹהַּ עֲשָׂרָה טְפָחִים אֵין מְטַלְטְלִין לַיָּם וְלֹא מִן הַיָּם לְתוֹכָהּ. פָּחוּת מִכֵּן מוּתָּר. מַה בֵּין סֶלַע וּמַה בֵּין סְפִינָה. סְפִינָה עוֹלָה וְיוֹרֶדֶת. סֶלַע בִּמְקוֹמָהּ הִיא. וְלֹא כַרְמְלִית הִיא. כְּלוּם הוּא מוּתָּר לְטַלְטֵל בְּכַרְמְלִית אֶלָּא בְאַרְבַּע אַמּוֹת. אָמַר רִבִּי אִילָא. עַל רֹאשָׁהּ. סֶלַע שֶׁבַּיָּם גָּבוֹהַּ עֲשָׂרָה טְפָחִים אֵין מְטַלְטְלִין מִתּוֹכָהּ לַיָּם וְלֹא מִן הַיָּם לְתוֹכָהּ. יוֹתֵר מִכֵּן נַעֲשִׂית כִּמְחִיצָה שֶׁהוּקְפָה זְרָעִים שֶׁאֵין מוּתָּר לְטַלְטֵל בָּהּ אֶלָּא בְאַרְבַּע אַמּוֹת. פָּחוּת מִכֵּן מְטַלְטְלִין מִתּוֹכָהּ לַיָּם וּמִן הַיָּם לְתוֹכָהּ וּמְטַלְטְלִין בָּהּ עַד בֵּית סָאתַיִם. רִבִּי בּוּן בַּר חִיָּיה בָּעֵי. מֵעַתָּה שְׁתֵּי כַרְמְלִיּוֹת סְמוּכוֹת זוֹ לְזוֹ מְטַלְטְלִין מִזּוֹ לְזוֹ. אָמַר רִבִּי חֲנַנְיָה בְרֵיהּ דְּרִבִּי הִלֵּל. מִכֵּיוָן שֶׁהַיָּם מַקִּיפָהּ מִכָּל־צַד כְּמִי שֶׁכּוּלָּהּ כַּרְמְלִית אַחַת.

[95]"From a ship in the sea higher than ten hand-breadths one moves neither from it to the sea nor from the sea into it. Rebbi Jehudah says, if its draught was more than ten hand-breadths but it does not extend higher than ten hand-breadths above the water one moves from it to the sea but not from the sea into it." Rebbi Abbahu said that Rebbi Johanan asked, why from it to the sea? Because it is not ten high. If it is so, even from the sea into it! Why from the sea into it is forbidden? Because it is ten deep. If it is so, even from it to the sea! Rebbi Abun said, why is it permitted from it to the sea? Because of danger[96].

From a rock in the sea higher than ten hand-breadths[97] one transports neither from it to the sea nor from the sea onto it. If it was less than this it is permitted. What is the difference between a rock and a ship? A ship rises and falls[98]; a rock stays in its place. But is it not *karmelit*? Is it permitted to move on *karmelit* only four cubits? Rebbi Ila said, it refers to the beginning: "from a rock in the sea higher than ten hand-breadths one moves neither from it to the sea nor from the sea onto it.[99]" If it was higher it becomes like a fence made for agriculture where inside one is permitted to transport only four cubits[100]. If it was lower one transports from it to the sea and from the sea onto it, and one transports up to two *bet se'ah*[101]. Rebbi Abun bar Ḥiyya asked, two adjacent *karmeliot*, may one transport from one to the other[102]? Rebbi Ḥananiah the son of Rebbi Hillel said, since the sea surrounds it from all sides it is considered as a single *karmelit*[103].

95 Tosephta 10:14 (ed. Liebermann).

96 It is true that the rules are inconsistent but pumping water from the wooden ship back into the ocean is necessary to protect the lives of the people on the ship, and cannot be forbidden. Since the sea is *karmelit*, the prohibitions are rabbinical and therefore it is reasonable to permit all transport from ship to sea.

97 This becomes a separate domain and transports from it to its surroundings are at least rabbinically forbidden. It is presumed that there be no dwelling (such as a light house) on the rock since a dwelling would make the rock an unrestricted private domain.

98 Therefore it may sometimes be higher and sometimes lower than ten hand-breadths.

99 In the opinion of S. Liebermann, one has to add here the statement that on a rock *higher* than ten hand-breadths above the sea one may carry without restriction only if its surface area does not extend over more than two *bet se'ah*.

A private domain either is for human dwelling when its size is not limited, or it is a corral for animals which is treated as private domain only up to the area for which two *se'ah* of seed grain are needed, standardized as 5'000 square cubits (cf. *Kilaim* Chapter 1, Note 195), the size of the enclosed area of the Tabernacle.

100 A field reserved for agricultural use cannot be a private domain. It is asserted here that a barren rock has the same status, but this contradicts all previous and following statements. The sentence should be deleted...

101 As noted before, this clause must refer to a rock higher than 10 hand-breadths without a human dwelling. Babli *Eruvin* 67b.

102 Since the sea is *karmelit* and so is the rock which is less than ten hand-breadths high, does this prove that transporting between two distinct *karmelit* domains is not rabbinically restricted?

103 The low rock is part of the sea for the rules of the Sabbath. It seems that this implies that transporting between two distinct *karmelit* domains is prohibited. While this is not found in the Babli, it is asserted by R. Hananel *ad* 100b, also quoted in Raviah §233 (p. 323, n. 24; cf. the sources quoted there).

(13b line 19) רַב הַמְנוּנָא אָמַר. נֶסֶר שֶׁהוּא חוּץ לַסְפִינָה וְאֵין בּוֹ רוֹחַב אַרְבַּע מוּתָּר לֵישֵׁב בּוֹ וְלַעֲשׂוֹת צְרָכָיו בַּשַּׁבָּת. אָמַר רִבִּי מָנָא. אִילּוּ אָמַר. תֵּיבָה פְתוּחָה. יֵאוּת. אָמַר רִבִּי אָבוּן. מָאן

דְּבָעֵי מֵיעֲבַד תַּקָּנָה לְאִילְפָא. מוֹצִיא נֶסֶר חוּץ לִשְׁלשָׁה שֶׁאֵין בּוֹ רוֹחַב אַרְבָּעָה וְאַתְּ רוֹאֶה אֶת הַמְּחִיצוֹת כְּאִילוּ עוֹלוֹת. רִבִּי יַעֲקֹב בַּר אָחָא בְּשֵׁם רַב הַמְנוּנָא. שֶׁכָּל־שְׁלשָׁה וּשְׁלשָׁה שֶׁהֵן סְמוּכִין לַמְּחִיצָה כִּמְחִיצָה הֵן. רִבִּי יִצְחָק בֵּירִבִּי אֶלְעָזָר מְפַקֵּד לְרִבִּי הוֹשַׁעְיָא בֵּירִבִּי שַׁמַּי דַּהֲוָה פָּרִישׁ. מֵיעֲבַד לֵיהּ סַל פָּחוּת.

Rav Hamnuna said, on a board outside the ship which is not four[91] wide one may sit and provide for his needs[104] on the Sabbath. Rebbi Mana said, if he had said an open box it would have been correct[105]. Rebbi Abun said, one who wants to provide for a boat makes outside of three [hand-breadths] a plank which is not four [hand-breadths] wide and one considers it as if partitions rose. [106]Rebbi Jacob bar Aḥa in the name of Rav Hamnuna: Because any three [hand-breadths] which are close to a partition are as if of the partition[107]. Rebbi Isaac ben Rebbi Eleazar commanded Rebbi Hoshaia ben Rebbi Shammai, who was a mariner, to make for himself a deficient container[108].

104 Usually this means, to relieve himself. It is assumed that the deck of the ship is at least 10 hand-breadths high, which makes it a private domain. In the parallel of Babli 100b, the question is of drawing water from the river.

105 To provide some privacy.

106 In the medieval quotes of this passage (Nahmanides and Rashba *ad* 100b) this is part of the preceding : "for R. Jacob bar Aḥa said in the name of Rav Hamnuna."

107 This is a general principle accepted in both Talmudim. For example, a *sukkah* must have walls. It is completely acceptable that the walls be planks fixed to poles; between the planks and between the highest plank and the roof there may be spaces of up to three hand-breadths width.

R. Abun recommends making an outhouse outside the ship but close enough so that it be counted as part of the private domain defined by the deck.

108 The quote in *Sefer Ha`ittim* p. 53 switches the adjectives פְּתוּחָה, פְּחוּתָה between box and container. The reading of the ms. is confirmed by Nahmanides and Rashba.

(13b line 27) ו'. כֵּינִי מַתְנִיתָא. וְהֵזִיד. וְקַשְׁיָא. אִילוּ יָרָה חֵץ לַהֲרוֹג בּוֹ אֶת הַנֶּפֶשׁ וְהִתְרוּ בּוֹ וְחָזַר בּוֹ. שֶׁמָּא כְּלוּם הוּא. הֱוֵי סוֹפָךְ מֵימַר. וְהֵזִיד.

רִבִּי יוֹסֵי בֶּן חֲנִינָה אָמַר. בְּשׁוֹגֵג בְּלֹא תַעֲשֶׂה. וּבְמֵזִיד בְּלֹא תַעֲשֶׂה. רִבִּי יְהוֹשֻׁעַ בֶּן לֵוִי אָמַר. בְּשׁוֹגֵג בְּהִיכָּרֵת. וּבְמֵזִיד בְּהִיכָּרֵת. תַּנֵּי רִבִּי שִׁמְעוֹן בֶּן יוֹחַי מְסַייֵעַ לְרִבִּי יְהוֹשֻׁעַ בֶּן לֵוִי. אֶת־יְ"יָ הוּא מְגַדֵּף וְנִכְרְתָה. הַגַּע עַצְמָךְ. אֲפִילוּ מֵזִיד בְּהִיכָּרֵת מַתְרִין בּוֹ וְלוֹקֶה וּמֵבִיא קָרְבָּן. רִבִּי אַבָּהוּ בְּשֵׁם רִבִּי יוֹחָנָן. הַשּׁוֹגֵג בְּחֵלֶב וּמֵזִיד בַּחַטָּאת מַתְרִין בּוֹ וְלוֹקֶה וּמֵבִיא קָרְבָּן.

תַּנֵּי. אֵין מִתְעַסְּקִין לֹא בַחֲלָבִים וְלֹא בָעֲרָיוֹת. הַמִּתְעַסֵּק בַּשַּׁבָּת פָּטוּר. בַּחֲלָבִים וּבָעֲרָיוֹת חַיָּיב. הֵיךְ עֲבִידָא. אָמַר. הֲרֵי אֲנִי קוֹצֵר חֲצִי גְרוֹגֶרֶת. וְקָצַר כִּגְרוֹגֶרֶת פָּטוּר. הֲרֵי אֲנִי אוֹכֵל חֲצִי זַיִת. וְאָכַל כְּזַיִת חַיָּיב. הֲרֵי אֲנִי מִתְחַמֵּם בָּהּ. וְהֶעֱרָה בָהּ חַיָּיב.

6[109] So is the Mishnah: "he acted intentionally.[110]" This is difficult. If somebody shot an arrow intending to kill a person, he was warned, and changed his intention; is that anything[111]? Finally you have to say that it was intentional[112].

Rebbi Yose ben Ḥanina said, unintentionally a prohibition, intentionally a prohibition[113]. Rebbi Joshua ben Levi said, unintentionally extirpation, intentionally extirpation[114]. Rebbi Simeon ben Yoḥai stated, a support of Rebbi Joshua ben Levi: *He blasphemes the Eternal and will be extirpated*[115]. Think of it; even if he was intentional in a matter of extirpation and he was warned and is being flogged, may he bring a sacrifice[116]? Rebbi Abbahu in the name of Rebbi Joḥanan: If he was unintentional about fat but intentional about the purification sacrifice one warns him and he is flogged[117].

It was stated: One experiments[118] neither with fat nor with incest or adultery. One who experiments on the Sabbath is not liable, with fat or with incest or adultery is liable. How is this? If he said, "am going to harvest the volume half of a dried fig" and then he harvested the volume of a dried fig, he is not liable. "I am going to eat half the volume of an olive" and ate the volume of an olive; he is liable. "I am going to arouse myself by her" and then touched her[119]; he is liable.

109 Here starts discussion of Mishnah 9.
110 After he realized that it was the Sabbath and that his throwing was a Sabbath violation he did not regret having thrown the object.
111 The sequence in the question is not quite correct. A person was warned not to shoot another (a requirement for future prosecution), nevertheless he shot but while the arrow was in the air he regretted the act. The fact that his victim was killed when he no longer wished to kill him does not shield the perpetrator from prosecution and conviction. In the case of the Mishnah, one cannot see what influence a temporary consciousness of the criminality of the deed should have on the legal status of the act.
112 Therefore one has to agree with the correction, that after the person realized that he was throwing on the Sabbath he was satisfied with what he had done, and an act which is started in oblivion but completed in consciousness cannot be atoned for by a sacrifice.

113 In his opinion, only if both the unintentional and the intentional acts are forbidden as simple prohibitions is there no liability for a purification sacrifice, but if the unintentional act is under a simple prohibition and the intentional is a deadly sin punishable by extirpation a sacrifice is due. This opinion is not otherwise found in the Talmudim.

114 This is the standard opinion, that a sacrifice is due only for sins for which the punishment is extirpation at least, and only if it was unintentional from beginning to end ('Babli 68b/69a, *Yebamot* 9a, *Horaiot* 8a, *Ševuot* 32b).

115 *Num.* 15:31; the basic text which bars the intentional sinner from offering a purification sacrifice. The quote clearly is elliptic; in *Sifry Num.* 112 the restriction to sins punishable at least with extirpation is stated in the name of R. Aqiba.

116 If the sin was under a simple prohibition if unintentional but subjects the perpetrator to extirpartion if intentional, if the act was prosecutable, he was flogged, and therefore is no longer subject to extirpation (Mishnah *Makkot* 3:17), should he still be liable for a sacrifice for the simple prohibition involved? This we never heard; therefore the position of R. Yose ben Ḥanina is untenable.

117 This sentence must read: Rebbi Abbahu in the name of Rebbi Johanan: If he was *intentional* about fat but *unintentional* about the purification sacrifice one warns him and he is flogged (*Terumot* 6:1, Notes 5,6; *Bava qamma* 7:3, Note 29, *Ševuot* 3:1, Note 9).

118 One acts without a particular aim.

119 His genitals touched the forbidden female's genitals (*Yebamot* 4:2 Note 59, 6:1 Note 11).

הבונה פרק שנים עשר

(fol. 13b) **משנה א**: הַבּוֹנֶה כַּמָּה יִבְנֶה וִיהֵא חַיָּב. הַבּוֹנֶה כָּל־שֶׁהוּא. הַמְסַתֵּת וְהַמַּכֶּה בַפַּטִּישׁ וּבַמַּעֲצָד הַקּוֹדֵחַ כָּל־שֶׁהוּא חַיָּב. זֶה הַכְּלָל כָּל־הָעוֹשֶׂה מְלָאכָה וּמְלַאכְתּוֹ מִתְקַיֶּימֶת בַּשַּׁבָּת חַיָּב. רַבָּן שִׁמְעוֹן בֶּן גַּמְלִיאֵל אוֹמֵר אַף הַמַּכֶּה בַקּוּרְנָס עַל הַסַּדָּן בִּשְׁעַת מְלָאכָה חַיָּב מִפְּנֵי שֶׁהוּא כִּמְתַקֵּן מְלָאכָה:

Mishnah 1: How much would a builder build to become liable? One who builds anything. One who chisels stone, and one who hits with a hammer or a hatchet[1], or who drills anything is liable. This is the principle: Anybody who performs work on the Sabbath and whose work has permanence is liable. Rabban Simeon ben Gamliel says, also one who hits with the back of his hammer on the anvil during work is liable because he improves the work[2].

משנה ב: הַחוֹרֵשׁ כָּל־שֶׁהוּא הַמְנַכֵּשׁ וְהַמְקַרְסֵם וְהַמְזָרֵד כָּל־שֶׁהוּא חַיָּב. הַמְלַקֵּט עֵצִים לְתַקֵּן כָּל־שֶׁהֵן. אִם לְהַסִּיק כְּדֵי לְבַשֵּׁל בֵּיצָה קַלָּה. הַמְלַקֵּט עֲשָׂבִים לְתַקֵּן כָּל־שֶׁהֵן אִם לִבְהֵמָה כִּמְלֹא פִי גְדִי:

Mishnah 2: He who ploughs any amount, who weeds, who prunes, or who thins[3] anything is liable. One who collects wood, if to improve in any amount, or if as firewood to cook an easily cooked egg[4]. One who collects grasses, if to improve in any amount, if for animals to fill a kid goat's mouth[4].

משנה ג: הַכּוֹתֵב שְׁתֵּי אוֹתִיּוֹת בֵּין בִּימִינוֹ בֵּין בִּשְׂמֹאלוֹ בֵּין מִשֵּׁם אֶחָד בֵּין מִשְּׁנֵי שֵׁמוֹת בֵּין מִשְּׁנֵי סִימָנִיּוֹת בְּכָל־לָשׁוֹן חַיָּב. אָמַר רַבִּי יוֹסֵי לֹא נִתְחַיְּיבוּ שְׁתֵּי אוֹתִיּוֹת אֶלָּא מִשּׁוּם רֹשֶׁם שֶׁכָּךְ הָיוּ רוֹשְׁמִין עַל קַרְשֵׁי הַמִּשְׁכָּן לֵידַע אֵי זֶהוּ בֶן זוּגוֹ. אָמַר רַבִּי יְהוּדָה מָצִינוּ שֵׁם קָטָן מִשֵּׁם גָּדוֹל שֵׁם מִשִּׁמְעוֹן וּמִשְּׁמוּאֵל נֹחַ מִנָּחוֹר. דָּן מִדָּנִיֵּאל גָּד מִגַּדִּיאֵל:

Mishnah 3: One who writes two letters is liable, whether with his right hand, or with his left hand[5], whether of one denomination or of two denominations[6], whether two signs of any language[7]. Rebbi Yose said, two letters create liability only as signs since they were making signs on the planks to know which belongs to which[8]. Rebbi Jehudah said, we find a short name from a long name, Sem from Simeon, Noah fron Naḥor, Dan from Daniel, Gad from Gadiel[9].

משנה ד: הַכּוֹתֵב שְׁתֵּי אוֹתִיּוֹת בְּהֶעְלֵם אֶחָד חַיָּב. כָּתַב בִּדְיוֹ בְּסַם בְּסִיקְרָא בְּקוֹמוֹס וּבְקַלְקַנְתּוֹם וּבְכָל־דָּבָר שֶׁהוּא רוֹשֵׁם עַל שְׁנֵי כוֹתְלֵי הַבַּיִת וְעַל שְׁנֵי דַפֵּי פִנְקָס וְהֵן נֶהְגִּין זֶה עִם זֶה חַיָּב. הַכּוֹתֵב עַל בְּשָׂרוֹ חַיָּב. וְהַמְסָרֵט עַל בְּשָׂרוֹ רַבִּי אֱלִיעֶזֶר מְחַיֵּב חַטָּאת וְרַבִּי יְהוֹשֻׁעַ פּוֹטֵר:

Mishnah 4: One who writes two letters in one oblivion is liable. He is liable if he wrote in ink, by chemicals[10], in vermilion, with gum[11], with vitriol of copper[12], with anything which leaves a record, on two walls of a house or two leaves of a wooden book[13] if they can be read together. One who writes on his body is liable. If he scratches[14] on his flesh, Rebbi Eliezer declares him liable but Rebbi Joshua declares him not liable.

משנה ה: כָּתַב בְּמֵי מַשְׁקִין בְּמֵי פֵירוֹת בַּאֲבַק דְּרָכִים בַּאֲבַק סוֹפְרִים וּבְכָל־דָּבָר שֶׁאֵינוֹ מִתְקַיֵּם פָּטוּר. לְאַחַר יָדוֹ בְּרַגְלוֹ בְּפִיו וּבְמַרְפֵּקוֹ. כָּתַב אוֹת אַחַת סָמוּךְ לַכְּתָב כָּתַב עַל גַּבֵּי כְתָב נִתְכַּוֵּן לִכְתּוֹב חֵית וְכָתַב שְׁנֵי זַיִנִין אֶחָד בָּאָרֶץ וְאֶחָד בַּקּוֹרָה עַל שְׁנֵי כוֹתְלֵי הַבַּיִת עַל שְׁנֵי דַפֵּי פִנְקָס וְאֵין נֶהְגִּין זֶה עִם זֶה פָּטוּר. כָּתַב אוֹת אַחַת נוֹטָרִיקוֹן רַבִּי יְהוֹשֻׁעַ בֶּן בְּתֵירָא מְחַיֵּב וַחֲכָמִים פּוֹטְרִין:

Mishnah 5: If he wrote with fluid of drinks, with fruit juice[15], with road dust, with scribe's dust, or with anything which is not permanent, he is not liable. With the back of his hand, with his foot, with his mouth, with his elbow[16]; if he wrote one letter adjacent to existing writing[17], wrote over existing writing, intended to write ח and wrote זז[18], one on the ground and one on a beam[19], on two walls of a house or two leaves of a wooden tablet if they cannot be read together, he is not liable. If he wrote one letter as abbreviation[20], Rebbi Joshua ben Bathyra declares liable but the Sages declare not liable.

משנה ו: הַכּוֹתֵב שְׁתֵּי אוֹתִיּוֹת בִּשְׁנֵי הֶעְלֵימוֹת אֶחָד שַׁחֲרִית וְאֶחָד בֵּין הָעַרְבַּיִם רַבָּן גַּמְלִיאֵל מְחַיֵּב וַחֲכָמִים פּוֹטְרִין:

Mishnah 6: One who wrote two letters in two periods of oblivion, one in the morning and one in the evening, Rabban Gamliel declares liable but the Sages declare not liable.

1 This one does not produce anything, but simply marks the end of the production process; cf. Chapter 7, Note 7.	2 A smith is used to hit also on an empty anvil to keep up the rhythm of his work. For the word קורנס cf. *Avodah zarah* Chapter 4,

Note 58.
3 Pruning is of last year's growth, thinning is from new growth.
4 One has to add, "is liable". An easily cooked egg is a chicken egg.
5 Even though the person is right handed it is not too difficult for him to write with his left hand.
6 The same letter twice or two different letters.
7 In any alphabet, not necessarily Hebrew.
8 Any sign (Greek σημεῖον, τό) which can be used to identify an object he considers to be the equivalent of a letter.
9 In his opinion, only combinations of letters which make sense are counted as writing.
10 According to Rashi yellow arsenic, according to Maimonides any coloring derived from roots.
11 Greek κόμμι, τό.
12 Greek χάλκανθος, ὁ,ἡ.
13 Greek πίναξ,-ακος, ὁ.

14 Without drawing blood, which would be a Sabbath violation of a different category.
15 A drink close to colorless.
16 The kinds of writing are too unusual; they cannot be classified as work.
17 Even though now a word can be read that did not exist before, the minimum for liability is two letters.
18 Since he intended to write one letter only, there can be no liability since the criminal intent was missing (Chapter 1, Note 52).
19 One letter is static, the other may be removed with the beam. This case is parallel to the one where one writes one letter each on walls in different rooms, which cannot be read together at one time.
20 Even though the letter is read as a word, it is only one letter. Writing shorthand in abbreviation was the principle of *Tironian notes*. Latin *scribere per notas* really means writing in cipher.

(13c line 3) הַבּוֹנֶה כַּמָּה יִבְנֶה וִיהֵא חַיָּיב כול׳. מַה בִּנְיָין הָיָה בַּמִּשְׁכָּן. שֶׁהָיוּ נוֹתְנִין קְרָשִׁים עַל גַּבֵּי אֲדָנִים. וְלֹא לְשָׁעָה הֱיָתָה. אָמַר רִבִּי יוֹסֵה. מִכֵּיוָן שֶׁהָיוּ נוֹסְעִים וְחוֹנִים עַל פִּי הַדִּיבֵּר כְּמִי שֶׁהוּא לְעוֹלָם. אָמַר רִבִּי יוֹסֵי בֵּירִבִּי בּוּן. מִכֵּיוָן שֶׁהִבְטִיחָן הַקָּדוֹשׁ בָּרוּךְ הוּא שֶׁהוּא מַכְנִיסָן לָאָרֶץ כְּמִי שֶׁהוּא לְעוֹלָם. הָדָא אָמְרָה. אֲפִילוּ מִן הַצַּד. הָדָא אָמְרָה. אֲפִילוּ נָתוּן עַל גַּבֵּי דָּבָר אַחֵר. הָדָא אָמְרָה. בִּינְיָין עַל גַּבֵּי כֵלִים בִּינְיָין. אֲדָנִים בַּקַּרְקַע הֵן.

תַּנֵּי. אֶחָד מֵבִיא אֶת הָאֶבֶן וְאֶחָד מֵבִיא אֶת הַטִּיט. הַמֵּבִיא אֶת הַטִּיט חַיָּיב. רִבִּי יוֹסֵה אוֹמֵר. שְׁנֵיהֶן חַיָּיבִין. סָבַר רִבִּי יוֹסֵי. אֶבֶן בְּלֹא טִיט בִּנְיָין. הַכֹּל מוֹדִין שְׁאִם נָתַן אֶת הַטִּיט תְּחִילָּה וְאַחַר כָּךְ נָתַן אֶת הָאֶבֶן שֶׁהוּא חַיָּיב. הַבַּנַּאי שֶׁיִּישֵּׁב אֶת הָאֶבֶן בְּרֹאשׁ הַדִּימוֹס חַיָּיב. לְמִי נִצְרְכָה. לְרַבָּנָן. וְהָהֵן דַּעֲבַד דַּפִּין וְהָהֵן דַּעֲבַד סַפִּינָין. חַיָּיב מִשּׁוּם בּוֹנֶה.

"How much would a builder build to become liable," etc. [21]What building was at the Sanctuary? They were putting the planks on top of the bases. But was this not temporary? Rebbi Yose says, because they were camping and travelling by the Word, it was as though permanent. Rebbi Yose ben Rebbi Abun said, since the Holy One, praise to Him, has promised them that He would bring them into the Land, it is as if it were permanent. This implies, even from the side. This implies even if it was put on top of something else. Does it imply that building on implements is building? The bases are like soil.

It was stated: "If one brings the stone and another one the mortar, he who brings the mortar is liable. Rebbi Yose says, both are liable." Rebbi Yose is of the opinion that stone without mortar is building. Everybody agrees that if one put up mortar first and someone then brought stone he is liable. "The builder who set the stone on top of the row is liable." For whom is this needed? For the rabbis. One who put up planks or one who put up adobe walls is liable because of building.

21   This text is from Chapter 7, Notes 437-446.

(13c line 15) וְהָהֵן דְּנָקַר כֵּיפִין כַּפִּין עָמוּדִין רֵחַיִּין. מְקַטֵּעַ פְּסָפָס. מְקַטֵּעַ בּוּלִין. חַייָב מְשׁוּם מְסַתֵּת. רַב יִרְמְיָה בְשֵׁם רַב. הַמַּרְכִּיב מִטָּה שֶׁלְּגִּילָה חַייָב מְשׁוּם בּוֹנֶה. אָמַר רִבִּי זְעוּרָא. אֵינוּ אֶלָּא כְנוֹטֵל מַלְבֵּן וְנוֹתְנוֹ עַל גַּבֵּי לְבֵנִים בַּשַּׁבָּת. רַב הַמְנוּנָא הוֹרֵי לְרֵישׁ גָּלוּתָא לְהַתִּיר שׁוּלְחָן שֶׁלְּפְרָקִים בַּשַּׁבָּת. אָמַר. רַב חוּנָה בַּר חִייָה הֲוָה עִמֵּיהּ. שָׁמַע רַב יְהוּדָה וְאָמַר. מָאן דְּהוֹרֵי לֵיהּ לָא יָלִיף וְלָא שִׁימֵּשׁ. אָמַר רִבִּי שַׁמַּי. מָאן דְּהוֹרֵי לֵיהּ כְּרַבָּן שִׁמְעוֹן בֶּן גַּמְלִיאֵל הוֹרֵי לֵיהּ. דְּתַנֵּי. לוּחִים שֶׁבַּסְּפִינָה וְשֶׁבַּעֲרִיסָה וְנִקְלִיטֵי הַמִּטָּה וְרֶגֶל הַשּׁוּלְחָן וְיַד הַסַּכִּין שֶׁבָּרֹאשׁוֹ הֲרֵי זֶה לֹא יַחֲזִיר. אִם הֶחֱזִיר הֲרֵי זֶה פָטוּר. וְעִם תָּקַע הֲרֵי זֶה חַייָב. רַבָּן שִׁמְעוֹן בֶּן גַּמְלִיאֵל אוֹמֵר. אִם הָיוּ רָפִים נוֹטֵל וּמַחֲזִיר. תַּנֵּי. תְּקוּעִים חִיבּוּר לְטוּמְאָה וּלְהַזָּיָה. קְבוּעִים חִיבּוּר לְטוּמְאָה וְאֵינוּ חִיבּוּר לְהַזָּיָה. הַנּוּטְלִין וְהַנּוֹתְנִין אֵינָן חִיבּוּר לֹא לְטוּמְאָה וְלֹא לְהַזָּיָה. וְהָכָא אַתְּ אָמַר הָכֵין. תַּמָּן דַּרְכָּן לִקָּבַע. לֹא לְקָבַע אֵינָן חִיבּוּר. בְּרַם הָכָא תְּקִיעָתָן הִיא גְּמַר מְלַאכְתָּן.

He who hollows out cliffs, cavities, pillars[22], millstones, or splits mosaic stones[23], splits blocks, is liable because of chiseling. One who puts together a Galilean bed[24] is liable because of building. Rebbi Ze`ura said, he only is like one who takes a brick and puts it on bricks on the Sabbath[25]. Rav Hamnuna instructed the Head of the Captivity to disassemble a composite table on the Sabbath. He said, Rav Huna bar Ḥiyya was with him. Rav Jehudah heard it and said, the one who instructed him did not study or serve. Rebbi Shammai said, the one who instructed him instructed following Rabban Simeon ben

Gamliel, as it was stated: Planking of a ship, or of a crib, and the posts of a bed[26], and the leg of a table[27], and the handle on the top of a knife one shall not return[28] but if one returned he is not liable. But if one pushed[29] in he is liable. Rabban Simeon ben Gamliel said, if they were loose he removes and returns. It was stated[30]: "Stuck together[31] they are a connection for impurity and sprinkling; nailed together they are a connection for impurity but not for sprinkling. Those which may be taken apart and put together again are connections neither for impurity nor for sprinkling." And here, you are saying so? There normally they are fixed; if not fixed there is no connection. But here sticking together is the end of its manufacture[32].

22   He chisels a pillar out of a rock.
23   Greek ψῆφος, ἡ.
24   This translation is a conjecture of R. Rabbinovicz (*Diqduqe Soferim Šabbat* p. 46 Note 6). In the Babli, 46b, the ms. sources give גלילתא, גלניתא, גלגניתא, ed. Bomberg גללניתא. The word also could describe a bed on wheels. In any case it is a bed which can be assembled and disassembled without any tools. {Cf. Greek χᾶλον, τό, "wood" (E. G.).}
25   Since the notion of building is not applicable to implements.
26   Greek τὰ ἀνάκλιτα "what is leaning to", two posts at head and end of the bed which hold a rod over which the mosquito net is spread.
27   Which can be disassembled.
28   Since one makes usable what was not usable at the start of the Sabbath.
29   If appropriately shaped pieces of wood (or in the case of the knife, metal and wood) are fitted together so that they become usable implements for permanent use without nails or glue, this is professional work and biblically forbidden. If the connection is not permanent, no biblical precept is violated.
30   Tosephta *Kelim Bava mesia*' 8:4.
31   Pieces of wood permanently stuck together form one piece. If any part becomes impure, the entire vessel is impure. If drops of water with ashes of the Red Cow are sprinkled on a part, it counts for the entire vessel. But if pieces of wood are nailed together, impurity spreads from one part to the other but sprinkling must be done for each part separately.
32   For the rules of the Sabbath the rules of impurity are irrelevant. If pieces of wood are stuck together it is a case of "hitting with a hammer" since the result is permanent.

‏(13c line 29) תַּנֵּי. רִבִּי סִימַיי אוֹמֵר. הַמַּרְכִּיב קֶרֶן עֲגוּלָה חַיָּיב. קֶרֶן פְּשׁוּטָה פָּטוּר. רִבִּי אֶלְעָזָר בֵּירְבִּי שִׁמְעוֹן אוֹמֵר. קְנֵי מְנוֹרָה חַיָּיב. קָנֶה שֶׁלְּצַיָּידָין (שֶׁלְסַסְיָידִין) פָּטוּר. קְנֵי מְנוֹרָה לָמָּה הוּא חַיָּיב. רִבִּי אַבָּהוּ בְשֵׁם רִבִּי יוֹחָנָן וְרַב חוּנָה תְּרֵיהוֹן אָמְרִין. מִשּׁוּם בּוֹנֶה. קָנֶה שֶׁלְּצַיָּידָין לָמָּה‏

הוּא פָּטוּר. מִפְּנֵי שֶׁהוּא מִלְמַעְלָן לְמַטָּן. הֵתִיבוּן. הֲרֵי הַחוֹפֵר בַּחוֹלוֹת הֲרֵי מִלְמַעְלָן לְמַטָּן הוּא. וְאַתְּ אָמַר. חַיָּיב. אָמַר רִבִּי שְׁמוּאֵל בַּר יוּדָן. כָּאן לְשָׁעָה כָּאן לִשְׁהוֹת.

It was stated[33]: "Rebbi Simai said, one who assembles a curved horn[34] is liable, with a straight horn he is not liable. Rebbi Eleazar ben Rebbi Simeon said, for the arms of a candelabra[35] he is liable; for a hunter's (whitewasher's)[36] rod he is not liable." Why is he liable for the arms of a candelabra? Rebbi Abbahu in the name of Rebbi Johanan and Rav Huna both say, because of building. Why is he not liable for a hunter's rod? Because it is from top to bottom. They objected, does not one who digs in the dunes work from top to bottom, and you are saying that he is liable[37]? Rebbi Samuel bar Yudan said, here temporarily, there permanent[38].

33 Tosephta 12:14 (ed. Liebermann; cf. *Tosefta ki-Fshutah Moed* pp. 194-195), Babli 47a; partially *Deut. rabba* 3.

34 A musical instrument (Geonic commentary to *Kelim* 11:7). These horns are composed of parts; curved horns can be made only by craftsmen but straight horns (shepherd's flutes) are easily put together by anybody. While the Babli does not recognize any building with implements and defines the liabilities noted in the Tosephta as "hitting with a hammer" (Rashi in Babli 47a), the Yerushalmi considers manufacturing which requires tools and skilled labor as building.

35 This also is both skilled work and intended to be permanent.

36 "Hunters" ציידין is the scribe's text (as well as two Tosephta mss.), "whitewashers" סיידין a gloss in the margin by the scribe's own hand, the Vienna ms. of the Tosephta, and the Venice Babli (other Babli texts have סייארין, ציארין). All these texts probably read צ as ss. A person whitewashing a wall will lengthen his rod to avoid using a ladder; this does not need any tools and is temporary.

37 If building is only making a structure against gravity then digging a cave in a dune or a mine shaft should be permitted on the Sabbath. It is asserted that these activities are a Sabbath violation.

38 The prior argument is dismissed. Building needs tools and permanence.

שְׁמוּאֵל אוֹמֵר. הַמַּלְחִים אֶת הַתִּירְצִין חַיָּיב מִשּׁוּם בּוֹנֶה. וְקַשְׁיָא. דָּבָר שֶׁאִילּוּ עֲשָׂאָה בַּשַׁבָּת חַיָּיב חַטָּאת בֵּית הַלֵּל מַתִּירִין אַף לְהַחֲזִיר. רִבִּי חֲנַנְיָא בְשֵׁם רִבִּי יוֹחָנָן. הִתִּירוּ סוֹפוֹ מִפְּנֵי תְחִילָּתוֹ. שֶׁאִם אָמַר אַתְּ שֶׁלֹּא יַחֲזִיר. אַף הוּא אֵינוֹ פּוֹתֵחַ. וְלֹא יִפְתַּח. אַף הוּא מְמַעֵט בְּשִׂמְחַת יוֹם טוֹב. אָמַר רִבִּי אָחָא. מַחֲזִיר. בִּלְבַד שֶׁלֹּא יַחֲזִיר כָּל־צָרְכּוֹ. אָמַר רִבִּי יוֹסֵי בַּר בּוּן. כְּשֶׁאֵין שָׁם פֶּתַח. אֲבָל אִם יֵשׁ שָׁם פֶּתַח מִשְׁתַּמֵּשׁ כְּנֶגֶד הַפָּתַח.

1 אומר | י אמ'   המלחים | י המלחם   התירצין | י התריסין ביום טוב   עשאה | י עשאו   2 חנניא | י חנניה   3 אמר | י אומ'   את | י את לו   4 צרכו | י צורכו   בר | י ביר'   כשאין | י בשאין   כנגד | י דרך

[39]Samuel said, anybody who tightly closes the shutters[40] is liable because of building. This is difficult. Something which if it was done on the Sabbath makes him liable for a purification sacrifice[41] the House of Hillel permit to restore[42]? Rebbi Ḥinena in the name of Rebbi Joḥanan: They permitted the end because of the start. For if you say that he cannot put them back he will not open. Don't let him open! Then he detracts from the enjoyment of the holiday. Rebbi Aḥa said, he may put them back on condition that he not restore completely[43]. Rebbi Yose ben Rebbi Abun said, if there is no door there. But if there is a door he uses the door[44].

39 This text is from *Beṣah* 1:5 and refers to Mishnah *Beṣah* 1:5: "The House of Shammai say, one may not remove store shutters on a holiday but the House of Hillel permit even to return them." The text is not the scribe's, but was added by the first corrector from a different ms.

The subject is a grocery store protected by an iron shutter which may be turned around an axle and serve as store counter. In the absence of refrigeration it may be essential for people to be able to buy food on holidays; this is permitted as long as no money changes hands on the holiday, no written records are made, nor is there exact weighing and measuring. Babli *Beṣah* 11b.

40 Modern Hebrew (Babli spelling) תריס. Greek θυρεός, ὁ "shield, armor". Here again ס and צ are interchangeable.

41 Following Samuel.

42 On the holiday.

43 Then the work is not professional and comparable to writing with the back of one's hand.

44 If customers can have access to the store without the owner removing the shutters, the House of Hillel will agree that the emergency permit is not valid.

(13c line 41) מַתְנִיתָא דְרִבִּי שִׁמְעוֹן. דְּתַנֵּי. הַגּוֹרֵד הַקּוֹדֵחַ הַקּוֹצֵץ כָּל־שֶׁהוּא בַּשַּׁבָּת חַיָּיב. רִבִּי שִׁמְעוֹן אוֹמֵר. הַגּוֹרֵד עַד שֶׁיְּגוֹר כָּל־צוֹרְכוֹ. הַקּוֹדֵחַ עַד שֶׁיִּקְדַּח כָּל־צָרְכוֹ. הַקּוֹצֵץ עַד שֶׁיְּקַצֵּץ כָּל־צָרְכוֹ. הָעוֹבֵד אֶת הָעוֹר עַד שֶׁיְּעַבֵּד כָּל־צוֹרְכוֹ. וְאָמַר רִבִּי יַעֲקֹב בַּר אָחָא. לֹא אַתְיָא אֶלָּא כְרִבִּי שִׁמְעוֹן. דְּרִבִּי שִׁמְעוֹן לֹא עָבַד מִקְצַת מְלָאכָה כְכוּלָּהּ. וְרַבָּנָן עֲבָדִין מִקְצַת מְלָאכָה כְכוּלָּהּ. וְקַשְׁיָא עַל דְּרַבָּן שִׁמְעוֹן בֶּן גַּמְלִיאֵל. אִילּוּ נָטַל לִקְצוֹר וְלֹא קָצַר שֶׁמָּא כְלוּם הוּא. אָמַר רִבִּי אָדָא. אַתְיָא דְרַבָּן שִׁמְעוֹן בֶּן גַּמְלִיאֵל כְּרִבִּי יְהוּדָה. דְּתַנֵּי. הַשּׁוֹבֵט וְהַמְקַטְקֵט עַל הָאָרִיג הֲרֵי זֶה חַיָּיב מִפְּנֵי שֶׁהוּא כִמְיַשֵּׁב בְּיָדוֹ. וְהָכָא מִפְּנֵי שֶׁהוּא כִמְיַשֵּׁב בְּיָדוֹ.

1 הגורד[45] | פ הגורר   2 שמעון | פ שמעון בן אלעזר   הגורד | פ הגורר   3 העובד | פ והמעבד   ואמ' | פ אמ'   4 ודבנן | פ ורבנין   5-6 ר' אדא | פ רב   6-7 הרי זה | פ -

[46]The Mishnah is Rebbi Simeon's, as it was stated[47]: "One who scratches[48], who drills, who chops anything is liable; Rebbi Simeon says, one who

scratches only if he scratches completely, one who drills only if he drills completely, one who chops only if he chopped completely, one who tans hides only if he tanned completely." And Rebbi Jacob bar Ada said, this only follows Rebbi Simeon since Rebbi Simeon did not treat partial work as whole work, but the rabbis do treat partial work as whole work[49].

And it is difficult about Rabban Simeon ben Gamliel. If one took [tools] to harvest but did not harvest, is that perhaps anything[50]? Rebbi Ada said, Rabban Simeon ben Gamliel parallels Rebbi Jehudah, as it was stated[51]: "One who hits or smooths[52] a piece of weaving is liable because he equalizes with his hand[53]." And here because he equalizes with his hand.

45 It is possible to read the words as גורר as in the parallel.
46 The paragraph is copied in *Pesahim* 6:1, 33b l. 10. The origin is here.
47 Tosephta 11:3 (ed. Liebermann).
48 One scratches off dirt from one's shoes on a rainy Sabbath (Tosephta 16:19, ed. Liebermann) or slags from a work-piece in preparation of use or sale.
49 The problem is the interpretation of the statement: "Anybody who performs work on the Sabbath and whose work has permanence is liable." For R. Simeon the work has permanence only if it does not need to be reworked; for the rabbis it has permanence if it cannot be undone. One might read the entire paragraph as a question: is the Mishnah R. Simeon's? R. Jacob bar Aha answers in the negative since even a small hole drilled cannot be undone

and causes liability according to the rabbis.
50 Why should hitting with a hammer on an empty anvil cause liability when nothing was accomplished by the action?
51 Babli 75b. There one reads מדקדק instead of מקטקט.
52 שובט is using a tool to keep the threads of the woof parallel to one another or press the threads of the warp down; מקטקט is using hands to straighten the warp and preparing it for the next layer. The dictionaries do not mention the Yerushalmi form which might be related to Arabic قطقط "to drizzle".
53 He makes liability not dependent on the use of a tool, only that it be skilled labor. Therefore also hitting with a hammer to get the correct rhythm for work induces liability.

(13c line 50) ב'. מַה חֲרִישָׁה הָיְתָה בַּמִּשְׁכָּן. שֶׁהָיוּ חוֹרְשִׁין לִיטַּע סִימָּנָיו. וְכַמָּה יַחֲרוֹשׁ וִיהֵא חַיָּיב. רִבִּי מַתַּנְיָה אָמַר. כְּדֵי לִיטַּע כְּרִישָׁה. רִבִּי בָּא בְשֵׁם רַב. כְּדֵי לִיטַּע זְכְרוּתָהּ שֶׁלְּחִיטָּה. תַּמָּן תַּנִּינָן. זֶרַע קִישׁוּאִין שְׁנַיִם. זֶרַע דִּילוּעִין שְׁנַיִם. תַּנֵּי. חִיטִּים מָדִיּוֹת שְׁתַּיִם. רִבִּי שְׁמוּאֵל בְּשֵׁם רִבִּי זְעוּרָה. חִיטִּין עַל יְדֵי שֶׁהֵן חֲבִיבוֹת עָשׂוּ אוֹתָן כִּשְׁאָר זֵרְעוֹנֵי גִינָּה שֶׁאֵינָן נֶאֱכָלִין. לָמָּה לִי לְתַקֵּן כָּל־שֶׁהוּא. לָמָּה לִי כִּמְלֹא פִּי גְּדִי.

2. [54]What kind of ploughing was in the Tabernacle? They ploughed to plant dyestuff. How much does one have to plough to become liable? Rebbi Mattaniah said, enough to plant a leek. Rebbi Aḥa bar Rav said, enough to plant a wheat sprout. There, we have stated: "Two green melon seeds make liable, two squash seeds." It was stated, two Median wheat kernels. Rebbi Samuel in the name of Rebbi Ze`ira: Since wheat was so much appreciated they treated it like garden vegetables that are not eaten.

Why do I need "to improve in any amount," why do I need "to fill a kid goat's mouth"[55]?

54 Chapter 7, Notes 224-226.
55 It teaches nothing that could not be   inferred from Mishnah 7:4.

(13c line 56) ג'. מָאן תַּנָּא. סִימָנִיּוֹת. רִבִּי יוֹסֵי. מָהוּ בְּכָל־לָשׁוֹן. אֲפִילוּ אֶלֶף אַלְפָּא. וְחָשׁ לוֹמַר. שֶׁמָּא יִתֵּן שֶׁלְּמַטָּן לְמַעְלָן שֶׁלְּמַעֲלָן לְמַטָּן. כְּמִין קוֹלְמוֹסִין הָיוּ עֲשׂוּיִן. וְחָשׁ לוֹמַר. שֶׁמָּא יִתֵּן שֶׁבִּפְנִים בַּחוּץ וְשֶׁבַּחוּץ בִּפְנִים. טַבָּעוֹת הָיוּ מוֹכִיחוֹת. וְחָשׁ לוֹמַר. שֶׁמָּא יַחֲלִיף. אָמַר רִבִּי אַחָא. לוּכְסוֹן הָיָה כָתוּב עֲלֵיהֶן. וְיַחֲלִיף. אָמַר רִבִּי אִימִי. וַהֲקֵמוֹתָ אֶת־הַמִּשְׁכָּן כְּמִשְׁפָּטוֹ. וְכִי יֵשׁ מִשְׁפָּט לָעֵצִים. אֶלָּא אֵי זֶה קֶרֶשׁ זָכָה לְהִינָּתֵן בַּצָּפוֹן יִינָּתֵן בַּצָּפוֹן. בַּדָּרוֹם יִינָּתֵן בַּדָּרוֹם.

אִילֵּין דְּרִבִּי הוֹשַׁעְיָה וּדְבַר פָּזִּי הֲווֹן שְׁאֵלִין בִּשְׁלָמֵיהּ דִּנְשִׂיָּיא בְּכָל־יוֹם. וַהֲווֹן דְּרִבִּי הוֹשַׁעְיָה עֲלִין קַדְמָאי וְנָפְקִין קַדְמָאי. אָזְלִין אִילֵּין דְּבַר פָּזִּי וְאִיתְחַתְּנוּן בִּנְשִׂיאוּתָא. אָתוֹן בָּעָיִין מֵיעוֹל קַדְמָאי. אִשְׁתָּאִילַת לְרִבִּי אִימִי. וַהֲקֵמוֹתָ אֶת־הַמִּשְׁכָּן כְּמִשְׁפָּטוֹ. וְכִי יֵשׁ מִשְׁפָּט לָעֵצִים. אֶלָּא אֵי זֶה קֶרֶשׁ זָכָה לְהִינָּתֵן בַּצָּפוֹן יִינָּתֵן בַּצָּפוֹן. בַּדָּרוֹם יִינָּתֵן בַּדָּרוֹם.

תְּרֵין זַרְעִין הֲווֹן בְּצִיפּוֹרִין בּוּלְווֹטַיָּא וּפַגָּנַיָּא. הֲווֹן שְׁאֵלִין בִּשְׁלָמֵיהּ דִּנְשִׂיָּיא בְּכָל־יוֹם. וַהֲווֹן בּוּלְווֹטַיָּא עֲלִין קַדְמָאי וְנָפְקִין קַדְמָאי. אָזְלִין פַּגָּנַיָּא וְזָכוֹן בְּאוֹרַיְיתָא. אָתוֹן בָּעוּ מֵיעוֹל קַדְמָאי. אִשְׁתָּאִילַת לְרִבִּי שִׁמְעוֹן בֶּן לָקִישׁ. שְׁאָלָהּ רִבִּי שִׁמְעוֹן בֶּן לָקִישׁ לְרִבִּי יוֹחָנָן. עָאַל רִבִּי יוֹחָנָן וּדְרָשָׁהּ בְּבֵי מִדְרָשָׁא דְּרִבִּי בְּנָיָה. אֲפִילוּ מַמְזֵר תַּלְמִיד חָכָם וְכֹהֵן גָּדוֹל עַם הָאָרֶץ. מַמְזֵר תַּלְמִיד חָכָם קוֹדֵם לְכֹהֵן גָּדוֹל עַם הָאָרֶץ: סָבְרִין מֵימַר. לִפְדּוֹת וְלִכְסוֹת וּלְהַחֲיוֹת. הָא לִישִׁיבָה לֹא. אָמַר רִבִּי אַבִּין. אַף לִישִׁיבָה. מַה טַעֲמָא: יְקָרָה הִיא מִפְּנִינִים. וַאֲפִילוּ מִי שֶׁהוּא נִכְנָס לִפְנַי וְלִפְנִים.

3. Who taught "signs"[56]? Rebbi Yose! What means "of any language"? Even אα[58]. Should one not be concerned that maybe one will put them upside down or bottom up[59]? They were made similar to reed pens[59]. Should one not be concerned that maybe one will put them inside out or outside in? The rings[60] did prove. Should one not be concerned that maybe one would

exchange? Rebbi Aha said, it was written slanted[61]. Why could they not be switched? Rebbi Immi said, *You shall erect the Tabernacle according to its ruling*[62]. Does there exist a ruling for wood? But the log which merited to be put in the North should be put in the North, in the South should be put in the South.

[63]Those of Rebbi Hoshaia and those of Bar Pazi went and greeted the Patriarch every day. Those of Rebbi Hoshaia went in first and left first. Those of Bar Pazi went and became related by marriage to the patriarchate. They came and wanted to enter first. They went and asked Rebbi Immi. *You shall erect the Tabernacle according to its ruling*[61]. Does there exist a ruling for wood? But the log which merited to be put in the North should be put in the North, in the South should be put in the South.

Two families were in Sepphoris, one of city councillors and one rural, who were greeting the Patriarch every day. The councillors went in first and left first. The rural ones went and acquired [knowledge in] Torah. They came and wanted to have precedence. It was asked before Rebbi Simeon ben Laqish. Rebbi Simeon ben Laqish asked it from Rebbi Johanan. Rebbi Johanan went up and preached in Rebbi Benaiah's house of study: "But if the bastard was learned and the High Priest ignorant, the learned bastard precedes the ignorant High Priest." They wanted to say, to be redeemed, for clothing, and for livelihood, but not for the Academy. Rebbi Abbin said, even for the Academy. What is the reason? *It is more precious than pearls*[63], even than he who enters into the Most Holy [of the Sanctuary.]

56 Writing is forbidden even if no letters are formed. Babli 103a.

57 The two letters do not have to be from the same alphabet.

58 Why is there a Sabbath violation only if two letters were written? R. Yose in the Mishnah reasons that the only writing in the construction of the Tabernacle was of signs which showed how the planks of the tabernacle had to be fitted together. This necessitates corresponding signs on adjacent planks, more than one at a time. Now it is asked whether not every single plank (which was a rectangular piece of wood 10 by ½ cubits) needed a sign which indicated what was top and what bottom? Then writing a single letter would be a Sabbath violation.

59 Thick at the bottom, thin at the top. In the Babli (98a) this is a matter of controversy.

60 Through which the interlocking rods were put. They all had to be on the same

side.	situated.
61 The corresponding signs on two adjacent planks were written at different heights and slanted so that they sat on one line only if the planks were correctly	62 *Ex.* 26:30. 63 The following two paragraphs are from *Horaiot* 3:7, Notes 328-336. 64 *Prov.* 3:15.

(13d line 1) תַּנֵּי. וְגַד מִגַּדִּיאֵל. מְתִיבִין לְרִבִּי יְהוּדָה. וַהֲלֹא אֵילוּ פְשׁוּטִים וְאֵילוּ כְפוּפִים. תַּנֵּי בְשֵׁם רִבִּי יוּדָה. כָּתַב שְׁנֵי אוֹתוֹת שָׁוִים וְהֵן שֵׁם חַיָּיב. כְּגוֹן שֵׁשׁ תֵּת גג רר חח. וְרַבָּנָן אֲמָרֵי. שְׁתֵּי אוֹתוֹת בְּכָל־מָקוֹם. אַשְׁכָּחַת אֲמַר. קַלַּת וְחוֹמְרַת עַל דְּרִבִּי יוּדָה. קַלַּת וְחוֹמְרַת עַל דְּרַבָּנָן. קַלַּת עַל דְּרִבִּי יוּדָה. כָּתַב שְׁתֵּי אוֹתִיּוֹת שָׁוִין וְהֵן שֵׁם. עַל דַּעְתֵּיהּ דְּרִבִּי יוּדָה חַיָּיב. עַל דַּעְתְּהוֹן דְּרַבָּנָן פָּטוּר. קַלַּת עַל דְּרַבָּנָן. שְׁתֵּי אוֹתוֹת מִכָּל־מָקוֹם אַף עַל פִּי שֶׁאֵינָן שֵׁם. עַל דַּעְתְּהוֹן דְּרַבָּנָן חַיָּיב. עַל דַּעְתֵּיהּ דְּרִבִּי יוּדָה פָּטוּר. מַחְלְפָה שִׁיטָתֵיהּ דְּרִבִּי יוּדָה. דְּתַנֵּי. יָכוֹל עַד שֶׁיִּכְתּוֹב אֶת כָּל־הַשֵּׁם. עַד שֶׁיֶּאֱרַג אֶת כָּל־הַבֶּגֶד. עַד שֶׁיַּעֲשֶׂה אֶת כָּל־הַנָּפָה. תַּלְמוּד לוֹמַר. מֵאַחַת. אִי מֵאַחַת יָכוֹל אֲפִילוּ כָּתַב אוֹת אַחַת. אֲפִילוּ אָרַג חוּט אֶחָד. אֲפִילוּ עָשָׂה בַּיִת אֶחָד בְּנָפָה וּבְכַבָּרָה. תַּלְמוּד לוֹמַר וְעָשָׂה אַחַת. הָא כֵיצַד. עַד שֶׁיַּעֲשֶׂה מְלָאכָה שֶׁכַּיּוֹצֵא מִזֶּה מִתְקַיֶּימֶת. וְהָכָא הוּא אֲמַר. הַשּׁוֹבֵט וְהַמְקַטְקֵט עַל הָאָרִיג הֲרֵי זֶה חַיָּיב מִפְּנֵי שֶׁהוּא כְמְיַשֵּׁב בְּיָדוֹ.

[65]It was stated, "and Gad from Gadiel"[66]. They objected to Rebbi Jehudah, are not these straight and those bent[67]?

It was stated in the name of Rebbi Jehudah: If he wrote two identical letters and they form a word he is liable, e. g.[68] חָח, רָר, גָּג, תֵּת, שָׁש. But the rabbis, two letters[69] anywhere. You are finding to say that there is leniency and stringency for Rebbi Jehudah, leniency and stringency for the rabbis. A leniency[70] for Rebbi Jehudah: If he wrote two identical letters and they form a word, in the opinion of Rebbi Jehudah he is liable, in the opinion of the rabbis he is not liable. Two letters anywhere even though they do not define a word, in the opinion of Rebbi Jehudah he is not liable, in the opinion of the rabbis he is liable.

The opinion of Rebbi Jehudah seems inverted, as it was stated[71]: "I could think only if he wrote the entire word, only if he wove the entire cloth, only if he made the entire sieve, the verse says, *of one*[72]. If *of one*, I could think even if he wrote one letter, even if he wove one thread, even if he made one loop on a fine or coarse sieve. The verse says, *he did one*[73]. How is this? Only if he made a work similar to one which is permanent." And here he says, "one who hits or smooths⁵² a weave is liable because he equalizes with his hand⁵³." And here because he equalizes with his hand⁷⁴.

65 Here starts discussion of Mishnah 3.
66 While this is in our Mishnah, the Halakhah presupposes a Mishnah which does not contain this clause. In the ms. it is an addition by the scribe on the margin. The clause also is missing in the Yerushalmi Mishnah edited by Lowe, in the Munich ms. of the Babli, and in the Merzbacher ms. of Alfasi. The clause is found in the Venice Babli, Maimonides's autograph Mishnah, and as *baraita* in *Sifra Hovah (Wayyiqra II) Pereq* 1(4).
67 The examples of the Mishnah are badly chosen since graphically שם is not part of שמואל or שמעון, nor דן of דניאל. No answer is given to the question. It may be that the question is considered correct, it also may be that final forms of letters are considered optional for use also in the middle of words. This is S. Liebermann's not universally accepted explanation (*Tarbiz* 4 p. 292) of a passage in *Megillah* 1:11 (71d l. 46). In any case, a final *mem* in the middle of a word is in the inscription of King Uziah's ossuary (published by A. L. Sukenik, *Tarbiz* 2 p. 290 ff.) The question is a major problem for the Babli, 104a.
68 Babli 103b; *Sifra Hovah (Wayyiqra II)*

Pereq 1(5).
69 The different letters.
70 In this and the following sentence, "leniency" has to be replaced by "stringency".
71 *Sifra Hovah (Wayyiqra II) Pereq* 1(4).
72 Lev. 4:2, introduction to the purification sacrifice of the anointed High Priest, *Sifra Hovah (Wayyiqra II) Pereq* 1(6).
73 Lev. 4:22, introduction to the purification sacrifice of the prince. It is presumed that the rules which trigger liability for a purification sacrifice are identical for everybody; therefore expressions used for different personalities have to be harmonized.
74 The question is difficult to understand since (1) both the *baraita* from *Sifra* and the one quoted from the discussion of Mishnah 2 are anonymous and (2) they are consistent in that they declare liability for minimal work if the results have permanence.

R. Jehudah requires the written letters to form an intelligible word, to be a completed action. In *Sifra*, the *baraita* 1(4) is anonymous but the quote of R. Jehudah in 1(5) also serves to underline R. Jehudah's consistency, for which he deserves praise.

(13d line 15) ד. כָּתַב בְּדָיוֹ עַל עֲלֵי יְרָקוֹת. בְּמַשְׁקִין וּבְמֵי פֵירוֹת עַל הַלּוּחַ. פָּטוּר. עַד שֶׁיִּכְתּוֹב דָּבָר שֶׁלְּקַיְימָא עַל דָּבָר שֶׁלְּקַיְימָא. רִבִּי יַעֲקֹב בַּר אֲחָא רִבִּי יָסָא בְשֵׁם רִבִּי אֶלְעָזָר. כָּתַב אוֹת אַחַת בְּטִיבֶּרְיָא וְאוֹת אַחַת בְּצִיפּוֹרִין חַייָב. וְהָא תַנִּינָן. אִם אֵינָן הֶהְגִּין זֶה עִם זֶה פָּטוּר. אָמַר רִבִּי אַבָּא בַּר מָמָל. בִּסְרָרָה.

4. If one wrote with ink on vegetable leaves, with drinks or fruit juice on a board, he is not liable unless he wrote with permanent material on

permanent material⁷⁵. Rebbi Jacob bar Aha, Rebbi Yasa in the name of Rebbi Eleazar: If he wrote one letter in Tiberias and one letter in Sepphoris he is liable⁷⁶. But did we not state, "if they cannot be read together, he is not liable"⁷⁷? Rebbi Abba bar Mamal said, ⁷⁸בסררה.

75 Cf. Tosephta 11:8 (ed. Liebermann).
76 Babli 104b.
77 If there is no liability if one writes two letters on walls in different rooms in the same house, there should be no liability if the letters were written in two different cities.
78 As it stands, "in deviation", the word makes no sense. The Medieval quotes (Rashba and Ritba on Babli 104b, *Maggid Mishneh*, R. Vidal of Toulouse on Maimonides 11:12) all read בסיד "with lime". S. Liebermann proposes to read בְּסִדְרָה "in sequence", making the statement of the Yerushalmi identical with Rashi's explanation in the Babli, *scil.,* that the two letters were written on the same sheet in two different cities.

(13d line 19) עֵדִים שֶׁאֵינָן יוֹדְעִין לַחְתּוֹם. רִבִּי שִׁמְעוֹן בֶּן לָקִישׁ אָמַר. רוֹשֵׁם לִפְנֵיהֶן בַּדְּיוֹ וְהֵן חוֹתְמִין בְּסִיקְרָא. בְּסִיקְרָא וְהֵן חוֹתְמִין בַּדְּיוֹ. אָמַר לֵיהּ רִבִּי יוֹחָנָן. מִפְּנֵי שֶׁאָנוּ עֲסוּקִין בְּהִילְכוֹת שַׁבָּת אָנוּ מַתִּירִין אֵשֶׁת אִישׁ. אֶלָּא מֵבִיא נְיָיר חָלָק וּמְקָרֵעַ לִפְנֵיהֶן וְהֵן חוֹתְמִין. וְלֹא כְתַב יָדוֹ שֶׁלְרִאשׁוֹן הוּא. מַרְחִיב לִפְנֵיהֶן אֶת הַקֶּרַע. רִבִּי מָנָא בָעֵי. וְלָמָּה לִי נָן אֲמְרִין. רוֹשֵׁם לִפְנֵיהֶן בַּמַּיִם. אִם בָּא וְעִרְעַר עִרְעוּרוֹ בָטֵל. הַקּוֹרֵעַ עַל הָעוֹר בְּתַבְנִית כְּתָב חַיָּיב. הָרוֹשֵׁם עַל הָעוֹר בְּתַבְנִית כְּתָב פָּטוּר. אָמַר לָהֶן רִבִּי אֱלִיעֶזֶר. וַהֲלֹא בֶּן סָטְדָא לֹא הֵבִיא כְשָׁפִים מִמִּצְרַיִם אֶלָּא בְכָךְ. אָמְרוּ לוֹ. מִפְּנֵי שׁוֹטֶה אֶחָד אָנוּ מְאַבְּדִין כַּמָּה פִיקְחִין.

⁷⁹If the witnesses do not know how to sign. Rebbi Simeon ben Laqish said, one sketches for them in ink and they sign with vermilion, or with vermilion and they sign in ink. Rebbi Johanan told him, because we are occupied with the rules of the Sabbath, should we permit a married woman? But he brings a blank sheet of paper and cuts it before them. Would it not be the first person's handwriting? One has to widen the cuts. Rebbi Mana asked, why do we not say that one sketches for them with water? If he would come and protest, his protest would be (invalid)⁸⁰.

⁸¹"If somebody tears into skin in the form of writing he is liable, if somebody sketches on skin in the form of writing it is not liable."

"Rebbi Eliezer told them, did not Ben Saṭda only in this way bring magic formulas from Egypt[82]? They said to him, because of one insane person should we condemn several sane ones[83]?"

79 This paragraph also is in *Gittin* 2:3, explained there in Notes 57-61.

80 With the text in *Gittin* read: valid.

81 This sentence is changed from *Gittin* to be adapted to the topic of Sabbath. Sketching on skin can be wiped off and is not permanent. The text in Tosephta 11:8 (ed. Liebermann) switches "liable" and "not liable", probably incorrectly, cf. *Gittin* Note 62.

82 In the Babylonian tradition (Babli 104b, Tosephta 11:15) this does not refer to writing on untanned hide but to writing on one's own skin (Mishnah 4). Since these two sentences are not in *Gittin*, the Yerushalmi seems to have the same tradition. In some sources (listed in *Tosefta ki-Fshutah Šabbat* p. 180) the name is סטרא, which Lieberman suggests is σωτήρ "savior", characterizing him as a false Messiah.

83 Since liability for erroneous acts means capital crime for intended actions. The definition of capital crime cannot be extended without a reliable tradition.

(13d line 34) כָּתַב. לֹא חֲקָק. וְכָתַב. לֹא הַמַּטִּיף. כָּתַב. לֹא הַשּׁוֹפֵךְ. וְכָתַב. לֹא חוֹקֵק. אִית תַּנָּיֵי תַנֵּי. אֲפִילוּ חוֹקֵק. אָמַר רַב חִסְדָּא. מָאן דְּאָמַר. לֹא חוֹקֵק. בְּבוֹלֵט מְקוֹם הַכְּתָב. מָאן דְּאָמַר. אֲפִילוּ חוֹקֵק. כְּגוֹן הָהֵן פִּינְקְסָא. וְכָתַב. לֹא הַמַּטִּיף. רִבִּי יוּדָן בֵּירִבִּי שָׁלוֹם וְרִבִּי מַתַּנְיָה. חַד אָמַר. בְּשֶׁלֹּא עֵירֵב נְקוּדוֹת. וְחוֹרָנָה אָמַר. אֲפִילוּ עֵירֵב נְקוּדוֹת. וְכָתַב. לֹא הַשּׁוֹפֵךְ. אָמַר רִבִּי חִייָה בַּר בָּא. אִילֵּין בְּנֵי מַדִינְחָא עֲרוּמִין סַגִּין. כַּד חַד מִינְּהוֹן בָּעֵי מִשְׁלְחָה מִילָה מִסְטְרִיקוֹן לְחַבְרֵיהּ הוּא כְתַב בְּמֵי מִילִין. וְהָהֵן דִּמְקַבֵּל כְּתָבַיָּיא הוּא שׁוֹפֵךְ דְּיוֹ שֶׁאֵין בָּהּ עֲפָץ וְהוּא קוֹלֵט מְקוֹם הַכְּתָב. עָשָׂה כֵן בַּשַּׁבָּת מָהוּ. רִבִּי יוֹחָנָן וְרִבִּי שִׁמְעוֹן בֶּן לָקִישׁ תְּרַוֵּיהוֹן אָמְרִין. וְהוּא שֶׁכָּתַב דְּיוֹ עַל גַּבֵּי דְיוֹ וְסִיקְרָא עַל גַּבֵּי סִיקְרָא. אֲבָל אִם כָּתַב דְּיוֹ עַל גַּבֵּי סִיקְרָא וְסִיקְרָא עַל גַּבֵּי דְיוֹ חַיָּיב. רִבִּי יִצְחָק בַּר מְשַׁרְשַׁיָּיא בְּשֵׁם רַבָּנָן דְּתַמָּן. חַיָּיב שְׁתַּיִם. מִשּׁוּם מוֹחֵק וּמִשּׁוּם כּוֹתֵב.

[84]*He shall write*[85], not engrave. *And he shall write*, not dropping points. *He shall write*, not pouring. *He shall write*, not engrave; some Tannaïm state, he even may engrave. Rab Ḥisda said, he who says not to engrave, if the writing is elevated. He who says even to engrave, as on a writing tablet. *And he shall write*, not dropping points; Rebbi Yudan ben Rebbi Shalom and Rebbi Mattaniah: One said, if he did not connect the points; the other said, even if he connected the points. *And he shall write*, not pouring. Rebbi Ḥiyya bar Abba said, those Orientals are very sophisticated. If one of them wants to

write a secret letter to another, he writes with juice of gall-nuts. The recipient pours ink without gall over it, which is absorbed at the place of writing. If one did that on the Sabbath, what? Rebbi Joḥanan and Rebbi Simeon ben Laqish both said, only if he wrote ink on ink and vermilion on vermilion. But if he wrote ink on vermilion or vermilion on ink, he is liable. Rebbi Isaac bar Mesharshia in the name of the rabbis there: He is liable twice, for erasing and for writing.

84 A slightly truncated copy of a text in *Gittin* 2:3, explained there in Notes 45-55. The text there makes it clear that the statement of R. Joḥanan and R. Simeon ben Laqish does not refer to the question asked about R. Ḥiyya bar Abba's statement but refers to Mishnah 5 which states that writing on top of writing does not induce liability.

85 *Deut.* 24:1,3. There it is emphasized twice that divorce can be effectuated only by a written document. In R. Aqiba's system, the additional *vaw* in each case counts for an additional mention, so that in all the requirement of writing is mentioned 4 times. Once it is needed for the fact that it is required; the other three mentionings may be read as restrictions.

(13d line 42) ה'. הָיָה צָרִיךְ לִכְתוֹב אֶת הַשֵּׁם וְנִתְכַּוֵּון לִכְתוֹב יְהוּדָה וְשָׁכַח וְלֹא כָתַב דָּלֶת. הֲרֵי הַשֵּׁם בִּמְקוֹמוֹ הוּא. מוֹחֲקוֹ וּמְקַיְּימוֹ הוּא בִּקְדוּשָׁה. רִבִּי יְהוּדָה אוֹמֵר. מַעֲבִיר אֶת הַקּוֹלְמוֹס עָלָיו וּמְקַיְּימוֹ. אָמְרוּ לוֹ. אַף הוּא אֵינוּ מִן הַמּוּבְחָר. מַחְלְפָה שִׁיטָתֵיהּ דְּרִבִּי יוּדָה. תַּמָּן הוּא אָמַר. אֵינוּ כְתָב. וְהָכָא הוּא אָמַר. כְּתָב הוּא. בְּשִׁיטָתוֹ הֱשִׁיבוּהוּ. בְּשִׁיטָתָךְ שֶׁאַתְּ אוֹמֵר. כְּתָב הוּא. אַף הוּא אֵינוּ מִן הַמּוּבְחָר. רִבִּי יַעֲקֹב בַּר זַבְדִּי בְשֵׁם רִבִּי אַבָּהוּ לֹא אָמַר כֵּן אֶלָּא מַחְלְפָה שִׁיטָתֵיהּ דְּרִבִּי יְהוּדָה. תַּמָּן הוּא אָמַר. אֵינוּ מִן הַמּוּבְחָר. הָא כָתַב כְּתָב הוּא. וְהָכָא הוּא אָמַר. כְּתָב עַל גַּבֵּי כְתָב אֵינוּ כְתָב. מָהוּ כְּתָב עַל גַּבֵּי כְתָב. חַד לְעֵיל מִן חַד. מַה טַּעֲמֵיהּ דְּרִבִּי יְהוֹשֻׁעַ בֶּן בְּתֵירָה. מֵאוֹת אַחַת אַתְּ לָמֵד כַּמָּה אוֹתוֹת.

5. [86]"If he had to write the Name[87] but intended to write Jehudah but forgot to write ד. Then the Name is at its proper place. He erases it and fixes it in holiness. Rebbi Jehudah says, he moves the pen over it and fixes it. They said to him, but this is not preferable." Rebbi Jehudah's argument seems inverted. There[88] he says, it is not writing. But here[89], he says, it is writing. They objected to him according to his opinion[90]. According to your opinion, since you say that it is writing, but this is not preferable. Rebbi Jacob bar Zavdi in the name of Rebbi Abbahu did not say so, but that Rebbi Jehudah's argument seems inverted. There[91] he says, it is not preferable,

therefore the writing is writing; but here he says, writing on top of writing is not writing[92]. What is writing on top of writing? One higher than the other[93].

What is Rebbi Joshua ben Bathyra's reason[94]? From one letter one may infer several letters.

86 Babli *Gittin* 20a, *Sopherim* 5:3.

87 The Tetragrammaton which may be written only in holy texts and only if the intention was that it should be holy.

88 Here in *Šabbat* Mishnah 5. While the statement is anonymous and therefore represents the majority opinion, since R. Jehudah is not on record to disagree one has to conclude that he agrees. A stronger argument can be made against the rabbis who in *Šabbat* declare writing on top of writing as nothing and in the matter of a scroll designate it only as undesirable, not invalid.

89 In the case of a biblical scroll where he agrees that the Name can be made legitimate by writing over writing.

90 Since Mishnah 5 is anonymous, it certainly represents the rabbis' opinion. They should have objected that his procedure is invalid. They note that for them the procedure is invalid but even for R. Jehudah it should at least he undesirable; he should not prescribe it.

91 For the scroll.

92 For the rules of the Sabbath.

93 He never accepts writing on top of writing as valid under any circumstance. He proposes that the Name should be written a second time in the empty space between the lines, higher than the erroneous word.

94 Who in the Mishnah under certain circumstances considers writing one letter as completed work for the rules of the Sabbath.

(53d line 53) ו'. וְקַשְׁיָא עַל דְּרַבָּן גַּמְלִיאֵל. אִילּוּ קָצַר כִּגְרוֹגֶרֶת בְּשַׁחֲרִית וְכִגְרוֹגֶרֶת בֵּין הָעַרְבַּיִם בְּהֶעְלֵם אֶחָד שֶׁמָּא אֵינוֹ חַיָּיב. כְּשֵׁם שֶׁאֵין הָעֲלֵימוֹת חוֹלְקוֹת כָּךְ לֹא יְצָרְפוּ. רִבִּי מָנָא אָמַר לָהּ סְתָם. רִבִּי אָבוּן בְּשֵׁם רִבִּי יוֹחָנָן. טַעֲמֵיהּ דְּרַבָּן גַּמְלִיאֵל תַּמָּן. אֵין יְדִיעָה לַחֲצִי מְלָאכָה. וְדִכְוָותָהּ. אֵין זָדוֹן לַחֲצִי זַיִת. אָכַל חֲצִי זַיִת בְּזָדוֹן וַחֲצִי זַיִת בִּשְׁגָגָה מַהוּ שֶׁיִּצְטָרְפוּ.

6[95]. It is difficult for Rabban Gamliel. If one harvested the volume of a dried fig in the morning and the volume of a dried fig in the evening in one oblivion, would he not be liable[96]? Since oblivions do not divide, so they should not combine! Rebbi Mana said it without attribution, Rebbi Abun in the name of Rebbi Johanan: The reason of Rabban Gamliel there is that there is no awareness for half a work[97], and similarly, there is no intent for half a work. If one ate half the volume of an olive intentionally and half the volume of an olive in error, would this combine[98]?

95 Here starts discussion of the last Mishnah.

96 It is clear that there is only one liability created for each work category during one period of oblivion. It seems illogical that Rabban Gamliel should combine actions occurring in different periods of oblivion.

97 Since in the interval between the two periods of oblivion there was no liability, this interval is disregarded.

98 If the question is not work on the Sabbath but eating forbidden food, would Rabban Gamliel combine intentional and unintentional acts? Since for the Sages they do not combine and practice does not follow Rabban Gamliel, no answer is given.

האורג פרק שלשה עשר

(fol. 13d) **משנה א**: רִבִּי אֱלִיעֶזֶר אוֹמֵר הָאוֹרֵג שְׁלֹשָׁה חוּטִין בַּתְּחִילָּה וְאֶחָד עַל הָאָרִיג חַיָּב. וַחֲכָמִים אוֹמְרִים בֵּין בַּתְּחִילָּה בֵּין בַּסּוֹף שִׁיעוּרוֹ שְׁנֵי חוּטִין:

Mishnah 1: Rebbi Eliezer says, he who weaves three threads to start or one on the weave is liable. But the Sages say, whether at the beginning or at the end its measure[1] is two threads.

משנה ב: הָעוֹשֶׂה שְׁנֵי בָתֵּי נִירִין בַּנִּירִין וּבַקֵּירוֹס וּבַנָּפָה וּבִכְבָרָה וּבַסַּל חַיָּב. הַתּוֹפֵר שְׁתֵּי תְפִירוֹת וְהַקּוֹרֵעַ עַל מְנָת לִתְפּוֹר שְׁתֵּי תְפִירוֹת:

Mishnah 2: He who makes two mashes, [attaching them] to the cross-pieces[2] or to the thrums[3], of for a fine or coarse sieve, or for a basket, is liable. One who sews two stitches or who tears in order to sew two stitches[4].

משנה ג: הַקּוֹרֵעַ בַּחֲמָתוֹ וְעַל מֵתוֹ וְכָל-הַמְקַלְקְלִין פְּטוּרִין. וְהַמְקַלְקֵל עַל מְנָת לְתַקֵּן שִׁיעוּרוֹ כִּמְתַקֵּן:

Mishnah 3: He who tears in his rage or about a deceased person[44], any who spoil are not liable. The measure[1] for one who spoils in order to repair is as for repairing.

משנה ד: שִׁיעוּר הַמְלַבֵּן וְהַמְנַפֵּץ הַצּוֹבֵעַ וְהַטּוֹוֶה שִׁיעוּרוֹ כִּמְלֹא רוֹחַב הַסִּיט כָּפוּל. הָאוֹרֵג שְׁנֵי חוּטִין שִׁיעוּרוֹ כִּמְלֹא הַסִּיט:

Mishnah 4: The measure[1] of one who bleaches, or who beats flax, who dyes, or who spins, is double the width of a span[5]. The measure for him who weaves two threads is the length of a span[6].

משנה ה: רִבִּי יְהוּדָה אוֹמֵר הַצָּד צְפוֹר לַמִּגְדָּל וּצְבִי לַבַּיִת חַיָּב. וַחֲכָמִים אוֹמְרִים צְפוֹר לַמִּגְדָּל וּצְבִי לַגִּינָּה וְלֶחָצֵר וְלַבֵּיבָרִין. רַבָּן שִׁמְעוֹן בֶּן גַּמְלִיאֵל אוֹמֵר לֹא כָל-הַבֵּיבָרִין שָׁוִין. זֶה הַכְּלָל כָּל-הַמְחוּסַּר צִידָה פָּטוּר וְשֶׁאֵינוֹ מְחוּסַּר צִידָה חַיָּב:

Mishnah 5: Rebbi Jehudah says, one who catches a bird for a cage or a deer for a house is liable, but the Sages say, a bird for a cage and a deer for a garden, or a courtyard, or a vivarium[7]. Rebbi Simeon ben Gamliel says, not all vivaria are equal. The principle: In every case where it still needs catching, he is not liable, if it does not need catching he is liable.

משנה ו: צְבִי שֶׁנִּכְנַס לַבַּיִת וְנָעַל אֶחָד בְּפָנָיו חַיָּב. אִם נָעֲלוּ שְׁנַיִם פְּטוּרִין. לֹא יָכוֹל אֶחָד לִנְעוֹל וְנָעֲלוּ שְׁנַיִם חַיָּבִין. וְרַבִּי שִׁמְעוֹן פּוֹטֵר:

Mishnah 6: If a deer enters a house, he who locked the house while it was there is liable. If two together locked, they are not liable. If one alone could not have locked it and two did it, they are liable; but Rebbi Simeon holds them not liable[8].

משנה ז: יָשַׁב אֶחָד עַל הַפֶּתַח וְלֹא מִילְאָהוּ וְיָשַׁב הַשֵּׁנִי וּמִילְאָהוּ הַשֵּׁנִי חַיָּב. יָשַׁב הָרִאשׁוֹן עַל הַפֶּתַח וּמִילְאָהוּ וּבָא הַשֵּׁנִי וְיָשַׁב לוֹ בְצִידוֹ אַף עַל פִּי שֶׁעָמַד הָרִאשׁוֹן וְהָלַךְ לוֹ הָרִאשׁוֹן חַיָּב וְהַשֵּׁנִי פָטוּר. לְמָה זֶה דוֹמֶה. לְנוֹעֵל אֶת בֵּיתוֹ לְשׁוֹמְרוֹ וְנִמְצָא צְבִי שָׁמוּר בְּתוֹכוֹ:

Mishnah 7: If one sat in the door opening but did not fill it[9] and a second person came and filled it, the second is liable. If the first one sat in the door and filled it when the second came and sat next to him, even though the first one got up and left, the first is liable and the second not liable. To what can this be compared? To one who locks his house in order to watch it and it turns out that a deer is kept inside[10].

1   The minimum which makes liable.
2   Where the warp is attached to the cross-beams.
3   Greek καῖρος, ὁ.
4   Is liable.
5   The distance between thumb and ring finger. The Kaliri in his composition on Yerushalmi talmudic measures (סלוק לפרשת שקלים) defines the *sit* as identical with the hand-breadth, the width of four thumbs, one sixth of a cubit or 1/48000 of a *parasang*.
6   Weaving a ribbon of at least one hand-breadth in width is counted weaving cloth.
7   The Mishnaic word is a transcription of the Latin.
   Animals trapped in a house are effectively caught. Animals held in a large enough vegetable garden or vivarium still have a chance to evade being grabbed.
8   For him no work done by more than one person ever creates liability.
9   In this case the deer could escape if it passed by the person sitting in the door opening. While this is unlikely, legally the deer is not caught.
10 If the door was locked without the person knowing that a deer was inside there could be no liability since there could be no intention.

(14a line 15) רִבִּי אֱלִיעֶזֶר אוֹמֵר הָאוֹרֵג כול׳. אָמַר רִבִּי עוּלָּא. טַעֲמֵיהּ דְּרִבִּי אֱלִיעֶזֶר. עַל יְדֵי שְׁלִישִׁי מְלַאכְתּוֹ מִתְקַיֶּימֶת. מַה רִבִּי אֱלִיעֶזֶר כְּרִבִּי יוּדָה. דְּתַנִּינָן תַּמָּן. רִבִּי יְהוּדָה אוֹמֵר עַד שְׁיְשַׁלֵּשׁ. הַשַּׂק וְהַקּוּפָּה מִצְטָרְפִין לַכִּלְאַיִם: אָמַר רִבִּי סִימוֹן. טַעֲמֵיהּ דְּרִבִּי אֱלִיעֶזֶר. תַּמָּן עַל יְדֵי שְׁלִישִׁי מְלַאכְתּוֹ מִתְקַיֶּימֶת. בְּרַם הָכָא פָּחוֹת מִיכֵּן מִיסְתַּתֵּר הוּא. אַשְׁכַּחַת אוֹמֵר עַל דְּרִבִּי

אֱלִיעֶזֶר. פְּעָמִים שְׁלשָׁה בַּתְּחִלָּה. פְּעָמִים שְׁנַיִם עַל גַּבֵּי אֶחָד אָרוּג מֵאֶתְמוֹל. פְּעָמִים שְׁנַיִם עַל גַּבֵּי אֶחָד אֲרוּגִים מֵאֶתְמוֹל.

"Rebbi Eliezer says, he who weaves," etc. [11]Rebbi Ulla said, the reason of Rebbi Eliezer is that by the third his work becomes permanent[12]. Does Rebbi Eliezer hold with Rebbi Jehudah? As we have stated there[13]: "Rebbi Jehudah says, only if there are three pin-stitches[14]. A sack and a chest bring together for *kilaim*.[15]" Rebbi Simon said, the reason of Rebbi Eliezer is there[16] that by the third his work becomes permanent, but here[17] it undoes itself. You conclude that according to Rebbi Eliezer, sometimes three to start out with, sometimes two additional to one woven yesterday, sometimes two additional to one woven yesterday[18].

11 The first part of this paragraph has a parallel (with R. Simon quoted before R. Ulla) in *Kilaim* 9:7, Notes 168-170.

12 For R. Eliezer work is only forbidden on the Sabbath if it practically is irreversible.

13 Mishnah *Kilaim* 9:10.

14 It is forbidden to put woolen and linen cloth together only if they are sewn together by at least three stitches (which do not have to be knotted at the ends).

15 This last clause also is a statement of R. Jehudah in the Mishnah but is irrelevant for the discussion here.

16 This statement is taken from *Kilaim* which is "here"; the statement of R. Eliezer in *Šabbat* is "there".

17 If two pieces of cloth are connected only by two open stitches, they will separate by themselves and cannot create *kilaim*.

18 It is clear from the plural used for "woven" that the last clause must read "sometimes one additional to two woven yesterday". This is Rashba's reading. R. Eliezer simply declares liability of a person who adds the third row on a loom, irrespective of the creation of the first two rows. Babli 105a.

(14a line 22) רַבָּנָן דְּקַיְסָרִין בְּעִינָן. מַהוּ אֶחָד עַל הָאָרִיג. אֶחָד עַל גַּבֵּי שְׁנַיִם. אֶחָד עַל גַּבֵּי שְׁלשָׁה. רַבָּנָן דְּהָכָא אָמְרֵי. אֶחָד עַל גַּבֵּי שְׁנַיִם. הָיְתָה טַלִּית אַחַת גְּדוֹלָה. בַּתְּחִילָּה עַד שֶׁיַּאֲרוֹג בָּהּ שְׁנַיִם חוּטִין וּבַסּוֹף אֲפִילוּ כָּל־שֶׁהוּא. הָאוֹרֵג שְׁנֵי חוּטִין עַל גַּבֵּי הַגַּב עַל גַּבֵּי אִימְרָא אֲפִילוּ כָּל־שֶׁהוּא חַיָּיב. לְמָה הַדָּבָר דּוֹמֶה. לְצִילְצוּל קָטָן שֶׁאֲרָג בָּהּ שְׁנֵי חוּטִים עַל רוֹחַב שְׁלשָׁה בָתִּים חַיָּיב. וּבְנֶפֶשׁ מַסֶּכֶת כְּמָאן דְּהוּא בַּתְּחִילָּה. וְהֵן בַּדָּא אֲפִילוּ בְּסוֹף כָּאָרִיג הוּא. וְהֵן לַסּוֹטָה אֲפִילוּ בְּסוֹף כָּאָרִיג הוּא.

The rabbis of Caesarea asked, what means "one on the weave"? One on top of two[19], one on top of three. The rabbis here[20] are saying, one on top of two. If there was one large toga, at the start until he weave two threads of it, and at the end the most minute amount[21]. [22]"One who weaves two threads on top of the back[23], on top of the seam[24], in the most minute amount[21] is liable. To what may this be compared? To a small belt where he is liable if he wove two threads in the width of three spaces[25]." And with woolen[26] warp[27] it is as at the start, and this cloth[28] even at the end it is weave, and this veil[29] even at the end it is weave.

19 In the quotes of this passages in Rashba and Ritba, in their commentaries on the Babli 105a, this clause is missing. On the other hand, since the sentence is formulated as a question, the text as given here can be sustained, meaning that the rabbis of Caesarea questioned whether For Rebbi Eliezer weaving a single thread constitutes a Sabbath violation if it is additional to two or three existing threads. The answer is given by the Academy of Tiberias.

20 Tiberias.

21 The "most minute amount" cannot be arbitrarily small even though it is noted in the Tosephta that it may be less than the hand-breadths stated in the Mishnah.

22 Tosephta 12:1 (ed. Liebermann), Babli 105a.

23 In the Tosephta: הגס "the thick part", the seam with which the cloth was started.

24 On the sides or the end.

25 A thread of the woof is counted fully if it covers three threads of the warp.

26 Arabic نفش "wool".

27 Cf. *Jud.* 16:13. Woolen warp always requires full three threads of woof to induce liability.

28 Straight cloth needs only one additional thread to induce liability.

29 Cf. Chapter 4, Note 45.

(14a line 29) הַכֹּל מוֹדִין בְּכוֹתֵב אֶת הַשֵּׁם עַד שָׁעָה שֶׁיַּשְׁלִים. כָּתַב אוֹת אַחַת לְהַשְׁלִים אֶת הַשֵּׁם וְאוֹת אַחַת לְהַשְׁלִים אֶת הַסֵּפֶר חַיָּיב. כָּתַב אוֹת אַחַת בַּחוֹל וְאוֹת אַחַת בַּשַּׁבָּת. רִבִּי אֱלִיעֶזֶר מְחַיֵּיב חַטָּאת וְרִבִּי יְהוֹשֻׁעַ פּוֹטֵר. לָמָּה. אוֹ מִשּׁוּם קִיּוּם מְלָאכָה אוֹ מִשּׁוּם שֶׁאֵינוֹ רָאוּי לְהִצְטָרֵף עִמּוֹ. אִיתָא חֲמֵי. אִילוּ אָרַג חוּט אֶחָד בַּחוֹל וְחוּט אֶחָד בַּשַּׁבָּת שֶׁמָּא אֵינוֹ פָטוּר. שֶׁמָּא אֵינוֹ רָאוּי לְהִצְטָרֵף עִמּוֹ. אֶלָּא מִשּׁוּם קִיּוּם מְלָאכָה. כַּהִיא דְּאָמַר רִבִּי יַעֲקֹב בַּר אָחָא רִבִּי יָסָא בְשֵׁם רִבִּי אֱלִיעֶזֶר. כָּתַב אוֹת אַחַת בְּטִיבֶּרְיָא וְאוֹת אַחַת בְּצִיפֵּרִין חַיָּיב. דְּלֹא כֵן כְּרִבִּי אֱלִיעֶזֶר. כָּתַב אוֹת אַחַת בַּשַּׁבָּת זוֹ וְאוֹת אַחַת בַּשַּׁבָּת הַבָּאָה. רִבִּי אֱלִיעֶזֶר מְחַיֵּיב חַטָּאת וְרִבִּי יְהוֹשֻׁעַ פּוֹטֵר. אָתָא חֲמֵי. אִילוּ כָתַב אוֹת אַחַת בַּחוֹל וְאוֹת אַחַת בַּשַּׁבָּת. רִבִּי אֱלִיעֶזֶר מְחַיֵּיב חַטָּאת. בֵּין בַּשַּׁבָּת זוֹ בֵּין בַּשַּׁבָּת הַבָּאָה לֹא כָּל־שֶׁכֵּן. מִפְּנֵי חֲכָמִים שֶׁהֵן פְּטוּרִין.

Everybody agrees that if he writes a word only at the moment when he finishes[30]. "One who wrote one letter to complete a word or one letter to complete a scroll is liable[31]." One who wrote one letter on a weekday and one letter on the Sabbath, Rebbi Eliezer makes him liable for a purification sacrifice but Rebbi Joshua declares him not liable. Why[32]? Either because of completion of the work or because it is not appropriate to be joined to it[33]. Come and see, is he not free from liability if he wove one thread on a weekday and one thread on the Sabbath, is it not appropriate to be joined to it[34]? But because of completion of the work, as Rebbi Jacob bar Aḥa said, Rebbi Yasa in the name of Rebbi Eleazar: If he wrote one letter in Tiberias and one letter in Sepphoris he is liable[35]. For if it were not so following Rebbi Eliezer. If he wrote one letter on this Sabbath and one letter on the next Sabbath, Rebbi Eliezer makes him liable for a purification sacrifice but Rebbi Joshua declares him not liable[36]. Come and see, if he wrote one letter on a weekday and one letter on the Sabbath, Rebbi Eliezer makes him liable for a purification sacrifice; not so much more if one letter on this Sabbath and one on the next! Because of the Sages[37] who declare not liable.

30 Since a Sabbath violation occurs only if the perpetrator's intent was executed. If he intended to write a longer word and did not finish it, his intent was not satisfied. But if he starts writing a longer text, the moment he finishes the first word which he intended to write he becomes liable.

31 Tosephta 11:7 (ed. Liebermann). For R. Eliezer he is liable since he finished a word, for R. Joshua and his followers because he finished, i. e., because of "hitting with a hammer".

32 The question is asked about R. Joshua.

33 The reason may be either that for him only writing two letters creates a Sabbath violation and therefore adding one letter is not "hitting with a hammer" or it is that it can be seen that the new letter was written at another time than the first, but if the difference were not visible he would declare liability because of "hitting with a hammer"?

34 Since cloth may be woven at different times without the interruption being visible, the reason must be that "hitting with a hammer" only applies to work done on the Sabbath itself.

35 Chapter 12, Note 76.

36 This *baraita* also is quoted in the Babli, *Keritut* 17a. Again R. Eliezer declares liable since an entire word was produced.

37 For R. Eliezer really the *baraita* is not needed; it only is needed for the Sages following R. Joshua who might make a distinction whether or not both letters were written on the Sabbath.

(14a line 41) ב'. בַּנִּירִין. נִירָיָא. בַּקֵּירוֹס. קִירוֹמָא. רִבִּי בָּא רַב יִרְמְיָה בְשֵׁם רַב. הַמְמַתֵּחַ צְדָדָיו בַּשַּׁבָּת חַיָּיב מְשׁוּם תּוֹפֵר. נֵימַר. מְשׁוּם תּוֹפֵר וּמְשׁוּם קוֹשֵׁר.

2[38]. "The cross pieces," the cross pieces[39]. "The thrums," καίρωμα[40]. [41]Rebbi Abba, Rav Jeremiah in the name of Rav: He who straightens out the sides on the Sabbath is liable because of sewing. He should have said, because of sewing and tying knots.

38 Discussion of Mishnah 2.	40 "Arrangement of slips or thrums."
39 The same word in Aramaic.	41 Copied from Chapter 7 (Note 416).

(14a line 43) ג'. בְּעוֹן קוֹמֵי רבִּי בָא. הֵיךְ מַה דְּאַתְּ אָמַר תַּמָּן. הַשּׁוֹחֵט חַטָּאתוֹ בַּשַּׁבָּת כִּיפֵּר וּמֵבִיא אֲחֶרֶת. וַאֲמַר אוּף הָכָא. לֹא יָצָא יְדֵי קָרְעוֹ. אֶלָּא כְּרִבִּי שִׁמְעוֹן. דְּרִבִּי שִׁמְעוֹן אָמַר. עַד שֶׁיְּהֵא לוֹ צוֹרֶךְ בְּגוּפוֹ שֶׁלַּדָּבָר. אֲמַר לוֹן. תַּמָּן הוּא גָּרַם לְעַצְמוֹ. בְּרַם הָכָא אַתְּ גְּרַמְתְּ לוֹ. אָמַר רבִּי יוֹסֵי. וַאֲפִילוּ תַמָּן אַתְּ גְּרַמְתְּ לוֹ. שֶׁאִילוּלֵי שֶׁאֲמַרְתְּ לוֹ שֶׁיָּבֹא הֵיאַךְ הָיָה מִתְכַּפֵּר לוֹ. הֱוֵי צוֹרֶךְ מֵימַר דְּרִבִּי שִׁמְעוֹן הִיא.

חֲבֶרַיָּיא בְּעוֹן קוֹמֵי רִבִּי יוֹסֵה. לֹא כֵן אָמַר רִבִּי יוֹחָנָן בְּשֵׁם רִבִּי שִׁמְעוֹן בֶּן יוֹצָדָק. מַצָּה גְזוּלָה אֵינוֹ יוֹצֵא בָהּ יְדֵי חוֹבָתוֹ בַּפֶּסַח. אֲמַר לוֹן. תַּמָּן גּוּפָהּ עֲבֵירָה. בְּרַם הָכָא הוּא עָבַר עֲבֵירָה. כָּךְ אָנוּ אוֹמְרִים. הוֹצִיא מַצָּה מֵרְשׁוּת הַיָּחִיד לִרְשׁוּת הָרַבִּים אֵינוֹ יוֹצֵא בָהּ יְדֵי חוֹבָתוֹ בַּפֶּסַח.

3. They asked before Rebbi Abba: Just as you are saying there[42], "one who slaughtered his purification sacrifice on the Sabbath did atone but has to bring another one[43]," so one should say also here[44], he did not accomplish his tearing. But it[45] must follow Rebbi Simeon, since Rebbi Simeon said, only if he needed the thing itself. He told them, there he caused it himself[46], but here you caused it to him[47]. Rebbi Yose said, and even there you caused it to him for had you not told him to come[48] how could it be atoning? Is there need to say that it follows Rebbi Simeon[49]?

The colleagues asked before Rebbi Yose, did not Rebbi Johanan say in the name of Rebbi Simeon ben Joṣadaq, on Passover one cannot fulfill one's obligation with a robbed *mazzah*? He told them, there in itself it is sinful, but here he committed a sin[50]. Would we say, if one brought a *mazzah* from a private to the public domain that he could not fulfill his obligation on Passover[51]?

42 Tosephta *Pesahim* 5:7, *Menahot* 5:3.	44 It is a rabbinic obligation to tear one's clothes in mourning for a close relative. The question is whether such tearing, which in
43 For the unintentional Sabbath violation.	

Mishnah 3 is declared not to induce liability for a purification sacrifice, satisfies the duty of tearing or whether another tearing will be needed after the end of the Sabbath.

45 Mishnah 3. The implication is that R. Jehudah would declare the person tearing his clothes a Sabbath violator since he declares liable for a Sabbath violation even if no particular intent was satisfied.

46 By unintentional sinning he created the liability for a sacrifice.

47 Either this means that the relative caused it by dying or the rabbis caused it by decreeing the duty to tear one's clothes.

48 Since a purification sacrifice cannot be brought voluntarily, the priests' court has to confirm his liability.

49 The Mishnah may as well be R. Jehudah's who also will agree that damaging actions are not sanctionable on the Sabbath.

50 The robbed or stolen *mazzah* is a forbidden object in his hand; neither the animal selected for the purification sacrifice nor the garment to be torn are intrinsically forbidden.

51 Since the Sabbath violation has no connection with the Passover obligation, it is obvious that the answer is negative.

(14a line 53) תָּנֵי. מַצָּה גְזוּלָה אָסוּר לְבָרֵךְ עָלֶיהָ. אָמַר רִבִּי הוֹשַׁעְיָה. עַל שֵׁם וּבוֹצֵעַ בֵּרֵךְ נִאֵץ יְיָ. אָמַר רִבִּי יוֹנָה. הָדָא דְאַתְּ אָמַר. בַּתְּחִילָה. אֲבָל בַּסוֹף לֹא דָמִים הוּא חַיָּיב לוֹ. רִבִּי יוֹנָה אָמַר. אֵין עֲבֵירָה מִצְוָה. רִבִּי יוֹסֵה אָמַר. אֵין מִצְוָה עֲבֵירָה. אָמַר רִבִּי אִילָא. אֵלֶּה הַמִּצְוֹת. אִם עֲשִׂיתָן כְּמִצְוָותָן הֵן מִצְוֹת. וְאִם לָאו אֵינָן מִצְוֹת.

2 דאת אמ' | ח דתימ'   3 יוסה | ח יוסי   אילא | ח הילא

[52]It was stated: It is forbidden to recite a benediction over a robbed *mazzah*. Rebbi Hoshaia said, because of *he who recites the blessing over a piece of bread blasphemes*[53]. Rebbi Jonah said, that is, originally. But in the end, does he not incur a monetary obligation[54]? Rebbi Jonah said, no sin can be a good deed[55]. Rebbi Yose said, no good deed can be a sin[56]. Rebbi Ila said, *these are the commandments*[57]. If you did them the way they were commanded they are a good deeds; otherwise they are not good deeds[58].

52 This is from *Hallah* 1:9 (ח), Notes 218-223. In the Babli (*Sanhedrin* 6b, *Bava Qamma* 94a) and in Yerushalmi *Sanhedrin* 1:1 (Notes 70-72) this is a tannaitic statement. Here, the argument is that a religious obligation, like eating *mazzah* on Passover, cannot be fulfilled in a sinful way. The Babli insists that not even the regular benedictions before and after eating can be recited if the food is stolen or robbed.

53 *Ps.* 10:3. Usually, the verse is read to mean: "Certainly, the wicked one praises his own desires; he who blesses unlawful gain slanders the Eternal! The Tosephta (*Sanhedrin* 1:2) explains the verse as referring to judges who do not follow the

rules.

54 The robber certainly cannot recite a benediction for robbed food, but after he ate it he acquired the food (or if he robbed flour he acquired it by baking) and is no longer required to return the robbed piece but has to pay. In that stage, the robber seems to be in the same position as a buyer who is slow in paying and one does not understand why he should not recite grace.

55 A good deed done by immoral means is no good deed at all and no religious obligation can be satisfied in this way. He declares his first argument faulty.

56 He accepts R. Jonah's original logic.

57 Lev. 27:34.

58 He sides with R. Jonah's final position against R. Yose.

(14a line 58) ד'. תַּמָּן תַּנִּינָן. הַמּוֹצִיא עֵצִים כְּדֵי לְבַשֵׁל בֵּיצָה קַלָּה. וְהָכָא אַתְּ אָמַר הָכֵן. תַּמָּן בְּמוֹצִיא לִצְבּוֹעַ. בְּרַם הָכָא בְּצוֹבֵעַ.

4. There, we have stated[59]: "One who brings out wood to cook an easily cooked egg," and here you are saying so? There one who brings out in order to dye, but here about him who dyes.

59 Mishnah 9:5. The question as usual is not about the sentence which was quoted, which is the beginning statement of the Mishnah, but about the later statement, "shells of walnuts, skins of pomegranates, isatis, and madder to dye a small tissue like a hair net." This is contrasted with the statement here in Mishnah 4 that tissue to be dyed creates liability already with three threads one hand-breadth long. The answer is that dyestuff and cloth to be dyed are different items.

(14a line 60) ה'. אָמַר רִבִּי חִינְנָא. מַתְנִיתָא דְלָא כְרִבִּי יְהוּדָה. דְּתַנִּינָן. הַצָּד צִפּוֹר לַמִּגְדָּל וּצְבִי לַבַּיִת חַיָּיב. הָא לְגִינָה וּלְבִיבָרִין פָּטוּר. מַחְלְפָה שִׁיטָתֵיהּ דְּרִבִּי יְהוּדָה. דְּתַנִּינָן תַּמָּן. אֵין צָדִין דָּגִים מִן הַבִּיבָרִין וְאֵין נוֹתְנִין לִפְנֵיהֶן מְזוֹנוֹת. הָא לְגִינָה וּלְבִיבָרִין פָּטוּר. מַחְלְפָה שִׁיטָתִין דְּרַבָּנִין. דְּתַנִּינָן. וַחֲכָמִים אוֹמְרִים צִפּוֹר לַמִּגְדָּל וּצְבִי לַגִּינָּה וְלֶחָצֵר וְלַבִּיבָרִין. וְתַנִּינָן תַּמָּן. אֲבָל צָדִין חַיָּה וָעוֹף מִן הַבִּיבָרִין וְנוֹתְנִין לִפְנֵיהֶן מְזוֹנוֹת. הָא לְגִינָה וּלְחָצֵר לֹא. כָּאן בְּחָצֵר מְקוּרָה. כָּאן בְּחָצֵר שֶׁאֵינוֹ מְקוּרָה. וְהָא תַנִּינָן. גִּינָּה. אִית לָךְ מֵימַר. גִּינָּה מְקוּרָה. אֶלָּא כָאן בִּגְדוֹלָה כָּאן בִּקְטַנָּה. רִבִּי עוּלָא אָמַר. בְּעוֹן קוֹמֵי רִבִּי אָחָא. מַה נִיתְנֵי. כָּל־הַמְחוּסָּר צִידָה חַיָּיב וְשֶׁאֵינוֹ מְחוּסָּר צִידָה פָּטוּר. אָמַר לוֹן. וְלֹא בִמְגַפֵּל לְתוֹכָהּ אֲנָן קַיָימִין. אֶלָּא כָּל־הַמְחוּסָּר צִידָה אָסוּר וְשֶׁאֵינוֹ מְחוּסָּר צִידָה מוּתָּר. אָמַר רִבִּי שְׁמוּאֵל אֲחוִי דְּרִבִּי בֶּרֶכְיָה. כָּל־שֶׁהוּא מְחוּסָּר נַשְׁבִּים מְחוּסָּר צִידָה וְשֶׁאֵינוֹ מְחוּסָּר נַשְׁבִּים אֵינוֹ מְחוּסָּר צִידָה.

1 דלא | י דילא   יהודה | י יודה   דתנינן | י דתנינן תמן. ר' יודה או'.   2 יהודה | י יודה   תמן | י -   3 שיטתין | י שיטתון   4 דרבנין | י דרבנן   דתנינן | י דתנינן תמן   ולביברין | י ולביברים   תמן | י -   6 שאינו | י שאינה   8 במגפל | י בנעל

שׁוֹחֲטִין מִן הַנְּגָרִין. אֵין שׁוֹחֲטִין לֹא מִן הַמִּכְמוֹרוֹת וְלֹא מִן הַמְצוּדוֹת. רִבִּי יוֹסֵי בַּר בּוּן בְּשֵׁם רִבִּי אִמִּי. מְצָדְתָּא דְשִׁיתָּאי. שְׁמוּאֵל. צַד הוּא בְּפִיתָם. רַב אָמַר. סִכְרָא דִנְהָרָא שָׁרֵי. אָמַר רִבִּי יוּדָן. כְּהַהִיא דְטַסִּים.

1 הנגרין | י הנגרים אין | י ואין המצודות | י המצדות בר | י ביר׳   2 אמי | י אימי מצדתא דשייתאי | י במצדתא דשיתייא שמואל | י שמואל אמ׳ בפיתם | י בפיטס סכרא | י סוכרא   3 דטסים | י דטסיס

5[60]. Rebbi Ḥinena said, our Mishnah[61] dos not follow Rebbi Jehudah, as we have stated: "[62]one who catches a bird for a cage or a deer for a house is liable;" therefore for a garden or a vivarium he is not liable[7]. The argument of Rebbi Jehudah is inverted since we have stated there[63]: "one does not catch fish from vivaria, one does not feed them," therefore for a garden or a vivarium he is not liable? The argument of the rabbis is inverted, as we have stated: "but the Sages say, a bird for a cage and a deer for a garden, or a courtyard, or a vivarium," and we have stated there[63], "but one catches wild animals and fowl from vivaria and feeds them," therefore not for a garden or a vivarium[64]? One for a covered courtyard, the other for a courtyard which is not covered[65]. But did we not state "a garden"? Can you say a covered garden[66]? But here a large one, there a small one[67]. Rebbi Ulla said, they asked before Rebbi Aḥa, how should one state? In any case where catching is still missing one is liable, but if catching is not missing one is not liable[68]? He answered them, do we not deal with the case that he corrals them into it? But "in any case where catching is still missing it is forbidden, but if catching is not missing it is permitted"[69]. Rebbi Samuel, Rebbi Berekhiah's brother, said: any which needs nets needs catching, what does not need nets does not need catching.

"One may slaughter from containers, one may not slaughter from fishermen's nets or from traps.[70]" Rebbi Yose bar Abun in the name of Rebbi Immi: a net of warp[71]. Samuel [said][72], one may catch with a barrel[732]. Rav said, the sluice of a water canal is permitted. Rebbi Yudan said, those between the plates[74].

60 This paragraph, referring to Mishnah 5, is a copy from Halakhah *Beṣah* 3:1. The references to the Mishnah *Beṣah* as "there" are almost correct.

61 The Mishnah in *Beṣah*.

62 Mishnah 5 here, a statement of R. Jehudah.

63 Mishnah *Beṣah* 3:1, an anonymous statement.

64 How can the rabbis forbid catching a

deer in a vegetable garden as a Sabbath violation but allow it on a holiday? This contradicts the statement (Mishnah *Megillah* 1:5) that the only difference between prohibited work on Sabbath and Holiday refers to the preparation of food. It is explained in *Beṣah* that preparation of meat starts with slaughter; anything preceding this is not exempt from the prohibition of work.

65 A courtyard covered by a roof is a house. The Babli 106b, *Beṣah* 24a restricts this answer to vivaria.

66 Nothing would grow in a vegetable garden devoid of sunlight. The answer cannot be correct.

67 A small garden is one where the deer can be taken without effort, a large one where one has to use tools to catch the deer; Babli 106b, *Beṣah* 24a. The question now arises how to define "small" and "large" for practical application.

68 This discussion refers to the last statement in Mishnah *Beṣah* 3:1. Should one say that for large vivaria, taking animals on a holiday is a biblical violation even though this seems to contradict the formulation of the first part Mishnah *Beṣah* 3:1.

69 This is the traditional formulation of the last statement in Mishnah *Beṣah* 3:1 in the name of Rabban Simeon ben Gamliel, in contrast to the formulation in *Šabbat* 13:5. The prohibition is rabbinic since animals in a corral are no longer wild. The next statement translates the criterion into a practical rule. The Babli *Beṣah* 24a has a different rule.

70 Tosephta *Beṣah* 3:1; Babli *Beṣah* 24b. This paragraph has no connection with the laws of the Sabbath. It was added to the ms. by the corrector, obviously from a ms. representing a different spelling tradition.

71 It does not have to be a real net with threads knotted crosswise; even a net of parallel threads or wires spanned between two rods is a tool whose use on a holiday is forbidden.

72 Added from *Beṣah*.

73 Greek πίθος, ὁ. Scooping up fish from an aquarium using a wide-belly clay vessel is not catching.

74 While one may not take fish from an open water canal, if part of it is closed off by planks on either side it was transformed into an aquarium from which fish may be taken.

(14a line 76) ו'. בַּעֲשׂוֹתָהּ. הַיָּחִיד שֶׁעֲשָׂהּ חַיָּב. שְׁנַיִם שְׁלֹשָׁה שֶׁעֲשׂוּ פְּטוּרִין. רַב חוּנָא אָמַר. הָיָה אֶחָד בָּרִיא וְאֶחָד תָּשׁ. נָעַל הַחוֹלֶה כָּל־צוֹרְכּוֹ וְלֹא נָעַל הַבָּרִיא כָּל־צוֹרְכּוֹ. הַחוֹלֶה חַיָּב וְהַבָּרִיא פָּטוּר. רִבִּי יוֹסֵי בֵּירִבִּי בּוּן בְּשֵׁם רַב חוּנָא. הָיָה צְבִי רָץ כְּדַרְכּוֹ וְנִתְכַּוֵּון לִנְעוֹל בַּעֲדוֹ. וְנָעַל בַּעֲדוֹ וּבְעַד הַצְּבִי. מוּתָּר. רִבִּי יוֹסֵי בֵּירִבִּי בּוּן בְּשֵׁם רַב חוּנָא. רָאָה תִּינוֹק מְבַעְבֵּעַ בַּנָּהָר וְנִתְכַּוֵּון לְהַעֲלוֹתוֹ וּלְהַעֲלוֹת נְחִיל שֶׁלְּדָגִים עִמּוֹ. מוּתָּר. רִבִּי יוֹסֵי בֵּירִבִּי בּוּן בְּשֵׁם רַב חוּנָא. הָיָה מְפַקֵּחַ בַּגַּל וְנִתְכַּוֵּון לְהַעֲלוֹתוֹ וּלְהַעֲלוֹת צְרוֹר שֶׁלְּזָהוּבִים עִמּוֹ. מוּתָּר.

6. *When she was doing it*[75]. The individual who did it is liable; two or three who were doing it are not liable.

Rav Huna said, if one was healthy and one weak. If the sick person locked completely[76] but the healthy one incompletely, the sick one is liable but the healthy one is not liable.

Rebbi Yose ben Rebbi Abun in the name of Rav Huna: If a deer was running normally and he intended to lock the door for himself and he locked for himself and the deer, it is permitted[77].

Rebbi Yose ben Rebbi Abun in the name of Rav Huna: If he saw a child gurgling in a river[78] and he intended to bring him up together with a school of fish, it is permitted.

Rebbi Yose ben Rebbi Abun in the name of Rav Huna: If he was digging in a pile[79] and was intending to bring him[80] up together with a hoard of gold coins, it is permitted.

75 *Lev.* 4:27. This paragraph is from Chapter 10, Note 49.
76 This refers to Mishnah 6. A deer ran into a house, the healthy person closed the door but did not lock it. The sick person locked the door; he is liable even if he could not have closed the door by himself since the healthy person stopped before he incurred liability.
77 If the deer was not chased and the person did not intend to catch it, the catch was unintentional and cannot be sanctioned.

78 The child was drowning. It is an obligation for the onlooker to save him; anything he does in saving the baby is privileged. The Babli, *Yoma* 84b, approves of catching the fish but not of intending to catch them.
79 The pile is the rubble from a collapsed house. There might be people buried under it alive. This is the same situation as the one described in the preceding case.
80 A person buried under the collapsed house.

(14b line 8) ז'. רִבִּי שַׁמַּי בָעֵי. מָהוּ לִיתֵּן לִפְנֵיהֶן מְזוֹנוֹת. יָבֹא כְהָהִיא דְתַנִּינָן תַּמָּן. אֵין נוֹתְנִין מַיִם לִפְנֵי דְבוֹרִים וְלִפְנֵי יוֹנִים שֶׁבַּשּׁוֹבָךְ. שֶׁאֵין עוֹשִׂין תַּקָּנָה לְדָבָר שֶׁאֵינוֹ מִן הַמּוּכָן. וְהָכָה כֵן. רִבִּי שַׁמַּי בָעֵי. מָהוּ לִכְפּוֹת עָלָיו כֵּלִי. יָבֹא כְהָהִיא דְאָמַר רִבִּי שִׁמְעוֹן בֵּירִבִּי יַנַּאי. אֲנִי לֹא שְׁמַעְתִּי מֵאַבָּא. אֲחוֹתִי אָמְרָה לִי מִשְּׁמוֹ. בֵּיצָה שֶׁנּוֹלְדָה בְיוֹם טוֹב סוֹמְכִין לָהּ כֵּלִי בִּשְׁבִיל שֶׁלֹּא תִתְגַּלְגֵּל. אֲבָל אֵין כּוֹפִין עָלֶיהָ כֵּלִי. שְׁמוּאֵל אָמַר. אַף כּוֹפִין עָלֶיהָ כֵּלִי. רִבִּי שַׁמַּי בָעֵי. מָהוּ לְקוֹשְׁרוֹ בְחֶבֶל. יָבֹא כְהָהִיא דְאָמַר רִבִּי שִׁמְעוֹן בֶּן אֶלְעָזָר. מוּתָּר לְהִשְׁתַּמֵּשׁ עַל צִדְדֵי בְהֵמָה בַּשַּׁבָּת. הִיא צִידְדֵי בְהֵמָה הִיא צִידְדֵי אִילָן. כָּל-שֶׁמּוּתָּר לְהִשְׁתַּמֵּשׁ עַל צִדְדֵי בְהֵמָה מוּתָּר לְקוֹשְׁרוֹ. כָּל-שֶׁאָסוּר לְהִשְׁתַּמֵּשׁ עַל צִדְדֵי בְהֵמָה אָסוּר לְקוֹשְׁרוֹ.

7. Rebbi Shammai asked, may one feed them[81]? It comes following what we have stated there[82]: "one does not provide water to bees and to pigeons in a dovecot," for one cannot provide for something which is not prepared[83]. And here it is the same.

Rebbi Shammai asked, may one put a vessel over it[84]? It comes following [85]what Rebbi Simeon ben Rebbi Yannai said: I did not hear from my father; my sister told me in his name. For an egg which was laid on the Sabbath one leans it against a vessel so it should not roll off. But one does not cover it with a vessel. But Samuel says, one even may cover it with a vessel.

Rebbi Shammai asked, may one tie it[86] with a rope? It comes following [87]what Rebbi Simeon ben Eleazar said, it is permitted to use the sides of an animal on the Sabbath. There is no difference between sides of an animal and sides of a tree. In any case where one is permitted to use the sides of an animal one is permitted to tie it; in any case where one is prohibited to use the sides of an animal one is prohibited to tie it.

81 In the interpretation of S. Liebermann, the three questions of R. Shammai refer to the three statements of R. Yose ben R. Abun in the name of Rav Huna. This first question is about caring for a wild animal legally caught on the Sabbath.

82 Mishnah *Šabbat* 24:3.

83 Anything which is not potential food on the Sabbath.

84 This refers to the third statement. If in rescuing a person from a collapsed house one finds a hoard of coins, may one cover these on the Sabbath?

85 Chapter 4, Notes 40-41. The parallel formulation in Babli 42b is not applicable to the question raised here.

86 The deer which was found in the house when it was locked.

87 Chapter 5, Notes 41-42. Babli 154b.

שמונה שרצים פרק ארבעה עשר

(fol. 14b) **משנה א**: שְׁמוֹנָה שְׁרָצִים הָאֲמוּרִין בַּתּוֹרָה הַצָּדָן וְהַחוֹבֵל בָּהֶן חַיָּב. וּשְׁאָר שְׁקָצִים וּרְמָשִׂים הַחוֹבֵל בָּהֶן פָּטוּר לְצוֹרֶךְ הַצָּדָן לְצוֹרֶךְ חַיָּב וְשֶׁלֹּא לְצוֹרֶךְ פָּטוּר. חַיָּה וָעוֹף שֶׁבִּרְשׁוּתוֹ הַצָּדָן פָּטוּר וְהַחוֹבֵל בָּהֶן חַיָּב:

Mishnah 1: The eight kinds of vermin mentioned in the Torah[1]: one who catches or injures them is liable. Other abominations[2] and vermin: one who injures them is not liable[3]; if he catches them for some need he is liable, otherwise he is not liable. Wild animals and fowl in his possession: if he catches them he is not liable but if he injures them he is liable[4].

משנה ב: אֵין עוֹשִׂין הִילְמִי בַשַּׁבָּת אֲבָל עוֹשֶׂה הוּא מֵי מֶלַח וְטוֹבֵל בָּהֶן פִּיתוֹ וְנוֹתֵן הוּא לְתוֹךְ הַתַּבְשִׁיל. אָמַר רִבִּי יוֹסֵי וַהֲלוֹא הוּא הִילְמִי בֵּין מְרוּבָּה וּבֵין מוּעֶטֶת. וְאִילּוּ הֵן מֵי מֶלַח הַמּוּתָּרִין נוֹתֵן שֶׁמֶן בַּתְּחִילָּה לְתוֹךְ הַמַּיִם אוֹ לְתוֹךְ הַמֶּלַח:

Mishnah 2: One makes no brine[5] on the Sabbath but he may make salt water[6], dips his bread in it, and adds it to a dish. Rebbi Yose said, is that not brine, whether strong or mild? But the following is permitted salt water: if he starts by adding oil to water or salt.

משנה ג: אֵין אוֹכְלִין אֵזוֹב יָוָן בַּשַּׁבָּת לְפִי שֶׁאֵינוֹ מַאֲכַל בְּרִיאִים אֲבָל אוֹכֵל הוּא אֶת יוֹעֶזֶר וְשׁוֹתֶה אַבּוּבְרוֹאָה. כָּל־הָאוֹכְלִין אוֹכֵל אָדָם לִרְפוּאָה וְכָל־הַמַּשְׁקִין הוּא שׁוֹתֶה חוּץ מִמֵּי דְקָרִין וְכוֹס הָעִיקָּרִין מִפְּנֵי שֶׁהֵן לִירוֹקָה. אֲבָל שׁוֹתֶה הוּא מֵי דְקָרִין לִצְמָאוֹ וְסָךְ שֶׁמֶן עִיקָּרִין שֶׁלֹּא לִרְפוּאָה:

Mishnah 3: One may not eat Greek hyssop[7] on the Sabbath because it is not food of healthy people, but one may eat true maiden hair[8] and drink shepherd's flute[9]. Any food may a person eat as medicine and any drink may he drink except piercing water[10] and a cup of roots[11] because these are for hepatitis. But one may drink piercing water for his thirst and rub oil of roots[12] not for healing.

משנה ד: הַחוֹשֵׁשׁ בְּשִׁינָּיו לֹא יִגְמַע בָּהֶן חוֹמֶץ אֲבָל מְטַבֵּל הוּא כְדַרְפּוֹ וְאִם נִתְרַפֵּא נִתְרַפֵּא. הַחוֹשֵׁשׁ בְּמָתְנָיו לֹא יָסוּךְ יַיִן וָחוֹמֶץ אֲבָל סָךְ הוּא אֶת הַשֶּׁמֶן וְלֹא שֶׁמֶן וֶרֶד. בְּנֵי

מְלָכִים סָכִין עַל מַכּוֹתֵיהֶן שֶׁמֶן וֶרֶד שֶׁכֵּן דַּרְכָּן בְּנֵי מְלָכִים לָסוּךְ בַּחוֹל. רִבִּי שִׁמְעוֹן אוֹמֵר כָּל־יִשְׂרָאֵל בְּנֵי מְלָכִים:

Mishnah 4: One whose teeth are aching may not sip[13] vinegar, but he may dip[14] as usual and if he is healed, he is healed. One whose hips are aching may not rub in oil and vinegar, but he may rub in oil, except for rose oil. Princes may rub rose oil on their injuries because they usually do this also on a weekday. Rebbi Simeon says, all of Israel are princes[15].

1 Lev. 11:29-30.
2 Worms, insects, and seafood.
3 An injury to any epidermis which cannot be tanned into leather is not considered a Sabbath violation.
4 Mammals and birds all have skin that can be tanned.
5 Greek ἅλμη, ἡ. The name is reserved for professionally prepared brine.
6 Made at home without special tools or ingredients.
7 Lavender (Maimonides).
8 *Adiantum Capillus Veneris L.*, definition of the Halakhah.
9 The pulp in the reeds from which shepherd's flutes are made dissolved in water.
10 Mineral water which hurts.
11 This seems to be any root extract. At other places, "cup of roots" refers to a concoction which was used by women to induce sterility.
12 Medicated oil rub.
13 The vinegar would be swallowed only after it was kept in the mouth around the aching tooth for some time.
14 Dipping his bread in vinegar (*Ru.* 2:14) and eating with the aching tooth.
15 What is permitted to some is permitted to all.

(14b line 52) שְׁמוֹנָה שְׁרָצִים כול׳. רִבִּי זְרִיקָן בְּשֵׁם רִבִּי אִימִּי. אִיתְפַּלְגוּן רִבִּי יוֹחָנָן וְרִבִּי שִׁמְעוֹן בֶּן לָקִישׁ. חַד אָמַר. דִּבְרֵי הַכֹּל. וְחוֹרָנָה אָמַר. בְּמַחֲלוֹקֶת. וְלָא יָדְעִין מַאן אֲמַר דָּא וּמַאן אֲמַר דָּא. אָמַר רִבִּי זְעִירָא. נָפְרָשׁ מִילֵּיהוֹן דְּרַבָּנָן מִן מִילֵּיהוֹן. דְּתַנִּינָן תַּמָּן. אִילּוּ שְׁעוּרוֹתֵיהֶן כִּבְשָׂרָן. עוֹר הָאָדָם וְעוֹר חֲזִיר שֶׁלְּיִישּׁוּב. רִבִּי יוֹסֵה אוֹמֵר. אַף עוֹר חֲזִיר שֶׁל בָּר. רִבִּי יוֹחָנָן אָמַר. לֹא שָׁנוּ אֶלָּא לְאִיסּוּר וּלְטוּמְאָה. אֲבָל לִלְקוֹת עוֹר הוּא וְאֵין לוֹקִים עָלָיו מִשּׁוּם נְבֵילָה. רִבִּי שִׁמְעוֹן בֶּן לָקִישׁ אָמַר. מִשְׁנָה תְּמִימָה שָׁנָה רִבִּי. בֵּין לְאִיסּוּר בֵּין לִלְקוֹת בֵּין לְטוּמְאָה. מַתְנִיתָא מְסַייְעָא לְדֵין וּמַתְנִיתָא מְסַייְעָא לְדֵין. מַתְנִיתָא מְסַייְעָא לְרִבִּי יוֹחָנָן. שְׁמוֹנָה שְׁרָצִים יֵשׁ לָהֶן עוֹרוֹת. אָמַר רִבִּי יוֹחָנָן בֶּן נוּרִי. לְפִיכָךְ אוֹמֵר אֲנִי. שְׁמוֹנָה שְׁרָצִים יֵשׁ לָהֶן עוֹרוֹת. מַתְנִיתָא מְסַייְעָא לְרִבִּי שִׁמְעוֹן בֶּן לָקִישׁ. הַחוֹבֵל בַּשְּׁרָצִים. אֶת שֶׁיֵּשׁ לָהֶן עוֹרוֹת חַייָב. וְאֶת שֶׁאֵין לָהֶן עוֹרוֹת פָּטוּר. רִבִּי יוֹחָנָן בֶּן נוּרִי אוֹמֵר. לְפִיכָךְ אוֹמֵר אֲנִי. כָּל־הַשְּׁרָצִים יֵשׁ לָהֶן עוֹרוֹת. רִבִּי יוֹסֵי בֵּירִבִּי בּוּן בְּשֵׁם רַב. עוֹר הוּא. וְאֵין לוֹקִין עֲלֵיהֶן מִשּׁוּם נְבֵילָה. וְאַתְיָא כְּהַהִיא דְּאָמַר רִבִּי יוֹחָנָן. הַצָּד זִיזִין זְבוּבִין חַגָּבִין יַתּוּשִׁין חַייָב. וְרִבִּי יְהוּדָה פוֹטֵר. וְכֵן הָיָה רִבִּי יְהוּדָה אוֹמֵר. אֵין חַייָבִין אֶלָּא

עַל דָּבָר שֶׁדַּרְכּוֹ לִיצוּד. הַצָּד חֲגָבִים בַּטַּל פָּטוּר. בַּשָּׁרָב חַיָּיב. אֶלְעָזָר בֶּן אַחְבַּאי אוֹמֵר. אַף בַּשָּׁרָב בְּשָׁעָה שֶׁמְקַלְּחִין פָּטוּר. הַצָּד צְבִי חִיגֵּר סוּמֵא חוֹלֶה קָטָן פָּטוּר. יָשֵׁן חַיָּיב. דּוּ קָמִיץ חָדָא וּפָתַח חָדָא.

"The eight kinds of vermin," etc. Rebbi Zeriqan in the name of Rebbi Immi: Rebbi Joḥanan and Rebbi Simeon ben Laqish disagreed. One said, this is everybody's opinion; the other said, it is in dispute[16]. We do not know who said what. Rebbi Ze`ira said, let us explain the rabbis' words from their own words, since we have stated there[17]: "these are the ones whose skins are like their flesh, human skin and domesticated pigskin. Rebbi Yose says, also wild pigskin." Rebbi Joḥanan said, they taught this only regarding prohibition and impurity. But with regard to flogging it is hide and one may not flog for it because of carcass meat[18]. Rebbi Simeon ben Laqish said, Rebbi taught a complete Mishnah, whether for prohibition, or for flogging, or for impurity. A *baraita* supports one, and a *baraita* supports the other. A *baraita* supports Rebbi Joḥanan: "The eight kinds of vermin have hides. Rebbi Joḥanan ben Nuri said, therefore I am saying that the eight kinds of vermin have hides.[19]" A *baraita* supports Rebbi Simeon ben Laqish. He who injures vermin, for those who have hides he is liable, for those who have no hides he is not liable. Rebbi Joḥanan ben Nuri said, therefore I am saying that all kinds of vermin have hides[20]. Rebbi Yose ben Rebbi Abun in the name of Rav: It is hide and one may not flog for it because of carcass meat. This follows what Rebbi Joḥanan said[21], "he who caught crickets[22], flies, *ḥagazin*[23], mosquitoes is liable, but Rebbi Jehudah declares not liable, for so did Rebbi Jehudah say, one is liable only for something which usually is hunted. One who catches locusts in dew is not liable, in dry time is liable. Eleazar ben Aḥbai says, even in heat one is not liable if it forms clusters[24]. One who catches a lame, blind, sick, young deer is not liable[25], for a sleeping one he is liable," for it closes one and opens one[26].

16 The statement that injury to one of the eight kinds of vermin constitutes a Sabbath violation is in one tradition a unanimous opinion, in another the object of a dispute between R. Joḥanan ben Nuri and the anonymous majority. As explained later, the problem really is which tradition of the statement of R. Joḥanan ben Nuri is correct.

17 Mishnah *Ḥulin* 9:2. The Mishnah implies that leather or fur is not subject to

impurity of food or animals (but is subject to *ṣoraat*, Lev. 13:47-59). But the epidermis of animals whose hide cannot be turned into leather is treated as like the rest of the body and is subject to all impurities spelled out in Lev. 11. The Mishnah singles out not only humans and pigs but later reports a disagreement about one of the eight species of vermin, with agreement about three others that their hides are subject to impurity; it ends with the statement of R. Joḥanan ben Nuri that all eight species of vermin have hides in this sense. The relevance for the discussion here is that if the hide is separate from the flesh, causing an ecchymosis under the skin is a Sabbath violation as derivative of threshing.

18 If somebody eats the hide of a forbidden animal without any flesh attached, he cannot be accused of eating forbidden food since what he ate was no food; the prohibition of hide is purely rabbinical. If one agrees with this point of view then the statement of R. Joḥanan ben Nuri also refers only to impurity and rabbinic prohibition and the majority will agree that for biblical prohibitions, including the Sabbath, the eight kinds of vermin have hides. This is R. Joḥanan's position. Babli 107a in the name of Rav.

19 Cf. Tosephta *Ḥulin* 8:17.

20 Babli 107b.

21 Cf. Tosephta 12:5 (ed. Liebermann); Babli 106b.

22 In Brelot's Arabic Dictionary (Beirut 1898), زيز is noted as Syrian dialect word for cricket.

23 An unexplained *hapax*. Probably misspelled for חגבים "locusts" mentioned in the Tosephta.

24 Explanation of Rashi. Also R. Ḥananel explains that according to Eleazar ben Aḥbai locusts may be taken on the Sabbath if they do not fly and can be caught effortlessly.

25 Tosephta 12:4 (ed. Liebermann).

26 *Cant. rabba* 8(16) also mentions the belief that deer sleep with one eye open (and, therefore, a healthy deer cannot easily be caught even when sleeping.)

(14b line 69) אָמַר רִבִּי יַנַּאי. מוּתָּר לַהֲרוֹג אֶת הַצְּרְעָה בַשַׁבָּת. וְתַנֵּי כֵן. חֲמִשָּׁה נֶהֱרָגִין בַּשַׁבָּת. זְבוּב הַמִּצְרִי וְצִירְעָה שֶׁבְּנִינְוֵה וְעַקְרָב שֶׁבְּהַדַּיָית וְנָחָשׁ שֶׁבְּאֶרֶץ יִשְׂרָאֵל וְכָלֶב שׁוֹטֶה שֶׁבְּכָל־מָקוֹם. מַעֲשֶׂה שֶׁנָּפַל נָחָשׁ בַּשַׁבָּת וְעָמַד נַפְתִּי אֶחָד וַהֲרָגוֹ. אָמַר רִבִּי. פָּגַע בּוֹ כְיוֹצֵא בוֹ. וְלֹא מִן הַדְּבָרִים הַנֶּהֱרָגִין בַּשַׁבָּת אִינּוּן. פָּתַר לָהּ בְּבָאִין לְהַזִּיק. תַּנֵּי. רִבִּי יַעֲקֹב אוֹמֵר. הָרוֹאֶה נָחָשׁ וְעַקְרָב בְּתוֹךְ אַרְבַּע אַמּוֹת רָאוּי הָיָה שֶׁיָּמוּת בָּהֶם. אֶלָּא שֶׁרַחֲמִים שֶׁלַּמָּקוֹם מְרוּבִּין. אָמַר רַבָּן שִׁמְעוֹן. בַּמֶּה דְבָרִים אֲמוּרִים. בִּזְמַן שֶׁלֹּא הֲרָגָן. אֲבָל אִם הֲרָגָן לֹא נִרְאוּ לוֹ אֶלָּא שֶׁיְּהָרְגֵם. וַחֲכָמִים אוֹמְרִים. בֵּין כָּךְ וּבֵין כָּךְ לֹא נִרְאוּ לוֹ אֶלָּא בִזְכוּת.

[27]Rebbi Yannai said, one is permitted to kill a wasp on the Sabbath[28]. And it was stated thus: "Five are killed on the Sabbath: an Egyptian fly, and a wasp in Niniveh[29], and a scorpion in Adiabene, and a snake in the Land of Israel, and a rabid dog anywhere. It happened that a snake fell[30] on the

Sabbath, when a Nabatean got up and killed it. Rebbi said, it met its match.³¹" But are they not of the ones which are killed on the Sabbath? Explain it if they come to do damage.

It was stated, Rebbi Jacob says, he who sees a snake or a scorpion within four cubits was destined to die by them³², only that the mercy of the Omnipresent is abundant. Rabban Simeon said, when has this been said? If he did not kill them. But if he killed them they appeared to him so he could kill them. In any case they appeared to him only by merit³³.

27 The entire paragraph has a parallel in the Babli, 121b.
28 Because its sting is dangerous.
29 This may either mean Assyria or Naveh in the Bashan plateau, cf. *Berakhot* 5:2, Note 81.
30 Babli: "in the house of study".
31 The Babli discusses whether this is praise or rebuke.
32 Ordinarily they would have bitten or stung them without him being aware of their presence.
33 Since they are ubiquitous but rarely seen.

(14c line 3) כָּתוּב שִׁמְעוּ־זֹאת כָּל־הָעַמִּים הַאֲזִינוּ כָּל־יֹשְׁבֵי חָלֶד: רִבִּי אָחָא אָמַר רִבִּי אַבָּהוּ וְרַבָּנָן. חַד אָמַר. לָמָּה הוּא מוֹשֵׁל כָּל־בָּאֵי הָעוֹלָם בְּחוּלְדָה. אֶלָּא לְפִי שֶׁכָּל־מָה שֶׁיֵּשׁ בַּיַּבָּשָׁה יֵשׁ בַּיָּם. הַרְבֵּה מִינִים בַּיָּם מַה שֶׁאֵין בַּיַּבָּשָׁה וְאֵין חוּלְדָה בַּיָּם. וְחוֹרָנָה אָמַר. לָמָּה הוּא מוֹשֵׁל כָּל־בָּאֵי הָעוֹלָם בְּחוּלְדָה. אֶלָּא מָה הַחוּלְדָה הַזֹּאת גּוֹרֶרֶת וּמַנַּחַת וְאֵינָה יוֹדַעַת לְמִי הִיא מַנַּחַת. כָּךְ הֵן כָּל־בָּאֵי הָעוֹלָם. גּוֹרְרִין וּמַנִּיחִין גּוֹרְרִין וּמַנִּיחִין וְאֵינָן יוֹדְעִין לְמִי הֵן מַנִּיחִין. יִצְבֹּר וְלֹא־יֵדַע מִי־אוֹסְפָם:

It is written, *hear this all nations, listen all who dwell like moles*³⁴. Rebbi Aha said, Rebbi Abbahu and the rabbis. One said, why does he compare all creatures to a mole? Only because everything that exists on dry land exists in the sea, but there are many species in the sea which are not on land, and there is no mole in the sea. But the other said, why does he compare all creatures to a mole? Like this mole which drags and deposits and does not know for whom it deposits, so are the creatures, they always drag and collect and do not know for whom they collect; *he piles up and does not know for whom he assembled it*³⁵.

34 *Ps.* 49:1. Usually the word חֶלֶד "world" is derived from חלד "to be permanent", not חלד "to burrow".
35 *Ps.* 39:7.

(14c line 10) חַיָּה וָעוֹף שֶׁבִּרְשׁוּתוֹ הַצָּדָן פָּטוּר וְהַחוֹבֵל בָּהֶן חַיָּב: לֹא אָמְרוּ אֶלָּא שֶׁבִּרְשׁוּת אָדָם. הָא אִם אֵינָן בִּרְשׁוּת אָדָם חַיָּב. אָמַר רִבִּי יוֹסֵה. הָדָא אָמְרָה. שׁוֹר שֶׁמָּרַד הַצָּדוֹ בַשַּׁבָּת חַיָּיב. רַבָּנָן דְּקַיְסָרִין בְּשֵׁם רַב אֲבִדָן. עוֹר עוֹף מוּתָּר לִכְתּוֹב עָלָיו מְזוּזָה.

"Wild animals and fowl in his possession: if he catches them he is not liable but if he injures them he is liable." They said this only if it is under the control of a human[36]. Therefore if it is not under the control of a human he is liable. Rebbi Yose said, this means that one who on the Sabbath catches an escaped bull is liable. The rabbis of Caesarea in the name of Rav Avidan: One is permitted to write a *mezuzah* on bird's skin[36].

35 What counts on the Sabbath is not the property right but actual control. A wild animal kept in a cage, which may not be personal property, is possession for the laws of the Sabbath but a herd of cattle roaming in the wild, while being property for civil law is not property for the Sabbath.

36 Since injuring fowl on the Sabbath is a violation, their skin is hide as explained in the first paragraph. Babli 108a.

(14c line 14) ב'. אֵין עוֹשִׂין הִילְמִי בַּשַּׁבָּת. מַה בֵּין הִילְמִי וּמַה בֵּין מֵי מֶלַח. הִילְמִי צְרִיכָה אוּמָן. מֵי מֶלַח אֵין צְרִיכָה אוּמָן. רַב חוּנָא אָמַר. כָּל־שֶׁנּוֹתְנִין לְתוֹכָהּ מֶלַח וְהִיא נְשָׁרֵית זוֹ הִיא מֵי מֶלַח. וְשֶׁאֵינָהּ נְשָׁרֵית זוֹ הִיא הִילְמִי. אָמַר רִבִּי אַבָּהוּ. כָּל־שֶׁנּוֹתְנִים לְתוֹכָהּ בֵּיצָה וְהִיא שׁוֹקַעַת זוֹ הִיא מֵי מֶלַח. וְשֶׁאֵינָהּ שׁוֹקַעַת זוֹ הִיא הִילְמִי.

עוֹשִׁין יֵינוֹמֵילִין בַּשַּׁבָּת. רִבִּי יָסָא בְשֵׁם רִבִּי יוֹחָנָן. יַיִן וּדְבַשׁ וּפִילְפְּלִין. רִבִּי יָסָא בְשֵׁם רִבִּי יוֹחָנָן. מוּתָּר לְעָרֵב וְאָסוּר לִשְׁחוֹק. רִבִּי יָסָא בְשֵׁם רִבִּי יוֹחָנָן. אֶת שֶׁהוּא מִשּׁוּם תַּעֲרוֹבֶת מוּתָּר. מִשּׁוּם שְׁחִיקָה אָסוּר. וְהָכָא. לֹא מִשּׁוּם תַּעֲרוֹבֶת אֲנָן קַיָּימִין. רִבִּי יְהוּדָה בֶּן טִיטַס רִבִּי יְהוּדָה בֶּן פָּזִי שִׁמְעוֹן בַּר בָּא בְשֵׁם רִבִּי יוֹחָנָן. שַׁנְיָיא הִיא הָכָא שֶׁהִיא גְמַר מְלָאכָה. רִבִּי אַבָּהוּ בְשֵׁם רִבִּי יוֹחָנָן. מוּתָּר לְשַׁבֵּר וְאָסוּר לְקַבֵּץ. רִבִּי אַבָּהוּ בְשֵׁם רִבִּי יוֹחָנָן. שׁוּם שֶׁשְּׁחָקוֹ. אִם הָיָה מְחוּסָּר שְׁחִיקָה אָסוּר. וְאִם לְעָרֵב אֶת שׁוּמָנָן מוּתָּר. תַּמָּן תַּנִּינָן. הַשּׁוּם וְהַבּוֹסֶר וְהַמְּלִילוֹת שֶׁרִיסְּקָן מִבְּעוֹד יוֹם. שֶׁהָיָה רִבִּי יִשְׁמָעֵאל אוֹמֵר. יִגְמוֹר מִשֶּׁתֶּחְשַׁךְ. וְרִבִּי עֲקִיבָא אוֹמֵר. לֹא יִגְמוֹר. רִבִּי יַעֲקֹב בַּר אָחָא רִבִּי שִׁמְעוֹן בַּר בָּא בְשֵׁם רִבִּי חֲנִינָא. לֹא נֶחְלְקוּ אֶלָּא בְחוּלִין. הַכֹּהֲנִים נָהֲגוּ בִתְרוּמָה כְרִבִּי יִשְׁמָעֵאל.

2. "One makes no brine on the Sabbath." What is the difference between brine and salt water? Brine needs a craftsman, salt water needs no craftsman. Rav Huna said, anything to which one adds salt and it dissolves is salt water, if it does not dissolve it is brine[37]. Rebbi Abbahu said, anything where one puts in an egg and it sinks is saltwater, if it does not sink it is brine[38].

One may make honeywine[39] on the Sabbath. Rebbi Yasa in the name of Rebbi Johanan: wine, honey, and pepper[40]. Rebbi Yasa in the name of Rebbi Johanan: one is permitted to mix but forbidden to grind. Rebbi Yasa in the name of Rebbi Johanan: Anything for mixing is permitted, for grinding is forbidden. But do we not deal here with mixing[41]? Rebbi Jehudah ben Titus, Rebbi Jehudah ben Pazi, Simeon bar Abba in the name of Rebbi Johanan: there is a difference here since it is completion of production[42].

Rebbi Abbahu in the name of Rebbi Johanan: one is permitted to break but forbidden to assemble[43]. Rebbi Abbahu in the name of Rebbi Johanan: ground garlic. If it needed grinding it is forbidden, but if to mix into fat it is permitted[44].

There, we have stated[45]: "About garlic, unripe grapes, and grain kernels which he squashed when it was still daylight, Rebbi Ismael used to say, he should finish after nightfall, Rebbi Aqiba said, he may not finish." Rebbi Jacob bar Aha, Rebbi Simeon bar Abba in the name of Rebbi Johanan: they disagreed only about profane food. "The Cohanim for heave used to follow Rebbi Ismael[46]."

37 Brine is only water saturated with salt.
38 He makes the definition dependent on the specific weight of the solution. Babli 108b.
39 οἰνόμελι, -ιτος, τό.
40 This is repeated in Chapter 20.
41 There seems to be no reason to forbid making brine of the Sabbath.
42 The prohibition has nothing to do with the rules of the preparation of food. Sine it was stated earlier that making brine is professional, completing the process is "hitting with a hammer."
43 One may break food apart but one may not put it together so that it becomes a new item. For example, one may not make a fig cake or string figs out of individual figs (Maimonides *Šabbat* 8:6).
44 Grinding garlic as garlic is forbidden, grating garlic into fat is permitted.
45 Mishnah *Idiut* 2:6, Tosephta *Idiut* 1:9.
46 Tosephta *Idiut* 1:9.

(14c line 29) ג'. חַד בַּר נָשׁ שָׁאַל לְרִבִּי שִׁמְעוֹן בַּר כַּרְסָנָא. מָהוּ מִישְׁתֵּי קָרִירְטוֹן בַּשַּׁבָּת. אָמַר לֵיהּ. אִם לְתַעֲנוּג מוּתָּר. אִם לִרְפוּאָה אָסוּר. וְלֹא מִן הַשָּׁפָה וְלִפְנִים הוּא. פָּתַר לָהּ. בִּלְבַד דָּבָר שֶׁהוּא שֶׁלְּסַכָּנָה.

3. A man asked Rebbi Simeon bar Karsana: May one drink claret[47] on the Sabbath? He said to him, if for enjoyment it is permitted, if as medicine it is forbidden. But is that not inside the lips[48]? Explain it, if there is danger[49].

47 The identification of קְרִירְטוֹן as late Latin *claretum* is Musaphia's.
48 As stated in *Avodah zarah* Chapter 2 (Note 109), "everything inside of the lips constitutes a danger to life." One might think that this constitutes a general permission to practice internal medicine on the Sabbath.
49 Only internal injuries are automatically declared as life-threatening. All other internal problems need medical evaluation.

(14c line 32) אֲבָל אוֹכֵל הוּא אֶת יוֹעֵזֶר. פּוֹלִיטְרִיכוֹן. וְשׁוֹתֶה אַבּוּב רוֹעֶה. כִּשְׁמוּעוֹ.

"But one may eat true maiden hair" πολύτριχον[50]. "And drink shepherd's flute[9]," as the simple meaning of the word.

50 *Adiantum Capillus Veneris L.*

(14c line 33) רִבִּי בָּא שְׁאַל לְרִבִּי יִרְמְיָה. מַה נִיתְנֵי. דְּקָרִין דְּקָלִין. אָמַר לֵיהּ. דְּקָרִין. שֶׁהֵן דּוֹקְרִין אֶת הַמָּרָה. אָמַר רִבִּי יוֹנָה. לֹא מִסְתַּבְּרָא אֶלָּא דְּקָלִין. שֶׁהֵן יוֹצְאִין מִבֵּין שְׁנֵי דְּקָלִין.
שִׁמְעוֹן בַּר בָּא בְּשֵׁם רִבִּי חֲנִינָה. זֶה שֶׁהוּא לוֹחֵשׁ נוֹתֵן שֶׁמֶן עַל גַּבֵּי רֹאשׁוֹ וְלוֹחֵשׁ. בִּלְבַד שֶׁלֹּא יִתֵּן לֹא בְּיָד וְלֹא בְּכֵלִי. רִבִּי יַעֲקֹב בַּר אִידִי רִבִּי יוֹחָנָן בְּשֵׁם רִבִּי יַנַּאי. נוֹתֵן בֵּין בְּיָד בֵּין בִּכְלִי. מַה בֵּינֵיהוֹן. מָאִיסָה. מָאן דְּאָמַר. נוֹתֵן בֵּין בְּיָד בֵּין בִּכְלִי. מָאוּס הוּא. מָאן דְּאָמַר. נוֹתֵן שֶׁמֶן עַל גַּבֵּי רֹאשׁוֹ. אֵינוֹ מָאוּס. אָמַר רִבִּי יוֹנָה. מַעֲשֵׂר שֵׁינִי בֵּינֵיהוֹן. נוֹתֵן בֵּין בְּיָד בֵּין בִּכְלִי. מַעֲשֵׂר שֵׁינִי אָסוּר. מָאן דְּאָמַר. נוֹתֵן שֶׁמֶן עַל גַּבֵּי רֹאשׁוֹ וְלוֹחֵשׁ. מַעֲשֵׂר שֵׁינִי מוּתָּר. אָמַר רִבִּי יוֹסֵה. וְכִי כָּל־שֶׁמּוּתָּר בַּשַּׁבָּת מוּתָּר בְּמַעֲשֵׂר שֵׁינִי וְכָל־שֶׁאָסוּר בַּשַּׁבָּת אָסוּר בְּמַעֲשֵׂר שֵׁינִי. וְהָא תַּנֵּי. מַדִּיחָה הִיא אִשָּׁה עַצְמָהּ וּבְנָהּ בְּיַיִן מִפְּנֵי הַזִּיעָה. בִּתְרוּמָה אָסוּר. הִיא תְּרוּמָה הִיא מַעֲשֵׂר שֵׁינִי. מַהִיא כְדוֹן. בִּלְבַד שֶׁלֹּא יַעֲשֶׂה בַּשַּׁבָּת כְּדֶרֶךְ שֶׁהוּא עוֹשֶׂה בַחוֹל.

1 חנינה | ד חנינא בלבד | ד ובלבד   4 ראשו | ד ראשו ולוחש   6 יוסה | ד יוסי   שמותר | ד שהוא מותר   7 שיני | ד שני   והא תני | ד והתני עצמה | ד -   ובנה | ד בנה   8 מהיא | ד מהו   בלבד | ד ובלבד   שהוא עושה | ד שעושה

לוֹחֲשִׁין לָעַיִן וּלְמֵעַיִים וְלִנְחָשִׁים וְלַעֲקְרַבִּים וּמַעֲבִירִין עַל הָעַיִן בַּשַּׁבָּת. מַעֲשֶׂה בְּרִבִּי עֲקִיבָה שֶׁאֲחָזַתּוּ הָעַיִן וְהֶעֱבִירוּ עָלָיו כֵּלִים בַּשַּׁבָּת.

Rebbi Abba asked Rebbi Jeremiah, how should we state, *deqarin, deqalin*? He said, *deqarin*, because it pierces the gall bladder. Rebbi Jonah said, it is more reasonable *deqalin*, because it gushes forth between two palm trees[51].

[52]Simeon bar Abba in the name of Rebbi Ḥanina: One who whispers[53] puts oil on his head and whispers, on condition that he use neither hand nor vessel[54]. Rebbi Jacob bar Idi, Rebbi Joḥanan in the name of Rebbi Yannai, he may use both hand or vessel[55]. What is the difference between them? Disgust. For him who says, he may use either hand or vessel, it is disgusting. For him who says, he puts oil on his head, it is not disgusting. Rebbi Jonah said, Second Tithe is the difference between them. For him who says, he may use either hand or vessel, Second Tithe is forbidden[56]. For him who says, he puts oil on his head and whispers, Second Tithe is permitted. Rebbi Yose said, is everything permitted on the Sabbath permitted with Second Tithe and everything forbidden on the Sabbath forbidden with Second Tithe? But was it not stated[57]: "A woman may douse herself and her son with wine because of sweat;" "[58]this is forbidden for heave." There is no difference between heave and Second Tithe. What about it? On condition that he not proceed on the Sabbath the way he proceeds on a weekday[59].

One recites spells for the eye, and for intestines, and for snakes[60], and for scorpions[61], and one puts things on the eye on the Sabbath. It happened that Rebbi Aqiba had an eye attack and they put vessels over his eye on the Sabbath.

51   Quoted in *Berakhot* 6:8 (Note 231).

52   The source of the text is *Ma`aser Šeni* 2:1, Notes 38-44 (ז); it is referred to in *Šabbat* 6, Notes 189-191.

53   A medical procedure where rubbing with oil is accompanied by whispered recitation of charms for illnesses of the eye, intestines, and snake and scorpion bites. The Babli (*Sanhedrin* 101a) approves whispered charms only for snake and scorpion bites; for eye and intestinal problems they approve only anointing and wrappings.

54   These rules are only given for the Sabbath when medical procedures are forbidden if there is no danger to the life of the patient.

55   "Hand" means to pour an amount of oil into one's palm and taking it from there by a finger of the other hand. "Vessel" is not the large container of the oil but a small cup containing just enough oil for the procedure. Its use is permitted on the Sabbath for people who would be repelled by the idea of dipping a finger into the jar of cooking oil.

56   It is forbidden to use Second Tithe oil for medical purposes; it is permitted to use it for anointing. It is suggested that just smearing oil on one's head with a finger is a form of anointing; this is rejected immediately.

57 Tosephta 12:13 (ed. Liebermann).	on the Sabbath and vice-versa.
58 Tosephta *Terumot* 9:15.	60 Snake bites. Cf. Babli *Sanhedrin* 101a.
59 What is the real reason for the rule of whispering? Anybody who does it with a vessel on weekdays has to do it without one	61 Scorpion stings.

(14c line 49) רַב וְרִבִּי חִייָה רַבָּה תְּרֵיהוֹן אָמְרִין. תִּשְׁעִים וְתִשְׁעָה מֵתִים בָּעַיִן וְאֶחָד בִּידֵי שָׁמַיִם. רִבִּי חֲנִינָה וּשְׁמוּאֵל תְּרֵיהוֹן אָמְרִין. תִּשְׁעִים וְתִשְׁעָה מֵתִים בְּצִינָּה וְאֶחָד בִּידֵי שָׁמַיִם. רַב אָמַר כְּדַעְתֵּיהּ וְרִבִּי חֲנִינָא אָמַר כְּדַעְתֵּיהּ. רַב עַל יְדֵי דַהֲוָה שָׁרֵי תַּמָּן דְּעֵיינָא בִּישָׁא שְׁכִיחָה תַּמָּן הֲוָה אֲמַר. תִּשְׁעִים וְתִשְׁעָה מֵתִים בָּעַיְינָא וְאֶחָד בִּידֵי שָׁמַיִם. רִבִּי חֲנִינָה עַל דַּהֲוָה שָׁרֵי בְּצִיפֵּרִין דְּצִיְנְּתָא תַּמָּן הֲוָה אֲמַר. תִּשְׁעִים וְתִשְׁעָה מֵתִים בְּצִינָה וְאֶחָד בִּידֵי שָׁמַיִם. רִבִּי שְׁמוּאֵל בַּר נַחְמָן בְּשֵׁם רִבִּי יוֹנָתָן. תִּשְׁעִים וְתִשְׁעָה מֵתִים בַּשָּׁרָב וְאֶחָד בִּידֵי שָׁמַיִם. וְרַבָּנִין אָמְרֵי. תִּשְׁעָה וְתִשְׁעָה מֵתִים בִּפְשִׁיעָה וְאֶחָד בִּידֵי שָׁמַיִם.

Rav and the Elder Rebbi Ḥiyya both say, ninety-nine die because of the eye and one by the hand of Heaven. Rebbi Ḥanina and Samuel both say, ninety-nine die because of cold and one by the hand of Heaven. Rav follows his opinion and Rebbi Ḥanina follows his opinion. Since Rav was living there[62], where the evil eye[63] is prevalent, he did say that ninety-nine die because of the eye and one by the hand of Heaven. Since Rebbi Ḥanina was living in Sepphoris, where it is cold, he did say that ninety-nine die because of cold and one by the hand of Heaven. Rebbi Samuel bar Naḥman in the name of Rebbi Jonathan: Ninety-nine die because of hot wind[64] and one by the hand of Heaven. But the rabbis say, ninety-nine die because of criminal negligence[65] and one by the hand of Heaven.

62 In Babylonia.	against magic spells.
63 Based on this statement, some Medieval authors explain that the treatment authorized in the preceding paragraph does not refer to ophthalmology but to action	64 The desert wind which is accompanied by extremely low relative humidity.
	65 Medical malpractice.

(14c line 58) רִבִּי חוּנְיָא יַעֲקֹב מֵעֲפַרְתַּיִם בְּשֵׁם רִבִּי. וְהֵסִיר יי מִמְּךָ כָּל־חוֹלִי. זוֹ שְׂרִיפָה. רִבִּי חוּנָה וְתַנֵּי לָהּ בְּשֵׁם רִבִּי אֱלִיעֶזֶר בֶּן יַעֲקֹב. וְהֵסִיר יי מִמְּךָ כָּל־חוֹלִי. זֶה רְעָיוֹן. דְּאָמַר רִבִּי אֶלְעָזָר. וְנָתַן עוֹל בַּרְזֶל עַל־צַוָּארֶךָ. זֶה רְעָיוֹן. אָמַר רִבִּי אָבוּן. וְהֵסִיר יי מִמְּךָ כָּל־חוֹלִי. זֶה יֵצֶר הָרָע

שֶׁרֹאשׁוֹ מָתוֹק וְסוֹפוֹ מַר. רִבִּי תַּנְחוּמָא בְשֵׁם רִבִּי אֶלְעָזָר רִבִּי מְנַחֲמָה בְשֵׁם רַב. וְהֵסִיר יְיָ מִמְּךָ כָּל־חוֹלִי. זֶה הַמָּרָה. דְּאָמַר רִבִּי אֶלְעָזָר. תִּשְׁעִים וְתִשְׁעָה מֵתִים בְּמָרָה וְאֶחָד בִּידֵי שָׁמַיִם.

Rebbi Onias, Jacob from Afartaim[66] in the name of Rebbi: *The Eternal will remove from you all sickness*[67], that is fever. Rebbi Huna who stated it in the name of Rebbi Eliezer ben Jacob, *the Eternal will remove from you all sickness*, that is worry, as Rebbi Eleazar said, *he will put an iron yoke on your neck*[68], this is worry. Rebbi Abun said, *the Eternal will remove from you all sickness*, that is the evil impulse whose start is sweet but whose end is bitter. Rebbi Tanhuma in the name of Rebbi Eleazar[69], Rebbi Menahema in the name of Rav: *The Eternal will remove from you all sickness*, that is the gall bladder[70], as Rebbi Eleazar said, ninety-nine die because of gall and one by the hand of Heaven.

66	This probably is biblical חֲפָרַיִם (*Jos.* 19:19).	68	*Deut.* 7:15.
		69	Babli *Bava mesia'* 107b.
67	*Deut.* 28:48.	70	Babli *Bava qamma* 92b.

(14c line 65) רוֹחֲצִין בְּיָם הַגָּדוֹל וּבְמֵי טִיבֶּרְיָא אַף עַל פִּי שֶׁהוּא מִתְכַּוֵּין לִרְפוּאָה. אֲבָל לֹא בְמֵי מִשְׁרָה וְלֹא בְמֵי סְדוֹם. אֵימָתַי. בִּזְמָן שֶׁהוּא מִתְכַּוֵּין לִרְפוּאָה. הָא לַעֲלוֹת מִטּוּמְאָה לְטָהֳרָה מוּתָּר. אָמַר רִבִּי שְׁמוּאֵל אָחוִי דְּרִבִּי בֶּרֶכְיָה. בִּלְבַד שֶׁלֹּא יִשְׁהֵא.

תַּנֵּי. סָכִין אֱלִינְתִּין לְחוֹלֶה בַשַּׁבָּת. אֵימָתַי. בִּזְמָן שֶׁטְּרָפוֹ בְעֶרֶב שַׁבָּת. אֲבָל אִם לֹא טְרָפוֹ מֵעֶרֶב שַׁבָּת אָסוּר. אָמַר רִבִּי שְׁמוּאֵל בֶּן אֶלְעָזָר. מַתִּיר הָיָה רִבִּי מֵאִיר לִטְרוֹף יַיִן וְשֶׁמֶן וְלָסוּךְ לְחוֹלֶה בַשַּׁבָּת. וּכְבָר חָלָה וּבִקַּשְׁנוּ לַעֲשׂוֹת לוֹ כֵן. וְלֹא הִנִּיחַ לָנוּ. אָמַרְנוּ לוֹ. רִבִּי. מְבַטֵּל אַתְּ דְּבָרֶיךָ בְחַיֶּיךָ. אָמַר לָהֶן. אַף עַל פִּי שֶׁהָיִיתִי אוֹמֵר כֵּן לֹא מְלָאַנִי לִבִּי מִיָּמַי לַעֲבוֹר עַל דִּבְרֵי חֲבֵרַיי.

[71]One may bathe in the ocean and in the waters of Tiberias even though one intends to do this for medical purposes, but not in water used for soaking flax or in the Dead Sea[72]. When? If he intended this for medical purposes; therefore to lift himself from impurity to purity it is permitted[73]. Rebbi Samuel, Rebbi Berekhiah's brother said, on condition that he not tarry[74].

It was stated[75]: One rubs *olentia*[76] on a sick person on the Sabbath; but only if it was mixed with oil and wine before Sabbath eve. But if he did not mix it before Sabbath eve it is forbidden. It was stated: Rebbi Simeon ben Eleazar said: Rebbi Meïr did allow to mix wine and oil and to rub it onto a sick person on Sabbath. When he fell sick, we wanted to prepare the same for him but he did not let us do it. We said to him: Our teacher, are you going to invalidate your words when your life is in danger? [77]He said to them: even though I did say so, I never intended to transgress the words of my colleagues.

71 Babli 109a.

72 Since everybody bathes both in the ocean or in the Sea of Galilee or the hot springs of Tiberias also on weekdays, nobody will notice that one bathes for medical reasons. But in a natural pond used to treat flax or in the Dead Sea one bathes only for medical reasons; this is rabbinically forbidden.

73 Using the pond or the Dead Sea as a *miqweh* cannot be forbidden since it is biblically justified.

74 Since immersion in a *miqweh* is done very quickly, staying in the water for more than a minimal time would be proof that the bathing was for medical purposes.

75 Tosephta 12:12 (ed. Liebermann); *Berakhot* 1:2 Note 126.

76 Latin "sweet smelling things" (E. G.) Cf. the text in *Berakhot* for a discussion of this translation.

77 This sentence is found in the Tosephta, a completely different one is given in *Berakhot*.

(14c line 73) ד׳. כָּתוּב כַּחוֹמֶץ לַשִּׁינַּיִם וְכֶעָשָׁן לָעֵינָיִם וְאַתְּ אָמַר הָכֵין. אָמַר רִבִּי שִׁמְעוֹן בַּר בָּא. כְּחוּמְצָן שֶׁלְּפֵּירוֹת הִיא מַתְנִיתָא. אָמַר רִבִּי אֶלְעָזָר בַּר יוֹסֵה. וְאָפִילוּ תֵימַר בְּמַתְנִיתִין. טַב לְבִישְׁתָּא וּבִישׁ לְטַבְתָּא.

4. It is written[78], *like vinegar for the teeth or like smoke for the eyes*, and you are saying so? Rebbi Simeon bar Abba said, the Mishnah is about fruit vinegar[79]. Rebbi Eleazar bar Yose[80] said, even if you are saying as our Mishnah, it is good for a bad situation and bad for a good one.

78 Prov. 10:26. The verse ends, *so is a lazy employee for his employer*. This implies that vinegar is bad for the teeth; how may the Mishnah recommend it to treat toothache?

79 And the verse in *Prov.* about wine vinegar. In the Babli 111a the explanation is attributed to R. Abbahu.

80 Since R. Simeon bar Abba was a third generation Amora, R. Eleazar bar Yose cannot be the Tanna R. Eleazar ben R. Yose; he must be a fourth or fifth generation Amora not otherwise mentioned in the Talmudim.

(14c line 76) תַּנֵּי. לֹא יְהֵא מְנַמְמֵא חוֹמֶץ וּפוֹלֵט. אֲבָל מְנַמְמֵא הוּא חוֹמֶץ וּבוֹלֵעַ. מַתְנִיתָא אָמְרָה שֶׁאָסוּר לְגַמּוֹת וְלִבְלוֹעַ. דְּתַנִּינָן. הַחוֹשֵׁשׁ שִׁינָּיו לֹא יְגַמֵּא בָּהֶן חוֹמֶץ. מָה הִיא כְדוֹן. אוֹ כְרִבִּי. אוֹ כְדִבְרֵי הַכֹּל בִּמְגַמֵּא חוֹמֶץ שֶׁלְּתרוּמָה אַחַר טִיבּוּלוֹ.

It was stated[81]: One should not sip vinegar and spit it out, but he may sip vinegar and swallow. The Mishnah says that it is forbidden to sip and to swallow, as we have stated, "One whose teeth are aching may not sip[13] vinegar." What about it? Either following Rebbi or following everyone who sips vinegar of heave after dipping[82].

81   Babli 111a, *Besah* 18b.

82   On the face of it one would be tempted to delete "of heave" but the reference is needed to explain the disagreement between Rebbi and the rabbis which is referred to in the next paragraph. It is clear that on the Sabbath one may not sip vinegar and then spit it out since this clearly indicates that the vinegar was not intended as food but as medicine. On the other hand, vinegar used to dip one's bread (Note 14) is food. The question is whether using bread to absorb an excessive amount of vinegar and then sucking the vinegar out of the bread to treat the toothache is permitted or forbidden.

This now is connected with a problem about heave, which must be eaten by a Cohen in purity. Consumption of heave by an unauthorized person not only is sinful but subjects the offender to a fine of 25% of the value of the food used illegitimately. If such a person uses heave vinegar to dip his bread he clearly uses food and is subject to the fine. If he uses the vinegar as medicine he sinned twice (he used heave illegitimately and he did not use it as food) but he is not subject to the fine. Sucking the vinegar out of the bread and using it for a toothache presents a problem similar to that of use on the Sabbath. Rebbi holds that it is food.

(14d line 3) רִבִּי אַבָּהוּ בְשֵׁם רִבִּי יוֹחָנָן הַכּוֹסֵס חִטֵּי כִלְאֵי הַכֶּרֶם לוֹקֶה. הַכּוֹסֵס חִיטֵּי תְרוּמָה לוֹקֶה. רִבִּי אַבָּהוּ בְשֵׁם רִבִּי יוֹחָנָן. הַמְגַמֵּא חוֹמֶץ שֶׁלתְרוּמָה לוֹקֶה. הַמְגַמֵּא חוֹמֶץ שֶׁלתְרוּמָה מְשַׁלֵּם אֶת הַקֶּרֶן וְאֵינוּ מְשַׁלֵּם אֶת הַחוֹמֶשׁ. הַכּוֹסֵס חִטִּים שֶׁלתְרוּמָה מְשַׁלֵּם אֶת הַקֶּרֶן וְאֵינוּ מְשַׁלֵּם אֶת הַחוֹמֶשׁ. רִבִּי אוֹמֵר. אוֹמֵר אֲנִי שֶׁהוּא מְשַׁלֵּם קֶרֶן וְחוֹמֶשׁ. רִבִּי יִרְמְיָה בְשֵׁם רִבִּי אִימִּי. מוֹדִין חֲכָמִים לְרִבִּי בִּמְגַמֵּא חוֹמֶץ שֶׁלתְרוּמָה אַחַר טִיבּוּלוֹ שֶׁהוּא מְשַׁלֵּם קֶרֶן וְחוֹמֶשׁ. שֶׁהַחוֹמֶץ מְיַישֵּׁב אֶת הַנֶּפֶשׁ.

1 הכוסס חטי | ו האוכל - | ו ר' אבהו בשם ר' יוחנן   2 המגמא (second occurrence) | ו המגמע   3 חטים שלתרומה | ו חיטי תרומה   5 אימי | ו אמי | ו במגמא | ו במגמע   טיבולו | ו טיבלו[83] שהוא | ו -   6 מיישב | ו מישב

[84]Rebbi Abbahu in the name of Rebbi Johanan: He who chews wheat grain of *kilaim* in a vineyard[85] is whipped[86]; he who chews wheat grain[87] of heave is whipped. Rebbi Abbahu in the name of Rebbi Johanan, he who sips vinegar of heave is whipped; he who sips vinegar of heave pays the principal but he does not pay the fifth[88]; he who chews wheat grain of heave pays the principal but he does not pay the fifth. Rebbi says, I am saying that he pays

principal and fifth. Rebbi Jeremiah in the name of Rebbi Immi: The rabbis agree with Rebbi about one who sips heave vinegar from his dipping that he pays principal and fifth since vinegar refreshes[89].

83 Clearly a misspelling.

84 The main source of this paragraph is *Terumot* 6:1, Notes 16-19, which is a parallel but not identical text. The present text is copied in *Yoma* 8:3 (45a l.58,ו). Babli *Yoma* 80b/81a.

85 Any non-vine produce in a vineyard is prohibited for usufruct.

86 If there are witnesses to the act, since he broke a biblical commandment. This corresponds to the term "is liable" used for Sabbath violations.

87 He spits out the grain after chewing; otherwise he would eat it and there would be no problem.

88 The fifth computed from the top which is a quarter from the bottom.

89 Even though vinegar in itself is neither food nor drink, when it was absorbed by bread it becomes food and stays food. For heave it remains subject to the fine, on the day of Atonement it remains forbidden drink, but on the Sabbath it may be used for a toothache.

(14d line 10) חֲבֵרַיָּיא בְשֵׁם רבִּי בָּא בַר זַבְדָא. כָּל־שֶׁהוּא מִן הַשָּׂפָה וְלִפְנִים מְרַפִּין אוֹתוֹ בַּשַּׁבָּת. הָתִיב רִבִּי זְעִירָא. הָתַנֵּי. הַחוֹשֵׁשׁ שִׁינָּיו לֹא יְגַמֵּא בָּהֶן חוֹמֶץ. וְלֹא מִן הַשָּׂפָה וְלִפְנִים הוּא. [רבִּי זְעִירָא] לֹא אָמַר כֵּן. אֶלָּא רִבִּי זְעוִרָא בְשֵׁם רבִּי בָּא בַר זַבְדָא. כָּל־שֶׁהוּא מִן הֶחָלָל וְלִפְנִים מְרַפִּין אוֹתוֹ. רִבִּי זְעִירָא רִבִּי בָּא בַר זוּטְרָא רבִּי חֲנִינָא בְשֵׁם רבִּי. מַעֲלִין עֶצֶם שֶׁלְרֹאשׁ בַּשַּׁבָּת. רִבִּי חִיָּיה בַּר מָדַיָּיה רִבִּי יוֹנָה רִבִּי זְעִירָא רַבָּא בַר זוּטְרָא רבִּי חֲנִינָא בְשֵׁם רבִּי. מַעֲלִין בְּנוֹת אָזְנַיִם בַּשַּׁבָּת. תַּמָּן אָמְרִין בְּשֵׁם רבִּי יוֹחָנָן. עַיִן שֶׁמָּרְדָה מְרַפִּין אוֹתוֹ בַּשַּׁבָּת. רִבִּי אַבָּהוּ בְשֵׁם רבִּי יוֹחָנָן. גַּבּוֹת יָדַיִם וְגַבּוֹת רַגְלַיִם סַכָּנָה. רִבִּי אַבָּהוּ בְשֵׁם רבִּי יוֹחָנָן. הָהֵן סִימוֹקָא סַכָּנָה. אָמַר רִבִּי אַבּוּן. לוֹקְטִין לוֹ עוּקֵץ עַקְרָב בַּשַּׁבָּת. רַב אָמַר. הָהֵן חַמְרָא לְבַר מִן עַיְינָא שָׁרֵי. לְגוּ מִן עַיְינָא אֲסִיר. שְׁמוּאֵל אָמַר. הָהֵן רוֹק תָּפֵל אָסוּר לִיתֵּן עַל גַּבֵּי הָעַיִן בַּשַּׁבָּת. מִינָהּ אַתְּ שְׁמַע לַחֲזִיתָא. רַבָּנָן דְּקַיְסָרִין אָמְרֵי. הָדָא אוּרְדְּעָנָא סַכָּנָה. רִבִּי חִזְקִיָּה עַפַּיָּיא בְשֵׁם רַבָּנָן דְּקַיְסָרִין. הָדָא עַכְשְׁמוּנִיתָא סַכָּנָה. אָמַר רִבִּי שְׁמוּאֵל בַּר רַב יִצְחָק. הָדָא גוּמַרְתָּא סַכָּנָה. אָמַר רִבִּי יִרְמִיָה. נוֹתְנִין עָלֶיהָ חֲמֵץ בַּפֶּסַח. הָהֵן בְּלָעָה שָׁרֵי מִיפְקַתֵּיהּ בְּשׁוּבְתָּא. אָמַר רִבִּי יוֹסֵה. מַתְנִיתָא אָמְרָה כֵן. מַחַט שֶׁל יָד לִטּוֹל בָּהּ אֶת הַקּוֹץ. דְּלָא כֵן. מַה בֵּין קוֹץ וּמַה בֵּין בָּלַע. וְהָהֵן דְּעַיְינָא שְׁאָלוּן לְרבִּי יִרְמִיָה. אָמַר לוֹן. הָא רִבִּי בָּא קוּמֵיכוֹן. שְׁאָלוּן לֵיהּ וְשָׁרָא. אֲמַר לוֹן. אוּף אֲנָא שָׁרֵי.

[90]The colleagues in the name of Rebbi Abba bar Zavda: Anything inside of the lips one heals on the Sabbath[91]. Rebbi Ze'ira objected, did we not state: "One whose teeth are aching may not sip[13] vinegar,"? Is this not inside from the lips? [Rebbi Ze'ira][92] did not say so, but Rebbi Ze'ira in the name of

Rebbi Abba bar Zavda: Anything inside a body cavity one heals on the Sabbath[93]. Rebbi Ze'ira, Rebbi Abba bar Zuṭra, Rebbi Ḥanina in the name of Rebbi: One treats the bone of the skull on the Sabbath[94]. Rebbi Ḥiyya the Mede, Rebbi Jona, Rebbi Ze'ira, Rebbi Abba bar Zuṭra, Rebbi Ḥanina in the name of Rebbi: One treats glands of the throat[95] on the Sabbath. Rebbi Abbahu in the name of Rebbi Joḥanan: One treats an infected eye[96] on the Sabbath. There, they say in the name of Rebbi Joḥanan: Tops of hands and feet are a danger[97]. Rebbi Abbahu in the name of Rebbi Joḥanan: Red color is dangerous[98]. Rebbi Abin said, one removes the sting of a scorpion on the Sabbath. Rav said, wine for exterior treatment of the eye is permitted, inside the eye it is forbidden. Samuel said, tasteless spittle is forbidden for the eye on the Sabbath[99] From this you infer for lichen[100]. The rabbis of Caesarea said, *ranula*[101] is dangerous. Rebbi Ḥizqiah from Acco in the name of the rabbis of Caesarea: spider sickness[102] is dangerous. Rebbi Samuel bar Rav Isaac: gangrene is dangerous. Rebbi Jeremiah said, one can put sour dough on it on Passover[103]. A boil is permitted.[104] Rebbi Yose said, the Mishnah says this[105]: "A small needle to remove a thorn." Otherwise, what is the difference between a thorn and a boil? Darkening of the eye[106], they asked Rebbi Jeremiah. He told them, is not Rebbi Abba available for you? They asked Rebbi Abba who permitted. He[107] told them, also I am permitting it.

90 From here to almost the end of the Halakhah the text is from *Avodah zarah* 2:2, Notes 83-137.

91 In the Babli *Avodah zarah* 28a, this is the position of Rebbi Immi. Since medical practice usually involves activities biblically forbidden on the Sabbath, such as compounding medicines and ointments or surgical interventions, also healing activities which do not involve these prohibitions are rabbinically forbidden on the Sabbath. However, if a condition is life-threatening, Sabbath prohibitions do not apply. A declaration that "one heals such-and-such a condition on the Sabbath" is the equivalent of declaring the condition as life-threatening.

92 Added from the text in *Avodah zarah*.

93 Babli 27b/28a, in the name of R. Joḥanan.

94 Any injury to the skull.

95 Babli *Avodah zarah* 28b. The translation used here of "daughters of the ear" is an interpretation of Rashi's explanation in the Babli: "Sinews of the ear which sometimes are lowered and keep the jaws open; then it is necessary to lift them and this is dangerous."

96 "An eye which rebelled": it feels as if the eye would leave its place. Babli *Avodah*

zarah 28b.
97 Any wounds at these places are considered life-threatening. Babli *Avodah zarah* 28a.
98 Dark red color of a wound is an indication of a life-threatening infection.
99 Babli 108b, with the names of Rav and Samuel switched. Since people sometimes put wine on their eyelids for non-medical reasons, it is permitted to do the same for minor aches for which medical intervention would be forbidden on the Sabbath.
100 A skin disease, purely external.
101 "Frog" (Aramaic), Latin *ranula,* an infection of the mouth.
102 This may either describe the bite of a spider or more likely a cancerous growth looking like a spider.
103 Using leavened matter on Passover is a deadly sin but for medical purposes in life-threatening situations it may be used without hesitation.
104 A boil filled with pus may be opened on the Sabbath.
105 Mishnah 17:2. As explained in Chapter 17 one may move a vessel on the Sabbath only if it is of any use on this day. A sewing needle cannot be used for its usual function on the Sabbath but may be used to remove a thorn in one's foot or to open a boil.
106 This may describe a cataract or glaucoma.
107 R. Jeremiah.

(14d line 29) רִבִּי אַבָּהוּ בְשֵׁם רִבִּי יוֹחָנָן. הָהֵן (סִפְדּוֹנָה) צִיפּוֹרְנָה סַכָּנָה. רִבִּי יוֹחָנָן מַטְתֵי כֵן וַהֲוָה מִיתְּסִי קוֹמֵי בְּרַתֵּיהּ דְּדֹמִיטְיָנִיס דְּטִיבְּרָיָא. בְּעָרוּבְתָא כְּפָתֵי רוּמְשָׁא סְלִק לְגַבָּהּ. אָמַר לָהּ. מִצְרָךְ אֲנָא כְּלוּם לִמְחָר. אָמְרָה לֵיהּ. לֹא. וְאִין צָרְכַתָּהּ סַב גַּלְעִינִין דְּתָמָרִין בְּפַלְגְּהוֹן וְקִידִין. וְאִית דְּאָמְרִין. דְּנִיקְלַבָס. וְעוֹר דִּשְׂעָרִין וְצוֹאָה דְּמַיְינוֹק יְבִישָׁה. שְׁחוֹק וּטְפוֹל. וְלָא תֵימַר קוֹמֵי בַר נַשׁ. לִמְחָר אָעַל וּדְרָשָׁהּ בְּצִיבּוּרָא. אִית דְּאָמְרִין דְּחֶנְקַת נַפְשָׁהּ. וְאִית דְּאָמְרִין דְּאִיתְגַּיְיָרַת. אַתְּ שְׁמַע מִינָהּ תְּלַת. אַתְּ שְׁמַע מִינָהּ. הָהֵן צִיפְדּוֹנָה סַכָּנָה. אַתְּ שְׁמַע מִינָהּ דְּכָל־שֶׁהוּא מִן הַשָּׂפָה וְלִפְנִים מְרַפְּין אוֹתוֹ. וְאַתְּ שְׁמַע מִינָהּ. הַהוּא דְּאָמַר רִבִּי יַעֲקֹב בַּר אָחָא בְּשֵׁם רִבִּי יוֹחָנָן. אִם הָיָה רוֹפֵא אוּמָּן מוּתָּר.

רִבִּי יְהוֹשֻׁעַ בֶּן לֵוִי הֲוָה לֵיהּ קוֹלוֹס. הוֹרוּן לֵיהּ רִבִּי חֲנִינָא וְרִבִּי יוֹנָתָן מִישְׁחוֹק תַּחְלוֹסִין בְּשׁוּבְתָא וּמֵיתָן גּוֹ חַמְרָא עַתִּיקָא וְיִשְׁתֵּי וְלָא יִסְכָּן.

[108]Rebbi Abbahu in the name of Rebbi Johanan. Scurvy[109] is dangerous. Rebbi Johanan had it; he was treated by the daughter of Domitianus of Tiberias. Friday evening he went up to her and asked her, will I need anything tomorrow? She said no, but if you need anything take date pits split and heated, some say of Nicolaus dates, skin[110] of barley grain, and dry excrement of a baby, grind it and apply it; do not tell this to anybody. The next day he went up and preached it in public. She heard it and strangled herself; but some say that she converted[111]. You understand from this three

things. You understand that scurvy is dangerous. You understand that anything inside of the lips one heals[91]. You understand what Rebbi Jacob bar Aha said in the name of Rebbi Joḥanan: If he was a professional healer it is permitted[112].

Rebbi Joshua ben Levy was suffering from colic[113]; Rebbi Ḥanina and Rebbi Jonathan instructed him to grind *taḥlusin*[114], put it in old wine and drink it to avoid becoming endangered[115].

108 Babli *Avodah zara* 28a.
109 This is the meaning of צִפְדִּינָה in modern Hebrew. Rashi in the Babli *Avodah zara* explains the word as French *muguet*, English thrush, a sickness producing a musk like smell of the mouth..
110 Bran.
111 Either she committed suicide because she lost her trade secret or she converted because she admired R. Joḥanan who made the recipe public and did not try to make money through his knowledge.
112 This refers to the statement in *Avodah zarah* that one may not use a Gentile healer. This is qualified now that a publicly approbated trained physician may be used.

113 Greek κόλον, τό, "large intestine; disease of the colon."
114 This probably is a plural of תּוּכְלָא "hard unripe date" which can be ground rather than תְּחֵלֵי "cress, nasturtium" which could be cut but not ground.
115 Since this is not a usual drink; its use on the Sabbath is rabbinically prohibited but to avoid future danger this prohibition can be waived. R. Joshua ben Levy was himself at least as qualified as the other two authorities to decide but he did not want to apply a leniency to himself on his own word.

(14d line 41) בַּר בְּרֵיהּ הֲוָה לֵיהּ בָּלַע. אֲתָא חַד וּלְחַשׁ לֵיהּ בִּשְׁמֵיהּ דְּיֵשׁוּ פַּנְטֵרָא וְאִינְשַׁם. כְּדִנְפִיק אֲמַר לֵיהּ. מָאן לְחַשְׁתְּ לֵיהּ. אֲמַר לֵיהּ. מִילַת פְּלָן. אֲמַר לֵיהּ. נִיחַ הֲוָה לֵיהּ אִילּוּ הֲוָה מַיֵּית וְלָא כֵן. וַהֲוָות לֵיהּ כֵּן כְּשִׁגְגָה שֶׁיּוֹצֵא מִלִּפְנֵי הַשַּׁלִּיט.

רִבִּי יַעֲקֹב בַּר אִידִי בְּשֵׁם רִבִּי יוֹנָתָן. בַּכֹּל מִתְרַפְּאִין. חוּץ מֵעֲבוֹדָה זָרָה וְגִילּוּי עֲרָיוֹת וּשְׁפִיכוּת דָּמִים. רִבִּי פִּינְחָס בָּעֵי. עַד כְּדוֹן כְּשֶׁאָמַר לוֹ. הָבֵא לִי עֵצִים מֵעֲבוֹדָה זָרָה. וְהֵבִיא לוֹ. אָמַר לוֹ. הָבֵא לִי עָלִים סְתָם. וְהֵבִיא לוֹ מֵעֲבוֹדָה זָרָה. נִשְׁמְעִינָהּ מִן הָדָא. רִבִּי יוֹנָה הֲוָה לֵיהּ צְמַרְמוֹרִין. אַייתוֹן לֵיהּ מִן זְכַרוּתֵיהּ דְּדוֹרִי וְשָׁתָה. רִבִּי אָחָא אַייתוֹן לֵיהּ וְלָא שָׁתָה. אָמַר רִבִּי מָנָא. אִילּוּ יָדַע רִבִּי יוֹנָה מַאן אַבָּא מְמַן הֲוָה לָא אִשְׁתָּתֵה.

אָמַר רִבִּי חוּנָא. מַתְנִיתָא אָמְרָה כֵן שֶׁאֵין מִתְרַפְּאִין מִגִּילּוּי עֲרָיוֹת. וְתַנֵּי כֵן. לְפִיכָךְ הוּתַּר מִכְּלַל שַׁבָּת וְלֹא הוּתַּר מִכְּלַל נַעֲרָה מְאוֹרָסָה. הוּתַּר מִכְּלַל שַׁבָּת. וְלֹא לְהִתְרַפְּאוֹת. וְדִכְוָותָהּ. לֹא הוּתַּר מִכְּלַל נַעֲרָה מְאוֹרָסָה. אֲפִילּוּ לְהִתְרַפְּאוֹת. וְלֹא סוֹף דָּבָר שֶׁאָמַר לוֹ. הָבֵא לִי אֵשֶׁת אִישׁ.

אֶלָּא אֲפִילוּ לִשְׁמוֹעַ אֶת קוֹלָהּ. כְּהָדָא חַד בַּר נָשׁ רְחַם אִיתָא בְּיוֹמוֹי דְּרִבִּי אֶלְעָזָר וְסִכֵּן. אֲתוֹן שְׁאֲלוּן לֵיהּ. מָהוּ תֵּיעֲבוֹר קוֹמוֹי וְיֵיחִי. אֲמַר. יָמוּת וְלֹא כֵן. מָהוּ יִשְׁמַע קוֹלָהּ וְלֹא יָמוּת. אֲמַר. יָמוּת וְלֹא כֵן. מַה הֲוָת. רִבִּי יַעֲקֹב בַּר אִידִי וְרִבִּי יִצְחָק בַּר נַחְמָן. חַד אֲמַר. אֵשֶׁת אִישׁ. וְחוֹרָנָה אֲמַר. פְּנוּיָה. מָאן דָּמַר. אֵשֶׁת אִישׁ. נִיחָא. וּמָאן דָּמַר. פְּנוּיָה. וְהָא בַּר כּוֹחָא נַגְרָא רְחַם אִיתָא בְּיוֹמוֹי דְּרִבִּי אֶלְעָזָר וְשָׁרָא לֵיהּ. כָּאן בִּפְנוּיָה כָּאן בְּאֵשֶׁת אִישׁ. וַאֲפִילוּ תֵּימַר. כָּאן וְכָאן בִּפְנוּיָה. תִּיפְתָּר שֶׁנָּתַן עֵינָיו בָּהּ עַד שֶׁהִיא אֵשֶׁת אִישׁ. אִית דְּבָעֵי מֵימַר. אִיתָהּ רוֹבָה הֲוָות וְלֹא מִנְסָבָה. וְכָל־מַה דַהֲוָה עָבַד בְּאִיסּוּר הֲוָה מֵעֲבַד. בְּגִין כֵּן אָסַר לֵיהּ.

אָמַר רִבִּי חֲנִינָה. מַתְנִיתָא אֲמָרָה כֵן שֶׁאֵין מִתְרַפִּין מִשְׁפִיכוּת דָּמִים. דְּתַנִּינָן תַּמָּן. יָצָא רוּבּוֹ אֵין נוֹגְעִין בּוֹ. שֶׁאֵין דּוֹחִין נֶפֶשׁ מִפְּנֵי נֶפֶשׁ. לֹא סוֹף דָּבָר שֶׁאָמַר לוֹ. הֲרוֹג אֶת פְּלוֹנִי. אֶלָּא אֲפִילוּ חֲמוֹס אֶת פְּלוֹנִי. תַּנֵּי. גּוֹי בְּיִשְׂרָאֵל אָסוּר. יִשְׂרָאֵל בְּגוֹי מוּתָּר. רַב חִסְדָּא בָּעֵי. מָהוּ לְהַצִּיל נַפְשׁוֹ שֶׁלְּגָדוֹל בְּנַפְשׁוֹ שֶׁלְּקָטוֹן. הָתִיב רִבִּי יִרְמְיָה. וְלֹא מַתְנִיתָא הִיא. יָצָא רוּבּוֹ אֵין נוֹגְעִין בּוֹ שֶׁאֵין דּוֹחִין נֶפֶשׁ מִפְּנֵי נֶפֶשׁ. רִבִּי יוֹסֵה בֵּירְבִּי בּוּן בְּשֵׁם רַב חִסְדָּא. שַׁנְיָיא הִיא תַּמָּן. שֶׁאֵין אַתְּ יוֹדֵעַ מִי הוֹרֵג אֶת מִי.

מַעֲשֶׂה בְּרִבִּי אֶלְעָזָר בֶּן דָּמָה שֶׁנְּשָׁכוֹ נָחָשׁ. וּבָא יַעֲקֹב אִישׁ כְּפַר סָמָא מִשֵּׁם שֶׁל יֵשׁוּ פַּנְדִּירָא לְרַפְּאוֹתוֹ וְלֹא הִנִּיחַ לוֹ רִבִּי יִשְׁמָעֵאל. אָמַר לוֹ. אֲנִי אָבִיא רְאָיָיה שֶׁיְּרַפְּאֵנִי. לֹא הִסְפִּיק לְהָבִיא רְאָיָיה עַד שֶׁמֵּת בֶּן דָּמָה. אָמַר לוֹ רִבִּי יִשְׁמָעֵאל. אַשְׁרֶיךָ בֶּן דָּמָה. שֶׁיָּצָאתָ בְּשָׁלוֹם מִן הָעוֹלָם וְלֹא פָרַצְתָּה גְדֵירָן שֶׁלַּחֲכָמִים. דִּכְתִיב וּפוֹרֵץ גָּדֵר יִשְּׁכֶנּוּ נָחָשׁ. וְלֹא נָחָשׁ נְשָׁכוֹ. אֶלָּא שֶׁלֹּא יִשְּׁכֶנּוּ נָחָשׁ לֶעָתִד לָבוֹא. וּמָה הֲוָה לֵיהּ לְמֵימַר. אֲשֶׁר יַעֲשֶׂה אוֹתָם הָאָדָם וָחַי בָּהֶם.

His[116] grandson suffered from choking; there came one, whispered something in the name of Jesus ben Pantera[117] and he could breathe. When he left, he asked him[118], what did you say over him? He answered, such and such words. He said, it would have been better for him had he died and not heard these words. It happened to him[119], *like an erroneous order from a ruler.*

Rebbi Jacob bar Idi in the name of Rebbi Johanan: One heals with anything except pagan worship, uncovering nakednesses, and spilling blood[120]. Rebbi Phineas asked: So far if he said, bring me leaves from pagan worship, and he brought him. If he said to him bring me leaves unspecified and he brought him from pagan worship? Let us hear from the following: Rebbi Jonah had a fever attack. They brought him from the penis of Dori[121] and he drank. They brought to Rebbi Aha and he did not drink. Rebbi Mana said, if my father Rebbi Jonah had known from where it was, he would not have drunk[122].

Rebbi Huna said, a *baraita* implies that one does not heal through uncovering nakedness[123], as it was stated: The Sabbath was permitted in exceptional cases; the betrothed maiden was never permitted in exceptional cases[124]. Was not the Sabbath permitted in exceptional cases for healing? The betrothed maiden was never permitted, not even for healing. Not only if one said to another, bring me a married woman, but even to hear her voice, as the following[125]: In the days of Rebbi Eleazar a man loved a woman and fell dangerously ill. They came and asked him, should she parade before him that he may live? He said, he should die but not this. May he hear her voice and live? He said, he should die but not this. How was it? Rebbi Jacob bar Idi and Rebbi Isaac bar Naḥman, one said, she was a married woman, but one said, she was single. One who said that she was a married woman we understand. But the one who said that she was single? Did not Bar Koḥa the carpenter[126] love a woman in the days of Rebbi Eleazar and he permitted him[127]? One case about a married woman and the other about a single one. Even you may say, here and here about a single one; explain it that he became infatuated with her when she still was married. Some want to say, she was a woman of substance and did not want to marry.[128] Everything which he did was forbidden; therefore he did permit nothing to him.

Rebbi Ḥanina said, a *baraita* implies that one does not heal through spilling blood, as we have stated there[129]: "If most of his body was outside one does not touch him, for one does not push aside one life before another life." Not only if one would say, kill this person, but even if he told him, injure that person. It was stated, a Gentile against a Jew, is prohibited[130]; a Jew against a Gentile is permitted[131]. Rav Hisda asked, may one save the life of an adult with the life of a minor? Rebbi Jeremiah objected, did we not state, "If most of his body was outside one does not touch him, for one does not push aside one life before another life"? Rebbi Yose ben Rebbi Abun in the name of Rav Ḥisda, there it is different for it is not known who is endangering whom.[132]

It happened that Eleazar ben Dama was bitten by a snake and Jacob from Kefar-Sama came to heal him in the name of Jesus ben Pandera, but Rebbi Ismael prevented him[133]. He told him, I shall bring a proof that he can heal me. He could not bring proof before he died. Rebbi Ismael said to him, you are blessed, ben Dama, that you left this world in peace and did not tear down the fences of the Sages, as it is written[134], *he who tears down a fence will be bitten by a snake*. But did not a snake bite him? But that it will not bite him in the Future World[135]. What could he have said? *Which a person should do and live by them*[136].

116 R. Joshua ben Levi's grandson.

117 This name (or *Pandera*) is unexplained. [Perhaps a distortion of Greek παντάρκης, Latin *Pantarces*, "all-helping", a surname of Jupiter (E. G.)].

118 R. Joshua ben Levi asked the Christian missionary.

119 The grandson died. (*Eccl.* 10:5).

120 In the Babli, *Pesahim* 25a, the tradition is by R. Abin (Abun) in the name of R. Johanan. The three sins are those which one is not permitted to commit even in order to save one's life. Since Christian faith healing is rejected before pagan healing is discussed it is clear that it is not rejected as pagan but as falsely claiming to be Jewish.

121 A pagan statue with a spout in form of a penis, like Brussel's Manneken Piss.

122 Therefore healing by idolatrous materials is forbidden even if not specifically asked for.

123 The technical term for criminal acts of a sexual nature, including but not restricted to incest and adultery.

124 The laws of the Sabbath are suspended in the Temple where the prescribed sacrifices are slaughtered and burned, actions which outside would be capital crimes. But a preliminarily married woman is absolutely forbidden for any man without exception.

125 Babli *Sanhedrin* 75a. R. Eleazar here is the Tanna, ben Shamua.

126 It is possible that Ben Koha is not a proper name but means "strongman".

127 R. Eleazar permitted the man to date the woman and to contract a marriage which was neither pre-arranged nor brokered.

128 In the Babli they hold that the man was not interested in marriage at all, only in sex.

128 Mishnah *Ahilut* 7:6. The Mishnah states that if a child during childbirth endangers the life of the mother one saves the mother's life by cutting the fetus into pieces. But if head and part of the body are already born so that the baby breathes on his own one may not harm him. Maimonides in his Mishnah Commentary notes "all this is obvious and does not need commentary."

129 Even though the baby might be stillborn (this includes the possibility that he might not live for a full thirty days after birth, in which case a person killing the baby could not be prosecuted for murder), if actually he is breathing on his own he must be treated as certainly being alive.

130 He can be prosecuted in a Jewish court based of Noahide law, *Gen*. 9:6.

131 He is not prosecutable in a court, only by the king's police powers (cf. *Sanhedrin* 6:5 Note 75). As S. Liebermann points out, this seems to be a truncated quote from Tosephta *Avodah zarah* 8:5 "a Gentile against a Jew, is liable; a Jew against a Gentile is not liable, if he robbed or stole."

132 Since it cannot be proven whether the

mother endangered the baby or the baby the mother, it is not known whose life is forfaited.

133 Babli *Avodah zara* 27b. According to this source, ben Dama was the son of R. Ismael's sister.

134 *Eccl.* 10:8. The fence is a stone wall without mortar with holes in which a snake may hide.

135 The mythical snake which seduced Eve.

136 *Lev.* 18:5.

(15a line 1) רִבִּי בָּא בַּר זַבְדָּא בְשֵׁם רַב. הֲלָכָה כְּרִבִּי שִׁמְעוֹן. דְּלֹא כֵן. מִי נָתַן שֶׁמֶן וֶרֶד לְעָנִי וְלֹא סָךְ.

אָמַר רִבִּי זְעוּרָה לְרִבִּי יוֹסֵי. חֲכִים רִבִּי לְבַר פְּדָיָה דְאַתְּ אֲמַר שְׁמוּעֲתָא מִן שְׁמֵיהּ. אֲמַר לֵיהּ. רִבִּי יוֹחָנָן אָמְרָן מִשְּׁמוֹ. אָמַר רִבִּי זְעוּרָה לְרִבִּי בָּא בַּר זַבְדָּא. חֲכִים רִבִּי לְרַב דְאַתְּ אֲמַר שְׁמוּעֲתָא מִן שְׁמֵיהּ. אֲמַר לֵיהּ. רַב אָדָא בַּר אַהֲבָה אַמְרִין מִשְּׁמוֹ.

Rebbi Abba bar Zavda in the name of Rav: Practice follows Rebbi Simeon, since otherwise, could anybody give rose oil to a poor person if he could not anoint himself[137]?

[138]Rebbi Ze`ira said to Rebbi Yose[139], does the Rabbi know Bar Pedaiah that you quote traditions in his name? He said to him, Rebbi Johanan quoted them in his name. Rebbi Ze`ira said to Rebbi Abba bar Zavda, does the Rabbi know Rav that you quote traditions in his name? He said to him, Rav Ada bar Ahavah quoted them in his name.

137 If it were true that common people never use rose oil except for medical reasons, nobody ever could give rose oil to a poor person. Since such a restriction is unknown, R. Simeon in Mishnah 4 must be correct.

138 This paragraph is from Chapter 1, Notes 190-191. It is quoted here because of the second question of R. Ze`ira.

139 The reading of Chapter 1, Yasa, is the correct one.

אילו קשרים פרק חמשה עשר

(fol. 15a) **משנה א**: אֵילוּ קְשָׁרִים שֶׁחַיָּיבִין עֲלֵיהֶן קֶשֶׁר הַגַּמָּלִין וְקֶשֶׁר הַסַּפָּנִים. וּכְשֵׁם שֶׁהוּא חַיָּיב עַל קִשְׁרָן כָּךְ הוּא חַיָּב עַל הֶתֵּירָן. רִבִּי מֵאִיר אוֹמֵר כָּל־קֶשֶׁר שֶׁהוּא יָכוֹל לְהַתִּירוֹ בְיָדוֹ אַחַת אֵין חַיָּיבִין עָלָיו:

Mishnah 1: The following are the knots for which one is liable: a camel driver's knot[1] and a mariner's knot[2]. Just as one is liable for knotting them so he is liable for untying them. Rebbi Meïr says, one is never liable for a knot which one can untie with one hand.

משנה ב: וְיֵשׁ לְךָ קְשָׁרִים שֶׁאֵין חַיָּיבִין עֲלֵיהֶן כְּקֶשֶׁר הַגַּמָּלִין וּכְקֶשֶׁר הַסַּפָּנִין. קוֹשֶׁרֶת אִשָּׁה מַפְתְּחֵי הַחֲלוּקָה וְחוּטֵי סְבָכָה שֶׁל פְּסִיקְיָא וּרְצוּעוֹת מִנְעָל וְסַנְדָּל וְנוֹדוֹת יַיִן וָשֶׁמֶן וּקְדֵירָה שֶׁל בָּשָׂר. רִבִּי אֱלִיעֶזֶר בֶּן יַעֲקֹב אוֹמֵר קוֹשְׁרִין לִפְנֵי בְהֵמָה בִּשְׁבִיל שֶׁלֹּא תֵצֵא. קוֹשְׁרִין דְּלִי בַּפְּסִיקְיָא אֲבָל לֹא בַחֶבֶל וְרִבִּי יְהוּדָה מַתִּיר. כְּלָל אָמַר רִבִּי יְהוּדָה כָּל־קֶשֶׁר שֶׁאֵינוֹ שֶׁל קַיָּימָא אֵין חַיָּיבִין עָלָיו:

Mishnah 2: But there are knots for which one is not liable as one is for a camel driver's knot and a mariner's knot. A woman may knot the openings of her garment[3], and the threads of the hair net, of the belt[4], and laces of shoe and sandal, wine and oil skins, and of a meat pot[5]. Rebbi Eliezer ben Jacob said, one may tie in front of an animal that it should not leave[6]; one may tie a pail to a belt but not to a rope[7], but Rebbi Jehudah permits it. Rebbi Jehudah stated a principle: One is never liable for a knot which is not permanent[8].

משנה ג: מְקַפְּלִין אֶת הַכֵּלִים אֲפִילוּ אַרְבָּעָה וַחֲמִשָּׁה פְעָמִים וּמַצִּיעִין אֶת הַמִּיטּוֹת מִלֵּילֵי שַׁבָּת לַשַּׁבָּת אֲבָל לֹא מִשַּׁבָּת לְמוֹצָאֵי שַׁבָּת. רִבִּי יִשְׁמָעֵאל אוֹמֵר מְקַפְּלִין אֶת הַכֵּלִים וּמַצִּיעִין אֶת הַמִּיטּוֹת מִיּוֹם הַכִּפּוּרִים לַשַּׁבָּת. חֶלְבֵי שַׁבָּת קְרֵיבִין לְיוֹם הַכִּפּוּרִים אֲבָל לֹא שֶׁל יוֹם הַכִּפּוּרִים קְרֵיבִין בַּשַּׁבָּת. רִבִּי עֲקִיבָה אוֹמֵר לֹא שֶׁל שַׁבָּת קְרֵיבִין לְיוֹם הַכִּפּוּרִים וְלֹא שֶׁל יוֹם הַכִּפּוּרִים קְרֵיבִין לַשַּׁבָּת:

Mishnah 3: One may fold garments even four or five times[9] and make the beds from Friday Night to the Sabbath Day, but not from Sabbath for after the Sabbath. Rebbi Ismael says, one folds garments and makes beds from the day of Atonement to the Sabbath[10]. The fats of the Sabbath[11] are brought on the

Day of Atonement but those of the Day of Atonement are not brought on the Sabbath. Rebbi Aqiba says, neither are those of the Sabbath brought on the Day of Atonement nor those of the Day of Atonement on the Sabbath.

1   The camel driver walks in front of the camels and leads them by a rope. The rope is tied through the camel's nose. Since this is a major operation it is done once only; the knot is permanent.

2   The knots which belong to the permanent rigging of the ship.

3   The garment was tied, not buttoned. Even if if was not necessary to untie all knots to undress, none of these is considered permanent and all of them may be tied or untied.

4   Latin *fascia, -ae, f.*

5   If the lid was fastened with a string before the pot was put into insulating material to keep it warm for the meal on Sabbath day.

6   One may leave the door of the barn or corral open but tie a rope across the opening which will force the cattle to remain inside. This obviously is a temporary device.

7   Since normally a rope is used, using a belt clearly makes it a temporary affair.

8   This is the guiding principle in this Chapter.

9   If he is not satisfied by the way his garments were folded, he may repeat the operation as many times as necessary.

10   Since the holiness of the Day of Atonement is less than that of the Sabbath. The statements presuppose that the Day of Atonement may fall on a Friday or a Sunday, which is avoided in today's computed calendar.

11   This refers to the Temple service. The left-over pieces of the sacrifices of one day have to be burned on the altar during the following night (*Lev.* 6:2,5). On the Sabbath, where burning is forbidden in general, only the sacrifice of the Sabbath (*Num.* 28:9-10) is permitted. Therefore it is clear that remainders from a Friday service of any kind cannot be burned in the following night. The question is about the service in the night from the Sabbath to Sunday, in case burning also is forbidden on Sunday. R. Aqiba follows his Mishnah (*Megillah* 1:5) that the only difference between Sabbath and the Day of Atonement is that violations of the Sabbath are criminal offenses while violations of the Day of Atonement are sins.

(15a line 33) אֵילוּ קְשָׁרִים כול'. מַה קְשִׁירָה הָיְתָה בַּמִּשְׁכָּן. שֶׁהָיוּ קוֹשְׁרִין אֶת הַמֵּיתָרִים. וְלֹא לְשָׁעָה הָיְתָה. אָמַר רִבִּי יוֹסֵה. מִכֵּיוָן שֶׁהָיוּ נוֹסְעִין וְחוֹנִין עַל פִּי הַדִּיבֵּר כְּמִי שֶׁהִיא לְעוֹלָם. אָמַר רִבִּי יוֹסֵי בֵּירִבִּי בּוּן. מִכֵּיוָן שֶׁהִבְטִיחָן הַקָּדוֹשׁ בָּרוּךְ הוּא שֶׁהוּא מַכְנִיסָן לָאָרֶץ כְּמִי שֶׁהוּא לְשָׁעָה. אָמַר רִבִּי פִּינְחָס. מִתוֹפְרֵי יְרִיעוֹת לָמְדוּ. נִפְסַק הָיָה קוֹשְׁרוֹ. חָזַר וְנִפְסָק. לַעֲשׂוֹתָן קְשָׁרִים קְשָׁרִים אֵי אֶיפְשָׁר. אֶלָּא חוֹזֵר וּמַתִּיר אֶת הָרִאשׁוֹן. אָמַר רִבִּי חִזְקִיָּה. הָהֵן חַייָטָא אוּמָנָא מְבַלֵּעַ תְּרֵין רֵישְׁיָיא. וְהַיְיְדָא אָמְרָה דָא. דְּאָמַר רִבִּי יוֹסֵי בֶּן חֲנִינָא. מֵאוֹרְגֵי יְרִיעוֹת לָמְדוּ. מַה טַעַם. אוֹרֶךְ הַיְרִיעָה הָאַחַת. כְּדֵי שֶׁתְּהֵא כוּלָּהּ אַחַת. נִפְסַק הָיָה קוֹשְׁרוֹ. מִכֵּיוָן שֶׁהָיָה מַגִּיעַ לָאָרִיג

הֲוָה שָׁרֵי לֵיהּ וּמְעַל לֵיהּ. רִבִּי תַנְחוּמָה בְשֵׁם רַב חוּנָא. אֲפִילוּ עָרֶב שֶׁבָּהּ לֹא הָיָה בּוֹ לֹא קֶשֶׁר וְלֹא תיָמֶת.

תַּנֵּי רִבִּי הוֹשַׁעְיָא. חוֹתָל שֶׁלִּתְמָרִים וְפָטִילַיָּיא שֶׁלִּתְמָרִים קוֹרֵעַ וּמַתִּיר. וּבִלְבַד שֶׁלֹּא יְקַשּׁוֹר.

"The following are the knots," etc. [12]What tying was in the Tabernacle? They were tying down the ropes. But was this not temporary? Rebbi Yose says, because they were travelling and camping by the Word, was it not permanent? Rebbi Yose ben Rebbi Abun said, since the Holy One, praise to Him, has promised them that he will bring them into the Land, it is as if it were temporary. Rebbi Phineas said, they learned it from the gobelin needle-workers. If a thread broke, he was tying it. If it broke again, it was impossible to make many knots but he would untie the first one. Rebbi Hizqiah said, an expert tailor merges the two heads. And where was this said? As Rebbi Yose ben Hanina said, they learned it from the weavers of the gobelins. What is the reason? *The length of one gobelin*, that it should be an entity. If [a thread] broke, he was tying it. When he came to the weave, he untied it and brought it in. Rebbi Tanhuma in the name of Rav Huna: Even on its warp there was neither knot nor connection.

Rebbi Hoshaia stated, a basket of palm leaves for dates or a plate of palm leaves one may tear and open, only one may not tie.

12   All this is in Chapter 7, Notes 394-408.

(15a line 45) ב'. אָמַר רִבִּי חִזְקִיָּה. בְּמַפְתֵּחַ אִימְרָא שֶׁהוּא מַדְבִּיקוֹ לַחֲלוּק. אָמַר רִבִּי יוֹסֵה. בְּמַפְתֵּחַ חָלוּק שֶׁהוּא עָשׂוּי כְּמִין שְׁנֵי דַפִּין. נִשְׁמְטוּ רְצוּעוֹת מִנְעַל וְסַנְדָּל נוֹטֵל וּמַחֲזִיר. וּבִלְבַד שֶׁלֹּא יְקַשּׁוֹר. חוֹטְמוֹ שֶׁנִּשְׁמָט. אִית תַּנָּיֵי תַנֵּי. מוּתָּר לְהַחֲזִיר. וְאִית תַּנָּיֵי תַנֵּי. אָסוּר לְהַחֲזִיר. הֲוֵון בָּעֵיי מֵימַר. מָאן דְּאָמַר. מוּתָּר. בְּשֶׁיֵּשׁ בּוֹ נֶקֶב אֶחָד. מָאן דְּאָמַר. אָסוּר. בְּשֶׁיֵּשׁ בּוֹ שְׁנֵי נְקָבִים. אָמַר רִבִּי יוֹסֵה בֵּירִבִּי בּוּן. בֵּין זֶה וּבֵין זֶה כְּמָאן דְּאָמַר. כְּשֶׁיֵּשׁ בּוֹ שְׁנֵי נְקָבִים. מָהוּ כְדוֹן. מָאן דְּאָמַר. מוּתָּר. בְּרָפִין. מָאן דְּאָמַר. אָסוּר. בָּאֲפוּצִים.

1 ב'. - E | במפתח E | במפתיח   2 חלוק E | חלוק חלוק[13]   3 שנשמט E | שנישמט ואית E | אית   4 הוון בעי מימר E | אמ' רב חסדא   מאן דאמ' E | מה דמר   מותר E | מותר להחזיר   מאן דאמ' E | מה דמר   אסור E | אסור להחזיר   5 נקבים E | נקבין   ביר' בון E | בר אבון   במאן דאמ' E | כמן דמר   נקבים E | נקבין   מהו E | מיי   6 מאן דאמ' E | מה דמר   באפוצים E | באפוצין

2. [14]Rebbi Hizqiah said, if one opens the hem which is connected to the garment[15]. Rebbi Yose said, if one opens a [split][16] garment which is made like two sheets. If shoe or sandal laces were dislocated, one removes and

returns them, only one may not knot them[17]. If its nose was dislocated[18], there are Tannaim who state, it is permitted to put it back, and there are Tannaim who state, it is forbidden to put it back. They wanted to say[19], he who says that it is permitted, if there is one hole; he who says that it is forbidden, if there are two holes. Rebbi Yose ben Rebbi Abun said, in both cases it is following him who says that there are two holes. What about it? He who says that it is permitted, if they are loose; he who says that it is forbidden, if they are squeezed[20].

13 I. e.., חָלוּק חָלוּק (J. N. Epstein).
14 From here to the middle of the discussion of Mishnah 16:1 there exists a Genizah fragment (E) edited by J. N. Epstein (*Tarbiz* 3, 1931, pp. 240-243).
15 Since it is obvious that one is permitted to dress and undress, the permission given in the Mishnah to untie knots must refer to situations where untying is not strictly necessary. R. Hizqiah constructs a rather artificial example where the garment is buttoned but the hem on which the buttonholes are is not sewn but tied to the garment. Instead of unbuttoning, one may untie.

16 Added from E, cf. Note 13. This describes a garment held together by a knot on each shoulder. Even though the woman could undress by untying one knot, she is permitted to untie both. Babli 112a.
17 One may put in new shoe laces; one is not permitted to repair the torn ones by tying the pieces together.
18 The strip in the middle of the sandal through which the laces are passing.
19 E: Rav Hisda said.
20 The first explanation is rejected since the standard is to have two holes. The lace may be replaced if and only if this can be done without using tools. Babli 112a.

(15a line 52) מַה חוֹלְקִין עַל רַבִּי אֱלִיעֶזֶר בֶּן יַעֲקֹב. מִן מַה דְּתַנֵּי. מוֹדִין חֲכָמִין לְרַבִּי מֵאִיר בְּחוֹתָמוֹת שֶׁבַּקַּרְקַע שֶׁמְּפַקְפְּקִין בּוֹ וּמַפְקִיעִין וּמַתִּירִין וְחוֹתְכִין. בַּשַּׁבָּת מְפַקְפְּקִין אֲבָל לֹא מַפְקִיעִין וְלֹא מַתִּירִין וְלֹא חוֹתְכִין. בַּכֵּלִים בַּשַּׁבָּת מוּתָּר. וְאֵין צָרִיךְ לוֹמַר בְּיוֹם טוֹב. הֲדָא אָמְרָה. אֵין חוֹלְקִין עַל רַבִּי אֱלִיעֶזֶר בֶּן יַעֲקֹב. אָמַר רִבִּי בָא. בְּחֶבֶל שָׁחוּל הִיא מַתְנִיתָא. חֶבֶל שֶׁהוּא מְשׁוּחָל.

1 חולקין E | חלוקין   2 בו E | -   3 צריך E | צורך   4 הדא E | הדה   4 אליעזר E | אלעזר   5 משוחל E | מושחל

Do they disagree with Rebbi Eliezer ben Jacob[21]? Since it was stated[22]: "The Sages agree with Rebbi Meïr about seals in the ground that one pushes aside, and removes, and unties, and cuts. On the Sabbath one pushes aside but one does not remove nor untie nor cut[23]. For implements on the Sabbath it is permitted[24]; it is not necessary to mention on a holiday." This implies that they do not disagree with Rebbi Eliezer ben Jacob. Rebbi Abba said, the Mishnah is about a rope hanging down, a rope tied hanging down[25].

21 Since he is mentioned by name, the implication would be that his is a minority opinion. On the other hand it is difficult to see why anybody should disagree with his opinion. Babli 113a.

22 A related text is in Tosephta *Yom Tov* 3:12.

23 If produce is stored in the ground and the door tied by a rope, the knot ("seal") is not permanent since produce is stored to be used eventually. If on a holiday one needs food, one may open the storage facility in any way one sees fit. In a similar case on the Sabbath one may push the rope to open a cleft through which one can take out some produce but rabbinically one may not otherwise remove the knot even though it is not permanent and removing it from an installation in the ground is not building or tearing down by biblical standards.

24 Since the notions of building and tearing down buildings does not apply to implements by biblical standards, there is no place for rabbinic restrictions.

25 R. Eliezer ben Jacob permits to tie a rope over the barn door opening if it already was tied to the door at one side and hanging down; then the knot to be made at the other side certainly is temporary. But if one would bring a new rope and tie it to both door posts there would be the possibility that after the Sabbath one would untie only one knot and the other would become permanent by default. If this was not intended originally no biblical liability is caused but there is reason to prohibit rabbinically. Babli 112b, bottom.

(15a line 57) בַּפְּסִיקְיָא אֲבָל לֹא בַחֶבֶל. רִבִּי יְהוּדָה מַתִּיר. הָא רַבָּנָן לֹא. אֶלָּא בְגִין דְּתַנִּינָן קַדְמַייָתָא בְּשֵׁם רִבִּי יְהוּדָה תַּנִּינָן אוֹף הָדָא בְשֵׁם רִבִּי יְהוּדָה. כְּלָל אָמַר רִבִּי יְהוּדָה כָּל־קֶשֶׁר שֶׁאֵינוֹ שֶׁלְקַיָּימָא אֵין חַייָבִין עָלָיו רִבִּי שְׁמוּאֵל בְּשֵׁם רִבִּי זְעוֹרָה. כֵּינִי מַתְנִיתָא. כָּל־קֶשֶׁר שֶׁאֵינוֹ שֶׁלְקַיָּימָא וְהוּא לְשָׁעָה אֵין חַייָבִין עָלָיו:

1 בפסיקיא E | בפיסקיא   2 קדמייתא E | וקדמיי]תה יהודה E | יודה (2)   3 זעורה E | זעירה

"To a belt but not to a rope, but Rebbi Jehudah permits it." Therefore the rabbis do not[26]? But because the earlier statement was in the name of Rebbi Jehudah, so also this is in the name of Rebbi Jehudah: "Rebbi Jehudah stated a principle: One is never liable for a knot which is not permanent." Rebbi Samuel in the name of Rebbi Ze'ira: So is the Mishnah: One is never liable for a knot which is not permanent and which is temporary[27].

26 This question is incomprehensible; since R. Jehudah disagrees with R. Eliezer ben Jacob and we have stated that the rabbis agree with the latter, it is obvious that the rabbis disagree with R. Jehudah. Also the reference to a prior statement is impossible

since the passage quoted is the first mention of R. Jehudah in the Chapter. Therefore it seems that the quote is incorrect both in the Leiden ms. and in E; with Nahmanides (*Novellae ad* 113a, ed Herschler col. 383) one has to read here also "Rebbi Jehudah stated a principle . . .". As explained earlier, already Mishnah 1 is based on the principle formulated by R. Jehudah which, therefore, is the majority opinion and should have been formulated as anonymous statement.

26 The intent, not the technique, is relevant. In contrast to R. Meïr, R. Jehudah proclaims liability for somebody who makes not a knot, but a tie, with the intent that it should be permanent.

(15a line 62) ג'. דְּבֵית רִבִּי יַנַּאי אָמְרֵי. קִיפּוּל בִּשְׁנַיִם אָסוּר. רִבִּי חַגַּי בְּשֵׁם רִבִּי שְׁמוּאֵל בַּר נַחְמָן. אֵין מְקַפְּלִין בַּשַּׁבָּת בִּשְׁנַיִם. וְהָהֵן דִּמְקַפֵּל עַל סִיפְסְלָה כְּמָאן דְּאִינּוּן תְּרֵין. רִבִּי חַגַּי בְּשֵׁם רִבִּי שְׁמוּאֵל בַּר נַחְמָן. לֹא נִיתְּנוּ שַׁבָּתוֹת וְיָמִים טוֹבִים אֶלָּא לַאֲכִילָה וְלִשְׁתִיָּיה. עַל יְדֵי שֶׁהַפֶּה זֶה (טְרִיחַ)²⁷ מֵרִיחַ²⁸ הִתִּירוּ לוֹ לַעֲסוֹק בָּהֶן בְּדִבְרֵי תוֹרָה. רִבִּי בְּרֶכְיָה בְּשֵׁם רִבִּי חִייָא בַּר בָּא. לֹא נִיתְּנוּ שַׁבָּתוֹת וְיָמִים טוֹבִים אֶלָּא לַעֲסוֹק בָּהֶן בְּדִבְרֵי תוֹרָה. מַתְנִיתָא מְסַייְעָה בֵּין לָדֵין בֵּין לָדֵין. כֵּיצַד הוּא עוֹשֶׂה. אוֹ יוֹשֵׁב וְאוֹכֵל אוֹ יוֹשֵׁב וְעוֹסֵק בְּדִבְרֵי תוֹרָה. כָּתוּב אֶחָד אוֹמֵר. שַׁבָּת הוּא לַיי. וְכָתוּב אַחֵר אוֹמֵר. עֲצֶרֶת לַיי אֱלֹהֶיךָ. הָא כֵּיצַד. תֵּן חֵלֶק לְתַלְמוּד תּוֹרָה וְחֵלֶק לֶאֱכוֹל וְלִשְׁתּוֹת. אָמַר רִבִּי אַבָּהוּ. שַׁבָּת לַיי. שְׁבוֹת כַּיי. מַה הַקָּדוֹשׁ בָּרוּךְ הוּא שָׁבַת מִמַּאֲמָר. אַף אַתְּ שְׁבוֹת מִמַּאֲמָר.

1 ג'. - E | . אמרי E | אמרין חגי E | חגיי 2 וההן E | והדן סיפסלא E | ספסילה דאינון תרין E | דהוא (דאינו) תריי חגי E | חגיי 3 שבתות וימים טובים E | ימים טובים ושבתות על E | ועל 4 חייא E | חייה 5 שבתות וימים טובים E | ימים טובים ושבתות בהן E | - בדברי | בדבריE | בדברי תורה E | תורה בחול על ידי שהוא טורח ואין לו פני לעסוק בדברי תורה ניתנו לו ימים טובים ושבתות לעסוק בהן בדברי תורה מסייעה E מסיעה 6 הוא E | היא 8 אבהו E | אבהוא כתוב ליי E | היא ליי

3. In the House of Rebbi Yannai they said, folding by two persons is forbidden[27]. Rebbi Haggai in the name of Rebbi Samuel bar Nahman: On the Sabbath, two together may not fold. If one folds on a footstool[28] it is as if two persons were folding[29]. Rebbi Haggai in the name of Rebbi Samuel bar Nahman: Sabbaths and holidays were given only for eating and drinking. Since this mouth [is bothersome][30] (is smelling), they permitted him to be occupied with words of the Torah. Rebbi Berekhiah in the name of Rebbi Hiyya bar Abba: Sabbaths and holidays were given only for being occupied with words of the Torah[31]. A *baraita* supports either one of them: What does one do? Either he sits down and eats or he sits and studies words of the Torah. One verse says, *it is a Sabbath for the Eternal*[32], and another verse says, *an assembly for the Eternal*[33], *your God*. How is that? Give part of it to

the study of Torah and part to eat and to drink. Rebbi Abbahu said, *a Sabbath for the Eternal*[34], rest like the Eternal. Since the Eternal rested from saying, you also should rest from saying[34].

27 Folding garments or bedsheets, as mentioned in Mishnah 3. Two people folding a sheet is professional work. Babli 113a (which has a list of further restrictons unknown to the Yerushalmi.)

28 Latin *subsellium, -ii, n.*

29 Since folding garments on a low bench is easier than folding when holding them in the air, the low bench has the status of a work tool which rabbinically cannot be used.

30 As E proves, this word, which was written by the Leiden scribe, is the correct expression. It was changed by the corrector into a word, reproduced in the Venice edition, which makes no sense in this context.

31 Here E has an explanatory addition which is attested to in some Medieval sources [*Sefer Ha'ittim* §198 p. 290; some mss. of *Meïri ad* 118b, ed. I. S. Lange p. 459, *Or zarua Šabbat* §89; it is missing in the quotes of the paragraph in *Šibbole Halleqet* (ed. S. Buber fol. 34a) and *Sefer Hamanhig* (ed I. Raphael p. 181)]: "on weekdays since he is occupied he has no free time to occupy himself with words of Torah; holidays and Sabbaths were given to him to occupy himself with words of Torah."

32 *Lev.* 23:3. This means totally to the Eternal.

33 *Deut.* 16:8. This means partially to the Eternal.

34 *Ex.* 20:10. E shows that probably the quote *Lev.* 23:3 is intended.

35 Unnecessary talk is forbidden on the Sabbath.

(15a line) מַעֲשֶׂה בְּחָסִיד אֶחָד שֶׁיָּצָא לְטַיֵּיל בְּכַרְמוֹ בַּשַּׁבָּת וְרָאָה שָׁם פִּירְצָה אַחַת וְחָשַׁב לְגַדְרוֹ בְּמוֹצָאֵי שַׁבָּת. אָמַר. הוֹאִיל וְחָשַׁבְתִּי לְגַדְרָהּ אֵינִי גוֹדְרָהּ עוֹלָמִית. מַה פָּעַל לוֹ הַקָּדוֹשׁ בָּרוּךְ הוּא. זִימֵּן לוֹ סוּכָה אַחַת שֶׁל נַצְפָּה וְעָלַת לְתוֹכָהּ וּגְדָרְתָהּ. מִמֶּנָּה הָיָה נִיזוֹן וּמִמֶּנָּה הָיָה מִתְפַּרְנֵס כָּל־יָמָיו.

[36]It happened that a pious person went to promenade in his vineyard on the Sabbath when he saw there a breach which he decided to repair after the Sabbath. He said, because I wanted to repair I shall never repair it. What did the Holy One, praise to Him, do for him? He prepared for him a tent of caper bush which grew there and mended it. From it he was fed and from there was his sustenance all his days.

36 This paragraph is not in the original text of the Yerushalmi; it was added by the corrector and is not in E. A Yerushalmi source of the story is *Lev. rabba* 34(15) at

the end. A slightly different version is in the Babli 150b. It is clear that the mention of a "tent" in this connection is a scribal error; maybe it should be שִׂיחַ "bush".

(15b line 2) אָמַר רִבִּי חֲנִינָא. מְדוֹחַק הִתִּירוּ לִשְׁאוֹל שָׁלוֹם בַּשַּׁבָּת. אָמַר רִבִּי חִיָּיא בַּר בָּא. רִבִּי שִׁמְעוֹן בֶּן יוֹחַי כַּד הֲוָה חֲמֵי לְאִימֵּיהּ מִשְׁתַּעְיָא סַגִּין הֲוָה אֲמַר לָהּ. אִימָּא. שׁוּבְתָּא הִיא. תַּנֵּי. אָסוּר לִתְבּוֹעַ צְרָכָיו בַּשַּׁבָּת. רִבִּי זְעוּרָה שָׁאַל לְרִבִּי חִיָּיה בַּר בָּא. מָהוּ מֵימַר. רְעֵינוּ פַרְנְסֵינוּ. אָמַר לֵיהּ. טוּפוֹס בְּרָכוֹת כָּךְ הֵן.

1 חנינא E | חנינה לשאול E | שאילת חייא E | חייה 2 משתעיא E | משתעיה סגין E | בגין 3 זעורה E | זעירה   4 טופוס E | טפוס

Rebbi Hanina said, with difficulty they permitted greeting on the Sabbath[37]. Rebbi Ḥiyya bar Abba said, when Rebbi Simeon ben Yoḥai saw that his mother enjoyed talking much, he said to her, mama, today is Sabbath. It was stated: It is forbidden to pray for his needs on the Sabbath. Rebbi Ze'ira asked Rebbi Ḥiyya bar Abba, may one say, "shepherd us, provide for us"[38]? He answered him, these are formulas[39] of benediction.

37 This is continuation of the statement that talking on the Sabbath is frowned upon. In the Babli, 12b, this is applied only to visits to the sick and mourners.

38 Expressions in the third benediction of Grace. (Cf. the author's *The Scholar's Haggadah*, p. 353.) The passage also is quoted in *Lev. rabba* 34 (Note 36).

(15b line 6) תַּנֵּי. מַדִּיחִין כּוֹסוֹת וּקְעָרוֹת וְתַמְחוּיִין מִלֵּילֵי שַׁבָּת לְשַׁחֲרִית לַחֲצוֹת וּמֵחֲצוֹת לְמִנְחָה. מִן הַמִּנְחָה וּלְמַעֲלָה אָסוּר. וּבְכוֹסוֹת מוּתָּר. שֶׁאֵין קָבַע לִשְׁתִיָּיה. רִבִּי יִרְמְיָה רִבִּי זְעוּרָה בְּשֵׁם רַב חִיָּיה בַּר אַשִׁי. אִשָּׁה פִּיקַּחַת מַדִּיחָה כּוֹס כָּאן קְעָרָה כָּאן תַּמְחוּי כָּאן. נִמְצֵאת מַרְבֶּצֶת בֵּיתָהּ בַּשַּׁבָּת.

It was stated: One rinses cups, pots, and plates from Friday Night to the morning, from morning to noon, from noon to afternoon[39]. After afternoon it is forbidden, only for cups it is permitted since drinking has no fixed times. Rebbi Jeremiah, Rebbi Ze'ira in the name of Rav Ḥiyya bar Ashi: An intelligent woman rinses a cup here, a pot there, a plate there; the result is that she waters down her house on the Sabbath[40].

39 One may cleanse dishes from one meal for the next; one is not required to have new dishes for every repast. Babli 118a.

40 If she has a one story house with a dirt floor, she washes different pieces at different places and so sprinkles all places.

(15b line 11) רִבִּי זְעוּרָה בְשֵׁם רַב חִסְדָּא. יוֹם הַכִּיפּוּרִים שֶׁחָל לִהְיוֹת בַּשַּׁבָּת אֵין תּוֹקְעִין. לְאַחַר הַשַּׁבָּת אֵין מַבְדִּילִין. מַה. כְּרִבִּי עֲקִיבָה. בְּרַם כְּרִבִּי יִשְׁמָעֵאל מַבְדִּיל. שֶׁכֵּן חֶלְבֵי שַׁבָּת קְרֵיבִין בְּיוֹם הַכִּיפּוּרִים. אָמַר רִבִּי עֶזְרָא קוֹמֵי רִבִּי מָנָא. אֲפִילוּ כְּרִבִּי יִשְׁמָעֵאל לֹא יַבְדִּיל. כְּלוּם הוּא מַבְדִּיל אֶלָּא לְהַתִּיר לוֹ דָּבָר שֶׁהוּא אָסוּר לוֹ. אִילוּ הִקְטִיר חֶלְבֵי שַׁבָּת בַּשַּׁבָּת שֶׁמָּא אֵינוּ מוּתָּר. אָמַר רִבִּי שְׁמוּאֵל אֲחוֹי דְרִבִּי בְּרֵכְיָה. וְיַבְדִּיל. שֶׁכָּךְ הוּא מַתִּיר לְהָדִיחַ כְּבָשִׁים וּשְׁלָקוֹת. אָמַר רִבִּי יוֹסֵה. כְּלוּם הוּא מוּתָּר לְהָדִיחַ כְּבָשִׁים וּשְׁלָקוֹת לֹא מִן הַמִּנְחָה וּלְמַעֲלָן. וְיַבְדִּיל מִן הַמִּנְחָה וּלְמַעֲלָן. מַה נַּפְשָׁךְ. כּוֹס אֵין כָּאן. נֵר אֵין כָּאן. בַּמֶּה הוּא מַבְדִּיל. אָמַר רִבִּי אָבוּן. בִּתְפִילָה.

2 מבדיל E | - 4 אילו E | אלו שמא E | שמה 5 שכך E | שכן מתיר E | מותר 9 בתפילה E | בתפלה

Rebbi Ze'ira in the name of Rav Ḥisda, if the Day of Atonement falls to be on the Sabbath[41] one does not blow[42], if after the Sabbath one does not make *havdalah*[43]. Why? Following Rebbi Aqiba. But following Rebbi Ismael he makes *havdalah* since the fats of the Sabbath[11] are brought on the Day of Atonement[44]. Rebbi Ezra said before Rebbi Mana, even according to Rebbi Ismael he should not make *havdalah*, since one only makes *havdalah* to permit things which were forbidden to him. If he would burn the fats of the Sabbath on the Sabbath, would that not be permitted? Rebbi Samuel the brother of Rebbi Berekhiah said, he should make *havdalah* since by it he permits to rinse pickled and parboiled [food][45]. Rebbi Yose said, he only is permitted to rinse pickled and parboiled [food] from the time of afternoon prayers or later. Could he make *havdalah* from the time of afternoon prayers or later? As you take it, there is no cup, there is no light[46], how can he make *havdalah*? Rebbi Abun said, in prayer[47].

41 It seems that this means that the Day of Atonement falls on Friday, as in the parallel in the Babli 114b.

42 A public blowing of a ram's horn on Friday afternoon towards evening at a fixed time before sundown to alert everybody to the coming of the Sabbath. The details of this Galilean procedure are found only in the Babli, 35b. If Friday is the Day of Atonement, nobody is working and the sounding of the horn is unnecessary and therefore rabbinically forbidden.

43 The required declaration of a "difference between Sabbath (or holiday) and weekday" after the end of the Sabbath or the holiday. Rabbinically, no work may be performed before some form of *havdalah*. But since everything forbidden on the Sabbath also is forbidden on the Day of Atonement (Mishnah *Megillah* 1:5), *havdalah* in this situation would make no sense. A special form of *havdalah* is required if Sunday is any other holiday since many things forbidden on the Sabbath are

permitted on a holiday.

44   It is implicit in his position as reported in Mishnah 3 that he considers the holiness of the Day of Atonement to be inferior to that of the Sabbath.

45   One is permitted to start preparing food for breaking the fast some time before the end of the day of Atonement even though in general one is prohibited to do anything on a Sabbath or holiday to prepare for the following weekday. (This exception holds true even if the day of Atonement is a Sabbath proper.)

46   The standard *havdalah* uses a cup of wine, a torch, and spices (the latter is not needed for holidays and the day of Atonement). *Berakhot* 5:2. On the Day of Atonement proper, neither a cup of wine nor fire is available.

47   The original form of *havdalah*, cf. *Berakhot* 5:2 Note 88.

כל כתבי הקודש פרק ששה עשר

(fol. 15b) **משנה א**: כָּל־כִּתְבֵי הַקּוֹדֶשׁ מַצִּילִין אוֹתָן מִפְּנֵי הַדְּלֵיקָה בֵּין שֶׁקּוֹרִין בָּהֶן וּבֵין שֶׁאֵינָן קוֹרִין בָּהֶן אַף עַל פִּי שֶׁכְּתוּבִים בְּכָל־לָשׁוֹן טְעוּנִים גְּנִיזָה. מִפְּנֵי מָה אֵין קוֹרִין בָּהֶן מִפְּנֵי בִיטּוּל בֵּית הַמִּדְרָשׁ.

Mishnah 1: One saves all holy Scriptures from a fire[1], whether they be used for reading or not used for reading[2]; even though they be written in any language they have to be hidden[3]. Why does one not read in them[4]? Because of neglect of the House of Study.

משנה ב: מַצִּילִין תִּיק הַסֵּפֶר עִם הַסֵּפֶר וְתִיק הַתְּפִילִּין עִם הַתְּפִילִּין אַף עַל פִּי שֶׁיֵּשׁ בְּתוֹכָן מָעוֹת. וּלְאֵיכָן מַצִּילִין אוֹתָן לְמָבוֹי שֶׁאֵינוֹ מְפוּלָּשׁ. בֶּן בְּתֵירָה אוֹמֵר אַף לַמְפוּלָּשׁ:

Mishnah 2: One saves the case of a scroll with the scroll, and the case of phylacteries with the phylacteries even if there are coins inside[5]. Where does one save it to? To a side street which is a dead end[6]; Ben Bathyra says, also one open on both ends[7].

משנה ג: מַצִּילִין מְזוֹן שָׁלֹשׁ סְעוּדוֹת הָרָאוּי לָאָדָם לְאָדָם הָרָאוּי לַבְּהֵמָה לַבְּהֵמָה. כֵּיצַד נָפְלָה דְלֵיקָה בְּלֵילֵי שַׁבָּת מַצִּילִין מְזוֹן שָׁלֹשׁ סְעוּדוֹת בַּשַּׁחֲרִית מַצִּילִין מְזוֹן שְׁתֵּי סְעוּדוֹת בַּמִּנְחָה מַצִּילִין מְזוֹן סְעוּדָה אַחַת. רִבִּי יוֹסֵה אוֹמֵר לְעוֹלָם מַצִּילִין מְזוֹן שָׁלֹשׁ סְעוּדוֹת:

Mishnah 3: One saves food for three meals; human food for humans and animal feed for animals. How is this? If the fire started Friday Night, one saves food for three meals, in the morning one saves food for two meals, in the afternoon one saves food for one meal. Rebbi Yose says, one always saves food for three meals.

משנה ד: מַצִּילִין סַל מָלֵא כִּכָּרוֹת אַף עַל פִּי שֶׁיֵּשׁ בּוֹ מֵאָה סְעוּדוֹת וְעִיגּוּל שֶׁל דְּבֵילָה וְחָבִית שֶׁל יַיִן וְאוֹמֵר לַאֲחֵרִים בּוֹאוּ וְהַצִּילוּ לָכֶם. אִם הָיוּ פִקְחִין עוֹשִׂין עִמּוֹ חֶשְׁבּוֹן לְאַחַר שַׁבָּת. וּלְאֵיכָן מַצִּילִין אוֹתָן לֶחָצֵר הַמְעוֹרֶבֶת. בֶּן בְּתֵירָה אוֹמֵר אַף לְשֶׁאֵינָהּ מְעוֹרֶבֶת:

Mishnah 4: One saves a bag full of loaves even if it contains food for a hundred meals, and loaves of dried figs, and wine amphoras[8], and one says to others, come and save for yourselves[9]. If they are intelligent[10] they settle accounts with him after the Sabbath. Where does one save to? To a courtyard with an *eruv*[11]. Ben Bathyra says, even if there is no *eruv*[12].

משנה ה: וּלְשָׁם הוּא מוֹצִיא אֶת כָּל־כֵּלָיו תַּשְׁמִישׁוֹ וְלוֹבֵשׁ כָּל־מַה שֶׁהוּא יָכוֹל לִלְבּוֹשׁ וְעוֹטֵף כָּל־מַה שֶׁהוּא יָכוֹל לַעֲטוֹף. רַבִּי יוֹסֵי אוֹמֵר שְׁמוֹנָה עָשָׂר כֵּלִים. וְחוֹזֵר וְלוֹבֵשׁ וּמוֹצִיא וְאוֹמֵר לַאֲחֵרִים בּוֹאוּ וְהַצִּילוּ עִמִּי:

Mishnah 5: There he also brings out all his utensils, and he puts on all he can wear and wraps around all he can wrap. Rebbi Yose says, 18 garments. He can come back and put on, and says to others: come and save with me[13].

משנה ו: רַבִּי שִׁמְעוֹן בֶּן נַנָּס אוֹמֵר פּוֹרְסִין עוֹר שֶׁל גְּדִי עַל גַּבֵּי שִׁידָּה תֵּיבָה וּמִגְדָּל שֶׁאָחַז בָּהֶם אֶת הָאוּר מִפְּנֵי שֶׁהוּא מְחָרֵךְ. עוֹשִׂין מְחִיצָה בְּכָל־הַכֵּלִים בֵּין מְלֵאִים בֵּין רֵיקָנִין בִּשְׁבִיל שֶׁלֹּא תַעֲבֹר הַדְּלֵיקָה. רַבִּי יוֹסֵי אוֹסֵר בִּכְלֵי חֶרֶס חֲדָשִׁים מְלֵאִים מַיִם שֶׁאֵינָן יְכוֹלִין לְקַבֵּל בָּהֶן אֶת הָאוּר וְהֵן מִתְבַּקְּעִין וּמְכַבִּין אֶת הַדְּלֵיקָה:

Mishnah 6: Rebbi Simeon ben Nanas says, one spreads kid leather over a chest, a box, or a cupboard which are on fire since it is singed[14]. One builds a wall out of vessels[15], whether full or empty, lest the fire cross over. Rebbi Yose forbids new clay vessels full of water since they cannot withstand the heat, spring leaks, and extinguish the fire[16].

משנה ז: נָכְרִי שֶׁבָּא לְכַבּוֹת אֵין אוֹמְרִים לוֹ כַּבֵּה אוֹ אַל תְּכַבֶּה מִפְּנֵי שֶׁאֵין שְׁבִיתָתוֹ עָלֶיךָ. אֲבָל קָטָן שֶׁבָּא לְכַבּוֹת אֵין שׁוֹמְעִין לוֹ שֶׁכֵּן שְׁבִיתָתוֹ עָלֶיךָ:

Mishnah 7: If a Gentile comes to extinguish one tells him neither to extinguish nor not to extinguish since you are not responsible for him resting. But if a minor comes to extinguish one may not listen to him since you are responsible for him resting[17].

משנה ח: כּוֹפִין קְעָרָה עַל גַּבֵּי הַנֵּר בִּשְׁבִיל שֶׁלֹּא תֶאֱחֹז בַּקּוֹרָה וְעַל צוֹאָה שֶׁל קָטָן וְעַל עַקְרָב שֶׁלֹּא תִּשֹּׁךְ. אָמַר רַבִּי יְהוּדָה מַעֲשֶׂה בָא לִפְנֵי רַבָּן יוֹחָנָן בֶּן זַכַּאי בָּעֲרָב וְאָמַר חוֹשְׁשַׁנִי אֲנִי לוֹ מֵחַטָּאת:

Mishnah 8: One may put a pot over a light lest it set fire to a beam[18], and over a child's excrement, and over a scorpion to prevent it from stinging. Rebbi Jehudah said, this happened before Rabban Johanan ben Zakkai in Arab and he said, I fear that he incurred liability for a purification sacrifice[19].

משנה ט: נָכְרִי שֶׁהִדְלִיק אֶת הַנֵּר מִשְׁתַּמֵּשׁ לְאוֹרוֹ יִשְׂרָאֵל. וְאִם בִּשְׁבִיל יִשְׂרָאֵל אָסוּר. מִילֵּא מַיִם לְהַשְׁקוֹת בְּהֶמְתּוֹ מַשְׁקֶה אַחֲרָיו יִשְׂרָאֵל וְאִם בִּשְׁבִיל יִשְׂרָאֵל אָסוּר. עָשָׂה גוֹי כֶּבֶשׁ

לֵירֵד בּוֹ יוֹרֵד אַחֲרָיו יִשְׂרָאֵל וְאִם בִּשְׁבִיל יִשְׂרָאֵל אָסוּר. מַעֲשֶׂה בְרַבָּן גַּמְלִיאֵל וּזְקֵנִים שֶׁהָיוּ בָּאִין בִּסְפִינָה וְעָשָׂה גוֹי כֶּבֶשׁ לֵירֵד בּוֹ וְיָרְדוּ בוֹ זְקֵנִים:

Mishnah 9: If a Gentile lit a candle[20], the Jew may use its light; but if he did it for the Jew it is forbidden. If he drew water[21] to let his animals drink, the Jew may let his animals drink, but if he did it for the Jew it is forbidden. If the Gentile built a ramp to descend on it, the Jew may descend after him, but if he did it for the Jew it is forbidden. It happened that Rabban Gamliel and the Elders arrived in a ship, the Gentile make the ramp to descend on it and the Elders descended on it[22].

1 Since making a fire is prohibited on the Sabbath, so is extinguishing a fire as long as no human lives are endangered by it. The Mishnah supposes that the houses are single family adobe houses separated from one another so that normally there is no danger of the fire spreading and endangering others.

2 For public readings. Scrolls of books of Scripture not for public readings are either Hagiographa or defective copies of Torah and Prophets.

3 If they are no longer usable they have to be disposed of in a dignified way; they may not be abandoned in garbage. Therefore even defective copies may be saved in a fire.

4 Hagiographa are not to be read on the Sabbath since this would interfere with people attending public lectures held for the benefit of people who during the week have no opportunity of Torah study.

5 Even if valuables which are not to be moved on the Sabbath are inside the boxes in which scrolls or phylacteries are kept. Since speed is of the essence, one does not have to investigate but without asking may carry *muqseh* articles with those one is authorized to move (cf. Chapter 3, Note 172).

6 Even if publicly owned and accessible to the public, a dead-end street never can be a public domain in the biblical sense for the rules of the Sabbath. For these rules, a dead-end street can be turned into common private domain of the dwellers in the street by an *eruv*; it may be used to deposit the scrolls even if there is no *eruv*. It is presumed that the dead-end street is bordered by walls of houses or courtyards on three sides.

7 A thoroughfare, even if very narrow and walled in on two sides, can never be turned into a private domain by an *eruv*. Therefore the majority does not permit the used of such a path on the Sabbath. Ben Bathyra permits its use as long as the street is walled in and is narrow enough (less than 16 cubits wide) to be disqualified as public domain for the rules of the Sabbath.

8 Again, since speed is of the essence, one may move packages of food irrespective of their size.

9 Even though he really wants the neighbors to help him save his property, he must invite them to save for themselves.

10 If they understand that the fire victim really did not want to donate his food to them, they either may in return give back the food to him or pay him something for the food which they took.

11 Since the neighbors are not threatened by the fire and are saving for themselves, they may take the things only to places in which they are authorized to carry.

12 He requires only that the place be potentially one where the neighbors could carry; but in this case he excludes the dead-end street into which the common courtyard opens.

13 Since everybody does wear clothing in the public domain; garments are not a load, and the owner may ask the neighbors to wear the clothes for him; he does not have to transfer ownership to them.

14 It is not usually burned in a fire; therefore covering utensils with hide is not supplying the fire with fuel.

15 Since vessels are not building material, moving amphoras together to hinder the spread of the fire is not building.

16 If it is a foregone conclusion that the vessels will break and douse the fire, using a subterfuge is forbidden as long as one cannot go and extinguish the fire directly as a danger to life.

17 An underage child has no religious obligations; only his parents have a responsibility to educate him for a life conforming to religious rules. But in matters of the Sabbath the Fourth Commandment holds the parent directly responsible for sons and daughters keeping the Sabbath.

18 To prevent the house being set on fire one may cause the flame to be ultimately extinguished once the oxygen in the vessel has been used up; this is indirect causation which only is rabbinically forbidden and can be waved in an emergency.

19 He was not sure whether the person putting the vessel over the scorpion was doing so in order to save people from being stung, in which case the action was permitted on the Sabbath, or whether he intended to use the scorpion for medical purposes after the Sabbath, in which case if would be a violation of biblical Sabbath rules.

20 For himself.

21 From a cistern or in the public domain inaccessible to the Jew on the Sabbath.

22 After the Gentile skipper had left the ship on the ramp, arriving in the harbor on the Sabbath.

(15b line 65) כָּל־כִּתְבֵי הַקּוֹדֶשׁ כול'. מָהוּ בֵּין שְׁקוֹרִין בָּהֶן וּבֵין שֶׁאֵין קוֹרִין בָּהֶן. בֵּין שֶׁיֵּשׁ בָּהֶן טָעִיּוֹת. בֵּין שֶׁאֵין בָּהֶן טָעִיּוֹת. וְהָא תַנֵּי. סֵפֶר שֶׁיֵּשׁ בּוֹ שְׁתַּיִם שָׁלשׁ טָעִיּוֹת בְּכָל־דַּף וְדַף מְתַקְּנוֹ וְקוֹרֵא בוֹ. אַרְבַּע אֵינוֹ קוֹרֵא בוֹ. מִן מַה דְּתַנֵּינָן. מִפְּנֵי מָה אֵין קוֹרִין בָּהֶן. מִפְּנֵי בִיטּוּל בֵּית הַמִּדְרָשׁ. הָדָא אָמְרָה. בֵּין תּוֹרָה לִנְבִיאִים. לְכִתְבֵי הַקּוֹדֶשׁ.

אֵין מַצִּילִין אוֹתָן מִפְּנֵי הַדְּלֵיקָה. מָאן דְּאָמַר. מְטַמְאִין אֶת הַיָּדַיִם. מַצִּילִין אוֹתָן מִפְּנֵי הַדְּלֵיקָה. וּמָאן דְּאָמַר. אֵין מְטַמְאִין אֶת הַיָּדַיִם. אֵין מַצִּילִין אוֹתָן מִפְּנֵי הַדְּלֵיקָה. הֲתִיבוּן. הֲרֵי עִבְרִי שֶׁכְּתָבוֹ תַרְגּוּם הֲרֵי אֵינוֹ מְטַמֵּא אֶת הַיָּדַיִם וּמַצִּילִין אוֹתוֹ מִפְּנֵי הַדְּלֵיקָה. מִן מַה דְּתַנֵּינָן. אַף עַל פִּי שֶׁכְּתוּבִין בְּכָל־לָשׁוֹן טְעוּנִין גְּנִיזָה. הָדָא אָמְרָה. שֶׁמַּצִּילִין אוֹתָן מִפְּנֵי

הַדְּלִיקָה. מַתְנִיתָה דְּרִבִּי שִׁמְעוֹן. דְּרִבִּי שִׁמְעוֹן אָמַר. אֵין דָּבָר מִשּׁוּם שְׁבוּת שֶׁעוֹמֵד בִּפְנֵי כִתְבֵי הַקּוֹדֶשׁ. מַה פְּלִיגִין. תַּמָּן מִפְּנֵי בִזְיוֹנָן. בְּרַם הָכָא כָּל־עַמָּא מוֹדֵיי שֶׁמַּצִּילִין אוֹתָן מִפְּנֵי הַדְּלִיקָה. לְמִי נִצְרְכָה. לְרַבָּן שִׁמְעוֹן בֶּן גַּמְלִיאֵל. אַף עַל גַּב דְּרַבָּן שִׁמְעוֹן בֶּן גַּמְלִיאֵל אָמַר. אַף בַּסְּפָרִים לֹא הִתִּירוּ שֶׁיִּכָּתְבוּ אֶלָּא יְוָונִית׃ מוֹדֵיי הוּא הָכָא שֶׁמַּצִּילִין אוֹתָן מִפְּנֵי הַדְּלִיקָה. מַעֲשֶׂה בְרַבָּן גַּמְלִיאֵל שֶׁהָיָה עוֹמֵד עַל הַבַּנָּיִין בְּהַר הַבַּיִת. וְהֵבִיאוּ לוֹ סֵפֶר אִיּוֹב כָּתוּב תַּרְגּוּם. וְאָמַר לַבַּנַּאי וְגָנְזוֹ תַּחַת הַנִּדְבָּךְ.

1 מאן דאמ' מטמאין | E מן דמר מטמי | 2 ומאן דאמ' אין מטמאין | E ומן דמר אין מטמין | 3 מן | E -
4 הדא | E הדה | 5 שעומד בפני כתבי הקודש | E עומד לפני כיתבי הקדש | 6 מודיי | E מודי | 7 בן גמליאל
| E - | 8 התירו | ק היתירו | 9 גמליאל | E שמעון בן גמליאל לבנאי | E לבניי

"All holy Scriptures," etc. What means "whether they are used for reading or not used for reading"? Whether they contain errors or do not contain errors. Was it not stated: If a scroll[23] contains two or three errors on every page, one corrects it and reads from it; with four one does not read from it[24]. Since we have stated, "why does one not read in them[4]? Because of neglect of the House of Study;" this implies that there is a difference between Torah and Prophets and Hagiographa[25].

One does not save from a fire[26]. For him who says, they render hands impure[27], one saves them from a fire; but for him who says, they do not render hands impure, one does not save them from a fire. They objected: Is there not a Hebrew book which was written in Aramaic[28]; it will not render hands impure but one saves it from a fire, since we have stated: "even though they are written in any language they have to be hidden." The Mishnah follows Rebbi Simeon, since Rebbi Simeon said, nothing forbidden only rabbinically stands in the way of Holy Scriptures[29]. Do they disagree[30]? There it is because of their degradation[31], but here everybody agrees that one saves them from a fire. For whom is it needed? For Rabban Simeon ben Gamliel. Even though Rabban Simeon ben Gamliel said[32], "also Hagiographa they permitted only that they could be written in Greek," would he agree here that one saves them from a fire? "It happened that Rabban [Simeon ben][33] Gamliel was supervising builders on the the Temple Mount when he an Aramaic version of Job was brought to him. He told the builder to hide it under a row of stones."

23 A Torah scroll.
24 Since the text is unreliable, one never can be sure that all errors were corrected.

The same statements *Megillah* 1:11, 71c l. 69. In the Babli, *Menaḥot* 29b, there is disagreement whether three errors on every page or only four are cause for disqualification.

25 Since Torah and Prophets have to be read in the synagogue on the Sabbath, the only candidates for books which should not be read on the Sabbath are Hagiographa.

26 This seems to be a truncated quote from a *baraita* which disagrees with the preceding argument and states that Hagiographa cannot be saved from a fire if this would involve transgressing rabbinic prohibitions.

27 Mishnah *Yadaim* 3:8 reports on disagreement whether touching a scroll of *Ecclesiastes* makes one's hands impure. There seems to be tacit agreement that *Esther* does not make the hands impure. This impurity is purely rabbinical; it was instituted so people should not store their heave, which is sanctified, with also holy Scripture, since this would attract rats which would attack the leather on which the scrolls were written. A scroll which does not render the hands impure is not holy; no rabbinic restrictions would have to be waved to save them from a fire.

28 Mishnah *Yadaim* 4:5.

29 Mishnah *Eruvin* 10:3. Only biblical prohibitions have to be observed when caring for Scripture on the Sabbath.

30 The mishnaic statements in *Yadaim* and *Eruvin*.

31 Lest rats be attracted to the scrolls, Note 27.

32 Mishnah *Megillah* 1:11. There do exist approved Aramaic versions of the Pentateuch and Jonathan ben Uziel's Aramaic paraphrase of Prophets but no recognized Aramaic versions of Hagiographa. The existing Aramaic versions of *Psalms, Proverbs, Job, Esther*, and *Chronicles* all seem to be post-Talmudic.

33 Added from E. From the context this seems to be the correct attribution, referring to Rabban Simeon ben Gamliel I, the head of the revolutionary government in the first war against the Romans. In the Babylonian parallels, Babli 115a, Tosephta 13:2 (ed. Liebermann) the name always is "Rabban Gamliel" I, the grandfather of Rabban Gamliel of Jabneh.

(15c line 7) אַף עַל פִּי שֶׁאָמְרוּ אֵין קוֹרִין בְּכִתְבֵי הַקּוֹדֶשׁ אֶלָּא מִן הַמִּנְחָה וּלְמַעְלָה. אֲבָל שׁוֹנִין וְדוֹרְשִׁין בָּהֶן. צָרַךְ דָּבָר נוֹטֵל וּבוֹדֵק. דַּלְמָא. רִבִּי וְרִבִּי חִייָא רַבָּא וְרִבִּי יִשְׁמָעֵאל בֵּירִבִּי יוֹסֵה הָיוּ יוֹשְׁבִין וּפוֹשְׁטִין בִּמְגִילַת קִינוֹת עֶרֶב תִּשְׁעָה בְאָב שֶׁחָל לִהְיוֹת בַּשַּׁבָּת מִן הַמִּנְחָה וּלְמַעְלָה. וְשִׁיְּירוּ בָהּ אֶלֶ"ף בֵּי"ת אֶחָד. אָמְרוּ. לְמָחָר אָנוּ בָאִין וְגוֹמְרִין אוֹתָהּ. עִם כְּשֶׁרִבִּי נִפְטַר לְבֵיתוֹ נִכְשַׁל בְּאֶצְבָּעוֹ וְקָרָא עַל גַּרְמֵיהּ רַבִּים מַכְאוֹבִים לָרָשָׁע. אָמַר לוֹ רִבִּי חִייָה. בְּחוֹבֵינוּ מַטְתָךְ כֵּן. דִּכְתִיב רוּחַ אַפֵּינוּ מְשִׁיחַ יְי נִלְכַּד בִּשְׁחִיתוֹתָם. אָמַר לוֹ רִבִּי יִשְׁמָעֵאל בֵּירִבִּי יוֹסֵי. אִילוּ לֹא הָיִינוּ עוֹסְקִין בָּעִנְיָין. עַל אַחַת כַּמָּה וְכַמָּה שֶׁהָיִינוּ עוֹסְקִין בָּעִנְיָין. וְעָלָה לְבֵיתוֹ וְנָתַן עָלֶיהָ סְפוֹג יָבֵשׁ וְקָשַׁר עָלֶיהָ גְּמִי מִבַּחוּץ. אָמַר רִבִּי יִשְׁמָעֵאל בֵּירִבִּי יוֹסֵי. מִמֶּנּוּ לָמַדְנוּ שְׁלֹשָׁה דְּבָרִים. סְפוֹג אֵינוֹ מְרַפֵּא אֶלָּא מְשַׁמֵּר. גְּמִי שֶׁהוּא מִן הַמּוּכָן. וְאֵין קוֹרִין בְּכִתְבֵי הַקּוֹדֶשׁ אֶלָּא מִן הַמִּנְחָה וּלְמַעְלָה.

1 בכתבי הקודש E | בכיתבי הקדש ולמעלה E ולמעלן   2 חייא רבא E | חחיה רבה ביר' | E בר   3 ערב |

E בערב   מן המנחה ולמעלה E | - | E | 4 אותה E | אתו   5 באצבעו E | בא[צב]ע   מכאובים E מכאובין
חייה E | חייה רבה   7 בעניין E | בעיניו כך   שהיינו E | עד שכנו   9 בכתבי הקודש E | בכיתבי הקדש   10
ולמעלה E | ולמעלן

מֵעַתָּה בְּמָקוֹם שֶׁיֵּשׁ בֵּית הַמִּדְרָשׁ אַל יִקְרָאוּ. בְּמָקוֹם שֶׁאֵין בֵּית הַמִּדְרָשׁ יִקְרָאוּ. לֵית לָךְ אֶלָּא כְהָדָא דְתַנֵּי רִבִּי נְחֶמְיָה. דְּתַנֵּי רִבִּי נְחֶמְיָה. מִפְּנֵי מָה אֵין קוֹרִין בְּכִתְבֵי הַקּוֹדֶשׁ אֶלָּא מִן הַמִּנְחָה וּלְמַעֲלָה. מִפְּנֵי שִׁטְרֵי הֶדְיוֹטוֹת. שֶׁאִם אוֹמֵר אַתְּ שֶׁהוּא מוּתָּר. אַף הוּא אוֹמֵר. מַה בְכָךְ שֶׁנִּתְעַסֵּק בִּשְׁטָרוֹתַיי. מִתּוֹךְ שֶׁאַתְּ אוֹמֵר לוֹ שֶׁהוּא אָסוּר. אַף הוּא אוֹמֵר. כִּתְבֵי הַקּוֹדֶשׁ אָסוּר. שִׁטְרֵי הֶדְיוֹטוֹת לֹא כָל־שֶׁכֵּן. הָדָא אָמְרָה. שֶׁהַמִּשְׁנָה קוֹדֶמֶת לַמִּקְרָא. וְדָא מְסַייְעָא לְהַהִיא דְתַנֵּי רִבִּי שִׁמְעוֹן בֶּן יוֹחַי. דְּתַנֵּי רִבִּי שִׁמְעוֹן בֶּן יוֹחַי. הָעוֹסֵק בַּמִּקְרָא מִידָּה שֶׁאֵינָהּ מִידָּה. הָעוֹסֵק בַּמִּשְׁנָה מִידָּה שֶׁנּוֹטְלִין מִמֶּנָּה שָׂכָר. הָעוֹסֵק בַּתַּלְמוּד אֵין לָךְ מִידָּה גְדוֹלָה מְזוֹ. לְעוֹלָם הֱוֵי רָץ אַחַר הַמִּשְׁנָה יוֹתֵר מִן הַתַּלְמוּד. אָמַר רִבִּי יוֹסִי בֵּירִבִּי בּוּן. הָדָא דְאַתְּ אָמַר עַד שֶׁלֹּא שִׁיקַע בּוֹ רֻבֵּי רוֹב מִשְׁנָיוֹת. אֲבָל מִשֶּׁשִּׁיקַע בּוֹ רִבִּי רוֹב מִשְׁנָיוֹת לְעוֹלָם הֱוֵי רָץ אַחַר הַתַּלְמוּד יוֹתֵר מִן הַמִּשְׁנָה.

1 יקראו E | אל יקראו   5 הדא E | הדה

Even though they said, one reads Hagiographa only after the afternoon prayers, nevertheless one studies and preaches about them[34]. If he needs it, he takes and checks[35]. [36]An example[37]: Rebbi, the Elder Rebbi Ḥiyya, and Rebbi Ismael ben Rebbi Yose were sitting and explaining the plain sense of a scroll of Lamentations on a Ninth of Av which fell on a Sabbath (after the afternoon prayers.)[38] They left over one alphabetic poem. They said, we shall come tomorrow and finish it. When Rebbi was on the way home, he hurt his finger and recited about himself, *many are the evildoer's hurts*[39]. [The Elder][40] Rebbi Ḥiyya said to him, it is our fault that this happened to you, as it is written, *our spirit, the Eternal's anointed, was caught by their corruption*[41]. Rebbi Ismael ben Rebbi Yose told him, that could have been said about us if we had not occupied ourselves with it; so much more since we did occupy ourselves with it. He went home, put a dry sponge[42] on it and tied it from the outside with bast. Rebbi Ismael ben Rebbi Yose said, from this we learned three things: A sponge does not heal but protects[43]; bast is prepared[44], and one recites from Hagiographa only after afternoon prayers[45].

Then at a place where there is a House of Study one should not read, at a place where there is no House of Study one should read[46]? You only have what Rebbi Nehemiah stated, as Rebbi Nehemiah stated, why may one only read Hagiographa after afternoon prayers? Because of persons' documents.

Because if you were telling him that it is permitted, then he would say, there is nothing wrong if I would occupy myself with my documents. Since you are telling him that it is forbidden, then he will say, since Hagiographa are forbidden, so much more private documents. This implies that Mishnah has precedence over Bible. This supports what Rebbi Simeon ben Yoḥai stated[46], as Rebbi Simeon ben Yoḥai stated, he who studies the written Torah does himself good that is not so good; he who studies Mishnah is occupied in an endeavor which deserves reward; he who studies Talmud could not endeavor anything greater than this, always a person should pursue Mishnah more than Talmud[47]. Rebbi Yose ben Rebbi Abun said, this was before Rebbi incorporated most of the Mishnah in the Talmud, but since Rebbi incorporated most of the Mishnah in the Talmud, a person should pursue Talmud more than Mishnah[48].

34 As Jacob Mann has pointed out, the classical *Midrashim*, which present sermon concepts, associate to pentateuchal texts not only texts from the Prophets but also from Hagiographa. This use is perfectly legitimate. (In legal contexts, קרא means not simply "reading" but "reading with correct accents"). The Babli, 117b, notes that in Babylonia one did neither preach nor study on Sabbath afternoon after prayers.

35 Checking the text for a sermon or similar use is appropriate at all times.

36 The following also is found in *Lev. rabba* 15(4), *Lament. rabbati* 4(25). It is quoted at length in *Sefer haMakhria*' (Isaias from Trani) §31 (Kohn & Klein, Munkacs 1900, col. 20a).

37 Greek δήλωμα, -ατος, τό.

38 The text in parentheses is missing in E, in the *editio princeps* of *Lev. rabba* and related mss. sources, and in the quote in *Sefer haMakhria*'. In *Lament. rabbati* it is replaced by "towards nightfall". As the following text shows, the three rabbis studied the text before the afternoon prayers; the text should be deleted.

39 *Ps.* 32:10. He referred to himself as evildoer because he read the text before the afternoon prayers for its simple meaning; had they used it as basis for sermons it would have been acceptable.

40 Added from E.

41 *Thr.* 4:20.

42 Greek σπόγγος, ὁ.

43 While healing not life-threatening situations is forbidden on the Sabbath, protecting a wound against infection is permitted. Babli 134b.

44 Bast is like string; it always is available when needed and never is *muqseh* because of uses which are forbidden on the Sabbath; therefore it may be used even for occasions which could not have been anticipated at the start of the Sabbath.

45 This statement shows that the text mentioned in Note 38 is to be deleted.

46 Cf. *Horaiot* 3:7, Notes 304-310.

47 One has to memorize the basic material of study before one studies and analyzes the details.

48 Since studying the Mishnah is now incorporated into Talmud study, it is possible to study on an elementary level appropriate for beginners.

In the opinion of Israel Levy in his *Introduction to the Yerushalmi Bava qamma* 1-6 (p. 19 Note 3) one should translate: "he who studies the written Torah does himself good that is not so good; he who studies tannaitic traditions is occupied in an endeavor which deserves reward; concerning him who studies Talmud there is no endeavor greater than this, a person should always pursue tannaitic tradition more than Talmud. Rebbi Yose ben Rebbi Abun said, this was before Rebbi incorporated most of tannaitic tradition (Mishnah and *baraitot*) in the Talmud, but since Rebbi incorporated most of the tannaitic material in the Talmud, a person should pursue Talmud more than Mishnah."

(15c line 32) בְּרָכוֹת שֶׁכָּתוּב בָּהֶן עִנְיָנוֹת הַרְבֵּה מִן הַתּוֹרָה אֵין מַצִּילִין אוֹתָן מִפְּנֵי הַדְּלֵיקָה. מִיכָּן אָמְרוּ. כּוֹתְבֵי בְרָכוֹת שׂוֹרְפֵי תוֹרָה. מַעֲשֶׂה בְאֶחָד שֶׁהָיָה כּוֹתֵב בְּרָכוֹת וְהָלַךְ רִבִּי יִשְׁמָעֵאל לְבוֹדְקוֹ. כֵּיוָן שֶׁהִרְגִּישׁ בְּקוֹל פַּעֲמוֹתָיו שֶׁלְּרִבִּי יִשְׁמָעֵאל נָטַל תַּכְרִיךְ שֶׁלִּבְרָכוֹת וּזְרָקָן לְתוֹךְ סָפָל שֶׁל מַיִם. כְּלָשׁוֹן זֶה אָמַר לוֹ. גָּדוֹל עוֹנֶשׁ הָאַחֲרוֹן מִן הָרִאשׁוֹן. אָמַר רִבִּי יְהוֹשֻׁעַ בֶּן לֵוִי. הָדָא אַגַּדְתָּא הַכּוּתְבָהּ אֵין לוֹ חֵלֶק. הַדּוֹרְשָׁהּ מִתְחָרֵךְ. הַשּׁוֹמְעָהּ אֵינוֹ מְקַבֵּל שָׂכָר.

"One does not save benedictions which contain pentateuchal materials from a fire[49]. Because of this, they said: Writers of benedictions are burners of the Torah[50]. It happened that there was a writer of benedictions; Rebbi Ismael went to check him out. When he noticed Rebbi Ismael's steps, he took a bundle of benedictions and threw them into a bowl of water. In the following formulation he spoke to him: The punishment for the later deed is worse than the one for the earlier[51]."

Rebbi Joshua ben Levi said, one who writes down sermons has no part, one who preaches them is going to be singed, one who listens to him is not rewarded[52].

49 Prayer texts which contain biblical quotes. The only prayer texts we have from Antiquity are Sadducee texts from Qumran. Rabbinic prayer books are known only from later Geonim, after the Arab conquest of Iraq. Prayer texts were considered part of oral tradition, to be memorized by following the reader in public service.

50 Since one is not permitted to disregard rabbinic prohibitions in order to save prayer texts, writing prayer texts is the equivalent of exposing the quoted verses to desctruction.

51 The disrespect shown to the holy text

is worse than making what is forbidden. Tosephta 13:4 (ed. Liebermann).

52   R. Joshua ben Levi was a renowned preacher. What he wants to say is that the preacher must present original thoughts; if he writes directions for other preachers he propagates dishonesty and as such has no part in the Future World; the person who buys from him preaches dishonestly and will be damaged in his soul; the persons who hear the sermon will not be moved; their time is wasted. *Soferim* 16:2.

(15c line 44) אָמַר רִבִּי יְהוֹשֻׁעַ בֶּן לֵוִי. אֲנָא מִן יוֹמוֹי לָא אִיסְתַּכְּלִית בְּסִפְרָא דַאֲגַדְתָּא. אֶלָּא חַד זְמַן אִסְתַּכְּלִית. אַשְׁכְּחִית כָּתוּב בָּהּ. מֵאָה וְשִׁבְעִים וַחֲמֵשׁ פַּרְשִׁיּוֹת שֶׁכָּתוּב בַּתּוֹרָה דִּבֶּר אֲמִירָה צִיוּוּי כְּנֶגֶד שְׁנוֹתָיו שֶׁלְאָבִינוּ אַבְרָהָם. דִּכְתִיב לָקַחְתָּ מַתָּנוֹת בָּאָדָם. וּכְתִיב הָאָדָם הַגָּדוֹל בָּעֲנָקִים. מֵאָה וְאַרְבָּעִים וְשִׁבְעָה מִזְמוֹרוֹת שֶׁכְּתוּבוֹת בַּתִּילִים כְּנֶגֶד שְׁנוֹתָיו שֶׁלְאָבִינוּ יַעֲקֹב. מְלַבַּד שֶׁכָּל־הַקִּילוּסִין שֶׁיִּשְׂרָאֵל מְקַלְּסִין לְהַקָּדוֹשׁ בָּרוּךְ הוּא כְּנֶגֶד שְׁנוֹתָיו שֶׁל יַעֲקֹב. שֶׁנֶּאֱמַר וְאַתָּה קָדוֹשׁ יוֹשֵׁב תְּהִלּוֹת יִשְׂרָאֵל: מֵאָה וְעֶשְׂרִים וּשְׁלֹשָׁה פְּעָמִים שֶׁיִּשְׂרָאֵל עוֹנִין הַלְלוּיָהּ. כְּנֶגֶד שְׁנוֹתָיו שֶׁלְאַהֲרֹן. הַלְלוּ יָהּ | הַלְלוּ־אֵל בְּקָדְשׁוֹ לְאַהֲרֹן קְדוֹשׁוֹ לְאַהֲרֹן קְדוֹשׁ יי. אֲפִילוּ כֵן אֲנָא מִתְבָּעִית בַּלֵּילְיָא.

רִבִּי חִיָּיה בַּר בָּא חֲמָא חַד סֵפֶר דַּאֲגָדָה. אֲמַר. אִי מַה כְּתַב טָבָאוּת. תִּקְטַע יָדָא דְכַתְבָהּ. אֲמַר לֵיהּ חַד. אֲבוִי דְהַהוּא גַבְרָא כַתְבָהּ. אֲמַר לֵיהּ. כֵּן אֲמָרִית. תִּקְטַע יָדָא דְכַתְבָהּ. וַהֲוַות לֵיהּ כֵּן כִּשְׁגָגָה שֶׁיּוֹצָא מִלִּפְנֵי הַשַּׁלִּיט:

[53]Rebbi Joshua ben Levi said, I never looked into a book of sermon concepts, except that once I looked, and I found written there: The 175 paragraphs where in the Torah is written speech, saying, commandment[54], correspond to the years of our father Abraham, as it is written, *you took gifts from Man*[55], and it is written, *the great Man among giants*[56]. The 147 songs written in Psalms[57] correspond to the years of our father Jacob. This teaches that all praises by which Israel praise the Holy One, praise to Him, correspond to the years of Jacob, as it is said, *You are Holy, throning over the praises of Israel*[58]. The 123 times Israel answer "halleluiah"[59] correspond to the years of Aaron, *Halleluiah, praise God by His holy one*[60], Aaron his holy one, *for Aaron, the Eternal's holy one*[61]. Nevertheless I was frightened in the night[62].

Rebbi Ḥiyya bar Abba saw a book of *agadah*. He said, even if what is written in there is good, the hand who wrote it should be amputated. A person told him, it was written by X's father. He said, I was saying, the hand who wrote it should be amputated. That happened to him, *as an error which is coming out from the ruler's mouth*[63].

53 Tactate *Soferim* 16:10. The piece is missing in Tactate *Soferim* in *Mahzor Vitry*.
54 The number of paragraphs which start with an expression of commandment.
55 *Ps.* 68:19. Traditionally the Psalm is read as describing the Exodus and the epiphany at Sinai. The gift is the Torah given to Moses.
56 *Jos.* 14:15.
57 The number of Psalms if Psalms 1-2, 9-10, 114-115 are combinred.
58 *Ps.* 22:4.
59 In the recitation of "Hallel" (Pss. 113-118) by the reader, the congregation answers every half-verse by "halleluiah". This form of recitation, described by Maimonides *Hilkhot Hanukkah* 3:12 (Babli *Sukkah* 38b), still is common among Yemenite congregations. The exact places of response are indicated in the Yemenite *Tikālil*.
60 *Ps.* 150:1.
61 *Ps.* 106:16.
62 Because of the sin he committed reading the book in which was written what only should be orally transmitted.
63 *Eccl.* 10:5.

(15c line 52) הַגִּילְיוֹנִים וְסִפְרֵי מִינִין. אִית תַּנָּיֵי תַנֵּי. קוֹרֵעַ אַזְכְּרוֹתֵיהֶן וְשׂוֹרְפָן. אִית תַּנָּיֵי תַנֵּי. שׂוֹרְפָן הֵן וְאַזְכְּרוֹתֵיהֶן. אָמַר רִבִּי טַרְפוֹן. אֲקַפַּח אֶת בָּנַיי שֶׁאִם יְבוֹאוּ לְבֵיתִי שֶׁאֲנִי שׂוֹרְפָן הֵן וְאַזְכְּרוֹתֵיהֶן. שֶׁאִם יִהְיֶה הָרוֹדֵף רוֹדֵף אַחֲרַיי שֶׁאֲנִי נִמְלָט לְתוֹךְ בָּתֵּיהֶן שֶׁלְעֲבוֹדָה זָרָה וְאֵינִי נִמְלָט לְתוֹךְ בָּתֵּיהֶן שֶׁלְמִינִין. שֶׁעוֹבְדֵי עֲבוֹדָה זָרָה אֵינָן מַכִּירִין אוֹתוֹ וְכוֹפְרִין בּוֹ. אֲבָל הַמִּינִין מַכִּירִין אוֹתוֹ וְכוֹפְרִין בּוֹ. וַעֲלֵיהֶן אָמַר דָּוִד הֲלוֹא־מְשַׂנְאֶיךָ יי׳ אֶשְׂנָא וגו׳. זֶה מִדְרָשׁ דָּרְשׁוּ. וּמָה אִם לְהַטִּיל שָׁלוֹם בֵּין אִישׁ לְאִשְׁתּוֹ אָמַר הַכָּתוּב. הַשֵּׁם שֶׁנִּכְתָּב בִּקְדוּשָּׁה יִמָּחֶה עַל הַמַּיִם. סִפְרֵי מִינִין שֶׁמַּטִּילִין אֵיבָה וְתַחֲרוּת וּמַחֲלוֹקֶת בֵּין יִשְׂרָאֵל לַאֲבִיהֶן שֶׁבַּשָּׁמַיִם אֵינוּ דִין שֶׁיִּשָּׂרְפוּ הֵן וְאַזְכְּרוֹתֵיהֶן.

[64]"Gospels[65] and books of heretics[66], some Tannaim say[67], one tears out the Names[68] and burns them; some Tannaim say[69], one burns them with their Names. Rebbi Tarphon said, I would hit my sons; if they came into my house I would burn them together with their Names. For if a persecutor would persecute me I would seek asylum in a pagan temple but would not seek asylum in heretics' houses, for the worshippers of idolatry do not know about Him, how could they disavow Him? But the heretics know Him and disavow Him; about them David said[70], *Your haters, o Eternal, I shall hate,* etc. This homily they[71] preached: If in order to bring peace between a man and his wife the verse commands that the Name written in holiness be erased[72], it is only logical that the books of heretics which propagate ill will and quarrel between Israel and their Father in Heaven should be burned with their Names."

64 Tosephta 13:5 (ed. Liebermann). Babli 116a.	67 The Divine Name in its forms which may not be erased as listed in *Megillah* 71d l. 59, Babli *Ševuot* 35a.
65 If written in Hebrew or Aramaic.	68 R. Yose the Galilean.
66 Usually this is applied to Ebionite literature. But since both prayer collections and written sermons on biblical texts, both of which were condemned in precedings paragraphs, were found in the Qumran caves, it is not excluded that the notion also includes the remainder of Sadducee/Essene literature in Tannaitic times.	69 R. Tarphon.
	70 *Ps.* 139:21.
	71 R. Ismael.
	72 In the ordeal which proves the innocence of a woman accused of adultery, *Num.* 5:23.

(15c line 62) מַתְנִיתִין בְּשֶׁאֵינוֹ טָפוּל לוֹ. אֲבָל אִם הָיָה טָפוּל לוֹ כְגוּפוֹ הוּא. נִיחָא תִּיק הַסֵּפֶר עִם הַסֵּפֶר. תִּיק תְּפִילִין עִם הַתְּפִילִין. רִבִּי חַגַּי בְּשֵׁם רִבִּי זְעִירָא שָׁמַע לָהּ מֵהָדָא. חוֹנֶה מַלְאַךְ־יְיָ סָבִיב לִירֵיאָיו וַיְחַלְּצֵם. וְכֵן הוּא אוֹמֵר. בֵּאדַיִן גּוּבְרַיָּא אִילֵּךְ כְּפִיתוּ בְּסָרְבָּלֵיהוֹן וגו'.

[73]Our Mishnah if it is not connected[74]; but if it is connected it is like its body. One understands the case[75] of the book with the book. The case of phylacteries with the phylacteries[76]? Rebbi Ḥaggai in the name of Rebbi Ze`ira understands it from the following: *The Eternal's angel is camping around those who fear Him and saves them*[77]. Similarly, it says. *then these men were bound in their coats*[78].

73 Discussion of Mishnah 2.	phylacteries from a case take more than a fraction of a second. The case is not part of the phylacteries since the owner removes them every weekday to put them on.
74 If the scroll is permanently fixed in the case the Mishnah is unnecessary since the case is an appurtenance of the scroll. Therefore it is permitted to remove the scroll in its case to places rabbinically forbidden even if the scroll only lies in the case and could be removed without effort.	
	77 *Ps.* 34:8. Just as everything around a God-fearing person is protected, so everything around his religious objects is protected. Cf. *Hagigah* 2:1 (77c l.12).
75 Greek θήκη, ἡ.	
76 In no case would removing the	78 *Dan.* 3:21. The coats also were saved.

(15c line 66) אַף עַל פִּי שֶׁיֵּשׁ בְּתוֹכָן מָעוֹת. יָבֹא כָיי דָּמַר רִבִּי יַעֲקֹב בַּר אֲחָא אָמַר חִינָּנָא קַרְתִּיגְנָאָה בְּשֵׁם רִבִּי הוֹשַׁעְיָה. דִּיסִיקְיָא שֶׁיֵּשׁ בְּתוֹכָהּ מָעוֹת נוֹתֵן עָלֶיהָ כִּכָּר וּמְטַלְטְלָהּ. וְלָאֵיכָן מַצִּילִין אוֹתָן. לְמָבוֹי שֶׁאֵינוֹ מְפוּלָּשׁ. הָא לִמְפוּלָּשׁ לֹא. בְּכָל־אֲתָר אַתְּ אָמַר. אֵין הַמְהַלֵּךְ כְּמַנִּיחַ. וְכָא אַתְּ אָמַר. הַמְהַלֵּךְ כְּמַנִּיחַ. אֶלָּא בְזוֹרֵק. תַּמָּן אַתְּ אָמַר. הַזּוֹרֵק פָּטוּר. וְכָא

אַתְּ אָמַר. הָאוּרָק חַיָּיב. רִבִּי חִזְקִיָּה בְשֵׁם רִבִּי אָחָא. בְּשֶׁלֹּא עֵירְבוּ אֲנָן קַייָמִין. בֶּן בְּתֵירָה כְרִבִּי יְהוּדָה. דְּתַנִינָן תַּמָּן. גְּשָׁרִים הַמְפוּלָּשִׁים מְטַלְטְלִין תַּחְתֵּיהֶן בַּשַּׁבָּת. דִּבְרֵי רִבִּי יוּדָה. וַחֲכָמִים אוֹסְרִין.

"Even if there are coins inside[5]." This parallels what Rebbi Jacob bar Aha said, Ḥinena from Cartagena in the name of Rebbi Hoshaia: On a saddle bag[79] full of coins one puts a loaf and may move it[80].

"Where does one save it to? To a side street which is a dead end." Therefore not to one which is a thoroughfare. Everywhere you are saying, one who is walking is not like one who is putting down, but here you are saying, one who is walking is not like one who is putting down[81]. But one who is throwing. Everywhere you are saying, one who throws is not liable, but here you are saying, one who throws is liable[82]. Rebbi Ḥizqiah in the name of Rebbi Aḥa: we are dealing with the case that they did not make an *eruv*[83].

Ben Bathyra is like Rebbi Jehudah, as we have stated there[84]: "One may move things under bridges which are thoroughfares, the words of Rebbi Jehudah, but the Sages prohibit."

79 Greek δισάκκιον, τό; modern Greek δισάκκι. Literally "double bag".
80 While the saddle bag is *muqseh*, anything *muqzeh* may be moved if it serves a basis for something which may be moved. Babli 142b.
81 If the house is adjacent to a thoroughfare one does not understand why the Sages opposed to ben Bathyra do not permit to carry the things into another house facing the same side street without stopping in the street since then there is no transport from a private domain to a non-private domain and therefore no biblical prohibition.
82 It is agreed that one may carry from the burning house into another house open to the same side street. The restriction to a dead-end street only applies to cases where one cannot carry but has to throw. But then Mishnah 11:1 states that the Sages declare not liable a person throwing from one private domain into another even over clearly public domain.
83 It is clear that the Mishnah would not be necessary if there were an *eruv*; the only question is whether there could have been an *eruv* or not.
84 Mishnah *Eruvin* 9:5. The argument is not only about the text quoted but mainly about the end of the Mishnah: "In addition, Rebbi Jehudah said, one may make an *eruv* for a side street which is a thoroughfare but the Sages forbid." The argument of R. Jehudah, endorsed by Ben Bathyra, is that any narrow strip bounded on two opposite sides, either under a bridge or on a narrow

thoroughfare, is a candidate for designation as a private domain.

It is asserted that Ben Bathyra permits moving to a thoroughfare because it could be unproblematic if there were an *eruv*; the Sages forbid since it never could be unproblematic.

(15c line 74) רִבִּי בּוּן בַּר חִיָּיא בְּשֵׁם רִבִּי בָּא בַּר מָמָל. דְּרִבִּי נְחֶמְיָה הִיא. דְּאָמַר. אֵינָן נִיטָּלִין אֶלָּא לְצוֹרֶךְ. אָמַר רִבִּי יוֹסֵה. טַעֲמוֹן דְּרַבָּנָן תַּמָּן. כָּל־מָה שֶׁיֵּשׁ בַּבַּיִת מִן הַמּוּכָן. בְּרַם הָכָא אִם אַתָּה אוֹמֵר כֵּן אַף הוּא מַצִּיל מִן הַיּוֹם לְמָחָר. מַתְנִיתִין דְּרִבִּי הוֹנְדְקֹס דְּאָמַר. לְעוֹלָם מַצִּילִין מָזוֹן שָׁלֹשׁ סְעוּדוֹת. תִּיפְתָּר שֶׁנָּפְלָה דְּלֵיקָה בְּלֵילֵי שַׁבָּת עַד שֶׁלֹּא אָכְלָהּ. בְּיוֹם הַכִּיפּוּרִים מַאי אִיכָּא לְמֵימַר. עַל דַּעְתְּהוֹן דְּרַבָּנָן לֹא יַצִּיל כְּלוּם. כָּל־עַמָּא מוֹדוֹ שֶׁמַּצִּילִין מָזוֹן סְעוּדָה אַחַת מִפְּנֵי הַסַּכָּנָה.

[85]Rebbi Abun bar Ḥiyya in the name of Rebbi Abba bar Mamal, this is Rebbi Nehemiah's who said, it can be taken only if necessary. Rebbi Yose said, the reason of the rabbis there is that everything in the house is prepared, but here if you would say so he would save from today for tomorrow[86]. The Mishnah is from Rebbi הונדקס[87] who said, one always saves food for three meals. Explain it if the fire started Friday evening before he ate[88]. What should one say on the day of Atonement? Should he not save anything following the rabbis[89]? Everybody agrees that one saves food for one meal because of the danger[90].

85 Discussion of Mishnah 3.
86 This refers to Mishnah 17:4 where it is asserted that all vessels may be used (and moved) on the Sabbath without establishing a need. R. Nehemiah disagrees and permits moving anything only for a genuine need. The first opinion wants to find in the Mishnah an endorsement of R. Nehemiah's position since it is presented as anonymous opinion which implies that it is practice to be followed. The need in this case is the obligation to consume three meals on the Sabbath. Since there is no reason to restrict using food on the Sabbath, limiting the moving of food out of the house to the three obligatory meals can be explained only following R. Nehemiah. The argument is rejected by R. Yose who explains the Mishnah here as a rabbinic restriction, to avoid preparing on a Sabbath for the needs of weekday. One still holds that nothing is *muqseh* which has not been explicitly removed from use on the Sabbath.

87 This name is a *hapax*; in the opinion of Krauss a Greek name ˝Ανδοκος. The quote of the passage in the Mishnah commentary of Salomo Adani reads חיקיים, another unexplained form. It is best to accept the interpretation of I. Löw (in Krauss's Dictionary) who sees in the statement of R. Hondikos not the statement of R. Yose in the Mishnah, but the statement in *Mekhilta*

dR. Ismael, ad Ex. 16:25, that the triple mention of "today" in the verse implies the obligation to eat three meals on the Sabbath. The name of the tradent in the Munich ms. of the Mekhilta is הנדקא (in the quote in *Leqaḥ ṭov, Pesiqta zuṭreta ad Ex.* 16:25, ed. S. Buber Note 119, הינדקא), which would mean *Indicus*. In the Babli 117b (a related but different statement) and the quote of the Mekhilta in *Midrash Wehizhir* ed. I. M. Freimann p. 18 the name is חידקא.

88 As noted before, the statement should be that there is an obligation to eat three meals on the Sabbath. Since one of them is the Friday evening meal, there should be only two needed for the Sabbath.

89 Since it is a fast day; there is no food needed on the day itself.

90 Since it would be dangerous not to break the fast in the evening, everybody agrees that the meal after the end of the fast is part of the needs of the day.

(15d line 5) תַּנֵּי. מַצִּילִין לַחוֹלֶה וּלְקָטָן וּלְבֵינוֹנִית. וּלְרַעֲבְתָן כְּדֵי מְזוֹנוֹ. מְעָרְבִין לַחוֹלֶה וּלְקָטָן כְּדֵי מְזוֹנוֹ. וּלְרַעֲבְתָן בְּבֵינוֹנִית.

תַּנֵּי. אֵין מַעֲרִימִין. רִבִּי יוֹסֵי בֵּירִבִּי בּוּן אָמַר. מַעֲרִימִין. אִית תַּנָּיֵי תַנֵּי. מַצִּיל וְאַחַר כָּךְ מְזַמֵּן. אִית תַּנָּיֵי תַנֵּי. מְזַמֵּן וְאַחַר כָּךְ מַצִּיל. מָאן דָּמַר. מַצִּיל וְאַחַר כָּךְ מְזַמֵּן. כְּמָאן דָּמַר. מַעֲרִימִין. וּמָאן דָּמַר. מַצִּיל וְאַחַר כָּךְ מְזַמֵּן. כְּמָאן דָּמַר. אֵין מַעֲרִימִין.

תַּנֵּי. אַף מְכַבִּין לְהַצִּיל. מַתְנִיתָה דְּרִבִּי שִׁמְעוֹן דְּאָמַר. אֵין דָּבָר מִשּׁוּם שְׁבוּת עוֹמֵד בִּפְנֵי כִתְבֵי הַקּוֹדֶשׁ.

תַּנֵּי. אַף מְטַמְּאִין לְהַצִּיל. וְהָתַנֵּי. בְּכָל־קוֹדֶשׁ לֹא־תִגָּע. לְרַבּוֹת הַתְּרוּמָה. הִיא תְּרוּמָה הִיא מַעֲשֵׂר שֵׁינִי. מַאי כְדוֹן. בִּלְבַד שֶׁלֹּא יַעֲשֶׂה בַשַּׁבָּת כְּדֶרֶךְ שֶׁעוֹשֶׂה בַחוֹל.

תַּנֵּי. כְּשֵׁם שֶׁמַּצִּילִין מִן הַדְּלֵיקָה כָּךְ מַצִּילִין מִיַּד הַגַּייִס וּמִיַּד הַנָּהָר וּמִיַּד הַמַּפּוֹלֶת וּמִיַּד כָּל־ דָּבָר שָׁאוּבֵד.

It was stated: One saves an average portion for a sick person and for a child, but for a glutton according to his wont. One prepares an *eruv* for a sick person or a child according to their wont but for a glutton an average portion[91].

It was stated[92] that one does not plan to circumvent the law. Rebbi Yose ben Rebbi Abun[93] said, one does plan to circumvent the law. Some Tannaim state, one saves and then invites; some Tannaim state, one invites and then saves[94]. He who says, one saves and then invites follows him who says, one does plan to circumvent the law. But he who says, one invites and then saves follows him who says, one does not plan to circumvent the law.

It was stated[95]: One extinguishes to save. This *baraita* follows Rebbi Simeon who said, nothing forbidden only rabbinically stands in the way of Holy Scriptures[29,96].

It was stated: One may cause impurity[97] to save. But was it not stated, *she may not touch anything holy*[98], including heave[99]? [100]There is no difference between heave and Second Tithe. What about it? On condition that he not proceed on the Sabbath the way he proceeds on a weekday.

91 Even though a sick person or a child eat less than a normal adult person, one may save a full portion for them. For a glutton one may increase the amount. For *eruv tehumin*, to allow a person to walk on the Sabbath further than the statutory 2000 cubits one deposits a symbolic amount of food at the Sabbath border before the start of the Sabbath. This then becomes the symbolic dwelling place of the person who has 2000 cubits in each direction (where a built-up area is counted as 4 cubits). One is interested to make the symbolic meal as small as possible.

92 Tosephta 13:7 (ed. Liebermann); Babli 117b.

93 Since R. Yose ben R. Abun is a very late Amora, this attribution is impossible, even though the reading is quoted by R. Hananel (Babli 120a). It must be either R. Yose ben Rebbi Jehudah as in the Babli, even though the Tosephta reports him to hold the opposite opinion, or R. Jehudah ben Laqish as reported in the Tosephta.

94 It is understood that the "three meals" quoted in the Mishnah are understood as 3 meals for every person in the house, including guests. Therefore according to the second opinion one may remove from the burning house a great amount of food and then invite neighbors to eat some of it.

95 Tosephta 13:6 (ed. Liebermann).

96 He holds that any work not intended for its own sake is only rabbinically forbidden. Extinguishing a fire in itself is biblically forbidden; extinguishing in order to save holy books would only be rabbinically prohibited.

97 The spelling of the scribe was מטמין; the corrector wrongly babylonized to מטמאין.

98 *Lev.* 12:4.

99 Since impure heave may not be eaten but must be burned, saving heave by making it impure would be futile.

100 This is inappropriate here; it is copied from Chapter 14, Note 59. Tithe is not like heave for impurity, *Sifra Tazria`Pereq* 1(8).

‏(15d line 16) מַתְנִיתִין דְּרבִּי יוֹסֵי דְּאָמַר. לְעוֹלָם מַצִּילִין מְזוֹן שָׁלשׁ סְעוּדּוֹת: מִכֵּיוָן שֶׁכּוּלָהּ גּוּף אֶחָד כְּמִי שֶׁכּוּלָהּ סְעוּדָה אַחַת.

‏וְאוֹמֵר לַאֲחֵרִים בּוֹאוּ וְהַצִּילוּ לָכֶם. שֶׁכֵּן דַּרְכָּן לְהַזְמִין אוֹרְחִין בַּשַּׁבָּת.

אִם הָיוּ פִּקְחִין עוֹשִׂין עִמּוֹ חֶשְׁבּוֹן לְאַחַר הַשַּׁבָּת. תַּמָּן תַּנִּינָן. מַנִּיחַ טַלִּיתוֹ אֶצְלוֹ וְעוֹשֶׂה עִמּוֹ חֶשְׁבּוֹן לְאַחַר שַׁבָּת. תַּמָּן אַתְּ אָמַר. מַשְׁכּוֹנֵיהּ גַּבֵּיהּ. הָכָא מַאי אִית לָךְ. אָמַר רִבִּי אַבָּא מָרִי. לְכָךְ שְׁנִינוּ. נִקְרָא פִּיקֵחַ.

[101]Does the Mishnah follow Rebbi Yose who said, "one always saves food for three meals"? Since all is one body, all of it counts as one meal.

"One says to others, come and save for yourselves[9]," since ordinarily one invites guests for the Sabbath[102].

"If they are intelligent[10] they settle accounts with him after the Sabbath.." There we have stated[103], "he leaves his toga with him and settles his account after the Sabbath." There you say, he has his pledge with him; here what do you have? Rebbi Abba Mari said, because of this we taught, "if they were intelligent"[104].

101 Discussion of Mishnah 4. Since an entire sack full of food can be saved, it should be forbidden even for R. Yose.
102 If the guests had been invited before the start of the fire it is obvious that their part of the food could be saved. Since it is possible to invite guests on Sabbath proper, even the Tanna who holds that one does not plan to circumvent the law will agree that they can be invited now.
103 Mishnah 23:1, speaking of a person who borrows from another on the Sabbath when he has no credit with the lender.
104 Since the original owner only has a moral, not a legal claim to the food which was taken by others.

(15d line 22) רִבִּי יוֹסֵי אוֹמֵר שְׁמוֹנָה עָשָׂר כֵּלִים. וְאֵילוּ הֵן. מִקְטוֹרֶן נִיקְלִי וּפוּנְדָּא וּפִילְיוֹן וּמַעֲפוֹרֶת וְקוֹלְבִּין שֶׁלְּפִשְׁתָּן וְחָלוּק שֶׁלְּצֶמֶר וּשְׁתֵּי אֶמְפְּלִיּוֹת שְׁנֵי סַבְרִיקִין וּשְׁנֵי אַבְרִיקִין שְׁנֵי מִנְעָלִין וְכוֹבַע שֶׁבְּרֹאשׁוֹ וַחֲגוֹר שֶׁבְּמָתְנָיו וְסוּדָרִין שֶׁעַל זְרוֹעוֹתָיו.

וְאוֹמֵר לַאֲחֵרִים בּוֹאוּ וְהַצִּילוּ עִמִּי. שֶׁכֵּן דַּרְכָּן לְהַשְׁאִיל כֵּלִים בַּשַּׁבָּת.

[105]Rebbi Yose says, 18 garments." And they are these: The burnus[106], arm cover[107], and money belt[108], and felt cap,[109] and a kafia[110], and a linen tunic[111], and a woolen shirt[112], and two felt stockings[113], two garters[114], and two breeches[115], two shoes, and the hat[116] on his head, and the belt on his hips[117], and shawls[118] on his arms.

"And says to others come and save with me," since ordinarily one lends garments on the Sabbath[102].

105 Discussion of Mishnah 5. The parallel is in the Babli 120a. R. Yose limits everybody to a maximum of 18 garments at a time.

106 Explanation of *Arukh*; Latin *amictorium* (a Medieval word, "loose garment, coat, wrap", classical Latin *amictus*). Rashi: *mantel* (modern French *manteau*). R. Hananel identifies with Hebrew מְעִיל "coat".

107 In the Babli אונקלי, explained as Greek ἀγκάλη, ἡ. Rashi: "A wide garment worn by Sarracens." R. Hananel: "A thin garment معرقة worn on the body to absorb the sweat."

108 Latin *funda*. This is worn on the outside. Rashi: A hollow belt worn over the garment. R. Hananel: In Persian *pesht*, is worn below the navel.

109 Latin *pilleus, -i, m.* In the Babli אפיליון. Rashi: A sheet to cover himself completely. R. Hananel does not comment on the term.

110 Rashi: to wrap around his head. The root is غفر "to cover".

111 Greek κολόβιον, τό "sleeveless or short-sleeved tunic". Rashi: *ganbeis*, which according to M. Katan were underpants worn under armor to protect the skin from the metal. R. Hananel: Undershirt which is called غلالة "tunic".

112 Rashi: *chemise* ("shirt") on his skin.

113 Greek ἐμπίλια, τά "felt shoes" (also bandage for horses' legs). Rashi: *calçones* (*chaussons*) of wool.

114 Rashi: "straps". R. Hananel: In Greek this means "trousers" but some say these are gloves with separate fingers. The Geonic commentary to *Tahorot* (*Kelim* 29:2) notes that "some say these are (Farsi) توبان ران (trousers)".

115 Latin *bracchia* (*bracchium, i, n.*).

116 Biblically this means "helmet".

117 Rashi: On his shirt inside.

118 Latin *sudarium, -ii,* n., "sweatcloth".

(15d line 27) כֵּינֵי מַתְנִיתָא. מִשֶּׁיֹּאחַז הָאוּר בָּהֶן. רִבִּי יִרְמְיָה רִבִּי בָּא בַּר מָמָל בְּשֵׁם רַב. סֵפֶר שֶׁאָחַז בּוֹ הָאוּר מִצַּד אֶחָד נוֹתֵן מַיִם מִצַּד הַשֵּׁינִי. וְאִם כָּבָה כָּבָה. אָחַז בּוֹ הָאוּר מִשְּׁנֵי צְדָדִין פּוֹשְׁטוֹ וְקוֹרֵא בוֹ. וְאִם כָּבָה כָּבָה. טַלִּית שֶׁאָחַז בּוֹ הָאוּר מִצַּד אֶחָד נוֹתֵן מַיִם מִצַּד הַשֵּׁינִי. וְאִם כָּבָה כָּבָה. אָחַז בּוֹ הָאוּר מִשְּׁנֵי צְדָדִין נוֹטְלוֹ וּמִתְעַטֵּף בָּהּ. וְאִם כָּבְתָה כָּבְתָה.

So is the Mishnah: Before they are on fire[119]. Rebbi Jeremiah, Rebbi Abba bar Mamal in the name of Rav: If a scroll started burning at one side one puts water on the other side[120]; if it was extinguished it was extinguished. If the fire burned on both sides one spreads it out and reads in it; if it was extinguished it was extinguished. [121]If a toga started burning at one side one puts water on the other side; if it was extinguished it was extinguished. If the fire burned on both sides one takes it and wraps oneself in it; if it was extinguished it was extinguished.

119 This refers to Mishnah 6. Ben Nanas only allows protecting the chest from the fire, not smothering it with a leather cover.

120 This is indirect causation of extinguishing which only is rabbinically forbidden and is tolerated in this case.

121 Babli 120a bottom.

(15d line 32) רִבִּי שְׁמוּאֵל בְּשֵׁם רִבִּי זֵירָא. דְּרִבִּי יוֹסֵה הִיא. אָמַר רִבִּי יוֹסֵה. הֲוָה סָבְרִין מֵימַר. מַה פְּלִיגִין מֵימַר רִבִּי יוֹסֵה וְרַבָּנָן. בְּשֶׁעָשָׂה מְחִיצָה שֶׁלְּכֵלִים. אֲבָל עָשָׂה מְחִיצָה שֶׁל מַיִם לֹא. מִן מַה דָּמַר רִבִּי שְׁמוּאֵל בְּשֵׁם רִבִּי זְעִירָא. דְּרִבִּי יוֹסִי הִיא. הָדָא אֲמָרָה. אֲפִילוּ עָשָׂה מְחִיצָה שֶׁלְּמַיִם הִיא הַמַּחֲלוֹקֶת.

[122]Rebbi Samuel in the name of Rebbi Ze'ira: This is Rebbi Yose's. We were of the opinion to say, where what Rebbi Yose says and the rabbis disagree? When he made a barrier of vessels. But not if he made a barrier of water. Since Rebbi Samuel said in the name of Rebbi Ze'ira: This is Rebbi Yose's, it implies that there is disagreement even if he made a barrier of water.

122 This is copied from the end of Chapter 3, Note 234.

(15d line 37) נָכְרִי שֶׁבָּא לְכַבּוֹת. בְּיֹמֵי רִבִּי אַמִי נָפְלָה דְלֵיקָה בַּכְּפָר. אַפִּיק רִבִּי אִימִי כְּרוֹז בְּשׁוּקֵי דַאֲרָמָאֵי וָמַר. מָאן דַּעֲבַד לָא מַפְסִיד. אָמַר רִבִּי אֶלְעָזָר בֵּירִבִּי יוֹסֵה קוֹמֵי רִבִּי יוֹסֵה. סַכָּנָה הַיְיתָה. אִם הָיְיתָה סַכָּנָה אֲפִילוּ רִבִּי אַמִי יַטְפֵי. וְלֹא כֵן תַּנֵּי. כָּל־דָּבָר שֶׁיֵּשׁ בּוֹ סַכָּנָה אֵין אוֹמְרִין. יֵיעָשׂוּ דְבָרִים הַלָּלוּ בַּנָּשִׁים וּבַקְטַנִּים. אֶלָּא אֲפִילוּ בִגְדוֹלִים אֲפִילוּ בְיִשְׂרָאֵל. מַעֲשֶׂה שֶׁנָּפְלָה דְלֵיקָה בַּחֲצַר יוֹסֵי בֶן סִימָאי בְּשִׁיחִין. וְיָרְדוּ בְנֵי קַיצְרָה שֶׁלְּצִיפּוֹרִין לְכַבּוֹת וְלֹא הִנִּיחַ לָהֶן. אָמַר לָהֶן. הַנִּיחוּ לַגַּבַּאי שֶׁיִּגְבֶּה חוֹבוֹ. מִיַּד קָשַׁר עָלָיו הֶעָנָן וְכִיבָּהוּ. בְּמוֹצָאֵי שַׁבָּת שָׁלַח לְכָל־חַד מֵהֶם סֶלַע וּלְאִיפַּרְכּוּס שֶׁלָּהֶן חֲמִשִּׁים דֵּינָר. לֹא הָיָה צָרִיךְ לַעֲשׂוֹת כֵּן. אָמְרוּ חֲכָמִים. חַד נַפְתִּי הֲוָה בִּמְגוּרָה דְּרִבִּי יוֹנָה. נְפִילַת דְלֵיקָה בִּמְגוּרָה דְּרִבִּי יוֹנָה. אֲזַל הַהוּא נַפְתָּיָיה בְעֵי מִטְפָּיְיתָהּ וְלָא שָׁבְקֵיהּ. אֲמַר לֵיהּ. בַּגְרָךְ מִדְלִי. אֲמַר לֵיהּ אִין. וְאִשְׁתְּזִיב כּוּלָּהּ. רִבִּי יוּדָן דִּכְפַר אִימִי פָּרַס גּוֹלְתֵּיהּ עַל גַּדִּישָׁא וְנוּרָה עָרְקָא מִינָּהּ.

1 בימי ר' | ר ביומוי דר' אפיק | ר ואפיק אימי | ר אמי   2 בשוקי | ר בשוקאי ומר | ר ואמ' מאן | ר כל מפסיד | ר מפסד יוסה | ר יוסי (2)   3 הייתה | ר הוית אם היתה סכנה | ר ואי סכנה הוית אמי | ר אימי ולא כן | ר לא שיש בו | ר -   4 דברים הללו בנשים | ר בגוים אפילו (2) | ר ואפי'   5 קיצרה | ר קצרה לכבות | ר לכבותו   6 להן | ר לון לכבות העבן | ר הענן וירדו גשמים   7 חד | ר אחד ואחד ולאיפרבוס | ר ולאפרכוס אמרו חכמ' | ר אמ' ר' חנינה היה | ר הוה   8 נפתי | ר כותיי במגורה | ר מגיריה במגורה | ר במגירותיה מפתייה | ר כותאה   9 מטפייתה | ר מיטפייה שבקיה | ר שבקיה ר' יונה ואישתזיב | ר ואישתזייב

[123]In the days of Rebbi Immi there was a fire in the village. Rebbi Immi sent a crier to the markets of the Gentiles saying: "He who works will not

lose.¹²⁴" Rebbi Eleazar ben Rebbi Yose said, that was danger to life. But if there was danger to life, Rebbi Immi himself should have fought the fire! Did we not state¹²⁵, in any case of danger to life one does not say that [the necessary work] be done by women¹²⁶ or minors, but [it should be done] even by adults, even by Jewish persons. "It happened that there was a fire in the courtyard of Yose ben Simai in Shiḥin, and the garrison of the barracks¹²⁷ of Sepphoris came to fight it but he did not let them fight it; he said, let the collector collect his due¹²⁸. Immediately there formed a cloud which extinguished it. After the Sabbath he sent to each of them a tetradrachma and to their commander¹²⁹ 50 denarii." The Sages¹³⁰ said, there was no need for him to do that. A Nabatean¹³¹ was in the neighborhood of Rebbi Jonah. There was a fire in Rebbi Jonah's neighborhood; the Nabatean wanted to fight it but Rebbi Jonah did not let him. He said to him, because of my property! He said, yes¹³². And everything was saved. Rebbi Jonah from Kefar-Immi spread his garment over the grain stack and the fire retreated from it.

---

123 Discussion of Mishnah 7. All fires mentioned here happened on a Sabbath. The text also is in *Nedarim* 4:9 (ר) Notes 104-113. It is difficult to decide which passage is the original.

124 One is permitted to assure people of their wages. In the Babli, 121a, R. Ammi (= Immi) says directly that suggesting payment is permitted in the case of a fire on the Sabbath.

125 Also in the Babli, Yoma 84b.

126 In Tosephta 15:15, *Nedarim* and *Yoma* 8:5 correctly: "Gentiles". This also is the quote from *Šabbat* in Medieval sources (*Raviah* p. 338, *Or zarua* 2 §38, *Roqeah* §109).

127 Latin *castra, -orum*, n. "military camp, barracks, fortress. "

128 Since the fire was on a Sabbath, he took it as divine punishment.

129 Greek ἔπαρχος, ὁ, equivalent of Latin *praefectus (castrorum)*. Tosephta 13:9 (ed. Liebermann).

130 In *Nedarim*: R. Hanina (the Chief Rabbi of Sepphoris in a later generation.) In the Babli 121a, this is the opinion of the Sages, while Yose ben Simai wanted to encourage them to fight Sabbath fires at Sepphoris. The mention of the Sages here may be a contamination from the Babli.

131 In *Nedarim*: "A Samaritan". Since a Samaritan as a Jew has to keep the Sabbath, the reading here is preferable.

132 R. Jonah agreed to be responsible for the Nabatean's loss if the fire reached his property.

(15d line 50) אֲבָל קָטָן שֶׁבָּא לְכַבּוֹת אֵין שׁוֹמְעִין לוֹ. וְלֹא כֵן תַּנֵּי. רָאוּ אוֹתוֹ יוֹצֵא וּמְלַקֵּט עֲשָׂבִים אֵין אַתְּ זָקוּק לוֹ. תַּמָּן אֵין לוֹ צוֹרֶךְ בַּעֲשָׂבִים. הָכָא יֵשׁ לוֹ צוֹרֶךְ כִּיבּוּי.

"But if a minor comes to extinguish one may not listen to him." But was it not stated, if one saw him going out and collecting grasses, one need not interfere? There he has no need for grasses; here he sees the need for fire fighting.

(15d line 52) כּוֹפִין קְעָרָה עַל גַּבֵּי הַנֵּר. יָבֹא כָיֵי דָּמַר רִבִּי שִׁמְעוֹן בֵּרִבִּי יַנַּאי. אֲנִי לֹא שָׁמַעְתִּי מֵאַבָּא. אֲחוֹתִי אָמְרָה לִי מִשְׁמוֹ. בֵּיצָה שֶׁנּוֹלְדָה בְיוֹם טוֹב סוֹמְכִין לָהּ בִּשְׁבִיל שֶׁלֹּא תִּתְגַּלְגֵּל. אֲבָל אֵין כּוֹפִין עָלֶיהָ אֶת הַכְּלִי. וּשְׁמוּאֵל אָמַר. אַף כּוֹפִין עָלֶיהָ כְּלִי.

"One may put a pot over a light." It comes following what [133]Rebbi Simeon ben Rebbi Yannai said: I did not hear from my father; my sister told me in his name. An egg which was laid on the Sabbath one props up against [a vessel] so it should not roll off. But one does not cover it with a vessel. But Samuel says, one may cover it with a vessel.

וְעַל צוֹאָה שֶׁל קָטָן. וְלֹא מַאֲכַל תַּרְנְגוֹלִין אִינּוּן. אָמַר רִבִּי עוּקְבָן. תִּפְתָּר בְּאִילֵּין רַכִּיכָה. שֶׁלֹּא יָבוֹאוּ לִידֵי מֵירוּחַ.

"And over a child's excrement." Is that not chicken feed[134]? Rebbi Uqban said, explain it if it is soft, that it should not be smeared around.

וְעַל עַקְרָב שֶׁלֹּא תִישָׁךְ. מַעֲשֶׂה בָא לִפְנֵי רַבָּן יוֹחָנָן בֶּן זַכַּאי בַּעֲרָב וְאָמַר חוֹשְׁשַׁנִי אֲנִי לוֹ מֵחַטָּאת. רִבִּי עוּלָּא אָמַר. שְׁמוֹנֶה עָשָׂר שָׁנִין עָבִיד הֲוֵי יָהִיב בַּהֲדָא עֲרָב וְלֹא אֲתָא קוֹמוֹי אֶלָּא אִילֵּין תְּרֵין עוֹבְדַיָּא. אָמַר. גָּלִיל גָּלִיל. שָׂנֵאתָ תּוֹרָה. סוֹפָךְ לַעֲשׂוֹת בְּמִסִּיקִין.

"And over a scorpion to prevent it from stinging." "This happened before Rabban Johanan ben Zakkai in Arab[135] and he said, I fear that he incurred liability for a purification sacrifice[19]." Rebbi Ulla said, eighteen years did he spend in Arab and only these two cases[136] came before him. He said, "Galilee, Galilee, you are hating Torah; in the end you will work for discharged veterans[137]."

133 This is copied from Chapter 4, Notes 40-41.

134 Therefore it should be obvious that it is not *muqseh* and should not be mentioned in Mishnah 8.

135 A village not far from Sepphoris.

136 The one mentioned in the Mishnah here and another case in Mishnah 22:3.

137 Latin *missicius, adj.* "discharged from military service", cf. *Bava qamma* 10:6, Note 60.

(15d line 62) לְצוֹרְכּוֹ וּלְצוֹרֶךְ יִשְׂרָאֵל. נִישְׁמְעִינָהּ מִן הָדָא. שְׁמוּאֵל אִיקַּבַּל גַּבֵּי חַד פַּרְסִיי. אִיטְפֵי בּוּצִינָא. אֲזַל הַהוּא פַּרְסִיי בְּעָא מִדְלַקְתֵּיהּ. וַהֲפַךְ שְׁמוּאֵל אַפּוֹי. כֵּיוָן דַּחֲזִיתֵיהּ מִתְעַסֵּק בִּשְׁטָרוֹתָיו יָדַע דְּלָא בְגִינֵיהּ אַדְלְקָהּ. וַהֲפַךְ שְׁמוּאֵל אַפּוֹי. אָמַר רִבִּי יַעֲקֹב בַּר אָחָא. הָדָא אָמְרָה. לְצוֹרְכּוֹ וּלְצוֹרֶךְ יִשְׂרָאֵל אָסוּר. אָמַר רִבִּי יוֹנָה. שַׁנְיָיא הִיא. שֶׁאֵין מַטְרִיחִין עַל הָאָדָם לָצֵאת מִבֵּיתוֹ. אָמַר רִבִּי אֱלִיעֶזֶר. מִשּׁוּם שֶׁאֵין מַטְרִיחִין עַל הָאָדָם לָצֵאת מִבֵּיתוֹ לָמָּה הֲפַךְ שְׁמוּאֵל אַפּוֹי.

For himself and for a Jew[138]? Let us hear from the following. Samuel was received at a Persian's. The light went out. The Persian went and wanted to light it; Samuel turned his face around[139]. When he saw[140] him occupied with his securities he knew that he did not light for him; Samuel again turned his face[141]. Rebbi Jacob bar Aḥa said, this implies that for himself and for a Jew it is forbidden[142]. Rebbi Jonah said, there is a difference since one does not bother a person to leave his house[143]. Rebbi Eliezer[144] said, if it is since one does not bother a person to leave his house, why did Samuel turn his face around[145]?

138 This refers to Mishnah 9, about a Gentile making light. If it is for himself, the Jew may use it. If it was done exclusively for the Jew, its use is forbidden. Nothing is said about the case that the light was lit for the benefit both of the Gentile and the Jew.

139 In order not to profit from the light which was lit on the Sabbath. Babli 122b.

140 While this is a Babylonian story where the use of the root חזי is legitimate, it is more likely that this is a Babylonism in a Galilean text since the quote by Rashba, ad 122b, uses the Galilean root חמי.

141 Samuel turned around and looked at the light because he realized that his host lit the light for business purposes, not in order to engage in conversation with him.

142 This also is the text of Rashba, who wants to amend "forbidden" to "permitted". The text should not be amended.

143 Samuel was at a stranger's house; in his own house he would not have turned around.

144 There is no Amora R. Eliezer known. With Rashba one might read "R. Yose".

145 Since also a visitor is not thrown out of the house which he is visiting; the argument of R. Jonah cannot be correct but R. Jacob bar Aḥa is.

(15d line 68) אָמְרוּ לוֹ. מָה אָנוּ לֵירֵד. אָמַר לָהֶן. הוֹאִיל וְלֹא בִשְׁבִילֵינוּ עָשָׂה מוּתָּרִין אָנוּ לֵירֵד.

[146]"They asked him, may we descend? He told them, since he did not do it for us we are permitted to descend."

146 This refers to the end of the Mishnah, discussion between Rabban Gamliel and the Elders. Tosephta 13:14 (ed. Liebermann); Babli 122a.

כל הכלים פרק שבעה עשר

(fol. 16a) **משנה א**: כָּל־הַכֵּלִים נִטָּלִין בַּשַּׁבָּת וְדַלְתוֹתֵיהֶן עִמָּהֶן אַף עַל פִּי שֶׁנִּתְפָּרְקוּ בַּשַּׁבָּת וְאֵינָן דּוֹמִין לְדַלְתוֹת הַבַּיִת לְפִי שֶׁאֵינָן מִן הַמּוּכָן:

Mishnah 1: All implements may be taken on the Sabbath and their doors with them, even if they were disassembled on the Sabbath[1]; they are not similar to doors of a house because the latter are not prepared[2].

משנה ב: נוֹטֵל אָדָם קוּרְנָס לְפַצּוֹעַ בּוֹ אֱגוֹזִים. קֻרְדּוֹם לַחְתּוֹךְ בּוֹ אֶת הַדְּבֵילָה. מְגֵירָה לָגוּר בָּהּ אֶת הַגְּבִינָה. מַגְרֵיפָה לִגְרוֹף בָּהּ אֶת הַגְּרוֹגְרוֹת. אֶת הָרַחַת וְאֶת הַמַּלְגֵּז לָתֵת עָלָיו לַקָּטָן. אֶת הַכּוּשׁ וְאֶת הַכַּרְכָּר לִתְחוֹב בּוֹ. מַחַט שֶׁל יָד לִיטּוֹל בָּהּ אֶת הַקּוֹץ וְשֶׁל סַקָּאִין לִפְתּוֹחַ בּוֹ אֶת הַדֶּלֶת:

Mishnah 2: A person may take a hammer to crack nuts, an axe to cut the fig cake, a saw to shave cheese with[3], a rake to rake with it dried figs, a spade or a pitchfork[4] to feed a child, a spindle or a spinning top to stick into something, a sewing needle to remove a thorn, and one of sack-clothiers to open a door.

משנה ג: קָנֶה שֶׁל זֵיתִים אִם יֵשׁ קֶשֶׁר בְּרֹאשׁוֹ מְקַבֵּל טוּמְאָה. וְאִם לָאו אֵין מְקַבֵּל טוּמְאָה. בֵּין כָּךְ וּבֵין כָּךְ נִטָּל בַּשַּׁבָּת:

Mishnah 3: If a stick used to stir olives[5] has a knot at its top it is an object of impurity, otherwise it is impervious to impurity. In any case it may be used on the Sabbath.

משנה ד: כָּל־הַכֵּלִים נִטָּלִין בַּשַּׁבָּת חוּץ מִן הַמַּסָּר הַגָּדוֹל וְיָתֵד שֶׁל מַחֲרֵישָׁה. כָּל־הַכֵּלִים נִטָּלִין לְצוֹרֶךְ וְשֶׁלֹּא לְצוֹרֶךְ. רְבִּי נְחֶמְיָה אוֹמֵר אֵין נִטָּלִין אֶלָּא לְצוֹרֶךְ:

Mishnah 4: All implements may be taken on the Sabbath except for the large saw and the blade of the plough[6]. All implements may be taken whether for a need or not for a need; Rebbi Nehemiah says, they may be taken only for a need[7].

משנה ה: כָּל־הַכֵּלִים הַנִּיטָּלִין בַּשַּׁבָּת שֶׁבְּרֵיהֶן נִטָּלִין וּבִלְבַד שֶׁיִּהְיוּ עוֹשִׂין מֵעֵין מְלָאכָה. שִׁבְרֵי עֲרֵיבָה לְכַסּוֹת בָּהֶן אֶת פִּי הֶחָבִית. וְשֶׁל זְכוּכִית לְכַסּוֹת בָּהֶן אֶת פִּי הַפַּךְ. רְבִּי יְהוּדָה

אוֹמֵר וּבִלְבַד שֶׁיִּהְיוּ עוֹשִׂין מֵעֵין מְלַאכְתָּן שִׁבְרֵי עֲרֵיבָה לָצוּק לְתוֹכָן מִקְפָּה. וְשֶׁל זְכוּכִית לָצוּק בְּתוֹכָן שֶׁמֶן:

Mishnah 5: Of all implements which may be taken on the Sabbath their breakage also may be taken as long as they are for some use: pieces from a trough to cover the top of an amphora, and of glass to cover the mouth of a phial. Rebbi Jehudah says, only if they can be used similarly to their original use: pieces from a trough to pour pap into them, and of glass to pour olive oil into them.

משנה ו: הָאֶבֶן שֶׁבַּקִּירוּיָא אִם מְמַלְאִין בָּהּ וְאֵינָהּ נוֹפֶלֶת מְמַלְאִין בָּהּ. וְאִם לָאו אֵין מְמַלְאִין בָּהּ. זְמוֹרָה שֶׁהִיא קְשׁוּרָה בַטָּפִיחַ מְמַלְאִין בָּהּ בַּשַּׁבָּת:

Mishnah 6: If the stone in a gourd-bottle[8] does not fall out when used to fill, one may fill with it; otherwise one may not fill with it. If a piece of vine is tied to a pail[9] one may use it to draw water on the Sabbath.

משנה ז: רִבִּי אֱלִיעֶזֶר אוֹמֵר פְּקַק הַחַלּוֹן בִּזְמַן שֶׁהוּא קָשׁוּר וְתָלוּי פּוֹקְקִין בּוֹ. וְאִם לָאו אֵין פּוֹקְקִין בּוֹ. וַחֲכָמִים אוֹמְרִים בֵּין כָּךְ וּבֵין כָּךְ פּוֹקְקִין בּוֹ:

Mishnah 7: Rebbi Eliezer says, if the window plug[9] is connected and hanging one may plug with it, otherwise one may not plug with it. But the Sages say, in any case one may plug with it.

משנה ח: כָּל־כִּסּוּיֵי הַכֵּלִים שֶׁיֵּשׁ לָהֶם בֵּית אֲחִיזָה נִטָּלִין בַּשַּׁבָּת. אָמַר רִבִּי יוֹסֵי בַּמֶּה דְבָרִים אֲמוּרִים בְּכִסּוּיֵי הַקַּרְקָעוֹת אֲבָל בְּכִסּוּיֵי הַכֵּלִים בֵּין כָּךְ וּבֵין כָּךְ נִטָּלִין בַּשַּׁבָּת:

Mishnah 8: All implement covers which have handles may be taken on the Sabbath. Rebbi Yose said, when has this been said? Covers of the ground[10]. But covers of implements in any case may be taken on the Sabbath.

1   Even if the lid was off the implement when the Sabbath started it does not lose its quality as part of a implement and is not *muqseh*. It is understood that tools are classified as implements for the Sabbath.

2   The door of a building is part of the building. While it may be moved to be opened or closed, it cannot be removed since this would be tearing down a building. If for some reason the door becomes unhinged on the Sabbath, it is *muqseh* since at the beginning of the Sabbath it was not prepared for its role as implement.

3   A very hard cheese like Parmesan. In all cases of the Mishnah the use of the implement is inappropriate; this is no reason to exclude their use on the Sabbath.

4   This also is the reading of the Mishnah in the Babli. In many Mishnah mss., including Maimonides's autograph, the reading is מַזְלֵג "fork". This is an acceptable reading since in Antiquity forks were not

used at meals but in the kitchen; it still describes inappropriate use.

5   Before being taken to the olive press the olives were kept in vats to soften. The rods with which they were stirred were then examined for signs of oil sticking to them. If the rod simply is straight, it is an implement for the rules of the Sabbath but not for those of impurity. If the top has some outcropping and holes, looking like a knot, to collect the oil drops, it is a implement both for the Sabbath and because of impurity.

6   Work tools which are expensive to replace cannot be taken for other uses. Since the intended use is forbidden on the Sabbath, they cannot be used on the Sabbath.

7   They can be moved either because the implement is needed or because it stands at a place which is needed for other things.

8   A large gourd which has been hollowed out and is used to draw water from a cistern. Since the gourd is light, it cannot be lowered into the water without ballast. If the ballast is a stone, which is not an implement and in itself would be *muqseh* on the Sabbath, it may be used only if the stone becomes part of the gourd as implement that in normal use will not fall from the gourd.

9   The window is a narrow cleft through which the wind blows. R. Eliezer considers the shutters as part of the house; he requires them to be part of the house at the beginning of the Sabbath. "Hanging" means that when not used as shutters they do not touch the ground. The anonymous majority considers them to be implements, not parts of the building.

10   If produce is stored underground, it can be accessed on the Sabbath only if its cover is made for easy removal; otherwise the cover would become part of the soil and the removal would be digging. But covers of implements certainly are more usable than broken implements; if broken implements can be used then so much more whole covers.

(16a line 30) כָּל־הַכֵּלִים נִטָּלִין בַּשַּׁבָּת כול׳. דַּלְתוֹת הַבַּיִת דְּרוּבָה וְדַלְתוֹת הַכֵּלִים דְּרוּבָן. דַּלְתוֹת הַבַּיִת דְּרוּבָה. שֶׁאַף עַל פִּי שֶׁנִּתְפָּרְקוּ מֵעֶרֶב שַׁבָּת אָסוּר לְטַלְטְלָן בַּשַּׁבָּת. דַּלְתוֹת הַכֵּלִים דְּרוּבָה שֶׁאַף עַל פִּי שֶׁנִּתְפָּרְקוּ בַּשַּׁבָּת נִטָּלִין בַּשַּׁבָּת.

"All implements may be taken on the Sabbath," etc. There is spelled out more for doors of a house and there is spelled out more for doors of implements[11]. There is spelled out more for doors of a house, for even if they were unhinged on Friday they may not be moved on the Sabbath. There is spelled out more for doors of implements, for even if they were unhinged on the Sabbath they may be used on the Sabbath[12].

11   E. g., of a chest or a cupboard.

12   Babli 122b.

(16a line 33) לְפִי שֶׁאֵינָן מִן הַמּוּכָן. וְאֵין תַּשְׁמִישָׁן אֶלָּא עַל גַּבֵּי קַרְקַע. רִבִּי אַבָּהוּ בְּשֵׁם רִבִּי אֶלְעָזָר. בָּרִאשׁוֹנָה הָיוּ כָּל־הַכֵּלִים נִיטָּלִין בַּשַּׁבָּת. כֵּיוָן שֶׁנֶּחְשְׁדוּ לִהְיוֹת מְחַלְּלִין יָמִים טוֹבִים וְשַׁבָּתוֹת. הָדָא הִיא דִכְתִיב בַּיָּמִים הָהֵמָּה רָאִיתִי בִיהוּדָה | דוֹרְכִים גִּתּוֹת בַּשַּׁבָּת וְעוֹמְסִים עַל־הַחֲמֹרִים וגו'. וְאֲסְרוּ לָהֶן הַכֹּל. כֵּיוָן שֶׁנִּגְדְּרוּ. הָיוּ מַתִּירִין לָהֶן וְהוֹלְכִין עַד שֶׁהִתִּירוּ לָהֶן אֶת הַכֹּל. חוּץ מִן הַמַּסָּר הַגָּדוֹל וְיָתֵד שֶׁלְּמַחֲרִישָׁה. רִבִּי יוֹסֵה אוֹמֵר. אַף הַצִּיפֹּרִין. רַבָּן שִׁמְעוֹן בֶּן גַּמְלִיאֵל אוֹמֵר. אַף הַהוֹגִין. מְדוּכָה. אִם יֵשׁ בָּהּ שׁוּם מְטַלְטְלִין אוֹתָהּ. וְאִם לָאו אֵין מְטַלְטְלִין אוֹתָהּ. רַבָּן שִׁמְעוֹן בֶּן גַּמְלִיאֵל אוֹמֵר. אִם הָיְתָה מְדוּכָה קְטַנָּה נִיתֶּנֶת עַל גַּבֵּי הַשּׁוּלְחָן הֲרֵי הִיא כִּקְעָרָה וּמְטַלְטְלִין אוֹתָהּ בַּשַּׁבָּת. רִבִּי יוֹסֵי רִבִּי אִילָא בְּשֵׁם רִבִּי אֶלְעָזָר. רִבִּי יַעֲקֹב בַּר אֲחָא בְּשֵׁם רִבִּי אֶלְעָזָר. קוֹדֶם לְהַתָּרַת כֵּלִים שָׁנוּ.

"Because the latter are not prepared," and they are used only connected to the ground[13]. Rebbi Abbahu in the name of Rebbi Eleazar: [14]"Originally all implements could be taken on the Sabbath. Because they were suspected of desecrating holidays and Sabbaths as it is written[15], *at that time I saw in Jehudah that they were working wine presses on the Sabbath . . .and loading on donkeys*, etc., they forbade them everything. After they were fenced[16] in they continued to permit to them until they permitted them everything except the big saw and the blade of the plough[6]. Rebbi Yose said, also the engraver's stylo[17]. Rabban Simeon ben Gamliel says, also the anchor[18]." [19]"A mortar, if there is garlic in it one may take it, otherwise one may not take it; Rabban Simeon ben Gamliel says, if it is a small mortar used at table then it is like a bowl and one moves it on the Sabbath." Rebbi Yose, Rebbi Ila in the name of Rebbi Eleazar, Rebbi Jacob bar Aḥa in the name of Rebbi Eleazar, they formulated before implements were permitted[20].

13 House doors are used only in connection with the house; they cannot be removed and used for other purposes.
14 Tosephta 14:1 (ed. Liebermann), Babli 123b.
15 *Neh.* 13:15.
16 When the Sabbath was universally kept publicly by rabbinic standards.
17 Definition of *Arukh, s. v.* צפורן. The root is Accadic *spr* "to be pointed".
18 Since a ship may not leave on the Sabbath.
19 Tosephta 13:17 (ed. Liebermann). Babli 123b.
20 Tosephta 13:17 is not Halakhah; any mortar may be moved even though grinding in a mortar is biblically a Sabbath violation.

(16a line 44) תַּמָּן תַּנִּינָן. קָלוֹסְטְרָא. רִבִּי יְהוֹשֻׁעַ אוֹמֵר. שׁוֹמְטָהּ מִפֶּתַח זוֹ וְתוֹלָהּ בַּחֲבֵירוֹ בַּשַּׁבָּת. רִבִּי טַרְפוֹן אוֹמֵר. הֲרֵי הִיא כְּכָל־הַכֵּלִים וּמִיטַּלְטֶלֶת בֶּחָצֵר: דְּבֵי רִבִּי יַנַּאי אָמְרִי. בְּחָצֵר שֶׁלֹּא עֵירְבָה הִיא מַתְנִיתָא. אִם בְּחָצֵר שֶׁלֹּא עֵירְבָה הָדָא הִיא דְתַנִּינָן. הֲרֵי הִיא כְּכָל־הַכֵּלִים וּמִיטַּלְטֶלֶת בֶּחָצֵר: רִבִּי יוֹסֵה בְשֵׁם רִבִּי יִרְמְיָה רִבִּי חֲנַנְיָה מַטֵּי בָהּ בְּשֵׁם רִבִּי אֶלְעָזָר. קוֹדֶם לְהַתָּרַת כֵּלִים שָׁנוּ. (אִי קוֹדֶם לְהַתָּרַת כֵּלִים שָׁנוּ) הָדָא הִיא דְתַנִּינָן. הֲרֵי הִיא כְּכָל־הַכֵּלִים וּמִיטַּלְטֶלֶת בֶּחָצֵר: כִּשְׁלֹשָׁה כֵלִים הַמִּיטַּלְטְלִין בֶּחָצֵר. וְאֵילוּ הֵן. סַכִּין קְטַנָּה וּמַקְצוּעַ שֶׁלִּדְבֵילָה וְזוֹמֵילִסְטְרָא.

חֲצוֹצֶרֶת. תּוֹקֵעַ הַשְּׁלִישִׁית בְּרֹאשׁ הַגַּג וּמַנִּיחָהּ בִּמְקוֹמָהּ. וְלֹא כְלִי הוּא. אָמַר רִבִּי יוּדָן. קוֹדֶם לְהַתָּרַת כֵּלִים שָׁנוּ

There, we have stated[21]: "A door-bolt[22], Rebbi Joshua says one may slip it off one door and hang it on another on the Sabbath[23]. Rebbi Tarphon says, it is like any other implement and may be moved in the courtyard[24]." In the House of Rebbi Yannai they say, the Mishnah is about a courtyard without an *eruv*[25]. If it is about a courtyard without an *eruv*, is that what we did state, "it is like any other implement and may be moved in the courtyard"[26]? Rebbi Yose in the name of Rebbi Jeremiah, Rebbi Ḥananiah reaches it in the name of Rebbi Eleazar: they formulated before implements were permitted. (If they formulated before implements were permitted,)[27] is that what we have stated: "it is like any other implement and may be moved in the courtyard"[28]? Like the[29] "three implements which can be carried in a courtyard: a small knife, the chopper of fig cake, and the soup ladle[30]."

The bugle, he blows a third time on the roof and puts it down at that spot[31]. Is it not a implement? Rebbi Yudan said, they formulated before implements were permitted.

21 Mishnah *Kelim* 11:4.
22 Latin *claustrum, n.* "door bolt, bar".
23 R. Joshua only allows drawing the bolt out, tying it to a string and drawing it on the string to another door opening to the same courtyard, since this is moving "as on the back of one's hand", unprofessional, and not biblically forbidden. If the bolt can be drawn out without using a tool, it cannot be destroying a building and is not forbidden.

24 He holds that a courtyard always is a domain by itself. It may not be part of the private domains of the houses opening into it; then without an *eruv* one may not carry from a house to the courtyard or from the courtyard to the house; but this does not limit one from carrying the bolt from one door to the next in the courtyard.
25 Babli 124a.
26 Since the door bolt was in the house,

not in the courtyard, at the start of the Sabbath, the argument of R. Tarphon seems pointless since without an *eruv* no implement can be moved from the house to the courtyard.

27 The text in parentheses is a mistaken correction by the corrector; it should be deleted.

28 The question raised (Note 26) has not been answered.

29 Tosephta 14:1 (ed. Liebermann), Babli 123b. It is asserted that there never was a rabbinic prohibition even in the days of Nehemiah which would have inhibited moving these implements in the courtyard, even from the house.

30 Greek ζωμήρυσις, -εως, ἡ.

31 The public announcement of the start of the Sabbath by blowing a horn; an institution common to Palestine and Babylonia but which in detail is only known from the Babli, 35b. One cannot understand why the horn must be put away immediately with the start of the Sabbath since a Tosephta (13:16; quoted Chapter 6 Note 62) notes that it may be used on the Sabbath as a baby bottle. This *baraita* clearly became obsolete with the permission to move all implements.

(16a line 54) רִבִּי זְעוּרָא בְשֵׁם רִבִּי אֶלְעָזָר. קָנִים וּמַקְלוֹת קוֹדֶם לְהַתָּרַת כֵּלִים שָׁנוּ. לוְוחִין שֶׁלִסְפִינָה אֵין מְטַלְטְלִין אוֹתָן בַּשַּׁבָּת. אִם הָיוּ מְכוּסִּין עַל גַּבֵּי כֵלִים אוֹ עַל גַּבֵּי אוֹכְלִין הֲרֵי הֵן כְּכִסוּיֵי כָּל־הַכֵּלִים וּמְטַלְטְלִין אוֹתָן בַּשַּׁבָּת. אָמַר רִבִּי לָא. אַף עַל גַּב דְּתֵימַר. כְּכִיסוּיֵי כֵלִים. וְהוּא שֶׁיְּהֵא עֲלֵיהֶן תּוֹאַר כָּלִי.

Rebbi Ze'ira in the name of Rebbi Eleazar: Half-pipes[32] and rods[33] were formulated before implements were permitted. One may not move planks[34] of a ship on the Sabbath. If they cover implements or food they are like covers of any implement and may be moved on the Sabbath. Rebbi La said, even although you are saying "like covers of implements", this is only if they have the designation of an implement[35].

32 The half-pipes mentioned in Mishnah *Menaḥot* 11:6 which separate between the loaves of the shew-bread, where it is mentioned that they cannot be removed or put in on the Sabbath. This clearly contradicts the Mishnah which declares that all implements may be moved on the Sabbath.

33 In Mishnah *Pesaḥim* 5:9 it is asserted by R. Eliezer that while on a weekday the Passover sacrifice is stripped of its hide while hanging on rods carried by two people, on the Sabbath one uses no sticks but two people stretch out their arms to replace the rods. In view of the Mishnah here there is no reason not to use the rods on the Sabbath. It would be easy to say that the practice does not follow R. Eliezer, but since he is a very reliable historical source there can be no doubt that he accurately reports Temple practice from his own experience. One has to conclude that the general

permission to use all implements (with the exception of expensive tools of trade) has to be dated to the council of Jabneh after the destruction of the Second Temple.

Babli 123b.

34 Planks used to cover the holds of the ship. These are not shaped as implements; in other circumstances they could be used as building materials.

35 The essence of an implement is that it is subject to impurity. Straight planks are impervious to impurity; they cannot be called "implements".

(16a line 59) כָּל־שֶׁנִּיטַּל בִּשְׁנַיִם מְטַלְטְלִין אוֹתָן. בִּשְׁנַיִם בְּאַרְבָּעָה וּבַחֲמִשָּׁה אָסוּר. אָמַר. רִבִּי זְעוּרָא. מִכֵּיוָן דְּאַתְּ אָמַר. בִּשְׁנַיִם מוּתָּר. אֲפִילוּ בְּאַרְבָּעָה וּבַחֲמִשָּׁה מוּתָּר. מַה דְּאָמַר רִבִּי מָנָא. (אָמַר) [בְּיוֹמֵי] 36 רִבִּי יוֹסֵה הֲווֹן טַלְיָיא טְעִינִין סַפְסְלָא דְּרִבִּי יוּדָה בַּר פָּזִי וְסַבַּיָּיא מְסַיְּיעִין לְהוֹן. רִבִּי לְעָזָר בְּשֵׁם רִבִּי חֲנִינָה. מַעֲשֶׂה הָיָה וְטִילְטְלוּ קָרוֹן שֶׁל בֵּית רִבִּי בַּשַׁבָּת. וְלֹאו כְּלִי הוּא. שֶׁלֹּא תֹאמַר. הוֹאִיל וְאֵין תַּשְׁמִישָׁן אֶלָּא עַל גַּב מְקוֹמָן אֵין מְטַלְטְלִין אוֹתָן בַּשַׁבָּת. רַב יְהוּדָה בְשֵׁם שְׁמוּאֵל. קוּפוֹת הַגְּדוֹלוֹת וְסוּגִין הַגְּדוֹלִים מְטַלְטְלִין אוֹתָן בַּשַׁבָּת. שֶׁלֹּא תֹאמַר. הוֹאִיל וְתַשְׁמִישָׁן בִּמְקוֹמָן אֵין מְטַלְטְלִין אוֹתָן. רִבִּי אַבָּא בְשֵׁם שְׁמוּאֵל. מַכְבֵּשׁ מִיטוֹת מְטַלְטְלִין אוֹתָן בַּשַׁבָּת. רִבִּי בָּא בְשֵׁם רַב. כּוֹבֶד הָעֶלְיוֹן וְהַתַּחְתּוֹן מְטַלְטְלִין אוֹתָן חוּץ מִן הָעוֹמְדִין. אָמַר רִבִּי בָּא. הָדָא דְּתֵימַר בְּעוֹמְדִין שֶׁשָּׁם. אֲבָל בְּעוֹמְדִין שָׁבָּן מוּתָּר. רִבִּי זְעוּרָה בְּשֵׁם רַב יְהוּדָה בְשֵׁם רַב. קָנִים וַחֲבָלִים שֶׁל קוֹרַיִיס מְטַלְטְלִין אוֹתָן בַּשַׁבָּת. מַה דְּרִבִּי יוֹסֵה אָמַר. רִבִּי יוֹחָנָן שָׁאַל לְרִבִּי יְהוּדָה בֶּן לֵוִי. מַהוּ לְטַלְטֵל כְּלֵי קוֹרַיִיס בַּשַּׁבָּת. אָמַר לֵיהּ. מְטַלְטְלִין. רִבִּי יוּדָה בֶּן פָּזִי לֹא אָמַר כֵּן אֶלָּא רִבִּי יוֹחָנָן שָׁאַל לְרִבִּי יְהוּדָה בֶּן לֵוִי. מַהוּ לְטַלְטֵל כְּלֵי קוֹרַיִיס בַּשַׁבָּת. אָמַר לֵיהּ. אֵין מְטַלְטְלִין. אָמַר לֵיהּ. לָמָּה. אָמַר לֵיהּ. מִפְּנֵי שֶׁאֵין מְטַלְטְלִין.

Anything which may be moved by two people may be moved by two; by four or five it is forbidden[37]. Rebbi Ze'ira said, since you are saying that by two it is permitted, even by four or five it is permitted[38]. That is what Rebbi Mana said, in the days of Rebbi Yose children were carrying Rebbi Jehudah ben Pazi's bench[39] and old men were helping them. Rebbi Eleazar in the name of Rebbi Hanina: It happened that they moved the carriage of Rebbi's house on the Sabbath. Is that not an implement? Lest you say that because one used only its place one could not move it on the Sabbath[40]. Rav Jehudah in the name of Samuel: Big boxes and big pails[41] may be moved on the Sabbath, lest you say because they are used only at their place one could not move them on the Sabbath[42]. Rebbi Abba in the name of Samuel: A bed press one may move on the Sabbath[43]. Rebbi Abba in the name of Rav: One may move the upper and lower cross-beams but not the vertical [beams][44].

Rebbi Abba said, this refers to installed vertical [beams]; but the vertical [beams] at rest[45] are permitted. Rods and ropes of the loom[46] one may move on the Sabbath; this is what Rebbi Yose said: Rebbi Joḥanan asked Rebbi Jehudah ben Levi, may one move appurtenances of a loom on the Sabbath? He told him, one may move. Rebbi Jehudah ben Pazi did not say so but: Rebbi Joḥanan asked Rebbi Jehudah ben Levi, may one move appurtenances of a loom on the Sabbath? He told him, one may not move. He asked him, why? He answered, because one may not move[47].

36 The word in parentheses was first written by the scribe, with the word in brackets on top of it. This seems to be a correction by the scribe himself; the word in parentheses should be deleted.

37 In this version nothing is said about moving by three people. Nahmanides (*Novellae ad* 121b, ed. M. Herschler col. 406) reads: "Anything which may be moved by two people may be moved by three; by four or five it is forbidden." *Meïri* (Commentary *ad* 123b, ed. I.S. Lange p. 484) reads as our text. Rashba (*Novellae ad* 123b) reads: "Anything which may be moved by two people may be moved by two; by three or five it is forbidden." Ritba (*Novellae ad* 122a, ed. M. Goldstein col. 776) paraphrases the text but it seems that he reads with Rashba, "by three or four or five it is forbidden." A connected text is Tosephta 14:3: "One does not carry on a yoke on the Sabbath, but two may carry together; three or four are forbidden."

"Forbidden" as always means rabbinically forbidden, not liable for a Sabbath violation.

38 Babli *Eruvin* 102a.
39 Latin *subsellium, -ii, n.*
40 Even though the carriage may not be used on the Sabbath to transport anything, if the place where it is parked is needed it may be moved on the Sabbath. Babli 124a.

41 Geonic commentary to Mishnah *Kelim* 16:3: "large containers, at least one *seah* large." Maimonides: "Large pails to transport wheat and flour."

42 Even if usually they are transported only using machinery, this does not make them *muqseh*.

43 I do not know what this expression means. *Pene Mosheh*: With which one presses the logs to equalize them. *Qorban haEdah* seems to read מוטות "yokes" or מטות "staffs" for מִטּוֹת "beds" and declares it an appurtenance of the loom.

44 Parts of the loom. A working loom may not be taken apart on the Sabbath by biblical standards but parts of a defective one may be moved even by rabbinic standards since the notions of building and tearing down do not apply to implements. Babli 113a.

45 Reading בן as equal to Arabic بِنّ "to rest at a place".

46 This seems to be Greek καῖρος, ὁ "weaving", short for כְּלֵי קוֹרייס "instruments needed for weave" used in the next sentence, for any implements needed for the

manufacture of textiles. Jastrow's identification as Latin *corius, corium* "leather, leather strap" (following Theodor) is inappropriate here, as are the additional meanings "upper surface (of a building), layer, stratum of earth".

47 It is a tradition. This answer is typical of R. Jehudah ben Levi, Babli *Niddah* 60a.

(16a line 75) נוֹטֵל אָדָם קוּרְנָס לִפְצוֹעַ בּוֹ אֱגוֹזִים. הָא שֶׁלֹּא לִפְצוֹעַ בּוֹ לֹא. מַתְנִיתָא דְרִבִּי נְחֶמְיָה. דְּאָמַר רִבִּי נְחֶמְיָה. אֵין נִיטָּלִין שֶׁלֹּא לְצוֹרֶךְ.

רִבִּי בָּא רִבִּי יוּדָא רִבִּי חִינָּנָא בַּר שְׁלֶמְיָה בְּשֵׁם רַב. מוֹדִין חֲכָמִים לְרִבִּי נְחֶמְיָה בְּזַייָרָא וּבְמְזוֹרָה וּבִמְכוֹנָה. בְּזַייָרָא. דּוּ עָצַר בֵּיהּ. בְּמְזוֹרָה. דּוּ חָבִיט בֵּיהּ. בְּמְכוֹנָה. דּוּ כָתִישׁ בֵּיהּ.

1 ר' יודא ר' | G • - חכמים | G חכמין בזיירא | י בזיירה G ביזירה   2 ובמזוורה ובמכונה | י ומזוורה ונוכנה G ומזורה ומוכנה בזיירא | G בזיירה במזוורה | G ומזוורה חביט | G חבט במכונה | י ובוכנה G ומוכנה כתיש | G כתת

כְּלִי הַמִּיוּחָד לְאִיסּוּר מְטַלְטְלִין אוֹתוֹ לְצוֹרֶךְ. לְהֵיתֵר בֵּין לְצוֹרֶךְ בֵּין שֶׁלֹּא לְצוֹרֶךְ. אָמַר רִבִּי יוֹסֵה. רְאֵה עַד אֵיכָן הֵיקִילוּ בַשַּׁבָּת. שֶׁאֲפִילוּ דְבָרִים שֶׁאֵין תַּשְׁמִישָׁן לְשֵׁם שַׁבָּת הִתִּירוּ אוֹתָן לְשֵׁם שַׁבָּת. דָּמַר רִבִּי לְעָזָר. דְּלוּפְקֵי לָמָּה הִיא טְמֵיאָה. מִפְּנֵי שֶׁהַשַּׁמָּשׁ אוֹכֵל עָלֶיהָ. בַּסִּיס דִּידֵיהּ לָמָּה הִיא טְמֵיאָה. מִפְּנֵי שֶׁהַשַּׁמָּשׁ עוֹמֵד עָלֶיהָ. רְאֵה עַד אֵיכָן הֶחֱמִירוּ בְטוּמְאָה. שֶׁאֲפִילוּ דְבָרִים שֶׁאֵין תַּשְׁמִישָׁן לְשֵׁם טַבְלָה. טִימְאוּ אוֹתָן לְשֵׁם טַבְלָה.

"A person may take a hammer to crack nuts." Therefore not to open nuts not[47]. Is the Mishnah Rebbi Nehemiah's, since Rebbi Nehemiah says, they may be taken only for a need? [48]Rebbi Abba (Rebbi Judah, Rebbi)[49] Hinena bar Shelemiah in the name of Rav: The Sages agree with Rebbi Nehemiah about the press, the plank, and the mace; the press with which he presses, the plank on which one beats them, the mace with which he smashes them[50]. An implement dedicated to a forbidden use may be moved only for a need; one for permitted use both with and without a need[51].

Rebbi Yose said, look how lenient they were on the Sabbath, that even things which are not to be used on the Sabbath they permitted for use on the Sabbath. As Rebbi Eleazar said, why is a tripod[52] impure? Because the waiter eats on it. Why is its base impure? Because the waiter stands on it. Look how stringent they were in impurity, that even things which are not used as a table they declared impure as a table[53].

47 The Mishnah seems to imply that while tools may be used for a purpose other than their customary use, they cannot be moved on the Sabbath without *some* purpose.

48 The following sentences are also found in *Beṣah* 1:5 (69c l.50, י), which also exists in a Genizah text edited by Ginzberg (p.

169,G) where the text is in better shape.

49 These words should be deleted with both witnesses from *Besah*. The title of Hinena bar Shelemiah was Rav, not Rebbi.

50 The items mentioned all belong to the wine press and represent considerable investment. The mace (in Babylonian form called בּוּכְנָה in י) is used to mash grapes on the plank put over the vat in the wine press.

51 Babli 124a. The definition of "need" will be taken up later.

52 Greek δελφική, ἡ, "Delphian", adjective used as a noun, Latin *delphica*

[scil. mensa]. This is a wooden tripod on which a wooden plate is laid to serve as table top. Since no volume is enclosed by any of its parts, one would have expected the tripod to be impervious to impurity. (A tripod used as a chair can become impure as a chair.)

53 In impurity an improvised table is treated as table; in the rules of the Sabbath, after the permission to use all kinds of implements, even tools of trade can be used for Sabbath purposes.

(17b line 10) אֶת הָרַחַת וְאֶת הַמַּלְגֵּז לָתֵת עָלָיו לַקָּטָן. הַכּוּשׁ וְהַכַּרְכָּר לִתְחוֹב בּוֹ. אָמַר רִבִּי סִימוֹן. שָׁרָא לִי רִבִּי אַבָּהוּ מֵיסַב קִילוֹרִית בַּשַּׁבָּת. רִבִּי בָּא בַּר כֹּהֵן בְּשֵׁם רַב שֵׁשֶׁת. מַתְנִיתָא אָמְרָה כֵן. מַחַט שֶׁל יָד לִיטּוֹל בָּהּ אֶת הַקּוֹץ. דְּלִכֵן מָה בֵין קוֹץ לָזֶה. רִבִּי בָּא בְּעָא קוֹמֵי רִבִּי מָנָא. מָהוּ מִיגְבְּלָתָהּ בְּיוֹם טוֹב. אָמַר לֵיהּ. אֵינוֹ אוֹכֶל נֶפֶשׁ.

"A spade or a pitchfork to feed a child, a spindle or a spinning top to stick into something." Rebbi Simon said, Rebbi Abbahu permitted me to apply eye salve[54] on the Sabbath[55]. Rebbi Abba bar Cohen in the name of Rav Sheshet: The Mishnah implies this, "a sewing needle to remove a thorn," since what would be the difference between this and a thorn? Rebbi Abba asked before Rebbi Mana, may one compound it on a holiday? He told him, it is not food[56].

54 Greek κολλύριον, τό, "salve", Latin *collyrium, -i*, n.

55 While compounding the salve on the Sabbath is a biblical violation, applying it externally is permitted.

56 The only actions prohibited on the Sabbath but permitted on a holiday are those needed to prepare food (Mishnah *Megillah* 1:5). Compounding lotions for external use is forbidden.

(17b line 15) דְּבֵי רִבִּי יַנַּאי אָמְרֵי. קָנֶה שֶׁהִתְקִינוֹ לִהְיוֹת בּוֹדֵק הַזֵּיתִין. כֵּיצַד הָיָה יוֹדֵעַ. אִם מְלוּכְלָךְ בְּמַשְׁקֶה בְּיָדוּעַ שֶׁנִּגְמְרָה מְלֶאכֶת הַמִּטְעָן. וְאִי לֹא. בְּיָדוּעַ שֶׁלֹּא נִגְמְרָה מְלֶאכֶת הַמִּטְעָן. אָמַר לֵיהּ רִבִּי מָנָא. לֹא תַנֵּי שְׁמוּאֵל אֶלָּא לִהְיוֹת שׁוֹלֶה בּוֹ הַזֵּיתִין. קָנֶה שֶׁהִתְקִינוֹ לִהְיוֹת פּוֹקֵק בּוֹ הַחַלּוֹן. נֵימַר. אִם הָיָה קָשׁוּר וְתָלוּי פּוֹקְקִין בּוֹ. וְאִילָּא אֵין פּוֹקְקִין בּוֹ. רַבָּן שִׁמְעוֹן בֶּן גַּמְלִיאֵל אוֹמֵר. מוּתָּקָן אַף עַל פִּי שֶׁאֵינוֹ קָשׁוּר וְתָלוּי. וְלֹא כֵן אָמַר רִבִּי יוֹחָנָן. מָשְׁכֵנִי

חִילְפַּיי וְהַרְאֵינִי נֶגֶר מְשֶׁל בֵּית רִבִּי קָשׁוּר אַף עַל פִּי שֶׁאֵינוֹ תָלוּי. אָמַר רִבִּי יוּדָן. מִכֵּיוָן שֶׁנִּיטְלוֹ וְנִיתְּנוֹ לְתוֹךְ יָדוֹ נַעֲשָׂה כְמַפְתֵּחַ.

[57]In the House of Rebbi Yannai they said, a stick which he prepared in order to check the olives. How did he know? If it was dirtied by fluid it was proof that the work of loading was completed; otherwise it was proof that the work of loading was not completed[5]. Rebbi Mana said to him, Samuel only stated that he was fishing out olives with it[58]. A stick which one prepared to close the window, should we say that he closes with it if it was tied and hanging, otherwise he may not close with it[59]? "Rabban Simeon ben Gamliel says, if it is prepared even if it is neither tied nor hanging." Did not Rebbi Johanan say, Hilfai pulled me and showed me a bolt of the House of Rebbi tied but not hanging[60]? Rebbi Yudan said, since he removed it and took it into his hand it becomes similar to a key[61].

57 This paragraph refers to Mishnah 3.
58 The modified rod is a implement, usable on the Sabbath and subject to impurity, if used for any purpose, not necessarily checking for softness.
59 Probably this is a text which appears in Babylonian sources (Babli 126a, Tosephta 14:3) as: "A stick which the home owner prepared to open or lock with, he uses to lock if it was tied and hanging (cf. Note 9), otherwise he may not use it. Rabban Simeon ben Gamliel says, if it is prepared even if it is neither tied nor hanging."
60 Therefore certainly not both requirements are necessary. The same text appears again in the discussion of Mishnah 7 and in *Eruvin* 10 (Note 131).
61 Which routinely is removed from the door. Therefore practice follows Rabban Simeon ben Gamliel.

(16b line 23) רַב יְהוּדָה בְשֵׁם רַב. הֲלָכָה כְּרִבִּי נְחֶמְיָה דְּאָמַר אֵין נִיטָּלִין אֶלָּא לְצוֹרֶךְ׃ רִבִּי יוֹחָנָן וְרַבָּנָן דְּתַמָּן. חַד אָמַר. לְצוֹרֶךְ. לְצוֹרֶךְ גּוּפוֹ. שֶׁלֹּא לְצוֹרֶךְ. שֶׁלֹּא לְצוֹרֶךְ גּוּפוֹ. רִבִּי נְחֶמְיָה אוֹמֵר אֵין נִיטָּלִין אֶלָּא לְצוֹרֶךְ גּוּפוֹ. וְחָרָנָה אָמַר. לְצוֹרֶךְ. לְצוֹרֶךְ גּוּפוֹ וּלְצוֹרֶךְ מְקוֹמוֹ. שֶׁלֹּא לְצוֹרֶךְ וְשֶׁלֹּא לְצוֹרֶךְ מְקוֹמוֹ. רִבִּי נְחֶמְיָה אוֹמֵר אֵין נִיטָּלִין אֶלָּא לְצוֹרֶךְ גּוּפוֹ וּלְצוֹרֶךְ מְקוֹמוֹ. תַּנֵּי. אָמַר רִבִּי יוּדָן. לֹא נֶחְלְקוּ בֵית שַׁמַּי וּבֵית הִלֵּל עַל הַמְּלֵאִין שֶׁמְּטַלְטְלִין אוֹתָן שֶׁלֹּא לְצוֹרֶךְ וְעַל הָרֵיקָנִין שֶׁיֵּשׁ בְּדַעְתּוֹ לְמַלּוֹתָן. וְעַל מַה נֶחְלְקוּ. עַל שֶׁאֵין בְּדַעְתּוֹ לְמַלּוֹתָן. שֶׁבֵּית שַׁמַּי אוֹסְרִין וּבֵית הִלֵּל מַתִּירִין. אַתְיָא דְבֵית שַׁמַּי כְּרִבִּי נְחֶמְיָה. אַתְּ אָמַרְתְּ. הֲלָכָה כְּרִבִּי נְחֶמְיָה. וְלֹא הֲלָכָה כְּבֵית שַׁמַּי.

Rav Jehudah in the name of Rav: Practice follows Rebbi Nehemiah who said, "they may be taken only for a need.[62]" Rebbi Johanan and the rabbis there. One said, for a need, for a need of itself; not for a need, not for a need of itself. Rebbi Nehemiah says, they may be taken only for a need of itself. But the other said, for a need, for a need of itself or of its place; not for a need, not for a need of itself or of its place. Rebbi Nehemiah says, they may be taken only for a need of itself or of its place⁶³. It was stated⁶⁴: Rebbi Jehudah said, the House of Shammai and the House of Hillel did not disagree that one moves full [containers] for no need and about empty [containers] which he intended to fill. Where did they disagree? About those which he has no intention to fill, where the House of Shammai prohibit and the House of Hillel permit. Does the House of Shammai come to parallel Rebbi Nehemiah? You say, practice follows Rebbi Nehemiah, but practice does not follow the House of Shammai⁶⁵.

62 Since the discussion in the Babli 124a concentrates on interpreting R. Nehemiah's opinion, it seems that the Babli agrees with this Babylonian statement.
63 Babli 124a.
64 A similar statement (by Rabban Simeon ben Gamliel instead of R. Jehudah) is in Tosefta *Yom Tov* 1:11, but where it is only agreed that full containers can be moved for a need.
65 If the "need" referred to by R. Nehemiah were only the use of the object itself then one would have to conclude that R. Nehemiah follows the teachings of the House of Shammai, which could not define practice in the presence of a contrary statement of the House of Hillel. It follows that R. Nehemiah accepts moving implements not only for a need of themselves but also to remove any item, which in itself could not be moved, if the place where it was standing was needed.

(16b line 33) תַּמָּן תַּנִּינָן. זְכוּכִית כְּדֵי לִגְרוֹד בּוֹ רֹאשׁ הַכַּרְכַּר. וְהָכָא אַתְּ אָמַר הָכֵן. רִבִּי אָחָא רִבִּי מַיְישָׁא בְּשֵׁם רַבָּנָן דְּקֵיסָרִי. כָּאן בְּעָבָה כָּאן בְּחַדָּה. וְאִית דְּבָעֵי מֵימַר. כָּאן בִּמְטַלְטֵל. כָּאן בְּמוֹצִיא.

⁶⁶"Glass to scrape the head of the weaver's beam." And here, you are saying so? Rebbi Aḥa, Rebbi Maisha, Rebbi Cohen in the name of the rabbis of Caesarea: Here if it is thick, there if it is sharp. Some want to say, here about moving, there about bringing out.

66 This is from Chapter 8, Notes 108-110.

(16b line 36) אֲנַן תַּנִּינַן. הָאֶבֶן בְּתוֹכָהּ. תַּנֵּי דְבֵי רִבִּי. וְהָאוֹכְלִין וְהָאֶבֶן בְּתוֹכָהּ. רִבִּי יַעֲקֹב בַּר זַבְדִי בְּשֵׁם רִבִּי אַבָּהוּ. אִיתְפַּלְגוּן רִבִּי חִייָה בַּר יוֹסֵף וְרִבִּי יוֹחָנָן. רִבִּי חִייָה בַּר יוֹסֵף כְּמַתְנִיתִין. רִבִּי יוֹחָנָן כְּהָדָא דְתַנֵּי דְבֵי רִבִּי. מַתְנִיתָא פְלִיגָא עַל רִבִּי יוֹחָנָן. הָאֶבֶן שֶׁבַּקִּירוּיָה אִם מְמַלִּין בָּהּ וְאֵינָהּ נוֹפֶלֶת. מְמַלִּין בָּהּ. כֵּיוָן שֶׁהִיא אֲפִיצָה לָהּ כְּגוּפָהּ הִיא. וְסֵיפָא פְלִיגָא עַל רִבִּי חִייָה בַּר יוֹסֵף. וְאִם לָאו אֵין מְמַלִּין בָּהּ. אָמַר רִבִּי יוּדָן. כֵּיוָן שֶׁהִיא עֲשׂוּיָה לְהַכְבִּיד נַעֲשָׂה כִּמְטַלְטֵל קִירוּיָא עַל גַּב הָאֶבֶן. מָה עָבַד לָהּ רִבִּי יוֹחָנָן. נַעֲשָׂה כִּמְטַלְטֵל קִירוּיָה עַצְמָהּ. מַתְנִיתָא פְלִיגָא עַל רִבִּי יוֹחָנָן. נוֹטֵל אָדָם בְּנוֹ וְהָאֶבֶן בְּיָדוֹ כַּלְכָּלָה וְהָאֶבֶן בְּתוֹכָהּ. וְתַנֵּי דְבֵי רִבִּי. הָאֶבֶן וְהָאוֹכְלִין בְּתוֹכָהּ. רִבִּי כֹהֵן בְּשֵׁם רַבָּנָן דְּתַמָּן. תִּינוֹק עָשׂוּ אוֹתוֹ כְּאוֹכְלִין. תַּמָּן אָמְרִין. עָשׂוּ הָאֶבֶן בְּיַד הַתִּינוֹק כְּקָמִיעַ מוּמְחֶה בְּיַד תִּינוֹק.

We have stated⁶⁷: "and a stone contained in it." In the House of Rebbi it was stated, "and food and a stone contained in it⁶⁸." Rebbi Jacob bar Zavdi in the name of Rebbi Abbahu: Rebbi Ḥiyya bar Joseph and Rebbi Joḥanan disagreed. Rebbi Ḥiyya bar Joseph as our Mishnah, Rebbi Joḥanan as stated by the House of Rebbi⁶⁹. The Mishnah disagrees with Rebbi Joḥanan: "If the stone in a gourd-bottle⁸ does not fall out when used to fill, one may fill with it.⁷⁰" Since it is squeezed in it it is like its body⁷¹. The final clause disagrees with Rebbi Ḥiyya bar Joseph: "otherwise one may not fill with it.⁷²" Rebbi Yudan said, since it is used as ballast, one carries the gourd on the stone. What does Rebbi Joḥanan do with this? He carries the gourd itself⁷¹. A Mishnah disagrees with Rebbi Joḥanan: "A person may carry his son with a stone in his hand, a basket and a stone in it,⁷³" and in the House of Rebbi it was stated, "and food and a stone contained in it." Rebbi Cohen in the name of the rabbis there: they treated a baby like food⁷⁴. There they are saying: they made the stone in the hand of the baby like an expert amulet in the hand of the baby⁷⁵.

---

67   As explained later, this is a quote from Mishnah 21:1. One may move a basket even though it only contains a stone which in itself could not be moved.

68   They disagree and hold that a stone in a basket makes the basket like a stone. Only if the basket contains something which may be moved then the stone may be disregarded.

69   This also is reported in the Babli 142a as R. Joḥanan's opinion.

70   Mishnah 6. Since the gourd may be moved when it is empty except for the stone in it, why may one not move a basket with only a stone in it?

71   If the stone does not fall out when the gourd is tilted to be filled with water it is safely lodged in the gourd's wall and is part

of the gourd *qua* bottle.

72 Mishnah 17:5 seems to contradict Mishnah 21:1.

73 Mishnah 21:1. It now becomes a problem, why do the rabbis of the House of Rebbi permit a baby to be carried with a stone in his hand but not a basket containing only a stone?

74 Since one may move a loaf of bread with a stone placed on it, one also may move a baby with a stone in his hand.

75 The stone is necessary to act as a pacifier; it is no different from a toy or a charm.

(16b line 48) אֵי זֶהוּ נֶגֶר הַנִּגְרָר. אָמַר רִבִּי יוֹחָנָן. קָשׁוּר אַף עַל פִּי שֶׁאֵינוֹ תָּלוּי. אָמַר רִבִּי יוֹחָנָן. מְשָׁכְנֵי חִילְפַיי וְהַרְאֵנִי נֶגֶר שֶׁלְּבֵית רִבִּי קָשׁוּר אַף עַל פִּי שֶׁאֵינוֹ תָּלוּי. אָמַר רִבִּי יוֹחָנָן. אַתְיָא דִּיחִידַיָּיא דְּהָכָא כִּסְתָמָא דְּתַמָּן. וִיחִידַיָּיא דְּתַמָּן כִּסְתָמָא דְּהָכָא. רִבִּי יוֹסֵי בָּעֵי קוֹמֵי רִבִּי יִרְמְיָה. הֵיךְ עָבְדִין עוֹבְדָא. אָמַר לֵיהּ. מִן דָּמַר רִבִּי יוֹחָנָן. מְשָׁכְנֵי חִילְפַיי וְהַרְאֵנִי נֶגֶר שֶׁלְּבֵית רִבִּי קָשׁוּר אַף עַל פִּי שֶׁאֵינוֹ תָּלוּי. הָדָא אָמְרָה כְּרִבִּי יוּדָן עָבְדִין עוֹבְדָא. אָתָא רִבִּי הוּנָא בְּשֵׁם רִבִּי שְׁמוּאֵל. כְּרִבִּי יְהוּדָה. עַד שֶׁיְּהֵא קָשׁוּר בַּדֶּלֶת. רִבִּי יַנַּאי רִבִּי אַמִּי אָמַר. עַד שֶׁיְּהֵא קָשׁוּר בַּדֶּלֶת בְּדָבָר שֶׁהוּא יָכוֹל לְהַעֲמִידוֹ. נִיגְרַיָּיא דְּרִבִּי לְעָזָר הֲוָה קָטִיר בְּגָמִי. נִשְׁמַט אָסוּר. נִקְמַז. רִבִּי יַעֲקֹב בַּר אָחָא בְּשֵׁם רַבָּנָן. מְדָרֵיהוּ בְּרָאשֵׁי עֶצְבָּעוֹתָיו.

⁷⁶What is a dragged bolt? Rebbi Johanan said, tied but not hanging. Rebbi Johanan said, Ḥilfai pulled me and showed me a bolt of the House of Rebbi tied but not hanging⁶⁰. Rebbi Johanan said, the single opinion here is parallel to the anonymous one there, and the anonymous there to the individual here⁷⁷. Rebbi Yose asked before Rebbi Jeremiah: how does one act in actuality? He said to him, since Rebbi Johanan said, Ḥilfai pulled me and showed me a bolt of the House of Rebbi tied but not hanging, this implies that one acts following Rebbi Jehudah . There came Rebbi Huna in the name of Rebbi Samuel, practice follows Rebbi Jehudah⁷⁸, except that it be tied to the door⁷⁹. Rebbi Yannai [the father-in-law of]⁸⁰ Rebbi Immi said, only if it is tied to the door by something which can fasten it. Rebbi Eleazar's bolt was tied with bast⁸¹. If it was detached it is forbidden; loose⁸¹? Rebbi Jacob bar Aha in the name of the rabbis, he supports⁸² it with his finger tips.

76 This paragraph is copied from *Eruvin* 10 (ı), where it is the discussion of Mishnah 10 (in the independent Mishnah mss., Mishnah 11) that a "dragged bolt", one which has no knob at the end which would turn it into a tool, may be used in the Temple on the Sabbath but not outside, but R. Jehudah says one lying on the ground, not connected to the door, may be used in the Temple and the dragged one everywhere. It is obvious that the prohibition is rabbinic.

77 The anonymous opinion in *Eruvin* parallels that of R. Eliezer in Mishnah 7 here; that of the Sages here corresponds to R. Jehudah's opinion there. Since practice is supposed to follow the anonymous opinion in the Mishnah, Rebbi in formulating the Mishnah text intentionally refrained from defining practice.

78 This sentence is not in *Eruvin* (nor in the text quoted by Raviah §390) and here is a marginal gloss by a different hand; it should be deleted since it interrupts R. Jeremiah's statement.

79 But it may lie on the ground. This can be read into R. Jehudah's statement in *Eruvin*.

80 Added from *Eruvin*; the addition is necessary since *the* R. Yannai lived two generations before R. Immi and cannot have spoken in the latter's name. In the Babli 102a the statement appears in the name of Babylonian authorities.

81 The translation follows Liebermann, p. 202. In the parallel in the Babli, *Eruvin* 102a, Rashi explains following Rav Hai Gaon: "the bolt fell and stuck in the ground" (cf. *Otzar ha-Gaonim*, vol. 3, p. 103). It also is possible to read the word as Arabic قمز "to take something with one's fingers", that the bolt is removed from the door but still held in by the fingers and not deposited anywhere.

82 The translation follows the *Eruvin* text. מדדה is what a woman does when she helps her toddler to learn how to walk. The word written here מדרה has no explanation.

(16b line 59) כָּל־כִּסוּיֵי הַכֵּלִים וכו'. אַבָּא בַּר כַּהֲנָא רַב חִיָּיה בַּר אַשִׁי בְּשֵׁם רַב. הֲלָכָה כְּרִבִּי יוֹסֵי.

1 כל כסויי הכלים וכו' | ז - אבא | ז ר' בא רב | ז ר'

"All implement covers," etc.[83] Abba bar Cahana, Rav Ḥiyya bar Ashi in the name of Rav, practice follows Rebbi Yose.

83 This header does not belong to the text of the mss. but is an added gloss. If it is genuine, the statement is about Mishnah 8 and the text in *Eruvin* is a copy from the text here even though the preceding paragraph clearly is copied from there. If the header is added in error then the reference is to the statement in Mishnah *Eruvin* 9(10), where R. Yose asserts that a key-bolt is a tool and may be moved on the Sabbath, a statement compatible with that of R. Jehudah in Mishnah 10(11).

מפנין פרק שמנה עשר

(fol. 16b) **משנה א**: מְפַנִּין אֲפִילוּ אַרְבַּע וְחָמֵשׁ קוּפּוֹת שֶׁל תֶּבֶן וְשֶׁל תְּבוּאָה מִפְּנֵי הָאוֹרְחִין וּמִפְּנֵי בִיטּוּל בֵּית הַמִּדְרָשׁ. אֲבָל לֹא אֶת הָאוֹצָר. מְפַנִּין תְּרוּמָה טְהוֹרָה וּדְמַאי וּמַעֲשֵׂר רִאשׁוֹן שֶׁנִּיטְּלָה תְרוּמָתוֹ וּמַעֲשֵׂר שֵׁנִי וְהֶקְדֵּשׁ שֶׁנִּפְדּוּ וְהַתּוּרְמוֹס הַיָּבֵשׁ מִפְּנֵי שֶׁהוּא מַאֲכָל לַעֲנִיִּים. אֲבָל לֹא אֶת הַטֶּבֶל וְלֹא אֶת מַעֲשֵׂר רִאשׁוֹן שֶׁלֹּא נִיטְּלָה תְרוּמָתוֹ וְלֹא אֶת מַעֲשֵׂר שֵׁנִי וְהֶקְדֵּשׁ שֶׁלֹּא נִפְדּוּ. לֹא אֶת הַלּוּף וְלֹא אֶת הַחַרְדָּל. רַבָּן שִׁמְעוֹן בֶּן גַּמְלִיאֵל מַתִּיר בַּלּוּף מִפְּנֵי שֶׁהוּא מַאֲכָל לָעוֹרְבִים:

Mishnah 1: One removes even four or five baskets of straw or of grain because of guests[1] or because of obstruction of the House of Study[2], but not the storehouse[3]. One removes pure heave, and *demay*[4], and First Tithe of which its heave was taken, and Second Tithe[5] or sancta which were redeemed, and dry lupines[6] because it is food of the poor; but not *tevel*[7], nor First Tithe whose heave was not taken, nor Second Tithe and sancta which were not redeemed, nor serpentary[8], nor mustard seed. Rabban Simeon ben Gamliel permits serpentary because it is food of ravens.

משנה ב: חֲבִילֵי קַשׁ וַחֲבִילֵי עֵצִים וַחֲבִילֵי זְרָדִין אִם הִתְקִינָן לְמַאֲכַל בְּהֵמָה מְטַלְטְלִין אוֹתָן. וְאִם לָאו אֵין מְטַלְטְלִין אוֹתָן. כּוֹפִין אֶת הַסַּל לִפְנֵי הָאֶפְרוֹחִין כְּדֵי שֶׁיַּעֲלוּ וְשֶׁיֵּרְדוּ. תַּרְנְגוֹלֶת שֶׁבָּרְחָה דּוֹחִין אוֹתָהּ עַד שֶׁתִּיכָּנֵס. וּמְדַדִּין עֲגָלִים וּסְיָחִים בִּרְשׁוּת הָרַבִּים וְהָאִשָּׁה מְדַדָּה אֶת בְּנָהּ. אָמַר רִבִּי יְהוּדָה אֵימָתַי בִּזְמַן שֶׁהוּא נוֹטֵל רַגְלוֹ אַחַת וּמַנִּיחַ אֶחָת. אֲבָל אִם הָיָה גּוֹרֵר אָסוּר:

Mishnah 2: One moves bundles of straw, and bundles of wood, and bundles of shoots if they were prepared as animal feed; otherwise one does not move them[9]. One turns over a basket before the chicks that they may climb up and down[10]. A chicken which escaped one may push until it re-enters. One helps calves and fillies to walk in the public domain and a woman may help her son to walk. Rebbi Jehudah said, when? If he lifts one foot and puts the other one down but if he draws them[11] it is forbidden.

משנה ג: אֵין מְיַלְּדִין אֶת הַבְּהֵמָה בְּיוֹם טוֹב אֲבָל מְסַעֲדִין. וּמְיַלְּדִין אֶת הָאִשָּׁה בַּשַּׁבָּת וְקוֹרִין לָהּ חֲכָמָה מִמָּקוֹם לְמָקוֹם וּמְחַלְּלִין עָלֶיהָ אֶת הַשַּׁבָּת. וְקוֹשְׁרִים אֶת הַטִּיבּוּר. רִבִּי יוֹסֵי אוֹמֵר אַף חוֹתְכִין. וְכָל־צָרְכֵי מִילָה עוֹשִׂין בַּשַּׁבָּת:

Mishnah 3: One does not use midwifery for animals on a holiday[12] but one helps[13]. One helps a woman in childbirth on the Sabbath, and calls a midwife for her from place to place[14], and desecrates the Sabbath for her, and ties the umbilical cord; Rebbi Yose says, also one cuts it. All that is necessary for circumcision one does on the Sabbath[15].

1 If one needs the space to accommodate visitors.

2 If more space is needed for all the listeners.

3 Since produce stored in a storehouse is not destined for immediate consumption, the containers are *muqseh*.

4 Produce which is suspected that tithes were not taken from it, see Introduction to Tractate *Demay*. Since one may give *demay* to the poor, it is food even though its consumption is forbidden to the well-to-do and it is forbidden to separate tithes on the Sabbath (Mishnah 2:7).

5 Second Tithe in Jerusalem is food. Outside of Jerusalem it is not food since it must be taken to the place of the Temple to be consumed in purity. But it may be redeemed and the sanctity transferred to the money which must then be spent for food in Jerusalem. Similarly, dedicated *sancta* are prohibited for all usufruct but except for sacrificial animals they may be redeemed and will regain profane status after redemption. While in a state of holiness they are *muqseh* on the Sabbath.

6 Greek θέρμος, ὁ.

7 Produce from which heave and tithes was not taken and which therefore is forbidden as food.

8 *Arum dracunculus L.* Arukh: *Arum Colocasia L.*

9 If they are collected as firewood they are *muqseh*.

10 Even though the chicks themselves are *muqseh*.

11 If the child does not try to walk on his own but lets himself be dragged by his mother.

12 Because this is an extraordinary exertion.

13 The permitted actions are described in the Halakhah.

14 Even from a place outside the Sabbath boundaries since a woman in childbirth automatically is defined as being in mortal danger.

15 This sentence is the introduction to the topic of the next Chapter.

(16c line 12) מִפַּנִּין אֲפִילוּ אַרְבַּע וְחָמֵשׁ קוּפוֹת כול'. רִבִּי זְעִירָא שָׁאַל לְרִבִּי יֹאשִׁיָּה. כַּמָּה הוּא שִׁיעוּר הַקּוּפוֹת. אָמַר לֵיהּ. נִלְמוֹד סָתוּם מִן הַמְפוֹרָשׁ. דְּתַנִּינָן תַּמָּן. בְּשָׁלֹשׁ קוּפוֹת שֶׁל שָׁלֹשׁ שָׁלֹשׁ סְאִין תּוֹרְמִין אֶת הַלִּשְׁכָּה.

"One removes even four or five baskets," etc. [16]Rebbi Ze'ira asked Rebbi Joshiah, what is the measure of baskets? He told him, let us infer the hidden from the explicit since we have stated there[17]: "The contributions for the Temple were removed in three baskets of three *seah* each."

תַּמָּן תַּנִּינָן. הַמּוֹצִיא יַיִן כְּדֵי מְזִיגַת הַכּוֹס. רִבִּי זְעִירָא שָׁאַל לְרִבִּי יֹאשִׁיָּה. כַּמָּה הוּא שִׁיעוּר הַכּוֹסוֹת. אָמַר לֵיהּ. נִלְמוֹד סָתוּם מִן הַמְפוֹרָשׁ. דְּתַנֵּי רִבִּי חִייָה. אַרְבָּעָה כוֹסוֹת שֶׁלְּפֶסַח יֶשְׁנָן רְבִיעִית יַיִן אִיטַלְקִי.

There, we have stated: "one who brings out wine to mix a cup," etc. Rebbi Ze'ira asked Rebbi Joshiah, what is the measure of cups? He told him, let us infer the hidden from the explicit since Rebbi Hiyya stated[18], the Four Cups of Passover add up to an Italic *quartarius* of wine.

16 This text is from Chapter 8, Notes 23-27.

17 Mishnah *Šeqalim* 3:2.

18 Cf. Tosephta *Pesahim* 10:1.

(16c line 18) מָהוּ לְפַנּוֹת מִן הָאוֹצָר כְּסֵדֶר הַזֶּה. נִשְׁמְעִינָהּ מִן הָדָא. וְשָׁוִין שֶׁלֹּא יִגַּע בָּאוֹצָר. אֲבָל עוֹשֶׂה הוּא שְׁבִיל וְנִכְנָס וְיוֹצֵא.

May one remove from the storehouse in this kind[19]? Let us hear from the following: They are of one opinion that one may not touch the storehouse but one may make a path to enter and leave[20].

19 This refers to a problem in the interpretation of Mishnah 1. Does "but not from the storehouse" mean nothing from there or only less than four baskets? An additional question is whether there is a difference if one had started to take produce from the storehouse before the Sabbath or not. Cf. Babli 126b-127a.

20 Quote from a *baraita* similar to one mentioned in the Babli 127a involving R. Aha and R. Simeon. Everybody agrees that even if the baskets in the storehouse are *muqseh* one may push them aside with his foot.

(16c line 20) אִית תַּנָּיֵי תַנֵּי. מְטַלְטְלִין אֶת הַדִּימוּעַ. אִית תַּנָּיֵי תַנֵּי. אֵין מְטַלְטְלִין. אָמַר רִבִּי לָעְזָר. מָאן דְּאָמַר. מְטַלְטְלִין. בִּמְדוּמָּע בִּתְרוּמָה טְהוֹרָה. וּמָאן דְּאָמַר. אֵין מְטַלְטְלִין.

בִּתְרוּמָה טְמֵיאָה. וּבְאוֹתוֹ שֶׁיֵּשׁ בּוֹ כְּדֵי לְהַעֲלוֹת. אֲבָל בְּאוֹתוֹ שֶׁאֵין בּוֹ כְּדֵי לְהַעֲלוֹת לֹא. מָאן תַּנָּא. מְטַלְטְלִין. רִבִּי אֱלִיעֶזֶר. דְּתַנִּינָן. רִבִּי אֱלִיעֶזֶר אוֹמֵר. סְאָה שֶׁנָּפְלָה הִיא סְאָה שֶׁעָלָת.

There are Tannaim who state, one moves *dema*'[21]. There are Tannaim who state, one does not move. Rebbi Eleazar said, he who said that one moves, if the heave was pure; but he who said that one does not move[22], if the heave was impure. Or about one where there was enough lift[23], but not about one where there was not enough lift. Who said that one moves? Rebbi Eliezer, as we have stated: "Rebbi Eliezer said, the *seah* which fell in is the *seah* which came up[24].

21 *Dema*' is produce containing both profane produce and heave.

22 Pure heave mixed with pure produce is food. As long as the produce stays mixed, it may be eaten only by Cohanim, but this does not change the fact that it is food. But if the heave is impure it must be burned; as long as it is mixture it is fuel, not food, and as such is *muqseh*.

23 If the amount of heave mixed with profane produce is less than 1% of the profane, it is possible to remove an amount equal to the heave that fell in and transfer the sanctity of the heave to the produce taken out; this is called "lifting" (Mishnah *Terumot* 5:1). In this case even if the heave was impure the produce remains food and may be moved on the Sabbath; but if the amount of impure heave was larger the situation cannot be remedied, and the produce is not food.

24 Mishnah *Terumot* 5:2. The problem is that it is forbidden to separate heave on the Sabbath (Mishnah 2:7). For R. Eliezer the heave was separated; one simply has to take it out; there is no problem on the Sabbath. For the Sages opposing him the heave was lost in the profane produce; one has to take new heave. Since this is forbidden on the Sabbath the mixture temporarily is not food and cannot be moved on the Sabbath.

(16c line 25) אָמַר רִבִּי אֱלִיעֶזֶר. אָדָם עוֹמֵד מֵעֶרֶב שַׁבָּת וְאוֹמֵר. הֲרֵי זוֹ תְרוּמָה לְמָחָר. וְאֵין אָדָם עוֹמֵד בַּשַּׁבָּת וְאוֹמֵר. הֲרֵי זוֹ תְרוּמָה לְמָחָר. רִבִּי יוֹסֵי בֵּירִבִּי בּוּן אוֹמֵר. אֵין אָדָם עוֹמֵד מֵעֶרֶב שַׁבָּת וְאוֹמֵר. הֲרֵי זוֹ תְרוּמָה לְמָחָר. מַתְנִיתָא פְלִיגָא עַל רִבִּי יוֹסֵי בֵּירִבִּי בּוּן. לָגִין טְבוּל יוֹם וּמִילְאָהוּ מִן הֶחָבִית מַעֲשֵׂר טֶבֶל. אִם אָמַר. הֲרֵי זוֹ תְּרוּמָה לְמָחָר מִשֶּׁתֶּחְשַׁךְ הֲרֵי זוֹ תְרוּמָה לְמָחָר. אִם אָמַר. הֲרֵי זֶה עֵירוּב. לֹא אָמַר כְּלוּם. פְּתַר לָהּ לְשֶׁעָבַר. וְהָתַנֵּי. רִבִּי חִייָה אוֹמֵר. אִית לָךְ מֵימַר לְשֶׁעָבַר. חָזַר בּוֹ רִבִּי יוֹסֵי בֵּירִבִּי בּוּן מֵהֲדָא. מַאי כְדוֹן. מִכְּבָר לִכְשֶׁאַפְרִישֶׁנָּה. הַגַּע עַצְמָךְ שֶׁהָיְתָה תְרוּמָה טְהוֹרָה. מִכְּבָר לִכְשֶׁאוֹכְלִינָּה. הַגַּע עַצְמָךְ שֶׁהָיְתָה תְרוּמָה טְמֵיאָה. מִכְּבָר לִכְשֶׁאַנִּיחֶנָּה בְּזָוִית.

1 אלעזר | ל יצחק בר אלעזר   2 בשבת | ל - -   3 לגין | ל לגין שהוא   4 תרומה למחר | ל תרומת מעשר   משתחשך הרי זו תרומה למחר | ל מחלל. אמ' הרי זו תרומה. מחלל   5 או' | ל אמ'   6 חזר | ל

ל וחזר בו | ל בה   ר' יוסי ביר' בון מהדא | ל -   מאי | ל מיי   7 מכבר | ל מככר   לכשאוכלינה | ל לכשאוכלנה
8 מככר | ל מככר

תַּנֵּי. מְטַלְטְלִין אֶחָד תְּרוּמָה טְהוֹרָה וְאֶחָד תְּרוּמָה טְמֵיאָה. אָמַר רִבִּי זְעִירָה. הָדָא אֲמְרָה.

טֶבֶל שֶׁיֵּשׁ עָלָיו. תְּנֵי. מוּתָּר לְטַלְטְלוֹ. כֵּיצַד עוֹשֶׂה. נוֹתֵן עֵינָיו בְּמִקְצָתוֹ וְאוֹכֵל הַשְּׁאָר.

1 מטלטלין | ל מטלטלה   זעירה | ל זעירא   2 תני | ל תניי   לטלטלו | ל לטלטלו בשבת   השאר | ל את השאר

[25]Rebbi [26]Eleazar said, a person can say on a Friday, this shall be heave tomorrow[27], but nobody can say on the Sabbath, this shall be heave tomorrow. Rebbi Yose ben Rebbi Abun said, nobody can say on a Friday, this shall be heave tomorrow. A Mishnah disagrees with Rebbi Yose ben Rebbi Abun:[28] "If a vessel[29] was immersed that day and somebody filled it from an amphora with *tevel* tithe, if he said[30], its contents should be heave [of the tithe] tomorrow, i. e., after nightfall, then this is heave. If he said, that should be *eruv*[31], he did not say anything." Explain it if he transgressed[32]. But Rebbi Hiyya stated: "He says,[33]" and you say, if he transgressed? Rebbi Yose ben Rebbi Abun retracted that. What is to be done[34]? "From before I shall separate it.[35]" Think about it, if it was pure heave, "from before I shall eat it.[36]" Think about it, if it was impure heave, "from before I shall deposit it in a corner.[37]"

It was stated: One may move[38] both pure and impure heave. Rebbi Ze'ira said, it means that one is permitted to move *tevel* that has a condition on it[39] on the Sabbath. What does he do[40]? He thinks about a part of it and eats the rest[41].

25 A slightly garbled version of this text is in *Demay* 7:5 (Notes 79-95, ל).

26 In *Demay*, R. Isaac bar Eleazar.

27 A person may not be pure for heave on Friday but he may be pure on the Sabbath. If his impurity (or that of his vessel) was removed by immersion in a *miqweh* he still contaminates holy things but not profane food until the next sundown (*Lev.* 22:7). Hence, he must keep his food in profane state until nightfall. But at nightfall it will be Sabbath and he will not be permitted to change the status of food and separate heave and tithes. He must make a declaration on Friday to separate heave on the Sabbath automatically.

28 *Tevul Yom* 4:4. The exact text of the Mishnah reads: "If a vessel which was immersed that day {and will be pure only after sundown} was filled from an amphora with *tevel* tithe, if he said that its contents should be heave of the tithe after nightfall, then this is heave of the tithe. If he said that it should be *eruv*, he did not say anything." Tithe can be *tevel* only if the heave of the tithe was not taken; hence, 'heave' in our text should always mean 'heave of the tithe" as in the Mishnah.

29 Greek λάγυνος, ὁ, "flask", Latin *lagena, lagaena, lagona, lagoena, -ae, f.* "large earthen vessel with neck and handles; flask, bottle".

30 On Friday.

31 Either an *eruv* to turn a common courtyard or dead-end street into a private domain or one to move the Sabbath boundary. The *eruv* must be deposited on Friday afternoon and be at the right spot at sundown, so that its owner can acquire the Sabbath rest at that spot. But in our case, at sundown the wine is still *tevel*; since it cannot be eaten it is not food, and the *eruv* is invalid.

32 R. Yose ben R. Abun would agree that if someone incorrectly followed R. Eleazar's prescription the declaration was valid.

33 There is a *baraita* in which R. Hiyya presents the text of the declaration to be recited in the case considered by R. Eleazar. R. Hiyya unconditionally permits the declaration.

34 What is the text of R. Hiyya's declaration?

35 When I separate it (on the Sabbath), the separation shall be valid from the moment of declaration (on Friday).

36 If a Cohen makes the declaration, he may say so since then he does not have to separate once it was declared to be heave. If another person makes the declaration, he may say: From the moment that a Cohen eats it.

37 Since impure heave must be burned, which is forbidden on the Sabbath, the only thing one can do with impure heave on the Sabbath is putting it away so that it should not be used.

38 On the Sabbath. Since impure heave cannot be used, one would expect that it could not be moved.

39 That heave is taken retroactively on the Sabbath to make the *tevel* edible. In that case, the *tevel* is food and certainly may be moved on the Sabbath.

40 This refers to Mishnah *Demay* 7:8 or to the declaration implied by R. Eleazar, *viz.*, that a person may say on Friday that a certain part of food shall become heave or heave of the tithe on the Sabbath without actually separating heave from profane food on Friday.

41 The part destined to be heave has to be kept in mind all the time while the rest is consumed.

(16c line 37) תַּנֵּי. מְטַלְטְלִין הַחַרְדָּל מִפְּנֵי שֶׁהוּא מַאֲכָל יוֹנִים. וְאֶת הֶחָצָב מִפְּנֵי שֶׁהוּא מַאֲכָל צְבָאִים. וְאֶת הַזְּכוּכִית מִפְּנֵי שֶׁהוּא מַאֲכָל נַעֲמִיּוֹת. אָמַר רִבִּי נָתָן. אִם כֵּן יְטַלְטְלוּ הַזְּמוֹרוֹת מִפְּנֵי שֶׁהַפִּילִין אוֹכְלִין אוֹתָן.

It was stated[42]: "One may move mustard seed because it is pigeon feed, and rue[43] because it is food for gazelles, and glass[44] because it is food for ostriches. Rebbi Nathan said, then one should be able to move shoots since elephants eat them[45]".

42 Babli 128a, Tosephta 14:8 (ed. Liebermann).

43 Gaonic identification (Gaonic commentary to *Kelim* 3:6).

44 Glass beads.

45 Since Mishnah 2 explicitly prohibits moving bundles of shoots which are not intended as feed for domestic animals, the entire argument based on the feeding habits of wild animals is unacceptable. In the Tosephta he adds a principle: One may move potential food if and only if it was *intended* either as food or as feed.

(16c line 41) רַבָּן שִׁמְעוֹן בֶּן גַּמְלִיאֵל מַתִּיר בַּלּוּף מִפְּנֵי שֶׁהוּא מַאֲכָל לָעוֹרְבִים: מָה אֲנָן קַיָּימִין. אִם בְּשֶׁיֵּשׁ לוֹ מֵאוֹתוֹ הַמִּין וְאוֹתוֹ הַמִּין מָצוּי בַּשּׁוּק. דִּבְרֵי הַכֹּל מוּתָּר. אִם בְּשֶׁאֵין לוֹ מֵאוֹתוֹ הַמִּין וְאֵין אוֹתוֹ הַמִּין מָצוּי בַּשּׁוּק. דִּבְרֵי הַכֹּל אָסוּר. אֶלָּא כִי נָן קַיָּימִין. בְּשֶׁיֵּשׁ לוֹ מֵאוֹתוֹ הַמִּין וְאֵין אוֹתוֹ הַמִּין מָצוּי בַּשּׁוּק. רַבָּנָן אָמְרִין. מִכֵּיוָן שֶׁאֵין אוֹתוֹ הַמִּין מָצוּי בַּשּׁוּק כְּמִי שֶׁאֵין לוֹ מֵאוֹתוֹ הַמִּין. וְרַבָּן שִׁמְעוֹן בֶּן גַּמְלִיאֵל אָמַר. מִכֵּיוָן שֶׁיֵּשׁ לוֹ מֵאוֹתוֹ הַמִּין כְּמִי שֶׁאוֹתוֹ הַמִּין מָצוּי בַּשּׁוּק.

"Rabban Simeon ben Gamliel permits serpentary because it is food of ravens." Where do we hold? If he keeps a certain kind and that kind is sold on the market, everybody agrees that it is permitted. If he does not keep a certain kind[46] and that kind is not sold on the market, everybody agrees that it is prohibited. But we must hold that he keeps a certain kind and that kind is not sold on the market. The rabbis said, since that kind is not sold on the market, it is as if he did not keep it. Rabban Simeon ben Gamliel said, since he keeps that kind it is as if that kind were sold on the market.

46 The kind of animal for which the feed is appropriate. This automatically restricts the statements made in the preceding paragraph to people owning the animals mentioned there.

(16c line 48) אָמַר רִבִּי זְעִירָה. לֹא אַתְיָא אֶלָּא כְרִבִּי חֲנִינָא. דְּאָמַר. עוֹלִין הָיִינוּ עִם רִבִּי לְחַמַּת גָּדֵר וְהָיָה אוֹמֵר לָנוּ. בַּחֲרוּ לָכֶם חֲלָקֵי אֲבָנִים וְאַתֶּם מוּתָּרִין לְטַלְטְלָם לְמָחָר. אָמַר רִבִּי יוֹסֵה. שַׁנְיָיא הִיא הָכָא שֶׁהוּא כְכִסֵּא. הָתִיב רִבִּי לְעָזָר. וְהָתַנִּינָן. חֲבִילֵי קַשׁ. וְקַשׁ לֹא כְמִפּוּיָּר הוּא.

[47]Rebbi Ze`ira said, this only follows Rebbi Ḥanina, as Rebbi Ḥanina said[48], we were ascending with Rebbi to the Hot Springs of Gadara when he said to us, choose smooth stones for yourselves; then you are permitted to move them tomorrow. Rebbi Yose said, there is a difference here because it is

like a chair⁴⁹. Rebbi Eleazar objected, did we not state "bundles of straw"? Is straw not as if dispersed⁵⁰?

47 Discussion of Mishnah 2.
48 Quote from Chapter 4, Note 62.
49 One only has to think about the stones, not actually taking them, since they are immediately usable without preparation.
50 Since bundles of straw also are usable to sit on, the Mishnah should not have made using them dependent on their being animal feed. The statement of R. Ze`ira is confirmed (but the attribution to R. Eleazar, a generation before R. Ze`ira, is impossible.)

(16c line 52) מַתְנִיתָא פְּלִיגָא עַל מָאן דָּמַר. כָּל־הַמְיוּחָד לְאִיסּוּר אִיסּוּר. דְּתַנֵּינָן. הָאֶבֶן שֶׁעַל פִּי הֶחָבִית מַטָּהּ עַל צִדָּהּ וְנוֹפֶלֶת. רִבִּי בָּא בְשֵׁם רַב חִייָה בַּר אַשִׁי. פָּתַר לָהּ בְּשׁוֹכֵחַ. מַתְנִיתָא פְּלִיגָא עַל מָאן דָּמַר. כָּל־הַמְיוּחָד לְאִיסּוּר אָסוּר. דְּתַנֵּינָן. כּוֹפִין סַל לִפְנֵי הָאֶפְרוֹחִין שֶׁיַּעֲלוּ וְשֶׁיֵּרְדוּ. וְתַנֵּי עֲלָהּ. עָלוּ מֵאֲלֵיהֶן אָסוּר לְטַלְטְלָהּ. אָמַר רִבִּי בּוּן בַּר חִייָה קוֹמֵי רִבִּי זְעִירָא. תִּיפְתָּר בְּמָאוּס. אָמַר לֵיהּ. וְהָתַנֵּי רִבִּי הוֹשַׁעְיָה. אֲפִילוּ סָאָה אֲפִילוּ תַּרְקַב. אִית לָךְ מֵימַר. סָאָה וְתַרְקַב מְאוּסִין הֵן.

⁵¹A Mishnah disagrees with him who said, anything which is specifically intended for something prohibited is prohibited, as we have stated: "If there is a stone on top of an amphora he tilts it on its side and it falls down." Rebbi Abba in the name of Rav Ḥiyya bar Ashi: He⁵² explained this about one who forgot. A Mishnah disagrees with him who said, anything which is specifically intended for something prohibited is prohibited, as we have stated: "one turns a basket upside down in front of the chicks that they may climb up and down." And it was stated about this, when they climbed on it by themselves it is forbidden to move it. Rebbi Abun bar Ḥiyya said before Rebbi Ze`ira, explain it if it is disgusting. He told him, did not Rebbi Hoshaia state, even a *seah*, even a *three-qab*. Can you say that *seah* and *three-qab* are disgusting?

51 This paragraph is from Chapter 3, Notes 189 ff.
52 In Chapter 3: Rav explained.

(16c line 59) אֵין מְיַילְּדִין אֶת הַבְּהֵמָה וכו'. אֵי זֶהוּ הַסִּיּוּעַ. מֵבִיא יַיִן וְנוֹפֵחַ לְתוֹךְ חוֹטְמוֹ. וְנוֹתֵן יָדוֹ לְמַטָּה וּמְקַבְּלוֹ. וְשׁוֹמֵט דַּדֶּיהָ וְנוֹתֵן לְתוֹךְ פִּיו. רַבָּן שִׁמְעוֹן בֶּן גַּמְלִיאֵל אוֹמֵר. אַף מְרַחֲמִין עַל הַבְּהֵמָה בְּיוֹם טוֹב. כֵּיצַד עוֹשָׂה. נוֹתֵן גּוּשׁ שֶׁלְּמֶלַח עַל רַחְמָהּ וְהִיא רוֹצָה לְהַנִּיק בְּנָהּ.

"One does not use midwifery for animals,⁵³" etc. What is help⁵⁴? "He brings wine and blows it into his nostrils, and puts his hand down and receives him, and moves her teats and puts in his mouth. Rabban Simeon ben Gamliel says, also one makes the animal love⁵⁵ on a holiday. How does one do that? One puts a block of salt on her belly and she wants to nurse her son."

53 Mishnah 3.	55 If the mother rejects the calf; Tosephta
54 Tosephta 15:2 (ed. Liebermann)	15:2.

(16 line 63) וְקוֹרִין לָהּ חֲכָמָה מִמָּקוֹם לְמָקוֹם. כָּיי דְתַנֵּינָן תַּמָּן. וְלֹא זוֹ בִלְבַד אֶלָּא אֲפִילוּ חֲכָמָה הַבָּאָה לְיַלֵּד.

"And one calls a midwife for her from place to place." As what we have stated there⁵⁶: "Not only these but even a midwife who comes to assist at a birth.⁵⁷"

וּמְחַלְּלִין עָלֶיהָ אֶת הַשַּׁבָּת. שְׁמוּאֵל אָמַר. עוֹשִׂין לָהּ מְדוּרָה אֲפִילוּ בִתְקוּפַת תַּמּוּז.

"And desecrates the Sabbath for her." Samuel says, one makes a bonfire for her even at the summer solstice⁵⁸.

וְקוֹשְׁרִים אֶת הַטִּיבּוּר. כְּהָדָא אַמְתֵּיהּ דְּבַר קַפָּרָא נַפְקָא מְיַילְדָה בַשַּׁבָּת. אֲתַת וּשְׁאָלַת לְרַבָּהּ. אָמַר לָהּ. אַזְלוֹן וּשְׁאָלוּן לַחֲיִיתָא. אָמְרָה לֵיהּ. לֵיכָּא חַיָּיא. אָמַר לָהּ. זִילִי עִיבִידִי כְּמִנְהָגֵךְ. אָמְרָה לֵיהּ. לֵיכָּא מִנְהָג. אָמַר לָהּ. אֵיזִילִי חַתִּיךְ. כְּרַבִּי יוֹסֵי.

"And ties the umbilical cord." As in the following: The slave girl of Bar Qappara expected to give birth on a Sabbath. She came and asked her master, who told her to go and ask the midwife. She said, there is no midwife. He said, go and follow your usage; she said, there is no usage. He said, go and cut it. This is like Rebbi Yose⁵⁹.

כֵּינִי מַתְנִיתָא. וְכָל־צָרְכֵי חַיָּה נַעֲשִׂין בַּשַּׁבָּת: תַּנֵּי: הַשִּׁילְיָא הַזֹּאת בַּשַּׁבָּת עֲשִׁירִין טוֹמְנִין אוֹתָן בַּשֶּׁמֶן. וְהָעֲנִיִּים טוֹמְנִין אוֹתָן בְּתֶבֶן וָחוֹל. אֵילּוּ וָאֵילּוּ טוֹמְנִין אוֹתָן בָּאָרֶץ כְּדֵי לִיתֵּן עֵרָבוֹן לָאָרֶץ.

So is the Mishnah: "Everything that is necessary for a woman in childbirth one does on the Sabbath.⁶⁰" It was stated:⁶¹ "Concerning the placenta on the Sabbath, the rich women hide it in oil, the poor ones hide it in straw and sand. Both hide it in the earth, to give a pledge to Earth⁶²."

56 Mishnah *Roš Haššanah* 2:5.

57 The witnesses of the New Moon and the midwife who leave their Sabbath boundaries to testify or to help are treated like the residents of the town in which they exercise their duty.

58 In his medical practice he insisted that the new mother always be kept warm. Babli 129a.

59 Therefore practice has to follow R. Yose. Babli 129b.

60 In this reading the Mishnah does not anticipate the topic of the next Chapter; also the statement of Mishnah 18:3 in the original text is repeated in 19:2.

61 Tosephta 15:3, Babli 129b. In these Babylonian sources the reason is given that the baby might catch a cold if the placenta remains exposed.

62 To ensure that Earth will have space ready for burial if the newborn should need it at the end of his life.

רבי אליעזר פרק תשעה עשר

(fol. 16d) **משנה א**: רִבִּי אֱלִיעֶזֶר אוֹמֵר אִם לֹא הֵבִיא כְלִי מֵעֶרֶב שַׁבָּת מְבִיאוֹ בַּשַׁבָּת מְגוּלֶּה וּבַסַּכָּנָה מְכַסֵּהוּ עַל פִּי עֵדִים. וְעוֹד אָמַר רִבִּי אֱלִיעֶזֶר כּוֹרְתִין עֵצִים לַעֲשׂוֹת פֶּיחָמִים לַעֲשׂוֹת בַּרְזֶל. כְּלָל אָמַר רִבִּי עֲקִיבָה כָּל־מְלָאכָה שֶׁאִיפְשָׁר לָהּ לַעֲשׂוֹת מֵעֶרֶב שַׁבָּת אֵינָהּ דּוֹחָה אֶת הַשַׁבָּת, מִילָה שֶׁאִי אִיפְשָׁר לָהּ לַעֲשׂוֹת מֵעֶרֶב שַׁבָּת דּוֹחָה אֶת הַשַׁבָּת:

Mishnah 1: Rebbi Eliezer says, if one did not bring the implement[1] before the Sabbath he brings it openly on the Sabbath and in times of danger[2] he brings it covered by the testimony of witnesses[3]. In addition, Rebbi Eliezer said, one cuts down trees to make charcoal to make iron[4]; Rebbi Aqiba stated a principle: Any work which he might have done on Friday does not push the Sabbath aside[5]; circumcision which is impossible to perform on Friday[6] pushes the Sabbath aside.

משנה ב: עוֹשִׂין כָּל־צוֹרְכֵי מִילָה מוֹלִין וּפוֹרְעִין וּמוֹצְצִין וְנוֹתְנִין עָלֶיהָ אִסְפְּלָנִית וְכַמּוֹן. אִם לֹא שָׁחַק מֵעֶרֶב שַׁבָּת לוֹעֵס בְּשִׁינָּיו וְנוֹתֵן. אִם לֹא טָרַף יַיִן וָשֶׁמֶן נוֹתֵן זֶה לְעַצְמוֹ וְזֶה לְעַצְמוֹ. אֵין עוֹשִׂין לָהּ חָלָק לְכַתְּחִילָה אֲבָל כּוֹרֵךְ עָלֶיהָ סְמַרְטוּט. אִם לֹא הִתְקִין מֵעֶרֶב שַׁבָּת כּוֹרֵךְ עַל אֶצְבָּעוֹ וּמֵבִיא אֲפִילוּ מֵחָצֵר אַחֶרֶת:

Mishnah 2: One does everything necessary for circumcision; one circumcises, and uncovers[7], and drains[8], and puts a bandage[9] and cumin[10] on it. If he did not grind on Friday he chews with his teeth and puts it on. If he did not mix wine and oil[11], he gives each one separately. One does not make a new dressing for it but binds a rag around it. If he did not prepare this on Friday he winds it around his finger and brings it even from another courtyard[12].

משנה ג: מַרְחִיצִין אֶת הַקָּטָן לִפְנֵי הַמִּילָה וּלְאַחַר הַמִּילָה וּמְזַלְפִין עָלָיו בַּיָּד אֲבָל לֹא בִּכְלִי. רִבִּי אֶלְעָזָר בֶּן עֲזַרְיָה אוֹמֵר מַרְחִיצִין אֶת הַקָּטָן בַּיּוֹם הַשְּׁלִישִׁי שֶׁחָל לִהְיוֹת בַּשַׁבָּת שֶׁנֶּאֱמַר וַיְהִי בַיּוֹם הַשְּׁלִישִׁי בִּהְיוֹתָם כּוֹאֲבִים. סָפֵק וְאַנְדְּרוֹגִינָס אֵין מְחַלְּלִין עָלָיו אֶת הַשַׁבָּת רִבִּי יְהוּדָה מַתִּיר בָּאַנְדְּרוֹגִינָס:

Mishnah 3: One bathes the baby before and after the circumcision by sprinkling on him with one's hand but not with a vessel[13]. Rebbi Eleazar ben Azariah says, one bathes the baby on the third day which falls on the Sabbath as it is said, *it was on the third day when they were hurting*[14]. One does not desecrate the Sabbath for a case of doubt[15] or for a hermaphrodite[16]; Rebbi Jehudah permits for the hermaphrodite[17].

משנה ד: מִי שֶׁהָיוּ לוֹ שְׁנֵי תִינוֹקוֹת אֶחָד לָמוּל עֶרֶב שַׁבָּת וְאֶחָד לָמוּל בַּשַּׁבָּת שָׁכַח וּמָל אֶת שֶׁל עֶרֶב שַׁבָּת בַּשַּׁבָּת חַיָּב. אֶחָד לָמוּל אַחַר הַשַּׁבָּת וְאֶחָד לָמוּל בַּשַּׁבָּת שָׁכַח וּמָל אֶת שֶׁל אַחַר הַשַּׁבָּת בַּשַּׁבָּת רִבִּי אֱלִיעֶזֶר מְחַיֵּב חַטָּאת וְרִבִּי יְהוֹשֻׁעַ פּוֹטֵר:

Mishnah 4: If one had two children to circumcise, one on Friday and one on the Sabbath. If he forgot and circumcised the one for Friday on the Sabbath he is liable[18]. One to circumcise on Sunday and one on the Sabbath; if he forgot and circumcised the one for Sunday on the Sabbath, Rebbi Eliezer makes him liable for a purification sacrifice but Rebbi Joshua declares him not liable[19].

משנה ה: קָטָן נִימּוֹל לִשְׁמוֹנָה לְתִשְׁעָה לַעֲשָׂרָה לְאַחַד עָשָׂר לִשְׁנֵים עָשָׂר לֹא פָחוֹת וְלֹא יוֹתֵר. כְּדַרְכּוֹ לִשְׁמוֹנָה. נוֹלַד בֵּין הַשְּׁמָשׁוֹת נִימּוֹל לְתִשְׁעָה. בֵּין הַשְּׁמָשׁוֹת עֶרֶב שַׁבָּת נִימּוֹל לַעֲשָׂרָה. יוֹם טוֹב לְאַחַר שַׁבָּת נִימּוֹל לְאַחַד עָשָׂר. שְׁנֵי יָמִים טוֹבִים שֶׁל רֹאשׁ הַשָּׁנָה נִימּוֹל לִשְׁנֵים עָשָׂר. קָטָן הַחוֹלֶה אֵין מוֹלִין אוֹתוֹ עַד שֶׁיַּבְרִיא:

Mishnah 5: A baby is circumcised on the eighth day, the ninth, the tenth, the eleventh, the twelfth, no less and no more. In the normal case, on the eighth. If he was born at dusk[20], on the ninth. In the twilight Friday evening, on the tenth. If there is a holiday on Sunday, on the eleventh[21]; the two days of the New Year on the twelfth. A sick baby one does not circumcise until he gets well.

משנה ו: אֵילוּ הֵן צִיצִים הַמְעַכְּבִין אֶת הַמִּילָה בָּשָׂר הַחוֹפֶה אֶת רֹב הָעֲטָרָה וְאֵינוֹ אוֹכֵל בִּתְרוּמָה. אִם הָיָה בַּעַל בָּשָׂר מְתַקְּנוֹ מִפְּנֵי מַרְאִית הָעַיִן. מָל וְלֹא פָרַע אֶת הַמִּילָה כְּאִילּוּ לֹא מָל:

Mishnah 6: The following are the fibers which invalidate a circumcision: the flesh which covers most of the corona; then he could not eat heave[22]. If he was fat one corrects him because of the bad impression[23]. If he circumcised but did not uncover[7] the circumcision it is as if he did not circumcise[24].

10 The knife for the circumcision.

2 When circumcision was forbidden, as in the Hadrianic persecution after the Bar Kochba rebellion.

3 That he could not be accused by other Jews of violating the Sabbath.

4 R. Eliezer holds that if the circumcision has to be performed on the Sabbath, all preparations are permitted, including the making of the knife.

5 He disputes R. Eliezer's assertion and holds that only what is prescribed by a verse may be done on the Sabbath but nothing else.

6 Since *Lev.* 12:3 is prescriptive: *On the eighth day, the prepuce of his flesh shall be circumcised*, even if the eighth day is a Sabbath. It is sinful to circumcise on the seventh day (but doing so does not create liability for a purification sacrifice since it is not a deadly sin.)

7 One has to cut the membrane under the prepuce to expose the penis's corona.

8 One drains the blood from the wound by sucking it out.

9 Greek σπληνίον, τό "pad, compress of linen laid on wound,"; Latin *splenium, -ii, n.* "plaster, patch".

10 Cumin powder as a blood clotting agent.

11 To be put on the wound as disinfectants.

12 Since this is also done by people who injured their finger it is clothing and R. Aqiba will agree that this kind of carrying through the public domain is permitted.

13 While it is permitted to wash the baby's entire body (which is not permitted for adults), it should be done differently than on weekdays. This is a purely rabbinic rule.

14 *Gen.* 34:25. This presumes that neonatal physiology is the same as the adult one.

15 When it is not clear which day is the 8th, as explained in the next Mishnah.

16 Greek ἀνδρόγυνος, ὁ "man-woman".

17 Since having a penis makes him a male, irrespective of other sex characteristics.

18 It is presumed that the child to be circumcised on the Sabbath was erroneously circumcised on Friday. Then there is no child at hand which must be circumcised on the Sabbath; what he does is an absolute Sabbath violation.

19 Since there is a baby at hand who has to be circumcised on the Sabbath, for R. Joshua he is under the obligation to violate the Sabbath. It he takes the wrong baby it is a sin, but not a deadly sin. For R. Eliezer it is a Sabbath desecration unless he circumcise the correct baby.

The Mishnah in the Babli switches the two cases. Maimonides's autograph Mishnah follows the Mishnah as given here.

20 It is intrinsically indeterminate whether the time between shortly after sundown and nightfall belongs to the previous or the following day (cf. *Berakhot* 1:1, Notes 23-47).

21 If the circumcision cannot be done on the Sabbath, it cannot be done on a holiday either.

22 If it looks as if he were uncircumcised there should be a cosmetic correction.

23 Since otherwise the circumcision is incomplete.

(16d line 36) רִבִּי אֱלִיעֶזֶר אוֹמֵר. אִם לֹא הֵבִיא כְלִי כּוֹל׳. אָמַר רִבִּי יוֹחָנָן. הֲוִינָן סָבְרִין מֵימַר. בְּכָל־הַדְּבָרִים חָלוּק רִבִּי אֱלִיעֶזֶר. מִמַּה שֶּׁצָּרַךְ רִבִּי אֱלִיעֶזֶר לִדְרוֹשׁ בִּיכּוּרִין. מַה בִּיכּוּרִין שֶׁנֶּאֱמַר

בְּעוֹמֶר דּוֹחִין הַשַּׁבָּת. אַף בִּיכּוּרִין שֶׁנֶּאֱמַר בִּשְׁתֵּי הַלֶּחֶם דּוֹחִין אֶת הַשַּׁבָּת. הָדָא אָמְרָה. לֹא בְכָל־הַדְּבָרִים חָלוּק רִבִּי אֱלִיעֶזֶר. אָמַר רִבִּי שְׁמוּאֵל בַּר רַב יִצְחָק. בְּכָל־הַדְּבָרִים חָלוּק רִבִּי אֱלִיעֶזֶר. וְלָמָּה צָרַךְ רִבִּי אֱלִיעֶזֶר לִדְרוֹשׁ בִּיכּוּרִין בִּיכּוּרִין. אֶלָּא עַל יְדֵי שֶׁעִיקָר דְּחִייָתָן שַׁבָּת וּמַכְשִׁירֵיהֶן מְלָאכָה. הֲתִיבוּן. וְהָתַנֵּי. לוּלָב וּמַכְשִׁירָיו דּוֹחִין אֶת הַשַּׁבָּת. אָמַר רִבִּי יוֹנָה. לַהֲבִיאוֹ מֵרֹאשׁ הַדֶּקֶל. וְהָתַנֵּי. שׁוֹפָר וּמַכְשִׁירָיו דּוֹחִין אֶת הַשַּׁבָּת. לַהֲבִיאוֹ מִחוּץ לַתְּחוּם. וְתַנֵּי כֵן. אֵין מְגָרְדִין וְלֹא מְגָרְדִין וְלֹא מְפָרְכִין. תַּנֵּי בְשֵׁם רִבִּי אֱלִיעֶזֶר. לוּלָב וּמַכְשִׁירָיו דּוֹחִין אֶת הַשַּׁבָּת. אָמַר רִבִּי יוֹנָה. סָלְקַת מַתְנִיתָא. תַּנֵּי. מַעֲשֶׂה הָיָה וְהוֹרָה רִבִּי כְּרִבִּי אֱלִיעֶזֶר. אָמַר רִבִּי יוֹחָנָן. חֲבוּרָה הָיְתָה מַקְשָׁה. מַה רָאָה רִבִּי לְהַנִּיחַ דִּבְרֵי חֲכָמִים וְלַעֲשׂוֹת כְּרִבִּי אֱלִיעֶזֶר. אָמַר רִבִּי הוֹשַׁעְיָה. שְׁאַלְנוּ אֶת רִבִּי יְהוּדָה הַגּוֹזֵר וְאָמַר לָנוּ. בְּמָבוֹי שֶׁאֵינוֹ מְפוּלָּשׁ. כְּהָדָא תַּנִּינָן. אָסוּר לְטַלְטֵל מִתּוֹכוֹ לַבָּתִּים וּמִן הַבָּתִּים לְתוֹכוֹ. אָמַר רִבִּי אַבָּהוּ. קַיַּימְתִּיהּ בְּתִינוֹק וּבְאִיזְמֵל שֶׁשָּׁבְתוּ בְּמָבוֹי. וְאֵינוֹ אָסוּר לְטַלְטְלוֹ בְּכָל־הַמָּבוֹי.

"Rebbi Eliezer says, if one did not bring the implement," etc. Rebbi Joḥanan said, we were of the opinion to say that Rebbi Eliezer disagrees in all cases[24]. Since Rebbi Eliezer needed to explain "first fruits;" since "first fruits" mentioned with the ʿomer push the Sabbath aside, so also "first fruits" mentioned with the Two Breads push the Sabbath aside[25]; this implies that Rebbi Eliezer does not disagree in all cases[26]. Rebbi Samuel ben Rav Isaac said, Rebbi Eliezer disagrees in all cases[27], and why did Rebbi Eliezer have to explain "first fruits" "first fruits"? Only because their essence pushes aside the Sabbath but their enabling actions are work[28]. They objected, did we not state, the *lulav* and its enabling actions push the Sabbath aside[29]? Rebbi Jonah said, to bring it from the top of the palm tree[30]. But did we not state, the *shofar* and its enabling actions push the Sabbath aside? To bring it from outside the Sabbath boundary[31]. And was it stated so: One does not scratch, and one does not scratch, and one does not break off[32]. It was stated in the name of Rebbi Eliezer: The *lulav* and its enabling actions push the Sabbath aside. Rebbi Jonah said, the *baraita* was finished[33]. It was stated: It happened that Rebbi instructed following Rebbi Eliezer. Rebbi Joḥanan said, the company was asking, what reason did Rebbi have to disregard the words of the Sages and to act following Rebbi Eliezer[34]? Rebbi Hoshaia said, we asked Rebbi Jehudah the circumciser and he told us, it was about a dead-end street, as we had stated that it is forbidden[35] to move from it into the houses and from the houses into it. Rebbi Abbahu said, I explained it about a baby and a knife being in the dead-end street on the Sabbath; and it is not forbidden to move in the entire dead-end street[36].

24 The question is whether R. Eliezer permits to perform preparations on the Sabbath which could have been made on Friday for circumcision only or in general for any action prescribed for the Sabbath even if it involves doing work which under other circumstances would be Sabbath violations.

25 The `omer is a measure, a tenth of an *epha*, about 3.5 liter, of new barley grain which is offered in the Temple to permit the consumption of grain from the new harvest. It has to be brought *on the day after the Sabbath* (*Lev.* 23:15) which in rabbinic tradition is the second day of the Feast of unleavened bread, in the Sadducee tradition of the Book of Jubilees the day following the Feast, and in Boethusian tradition on the Sunday in the Feast. The common testimony of Philo and Josephus shows that rabbinic tradition was followed in the Temple service. The `omer had to be brought to the Temple on a fixed date, even if this date was a Sabbath (except for Boethusians for which this never could happen.) Therefore it is clear that there is a biblical prescription to cut the barley on the Sabbath if that is the day on which the grain has to be offered.

The Two Breads are the only leavened bread ever permitted in the Temple precinct; they have to be presented to the altar (but not offered on it) on the festival of Weeks (*Lev.* 23:17), which falls on the 50th day after the `omer, on the same day of the week as the `omer. These Two Breads permit the use of new wheat in the Temple service. R. Eliezer concludes from an argument of "equal cut", since both the `omer and the Two Breads are referred to in the verse as "first fruits" that they follow the same rules and, therefore, if the two loaves were not baked before the Sabbath they may be baked on the Sabbath.

26 If it were understood that in all cases of a prescribed action on the Sabbath the preparation also can be done on the Sabbath the argument of "equal cut" would be unnecessary. Babli 131a.

27 This sentence is missing in modern editions of the Yerushalmi.

28 R. Johanan's argument is not convincing. For the `omer the action of harvesting is prescribed on the day of the sacrifice (*Lev.* 23:10); the grain must be roasted (*Lev.* 2:14) and part of it burned on the altar. This means that both the preparation and the offering involve actions that are violations of Sabbath prohibitions. But the Two Breads are simply presented to the altar; no part of them may be burned on the altar (*Lev.* 2:12); they have to be eaten by the priests in the Temple precinct. This means that the offering itself does not imply any Sabbath violation; there is no intrinsic reason which would allow baking the breads on the Sabbath.

29 Babli 131a,b. *Lev.* 23:40 requires that on the first day of Tabernacles one has to take four kinds of greenery tied to a palm branch, the *lulav*. Since this is required at a fixed day of the calendar, it has precedence

over the rules of the Sabbath. For R. Eliezer cutting the plants may be done on the Sabbath. The statement has to be dated before the destruction of the Temple since in Rabban Johanan ben Zakkai's reconstruction of rabbinic Judaism at Jabneh, in imitation of a Temple ceremony the obligation to take the "four kinds" was extended to all seven days of Tabernacles which automatically re-instituted the rules of the Sabbath as preeminent. Here the situation is completely parallel to that of the Two Breads in that taking the Four Kinds on the holiday does not involve any Sabbath desecration; but the preparation involves forms of harvesting which are forbidden on the Sabbath.

30 It is possible to explain that R. Eliezer in this case permits only rabbinic prohibitions, not work by biblical standards.

31 This statement also refers to the time before the reforms of Rabban Johanan ben Zakkai which permanently extended the holiday of the New Year to two days, thereby eliminating the power of the duty to sound the *shofar* to override the rules of the Sabbath (including rabbinic rules). The prohibition to bring anything from outside the Sabbath boundaries (at least if the distance is less than three *parasang*) certainly is rabbinic,

32 This text seems corrupt. S. Liebermann reads מגדד "one cuts" instead of the second מגרד. It is not clear whether the topic is preparing a ram's horn for use as a *shofar* or the preparation of the Four Kinds. מפרך means breaking off outcroppings to produce smooth surface.

33 The *baraita* about not scraping, not cutting, etc., is separate from the statement attributed to R. Eliezer about the *lulav*.

34 Such an act contradicts all our rules for determining practice.

35 Rabbinically.

36 As explained in the next paragraph, this is a matter of different interpretations of rabbinic rules. Since R. Eliezer allows biblical rules to be broken, saying that Rebbi instructed following R. Eliezer is a misrepresentation of what he did.

(16d line 51) בְּעוֹן קוֹמֵי רִבִּי יוֹסֵה. כָּמָה דְאַתְּ מַר בְּכֵלִים שֶׁשָּׁבְתוּ בְּכָל־הֶחָצֵר מְטַלְטְלִין אוֹתָן בְּכָל־הֶחָצֵר. וְדִכְוָותָהּ כֵּלִים שֶׁשָּׁבְתוּ בְּמָבוֹי מְטַלְטְלִין אוֹתָן בְּכָל־הַמָּבוֹי. בְּשַׁבָּת שֶׁאָלוֹן לֵיהּ וְלֹא אֲגִיבוֹן. דְּלֹא הֲוָה רִבִּי יוֹסֵי אָמַר אֶלָּא כָּל־מִילָּה בְּאַתְרָהּ. כַּד אֲתוֹן לְעֵירוּבִין אָמַר לוֹן בְּשֵׁם רִבִּי יוֹחָנָן. כֵּלִים שֶׁשָּׁבְתוּ בְּמָבוֹי מְטַלְטְלִין אוֹתָן בְּכָל־הַמָּבוֹי. וְדִכְוָותָהּ כֵּלִים שֶׁשָּׁבְתוּ בְּחָצֵר מְטַלְטְלִין אוֹתָן בְּכָל־הֶחָצֵר. רַב אָמַר. אֵין מְטַלְטְלִין אוֹתָן אֶלָּא בְאַרְבַּע אַמּוֹת. אָמַר רִבִּי יוֹסֵה בֵּירִבִּי בּוּן. רַב כְּדַעְתֵּיהּ וְרִבִּי יוֹחָנָן כְּדַעְתֵּיהּ. רִבִּי יוֹחָנָן דּוּ אָמַר. קוֹרָה בְלֹא שִׁיתּוּף מַתֶּרֶת. הוּא דְאָמַר. מְטַלְטְלִין אוֹתָן בְּכָל־הַמָּבוֹי. רַב דּוּ אָמַר. אֵין קוֹרָה מַתֶּרֶת בְּלֹא שִׁיתּוּף. הוּא דְאָמַר. אֵין מְטַלְטְלִין אוֹתָן אֶלָּא בְאַרְבַּע אַמּוֹת. עַל דַּעְתֵּיהּ דְּרִבִּי יוֹחָנָן לְאֵי זֶה דָבָר מִשְׁתַּתְּפִין בְּכָל־הַמָּבוֹי. אָמַר רִבִּי יוֹסֵה בֵּירִבִּי בּוּן. כְּדֵי לַעֲשׂוֹת כָּל־הָרְשׁוּיוֹת אַחַת.

1 קומי | ז קומוי יוסה | ז יסא   כמה | ז היך מה   מר | ז מר תמן   בכל החצר | ז בחצר   2 בכל החצר | ז בחצר   בכל המבוי | ז במבוי   בשבת | ז ובשבת שאלון | ז שואלין   3 הוה | ז -   יוסי | ז יסא   מילה | ז מלא ימלא   כד אתון | ז כך דאתון   4 בכל המבוי | ז במבוי   6 בלא שיתוף מתרת | ז מתרת בלא שיתוף   7 הוא דאמ' | ז הוי דו אמ' אותן | ז -   הוא דאמ' | ז הוי דו אמ'   8 אותן | ז בו משתתפין | ז משתתף   9 אחת | ז כאחת

³⁶They asked before Rebbi Yose³⁷: Since you say about implements which were resting anywhere in the courtyard one may move them in the entire courtyard³⁸, similarly concerning implements which were resting anywhere in a dead-end street, may one move them in the entire dead-end street? They asked him in *Šabbat*³⁹ and he did not answer since Rebbi Yose³⁷ said each matter only at its place. When they came to *Eruvin*⁴⁰ he told them in the name of Rebbi Joḥanan: one may move implements which were resting anywhere in a dead-end street in the entire dead-end street; similarly implements which were resting in a courtyard one may move in the entire courtyard; Rav said, one may move them only four cubits⁴¹. Rebbi Yose ben Rebbi Abun said, Rav is consistent and Rebbi Joḥanan is consistent. Since Rebbi Joḥanan says that a beam permits without participation⁴², it is he who says that one may move in the entire dead-end street. Since Rav said that a beam does not permit without participation⁴², it is he who says that one may move them only within four cubits. In Rebbi Joḥanan's opinion, why does one participate in the entire dead-end street? Rebbi Yose ben Rebbi Abun said, to make all domains one⁴³.

36 This paragraph is copied from *Eruvin* 6 (Note 154), ו.

37 With ו read: Yasa (third generation), not Yose (fifth generation).

38 A courtyard, with only one exit to the street, common to several houses for which no *eruv* was made. The courtyard essentially is private property where one may carry. But since no *eruv* was made it is rabbinically forbidden to move things from the houses to the courtyard and vice-versa. In the courtyard itself one may move things since it is not public domain in any sense.

39 When studying the Mishnah Tractate *Šabbat*.

40 When studying the Mishnah Tractate *Eruvin*.

41 This is the only opinion reported in the Babli, 130b.

42 A dead-end street which is bordered on three sides by the walls of houses together with the courtyards opening into it can be turned for the laws of the Sabbath into a single private domain by 1) symbolically turning the opening of the dead-end street into a thoroughfare into a door either by installing a horizontal beam (קוֹרָה) over the entrance or a vertical strip (לְחִי) at the entrance symbolizing a doorpost; and 2) depositing a meal in some house opening to a courtyard which opens to the dead-end-street to which each house adjacent to the dead-end street contributed something. The latter is called שִׁיתּוּף "participation".

R. Joḥanan holds that the two required

actions are for two distinct reasons. Installing the beam turns the dead-end street into a private domain but without participation it is forbidden to move from the courtyards into the street or from the street into the courtyards, just as without *eruv* one may not move between courtyard and adjacent houses.

43 He does not split the action into two; if both conditions are satisfied one may freely transport between houses and dead-end street, with only one the dead-end street remains public domain. Babli *Eruvin* 5a, 73b.

44 If there is participation one does not need separate *eruvin* for the different courtyards.

(16d line 62) רִבִּי סִימוֹן בְּשֵׁם רִבִּי יְהוֹשֻׁעַ בֶּן לֵוִי. סַכִּין שֶׁלְּמִילָה עוֹשֶׂה לָהּ חוֹלָה וּמְבִיאָהּ. בַּר מָרִינָה הֲוָה לֵיהּ עוֹבְדָא. שָׁאִיל לְרִבִּי סִימוֹן וּשְׁרָא. שָׁאַל לְרִבִּי אִמִּי וַאֲסַר. וְאִיקְפִּיד רִבִּי סִימוֹן. וְלֹא כֵן תַּנֵּי. נִשְׁאַל לְחָכָם וְהִתִּיר. יִשְׁאַל לְחָכָם אַחֵר שֶׁמָּא יֶאֱסוֹר. אָמַר רִבִּי יוּדָן. הָכֵין הֲוָה עוֹבְדָא. שָׁאַל לְרִבִּי אִמִּי וַאֲסַר לֵיהּ. לְרִבִּי סִימוֹן וּשְׁרָא. אִיקְפִּיד רִבִּי אִמִּי. כְּהָדָא דְתַנֵּי. נִשְׁאַל לְחָכָם וְאָסַר. אַל יִשְׁאַל לְחָכָם אַחֵר שֶׁמָּא יַתִּיר.

Rebbi Simon in the name of Rebbi Joshua ben Levi: For the knife for circumcision one makes walls of people[45] and brings it. There was a case for Bar Marinus. He asked Rebbi Simon who permitted. He asked Rebbi Immi who forbade. Rebbi Simon was offended. But was it not stated, if one asked a Sage who permitted, one may ask another one who might forbid[46]? Rebbi Yudan said, the case was as follows: He asked Rebbi Immi who forbade, Rebbi Simon who permitted. Rebbi Immi was offended, following what was stated, if one asked a Sage who forbade, one may not ask another one who might permit[47].

45 In the public domain one forms two parallel rows of people with a narrow passageway between them. The rows are treated as walls, the passageway becomes a private domain where moving the knife is permitted. The word חולה seems to be جوَال "who puts himself between two obstacles."

46 This is not mentioned anywhere else.

47 Babli *Berakhot* 63b, *Avodah zarah* 7a.

(16d line 68) בִּימֵי רִבִּי יִרְמְיָה אִנְשׁוֹן מַפְתְּחֵיָּיהּ דְּסִדְרָא רוֹבָה. אָתוֹן וְשָׁאֲלוֹן לֵיהּ. אָמַר לוֹן. כַּד תֶּחֱמוֹן שְׁטָפָא עָבַר אַיְיתִינוֹן דֶּרֶךְ חוֹלָה. חֵילֵיהּ דְּרִבִּי יִרְמְיָה מֵהָדָא. כָּל־חוֹלָה שֶׁנַּעֲשִׂית בֵּין לְדַעַת בֵּין שֶׁלֹּא לְדַעַת הֲרֵי זוֹ חוֹלָה.

רִבִּי יוּדָה בֶּן פָּזִי רִבִּי יִרְמְיָה לַהֲבִיאָן דֶּרֶךְ מִנְעָלָיו. רִבִּי חִינְנָא בַּר פַּפָּא הוֹרֵי לַעֲשׂוֹת חוֹלָה וְלַהֲבִיאָן דֶּרֶךְ מִנְעָלָיו. רִבִּי שְׁמוּאֵל בַּר אַבְדּוּמָא הֲוָה לֵיהּ עוֹבְדָא לְמִיגְזוֹר לְרַב שִׁשְׁעָה בְּרֵיהּ.

אִינְשׁוֹן מַייתֵי אוּזְמֵל. שָׁאַל לְרִבִּי מָנָא. אָמַר לוֹ. יִדָּחֶה לְמָחָר. שָׁאַל לְרִבִּי יִצְחָק בַּר אֶלְעָזָר. אָמַר לוֹן. מִישְׁחוֹק קוֹנְדִיטוֹן לָא אַנְשִׁיתוֹן וּמַייתֵי אוּזְמֵיל אַנְשִׁיתוֹן. יִדָּחֶה לְמָחָר.

In the days of Rebbi Jeremiah they forgot the keys to the great study hall[48]. They came and asked him, who told them: if you see a great mass of people passing by bring it by walls of people[49]. The strength of Rebbi Jeremiah is from the following: A wall of people made with or without the knowledge of the participants is a wall of people[50].

Rebbi Jehudah bar Pazi instructed to bring it in shoes[51]. Rebbi Ḥinena bar Pappos instructed to make a wall of people and to bring it in shoes[52]. Rabbi Samuel ben Eudaimon had a case to circumcise his son, Rav Shishaa. They forgot to bring the knife. He asked Rebbi Mana who said, it should be deferred until tomorrow[53]. He asked Rebbi Isaac ben Eleazar who told them, you did not forget to mix spiced wine[54], but to bring a knife you forgot; it should be deferred until tomorrow.

48 Where the rabbi was preaching on the Sabbath.
49 Since he instructed them in Aramaic, he showed that he considered them uneducated. Cf. Babli *Eruvin* 43b, bottom.
50 Babli 101b.
51 Since this is not how carrying is usually done it cannot be biblically prohibited (Mishnah 10:3).
52 Two ways to make sure no biblical prohibition is violated.
53 He follows R. Aqiba in Mishnah 1 who states that anything that could have been done on Friday may not be done on the Sabbath. This is applied even to rabbinic prohibitions. [The text is quoted in this form by all Medieval authorities who refer to it except Ravan, who has R. Mana stating that the circumcision should not be deferred until Sunday. This would conform to the statement of the preceding paragraph that one is permitted to ask a second authority only if the first was permissive. S. Liebermann and most authorities declare the text of Ravan either a scribal error in the underlying ms. (now lost) or a printer's error in the Prague edition (1610, §370).] In any case, practice is determined by this story as following R. Aqiba.
54 Latin [*vinum*] *conditum*. In this version, subterfuges which might circumvent both biblical and rabbinic prohibitions are rejected as a punishment for preferring the party following the circumcision to the religious act.

(17a line 1) רִבִּי יוֹסֵה בֵּירִבִּי בּוּן בְּשֵׁם רַב חוּנָה. מַתְנִיתִין אָמְרָה כֵן שֶׁאָסוּר לַעֲשׂוֹת חוּלָה. דְּתַנִּינָן. רִבִּי אֱלִיעֶזֶר אוֹמֵר אִם לֹא הֵבִיא כְלִי מֵעֶרֶב שַׁבָּת מְבִיאוֹ בַשַּׁבָּת מְגוּלָּה. שֶׁאִם אוֹמֵר אַתְּ כֵּן שֶׁמּוּתָּר לַעֲשׂוֹת. אַף הוּא אֵינוֹ מוֹצֵא לַעֲשׂוֹת חוּלָה וּמְבִיאוֹ.

Rebbi Yose ben Rebbi Abun in the name of Rav Huna: Our Mishnah implies that it is forbidden to make walls of people, as we have stated: "Rebbi Eliezer says, if one did not bring the implement[1] before the Sabbath he brings it openly on the Sabbath." For if you are saying that one may make, could he not find it possible to make and bring it[55]?

55 The argument is not from the statement of Rebbi Eliezer which is quoted here but from R. Aqiba's opposition to this teaching. If R. Aqiba, whom practice follows, would agree that two walls formed by people turn the public domain into a private one he could simply have added the requirement that the open transport required by R. Eliezer should be through such walls. Since he categorically denies the possibility of bringing the knife on the Sabbath, he rejects the idea of human walls.

(17a line 4) שָׁאֲלוּ לְהִלֵּל הַזָּקֵן. מַה לַעֲשׂוֹת לָעָם שֶׁלֹּא הֵבִיאוּ סַכִּינֵיהֶן עִמָּהֶם. אָמַר לָהֶן. הֲלָכָה שָׁמַעְתִּי וְשָׁכַחְתִּי. אֶלָּא הַנִּיחוּ לָהֶן לְיִשְׂרָאֵל. אִם אֵינָן נְבִיאִים בְּנֵי נְבִיאִים הֵן. מִיָּד כָּל־מִי שֶׁהָיָה פִסְחוֹ טָלֶה הָיָה תּוֹחֲבָהּ בְּגִיזָּתָהּ. גְּדִי הָיָה קוֹשְׁרוֹ בְקַרְנָיו. וְנִמְצְאוּ פִסְחֵיהֶן מְבִיאִין סַכִּינֵיהֶן עִמָּהֶן. כֵּיוָן שֶׁרָאָה מַעֲשֶׂה נִזְכַּר הֲלָכָה. אָמַר לָהֶן. כָּךְ שָׁמַעְתִּי מִפִּי שְׁמַעְיָה וְאַבְטַלְיוֹן.

2 הלכה | פ הלכה זו לחן | פ - | 3 בגייתה | פ בגייתו בקרניו | פ בין קרניו ונמצאו | פ נמצא | 4 מעשה | פ את המעשה הלכה | פ את ההלכה לחן | פ מפי שמעיה | פ משמעיה

רִבִּי וְעֵירָה בְּשֵׁם רִבִּי אֱלִיעֶזֶר. כָּל־תּוֹרָה שֶׁאֵין לָהּ בֵּית אָב אֵינָהּ תּוֹרָה. רָכַב עָלֶיהָ. נָשַׁע עָלֶיהָ. נְתָלָה עָלֶיהָ. עָבַר בָּהּ נָהָר. קִיפֵּל עָלֶיהָ הַמּוֹסֵירָה. נָתַן טַלִּיתוֹ עָלֶיהָ. פְּסוּלָה. הָדָא יַלְפָּה מֵהַהִיא וְהַהִיא יַלְפָּה מֵהֲדָא. הָדָא יַלְפָּה מֵהֲדָא. שֶׁאִם תָּלָה בָהּ סַכִּין לְשׁוֹחֲטָהּ כְּשֵׁירָה. וְהַהִיא יַלְפָּה מֵהֲדָא. שֶׁבְּפַר־עֲבוֹדָה שֶׁהִיא לְשֵׁם קָדָשִׁים אֵינָהּ עֲבוֹדָה. וְיִתִּירוּ לָהֶן עַל יְדֵי חוּלָה. אֶלָּא כְרִבִּי אָמִי. וַאֲפִילוּ תֵימַר כְּרִבִּי סִימוֹן. כְּשֵׁם שֶׁנֶּעֶלְמָה זוֹ כָּךְ נֶעֶלְמָה זוֹ. אָמַר רִבִּי אָבִין. וַהֲלֹא אִי אֶיפְשָׁר לִשְׁנֵי שָׁבוּעוֹת שֶׁלֹּא חָל אַרְבָּעָה עָשָׂר לִהְיוֹת בְּשַׁבָּת. וְלָמָּה נֶעֶלְמָה הֲלָכָה מֵהֶן. כְּדֵי לִיתֵּן גְּדוּלָּה לְהִלֵּל.

2 עליה | פ ובגנב נהר | פ את הנהר המוסירה | פ את המוסירה פסולה | פ In the Leiden ms. a corrector added here the remainder of the Mishnah; a text also missing in Ginze Schechter 3 הדא | ג הדה מהחיא | פג מן החיא ילפה | ג - מהדא | פ מן הדא ג מן הדה הדא | ג הדה 4 כשירה | פ כשרה ג שהיא... מהדא | פ מן הדא ג מן הדה ויתירו | פג ויתיר 5 אמי | פ אימי כשם | ג כיון 6 אבין | פ אבון אי - פג 56 שבועות | פ שביעית שלא חל | פג שיחול נעלמה | פ ונתעלמה

They asked Hillel the Elder: What to do with people who did not bring their knives with them[57]? [58]He told them, I was informed of the practice but I forgot. But let Israel act; if they are not prophets they are descendants of prophets. Then everybody whose Passover sacrifice was a lamb stuck it in its fleece, for a kid goat he bound it to its horns; it turned out that the Passover sacrifices brought their knives with them. When he saw the action he remembered the practice. He told them, this is what I heard from Shemaya and Abtalion.

Rebbi Ze'ira in the name of Rebbi Eleazar. Any teaching which has no pedigree is no teaching[59]. There, we have stated[60]: "If he rode on it, leaned on it, hung on it, used it to cross a river, folded the bridle on it, put his toga on it, it is disqualified.[61]" This learns from that and that learns from this. This learns from that that if he hung on it a knife to slaughter it[62] it remains qualified. That learns from this, that any action which is done for *sancta* is not work[63]. Why did they not allow it to them by means of walls of people? It must follow Rebbi Immi. Even if you are saying following Rebbi Simon, just as they could not remember this so they did not remember that. Rebbi Abbin said, but it is impossible that in two Sabbatical periods there should be no 14th which falls on the Sabbath[64]! How could they not have remembered? To confer greatness on Hillel[65].

56 The word is missing in *Ginze Schechter*; it is added in the Leiden codex of *Pesahim* by the corrector. It is correctly missing since in Yerushalmi spelling אֶפְשַׁר means "possible", אִיפְשַׁר "impossible".

57 This is taken from *Pesahim* 6:1 treating of the Passover sacrifice if the 14th of Nisan is a Sabbath. It is presumed that Jerusalem is public domain and, therefore, carrying a knife to slaughter the Passover sacrifice in the Temple was not possible. For sacrifices all actions starting with receiving the blood from the slaughtered victim had to be performed by priests but the slaughter itself was possible by laymen and the Temple did not have enough slaughterers to serve the multitude coming on Passover eve. Since the day of the sacrifice is determined by the verse, it may not be moved even if it falls on a Sabbath.

58 From here on, the paragraph and the next are copied from *Pesahim* 6:1 (33a l. 40, פ). For the second paragraph a copy of the *Pesahim* text exists from the Cairo *Genizah*, edited by L. Ginzberg in *Ginze Schechter* 1, New York NY 1928, pp. 447-448 (ג). Cf. Babli *Pesahim* 66a.

59 This is the conclusion of a lengthy story in *Pesahim*, where it is mentioned that the Elders of Bathyra, at that time the heads of the Synhedrion, did not know how to proceed if the 14th of Nisan was a Sabbath and that they were not convinced by any logical arguments presented by Hillel until he affirmed that what he said conformed to the teachings of their predecessors in the

Synhedrion.
60 Mishnah *Parah* 2:3.
61 "It" is the Red Cow which *never had borne a yoke* (*Num.* 19:2.) The Mishnah continues with examples of loads which do not qualify and ends with the statement: "Anything done for its needs leaves it qualified; for extraneous purposes disqualifies."
62 The Red Cow.
62 The Mishnah had stated earlier that "anything which disqualifies sacrifices disqualifies the Red Cow and vice-versa."
63 From the moment that an animal is dedicated as sacrifice any use of it other than sacrificing is forbidden.
64 This is difficult to verify. In the current computed calendar (whose algorithm has a built-in bias against placing the New Year's Day on a Tuesday which puts the Feast of Unleavened Bread on a Sunday and the 14th of Nisan on a Sabbath) there are intervals of 20 years possible between two such occurrences. If the Mishnaic calendar was implemented as presented in the Babli (*Arakhin* 8b-10a) then R. Abbin's statement seems justified, if no precautions were taken to avoid the Day of Atonement falling on Friday or Sunday; cf. the Appendix of the author's *Seder Olam* (Northvale 1998). If R. Abbin quoted here is R. Abun as stated in *Pesahim* he would be a contemporary of R. Yose, who published the algorithm for the current calendar; then his assertion has to be questioned. (It is not certain that the calendar rules described by Abraham ben Hiyya, the source of the currently used algorithm, are totally identical with those promulgated by R. Yose.)
65 Who following his performance in this case rose to be the head of the Synhedrion.

(17a line 16) תָּנֵי. רִבִּי אֱלִיעֶזֶר אוֹמֵר. כְּשֵׁם שֶׁהַשְּׁחִיטָה דוֹחָה שַׁבָּת כָּךְ מַכְשִׁירֵי שְׁחִיטָה דוֹחִין אֶת הַשַּׁבָּת. אָמַר לוֹ רִבִּי עֲקִיבָה. לֹא. אִם אָמַרְתָּ בִשְׁחִיטָה שֶׁאֵי אֶיפְשָׁר לַיעֲשׂוֹת מֵעֶרֶב שַׁבָּת. תֹּאמַר בְּמַכְשִׁירֵי שְׁחִיטָה שֶׁאֵיפְשָׁר לַעֲשׂוֹתָן מֵעֶרֶב שַׁבָּת. אָמַר לוֹ רִבִּי אֱלִיעֶזֶר. אֵימוֹרֵי צִיבּוּר יוֹכִיחוּ. שֶׁיָּכוֹל לַעֲשׂוֹתָן מֵעֶרֶב שַׁבָּת וְדוֹחִין אֶת הַשַּׁבָּת. מַה לִּי מַכְשִׁירֵי שְׁחִיטָה לִפְנֵי שְׁחִיטָה. מַה לִּי מַכְשִׁירֵי שְׁחִיטָה לְאַחַר שְׁחִיטָה. אָמַר לוֹ רִבִּי עֲקִיבָה. מַה לִּי מַכְשִׁירֵי שְׁחִיטָה לְאַחַר שְׁחִיטָה שֶׁכְּבָר דָּחָה שְׁחִיטָה אֶת הַשַּׁבָּת. יִדָּחוּ מַכְשִׁירֵי שְׁחִיטָה לִפְנֵי שְׁחִיטָה שֶׁעֲדַיִין לֹא דָחָה שְׁחִיטָה אֶת הַשַּׁבָּת. דָּבָר אַחֵר. שֶׁמָּא יִמָּצֵא הַזֶּבַח פָּסוּל וְנִמְצָא דוֹחֶה שַׁבָּת בְּלֹא שְׁחִיטָה.

1 אליעזר | פ ליעזר   2 ליעשות | פ ליעשות   3 לעשותן | פ לעשות | פ לחם ליעשות   - | פ אין דוחין את השבת   4 שיכול | פ שהיא יכול   מערב | פ מוצאי   ודוחין | פ והרי הן   5 לי מכשירי | פ למכשירי   6 דחה | פ דחת   שעדיין | פ ואדיין   דחה | פ דחת

גַּבֵּי תִינוֹק מַה אִית לָךְ. שֶׁמָּא יִחֱלֶה תִּינוֹק וְנִמְצָא דוֹחֶה שַׁבָּת בְּלֹא מִילָה. הֲתִיבוּן. הֲרֵי מִזְבֵּחַ שֶׁנִּפַּל בַּשַּׁבָּת הֲרֵי אֵינוֹ רָאוּי לִיבָּנוֹת בַּשַּׁבָּת. מִין מִזְבֵּחַ רָאוּי לִיבָּנוֹת מֵאֶתְמוֹל. הַגַּע עַצְמָךְ שֶׁנּוֹלְדָה לוֹ יַבּוֹלֶת. הֲרֵי אֵינוֹ רָאוּי לַחֲתוֹכָהּ בַּשַּׁבָּת. מִין יַבּוֹלֶת רְאוּיָה לֵיחָתֵךְ מֵאֶתְמוֹל. הַגַּע עַצְמָךְ שֶׁחָל אַרְבָּעָה עָשָׂר לִהְיוֹת בַּשַּׁבָּת. הֲרֵי אֵינוֹ רָאוּי לְהַזֹּאת בַּשַּׁבָּת. מִין הַזָּיָה רְאוּיָה לְהַזֹּאת מֵאֶתְמוֹל.

[66]It was stated: "Rebbi Eliezer says, just as slaughter pushes the Sabbath aside[67] so the preparations of slaughter[68] push the Sabbath aside. Rebbi Aqiba said to him, no. If you speak about slaughter which is impossible to be done on Friday, what can you infer about preparations of slaughter than can be done on Friday? Rebbi Eliezer said to him, the public parts[69] shall prove which he could make on (Friday)[70] which nevertheless push aside the Sabbath. What is the difference between preparations of slaughter before the slaughter and preparations of slaughter after slaughter[71]? Rebbi Aqiba said to him, about preparations of slaughter after slaughter when the slaughter already had pushed away the Sabbath, what does this imply for preparations of slaughter before slaughter when the slaughter not yet had pushed away the Sabbath? Another explanation: Maybe the sacrifice would be found disqualified, then it turned out that the Sabbath was pushed aside without a slaughter[72]."

What can you say about a baby[73]? Maybe the baby would become sick; then the Sabbath would be pushed aside without circumcision. They objected: If the altar collapsed on the Sabbath, it will not be possible to build on the Sabbath[74]! A kind of altar can be built the day before. Think of it, if it developed a wart[75]? It cannot be cut on the Sabbath! Warts can be cut on the day before. Think of it, if the fourteenth falls on a Sabbath, there cannot be sprinkling on the Sabbath[76]! Sprinkling is done on the day before.

66 These paragraphs are from *Pesahim* 6:4, on the Mishnah in which R. Aqiba states his principle as here in Mishnah 1 (33c l. 9, פ). The text of the first paragraph is Tosephta *Pesahim* 5:1; partially reproduced in Babli *Pesahim* 69a. The second paragraph, while clearly originating in *Pesahim*, is copied there in very defective form but a Genizah fragment shows that it should read exactly as formulated here.

67 Of the Passover sacrifice if the 14th of Nisan is a Sabbath, and all sacrifices obligatory on a Sabbath.

68 In particular, bringing a knife for the required slaughter.

69 Greek μηρία, τά, "thigh bones", the parts of a sacrifice which have to be burned on the altar. This does not refer to the Passover sacrifice, of which nothing is burned on the altar, nor the regular Sabbath sacrifice which is a holocaust of which nothing is separated for the altar. It must refer to the public purification offering required on holidays, of which only parts are burned. If the holiday is on a Sabbath, all sacrifices or parts destined for the altar have to be burned either on the holiday or the following night. There is no requirement to wait until nightfall, after the end of the Sabbath, for any of these.

| 70 With the text in *Pesahim* read: Sunday.
71 Since it would be sinful not to burn the parts taken from the sacrifice, the burning of the parts is as necessary as the bringing of the knife.
72 This is the main argument why practice follows R. Aqiba.
73 This now refers to the Mishnah in *Šabbat* where R. Aqiba forbids bringing a knife for a circumcision on the Sabbath. What could go wrong in this case?
74 Since there can be no sacrifice without an altar, R. Eliezer would permit to rebuild one on the Sabbath. The question is whether R. Aqiba would prohibit and why. The answer is that while this altar could not have been rebuilt the day before since it was still standing, he will prohibit since building is a common weekday practice.
75 A wart on a sacrificial animal disables it (*Lev.* 22:22). A Passover sacrifice which develops a wart in the night from the 13ᵗʰ to the 14ᵗʰ of Nisan cannot be brought if the latter day is a Sabbath even though the wart was nonexistent the day before, for the same reason, that in general warts are cut on weekdays.
76 A person who was impure by the impurity of the dead, who needs to be sprinkled with water containing ashes of the Red Cow on the 3ʳᵈ and 7ᵗʰ days of his impurity, according to R. Aqiba cannot eat from the Passover sacrifice if the 7ᵗʰ day happens to be the 14ᵗʰ of Nisan which is a Sabbath, even though the prohibition of sprinkling on the Sabbath is rabbinic only.

(17a line 31) הִמּוֹל | יִמּוֹל. מִיכָּן לִשְׁנֵי מִילוֹת. אַחַת לַמִּילָה וְאַחַת לַפְּרִיעָה. אַחַת לַמִּילָה וְאַחַת לַצִּיצִים. עַד כְּדוֹן לְרַבִּי עֲקִיבָה דּוּ אָמַר. לְשׁוֹנוֹת רִיבּוּיִין הֵן. כְּרַבִּי יִשְׁמָעֵאל דּוּ אָמַר. לְשׁוֹנוֹת כְּפוּלוֹת הֵן. הַתּוֹרָה דִבְּרָה כְדַרְכָּהּ. הָלוֹךְ הָלַכְתְּ. נִכְסֹף נִכְסַפְתָּה. גֻּנֹּב גֻּנַּבְתִּי. מְנָן לֵיהּ. אָמַר רִבִּי יוּדָה בֶן פָּזִי. אָז אָמְרָה חֲתַן דָּמִים לַמּוּלוֹת: מִיכָּן לִשְׁנֵי מִילוֹת. אַחַת לַמִּילָה וְאַחַת לַפְּרִיעָה. אַחַת לַמִּילָה וְאַחַת לַצִּיצִים. רַב אָמַר. הִמּוֹל | יִמּוֹל. מִיכָּן לְנוֹלַד כְּשֶׁהוּא מָהוּל שֶׁצָּרִיךְ לְהַטִּיף מִמֶּנּוּ דַּם בְּרִית. הִמַּל יִמּוֹל. מִיכָּן לְיִשְׂרָאֵל עָרֵל שֶׁלֹּא יִמּוֹל. וְאֵין צָרִיךְ לוֹמַר גּוֹי עָרֵל. אָמַר רִבִּי לֵוִי. כָּתוּב וְאַתָּה אֶת־בְּרִיתִי תִשְׁמֹר. כָּל־כִּיּוֹצֵא בָךְ.

1 מיכן | א גזירה לשני | א לשתי אחת | א אחד ואחת | א ואחד למילה | א לפריעה 3 כפולות | א כפולין
נכסף | א כי נכסף גנבת | א גנבתי מנן ליה | א מנלן 4 לשני | א לשתי 5 לציצים | א לציצין 6 המל | א
המול ימול | א ימול עד שימול 7 כל | א אתה וכל

⁷⁷*Circumcising he shall circumcise*⁷⁸. A decision for two circumcisions, one for the circumcision, the other for uncovering⁷. One for circumcision, the other for the fibers⁷⁹. So far following Rebbi Aqiba who said, these are expressions of additions⁸⁰. From where for Rebbi Ismael who said, these are double expressions in the style of the Torah, *going I went, desiring you desired*⁸¹, *stealing (you were) stolen*⁸²? Rebbi Judah ben Pazi said, *then she said, a blood bridegroom for circumcisions*⁸³, from there that there are two circumcisions, one for the circumcision, the other for uncovering; one for

circumcision, the other for the fibers. Rav said, *circumcising he shall circumcise*, from here that one has to draw a drop of covenant blood from one born circumcised[84]. *Circumcising he shall circumcise*, from here that an uncircumcised Jew cannot circumcise; not to speak of an uncircumcised Gentile[85]. Rebbi Levi said, it is written: *But you have to keep My Covenant*[86], you and yours[87].

77 This and the following paragraph also are in *Yebamot* 8:1 (Notes 67-84,א). Here they appear as discussions of Mishnah 2.
78 Gen. 17:13.
79 Cf. Mishnah 6.
80 This interpretation of double expressions is also attributed to R. Aqiba in the Babli, *Ševuot* 27b. Cf. *Sotah* 7:5 (21d l. 66), 8:1 (22b l. 34), *Nedarim* 1:1 (36c l. 35).
81 Gen. 31:30, a speech of Laban without legal implications; this proves that the repetitions are literary devices to express emphasis. Babli *Avodah zarah* 27a.
82 Gen. 40:15, Josef's speech to the cup bearer. Incorrectly copied here by the corrector.
83 Ex. 4:26.
84 Babli *Yebamot* 71a.
85 Gen. rabba 46(8).
86 Gen. 17:9.
87 Gen. rabba 46(8); Babli *Avodah zarah* 27a.

(17a line 40) תָּנֵי. יִשְׂרָאֵל מָל אֶת הַכּוּתִי. וְכוּתִי אֵינוֹ מָל אֶת יִשְׂרָאֵל. מִפְּנֵי שֶׁמִּתְכַּוֵּין לְשֵׁם הַר גְּרִיזִים. דְּבָרֵי רִבִּי יוּדָן. אָמַר רִבִּי יוֹסֵי. וְכִי הֵיכָן מָצִינוּ שֶׁמִּילָה צְרִיכָה כַוָּנָה. יְהֵא מָל וְהוֹלֵךְ לְשֵׁם הַר גְּרִיזִים עַד שֶׁתֵּצֵא נַפְשׁוֹ.

1 שמתכוין | א שהוא מהול   2 יודן | א יודה אמ' | ט אמ' לו יוסי | א יוסה היכן | א איכן מצינו | א מצינו בתורה שמילה | א שהמילה יהא | א אלא יהא

הַמָּשׁוּךְ לֹא יִמּוֹל. שֶׁלֹּא יָבוֹא לִידֵי סַכָּנָה. דְּבָרֵי רִבִּי יוּדָה. אָמַר לוֹ רִבִּי יוֹסֵי. הַרְבֵּה מְשׁוּכִין הָיוּ בִּימֵי בֶּן כּוֹזִיבָא וְכוּלָּם מָלוּ וְחָיוּ וְהוֹלִידוּ בָּנִים וּבָנוֹת. וְהַמָּשׁוּךְ וְשֶׁנּוֹלַד שָׁמוּל וְגֵר שֶׁנִּתְגַּיֵּיר כְּשֶׁהוּא מָהוּל צָרִיךְ לְהַטִּיף מִמֶּנּוּ דַּם בְּרִית. תָּנֵי. אָמַר רִבִּי שִׁמְעוֹן בֶּן אֶלְעָזָר. לֹא נֶחְלְקוּ בֵית שַׁמַּי וּבֵית הִלֵּל עַל הַנּוֹלַד מָהוּל שֶׁצָּרִיךְ לְהַטִּיף מִמֶּנּוּ דַּם בְּרִית. שֶׁהִיא עָרְלָה כְבוּשָׁה. עַל מַה נֶּחְלְקוּ. עַל שֶׁנִּתְגַּיֵּיר מָהוּל. שֶׁבֵּית שַׁמַּי אוֹמְרִים שֶׁצָּרִיךְ לְהַטִּיף מִמֶּנּוּ דַּם בְּרִית. וּבֵית הִלֵּל אוֹמְרִים. אֵינוֹ צָרִיךְ לְהַטִּיף מִמֶּנּוּ דַּם בְּרִית. רִבִּי יִצְחָק בְּשֵׁם רִבִּי הוֹשַׁעְיָה. הֲלָכָה כְדִבְרֵי הַתַּלְמִיד. אָתָא עוֹבְדָא קוֹמֵי רַב נָמָר. מִן מַה דְתַנִּינָן. מִפְּנֵי שֶׁהִיא עָרְלָה כְבוּשָׁה. הָדָא אָמְרָה. עָרֵל בָּרוּר הוּא וְדוֹחִין עָלָיו אֶת הַשַּׁבָּת. רִבִּי אַבָּהוּ אָמַר. אֵין דּוֹחִין עָלָיו אֶת הַשַּׁבָּת וְצָרִיךְ לְהַטִּיף מִמֶּנּוּ דַּם בְּרִית. רִבִּי אָדָא בַּר אַהֲבָה אִיתְיְלִיד לֵיהּ חַד בַּר. כֵּוָן מִיסְמַיס בֵּיהּ מִית. רִבִּי אַבִּין אָמַר. נַעֲשָׂה פָצוּעַ דַּכָּה וְנִתְעַנָּה עָלָיו וָמִית. רַבָּנָן דְּקַיְסָרִין מָרִין. כְּרוּת שָׁפְכָה נַעֲשָׂה וְנִתְעַנָּה וָמִית.

2 והמשוך | א המושך ושנולד | א והנולד וגר שמתגייר כשהוא מהול | א והמל עד שלא נתגייר   3 אמ' | א -
4 הנולד | | א שנולד שהיא | א מפני שהיא   5 על | א על גר שצריך | א צריך   6 אינו | א אין   7 ומר | א

ואמ' מה | א הא דתנינן | א דתני 9 אהבה | א אחווה איתיליד | א אתליד בר | | א בר נש בן כו מיסמיס ביה | א | מי מסמס בה ר' אבין אמ' | א אמ' ר' אבין 10 פצוע דכא | א כרות שפכה ומית | א שימות רבנן | א רבנין מרין | א אמרין כרות שפכה | א פצוע דכא ומית | א שימות

It was stated[88]: "A Jew may circumcise a Samaritan but a Samaritan may not circumcise a Jew since he circumcises in the name of Mount Gerizim, the words of Rebbi Jehudah. Rebbi Yose said to him, where do we find that circumcision needs intent? Let him continue to circumcise in the name of Mount Gerizim until he dies!" "The drawn[89] should not circumcise lest he get into danger, the words of Rebbi Jehudah. Rebbi Yose said to him, many drawn ones were in the days of Ben Koziba[90], they all circumcised, lived, and begat sons and daughters. One has to draw a drop of covenant blood from the drawn, the one born circumcised, and the circumcised convert. Rebbi Simeon ben Eleazar stated: The House of Shammai and the House of Hillel did not disagree that one has to draw a drop of covenant blood from the one born circumcised; because that is a compressed prepuce; what did they disagree about? About the convert who converted when already circumcised, for the House of Shammai said one has to draw a drop of covenant blood from him, but the House of Hillel say, one does not have to draw a drop of covenant blood from him." Rebbi Issac bar Nahman said in the name of Rebbi Hoshaia[91]: Practice follows the words of the student[92]. There came a case before Rav, who said: Since we have stated that it is a compressed prepuce[93], it is implied that he certainly is uncircumcised and one pushes the Sabbath away for him[96]. Rebbi Abbahu said, one does not push the Sabbath away for him but one has to draw a drop of covenant blood from him[95]. A son was born to Rav Ada bar Ahava in that condition[96]. He squeezed it, he died. Rebbi Abin said, testicles became injured and he fasted for him; he died. The rabbis of Caesarea said, his penis was damaged and he fasted for him; he died.

88 Babli *Avodah zarah* 27a, Tosephta *Avodah zarah* 3:13.

89 People originally circumcised who manipulated their penises (or had plastic surgery) to appear uncircumcised. They might have been forcibly circumcised in the general conscription ordered by Bar Kokhba.

90 Bar Kokhba.

91 *Sifra Tazria' Pereq* 1(7); also Tosephta *Šabbat* 15:9; Babli *Šabbat* 135a; *Gen. rabba* 46(9).

92 R. Simeon ben Eleazar, a student of R. Jehudah who is quoted in a *baraita* in the Babli as stating that the Houses of Shammai and Hillel disagree about the child born

without prepuce.

93 Also in the Babli, *Šabbat* 135a, he is quoted as deciding practice following R. Jehudah.

94 The statement of R. Simeon ben Eleazar, who asserts flatly that the baby apparently without prepuce has a compressed prepuce, not that possibly he has one. Therefore blood is drawn from a baby born on the Sabbath with no apparent prepuce on the Sabbath following

95 This is the uncontested anonymous decision of the Babli.

96 Babli *Šabbat* 135a. There, R. Ada bar Ahava accused himself of being punished for not following the ruling of his teacher Rav.

(19a line 58) רִבִּי יוֹחָנָן בַּר מַרְיָיה בָּעֵי. נִתְעָרְבוּ מִלְמַטָּן מָהוּ לַחֲזוֹר וְלַעֲרוֹת עֲלֵיהֶן מִלְמַעֲלָן.

Rebbi Johanan bar Marius asked, if it was mixed at the bottom, may one again stir on top[97]?

97 This refers to the statement in Mishnah 2 that if one did not prepare a mixture of wine and oil on Friday one has to apply wine and oil separately on the Sabbath. He asks what happens if one prepared a mixture on Friday but the components separated during the night and now appear separated while at the bottom of the vessel some mixture is still there. No answer is given.

(17a line 59) אֲנָן תַּנֵּינָן. מַרְחִיצִין אֶת הַקָּטָן. תַּנֵּי דְבֵית רַב. מַרְחִיצִין אֶת הַמִּילָה. רִבִּי אַבָּהוּ בְּשֵׁם רִבִּי יוֹחָנָן. הֲלָכָה כְּמִי שֶׁהוּא אוֹמֵר. מַרְחִיצִין אֶת הַקָּטָן. אָמַר רִבִּי יוֹסֵה. עַל כּוֹרְחָךְ אַתְּ אוֹמֵר. מַרְחִיצִין אֶת הַקָּטָן. תַּנֵּי שְׁמוּאֵל. אֵין מוֹנְעִין לֹא שֶׁמֶן וְלֹא חַמִּין מֵעַל גַּבֵּי מַכָּה בַשַּׁבָּת. אָמַר רִבִּי יוֹסֵי. כָּל־שָׁעָה רִבִּי זְעִירָא רִבִּי בָּא אָמַר לִי. תְּנִי מַתְנִיתָךְ. וְלֹא עוֹד אֶלָּא שֶׁמְּזַלְּפִין מַיִם עַל גַּבֵּי מַכָּה בַשַּׁבָּת. אִם אוֹמֵר אַתְּ שֶׁמַּרְחִיצִין אֶת הַמִּילָה. מַה בֵּין מַכָּתוֹ שֶׁל גָּדוֹל לְמַכָּתוֹ שֶׁל קָטָן.

[98]We have stated: "One washes the baby." It was stated in the House of Rebbi: "One washes the circumcision." Rebbi Abbahu in the name of Rebbi Johanan: Practice follows him who says, "one washes the baby". Rebbi Yose said, you are forced to say, one washes the baby. Samuel stated, one never withholds either oil or warm water from a wound on the Sabbath. Rebbi Yose said, my teacher Rebbi Ze`ira always was coming to say to me, state in your Mishnah, not only this but one sprinkles warm water on a wound on the Sabbath. If you are saying, "one washes the circumcision", what is the difference between an adult and a baby?

רִבִּי אַבָּהוּ בְשֵׁם רִבִּי אֶלְעָזָר. הֲלָכָה כְּרִבִּי אֶלְעָזָר בֶּן עֲזַרְיָה. רִבִּי בּוּן בְּשֵׁם רִבִּי אַבָּהוּ. טַעֲמָא דְּרִבִּי אֶלְעָזָר בֶּן עֲזַרְיָה. וַיְהִי בַיּוֹם הַשְּׁלִישִׁי בִּהְיוֹתָם כּוֹאֲבִים. בִּהְיוֹתוֹ כּוֹאֵב אֵין כָּתוּב כָּאן אֶלָּא בִּהְיוֹתָם כּוֹאֲבִים. מְלַמֵּד שֶׁכָּל־אֵיבָרֵיהֶם כּוֹאֲבִים עֲלֵיהֶן. רִבִּי יַעֲקֹב בַּר אֲחָא אָמַר. רִבִּי אֶלְעָזָר וְרִבִּי יוֹחָנָן מְפַקְּדִין לַחַיָּיתָא. כָּל־שִׁיקוּיִין דְּעָבְדִין לַחוֹלֶה בְּשַׁבְּתָא. עָבְדִין אֲפִילוּ בַיּוֹם הַשְּׁלִישִׁי שֶׁחָל לִהְיוֹת בַּשַּׁבָּת. שְׁמוּאֵל אָמַר. מִפְּנֵי הַסַּכָּנָה. רִבִּי יוֹסֵי בַּר בּוּן בְּשֵׁם רַבָּנִין דְּתַמָּן. מְחַמִּין לוֹ חַמִּין בַּשַּׁבָּת. וְתַנֵּי כֵן. מְחַמִּין הוּא אָדָם אֲלוּנְטִית וְנוֹתְנָהּ עַל גַּבֵּי מֵעַיִם בַּשַּׁבָּת. לֹא יִטּוֹל אָדָם עֲרִיבָה מְלֵיאָה חַמִּין וְיִתְּנֶנָּה עַל גַּבֵּי מֵעַיִם בַּשַּׁבָּת. רִבִּי יְהוֹשֻׁעַ בֶּן לֵוִי אָמַר. לֵית כָּאן אֶלָּא מוּתָּר.

Rebbi Abbahu in the name of Rebbi Eleazar. Practice follows Rebbi Eleazar ben Azariah. Rebbi Abun in the name of Rebbi Abbahu, the reason of Rebbi Eleazar ben Azariah: *it was on the third day when they hurt*[11]. It does not say, "when it hurt", but *when they hurt*, at a time when all their limbs hurt them. Rebbi Jacob bar Aḥa said, Rebbi Eleazar and Rebbi Johanan ordered for the women having newborns, that all treatments which you give to a sick person on the Sabbath should be given if the third day falls on a Sabbath. Samuel said, because of the danger. Rebbi Yose asked, if it is because of the danger one heats hot water for him! Rebbi Yose ben Rebbi Abun in the name of the rabbis there: One heats hot water for him. And it was stated thus: A person heats a linen cloth and puts it on his belly on the Sabbath. A person may not take a bottle full of hot water and put it on his belly on the Sabbath. Rebbi Joshua ben Levi said, on the contrary it is permitted.

98 This and the next paragraph are from Chapter 9, Notes 109 ff.

(19b line 1) סָפֵק וְאַנְדְּרוֹגִינָס אֵין מְחַלְּלִין עֲלֵיהֶן אֶת הַשַּׁבָּת. רִבִּי יְהוּדָה מַתִּיר בָּאַנְדְּרוֹגִינָס. תַּמָּן תַּנִּינָן. הַכֹּל חַיָּיבִין בָּרְאִיָּה חוּץ מֵחֵרֵשׁ שׁוֹטֶה וְקָטָן טוּמְטוּם וְאַנְדְּרוֹגִינָס.

מָה אָמַר בָּהּ רִבִּי יוּדָה. נִשְׁמְעִינָהּ מִן הָדָא. רִבִּי יוֹחָנָן בֶּן דְּהֲבַאי אָמַר מִשּׁוּם רִבִּי יְהוּדָה. אַף הַסּוּמָא. וְלֵית בַּר נַשׁ אָמַר אַף אֶלָּא מִכְּלָל דּוּ מוֹדֵי עַל קַדְמִיתָא. מַחְלָפָה שִׁיטַת רִבִּי יְהוּדָה. תַּמָּן הוּא אוֹמֵר. פְּרָט. וָכָה הוּא אוֹמֵר. לְרַבּוֹת. רִבִּי יְהוּדָה וְרַבָּנָן מִקְרָא אֶחָד דָּרְשׁוּ. רִבִּי יְהוּדָה דָּרַשׁ זָכָר. וְרַבָּנָן דָּרְשֵׁי עָרֵל. מַה תַּלְמוּד לוֹמַר זָכָר. עַד שֶׁיְּהֵא כּוּלוֹ זָכָר. וְרִבִּי יְהוּדָה דָּרַשׁ זָכָר. מַה תַּלְמוּד לוֹמַר עָרֵל. אֲפִילוּ מִקְצָתוֹ עָרֵל. בְּרַם הָכָא כָּל־זְכוּרְךָ. פְּרָט לְאַנְדְּרוֹגִינָס.

1 בה | צ כא יודה | צ יהודה ר' | צ - אמ' | צ - משום | צ משם יהודה | א יודה   2 ולית | א ליתי מכלל | צא - דו | צ דהוא קדמיתא | צא קדמייתא שיטת ר' | צא שיטתיה דר' יהודה | א יודה   3 הוא | א - או' | צא אמ' | וכה | צא והכא יהודה | צא יודה דרשו | צא דרשו   4 ר' יהודה דרש זכר | צא - ורבנן | צ רבנן דרשין | צא דרשין זכר | צא ערל זכר ור' יהודה | צא ר' יודה   5 אפילו | צא ואפילו

"One does not desecrate the Sabbath for a case of doubt[15] or for a hermaphrodite[16]; Rebbi Jehudah permits for the hermaphrodite[17]." There, we have stated[99]: "Everybody is liable to be seen[100] except the deaf-and-dumb, the insane, the minor[101], the sexless[102], and the hermaphrodite."

[103]What does Rebbi Jehudah say in this case? Let us hear from the following: Rebbi Johanan ben Dahavai said in the name of Rebbi Jehudah, neither does the blind one[104]. Nobody says "neither" unless he agree with the preceding statement[105]. The argument of Rebbi Jehudah seems to be inverted. There[106] he says except, but here he says including. Rebbi Jehudah and the rabbis explain the same verse[107]. Rebbi Jehudah emphasizes *male*, the rabbis emphazise *uncircumcised*. Why does the verse add *male*[108]? Only if he be totally male. But Rebbi Jehudah emphasizes *male*, why does the verse add *uncircumcised*? Even if he is only partially uncircumcised. But here[109], *all your maleness*, except the hermaphrodite.

99 Mishnah *Hagigah* 1:1.
100 This refers to the duty of pilgrimage, Ex. 23:17: *Three times a year all your male population should be seen before the Lord, the Eternal.*
101 The first three categories are exempt from all religious duties.
102 He has neither male nor female characteristics.
103 This paragraph also appears in *Hagigah* 1:1 (76a l. 31, צ) in addition to *Yebamot* 8:1. It is difficult to establish which text is the original since both "there" and "here" are used to point to Mishnah *Hagigah*.
104 Tosephta *Hagigah* 1:1. Babli *Hagigah* 2a, *Sanhedrin* 4b, *Arakhin* 2b.
105 The Babylonian texts do not support the interpretation given here.
106 In *Hagigah*.
107 Gen. 17:14: *An uncircumcised male who refuses to circumcise the prepuce of his flesh....*
108 This interpretation disregards the existence of societies practicing female circumcision.
109 In *Hagigah*.

(17b line 10) מִי שֶׁהָיוּ לוֹ ב' תִּינוֹקוֹת כּוּל'. אָמַר רִבִּי יוֹחָנָן. דְּרִבִּי מֵאִיר הִיא. דְּאָמַר. דָּבָר שֶׁעֲשִׂיָּיתוֹ מִצְוָה פָּטוּר. וְשֶׁאֵין בַּעֲשִׂיָּיתוֹ מִצְוָה חַיָּיב בְּמַחֲלוֹקֶת. רִבִּי שִׁמְעוֹן אוֹמֵר. דָּבָר שֶׁיֵּשׁ בַּעֲשִׂיָּיתוֹ מִצְוָה חַיָּיב. וְשֶׁאֵין בַּעֲשִׂיָּיתוֹ מִצְוָה פָּטוּר בְּמַחֲלוֹקֶת. רִבִּי יוֹסֵי בְשֵׁם רִבִּי יוֹחָנָן. דִּבְרֵי רִבִּי מֵאִיר וְהוּא שֶׁיְּהֵא שֶׂה תָמִים וּבֶן שָׁנָה וּשְׁלָמִים וְרָאוּי לְהִשְׁתַּנּוֹת לְשֵׁם פֶּסַח. אַתְּ שְׁמַע מִינָהּ תְּלַת. שְׁמַע מִינָהּ. דָּבָר שֶׁאֵין לוֹ קִיצְבָּה. וְדָבָר שֶׁאֵין דַּרְכּוֹ לְהִתְחַלֵּף. וְדָבָר שֶׁיֵּשׁ בַּעֲשִׂיָּיתוֹ מִצְוָה. מָה אִית לָךְ דָּבָר שֶׁאֵין לוֹ קִיצְבָּה. רִבִּי יִרְמְיָה סְבַר מֵימַר. שֶׁלֹּא נִיתְּנָה הַתּוֹרָה קִיצְבָּה

כַּמָּה פְּסָחִים יִדָּחוּ אֶת הַשַּׁבָּת בְּכָל־שָׁנָה. רִבִּי יוֹסֵי סָבַר מֵימַר. שֶׁאֵין אַתְּ יָכוֹל לַעֲמוֹד עַל מִנְיָינָן. רִבִּי יוֹסֵה כַּד הֲוֵי מַטֵּי לְאִילֵּין נִיתְנָה הַתּוֹרָה קִיצְבָּה כַּמָּה פְּסָחִים יִדָּחוּ אֶת הַשַּׁבָּת בְּכָל־הַשָּׁנָה. רַב חִסְדָּא אָמַר. דִּבְרֵי רִבִּי שִׁמְעוֹן תִּיפְתָּר שֶׁהָיְתָה שָׁם חֲבוּרָה אַחַת שֶׁלֹּא שָׁחֲטָה. אָמַר רִבִּי זְעִירָא. מִילְּתֵיהּ דְּרִבִּי יַנַּאי אָמְרָה. וְהוּא שֶׁשָּׁכַח וּמָל אֶת שֶׁלַּשַּׁבָּת בְּעֶרֶב שַׁבָּת. מָלוֹ בְּשַׁחֲרִית. רִבִּי זְעוּרָה אָמַר. סָבַר רִבִּי יַנַּאי פָּטוּר. רִבִּי בָּא אָמַר. חַיָּיב. וּלְיֵי דָא מִילָה אָמְרָהּ רִבִּי יַנַּאי. בָּא לְהוֹדִיעֲךָ אֵיכָן דֶּרֶךְ הַתִּינוֹקוֹת לַחֲלַף. עַל דַּעְתֵּיהּ דְּרִבִּי זְעוּרָה כְּרַבִּי יַנַּאי. עַל דַּעְתֵּיהּ דְּרַב כְּרִבִּי מֵאִיר. אָמַר רִבִּי מָנָא קוֹמֵי רִבִּי יוֹסֵי. מַה דָּמַר רַב חִסְדָּא כְּרִבִּי שִׁמְעוֹן. וּמָה דָּמַר רִבִּי יַנַּאי כְּרִבִּי מֵאִיר. וּמְשִׁיבִין דָּבָר בֵּין רִבִּי מֵאִיר לְרִבִּי שִׁמְעוֹן. וְאַשְׁכְּחָן פְּלִינָא בֵּין רִבִּי מֵאִיר לְבֵין רִבִּי שִׁמְעוֹן בְּשִׁיוּר. אִילּוּ הַתִּינוֹקוֹת סְפֵיקוֹת מַה אַתְּ עָבִיד לוֹ. כִּדְבָר שֶׁיֵּשׁ לוֹ קִיצְבָּה אוֹ כִדְבָר שֶׁאֵין לוֹ קִיצְבָּה. אֵין תַּעֲבְדִינוּן כִּדְבָר שֶׁיֵּשׁ לוֹ קִיצְבָּה. וְהוּא שֶׁיְּהֵא שָׁם תִּינוֹק אַחֵר לָמוּל. אָמַר רִבִּי יוֹסֵה. מִילֵּיהוֹן דְּרַבָּנָן עַבְדִּין לוֹן כִּדְבָר שֶׁאֵין לוֹ קִיצְבָּה. וְהוּא שֶׁיְּהֵא שָׁם תִּינוֹק אַחֵר לָמוּל. אִיתָא חֲמֵי. הַקְּדִים זְמַנּוֹ פָּטוּר. אִיחֵר זְמַנּוֹ חַיָּיב. רַב הוּנָא אָמַר. חִילוּפִין הִיא מַתְנִיתָא. דְּתַנֵּי אָמַר רִבִּי שִׁמְעוֹן. לֹא נֶחְלְקוּ רִבִּי אֱלִיעֶזֶר וְרִבִּי יְהוֹשֻׁעַ עַל מִי שֶׁהָיָה לָמוּל אַחַר שַׁבָּת וּמָלוֹ בַּשַּׁבָּת שֶׁחַיָּיב. וְעַל. מִי שֶׁהָיָה לוֹ לָמוּל בְּעֶרֶב שַׁבָּת וּמָלוֹ בַּשַּׁבָּת. שֶׁרִבִּי אֱלִיעֶזֶר מְחַיֵּיב חַטָּאת וְרִבִּי יְהוֹשֻׁעַ פּוֹטֵר. אָמַר רִבִּי יוֹסֵי בֵּירִבִּי בּוּן. מִן קוּשְׁיֵי מַקְשֵׁי לַהּ לְרִבִּי יַנַּאי. וְהוּא שֶׁשָּׁכַח וּמָל אֶת שֶׁלַּשַּׁבָּת בְּעֶרֶב שַׁבָּת. רַב אָדָא בַּר אַהֲבָה אָמַר. זוֹ דִּבְרֵי רִבִּי מֵאִיר וְרִבִּי שִׁמְעוֹן. אֲבָל דִּבְרֵי רִבִּי יוֹסֵי. אֲפִילוּ דָבָר שֶׁאֵין בַּעֲשִׂייָתוֹ מִצְוָה הוֹאִיל וְטוֹעֶה בּוֹ לְשֵׁם מִצְוָה פָּטוּר.

פֵּירַשׁ אֵינוֹ חוֹזֵר אֶלָּא עַל צִיצִין הַמְעַכְּבִין אֶת הַמִּילָה. אָמַר רִבִּי יוֹחָנָן. דִּבְרֵי רִבִּי יוֹסֵי. אֲפִילוּ פֵּירַשׁ חוֹזֵר אֲפִילוּ עַל צִיצִין שֶׁאֵין מְעַכְּבִין אֶת הַמִּילָה. הֵיי דֵין רִבִּי יוֹסֵי. הֵיי דְּתַנִּינָן תַּמָּן. רִבִּי יוֹסֵי אוֹמֵר. יוֹם טוֹב הָרִאשׁוֹן שֶׁלַּחַג שֶׁחָל לִהְיוֹת בַּשַּׁבָּת. שָׁכַח וְהוֹצִיא אֶת הַלּוּלָב לִרְשׁוּת הָרַבִּים. פָּטוּר. מִפְּנֵי שֶׁהוֹצִיאוֹ בִרְשׁוּת: אַף בְּסַכִּין שֶׁלַּמִּילָה וְאַף בְּמִילָה כֵּן. מִמַּה דָּמַר רִבִּי יוֹחָנָן. דִּבְרֵי רִבִּי יוֹסֵי. אֲפִילוּ פֵּירַשׁ חוֹזֵר אֲפִילוּ עַל צִיצִין שֶׁאֵין מְעַכְּבִין אֶת הַמִּילָה. הָדָא אָמְרָה. אֲפִילוּ בְּסַכִּין שֶׁלַּמִּילָה כֵּן. אֲפִילוּ בְּמִילָה כֵּן.

2 חזור | פ יחזור אפי' | פ אף ציצין | פ הציצין היי דין | א היי דן היי | פ ההוא א ההיא   4 ואף | פ כן. אף במילה | פא במצה   ממה | פ מן מה   5 יוסי | א יוסה ציצין | א הציצין   6 במילה | פא במצה

[110]"If one had two children," etc. [111]Rebbi Joḥanan said, it is Rebbi Meïr's who said, for something where there is a commandment performed one is not liable, but if no commandment is performed whether he is liable is disputed[112]. Rebbi Simeon says, where there is a commandment performed one is liable, but if no commandment is performed whether he is not liable is disputed[113]. Rebbi Yose in the name of Rebbi Joḥanan: The word of Rebbi Meïr is, on condition that it be a sheep without blemish, a yearling, and a well-being sacrifice fit to be changed into a Passover sacrifice[114]. One understands from this three consequences. One understands something which is not a fixed

number[115]. And which is not usually exchanged[116]. And doing something which fulfills a commandment[117]. What means "something which is not a fixed number"? Rebbi Jeremiah wanted to say that the Torah did not specify how many Passover sacrifices should push the Sabbath aside in any given year. Rebbi Yose wanted to say, where you cannot determine the amount. When Rebbi Yose came to these [118]["children in doubt"[119] he used to say, Rebbi Jeremiah taught us correctly. Could you say that you cannot determine the amount[120]? But the Torah did not] specify[121] how many Passover sacrifices should push the Sabbath aside in any given year. Rav Hisda said, one may explain the words of Rebbi Simeon if a group was there which did not slaughter[122]. Rebbi Ze`ira said, the word of Rebbi Yannai[123] implies that he forgot and circumcised the one for the Sabbath on Friday. It he circumcised him in the morning, Rebbi Ze`ira said that Rebbi Yannai was of the opinion that he is not liable[124]. Rebbi Abba said, he is liable[125]. In relation to what did Rebbi Yannai say it? He comes to tell you in which cases can there be a switching of children[126]. In Rebbi Ze`ira's opinion following Rebbi Yannai Rav followed Rebbi Meïr[127]. Rebbi Mana said before Rebbi Yose, what Rav Hisda said follows Rebbi Simeon, and what Rebbi Ze`ira said follows Rebbi Meïr. Can one object anything between Rebbi Meïr and Rebbi Simeon[128]? Do we find a difference between Rebbi Meïr and Rebbi Simeon about the remainder[129]? How do you treat the babies in doubt? Like something which is a fixed amount or something which is not a fixed amount[130]? If you are treating it like something which is a fixed amount . . . only if there remains another baby to circumcise[131]. Rebbi Yose said, the words of the rabbis make the case like something which is not a fixed amount: only if there remains another baby to circumcise. Come and see: If he anticipated his time he is not liable, if he delayed his time he is liable[132]? Rav Huna said, the Mishnah is the other way around, as it was stated[133]: Rebbi Simeon said, Rebbi Eliezer and Rebbi Joshua did not disagree about one which was to be circumcised after the Sabbath if he circumcised him on the Sabbath that he is liable, but one who was to be circumcised before the Sabbath if he circumcised him on the Sabbath where Rebbi Eliezer makes him liable for a purification sacrifice and Rebbi Joshua declares him not liable. Rebbi Yose ben Rebbi Abun said, because of this objection it was difficult for Rebbi Yannai, only if he forgot and circumcised the one of the Sabbath on Friday[134]. Rebbi Ada bar Ahavah said, these are the words of Rebbi Meïr and Rebbi Simeon, but the words of Rebbi Yose [are]: Even if no commandment is performed he is not liable since he erred on behalf of a commandment[135].

[136]If he finished he can return only for fibers which would invalidate the circumcision[137]. Rebbi Johanan said, the words of Rebbi Yose, even if he finished he may even return for fibers which do not invalidate the circumcision[138]. Which [statement of] Rebbi Yose? That which we stated there[139]: "Rebbi Yose says, if the first day of Tabernacles falls on a Sabbath[140], if he forgot and took the *lulav* out into the public domain he is not liable because he took it out with permission." Does the same hold for a knife for circumcision, the same for (circumcision) [unleavened bread][141]? Since Rebbi Johanan said, the words of Rebbi Yose, even if he finished he may even return for fibers which do not invalidate the circumcision, this implies the same even for a knife for circumcision, the same for (circumcision) [unleavened bread].

110 This entire piece is also found in *Pesahim* 6:7 (33d l. 63). It is not clear where the paragraph belonged originally. The text here has some lacunae, the one there has some places where the order of the sentences may be questioned. While it is clear that both are based on the same original, in their present shape they do not seem to be copies of one another. The text is unusually difficult.

111 The main problem discussed in the paragraph is the correct reading in Mishnah 4. The Mishnah printed in the Venice edition of the Yerushalmi and reproduced at the start of this Chapter (not from the Leiden ms.) states liability if the baby scheduled for Friday was circumcised on the Sabbath and notes a controversy if the one scheduled for Sunday was circumcised on the Sabbath. In the Babli 137a this version is attributed to R. Hiyya (the Elder). The Mishnah in the Babli switches the two cases. A *baraita* in the Babli 137a in the name of R. Meïr keeps the order of the Mishnah of the Yerushalmi but states "not liable" in the first case. In the following, different authorities seem to accept different readings. The interpretation given here in general follows S. Liebermann.

112 It seems that R. Johanan reads in the Mishnah a text similar to that attributed to R. Meïr in the Babli. If he circumcises the baby scheduled for Sabbath on Friday he violates a positive commandment, *viz.*, to circumcise on the eighth day, but no liability for a sacrifice is created. If then he circumcises the one scheduled for Friday on the Sabbath, he violates the Sabbath but in the act satisfies a commandment; according to R. Meïr this frees him from liability.

113 R. Simeon reads the Mishnah as given at the start of this Chapter. The fact that the baby scheduled for Friday had to be circumcised and the circumcision on the Sabbath accomplished this does not free from liability for the desecration of the Sabbath.

Since the text in *Pesaḥim* confirms the text here there is no possibility to emend "liable" into "not liable" as proposed by the classical commentaries.

114 This refers to Mishnah *Pesaḥim* 6:9 (6:5 in most independent Mishnah mss.) where in a discussion of liability if a Passover sacrifice was slaughtered incorrectly on a Sabbath which was a 14th of Nisan, R. Eliezer notes that obligatory sacrifices must be slaughtered on the Sabbath but that a person slaughtering a private sacrifice in the name of a public one on the Sabbath is liable but R. Meïr declares him not liable. R. Joshua rejects a comparison of public and private sacrifices since public sacrifices are prescribed in number but the number of private ones is unlimited.

R. Johanan notes that R. Meïr exempts from liability only if the error was excusable. A Passover sacrifice must be without blemish, male, and a yearling (*Ex.* 12:5). A blemished animal cannot be a sacrifice at all; slaughtering a blemished animal as a sacrifice is an inexcusable error. A well-being sacrifice may be male or female and of almost any age (more than 8 days old). Such an animal can be a candidate for Passover sacrifice only if it is a male yearling. If the three conditions are satisfied an illegal switching between the categories is excusable.

115 This excludes sacrificing privately in the name of public sacrifices.

116 This seems to contradict the prior statement that only well-being sacrifices are exempt from liability if they are fit to be Passover sacrifices. Therefore the commentaries emend the statement to read: And which usually is exchanged. Since the statement is not discussed further in the Halakhah, there is no certainty achievable but since the text is identical in both sources one would have to assume a corruption in the original common source. There is no difficulty explaining the text as it stands. If it were something that routinely can be changed, such as excess Passover animals reclassified as animals for well-being sacrifices, and if the slaughter were legitimate for the new denomination, there would be universal agreement that everything is legitimate and there is merit, never liability. The question of liability can arise only if such a reclassification is unusual and has not been effected.

117 As offering the Passover in the case of sacrifices and circumcising in the case of Mishnah *Šabbat*.

118 The text in brackets is added from *Pesaḥim*; it is essential for the understanding of the argument:

ר' יוסי כד הוי מטי לאילין [תינוקות ספיקות היה אמ'. יפה לימדנו ר' ירמיה. אית לך מימר. שאין את יכול לעמוד על מיניינן. אלא שלא] ניתנה ...

119 Mishnah *Šabbat* 19:4.

120 After the fact one always can count how many sacrifices were offered in the Temple.

121 There is not an *a priori* limit on the numbers.

122 Since in *Šabbat* the disagreement between R. Eliezer and R. Joshua is whether

there still is a baby to be circumcised, so in parallel their disagreement in *Pesahim* must refer to a case where a Passover sacrifice has still to be slaughtered.

123 As given in the next sentence.

124 This is based on the Mishnah as given at the start of the Chapter. If he correctly circumcised the baby scheduled for the Sabbath on the morning of the Sabbath and later the same day wrongly circumcised the baby scheduled for Sunday, is he not liable because Sabbath already was being pushed aside for the first circumcision?

125 He disagrees with R. Ze'ira and states that R. Yannai in this case holds that R. Joshua also would find him liable.

126 He only comes to explain how it could happen that the baby scheduled for Sunday would be circumcised on the Sabbath and no other baby still had to be circumcised.

127 The language is elliptic (but, as S. Liebermann has pointed out, it also appears otherwise in the Yerushalmi, cf. *Eruvin* 6, 23c l. 65). R. Ze'ira asserts that accepting the interpretation of the Mishnah given by R. Yannai, there exists a (not otherwise reported) decision by Rav which follows the reading of the Mishnah ascribed to Rav, which therefore decides practice.

128 The two opinions are based on two different readings of the Mishnah; there should be no need to try to harmonize the opinions. It is not explained who tried to harmonize them.

129 Both agree that there must be a baby left to be circumcised, or a sacrifice to be slaughtered, to lift liability from an untimely circumcision or slaughter.

130 How can one apply the arguments from the Mishnah in *Pesahim* to the case in *Šabbat*?

131 The text in *Pesahim* adds:
אפי׳ אין שם תינוק אחד למול. ואין תעבדינון כדבר שאין לו קיצבה.
"even if there is not one baby to be circumcised. But if you are treating it like something which is not a fixed amount," and one has to read this text here also. In *Pesahim* one infers that R. Joshua agrees with R. Eliezer that in matters of public sacrifices, which are fixed in numbers, there is no excuse for additional slaughter and any error will result in liability. But in matters of private offerings (excluding purification and reparation offerings, which follow the rules of public sacrifices) where the numbers are indefinite, he denies liability for additional infractions of the rules of the Sabbath. Therefore in the case here he might agree to liability if the baby scheduled for Friday was circumcised on the Sabbath only if the case is compared to public sacrifices.

132 The position of R. Joshua in the Mishnah does not seem reasonable (assuming R. Meïr's argument.) By circumcising the baby scheduled for Friday on the Sabbath he fulfills a commandment (even though a day late) and is declared liable; but by circumcising the baby scheduled for Sunday on the Sabbath he does not fulfil a commandment (since its time has not yet arrived) but is declared not liable!

133 Babli 137a.

134 The explanation given in Note 18 is necessary; if both babies are still uncircumcised on the Sabbath R. Joshua will declare him not liable even if the one scheduled for Friday is circumcised first.

135 For example, if on Passover he slaughtered a defective animal as sacrifice when no commandment could be fulfilled with it.

136 This paragraph is found not only in *Pesahim* (ס), but also in *Yebamot* 8:1 (Notes 106-107, א) and is repeated at the end of the present Halakhah. Most of the remaining parts of the Halakhah are also found there.

137 If the circumcision is done on a Sabbath, once he is finished he can return only to correct a defect as described in Mishnah 6 but not for cosmetic adjustments. Babli 133b.

138 This is a straight application of R. Yose's (the Tanna) position, Note 135.

139 Mishnah *Sukkah* 3:14.

140 R. Yose holds that since the Torah requires one to take a palm branch on the first day of Tabernacles (*Lev.* 23:40), even taking it out on the Sabbath cannot be punishable. The same then holds for the knife for a circumcision which must be performed on the Sabbath and the unleavened bread which must be eaten during the first night of the Feast of Unleavened Bread even if that happens to be on a Sabbath. (During the remainder of the Feast of Unleavened Bread, leavened matter is forbidden but consumption of unleavened bread is not obligatory.)

141 The text in parentheses is from *Šabbat*, the [correct] text in brackets is from *Pesahim* and *Yebamot*; it is confirmed by the text here at the end of the Halakhah.

(17b line 43) יֵשׁ קָטָן נִימוֹל לְיוֹמוֹ. הֵיךְ עֲבִידָא. יָלְדָה וְאַחַר כָּךְ נִתְגַּיְּירָה נִימוֹל לְיוֹמוֹ. נִתְגַּיְּירָה וְאַחַר כָּךְ יָלְדָה נִימוֹל לִשְׁמוֹנָה. יַעֲקֹב אִישׁ כְּפַר נָבוֹרַיָּא שָׁאַל לְרִבִּי חַגַּיי. מֵעַתָּה נוֹלַד בֵּין הַשְּׁמָשׁוֹת נִימוֹל בֵּין הַשְּׁמָשׁוֹת. אָמַר לֵיהּ. אִילּוּ הֲוֵינָן אֲנָא וְאַתְּ עָלִין בְּחַד תִּרְעָא דִּלְמָא הֲוֵינָן יְכֹלִין מְכַוְּונָה.

¹⁴²It is possible that a child is circumcised on his first day. How is this possible? If she gave birth and then converted, he is circumcised on his first day. If she converted and then gave birth, he is circumcised on his eighth day¹⁴³. Jacob from Kefar-Naboraia asked Rebbi Ḥaggai, then if he was born during twilight, should he not be circumcised at twilight¹⁴⁴? He told him, if I and you were entering the same door, could we make it simultaneous¹⁴⁵?

142 Here starts discussion of Mishnah 5.

143 In the first case he is a convert, in the second the child of a Jewish mother. Cf. Babli 135a,, Rashi *s. v.* כל שאין אמו טמאה לידה.

144 If the boy was born Friday night at twilight, the Mishnah states that he is circumcised on Sunday since it is not knowable whether he was born on Friday or on the Sabbath, Note 20. Why could the child not be circumcised exactly 8 times 24 hours afterwards, when it would be irrelevant which day it was?

145 Since simultaneity is not realizable under normal circumstances, the identical

moment cannot be reproduced, not to mention the variations in the astronomical data.

(17b line 52) שְׁמוּאֵל אָמַר. אֲחָזַתּוֹ חַמָּה מַמְתִּינִין לוֹ שְׁלֹשִׁים יוֹם. אוֹתָן שְׁלֹשִׁים יוֹם מַהוּ לְהַאֲכִילוֹ חָלָב תְּרוּמָה. מַהוּ לְסוֹכוֹ שֶׁמֶן תְּרוּמָה. נִשְׁמְעִינָהּ מִן הָדָא. הֶעָרֵל וְכָל־הַטְּמֵאִים לֹא יֹאכְלוּ בַּתְּרוּמָה. נְשֵׁיהֶן וְעַבְדֵּיהֶן יֹאכְלוּ. רִבִּי אָחָא בְּשֵׁם רִבִּי תַּנְחוּם בַּר חִיָּיה. אֵין עוֹרְלָה אֶלָּא מִיּוֹם הַשְּׁמִינִי וּלְהַלָּן. וְתַנֵּי כֵן. כָּל־שְׁלֹשִׁים יוֹם אָסוּר לְהַאֲכִילוֹ חָלָב תְּרוּמָה וּלְסוֹכוֹ שֶׁמֶן תְּרוּמָה. לֵילֵי שְׁמִינִי מָה אַתְּ עָבַד לֵיהּ. מִמַּה דְּתַנֵּי. לֵילֵי שְׁמִינִי בְּנִכְנַס לְדִיר לְהִתְעַשֵּׂר. הָדָא אָמְרָה. לֵילֵי שְׁמִינִי כַּשְּׁמִינִי. וְתַנֵּי כֵן. כָּל־שִׁבְעַת הַיָּמִים מוּתָּר לְהַאֲכִילוֹ חָלָב תְּרוּמָה וּלְסוֹכוֹ שֶׁמֶן תְּרוּמָה.

1 אחזתו | א אפילו אחזתו חמה | א חמה שעה אחת לו | א לו עד אותן | א ואותן   2 חלב תרומה | א מחלבה שלתרומה תרומה | א שלתרומה   3 נשיהן | א ונשיהם בר | א ביר' עורלה | א ערלה   4 ולהלן | א והלאה להאכילו | א להאכילה תרומה | א שלתרומה ולסוכו | א ולסוכו ואסור לסוכו שמן | א בשמן   5 תרומה | א שלתרומה ליה | א לה ממה | א מן מה בנכנס | א הנכנס   6 כשמיני | א כשמיני הוא הימים | א ימים חלב תרומה | א חלבה שלתרומה   7 שמן תרומה | א בשמן שלתרומה

[146]Samuel said, if he runs a fever [for one hour][147] one waits with him one month[148]. May one feed him with milk-substitute[149] from heave? May one rub him with heave oil? Let us hear from the following: "The uncircumcised and any impure persons may not eat heave; their wives and slaves may eat." Rebbi Aḥa in the name of Rebbi Tanḥum bar Ḥiyya: The prepuce is counted only from the eighth day onward[150]. It was stated so: For the entire thirty days it is forbidden to feed him with milk-substitute from heave and forbidden to rub him with heave oil. How do you treat the night of the eighth day? Since it was stated: In the night of the eighth day it enters the corral to be tithed[151], that means that the night of the eighth is treated like the eighth day. And it was stated so: All seven days long one is permitted to feed him with milk-substitute from heave and permitted to rub him with heave oil.

146 The parallel is in *Yebamot* 8:1, Notes 97-100. The original seems to be there since Samuel's statement here is missing an essential part.

147 Added from *Yebamot*.

148 In the Babli, *Yebamot* 71a and *Šabbat* 137a, he gives a minimum of 7 times 24 hours.

149 Some baby food made from heave grain. There is no heave milk.

150 The Babli, *Yebamot* 71a, asserts the opposite, that uncircumcised babies of Cohanim may not be fed heave products. The argument here is that since for the first 7 days there is no obligation to circumcise, there can be no disability connected to this fact either.

151 A newborn animal is acceptable as

sacrifice only after eight days (*Lev.* 22:27)). If a calf can be counted for tithing already in the night of the eighth day, to be chosen as tithe sacrifice, this proves that one does not have to wait until it is daytime; Babli *Zebahim* 12a. Therefore, the baby may not be fed heave products between nightfall of the eighth day and the time of circumcision on the next morning.

(17b line 61) אֵילוּ צִיצִין הַמְעַכְּבִין אֶת הַמִּילָה. רִבִּי אֲבוּנָא בְשֵׁם רַב יִרְמְיָה. בְּחוֹפָה רוֹב גּוּבְהָהּ שֶׁלְעֲטָרָה. רִבִּי יוֹסֵה בֶּן חֲנִינָא אוֹמֵר. בְּחוֹפָה רוֹב גּוּבָהּ עֲטָרָה. רִבִּי טְבַיי בְּשֵׁם שְׁמוּאֵל. בּוֹדְקִין אוֹתוֹ בְּשָׁעָה שֶׁמִּתְקַשֶּׁה.

1 אבונא | א אבינא רב | א ר'   2 חנינה | א יוסי עטרה | א שלעטרה טביי | א טבי   3 שמתקשה | א שהיא מקשה

"The following are the fibers which invalidate a circumcision.[152]" Rebbi Avuna in the name of Rav Jeremiah[153]: If it covers most of the height of the corona[154]. Rebbi Yose ben Hanina[155] said, if it covers most of the top of the corona. Rebbi Tebi in the name of Samuel: One checks at the time of an erection[156].

152 Mishnah 6.
153 In *Yebamot*: R. Abinna in the name of Rebbi Jeremiah. The text here is correct since also in the Babli, *Šabbat* 137b, this is a statement of Rebbi Abinna in the name of the Babylonian *Rav* Jeremiah bar Abba and R. Avina lived two generations before *Rebbi* Jeremiah (cf. Berakhot Chapter 6, Note 148).
154 Making clear that "most" in the Mishnah refers to the vertical, not the horizontal.
155 In *Yebamot*: Yose ben Yose. This also was the version of the scribe here, "Hanina" is the scribe's own correction. But it seems that the *Yebamot* version is correct and the late Galilean Amora R. Yose ben Yose endorses the earlier Babylonian ruling.
156 This refers to the fat baby mentioned in the Mishnah; if only the uncovered part of his corona is visible, nothing has to be done. In the Babli 137b this is a statement of Samuel, modifying a tannaitic statement of Rabban Simeon ben Gamliel (Tosephta Shabbat 15:9, ed. Liebermann).

(17b line 64) מָל וְלֹא פָרַע אֶת הַמִּילָה כְּאִילוּ לֹא מָל: תַּנֵּי. וְאָנוּשׁ כָּרֵת. רִבִּי אָחָא בְשֵׁם רִבִּי אַבָּהוּ. הָדָא דְתֵימַר בְּשֶׁאֵין בּוֹ כְדֵי לְמָרֵק. אֲבָל אִם יֶשׁ בּוֹ כְדֵי לְמָרֵק מְמָרֵק וְאֵינוֹ חוֹשֵׁשׁ. תַּנֵּי. כָּל־שָׁעָה שֶׁעוֹסֵק בְּמִילָה חוֹזֵר בֵּין עַל צִיצִין הַמְעַכְּבִין בַּמִּילָה בֵּין עַל צִיצִין שֶׁאֵין מְעַכְּבִין. פֵּירֵשׁ. אֵינוֹ חוֹזֵר אֶלָּא עַל צִיצִין הַמְעַכְּבִין בַּמִּילָה. אָמַר רִבִּי יוֹחָנָן. דִּבְרֵי רִבִּי יוֹסֵי. אֲפִילוּ עַל צִיצִין שֶׁאֵין מְעַכְּבִין בַּמִּילָה. אִם פֵּירֵשׁ חוֹזֵר. הֵיי דֵין רִבִּי יוֹסֵי. הֵיי דְתַנִּנֵן תַּמָּן. רִבִּי יוֹסֵי אוֹמֵר. יוֹם טוֹב הָרִאשׁוֹן שֶׁלְחַג שֶׁחָל לִהְיוֹת בַּשַּׁבָּת. וְשָׁכַח וְהוֹצִיא אֶת הַלּוּלָב לִרְשׁוּת הָרַבִּים. פָּטוּר.

מִפְּנֵי שֶׁהוֹצִיאוּ בִרְשׁוּת: אַף בְּסַכִּין שֶׁלְמִילָה אַף בְּמַצָּה כֵן. מִמַּה דָמַר רִבִּי יוֹחָנָן. דִּבְרֵי רִבִּי יוֹסֵי. אֲפִילוּ עַל צִיצִין שֶׁאֵין מְעַכְּבִין בַּמִּילָה. אִם פִּירֵשׁ חוֹזֵר. הָדָא אָמְרָה. אֲפִילוּ בְּסַכִּין שֶׁלְמִילָה וְאַף בְּמַצָּה כֵן

1 כאלו | א כילו   2 בו | א ביום   ¹⁵⁷(2) | א ביום   3 שעוסק | א שהוא עוסק במילה | א את המילה   - | א את המילה 4 במילה | א את המילה אפילו | א אפילו פירש חוזר אפילו   5 במילה | א את המילה אם פירש חוזר | א - היי | א ההיא   6 לרשות | א ברשות   7 אף | א כן ואף   ממה | א מן מה   8 אפילו | א אפילו אם פירש חוזר אם פירש חוזר | א -   9 ואף | א כן אף

¹⁵⁸"If he circumcised but did not uncover⁷ the circumcision it is as if he did not circumcise²⁴." It was stated: He is subject to divine extirpation¹⁵⁹. Rebbi Aḥa in the name of Rebbi Abbahu: That is to say if there is no time left [in the day]¹⁵⁷ to correct it. But if there is time left [in the day] to correct, he corrects without hesitation.

¹⁶⁰It was stated: As long as he is occupied with the circumcision, he may return both to fibers which invalidate the circumcision as also to fibers that do not invalidate the circumcision. Once he has stopped, he may return only to fibers which invalidate the circumcision. Rebbi Johanan said, the words of Rebbi Yose imply that even after he has stopped he may return even to fibers that do not invalidate the circumcision. Which [statement of] Rebbi Yose? That which we had stated there: "Rebbi Yose said, if the first day of Tabernacles falls on a Sabbath and somebody forgot [that it was the Sabbath] and took the palm branch into the public domain he is not liable since he took it out with permission." Is it the same for the knife of circumcision, for a mazzah? Since Rebbi Johanan said, the words of Rebbi Yose imply that even after he has stopped he may return even to fibers that do not invalidate the circumcision, that means the same holds for the knife of circumcision, for a mazzah.

157 Probably the original version was the composite בּוֹ בָּיוֹם "on the same day". The scribe originally wrote ביום and corrected to בו.

158 The parallel is in *Yebamot* 8:1 (Notes 104 ff., 9a l. 43, א).

159 The person incorrectly circumcising on the Sabbath.

160 This paragraph is repeated from above, Notes 136 ff.

תולין פרק עשרים

(fol. 17c) **משנה א**: רִבִּי אֱלִיעֶזֶר אוֹמֵר תּוֹלִין אֶת הַמְשַׁמֶּרֶת בְּיוֹם טוֹב וְנוֹתְנִין לַתְּלוּיָה בַּשַּׁבָּת. וַחֲכָמִים אוֹמְרִים אֵין תּוֹלִין אֶת הַמְשַׁמֶּרֶת בְּיוֹם טוֹב וְאֵין נוֹתְנִין לַתְּלוּיָה בַּשַּׁבָּת. אֲבָל נוֹתְנִין לַתְּלוּיָה בְּיוֹם טוֹב:

Mishnah 1: Rebbi Eliezer says, one hangs the yeast-sieve[1] on a holiday and one uses one hanging on the Sabbath[2]. But the Sages say, one may not hang a yeast-sieve on a holiday[3] and may not use a hanging one on the Sabbath[4] but one may use a hanging one on a holiday[5].

משנה ב: נוֹתְנִין מַיִם עַל גַּבֵּי שְׁמָרִים בִּשְׁבִיל שֶׁיִּצַּלּוּ וּמְסַנְּנִין אֶת הַיַּיִן בְּסוּדָרִים וּבִכְפִיפָה מִצְרִית. נוֹתְנִין בֵּיצָה בְּמְסַנֶּנֶת שֶׁל חַרְדָּל וְעוֹשִׂין יֵינוֹמֵלִין בַּשַּׁבָּת. רִבִּי יְהוּדָה אוֹמֵר בַּשַּׁבָּת בַּכּוֹס וּבְיוֹם טוֹב בַּלָּגִין וּבַמּוֹעֵד בֶּחָבִית. רִבִּי צָדוֹק אוֹמֵר הַכֹּל לְפִי הָאוֹרְחִין:

Mishnah 2: One may add water to the yeast to clear it[6]; one may sift wine through sheets[7] or a Egyptian basket[8]. One may break an egg into the sieve of mustard seed[9], and make honey-wine[10] on the Sabbath. Rebbi Jehudah says, on the Sabbath in a cup, on a holiday in a pitcher[11], and during a holiday week[12] in an amphora. Rebbi Sadoq says, everything according to the number of guests[13].

משנה ג: אֵין שׁוֹרִין אֶת הַחִלְתִּית בְּפוֹשְׁרִין אֲבָל נוֹתְנָהּ לְתוֹךְ הַחוֹמֶץ. אֵין שׁוֹרִין אֶת הַכַּרְשִׁינִין וְלֹא שָׁפִין אוֹתָן. אֲבָל נוֹתֵן הוּא לְתוֹךְ הַקְּעָרָה אוֹ לְתוֹךְ הַכַּלְכָּלָה. אֵין כּוֹבְרִין אֶת הַתֶּבֶן בִּכְבָרָה וְלֹא יִתְּנֶנּוּ בְּמָקוֹם גָּבוֹהַּ בִּשְׁבִיל שֶׁיֵּרֵד הַמּוֹץ אֲבָל נוֹטֵל בִּכְבָרָה וְנוֹתֵן לְתוֹךְ הָאֵבוּס:

Mishnah 3: One does not soak asafoetida[14] in lukewarm water but one may add it to vinegar[15]. One does not soak vetch[16] and does not smooth it, but one may put it into a pot or into a bag[17]. One does not shake straw in a sieve[18] and does not expose it on an elevated place to cause the chaff to fall down, but one may take it in a sieve to put it into a trough[19].

משנה ד: גּוֹרְפִין מִלִּפְנֵי הַפִּטָּם וּמְסַלְּקִין לַצְּדָדִין מִפְּנֵי הָרְעִי דִּבְרֵי רִבִּי יוֹסֵה. וַחֲכָמִים אוֹסְרִין. נוֹטְלִין מִלִּפְנֵי בְהֵמָה זוֹ וְנוֹתְנִין לִפְנֵי בְהֵמָה זוֹ בַּשַּׁבָּת:

Mishnah 4: One cleans up after an animal to be fattened[20], and one removes it[21] to the sides for one grazing, the words of Rebbi Dosa, but the Sages forbid. One may take from before one animal and put it before another one on the Sabbath[22].

משנה ח הַקַּשׁ שֶׁעַל גַּבֵּי הַמִּטָּה לֹא יְנַעְנְעֶנּוּ בְיָדוֹ אֲבָל מְנַעְנְעוֹ בְגוּפוֹ אִם הָיָה מַאֲכַל בְּהֵמָה אוֹ שֶׁהָיָה עָלָיו כַּר אוֹ סָדִין מְנַעְנְעוֹ בְיָדוֹ. מַכְבֵּשׁ שֶׁל בַּעֲלֵי בָתִּים מַתִּירִין אֲבָל לֹא כוֹבְשִׁין. וְשֶׁל כּוֹבְסִין לֹא יִגַּע בּוֹ. רַבִּי יְהוּדָה אוֹמֵר אִם הָיָה מוּתָּר מֵעֶרֶב שַׁבָּת מַתִּיר אֶת כֵּלָיו וְשׁוֹמְטָן:

Mishnah 5: Straw on a bed[23] one may not move with his hands[24] but he may move it with his body; if it was animal feed or there was a pillow or a sheet[25] one may move it with his hand. One may open a clothes press[26] in a private home but one may not close it; a washer's one may not be touched. Rebbi Jehudah said, if it was open from before the Sabbath he removes the clothes and lets it[27] drop.

1 Since on a holiday the preparation of food is permitted (*Lev.* 12:16), R. Eliezer also permits installation of the necessary implements. If the wine was stored in the amphora in which it was made, he permits to install a sieve on top of a pitcher to remove the yeast from the fluid actually to be served for the holiday meal.

2 Even though sifting is one of the 39 forbidden actions, R. Eliezer restricts this to solid food as described in Mishnah 7:2.

3 They do not permit installations on the holiday. Even though putting a sieve on a pitcher is not making a tent, it is close enough to be rabbinically prohibited as tent making.

4 Since this is classified either as selecting or sifting; both biblically prohibited.

5 Since the sifting is necessary to make the wine acceptable to everybody, it is legitimate preparation of food on the holiday.

6 If the yeast is in the sieve from before the Sabbath, no biblical prohibition is involved.

7 Latin *sudarium, -ii, n.* "sweat cloth". This is not professional work.

8 A basket woven from palm leaves.

9 To give it color. The biblical prohibition of painting on the Sabbath does not apply to food.

10 Greek οἰνόμελι.

11 Cf. Chapter 18 Note 29.

12 The semi-holidays in the weeks of the Feast of Unleavened Bread and Tabernacles.

13 For a big party one may even prepare a full barrel on the Sabbath.

14 To use as spice or for medical reasons.

15 As a spice.

16 Cf. Mishnah 1:8, Note 13. This Mishnah is not a complete repetition of Mishnah 1:8 since here one also forbids short-term immersion in water to separate

the vetch from the chaff, which would be a violation of the biblical prohibition of selecting the good out of a mixture of good and bad.

17 Since shaking grain in a sieve is a biblical prohibition (Mishnah 7:2); the corresponding motion is forbidden for all kinds of produce.

18 Since this is biblically forbidden.

19 Since there is an obligation to feed one's animals, one may use a vessel to move the animal feed in such a way that automatically much chaff will be blown away without the action of a rabbi.

20 Food outside the barn.

21 The remaining food, but one may not clean the barn.

22 Inside one trough or inside the barn.

23 The bed is a wooden plank, the straw serves as a mattress.

24 If the straw never was used as a mattress before it is produce and cannot be used as an implement; it is *muqseh*.

25 Lying on it from before the Sabbath; then the straw is a mattress and may be moved as an implement.

26 Used for what today would be done by ironing.

27 Since each part of the press is an implement and may be moved on the Sabbath.

(17c line 27) רִבִּי אֱלִיעֶזֶר אוֹמֵר תּוֹלִין אֶת הַמְשַׁמֶּרֶת כול׳. תַּנֵי. לֹא נֶחְלַק רִבִּי אֱלִיעֶזֶר וַחֲכָמִים שֶׁנּוֹטְעִין אוֹהָלִין בַּתְּחִילָה בַּשַּׁבָּת. וְעַל מַה נֶחְלָקוּ. עַל מוֹסִיפִין. שֶׁרִבִּי אֱלִיעֶזֶר אוֹמֵר. מוֹסִיפִין בְּיוֹם טוֹב וְאֵין מוֹסִיפִין בַּשַּׁבָּת. וַחֲכָמִים אוֹמְרִים. אֵין מוֹסִיפִין בְּיוֹם טוֹב וְאֵין צָרִיךְ לוֹמַר בַּשַּׁבָּת. וְכָא לֹא בְתוֹסֶפֶת אֲנָן קַייָמִין. אָמַר רִבִּי אַבִּין בַּר כַּהֲנָא. תִּיפְתָּר בִּמְשַׁמֶּרֶת חֲדָשָׁה שֶׁמַּכְשִׁירָהּ לִכְלִי. כָּל־שֶׁכֵּן.

"Rebbi Eliezer says, one hangs the yeast-sieve," etc. It was stated[28]: "Rebbi Eliezer and the Sages did not disagree that one sets up new tents on the Sabbath. Where do they disagree? About extending, for Rebbi Eliezer says one adds on a holiday but one does not add on a Sabbath, but the Sages say, one does not add on a holiday, and it is not necessary to say on a Sabbath." Do we not deal here with an addition[29]? Rebbi Abbin bar Cahana said, explain it about a new yeast-sieve which he turns into an implement[30]. *A fortiori*[31].

28 It seems that the text is corrupt and the correct version is in Tosephta 12:14 (ed. Liebermann) and *Sukkah* 1:8: "The Sages agree with R. Eliezer that one *does not make new tents* on an holiday, not to mention on a Sabbath. Where did they disagree? Whether one adds, for R. Eliezer said, one does *not* add on a holiday, not to mention the Sabbath, but the Sages say, one *may* add on a Sabbath, not to mention the holiday."

29 The question is directed to the Sages based on the version of the Tosephta: Even

if we say that hanging a sieve over a wine-barrel is adding to a tent, how can the Sages forbid what they permit in the Tosephta?

30 The Sages forbid not because of making a tent, which it is not, but because of "hitting with a hammer".

31 If the explanation is correct, the question remains why R. Eliezer disagrees.

Here starts a new Genizah fragment edited by J. N. Epstein in *Tarbiz* 3 (E). It reads לא כל שכן "not so much more?" which is difficult to understand and possibly a scribal error since the expression לא כל שכן is much more frequent than כל שכן and also appears in the next sentence.

(17c line 32) מִחֲלָפָה שִׁיטָתֵיהּ דְּרִבִּי אֱלִיעֶזֶר. מָה אִם תַּמָּן שֶׁמַּכְשִׁירָהּ לִכְלִי אַתְּ אָמַר. מוּתָּר. כָּאן שֶׁאֵינוֹ מַכְשִׁירָהּ לִכְלִי לֹא כָל־שֶׁכֵּן. אָמַר רִבִּי חִינְנָא. אַתְיָא דְּרִבִּי אֱלִיעֶזֶר כְּרִבִּי יְהוּדָה. דְּתַנֵּי בְשֵׁם רִבִּי יְהוּדָה. אַף בְּמַכְשִׁירֵי אוֹכֶל נֶפֶשׁ הִתִּירוּ. רִבִּי אָחָא בְשֵׁם רִבִּי בָא. כְּדִבְרֵי הַמַּכְשִׁיר. וּבִלְבַד מִלְמַעְלָן. כְּהָדָא בִּימֵי רִבִּי יוּדָה בֶּן פָּזִי הֲוָה רִיבְעָה בְבֵי מִדְרָשָׁא. וְהָוֹון פְּרָסִין קִילְעִיהּ מֵאִתְמוֹל בְּאַרְבַּע אַמּוֹת וּלְמָחָר הֲווֹ פָּרְסִין כּוּלְּהוֹן. סָבְרוּן מֵימָר. מִדְּבָרֵי רִבִּי יוּדָה בֶּן פָּזִי. בְּדָקוּן וְאַשְׁכְּחוּן דְּלָאוּ מִדַּעַת רִבִּי יוּדָה בֶּן פָּזִי עַד שֶׁיִּפְרוֹס רוּבָּן. רִבִּי חִייָה בְשֵׁם רִבִּי יוֹחָנָן. הַנּוֹטֵעַ אוֹהָלִין בַּשַּׁבָּת חַיָּיב מִשּׁוּם בּוֹנֶה. אָמַר רִבִּי זְעִירָא. אֵינוֹ אֶלָּא כְפוֹרְסָן וּמְקַפְּלָן בַּשַּׁבָּת. רִבִּי בָּא בַּר כֹּהֵן בָּעָא קוֹמֵי רִבִּי יוֹסֵי. הָהֵן כִּילָה דְּעַל אָרוֹנָא מָהוּ. אָמַר לֵיהּ. כֵּיוָן דְּהִיא פְרוּסָה מֵאִתְמוֹל נַעֲשָׂה כְפוֹתֵחַ וְנוֹעֵל בַּשַּׁבָּת.

1 שיטתיה E | שטתיה   שמכשירה E | שהוא מכשירה   כאן E | כן   2 חיננא E | חננה   אתיא E | איתיה   אליעזר E | ליעזר   יהודה E | יודה   3 יהודה E | יודה   המכשיר E | מי שהוא מכשיר   4 כהדא E | כהדה   בימי ר' E | ביומוי דר'   בן E | בר   רבעה E | דבעה קילעיה E | קילעיא   5 מאתמול E | מן איתמל   הוו E | הוון   סברון E | סבריו   מדברי E | מן דעתיה   דר' E | בן   E | בר   6 מדעת E | מן דעתיה ר' E | דר'   7 אוהלין E | אהלין   זעירא E | זעירה   8 כהן E | כוהן   מהו E | מה הוא   כיון E | מכיון   9 מאתמול E | מן איתמל

The argument of Rebbi Eliezer seems inverted. Since there[32], where he qualifies it as an implement, you say that it is permitted, here, where he does not qualify it as an implement, not so much more? Rebbi Ḥinena said, Rebbi Eliezer parallels Rebbi Jehudah[33], as it was stated in the name of Rebbi Jehudah: Also they permitted preparations for making food[34].

Rebbi Aḥa in the name of Rebbi Abba: Following him who permits, only from above[35]. As the following: In the days of Rebbi Jehudah ben Pazi there was a festive meal[36] in the House of Study. They spread a canopy the day before over four cubits[37]; the next day they were extending it over everything. They were of the opinion that this followed the words of Rebbi Jehudah ben Pazi. They investigated and found that it was not according to Rebbi Jehudah ben Pazi's opinion unless it was spread over most of it[38].

Rebbi Ḥiyya in the name of Rebbi Joḥanan: He who sets up tents on the Sabbath is liable because of building[39]. Rebbi Ze'ira said, he only is spreading and folding it on the Sabbath. Rebbi Abba bar Cohen asked before Rebbi Yose, what is the rule for a spread over a chest? He told him, since it was spread the day before he is like one who unlocks and locks on the Sabbath.

32 It seems that this argument should be placed in Chapter 17 since "there" refers to the Mishnah 20:1 here, but "here" refers to Mishnah 17:7. Since it was determined at the end of the preceding paragraph that R. Eliezer refers to a new sieve, which is used for the first time on the holiday, he should be more restrictive in this case than with regard to the closure of the window which was tied there from before the holiday.

33 Since R. Jehudah was the student of his father R. Ilai who had been R. Eliezer's student, the chronologically correct statement would be that R. Jehudah formulated the teachings of R. Eliezer. Babli 137b.

34 Since Mishnah 20:1 speaks about preparation of food, the disagreement between R. Eliezer and the Sages has nothing to do with the rules of the Sabbath; it is about the rules of the holiday, whether the biblical permission to prepare food is to be interpreted strictly as allowing only preparation of food or also preparations of utensils used for the preparation of food.

35 This refers back to the Tosephta quoted in the preceding section. It is forbidden to erect a tent, but on a holiday it is permitted to lower the cover but not to spread it higher; cf. Babli *Eruvin* 101a.

36 Aramaic רבע corresponds to Hebrew רבץ "to lie down comfortably"; a dinner served on couches, not in a house but under a portico, which needs a shield from the sun.

37 4 cubits wide over the portico.

38 Then it is no longer considered making a tent but rather extending a cover.

39 Babli 138a.

(17c line 43) רִבִּי זְעִירָה רַב חִייָה בַּר אַשִׁי בְּשֵׁם שְׁמוּאֵל. הַמְשַׁמֵּר חַיָּיב מִשּׁוּם בּוֹרֵר. אָמַר רִבִּי זְעִירָא. לֹא מִסְתַּבְּרָא דְלֹא מִשּׁוּם מְרַקֵּיד. רִבִּי יוֹסֵי וְרִבִּי יוֹנָה תְּרֵיהוֹן אָמְרִין. בְּקַדְמִיתָא הֲוֵינָן אָמְרִין. יָאוּת אָמַר רִבִּי זְעִירָא. וּמַה הַמְרַקֵּד קָמַח לְמַטָּן וְסוֹלֶת לְמַעֲלָן. אַף הַמְשַׁמֵּר יֵין לְמַטָּן וּשְׁמָרִים לְמַעֲלָן. וְלֹא הֲוֵינָן אָמְרִין כְּלוּם. לָמָּה. שֶׁהוּתַר מִכְּלַל בְּרֵירָה הוּתַּר מִכְּלַל שִׁימוּר. הוּתַּר מִכְּלַל בְּרֵירָה בּוֹרֵר כְּדַרְכּוֹ בְּחֵיקוֹ וּבְתַמְחוּי. הוּתַּר מִכְּלַל שִׁימוּר נוֹתְנִין לַתְּלוּיָה בְּיוֹם טוֹב: וְלֹא הוּתָּר מִכְּלַל הַרְקָדָה. דָּמַר רִבִּי חֲנִינָה בְּרוֹקָה בְּשֵׁם רַב יְהוּדָה. אֵין שׁוֹנִין אֶת הַקֶּמַח אֲבָל מַרְקִידִין לַאֲחוֹרֵי נָפָה. אֵין תֵּימַר. מִשּׁוּם מְרַקֵּיד הוּא. יְהֵא אָסוּר. אָמַר רִבִּי יוֹסֵה בֵּירִבִּי בּוּן. וּדְלֹא כְרִבִּי יוּדָה. דְּתַנֵּי בְשֵׁם רִבִּי יוּדָה. אַף מַכְשִׁירֵי אוֹכֶל נֶפֶשׁ הִתִּירוּ. בְּעַיָּיא דָא מִילְּתָא. מָהוּ לְשַׁנּוֹת קֶמַח לַאֲחוֹרֵי הַנָּפָה כְּרַבָּנָן.

⁴⁰Rebbi Ze'ira, Rav Hiyya bar Ashi in the name of Samuel: One who filters yeast is liable because of selecting. Rebbi Ze'ira said, it is more reasonable that it should be because of sifting. Rebbi Yose and Rebbi Jonah both said, at the start we were saying that Rebbi Ze'ira said it correctly, since as in sifting the flour is below and the farina on top, so in filtering wine the wine as at the bottom and the yeast on top; but we were not saying anything. Why? Because the category of selecting was permitted, the category of filtering was permitted. The category of selecting was permitted: "he selects normally, on his chest, or from a pot". ⁴¹Also the category of filtering was permitted, "on a holiday one puts into one which was hanging". But the category of sifting was not permitted. As Rebbi Hanina Beroqa said in the name of Rav Jehudah, One does not re-sift the flour but one may pass it through the back of the sieve. If you say it is because of sifting, it should be forbidden. Rebbi Yose ben Rebbi Abun said, it does not follow Rebbi Jehudah, for it was stated in the name of Rebbi Jehudah, they also permitted preparations for making food. There is a question about the following: following the rabbis, may one re-sift the flour through the back of the sieve?

40	From Chapter 7, Notes 335-342.	in Chapter 7); it is also missing in the ms.
41	This sentence is missing in E (as noted	text here but was added by the corrector.

(17c line 55) נוֹתְנִין מַיִם עַל גַּבֵּי שְׁמָרִים כו׳. רִבִּי בָּא בְשֵׁם רַב יְהוּדָה בְשֵׁם רַב. וּבִלְבַד שֶׁלֹּא יַעֲשֶׂה אוֹתָהּ כְּמִין חֵיק. בְּעָיָא דָא מִילְתָא. מָהוּ לְכַפּוֹתָן וְנַעֲשִׂית חֵיק מֵאֵילֶיהָ. אָמַר רִבִּי מַתַּנְיָה. מַטָּה אוֹתָהּ עַל צִידָהּ וּבִלְבַד שֶׁלֹּא יַעֲשֶׂה בַשַּׁבָּת כְּשֶׁעוֹשֶׂה בַחוֹל.

1 נותנין מים על גבי שמרים וכו' E | בשם ⁴²בשם E | - E | בעייא 2 | בעייה E | מהו E | מהוא לכפותן E לכפותה והיא נעשית E | נעשה 3 | כשעושה E | כדרך שהוא עושה

"One may add water to the yeast," etc. Rebbi Abba in the name of Rebbi Jehudah in the name of Rav: Only he should not make it like a bosom⁴³. There is a question about the following: May one turn it over that the bosom is made by itself? Rebbi Mattaniah said, one may turn it on its side on condition not to do it on the Sabbath the way he does it on a weekday.

42	The quote from Mishnah 2 is a corrector's addition. It is missing in E	where בשם ר׳ בא is a scribal error for ר׳ בא בשם.

43 One should be careful not to make a hollow in order not to follow a weekday routine (Babli 139b, Rashi's explanation).

(17c line 58) כֵּינִי מַתְנִיתָהּ. מְפָרְדִין בֵּיצָה בִּמְסַנֶּנֶת שֶׁלְחַרְדָּל. גּוּשׁ שֶׁלְחַרְדָּל. רִבִּי יוֹסֵי בְּשֵׁם רִבִּי אֶלְעָזָר. מְמָעֵךְ בְּיָד אֲבָל לֹא בִכְלִי. רִבִּי יַעֲקֹב בַּר אָחָא רִבִּי יוֹחָנָן בְּשֵׁם רִבִּי יַנַּאי. מְמָעֵךְ בֵּין בְּיָד בֵּין בִּכְלִי. אָמַר לוֹ רִבִּי יוֹחָנָן. וַהֲלֹא הַכְּלָבִים אֵין עוֹשִׂין אוֹתָהּ כֵּן. רִבִּי חִזְקִיָּה רִבִּי אַבָּהוּ בְּשֵׁם רִבִּי יוֹחָנָן. מְמָעֵךְ בֵּין בְּיָד בֵּין בִּכְלִי.

1 מפרדין E | במפרכת⁹ יוסי E | יוסה   2 אחא E | אידי   3 לו E | ליה אין E | אינו אותה E | - E | ר' E | אתא אבהו E | אבהוא

וְעוֹשִׂין יֵינוֹמֵילִין בַּשַּׁבָּת. רִבִּי יָסָא בְשֵׁם רִבִּי יוֹחָנָן. יַיִן וּדְבַשׁ וּפִילְפָּלִין.

1 יינומילין E | עמילין   יסא E | יסה   ופילפלין E | ופלפלין

So is the Mishnah: One separates[44] an egg in the sieve of mustard seed. A lump of mustard seed? Rebbi Yose in the name of Rebbi Eleazar, one squeezes by hand but not with a tool. Rebbi Jacob bar Aḥa, Rebbi Joḥanan in the name of Rebbi Yannai: One may squeeze both by hand and with a tool. Rebbi Joḥanan objected to him, do not the dogs make it so[45]? [There came][46] Rebbi Ḥizqiah, Rebbi Abbahu in the name of Rebbi Joḥanan: One may squeeze both by hand and with a tool.

"And one makes honey-wine on the Sabbath." Rebbi Yasa in the name of Rebbi Joḥanan: Wine and honey and pepper[47].

44 Separating the egg white from the yolk. As the Babli explains (140a, first line), since both egg white and yolk are consumed, this separation is not separating food from chaff and therefore not a derivative of selecting, which is forbidden on the Sabbath.

45 The original text of the ms. was: Do not the dogs eat it? The Babli 140a calls raw mustard seed "donkey feed". According to this argument one should prefer a tool on the Sabbath, so as not to act in a weekday manner.

46 Added from E.

47 Babli 140a.

(17c line 64) אָמַר רִבִּי מָנָא. כֵּינִי מַתְנִיתָהּ. אֲבָל נוֹתְנָהּ לְפָנָיו לְתוֹךְ הַחוֹמֶץ. רַב הוּנָא אָמַר. לֹא שָׁנוּ אֶלָּא בְּפוֹשְׁרִין. הָא בְצוֹנֵין מוּתָּר. רִבִּי יוֹחָנָן בְּשֵׁם רִבִּי יַנַּאי. אֲפִילוּ בְצוֹנִין אָסוּר. אָמַר לוֹ רִבִּי יוֹחָנָן. וַהֲלֹא לֹא שָׁנוּ אֶלָּא בְּפוֹשְׁרִין. אֶלָּא עַל חַם יָנֵעוּנוּ.

1 הונא E | חונא   2 ינאי E | יניי   בצונין E | בצון   3 אלא E | אמ' ליה

רַב הוּנָא אָמַר. מֵי חִילְתִּית מוּתָּר לִשְׁתּוֹתָהּ בַּשַּׁבָּת. שְׁמוּאֵל אָמַר. חִילְתִּית עַצְמָהּ מַיֲכַל בְּרִיאִים (הוּא) [הִיא]. רַב הוּנָא אָמַר. מָאן דַּאֲכַל מַתְקַל זוּזָא מִינֵּיהּ מִסְתַּכֵּן וְעוֹרוֹ נֶחֱלָץ. רִבִּי בָּא אֲכַל מַתְקַל זוּזָא מִינָהּ וּפְרַשׁ לְנַהֲרָא.

1 הונא E | חונא לשתותה E | לשתותו   2 הונא E | חונא   3 ופרש לנהרא E | ופירש לנהרה

Rebbi Mana said, so is the Mishnah: But one may put it in vinegar in his presence[48]. Rav Huna said, they taught only lukewarm water; therefore it is permitted in cold water. Rebbi Joḥanan in the name of Rebbi Yannai, even in cold water it is forbidden[49]. Rebbi Joḥanan said to him, did they not teach only lukewarm water? (But) {He said to him][50], did we exert ourselves for nothing[51]

Rav Huna said, one is permitted to drink *asa foetida* water on the Sabbath. Samuel said, *asa foetida* in itself is healthy persons' food[52]. Rav Huna said, he who eats the weight of a *zuz*[53] from it is in danger and his skin is loosened. Rebbi Abba ate the weight of a *zuz* from it and jumped in the river[54].

48   This refers to Mishnah 3. In no case may one soak for an extended period; even into vinegar one may put *asa foetida* only for immediate use.
49   Babli 140a.
50   The text of E [in brackets] is preferable to the text of the Leiden ms. (in parentheses).
51   As the Babli explains, the mention of lukewarm water only is R. Yose (ben Halafta's) opinion which in this case is a minority opinion, rather than practice.
52   Therefore the water is not qualified as exclusively used as medicine and as not forbidden on the Sabbath.
53   Half a *sheqel*, in talmudic times identified with the Roman *denarius*, approximately 3.6 g.
54   To counteract the sedative effect of the drug.

(17c line 70) אֵין שׁוֹרִין אֶת הַכַּרְשִׁינִין. מִשּׁוּם בּוֹרֵר. וְאֵין שָׁפִין אוֹתָן. מִשּׁוּם דָּשׁ. אֵין כּוֹבְרִין אֶת הַתֶּבֶן בַּכְּבָרָה וְלֹא יִתְּנֶנָּה בְּמָקוֹם גָּבוֹהַּ בִּשְׁבִיל שֶׁיֵּרֵד הַמּוֹץ. מִשּׁוּם מְרַקֵּיד.

1 אין E | תני אין   משום E | משם   2 במקום E | על גבי מקום   משום E | משם

[It was stated:][55] "One does not soak vetch," because of selecting; "and does not smooth it," because of threshing. "One does not shake straw in a sieve and does not expose it on an elevated place to cause the chaff to fall," because of sifting[56].

55   Added from E.
56   Since these activities can be classified under some of the forbidden 39 categories of work, the prohibitions are biblical.

(17c line 73) גּוֹרְפִין מִלְּפְנֵי הַפְּטָם וכו'. מִפְּנֵי שֶׁהַפְּטָם מוֹתִיר הָרֹעִי אוֹכֵל. בְּעָיָא דָא מִילְתָא. מָהוּ לִיטוֹל מִלְּפְנֵי בְהֵמָה זוֹ וְלִיתֵּן לִפְנֵי בְהֵמָה זוֹ. וְלֹא מַתְנִיתָהּ הִיא. נוֹטְלִין מִלְּפְנֵי בְהֵמָה זוֹ וְנוֹתְנִין לִפְנֵי בְהֵמָה זוֹ בַּשַּׁבָּת: מַתְנִיתָהּ מִין בְּמִינוֹ. צְרִיכָה לֵיהּ מִין בְּשֶׁאֵינוֹ מִינוֹ. תַּנֵּי. נוֹטֵל אָדָם מִלְּפְנֵי הַחֲמוֹר וְנוֹתֵן לִפְנֵי פָרָה. מִלְּפְנֵי בְהֵמָה שֶׁפִּיהָ רַע וְנוֹתֵן לִפְנֵי בְהֵמָה שֶׁפִּיהָ יָפָה.

1 גורפין מלפני הפטם וכו'. - E | מפני E | מה E | הרעי E | הריעי בעיא E | ב[עייה   The remainder of the paragraph is not legible.

"One cleans up after an animal to be fattened," etc.[57] Because what the animal to be fattened leaves over, the grazing one eats[58]. The following is in question: May one take from before one animal and give it before another animal? Is that not the Mishnah, "one may take from before one animal and put it before another on the Sabbath"? The Mishnah is about the same kind; what he asks is about another kind. It was stated, a person may take from before a donkey and put before a cow; from before an animal whose mouth is repelling to an animal whose mouth is nice[59].

57 Addition of the corrector in the ms.; missing in E.
58 Explanation of *Ritba* (ed. M. Goldstein, Jerusalem 1990, col. 915). Since it remains animal feed it cannot become *muqseh*.
59 In this form the second statement contradicts the Babli 140b. Since also it contradicts the first statement, probably one should switch the terms "repelling" and "nice" (it is not impossible that this was E's reading.) As the Babli explains, a donkey eats in a orderly manner, therefore food taken from before the donkey and put before a cow will be eaten. But cattle eat in a very disorderly way from a trough; the cow's spittle in the grain will make it repellent to a donkey. Since remainders of cow feed are not donkey feed, one may not take food from before a cow and put it before a donkey.

(17d line 1) הַקַּשׁ שֶׁעַל הַמִּטָּה. מַתְנִיתָהּ בְּשֶׁלֹּא יָשַׁן עָלָיו מֵאֶתְמוֹל. אֲבָל אִם יָשַׁן עָלָיו מֵאֶתְמוֹל כְּגוּפוֹ הִיא. אָמַר רִבִּי יַעֲקֹב בַּר אִידִי. רִאשׁוֹנִים הָיוּ שׁוֹאֲלִין. מָהוּ שֶׁיְּעַנְעֶנּוּ דֶּרֶךְ אֲצִילֵי יָדָיו. אָמַר רִבִּי יַנַּאי. קֵרוֹחַ קְרִיחָה קִפּוּחַ קַפִּיחָה שָׂפוֹד צְנִינִים עַל מָאן דְעָדֵי לֵיהּ. נָפַל בֵּיתֵיהּ עַל מָאן דְרוֵיהּ עֲלֵיהּ. תַּנֵּי רִבִּי חִייָה. הָדֵין דִּין לְעָנִי.

2 היא E | הוא אידי E | אדי מהו E | מהוא שיענענו E | שיעננו   3 ינאי E | יניי דעדי E | דערי ביתיה | E ביתיה   4 דרויה E | דרייה הדין דין E | הדן דן

וְהָתַנֵּי. מוֹדִין חֲכָמִים לְרִבִּי מֵאִיר בְּחוּתָמוֹת שֶׁבַּקַּרְקַע שֶׁמְּפַקְפְּקִין וּמַפְקִיעִין וּמַתִּירִין וְחוֹתְכִין. בַּשַּׁבָּת מְפַקְפְּקִין אֲבָל לֹא מַפְקִיעִין וְלֹא מַתִּירִין וְלֹא חוֹתְכִין. בְּכֵלִים. בַּשַּׁבָּת מוּתָּר וְאֵין צוֹרֶךְ בְּיוֹם טוֹב. מַכְבֵּשׁ אָמְרָה. הָדָא אָמְרָה. עָשׂוּ אוֹתוֹ כְּקַרְקַע. אָמַר רִבִּי יוֹסֵי. מַתְנִיתָהּ אָמְרָה כֵן. שֶׁל כּוֹבָסִין לֹא יִגַּע בּוֹ.

1 וחתני | E והא תני | 2 בכלים | E ובכלים | 3 צורך | E צריך לומר הדא | E הדה יוסי | E - | 4 של כובסין | E שלן(כ]בוסין

"Straw on a bed." Our Mishnah: if he did not sleep on it yesterday; but if he slept on it yesterday it is like its body[60]. Rebbi Jacob bar Idi said, the earlier generations were asking, may he stir it by his fingertips[61]? Rebbi Yannai said, the balding is bald, the deprived is deprived, pour cold water on the shivering[63], the house fell on the dweller in it[64]. Rebbi Ḥiyya stated, this is the rule for the poor man[65].

But was it not stated, "the Sages agree with Rebbi Meïr about seals in the ground that one pushes aside, and removes, and unties, and cuts. On the Sabbath one pushes aside but one does not remove nor untie nor cut. For implements on the Sabbath it is permitted; it is not necessary [to mention][67] on a holiday."[68]. This implies that they treated the clothes press as if it were in the ground. Rebbi Yose said, the Mishnah said so, "a washer's one may not be touched."

60 It is part of the bed which as an implement may be moved. Tosephta 15:5 (ed. Liebermann). One also could translate "it is like his (own) body".

61 That it may be moved, only not in the way this is done on weekdays. No answer is given.

63 Translation of the text of E. The word in the Leiden ms. is incomprehensible.

64 This seems to be a popular saying that one misfortune produces another. Since the Mishnah declares difficulties only for the poor person who has no pillow on his bed, the poor is compared to the balding who immediately is characterized as bald, one discriminated against in one matter who is discriminated against in everything, the person shivering in the cold on whom cold water is poured, or the dweller in a collapsing house.

65 But the rich person can make his bed at will.

66 Seals on storage of produce in the ground. On the Sabbath one may not change anything there since it would be building or tearing down. On a holiday it is permitted to reach the food which is stored there. Babli *Besah* 31b, Tosephta *Besah* 3:12; cf. Chapter 15, Notes 22-24.

67 Added from E.

68 Since a clothes press is an implement it should be possible to move it on the Sabbath.

נוטל פרק עשרים ואחד

Note in the *editio princeps*:

באלו הארבעה פרקים שלפנינו לא מצאנו להם ברייתות בארבעה העתקות ישנות שהיו לפנינו

For the remaining four Chapter we did not find *beraitot* in the four old copies at our disposal.

Note in Manuscript E:

חסרה מסכתא זו ארבעה פר[קים]

This Tractate is missing four Chapters.

משנה א: נוֹטֵל אָדָם אֶת בְּנוֹ וְהָאֶבֶן בְּיָדוֹ כַּלְכָּלָה וְהָאֶבֶן בְּתוֹכָהּ. מְטַלְטְלִין תְּרוּמָה טְמֵאָה עִם הַטְּהוֹרָה וְעִם הַחֻלִּין. רַבִּי יְהוּדָה אוֹמֵר אַף מַעֲלִין אֶת הַמְדוּמָע בְּאֶחָד וּמֵאָה:

Mishnah 1: A person may lift his son with a stone in the latter's hand, or a basket with a stone in it[1]. One may move impure heave together with pure one or with profane food. Rebbi Jehudah says, one also may lift *demaʿ* by 101[2].

משנה ב: הָאֶבֶן שֶׁעַל פִּי הֶחָבִית מַטָּהּ עַל צִדָּהּ וְהִיא נוֹפֶלֶת. הָיְתָה בֵּין הֶחָבִיּוֹת מַגְבִּיהָהּ וּמַטָּהּ עַל צִדָּהּ וְהִיא נוֹפֶלֶת. מָעוֹת שֶׁעַל הַכַּר נוֹעֵר אֶת הַכַּר וְהֵן נוֹפְלוֹת. הָיְתָה עָלֶיהָ לִשְׁלֶשֶׁת מְקַנְּחָהּ בִּסְמַרְטוּט. הָיְתָה שֶׁל עוֹר נוֹתְנִין עָלֶיהָ מַיִם עַד שֶׁתִּיכָלֶה:

Mishnah 2: An amphora covered by a stone: one tilts it and the stone falls down[3]. If it was between amphoras one lifts it[4], tilts it and the stone falls down. Coins on a pillow: one shakes the pillow and they fall down. If chicken droppings were on it, one cleans it with a rag[5]. If it was of leather, one pours water on it[6] until it disappears.

משנה ג בֵּית הִלֵּל אוֹמְרִים מַעֲבִירִין מֵעַל הַשֻּׁלְחָן עֲצָמוֹת וּקְלִיפִּין וּבֵית שַׁמַּאי אוֹמְרִים מְסַלֵּק אֶת הַטַּבְלָה כֻּלָּהּ וְנוֹעֲרָהּ. מַעֲבִירִין מֵעַל הַשֻּׁלְחָן פֵּירוּרִין פָּחוֹת מִכַּזַּיִת. שִׁיעַר שֶׁל אֲפוּנִים וְשֶׁל עֲדָשִׁים מִפְּנֵי שֶׁהוּא מַאֲכַל בְּהֵמָה סְפוֹג אִם יֵשׁ לוֹ עוֹר בֵּית אֲחִיזָה מְקַנְּחִין בּוֹ. וְאִם לָאו אֵין מְקַנְּחִין בּוֹ. וַחֲכָמִים אוֹמְרִים בֵּין כָּךְ וּבֵין כָּךְ נִיטָּל בַּשַּׁבָּת וְאֵינוֹ מְקַבֵּל טוּמְאָה:

Mishnah 3: The House of Hillel say, one removes from the table bones and shells[7], but the House of Shammai say, one removes the entire table and shakes it[8]. One removes from the table crumbs less than olive size, hair[9] of chick-peas and lentils, since it is animal feed. One cleans with a sponge[10] if it has a leather handle; otherwise one does not clean with it[11]. The Sages say in any case it may be taken on the Sabbath[12] and is impervious to impurity[13].

1   It is possible to carry *muqseh* items with other things which may be moved on the Sabbath. Chapter 3, Note 219; Chapter 17, Note 67.

2   Profane food mixed with less than 1% of heave becomes permitted to lay people if a replacement heave is taken from it; cf. *Terumah* 4:7, *Orlah* 2:1.

3   Since the amphora may be moved with the stone but the stone by itself is *muqseh*, the stone cannot be lifted from the mouth of the amphora but must be removed by moving the amphora. The same argument applies to coins on a pillow.

4   One lifts the entire amphora and puts it down at a place where it can be tilted.

5   Pouring water on textiles is forbidden as washing; therefore only rubbing off dry is possible on the Sabbath.

6   While washing leather is also forbidden as washing, simply pouring water on it without rubbing is not considered washing and is permitted.

7   These belong to the garbage and as such should be *muqseh*. The House of Hillel follow R. Simeon who restricts the notion of *muqseh* to things not usable at the start of the Sabbath. (The Mishnah in the Babli switches the statement of the Houses of Hillel and Shammai, but this is immediately corrected in the Babli's Halakhah.)

8   Latin *tabula, -ae, f.* Since the table (or the table top if not attached to the legs) may be moved on the Sabbath, the statement of the House of Shammai follows the rule established in Mishnah 1.

9   The shell.

10   Greek σπόγγος, ὁ.

11   Since squeezing water out of the sponge would be biblically forbidden, one may clean the table only with a sponge that has a handle and was not wetted, when it is presumed that cleansing without squeezing is possible.

12   Even if it has no handle it is an implement and can be moved on the Sabbath.

13   The sponge is neither wood, nor metal, nor earthenware, nor textile, and therefore not of material susceptible to impurity.

חבית פרק עשרים ושנים

משנה א חָבִית שֶׁנִּשְׁבְּרָה מַצִּילִין מִמֶּנָּה מְזוֹן שָׁלֹשׁ סְעֻדּוֹת וְאוֹמֵר לַאֲחֵרִים בּוֹאוּ וְהַצִּילוּ לָכֶם וּבִלְבַד שֶׁלֹּא יִסְפֹּג. אֵין סוֹחֲטִין אֶת הַפֵּרוֹת לְהוֹצִיא מֵהֶן מַשְׁקִין וְאִם יָצְאוּ מֵעַצְמָן אֲסוּרִין. רַבִּי יְהוּדָה אוֹמֵר אִם לְאוֹכְלִין הַיּוֹצֵא מֵהֶן מֻתָּר. וְאִם לְמַשְׁקִין הַיּוֹצֵא מֵהֶן אָסוּר. חַלּוֹת דְּבַשׁ שֶׁרִסְּקָן מֵעֶרֶב שַׁבָּת יָצְאוּ מֵעַצְמָן אֲסוּרִין וְרַבִּי אֱלִיעֶזֶר מַתִּיר:

Mishnah 1: If an amphora broke, one saves from it food for three meals and tells others: come and save for yourselves[1]; only one may not absorb it in a sponge[2]. One does not squeeze fruits to extract their juice[3] and if it seeped out by itself it is forbidden. Rebbi Jehudah says, if they are solid food, what comes from them is permitted[4], but if they are for drinks, what comes from them is forbidden. What flows from itself from honeycombs which he crushed on Friday is forbidden, but Rebbi Eliezer permits it[5].

משנה ב כָּל־שֶׁבָּא בְחַמִּין מֵעֶרֶב הַשַּׁבָּת שׁוֹרִין אוֹתוֹ בְּחַמִּין בַּשַּׁבָּת. וְכָל־שֶׁלֹּא בָא בְחַמִּין מֵעֶרֶב שַׁבָּת מְדִיחִין אוֹתוֹ בְּחַמִּין בַּשַּׁבָּת חוּץ מִן הַמָּלִיחַ הַיָּשָׁן וְדָגִים מְלוּחִים קְטַנִּים וְקוּלְיָס הָאִסְפָּנִין שֶׁהֲדָחָתָן זוֹ הִיא גְּמַר מְלַאכְתָּן:

Mishnah 2: Everything which was in hot water[6] on Friday one soaks[7] in hot water on the Sabbath but anything which was not in hot water on Friday one rinses[7] in hot water on the Sabbath except for old salted fish and anchovies in salt and Spanish mackerel[8], for which rinsing is the end of preparation[9].

משנה ג שׁוֹבֵר אָדָם אֶת הֶחָבִית לֶאֱכוֹל מִמֶּנָּה גְּרוֹגָרוֹת וּבִלְבַד שֶׁלֹּא יִתְכַּוֵּן לַעֲשׂוֹתָהּ כֶּלִי. אֵין נוֹקְבִין מְגוּפָה שֶׁל חָבִית דִּבְרֵי רַבִּי יְהוּדָה. רַבִּי יוֹסֵי מַתִּיר. לֹא יִקְּבֶנָּה מִצִּדָּהּ וְאִם הָיְתָה נְקוּבָה לֹא יִתֵּן עָלֶיהָ שַׁעֲוָה מִפְּנֵי שֶׁהוּא מְמָרֵחַ. אָמַר רַבִּי יְהוּדָה מַעֲשֶׂה בָא לִפְנֵי רַבָּן יוֹחָנָן בֶּן זַכַּאי בַּעֲרָב וְאָמַר חוֹשֵׁשׁ אֲנִי לוֹ מֵחַטָּאת:

Mishnah 3: A person may break open an amphora[10] to eat dried figs from it; only he may not intend to make it into a vessel. One does not drill a hole in the plug of an amphora, the words of Rebbi Jehudah[11], but Rebbi Yose permits. One may not drill a hole in its[12] side, and if it has a hole one may not close it with wax because he smears[13]. Rebbi Jehudah said, a case came before Rabbon Joḥanan ben Zakkai in Arab and he said, I fear that he incurred liability for a purification sacrifice[14].

משנה ד נוֹתְנִין תַּבְשִׁיל לְתוֹךְ הַבּוֹר בִּשְׁבִיל שֶׁיְּהֵא שָׁמוּר וְאֶת הַמַּיִם הַיָּפִים בָּרָעִים בִּשְׁבִיל שֶׁיִּצַּנּוּ וְאֶת הַצּוֹנִין בַּחַמִּין בִּשְׁבִיל שֶׁיֵּחַמּוּ. מִי שֶׁנָּשְׁרוּ כֵלָיו בַּדֶּרֶךְ מְהַלֵּךְ בָּהֶן וְאֵינוֹ חוֹשֵׁשׁ. הִגִּיעַ לֶחָצֵר הַחִיצוֹנָה שׁוֹטְחָן בַּחַמָּה אֲבָל לֹא כְּנֶגֶד הָעָם:

Mishnah 4: One may put food in a cistern for preservation[15], and potable water into bad one to cool, and cold water into hot to warm it. One whose garments became soaked on the road walks in them without worry[16]. If he comes to an outer courtyard he puts them out to dry in the sun[17] but not in public[18].

משנה ה הָרוֹחֵץ בְּמֵי מְעָרָה אוֹ בְמֵי טִיבָּרְיָה מִסְתַּפֵּג אֲפִילוּ בְעֶשֶׂר לוּנְטִיּוֹת וְלֹא יְבִיאֵם בְּיָדוֹ. אֲבָל עֲשָׂרָה בְנֵי אָדָם מִסְתַּפְּגִין בְּלוּנְטִית אַחַת פְּנֵיהֶן יְדֵיהֶן וְרַגְלֵיהֶן וּמְבִיאִין אוֹתוֹ בְּיָדָם:

Mishnah 5: One who bathes in the waters of a cave or in the waters of Tiberias dries himself even with ten towels[19] but may not bring them in his hand[20]. But ten people dry with one towel their faces, and their hands, and their feet, and bring it in their hands[21].

משנה ו סָכִין וּמְמַשְׁמְשִׁין בִּבְנֵי מֵעַיִם אֲבָל לֹא מִתְעַמְּלִין וְלֹא מִתְגָּרְדִין. אֵין יוֹרְדִין לְפִילוֹמָא. וְאֵין עוֹשִׂין אַפּוּקְטְפִיזִין בַּשַּׁבָּת וְאֵין מְעַצְּבִין אֶת הַקָּטָן וְלֹא מַחֲזִירִין אֶת הַשֶּׁבֶר. מִי שֶׁנִּפְרְקָה יָדוֹ אוֹ רַגְלוֹ לֹא יִטְרְפֵם בְּצוֹנֵן אֲבָל רוֹחֵץ הוּא כְדַרְכּוֹ וְאִם נִתְרַפָּא נִתְרַפָּא:

Mishnah 6: One anoints and massages the belly but one does not exercise or scratch[22]. One does not go to a mud-bath[23], nor does one make an emetic[24] on the Sabbath, nor does one stretch a baby, nor set a fracture. If somebody's hand or foot became dislocated he cannot force it back with cold water but he may wash in his usual way and if this healed him, he was healed.

1   Cf. Mishnah 16:3. The object is an amphora filled with wine or olive oil.

2   In itself this is not forbidden, but it is rabinically prohibited since we are afraid that he will squeeze the sponge on the Sabbath to recoup his wine.

3   This is forbidden under the category of threshing.

4   If the fruit is to be eaten, the juice which seeps from it is permitted since there is no reason rabbinically to forbid since nobody will want to squeeze it. But for fruits used to make juice the seepage is rabbinically forbidden.

5   He does not suspect people to crush honeycombs on the Sabbath.

6   Cooked or soaked in hot water.

7   Soaking is for an extended period, rinsing is short term.

8   Greek κολίας, -ου, τό.

9   Therefore this is biblically forbidden as "hitting with a hammer".

10   If the amphora is tightly closed with clay that sticks to its walls, one may open it by damaging the vessel even though the intent is for a positive action.

11   He insists that the only way is to remove the entire cover, not to drill a hole into it.

12   The cover's side.

13   This is forbidden under the header "rubbing clean", cf. Chapter 7, Note 5.

14   Cf. Chapter 16, Notes 133-137.

15   In all cases mentioned in this sentence, the materials to be cooled or warmed are in a separate container.

16   The water absorbed by his garments are part of the garment, not a load.

17   Even though drying by artificial means is forbidden.

18   That it should not look as if he washed on the Sabbath.

19   Latin *linteum, -i, n.,* "linen" (*scil.* cloth".

20   Even at a place where carrying is permitted, since one suspects that he will squeeze the water out of his towel.

21   If carrying is permitted at the place, a group may bring a single towel since they are many and can check on one another.

22   The latter are exertions inappropriate for the Sabbath.

23   Greek πήλωμα, -ατος, τό, "mud".

24   S. Liebermann (*Tosefta ki-Fshutah Šabbat* p. 279) notes "almost certainly this is ἐπὶ καταφυσᾶν" "to throw up".

שואל פרק עשרים ושלשה

משנה א שׁוֹאֵל אָדָם מֵחֲבֵירוֹ כַּדֵּי יַיִן וְכַדֵּי שֶׁמֶן וּבִלְבָד שֶׁלֹּא יֹאמַר לוֹ הַלְוֵינִי. וְכֵן אִשָּׁה לַחֲבִירְתָּהּ כִּכָּרוֹת וְאִם אֵינוֹ מַאֲמִינוֹ מַנִּיחַ טַלִּיתוֹ אֶצְלוֹ וְעוֹשֶׂה עִמּוֹ חֶשְׁבּוֹן לְאַחַר הַשַּׁבָּת. וְכֵן עֶרֶב פְּסָחִים בִּירוּשָׁלַיִם שֶׁחָל לִהְיוֹת בַּשַּׁבָּת מַנִּיחַ טַלִּיתוֹ אֶצְלוֹ וְאוֹכֵל אֶת פִּסְחוֹ וְעוֹשֶׂה עִמּוֹ חֶשְׁבּוֹן לְאַחַר יוֹם טוֹב:

Mishnah 1: A person may ask from a neighbor wine jugs and oil jugs, only he may not say to him: lend me[1]; and similarly a woman loaves from her neighbor. If that one does not trust him he may leave his toga with him and settle the account after the Sabbath[2]. Similarly, on a Passover eve in Jerusalem which happens on a Sabbath he leaves his toga with him[3], eats his Passover sacrifice, and settles the account after the holiday.

משנה ב מוֹנֶה אָדָם אֶת אוֹרְחָיו וְאֶת פַּרְפְּרוֹתָיו מִפִּיו אֲבָל לֹא מִן הַכְּתָב. מֵפִיס אָדָם עִם בָּנָיו וְעִם בְּנֵי בֵיתוֹ עַל הַשּׁוּלְחָן וּבִלְבַד שֶׁלֹּא יִתְכַּוֵּן לַעֲשׂוֹת מָנָה גְדוֹלָה כְּנֶגֶד קְטַנָּה מִשּׁוּם קוּבְיָא. מְטִילִין חֲלָשִׁין עַל הַקֳּדָשִׁים בְּיוֹם טוֹב אֲבָל לֹא עַל הַמָּנוֹת:

Mishnah 2: A person counts his guests and his desserts orally but not from a written list[4]. A person may make a lottery with his children and his family on the table on condition that he not make portions large or small, because of gambling[5]. One casts lots on *sancta* on the holiday[6] but not on portions[7].

משנה ג לֹא יִשְׂכּוֹר אָדָם פּוֹעֲלִים בַּשַּׁבָּת וְלֹא יֹאמַר אָדָם לַחֲבֵירוֹ לִשְׂכּוֹר לוֹ פּוֹעֲלִים וְאֵין מַחְשִׁיכִין עַל הַתְּחוּם לִשְׂכּוֹר פּוֹעֲלִים וּלְהָבִיא פֵּירוֹת. אֲבָל מַחְשִׁיךְ הוּא לִשְׁמוֹר וּמֵבִיא פֵּירוֹת בְּיָדוֹ. כְּלָל אָמַר אַבָּא שָׁאוּל כָּל־שֶׁאֲנִי זַכַּאי בַּאֲמִירָתוֹ רַשַּׁאי אֲנִי לְהַחְשִׁיךְ עָלָיו:

Mishnah 3: A person may not hire workers on the Sabbath[8] and not say to another to hire workers for him. One does not wait for nightfall at the Sabbath boundary[9] to hire workers and to bring produce, but one may wait for nightfall to watch[10] and to bring produce in his hand[11]. Abba Shaul formulated a principle: For anything which I am permitted to talk about I am permitted to wait for nightfall[12].

משנה ד מַחְשִׁיכִין עַל הַתְּחוּם לְפַקֵּחַ עַל עִיסְקֵי כַלָּה וְעַל עִיסְקֵי הַמֵּת לְהָבִיא לוֹ אָרוֹן וְתַכְרִיכִין. גּוֹי שֶׁהֵבִיא חֲלִילִין בַּשַּׁבָּת לֹא יִסְפּוֹד בָּהֶן יִשְׂרָאֵל אֶלָּא אִם כֵּן בָּאוּ מִמָּקוֹם קָרוֹב. עָשׂוּ לוֹ אָרוֹן וְחָפְרוּ לוֹ קֶבֶר יִקָּבֵר בּוֹ יִשְׂרָאֵל וְאִם בִּשְׁבִיל יִשְׂרָאֵל לֹא יִקָּבֵר בּוֹ עוֹלָמִית:

Mishnah 4: One waits for nightfall at the Sabbath border to oversee preparations for a wedding or preparations for a burial[13], to bring a casket and shrouds. If a Gentile brought fifes on the Sabbath, a Jew should not use them for dirges unless they came from a nearby place[14]. If they made for him[15] a casket and dug him a grave a Jew may be buried in it; but if it was made for a Jew he never should be buried in it.

משנה ח עוֹשִׂין כָּל־צָרְכֵי הַמֵּת סָכִין וּמְדִיחִין אוֹתוֹ וּבִלְבַד שֶׁלֹּא יָזִיז בּוֹ אֵבֶר. שׁוֹמְטִין אֶת הַכַּר מִתַּחְתָּיו וּמַטִּילִין אוֹתוֹ עַל הַחוֹל בִּשְׁבִיל שֶׁיַּמְתִּין. קוֹשְׁרִים אֶת הַלֶּחִי לֹא שֶׁיַּעֲלֶה אֶלָּא שֶׁלֹּא יוֹסִיף. וְכֵן קוֹרָה שֶׁנִּשְׁבְּרָה סוֹמְכִין אוֹתָהּ בְּסַפְסָל אוֹ בַאֲרוּכוֹת הַמִּטָּה לֹא שֶׁתַּעֲלֶה אֶלָּא שֶׁלֹּא תוֹסִיף. אֵין מְאַמְּצִין אֶת הַמֵּת בַּשַּׁבָּת וְלֹא בַחוֹל עִם יְצִיאַת הַנֶּפֶשׁ. וְכָל־הַמְאַמֵּץ עִם יְצִיאַת נֶפֶשׁ הֲרֵי זֶה שׁוֹפֵךְ דָּמִים:

Mishnah 5: One does all that is needed for a corpse[16], one anoints, and rinses, on condition that none of his limbs be moved[17]. One takes away the pillow under him[18] and lays him on sand so he can wait[19]. One ties the jaw, not to lift it but lest it descend. Similarly, if a beam broke one supports it by a bench or the long logs of a bed-frame, not to lift it but lest it descend[20]. One does not close the eyelids of a corpse on the Sabbath, nor on a weekday at the moment of death[21]. Anybody who closes the eyes at the moment of death is spilling blood.

1 Since this is a weekday occupation.
2 Chapter 16, Note 103.
3 The person who is in Jerusalem but failed to buy a Passover lamb before Sabbath may take one from a sheep merchant and settle the account on Monday, after the holiday on Sunday.
4 That he might not take a pencil and make modifications to the list.
5 If the portions are more or less equal, one may make a competition or lottery to determine who gets what; but if the portions are unequal it would become a game of chance forbidden even on weekdays.
6 As described in *Yoma* Chapter 4.
7 Parts from the previous day may not be given away in a competition on the Sabbath.
8 To work for him after the Sabbath. Doing so would violate a prophetic injunction, *Is.* 58:13.
9 To move outside immediately on the first occasion. This is a rabbinic prohibition.

10 To watch over his fields outside the Sabbath boundary since it is permitted to watch over one's property inside the Sabbath boundary on the Sabbath proper.
11 If he waited at the border for a legitimate cause he can bring some produce with him when returning.
12 Anything one may ask another Jew to do for him on the Sabbath he is permitted to wait for at the Sabbath border at the end of the Sabbath.
13 Since organizing either a wedding or a burial are meritorious deeds, one may talk about these to others on the Sabbath and therefore, following Abba Shaul, wait at the Sabbath boundary at the end of the Sabbath.
14 From within the Sabbath boundary.
15 The Gentile.
16 On the Sabbath.
17 Since the corpse is *muqseh*, it may not be moved but can be touched.
18 Since the pillow is an implement, it may be moved under all circumstances.
19 Be cooled to deter decomposition.
20 To avoid its breaking.
21 Since this gives a signal to the dying person that he is considered dead; this may destroy his will to live and shorten his life, even if it is only for a few seconds.

מי שהחשיך פרק עשרים וארבעה

משנה א מִי שֶׁהֶחְשִׁיךְ בַּדֶּרֶךְ נוֹתֵן כִּיסוֹ לַנָּכְרִי וְאִם אֵין עִמּוֹ נָכְרִי מַנִּיחוֹ עַל הַחֲמוֹר. הִגִּיעַ לֶחָצֵר הַחִיצוֹנָה נוֹטֵל אֶת הַכֵּלִים הַנִּיטָּלִין בַּשַּׁבָּת וְשֶׁאֵינָן נִיטָּלִין מַתִּיר אֶת הַחֲבָלִים וְהַשַּׂקִּין נוֹפְלִין.

Mishnah 1: If somebody is caught on the road when it gets dark[1], he gives his wallet to a Non-Jew; if no Non-Jew is with him he puts it on the donkey[2]. If he comes to an outer courtyard[3] he removes the implements which may be moved on the Sabbath. For those which may not be moved he unties the rope and the sacks fall down by themselves.

משנה ב מַתִּירִין פְּקִיעֵי עָמִיר לִפְנֵי בְהֵמָה וּמְפַסְפְּסִים אֶת הַכִּיפִין אֲבָל לֹא אֶת הַזִּירִין. אֵין מְרַסְּקִין לֹא אֶת הַשַּׁחַת וְלֹא אֶת הֶחָרוּבִין לִפְנֵי בְהֵמָה בֵּין דַּקָּה בֵּין גַּסָּה. רַבִּי יְהוּדָה מַתִּיר בֶּחָרוּבִין לַדַּקָּה:

Mishnah 2: One unties bundles of straw for animals and one separates packages but not sheaves. One does not crush green stalks or carob for animals whether small or large; Rebbi Jehudah permits carob for small animals[4].

משנה ג אֵין אוֹבְסִין אֶת הַגָּמָל וְלֹא דוֹרְסִין אֲבָל מַלְעִיטִין. אֵין מַמְרִין אֶת הָעֲגָלִים אֲבָל מַלְעִיטִין אוֹתָן. מְהַלְקְטִין לַתַּרְנְגוֹלִים וְנוֹתְנִין מַיִם עַל גַּבֵּי הַמּוּרְסָן אֲבָל לֹא גוֹבְלָן וְאֵין נוֹתְנִין מַיִם לִפְנֵי דְבוֹרִים וְלִפְנֵי יוֹנִים שֶׁל שׁוֹבָךְ אֲבָל נוֹתְנִין לִפְנֵי אֲוָזִים וְתַרְנְגוֹלִין וְלִפְנֵי יוֹנִים הַיְרוֹדְסִיּוֹת:

Mishnah 3: One does not stuff[5] a camel, nor force-feed[6], but puts food in its mouth[7]. One does not stuff calves but gives food into their mouths. One hand-feeds chickens and adds water to bran but does not give water to bees and pigeons of the dovecote[8], but gives to geese and chicken and for Herodes[9] pigeons.

משנה ד מְחַתְּכִין אֶת הַדִּילוּעִין לִפְנֵי הַבְּהֵמָה וְאֶת הַנְּבֵילָה לִפְנֵי הַכְּלָבִים. רַבִּי יְהוּדָה אוֹמֵר אִם לֹא הָיְתָה נְבֵילָה מֵעֶרֶב שַׁבָּת אֲסוּרָה לְפִי שֶׁאֵינָהּ מִן הַמּוּכָן:

Mishnah 4: One cuts squash for animals and a cadaver for dogs[10]. Rebbi Jehudah says, if it was not a cadaver before the Sabbath it is forbidden since it is not prepared.

משנה ח מְפִירִין נְדָרִים בַּשַׁבָּת וְנִשְׁאָלִין נְדָרִים שֶׁהֵן לְצֹרֶךְ הַשַׁבָּת. פּוֹקְקִין אֶת הַמְּאוֹר וּמוֹדְדִין אֶת הַמַּטְלִית וְאֶת הַמִּקְוָה. מַעֲשֶׂה בִימֵי אָבִיו שֶׁל רִבִּי צָדוֹק וּבִימֵי אַבָּא שָׁאוּל בֶּן בָּטְנִית שֶׁפָּקְקוּ אֶת הַמְּאוֹר בְּטָפִיחַ וְקָשְׁרוּ אֶת הַמַּקֵּידָה בְגֶמִי לֵידַע אִם יֵשׁ בַּגִּגִית פּוֹתֵחַ טֶפַח אִם לָאו. מִדִּבְרֵיהֶן לָמַדְנוּ שֶׁפּוֹקְקִין וּמוֹדְדִין וְקוֹשְׁרִין בַּשַׁבָּת:

Mishnah 5: One dissolves vows on the Sabbath[11] and one may ask about vows[12] if it is a need for the Sabbath. One plugs the skylight and measures a rag[13] and a *miqweh*[14]. It happened in the days of Rebbi Ṣadoq's father and in the days of Abba Shaul ben Botnit, that they plugged the skylight with a jar and[15] tied a dish to bast to know whether a barrel[17] had a hand-breadth width opening or not[17]. From their words we infer that one plugs, and measures, and ties on the Sabbath.

1   Friday evening.
2   He may not increase his donkey's load if a Non-Jew is available since he is responsible for the Sabbath rest of his animal.
3   The first place where his property may be guarded until the end of the Sabbath.
4   Since small animal cannot chew the very hard carob pods, crushing carob for small animals is parallel to opening bundles of hay or straw for cattle.
5   Making it eat more than its need to fatten it; in the case of a camel to prepare it for a trip to the desert where it will be able to survive on minimal rations.
6   Pushing the food down its throat.
7   Without forcing.
8   These are flying larger distances and easily find water by themselves.
9   This translation is very tentative. It is not known which kind of pigeons were kept in cages and therefore had to be fed every day. Maimonides reads רודסיות "from Rhodes" but explains "Herodes". In the Babli one finds הרדסיות, הדרסיות, דורסאית, דורסיות, cf. *Diqdude Soferim Šabbat* p. 380 Note ד.
10   Even if the squash had not been cut from its vine or the animal had not died before the Sabbath.
11   Since the power of the father to dissolve the vows of his underage daughter or the husband to dissolve the vows of his wife ends with sundown of the day on which he is informed.
12   Since the power of a court or of a duly ordained Sage to revoke vows is not limited in time, they may be asked only about vows which interfere with the keeping of the Sabbath.
13   Whether it has the minimal dimensions which make it susceptible to impurity.
14   Whether it contains the required 40

se`ah of water to purify by immersion.

15   Of a house where a corpse was lying in order to allow Cohanim to be on the roof, the skylight had to be closed. If it was built without a shutter, it may be temporarily closed by any object which may be moved on the Sabbath.

16   Maimonides translates "chandelier".

17   The explanation given by the Babli (157a/b) is that there was a corpse in one house, and a window between this and an adjacent house. An open window transmits tent-impurity if it is at least (1 handbreadth)[2]. The window was partially blocked and it was impossible to measure the size of the open hole directly. They tied a dish to a flimsy piece of bast (so the knot should not be permanent), lowered it in front of the hole so a well defined part of it covered the hole, and then measured that part to know whether impurity was transferred to the second house.

מבוי פרק ראשון עירובין

(fol.18a) **משנה א**: מָבוֹי שֶׁהוּא גָבוֹהַּ מֵעֶשְׂרִים אַמָּה יְמַעֵט. רִבִּי יְהוּדָה אוֹמֵר אֵינוֹ צָרִיךְ. וְהָרָחָב מֵעֶשֶׂר אַמּוֹת יְמַעֵט. אִם יֶשׁ לוֹ צוּרַת פֶּתַח אַף עַל פִּי שֶׁהוּא רָחָב מֵעֶשֶׂר אַמּוֹת אֵינוֹ צָרִיךְ לְמַעֵט:

Mishnah 1: An alley which is higher than twenty cubits should be reduced; Rebbi Jehudah says, this is not necessary[1]. If it is wider than ten cubits it should be reduced[2]; if there is a door-frame even though it is wider than ten cubits there is no need to reduce[3].

משנה ב: הָכְשֵׁר הַמָּבוֹי בֵּית שַׁמַּאי אוֹמְרִין לֶחִי וְקוֹרָה. וּבֵית הִלֵּל אוֹמְרִין אוֹ לֶחִי אוֹ קוֹרָה. רִבִּי אֱלִיעֶזֶר אוֹמֵר לְחָיַיִם. מִשּׁוּם רִבִּי יִשְׁמָעֵאל אָמַר תַּלְמִיד אֶחָד לִפְנֵי רִבִּי עֲקִיבָה לֹא נֶחְלְקוּ בֵית שַׁמַּאי וּבֵית הִלֵּל עַל מָבוֹי שֶׁהוּא פָחוֹת מֵאַרְבַּע שֶׁהוּא אוֹ בְלֶחִי אוֹ בְקוֹרָה וְעַל מַה נֶחְלְקוּ עַל רוֹחַב מֵאַרְבַּע אַמּוֹת וְעַד עֶשֶׂר שֶׁבֵּית שַׁמַּאי אוֹמְרִים לֶחִי וְקוֹרָה וּבֵית הִלֵּל אוֹמְרִין אוֹ לֶחִי אוֹ קוֹרָה. אָמַר רִבִּי עֲקִיבָה עַל זֶה וְעַל זֶה נֶחְלְקוּ:

Mishnah 2: The legitimization of an alley: the House of Shammai say by lath and beam[4]; but the House of Hillel say, either by lath or by beam; Rebbi Eliezer says, two laths[5]. A student[6] said before Rebbi Aqiba in the name of Rebbi Ismael that the Houses of Shammai and Hillel did not disagree about an alley which is less that four [cubits wide] that it is [permitted] either by lath or by beam; about what did they disagree? About one wider than four [cubits] up to ten[7] where the House of Shammai say by lath and beam; but the House of Hillel say, either by lath or by beam. Rebbi Aqiba said, they disagree in both cases.

משנה ג: קוֹרָה שֶׁאָמְרוּ רְחָבָה כְּדֵי לְקַבֵּל אָרִיחַ וְהָאָרִיחַ חֲצִי לְבֵינָה שֶׁל שְׁלֹשָׁה טְפָחִים דַּיָּיה לַקּוֹרָה שֶׁתְּהֵא רְחָבָה טֶפַח כְּדֵי לְקַבֵּל אָרִיחַ לְאָרְכּוֹ:

Mishnah 3: The beam about which they spoke must be wide enough to carry a tile which is half a brick of three hand-breadths[8]; therefore it is sufficient for a beam to be one hand-breadth wide to accept the tile lengthwise[9].

משנה ד: רְחָבָה לְקַבֵּל אָרִיחַ וּבְרִיאָה לְקַבֵּל אָרִיחַ. רַבִּי יְהוּדָה אוֹמֵר רְחָבָה אַף עַל פִּי שֶׁאֵינָהּ בְּרִיאָה:

Mishnah 4: Wide enough to carry a tile and strong enough to carry a tile. Rebbi Jehudah says, wide enough even if not strong enough[10].

משנה ה: הָיְתָה שֶׁל קַשׁ אוֹ שֶׁל קָנִים רוֹאִין אוֹתָהּ כְּאִלּוּ הִיא שֶׁל מַתֶּכֶת. עֲקוּמָה רוֹאִין אוֹתָהּ כְּאִלּוּ הִיא פְשׁוּטָה. עֲגוּלָּה רוֹאִין אוֹתָהּ כְּאִלּוּ הִיא מְרוּבַּעַת. אִם יֵשׁ בְּהֶקֵּפָהּ שְׁלֹשָׁה טְפָחִים יֵשׁ בָּהּ רוֹחַב טֶפַח:

Mishnah 5: If it was made of straw or reeds, one considers it as if of metal[11], curved as if it were straight[12]; round one considers it as if square[13]. If its circumference is three hand-breadths its width is one hand-breadth[14].

משנה ו: לְחָיַיִם שֶׁאָמְרוּ גּוֹבְהָן עֲשָׂרָה טְפָחִים רוֹחְבָּן וְעוֹבְיָין כָּל־שֶׁהֵן. רַבִּי יוֹסֵי אוֹמֵר רָחְבָּן שְׁלֹשָׁה טְפָחִים:

Mishnah 6: The laths[15] about which they spoke, their height ten hand-breadths, their width and thickness arbitrarily small; Rebbi Yose said, their width three hand-breadths.

משנה ז: בַּכֹּל עוֹשִׂין לְחָיַיִם אֲפִילוּ בְדָבָר שֶׁיֵּשׁ בּוֹ רוּחַ חַיִּים רַבִּי מֵאִיר אוֹסֵר. וּמְטַמֵּא מִשּׁוּם גּוֹלֵל וְרַבִּי מֵאִיר מְטַהֵר. כּוֹתְבִין עָלָיו גִּטֵּי נָשִׁים וְרַבִּי יוֹסֵי הַגְּלִילִי פּוֹסֵל:

Mishnah 7: One may use anything for laths, even living things[16]; Rebbi Meïr forbids this. And it makes impure because of a cover stone[17], but Rebbi Meïr declares it pure. One writes on it divorce documents[18] but Rebbi Yose the Galilean disqualifies.

משנה ח: שְׁיָרָא שֶׁחָנַת בַּבִּקְעָה וְהִקִּיפוּהָ כְּלֵי בְהֵמָה מְטַלְטְלִין בְּתוֹכָהּ וּבִלְבַד שֶׁיְהֵא גָדֵר גָּבוֹהַּ עֲשָׂרָה טְפָחִים וְלֹא יְהוּ פְרָצוֹת יְתֵירוֹת עַל הַבִּנְיָן. כָּל־פִּרְצָה שֶׁהִיא כְעֶשֶׂר אַמּוֹת מוּתֶּרֶת מִפְּנֵי שֶׁהִיא כְּפֶתַח יוֹתֵר מִכָּאן אָסוּר:

Mishnah 8: If a caravan rested in an area of difficult access[19] which they surrounded by the implements of animals[20] one may move things inside on condition that the fence be ten hand-breadths high and the openings not be more than the built-up part[21]. Any opening up to ten cubits is permitted since it is like a door; more than that is forbidden.

משנה ט: מַקִּיפִין שְׁלֹשָׁה חֲבָלִים זֶה לְמַעְלָה מִזֶּה וְזֶה לְמַעְלָה מִזֶּה וּבִלְבַד שֶׁלֹּא יְהֵא בֵּין חֶבֶל לַחֲבֵירוֹ שְׁלֹשָׁה טְפָחִים. שִׁעוּר חֲבָלִים וְעוֹבְיָן יוֹתֵר עַל טֶפַח שֶׁיְהֵא הַכֹּל עֲשָׂרָה טְפָחִים:

Mishnah 9: One may surround by three ropes, one higher than the other, on condition that the distance between one rope and the next be less than three hand-breadths and the measure and their thickness be more than a hand-breadth so that together it be more than ten hand-breadths[22].

משנה י׃ מַקִּיפִין בַּקָּנִים וּבִלְבַד שֶׁלֹּא יְהֵא בֵּין קָנֶה לַחֲבֵירוֹ שְׁלֹשָׁה טְפָחִים. בַּשְׁיָרָא דִיבְּרוּ, דִּבְרֵי רִבִּי יְהוּדָה. וַחֲכָמִים אוֹמְרִין לֹא דִיבְּרוּ חֲכָמִים בַּשְׁיָרָא אֶלָּא בַהֹוֶה. כָּל־מְחִיצָה שֶׁאֵינָהּ שֶׁל שְׁתִי וָשֶׁל עֵרֶב אֵינָהּ מְחִיצָה דִּבְרֵי רַבִּי יוֹסֵי בֵּי רִבִּי יְהוּדָה וַחֲכָמִים אוֹמְרִין אֶחָד מִשְּׁנֵי דְבָרִים. אַרְבָּעָה דְבָרִים פָּטְרוּ בַּמַּחֲנֶה מְבִיאִין עֵצִים מִכָּל־מָקוֹם וּפְטוּרִים מֵרְחִיצַת יָדַיִם וּמִדְּמַאי וּמִלְעָרֵב׃

Mishnah 10: One surrounds with sticks, on condition that between one stick and the next there be less than three hand-breadths[23]. They spoke about a caravan, the words of Rebbi Jehudah[24], but the Sages say that the Sages mentioned a caravan only as an example. Any partition which is not woof and warp is no partition, the words of Rebbi Yose ben Rebbi Jehudah; but the Sages say, one of these two[25]. Of four matters they freed a military camp[26]: One may bring wood from anywhere[27], and they are not liable for washing their hands[28], and from *demay*[29], and from making an *eruv*[30].

1   Cf. *Šabbat* 1, Note 142. The status of an alley, a narrow public road bordered by walls of houses, essentially is that of a *karmelit*. Since such an alley is not a thoroughfare, it is customary that under certain circumstances the dwellers in houses opening on the alley can turn it into their common private domain. A prior condition is that the alley be a dead-end street; an alley open at both ends, while not a public domain in the technical sense, does not qualify directly. The second condition, mentioned only in Mishnah 2, is that the entrance to the alley must be well defined and immediately recognizable; this is done either by placing a horizontal beam over the entrance (קוֹרָה) or placing there a vertical lath (לֶחִי). The Mishnah presumes that a beam was used; the majority holds that a beam placed higher than 20 cubits is not noticed whereas R. Jehudah holds that it always is noticed.

2   The entrance to the alley should not be wider than 10 cubits.

3   If there are two door-posts and a beam from one to the other, even if there are no doors, it is clear that the domain is visibly separated from the thoroughfare onto which it opens.

4   A beam must have a minimal width as indicated in Mishnah 3, there is no requirement of minimal thickness or strength for the lath, which is only needed to indicate the place up to where the dwellers in the alley may carry on the Sabbath.

5   On both sides of the alley.

6   According to the Babli, this was R. Meïr, the only Sage of whom it is known that he studied first under R. Ismael and then under R. Aqiba.

7   Since for alleys wider than 10 cubits both Houses agree that one needs "a shape of a door," i. e., two laths and a beam over them.

8   Therefore the tile is 1.5×3 hand-breadths[2].

9   Since a hand-breadth is counted as 4 thumb-breadths, the tile will extend over the beam by one thumb-breadth on each side.

10   Since the only function of the beam is to indicate the boundary of the private domain in the alley, only size but not structural stability is required.

11   This Mishnah follows R. Jehudah in the previous Mishnah which thereby is declared practice to be followed. The beam does not need to be able to carry any load.

12   If the beam is not a straight log but is curved.

13   If the beam is a round log then while it might be strong enough to carry a tile it is impossible to fasten one on it permanently.

14   This defines π as 3, from an interpretation of *1K.* 7:23 (presuming that עגל means "circular" not "oval").

15   The plural indicates that the statement is valid also in R. Eliezer's opinion.

16   One may tie an animal which is at least ten hand-breadths high to the entrance of an alley as a symbolic lath. R. Meïr requires the lath to be permanently fixed.

17   If an animal is used to cover a grave, it acts as a grave stone and touching it transmits the severe impurity of the dead. For R. Meïr a living animal cannot play the role of a grave stone, therefore its body is a roof over the corpse and acts as a shield against transmission of impurity.

18   The husband may write the text of the divorce document and have the witnesses sign on the horns of a cow and hand over the cow to the wife, Mishnah *Gittin* 2:3, where R. Yose the Galilean also rejects foodstuffs as writing material for divorce documents.

19   Which therefore is *karmelit*, where carrying is forbidden only rabbinically and which therefore can be turned into a kind of private domain by an improvised wall.

20   The bags on the beasts of burden may be used as temporary walls for the Sabbath.

21   The bags used for the wall need not touch one another but the openings must be smaller than the lengths of the bags, and no opening may be more than 10 cubits.

22   Instead of making a wall of camel or donkey bags the caravan may delineate its resting place by putting up some poles and stretching ropes from one to the other. This then is considered a wall if the distances from the ground to the first rope and between the ropes each are less than 3 hand-breadths. If such a distance is denoted by 3-ε, the entire open space is 9-3ε. Therefore the ropes have to cover a width of at least 1+3ε to insure that the top of the third rope be 10 hand-breadths above ground.

23   Instead of using horizontal ropes one may use vertical sticks following the same rules.

24   He accepts the imitation of a fence by either horizontal or vertical components only for a caravan camping in an uninhabited area; whereas the majority accepts the rules as universally valid.

25 R. Yose ben R. Jehudah disagrees with his father and rejects any fence not showing material in two directions perpendicular to one another.
26 In wartime.
27 They can collect fire wood from anywhere and it is not considered robbery.
28 Before eating profane food (with bread).
29 Provisions delivered to the army by not strictly observant persons may be eaten by strictly observant soldiers without setting heave of the Tithe apart, since it is only a suspicion, not a fact, that tithes were not taken from the provisions; cf. Introduction to Tractate *Demay*.
30 In a camp in a *karmelit* situation one may carry freely once the boundary fence was established without going through an *eruv* ceremony as explained in Chapter 3.

(18b line 19) מָבוֹי שֶׁהוּא גָבוֹהַּ מֵעֶשְׂרִים כּוֹל׳. רִבִּי יוֹסֵה אָמַר לָהּ סְתָם. רִבִּי אָחָא בְשֵׁם רַב. רַבָּנָן יַלְפִין לָהּ מִפִּתְחוֹ שֶׁלְהֵיכָל. וְרִבִּי יוּדָה יָלִיף לָהּ מִפֶּתַח הָאוּלָם. אִם מִפֶּתַח הָאוּלָם דַּייוֹ אַרְבָּעִים אַמָּה. דְּתַנִּינָן תַּמָּן. פֶּתַח הָאוּלָם גָּבוֹהַּ אַרְבָּעִים אַמָּה וְרוֹחַב עֶשְׂרִים אַמָּה. תַּנֵּי רִבִּי חִייָה. אֲפִילוּ אַרְבָּעִים חֲמִשִּׁים אַמָּה. תַּנֵּי בַּר קַפָּרָא. אֲפִילוּ מֵאָה אַמָּה. אָמַר רִבִּי אָבִין. רִבִּי יוּדָה כְּדַעְתֵּיהּ וְרַבָּנָן כְּדַעְתְּהוֹן. דְּתַנִּינָן תַּמָּן. וְכֵן גְּשָׁרִים הַמְפוּלָּשִׁין מְטַלְטְלִין תַּחְתֵּיהֶן בַּשַּׁבָּת. דִּבְרֵי רִבִּי יוּדָה. וַחֲכָמִים אוֹסְרִין. הֵיךְ מַה דְתֵימַר תַּמָּן. אַתְּ רוֹאֶה אֶת הַמְּלַתֵּירָה כִּילוּ יוֹרֶדֶת וְסוֹתֶמֶת. אוּף הָכָא אַתְּ רוֹאֶה אֶת הַתִּיקְרָה כִּילוּ יוֹרֶדֶת וְסוֹתֶמֶת. הִיא דַעְתֵּיהּ דְּרִבִּי יוּדָה בָּסוּכָה. הִיא דַעְתֵּיהּ בְּמָבוֹי. הִיא דַעְתְּהוֹן דְּרַבָּנָן בְּסוּכָּה. הִיא דַעְתְּהוֹן בְּמָבוֹי. וְלֹא דָמְיָיא. יֵשׁ דְּבָרִים כְּשֵׁירִים בַּסּוּכָּה וּפְסוּלִין בְּמָבוֹי. כְּשֵׁירִין בְּמָבוֹי וּפְסוּלִין בַּסוּכָּה. דּוּקְרָנִין כְּשֵׁירִין בַּסּוּכָּה וּפְסוּלִין בְּמָבוֹי. וְתַנֵּי כֵן. הֵבִיא אַרְבָּעָה דִיקְרָנִין וְסִיכֵּךְ עַל גַּבֵּיהֶן. סוּכָּה כְשֵׁירָה מָבוֹי פָּסוּל. הָדָא דְתֵימַר. בְּגוּבְהוֹהִין שְׁלֹשָׁה לְמַעְלָה מִכּוֹתְלֵי הַמָּבוֹי. אֲבָל אִם אֵינָן גְּבוֹהִין שְׁלֹשָׁה מִכּוֹתְלֵי הַמָּבוֹי כָּשֵׁר. בְּשֶׁאֵין בָּהֶן רוֹחַב אַרְבָּעָה. אֲבָל אִם יֵשׁ בָּהֶן רוֹחַב אַרְבָּעָה אֲפִילוּ גְּבוֹהִין כַּמָּה כָּשֵׁר. דְּפָנוֹת כְּשֵׁירוֹת בַּסּוּכָּה וּפְסוּלוֹת בְּמָבוֹי. וְתַנֵּי כֵן. שְׁתַּיִם כְּהִילְכָתָן וּשְׁלִישִׁית אֲפִילוּ טֶפַח כָּשֵׁר. רִבִּי חִייָה בְשֵׁם רִבִּי יוֹחָנָן. שְׁתַּיִם שֶׁל אַרְבָּעָה אַרְבָּעָה טְפָחִים וּשְׁלִישִׁית אֲפִילוּ טֶפַח כָּשֵׁר. וּבְמָבוֹי עַד שֶׁיְּהֵא מְגוּפָּף מֵאַרְבַּע רוּחוֹתָיו. רַחַב מֵעֶשֶׂר סוּכָּה כְשֵׁרָה וּמָבוֹי [31]פָּסוּל. הִדְלָה עָלֶיהָ אֶת הַגֶּפֶן וְאֶת הַדְּלַעַת. הָדָא דְתִימָא. עַל בֵּית סָאתַיִם. אֲבָל יְתִיר מִבֵּית סָאתַיִם נַעֲשֵׂית כִּמְחִיצָה שֶׁהוּקְפָה זְרָעִים. שֶׁאֵין מְטַלְטֵל בָּהּ אֶלָּא בְּאַרְבַּע אַמּוֹת. חֲמָתָהּ מְרוּבָּה מִצִּילָּתָהּ בַּסּוּכָּה פְּסוּלָה וּבְמָבוֹי כָּשֵׁר. סוּכָּה מְקוּרָה פְסוּלָה. מָבוֹי מְקוּרָה כָשֵׁר. רִבִּי אִמִּי בְשֵׁם רַב אוֹשַׁעְיָה. לֹא סוֹף דָּבָר מְקוּרָה. אֶלָּא נָתַן מִלְתְּרָא וְיֵשׁ בּוֹ רָחַב אַרְבָּעָה טְפָחִים. מַתֶּרֶת אֶת הַמָּבוֹי.

1 יוסה | ס יוסי   2 רבנן | ס ורבנן   מפתחו | ס מפיתחו   מפתח האולם | ס מפתחו שלאולם (2)   דייו | ס דיו
3 פתח האולם | ס פתחו שלאולם   גבוה | ס גובהו   ורוחב | ס ורוחבו[32]   5 יודה | ס יהודה   דתימר | ס דאת
אמר   המלתירה | ס התיקרה   כילו | ס כאילו   7 אוף | ס כך את אמר   התיקרה | ס המלתירה   כילו | ס כאילו
היא   9 ופסולין | ס ופסולים   כשירין | ס כשירים   ופסולין | ס ופסולים   כשירין | ס כשירים   10 דיקרנין | ס
דקרנין   סוכה כשירה | ס בסוכה כשר   מבוי | ס ובמבוי   11 דתימר | ס דאת אמר   12 מכותלי | ס
למעלה מכותלי   13 ושלישית | ס והשלישית   14 כשר | ס -   ושלישית | ס והשלישית   15 מעשר | ס
מעשר אמות   סוכה כשירה | ס בסוכה כשר   ומבוי | ס ובמבוי   16 והדלעת | ס והדלעת ואת הקיסוס וסיכך

על גביו פסולה | דתימא | ס דאת אמר סאתיים | ס סאתים יתיר | ס יותר סאתיים | ס סאתים 17
מטלטל | ס מותר לטלטל 18 ובמבוי | ס במבוי אמי | ס אחא רב | ס ר' 20 אושעי' | ס הושעיה אלא |
ס אלא אפי' בו | ס בה רחב | ס רוחב

"An alley which is higher than twenty," etc. [35]Rebbi Yose said it without attribution, Rebbi Aḥa in the name of Rav: The rabbis inferred it from the door of the Sanctuary, but Rebbi Jehudah inferred it from the door of the Hall[36]. An argument from the door of the Hall is sufficient only up to forty cubits, as we have stated there[37]: "The door of the Hall was forty cubits high and twenty cubits wide." Rebbi Ḥiyya stated, even forty or fifty cubits; Bar Qappara stated, even a hundred cubits[38]. Rebbi Abin said, Rebbi Jehudah follows his opinion and the rabbis follow their opinion, as we have stated there[39], "and similarly one carries under panelled bridges on the Sabbath, the words of Rebbi Jehudah, but the Sages forbid it.[40]" As you are saying there, one considers the cross-beam[41] as if it came down[42] and closed, here also one considers the roof as if it came down and closed. This is the opinion of Rebbi Jehudah in the case of a *sukkah*, this is his opinion in the case of an alley. Also the opinion of the rabbis in the case of a *sukkah* is their opinion in the case of an alley. But they do not compare[43]. There are items qualified for a *sukkah* which are disqualified for an alley and those qualified for an alley but disqualified for a *sukkah*. Double pointed stakes[44] are qualified for a *sukkah* but disqualified for an alley, and it was stated thus: If he brought four double pointed stakes and thatched over them it is qualified as a *sukkah*[45] but disqualified for an alley[46]. That is, if they are higher by more than three [hand-breadths] than the walls of the alley. But if they are not higher by more than three [hand-breadths] than the walls of the alley it is qualified. If they are not, but if they are four [hand-breadths] wide they are qualified even if arbitrarily high[47]. Walls may be qualified for a *sukkah* but disqualified for an alley, and it was stated thus: "Two regular and the third even one hand-breadth is qualified[48]." Rebbi Ḥiyya in the name of Rebbi Johanan: Two of four hand-breadths each and the third even one hand-breadth is qualified[49]. But for an alley only if it is closed in its four directions[50]. Wider than ten cubits is qualified for a *sukkah* but disqualified for an alley[51]. "If he drew a vine or squash.[52]" That means, up to an area of two *bet se'ah*. But more than an area of two *bet se'ah* it is a partition made for agriculture where one may transport only four cubits[53]. If its sunshine is more than its shadow it is disqualified as *sukkah*[54] but qualified for an alley. A roofed *sukkah* is disqualified, a roofed alley is qualified[55]. Rebbi Immi in the name of Rav Oshaia:[56] Not only roofed, but if he put there a cross beam four hand-breadths wide, it makes the alley permitted[57].

31 From here on the text was added by the corrector from a source parallel to the *Sukkah* text.

32 The text in *Sukkah* follows the Mishnah text closer than the text in *Eruvin*.

33 The quote of Mishnah *Sukkah* 1:4 is shortened, becoming unintelligible in *Eruvin*.

34 Babylonian Aramaic, a corrector's error.

35 The same text also is the introduction to Tractate *Sukkah* 1:1 (ט).

36 The rabbis hold that one does not realize that a beam is there to indicate a door if it is higher than 10 cubits since the entrance door to the Herodian Temple was 10 cubits. R. Jehudah disputes this since the inner door between the antechamber and the main room, visible only to the officiating priests, was larger. The biblical accounts of Solomon's Temple (*1K.* 6:2-3, *2Chr.* 3:3-4) do not give measurements of the doors. Babli 2a.

37 Mishnah *Middot* 3:4.

38 He disputes any connection with Temple measurements since R. Jehudah rejects height limitations in general. Babli 2b.

39 Mishnah 9:5.

40 The bridge is supported by a structure of beams underneath with beams running lengthwise on both sides. R. Jehudah holds that the boundary of the space below the bridge is clearly indicated if there are virtual walls hanging down from the beams enclosing the space which therefore assumes the role of a house. The rabbis accept only real walls.

41 Greek μέλαθρον, τό. This is a substantial load-carrying beam used in construction.

42 As a virtual wall, Note 40.

43 The fact that the rabbis take 20 cubits as upper height limit for both the entrance to an alleyway and a *sukkah* is accidental since the rules in both cases diverge widely.

44 Greek δίκρανον, τό.

45 One may make a *sukkah* by putting up four poles carrying a frame on which one thatches a roof on condition that the poles qualify as walls, i. e., each of them is at least 4 hand-breadths wide. Otherwise one would have to make makeshift walls between the poles as described in Mishnah 9.

46 The poles carrying the cross beam may not be much higher than the walls of the alley (or the cross beam cannot be fastened to the tops of the poles, Babli 9a top).

47 If a pole qualifies as a wall it is clear that it may be 20 cubits high for the rabbis and arbitrarily high for R. Jehudah.

48 Tosephta *Sukkah* 1:13. A *sukkah* must be at least 10 hand-breadths high and the sides have to be at least 7 hand-breadths wide.

49 As explained in Mishnah 9, a space of

slightly less that 3 hand-breadths is disregarded. Therefore a wall qualifies as being 7 hand-breadths wide if the actual material wall extends to slightly more than 4 hand-breadths.

50 It must have three actual walls and a symbolic door on the fourth side.

51 Mishnah 1 for the alley. There are no limitations on the surface area covered by a *sukkah*.

52 This may refer either to Mishnah *Sukkah* 1:4 or to Tosephta *Eruvin* 1:7; shortened to leave out all of the argument. The thatched roof of a *sukkah* must be vegetal material not connected to the ground. Therefore vine or squash are disqualified to be used for thatching. But a vine growing in an arch over the entrance of an alley is as good as a beam to mark the entrance.

53 A vine used to designate the entrance to an alley may be used only if the total area of the alley does not exceed 5'000 square cubits since this is the maximal size of farming or ranching corrals permitted for Sabbath use. Babli 23b.

54 Mishnah *Sukkah* 1:1. Since alleys usually have no roof, they are not expected to provide shade.

55 The essence of a *sukkah* is its makeshift thatched roof; it is not a *sukkah* if it has a waterproof roof. But if the entrance to an alley passes under a permanent roof at least 4 hand-breadths wide it does not need any other sign at the entrance. If the alley is open at both ends and one end is roofed, it is considered a dead-end alley. Cf. S. Liebermann, *Tosephta ki-Fshutah* part 3, p. 309, on Tosephta 1:7.

56 It is difficult to decide between this reading, quoting Babylonians, and ס "R. Aha in the name of R. Hoshaia", quoting Galileans. In the Babli 3a the rule is given in the name of other Babylonian Amoraim.

57 A cross-beam 4 hand-breadths wide is a roof and not subject to any restrictions imposed on beams or laths in order to permit carrying in an alley.

(fol. 18b line 46) רִבִּי אָחָא רִבִּי חִינָּנָא בְּשֵׁם כַּהֲנָא. [אֵין] הֲלָכָה כְּרִבִּי יוּדָה. דְּלֹא כֵן מָה אָנָן אָמְרִין. רִבִּי יוּדָה וַחֲכָמִים תְּהֵא הֲלָכָה כְּרִבִּי יוּדָה. אֶלָּא בְּגִין דְּאָמַר רִבִּי יַעֲקֹב בַּר אִידִי בְּשֵׁם רִבִּי יְהוֹשֻׁעַ בֶּן לֵוִי. הֲלָכָה כְּדִבְרֵי הַמֵּיקַל בְּהִילְכוֹת עֵירוּבִין. וְאָמַר רִבִּי נַחְמָן בַּר יִצְחָק בְּשֵׁם רִבִּי יְהוֹשֻׁעַ בֶּן לֵוִי. הֲלָכָה כְּרִבִּי יוֹחָנָן בֶּן נוּרִי. וּמַקְשִׁינָן עֲלֵיהּ. לֹא כֵן אָמַר רִבִּי יַעֲקֹב בַּר אִידִי בְּשֵׁם רִבִּי יְהוֹשֻׁעַ בֶּן לֵוִי. הֲלָכָה כְּדִבְרֵי הַמֵּיקַל בְּהִילְכוֹת עֵירוּבִין. לֹא כֵן אָמַר רִבִּי יִצְחָק בַּר נַחְמָן בְּשֵׁם רִבִּי יְהוֹשֻׁעַ בֶּן לֵוִי. הֲלָכָה כְּרִבִּי יוֹחָנָן בֶּן נוּרִי. וְקַשְׁיָינָן עֲלֵיהּ. סָבְרִין מֵימַר. יָחִיד אֵצֶל יָחִיד. הָא יָחִיד אֵצֶל חֲכָמִים לֹא. אֲתָא רִבִּי יַעֲקֹב בַּר אָחָא. רִבִּי יַעֲקֹב בַּר אִידִי בְּשֵׁם רִבִּי יְהוֹשֻׁעַ בֶּן לֵוִי. הֲלָכָה כְּרִבִּי יוֹחָנָן בֶּן נוּרִי וַאֲפִילוּ חֲכָמִים הַחֲלוּקִין עָלָיו. וְכָא תָהֵא הֲלָכָה כְּרִבִּי יוּדָה וַאֲפִילוּ חֲכָמִים הַחֲלוּקִין עָלָיו. שְׁמוּאֵל אָמַר. הֲלָכָה כְּדִבְרֵי הַמֵּיקַל בְּעֵירוּבִין. אֲמַר לֵיהּ רַב חִייָה בַּר אָשִׁי. כְּגוֹן הַהִיא דִּתְנִינָן תַּמָּן. וְכֵן גְּשָׁרִים הַמְפוּלָּשִׁים מְטַלְטְלִין תַּחְתֵּיהֶן בַּשַּׁבָּת. דִּבְרֵי

רִבִּי יוּדָה. וַחֲכָמִים אוֹסְרִין. אָמַר לֵיהּ. לֹא עֵירוּבִין אָמַרְתִּי אֶלָּא מְחִיצוֹת. סָבַר כַּהֲנָה כְּהָדָא דִשְׁמְקֵל. לְפוּם כֵּן צָרַךְ מֵימַר. אֵין הֲלָכָה כְּרִבִּי יוּדָה.

[58]Rebbi Aha, Rebbi Hinena in the name of Cahana: Practice does [not][59] follow Rebbi Jehudah. If it were not so what would we say? Rebbi Jehudah versus the Sages, practice should follow Rebbi Jehudah[60]? But since Rebbi Jacob bar Idi said in the name of Rebbi Joshua ben Levi, practice follows the lenient opinion in *Eruvin*, and Rebbi Nahman bar Isaac[61] said in the name of Rebbi Joshua ben Levi, practice follows Rebbi Johanan ben Nuri[62]. (We asked about it, did not Rebbi Jacob bar Idi say in the name of Rebbi Joshua ben Levi, practice follows the lenient opinion in *Eruvin*, and Rav Nahman bar Isaac said in the name of Rebbi Joshua ben Levi, practice follows Rebbi Johanan ben Nuri.)[63] We asked about it, we would think this[64] refers to an individual versus an individual but not an individual versus the Sages. There came Rebbi Jacob bar Aha, Jacob bar Idi said in the name of Rebbi Joshua ben Levi, practice follows Rebbi Johanan ben Nuri even though the Sages disagree with him. Why should practice not follow Rebbi Jehudah even though the Sages disagree with him[65]? Samuel said, practice follows the lenient opinion in *Eruvin*. Rav Hiyya bar Ashi said to him, for example what we have stated there, "and similarly one carries under panelled bridges on the Sabbath, the words of Rebbi Jehudah, but the Sages forbid it[40]"? He told him, did I not say *Eruvin* but partitions[66]? Cahana shares Samuel's opinion[67]. Therefore it was necessary to say that practice does not follow Rebbi Jehudah.

58 The text is copied by Nachmanides in his *Novellae* to *Eruvin* Chapter 4 (col. 596-597 in the edition Jerusalem 1973); a parallel for the entire paragraph is in the Babli 46a. A defective copy (by the corrector) also is in Chapter 6, Note 33.

59 The scribe wrote "not" and then [erroneously] crossed it out. Therefore it is missing in the printed editions.

60 It should not be necessary to mention that practice does not follow the lone dissenter.

61 Read with the later text and the quote in Nachmanides: R. Isaac bar Nahman.

62 In Mishnah 4:5, about a person who fell asleep in an uninhabited area on Friday afternoon and was sleeping during twilight, the Sages hold that since he did not consciously determine his place of rest at sundown he only can move inside 4 cubits from the place where he slept, but R. Johanan ben Nuri lets him move 2'000 cubits in every direction.

63 The text in parentheses is duplicated afterwards; it is not in Nachmanides.

64 That one follows the lenient opinion.

65   If practice follows R. Johanan ben Nuri as a matter of principle, it also should follow R. Jehudah in Mishnah 1:1.

66   The case of a bridge is not a case of *turning* a common domain into private domain but whether the space under a bridge automatically has the status of a permanent dwelling which does not need any *eruv*.

67   He agrees with Samuel not only that in matters of *eruv* one follows the lenient opinion but also that the principle does not apply to questions of partitions. In the matter of an alley he holds that turning it into a private domain needs two things, first the fixation of the entrance partition described in Mishnah 1:1 to which the principle does not apply, and the collection of an *eruv* as described in Chapter 2, to which the principle does apply.

(18b line 62) לֹא אָמַר אֶלָּא לְמַעְלָה מֵעֶשְׂרִים. הָא בְסוֹף עֶשְׂרִים כָּשֵׁר. וַתְיָיא כְרַב דְּרַב אָמַר. סוֹף שִׁיעוּרִין לְהָקֵל. רִבִּי יוֹחָנָן אָמַר. סוֹף שִׁיעוּרִין לְהַחֲמִיר. רִבִּי חִייָה בְשֵׁם רִבִּי יוֹחָנָן. מָבוֹי שֶׁקּוֹרָתוֹ לְמַעְלָה מֵעֶשְׂרִים נוֹתֵן קוֹרָה בְתוֹךְ עֶשְׂרִים וּמְמַעֵט בְּתוֹךְ עֶשְׂרִים. אָמַר רִבִּי יוֹסֵה. וְהוּא שֶׁיְּהֵא כָל־הֶכְשֵׁר קוֹרָה בְתוֹךְ עֶשְׂרִים. רִבִּי חִלְקִיָּה אָמַר בְּשֵׁם רִבִּי אֲחָא. וַאֲפִילוּ כְרַב אַתְיָא הִיא. דְּרַב אָמַר. שְׁחִיטָה מֶחֱצָה לְמֶחֱצָה כְּשֵׁירָה. וְלָמָּה אָמְרוּ. פְּסוּלָה. מִפְּנֵי מַרְעִית הָעַיִן. שֶׁאִם תֵּימַר שֶׁיִּתֵּן בְּתוֹךְ עֶשְׂרִים. אַף הוּא נוֹתֵן לְמַעְלָה מֵעֶשְׂרִים.

They only said "higher than twenty". Therefor at the end of twenty it is qualified. This follows Rav who said that the end of measurements is for leniency; Rebbi Johanan said that the end of measurements is for restriction[68]. Rebbi Hiyya in the name of Rebbi Johanan: For an alley whose beam is higher than twenty he puts another beam within twenty and this reduces to less than twenty[69]. Rebbi Yose said, on condition that the entire qualification beam be within twenty[70]. Rebbi Hilqiah said in the name of Rebbi Aha, even this comes following Rav, as Rav said that slaughter half by half is qualified, and why did they say that it is disqualified? Because of the visual impression[71]. For if you say that he has to put it within twenty, he would put it higher than twenty[73].

68   As a general principle, every rabbinic statement that a quantity *x* is qualified up to a limit *a* is read by Rav as "*x* less or equal to *a*" whereas R. Johanan reads it as "*x* strictly less than *a*". In the Babli, 3a (last line), the position of Rav is represented by the Babylonian Rava, that of R. Johanan by the Galilean Ulla.

69   Babli 3b.

70   The upper rim of the beam must be less than 20 cubits from the ground.

71   Even though Rav said that the upper bound is qualified in theory, in practice he will agree with R. Johanan that to avoid

errors one has to be restrictive. His example is the rule that ritual slaughter requires that as biblical requirement half of both windpipe and esophagus of the animal have to be cut in slaughter. Nevertheless as a practical rule, since 50-50 is not exactly determinable by visual inspection, one requires that clearly more than half be cut in one stroke; Babli *Hulin* 29a.

72   If you say the the beam may reach 20 cubits above ground, it might reach higher. In Medieval sources one reads in RAVIAH *Hulin* § 1086: "We read in the Yerushalmi, first Chapter of *Eruvin*: slaughter half by half is not more than half, for if you told him it is qualified he would cut less than half." In *Or zarua* (Part One, §370) one reads: "Rav said that slaughter half by half is qualified, and why did we say only if he cuts most of it? For if you tell him that he has to cut half, he would cut less than half. But if you are telling him to cut most of it, he will not cut less than half." A text similar to these has to be inserted here.

(18b line 70) יְמַעֵט. כֵּיצַד יְמַעֵט. עוֹשֶׂה אִיסְטַבָּה עַל פֶּתַח הַמָּבוֹי וּמַתִּיר הַמָּבוֹי. כַּמָּה יְהֵא בָהּ. רִבִּי אָחָא בְשֵׁם רִבִּי הוֹשַׁעְיָה. אַרְבָּעָה טְפָחִים כְּדֵי מָבוֹי. רִבִּי יוֹסֵה אוֹמֵר. טֶפַח כְּדֵי קוֹרָה. חֲבֵרַיָּיא אָמְרִין. כָּל־שֶׁהוּא. הֲרֵי אֵין כָּאן גּוֹבַהּ עֶשְׂרִים עַל רוֹחַב טֶפַח.

לֹא הָיָה גָבוֹהַּ עֲשָׂרָה טְפָחִים צָרִיךְ לָחוֹק. כַּמָּה יְחוֹק. רִבִּי אָחָא אָמַר. אַרְבַּע אַמּוֹת כְּדֵי מָבוֹי. רִבִּי יוֹסֵה אָמַר. אַרְבָּעָה טְפָחִים כְּדֵי מָקוֹם. רִבִּי יַעֲקֹב בַּר אָחָא רִבִּי יוֹסֵה בְשֵׁם רִבִּי יוֹחָנָן. עוֹשֶׂה חָרִיץ עַל פֶּתַח הַמָּבוֹי עָמוֹק עֲשָׂרָה וְרָחָב אַרְבָּעָה וּמַתִּיר הַמָּבוֹי בֵּין מִבִּפְנִים בֵּין מִבַּחוּץ. וְהוּא שֶׁיְּהֵא בְתוֹךְ שְׁלֹשָׁה לְכָתְלֵי הַמָּבוֹי. וַאֲפִילוּ לְמָאן דָּמַר תַּמָּן אַרְבָּעָה. מוֹדֵי הָכָא בִשְׁלֹשָׁה. תַּמָּן חוּץ לַמָּבוֹי. בְּרַם הָכָא בְתוֹךְ הַמָּבוֹי.

עָשָׂה גָדֵר בְּפֶתַח הַמָּבוֹי גָּבוֹהַּ עֲשָׂרָה וְרָחָב אַרְבָּעָה וּמַתִּיר הַמָּבוֹי בֵּין מִבִּפְנִים בֵּין מִבַּחוּץ. הָיָה שָׁם גָּדֵר. אִם מִתְלַקֵּט הוּא עֲשָׂרָה טְפָחִים מִתּוֹךְ שְׁלֹשָׁה צָרִיךְ קוֹרָה. וְאִם לָאו אֵין צָרִיךְ. אִית תַּנָּיֵי תַנֵּי. מִתּוֹךְ אַרְבַּע. מָאן דָּמַר. מִתּוֹךְ שָׁלֹשׁ. רַבָּנָן. מָאן דָּמַר. מִתּוֹךְ אַרְבַּע. רִבִּי מֵאִיר. הָיָה מוּנְדְּרָן בְּאֶמְצַע הַמָּבוֹי. לָעֶלְיוֹנִים נִידּוֹן מִשּׁוּם חָרִיץ. וּלְתַחְתּוֹנִים מִשּׁוּם גָּדֵר.

"It should be reduced." How does one reduce? He makes a platform[73] at the entrance of the alley and permits the alley. How much must it be? Rebbi Aha in the name of Rebbi Hoshaia: Four hand-breadths for an alley[74]. Rebbi Yose says, one hand-breadth corresponding to the beam[75]. The colleagues say, anything, since here is no longer a height of twenty cubits in the widths of a hand-breadth[76].

If its height was less than ten hand-breadths one has to dig out. How much does he have to dig? Rebbi Aha said, four cubits as an alley[77]. Rebbi Yose said, four hand-breadths as a space. Rebbi Jacob bar Aha, Rebbi Yose[78] in the name of Rebbi Johanan, he makes a ditch at the entrance of the alley, ten [hand-breadths] deep and four wide; this permits the alley from inside and out[79], on condition that it be within three [hand-breadths] of the walls of the alley[80]. And even he who says there four, here he agrees with three. There it is outside of the alley, but here within the alley[81].

If he made a stone fence at the entrance to the alley, ten [hand-breadths] high and four wide, it permits the alley from inside and out[82]. If there had been a stone fence, if it reduces to ten hand-breadths within three[83] it needs a beam, otherwise it does not need a beam. There are Tannaim who state, within four [cubits]. He who says, within three [cubits], the rabbis. He who says, within four [cubits], Rebbi Meïr[84]. If there was a slope in the middle of the alley, for those at the high end it acts as a ditch, for those at the low end as a stone fence[85].

73 It is possible to read מסטבה.

74 This statement is difficult. Rashba (*Novellae* to *Eruvin*, first paragraph) reads: כדי מקום "as a space", an expression also used in the next paragraph. An area of four by four hand-breadths is a space for itself; cf. Mishnah Šabbat 11:3. Babli 10a, top.

75 Since the Mishnah only requires that the beam not be higher than 20 cubits above ground, it is necessary to lift the ground only directly below the beam.

76 This follows R. Johanan in the preceding paragraph and refers to the case that the beam is exactly 20 cubits above ground everywhere. Then lifting the ground by an arbitrarily small amount at an arbitrarily small area satisfies the requirement of the Mishnah.

77 Since 4 cubits is the maximum one is permitted to carry in the public domain, it is the minimum for an alley to require an *eruv*.

78 For chronological reasons one has to read "Yasa" instead of "Yose".

79 From the outside the ditch hinders the access from the public domain; from the inside the ditch is as good as a fourth wall which would turn the alley into a courtyard.

80 Since a distance of less than 3 hand-breadths always is disregarded.

81 The reference to 3 and 4 hand-breadths is to a text close to Tosephta 1:6, a case where there is not one beam crossing from one wall to the one on the other side of the alley but short beams sticking out from either wall. If the distance between these beams is less than 3 hand-breadths for the rabbis and 4 for Rabban Simeon ben Gamliel, the beams are considered adjacent and qualify as one beam. It is noted that Rabban Simeon ben Gamliel also will agree that a ditch, which is not dug as a marker but to qualify for the minimal height of the alley walls, cannot be farther than 3 hand-breadths from a wall.

81 Same argument as in Note 78.

82 There had been a stone fence but it collapsed and now the heap is not 10 hand-breadths high on a basis 3 cubits wide; it

does not qualify as a wall but is part of the alley. Cf. Babli *Šabbat* 100a.

83 It is not known where to find a relevant statement of R. Meïr.

84 If the incline covers a height of at least 10 hand-breadths the dwellers in the two parts of the alley may make separate *eruvim* without additional beam or lath. Ravia §271 (ed. A. Aptowitzer p. 401 Note 13.)

(18c line 9) הָרָחָב מֵעֶשֶׂר אַמּוֹת יְמַעֵט. כֵּיצַד מְמַעֵט. נוֹתֵן מְלַתֵּרָה בְּפֶתַח הַמָּבוֹי וּמַתִּיר הַמָּבוֹי. לְרוֹחַב אִיתְאָמְרַת. וְרַבָּנָן עָבְדִין לָהּ אֲפִילוּ בַגְבוֹהּ. וְלֹא כְפָרוּץ לִמְלוֹאוֹ הוּא. נַעֲשִׂית כְּאַכְסַדְרָה. רִבִּי מַתִּיר אַכְסַדְרָה בְּבֵית שָׁרֵיי. כַּמָּה עַמּוּדִין הָיָה בָהּ. רִבִּי יַעֲקֹב בַּר אָחָא אָמַר רִבִּי חִייָה רִבִּי יוֹסֵה. חַד אָמַר. שִׁשָּׁה. וְחַד אָמַר. שְׁמוֹנָה. אָמַר רִבִּי יַעֲקֹב בַּר אָחָא. וְלֹא פְלִיגִי. מָאן דָּמַר שִׁשָּׁה. לֹא מְחַשֵּׁב אִילֵּין תְּרֵין בָּרַייָא. מָאן דָּמַר שְׁמוֹנָה. מְחַשֵּׁב אִילֵּין תְּרֵין בָּרַייָא. רִבִּי יַעֲקֹב בַּר אָחָא בְשֵׁם רִבִּי אֶלְעָזָר. לֹא סוֹף דָּבָר שִׁשָּׁה לֹא סוֹף דָּבָר שְׁמוֹנָה. אֶלָּא אִם הָיוּ הָרַבִּים בּוֹקְעִין בָּהּ. אֲפִילוּ שְׁנַיִם יְהוּ אֲסוּרִין. אִם אֵין הָרַבִּים בּוֹקְעִין בּוֹ. אֲפִילוּ כַּמָּה יְהוּ מוּתָּרִין. מַה דַּהֲוָה עֲבָדָא הַוְיָא עֲבָדָא.

"If it is wider than ten cubits it should be reduced." How does one reduce? He puts a cross-beam[41] on the entrance of the alley and permits the alley[85]. This was said for width; the rabbis also apply it to height[86]. Is it not as if opened in its length[87]? It is turned into a porch[88]. Rebbi permitted a porch in Bet Shearim. How many pillars did it have? Rebbi Jacob bar Aha said, Rebbi Hiyya and Rebbi Yose[78], one said, six, but the other one said, eight. Rebbi Jacob bar Aha said, they do not disagree. He who said six does not count the two outer ones[89], he who said eight does count the two outer ones. Rebbi Jacob bar Aha in the name of Rebbi Eleazar: Six is not important, eight is not important. But if it was used by the public even with two it will be forbidden[90], if it is not used by the public even with many it will be permitted. The case which happened was as it happened.

85 A short pillar which reduces the width of the entrance to 10 cubits allows an *eruv* for the alley.

86 A pillar at the entrance of the alley is a distinctive sign which separates the alley from the public domain and permits an *eruv*.

87 If the entrance is too wide, what is the use of a vertical beam? The Babli 11a requires not only a vertical beam but a full door frame. It is impossible to read this into the Yerushalmi text.

88 Greek ἐξέδρα, ἡ, a covered walkway. While this is a well-defined space, it has no walls. In order to treat it by the rules of an alley one has to hold that the beams which form the frame for the roofing (which may be either a full roof or simply lattice work) define virtual walls around the walkway.

89 The two door posts with the beam connecting them which forms the entrance door frame and is necessary to define the space of the alley.

90 Since an alley can be permitted as private space only if it is used exclusively by the inhabitants of the houses opening into it and their guests, the same must hold for a virtual alley.

(18c line 19) אַכְסַדְרָה שֶׁנִּפְרְצָה לִמְלוֹאָהּ לִרְשׁוּת הָרַבִּים. רִבִּי לָא [רַב] וְרִבִּי יוֹחָנָן תְּרֵיהוֹן אָמְרִין. מְטַלְטְלִין בְּכוּלָּהּ. שְׁמוּאֵל אָמַר. אֵין מְטַלְטְלִין בָּהּ אֶלָּא בְּאַרְבַּע אַמּוֹת. אָמַר רִבִּי יוֹסֵי. וְלֹא מוֹדֵי שְׁמוּאֵל בְּמָבוֹי שֶׁהוּא מְקוֹרֶה לְמַעֲלָה מֵעֶשְׂרִים אַמָּה שֶׁהוּא כָשֵׁר. אֶלָּא מִיסְבּוֹר סְבַר שְׁמוּאֵל. וְהוּא שֶׁיְּהֵא הֶכָשֵׁר קוֹרָה בְּתוֹךְ עֶשְׂרִים. אָתָא רִבִּי אָחָא רִבִּי חִינְנָא בְּשֵׁם רִבִּי הוֹשַׁעְיָה. וְהוּא שֶׁיְּהֵא הֶכָשֵׁר קוֹרָה בְּתוֹךְ עֶשְׂרִים. אָמַר רִבִּי יוֹסֵי. וַאֲפִילוּ דְסָבַר שְׁמוּאֵל בְּמָבוֹי הַמְקוֹרֶה לְמַעֲלָה מֵעֶשְׂרִים אַמָּה שֶׁהוּא כָשֵׁר. לֹא דָמִי מָבוֹי לְאַכְסַדְרָה. מָבוֹי נַעֲשָׂה לְתַשְׁמִישׁ בָּתִּים. אַכְסַדְרָה לֹא נַעֲשִׂית אֶלָּא לְתַשְׁמִישׁ דָּבָר. אִילּוּ מָבוֹי שֶׁאֵינוּ מְקוֹרֶה וְנָתַן הַקּוֹרָה בְּתוֹךְ עֶשְׂרִים שֶׁמָּא אֵינוּ כָשֵׁר. אִילּוּ אַכְסַדְרָה שֶׁאֵינָהּ מְקוֹרֶה וְנָתַן הַקּוֹרָה בְּתוֹךְ עֶשְׂרִים שֶׁמָּא כְלוּם הוּא.

If a porch was totally open to the public domain[91], Rebbi La: [Rav][92] and Rebbi Johanan both are saying, one may carry in its entirety; Samuel said, one may carry in it only four cubits. Rebbi Yose said, does not Samuel agree that an alley roofed higher than twenty cubits is qualified[93]? But Samuel must hold, only if the qualifying beam be within twenty cubits. There came Rebbi Aha, Rebbi Hinena in the name of Rebbi Hoshaia, only if the qualifying beam be within twenty cubits. Rebbi Yose said, even if Samuel would think that an alley roofed higher than twenty cubits is qualified, an alley is not comparable to a porch. An alley is made for the use of the adjacent houses, a porch is made for the use (of a thing)[94]. If an alley is not roofed but there is a beam within twenty cubits, would it not be qualified? But if a porch is not roofed although there is a beam within twenty cubits, would that mean anything[95]?

91 The Babli 94b calls this "a porch in an agricultural domain". Since the porch has a roof it is a well-defined domain and should have the status of a house.

92 The word was written by the scribe but erroneously deleted by the corrector, as shown by the parallel in *Sukkah* 1:1, 51d l. 13; Babli *Eruvin* 94b.

93 Since in a house one does not require that the ceiling be lower than 20 cubits.

94 Since this is difficult to understand, S. Liebermann proposes to read אבר "air" instead of דבר "thing". The *exedra* is made so one may sit outside in the shade.

95 A space delineated by four poles connected by horizontal beams is a private space only under very restricted circumstances, e. g., around a cistern or a

well (Mishnah 2:1).

(18c line 29) הָיָה רָחָב בְּתוֹךְ חֲמֵשׁ עֶשְׂרֵה אַמָּה. רִבִּי בָּא וְרַב הוּנָא בְשֵׁם רַב. עוֹשֶׂה פַס שֶׁלְּשָׁלֹשָׁה אַמּוֹת וְכָל־שֶׁהוּא. מַרְחִיקוֹ מִן הַכּוֹתֶל שְׁתֵּי אַמּוֹת. אוֹתוֹ וְכָל־שֶׁהוּא נִידּוֹן לְשֵׁם לֶחִי וְהַשְּׁאָר. וְהוּא שֶׁיְּהֵא הָעוֹמֵד רָבָה עַל הֶחָלָל. וְיַעֲשֶׂה פַס אַרְבָּעָה טְפָחִים. וְלֹא כֵן תַּנֵּי. עוֹשֶׂה פַס שֶׁל אַרְבָּעָה טְפָחִים. אָמַר רִבִּי בָּא בַּר פַּפֵּי. כְּדֵי לְהַתִּיר שְׁנֵיהֶן בְּלֹא קוֹרָה. אִית תַּנָּיֵי תַנֵּי. מַעֲמִיד קָנֶה וְדִוּקְרָן. אִית תַּנָּיֵי תַנֵּי. עוֹשֶׂה פַס שֶׁל אַרְבָּעָה טְפָחִים. אָמַר רִבִּי יוֹסֵה. הֲלָכָה כְּאוֹמֵר עוֹשֶׂה פַס אַרְבָּעָה טְפָחִים.

If it was wide within fifteen cubits, Rebbi Abba and Rav Huna in the name of Rav: He makes a plank of slightly more than three hand-breadths and removes it two cubits from the wall[96]. The slight addition is treated as lath, and it is permitted[97] on condition that what is standing be more than the empty space[98]. Should he not make a plank four hand-breadths wide? Did we not state, he makes a plank four hand-breadths wide? Rebbi Abba bar Pappai said, in order to permit both parts without beam[99]. Some Tannaim state, he puts up a stick and a double-pointed stake[44]; some Tannaim state, he makes a plank four hand-breadths wide. Rebbi Yose said, practice follows him who said, he makes a plank four hand-breadths wide.

96 If the entrance to the alley is rather more than 10 cubits wide, up to 15 cubits one puts up a plank which divides the entrance into two parts. The main part is ten wide, the plank is chosen to be slightly wider than three cubits and the second opening is 2 cubits wide. Then since the width of the opening is less the width of the plank, the opening is disregarded. The small amount by which the plank is wider than 3 cubits is used as lath to qualify the larger opening as entrance to the alley. (One uses 3 and 2 cubits to be on the safe side. As explained in Note 71, as a precaution one does not say that the plank has to be 2+ε and the opening 2-ε for some arbitrarily small ε > 0.) Babli 10b.

97 Reading with Rashba (Novellae to Eruvin, ad 10a, col. 71) ושרי instead of והשאר "and the remainder."

98 A general principle in constructing separations for the rules of the Sabbath, cf. Mishnah 1:8.

99 If the plank is 4 cubits wide it can be put anywhere in the opening as long as no empty stretch is wider than 10 cubits. Then the rims of the plank on both sides act as laths; it no longer is necessary that the second opening be less than the width of the plank, and neither entrance needs a beam.

(18c line 37) תַּנֵּי. רַבָּן שִׁמְעוֹן בֶּן גַּמְלִיאֵל אוֹמֵר. מָבוֹי שֶׁיֶּשׁ לוֹ שְׁנֵי פְתָחִים נוֹתֵן קוֹרָה בְּאֶחָד מֵהֶן וּמַתִּיר. רִבִּי אָחָא בְשֵׁם רִבִּי לֵוִי. אֵין הֲלָכָה כְרַבָּן שִׁמְעוֹן בֶּן גַּמְלִיאֵל. אָמַר רִבִּי בָּא. וְהוּא שֶׁהֶעֱמִיד קָנֶה וְדוּקְרָן. אֲבָל אִם עָשָׂה פַס אַרְבָּעָה טְפָחִים הֲלָכָה כְרַבָּן שִׁמְעוֹן בֶּן גַּמְלִיאֵל. וְתַנֵּי כֵן. מָבוֹי שֶׁיֶּשׁ לוֹ אַרְבָּעָה פְתָחִים נוֹתֵן קוֹרָה בְּאֶחָד מֵהֶן וּמַתִּיר. אָמַר רִבִּי יוֹסֵי. וְהוּא שֶׁנְּתָנוֹ עַל הָאֶמְצָעִי. אֲבָל אִם נָתַן עַל הַחִיצוֹן נִיחָא עוֹמֵד שֶׁכָּאן מַתִּיר פִּירְצָה שֶׁכָּאן. וּמִי מַתִּיר פִּירְצָה שֶׁלְּהַלָּן. אָמַר רִבִּי שַׁמַּי. תִּיפְתָּר כְרַבָּן שִׁמְעוֹן בֶּן גַּמְלִיאֵל וְלֵית אַתְּ שְׁמַע מִינָּהּ כְּלוּם.

It was stated: Rabban Simeon ben Gamliel says, if an alley has two entrances[100], he puts a beam over one of them and permits it. Rebbi Aha in the name of Rebbi Levi: Practice does not follow Rabban Simeon ben Gamliel. Rebbi Abba said, only if he put up a stick and a doubly pointed stake; but if he made a plank four hand-breadths wide,[101] practice follows Rabban Simeon ben Gamliel, as it was stated thus: If an alley has four entrances[102], he puts a beam over one of them and permits it. Rebbi Yose said, only if he does it for a middle one[103]. But if he put it on an outer one could it be that what is standing here would permit what is open there? What would permit that which is open there? Rebbi Shammai said, explain it that it follows Rabban Simeon ben Gamliel and you cannot infer anything[104].

100 Not that the alley had exits at opposite ends, since then it would be a thoroughfare which cannot be turned into a private domain, but at one end it is open to the public road and nearby it has a second entry point where a piece of side wall is missing.

101 The second entrance is partially blocked by a vertical plank 4 hand-breadths wide, so that it appears as a hole in the wall but not an entry point.

102 Rashba (ad 10a, col. 93) reads: "4 hand-breadths".

103 The plank must be for the secondary opening, not for the outer opening to the road. The argument proves Rashba's reading since if there are 4 openings there is no middle one.

104 Practice still requires a beam or a lath for each of the entrances.

(18c line 45) מָבוֹי עָקוּם וּמְפוּלָּשׁ. רִבִּי יוֹחָנָן אָמַר. נוֹתֵן לֶחִי וְקוֹרָה מִיכָּן וְעוֹשֶׂה צוּרַת הַפֶּתַח מִיכָּן. רֵישׁ לָקִישׁ אָמַר. נוֹתֵן לֶחִי אוֹ קוֹרָה וּמַתִּיר. עַל דַּעְתֵּיהּ דְּרֵישׁ לָקִישׁ. בְּקֹשִׁי לַעֲשׂוֹת לָהֶן תַּקָּנָה. אֵילּוּ מִשְׁתַּמְּשִׁין עַד מְקוֹם הַכּוֹתֶל וְאֵילּוּ מִשְׁתַּמְּשִׁין עַד מְקוֹם הַכּוֹתֶל. וְלֹא נִמְצְאוּ שְׁתֵּי רְשׁוּיוֹת מִשְׁתַּמְּשׁוֹת בִּרְשׁוּת אַחַת. אֶלָּא אֵילּוּ מִשְׁתַּמְּשִׁין דֶּרֶךְ עֲקַמּוּמִיּוֹת וְאֵילּוּ מִשְׁתַּמְּשִׁין דֶּרֶךְ עֲקַמּוּמִיּוֹת וְלֹא נִמְצְאוּ שְׁתֵּי רְשׁוּיוֹת מִשְׁתַּמְּשׁוֹת בִּרְשׁוּת הָאֲסוּרָה לָהֶן. רַב וּשְׁמוּאֵל. רַב כְּרִבִּי יוֹחָנָן וּשְׁמוּאֵל כְּרֵישׁ לָקִישׁ.

רִבִּי יוֹחָנָן וְרֵישׁ לָקִישׁ הֲווֹ שָׁרְיָין בִּשְׁקָקָה דְּרִבִּי יִצְחָק. רֵישׁ לָקִישׁ טִילְטֵל. כְּדַעְתֵּיהּ. רִבִּי יוֹחָנָן לֹא אָסַר וְלֹא טִילְטֵל. אָמַר רִבִּי יוֹחָנָן. הַנִּיחוּ לִבְנֵי מָבוֹי שֶׁיְּהוּ שׁוֹגְגִין וְאַל יְהוּ מֵזִידִין. מָה. טִילְטֵל לֹא טִילְטֵל. אִין תֵּימַר. טִילְטֵל. מַחְלָפָה שִׁיטַת רִבִּי יוֹחָנָן. אִין תֵּימַר. לֹא טִילְטֵל. יוֹאַסַּר לִבְנֵי הַמָּבוֹי. רִבִּי יוֹחָנָן בִּיטֵּל רְשׁוּתוֹ. אָמַר רִבִּי אָחָא. כָּף רֵישׁ לָקִישׁ לְרִבִּי יוֹחָנָן וְטִילְטֵל. אָמַר רִבִּי מַתַּנְיָה. וְיָאוּת. מַה טַעֲמֵיהּ דְּרִבִּי מֵאִיר. עָשׂוּ אוֹתוֹ כְשׁוֹגֵג אֶצֶל מֵזִיד. מַה טַעֲמוֹן דְּרַבָּנָן. מִכֵּיוָן שֶׁחֲשׁוּדִין הֵן לְטַלְטֵל. כְּמֵזִידִין הֵן. אָמְרִין לֵיהּ. אִין כֵּינִי. יֵעָשֶׂה שׂוֹנְאָיו שֶׁל רִבִּי יוֹחָנָן כִּצְדוּקִי אֵצֶל בְּנֵי הַמָּבוֹי וְיוֹאַסֵּר לִבְנֵי הַמָּבוֹי. אָמַר רִבִּי יוֹסֵי בֵּירְבִּי בּוּן. צְדוּקִי חָשׁוּד לְטַלְטֵל. וָכָא מָה אִית לָךְ. מַה נָּפַק מִבֵּינֵיהוֹן. הָיָה עָשׂוּי כְּמִין כִּי. רִבִּי יוֹחָנָן אָמַר. נוֹתֵן לֶחִי וְקוֹרָה מִיכָּן וְעוֹשֶׂה צוּרַת פֶּתַח מִיכָּן. רֵישׁ לָקִישׁ אָמַר. אֲפִילּוּ כַמָּה קוֹרוֹת אֵינָן מַתִּירִין אוֹתוֹ.

A curved and open alley[105]. Rebbi Johanan said, he puts a beam or a lath on one side and makes a door frame on the other side[106]. Rebbi Simeon ben Laqish said, he puts a beam or a lath there which permits[107]. In Rebbi Simeon ben Laqish's opinion, if they wanted to fix it so that each side may use it up to the closing wall, would not two domains use a common domain? But one may use it up to the bend and the other may use it up to the bend[108]. Would not two domains use a domain forbidden to them? Rav and Samuel, Rav like Rebbi Johanan and Samuel like Rebbi Simeon ben Laqish[109].

Rebbi Johanan and Rebbi Simeon ben Laqish were staying in Rebbi Isaac's street[110]. Rebbi Simeon ben Laqish carried, according to his opinion, Rebbi Johanan did not carry, according to his opinion. Rebbi Johanan neither forbade nor carried; he said, let the dwellers in the alley be in error, lest they be intentional. What, did he carry or did he not carry? If you say that he carried, then Rebbi Johanan's opinion did change. If you say that he did not carry, it should be forbidden to the dwellers in the alley[111]. Rebbi Johanan annulled his rights[112]. Rebbi Aha said, Rebbi Simeon ben Laqish forced Rebbi Johanan and he carried. Rebbi Mattaniah said, this is correct. What is Rebbi Meïr's reason[113]? They considered him as unintentional compared to intentional[114]. What is the rabbis' opinion? Since they are suspected of carrying they are as if intentional. They told him, if this be so then the haters of Rebbi Johanan should be considered like a Sadducee for the dwellers in the alley and it should become forbidden for the dwellers in the alley[115]. Rebbi Yose ben Rebbi Abun said, a Sadducee is suspected of carrying[116]; here what can you say? What is the difference between them? If it was built like a χ.

Rebbi Johanan said, he puts a beam or a lath on one side and makes a door frame on the other side[117]. Rebbi Simeon ben Laqish said, even many beams do not make it permitted[118].

105 As S. Liebermann has pointed out, the correct interpretation is in Raviah §379, p. 401 (Notes 16 ff.). The alley is L-shaped but open at both ends. It cannot get an *eruv* in its entirety since it is open at both sides. But it can be turned into two separate private domains, each for one straight leg.

106 A beam or lath at the entrance from the public road and a door frame at the bend, to indicate that the common area in the alley ends here.

107 The sharp corner in itself is enough of a sign that the common area stops here.

108 The square area at the bend which is common to both legs as straight rows is forbidden to the dwellers in both legs whereas in R. Johanan's way of doing it the door-frame is the border between the two domains and all inhabitants may use their respective domains up to the door frame.

109 Babli 6b.

110 Which was an L-shaped alley, one leg of which was turned into a private domain for the purposes of the Sabbath following R. Simeon ben Laqish.

111 As a matter of principle, a common courtyard or an alley may be turned into a private domain only if all residents there agree to the operation. A single dissent makes the *eruv* illegal.

112 If the dissenting person agrees not to be counted as a dweller there, and therefore, not to use the common space, the *eruv* may be established without him.

113 This refers to Mishnah 6:1 where R. Meïr states that a single dissenting person makes an *eruv* impossible even if that person either is a Gentile for whom the Sabbath rules do not exist or a Sadducee who objects to the notion of *eruv* as not biblical. Cf. Babli 62a.

114 While a Sadducee willfully disregards rabbinical rules, it is not because he is intent of breaking them but because he does not accept their validity. Since for him breaking the rules excludes criminal intent, it cannot be considered as equivalent of intentionally breaking the rules.

115 If he refuses to recognize the *eruv* he will be unable to contribute to it and thereby make the entire *eruv* impossible.

116 Since the Sadducee does recognize only the biblical text as authoritative and strictly refrains from carrying anything in the public domain but objects to the notion of *eruv* as a rabbinic invention (CD xi), it is quite possible that he might consider a dead-end alley as not a public domain and permitted area for carrying without an *eruv*.

117 He considers an X-shaped configuration of alleys as a combination of two V-shaped ones, each one of which is treated according to the rules of L-shaped alleys where each leg can be turned into an private domain by putting a door frame at the bend.

117 He considers the X as combination of two straight open-ended alleys which cannot possibly be turned into a private domain.

(18c line 64) רַב יִרְמְיָה בְשֵׁם רַב. מָבוֹי שֶׁנִּפְרַץ מִכְּנֶגְדּוֹ אַרְבָּעָה. מִן הַצַּד יוֹתֵר מֵעֶשֶׂר. חֲבֵרַיָּיא בְשֵׁם רַב. לֹא שַׁנְיָיא. בֵּין שֶׁכְּנֶגְדּוֹ בֵּין מִן הַצַּד אַרְבָּעָה. הֲווֹן בָּעַיי מֵימַר. מָאן דָּמַר. מִן הַצַּד יוֹתֵר מֵעֶשֶׂר. הָא עֶשֶׂר מוּתָּר. בְּשֶׁיֵּשׁ שָׁם רוֹחַב אַרְבָּעָה. מָאן דָּמַר. בֵּין שֶׁכְּנֶגְדּוֹ בֵּין מִן הַצַּד אַרְבָּעָה. בְּשֶׁאֵין שָׁם רוֹחַב אַרְבָּעָה. לֹא כֵן סָבְרִינָן מֵימַר. רַב כְּרִבִּי יוֹחָנָן. אָמַר רִבִּי יוֹסֵי בֵּירִבִּי בּוּן. כְּדַי לַעֲשׂוֹת כָּל־הָרְשׁוּת כְּאַחַת.

מָבוֹי שֶׁנִּפְרַץ מִצִּידוֹ כְּלַפֵּי רֹאשׁוֹ. רַבָּנָן דְּקַיְסָרִין אָמְרִי רִבִּי חִייָה רִבִּי יוֹסֵה. אִם יֵשׁ שָׁם עוֹמֵד אַרְבָּעָה צָרִיךְ קוֹרָה. וְאִי לֹא לֹא צָרִיךְ. מַה בֵּינוֹ לְמָבוֹי שֶׁיֵּשׁ לוֹ שְׁנֵי פְתָחִים. אִילוּ מָבוֹי שֶׁיֵּשׁ לוֹ שְׁנֵי פְתָחִים שֶׁמָּא אֵינוֹ נוֹתֵן קוֹרָה עַל אַחַת מֵהֶן וּמַתִּיר. אָמַר רַב נַחְמָן בַּר יַעֲקֹב. וּמָבוֹי שֶׁיֵּשׁ לוֹ שְׁנֵי פְתָחִים אֵין דֶּרֶךְ בְּנֵי אָדָם לִיכָּנֵס בְּפֶתַח הַזֶּה וְלָצֵאת בָּזֶה. בְּרַם הָכָא דֶּרֶךְ בְּנֵי אָדָם לִיכָּנֵס בְּפֶתַח זֶה וְלָצֵאת בַּפִּירְצָה.

Rav Jeremiah in the name of Rav: An alley which was broken at its end into four [hand-breadths], at a side more than ten [cubits][118]. The colleagues in the name of Rav, there is no difference, whether at its end or at a side four [hand-breadths]. They wanted to say, he who says that "at a side more than ten [cubits]," therefore ten are permitted if it is four [hand-breadths] wide[119]. He who says, "whether at its end or at a side four [hand-breadths]," if it is not four hand-breadths wide[120]. Were we not of the opinion that Rav is like Rebbi Johanan[121]? Rebbi Yose ben Rebbi Abun said, to unify the entire domain[122].

An alley which was broken at its side towards the entrance[123], the rabbis of Caesarea said, Rebbi Ḥiyya and Rebbi Yose[78]. If four [hand-breadths] wide was standing it needs a beam[124], otherwise it does not need one. What is the difference between this and an alley which has two openings[125]? If an alley has two openings, does he not put a beam over one of them and permits? Rav Nahman bar Jacob said, if an alley has two openings, is it not usual that people enter by one and leave by the other? But is it usual that people enter by one and leave by the breach?

118 The explanation follows Rashi to Babli 6a, top. The entrance to the alley is ten cubits wide; the alley itself is wider. If the wall reducing the entrance to 10 cubits is broken in the length of 4 hand-breadths the alley becomes one with two entrances and needs a beam over one and a door frame for the other. The same is true if one of the side walls of the alley is broken for more than 10 cubits (but not if there are framed entrances to courtyards opening into the alley.)

119 If the additional wall at the entrance is at least 4 hand-breadths wide, any breach at a side wall up to 10 cubits can be left

untreated..

120 If the standing wall at the entrance is less than 4 hand-breadths wide, the breach at the side follows the rules of a breach in the front.

121 Since R. Johanan always requires a beam or a lath at the main entrance and a door frame at the other entrance, how can Rav make it dependent on the size of the breach?

122 In the case of the L-shaped alley he requires a door frame to equally permit *eruvim* for both legs of the L. But here we have a breach, not a door, and if it is larger than 10 cubits there is no way of turning the alley into a private domain.

123 The entrance is ten cubits wide; near the entrance there is a hole in one of the walls bordering the alley.

124 Because it is a separate entrance it does not follow the rules of a breach in the wall further away from the entrance.

125 The rules for an L-shaped alley do not depend on width or length.

(18d line 1) קוֹרָה אַחַת מָהוּ שֶׁתַּתִּיר שְׁנֵי מָבוֹאוֹת. רִבִּי יִרְמְיָה אָמַר. רִבִּי זֵירָא וְרִבִּי אַבָּהוּ. חַד אָמַר. אָסוּר. וְחַד אָמַר. מוּתָּר. מָאן דָּמַר. אָסוּר. בְּנוֹתְנִין לְמַעֲלָה מִשְּׁלֹשָׁה לְכוֹתְלֵי הַמָּבוֹי. מָאן דָּמַר. מוּתָּר. בְּנוֹתְנִין לְמַטָּה מִשְּׁלֹשָׁה לְכוֹתְלֵי הַמָּבוֹי.

רִבִּי זוֹעֵירָה בָּעֵי. חָצֵר בְּמָה הִיא נִיתֶּרֶת. אַשְׁכָּח תַּנֵּי. רִבִּי אוֹמֵר. בְּפַס אֶחָד. וַחֲכָמִים אוֹמְרִים. בִּשְׁנֵי פַסִּין. רַב יִרְמְיָה בְשֵׁם רִבִּי חִייָה. הֲלָכָה כְדִבְרֵי הָאוֹמֵר. בִּשְׁנֵי פַסִּים. וּבִלְבַד פַּס שֶׁלְאַרְבָּעָה טְפָחִים מִיכָּן וּפַס שֶׁלְאַרְבָּעָה טְפָחִים מִיכָּן. רִבִּי יוֹסֵה בְשֵׁם רִבִּי יוֹחָנָן. הֲלָכָה כְדִבְרֵי הָאוֹמֵר. בִּשְׁנֵי פַסִּין. וַאֲנִי אוֹמֵר. בְּפַס אֶחָד. וּבִלְבַד פַּס שֶׁלְאַרְבָּעָה טְפָחִים מִיכָּן וּפַס שֶׁלְאַרְבָּעָה טְפָחִים מִיכָּן. וְאֵין כָּאן אֶלָּא שְׁלֹשָׁה טְפָחִים מִיכָּן וּשְׁלֹשָׁה טְפָחִים מִיכָּן. הֲוֵי דוּ אָמַר בְּשֵׁם רִבִּי יוֹחָנָן. פַּס וְכָל־שֶׁהוּא מִיכָּן וּפַס וְכָל־שֶׁהוּא מִיכָּן.

May one beam permit two alleys? Rebbi Jereniah said, Rebbi Ze'ira[126] and Rebbi Abbahu, one said, it is forbidden, the other said, it is permitted. He who said, it is forbidden, if it was put higher than three [hand-breadths] than the walls of the alley; he who said, it is permitted, if it was put lower than three [hand-breadths] than the walls of the alley[127].

Rebbi Ze'ira said, by what can a courtyard become permitted[128]? It was found stated, with one plank[129], the words of Rebbi, but the Sages say, with two planks. Rav[130] Jeremiah in the name of Rebbi Hiyya, practice follows him who said, by two planks on condition that there be a plank of four hand-breadths on each side. Rebbi Yose in the name of Rebbi Johanan, practice follows him who said, by two planks, but I am saying, by one plank. On condition that there be a plank of four hand-breadths on each side? But there are only planks of three hand-breadths on each side[131], and what he said in the name of Rebbi Joḥanan, a plank of any thickness on each side[132].

126 This is the Babylonian spelling. Since in the next paragraph his name is spelled in the original Galilean form זעורה, the spelling here probably is a copyist's mistake.

127 Two diverging alleys whose entrances are close to one another but whose walls have different heights. If the walls have equal heights there is no problem since then one very long beam simply can be considered as two beams, one for each alley. The only problem arises if the beam is appropriate for one alley but not quite so for the other. Then one follows the principle stated earlier (cf. Note 22) that distances of less than three hand-breadths are disregarded.

128 A courtyard wall separating it from the public road was breached. The length of the breach must be less than 10 cubits; otherwise one may not carry in the courtyard on the Sabbath until the wall is repaired.

129 The practical difference between a lath לחי and a plank פס is that a lath has a minimal length but no minimal width or thickness whereas the plank has minimal length and width (4 hand-breadths) but no minimal thickness (cf. Tosephot 12a, s. v. בפסי). On both ends of the breach one has to put up planks as a minimal indication of a door.

130 Read: "Rebbi". The R. Hiyya quoted here is R. Hiyya bar Abba.

131 In keeping with the requirement of R. Yose in Mishnah 6.

132 As for the laths used to permit an alley. Babli 12a.

(18d line 11) רִבִּי זְעוּרָא רַב חוּנָא בְשֵׁם רַב. מָבוֹי שֶׁאָרְכּוֹ וְרָחְבּוֹ שָׁוִין אֵינָן נִיתָּרוֹת בְּלֶחִי וְקוֹרָה אֶלָּא בְפַסִּים כְּחָצֵר. שְׁמָעָהּ שְׁמוּאֵל מִינֵּיהּ וּלְעָתָהּ בַּתְרֵיהּ אַרְבָּעִין זִמְנִין. רַבָּנִין דְּקַיְסָרִין לָא אֳמְרִין כֵּן. אֶלָּא שְׁמוּאֵל שְׁאִיל לְרַב. כַּמָּה יְהֵא אוֹרְכָּן יוֹתֵר עַל רָחְבָּן. אַגִּיב וַאֲמַר לֵיהּ. כָּל־שֶׁהוּא. וּלְעִיתָהּ בַּתְרֵיהּ אַרְבָּעִין זִמְנִין. דְּאַתְּ מִבָּעֵי רַב וְלֹא מַשְׁכַּח יָתֵיהּ.

Rebbi Ze`ira, Rav Huna in the name of Rav: An alley whose length and width are equal is not permitted by lath or beam but by planks like a courtyard[133]. Samuel heard this from him and exerted himself after him 40 times[134]. The rabbis of Caesarea do not say so but rather that Samuel asked Rav, by how much must their length exceed their width? He responded and told him, anything[135]. For this he exerted himself after him 40 times, for one might need Rav and not find him.

133 Babli 12b.
134 He repeated in order to memorize.
135 In the Babli Rav attributes the ruling to his uncle R. Ḥiyya.

(18d line 16) תַּמָּן תַּנִּינָן: שֶׁהַמָּבוֹי לַחֲצֵירוֹת כֶּחָצֵר לַבָּתִּים: כַּמָּה חֲצֵירוֹת יְהוּ בְמָבוֹי. רַב וּשְׁמוּאֵל תְּרַוֵּויהוֹן אֲמָרִין. אֵין לְהֶן פָּחוּת מִשְׁתַּיִם. רִבִּי יַעֲקֹב בַּר אֲחָא בְשֵׁם רִבִּי יוֹחָנָן. אֲפִילוּ חָצֵר אַחַת מִיכָּן וְחָצֵר אַחַת מִיכָּן. רִבִּי אֲחָא רִבִּי חִינְנָא בְשֵׁם רִבִּי יוֹחָנָן אָמַר. אֲפִילוּ חָצֵר מִיכָּן וּבַיִת מִיכָּן. בַּיִת מִיכָּן וְחָנוּת מִיכָּן. רַב נַחְמָן בַּר יַעֲקֹב (בָּעֵי) [בְּשֵׁם רִבִּי יוֹחָנָן]. מָבוֹי אֵין פָּחוּת מִשְּׁנֵי חֲצֵירוֹת. חָצֵר אֵינָה פְחוּתָה מִשְּׁנֵי בָתִּים. מָבוֹי שֶׁאָרְכּוֹ וְרָחְבּוֹ שָׁוִין אֵינָן נִיתָּרוֹת בְּלֶחִי וְקוֹרָה אֶלָּא בְפַסִּים כֶּחָצֵר. שְׁמוּאֵל שָׁאַל לְרַב. כַּמָּה יְהֵא אָרְכּוֹ יָתֵר עַל רָחְבּוֹ. וְהוּא אָמַר לֵיהּ. כָּל־שֶׁהוּא. הָהֵין דָּרַייָּא דְאַרְעָא דְיִשְׂרָאֵל מְרַבְּעוּ. חֲמִשָּׁה מְבוֹאוֹת פְּתוּחִין לַמָּבוֹי. עוֹמֵד מְרוּבֶּה עַל הַפָּרוּץ וּפָרוּץ מְרוּבֶּה עַל הָעוֹמֵד אֵינוֹ צָרִיךְ קוֹרָה. אִם יֵשׁ בֵּינֵיהֶן אַרְבַּע אַמּוֹת הוּפְלַג.

There we have stated[136]: "Because the relation of the alley to courtyards is like that of a courtyard to houses." How many courtyards must there be for an alley[137]? Rav and Samuel both are saying, there cannot be less than two. Rebbi Jacob bar Aha in the name of Rebbi Johanan, even one courtyard on each side. Rebbi Aha, Rebbi Ḥinena in the name of Rebbi Johanan said, even a courtyard on one side and a house on the other side, a house on one side and a store on the other side. Rav Naḥman bar Jacob (asked) [in the name of Rebbi Johanan][138]: An alley cannot have less than two courtyards, a courtyard cannot have less than two houses[139]. An alley whose length and width are equal is not permitted by lath or beam but by planks like a courtyard[133]. Samuel asked Rav, by how much must its length exceed its width? He told him, anything[135]. The dwellers of the Land of Israel make theirs square. If five alleys open into one alley. Whether what is standing is more than what is breached or what is breached is more than what is standing, it does not need a beam[140], if they are distant four cubits[141].

136 Mishnah 6:8. The rules which make a multi-party courtyard accessible to all parties are completely parallel to those which make a multi-courtyard alley accessible to all courtyard dwellers.

137 That the alley can be turned into private domain for the rules of the Sabbath.

138 The text in parentheses was written by the scribe; it was changed into the text in brackets by the corrector. The first text is quoted by the Sephardic Rashba (ad 12b, col. 97) but the second by the Ashkenazic Sefer Miṣwot Gadol (Hilkhot Eruvin, fol. 245a in the Venice edition). R. Naḥman bar Jacob is not known to have had contact with R. Johanan.

139 There is a difference in that an alley with only one courtyard cannot be turned into a private domain but a courtyard belonging to only one one-family dwelling automatically is private domain.

140 A dead-end alley with five side arms becomes permitted by beam or lath at the entrance from the public road and does not

need anything for the side arms (assuming that all dwellers there participate in the *eruv*) even if the total length of the openings into the side alleys is larger than the total length of the walls bordering the main alley. 141 The meaning of this clause is unknown.

(18d line 26) תַּנֵּי רִבִּי הוֹשַׁעְיָה. פְּתָחִים פְּתוּחִין לִרְשׁוּת הָרַבִּים. נִפְתָּחִים נַעֲשָׂה מְקוֹמָם רְשׁוּת הָרַבִּים. נִנְעָלִים נַעֲשָׂה מְקוֹמָם רְשׁוּת הַיָּחִיד. מְבוֹאוֹת הַמְפוּלָּשׁוֹת לַיָּם כִּמְפוּלָּשִׁין לְבִקְעָה. וְהָהֵן שְׁקָקָה דְּרִבִּי חָנִין לֹא צָרִיךְ צוּרַת פֶּתַח. שֶׁהוּא כְּמִתְלַקֵּט עֲשָׂרָה טְפָחִים מִתּוֹךְ שָׁלֹשׁ. תְּקָנָה תִּיקְּנוּ בּוֹ כְּדֵי לְהַתִּיר בָּתִּים שֶׁלְּמַטָּן.

Rebbi Hoshaia stated: Doors which open on the public road, if they are open their place becomes public domain, if they are locked their place becomes private domain[142]. Alleys that open on the sea are like alleys open to an agricultural area[143]. The street of Rebbi Ḥanin does not need a door frame since it descends ten hand-breadths within three [cubits][144]. They made an arrangement to allow the lower-lying houses.

142 This is another way to describe a platform in front of a door opening to the public road; cf. *Šabbat* 1, Notes 172-173.
143 The alley is not a dead-end street since the sea does not act as a wall. On the other hand it is not a thoroughfare since it ends in *karmelit*, not the public domain. Therefore it can become permitted on the Sabbath if it receives a beam or lath at the opening to the public road and a door frame towards the sea like any other alley open on both sides.

144 His alley did open to the sea and it did descend 10 hand-breadths within 3 cubits. The dwellers in the upper part can use the declivity as a wall (Note 85) but then the lower part of the alley is not private domain for the Sabbath. But a door frame at the end pointing to the sea together with a beam at the entrance from the street turns the entire length of the alley into potential private domain.

(18b line 31) אִם יֵשׁ לוֹ צוּרַת פֶּתַח אַף עַל פִּי שֶׁהוּא רָחָב מֵעֶשֶׂר אַמּוֹת אֵינוֹ צָרִיךְ לְמַעֵט: חֲנַנְיָה בַּר שִׁלְמְיָא הֲוָה יְתִיב מַתְנֵי לְחִייָה בְּרֵיהּ דְּרַב. אַפִּיק רַב רֵישֵׁיהּ מִן כַּוַּותָא. אָמַר לֵיהּ. לֵית כֵּן. אָמַר לֵיהּ. וְלָא נִיתַנְיֵיהּ כֵּן. אֲמַר לֵיהּ. דְּתַנִּיתֵיהּ וְאוֹדְעֵיהּ דְּלֵית כֵּן.

אַבָּא בַּר הוּנָא אָמַר. צוּרַת פֶּתַח שֶׁאָמְרוּ קָנֶה מִיכָּן וְקָנֶה מִיכָּן וְגוּמְיָא עַל גַּבֵּיהוֹן. רִבִּי יַנַּאי בֵּירִבִּי יִשְׁמָעֵאל בְּשֵׁם רִבִּי שִׁמְעוֹן בֶּן לָקִישׁ. צִיר וּבֶן צִיר לֹא יְהֵא מְחוּסָּר אֶלָּא דֶלֶת.

תַּנֵּי רִבִּי חִייָה. כֵּיצַד מַתִּירִין רְשׁוּת הָרַבִּים. רִבִּי יְהוּדָה אוֹמֵר. לֶחִי מִיכָּן וְלֶחִי מִיכָּן. קוֹרָה מִיכָּן וְקוֹרָה מִיכָּן. וַחֲכָמִים אוֹמְרִים. לֶחִי וְקוֹרָה מִיכָּן וְעוֹשֶׂה צוּרַת פֶּתַח מִיכָּן. רִבִּי יִרְמְיָה בְּשֵׁם רִבִּי שְׁנוּאֵל בַּר רַב יִצְחָק. צִיר וּבֶן צִיר לֹא יְהֵא מְחוּסָּר אֶלָּא דֶלֶת. אֲמָרָהּ רִבִּי יִרְמְיָה קוֹמֵי

רִבִּי זְעִירָה. אָמַר לֵיהּ. וּמָה בְיָדָךְ. רִבִּי אִילָא בְשֵׁם רִבִּי יוֹחָנָן. צוּרַת הַפֶּתַח שֶׁאָמְרוּ קָנֶה מִיכָּן וְקָנֶה מִיכָּן וְגָמִי עַל גַּבֵּיהוֹן. אָמַר רִבִּי יוֹסֵה. רַבָּנִין דְּהָכָא כְּדַעְתּוֹן וְרַבָּנִין דְּתַמָּן כְּדַעְתּוֹן. רַבָּנִין דְּתַמָּן דְּאִינּוּן אָמְרִין. צוּרַת הַפֶּתַח שֶׁאָמְרוּ. קָנֶה מִיכָּן וְקָנֶה מִיכָּן וּגְמִייָא עַל גַּבֵּיהֶן. וְאִינּוּן אָמְרִין. לֵית כֵּן. וְרַבָּנָן דְּהָכָא דְּאִינּוּן אָמְרִין. צִיר וּבֶן צִיר לֹא יְהֵא מְחוּסָּר אֶלָּא דֶלֶת. וְאִינּוּן אָמְרִין. דְּאִית כֵּן.

חֲנַנְיָה בֶּן אֲחִי רִבִּי יְהוֹשֻׁעַ אוֹמֵר. בֵּית שַׁמַּי אוֹמְרִים. דֶּלֶת מִיכָּן וְדֶלֶת מִיכָּן. וּכְשֶׁהוּא מַכְנִיס מוֹצִיא וְנוֹעֵל. וּבֵית הִלֵּל אוֹמְרִים. דֶּלֶת מִיכָּן וְצוּרַת פֶּתַח מִיכָּן. אָמַר שְׁמוּאֵל. הֲלָכָה כַּחֲנַנְיָה בֶּן אֲחִי רִבִּי יְהוֹשֻׁעַ. וְלֹא דָא הִיא קַדְמִייָתָא. אָמַר רִבִּי בָּא. עַל יְדֵי דֶלֶת הוּא נִנְעוֹל. הוֹרֵי רִבִּי אָחָא בְהֶן דַּעֲבַד צוּרַת פֶּתַח שֶׁהוּא צָרִיךְ לְהִיכָּנֵס לְפָנִים מֵאַרְבַּע אַמּוֹת. רִבִּי אַיְיבוֹן הוֹרֵי כְהֶן.

"If there is a door-frame even though it is wider than ten cubits there is no need to reduce³." Hananiah bar Shelemia was sitting stating this to Hiyya, Rav's son. Rav put out his head from the window and said, it is not so. He told him, but was it not stated so? He said to him, if you state this to him you have to inform him that it is not so¹⁴⁵.

Abba bar Huna¹⁴⁶ said, the door frame about which they spoke is a stick on each side and bast over them. Rebbi Yannai the son of Rebbi Ismael in the name of Rebbi Simeon ben Laqish: A hinge and its fastener; nothing should be missing but the door.

Rebbi Hiyya stated: How does one permit public domain¹⁴⁷? Rebbi Jehudah says, a lath on each side or a beam on each side, but the Sages say, a lath and a beam on one side and he makes a door frame on the other side. Rebbi Jeremiah in the name of Rebbi Samuel bar Rav Isaac: A hinge and its fastener; nothing should be missing but the door. Rebbi Jeremiah said this before Rebbi Ze`ira, who told him, what do you have in your hand¹⁴⁸? Rebbi Ila in the name of Rebbi Johanan, the door frame about which they spoke is a stick on each side and bast over them. Rebbi Yose said, the rabbis here follow their opinion and the rabbis there follow their opinion. Since the rabbis there are saying, the door frame about which they spoke is a stick on each side and bast over them; they are those who say, it is not so¹⁴⁹. But the rabbis here who are saying, a hinge and its fastener; nothing should be missing but the door, they are those who say, it is so.

Hanania the son of Rebbi Joshua's brother¹⁵⁰ says, the House of Shammai say, a door on each side. When he enters he closes and locks. But the House of Hillel say, a door on one side and a door frame on the other side. Samuel said, practice follows Hanania the son of Rebbi Joshua's brother[151]. Is that not the same as the earlier statement? Rebbi Abba said, if there is a door it can be locked[152].

Rebbi Aha instructed one who made a door frame that he had to make it inside of four cubits[153]. Rebbi Aybun instructed in this sense.

145 Babli 2b/3a, 11a.
146 A Babylonian Amora of the second generation, student of his father Rav Huna. He exemplifies the Babylonian tradition, in contrast to the restrictive Galilean tradition which requires a door frame which is ready to have a door placed in it.
147 This refers to an alley between walls which is open at both ends. Turning parts of a public road into private domain, for the owner of houses opposite one another on a street, is mentioned in the Babli (6a/b, Šabbat 6a,117a) but rejected.
148 This is nothing new since it already was stated by R. Simeon ben Laqish and is rejected by the Babylonian R. Ze`ira who quotes R. Johanan as adopting the Babylonian position.
149 They follow Rav in rejecting the Mishnah since their "door frame" is flimsy. The Mishnah is accepted as practice in Galilee where a solid frame is required.
150 His name was Hanania ben Hanania, the unlucky form indicating a posthumous child.
151 Babli 6b.
152 The difference between the rule of Hanania following the House of Hillel and the rule stated earlier in the name of the Sages is that Hanania requires a door on one side which could be locked even if actually it never will be locked.
153 The door frame has to be made between walls, not at their end.

(18d line 52) רִבִּי זְעִירָה בְשֵׁם רַב חִסְדָּא. יְתֵידוֹת הַיּוּצָאוֹת מִכּוּתְלֵי הַמָּבוֹי אָדָם נוֹתֵן עֲלֵיהֶן אֶת הַקּוֹרָה וּמַתִּיר אֶת הַמָּבוֹי. וְהֵן שֶׁיְּהוּ בְתוֹךְ שְׁלֹשָׁה לְכוּתְלֵי הַמָּבוֹי. תְּרֵין אֲמוֹרִין. חַד אָמַר. וְהֵן שֶׁיְּהִיוּ בְּרִיאוֹת כְּדֵי לְקַבֵּל אֶת הַקּוֹרָה וְאָרִיחֶיהָ. וְחָרָנָה אָמַר. אֲפִילוּ אֵינָן בְּרִיאוֹת כְּדֵי לְקַבֵּל אֶת הַקּוֹרָה וְאָרִיחֶיהָ. רִבִּי זְעִירָה בָעֵי. תַּחַת הַקּוֹרָה אָסוּר וּמַתִּיר אֶת הַמָּבוֹי. אָמַר רִבִּי אָחָא בַּר עוּלָּה. וְלָמָּה לֹא אָמַר לֵיהּ. וְלֹא אַשְׁכַּחְנָן כֵּן עַל דִּשְׁמוּאֵל. דְּאָמַר שְׁמוּאֵל. תַּחַת הַקּוֹרָה אָסוּר וּמַתִּיר אֶת הַמָּבוֹי. רִבִּי זְעִירָה בְשֵׁם שְׁמוּאֵל. תַּחַת הַקּוֹרָה וּבֵין לְחָיִים נִידוֹן כְּאַסְקוּפָּה. רִבִּי זְעִירָא בָעֵי. כְּהֵיידָא אַסְקוּפָה. כְּאַסְקוּפָּה מוּתֶּרֶת אוֹ כְּאַסְקוּפָּה אֲסוּרָה. אָמַר רִבִּי זֵירָא. עַד דַּאֲנָא תַמָּן אִיצְטָרְכַת לִי. וְכַד סְלִיקַת לְהָכָא שְׁמָעִית רִבִּי יָסָא בְשֵׁם רִבִּי יוֹחָנָן. אִיסְקוּפָּה הַגְּבוֹהָה עֲשָׂרָה וְאֵין רְחָבָה אַרְבָּעָה מוּתָּר לְכָאן וּמוּתָּר לְכָאן. וּבִלְבָד שֶׁלֹּא יַחֲלִיף. אָמַר רִבִּי מָנָא קוֹמֵי רִבִּי יוֹסֵי. חֲמִי מָה אָמַר. לֹא אָמַר אֶלָּא בְּשֶׁאֵין שָׁם רוֹחַב אַרְבָּעָה. אֲבָל יֵשׁ שָׁם רוֹחַב אַרְבָּעָה. אֲסוּרָה. אָמַר לֵיהּ. וְהָדָא הִיא אַמְלַתֶּרָה. אִילּוּ מְלַתֶּרָה שֶׁמָּא אֵינָהּ מוּתֶּרֶת. רִבִּי

זְעִירָא אָמַר. שְׁמוּאֵל וְרִבִּי יוֹחָנָן. שְׁמוּאֵל אָמַר. תַּחַת הַקּוֹרָה אָסוּר. וְרִבִּי יוֹחָנָן אָמַר. מוּתָּר. הַכֹּל מוֹדִין עַל בֵּין לְחָיַיִם שֶׁאָסוּר. וְתַנֵּי כֵן. מָבוֹי הֶעָשׂוּי לְחָיַיִם לְחָיַיִם. אִם יֵשׁ בֵּין זוֹ לָזוֹ אַרְבָּעָה טְפָחִים. מְטַלְטְלִין עַד הַחִיצוֹן. וְאִם לָאו. מְטַלְטְלִין עַד הַפְּנִימִי. רַבָּנָן דְּקַיְסָרִין בְּשֵׁם רִבִּי עוּקְבָה. בְּשֶׁאֵין הַחִיצוֹן עוֹדֵף. אֲבָל אִם הָיָה הַחִיצוֹן עוֹדֵף מְטַלְטְלִין עַד הַחִיצוֹן.

Rebbi Ze'ira[154] in the name of Rav Ḥisda: If pegs stick out from the walls of an alley, a person places a beam on them and allows the alley[155], on condition that they be within three [hand-breadths] of the alley. Two Amoraim, one said, only if they are strong enough to carry the beam and its tiles, but the other said, even if they are not strong enough to carry the beam and its tiles[156].

Rebbi Ze'ira asked: under the beam it is forbidden but it permits the alley[157]? Rebbi Aḥa ben Rebbi Ulla said, why did one not say to him,[158] did we not find this for Samuel? As Samuel said, under the beam[159] it is forbidden but it permits the alley. Rebbi Ze'ira in the name of Samuel: Under the beam and between the laths it is judged like a threshold[160]. Rebbi Ze'ira asked, what kind of threshold[161]? Like a permitted threshold or a forbidden threshold? Rebbi Ze'ira said, when I was still there it was questionable for me, but when I came here I heard Rebbi Yasa in the name of Rebbi Joḥanan: If a threshold is ten [hand-breadths] high but less than four wide it is permitted for both domains; only one should not exchange[162]. Rebbi Mana said before Rebbi Yose, look what he is saying! He only said, if it is less than four wide. But if it is four wide it is forbidden. He said to him, is that not the case of a cross-beam[41,163]? Is it not permitted under a cross-beam?

Rebbi Ze'ira said, Samuel and Rebbi Joḥanan. Samuel said, under the beam it is forbidden[159], but Rebbi Joḥanan said, it is permitted. Everybody agrees that between laths it is forbidden[164], and it was stated thus: If an alley is made of laths, if between one and the next are four hand-breadths one carries up to the outer one; otherwise one carries up to the inner one[165]. The Rabbis of Caesarea in the name of Rebbi Uqba, unless the outer one is wider. But if the outer one was wider one carries up to the outer one[166].

154 The great variability of the spelling of this name, זעירה, זעירא, זירא raises questions about the homogeneity of the following portion.

155 The pegs stick out in front of the alley into the public road. A beam placed there

indicates that the alley should be considered a private road even though under the beam there is public road. Only the beam must be within 3 hand-breadths of the alley walls so it may be considered having no distance from them. Babli 8b.

156 This is a question which can be raised for all beams, whether they only have to be wide enough to support a tile or also strong enough. Babli 14a.

157 Since the beam is clearly outside the alley, lying over public domain, how can it serve to turn the alley into a quasi-private domain?

158 This is the corrector's text. The scribe's was ולמה לא. ולא אשכחנן "why not? Did we not find . . .". This is a better text.

159 This now refers to a normal beam lying between the walls of the alley. Since the beam represents the lintel of an imaginary door at the inside of the beam, the space under the beam belongs to the outside. Babli 8b.

160 Cf. *Šabbat* 1, Note 66.

161 If the threshold is ten hand-breadths above street level and is large enough to be a domain in its own right, it would be forbidden to carry there both from inside the house of from the outside.

162 One may not carry anything from the inside to the threshold, put it down, and take it up again moving to the public domain.

163 It is implied here that a μέλαθρον is at least four hand-breadths wide (quoted by R. Hananel *ad* Babli 3a). Then the space under it is roofed, clearly not in the public domain and, therefore, permitted to the dwellers in the alley.

164 Since this is a flimsy sign and is neither roof nor door, it belongs to the outside. Babli 9a.

165 There is a path but not between walls. If the walls are represented by laths and between one lath and the next are less than 4 hand-breadths, then according to what had been said before the laths are virtually touching, they all form one lath and by the rule just stated the entire length belongs to the outside. But if the distances are larger, only the lath designating the exit to the public road falls under this rule. Cf. Babli 9a.

166 If the width of the alley at the outermost lath is larger than at the nearby inner laths, it is separate and cannot be counted with the others.

(18d line 72) הֶכְשֵׁר מָבוֹי כול". מַה לְחָיַיִם. לְחָיַיִם וְקוֹרָה כְּבֵית שַׁמַּי. לְחָיַיִם וְלֹא קוֹרָה כְּבֵית הִלֵּל. שְׁלֹשָׁה כְּרַבִּי יוֹסֵי. כָּל־שֶׁהוּא כְּרַבָּנִין. נִישְׁמְעִינָהּ מִן הָדָא. מַעֲשֶׂה שֶׁהָלַךְ רַבִּי אֱלִיעֶזֶר אֵצֶל רַבִּי יוֹסֵי בֶּן פְּרוֹרָה תַלְמִידוֹ לְאוֹבְלִין. וְהִרְאֵהוּ מָבוֹי אֶחָד. וְלֹא הָיָה בּוֹ אֶלָּא לֶחִי אֶחָד בִּלְבָד. אָמַר לוֹ. עֲשֵׂה לוֹ לְחָיַיִם. אָמַר לוֹ. מָה. אַתְּ אָמַר לִי לְסוֹתְמוֹ. אָמַר לוֹ. יִסְתֵּם. וְכִי מַה רְאָיָיה רְשׁוּת לְשַׁבָּת לָבוֹא לְכָאן. הָדָא אָמְרָה. שְׁלֹשָׁה כְּרַבִּי יוֹסֵי. אִין תֵּימַר. כָּל־שֶׁהוּא כְּרַבָּנָן. כָּל־שֶׁהוּא סוֹתֵם.

תַּנֵּי. וַהֲלָכָה כְּדִבְרֵי הַתַּלְמִיד. דְּל כֵּן מָה נָן אָמְרִין. כְּבֵית שַׁמַּי. וְיֵשׁ הֲלָכָה כְּבֵית שַׁמַּי וְלֹא כְבֵית הִלֵּל. אֶלָּא בְגִין דְּתַנֵּי. רַבָּן שִׁמְעוֹן בֶּן גַּמְלִיאֵל אוֹמֵר. מָבוֹי שֶׁאֵין בּוֹ אַרְבָּעָה טְפָחִים אֵינוֹ

צָרִיךְ קוֹרָה. דִּבְרֵי חֲכָמִים. רַב חוּנָא בְשֵׁם רַב. מָבוֹי שֶׁהוּא פָּחוּת מֵאַרְבַּע אַמּוֹת אֵינוֹ צָרִיךְ כְּלוּם.

"The legitimization of an alley," etc. What laths[167]? Two laths and beam following the House of Shammai? Laths but no beam following the House of Hillel? Three [hand-breadths wide] following Rebbi Yose? Arbitrarily small following the rabbis? Let us hear from the following[168]: "It happened that Rebbi Eliezer went to his student Rebbi Yose ben Perora at Oblin. He showed him an alley where there was only one lath. He told him, make it two laths. He said to him, what? Are you telling me to close it off? He told him, let it be closed; there is an argument for the domains of the Sabbath in this respect[169]?" This implies three following Rebbi Yose. If you would say, arbitrarily small following the rabbis, does arbitrarily small close off[170]?

It was stated, practice follows the student, for if it were not so, would we say following the House of Shammai[171]? Could practice follow the House of Shammai rather than the House of Hillel? But since it was stated[172], "Rabban Simeon ben Gamliel says, an alley which is not four hand-breadths deep does not need a beam." The words of the Sages? Rav Huna in the name of Rav: An alley which is less than four cubits does not need anything[173].

167 This refers to R. Eliezer who in Mishnah 2 requires two laths to permit an alley. The first question is whether he also requires a beam following the House of Shammai or no beam following the House of Hillel. Even though in the Babli R. Eliezer is called a Shammaite, it seems that in general he was extremely conservative and objected to all innovations. Therefore his opinion might show what practice was before schools developed in Pharisaic Judaism. The second question refers to Mishnah 6, where R. Yose sets minimal standards for the width of laths but is opposed by the majority.

168 Tosephta 1:2, Babli 11b/12a. In the Babli and one Tosephta ms. the name is ben Perida; the other sources have פרורה, פירה, פריד.

169 The objection was that since the alley, while not a thoroughfare, is public property, it is not possible to close it off as private property. R. Eliezer's answer is that property rights are no argument for the rules of the Sabbath which are only based on use.

170 Since R. Eliezer agrees that two laths put at right angles to the roadway would in effect close it off it is clear that these cannot be of negligible width.

171 Since the student in Mishnah 2 affirms the tradition of the House of Hillel and only gives a new interpretation of the position of the House of Shammai, there should be no question of practice which is not supposed

to follow the House of Shammai.
172 Babli 12a (middle). In Tosephta 1:3 (and the first version in the Babli) the reading is "four cubits". The reference is to the width of the alley.
173 In general the majority of the Sages has to be followed against Rabban Simeon ben Gamliel (in the theory of the Babli, except for Rabban Simeon ben Gamliel quoted in the Mishnah); but in this case it was stated that practice follows the student who required either lath or beam for any alley irrespective of width.

(19a line 8) קוֹרָה שֶׁאָמְרוּ כול'. אָמַר רִבִּי בָּא. כְּדֵי לְקַבֵּל עָלָיו דּוֹמוֹס שֶׁלְאָרְחִין לְאוֹרְכּוֹ. תַּנֵּי. רַבָּן שִׁמְעוֹן בֶּן גַּמְלִיאֵל אוֹמֵר. כְּדֵי לְקַבֵּל עָלָיו דּוֹמוֹס שֶׁלְאָרְחִין לְרוֹחְבּוֹ. מַה בֵּינֵיהֶן. אָמַר רִבִּי שִׁיָן. בְּרִיּוּת בֵּינֵיהֶן. עַל דַּעְתֵּיהוֹן דְּרַבָּנָן. אַרְבָּעִין אָרְחִין. עַל דַּעְתֵּיהּ דְּרַבָּן שִׁמְעוֹן בֶּן גַּמְלִיאֵל עֶשְׂרִין אָרְחִין.

שְׁתֵּי קוֹרוֹת. בְּזוֹ חֲצִי טֶפַח וּבְזוֹ חֲצִי טֶפַח. כַּמָּה יְהֵא בֵּינֵיהֶן. רִבִּי זְעִירָא אָמַר. חֲצִי טֶפַח. מַה בֵּין חֲצִי טֶפַח מִיכָּן וַחֲצִי טֶפַח מִיכָּן וְחֲצִי טֶפַח בָּאֶמְצַע. תַּנֵּי רִבִּי הוֹשַׁעְיָה. טֶפַח. שְׁתֵּי קוֹרוֹת. בְּזוֹ שְׁלִישׁ וְכָל־שֶׁהוּא וּבְזוֹ שְׁלִישׁ וְכָל־שֶׁהוּא וּבֵינֵיהֶן פָּחוּת מִשְּׁלִישׁ. יָבוֹא כַּיי דְּמַר רִבִּי יוֹחָנָן. הָעוֹמֵד וְחָלָל מִטְטַרְפִין בָּאַרְבָּעָה. וְהוּא שֶׁיְּהֵא הָעוֹמֵד רָבָה עַל חָלָל.

"The beam about which they spoke," etc. Rebbi Abba said, to accommodate a row[174] of tiles lengthwise. It was stated: Rabban Simeon ben Gamliel says, to accommodate a row of tiles crosswise. What is the difference between them? Rebbi Ashian said, strength is between them. In the opinion of the rabbis, forty tiles. In the opinion of Rabban Simeon ben Gamliel, twenty tiles[175].

Two beams, on each one half of a hand-breadth; how much can be between them? Rebbi Ze'ira said, half a hand-breadth. What is the difference between half a hand-breadth on either side and half a hand-breadth in the middle[176]? Rebbi Hoshaia stated, a hand-breadth. Two beams, on each a little more than a third of a hand-breadth and between them less than a third of a hand-breadth[177]. This parallels what Rebbi Johanan said, what is standing and empty space combine for four [hand-breadths], on condition that what is standing be more than the empty space[178].

174 Greek δόμος, ὁ.
175 The formulation seems self-contradictory. The length of the beam is assumed to be the standard 10 cubits which is 60 hand-breadths. A tile is 3 hand-breadths long and 1.5 hand-breadths wide. If the tiles are put on the beam lengthwise, the beam has to carry 20 tiles, if crosswise, there are 40 tiles.

Of the medieval commentators, Rashba (col. 105, Note 446) quotes the text as given here but adds "it seems that the formulation is slightly corrupt." His student Ritba (*ad* 13b, ed. Warsaw 22a) switches the places of 40 and 20. The same is true for Meïri (ed. Herschler, col. 68a) but since he gives a paraphrase rather than a copy of the text it is not clear how he read it. In any case, the Babli disagrees, 14a.

176 This follows the rabbis in the preceding paragraph. If two beams protrude from the walls on each side, they can be counted as one only if 20 tiles can be put on them. Therefore the gap between them must be bridged by one tile which according to R. Ze`ira must lie safely on both sides but according to R. Hoshaia only minimally.

177 This is a more restrictive interpretation of the preceding. As explained in the following sentence, we have a general rule that gaps can be disregarded if they are minor (for walls less that 3 or 4 hand-breadths) and in addition the solid material is wider than the gap. When applied to beams, the author of the present statement holds that on each side the solid part must be larger than the gap. To accommodate one hand-breadth, on each side one needs $1/3+\varepsilon$ of solid material to justify a gap of $1/3 -\varepsilon$ for arbitrary $\varepsilon>0$.

178 This refers to walls; cf. Chapter 7(24b l.55), Chapter 8(25a l.32), Babli 16a.

(19a line 18) קוֹרָה שֶׁהִיא יוֹצְאָה מִכּוֹתָל זֶה וְאֵינָהּ נוֹגַעַת בַּכּוֹתָל הַשֵּׁינִי. אוֹ שֶׁהָיוּ שְׁתַּיִם זוֹ כְנֶגֶד זוֹ. אִם יֵשׁ בֵּין זוֹ לְזוֹ שְׁלֹשָׁה טְפָחִים צָרִיךְ קוֹרָה. וְאִם לָאו אֵין צָרִיךְ קוֹרָה. אִית תַּנָּיֵי תַּנֵּי. אַרְבָּעָה. מָאן דָּמַר. שְׁלֹשָׁה. כְּדֵי עֲבִירַת אָדָם. מָאן דָּמַר. אַרְבָּעָה. כְּדֵי מָקוֹם. קוֹרָה שֶׁרֹאשָׁהּ אֶחָד לְמַעֲלָה מֵעֶשְׂרִים אַמָּה וְרֹאשָׁהּ אֶחָד לְמַטָּה מֵעֶשְׂרִים אַמָּה. רוֹאִין שֶׁאִילּוּ יָגוּד בְּתוֹךְ שְׁלֹשָׁה טְפָחִים וְהִיא נִרְאֵית בְּתוֹךְ עֶשְׂרִים אַמָּה מוּתָּר. וְאִם לָאו אָסוּר. קוֹרָה שֶׁרֹאשָׁהּ אֶחָד לְמַעֲלָה מֵעֲשָׂרָה טְפָחִים וְרֹאשָׁהּ אֶחָד לְמַטָּה מֵעֲשָׂרָה טְפָחִים. רוֹאִין שֶׁאִילּוּ יָגוּד בְּתוֹךְ שְׁלֹשָׁה וְהִיא נִרְאֵית בְּתוֹךְ עֲשָׂרָה טְפָחִים מוּתָּר. וְאִם לָאו אָסוּר.

If a beam protrudes from one wall but does not touch the second wall, or there were two opposite ones, if the gap between one and the other is three hand-breadths it needs another beam, otherwise it does not need another beam. There are Tannaim who state, four. He who says three, that a human may pass through. He who says four, that it be a place[179].

If one of the heads of a beam is higher that twenty cubits and the other lower than twenty cubits, one looks that if one would cut within three hand-breadths it would be seen lower than twenty cubits it is permitted[180], otherwise it is forbidden. If one of the heads of a beam is lower than ten hand-breadths and the other higher than ten hand-breadths, one looks that if one would cut within three hand-breadths it would be seen lower[181] than ten hand-breadths it is permitted, otherwise it is forbidden.

179 This explains the general disagreement whether one may disregard a gap only up to 3 or up to 4 hand-breadths, cf. Notes 80,81. 3 hand-breadths is the minimum width of an adult; 4 hand-breadth everywhere is the minimal size of a domain in the rules of the Sabbath, cf. Note 74. Babli 14a.

180 If the beam except the last 3 hand-breadths near the second wall is below 20 cubits the beam is acceptable since the higher part could be cut and it still would be qualified under the rule of the preceding paragraph. Since the rules of *Eruvin* are rabbinic, the possibility alone is sufficient for qualification.

181 Obviously one has to read: higher. Then the argument is parallel to that of the preceding sentence.

(19a line 37) שְׁתֵּי קוֹרוֹת זוֹ לְמַעֲלָה מְזוֹ. רִבִּי יוֹסֵי בֵּירִבִּי יוּדָה אוֹמֵר. רוֹאִין אֶת הַתַּחְתּוֹנָה כְּאִילוּ הִיא לְמַעְלָן וְהָעֶלְיוֹנָה כְּאִילוּ הִיא לְמַטָּה. וּבִלְבַד שֶׁלֹּא תְהֵא הָעֶלְיוֹנָה לְמַעְלָה מֵעֶשְׂרִים אַמָּה וְהַתַּחְתּוֹנָה לְמַטָּה מֵעֲשָׂרָה טְפָחִים. אַשְׁכָּח תַּנֵּי. רִבִּי יוֹסֵה בֵּירִבִּי יוּדָה בְּשִׁיטַת אָבִיו וְחָלוּק עַל אָבִיו. בְּשִׁיטַת אָבִיו. דּוּ אָמַר. רוֹאִין אֶת הַתַּחְתּוֹנָה כְּילוּ הִיא לְמַעְלָן וְהָעֶלְיוֹנָה כְּילוּ הִיא לְמַטָּן. וְחָלוּק עַל אָבִיו. דּוּ אָמַר. וּבִלְבַד שֶׁלֹּא תְהֵא הָעֶלְיוֹנָה לְמַעְלָה מֵעֶשְׂרִים אַמָּה וְהַתַּחְתּוֹנָה לְמַטָּה מֵעֲשָׂרָה טְפָחִים. בְּשִׁיטַת אָבִיו הוּא. אֵין תֵּימַר. אֲפִילוּ לְמַעְלָה מִכַּמָּה. רִבִּי יוֹסֵה חִינְנָא בַּר שְׁלָמְיָא רִבִּי יוּדָן. חִינְנָא בַּר שִׁילְמְיָא בְּשֵׁם רַב. וְהִיא שֶׁתְּהֵא הָעֶלְיוֹנָה בְּתוֹךְ שְׁלֹשָׁה טְפָחִים לַתַּחְתּוֹנָה.

If two beams are one on top of the other. Rebbi Yose ben Rebbi Jehudah says, one looks at the lower one as if it were higher or the higher one as if it were lower, on condition that the upper one not be higher than twenty cubits and the lower not be lower than ten hand-breadths[182]. It was found stated that Rebbi Yose ben Rebbi Jehudah follows his father's argument and disagrees with him. He follows his fathers argument since he says, one looks at the lower one as if it were higher or the higher one as if it were lower[183]. He disagrees with him since he says, on condition that the upper one not be higher than twenty cubits and the lower not be lower than ten hand-breadths. If you would say that he follows his father's opinion it could be arbitrarily high[184]. Rebbi Yose, Ḥinena bar Shelemiah, Rebbi Yudan; Ḥinena bar Shelemiah in the name of Rav: Only if the upper one be within three hand-breadths of the lower one[185].

182 Babli 14a, Tosephta 1:5. Mishnah 3 requires that the beam be wide enough for a tile to be placed there. The case considered here is of two beams, each one too narrow, but which would be acceptable if they were parallel on the same level. R. Yose ben R. Jehudah asserts that if the beams could be imagined to be moved vertically to become parallel they are acceptable even if on different height levels.

183 Since R. Jehudah in Mishnah 4 is explicit that the beams do not have to be strong he is the author of Mishnah 5 which introduces the principle of "one looks as if" used by his son.

184 Mishnah 1.

185 He permits the argument of R. Yose ben R. Jehudah if the difference in level of the two beams is negligible, i. e., smaller than 3 hand-breadths.

(19a line 36) רְחָבָה לְקַבֵּל אָרִיחַ כול׳. תַּנֵּי. רִבִּי שִׁמְעוֹן אוֹמֵר. בְּרִייָה אַף עַל פִּי שֶׁאֵינָהּ רְחָבָה. רַה הוּנָא בְשֵׁם רַב. הֲלָכָה כְּרִבִּי מֵאִיר. שְׁמוּאֵל אָמַר. הֲלָכָה כְּרִבִּי יוּדָה. רִבִּי יְהוֹשֻׁעַ בֶּן לֵוִי אָמַר. הֲלָכָה כְּרִבִּי שִׁמְעוֹן. אָמַר רִבִּי שִׁמְעוֹן בַּר כַּרְסָנָא. מִכֵּיוָן דְּתֵימַר. הֲלָכָה כְּהָדֵין וַהֲלָכָה כְּהָדֵין. מָאן דַּעֲבַד הָכֵין לָא חֲשָׁשׁ וּמָאן דַּעֲבַד הָכֵין לָא חֲשָׁשׁ. אָנַר רִבִּי מָנָא. מִכֵּיוָן דְּאִיתְמַר הֲלָכָה כְּרַבָּנָן. שָׁבְקִין לְיָחִיד וְעָבְדִין כְּרַבָּנָן.

רַב אֲזַל לְחַד אֲתַר. חָמָא חַד מָבוֹי שְׁרִיתֵיהּ בְּלֵיחַיָּא. יְהַב לָהּ חוּטְרָא וְאַפְלָהּ. אָמַר לֵיהּ רַב חוּנָא. דִּיקְלָא קָאִים. אָמַר לֵיהּ רַב. עֵינוֹי דְּרַב חוּנָא גָּבַהּ. וְעֵינוֹי דְּרַב לֵית אִינּוּן גָּבַהּ. אֶלָּא הֲרֵינִי אוֹסֵר לָהֶן מִשּׁוּם קוֹרָה. וּלְשַׁבָּת הַבָּאָה אֲנִי מַתִּיר לָהֶן מִשּׁוּם לֶחִי. שֶׁיִּהְיוּ יוֹדְעִין יָנָטַל הַדֶּקֶל שֶׁהוּא אָסוּר לְטַלְטֵל. וְאִית בָּעֵי מֵימַר. דְּלָא יְהַוּוּן סָבְרִין כְּרִבִּי יוּדָה. דְּרִבִּי יוּדָה אָמַר. רְחָבָה אַף עַל פִּי שֶׁאֵינָהּ בְּרִייָה׃

דְּרִבִּי חִינָּנָא לֹא אָמַר כֵּן. אֶלָּא רַב אֲזַל לְחַד אֲתַר. חָמָא חַד מָבוֹי שֶׁנִּיטַּל קוֹרָתוֹ וְאָסַר לָהּ. אָמַר לֵיהּ רַב חוּנָא. דִּיקְלָא קָאִים. אָמַר לֵיהּ רַב. עֵינוֹי דְּרַב חוּנָא גָּבַהּ. וְעֵינוֹי דְּרַב לֵית אִינּוּן גָּבַהּ. אֶלָּא הֲרֵינִי אוֹסֵר לָהֶן מִשּׁוּם קוֹרָה. וּלְשַׁבָּת הַבָּאָה אֲנִי מַתִּיר לָהֶן מִשּׁוּם לֶחִי. שֶׁיִּהְיוּ יוֹדְעִין שֶׁאִם יִנָּטֵל הַדֶּקֶל שֶׁהוּא אָסוּר לְטַלְטֵל. אִית דְּבָעֵי מֵימַר. דְּלָא יְהַוּוּן סָבְרִין כְּרִבִּי יוּדָה. דְּתַנֵּינָן תַּמָּן. אֵיזֶהוּ קַרְפֵּף. כָּל־שֶׁהוּא סָמוּךְ לָעִיר. דִּבְרֵי רַבִּי יְהוּדָה. וְהָכָא הוּא אוֹמֵר אָכֵן. אָמַר רִבִּי מָנָא. כְּבֵית דִּירָה עֲבַד לָהּ רִבִּי יוּדָה.

"Wide enough to carry a tile,[186]" etc. It was stated: Rebbi Simeon says, strong even if it is not wide. Rav Huna in the name of Rav: Practice follows Rebbi Meïr[187]. Samuel said, practice follows Rebbi Jehudah. Rebbi Joshua ben Levi said, practice follows Rebbi Simeon. Rebbi Simeon bar Carsana said, since you are saying that practice follows this one and that one, one may follow this one or that one without worry. Rebbi Mana said, since it was said that practice follows the rabbis, one disregards individuals and acts following the rabbis.

Rav went to a certain place; he saw a certain alley, he understood that [the beam] was [rotten][188], he hit it with a stick and felled it. Rav Huna said to him, the date palm stands[189]. Rav told him, the eyes of Rav Huna are high, the eyes of Rav are not high; but I am forbidding it for them because of a beam[190] and the next Sabbath I am permitting it to them because of a lath[191], that they should know that if the palm tree were removed they would be forbidden to carry. Some want to say, that they should not think following Rebbi Jehudah, as Rebbi Jehudah said, "wide enough even if not strong enough.[186]"

Rebbi Ḥinena did not say so but: [192]Rav went to a certain place; he saw a certain alley whose beam had been removed, and forbade it. Rav Huna said to him, the date palm stands. Rav told him, the eyes of Rav Huna are high, the eyes of Rav are not high; but I am forbidding it for them because of a beam, and the next Sabbath I am permitting it to them because of a lath, that they should know that if the palm tree were removed they would be forbidden to carry. Some want to say, that they should not think following Rebbi Jehudah, [193]as we have stated there, "what is a corral? Anything close to a village, the words of Rebbi Jehudah." And here he says so? Rebbi Mana said, Rebbi Jehudah treated it[194] as a house.

186 Mishnah 4.
187 The presumed author of the anonymous Mishnah. Since the editor of the Mishnah formulated it without mentioning a name, he indicated that his opinion was practice to be followed.
188 With Rashba (*ad* 15a, col. 112) read בלייה. The action must have been on a Sabbath; Rav prohibited carrying in the alley.
189 A date palm was standing at the entrance of the alley; it could be used as lath following Mishnah 7.
190 Since he stated that practice follows R. Meïr there was no valid *eruv* to start with.
191 The date palm can be used as lath but it must be so in the preparation for the Sabbath. No *eruv* can be made on the day of Sabbath.
192 This is the version alluded to in the Babli, 15a.
193 The following should be replaced by the text of the preceding paragraph. The text here is taken from Chapter 2 (Note 93) and *Beṣah* 4:2 (62c l. 17) and has no connection with the present topic. The problem is that in Mishnah 2:6 R. Jehudah allows carrying in a corral only if it contains at least a cistern, or a water ditch, or a cave, but in Mishnah *Beṣah* 4:2 he permits taking anything from any corral which is defined as fenced-in area close to a village.
194 The cistern or cave is treated as a house and the corral as the house's yard

where carrying is permitted.

(19a line 55) הָיְתָה שֶׁל קַשׁ אוֹ שֶׁלְּקָנִים כול'. לְמִי נִצְרְכָה. לְרִבִּי יוּדָה. דְּרִבִּי יוּדָה אָמַר. רְחָבָה אַף עַל פִּי שֶׁאֵינָהּ בְּרִיאָה׃

עֲקוּמָּה רוֹאִין אוֹתָהּ כְּאִילוּ הִיא פְשׁוּטָה. רִבִּי אָחָא בְשֵׁם רִבִּי זְעִירָא. רִבִּי יוּדָה הִיא. רִבִּי יוֹסֵה בְשֵׁם רִבִּי זְעִירָא. דִּבְרֵי הַכֹּל הִיא. וְהוּא שֶׁתְּהֵא עֲקַמוּמִיֵּת מִן הַצַּד. עֲקַמוּמִיֵּת שֶׁאֵינָה מְעַכֶּבֶת אֶת הַמָּבוֹי. אֲבָל עֲקַמוּמִיֵּת שֶׁהִיא מְעַכֶּבֶת אֶת הַמָּבוֹי הֲרֵי זוֹ אֲסוּרָה. וְאֵי זֶהוּ עֲקַמוּמִיֵּת שֶׁהִיא מְעַכֶּבֶת אֶת הַמָּבוֹי. כָּל־שֶׁאִילוּ יָגוּד וְאֵין בֵּין זוֹ לְזוֹ שְׁלֹשָׁה.

"If it was made of straw or reeds,[195]" etc. For whom was this needed? For Rebbi Jehudah, as Rebbi Jehudah said, "wide enough even if not strong enough.[196]"

"Curved one considers it as if it were straight.[195]" Rebbi Aha in the name of Rebbi Ze'ira: This is Rebbi Jehudah's. Rebbi Yose in the name of Rebbi Ze'ira: It is everybody's opinion, but only if the curvature be at the side, a curvature which does not obstruct the alley. But a curvature which impedes the alley makes it forbidden. What is a curvature which obstructs[197] the alley? Any which if you excise it there is less than three [hand-breadths] between the pieces[198].

195 Mishnah 5.
196 Since for the majority a bundle of straw never can carry the load of tiles.
197 Obviously one has to read: "does not obstruct". Noted by Rashba, col. 109.
198 If one eliminates the curved parts the gap created in the straight segment is less than 3 hand-breadths. Babli 14a.

(19a line 62) עֲגוּלָּה רוֹאִין אוֹתָהּ כְּאִילוּ הִיא מְרוּבַּעַת. עוֹד הִיא דְּרִבִּי יוּדָה. מִן הַיָּם לָמְדוּ. וַיַּעַשׂ אֶת־הַיָּם מוּצָק עֶשֶׂר בָּאַמָּה וגו'. אִיפְשָׁר לוֹמַר עָגוּל. שֶׁכְּבָר נֶאֱמַר מְרוּבָּע. אִיפְשָׁר לוֹמַר מְרוּבָּע. שֶׁכְּבָר נֶאֱמַר עָגוּל. אֵין תֵּימַר עָגוּל. נִמְצֵאתָ אוֹמֵר. מֵאָה וְשִׁשִּׁים יָדוֹת טַהֲרָה הוּא מַחֲזִיק. אֵין תֵּימַר מְרוּבָּע. נִמְצֵאתָ אוֹמֵר. מֵאָה וְעֶשְׂרִים וּשְׁתֵּי יָדוֹת טַהֲרָה הָיָה מַחֲזִיק. אֱמוֹר מֵעַתָּה. שְׁתֵּי אַמּוֹת הָעֶלְיוֹנוֹת עֲגוּלוֹת הָיוּ. שָׁלֹשׁ אַמּוֹת הַתַּחְתּוֹנוֹת מְרוּבָּעוֹת הָיוּ. נִמְצֵאתָ אוֹמֵר. מֵאָה וַחֲמִשִּׁים יָדוֹת טַהֲרָה הָיָה מַחֲזִיק. כָּתוּב אֶחָד אוֹמֵר אַלְפַּיִם בַּת יָכִיל. וְכָתוּב אֶחָד אוֹמֵר מַחֲזִיק בַּתִּים שְׁלֹשֶׁת אֲלָפִים יָכִיל. אִיפְשָׁר לוֹמַר אַלְפַּיִם. שֶׁכְּבָר נֶאֱמַר שְׁלֹשֶׁת אֲלָפִים. אִיפְשָׁר לוֹמַר שְׁלֹשֶׁת אֲלָפִים. שֶׁכְּבָר נֶאֱמַר בַּת. נִמְצֵאתָ אוֹמֵר. אַלְפַּיִם בְּלַח שֶׁהֵן שְׁלֹשֶׁת אֲלָפִים בְּיָבֵשׁ. מִיכָּן לָמְדוּ חֲכָמִים. אַרְבָּעִים סְאָה בְלַח שֶׁהֵן כּוֹרַיִים בְּיָבֵשׁ.

"Round, one considers it as if square.[195]" Again this is Rebbi Jehudah's[199]. They inferred it from the sea[200]. *He made the sea cast, ten cubits*[201]. It is impossible to say "circular" since already it was said "square"[202]. It is impossible to say "square" since already it was said "circular". If you said circular, it would turn out to contain 160 times the measure of purity. If you said square, it would turn out to contain 122 times the measure of purity. Therefore you have to say that the upper two cubits were circular, the lower three cubits were square and it turns out that it contained 150 times the measure of purity[203]. One verse says, *it contained 2'000 bat*[204], but another verse says, *it contained a volume of 3'000 bat*[205]. It is impossible to say 2'000 since already it says 3'000 and it is impossible to say 3'000 since already it says 2'000. Therefore you have 2'000 in fluid measure which are 3'000 in dry measure. From here the Sages learned that 40 *seah* in fluid measure are two *kor* in dry measure[205].

199 Since tiles cannot be laid on a round beam, the round beam is unacceptable for the majority.

200 The water container in Solomon's temple. Since the verse there states that its diameter was 10 cubits and its circumference 30, it is inferred that for halakhic computations the ratio of circumference of a circle to diameter is 3 (even though it is obvious that for other computations this cannot be correct since it is the ratio of the circumference of the regular hexagon to the diameter).

201 *1K.* 7:23.

202 The verse notes that the "sea" at the top was circular, diameter 10 and circumference 30. But in v. 24 it says that below it was adorned by flower buds, 10 cubits at each side. This implies that the bottom was square.

203 The numbers are impossible; to make them approximately intelligible one has to switch the positions of "square" and "circular". The height of the "sea" was 5 cubits. The "measure of purity" is the minimum size of a *miqweh* which is $3(cubits)^3$. If the "sea" were cubical, the outer volume would be $500(cubits)^3 = 166^2/_3$ *miqwaot*. Since the verse asserts that the walls were 1 hand-breadth wide ($^1/_6$ cubit) the actual inner volume was $4^5/_6 (9^2/_3)^2 = 451.6481 (cubits)^3 = 150.54$ *miqwaot*. The fractional part should be disregarded. If the "sea" were a right circular cylinder, with the prescribed value of $\pi=3$ the outer volume would be $375(cubits)^3 = 125$ *miqwaot*; the inner volume $338.7361 (cubits)^3 = 122.91$ *miqwaot*. In v. 26 it is stated that the volume contained in the "sea" was 2'000 *bat* which is 6'000 *se`ah* or 150 *miqwaot* (Babli 14a, *Pesahim* 109b). This volume also is the sum of the volumes of a rectangular solid of edge legths 3,10,10 and a right circular cylinder of radius 5 and height 3, as

stated in the text. The problem is that these are outer measures; the inner measures are consistently disregarded.	204 *1K.* 7:26. 205 *2Chr.* 4:5. 206 Babli 14b, Targum *2Chr.* 4:5.

(19a line 74) לְחָיַיִם שֶׁאָמְרוּ כול׳. מַתְנִיתָא בְמָשׁוּכִין מִן הַכּוֹתָל. אֲבָל אִם הָיוּ סְמוּכִין לַכּוֹתָל אוֹף רִבִּי יוֹסֵי מוֹדֶה. וְתַנֵּי כֵן. עָשָׂה לְחָיַיִם לַמָּבוֹי. אִם גְּבוֹהִין מִן הָאָרֶץ פָּחוֹת מִשְּׁלֹשָׁה. אוֹ שֶׁהָיוּ סְמוּכִין לַכּוֹתָל פָּחוֹת מִשְּׁלֹשָׁה. מוּתָּר. שְׁלֹשָׁה. וְהוּא שֶׁיְּהֵא הָעוֹמֵד רָבָה עַל הֶחָלָל.

"The laths[15] about which they spoke," etc. The Mishnah if they were distant from the wall. But if they were leaning against the wall even Rebbi Yose will agree[207]. And it was stated thus: If one made laths for an alley, if they are less than three [hand-breadths] from the ground or they were within three [hand-breadths] from the wall, it is permitted. Three only if what is standing be more than the empty space[208].

207 A lath plastered on the wall may be narrower than 3 hand-breadths.
208 In the tradition of the Babli 14b a space of full 3 hand-breadths never is negligible.

(19b line 2) אַבְנֵי הַבִּנְיָין הַיּוֹצְאוֹת מִן הַבִּנְיָן. אִם אֵין בֵּין אַחַת לַחֲבֵירָתָהּ שְׁלֹשָׁה טְפָחִים. נִידּוֹן כִּלְחָיַיִם. קֶרֶן זָוִית יוֹצֵא מִיכָּן וְקֶרֶן זָוִית מִיכָּן נִידּוֹן כִּלְחָיַיִם. כּוֹתָל הַנִּכְנָס וְנִרְאֶה כְפַס מִבִּפְנִים וְשָׁוֶה מִבַּחוּץ. אוֹ שֶׁנִּרְאָה כְפַס מִבַּחוּץ וְשָׁוֶה מִבִּפְנִים. נִידּוֹן כִּלְחָיַיִם. הָיָה מָשׁוּךְ. אַבָּא בַּר רַב חוּנָה אוֹמֵר. רוֹאִין אוֹתוֹ כִּילּוּ הוּא כָנוּס. הָתִיב רַב חִסְדַּאי. וְהָתַנִּינָן. חָצֵר גְּדוֹלָה שֶׁנִּפְרְצָה לִקְטַנָּה. הַגְּדוֹלָה מוּתֶּרֶת וְהַקְּטַנָּה אֲסוּרָה. וְיֵיעָשׂוּ כוֹתְלֵי גְדוֹלָה כִלְחָיַיִם אֵצֶל כוֹתְלֵי קְטַנָּה וְהוּתְּרָה קְטַנָּה. אָמַר לֵיהּ. אַבָּא בַּר רַב חוּנָה. תִּיפְתָּר בְּמָשׁוּכִין יוֹתֵר מֵעֶשֶׂר. תַּנֵּי רִבִּי שַׁיָּין קוֹמֵי רִבִּי אָחָא. בִּגְדוֹלָה אַחַת עֶשְׂרֵה וּבִקְטַנָּה עֶשֶׂר. אִיתְבְּעַת מַתְנִיתָא וְלֹא אִישְׁתַּכְּחַת. אָמַר לֵיהּ אָחָא. כֵּן אָמַר רִבִּי שִׁמְעוֹן בֶּן לָקִישׁ. כָּל־מִשְׁנָה שֶׁלֹּא נִכְנְסָה לַחֲבוּרָה אֵין סוֹמְכִין עֲלֶיהָ. אָמַר רִבִּי יוֹסֵה. אַתְיָיא כְּמָאן דָּמַר. חָצֵר נִיתֶּרֶת בִּשְׁנֵי פַסִּין וּבִלְבָד פַּס שֶׁלְּאַרְבָּעָה טְפָחִים מִיכָּן וּפַס שֶׁלְּאַרְבָּעָה טְפָחִים מִיכָּן. אָמַר רִבִּי יוֹסֵה בֵּירִבִּי בּוּן. וַאֲפִילוּ תֵימַר כֵּן אַתְיָא כְּמָאן דָּמַר. חָצֵר נִיתֶּרֶת בִּשְׁנֵי פַסִּים. וּבִלְבַד פַּס שֶׁלְּאַרְבָּעָה טְפָחִים מִיכָּן וּפַס שֶׁלְּאַרְבָּעָה טְפָחִים מִיכָּן. רַב עוּקְבָה בְּשֵׁם רַבָּנָן דְּתַמָּן. לִגְדוֹלָה הֵן נִידּוֹנוֹת וְאֵינָן נִידּוֹנוֹת לִקְטַנָּה.

1 ליה G | לה אחא G | ר' אחא נכנסה G | ניכנסה 2 אתייא G | ואתייה כמאן G | כמו ניתרת G | ניתורת 3 טפחים G | טפחין (2) תימר G | תמר אתיא G | אתייה 4 כמאן G | כמו ניתרת G | ניתורת טפחים | G טפחין 5 טפחים G | טפחין רב עוקבה G | ר' אמר [עו]קבן

Building stones which protrude from the building, if between one and the other is less than three hand-breadths they are considered as laths[209]. Corners sticking out at each side are considered as laths[210]. A wall which is indented and looks like a plank from inside but even on the outside or looks like a plank from outside but even on the inside is considered as laths[211]. If it was prolonged, Abba bar Rav Huna said, one looks at it as if indented[212]. Rav Hisdai objected, did we not state[213], "if a large courtyard collapsed into a small one, the large one is permitted but the small one forbidden." Should not the walls of the large one be like laths for the walls of the small one and the small one be permitted? Abba bar Rav Huna told him, explain it if they were extended more than ten[214]. Rebbi Ashian stated before Rebbi Aha, if the large one is eleven but the small one ten. The *baraita* was searched for but not found. [215][Rebbi] Aha told him, so says Rebbi Simeon ben Laqish: One does not use as support any Mishnah which is not accepted by a group[216]. Rebbi Yose said, it follows him who said, a courtyard becomes permitted by two planks on condition that there be a plank of four hand-breadths on each side[129]. Rebbi Yose ben Rebbi Bun said, even you have to say that it follows him who said, a courtyard becomes permitted by two planks on condition that there be a plank of four hand-breadths on either side. (Rav) [Rebbi Mar][217] Uqba in the name of the rabbis there: They are considered only for the large one but are not considered for the small one[218].

209 Babli 15a, Tosephta 1:9.

210 The entrance to the alley is slightly narrower than the alley itself because on both sides the walls of the alley end in convex corners. This is enough of a hint of a door frame.

211 Babli 15a, Tosephta 1:10; the thin wall is considered as door frame.

212 A small continuation of a wall of the alley is built into the street into which the alley opens. The extension represents a door frame.

213 Mishnah 9:2. The breach happened on the Sabbath. The large courtyard may continue to be used to move things since the breach acts like a door and is not open into public domain. The small yard cannot be used since the breach turns it into an appendix of the large one and its dwellers did not contribute to the *eruv* of the large one.

214 It is clear that the breach can be at most 10 cubits wide since it is considered a door. If only one cubit of the wall is left standing, 3 hand-breadths on each side, they should be considered as laths for the small one and its *eruv* should continue to be valid. If more of the wall is standing the total sum of the standing wall has to be more than 10 cubits.

215 Here starts a Genizah fragment edited by Ginzberg, p. 93 (G). The title in brackets is added from G.

216 The explanation of R. Ashian is

without foundation.
217 The text in parentheses is the Leiden ms.'s, the one in brackets from G.
218 The Babylonian rabbis essentially accept R. Ashian's objection that the smaller courtyard also be permitted but explain that the Mishnah refers to a special configuration where the walls of the large courtyard could not be used for the smaller one. Babli 9b.

(19b line 19) כּוֹתָל שֶׁצִּידוֹ אֶחָד יוֹצֵא וְצִידוֹ אֶחָד כָּנוּס. נוֹתֵן אֶת הַקּוֹרָה לוֹכְסָן וּמִשְׁתַּמֵּשׁ לוֹכְסָן. כַּהֲנָא אָמַר. נוֹתֵן אֶת הַקּוֹרָה לוֹכְסָן וּמִשְׁתַּמֵּשׁ לוֹכְסָן. רִבִּי אָחָא בְשֵׁם כַּהֲנָא. וּבִלְבַד שֶׁלֹּא תְהֵא הַקּוֹרָה מְשׁוּכָה יוֹתֵר מֵעֶשֶׂר. וּמִדְּרִבִּי יוֹסֵי. קַייָמָהּ רַב אֲבַדְיָמֵי נְחִיתָה. וּבִלְבַד שֶׁלֹּא תְהֵא הַקּוֹרָה מְשׁוּכָה יוֹתֵר מֵעֶשֶׂר. רִבִּי אָחָא בְשֵׁם רִבִּי שִׁמְעוֹן בֶּן לָקִישׁ. וּבִלְבַד שֶׁלֹּא יְהֵא הַכּוֹתֶל מָשׁוּךְ יוֹתֵר מֵאַרְבַּע. אַשְׁכַּחַת אָמַר. מַה דִּצְרִיכָה לְהֶן פְּשִׁיטָא לְהֶן.

1 אמ' | G - | 2 ומשתמש | G ומישתמש 3 ומדר' | G אמר ר' יוסי | G יוסה אבדימי | G אבודמא שלא | G שלוא 4 יותר | G יתר שלא | G שלוא 5 יותר | G יתר אשכחת | G ר' יוסה ר' אילא ר' אחא ובלבד שלוא יהא משוך הכותל יתר מארבע אשכחת להן | G להן ומה דצריכה להן פשיטא להן

אָמַר רִבִּי עוּלָּא. מִשְׁלֹשָׁה עַד אַרְבָּעָה הִיא מַתְנִיתָהּ. פָּחוּת מִשְּׁלֹשָׁה אֲפִילוּ יוֹתֵר מֵעֶשֶׂר מוּתָּר. אַרְבָּעָה אֲפִילוּ פָּחוּת מֵעֶשֶׂר אָסוּר. אֶלָּא אִם כֵּן אָנָן קַייָמִין מִשְּׁלֹשָׁה עַד אַרְבָּעָה.

1 משלשה | G משלושה (2) 2 אם | G -

If a wall on one side is extended and on the other side is shortened. Cahana said, he puts the beam obliquely and uses it obliquely[219]. Rebbi Aḥa in the name of Cahana: he puts the beam in the diagonal and uses in the diagonal, but only on condition that the beam not be extended more than ten? (From) Rebbi Yose [said][220], Rav Eudaimon the emigrant confirmed it, on condition that the beam not be extended more than ten[221]. Rebbi Aḥa in the name of Rebbi Simeon ben Laqish: On condition that the wall not be extended more than four [cubits][222]? [Rebbi Yose, Rebbi Ila, Rebbi Aḥa[223] in the name of Rebbi Simeon ben Laqish: On condition that the wall not be extended more than four [cubits].] You conclude to say, what was problematic for the one was obvious for the other [and what was problematic for the other was obvious for the one].

[224]Rebbi Ulla said, the Mishnah is from three to four [hand-breadths]. Less than three even more than ten [cubits] is permitted, four even less than ten [cubits] is prohibited. Where do we hold? From three to four.

219 If the walls bordering on the alley do not end at equal distances from the road, one may use a beam going from the end of the wall at one side to the end of the wall at the other. Greek λοξός, -ή, -όν "oblique".
220 The text of the Leiden ms. in

221 Since the beam represents the entrance door and no door may be more than 10 cubits wide, the restriction also applies to the oblique beam. It needed the inquiry of an emigrant to Babylonia to ascertain the tradition of the Babylonian Cahana.

222 May the longer wall extend more than 4 cubits over the shorter one, or do more than 4 cubits at one side define a domain different from the alley?

223 If one does not read the additions from G, the preceding question was declarative, not a question, and in the end only the first question of R. Aha was obvious for R. Yose. If one reads the additions, the name tradition here is thoroughly garbled since R. Aha, a contemporary of R. Yose, cannot have been the source of the earlier R. Ila. In addition, at the end it is asserted that what was problematic for R. Aha was obvious for R. Yose and vice-versa. Therefore in the previous sentence one has to replace "Aha" by "Yose", and read here "R. Aha, R. Ila" as recognized by S. Liebermann.

224 The meaning of this is totally unknown. Similar language is used in Chapter 8, on Mishnah 3 (25a l.36).

(9b line 28) בַּכֹּל עוֹשִׂין לְחָיַיִם כול'. תַּנֵּי. כָּל־דָּבָר שֶׁיֵּשׁ בּוֹ רוּחַ חַיִּים עוֹשִׂין אוֹתוֹ דוֹפָן וְאֵין עוֹשִׂין אוֹתוֹ לֶחִי. דִּבְרֵי רִבִּי מֵאִיר. וַחֲכָמִים אוֹמְרִים. אֵין עוֹשִׂין אוֹתוֹ דוֹפָן אֲבָל עוֹשִׂין אוֹתוֹ לֶחִי. אָמַר רִבִּי אָחָא. חַד תַּנָּא הוּא. מָאן דָּמַר. עוֹשִׂין אוֹתוֹ דוֹפָן. עוֹשִׂין אוֹתוֹ לֶחִי. וּמָאן דָּמַר. אֵין עוֹשִׂין אוֹתוֹ דוֹפָן. אֵין עוֹשִׂין אוֹתוֹ לֶחִי. אָמַר רִבִּי יוֹסֵה. תְּרֵין תַּנָּאִין אִינּוּן. וְלָמָּה עוֹשִׂין אוֹתוֹ דוֹפָן. שֶׁאִילּוּ יִשָּׁמֵט אֵינוֹ מַרְגִּישׁ. וְאֵין עוֹשִׂין אוֹתוֹ לֶחִי. שֶׁאִילּוּ יִשָּׁמֵט הוּא מַרְגִּישׁ. קָם רִבִּי יְהוֹשֻׁעַ דְּרוֹמַיָּא עִם תַּלְמִידוֹי דְּרִבִּי אָחָא. אָמְרוּ לוֹ. אָמְרִין דְּבַתְרֵיהּ. דְּהִיא פְּלִיגָא עַל רַבְכוֹן. וַחֲכָמִים אוֹמְרִים. אֵין עוֹשִׂין אוֹתוֹ דוֹפָן אֲבָל עוֹשִׂין אוֹתוֹ לֶחִי. מַה אִם בְּשָׁעָה שֶׁאִילּוּ יִשָּׁמֵט אֵינוֹ מַרְגִּישׁ אַתְּ אָמַר. מוּתָּר. כָּאן שֶׁאִילּוּ יִשָּׁמֵט הוּא מַרְגִּישׁ. לֹא כָל־שֶׁכֵּן. הֲוֵי. תְּרֵין תַּנָּיִין אִינּוּן עַל דְּרִבִּי אָחָא. הֵיכְמָה דְתֵימַר תַּמָּן. תְּרֵין תַּנָּיִין אִינּוּן עַל דְּרִבִּי יוֹסֵי. כֵּן אַתְּ אָמַר אוֹף הָכָא. תְּרֵי תַנָּיִין אִינּוּן עַל דְּרִבִּי אָחָא.

1 לחיין G | לחיי 3 תנא G | תני 4 תנאין G | תניי 6 יושוע G | ישו דרומיא G | דרומייה אמרו לו | G אמ' לון אמרין G | אמרון דבתריה G | דבתרה פליגא G | פליגה 7 רבכון G | רבכן 8 כאן G | כן לא כל | G לכל הוי | G הוו 9 דר' | G ר' היכמה G | היכמא כחמה G | יוסי יוסה G | יוסה 10 הכא G | הכה

"One may use anything for laths," etc. It was stated: Anything alive one makes into a sidewall[225] but one does not make it into a lath, the words of Rebbi Meïr, but the Sages say, one does not make it into a sidewall but makes it into a lath. Rebbi Aḥa said, there is one Tanna; for him who says that one makes it into a sidewall one makes it into a lath, and for him who says that one does not make it into a sidewall one does not make it into a lath[226]. Rebbi Yose said, there are two Tannaim. Why could one make it into a sidewall? For if it would slip off, would he not notice? Why does one not make it into a lath? For if it would slip off, would he notice[227]? Rebbi Joshua the Southerner was standing with students of Rebbi Aḥa. (They said to him) [He said to them][228], it is said at the end what disagrees with your teacher: But the Sages say, one does not make it into a sidewall but makes it into a lath. Since in a situation where he would not notice in case it slipped off you are saying that it is permitted, here where he would notice in case it slipped off not so much more? Therefore there must be two Tannaim according to Rebbi Aḥa[229]. Since you are saying that there are two Tannaim according to Rebbi Yose, so you also have to say here, there are two Tannaim according to Rebbi Aḥa.

225 The wall of a booth for Tabernacles.

226 He asserts that both for R. Meïr and for the Sages there is no difference between the rules for *Sukkah* and *Eruvin* as far as use of animals is concerned; their only difference is whether such use is permitted or not. One statement covers both cases.

227 There is a reason to differentiate between the rules of *Sukkah* and *Eruvin*. A person using the booth will immediately notice if a wall is missing; if the animal runs away he will not use the booth. But a person using the alley may not see the place of the lath; if the animal runs away he might use the alley to carry when it is forbidden to do so.

228 The reading of [G] is preferable over that of (the Leiden ms.)

229 Since R. Yose has shown that it is unreasonable to allow animals to be used for *eruvin*, the only question is whether the use is permitted for a *sukkah* or not.

(19b line 41) רִבִּי שִׁמְעוֹן בַּר כַּרְסָנָא בְשֵׁם רִבִּי אָחָא. רִבִּי מֵאִיר וְרִבִּי יוֹסֵה וְרִבִּי אֶלְעָזָר בֶּן עֲזַרְיָה שְׁלָשְׁתָּן אָמְרוּ דָבָר אֶחָד. רִבִּי מֵאִיר דְּלְחָיַיִם. מְטַמֵּא מִשּׁוּם גּוֹלֵל. רַבִּי מֵאִיר מְטַהֵר. רִבִּי יוֹסֵה דָּאֲהִילוֹת. רַבִּי יוֹסֵה אוֹמֵר. הַבַּיִת שֶׁבַּסְּפִינָה אֵינוֹ מֵבִיא אֶת הַטּוּמְאָה׃ רִבִּי אֶלְעָזָר בֶּן עֲזַרְיָה. דְּתַנֵּי. מַעֲשֶׂה בְּרִבִּי אֶלְעָזָר בֶּן עֲזַרְיָה וְרִבִּי עֲקִיבָה שֶׁהָיוּ בָאִין בִּסְפִינָה. וְעָשָׂה רִבִּי עֲקִיבָה סוּכָּה בְרֹאשׁ הַסְּפִינָה. וּבָאַת הָרוּחַ וְהִפְרִיחָתָהּ. אָמַר לוֹ רִבִּי אֶלְעָזָר בֶּן עֲזַרְיָה. עֲקִיבָה. הֵיכָן סוּכָּתָךְ.

1 אלעזר G | לעזר 2 דלחיים G | דלחיין - | ס דתנינן גולל G | גוליל 3 ר' | ס ור' ר' | ס דר' או' | G דהוא אמר שבסםפינה G | שביספינה אלעזר | G לעזר 4 עזריה G | עזרייה אלעזר |G אלעזר | ס לעזר עזריה | G עזרייה באין | G באים ועשה | Gס ועשה לו 5 הרוח G | רוח והפריחתה | G והפריחתה אלעזר | G לעזר עזריה G | עזרייה היכן G | אייה ס איה

[230]Rebbi Simeon bar Carsana in the name of Rebbi Aḥa: Rebbi Meïr, and Rebbi Yose, and Rebbi Eleazar ben Azariah, all three said the same. Rebbi Meïr of the laths, "it makes impure because of a cover stone[17], but Rebbi Meïr declares it pure.[231]" Rebbi Yose of *Ahilut*, "Rebbi Yose said, the house on a

ship does not transmit impurity[232]." Rebbi Eleazar ben Azariah, as it was stated: It happened that Rebbi Eleazar ben Azariah and Rebbi Aqiba came in a ship, and Rebbi Aqiba made himself a *sukkah* on the ship's deck. There came a wind which blew it away. Rebbi Eleazar ben Azariah said to him, Aqiba, where is your *sukkah*[233]?

230 This paragraph also is in *Sukkah* 2:4 (52d l.60, ס).

231 As explained in the previous paragraph, an animal may run away and therefore is not under the rules of a stone in any way.

232 Since the house is built to be moved all the time it does not qualify as "tent" and the rules of "tent impurity" do not apply to it.

233 R. Eleazar ben Azariah did not make a *sukkah* on the ship since he holds that since such a *sukkah* is not guaranteed to stay for the 8 days of Tabernacles it is not qualified even if the wind does not blow it away.

(19b line 48) מַה טַּעֲמָא דְּרִבִּי יוֹסֵי הַגְּלִילִי. סֵפֶר. מַה סֵּפֶר מְיוּחָד שֶׁאֵין בּוֹ רוּחַ חַיִּים. אַף כָּל־דָּבָר שֶׁאֵין בּוֹ רוּחַ חַיִּים. מַה סֵּפֶר מְיוּחָד דָּבָר מְיוּחָד שֶׁאֵינוֹ אוֹכֵל. אַף כָּל־שֶׁאֵינוֹ אוֹכֵל. מַה טַעֲמוֹן דְּרַבָּנָן. מַה סֵּפֶר מְיוּחָד שֶׁהוּא בְתָלוּשׁ. אַף כָּל־דָּבָר שֶׁהוּא בְתָלוּשׁ. עַל דַּעְתֵּיהּ דְּרִבִּי יוֹסֵי הַגְּלִילִי יָדוֹת אוֹכְלִין כְּאוֹכְלִין. נִישְׁמְעִינָהּ מִן הָדָא. כְּתָבוֹ עַל קֶרֶן הַצְּבִי וּגְדָדוֹ וַחֲתָמוֹ וּנְתָנוֹ לָהּ. כָּשֵׁר. מִפְּנֵי שֶׁגְּדָדוֹ וְאַחַר כָּךְ חֲתָמוֹ. הָא אִם חֲתָמוֹ וְאַחַר כָּךְ גְּדָדוֹ. לֹא. רִבִּי אָחָא בְּשֵׁם רִבִּי מְיָישָׁא. וְהוּא שֶׁכָּתַב עַל זִכְרוּתוֹ שֶׁלְּקֶרֶן. אֲבָל אִם כָּתַב עַל נַרְתֵּיקוֹ. כְּפָרוּשׁ הוּא וְכָשֵׁר. רִבִּי יוֹנָה בָּעֵי. אַף לְעִנְיָין הֶכְשֵׁר זְרָעִים כֵּן. הֵיךְ עֲבִידָא. חִישֵּׁב עֲלֵיהֶן שֶׁיֵּרְדוּ עַל הַבְּהֵמָה וּמִן הַבְּהֵמָה עַל הָאוֹכְלִין. תַּמָּן אָמַר רִבִּי יוֹסֵי הַגְּלִילִי. סֵפֶר. מַה סֵּפֶר מְיוּחָד שֶׁאֵין בּוֹ רוּחַ חַיִּים. אַף כָּל־דָּבָר שֶׁאֵין בּוֹ רוּחַ חַיִּים. אוֹף הָכָא כֵן. אוֹ שַׁנְיָיא הִיא. דִּכְתִיב וְכָל־מַשְׁקֶה אֲשֶׁר יִשָּׁתֶה בְּכָל־כְּלִי יִטְמָא. מֵעַתָּה אֲפִילוּ חִישֵּׁב שֶׁיֵּרְדוּ לַבּוֹרוֹת שִׁיחִין וּמְעָרוֹת. שַׁנְיָיא הִיא הָכָא. דִּכְתִיב כְּלִי.

1 מה G | ומה חיים G | חיין 2 חיים G | חיין G | מה חיין G | ומה 3 דרבנן G | דרבנין 4 אוכלין כאוכלין G | האוכלין כהאוכלין נישמעינה G | נישמעינא הדא | הדה וחתמו G | וחיתמו 5 שגדדו G | שגררו חתמו G | חיתמו האG | אבל גדדו G | גררו 6 וכשר G | והיא כשר 7 עבידא G | עבודה חישב עליהן G | חשב 8 האוכלין G | האכלין יוסי G | יוסה חיים G | חיין 9 חיים G | חיין הכא G | הכה שנייא G | שנייה וכל משקה אשר ישתה G | משקה 10 יטמא G | יטמא משק א בכל יטמא שיחין ומערות G | ולשיחין ולמערות שנייא G | שנייה

[234]What is Rebbi Yose the Galilean's reason? *Scroll*. Since a scroll is special in not being a living being, so no living being. Since a scroll is special in not being food, so no food. What is the rabbis' reason? *Scroll* Since a scroll is detached, so everything being detached. Are stalks of food in Rebbi Yose the Galilean's opinion like food? Let us hear from the following: If he

wrote it on a deer's antlers, shaved it off, had it signed, and gave it to her, it is valid. Because he shaved it off before he had it signed. Therefore, not if he had it signed and afterwards shaved it off. Rebbi Aḥa in the name of Rebbi Miasha: Only if he wrote on the male horn. But if he wrote on the sheath[235] it is as if separated and is valid. Rebbi Jonah asked: Is that the same for preparation of produce? If he desired that it should rain on an animal and [the rain] dripped from the animal onto food. There, Rebbi Yose said *scroll*, since a scroll is special in not being a living being, so no living being; and here, does he say so? There is a difference since it is written[236], *any drinkable drink in any vessel shall be impure*. Then also if it rained into cisterns, ditches and caves? There is a difference here, for it is written: *a vessel*.

---

234 The entire paragraph, dealing with divorce documents, is from *Gittin* 2:3, explained there in Notes 83-97.

235 Greek νάρθηξ, -ηκος, ὁ.

236 *Lev.* 11:34.

(19b line 62) שְׁיָרָא שֶׁחָנַת בַּבִּקְעָה כול'. רִבִּי אֲחָא בְּשֵׁם רִבִּי חִסְדַּיי. לְמִי נִצְרְכָה. לְרִבִּי יוֹסֵה בֵּירִבִּי יוּדָה. דְּרִבִּי יוֹסֵה בֵּירִבִּי יוּדָה אוֹמֵר. כָּל־מְחִיצָה שֶׁאֵינָהּ שְׁלֹשְׁתֵי וְשֶׁלְעָרֶב אֵינָהּ מְחִיצָה. (דִּבְרֵי רִבִּי יוֹסֵה בֵּירִבִּי יוּדָה.) וּמוֹדֶה הוּא הָכָא. וְתַנֵּי כֵן. בַּכֹּל עוֹשִׂין מְחִיצוֹת. אֲפִילוּ אוּכָּפִין אֲפִילוּ עֲבִיטִין אֲפִילוּ גְמָלִים. וּבִלְבַד שֶׁלֹּא יְהֵא בֵין אִיכּוּף לְאִיכּוּף מְלֹא אִיכּוּף. בֵּין עָבִיט לַעֲבִיט מְלוֹא עָבִיט. בֵּין גָּמָל לְגָמָל כִּמְלוֹא גָמָל. וּבִלְבַד שֶׁלֹּא יְהֵא עוֹמֵד כְּנֶגֶד עוֹמֵד וּפָרוּץ כְּנֶגֶד פָּרוּץ. אֶלָּא עוֹמֵד כְּנֶגֶד פָּרוּץ וּפָרוּץ כְּנֶגֶד עוֹמֵד.

1 ר' חסדיי G | רב חסדא נצרכה G נצרכה 2 יוסה G יוסי או' G אמ' G | ושלערב G או שלע(ר)ב - 3 | א' | ומודה G מודה הכא G הכה ותני G תני 4 עביטין G ע(ב)ניטי(ם) G עבִיטים גמלים G גמלין שלא G | שלוא איכוף G אכוף (2)

"If a caravan rested in an area of difficult access[19]," etc. Rebbi Aḥa in the name of (Rebbi Ḥasdai) [Rav Ḥisda][237]: For whom was this needed? For Rebbi Yose ben Rebbi Jehudah, since Rebbi Yose ben Rebbi Jehudah says[238], any partition which is not woof and warp is no partition, (the words of Rebbi Yose ben Rebbi Jehuda.)[239] But he agrees here, and it was stated thus[240]: One makes partition with everything, even camel saddles, even tubs, even camels, on condition that between two saddles there not be space for a saddle, between two tubs there not be space for a tub, between two camels there not be space for a camel, and on condition that no standing wall be opposite standing wall and breach opposite breach[241], but a standing wall opposite a breach and a breach opposite a standing wall.

237 Since no R. Hasdai is otherwise known in the Talmudim, the reading of [G] is preferable to that of the (Leiden ms.).
238 Mishnah 10.
239 This quote from the Mishnah is inappropriate here; it was deleted by the corrector in the ms. But G shows that it belongs to the original text.
240 Babli 15b/16a.

241 Not only is it required that the length of the wall be strictly greater than the opening (a matter of dispute in the Babli 15b) but also, and this is accepted in the Babli, that there can be no straight path from an opening on one side to that on the other side. This implies that if the caravan is camping on a road, the roadway has to be blocked at least on one side.

(19b line 69) נִמְצֵאתָ אוֹמֵר לְעִנְיָין כִּלְאַיִם. כָּל־הַפְּחוּתוֹת מִשְׁלֹשָׁה כְּסָתוּם. מִשְׁלֹשָׁה וְעַד אַרְבָּעָה. אִם הָעוֹמֵד רָבָה עַל הַפָּרוּץ מוּתָּר. וְאִם הַפָּרוּץ רָבָה עַל הָעוֹמֵד אָסוּר. מד' וְעַד עֶשֶׂר. אִם הָעוֹמֵד רָבָה עַל הַפָּרוּץ מוּתָּר. אִם הַפָּרוּץ רָבָה עַל הָעוֹמֵד. כְּנֶגֶד הָעוֹמֵד מוּתָּר. כְּנֶגֶד הַפָּרוּץ אָסוּר. יוֹתֵר מֵעֶשֶׂר. אַף עַל פִּי שֶׁהָעוֹמֵד רָבָה עַל הַפָּרוּץ. כְּנֶגֶד הָעוֹמֵד מוּתָּר. כְּנֶגֶד הַפָּרוּץ אָסוּר.

1 נמצאת | G נימצאתה או' | כ אמר לעניין | G לעניין כלאים | G כלאין משלשה | G משלושה   2 מד' |
G מארבעה כ מארבע[242]   3 רבה | כ מרובה[242]   מיתר | G -   אם | G ס ואם   רבה | כ מרובה[242]   4 יותר | G
יתר

אֲבָל לְעִנְיָין שַׁבָּת. כָּל־הַפְּחוּתוֹת מִשְׁלֹשָׁה כְּסָתוּם. מִשְׁלֹשָׁה וְעַד אַרְבָּעָה מֵאַרְבָּעָה וְעַד עֶשֶׂר. אִם הָעוֹמֵד רָבָה עַל הַפָּרוּץ מוּתָּר. אִם הַפָּרוּץ רָבָה עַל הָעוֹמֵד אָסוּר. יוֹתֵר מֵעֶשֶׂר. אַף עַל פִּי שֶׁהָעוֹמֵד רָבָה עַל הַפָּרוּץ אָסוּר. רִבִּי חֲנַנְיָה רִבִּי יוּדָה בַּר פָּזִי בְּשֵׁם רִבִּי יוֹחָנָן. לֵית כָּאן מִשְׁלֹשָׁה וְעַד אַרְבָּעָה. יֵשׁ כָּאן פִּרְצָה שְׁלֹשָׁה. אֵין כָּאן מְקוֹם אַרְבָּעָה.[243] הָתִיב רִבִּי מָנָא. וְהָתַנִינָן. מַקִיפִין בַּקָּנֶה. וְקָנֶה יֶשׁ לוֹ מָקוֹם. אָמַר לֵיהּ. לָא תִתְיבִינֵי פְּחוּת מִשְׁלֹשָׁה. שֶׁכָּל־הַפְּחוּתוֹת מִשְׁלֹשָׁה כְּסָתוּם. רִבִּי יוֹסֵי בֵּירִבִּי בּוּן בְּשֵׁם רַב. מִכָּל־מָקוֹם. מִכֵּיוָן שֶׁהָעוֹמֵד רָבָה עַל הַפָּרוּץ מוּתָּר.

1 אבל | סכ -   לעניין | G לעניין הפחות | G פחות משלשה | G משלושה   2 אם | G ס ואם יותר | G ס
יתר   3 כאן | G כן משלשה | G משלושה   4 כאן | G כן פרצה | סכ פירצה שלשה | G שלושה אין | G
ואין התיב | סכ מתיב[244]   5 בקנה | סכ בקנים[245]   6 כסתום | סכ כסתום היא

[246]It turns out that concerning *kilaim* everything less than three [handbreadths] is considered closed[247]. From three to four, if what is standing is more than what is torn down it is permitted, but if what is torn down is more than what is standing, it is forbidden. From four [hand-breadths] to ten [cubits], if what is standing is more than what is torn down, it is permitted; but

if what is torn down is more than what is standing it is permitted where it is standing[248], forbidden where it is torn down.

Concerning the Sabbath, everything less than three [handbreadths] is considered closed. From three to four, and from four [hand-breadths] to ten [cubits], it is permitted if what is standing is more than what is torn down, but forbidden if what is torn down is more than what is standing. More than ten, it is forbidden even though what is standing is more than what is torn down. Rebbi Ḥananiah, Rebbi Judah bar Pazi, in the name of Rebbi Joḥanan: There is no "from three to four.[249]" There is a hole of three and no place of four! Rebbi Mana objected: Did we not state: "One surrounds with sticks," does a stick form a place[250]? He said to him, do not object to me from a breach less than three hand-breadths, since anything less than three is considered closed! Rebbi Yose ben Rebbi Abun in the name of Rav: In any case, since what is standing is more than what is torn down, it is permitted[251].

242 The deviations in *Kilaim* are corrector's errors.
243 Here ends G.
244 Babylonian spelling.
245 Correct quote from Mishnah 10.
246 This paragraph from *Kilaim* 4:4 (Notes 82-87,כ), it also is found in *Sukkah* 1:1 (52a l. 74,ט) The baraita is similar to Tosephta Kilaim 4:6 quoted also in Babli *Eruvin* 16a. The main difference between Yerushalmi and Babli-Tosephta is that in the latter source, each breach has to be smaller than the surrounding wall whereas in the Yerushalmi only the total length of standing wall has to be larger than the total length of the missing parts.

The problem of *kilaim* addressed here is that grain must be separated from vines by at least 4 cubits. If the farmer wants to sow grain close to his vineyard, he has to fence off the vineyard by a wall. The question is, what is called a wall?

247 As noted before, an opening of less than three hand-breadths in a wall is disregarded; in computing the total length of the torn-down parts, breaches smaller than three hand-breadths in width are disregarded.

248 The Babli notes that not only are breaches up to three hand-breadths long disregarded as holes, but also standing pieces of wall up to three hand-breadths wide are disregarded as walls. This is the background of the discussion later in this paragraph.

249 R. Johanan wants to eliminate the middle part of the baraita, the one dealing with breaches of between three and four hand-breadths, in case that the standing walls also are in pieces less than four hand-breadths wide. While a hole wider than three hand-breadths is considered a breach, a wall narrower than four hand-breadths is

not a wall. In that case, there are only holes and no wall at all; the entire wall should be considered as non-existent! He requires in this case that any sown field should be at least four cubits distant from the vineyard.

250 Mishnah 1:10. Since the sticks are counted and no stick is even one hand-breadth wide, any piece of wall should be considered a wall. The answer is that as long as no two sticks are three hand-breadths distant from each other, the entire dividing fence is considered a solid wall.

251 This explicitly rejects the text of Babli/Tosephta, that no single hole may be wider than both adjacent pieces of standing wall; the wall is valid as long as the combined length of standing wall (of at least 4 hand-breadths length) is larger than the combined length of the breaches.

(19c line 7) מַקִּיפִין שְׁלֹשָׁה חֲבָלִים כול׳. אָמַר רִבִּי זְעִירָא. לא אָמְרוּ אֶלָּא בְעֶשֶׂר וּבְיוֹתֵר מֵעֶשֶׂר. הָא פָּחוֹת מִיכֵּן לֹא. וְתַנֵּי כֵן. הֵבִיא דוֹפָן שֶׁלְשִׁבְעָה טְפָחִים וְהִגְבִּיהוֹ מִן הָאָרֶץ פָּחוֹת מִשְּׁלֹשָׁה מוּתָּר. תַּמָּן אַתְּ אֲמַר. כָּל־פָּחוֹת מִשְּׁלֹשָׁה כְסָתוּם. וְכָא אַתְּ אֲמַר. כָּל־פָּחוֹת מִשְּׁלֹשָׁה כְסָתוּם. אִין אַתְּ בָּעֵי מַקְשִׁייָא הָכֵין קָשֵׁי. הֵבִיא דוֹפָן שֶׁל (אַרְבָּעָה) [שִׁבְעָה] טְפָחִים וְכָל־שֶׁהוּא. וְהִגְבִּיהוֹ מִן הָאָרֶץ שְׁנֵי טְפָחִים חָסֵר כָּל־שֶׁהוּא. יֵיבָא כַּיי דְּמַר רִבִּי יוֹחָנָן. הָעוֹמֵד וְהֶחָלָל מִצְטָרְפִין בְּאַרְבָּעָה. וְהוּא שֶׁיְּהֵא הָעוֹמֵד רָבָה עַל הֶחָלָל.

"One may surround by three ropes," etc. Rebbi Ze`ira said, they said this only about ten or more than ten[252]; therefore no less than ten. But was it stated thus? If one brought a wall of seven hand-breadths and raised it less than three from the ground, is it permitted[253]? There you are saying, everything less than three [handbreadths] is considered closed, and here you should be saying, everything less than three [handbreadths] is considered closed. If you want to object, object to the following: If one brought a wall of slightly more than (four) [seven][254] hand-breadths and raised it less than two hand-breadths from the ground[255], should it come following what Rebbi Johanan said, what is standing and empty space combine for four hand-breadths, on condition that what is standing be more than the empty space[98].

252 The Mishnah requires a wall for the Sabbath to be at least 10 hand-breadths high; similarly Mishnah *Sukkah* 1:10 requires walls of a least 10 hand-breadths. R. Ze`ira states that in contrast to the rules of the Sabbath where only slightly more than 50% actually must be wall, the rules for a *sukkah* for which walls are hanging down actually require 10 hand-breadths. The consensus of all commentators is to read here "10" in the masculine even though it is written in the feminine since "10 cubits" would make no sense at all.

253 Since דוֹפָן always is used for walls of a

sukkah, the *baraita* refers to a *sukkah*. It is stated that if the wall almost reaches to the roof but is almost 3 hand-breadths from the ground, it is considered a wall standing on the ground since distances of less than 3 hand-breadths are disregarded. The text is repeated in Chapter 7, Note 44.

254 The text in (parentheses) was written by the scribe, the one in [brackets] is the corrector's. The correction is erroneous.

255 If the rules of the Sabbath were applicable to *Sukkah*, this should qualify as a wall since its upper rim is 7 hand-breadths from the ground, and be acceptable for a roof 10 hand-breadths high. R. Ze`ira disqualifies it since the rules were meant only for the ground, not the roof.

(19c line 15) רִבִּי שִׁמְעוֹן בֶּן לָקִישׁ בְּשֵׁם רִבִּי יוּדָה בֶּן חֲנַנְיָה. נָעַץ אַרְבָּעָה קָנִים בְּאַרְבַּע זָוִיּוֹת הַכֶּרֶם וְקָשַׁר גֶּמִי מִלְמַעְלָה. מַצִּיל מִשּׁוּם פֵּיאָה. אָמַר רִבִּי יוֹחָנָן. כִּמְחִיצַת שַׁבָּת כֵּן מְחִיצַת כִּלְאַיִם. אָמַר רִבִּי יוֹחָנָן. מַעֲשֶׂה שֶׁהָלַךְ רִבִּי יְהוֹשֻׁעַ בֶּן קָרְחָה אֶצֶל רִבִּי יוֹחָנָן בֶּן נוּרִי לְנַגְנְגַד וְהִרְאֵהוּ שָׂדֶה אַחַת וּבֵית חֲבֵירָתָהּ הָיְתָה נִקְרֵאת. וְהָיוּ שָׁם פְּרָצוֹת יוֹתֵר מֵעֶשֶׂר. וְהָיָה נוֹטֵל עֵצִים וְסוֹתָם. דּוּקְרָנִין וְסוֹתָם. עַד שֶׁמִּיעֲטָן פָּחוּת מֵעֶשֶׂר. אָמַר. כְּזוֹ כֵן מְחִיצַת שַׁבָּת. אָמַר רִבִּי זְעִירָא. מוֹדֶה רִבִּי שִׁמְעוֹן בֶּן לָקִישׁ לְעִנְיָין שַׁבָּת. שֶׁאֵין פֵּיאָה מַצֶּלֶת יוֹתֵר מֵעֶשֶׂר. אָמַר רִבִּי חַגַּיי. מַתְנִיתָא אָמְרָה כֵן. מַקִּיפִין שְׁלֹשָׁה חֲבָלִים זֶה לְמַעְלָה מִזֶּה. אִם אוֹמֵר אַתְּ שֶׁהַפֵּיאָה מַצֶּלֶת יוֹתֵר מֵעֶשֶׂר. כְּמוֹ כֵן חֶבֶל אֶחָד.

1 חנניה | כ חנינה ס חנינא ארבעה | ס ארבע בארבע | כ בארבעה 2 הכרם | כ שבכרם ס של כרם מלמעלה | ס מלמעלן יוחנן | כ יונה 3 לנגנגד | כ לנגניגר ס לנגינר 4 והראהו | כ הראהו חבירתה | ס רתה 5 אעים | כ אעין דוקרנין | ס ודוקרמים כזו | כס כזה 6 זעירא | ס זעורה לעניין | כס לעניין שאין פיאה | כ שהפיאה²⁵⁶ 7 חגיי | כ חגי זו | כס זה מזו | כס מזה או' | כ אמ' 8 כמו כן | כס דייו

²⁵⁷Rebbi Simeon ben Laqish in the name of Rebbi Judah ben Haninah²⁵⁸: If one put in four poles at the four corners of a vineyard and connected them with a bast string on top, this saves as a symbolic fence²⁵⁹. Rebbi Johanan said, the rules of separation walls for the Sabbath are the rules for *kilaim*²⁶⁰. Rebbi Johanan said, it happened that Rebbi Joshua ben Qorhah went to Rebbi Johanan ben Nuri at Nagnigar²⁶¹; he showed him a field called *bet haverata* whose wall had parts torn down more than ten [cubits] wide. He took wood to insert, forked poles⁴⁴ to insert, until he reduced to less than ten. He said, just like that is a dividing wall for the Sabbath. Rebbi Ze`ira said, Rebbi Simeon ben Laqish agrees that on the Sabbath, a symbolic fence does not save more than ten²⁶². Rebbi Haggai said, the Mishnah says so: "One may surround by three ropes one higher than the other." If you say that the string saves, one rope would be sufficient²⁶³.

רִבִּי יוֹנָה אָמַר. רַב הוֹשַׁעְיָה בָעֵי. הָדָא פֵּיאָה אֲמָה אִיתְאָמַר. מִלְמַעְלָן מִן הַצַּד. אִין תֵּימַר מִלְמַעְלָן. כָּל־שֶׁכֵּן מִן הַצַּד. אִין תֵּימַר מִן הַצַּד. הָא מִלְמַעְלָה לֹא. אִין תֵּימַר מִלְמַעְלָן. יָאוּת אָמַר רִבִּי חַגַּיי. אִין תֵּימַר מִן הַצַּד. לֹא אָמַר רִבִּי חַגַּיי כְּלוּם. מַה נַפְשָׁךְ. אִם מִלְמַעְלָן. מִלְמַעְלָן. אִם מִן הַצַּד. הֲרֵי מִן הַצַּד. רַבָּנָן דְּקַיְסָרִין בְּשֵׁם רִבִּי יִרְמְיָה. תִּיפְתָּר בְּשֶׁעֲשׂוּיִין כְּמִין דְּקָרן.

1 רב הושעיה | כ ר' יאשיה   אמה איתאמר | סכ מה את אמרת   2 כל | כ הא כל   מלמעלה | סכ מלמעלן   3 יאית אמ' ר' חגיי. אין תימר מן הצד | כ -   3-4 מה נפשך. הרי למעלן. אם למעלן. אם מן הצד. הרי מן הצד | ס -   4 אם | כ אי   רבנן | כ רבנין   בשעשויין | סכ בעשויין   5 דקרן | ס דקרים כ דוקרן

Rebbi Jonah said: Rebbi Hoshaia asked, what do you say[264] about that symbolic fence, on top or at the sides[265]? If you say on top, so much more on the sides. If you say on the sides, then not on the top. If you say on the top, Rebbi Ḥaggai said it correctly[266]. If you say from the sides, Rebbi Ḥaggai did not say anything[267]. What do you want to say[268], if on top, it must be on top. Or from the sides, it is on the sides. The rabbis of Caesarea in the name of Rebbi Jeremiah: Explain it if they were strung on forked poles[269,44].

רִבִּי זְעִירָא רִבִּי אֲבְדִּימִי דְחֵיפָה בְּשֵׁם רִבִּי שִׁמְעוֹן בֶּן לָקִישׁ. לְגוֹבַהּ אֲפִילוּ עַד מֵאָה אַמָּה. אָמַר רִבִּי יוּדָן. הָדָא דְּתֵימַר לְעִנְיָין כִּלְאַיִם. אֲבָל לְעִנְיָין שַׁבָּת לֹא תְהֵא פֵּיאָה גְבוֹהָה מִן הַקּוֹרָה. אָמַר רִבִּי יוֹסֵה אָמַר רִבִּי. הִיא כִלְאַיִם הִיא שַׁבָּת. עַל דַּעְתֵּיהּ דְּרִבִּי. מַה בֵּין קוֹרָה מַה בֵּין פֵּיאָה. קוֹרָה מַצֶּלֶת מֵרוּחַ אַחַת. פֵּיאָה אֵינָהּ מַצֶּלֶת עַד שֶׁתְּהֵא מְגוּפֶפֶת מֵאַרְבַּע רוּחוֹתֶיהָ. וַתְיָא כַּיי דָּמַר רִבִּי זְעִירָא בְּשֵׁם רַב הַמְנוּנָא. פֵּיאָה אֵינָהּ מַצֶּלֶת עַד שֶׁתְּהֵא מְגוּפֶפֶת מֵאַרְבַּע רוּחוֹתֶיהָ.

1 זעירא | ס זעורא   אבדימי | סכ אבודמא   לגובה | ס לגבוה   2 דתימר | סכ דאת אמר   שבת | ס פיאה   גבוהה | כ גדולה   3 יוסה | ס יוסי אמ' ר' | סכ -   דר' | ס דר' יוסה כ דר' יוסי   קורה | ס פיאה   4 פיאה | ס קורה | -   כ פיאה אינה מצלת מרוח אחת עד שתהא מגופפת מארבע רוחותיה   5 ותייא | סכ ואתיא   כיי | ס כהיא כ בההיא   דמר | ס דאמ'   זעירא | ס זעורה   פיאה | ס הפיאה

Rebbi Zeʿira, Rebbi Eudaimon of Haifa, in the name of Rebbi Simeon ben Laqish: In height even one hundred cubits[270]. Rebbi Judan said, that is, for *kilaim*, but as regards the Sabbath, a symbolic fence should not be better than a beam. Rebbi Yose said (in the name of Rebbi)[271], it is the same for *kilaim* and Sabbath. According to Rebbi [Yose][272], what is the difference between a beam and a symbolic fence? A beam saves in one direction[273]; a symbolic fence does not save from one side unless it is used to close all four sides;. This follows what Rebbi Zeʿira said in the name of Rav Hamnuna: A symbolic fence does not save unless it seals all four sides[274].

אָמַר רִבִּי בָּא בַּר מָמָל. טְטְרַפְלִיּוֹת שֶׁבִּכְרָמִים אָסוּר לְטַלְטֵל תַּחְתֵּיהֶן מִפְּנֵי שֶׁהֵן סוֹף תִּקְרָה. וְאֵין סוֹף תִּקְרָה מַצִּיל מִשּׁוּם פֵּיאָה. אָמַר רִבִּי פִּינְחָס. אָתָא עוּבְדָא קוֹמֵי רִבִּי יִרְמְיָה בְּאַרְבָּעָה עֲמוּדִים וַעֲלֵיהֶם אַרְבַּע פְּצְטְלִיּוֹת. וְהִתִּיר לְטַלְטֵל מִשּׁוּם פֵּיאָה. רִבִּי בּוּן וְרִבִּי בּוּן בְּעוֹן קוֹמֵי רִבִּי זְעִירָא. פֵּיאָה מַהוּ שֶׁתַּצִּיל בְּסוּכָּה. אָמַר לוֹן. פֵּיאָה מַצֶּלֶת בְּסוּכָּה. סוֹף סְכָךְ מָהוּ שֶׁתַּצִּיל בְּסוּכָּה. אָמַר לוֹן. אֵין סוֹף סְכָךְ מַצִּיל בְּסוּכָּה. מַה בֵּין זֶה לָזֶה. זֶה נַעֲשָׂה לְכָאן. וְזֶה נַעֲשָׂה לְכָאן. אָמַר רִבִּי אַבָּהוּ. כָּל־אִילֵּין מִילַּיָּא לְעִנְיָין מֵיסַב וּמִיתַּן. הָא לְהוֹרוֹת אָסוּר. לְהוֹרוֹת. מָה אִם סוּכָּה קַלָּה אַתְּ אָמַר. אָסוּר. שַׁבָּת הַחֲמוּרָה לֹא כָּל־שֶׁכֵּן. רִבִּי בּוּן בַּר חִיָּיא בְּעָא קוֹמֵי רִבִּי זְעִירָא. מָאן תַּנָּא. פֵּיאָה מַצֶּלֶת. לֹא רִבִּי יוֹחָנָן בֶּן נוּרִי. אָמַר לֵיהּ. אַדָא תַנָּה.

1 טטרפליות | כ טיטרפליות שבכרמים | ס(כ)²⁷⁵ שבכרכים 2 בארבעה | ס בארבע 3 ארבע | סכ ארבעה פצטליות | סכ פיסטליות משום | סכ תחתיהן משום ור' בון | כ ור' בנין 4 זעירה | סכ זעירא שתציל | ס שיציל 5 לכאן | סכ לכך וזה | סכ לכך 6 לכאן | סכ וזה אינו 6 לכאן | סכ לכך מיסב ומיתן | סכ משא ומתן 7 חייא | סכ חייה 8 זעירא | ס זעורה אדא | ס אדהי

Rebbi Abba bar Mamal said, it is forbidden to carry under the four-gated bowers[276] in vineyards[277] since they form the end of the roof and the end of a roof cannot save as a symbolic fence. Rebbi Phineas said, a case came before Rebbi Jeremiah of four pillars and on them four beams[278]; he permitted to carry under them because of a symbolic fence. Rebbi Abun and Rebbi Abun[279] asked before Rebbi Ze`ira, does a symbolic fence save in a *sukkah*[280]? He said to them, a symbolic fence saves in a *sukkah*. Does the end of the roofing save in a *sukkah*[281]? He said to them, the end of the roofing does not save in a *sukkah*. What is the difference between them? One is made for the purpose, the other one is [not][281] made for the purpose. Rebbi Abbahu said, all these things[283] are for discussion's sake, but as far as teaching, it is forbidden to teach it. If this is forbidden for the minor commandment of *sukkah*, so much more for the strict commandment of Sabbath! Rebbi Abun bar Ḥiyya asked before Rebbi Ze`ira: Is not the Tanna, according to whom a symbolic fence saves, Rebbi Joḥanan ben Nuri? He said to him, that is the Tanna[284].

256 But the Rome ms. of *Kilaim* reads with the other sources.

257 The following text is both in *Kilaim* 4:4 (Notes 51-81,כ) and in *Sukkah* 1:1 (52a l. 50,ס). Cf. Babli 11a.

258 This is the correct name as given in the parallels.

259 In Tractates *Kilaim* and *Eruvin* the word פֵּיאָה does not mean "corner" as in biblical Hebrew and in Tractate *Peah* but a wire or string strung as a symbolic fence around a field or a vineyard to separate it from the neighboring one, or around a town to make it a "walled" town for the rules of

the Sabbath. The imaginary fence represented by the string "saves" from the prohibition of *kilaim*.

260 In the Babli 11a/b, the statement of R. Simeon ben Laqish in the name of R. Judah ben Haninah explicitly excludes the expedient of the bast rope for the Sabbath, but R. Johanan excludes it also for *kilaim*. R. Simeon ben Laqish is reported there to accept for himself the statement attributed here to R Johanan, that the rules for Sabbath and *kilaim* are identical, whereas R. Johanan rejects this in general. The position of the Babli is that R. Simeon ben Laqish only reports the opinion of R. Judah ben Haninah without accepting it himself, and that R. Johanan prohibits the use of a rope for openings wider than 10 cubits, see Note 262. The Yerushalmi accepts R. Simeon ben Laqish's statement as describing his own position.

261 A place in lower Galilee of unknown location.

262 The string represents a gate, not a wall.

263 The caravan clearly wants more space for animals and people than 10 by 10 cubits; if they park some camel loads at the four corners of their camp, they need a surrounding wall, not a surrounding gate. If it is possible to symbolize a wall with one rope, why does one need three?

264 The translation follows the parallel sources. איתאמר is Babli spelling.

265 If four poles are put up at the four sides of the vineyard, does the string have to go from top to top, to create the impression of a gate, or is it strung at half height between the poles, to give the impression of a wall?

266 Since Mishnah 9 does not require the lowest rope to be within three hand-breadths of the ground, it is clear that even if the rows are strung high one needs three ropes rather than just one.

267 If the rope must be low, the case of פִּאָה is different from that of the Mishnah.

268 A technical term, indicating that the desired result can be inferred from both hypotheses. The inference here is that R. Haggai is correct in both cases, since the Mishnah is formulated to apply to both of them.

269 If the poles have separate hooks so that each side has a complete arrangement of poles and rope, then even R. Ze`ira will admit that the rope forms a valid enclosure for the Sabbath. In this case, by necessity the rope is on top only. In this, the Yerushalmi parallels the final explanation of the Babli 11b, rejecting symbolic walls but accepting symbolic gates.

270 If a rope is drawn from the top of one pole to the next, there are no height limitations (except, naturally, that it cannot be lower than 10 hand-breadths.)

271 An addition of the text here, missing in the parallels, to be deleted.

272 Necessary addition from the parallels, missing here.

273 Beam or lath are needed only at the entrance to the alley.

274 The problem is not discussed in the Babli.

275 Reading of the Rome ms.

276 Greek τετράπυλον, τό, "archway entered from four sides." Bowers erected at the crossing of two paths, with only the posts and the connecting beams built, and

the roof formed by plants climbing on the poles. Rebbi Abba bar Mamal considers these beams as קוֹרָה under which one may not carry in a dead-end street (Note 159).

277 The vineyard in question is not enclosed by a wall, or it is enclosed but too large (larger than 5000 square cubits) to be considered a courtyard for the rules of Sabbath; hence, one may carry under the roof of the bower but not outside.

278 Greek ἐπιστύλιον, τό, "architrave."

279 In *Kilaim* "R. Bun and the rabbis." S. Liebermann points out that in *Terumot* 11:4 (Note 88) for the Leiden text "R. Abun asked (verb in plural)" the Rome ms. reads: "R. Abun and R. Abin asked". This probably should be read here also.

280 The hut one builds to live in on the festival of Tabernacles must have roofing of plant material. The walls may be made of any material. The question is whether a virtual wall is permitted.

281 Since the roofing must have some support, the four corner posts of the *sukkah* must have some connection on which the roofing may rest. Can these connections be considered as *peah*, following R. Jeremiah in the preceding case?

282 Added from the parallels, necessary for understanding the text.

283 The rulings of R. Ze'ira. Building a *sukkah* is a positive commandment but neglecting it is not punishable in court. But desecrating the Sabbath is a capital crime.

284 Hence, in regard to the Sabbath this is the opinion of a minority of one, which cannot be operational practice.

(19c line 49) מַקִּיפִין בַּקָּנִים בִּלְבַד כול'. מַקִּיפִין בַּקָּנִים לַשַּׁיָּירָא. דִּבְרֵי רִבִּי יוּדָה. הָא יָחִיד צָרִיךְ שְׁתִי וָעֵרֶב. וְהָא רִבִּי יוּדָה מַאי שְׁנָא²⁸⁵ בֵּין יָחִיד לַשַּׁיָּירָא. וְרַבָּנָן לָא מְהַשְׁנֵיי בֵּין יָחִיד לַשַּׁיָּירָא. נִישְׁמְעִינָהּ מִן הָדָא. שִׁיָּירָא שֶׁחָנָת בְּתֵל שֶׁהוּא גְבוֹהָה עֲשָׂרָה. בְּנֶקַע שֶׁהוּא עָמוֹק עֲשָׂרָה. בְּגִינָה שֶׁהִיא מוּקֶּפֶת גָּדֵר. מְטַלְטְלִין בָּהּ אֲפִילוּ כּוֹר אֲפִילוּ כּוֹרַיִים. מְטַלְטְלִין בָּהּ עַד בֵּית סָאתַיִם. וּבִלְבַד שֶׁלֹּא יְשַׁיְּירוּ בָהּ בֵּית סָאתַיִם פָּנוּי. רִבִּי אָחָא בְּשֵׁם רִבִּי חִינָּנָה. אֲפִילוּ אוּכָּפוֹת אֲפִילוּ עֲבִיטִין. מִילְתֵיהּ דְּרַב הוּנָא אָמְרָה. וּבִלְבַד אָדָם. דָּמַר רִבִּי בָּא בְּשֵׁם רַב חוּנָה. אֶחָד אוֹ שְׁנַיִם נוֹתְנִין לָהֶן בֵּית סָאתַיִם. שְׁלֹשָׁה נוֹתְנִין לָהֶן בֵּית שֵׁשֶׁת סָאִין. מִיכָּן וָהֵילֵךְ לְפִי חֶשְׁבּוֹן.

"One surrounds with sticks, on condition," etc. One surrounds with sticks for a caravan, the words of Rebbi Jehudah. This implies that an individual needs woof and warp[25]. So Rebbi Jehudah differentiates between an individual and a caravan; do the rabbis not differentiate between an individual and a caravan[285]? Let us hear from the following:[286] "If a caravan rested on a hill ten [hand-breadths] high, or in a depression ten [hand-breadths] deep[287], or in a garden fenced in by a stone wall, one carries in it even if it is a *kor*[288] or two *kor*, (one carries in it up to two *bet se'ah*)[289], on condition that they do not leave an area of two *bet se'ah* unoccupied." Rebbi Aḥa in the name of Rebbi Ḥinena: even with camel saddles, even with tubs. The word of Rav Huna implies, only by humans. For Rebbi Abba said in the name of Rav Huna, to one or two one gives two *bet se'ah*, to three one gives six *bet se'ah*, from there on by proportion[290].

285 In Mishnah 10 the majority permits walls of sticks also for individuals; do they never differentiate between rules for individuals and for groups?
286 Tosephta 2:3.
287 Since these places are naturally separated from their surroundings, they do not need to be fenced in to become separate domains for the Sabbath.
288 *Kor* is a measure of dry volume, of 30 *se'ah*. What it really should have said is "*bet kor*", the area which can be sown with a *kor* of seed grain. Based on the standard definition of a *bet se'ah* as 2500 square cubits, a *bet kor* is 75'000 square cubits.
289 The clause in parentheses is not in the Tosephta. Since it contradicts the statements preceding and following it should be deleted. One may conjecture that the sentence originally was a marginal gloss by a reader who did not understand the thrust of the argument, which then was copied into the text.

Two *bet seah* is the maximal area allowed for carrying on the Sabbath in a corral which is not used for human dwelling. But the camping caravan is temporary home to the travelers, therefore its domain is used for human dwelling.
290 The statement of the Tosephta is qualified (cf. Babli 16b). As noted in the next paragraph, groups of 3 or more people are defined as caravans. A caravan of n travelers can spend the Sabbath in a camp measuring $2n$ *bet se'ah* (in fact, it can be $2(n+1)-\varepsilon$ since an additional $(2-\varepsilon)$ *bet se'ah* is authorized in the Tosephta.)

(19c line 59) אֵין שְׁיָירָה פָּחוּת מִשְּׁלֹשָׁה. אֵין הַגּוֹי מַשְׁלִים בַּשְּׁיָירָה. קָטָן מָהוּ שֶׁיַּשְׁלִים בַּשְּׁיָירָה. הֵיךְ עֲבִידָא. הָיוּ שְׁנַיִם וְעֵירְבוּ עֵירוּב אֶחָד. וּבָא הַגּוֹי וְהוֹסִיף. כְּבָר נִכְנְסָה שַׁבָּת בְּאִסּוּר. הָיוּ שְׁלֹשָׁה וְעֵירְבוּ שְׁנֵי עֵירוּבִין. וּבָא הַגּוֹי וּפָתַח. כְּבָר נִכְנְסָה שַׁבָּת בְּהֶיתֵר. רִבִּי רְדִיפָה אָמַר. רִבִּי נִיסָא שָׁאַל. מָהוּ לִיתֵּן לָהֶן שְׁלֹשָׁה רָאשֵׁי תוֹרִין. שֶׁיְּהֵא זֶה מְטַלְטֵל בְּתוֹךְ סָאתַיִם שֶׁלָּזֶה. וְזֶה מְטַלְטֵל בְּתוֹךְ סָאתַיִם שֶׁלָּזֶה.

A caravan is no less than three people[291]. The Gentile does not complement a caravan[292]. Does an underage person complement a caravan[293]? [294]How is this? If there were two and they established one *eruv*, and a Gentile came and added; the Sabbath already had started in prohibition. If there were three but they established two *eruvim* and a Gentile came and opened; the Sabbath already had started in permission. [295]Rebbi Redifa said that Rebbi

Nisa asked, may they have three ox heads so that each of them may enter the two *se'ah* of another?

291 In the language of the Babli 16b three people travelling together automatically form a caravan.

292 Since he is not obligated to keep the Sabbath he cannot be a mitigating influence.

293 He is not obligated now but his parents are obligated to teach him the laws of the Sabbath. The question is not resolved.

294 This is copied word by word in Chapter 6, discussion of Mishnah 4. The first case refers to the situation here. If two people were in an uninhabited area at the start of the Sabbath and enclosed an area of two *bet se'ah*, if on the Sabbath a Gentile came and enlarged that area they could not carry in the enlarged area since it already was forbidden to them at the start of the Sabbath (a matter of controversy in the Babli, 17a). The next case belongs to Chapter 6. People in adjacent courtyards made separate *eruvim*. If on the Sabbath a Gentile opened a passage between the two domains, they continue using their courtyards since the legal status cannot be changed on the Sabbath even though if the passage had existed before the Sabbath they would not have been able to have separate *eruvim*. In these situations the Gentile is mentioned not because he is not obligated but because he is able to do work forbidden to Jews on the Sabbath.

295 "Ox head" or "top of the line" means "vertex of a triangle" (*Kilaim* 1:9 Note 202, 2:7 Note 101). The configuration envisaged seems to be that of three triangular domains sharing a common vertex. By the rules of *Kilaim*, fields sown with different crops but sharing only a vertex do not need any real or symbolic separation. The question is raised whether the same holds true for the rules of the Sabbath. Since the question is not answered, the details of the configuration are not discussed.

(19c line 65) רִבִּי אָחָא בְּשֵׁם רַב חַסְדַּיי. אַתְיָיא דְּרִבִּי יוֹסֵי בֵּירִבִּי יוּדָה בְּשִׁיטַת אָבִיו וְחָלוּק עַל אָבִיו. בְּשִׁיטַת אָבִיו. בְּיָחִיד יָתֵר מִבֵּית סָאתַיִם. וְחָלוּק עַל אָבִיו. בְּשִׁייָרָה פָּחוּת מִבֵּית סָאתַיִם. וְהֵן אַשְׁכַּחְנָן דְּרִבִּי יוּדָה אָמַר. בְּיָחִיד יוֹתֵר מִבֵּית סָאתַיִם צָרִיךְ שְׁתִי וָעֵרֶב. נִישְׁמְעִינָהּ מִן הָדָא. דָּמַר רִבִּי אָחָא תַּנָא רִבִּי חָנִין רִבִּי יוֹסֵה בְּשֵׁם רַב שֵׁשֶׁת. כְּשֵׁם שֶׁחֲלוּקִין כָּאן כָּךְ חֲלוּקִים בְּכִלְאַיִם. וְכִלְאַיִם לֹא אֲפִילוּ הִיא בֵּית רוֹבַע.

Rebbi Aḥa in the name of Rav Ḥasdai: Rebbi Yose ben Rebbi Jehudah follows the argument of his father and disagrees with his father. The argument of his father, about an individual more than two *bet se'ah*[296]. And disagrees with his father, about a caravan less than two *bet se'ah*[297]. Did we not hear that Rebbi Jehudah said, an individual for more than two *bet se'ah* needs woof and warp[298]? Let us hear from the following, that Rebbi Aḥa the

Tanna, Rebbi Ḥanin, Rebbi Yose in the name of Rav Sheshet: Just as they differ here so they are differing about *kilaim*. And in *Kilaim* not even if it is a *bet rova*[299]?

296 In Mishnah 10 they agree that an individual only may fence in an area appropriate for a caravan only by a fence with both vertical and horizontal material.

297 R. Jehudah only says that the one-directional fence is authorized only for a caravan, which gets several *bet se'ah*. It is asserted here that for smaller domains R. Jehudah authorizes one-directional fences for individuals while it is clear from the Mishnah that his son never admits them. Babli 17a

298 In Mishnah 10.

299 The *rova'* is a quarter *qab*, a *qab* being a sixth of a *se'ah*. If they disagree for *kilaim* it follows that R. Jehudah must permit one-directional fences for small domains.

(19c line 72) כַּמָּה הִיא מַחֲנֶה. רִבִּי חֲנַנְיָה אָמַר. מֵאָה. וַיָּבֹא גִדְעוֹן וּמֵאָה־אִישׁ אֲשֶׁר־אִתּוֹ בִּקְצֵה הַמַּחֲנֶה. רִבִּי אָבוּנָה בָעֵי. אִילּוּ אָמַר מַחֲנֶה וַאֲנָשִׁים אֲשֶׁר־אִתּוֹ מֵאָה. יָאוּת. רִבִּי יוֹחָנָן אָמַר. עֲשָׂרָה. וַיָּבֹאוּ נַעֲרֵי דָוִד וַיְדַבְּרוּ אֶל־נָבָל וגו'. מָהוּ וַיָּנִיחוּ. רִבִּי יוּסְטָא בַּר שׁוּנֶה אָמַר. נַעֲשׂוּ מַחֲנֶה. רִבִּי יוּדָה בַּר פָּזִי אָמַר. עֲשָׂרָה. עַד־לְמַחֲנֶה גָדוֹל כְּמַחֲנֵה אֱלֹהִים׃ וְכַמָּה מַחֲנֵה אֱלֹהִים. עֲשָׂרָה. תַּנֵּי בְשֵׁם רִבִּי יוּדָה. שְׁנַיִם עָשָׂר אֶלֶף כְּמַחֲנֶה יִשְׂרָאֵל הַיּוֹצְאִים לְמִלְחֶמֶת הָרְשׁוּת מוּתָּרִין בְּגֶזֶל עֵצִים לַחִין וַאֲסוּרִין בְּגֶזֶל עֵצִים יְבֵישִׁין. הַיּוֹצְאִים לְמִלְחֶמֶת חוֹבָה מוּתָּרִין בְּגֶזֶל עֵצִים יְבֵישִׁין וְלַחִין. רִבִּי דָּנִיאֵל בְּרֵיהּ דְּרַב קָטָנָא בְשֵׁם רַב חוּנָה. אִם הָיוּ עֲשׂוּיִין חֲבִילָה אָסוּר. עַד כְּדוֹן בְּשֶׁאֵינָן סְמוּכִין לַחוֹרֵשׁ. וַאֲפִילוּ סְמוּכִין לַחוֹרֵשׁ. עַד כְּדוֹן בְּשֶׁאֵינָן סְמוּכִין לַמַּעֲיָן. וַאֲפִילוּ סְמוּכִין לַמַּעֲיָן. נִכְנְסוּ עִמָּהֶן לָעִיר כְּבָר נִפְטְרוּ. יָצְאוּ עִמָּהֶן מֵעִיר כְּבָר נִתְחַיְּיבוּ בִדְמַאי. רִבִּי יוֹסֵה בְשֵׁם רִבִּי אַבָּהוּ אָמַר רִבִּי חִזְקִיָּה בְשֵׁם רִבִּי יוּדָה בֶּן פָּזִי. דְּמַייִ תָּקֵן לֹא תָקֵן.

How many form a camp? Rebbi Ḥananiah said, one hundred. *Gideon came with the hundred men who were with him to the border of the camp*[300]. Rebbi Abuna asked, if it had said, "the camp of a hundred men who were with him" it would be acceptable[301]. Rebbi Joḥanan said, ten: *David's servants came and spoke to Nabal*[302], etc. What means *and they rested*[302]? Rebbi Justus bar Shune said, they made a camp. Rebbi Jehudah ben Pazi said, ten: *Until the camp was large like God's camp*[303]. How many are "God's camp"? Ten[304].

It was stated in the name of Rebbi Jehudah: 12'000 who are marching off as camp of Israel in a war of choice are permitted to rob moist wood but are forbidden to rob dry wood. Those who march out in a war of obligation are permitted to rob both dry and moist wood[305]. Rebbi Daniel the son of Rav Qatina in the name of Rav Huna: If they were made into bundles it is forbidden. So far if it was not close to a forest; even if it was close to a forest. So far if it was not close to a spring; even if it was close to a spring. [306]If they brought it with them to a town, they already are freed from liability. What they took out with them from a town already is liable for *demay*. Rebbi Yose in the name of Rebbi Abbahu, Rebbi Hizqiah said in the name of Rebbi Jehudah ben Pazi: *Demay* was put in order or not in order[307].

300 *Jud.* 7:19.
301 Since the camp was the enemy's the quote does not prove anything.
302 *IS.* 25:9. It had been stated in v. 5 that they were ten.
303 *1Chr.* 12:22.
304 The source of this statement is unknown. Rashba col. 124, who quotes this statement, does not comment on it.
305 Details of the statement in Mishnah 10. The Babli disagrees about the kind of wood, 17a, Tosephta 2:6.

The source of the number 12'000 is unknown. In *Midrash Shemuel* (ed. Buber 23(9)) the quote is "12'000 like the camp of Midyan." This cannot be correct since the escapees from Gideon's attack were about 15'000 (*Jud.* 8:10). Our text is confirmed by R. Hananel (*ad* 17a).
306 This refers to the statement in Mishnah 10 that in a camp one is not liable for *demay*. It is specified that food delivered to the camp is not liable even in a town but food acquired in town remains liable even if taken out to camp.
307 Cf. *Šabbat* 2, Note 238.

(19d line 9) וּמִלְּעָרֵב. רַב חִיָּיה בַּר אַשִּׁי אָמַר. הָדָא דְּאַתְּ אָמַר בְּעֵירוּבֵי חֲצֵירוֹת. אֲבָל בְּעֵירוּבֵי תְחוּמִין דְּבַר תּוֹרָה הֵן. וְיֵשׁ חֲצֵירוֹת בַּמַּחֲנֶה. לִסְתּוֹר אוֹהָלִים שֶׁבַּמַּחֲנֶה. כְּהָדָא דְּתַנֵּי. אוֹהָלִים שֶׁבַּמַּחֲנֶה צְרִיכִין עֵירוּב. אוֹהָלִים שֶׁבִּשְׁיָירָה אֵינָן צְרִיכִין עֵירוּב. יְהוּדָה בֶּן תֵּימָא אוֹמֵר. אַף חוֹנִים בְּכָל־מָקוֹם. וּבִמְקוֹם שֶׁיֵּשׁ נֶהֱרָגִין שָׁם נִקְבָּרִין. שֶׁלֹּא תֹאמַר. יָצְאוּ כְהָרוּגֵי פְלַמּוֹסִיּוֹת. אִית תַּנָּיֵי תַנֵּי. אָסוּר לְפַנּוֹתָן. וְאִית תַּנָּיֵי תַנֵּי. מוּתָּר לְפַנּוֹתָן. אָמַר רַב חִסְדַּאי. מָאן דָּמַר. מוּתָּר לְפַנּוֹתָן. בִּמְכוּנָסִין. וּמָאן דָּמַר. אָסוּר לְפַנּוֹתָן. בִּמְפוּזָּרִין. כְּשֵׁם שֶׁבַּהֲלִיכָתָן פְּטוּרִין מֵאַרְבָּעָה דְבָרִים. כָּךְ בַּחֲזִירָתָן פְּטוּרִין מֵאַרְבָּעָה דְבָרִים. רִבִּי יוֹסֵי בֵּירִבִּי בּוּן שָׁמַע לָהּ מִן הָדָא מִי־יָרֵא וְחָרֵד יָשׁוֹב וְיִצְפּוֹר מֵהַר הַגִּלְעָד. וְלָמָּה הֵן חוֹזְרִין בְּאַפִּירָה. מִפְּנֵי הַשּׁוֹנְאִין. רִבִּי יוֹסֵי בֵּירִבִּי בּוּן בְּשֵׁם רַב. כְּשֵׁם שֶׁבַּהֲלִיכָתָן פְּטוּרִין מֵאַרְבָּעָה דְבָרִים. כָּךְ בַּחֲזִירָתָן פְּטוּרִין מֵאַרְבָּעָה דְבָרִים.

"And from making an *eruv*". Rav Hiyya bar Ashi said, this refers to *eruv* of courtyards[30]. But *eruv* of ranges is a matter of biblical law[308]. Are there courtyards in a camp? To disassemble[309] tents in a camp, as it was stated: "[310]Tents in a camp need an *eruv*, tents of a caravan do not need an *eruv*.

"Jehudah ben Tema says, also they may camp anywhere and at the place where they are killed they are buried, lest you say that they should be treated like war[311] dead." There are Tannaim who state that it is forbidden to remove them; there are Tannaim who state that it is permitted to remove them. He who said that it is permitted to remove them, if they are together[312]; he who said that it is forbidden to remove them, if they are dispersed.

Just as they are exempt from four matters when they are marching out, so they are exempt from four matters when they are returning. Rebbi Yose ben Rebbi Abun understood this from the following[313]: *Anybody who is fearful and anxious should return and sneak away from Mount Gilead.* Why did they have to return sneaking? Because of the enemies[314]. Rebbi Yose ben Rebbi Abun in the name of Rav: Just as they are exempt from four matters when they are marching out, so they are exempt from four matters when they are returning.

---

308 Babli 17b. It is agreed that *Ex.* 16:29 implies that leaving one's place on the Sabbath, even if one does not carry anything, is prohibited. It is only the definition of "one's place" which is a matter of rabbinic interpretation.

309 It is unclear what this means. Meïri (79b), Rashba (col. 125) and Ritba (28a) read "to permit".

310 Tosephta 2:5-6, partially quoted in Babli 17a. In the Tosephta (ed. Liebermann p. 93) 3 out of 4 sources read: Tents in a camp *do not need* an *eruv*, tents of a caravan *need* an *eruv*. While the Medieval authors agree in substance with the majority of the Tosephta mss., the explicit quotes of Meïri and Rashba (loc. cit. Note 309) confirm the Yerushalmi text; only Ritba reads the Tosephta text in the Yerushalmi.

Maimonides in *Hilkhot Eruvin* 1:3 follows the Yerushalmi text but in *Hilkhot Melakhim* 6:13 he only requires that the camp be enclosed by a fence 10 handbreadths high without *eruv* following the Babli. There is no reason to emend the text.

311 Greek πόλεμος, ὁ. This must refer to Gentile fallen soldiers.

312 A mass grave. In *Masekhet Semahot* 14:4: "In times of war there is no permanence to graves"; it is implied that they always may be re-buried in a Jewish cemetary.

313 *Jud.* 7:3.

314 Since there always is danger, there is no reason to abrogate the exemption.

עושין פסין פרק שני

(fol.19d) **משנה א**: עוֹשִׂין פַּסִּין לַבֵּירָאוֹת אַרְבָּעָה דְיוֹמְדִין נִרְאִין כִּשְׁמוֹנָה דִּבְרֵי רִבִּי יְהוּדָה. רִבִּי מֵאִיר אוֹמֵר שְׁמוֹנָה נִרְאִין כִּשְׁנֵים עָשָׂר. אַרְבָּעָה דְיוֹמְדִין וְאַרְבָּעָה פְּשׁוּטִין גּוֹבְהָן עֲשָׂרָה טְפָחִים וְרוֹחְבָּן שִׁשָּׁה וְעוֹבְיָין כָּל־שֶׁהוּא וּבֵינֵיהֶן כִּמְלוֹא שְׁתֵּי רְבָקוֹת שֶׁל שָׁלֹשׁ שָׁלֹשׁ בָּקָר דִּבְרֵי רִבִּי מֵאִיר. רִבִּי יְהוּדָה אוֹמֵר שֶׁל אַרְבַּע אַרְבַּע קְשׁוּרוֹת וְלֹא מוּתָּרוֹת אַחַת נִכְנֶסֶת וְאַחַת יוֹצֵאת:

Mishnah 1: One makes planks for wells, four double columns[1] which look like eight, the words of Rebbi Jehudah. Rebbi Meïr says eight which look like twelve, eight double columns and four simple ones, their height ten [hand-breadths], and their width six, and their thickness arbitrary. And between them the width of two teams of three cattle each, the words of Rebbi Meïr; Rebbi Jehudah says of four each, tied together rather than loose, one entering and one leaving[2].

משנה ב: מוּתָּר לְהַקְרִיב לַבְּאֵר וּבִלְבַד שֶׁתְּהֵא פָּרָה רֹאשָׁהּ וְרוּבָּהּ בִּפְנִים וְשׁוֹתָה. מוּתָּר לְהַרְחִיק כָּל־שֶׁהוּא וּבִלְבַד שֶׁיַּרְבֶּה בַּפַּסִּים:

Mishnah 2: It is permitted to make them close to the well on condition that the head and most of the cow be inside when she drinks. It is permitted to put them arbitrarily far away on condition to add planks[3].

משנה ג: רִבִּי יְהוּדָה אוֹמֵר עַד בֵּית סָאתַיִם. אָמְרוּ לוֹ לֹא אָמְרוּ בֵית סָאתַיִם אֶלָּא בְגִנָּה וּבְקַרְפֵּף. אֲבָל אִם הָיָה דִּיר אוֹ סַהַר אוֹ מוּקְצֶה אוֹ חָצֵר אֲפִילוּ בֵית חֲמֵשֶׁת כּוֹרִין אֲפִילוּ בֵית עֲשֶׂרֶת כּוֹרִין מוּתָּר וּמוּתָּר לְהַרְחִיק כָּל־שֶׁהוּא וּבִלְבַד שֶׁיַּרְבֶּה בַפַּסִּין:

Mishnah 3: Rebbi Jehudah says, up to two *bet se'ah*[4]. They said to him, two *bet se'ah* were said only for a garden patch[5] and a corral[6]. But if there was a sheep-pen, or a sheep corral, or a backyard, or a front yard, even five *bet kor*[7], even ten *bet kor* are permitted and it is permitted to put them arbitrarily far away on condition to add planks[3].

משנה ד: אִם הָיְתָה דֶּרֶךְ הָרַבִּים מַפְסַקְתָּהּ יְסַלְּקֶנָּה לַצְּדָדִין. וַחֲכָמִים אוֹמְרִין אֵינוֹ צָרִיךְ. אֶחָד בְּאֵר הָרַבִּים וּבוֹר הָרַבִּים וּבְאֵר הַיָּחִיד עוֹשִׂין לָהֶן פַּסִּים. אֲבָל לְבוֹר הַיָּחִיד עוֹשִׂין לוֹ

מְחִצָּה גְבוֹהָה עֲשָׂרָה טְפָחִים דִּבְרֵי רִבִּי עֲקִיבָה. רִבִּי יְהוּדָה בֶּן בָּבָא אוֹמֵר אֵין עוֹשִׂין פַּסִּים אֶלָּא לִבְאֵר הָרַבִּים בִּלְבַד. וְלַשְּׁאָר עוֹשִׂין חֲגוֹרָה גְבוֹהָה עֲשָׂרָה טְפָחִים:

Mishnah 4: If a public road interrupts them he should divert it around it, but the Sages say that this is unnecessary[8]. One makes planks both for a public cistern, a public well, and a private well, but for a private cistern one makes a partition of ten hand-breadths[9], the words of Rebbi Aqiba. Rebbi Jehudah ben Bava said, one makes planks only for a public well; for everything else one makes a belt[10] ten hand-breadths high.

משנה ה: וְעוֹד אָמַר רִבִּי יְהוּדָה בֶּן בָּבָא הַגִּינָה וְהַקַּרְפֵּף שֶׁהֵן שִׁבְעִים אַמָּה וְשִׁירַיִם עַל שִׁבְעִים אַמָּה וְשִׁירַיִם מוּקֶּפֶת גָּדֵר גָּבוֹהַּ עֲשָׂרָה טְפָחִים מְטַלְטְלִין בְּתוֹכָהּ וּבִלְבַד שֶׁיְּהֵא בָהּ שׁוֹמֵירָה אוֹ בֵית דִּירָה אוֹ שֶׁתְּהֵא סְמוּכָה לָעִיר.

Mishnah 5: In addition, Rebbi Jehudah ben Bava said, if a garden patch or a corral are seventy cubits and a remainder by seventy cubits and a remainder surrounded by a wall ten hand-breadths high[11] one carries inside on condition that it contain a watchman's hut or a dwelling or be close to a village[12]

משנה ו: רִבִּי יְהוּדָה אוֹמֵר אֲפִילוּ אֵין בָּהּ אֶלָּא בּוֹר וְשִׁיחַ וּמְעָרָה מְטַלְטְלִין בְּתוֹכָהּ. רִבִּי עֲקִיבָה אוֹמֵר אֲפִילוּ אֵין בָּהּ אַחַת מִכָּל־אֵילּוּ מְטַלְטְלִין בְּתוֹכָהּ וּבִלְבַד שֶׁתְּהֵא שִׁבְעִים אַמָּה וְשִׁירַיִם עַל שִׁבְעִים אַמָּה וְשִׁירַיִם.

Mishnah 6: Rebbi Jehudah says, even if it only contains a cistern, or an irrigation ditch, or a cave, one carries in it. Rebbi Aqiba says, even if none of these is there one carries in it on condition that it be seventy cubits and a remainder by seventy cubits and a remainder[11].

משנה ז: רִבִּי אֶלְעָזָר אוֹמֵר הָיָה אוֹרְכָּהּ יוֹתֵר עַל רָחְבָּהּ אֲפִילוּ אַמָּה אַחַת אֵין מְטַלְטְלִין בְּתוֹכָהּ. רִבִּי יוֹסֵה אוֹמֵר אֲפִילוּ אוֹרְכָּהּ כִּשְׁנַיִם בְּרוֹחְבָּהּ מְטַלְטְלִין בְּתוֹכָהּ:

Mishnah 7: Rebbi Eliezer says, if its length exceeds its width even by one cubit one may not carry there[13]. Rebbi Yose says, even if its length is twice its width one carries in there.

משנה ח: אָמַר רִבִּי אִלְעַאי שָׁמַעְתִּי מֵרִבִּי אֱלִיעֶזֶר אֲפִילוּ הִיא כְבֵית כּוֹר. וְכֵן שָׁמַעְתִּי מִמֶּנּוּ אַנְשֵׁי הֶחָצֵר שֶׁשָּׁכַח אֶחָד מֵהֶן וְלֹא עֵירַב בֵּיתוֹ אָסוּר מִלְּהַכְנִיס וּמִלְּהוֹצִיא לוֹ אֲבָל לָהֶן מוּתָּר. וְכֵן שָׁמַעְתִּי מִמֶּנּוּ שֶׁיּוֹצְאִין בְּעִקְרְבָנִין בַּפֶּסַח וְחִיזַּרְתִּי עַל כָּל־תַּלְמִידָיו וּבִיקַּשְׁתִּי לִי חָבֵר וְלֹא מָצָאתִי:

Mishnah 8: Rebbi Illai said, I heard from Rebbi Eliezer: Even if it is a *bet kor*[97], and I also heard from him that if one of the dwellers in a courtyard had forgotten to make an *eruv* he is forbidden to bring into or bring out of his house but to others it is permitted[14]. I also heard from him that one may satisfy one's obligation on Passover with white stone-crop[15]. I asked around among all his students to find support but did not find any[16].

1   The word seems to be a Greek-Hebrew hybrid, δύο-עַמוּדִים "double column". The circular well is in the middle of a square; at each corner one erects planks 10 hand-breadths high and on each side 6 wide. Since from each side one sees two planks, these are "4 looking like 8". Since the opening between two planks, space in excess of the width of 6 cows for R. Meïr or eight for R. Jehudah, is more than what is permitted as opening of a wall of a private domain, special rules are needed to permit grazing animals to drink from a well. Even though the meadows on which they are grazing is public domain or *karmelit*, the well or cistern is private domain if it is at least 10 hand-breadths deep. Therefore one has to see to it that the animals drink in a private domain. R. Meïr requires a straight plank (of indeterminate width) after a 5 cubits opening.

2   As explained at the end of the discussion of this Mishnah, the space between two planks can be 10 cubits for R. Meïr and almost 14 for R. Jehudah.

3   The distances between two planks cannot be greater than those described in Mishnah 1, 5 cubits for R. Meïr and 14 for R. Jehudah.

4   In his opinion the maximal size of domain for which double planks are authorized are the standard 5'000 square cubits.

5   An irrigated vegetable garden.

6   For cattle.

7   A *kor* is 30 *se'ah*; a *bet kor* 75'000 square cubits.

8   The first clause in this sentence is R. Jehudah's (and is stated as such in the independent Mishnah mss., the Mishnah in the Babli, and the quote in the Halakhah). He holds that enclosures which trespass on a public road are unauthorized.

9   Since the double planks are authorized only for the benefit of animals, once a cistern runs dry the double planks lose their utility and it would be forbidden to carry there. Therefore for a non-public cistern he requires a regular enclosure where one may carry regardless of the amount of water available.

10   Possibly by the standards of Mishnah 1:9.

11   Since $70.71...^2 = 5'000$, the area enclosed is 2 *bet se'ah*. In an enclosed area of up to 2 *bet se'ah* one may carry. One of more than 2 *bet se'ah* may be turned into a domain for carrying only if it is used for human dwelling.

12   Within 70.71 cubits of the village.

13   His reason is unknown. The statement is rejected in the Babli.

14   Whereas for the majority nobody may carry in and out of the courtyard unless the

non-participant annulled his rights (Chapter 1, Note 112).

15 A medicinal plant which he authorizes as "bitter herb" for the Seder night.

16 Therefore these statements are not authoritative.

(19d line 66) עוֹשִׂין פַּסִּין לַבֵּירָאוֹת כול'. לְפִי שֶׁהַפָּרוּץ רָבָה עַל הָעוֹמֵד הוּא עוֹשֶׂה דִיוֹמְדִין. אֲבָל לֹא פְשׁוּטִין. אוֹף הוּא מוֹכִיחַ עַל עַצְמוֹ מִשּׁוּם הוֹלֶכֶת הַבְּאֵר. רִבִּי זְעִירָא בְשֵׁם רִבִּי אֶלְעָזָר. הִגִּיעוּךָ סוֹף תְּחוּמֵי שַׁבָּת עַד אֵיכָן הֵן. שֶׁאִם עָשָׂה כֵן בְּמָקוֹם אֶחָד וְחָזַר וְזָרַק אַרְבַּע אַמּוֹת בִּרְשׁוּת הָרַבִּים. חַיָּיב. אָמַר רִבִּי יוֹסֵה. לְפִי שֶׁבְּכָל־מָקוֹם עוֹמֵד רָבָה עַל הַפָּרוּץ. וְכָאן הֵיקַלְתָּה עָלָיו שֶׁיְּהֵא הַפָּרוּץ רָבָה עַל הָעוֹמֵד. הֶחֱמַרְתָּה עָלָיו בְּדָבָר אַחֵר. שֶׁבְּכָל־מָקוֹם עוֹשֶׂה פַס שֶׁלְאַרְבַּע טְפָחִים וְכָאן עוֹשֶׂה פַס שֶׁלְשִׁשָּׁה טְפָחִים.

"One makes planks for wells," etc. Since what is breached is more than what is standing he makes double columns but not simple ones, which proves by itself that it is because of access to the well. Rebbi Ze`ira in the name of Rebbi Eleazar: You are reaching here what are the limits of domains of the Sabbath, for if he did so at (one)[17] place and then threw there four cubits in the public domain he would be liable. Rebbi Yose said, since you were lenient with him about what is breached may be more than what is standing, you are strict with him in another matter since everywhere else one makes a plank of four hand-breadths but here he makes a plank of six hand-breadths[18].

17 With the later prints of the Yerushalmi one has to read here אַחֵר "another". If one puts up four double-planks anywhere else so that the opening is wider than the standing walls it does not mean anything. If within this space one throws something more than 4 cubits it is throwing in the public domain and a Sabbath violation. The Babli 20a reads differently.

18 Both aspects, the corner planks and their width, are required to make it clear that these rules are valid exclusively for water sources but nothing else.

(19d line 73) רַב יִרְמְיָה בְשֵׁם רַב. לֹא הִתִּירוּ פַסֵּי בֵירָאוֹת אֶלָּא לְעוֹלֵי רְגָלִים בִּלְבָד. רַב אַבִּין אָמַר. בְּשַׁעַת עוֹלֵי רְגָלִים. רִבִּי יִרְמְיָה בְשֵׁם רִבִּי שְׁמוּאֵל בֶּן רַב יִצְחָק. מִפְּנֵי עוֹלֵי רְגָלִים. אָמַר רִבִּי עֶזְרָא קוֹמֵי רִבִּי מָנָא. מַתְנִיתָא אָמְרָה כֵן. עוֹשִׂין פַּסֵּי לַבֵּירִיּוֹת בַּזְּמַן הַזֶּה. וְהָא תַנִּינָן. מְמַלִּים מִבּוֹר הַגּוֹלָה בַּגַּלְגַּל בַּשַּׁבָּת מִבּוֹר הַגָּדוֹל כול'. מִפְּנֵי מַה מְמַלִּים מִבְּאֵר הַקַּר בַּגַּלְגַּל בְּיוֹם טוֹב. אֶלָּא בְּשָׁעָה שֶׁעָלָה מִן הַגּוֹלָה וְחָנוּ עַל אוֹתָהּ הַבְּאֵר. וְהִתְנוּ עִמָּהֶן הַנְּבִיאִים שֶׁבֵּינֵיהֶן שֶׁיְּהוּ מְמַלִּים מִבְּאֵר הַקַּר בַּגַּלְגַּל בְּיוֹם טוֹב. לֹא כָל־בְּאֵרוֹת הַקַּר הִתִּירוּ. אֶלָּא אוֹתָהּ

בְּאֵר שֶׁחָנוּ עָלֶיהָ בִּלְבָד. כְּמָה דְּאַתְּ אָמַר תַּמָּן. מַה שֶּׁהוּתָּר הוּתָּר וְכֹה שֶׁהוּתָּר הוּתָּר. רִבִּי אַבְדִּימָא דְחֵיפָה הוֹרֵי בְחֵיפָה. רִבִּי יִרְמְיָה הוֹרֵי בְחֶלֶף בְּפַסֵּי בֵירָאוֹת בַּזְּמָן הַזֶּה.

Rav Jeremiah in the name of Rav: They permitted planks for wells only for pilgrims[19]. Rav Abin said, at the time of pilgrimage[20]. Rebbi Jeremiah in the name of Rebbi Samuel bar Rav Isaac: Because of the pilgrims[21]. Rebbi Ezra said before Rebbi Mana, the Mishnah implies that one makes planks for wells in the present time[22]. But did we not state[23], "one fills from the cistern of the diaspora with a wheel on the Sabbath, from the large cistern, etc." Why "may one fill from the cold well[24] with a wheel on the holiday"? But at the time when Israel came from the diaspora and camped at this well, the prophets among them stipulated that that one could fill from the cold well with a wheel on the holiday[25]. They did not permit all cold wells, only this well at which they camped. As you are saying there, what was permitted was permitted, and here what was permitted was permitted. Rebbi Eudaimon from Haifa instructed in Haifa, Rebbi Jeremiah instructed in Ḥelef about planks for wells in the present time[26].

19 The three yearly pilgrimages to the Temple. This implies that after the destruction of the Temple all the rules of the present Chapter became obsolete. Babli 20b as accepted doctrine.

20 The suspension of the universal requirement that "what is standing must be more than what is breached" is authorized only temporarily for the needs of actual pilgrims.

21 But along the pilgrim's route from Babylonia to Jerusalem the installations are permanent.

22 Since the Mishnah is formulated in the present it must be valid in the present, after the destruction of the Temple and the end of pilgrimages.

23 Mishnah 10:12.

24 While the cisterns mentioned in the Mishnah were on the Temple Mount, the well was somewhere on the pilgrims' route. Using a mechanical contraption is rabinically forbidden on the holiday since one might be tempted to fix it in case it broke on the holiday.

25 Babli 104b. Tosephta 8:22.

26 The Babylonian point of view is rejected.

(20a line 7) הֲוֹון בָּעֵיי מֵימַר. רִבִּי מֵאִיר יוֹדֶה לְרִבִּי יוּדָה. רִבִּי יוּדָה לֹא יוֹדֶה לְרִבִּי מֵאִיר. רִבִּי מֵאִיר יוֹדֶה לְרִבִּי יוּדָה. רִבִּי מֵאִיר אִית לֵיהּ דְּיוֹמְדִין פְּשׁוּטִין וְאַתְּ אָמַר הָכֵין. מִתּוֹךְ שֶׁאַתְּ עוֹשֶׂה דְּיוֹמְדִין אֲבָל לֹא פְּשׁוּטִין אַף הוּא סָבוּר לוֹמַר. שָׁמָּה מְחִיצַת שַׁבָּת כָּךְ הוּא. וְהוּא הוֹלֵךְ וְעוֹשֶׂה כֵן בְּמָקוֹם אַחֵר וּמִתְחַיֵּיב. רִבִּי אָחָא בְּשֵׁם רִבִּי חִינְנָא. לָא דַיִין מוֹדִי לְדַיִין וְלָא דַיִין מוֹדֵי לְדַיִין.

אָמַר רִבִּי מָנָא. אַף עַל גַּב דְּלָא אָמַר רִבִּי יוֹסֵה דְּכִי הָדָא מִילְתָא. אֲמָרָהּ דִּכְוָותָהּ. רִבִּי בּוּן וְרִבִּי בּוּן בְּעוֹן קוֹמֵי רִבִּי זְעִירָא. כַּמָּה יְהֵא דְיוֹמַד אָרוֹךְ וְלֹא יְהֵא צָרִיךְ פָּשׁוּט. אָמַר לֵיהּ. פָּחוּת מִשְּׁלֹשָׁה כְּסָתוּם. יוֹתֵר מֵחֲמִשָּׁה מוּפְלָג. אֶלָּא כֵן אָנָן קַיָּימִין מִשְּׁלֹשָׁה וְעַד אַרְבָּעָה. אִין תֵּימַר. רִבִּי מֵאִיר יוֹדֶה לְרִבִּי יוּדָה. וְיַעֲשֶׂה בְדְיוֹמַד אָרוֹךְ וְלֹא יְהֵא צָרִיךְ פָּשׁוּט. אָמַר רִבִּי בָּא בַּר מָמָל. לֹא נִצְרַךְ רִבִּי מֵאִיר לַפְּשׁוּטִים אֶלָּא בְשִׁיטַת רִבִּי יוּדָה. אָמַר רִבִּי יוֹסֵה. וַאֲפִילוּ מִשִּׁיטָתֵיהּ. מִכָּל־מָקוֹם אֵין הָעוֹמֵד רָבָה עַל הַפָּרוּץ. מִכֵּיוָן שֶׁהָעוֹמֵד רָבָה עַל הַפָּרוּץ צָרִיךְ פָּשׁוּט.

They wanted to say that Rebbi Meïr would admit to Rebbi Jehudah, Rebbi Jehudah will not admit to Rebbi Meïr[27]. Rebbi Meïr will admit to Rebbi Jehudah? Does not Rebbi Meïr have simple poles, and you are saying so? If you are making double columns but no straight poles, he[28] would think, perhaps a partition for the Sabbath is made in this way; he would make it in other places and become liable. Rebbi Aḥa in the name of Rebbi Ḥinena: Neither of them yields to the other. Rebbi Mana said, even though Rebbi Yose (about)[29] did not say this, he said something similar. Rebbi Bun and Rebbi Bun[30] asked before Rebbi Ze`ira: How far away does a double column have to be so it would not need a straight [plank][31]? He told him, less than three [hand-breadths] is considered closed, more than six is far away[32]. Therefore we have to consider from three to four. If you would say that Rebbi Meïr yields to Rebbi Jehudah, should he not make a double column far away and not need a simple [plank][33]? Rebbi Abba bar Mamal said, Rebbi Meïr requires simple [planks] only according to Rebbi Jehudah's method[34]. Rebbi Yose said, even according to his own method, since in any case what is standing is not more than what is breached. Since what is standing should be more than what is breached it needs a simple [plank][35].

27 Since R. Jehudah permits a wider opening, he cannot agree to R. Meïr's lower limit. But R. Meïr could agree that R. Jehudah is correct in principle; only for practical reasons he prescribes a narrower opening.

28 An uninformed person who sees the surroundings of a well turned into a private domain by 4 double poles would think that any domain might be turned into one where carrying is permitted by the same device. But since he sees that at regular intervals simple planks are required he will inquire about the rules and be told that in all other cases the length of the walls has to exceed the lengths of the openings.

29 For דכי read רבי "my teacher Rebbi Yose said".

30 Read "R. Abun and R. Abin", cf. Chapter 1, Note 279.

31 When would R. Meïr dispense with straight planks? Babli 19b.

32 As long as one can disregard a distance of 3-ε on each side, nothing additional is required.

33 This quote of R. Ze`ira's explanation is R. Mana's proof that R. Ze`ira also holds that R. Meïr cannot agree with R. Jehudah in principle since he would have to indicate how it would be possible to make the enclosure without straight planks.

34 He wants to split the Mishnah into two parts and indicate that straight planks are needed only for a large width following R. Jehudah.

35 Since the Mishnah about enclosing a well in any case contradicts our principle that "what is standing must be more than what is breached", R. Meïr's insistence on straight planks is one of principle, not of practical consideration as suggested at the start of this discussion.

(20a line 20) הָיְתָה אֶבֶן אַחַת גְּדוֹלָה. רוֹאִין שֶׁאִם תֵּיחָלֵק וְיֵשׁ בָּהּ שִׁשָּׁה לְכָאן וְשִׁשָּׁה לְכָאן נִידּוֹן מִשּׁוּם דְּיוֹמָד. אִית תַּנָּיֵי תַנֵּי. שֶׁאִם תֵּיחָקֵק. הָווֹן בָּעֵי מֵימַר. מָאן דָּמַר. שֶׁאִם תֵּיחָקֵק. מוֹדֶד מִבִּפְנִים. מָאן דָּמַר. שֶׁאִם תֵּיחָלֵק. מוֹדֶד מִבַּחוּץ. אָמַר רִבִּי יוֹסֵה. וְלֹא עוֹד כִּקְלִיפַת הַשּׁוּם הַחִיצוֹנָה אַתְּ עָתִיד לְהַעֲמִידָהּ. הֲוֵי. לָא שַׁנְיָיא בֵּין כְּמָאן דְּאָמַר. שֶׁאִם תֵּיחָלֵק. בֵּין כְּמָאן דָּמַר. שֶׁאִם תֵּיחָקֵק. מוֹדֶד מִבִּפְנִים. מָאן דָּמַר. שֶׁאִם תֵּיחָקֵק. בַּעֲגוּלָה. וּמָאן דָּמַר. שֶׁאִם תֵּיחָלֵק. בִּמְרוּבַּעַת. תֵּדַע לָךְ שֶׁהוּא כֵן. דְּכֵן תַּנָּיָה מֵתִיב לְחַבְרֵיהּ. אֵין בֵּין דְּבָרַיי לִדְבָרֶיךָ אֶלָּא שֶׁאַתָּה אוֹמֵר בַּעֲגוּלָה וַאֲנִי אוֹמֵר בִּמְרוּבַּעַת.

"If one big stone was there one sees that if it is split and there be six [hand-breadths] in both directions it is considered a double column.[36]" Some Tannaim state, if it is hollowed out. They wanted to say that he who says, if it is hollowed out, measures from the inside while he who says, if it is split, measures from the outside. Rebbi Yose said, would you not let it stand if it was like garlic skin[37]? This implies that both he who says that it is split as also he who says it is hollowed out measures from the inside. He who says, if it is hollowed out, if it is round[38]; he who says, if it is split, if it is square. You should know that it is so since one Tanna said to the other, the only difference between my formulation and yours is that you are speaking of a round one but I about a square one.

36 Tosephta 1:12, Babli 19b. If the stone has a square base and each side is six hand-breadths long it is counted as double column.

37 Since the Mishnah does not prescribe depth of columns or planks there is no practical difference whether one measures from the outside or from the inside of an arbitrarily thin membrane.

38 If the base of the stone is circular the

radius, not the diameter, must be 6 handbreadth (1 cubit). In Babli and Tosephta this is an explicit statement by R. Ismael ben R. Johanan ben Beroqa.

(20a line 29) הָיָה שָׁם חָרִיץ עָמוֹק עֲשָׂרָה וְרָחָב אַרְבָּעָה וְיֵשׁ בּוֹ שִׁשָּׁה לְכָאן שִׁשָּׁה לְכָאן. נִידוֹן מִשּׁוּם דְּיוֹמַד. לֹא סוֹף דָּבָר חָרִיץ אֶלָּא אֲפִילוּ גַּבְשׁוּשִׁית. מִקְצָתוֹ חָרִיץ וּמִקְצָתוֹ גַבְשׁוּשִׁית. הָיוּ חֲמִשָּׁה קָנִים וְאֵין בֵּין זֶה לָזֶה שְׁלֹשָׁה. וְיֵשׁ בָּהֶן שִׁשָּׁה לְכָאן שִׁשָּׁה לְכָאן. נִידוֹנִין מִשּׁוּם דְּיוֹמַד. שְׁלֹשָׁה וְקָשַׁר גֶּמִי מִלְּמַעְלָן מָהוּ שֶׁיַּצִּיל מִשּׁוּם פֵּיאָה. כְּלוּם פֵּיאָה מַצֶּלֶת עַד שֶׁתְּהֵא מוֹכַחַת מִכָּל־צְדָדֶיהָ. אֶלָּא כָּהֵן דַּעֲגָלִין כְּסָתוּם הוּא. הֵיךְ מַה דְּאַתְּ אָמַר תַּמָּן. רוֹאִין שֶׁאִם תֵּיחָלֵק וְיֵשׁ בָּהּ שִׁשָּׁה לְכָאן וְשִׁשָּׁה לְכָאן נִידוֹן מִשּׁוּם דְּיוֹמַד. יָמַר אוּף הָכָא כֵן. תַּמָּן עַד קְלִיפַת הַשּׁוּם הַחִיצוֹנָה אַתְּ עָתִיד לְהַעֲמִידָהּ. וְהָכָא מָה אִית לָךְ. אִם אוֹמֵר אַתְּ כֵּן בְּטַלְתָּהּ הִילְכוֹת פֵּיאָה.

If there was a ditch ten [hand-breadths] deep and four wide, and it extends six in each direction[39], it is judged to be a double column. Not only a ditch but also a heap[40]. Partially a ditch and partially a heap? If there were five sticks with less than three [hand-breadths] between them which together cover six [hand-breadths] in each direction, they are judged to be a double column[41]. If there were three[42] and he tied bast on top, would this save as symbolic fence? Does not a symbolic fence save only if it is proven from each side[43]? Then what was tied around is as if blocked. Similar to what you are saying there, one sees that if it is split and there would be six [hand-breadths] in both directions it is considered a double column, could you say the same here? There would you not let it stand if it was like garlic skin; here what can you say? If you would say so you would abrogate the rules of symbolic fences[44].

39 At a corner two ditches, 1 cubit long, $2/3$ cubits wide and $1\,2/3$ cubits deep are the replacement of a double column erected there.

40 A rudimentary wall also counts if it has the necessary dimensions.

41 Since any opening of less than 3 hand-breadths is disregarded, the five sticks (two at each side and one at the right angle) stand for solid walls of 1 cubit length in each direction.

42 Three sticks at ABC form an isosceles right angled triangle with vertex B and edge length 6 hand-breadths.

43 Chapter 1 Note 274.

44 There are no exceptions to the rule indicated in the preceding Note.

(20a line 39) הַכּוֹתֶל וְהָאִילָן וַאֲגוּדַּת קָנִים נִידּוֹנִין מִשּׁוּם דְּיוֹמַד. עָלוּ מֵעֲלֵיהֶן מְטַלְטְלִין בָּהֶן עַד בֵּית סָאתָיִם. אֲשָׁעָן בְּיָד מְטַלְטְלִין בָּהֶן אֲפִילוּ כּוֹר אֲפִילוּ כּוֹרַיִים. הָיְתָה בְּאֵר אַחַת גְּדוֹלָה.

לַחֲצָיָה עָשָׂה וּלְחֶצְיָה לֹא עָשָׂה. לְחֶצְיָה שֶׁעָשָׂה מוּתָּר. וּלְחֶצְיָה שֶׁלֹּא עָשָׂה אָסוּר. הָיוּ שְׁתַּיִם. הָאֶמְצָעֵי מָהוּ שֶׁיִּדּוֹן לְכָאן וּלְכָאן. מַה צְּרִיכָה לֵיהּ. כְּשֶׁהָיוּ שְׁנַיִם מְמַלִּין. אֲבָל אִם הָיָה אֶחָד מְמַלֵּא נִידּוֹן לְכָאן וּלְכָאן.

A wall, and a tree, and a copse of reeds are counted as double columns[45]. If they grew by themselves one may carry there up to an area of two *bet se'ah*. If he planted them with his hands one may carry there even one or two *bet kor*[46]. If there was one large well and he made [the double columns] for one half but not for the other half. For the half for which he made it it is permitted, for the half for which he did not make it it is forbidden. If there were two, could the space in-between be considered for both sides? What is his problem? If both were used to fill; but if only one was used to fill it is usable for both sides[47].

45 Babli 15a, 19b, *Šabbat* 24b.
46 Chapter 1, Note 288.
47 If separate symbolic enclosures were made for two adjacent wells and one set of double columns serves for both enclosures, it is clear that one may not simultaneously draw water from both wells since this would use the middle double pillars in two contradictory ways. (This implies that they were double, not triple, i. e., shaped like a Γ but not a T.) But if at one time only one well is used, the next time the other well may be used, even on the same Sabbath.

(20a line 46) חָצֵר שֶׁהִיא פְתוּחָה לַפַּסִּים מְטַלְטְלִין מִן הֶחָצֵר לַפַּסִּים אֲבָל לֹא מִן הַפַּסִּים לֶחָצֵר. הָא שְׁתַּיִם אֲסוּר. אָמַר רִבִּי בָּא. לֹא סוֹף דָּבָר שְׁתֵּי חֲצֵירוֹת. אֶלָּא אֲפִילוּ חָצֵר אַחַת וּבָהּ שְׁנֵי בָתִּים. סָבְרִין מֵימַר. בְּשֶׁלֹּא עֵירְבוּ. הָא אִם עֵירְבוּ מוּתָּרִין. רִבִּי דָּנִיאֵל בְּרֵיהּ דְּרַב קְטִינָה בְּשֵׁם רַב חוּנָה. אֲפִילוּ עֵירְבוּ אֲסוּרוֹת. שֶׁאֵין עֵירוּב עוֹשֶׂה אוֹתָן אַחַת. רַב חוּנָה כְדַעְתֵּיהּ. דְּאִיתְפַּלְגוּן. מָבוֹי שֶׁצִּידּוֹ אֶחָד גּוֹי וְצִידּוֹ אֶחָד יִשְׂרָאֵל. רַב חוּנָה בְשֵׁם רַב אָמַר. אִם עֵירוּבוֹ דֶּרֶךְ פְּתָחִים הַגּוֹי אוֹסֵר עֲלֵיהֶן. אַבָּא בַּר חָנָה בְּשֵׁם רִבִּי יוֹחָנָן. אֲפִילוּ עֵירוּבוֹ דֶּרֶךְ חַלּוֹנוֹת אֵין הַגּוֹי אוֹסֵר עֲלֵיהֶן. וַאֲפִילוּ דְיִסְבּוֹר רַב חוּנָא כְרִבִּי יוֹחָנָן. תַּמָּן מוּתָּר. מוֹדֶה הוּא הָכָא שֶׁהוּא אָסוּר. תַּמָּן שְׁמָא לְמָחָר תֵּחָרֵב הַבְּאֵר. אַף הוּא סָבוּר לוֹמַר. שֶׁמָּא עֵירוּב מוֹעִיל בְּפַסִּים בֵּירָאוֹת. וְאֵין מוֹעִיל עֵירוּב בְּפַסֵּי בֵירִיּוֹת.

From a courtyard open to planks one carries from the courtyard to the planks but not from the planks to the courtyard[48]. Therefore two are forbidden[49]. Rebbi Abba said, not only two courtyards but even a single courtyard and in it two houses[50]. They thought to say if they did not make an *eruv*; therefore if they made an *eruv* it would be permitted. Rebbi Daniel the son of Rav Qatina in the name of Rav Huna: even if they made an *eruv* it is forbidden, for the *eruv* does not make them one[51]. Rav Huna follows his opinion, as they disagreed: An alley in which on one side dwelt a Gentile and on the other a Jew, Rav Huna in the name of Rav: even if they made an *eruv* through doors the Gentile prohibits it for them[52]. Abba bar bar Hana in the name of Rebbi Johanan, even if they made the *eruv* through windows the Gentile does not prohibit for them[53]. Even if Rav Huna would hold with Rebbi Johanan that there it is permitted, here he has to agree that it is forbidden. There, maybe tomorrow the well will run dry and then he would think that perhaps an *eruv* is efficient for the planks of wells when an *eruv* is not efficient for the planks of wells[54].

48 Tosephta 1:15 and Babli 20a disagree with this Yerushalmi in principle. The courtyard is walled in according to the rules that what is standing must be more than what is open; there one carries according to the general rules. It is open to a place where carrying is permitted only for the needs of animals; this place is an appendix of the courtyard but the courtyard is not an appendix to the place.

49 If two different courtyards open on the well, the well cannot belong to two different domains; therefore it belongs to neither of them.

50 And each of the houses has a backdoor opening on the well.

51 The permission to use the well is given only if there is a single opening from the courtyard to the well.

52 Since the Gentile is not subject to the laws of the Sabbath he cannot agree to a change of status of the alley for the Sabbath even if otherwise the *eruv* was totally conforming to the rules.

53 In his opinion the Gentile is irrelevant for the rules of the Sabbath even if the houses which are united by the *eruv* share only windows, not full door openings.

54 The prohibition of a well which is accessible from two different courtyards is based on a practical problem rather than a legal principle; one has to avoid giving the impression that courtyards joined in an *eruv* have any impact on the rules of wells surrounded by double columns. If the well runs dry before the Sabbath the double columns lose all their meaning.

(20a line 58) אָמַר רְבִּי יוֹסֵי בֵּירְבִּי בּוּן. לֹא הִתִּירוּ פַּסֵּי בִירִיּוֹת אֶלָּא לְמַלְּאוֹת בָּהֶן מַיִם בִּלְבָד. בָּאוּ מַיִם בַּשַּׁבָּת. כְּבָר נִכְנְסָה שַׁבָּת בְּאִיסוּר. חֲרָבָה הַבְּאֵר כְּבָר נִכְנְסָה שַׁבָּת בְּהֶיתֵר. רִבִּי יוֹנָה אָמַר. רִבִּי נָסָא שָׁאַל. מָהוּ לְטַלְטֵל בֵּין הַפַּסִּים. נֵימַר. אִם יֵשׁ בֵּין זֶה לָזֶה אַרְבָּעָה טְפָחִים כְּאִסְקוּפָּה אֲסוּרָה. וְאִם לָאו כְּאִיסְקוּפָּה מוּתֶּרֶת. מוּתָּר לְכָאן וּמוּתָּר לְכָאן. וּבִלְבַד שֶׁלֹּא יַחֲלִיף.

תַּנֵּי. יֵשְׁנָן כְּעֶשֶׂר אַמּוֹת. דִּבְרֵי רִבִּי מֵאִיר. רִבִּי יוּדָה אוֹמֵר. כְּשָׁלֹשׁ עֶשְׂרֵה וּכְאַרְבַּע עֶשְׂרֵה פָּרָא. אַמָּה מֶחֱצָה וְאַמָּה בֵּינַיִין.

Rebbi Yose ben Rebbi Abun said, they permitted the planks of wells only to draw water[55]. If water came on the Sabbath, the Sabbath already came with prohibition. If the well dried out, the Sabbath already came with permission[56]. Rebbi Jonah said that Rebbi Nasa asked, may one carry between the planks[57]? We should say that if there are four hand-breadths between one and the other it is like a prohibited threshold, otherwise like a permitted threshold, permitted for both domains; only one should not exchange[58].

It was stated, there are about ten cubits, the words of Rebbi Meïr; Rebbi Jehudah says, like thirteen or fourteen minus[2,59]: a cubit, a half, and one cubit interspace[60].

55 Babli 21a.
56 Babli 20a disagrees in both cases.
57 He questions R, Yose ben R. Abun's statement.
58 Chapter 1, Note 162.
59 Both R. Meïr and R. Jehudah presume that an average cow is 1.5 cubits wide and between the two teams one leaves 1 cubit of space. R. Meïr permits space for 6 cows, 9 cubits, + 1 cubit. R. Jehudah for 8 cows, 12 cubits, + 1 cubit, for a width of 13 cubits. He admits a wider room for moving of the cows and accepts any distance less than 14 cubits.

פרא is Latin *parum* "too little, not enough". In *Demay* 5:2 the expression is פָּרָא צִיבְחַר "less a little bit."

(20a line 65) מוּתָּר לְהַקְרִיב לַבְּאֵר כול'. רִבִּי יִרְמְיָה בְּשֵׁם רִבִּי שְׁמוּאֵל בַּר רַב יִצְחָק. וְהוּא שִׁיעוּרָא. כְּשִׁיעוּר הַזֶּה אֲפִילוּ גָּמָל כּוּלּוֹ מִבַּחוּץ מוּתָּר. פָּחוּת מִכְּשִׁיעוּר הַזֶּה אֲפִילוּ גְּדִי כּוּלּוֹ מִבִּפְנִים אָסוּר. תַּנֵּי. רִבִּי שִׁמְעוֹן בֶּן אֶלְעָזָר אוֹמֵר. מְלֹא גָּמָל וְגַמָּלוֹ. מַה וּפְלִיג. כָּל־מַה שֶׁהַפָּרָה פוֹשֶׁטֶת צַוָּארָהּ הַגָּמָל עוֹקֵם צַוָּארוֹ. מָה אַתְּ בָּעֵי. וְאֵין הַפָּרָה עוֹמֶדֶת בִּרְשׁוּת הָרַבִּים וְאוֹכֶלֶת בִּרְשׁוּת הַיָּחִיד. אָמַר רִבִּי יוֹסֵה. תַּמָּן בָּהוּא דְּמַפְסִיק לֵיהּ. בְּרַם הָכָא בְּאוֹכֶלֶת מֵאֵילֶיהָ.

עַל דַּעְתֵּיהּ דְּרִבִּי מֵאִיר דְּיוֹמְדִין פְּשׁוּטִין. עַל דַּעְתֵּיהּ דְּרִבִּי יוּדָה דְּיוֹמְדִין אֲבָל לֹא פְּשׁוּטִין.

"It is permitted to make them close to the well,"[60] etc. Rebbi Jeremiah in the name of Rebbi Samuel ben Rav Isaac: This is its measure[61]. With this measure even though the camel is entirely outside it is permitted. Less than this measure even if the kid goat is entirely inside it is forbidden. It was stated: Rebbi Simeon ben Eleazar said, enough for a camel and its camel driver[62]. Does he disagree? In every case where the cow stretches its neck, the camel bends its neck. Why do you want this[63]? Could not the cow stand in the public domain and eat in a private domain? Rebbi Yose said, there it is about one who [provides][64] for it, but here if it eats by itself[654].

In Rebbi Meïr's opinion, double columns and single ones; in Rebbi Jehudah's opinion double columns but no single ones[66].

60   Discussion of Mishnah 2.
61   The Mishnah prescribes that the poles must be far enough away that a cow's head and most of its body be inside. This is part of the rabbinic institutions, it is permitted even for camels which are much longer and must be observed even for a herd of goats which are much shorter.
62   A minimal domain around a well may be used for camels only if it is wide enough to allow the camel driver to be completely inside with his camel.
63   The explanation is not satisfactory since neither cow nor camel are required to observe the distinction between public and private domain; this is only for humans. Why is space for the camel driver needed?
64   Reading דמספיק for דמפסיק "who interrupts".
65   The camel needs its camel driver while the cow does not need its master. Therefore humans are not mentioned by RR. Meïr and Jehudah who define everything referring to cattle. Babli 20b.
66   If the area around the well is extended, then the additional planks required by the Mishnah are simple planks of arbitrary size for R. Meïr but double planks (2 times 6 hand-breadths straight) for R. Jehudah.

(20a line 73) עַל דַּעְתֵּיהּ דְּרִבִּי יוּדָה בְּאֵר מָהוּ שֶׁתַּעֲלֶה מִמִּדַּת סָאתַיִם. נִשְׁמְעִינָהּ מִן הָדָא. רִבִּי שִׁמְעוֹן בֶּן אֶלְעָזָר אוֹמֵר. בְּאֵר שֶׁיֵּשׁ בָּהּ מִידַּת סָאתַיִם אֵינוֹ צָרִיךְ לְהַרְחִיק מִמֶּנּוּ אֶלָּא מְלֹא רֹאשָׁהּ וְרוּבָּהּ שֶׁלְפָּרָה. הָדָא אֲמָרָה שֶׁהַבְּאֵר עוֹלָה מִמִּדַּת סָאתַיִם.

According to Rebbi Jehudah, is the well included in the measure of two [*bet*] *se'ah*[67]? Let us hear from the following[68]: If a well is two *bet se'ah* one may not go farther away than for the head and most of the body of a cow. This implies that the well is included in the measure of two [*bet*] *se'ah*.

67   Who in Mishnah 3 restricts the area around the well to this size.
68   Tosephta 1:13, Babli 22a.

(20b line 1) פיס׳. רִבִּי יְהוּדָה אוֹמֵר עַד בֵּית סָאתַיִם כול׳. אָמַר רִבִּי יוֹחָנָן. מְחַלְפָה שִׁיטָתֵיהּ דְּרִבִּי יוּדָה. דְּתַנִּינָן תַּמָּן. וְכֵן גְּשָׁרִים הַמְפוּלָּשִׁין מְטַלְטְלִין תַּחְתֵּיהֶן בַּשַׁבָּת. דִּבְרֵי רַבִּי יְהוּדָה. וַחֲכָמִים אוֹסְרִין. אָמַר רִבִּי אֶלְעָזָר. אֵינָהּ מוּחְלֶפֶת. אָמַר רִבִּי יִרְמְיָה. דִּי סְבַר כְּרַב יְהוּדָה. דְּמַר רַב יְהוּדָה. הָדָא דְתֵימַר בִּמְפוּלָּשִׁין לְבִקְעָה. אֲבָל אִם הָיוּ מְפוּלָּשִׁין לִרְשׁוּת הָרַבִּים אָסוּר. אָמַר

רִבִּי יוֹסֵה. בְּכָל־אָתָר רִבִּי לֶעְזָר סָמִיךְ לְרִבִּי חִיָּיה רוֹבָה. תַּנֵּי רִבִּי חִיָּיה. כֵּיצַד מַתִּירִין רְשׁוּת הָרַבִּים. רִבִּי יוּדָה אוֹמֵר. לֶחִי מִיכָּן וְלֶחִי מִיכָּן. קוֹרָה מִיכָּן וְקוֹרָה מִיכָּן. וַחֲכָמִים אוֹמְרִים. לֶחִי וְקוֹרָה מִיכָּן. וְיַעֲשֶׂה צוּרַת הַפֶּתַח מִיכָּן. וְכָא אָמַר הָכֵין. כָּאן בְּעֶשֶׂר. וְכָאן בִּשְׁלֹשׁ עֶשְׂרֵה. מִילֵּיהוֹן דְּרַבָּנָן פְּלִיגִין. רִבִּי אָחָא אָמַר. רַב הוֹשַׁעְיָה שָׁאַל לְאַבָּא. כַּמָּה תְהֵא פִירְצַת הַמָּבוֹי עַל דַּעְתֵּיהּ דְּרִבִּי יוּדָה. וְהוּא אָמַר לֵיהּ. מְשַׁלֹשׁ עֶשְׂרֵה. וְהָכָא אָמַר הָכֵין. דְּרַבָּנָן דְּקַיְסָרִין אֲמְרִין. תַּמָּן עוֹמֵד רָבָה עַל הַפָּרוּץ. בְּרַם הָכָא. פָּרוּץ רָבָה עַל הָעוֹמֵד.

Paragraph. "Rebbi Jehudah says, up to two *bet se'ah*,"[69] etc. Rebbi Johanan said, the argument of Rebbi Jehudah is inverted, as we have stated there: "And similarly one carries under panelled bridges on the Sabbath, the words of Rebbi Jehudah, but the Sages forbid it[70]". Rebbi Eleazar said, it is not inverted. Rebbi Jeremiah said, for he is of Rav Jehudah's opinion, as Rav Jehudah said, that is if it is open to a domain of difficult access. But if it was open to the public domain it is forbidden[71]. Rebbi Yose said, everywhere Rebbi Eleazar seeks support from the Elder Rebbi Hiyya[72]. Rebbi Hiyya stated, how does one permit public domain? Rebbi Jehudah says, a lath on each side or a beam at each side but the Sages say a lath and a beam on one side and he shall make a door frame on the other side. And here he says so[73]? Here about ten [cubits], there about thirteen[74]. The words of the rabbis disagree. Rebbi Aha said, Rav Hoshaia asked my father, how large can the breach of an alley be in the opinion of Rebbi Jehudah? And he told him, thirteen [cubits]. And here he says so[75]? The Rabbis of Caesarea say, there what is standing is more than what is breached but here what is breached is more than what is standing[76].

69 Even though the quote is from Mishnah 3, the discussion is about Mishnah 4 where R. Jehudah prohibits using part of a thoroughfare as enclosure of a well.

70 Mishnah 9:5, explained in Chapter 1, Note 40.

71 A quote from the end of Chapter 9. Since R. Jehudah in Mishnah 9:5 accepts virtual walls only for *karmelit*, that Mishnah is consistent with Mishnah 2:4.

72 Cf. *Yebamot*, end of Halakhah 2:3.

73 There he permits turning parts of a public road, i. e., an alley open at both ends, into a private domain but here he forbids. Babli 22a.

74 A roadway cannot have the status of an alley if it is wider than 10 cubits (Mishnah 1:1) but the enclosure of a well can be 13.

75 Since it was stated just before that only a breach up to 10 cubits is acceptable.

76 The two situations cannot be

compared. 13 cubits are permitted only in the situation of the enclosure of a well which is made for the benefit of animals, not humans.

(20b line 15) פיס'. רִבִּי יְהוּדָה אוֹמֵר. אִם הָיְתָה דֶּרֶךְ הָרַבִּים מַפְסַקְתָּהּ כול'. מַה בֵּין בּוֹר הָרַבִּים וּמַה בֵּין בּוֹר הַיָּחִיד. בּוֹר הָרַבִּים יֵשׁ לוֹ קוֹל. בּוֹר הַיָּחִיד אֵין לוֹ קוֹל. מֵאַתָּה אֲפִילוּ לִבְאֵרוֹ. אֶלָּא בּוֹר הָרַבִּים מֵימָיו מְצוּיִין לְכָלוֹת. בּוֹר הַיָּחִיד אֵין מֵימָיו מְצוּיִין לְכָלוֹת.

רִבִּי יַעֲקֹב בַּר אָחָא עַמְרָם רַב יְהוּדָה בְשֵׁם שְׁמוּאֵל. הֲלָכָה כְרִבִּי יוּדָה בֶּן בָּבָא. אָמַר רִבִּי יוּדָה אָבוֹי דְרִבִּי מַתַּנְיָה. מַתְנִיתָא אָמְרָה כֵּן. עוֹשִׂין פַּסִּין לַבֵּירִיּוֹת. וְלֹא לַבּוֹרוֹת. וְהָא תַנִּינָן. אֲבָל לַבּוֹר הַיָּחִיד עוֹשִׂין לוֹ מְחִצָּה גְּבוֹהָה עֲשָׂרָה טְפָחִים. דִּבְרֵי רִבִּי עֲקִיבָה. אֶלָּא כֵן אָנוּ קַיָּימִין לְבוֹר הָרַבִּים. וְדִכְוָותָהּ עוֹשִׂין פַּסִּין לַבֵּירִיּוֹת. לַבְּאֵר הָרַבִּים.

Paragraph. "Rebbi Jehudah says[8], if a public road interrupts them," etc. What is the difference between a public cistern and a private cistern[9]? A public cistern has publicity[77], a private cistern has no publicity. Then even for his well[78]! But a public well can be expected to run dry, a private well is not expected to run dry[79].

Rebbi Jacob bar Aha, Amram, Rav Jehudah in the name of Samuel: Practice follows Rebbi Jehudah ben Bava[80]. Rebbi Jehudah the father of Rebbi Mattaniah said, the Mishnah says so, "one makes planks for wells," not for cisterns. But did we not state, "but for a private cistern one makes a partition of ten hand-breadths[9], the words of Rebbi Aqiba"? But therefore we must deal with public cisterns, and similarly "one makes planks for wells," for public wells.

77 It is common knowledge when a public cistern runs dry and the enclosure may not be used, whereas for a private cistern he might start using the enclosure and discover only belatedly that he was carrying there in violation of the Sabbath laws.
78 Why are enclosures permitted for private wells whose status is not monitored?

79 Only public wells are subject to permanent overuse.
80 Babli 23a.
Since R. Aqiba permits flimsy enclosures only for public cisterns and he otherwise treats cisterns and wells according to the same rules, he must refer to public wells in Mishnah 1.

(20b line 23) פיס'. וְעוֹד אָמַר רִבִּי יְהוּדָה בֶּן בָּבָא כול'. רִבִּי שְׁמוּאֵל בַּר נַחְמָן בְּשֵׁם רִבִּי יוֹנָתָן. מֵחֲצַר הַמִּשְׁכָּן לָמְדוּ. אוֹרֶךְ הֶחָצֵר מֵאָה בָאַמָּה וְרוֹחַב חֲמִשִּׁים בַּחֲמִשִּׁים. וְחַמְשִׁין זִימְנִין מוֹ

מֵאָה הָא חֲמִשָּׁה אַלְפִין. שׁוּבְעִין מִן שׁוּבְעִין הָא חֲמִשָּׁה אַלְפִין פָּרָא מֵאָה. וְתַנִּינַן שִׁבְעִים אַמָּה וְשִׁירַיִים. וְתַנֵּי שְׁמוּאֵל. אַמָּה וּשְׁנֵי שְׁלִישֵׁי אַמָּה שָׁנוּ. שׁוּבְעִין זִימְנִין מִן תְּרֵין תִּלְתּוֹתִין וְשׁוּבְעִין זִימְנִין מִן תְּרֵין תִּלְתּוֹתִין דְּעָבְדִין מֵאָה וְאַרְבָּעִים תִּלְתּוֹתִין מֵאָה וְאַרְבָּעִים תִּלְתּוֹתִין שֶׁהֵן תִּשְׁעִים וְשָׁלֹשׁ אַמָּה וּשְׁלִישׁ. צֵא מֵהֶן אַרְבָּעָה תְשׁוּעִין לְאַרְבַּע רוּחוֹת. נִשְׁתַּיֵּיר שָׁם תִּשְׁעָה עָשָׂר תִּלְתּוֹתִין חָסֵר תְּשׁוּעַ. כְּהָדָא דְתַנֵּי. יֵשׁ כָּאן דָּבָר קַל וְלֹא יָכְלוּ חֲכָמִים לַעֲמוֹד עָלָיו.

Paragraph. "In addition, Rebbi Jehudah ben Bava said," etc. Rebbi Samuel bar Naḥman in the name of Rebbi Jonathan, they inferred it from the courtyard of the Tabernacle: *the length of the courtyard 100 cubits wide 50 by 50*[81]. 50 times 100 are 5'000. 70 by 70 are 5'000 minus 100, and we have stated "seventy cubits and a remainder." And Samuel stated, they stated cubits and two thirds of a cubit. Seventy times two thirds and seventy times two thirds make 140 thirds each; 140 thirds and 140 thirds are $93^1/_3$. There is missing from there $^4/_9$ for the corner, there remain nineteen thirds minus one ninth. As we have stated, there is a slight difference which the Sages could not compute[82].

---

81 *Ex.* 27:18. Babli 23b. The expression "50 by 50" is read as meaning that the standard measure of area shall be a square of 5'000 square cubits.

82 Since $70^2 = 4900$ and $71^2 = 5041$ the square root of 5'000 is between 70 and 71. In order to compute $70^2/_3{}^2$ one uses the binomial formula in its geometric form: A square of sides $70^2/_3$ is composed of a square of sides 70 + two rectangles 70 by $^2/_3$ + a square of area $^4/_9$ for a total of $4993^7/_9$. The difference to 5000 is $6^2/_9 = {}^{19}/_3 - {}^1/_9$. The additional correction was a problem. Not only is the square root of 5000 irrational, not expressible as a fraction, but of the two square root algorithms used in Antiquity, the Babylonian, using a kind of Newton approximation, is an approximation from above and the Hellenistic, using an equivalent of modern continued fractions, starts with an approximation from above, when the legal situation here demands an approximation from below. $70^2/_3$, is a reasonable rational approximation from below to $\sqrt{5000}$ since $70^7/_9{}^2$ already is >5009. The second term of the continued fraction development is an approximation from below, $70^{140}/_{197}$, not a practical expression. The systematic approximation of square roots from below which used to be taught in our schools is essentially dependent on the notion of place values underlying Indian-Arabic numerals. The first approximation of $\sqrt{5000}$ both in the Babylonian and the Hellenistic methods, $70^5/_7$, is an exceedingly good low-denominator approximation from above, $(70^5/_7)^2 = 5000^{25}/_{49}$, and therefore not usable in this context. The approximation of $70^2/_3$ cubits allows a measuring error of 1 digit without exceeding $\sqrt{5000}$. Tosephta 4:9.

(20b line 33) קַרְפֵּף שֶׁיֵּשׁ בּוֹ מִידַת סָאתַיִם אֵינוֹ מוּתָּר לְטַלְטֵל בּוֹ אֶלָּא בְאַרְבַּע אַמּוֹת. הָיוּ שְׁנַיִם. בָּזֶה בֵית סְאָה וּבָזֶה בֵית סְאָה חָסֵר אַרְבַּע אַמּוֹת. רִבִּי זְעִירָה בְשֵׁם רִבִּי יוֹחָנָן. מְטַלְטְלִין בִּשְׁנֵי תַשְׁלוּמִין לָרִאשׁוֹן. רִבִּי לָא בְשֵׁם רִבִּי יוֹחָנָן. אֵין מְטַלְטְלִין בִּשְׁנֵי תַשְׁלוּמִין לָרִאשׁוֹן. אָמַר רִבִּי זְעִירָא. מוֹדֶה רִבִּי לָא שֶׁאִם הָיוּ שְׁלֹשָׁה. בָּזֶה בֵית סְאָה וּבָזֶה בֵית סְאָה וּבָזֶה בֵית סְאָה. מוֹדִין שֶׁמְטַלְטְלִין בַּשְּׁנֵי תַשְׁלוּמִין לָרִאשׁוֹן.

קַרְפֵּף שֶׁיֵּשׁ בּוֹ עַד בֵּית סָאתַיִם. אָמַר רִבִּי אַבָּהוּ. הוֹאִיל וְהוּא רָאוּי לַתִּיר עַל יְדֵי שְׁיָיָרָה וְזָרַק מֵרְשׁוּת הָרַבִּים לְתוֹכוֹ. חַיָּיב. רִבִּי שְׁמוּאֵל בַּר רַב יִצְחָק בָּעֵי. (לֹא לִכְשֶׁתִּיְרֶנּוּ) [לִכְשֶׁתִּיְרְצוּ] שְׁיָיָרָה. לֵאָסוֹר אָסוּר. הָא חַיָּיב חַטָּאת אֵין כָּאן. מֵעַתָּה מָבוֹי שֶׁקּוֹרָתוֹ לְמַעְלָה מֵעֶשְׂרִים. הוֹאִיל וְהוּא כָשֵׁר עַל דַּעְתֵּיהּ דְּרִבִּי יוּדָה מִשָּׁלֹשׁ עֶשְׂרֵה וְזָרַק מֵרְשׁוּת הָרַבִּים לְתוֹכוֹ. וְחַיָּיב. מָבוֹי שֶׁנִּפְרַץ יוֹתֵר מֵעֶשֶׂר. הוֹאִיל וּפִירְצַת הַמָּבוֹי עַל דַּעְתֵּיהּ דְּרִבִּי יוּדָה מִשָּׁלֹשׁ עֶשְׂרֵה וְזָרַק מֵרְשׁוּת הָרַבִּים לְתוֹכוֹ. חַיָּיב.

חָצֵר שֶׁהִיא פְתוּחָה לַקַּרְפֵּף. מְטַלְטְלִין מִן הֶחָצֵר לַקַּרְפֵּף. אֲבָל לֹא מִן הַקַּרְפֵּף לֶחָצֵר. רִבִּי יוּדָן עַנְתּוֹדְרַיָּא שָׁאַל. מַהוּ לְטַלְטֵל מִקַּרְפֵּף לְקַרְפֵּף דֶּרֶךְ חָצֵר. מַחְלְפָה שִׁיטָתֵיהּ דְּרִבִּי יוּדָה. דְּתַנִּינָן תַּמָּן. אֵיזֶהוּ קַרְפֵּף. כָּל־שֶׁהוּא סָמוּךְ לָעִיר. דִּבְרֵי רִבִּי יוּדָה. וְכָא הוּא אוֹמֵר הָכֵין. אָמַר רִבִּי מָנָא. כְּבֵית דִּירָה עֲבִיד לָהּ רִבִּי יוּדָה.

In a corral which covers two *bet se'ah* one is permitted only to carry a distance of four cubits[83]. If there were two, each one a *bet se'ah* minus four cubits; Rebbi Ze'ira in the name of Rebbi Johanan: one carries in the second as complement of the first[84]. Rebbi La in the name of Rebbi Johanan, one may not carry in the second as complement of the first. Rebbi Ze'ira said, Rebbi La agrees that if there were three[85]. Each of the three a *bet se'ah*, one agrees that one carries in the second as complement of the first[86].

A corral which covers up to two *bet se'ah*. Rebbi Abbahu said, since it can be permitted by a caravan, if somebody threw from the public domain into it he is liable[87]. Rebbi Samuel bar Rav Isaac asked, (not after it was permitted) [if it was chosen by][88] the caravan it becomes forbidden in a prohibition; therefore here is no liability for a purification sacrifice[89]. By the same argument, an alley whose beam is higher than twenty cubits since it is qualified in the opinion of Rebbi Jehudah (more than thirteen)[90], if somebody threw from the public domain into it would he be liable? An alley which was breached more than ten [cubits], since a breach of an alley in the opinion of Rebbi Jehudah is more than thirteen, if somebody threw from the public domain into it would he be liable?

If a courtyard is open into a corral one may carry from the courtyard to the corral but not from the corral to the courtyard[91]. Rebbi Judah from Anthodriya asked, may one carry from one corral to another corral through the courtyard[92]? [93]The opinion of Rebbi Jehudah seems inverted, as we have stated there, "what is a corral? Anything close to a village, the words of Rebbi Jehudah." And here he says so? Rebbi Mana said, Rebbi Jehudah treated it as a house.

83 This refers to areas enclosed by a makeshift fence such as is authorized for a caravan. The moment it is a full two *bet se'ah* one requires a wall or a fence with woof and warp (Mishnah 5).

84 Cf. Babli 93a. Two people enclosed adjacent areas with makeshift fences. R. La notes that they cannot combine their areas to one authorized for caravans, cf. Chapter 1 Note 296.

85 Three people camping together form a caravan and follow the rules explained in Chapter 1.

86 Since as member of a caravan he has two *bet se'ah* at his disposal.

87 Even though the enclosure made by a caravan does not qualify as wall of a private domain under normal circumstances, the area becomes a private domain for the rules of the Sabbath.

88 The text in parentheses was originally written by the scribe, the text in brackets is the corrector's. The original text is preferable.

89 R. Abbahu's statement is refuted. Since the entire arrangement is rabbinical, no biblical liability is possible.

90 The text in parentheses should be deleted; it is appropriate only in the next sentence.

Since practice does not follow R. Jehudah, the rules of private domain cannot be applied to areas which may become private domains only according to him.

91 Courtyard and corral must have a common owner. Since the corral (enclosed by a makeshift fence) is an appendix to the courtyard but not vice-versa, cf. Note 48, Mishnah 9:2.

92 Since from courtyard to corral is permitted, may one move from one corral to the other without stopping in the courtyard? The question is not answered since if half of the way is forbidden the entire way cannot be permitted.

93 Chapter 1, Note 194.

(20b line 52) פיס'. רִבִּי יוּדָה אוֹמֵר אֲפִילוּ אֵין בָּהּ אֶלָּא בּוֹר כּוֹל'. תַּנֵּי. רִבִּי לְעָזָר אוֹמֵר הָיָה אָרְכָּהּ יוֹתֵר עַל רָחְבָּהּ אֲפִילוּ אַמָּה אַחַת אֵין מְטַלְטְלִין מְתוֹכָהּ. וְהָדָא פְלִיגָא עַל דְּרִבִּי יוֹנָתָן. רִבִּי יוֹסֵה אוֹמֵר. אֲפִילוּ אָרְכָּהּ כִּשְׁנַיִם בְּרָחְבָּהּ מְטַלְטְלִין בְּתוֹכָהּ׃ הָדָא מְסַיְּיעָה לְרִבִּי יוֹנָתָן. וְהָא תַנֵּי. כִּלְאַיִם בְּרוּבָּהּ. רִבִּי יוֹסֵה אוֹמֵר. אֲפִילוּ אָרְכָּהּ כִּשְׁנַיִם בְּרָחְבָּהּ.

Paragraph. "Rebbi Jehudah says, even if it only contains a cistern," etc. It was stated, "Rebbi Eliezer says, if its length exceeds its width even by one cubit one may not carry there[13]." This disagrees with R. Jonathan[94]. "Rebbi Yose says, even if its length is twice its width one carries in there," this agrees with Rebbi Jonathan. We also have stated[95], "*Kilaim* in a quarter[96]. Rebbi Yose says, even if its length is twice its width."

94 Who said earlier (Note 81) that one inferred from the courtyard of the Tabernacle whose sides were in ratio 1:2.

85 The reference is to a statement close to Tosephta *Kilaim* 2:6: "How much is a *bet rova*'? 10.5 cubits square, Rebbi Yose says even if its length is twice its width." The quarter is a quarter *qav*, 1/24 of a *se'ah*.

Therefore a *bet qav* = 2500/24 = 104.1667 square cubits or 10.206^2, somewhat less than the 10.5^2 given in the Tosephta. The quote shows that R. Yose consistently considers "squares" mentioned in legal contexts as measures of area, rather than geometric squares.

96 Read רובע for רובה.

(20b line 57) פיס'. אָמַר רִבִּי אֶלְעַאי שָׁמַעְתִּי מֵרִבִּי לִיעֶזֶר. רִבִּי אַבָּהוּ בְשֵׁם רִבִּי אֶלְעָזָר. בְּמִתְלַקֶּטֶת סָאתַיִם מִבֵּית כּוֹר הִיא מַתְנִיתָא.

וְכֵן שָׁמַעְתִּי מִמֶּנּוּ. אַנְשֵׁי חָצֵר שֶׁשָּׁכַח אֶחָד מֵהֶן וְלֹא עֵירֵב. בֵּיתוֹ אָסוּר. תַּמָּן רַבָּנָן. בְּרַם הָכָא רִבִּי אֱלִיעֶזֶר. רַבָּנָן אֲמָרִי. אָדָם מְבַטֵּל רְשׁוּת בֵּיתוֹ וְאֵין אָדָם מְבַטֵּל רְשׁוּת חֲצֵירוֹ. רִבִּי אֱלִיעֶזֶר אוֹמֵר. כְּשֵׁם שֶׁאָדָם מְבַטֵּל רְשׁוּת בֵּיתוֹ כָּךְ מְבַטֵּל רְשׁוּת חֲצֵירוֹ. עַל דַּעְתֵּיהּ דְּרִבִּי אֱלִיעֶזֶר יֵיעָשֶׂה כְּאַכְסְנַאי וִיהֵא מוּתָּר. רִבִּי חִייָה בַּר אָדָא בְשֵׁם רִבִּי שִׁמְעוֹן בֶּן לָקִישׁ. קָנַס קְנָסוֹ רִבִּי אֱלִיעֶזֶר. רִבִּי שַׁמַּי בָעֵי. דָּבָר מִדִּבְרֵיהֶן קוֹנְסִין לוֹ בְשׁוֹגֵג כְּרִבִּי לִיעֶזֶר. רִבִּי בָּא בְּרֵיהּ דְּרַב פַּפֵּי בָעֵי. אָמַר. הֲרֵינִי מְבַטֵּל רְשׁוּת בֵּיתִי. אוֹף רַבָּנָן מוֹדֵיי. אָמַר. הֲרֵינִי מְבַטֵּל רְשׁוּת חֲצֵירִי. אוֹף רִבִּי לִיעֶזֶר מוֹדֵיי.

וְכֵן שָׁמַעְתִּי מִמֶּנּוּ שֶׁיּוֹצְאִין בְּעַקְרַבָּנִין בַּפֶּסַח. הֲוֵינָן סָבְרִין מֵימַר. בְּעַקְרַבָּנִין. אַשְׁכַּח תַּנֵּי. עַל כּוּלְּהוֹן.

Paragraph. "Rebbi Illai said, I heard from Rebbi Eliezer:" Rebbi Abbahu in the name of Rebbi Eleazar, this Mishnah is about two *bet seah* collected from the *bet kor*[97].

"And also I heard from him that if one of the dwellers in a courtyard had forgotten to make an *eruv* he is forbidden [to bring into] his house." There it follows the rabbis, here Rebbi Eliezer[98]. The rabbis say, a person may annul his right to his house but not his right to his courtyard[99]. Rebbi Eliezer says, just as a person may annul his right to his house so he may annul his right to his courtyard. According to Rebbi Eliezer, could he not be treated like a guest[100] and be permitted? Rebbi Ḥiyya bar Ada in the name of Rebbi Simeon ben Laqish: Rebbi Eliezer fined him[101]. Rebbi Shammai asked, according to Rebbi Eliezer, does one fine anybody in error about a matter of their words[102]? Rebbi Abba the son of Rav Pappai asked, if somebody said, I am annulling the right to my house, would the rabbis agree? If somebody said, I am annulling the right to my courtyard, would Rebbi Eliezer agree?

"Also I heard from him that one may satisfy one's obligation on Passover with white stone-crop[15]." They were of the opinion to say, about white stone-crop. It was found stated, about all of them[103].

97 R. Eliezer never permitted carrying in a corral which does not contain a human dwelling and which is larger than two *bet se'ah*. If the entire area was fenced in and there was an area smaller than two *bet se'ah* somehow separated from the entire area, such as a hill, or a depression, or a cave, one may carry in that separate area because of the fence around the entire area.

98 The rabbis in Mishnah 6:3 forbid his house to him and everybody else and permit other houses opening to the same courtyard to him and everybody else.

99 This has to read: "The rabbis say, a person may annul his right to his courtyard but not his right to his house." In the matter of *eruvin*, "annulling one's right" means asking not to be counted. This permits the other parties to establish an *eruv* without his participation; he will have no right to use the *eruv*.

100 An Aramaic word derived from Greek ξένος, ὁ "stranger". A guest who has no property rights in the courtyard is irrelevant for the *eruv*.

101 The answer to the question in theory is positive but R. Eliezer holds that the person forgetting an *eruv* should be fined.

102 Since by biblical law one could carry in the common courtyard, R. Eliezer's restriction seems to be contrary to the rules.

103 All statements of R. Illay are unsupported.

בכל מערבין פרק שלישי

(fol.20c) **משנה א**: בַּכֹּל מְעָרְבִין וּמִשְׁתַּתְּפִין חוּץ מִן הַמַּיִם וּמִן הַמֶּלַח. וְהַכֹּל נִלְקָח בְּכֶסֶף מַעֲשֵׂר חוּץ מִן הַמַּיִם וּמִן הַמֶּלַח. הַנּוֹדֵר מִן הַמָּזוֹן מוּתָּר בַּמַּיִם וָמֶלַח. מְעָרְבִין לַנָּזִיר בַּיַּיִן וּלְיִשְׂרָאֵל בִּתְרוּמָה. סוּמָכוֹס אוֹמֵר אַף בַּחוּלִין לַכֹּהֵן בְּבֵית הַפְּרָס. רִבִּי יְהוּדָה אוֹמֵר אֲפִילוּ בֵין הַקְּבָרוֹת מִפְּנֵי שֶׁהוּא יָכוֹל לַחוֹץ וְלוֹכַל:

Mishnah 1: With anything one may make an *eruv* or participate except with water or salt[1]. Anything may be bought with money of [Second] Tithe[2] except water and salt. One who vows not to eat food is permitted water and salt. One may make an *eruv* for a *nazir* with wine and for an Israel with heave[3]. Symmachos says, also with profane food for a Cohen in a *bet happeras*[4]. Rebbi Jehudah says among the graves since he could be shielded and eat.

משנה ב: מְעָרְבִין בַּדְּמַאי וּבְמַעֲשֵׂר רִאשׁוֹן שֶׁנִּיטְּלָה תְרוּמָתוֹ וּבְמַעֲשֵׂר שֵׁנִי וְהֶקְדֵּשׁ שֶׁנִּפְדּוּ. הַכֹּהֲנִים בַּחַלָּה וּבִתְרוּמָה. אֲבָל לֹא בַטֶּבֶל וְלֹא בְמַעֲשֵׂר רִאשׁוֹן שֶׁלֹּא נִיטְּלָה תְרוּמָתוֹ וְלֹא בְמַעֲשֵׂר שֵׁנִי וְהֶקְדֵּשׁ שֶׁלֹּא נִפְדּוּ. הַשּׁוֹלֵחַ אֶת עֵירוּבוֹ בְּיַד חֵרֵשׁ שׁוֹטֶה וְקָטָן אוֹ בְיַד מִי שֶׁאֵינוֹ מוֹדֶה בָעֵירוּב אֵינוֹ עֵירוּב. אִם אָמַר לְאַחֵר לְקַבְּלוֹ מִמֶּנּוּ הֲרֵי זֶה עֵירוּב:

Mishnah 2 One may make an *eruv* with *demay*[5], and with First Tithe from which heave has been taken[6], and Second Tithe or dedicated [food][7] which was redeemed; Cohanim with *hallah* and with heave. But not with *tevel,* nor with First Tithe from which heave was not taken, and Second Tithe or dedicated [food] which was not redeemed. If somebody sends his *eruv*[8] through a deaf-and-dumb or insane person, or a minor, or by somebody who does not accept *eruvin*[9], it is not an *eruv*. If he told a third person to receive it from him it is an *eruv*[10].

משנה ג: נְתָנוֹ בָאִילָן לְמַעְלָה מֵעֲשָׂרָה טְפָחִים אֵינוֹ עֵרוּב. לְמַטָּה מֵעֲשָׂרָה טְפָחִים הֲרֵי זֶה עֵרוּב. נְתָנוֹ בַבּוֹר אֲפִילוּ עָמוֹק מֵאָה אַמָּה הֲרֵי זֶה עֵרוּב. נְתָנוֹ בְרֹאשׁ הַקָּנֶה אוֹ בְרֹאשׁ הַקּוּנְטָס כָּל־זְמַן שֶׁהוּא תָלוּשׁ וְנָעוּץ אֲפִילוּ גָבוֹהַּ מֵאָה אַמָּה הֲרֵי זֶה עֵרוּב. נְתָנוֹ בַּמִּגְדָּל וְנָעַל בְּפָנָיו וְאָבַד הַמַּפְתֵּחַ הֲרֵי זֶה עֵרוּב. רִבִּי אֱלִיעֶזֶר אוֹמֵר אִם אֵין יָדוּעַ שֶׁהַמַּפְתֵּחַ בִּמְקוֹמוֹ אֵינוֹ עֵירוּב:

Mishnah 3: If he deposited it in a tree higher than ten hand-breadths it is not an *eruv*; below ten hand-breadths it is an *eruv*[11]. If he put it in a cistern even 100 cubits deep it is an *eruv*[12]. If he put it on top of a stick or a pole[13] as long as it was uprooted and inserted it is an *eruv* even if 100 cubits high. If he put it into a tower it is an *eruv* even if the key was lost. Rebbi Eliezer said, if it is not known that the key is in its place it is no *eruv*[14].

משנה ד: נִתְגַּלְגֵּל חוּץ לַתְּחוּם נָפַל עָלָיו גַּל אוֹ נִשְׂרַף אוֹ תְרוּמָה וְנִטְמֵאת מִבְּעוֹד יוֹם אֵינוֹ עֵירוּב. מִשֶּׁחֲשֵׁיכָה הֲרֵי זֶה עֵירוּב. אִם סָפֵק רִבִּי מֵאִיר וְרִבִּי יְהוּדָה אוֹמֵר הֲרֵי זֶה חַמָּר גַּמָּל. רִבִּי יוֹסֵי וְרִבִּי שִׁמְעוֹן אוֹמֵר סְפֵק הָעֵירוּב כָּשֵׁר. אָמַר רִבִּי יוֹסֵי הֵעִיד אַבְטוֹלָס מִשֵּׁם חֲמִשָּׁה זְקֵנִים שֶׁסְּפֵק הָעֵירוּב כָּשֵׁר:

Mishnah 4: If it rolled outside the Sabbath boundary, if a pile fell on it, or it was burned or heave which became impure on Friday afternoon it is not *eruv*. After dark it is an *eruv*[15]. If it is a matter of uncertainty, Rebbi Meïr and Rebbi Jehudah say, he is a donkey driver-camel driver[16]. Rebbi Yose and Rebbi Simeon say that in case of doubt an *eruv* is qualified. Rebbi Yose said, Autolas[17] testified in the name of five Elders that in case of a doubt an *eruv* is qualified[18].

משנה ה: מַתְנֶה אָדָם עַל עֵירוּבוֹ וְאוֹמֵר אִם בָּאוּ גוֹיִם מִן הַמִּזְרָח עֵירוּבִי לַמַּעֲרָב. וְאִם בָּאוּ מִן הַמַּעֲרָב עֵירוּבִי לַמִּזְרָח. אִם בָּאוּ מִכָּאן וּמִכָּן לְמָקוֹם שֶׁאֶרְצֶה אֵלֵךְ. לֹא בָאוּ לֹא מִכָּן וְלֹא מִכָּן הֲרֵינִי כִבְנֵי עִירִי.

Mishnah 5: A person may make his *eruv* conditional and say, if Gentiles come from the East my *eruv* shall be in the West, but if they come from the West my *eruv* shall be in the East, if they come from both sides I shall be able to go where I want, if they come from neither side I shall be like the people of my village[19].

משנה ו: אִם בָּא חָכָם מִן הַמִּזְרָח עֵירוּבִי לַמִּזְרָח בָּא מִן הַמַּעֲרָב עֵירוּבִי לַמַּעֲרָב בָּא מִכָּן וּמִכָּן לְמָקוֹם שֶׁאֶרְצֶה אֵלֵךְ לֹא בָא לֹא מִכָּן וְלֹא מִכָּן הֲרֵינִי כִבְנֵי עִירִי.

Mishnah 6 If a Sage comes from the East my *eruv* shall be to the East, if he comes from the West my *eruv* shall be to the West, on both sides I shall be able to go where I want[20], if they come from neither side I shall be like the people of my village.

משנה ז: רִבִּי יְהוּדָה אוֹמֵר אִם הָיָה מֵהֶן אֶחָד רַבּוֹ יֵלֵךְ אֵצֶל רַבּוֹ. שְׁנֵיהֶן רַבּוֹתָיו לְמָקוֹם שֶׁיִּרְצֶה יֵלֵךְ:

Mishnah 7: Rebbi Jehudah says, if one of them was his teacher he has to go to his teacher[21], if both were his teachers he may go to where he wants.

משנה ח: רִבִּי אֱלִיעֶזֶר אוֹמֵר יוֹם טוֹב שֶׁהוּא סָמוּךְ לַשַּׁבָּת בֵּין מִלְּפָנֶיהָ וּבֵין מִלְאַחֲרֶיהָ מְעָרֵב אָדָם שְׁנֵי עֵירוּבִין וְאוֹמֵר עֵירוּבִי הָרִאשׁוֹן לַמִּזְרָח וְהַשֵּׁנִי לַמַּעֲרָב. הָרִאשׁוֹן לַמַּעֲרָב וְהַשֵּׁנִי לַמִּזְרָח. עֵירוּבִי הָרִאשׁוֹן וְהַשֵּׁנִי כִּבְנֵי עִירִי וְהָרִאשׁוֹן כִּבְנֵי עִירִי.

Mishnah 8: Rebbi Eliezer says, if a holiday is next to a Sabbath either before or after, a person may make two *eruvin* and say: my first *eruv* shall be to the East and the second to the West, the first to the West and the second to the East, my first *eruv* but on the second like the people of my town. My *eruv* for the first [day], but the second like the people of my town; the second [day], but the first like the people of my town.[22]

משנה ט: וַחֲכָמִים אוֹמְרִים מְעָרֵב לְרוּחַ אַחַת אוֹ אֵינוֹ מְעָרֵב כָּל־עִקָּר אוֹ מְעָרֵב לִשְׁנֵי יָמִים אוֹ אֵינוֹ מְעָרֵב כָּל־עִקָּר. כֵּיצַד יַעֲשֶׂה מוֹלִיכוֹ בָּרִאשׁוֹן וּמַחְשִׁיךְ עָלָיו וְנוֹטְלוֹ וּבָא לוֹ וּבַשֵּׁנִי מַחְשִׁיךְ עָלָיו וְאוֹכְלוֹ וּבָא לוֹ וְנִמְצָא מִשְׂתַּכֵּר בַּהֲלִיכָתוֹ וּמִשְׂתַּכֵּר בְּעֵירוּבוֹ. נֶאֱכַל בָּרִאשׁוֹן עֵירוּב לָרִאשׁוֹן וְאֵינוֹ עֵירוּב לַשֵּׁנִי. אָמַר לָהֶן רִבִּי אֱלִיעֶזֶר מוֹדִין אַתֶּם לִי שֶׁהֵן שְׁתֵּי קְדֻשּׁוֹת:

Mishnah 9 But the Sages say, either one makes an *eruv* to one side or one does not make an *eruv* at all; one makes an *eruv* for both days or one does not make an *eruv* at all[22]. What should he do? He brings it on the first day, stays there when it gets dark, takes it and goes home, On the second day he brings it, stays there when it gets dark, eats it and goes home[23]. It turns out that he profits from his going and his *eruv*. If it is eaten on the first day, it is an *eruv* for the first but is not an *eruv* for the second. Rebbi Eliezer told them, you agree with me that they are two kinds if sanctities[24].

משנה י: רִבִּי יוּדָה אוֹמֵר רֹאשׁ הַשָּׁנָה שֶׁהָיָה יָרֵא שֶׁמָּא תִתְעַבֵּר מְעָרֵב אָדָם שְׁנֵי עֵירוּבִין וְאוֹמֵר עֵירוּבִי הָרִאשׁוֹן לַמִּזְרָח וְהַשֵּׁנִי לַמַּעֲרָב הָרִאשׁוֹן לַמַּעֲרָב וְהַשֵּׁנִי לַמִּזְרָח עֵירוּבִי הָרִאשׁוֹן וְהַשֵּׁנִי כִּבְנֵי עִירִי הַשֵּׁנִי וְהָרִאשׁוֹן כִּבְנֵי עִירִי וְלֹא הוֹדוּ לוֹ חֲכָמִים:

Mishnah 10: Rebbi Jehudah said, if a person was afraid that the New Year's Day might be complemented[25], he makes two *eruvin* and says, my first *eruv* should be to the East and the second to the West, the first to the West and the second to the East, my *eruv* for the first day and on the second like the people of my village, for the second day but the first day like the people of my village. But the Sages did not agree with him.

משנה יא: וְעוֹד אָמַר רִבִּי יְהוּדָה מַתְנֶה אָדָם עַל הַכַּלְכָּלָה בְּיוֹם טוֹב הָרִאשׁוֹן וְאוֹכְלָהּ בַּשֵּׁנִי וְכֵן בֵּיצָה שֶׁנּוֹלְדָה בָרִאשׁוֹן תֵּאָכֵל בַּשֵּׁנִי וְלֹא הוֹדוּ לוֹ חֲכָמִים:

Mishnah 11: In addition, Rebbi Jehudah says that a person may stipulate about a basket on the first day[26] and eat from it on the second; similarly an egg which was laid on the first may be eaten on the second[27]; but the Sages did not agree with him[28].

משנה יב: רִבִּי דוֹסָא בֶּן אַרְכִּינָס אוֹמֵר הָעוֹבֵר לִפְנֵי הַתֵּבָה בְּיוֹם טוֹב שֶׁל רֹאשׁ הַשָּׁנָה אוֹמֵר הַחֲלִיצֵנוּ ה' אֱלֹהֵינוּ אֶת יוֹם רֹאשׁ הַחֹדֶשׁ הַזֶּה אִם הַיּוֹם אִם לְמָחָר וּלְמָחָר הוּא אוֹמֵר אִם הַיּוֹם אִם לְאֶמֶשׁ וְלֹא הוֹדוּ לוֹ חֲכָמִים:

Mishnah 12: Rebbi Dosa ben Hyrkanos said, the reader[29] on New Year's Day says "save us, Eternal, our God, on this Day of the New Moon, whether it be today or tomorrow." The next day he says, "whether it be today or was yesterday"; but the Sages did not agree with him.

1 An עֵרוּב חֲצֵרוֹת which allows carrying in and to a multi-family courtyard is made by depositing food from all inhabitants of the courtyard in one of the houses belonging to it. An עֵרוּב תְּחוּמִים is made by a single person who wants to move his Sabbath domain in a certain direction by depositing food for a meal near the border of his regular Sabbath domain before the start of the Sabbath with the intention that the place of this food be the center of his Sabbath rest, which gives him 2'000 cubits in every direction from his new place. שִׁיתּוּף מְבוֹאוֹת makes a dead-end alley (duly marked by beam or lath) a common Sabbath domain of its dwellers by deposition of food common to inhabitants of the alley in one of the houses belonging to it. The rules for *eruv* of courtyards and participation of alleys are identical.

2 Second Tithe is the property of the farmer and should be eaten in purity in Jerusalem. The tithe may be redeemed for money and the money spent on food at the place of the Temple (*Deut.* 24:16). Edibles without calories are not considered food.

3 Even though the *nazir* is forbidden wine and the non-Cohen heave, wine is food appropriate for people who may consume it.

4 A place where a source of impurity is known but its location is unknown. The Cohen may not enter by rabbinic decree but he could be carried there in a wooden box which shields against the impurity of the dead. The food may not be heave since heave in a *bet happeras* is at least rabbinically impure and must be burned; it is no longer food.

5 *Demay* is produce of which one may assume that heave was taken but one

suspects that it was not tithed. While a scrupulous person will not eat *demay* it may be given to the poor and the traveler and therefore is edible food.

6   Any food of which heave was not taken is *tevel* and forbidden for consumption; it is not food. First Tithe of which Heave of the Tithe was taken is wholly profane.

7   Donated to the Temple to be sold and the proceeds used for the upkeep of the Temple.

8   For an *eruv tehumim*, if the person wanting to change his Sabbath domain does not go by himself to deposit the food, he must send it by a legally competent person.

9   A Sadducee who as a matter of principle denies the possibility of an *eruv*, cannot be an agent for its creation.

10 In this case the identity of the carrier is irrelevant.

11 If the tree is standing in the public domain and the place where the *eruv* is deposited is at least 4-by-4 hand-breadths wide, this place is a separate domain. Since it is standing in the public domain the intent of the person making the *eruv* is to spend the Sabbath in the public domain. But then the *eruv* is in a separate private domain if it is at least 10 hand-breadths high. Since climbing on trees is rabbinically forbidden on the Sabbath there is no possibility that the person keep the Sabbath at the place of his *eruv*.

12 This is a private domain by construction even if built in the public domain.

13 Greek κοντός, ὁ. Since stick or pole are not 16 hand-breadths[2] wide at the top they cannot form a separate domain.

14 The rabbis hold that one can break into the tower even without a key. R. Eliezer holds that one needs a key. If the owner forgot where he put the key it is no obstacle but if the key might be lost it is.

15 The food must be available at the beginning of the Sabbath. Since it is a symbolic Sabbath meal it may be eaten at any time on the Sabbath; therefore if it is lost during the Sabbath the *eruv* remains in force.

16 The donkey driver walks behind his animal, the camel driver in front of it. The donkey-camel driver is in an impossible situation, by analogy his situation is impossible; the person's Sabbath rest is not at his home since he made an *eruv*; it is not at the place of the *eruv* since the latter might be invalid. He might be able to walk between house and *eruv* but at each endpoint not one step further.

17 In other sources the name is אבטולמוס (Ptolemaios).

18 Since the *eruv* is a rabbinic institution to allow carrying in or walking to places biblically permitted, in cases of doubt one has to permit.

19 He can make two *eruve tehumim*, deposit each one at an appropriate place and determine on Sabbath morning which one to use. While we do not accept retroactive determinations for biblical commandments, they are acceptable for rabbinic institutions.

20 He has no preacher at his place; he intends to go to any place where there is instruction. If two preachers come he may choose which lecture to attend.

21 Since we presume that his intention is to hear his teacher, the second *eruv* becomes void automatically.

22 Since on a holiday one may carry, by

necessity this refers to *eruv tehumim*. R. Eliezer holds that since Sabbath and holiday are distinct entities, one may make different *eruvim* for the two days. The Sages agree but they hold that an *eruv* can be made only in preparation on a working day; therefore a different *eruv* for the second day can never become effective.

23   This works only if Friday is a holiday. He brings the *eruv* on Thursday to the place he has selected, waits there for the start of the holiday to enter into force and takes the *eruv* home lest it become lost. On Friday he brings the *eruv* back to the place he chose the day before, waits for the start of the Sabbath but then, since he is forbidden to carry on the Sabbath, eats the *eruv* before returning to his house.

24   Since the Sages agree that the *eruv* must exist at the beginning of the Sabbath they imply that the Sabbath is not the extension of the holiday.

25   This refers to the times when the calendar was not computed but the day of the New Moon was determined by observation. Outside the seat of the Synhedrion the day of the New Moon of Tishre, which is New Year's Day in the Baylonian calendar, had to be observed for two days since it could be either the 30th or the 31st of Elul. This is the only holiday falling on a New Moon. While the holiday lasts two days, it is clear that this is not a question of two distinct sanctities but in fact one of the days is really a weekday, the other a holiday, only it is not known which is which. Rebbi Jehudah, the student of R. Eliezer's student, follows R. Eliezer and permits two different *eruvin*. The Sages hold that the two days are legally one long holiday.

26   Still about New Year's day. *Tevel* may not be eaten; heave and tithes may not be taken on a holiday. R. Jehudah permits to designate heave and tithes on the first day after a declaration that heave and tithe are designated if and only if the day was a weekday. If the same declaration is repeated on the second day, exactly one of them is valid and the remainder of the produce in the basket may be consumed.

27   Since the egg either was laid or consumed on a weekday.

28   Since the two days are legally one long holiday and the egg was not food at the start of the holiday.

29   Who leads the congregation in prayer and has to mention the holiday. The Sages reject conditional prayers and therefore hold that the New Moon should not be mentioned in the prayers of New Year's day.

(20c line 55) בַּכֹּל מְעָרְבִין וּמִשְׁתַּתְּפִין כול׳. אָמַר רִבִּי אָחָא. דְּרִבִּי אֱלִיעֶזֶר הִיא. דְּתַנִּינָן תַּמָּן. בַּכֹּל מְעָרְבִין וּמִשְׁתַּתְּפִין חוּץ מִן הַמַּיִם וּמִן הַמֶּלַח. דִּבְרֵי רִבִּי אֱלִיעֶזֶר. אָמַר רִבִּי יוֹסֵה. דִּבְרֵי הַכֹּל הִיא. מְעָרְבִין בַּחֲצֵירוֹת וּמִשְׁתַּתְּפִין בֵּין בַּחֲצֵירוֹת בֵּין בַּתְּחוּמִין. מַתְנִיתָא דְּרִבִּי מֵאִיר. דְּתַנֵּי. כָּל־דָּבָר שֶׁהוּא נֶאֱכָל חַי כְּמוֹת שֶׁהוּא מְעָרְבִין בּוֹ. עִם הַפַּת. אֵין מְעָרְבִין בּוֹ. הַשׁוּם וְהַבְּצָלִים. עַל דַּעְתֵּיהּ דְּרִבִּי מֵאִיר אֵין מְעָרְבִין בּוֹ. דְּתַנֵּי. אָמַר רִבִּי יוּדָה. מַעֲשֶׂה שֶׁשָּׁבַת רִבִּי מֵאִיר בְּאַרְדַּקְסַם וּבָא אֶחָד וְאָמַר. עִירַבְתִּי עַל יְדֵי בְצָלִים. וְהוֹשִׁיבוֹ רִבִּי מֵאִיר בְּאַרְבַּע אַמּוֹת

שָׁלוּ. אַף עַל גַּב דְּרִבִּי מֵאִיר אָמַר. בַּכֹּל מְעָרְבִין וּמִשְׁתַּתְּפִין חוּץ מִן הַמַּיִם וּמִן הַמֶּלַח. וּבִלְבַד דָּבָר שֶׁהוּא נֶאֱכָל חַי כְּמוֹת שֶׁהוּא. הַלּוּף וְהַקּוֹלְקָס. עַל דַּעְתִּין דְּרַבָּנָן אֵין מְעָרְבִין בָּהֶן.

"With anything one may make an *eruv* or participate," etc. Rebbi Aḥa said, this is Rebbi Eliezer's, as we have stated there[30], "with anything one may make an *eruv* or participate except with water or salt, the words of Rebbi Eliezer." Rebbi Yose said, it is everybody's opinion. One makes an *eruv* for courtyards and participates both for courtyards and for domains[31]. Our Mishnah is Rebbi Meïr's, as it was stated: one may make an *eruv* with anything eaten raw as is; with bread, one does not make an *eruv* with it[32]. Garlic and onions, in the opinion of Rebbi Meïr one does not make an *eruv* with them[33], as it was stated: Rebbi Jehudah said, it happened that Rebbi Meïr spent a Sabbath at Ardaksam[34]; there came a person who said, I made an *eruv* with onions and Rebbi Meïr restricted him to his four cubits[35]. Even though Rebbi Meïr said, with everything one may make an *eruv* or participate except with water or salt, on condition that it be something eaten raw as is. Arum and colocasia: in the rabbis' opinion one does not make an *eruv* with[36].

30 Mishnah 7:10, detailing the rules for *eruvin* of courtyards, where R. Joshua disagrees and asserts that a single loaf of bread is a valid *eruv*. It follows that Mishnah 3:1 refers to *eruv tehumim*, an *eruv* of domains. (Note by Rashba).

31 This sentence makes no sense as it stands since one makes an *eruv* both for courtyards and domains and participates for alleys. A possible emendation would be to delete the first mention of "courtyards"; S. Liebermann proposes to read כן for בין "by the same rules one makes *eruv* or participates for courtyards and domains."

32 Obviously a reference "the words of R. Meïr" is missing here. For an *eruv tehumim* which represents two meals at a place where there are no cooking facilities, he requires food that can be eaten as is without any additions. He excludes vegetables eaten only with bread.

33 Since they are eaten raw only with bread, or because they cause bad mouth odor, see below.

34 In the Babli 29a the place is ערדיסקא. It must have been in lower Galilee not far from Tiv'on.

35 Tosephta 6:4. If he came from another place to hear R. Meïr on basis of an invalid *eruv*, he voluntarily left his Sabbath domain and is restricted to his 4 cubits as explained in Chapter 4.

36 Since they are not edible when raw.

(20c line 65) תַּנֵּינָן תְּרֵין כְּלָלִין וְלָא דָמְיָין חַד לְחַד. בַּכֹּל מְעָרְבִין וּמִשְׁתַּתְּפִין חוּץ מִן הַמַּיִם וּמִן הַמֶּלַח. בֵּין בְּדָבָר שֶׁהוּא נֶאֱכַל חַי כְּמוֹת שֶׁהוּא. בֵּין בְּדָבָר שֶׁאֵינוֹ נֶאֱכַל חַי כְּמוֹת שֶׁהוּא. וְהַכֹּל נִלְקַח בְּכֶסֶף מַעֲשֵׂר חוּץ מִן הַמַּיִם וּמִן הַמֶּלַח. וּבִלְבַד דָּבָר שֶׁהוּא נֶאֱכַל חַי כְּמוֹת שֶׁהוּא. בַּכֹּל מְעָרְבִין וּמִשְׁתַּתְּפִין חוּץ מִן הַמַּיִם וּמִן הַמֶּלַח. בֵּין כְּרִבִּי עֲקִיבָה בֵּין כְּרִבִּי יִשְׁמָעֵאל. וְהַכֹּל נִלְקַח בְּכֶסֶף מַעֲשֵׂר חוּץ מִן הַמַּיִם וּמִן הַמֶּלַח. כְּרִבִּי עֲקִיבָה. בְּרַם כְּרִבִּי יִשְׁמָעֵאל.

תַּנֵּי רִבִּי יִשְׁמָעֵאל. וְנָתַתָּה הַכֶּסֶף בְּכֹל אֲשֶׁר־תְּאַוֶּה נַפְשְׁךָ הֲרֵי זֶה כְּלָל. בַּבָּקָר וּבַצֹּאן וּבַיַּיִן וּבַשֵּׁכָר הֲרֵי זֶה פְּרָט. וּבְכֹל אֲשֶׁר תִּשְׁאָלְךָ נַפְשֶׁךָ הֲרֵי זֶה כְּלָל אַחֵר. כְּלָל וּפְרָט וּכְלָל וְאֵין אַתָּה דָן אֶלָּא כְעֵין הַפְּרָט. לוֹמַר. מַה הַפְּרָט מְפוֹרָשׁ דָּבָר שֶׁהוּא וְוֶלֶד וְוַלְדוֹת הָאָרֶץ. אַף אֵין לִי אֶלָּא דָבָר שֶׁהוּא וָוֶלֶד וְוַלְדוֹת הָאָרֶץ. רִבִּי עֲקִיבָה מְפָרֵשׁ. מַה הַפְּרָט מְפָרֵשׁ שֶׁהוּא פְּרִי כְּווֶלֶד פְּרִי וּמַכְשִׁירֵי פְּרִי. אַף אֵין לִי אֶלָּא דָבָר שֶׁהוּא פְּרִי וָוֶלֶד פְּרִי וּמַכְשִׁירֵי פְּרִי. מַה נָפַק מִבֵּינֵיהוֹן. דָּגִים וַחֲגָבִים כְּמֵיהִין וּפִטְרִיּוֹת. כְּרִבִּי עֲקִיבָה נִלְקָחִין בְּכֶסֶף מַעֲשֵׂר. כְּרִבִּי יִשְׁמָעֵאל אֵינָן נִלְקָחִין.

2 הרי זה | ד - תשאלך | ד תאוה זה | ד - אחר | ד - ואין | ד אי 3 לומר | ד לומר לך 4 מפרש | ד מפורש דבר כוולד | ד וולד 5 נפק מביניהון | ד נפיק מן ביניהון דגים | ד דגין 6 וחגבים | ד וחגבין נלקחין | ד ניקחין כר' ישמאל אינו נלקחין | ד -

We have stated two principles which are not comparable one with the other. "With anything one may make an *eruv* or participate except with water or salt," whether it is something eaten raw as is or something which is not eaten raw. "Anything may be bought with money of [Second] Tithe except water and salt," but only something eaten raw as is[37]. "With anything one may make an *eruv* or participate except with water or salt," both according to Rebbi Aqiba and Rebbi Ismael. "Anything may be bought with money of [Second] Tithe except water and salt," according to Rebbi Aqiba. But according to Rebbi Ismael?

[38]Rebbi Ismael stated: [39]*Spend the money on anything you want*, this is a general clause. *For cattle and sheep, wine and intoxicating drink*, this is detail. *And anything you want*, another general clause. General, detail, and general, you may judge only in light of the detail[40]. Just as the detail is explained as born from what is born from the earth, so only what is born from what is born from the earth[41]. Rebbi Aqiba explains[42]: Just as the detail is explained as fruit, born from a fruit, or what prepares fruit, so only what is fruit, born from a fruit, or what prepares fruit[43]. What is the difference between them? Fish, locusts, truffles, and mushrooms which may be bought with tithe money following Rebbi Aqiba, following Rebbi Ismael they may not be bought[44].

37 This text makes sense only if one switches the statements: For an *eruv* (*tehumim*) only produce eaten raw is acceptable, for Second Tithe all produce.
38 This text also is in *Ma`aser Šeni* 1:4 (Notes 144-151,‫ד‬). Parallels in *Sifra* Introduction (8), Babli *Eruvin* 27b, *Bava Qamma* 54b,36a; in slightly different version *Nazir* 35b.
39 *Deut.* 14:26.
40 One of the hermeneutical principles of R. Ismael. *Sifra,* Introduction.
41 Anything grown by sexual reproduction from plant or animal living on the land.
42 In detail explained *Sifry Deut.* 107 naturally without reference to R. Ismael's rule.
43 In *Sifry* called משביחי אכילה "food enhancers", such as costus, amomum, other spices, benjamin, asa foetida, peppers, and saffron.
44 In *Sifra*, R. Ismael explicitly excludes truffles and mushrooms.

(20d line 3) בַּכֹּל מְעָרְבִין וּמִשְׁתַּתְּפִין חוּץ מִן הַמַּיִם וּמִן הַמֶּלַח. אָמַר רִבִּי יָסָא. לְפִי שֶׁאֵין הַגּוּף נִיזוֹן מֵהֶן. אָמַר רִבִּי לֵוִי. שֶׁהֵן מִין קְלָלָה. אָמַר רִבִּי אֶלְעָזָר. עֲשָׂאָן מֵי מֶלַח נִלְקָחִין בְּכֶסֶף מַעֲשֵׂר. רִבִּי אָחָא בְשֵׁם רִבִּי מְיַישָׁא. וְהוּא שֶׁנָּתַן בְּתוֹכוֹ שֶׁמֶן. רִבִּי יוֹסֵה בָעֵי. מֵעַתָּה לֹא יְעָרֵב אֶלָּא לְפִי חֶשְׁבּוֹן שֶׁבָּהֶן.

תַּמָּן תַּנִּינָן. חֲצִי לוֹג יַיִן. רַבִּי עֲקִיבָה אוֹמֵר רְבִיעִית. אָמַר רִבִּי אֶלְעָזָר. וְכֵן לְעֵירוּב. אָמַר רִבִּי חִינְנָא. הָדָא דְתֵימַר בְּיַיִן. אֲבָל לֹא בְשֶׁמֶן. מְעָרְבִין מָזוֹן שְׁתֵּי סְעוּדוֹת. תַּנֵּי. מְעָרְבִין בְּחוֹמֶץ מָזוֹן שְׁתֵּי סְעוּדוֹת. תַּנֵּי. מְעָרְבִין בְּשֶׁמֶן מָזוֹן שְׁתֵּי סְעוּדוֹת. רִבִּי יִרְמְיָה בְשֵׁם רִבִּי שְׁמוּאֵל בַּר רַב יִצְחָק. כְּדֵי לִטְבַּל יָרָק הַנֶּאֱגָד מָזוֹן שְׁתֵּי סְעוּדוֹת. רִבִּי יִצְחָק עֲטוּשִׁיָּא אָמַר קוֹמֵי רִבִּי זְעִירָא מִשּׁוּם דְּבֵית רִבִּי יַנַּאי. אֲפוּנִים חַיִים מְעָרְבִין בָּהֶן. לְמִי נִצְרָכָה. לְרִבִּי מֵאִיר. שֶׁלֹּא תֹאמַר. הוֹאִיל וְהֵן מַסְרִיחִין אֶת הַפֶּה אֵין מְעָרְבִין בָּהֶן. דָּג מָלִיחַ מְעָרְבִין בּוֹ. בָּשָׂר מָלִיחַ מְעָרְבִין בּוֹ. בָּשָׂר חַי מְעָרְבִין בּוֹ. דְּתַנִּינָן. הַבַּבְלִיִּים אוֹכְלִין אוֹתוֹ כְּשֶׁהוּא חַי. מִפְּנֵי שֶׁדַּעְתָּן יָפָה: רִבִּי יוּדָן בָּעֵי. הָדָא כְלֹבוּדָא הוֹאִיל וְאִילֵּין כּוּתָאֵי אָכְלִין מִינָהּ חַיָּיא מְעָרְבִין בָּהּ. שְׁמוּאֵל בַּר שִׁילַת בְּשֵׁם רַב. פַּעֲפּוּעִין וְגִדְגְּנִיּוֹת וַחֲלוּגְלוּגוֹת מְעָרְבִין בָּהֶן. בָּעוֹן קוֹמוֹי. אִילֵּין אִינּוּן. אָמַר לוֹן. קַקוּלֵּי וְהִנְדְּקוּקֵי וּפַרְפָּחִינֵיהּ.

1 אלעזר | ק לעזר   2 לא | ק -   מזון | ק בו מזון   4 לטבל | ק לטבול   ירק | ק בירק   מזון | ק -   5 משום דבית | ק בשם דבי   אפונים חיים | ק אפונין חיין   בהן | ק בהן מזון שתי סעודות   7 מערבין בו | ק -   אוכלין | ק - אוכלים יפה | ק מקולקלת   8 כלבודא | ק כלקידא   הוא   חייא | ק חייה   9 אילין | ק היידן

"With anything one may make an *eruv* or participate except with water or salt." Rebbi Yasa said, because the body is not fed by them. Rebbi Levi said, because they are agents of curse[45]. Rebbi Eleazar said, if he made them into brine it may be bought with Tithe money[46]. Rebbi Aha in the name of Rebbi Miasha: only if he mixed oil into it. Rebbi Yose asked, then should he be able to use it for *eruv* only in proportion[47]?

[48]There we had stated:[49] "Half a *log* of oil. Rebbi Aqiba said, a quarter." Rebbi Eleazar said, and so it is for an *eruv*. That is for wine, but not for oil, for which one makes an *eruv* with food for two meals[50]. It was stated: One makes an *eruv* with vinegar as food for two meals. Rebbi Jeremiah in the name of Rebbi Samuel ben Rebbi Issac, enough to dip bundles of vegetable as food for two meals. Rebbi Isaac of Atosha said before R. Ze'ira in the name of the House of Rebbi Yannai: one may make an *eruv* with raw peas. For whom is this necessary? For Rebbi Meïr, lest you say, because they generate bad mouth odor one may not use them for *eruv*. One may make an *eruv* with salted fish. One may make an *eruv* with salted meat. One may make an *eruv* with raw meat. There, we have stated[51]: "The Babylonians eat it raw because their taste is refined." Rebbi Yudan asked, may one use χαλκίς[52] for *eruv* since the Samaritans eat it raw? Samuel bar Shilat in the name of Rav: One may use for *eruv pa'apu'in, gudganiot,* and *haluglugot.* They asked him, what are these? He said to them, καυκαλίς[53], melilot[54], and purslain[55].

45 Water at the deluge; salt is mentioned *Deut.* 29:22.

46 Babli 27a.

47 Since in the following a minimal quantity of oil for a valid *eruv* is determined, brine should be acceptable only if it contains that quantity of oil. Then the mention of brine would be unnecessary.

48 The following paragraph also is in *Peah* 8:5 (Notes 56-64,פ); a parallel is in the Babli 29a.

49 Mishnah *Peah* 8:5 detailing minimal amounts of produce to be given as tithe of the poor.

50 Tosephta 6:3.

51 Mishnah *Menahot* 11:7, referring to the ram brought as sin-offering on a Day of Atonement that falls on the Sabbath; it must be eaten by the priests before the next morning but cannot be cooked. The priests from Babylonia (in the opinion of the Babli, those from Alexandria) ate it raw after the fast. The text of our Mishnah, "because their taste is refined" is a euphemism.

52 χαλκίς, -ίδος, ἡ, a kind of herring or sardine. This translation follows the text in *Peah*; the word here has not been identified. In the Babli (*Avodah zarah* 39b, Tosephta *Avodah zarah* 4:11) the word appears as כילבית or כילכית , identified as a kind of sardine.

53 A plant, *melilotus officinalis.* In Arabic فقل is cardamom, قاقلى an alkaline plant.

54 Arabic حندقوقا, a kind of tall clover, only barely digestible.

55 Arabic فرفخ.

(20d line 20) פיס'. הַנּוֹדֵר מִן הַמָּזוֹן מוּתָּר בַּמַּיִם וּבַמֶּלַח. תַּמָּן תַּנִּינָן. הַנּוֹדֵר מִן הַמְבוּשָּׁל מוּתָּר בַּצֲלִי וּבַשָּׁלוּק. מַתְנִיתָא אָמְרָה כֵן. שֶׁהַשָּׁלוּק קָרוּי מְבוּשָּׁל. דְּתַנִּינָן. הָיָה מְבַשֵּׁל אֶת הַשְּׁלָמִים אוֹ שׁוֹלְקָן. וּקְרָייָא אָמַר שֶׁהַצֲלִי קָרוּי מְבוּשָּׁל. שֶׁנֶּאֱמַר וַיְבַשְּׁלוּ אֶת הַפֶּסַח בָּאֵשׁ. אִין תֵּימַר. שֶׁלֹּא כַהֲלָכָה. רִבִּי יוֹנָה בּוֹצְרָייָה אָמַר כַּמִּשְׁפָּט. מַתְנִיתָא שֶׁהַשָּׁלוּק קָרוּי מְבוּשָּׁל. וּקְרָייָא אָמַר שֶׁהַצֲלִי קָרוּי מְבוּשָּׁל. וְתַנִּינָן. הַנּוֹדֵר מִן הַמְבוּשָּׁל מוּתָּר בַּצֲלִי וּבַשָּׁלוּק. אָמַר רִבִּי יוֹחָנָן. הִילְכוּ בִנְדָרִים אַחַר לְשׁוֹן בְּנֵי אָדָם. אָמַר רִבִּי יֹאשִׁיָּה. הִילְכוּ בִנְדָרִים אַחַר לְשׁוֹן תּוֹרָה. מַה נְּפַק מִבֵּינֵיהוֹן. אָמַר. קוֹנָם יַיִן שֶׁאֲנִי טוֹעֵם בָּחָג. עַל דַּעְתֵּיהּ דְּרִבִּי יוֹחָנָן אָסוּר בְּיוֹם טוֹב הָאַחֲרוֹן. עַל דַּעְתֵּיהּ דְּרִבִּי יֹאשִׁיָּה מוּתָּר. אוֹף רִבִּי יֹאשִׁיָּה מוֹדֶה שֶׁהוּא אָסוּר. לֹא אָמַר רִבִּי יֹאשִׁיָּה אֶלָּא לְחוֹמְרָן.

אָמַר רִבִּי חִייָא בַּר בָּא. רִבִּי יוֹחָנָן אָכַל חֲלִיטִין וְאָמַר. לֹא טְעָמִית מִידֵי בְּהַהוּא יוֹמָא. וְתַנִּינָן. הַנּוֹדֵר מִן הַמָּזוֹן מוּתָּר בַּמַּיִם וּמֶלַח. פָּתַר לָהּ כְּרִבִּי יֹאשִׁיָּה. דְּרִבִּי יֹאשִׁיָּה אָמַר. הִילְכוּ בִנְדָרִים אַחַר לְשׁוֹן תּוֹרָה. וּמִנַּיִין שֶׁכָּל־הַדְּבָרִים קְרוּיִין מָזוֹן. רִבִּי אָחָא בְּיִרְבִּי עוּלָּא אָמַר. וַעֲשֶׂר אֲתוֹנוֹת נוֹשְׂאוֹת בַּר וָלֶחֶם וּמָזוֹן. מַה תַּלְמוּד לוֹמַר וּמָזוֹן. אֶלָּא מִיכָּן שֶׁכָּל־הַדְּבָרִים קְרוּיִין מָזוֹן.

Paragraph. "One who vows not to eat food is permitted water and salt." There, we have stated[56]: "One who made a vow to abstain from cooked food is permitted roasted and scalded food." [57]A Mishnah states that scalding is called cooking, as we have stated[58]: "If he cooked the well-being offering or scalded it." A verse states that "roasted" is called "cooked" as it is said[59]: *They cooked the Pesaḥ in fire.* If you say, against the rules, Rebbi Jonah from Bostra said, *as is the rule*[60]. A Mishnah [states] that scalded is called cooked, and a verse that roasted is called cooked; but did we not state: "One who makes a vow to abstain from cooked food is permitted roasted and scalded food"? Rebbi Joḥanan said, in matters of vows one follows common usage. Rebbi Joshia said, in matters of vows one follows biblical usage. What is the difference between them? If one said, a *qonam*[61] that I shall not taste wine on Tabernacles. In the opinion of Rebbi Joḥanan he is forbidden on the last day of the holiday[62]. In the opinion of Rebbi Joshia, is he permitted? Also Rebbi Joshia agrees that he is prohibited. Rebbi Joshia said it only for restrictions.

Rebbi Ḥiyya bar Abba said, Rebbi Joḥanan ate bake-meats and said, I did not taste (anything) [food][63] on that day. But did we not state: "He who made a vow not to eat food is permitted water and salt"? Explain it following Rebbi Joshia, who said, in matters of vows one follows biblical usage. And from where that everything is called food? Rebbi Aḥa bar Ulla said[64]: *And ten female donkeys carrying grain, bread, and food.* Why does the verse say, *and food*? From here that everything is called food[65].

56 Mishnah *Nedarim* 6:1.
57 This paragraph and the next are also in *Nedarim* 6:1 (Notes 6-14) and *Nazir* 6:11 (Note 225), cf. Babli *Nedarim* 49a.
58 Mishnah *Nazir* 6:11. The verse *Num.* 6:18 requires the sacrifice to be cooked.
59 *2Chr.* 35:13.
60 *Roasted in fire, Ex.* 12:9. Cooked would be on the fire, not in it.
61 The Phoenician equivalent of Hebrew *qorbān*, "(forbidden like) sacrifice" which people were afraid to pronounce in vows. Cf. Introduction to Tractate *Nedarim*.
62 Which in popular consciousness is the last day of *Sukkot* but legally is a separate holiday with its own rules.
63 The text of *Eruvin* (in parentheses) has to be emended to the text in *Nedarim* and *Nazir* [in brackets] to make sense. Babli *Berakhot* 44a.
64 *Gen.* 45:23.
65 Babli *Berakhot* 35b.

(20d line 36) נָדַר מִן הַכִּכָּר מְעָרְבִין בּוֹ. הִקְדִּישׁוֹ אֵין מְעָרְבִין בּוֹ. נָדַר מִן הַכִּכָּר מְעָרְבִין בּוֹ. שֶׁכֵּן אַחֵר רָאוּי לְאוֹכְלוֹ. הִקְדִּישׁוֹ אֵין מְעָרְבִין בּוֹ. שֶׁלֹּא הוּא וְלֹא אַחֵר רְאוּיִין לְאוֹכְלוֹ. רְבִּי אֲחָא בָּעֵי. וְאֵין אָדָם נִשְׁאַל עַל הֶקְדֵּישׁוֹ. רְבִּי אֲחָא אָמַר. רְבִּי מְיָישָׁא בָּעֵי. תַּמָּן אָמַר רְבִּי שִׁמְעוֹן חִייָה בְּרֵיהּ דְּרַב אָמַר. עֲבוֹדָה זָרָה שֶׁעֲשָׂאָהּ לְחִי לַמָּבוֹי מַתֶּרֶת אֶת הַמָּבוֹי. וְהָכָא אַתְּ אָמַר הָכֵין. אָמַר רְבִּי אֶלְעָזָר. תַּמָּן מִכָּל־מָקוֹם נִסְתַּם הַמָּבוֹי. וְהָכָא מָה אִית לָךְ. מְעָרְבִין לַנָּזִיר בַּיַּיִן. שֶׁכֵּן אַחֵר רָאוּי לִשְׁתוֹתוֹ. וּלְיִשְׂרָאֵל בַּתְּרוּמָה. שֶׁכֵּן כֹּהֵן רָאוּי לְאוֹכְלָהּ. וְלַכֹּהֵן בְּבֵית הַפְּרָס. מַתְנִיתָא דְּבֵית שַׁמַּי. דְּבֵית שַׁמַּי אָמְרִין. אֵין מְעָרְבִין לְאָדָם אֶלָּא אִם כֵּן הָיוּ כָלָיו תַּשְׁמִישׁוֹ שָׁם. סוּמְכוּס כְּבֵית שַׁמַּי. דְּתַנִּינָן. סוּמְכוּס אוֹמֵר. אַף בַּחוּלִין לַכֹּהֵן בְּבֵית הַפְּרָס. מֵעַתָּה אֲפִילוּ בֵין הַקְּבָרוֹת. רָאוּי הוּא לַעֲבוֹר עַל הַשְּׁבוּת וְלוֹכַל. שֶׁכֵּן הוּא רָאוּי לִיכָּנֵס בְּשִׁידָה תֵיבָה וּמִגְדָּל וְלַעֲשׂוֹת לוֹ חוֹר מְטֻפָּח וְלִתְחוֹב בְּכוֹשׁ וּבְקֵיסָם וְלֶאֱכוֹל.

5 אלעזר G | לעזר נסתם G | ניסתם 6 ולכהן G | ולכוהן 7 שמי G | שמיי לאדם G | לאדן 8 שמי G | שמיי בין G | בן 9 ולוכל G | ול[אכל ליכנס G | להיכנס תיבה G | ובתיבה 10 ולאכול G | ו[ל]אכל

If he forbade himself a loaf by a vow it may be used as *eruv*, if he dedicated it it may not be used as *eruv*. If he forbade himself a loaf by a vow it may be used as *eruv*, since another person may eat it. If he dedicated it it may not be used as *eruv*, since neither he nor another person may eat it[66]. Rebbi Aḥa asked, may not a person ask about his dedication[67]? Rebbi Aḥa said that Rebbi Miasha asked: There Rebbi Simeon[68] said that Ḥiyya the son of Rav said, if one used idolatry[69] to make a lath it permits the alley, and here you are saying so? Rebbi Eleazar said, there in any case the alley was closed; here what do you have[70]?

[71]"One may make an *eruv* for a *nazir* with wine" for another person may drink it. "And for an Israel with heave," for a Cohen may eat it. For a Cohen in a *bet happeras*[72]? The Mishnah follows the House of Shammai, for the House of Shammai say that one may not make an *eruv* for a person unless his personal vessels may be there[73]. Symmachos follows the House of Shammai as we have stated: "Symmachos says, also with profane food for a Cohen in a *bet happeras*[4]." Then also between the graves? He might transgress a rabbinic prohibition and eat there[74]. For he could enter on a bench[75], in a box or a chest, make a hole less than a hand-breadth [wide][76], stick a spindle or a splinter into it, and eat it.

66 Babli 30a.
67 Since a dedication to the Temple is a vow, a dedication may be removed by rabbinic authority like any other vow. Then the dedicated item reverts to profane status and therefore always was potential food. Naturally the dedicated object should be redeemed and returned to profane status but this is not possible on the Sabbath and therefore not an option to validate an *eruv* on the Sabbath. The Babli notes that the disregard of possible removal of dedication is a separate rabbinic decree.
68 This must refer to R. Simeon ben Laqish.
69 Wood from an *ashera* or an idol, forbidden for all usufruct.
70 Since the lath has no required minimal depth it is a sign, not a material presence. The material could not be used for a beam which has to be three-dimensional material.
71 Here starts a Genizah fragment edited by Ginzberg (pp. 95-101,G).
72 In the Mishnah in the Babli and in Maimonides's autograph Mishnah this is a separate declarative sentence, independent of Symmachos's statement who there forbids heave for the Israel and requires strictly profane food. In the Yerushalmi Mishnah Symmachos adds to the statement of the anonymous Tanna but he does not disagree with him. Therefore it is impossible to read the Babli's Mishnah in the Yerushalmi text.
73 In the interpretation of the Babli this means that for the House of Shammai an *eruv tehumin* is possible only if a person transports his bed to the place of the *eruv*.
74 This sentence should be read before the preceding one. Since the prohibition of the *bet happeras* is rabbinical, the Cohen could disregard the prohibition without defiling himself biblically.
75 Arabic سكّة. It is presumed that the bench is fixed to a flat wooden plank. Since wooden implements which do not enclose a volume are impervious to impurity, the Cohen sitting on the bench can be transported through the cemetery without violating the biblical prohibition of defiling himself with the impurity of the dead.
75 Such a hole does not transmit the impurity of the dead. Babli 30b.

(20d line 50) פיס'. מְעָרְבִין בַּדְּמַאי וּבְמַעֲשֵׂר רִאשׁוֹן כול'. רִבִּי יַעֲקֹב דְּרוֹמָיָא בָּעֵי. מַתְנִיתָהּ דְּלֹא כְבֵית שַׁמַּי. דְּתַנִּינָן. וְשֶׁלַּדְּמַאי. בֵּית שַׁמַּי פּוֹסְלִין וּבֵית הִלֵּל מַכְשִׁירִין. וְשֶׁלְּמַעֲשֵׂר שֵׁנִי בִּירוּשָׁלַיִם לֹא יִטּוֹל. וְאִם נָטַל. כָּשֵׁר:

1 דרומיא G | [דרו[מייה   2 שמיי G | שמיי   ובית G | בית

רַב שֵׁשֶׁת בְּשֵׁם רִבִּי חִייָה רִבָּה. טֶבֶל שֶׁיֵּשׁ עָלָיו תְּנַיי מוּתָּר לְטַלְטְלוֹ. כֵּיצַד הוּא עוֹשֶׂה. נוֹתֵן עֵינָיו בְּמִקְצָתוֹ וְאוֹכֵל אֶת הַשְּׁאָר. וְתַנֵּי. בֵּית שַׁמַּי אוֹמְרִים. אֵין מְעָרְבִין בְּמַעֲשֵׂר שֵׁנִי בִּירוּשָׁלַיִם. אָמַר רִבִּי יִרְמְיָה. הָדָא דְאַתְּ אָמַר. בְּעֵירוּבֵי חֲצֵירוֹת. אֲבָל בְּעֵירוּבֵי תְחוּמִין (בְּקַר)תְנֵי שֶׁנָּתַן עֵירוּבוֹ בִּירוּשָׁלַיִם שֶׁהוּא יָכוֹל לַעֲלוֹת וּלְאוֹכְלוֹ שָׁם.

1 רבה G | רובא   2 שמיי G | שמיי   3 בעירובי G | בעירובו

שְׁמוּאֵל אָמַר. כְּבֶן תֵּשַׁע כְּבֶן עֶשֶׂר עֵירוּבוֹ עֵירוּב. אָמַר רִבִּי יוֹסֵה. הָדָא דְתֵימַר. בְּעֵירוּבֵי תְחוּמִין. אֲבָל בְּעֵירוּבֵי חֲצֵירוֹת אֲפִילוּ קָטָן. אָמַר רִבִּי יְהוֹשֻׁעַ. מִפְּנֵי מַה מְעָרְבִין בַּחֲצֵירוֹת. מִפְּנֵי דַרְכֵי שָׁלוֹם. מַעֲשֶׂה בְּאִשָּׁה אַחַת שֶׁהָיְתָה דְבוּבָה לַחֲבֶירְתָּהּ וְשָׁלְחָה עֵירוּבָהּ גַּבֵּי בְרָהּ. נַסְתֵּיהּ וְגָפַפְתֵּיהּ וּנְשָׁקַתֵּיהּ. אֲתָא וַאֲמַר קוֹמֵי אִימֵּיהּ. אָמְרָה. הָכֵין הֲוַת רַחֲמָה לִי וְלָא הֲוֵינָא יָדְעָה. מִתּוֹךְ כָּךְ עָשׂוּ שָׁלוֹם. הָדָא הוּא דִכְתִיב דְּרָכֶיהָ דַרְכֵי־נוֹעַם וְכָל־נְתִיבוֹתֶיהָ שָׁלוֹם:

1 כבן G | כבין כבן G | וכבין הדא G | הדה דתימר G | דאת אמר 2 תחומין G | תחומים יהושע G7 יהושוע בן לוי 3 ושלחה G | שלחה גבי | 7 ביד   4 וגפפתיה ונשקתיה G | ונשקתיה וגפ[פ]תיה 7 וכפפתיה ונשקתיה ואמר | 7 אמר קומי אימיה | 7 לאימיה ולא G | ואנא לא   הוינא | 7 חוות

Paragraph. "One may make an *eruv* with *demay*[5], and with First Tithe." Rebbi Jacob the Southerner asked, is our Mishnah not following the House of Shammai? As we have stated[76], "of *demay*, the House of Shammai declare invalid but the House of Hillel declare valid[77]. Of Second Tithe in Jerusalem one should not take but if he took it is valid[78]."

Rav Sheshet in the name of the Elder Rebbi Ḥiyya: It is permitted to move *tevel*[6] which has a condition on it[79]. How does he do it? He puts his eyes on a small part and eats the remainder. And it was stated: The House of Shammai say, one does not use Second Tithe as *eruv* in Jerusalem. Rebbi Jeremiah said, this you are saying about *eruv* of courtyards[80]. But for an *eruv* of domains, a villager[81] who deposits his *eruv* at Jerusalem can go there and eat it.

Samuel said, if he is nine or ten years old his *eruv* is an *eruv*[82]. Rebbi Yose said, this you are saying about *eruv* of domains. But for an *eruv* of courtyards, even if he is small. [83] Rebbi Joshua [ben Levi][84] said, why does one make *eruv* of courtyards[85]? Because of peaceful relations. It happened that a woman was hostile to another and sent her her *eruv* through her son. She took him, embraced him, and kissed him. He went and told it before his mother. She said, obviously she loves me and I did not know it. As a consequence they made peace. That is what is written, *its ways are ways of pleasantness and all its paths peace*[86].

76 Mishnah *Sukkah* 3:5. The topic of the Mishnah is the *etrog*, C *itrus medica*, a fruit which is part of the "four kinds" of plants carried on Tabernacles.

77 Since *demay* may not be eaten, for the House of Shammai it is not a fruit and therefore cannot be part of the "four kinds". By analogy it should be forbidden to use *demay* as food for *eruv*. For the House of Hillel *demay* can always be turned into food even on Sabbath and holidays as explained later by the Elder R. Hiyya; therefore it is food in all respects.

78 Second tithe has to be consumed in Jerusalem; it is food there. But the use of the *etrog* for a religious ceremony is not consumption; while it is permitted it is inappropriate.

79 *Tevel* is neither food nor an implement and therefore is *muqseh*. But if heave and tithes are mentally removed, it becomes food and may be moved and eaten. If one decides on the Sabbath to give after the Sabbath heave and tithes from a certain part of the *tevel* produce, the remainder may be eaten. Cf. *Šabbat* 18, Notes 25 ff.

80 This is inappropriate use of Second Tithe since the *eruv* of courtyards represents a symbolic meal not an actual one. But the *eruv* of domains is to be eaten on the Sabbath; this is appropriate use.

81 G shows that the correct text is בקרתני. This also was the text of the scribe, erroneously changed by the corrector into תני "it was stated", which is the version of all printed editions but makes no sense here.

82 Since at this age he is able to legally buy in a grocery store (Mishnah *Gittin* 5:8, Halakhah 5:9 Notes 234 ff.) he is able to place his food. While a smaller child is not able to do anything of legal consequence, an *eruv* of courtyards is controlled by the recipient of the foodstuffs and for such a small distance an underage child may be used. Babli 31b.

83 The following also is in Chapter 7 (24c l. 74, Note 94, 7).

84 Added from G, 7, and its frequent quotes in Medieval sources.

85 Assuming that the courtyard participated in an alley, a separate *eruv* for courtyards essentially is superfluous. It is required because it is required if there is no alley and because it helps neighborly relations.

86 *Prov.* 3:17.

(20d line 65) פיס'. הַשּׁוֹלֵחַ אֶת עֵירוּבוֹ בְּיַד חֵרֵשׁ שׁוֹטֶה וְקָטָן כול'. אָמַר רִבִּי לְעָזָר. וְצָרִיךְ לַעֲמוֹד עִמּוֹ. תַּמָּן אָמַר רִבִּי יוֹסֵה בְשֵׁם רַב שֵׁשֶׁת רִבִּי לְעָזָר בְּרִבִּי יוֹסֵי בְשֵׁם רִבִּי אָבוּן. בָּאוֹמֵר לַחֲבֵירוֹ. הֲרֵי אֲנִי מְעַשֵּׂר עַל יָדָךְ. אֵינוֹ צָרִיךְ לַעֲמוֹד עִמּוֹ. וְהָכָא אַתְּ אָמַר הָכֵין. אָמַר רִבִּי חִיָּיה בַּר אָדָא. כָּאן בְּגָדוֹל וְכָאן בְּקָטָן. רִבִּי אָחָא בְשֵׁם רִבִּי חִינְנָא. וַאֲפִילוּ תֵימַר. כָּאן וְכָאן בְּגָדוֹל

וְכָאן בְּקָטוֹן. תַּמָּן בָּאוֹמֵר לוֹ. הֲרֵי אֲנִי מְעַשֵּׂר עַל יָדָךְ. שֶׁאֵינוֹ צָרִיךְ לַעֲמוֹד עִמּוֹ. בְּרַם הָכָא בָּאוֹמֵר לוֹ. עֲרֵב עַל יָדִי. הָדָא יַלְפָא מִן הַהִיא וְהַהִיא יַלְפָא מִן הָדָא. הָדָא יַלְפָא מִן הַהִיא. שֶׁאִם אָמַר לוֹ. אֲנִי מְעַשֵּׂר עַל יָדָךְ. שֶׁאֵינוֹ צָרִיךְ לַעֲמוֹד עִמּוֹ. וְהַהִיא יַלְפָא מִן הָדָא. שֶׁאִם אָמַר לוֹ. עֲרֵב עַל יָדִי. שֶׁהוּא צָרִיךְ לַעֲמוֹד עִמּוֹ.

2 עמו G | עימו   4 בקטון | בקטון G | בקטון חיננא G | חננא   5 וכאן G | כאן וכאן | בקטון | בקטון G | בקטן הכא G הכה   6 הדא G הדה (3) ילפא | ילפה G (3) ילפא   7 ילפא G | ילפה   8 עמו G | עימו

Paragraph. "If somebody sends his *eruv*[8] through a deaf-and-dumb or insane person, or a minor," etc. [87]Rebbi Eleazar said, he has to be with him. There Rebbi Yose said in the name of Rebbi Sheshet, Rebbi Eleazar the son of Rebbi Yose in the name of Rebbi Abun[88]: If somebody says to another I shall tithe for you, he does not have to be with him. And here, you say so? Rebbi Ḥiyya bar Ada said, here about an adult, there about a minor. Rebbi Aḥa said in the name of Rebbi Ḥinena[89], you may even say in both cases we deal with an adult or in both cases we deal with a minor. There, when he says, I shall tithe for you, he does not have to be with him. But here, he says make an *eruv* for me! This learns from that and that learns from this. This learns from that, if he says I shall tithe for you, he does not have to be with him. That learns from this, if he says make an *eruv* for me, he has to be with him[90].

87 A somewhat differently organized parallel to this paragraph is in *Ma`serot* 2:1 (Notes 39-43).

88 In *Ma`serot*: Abin.

89 In *Ma`serot*: R. Hanania in the name of R. Hanina.

90 Since these are the statements one started out with it is clear that with the text in *Ma`serot* one has to read: "This learns from that, if he says I shall make an *eruv* for you, he does not have to be with him. That learns from this, if he says tithe for me, he has to be with him." In any case if the initiative is from the other side he does not have to be there to check but if the initiative is his he has to supervise the minor. Cf. Tosaphot 31b *s. v.* כאן.

(20d line 76) פִּיס'. נְתָנוֹ בָּאִילָן לְמַעְלָה מֵעֲשָׂרָה טְפָחִים כול'. הֲרֵי זֶה עֵירוּב וְאָסוּר לְטַלְטְלוֹ. לְמַטָּה מִשְּׁלֹשָׁה מוּתָּר. וְקַשְׁיָא. אִם עֵירוּבוֹ עֵירוּב יְהֵא מוּתָּר לְטַלְטְלוֹ. אִם אָסוּר לְטַלְטְלוֹ לֹא יְהֵא עֵירוּבוֹ עֵירוּב. רָאוּי הוּא לַעֲבוֹר עַל הַשְּׁבוּת וְלֶאֱכוֹל. מֵעַתָּה אֲפִילוּ לְמַעְלָה מֵעֲשָׂרָה. רַב יְהוּדָה בְשֵׁם שְׁמוּאֵל. תִּיפְתָּר שֶׁהָיִיתָה כּוּרָתוֹ אַרְבָּעָה. אָמַר רִבִּי מָנָא. וְהוּא שֶׁתְּהֵא רְשׁוּת הָרַבִּים מַקֶּפְתּוֹ מִכָּל־צַד. בָּאוֹמֵר. שְׁבִיתָתִי תַחְתָּיו. תַּנֵּי. נְתָנוֹ בַּכַּלְכָּלָה וּתְלָייוֹ בָּאִילָן. לְמַעְלָה מֵעֲשָׂרָה טְפָחִים אֵינוֹ עֵירוּב. לְמַטָּה מֵעֲשָׂרָה טְפָחִים עֵירוּבוֹ עֵירוּב וְאָסוּר לְטַלְטְלוֹ. לְמַטָּה מִשְּׁלֹשָׁה מוּתָּר. וְקַשְׁיָא. אִם עֵירוּבוֹ עֵירוּב יְהֵא מוּתָּר לְטַלְטְלוֹ. אִם אָסוּר לְטַלְטְלוֹ לֹא יְהֵא

עֵירוּבוֹ עֵירוּב. רִבִּי אָחָא בְּשֵׁם רִבִּי חִינְנָא. רָאוּי הוּא לְהוֹפְכָהּ וּלְבַטֵּל רְשׁוּת הַיָּחִיד שֶׁבָּהּ. אָמַר רִבִּי יוֹסֵה. הָדָא אָמְרָה. סַפְסָל שֶׁהוּא נָתוּן בִּרְשׁוּת הָרַבִּים גָּבוֹהַּ עֲשָׂרָה וְרָחַב אַרְבָּעָה. מִכֵּיוָן שֶׁהוּא רָאוּי לְהוֹפְכוֹ וּלְבַטֵּל רְשׁוּת הַיָּחִיד שֶׁבּוֹ. הָדָא אָמְרָה שֶׁעֵירוּבוֹ עֵירוּב וּמוּתָּר לְטַלְטְלוֹ.

1 פיס' | G חסלת: טפחים כול' | G טפחין אינו עירוב למטה מעשרה טפחין   הרי זה | G **ס** עירובו   2 משלשה | G מישלושה וקשיא | G וקשייא אם | G **ס** ואם   3 לעבור | G לעבר ולאכול | **ס** ולוכל   4 תיפתר | G תפתר כורתו | **ס** בכרתו   5 הרבים | G הרבין ותלייו | G ותליו   6 טפחים | G טפחין (2)   7 משלשה | G מישלושה וקשיא | G וקשייא אם | **ס** ואם לטלטלו | G לטלטל   8 חיננא | G חננא להופכה | **ס** להפכה 9 הדא | G הדא   מיכיוון | G מיכיון   10 להופכו | **ס** להפכו   הדא | G הדה

Paragraph. "If he deposited it in a tree more than ten hand-breadths high," etc. [91]It is an *eruv* but it is forbidden to move it[92]; below three it is permitted[93]. This is difficult. If his *eruv* is a [valid] *eruv* one should be permitted to move it. If one is forbidden to move it his *eruv* should not be a [valid] *eruv*. He might transgress the rabbinic prohibition and eat. Then also higher than ten [hand-breadths][94]? Rav Jehudah in the name of Samuel, explain it if its stem was four [hand-breadths][11]. Rebbi Mana said, only if the public domain surrounds it on all sides; he says my Sabbath rest shall be below it[95]. It was stated: If he put it in a basket and hung it on a tree, higher than ten hand-breadths high it is not an *eruv*; below ten hand-breadth it is an *eruv* but it is forbidden to move it; below three it is permitted. This is difficult. If his *eruv* is a [valid] *eruv* one should be permitted to move it. If one is forbidden to move it his *eruv* should not be a [valid] *eruv*. Rebbi Aḥa in the name of Rebbi Ḥinena: He might turn it upside down and annul the private domain created by it[96]. Rebbi Yose said, this implies that a bench in the public domain high ten and wide four [hand-breadths], since one may tilt it and annul the private domain created by it, it implies that his *eruv* is a [valid] *eruv* and it is permitted to move it[97].

91 This paragraph also is in *Sukkah* 2:4 (52d l. 66, **ס**). The next one also is found there but rearranged that "here" and "there" correctly point to *Sukkah* and *Eruvin*.
92 As is clear from G, this refers to an *eruv* placed on a tree less than ten hand-breadths high. The prohibitions here are rabbinic ("forbidden" but not "liable").
93 Anything below 3 hand-breadths is as lying on the ground, not on the tree. Babli 33a, Tosephta 2:13.
94 If one entertains the possibility that people would disregard rabbinic prohibitions, why would an *eruv* placed higher than 10 hand-breadths be invalid since one could climb the tree in violation of the rabbinic prohibition.
95 Not all *eruvim* placed 10 hand-breadths high are invalid; only if the tree is in the public domain, the place of the *eruv*

forms a separate private domain of 4-by-4 hand-breadths, and the person making the *eruv* does not intend to climb the tree at sundown (which would be permitted).

96 Since the basket can be turned and emptied while hanging on the tree it is not moved from its place, the food is accessible,

and the *eruv* valid. Babli 33a,b.

97 If the food is on the bench, one may tilt the bench, the food falls down and is accessible. In this and the preceding case the prohibition of transporting cannot apply to the food.

(21a line 14) תַּמָּן תַּנִּינָן. שְׁתַּיִם בִּידֵי אָדָם וְאַחַת בָּאִילָן. אוֹ שְׁתַּיִם בָּאִילָן וְאַחַת בִּידֵי אָדָם. כְּשֵׁירָה. וְאֵין עוֹלִין לָהּ בְּיוֹם טוֹב. וְהָכָא אַתְּ אָמַר. עֵירוּבוֹ עֵירוּב וּמוּתָּר לְטַלְטְלוֹ. אָמַר רִבִּי יִרְמְיָה. כָּאן לְמַעֲלָן וְכָאן מִן הַצַּד. הָדָא יַלְפָא מִן הַהִיא וְהַהִיא יַלְפָא מִן הָדָא. הָדָא יַלְפָא מִן הַהִיא. שֶׁאִם הָיוּ שְׁתֵּי יְתֵידוֹת יוֹצְאוֹת וְסִיכֵּךְ עַל גַּבֵּיהֶן שֶׁהִיא כְשֵׁירָה וְעוֹלִין לָהּ בְּיוֹם טוֹב. וְהַהִיא יַלְפָא מִן הָדָא. שֶׁאִם הָיָה נָתוּן בָּאִיבוֹ שֶׁלְּאִילָן שֶׁעֵירוּבוֹ עֵירוּב וְאָסוּר לְטַלְטְלוֹ. אָמַר רִבִּי יוֹסֵה. בֵּין הָכָא בֵּין תַּמָּן מִן הַצַּד הִיא. מַאי כְדוֹן. כַּיי דָמַר רִבִּי יַעֲקֹב בַּר אָחָא בְּשֵׁם רִבִּי זְעִירָא. דְּרִבִּי שִׁמְעוֹן בֶּן אֶלְעָזָר הוּא. דְּתַנִּי. רִבִּי שִׁמְעוֹן בֶּן אֶלְעָזָר אוֹמֵר. מוּתָּר לְהִשְׁתַּמֵּשׁ עַל צִדְדֵי בְהֵמָה בַשַּׁבָּת. הִיא צִדְדֵי בְהֵמָה הִיא צִדְדֵי אִילָן.

1 אדם G | אדן (2)   2 עולין G | עולים   והכא G | הכה   את אמר G | אתןמר כשירה ואין עו]לין לה ביום טוב וכה אתמר עירוב עירובו G | עירובו   3 למעלן G | מלמעלן   וכאן G | וכן   הדא G | הדה   ילפא G | ילפה (3)   4 כשירה G | כשרה ועולין G | ועולים   5 ילפא G | ילפה הדא G | הדה   6 מאי G | ומיי כיי G | כהיא דמר דאמר G | אלעזר   7 אלעזר G | לעזר להשתמש G | לישתמש   8 צדדי G | צידדי

There, we have stated[98]: "Two human-made and one a tree, or two as trees and one human-made is valid but one may not enter it on the holiday." [Here you are saying it is valid but one may not enter it on the holiday][99] but there you are saying his *eruv* is a [valid] *eruv* and it is permitted to move it[97]. Rebbi Jeremiah said, one on top, the other at the side[100]. This learns from that and that learns from this. This learns from that, if there were two pegs protruding and he thatched over them it is valid and one uses it on the holiday[101]. That learns from this, if he put it on a tree branch his *eruv* is a [valid] *eruv* and it is forbidden to move it[102]. Rebbi Yose said, in both cases it is at the side. How is that? As Rebbi Jacob bar Aḥa said in the name of Rebbi Ze`ira: This is Rebbi Eleazar ben Simon's, as Rebbi Eleazar ben Simon says, one is permitted to use the sides of an animal on the Sabbath. There is no difference between sides of an animal and sides of a tree[103].

98 Mishnah *Sukkah* 2:4. A booth (*sukkah*) for Tabernacles must have a thatched roof and at least three walls. Up to

two walls can be tree trunks. Since biblically one is forbidden to cut or pluck anything from a tree on a holiday,

rabbinically one is forbidden to climb on it. The Mishnah permits the use of the trunks as walls on the intermediate days of Tabernacles but not on the holiday.
99 Added from G (and the parallel in *Sukkah*).
100 Since the roof must be on top of the walls, in the case of the Mishnah it must rest on the top of the trees (or top of branches) which is rabbinically forbidden. But the basket is on the side of the trunk and the statement follows the opinion that the sides of tree trunks may be used on Sabbaths and holidays.
101 *Šabbat* Chapter 5 Notes 39-43. Cf. Babli *Šabbat* 154b.

(21a line 24) אֵיךְ אַתְּ רוֹאֶה עָמוֹק כְּגָבוֹהַּ. אַבָּא בַּר רַב חוּנָה אָמַר. בְּאוֹמֵר. שְׁבִיתָתוֹ תַּחְתָּיו.

How[102] can you consider deep as high? Abba bar Rav Huna said, if one said, my Sabbath rest is below[103].

102 This is the corrector's text. The scribe wrote correctly אין "you cannot consider ...".
103 This refers to the statement in Mishnah 3 that an *eruv* in a cistern always is valid. If the cistern is surrounded by public domain, it is a separate private domain. How can anybody have an *eruv* in a domain different from where he would be on the Sabbath? The answer is that the cistern must be dry and he intends to take the bottom of the cistern as his place of Sabbath rest.

(21 line 25) נְתָנוֹ בְראֹשׁ הַקָּנֶה אוֹ בְראֹשׁ הַקּוּנְטֵס. כָּל־זְמַן שֶׁהוּא תָלוּשׁ וְנָעוּץ אֲפִילוּ גָּבוֹהַּ מֵאָה אַמָּה הֲרֵי זֶה עֵירוּב. מִפְּנֵי שֶׁהוּא תָלוּשׁ וְנָעוּץ. הָא אִם אֵינוֹ תָלוּשׁ וְנָעוּץ אֵין עֵירוּבוֹ עֵירוּב. לֵית פְּלִיגָא עַל שְׁמוּאֵל. דָּמַר רַב יְהוּדָה בְשֵׁם שְׁמוּאֵל. תִּיפְתָּר בְּשֶׁהָיְתָה כּוֹרָתוֹ אֲרֻבָּעָה. אָמַר רִבִּי מָנָא. וְהוּא שֶׁתְּהֵא טַבְלָה נְתוּנָה בְראֹשׁוֹ.

תַּנֵּי. רִבִּי לִיעֶזֶר אוֹמֵר. אִם בַּשָּׂדֶה אָבַד אֵין עֵירוּבוֹ עֵירוּב. אִם בָּעִיר אָבַד הֲרֵי זֶה עֵירוּב. אִם בַּשָּׂדֶה אָבַד אֵין עֵירוּבוֹ עֵירוּב. שֶׁאֵינוֹ יָכוֹל לַהֲבִיאוֹ דֶּרֶךְ שְׁבִיתָתוֹ. אִם בָּעִיר אָבַד הֲרֵי זֶה עֵירוּב. שֶׁהוּא יָכוֹל לַהֲבִיאוֹ דֶּרֶךְ פָּטוּר. יָאוּת אָמַר רִבִּי אֶלְעָזָר. מַה טַעֲמֵיהּ דְּרַב. אָמַר רִבִּי בָּא בְרֵיהּ דְּרַב פַּפִּי. דְּרִבִּי מֵאִיר הִיא. דְּרִבִּי מֵאִיר אָמַר. אַף פּוֹחֵת הוּא כַתְּחִלָּה וְנוֹטֵל. כְּלוּם אָמַר רִבִּי מֵאִיר לֹא בְיוֹם טוֹב. דִּלְמָא בְשַׁבָּת. וְהָכָא בְשַׁבָּת אֲנַן קַייָמִין. אָמַר רִבִּי אַבָּמְרִי. דְּרִבִּי אֱלִיעֶזֶר בֶּן יַעֲקֹב הִיא. דְּתַנִּינָן תַּמָּן. רִבִּי אֱלִיעֶזֶר בֶּן יַעֲקֹב אוֹמֵר. קוֹשְׁרִין לִפְנֵי בְהֵמָה בִּשְׁבִיל שֶׁלֹּא תֵצֵא. הִיא קְשִׁירָה הִיא נְעִילָה. הָדָא דְתֵימַר. בְּמִגְדָּל שֶׁלְּאֶבֶן. אֲבָל בְּמִגְדָּל שֶׁלְּעֵץ נַעֲשָׂה כְּשׁוֹבֵר אֶת הֶחָבִית לוֹכַל מִמֶּנָּה גְרוֹגְרוֹת.

1 ליעזר G | לעזר 3 אלעזר G | לעזר טע' דרב G | טעמון דרבנין בא G | אבא 4 היא G | הוא 5 והכא G | והכה קיימין G | קימין אבומרי G | אבמרי 6 אליעזר G | ליעזר (2) 7 הדא G | הדה

"If he put it on top of a stick or a pole[13] as long as it was uprooted and inserted it is an *eruv* even if 100 cubits high." Because it was uprooted and inserted; therefore if it was not uprooted and inserted his *eruv* is not a [valid]

eruv. Does this not disagree with Samuel[104], as Rav Jehudah said in the name of Samuel, explain it if its stem was four [hand-breadths]? Rebbi Mana said, only if a table was put on its top[105].

It was stated:[106] "Rebbi Eliezer[107] says, if it was lost in the field his *eruv* is not a [valid] *eruv*; if it was lost in town his *eruv* is a [valid] *eruv*." If it was lost in the field his *eruv* is not a [valid] *eruv*, for he cannot bring it[108] in a Sabbath way. If it was lost in town his *eruv* is a [valid] *eruv*, for he can bring it through exempt space[109]. Rebbi Eleazar said it correctly: what is the reason (of Rav) [of the rabbis][110]? Rebbi Abba the son of Rav Pappai said, it is Rebbi Meïr's since Rebbi Meïr said, "he even originally reduces and takes.[111]" Rebbi Meïr said this only for a holiday, maybe for the Sabbath[112]? But here we are concerned with the Sabbath! Rebbi Abba Mari said, it is Rebbi Eliezer ben Jacob's, as we have stated there[113], "Rebbi Eliezer ben Jacob said, one may tie in front of an animal that it should not leave." There is no difference between tying and locking. That means, about a stone tower. But for a wooden tower he is like one who breaks the amphora to eat dried figs from it[114].

104 He explained earlier (Note 95) that the *eruv* becomes invalid only if it is in an isolated private domain in the public domain. This has nothing to do with the difference between a tree and a pole. A different explanation in the Babli, 34b.

105 If the pole or column was topped by a table measuring at least 4-by-4 hand-breadths, the *eruv* deposited there would be as invalid as one deposited in a tree.

106 Tosephta 2:15, about the *eruv* deposited in a tower when the key was lost.

107 With G and the Tosephta read: Eleazar.

108 A replacement key.

109 Since the roofs of houses are exempt space (*Šabbat* 1 Note 109), in theory one may move things there even without an *eruv* by climbing over rooftops.

110 The correct reading is that of G [in brackets]. The rabbis are the opponents of R. Eleazar in the Tosephta.

111 Mishnah *Besah* 4:3. If produce is stored in a makeshift building formed by bricks without mortar, R. Meïr permits removing bricks to create an opening to get to the produce.

112 It is true that removing bricks which were laid without mortar cannot be classified as destroying a building by biblical standards, but this does not imply that the rabbinic prohibition of this activity was waved on a Sabbath where preparation of food is forbidden.

113 Mishnah *Šabbat* 15:2, Note 6.

114 Which is permitted on the Sabbath,

Mishnah *Šabbat* 22:3. Quoted Tosaphot 34b   *s. v.* ואמאי.

(21a line 40) פיס'. נִתְגַּלְגֵּל חוּץ לַתְּחוּם כול'. לֹא אָמְרוּ אֶלָּא וְנִטְמֵאת. סָפֵק נִיטְמֵאת מִבְּעוֹד יוֹם סָפֵק נִיטְמֵאת מִשֶּׁחָשֵׁיכָה. אֲבָל אִם הָיְתָה סָפֵק טְהוֹרָה סָפֵק טְמֵיאָה מְעָרְבִין בָּהּ. רִבִּי שְׁמוּאֵל בַּר נַחְמָן בְּשֵׁם רִבִּי יוֹנָתָן. אַחַר חֲזָקוֹת הָלְכוּ.

1 פיס'. G | הלכ'   2 טהורה G | טמאה טמיאה G | טהורה מערבין G | מערבים   3 הלכו G | הילכו

מַתִיבִין רִבִּי מֵאִיר וְרִבִּי יוּדָה לְרִבִּי יוֹסֵי וּלְרִבִּי שִׁמְעוֹן. אִילוּ נֶאֱכַל מִבְּעוֹד יוֹם שֶׁמָּא אֵינוֹ אָסוּר. לְעוֹלָם הוּא בְהֶיתֵּירוֹ עַד שֶׁיִּוָּדַע לוֹ שֶׁהוּא אָסוּר. מַתִיבִין רִבִּי יוֹסֵי וְרִבִּי שִׁמְעוֹן לְרִבִּי מֵאִיר וּלְרִבִּי יוּדָה. אִילוּ נֶאֱכַל מִשֶּׁחָשֵׁיכָה שֶׁמָּא אֵינוֹ מוּתָּר. לְעוֹלָם הוּא בְאִיסוּרוֹ עַד שֶׁיִּוָּדַע לוֹ שֶׁהוּא מוּתָּר.

1 שמא G | שמה   2 אסור G | מותר יוסי G | יוסה   3 שמא G | שמה מותר G | אסור שיוודע G | שיודע

Paragraph. "If it rolled outside the Sabbath boundary," etc. They said only "if it became impure.[115]" A doubt whether it became impure when it still was daylight, a doubt whether it became impure in the night. But if there was a doubt whether it was pure or impure one may use it for an *eruv*[116]. Rebbi Samuel bar Nahman in the name of Rebbi Jonathan: They followed the *status quo ante*[117].

Rebbi Meïr and Rebbi Jehudah objected to Rebbi Yose and Rebbi Simeon[118]: If it had been eaten when it still was daylight (could it be permitted?) [would it not be forbidden?][119] It remains in its permitted state until it becomes known to you that it is forbidden. Rebbi Yose and Rebbi Simeon objected to Rebbi Meïr and Rebbi Jehudah: If it had been eaten after nightfall (could it be prohibited?) [would it not be permitted?][119] It remains in its prohibited state until it becomes known to you that it is permitted.

115 Mishnah 4, the case of an *eruv* made with heave, which is food only if pure. The Mishnah only deals with the case that there is certainty that the heave became impure, the only question is when it happened. The *eruv* is valid if and only if the heave was pure at the beginning of the Sabbath at sundown or in early twilight. Babli 36a.
116 If the *eruv* was deposited in the public domain, any doubt whether there is purity has to be resolved in favor of purity (cf. *Sotah* 1:2 Note 88). The Babli 36a disagrees.
117 Both groups, R. Meïr and R. Jehudah who are restrictive and R. Yose and R. Simeon who are lenient agree with the principle that in cases of doubt one presumes the permanence of the prior state; cf. *Gittin* 6:3 (Note 87).
118 R. Meïr and R. Jehudah define the prior state by the fact that a person is prohibited from leaving his place on the Sabbath. This prohibition can only be lifted

if it is certain that there was a valid *eruv*. R. Yose and R. Simeon define the prior state by the fact that a valid *eruv* was made sometime on Friday; it may be invalidated only by the certain knowledge that it was invalid at the beginning of twilight. An *eruv tehumim* may be eaten immediately after nightfall.

119 The text in parentheses is that of the scribe of L and of G, which has to be accepted as the original text. The text in brackets is the corrector's and all printed editions. The meaning is the same; the original text had two rhetorical questions, the corrected text two correct statements.

(21a line 48) מָהוּ לִיתֵּן לוֹ אַלְפַּיִים מֵעֵירוּבוֹ לְבֵיתוֹ. רִבִּי בָּא בַּר מָמָל אָמַר. נוֹתְנִין לוֹ. רִבִּי שְׁמוּאֵל בַּר רַב יִצְחָק אָמַר. אֵין נוֹתְנִין לוֹ. רִבִּי שַׁמַּי אָמַר קוֹמֵי רִבִּי יוֹסֵה בְּשֵׁם רִבִּי אָחָא. מַה פְלִיגִין כְּרִבִּי מֵאִיר. בְּרַם כְּרִבִּי יוּדָה כָּל־עַמָּא מוֹדַיי שֶׁנּוֹתְנִין לוֹ. וְלֹא דָמֵי חַמָּר גַּמָּל דְּרִבִּי מֵאִיר לְחַמָּר גַּמָּל דְּרִבִּי יוּדָה. חַמָּר גַּמָּל דְּרִבִּי מֵאִיר בְּעֵירוּבוֹ אֵינוּ. שֶׁלֹּא זָכָה לוֹ עֵירוּבוֹ. לַעֲקוֹר אֶת רַגְלָיו מִבְּנֵי עִירוֹ. חַמָּר גַּמָּל דְּרִבִּי יוּדָה שֶׁנָּתַן דַּעְתּוֹ לַעֲקוֹר רַגְלָיו מִבְּנֵי עִירוֹ.

1 מהו G | מהוא לו | G - | מעירובו לביתו G | אמה מעירוב נותניו G | נותנים   2 נותניו G | נותנים   3 שנותניו G | שנותנים   4 שלא G | שלוא   5 לעקור G | לעקור את

Does one give him the 2'000 [cubits] to his house[120]? Rebbi Abba bar Mamal said, one gives him. Rebbi Samuel bar Rav Isaac said, one does not give him. Rebbi Shammai said before Rebbi Yose in the name of Rebbi Aha: They disagree following Rebbi Meïr, but following Rebbi Jehudah everybody agrees that one gives him. The donkey driver-camel driver of Rebbi Meïr cannot be compared to the donkey driver-camel driver of Rebbi Jehudah. The donkey driver-camel driver of Rebbi Meïr cannot use his *eruv* since his *eruv* did not have the power to pull out his feet away from the people of his place; the donkey driver-camel driver of Rebbi Jehudah was thinking to pull out his feet away from the people of his place.

120 As explained in Note 16, the question is whether he may walk in the domain which is common to the Sabbath domain of his house and the Sabbath domain defined by his *eruv*. The distinction between the argument of R. Meïr and that of R. Jehudah refers to Mishnah 4:10 about a person who was going to another place and promised to make an *eruv* on the way for the townspeople but then did not keep his word, where R. Jehudah lets him go since by his action he has shown that he does not want to be counted with the townspeople, whereas R. Meïr makes him donkey-camel driver with only 4 cubits to move in. A different version is given later (Chapter 4, Note 21); *Qiddušin* 3:3 (Note 128): R. Yose said, R. Meïr said this only as a restriction. In this version, he agrees in principle with R. Jehudah but fines people acting stupidly.

(21a line 55) תַּמָּן תַּנִּינָן. סְפֵקוֹ טָהוֹר. רִבִּי יוֹסֵי מְטַמֵּא. אָמַר רִבִּי יוֹנָה. לֹא טִימֵּא רִבִּי יוֹסֵה אֶלָּא מִשּׁוּם הוֹכֵחַ. אָמַר רִבִּי יוֹנָה. וַאֲפִילוּ מָקוֹם אֶחָד רִבִּי יוֹסֵי מְטַמֵּא. מַחְלָפָה שִׁיטָתֵיהּ דְּרִבִּי יוֹסֵה. דְּתַנִּינָן. אָמַר רִבִּי יוֹסֵה. הֵעִיד אַבְטוֹלַס בְּשֵׁם חֲמִשָּׁה זְקֵנִים שֶׁסְּפֵק הָעֵירוּב כָּשֵׁר. וְכָא אַתְּ אָמַר הָכֵין. תַּמָּן בְּשֵׁם גַּרְמֵיהּ. בְּרַם הָכָא בְּשֵׁם חֲמִשָּׁה זְקֵנִים. הֲוֹון בָּעֲיי מֵימַר. מַאן דָּמַר תַּמָּן טָהוֹר אָמַר הָכָא מוּתָּר. מַאן דָּמַר תַּמָּן טָמֵא אָמַר הָכָא אָסוּר. וַאֲפִילוּ כְּמַאן דָּמַר תַּמָּן טָמֵא. מוֹדִי הוּא הָכָא שֶׁהוּא מוּתָּר. אָמַר רִבִּי חִינְנָא. כְּלוּם אִינּוּן פְּלִיגִין תַּמָּן לֹא מִדִּבְרֵיהֶן. וּסְפֵק דִּבְרֵיהֶן לְהָקֵל. וְעֵירוּב דְּבַר תּוֹרָה. וּסְפֵק דְּבַר תּוֹרָה לְהַחְמִיר. וְעֵירוּב דְּבַר תּוֹרָה. רִבִּי יוֹנָתָן אָמַר קוֹמֵי רִבִּי חִייָה רוֹבָה בְּשֵׁם רִבִּי שִׁמְעוֹן בֵּירִבִּי יוֹסֵי בֶּן לַקוּנְיָא. לוֹקִין עַל תְּחוּמֵי שַׁבָּת דְּבַר תּוֹרָה. אָמַר לֵיהּ רִבִּי חִייָה רוֹבָה. וַהֲלֹא אֵין בַּשַּׁבָּת אֶלָּא סְקִילָה וְכָרֵת. אָמַר לֵיהּ. וְהָכְתִיב אַל־תֵּֽאכְלוּ מִמֶּנּוּ נָא. אָמַר לֵיהּ מַה כְּתִיב לֹא. אַל כְּתִיב. וְהָכְתִיב שְׁבוּ | אִישׁ תַּחְתָּיו אַל־יֵ֥צֵא אִ֛ישׁ מִמְּקֹמ֖וֹ בַּיּ֥וֹם הַשְּׁבִיעִֽי׃ אָמַר לֵיהּ. מַה כְּתִיב לֹא. אַל כְּתִיב. אָמַר רִבִּי יוֹסֵי בֵּירִבִּי בּוּן. אַף עַל פִּי כֵן זֶה עוֹמֵד בִּשְׁמוּעָתוֹ וְזֶה עוֹמֵד בִּשְׁמוּעָתוֹ. אָמַר רִבִּי שְׁמוּאֵל בַּר סוֹסַרְטָא. עֵירוּב עָשׂוּ אוֹתוֹ כִּסְפֵק חֶרֶשׁ. רִבִּי יִרמְיָה בָּעֵי. עַד כְּדוֹן בְּקַיָּים. וַאֲפִילוּ נִשְׂרָף. אָמַר רִבִּי יוֹסֵה. קַיָּימְתִּיהָ כַּיי דָּמַר רִבִּי הוֹשַׁעְיָה. הִגִּיעוּךָ סוֹף תְּחוּמֵי שַׁבָּת שֶׁאֵינָן מְחוּוָּרִין מִדְּבַר תּוֹרָה. רִבִּי מָנָא בָּעֵי. נִיחָא אַלְפַּיִים אַמָּה אֵינוֹ מְחוּוָּר. אַרְבַּעַת אֲלָפִים מְחוּוָּר הוּא. רִבִּי שִׁמְעוֹן בַּר כַּרְסָנָא בְּשֵׁם רִבִּי אָחָא. אֵין לְךָ מְחוּוָּר מִכּוּלָּם אֶלָּא תְּחוֹם שְׁנֵים עָשָׂר מִיל כְּמַחֲנֵה יִשְׂרָאֵל.

1 יוֹסֵי G | יוֹסֵה טימא G | טימא אותו 2 הוכח G | הוכיחו מקום אחד G | מקווה אחד יוֹסֵי G | יוֹסֵה 3 אבטולס G | אכטלס בשם G | משם וכא G | והכה 4 מאן G | מן 5 מאן G | מן אמ' מוֹדי G | מוֹדה הכא G | הכח 6 מדבריהן G | מדברהון 7 לקוניא G | בר בן לקוניא G | בר לקונייה לוֹקין G | לוֹקים 8 רובה G | רבה ביר' G | בירבי 9 רובה G | רבה 10 והכת' G | והא כתיב לֵיהּ G | לה אל G | לֹא אל לֵיהּ G | לה והכת' G | והא כתיב 11 לֵיהּ G | לה אל G | לֹא אל יוֹסֵי G | יוֹסֵה 12 עוֹמֵד G | עָמַד (2) 13 כספק חרש G | כיספיק חיריש 14 קיימתיה G | קיימתיה כיי דאמר ר' G | דמר כההיא G | רב 16 אחא G | אחה מכולם G | מיכולם

There, we have stated[121]: "If there is a doubt, it is pure; Rebbi Yose declares it impure." Rebbi Jonah said, Rebbi Yose declared it impure only because of proof[122]. And Rebbi Jonah said, Rebbi Yose declares impure even (one place) [one *miqweh*][123]. The argument of Rebbi Yose seems inverted, as we have stated: "Rebbi Yose said, Autolas[17] testified in the name of five Elders that in case of a doubt an *eruv* is qualified[18]." And here you are saying so? There in his own name, but here in the name of five Elders. They wanted to say that he who says there "pure" says here "permitted"; he who says there "impure" says here "prohibited". But even he who says there "impure" agrees here that it is permitted[124]. Rebbi Hinena said, do they not only disagree about their words? And a doubt about their words is for leniency[125]. But an *eruv* is a word of Torah; and a doubt about a word of the Torah is for restriction[126] But is *eruv* a word of the Torah? Rebbi Jonathan said before the

Elder Rebbi Ḥiyya in the name of Rebbi Simeon ben Rebbi Yose ben Laqonia: One whips because of Sabbath domains as word of the Torah[127]. Rebbi Ḥiyya the Elder said to him, but for Sabbath there is only stoning or extirpation[128]? He said to him, is there not written[129], *do not eat from it raw*? He said to him, is there written לא? No, it is written אַל! He said to him, is there not written[130], *stay everybody where he is, no person shall leave his place on the Seventh day*? He said to him, is there written לא? No, it is written אַל. Rebbi ben Rebbi Abun said, nevertheless each one kept to his tradition[131]. Rebbi Samuel bar Sosarta said, they treated *eruv* as a doubt involving a deaf-mute person[132]. Rebbi Jeremiah asked, so far if it exists, or even if it was burned[133]? Rebbi Yose said, I confirmed this following what Rebbi[134] Hoshaia said: You must conclude that the boundaries of Sabbath domains are not clear in the words of the Torah. Rebbi Mana asked, it is accepted that 2'000 cubits is not clear[135]. Are 4'000 cubits not clear? Rebbi Simeon bar Carsana in the name of Rebbi Aḥa: The only clear case among all of them is the domain of twelve *mil* of the camp of Israel[136].

121 Mishnah *Miqwaot* 2:2. The Mishnah states that if a person was impure by biblical standards he can be purified only by immersion in a *miqweh* which is unquestionably valid. But if his impurity is rabbinic, immersion in a *miqweh* will purify him unless the *miqweh* is unquestionably invalid. R. Yose disagrees and holds that the principle of permanence of the *status quo ante* also applies to rabbinic impurity and the *miqweh* must be unquestionably valid.

122 If there are a group of items, the status of one is certain but that of the others is uncertain, one may assume that the other items share the status of the certain one unless proven otherwise (cf. *Demay* 2:1 2nd paragraph; *Terumot* 4:8 Note 83.) The Mishnah quotes the case that there be two *miqwaot*, one of them known to be invalid, while the other might be valid. If the person does not know in which of the two he immersed, R. Yose holds that it must have been the invalid one.

123 The text in parentheses is from L, that in brackets from G. The preceding argument is rejected, R. Yose applies the principle of permanence of the *status quo ante* even if nothing is certain and there is only one item.

124 The two cases cannot be compared. The rules of impurity are biblical even if they are extended to cover cases of only rabbinic impurity. The rules of *eruv* are all rabbinic.

125 He holds the opposite view. The Mishnah *Miqwaot* clearly distinguishes between biblical and rabbinic impurity and decrees leniency only for rabbinic cases; for

him the rules of *eruv tehumim* are all biblical; only *eruv haserot* is rabbinical.

126 A generally recognized principle, cf. *Ketubot* 1:1 Note 21.

127 Babli 17b. This proves at least that leaving one's Sabbath domain is a biblical violation.

128 A Sabbath violation of one of the 39 forbidden categories of work is punishable by stoning if there are witnesses or divine extirpation otherwise. We do not find flogging as punishment for any Sabbath violation.

129 *Ex.* 12:9.

130 *Ex.* 16:29. Even though this is the sequence of the sentences also in G, it is clear that the order has to be inverted. R. Jonathan first quoted *Ex.* 16:29 as proof that leaving one's domain on the Sabbath is a biblical violation. Since no punishment is stated, the standard sanction of flogging applies. To this R. Hiyya replies that the standard sanction applies only to prohibitions introduced by לא, not to admonitions formulated with אַל. R. Jonathan retorts that this explanation is impossible since eating the Passover sacrifice raw is a punishable transgression forbidden by אַל.

131 It is unresolved whether leaving one's domain on the Sabbath is a transgression punishable in court. But the institution of *eruv* certainly is a rabbinic interpretation of the rules.

132 In the interpretation of biblical prohibitions, matters of doubt are treated differently when a person is involved who can be interrogated about the situation. Then the rules of resolution of doubts can be invoked only after the facts have been investigated. But if the person involved is deaf mute and unable to communicate by sign language the rules are applied immediately.

133 The preceding makes sense if the *eruv* still exists. But if it was burned (as mentioned in the Mishnah) it should be impossible to invoke a principle of permanence of the *status quo ante*.

134 This is the text of L which probably is correct. In G: Rav.

135 The 2'000 cubits counted from the city walls are in imitation of the suburban space allotted to the levitic cities (*Num.* 35:5) where the Sabbath is not mentioned. The measure therefore has only rabbinic status. Babli 36a, *Beṣah* 36b. The Sadducee Damascus Document (CD A x) accepts a limit of 1'000 cubits (*Num.* 35:4) for humans and 2'000 cubits for animals (CD A xi) as biblical.

136 This is the general tradition that the diameter of the encampment of the Israelites as described in *Num.* 2 was 3 *parsah* (12 *mil* or 90 itinerant *stadia*): *Ševi'it* 6:1 (Note 28), copied in *Gittin* 1:2 (Note 94), Babli *Berakhot* 54b, *Eruvin* 53b, *Yoma* 75b.

(21b line 1) פיס'. מַתָּנָה אָדָם עַל עֵירוּבוֹ כול'. כֵּינֵי מַתְנִיתָה. עַל עֵירוּבָיו. אָמַר רִבִּי לָעֳזָר. מָאן תַּנָּא. אִם בָּאוּ. אִם לֹא בָאוּ. רִבִּי מֵאִיר. הַיְידָן רִבִּי מֵאִיר. חֲבֵרַיָּיא אָמְרִין. רִבִּי מֵאִיר דְּקִידּוּשִׁין. דְּתַנֵּי. הָאוֹמֵר לָאִשָּׁה. הֲרֵי אַתְּ מְקוּדֶּשֶׁת לִי עַל מְנָת שֶׁיֵּרְדוּ גְשָׁמִים. יָרְדוּ גְשָׁמִים מְקוּדֶּשֶׁת. וְאִם לָאו אֵינָהּ מְקוּדֶּשֶׁת. רִבִּי מֵאִיר אוֹמֵר. בֵּין יָרְדוּ בֵין לֹא יָרְדוּ מְקוּדֶּשֶׁת עַד

שֶׁיַּכְפִּיל תְּנָאוֹ. הַכֹּל מוֹדִין שֶׁאִם אָמַר הֲרֵי אַתְּ מְקוּדֶּשֶׁת לִי לְאַחַר שֶׁיֵּרְדוּ גְשָׁמִים. יָרְדוּ גְשָׁמִים מְקוּדֶּשֶׁת. וְאִם לָאו אֵינָהּ מְקוּדֶּשֶׁת. בְּרַם כְּרַבָּנָן בֵּין שֶׁיֵּרְדוּ בֵין שֶׁלֹּא יָרְדוּ מְקוּדֶּשֶׁת. רִבִּי יוֹסֵה אָמַר. רִבִּי מֵאִיר דְּעֵירוּבִין. דְּתַנִּינָן. אִם סָפֵק. רִבִּי מֵאִיר וְרִבִּי יוּדָה אוֹמְרִין. הֲרֵי זֶה חַמָּר גַּמָּל. רִבִּי יוֹסֵי וְרִבִּי שִׁמְעוֹן אוֹמְרִין סְפֵק הָעֵירוּב כָּשֵׁר. אָמַר רִבִּי יוֹסֵה. לֹא אָמַר רִבִּי מֵאִיר אֶלָּא לַחוֹמְרִין. אָמַר רִבִּי מָנָא. וְיֵאוּת. בְּעֵירוּבוֹ אֵינוֹ. שֶׁלֹּא זָכָה לוֹ עֵירוּבוֹ. לַעֲקוֹר אֶת רַגְלָיו מִבְּנֵי עִירוֹ. וְהָכָא לָרִאשׁוֹן אֵינָהּ מְקוּדֶּשֶׁת שֶׁלֹּא יָרְדוּ גְשָׁמִים. וְלַשֵּׁנִי אֵינָהּ מְקוּדֶּשֶׁת שֶׁלֹּא כָּפַל הָרִאשׁוֹן אֶת תְּנָאָיו. רִבִּי חַגַּי בְּעָא קוֹמֵי רִבִּי יוֹסֵה. הָהֵן אִם לֹא חַד הוּא. אָמַר. שַׁנְיָיא הִיא. שֶׁהָיְתָה הָאָרֶץ לִפְנֵיהֶן וְהוּא מְבַקֵּשׁ לְהוֹצִיאָהּ מִיָּדָן.

1 אדם G | אדן כול' G | - | כיני G | כני 2 תנא G | תנה היידן G | הידן חברייא G | חברייה 3 דקידושין G | דקידושים 4 ירדו G | שירדו לא G | שלא עד G | על 5 תנאו | תניין G תנו[י]יה [138] הרי את מקודשת לי G | - 6 ברם כרננו בין שירדו גשמים בין שלא ירדו מקודשת G | - 7 דתנינן G | דתנינן אם ספק 7-8 ר' יוסי ור' שמעון אומ' ספיק העירוב כשר G | - 9 בעירובו G | תמן בעירובו שלא G | שלו והכא G | והכה 11 תנייו | תניו בעא G | בעה ההן G | והן אם G | ואם חד G | כי לאחד אמ' G | אמר לה שנייא G | שנייה 12 להוציאה G | להוצאה

[137]Paragraph. "A person may make his *eruv* conditional," etc. So is the Mishnah: "A person can impose a condition on his `eruvin." Rebbi Eleazar said, who is the Tanna of "if they came", "if they did not come"? Rebbi Meïr! Which Rebbi Meïr? The colleagues say, Rebbi Meïr of *Qiddušin*. As it was stated: If somebody say to a woman: You are preliminarily married to me on condition that there will be rain. If rain fell, she is preliminarily married, otherwise she is not preliminarily married. Rebbi Meïr says, she is preliminarily married whether or not rain fell unless he doubled his condition. Everybody agrees that if he said, after rainfall, if it rained she is preliminarily married, otherwise she is not preliminarily married. (But following the rabbis she is preliminarily married whether rain fell or not.)[138A] Rebbi Yose said, it follows Rebbi Meïr in *Eruvin*, as we have stated there: "If it is a matter of uncertainty,, Rebbi Meïr and Rebbi Jehudah say, he is a donkey driver-camel driver." Rebbi Yose said, Rebbi Meïr said this only as a restriction. Rebbi Mana said, that is correct. He cannot acquire his `eruv since he is not able to enjoy it. [Why not] like the people of his place? If he had decided to leave his place. And here, she is not preliminarily married to the first, since no rain came. She is not preliminarily married to the second, since the first did not double his condition. Rebbi Ḥaggai asked before Rebbi Yose: Is this "if" not a reaction? He answered, there is a difference since the land was in their hand and he wanted to take it away from them.

137 This paragraph and the next are from *Qiddušin* 3:3, explained there in Notes 116-131. It is clear that the text here is a copy from there since in the text "here" refers to *Qiddušin* and the discussion between R. Haggai and R. Yose at the end of the paragraph has absolutely nothing to do with the Mishnah in *Eruvin* but asks why the conditional distribution of land to the tribes of Gad and Reuben (*Num.* 32:29-30) required a double condition, both positive and negative; this is relevant only for *Qiddušin*. Similarly the next paragraph has no connection with the topics of *Eruvin*.
138 Cf. *Qiddušin* Note 116.
138A To be deleted with G and *Qiddušin*.

(21c line 17) רִבִּי יוּדָה בֶּן שָׁלוֹם רִבִּי יוּדָה בֶּן פָּזִי בְשֵׁם רִבִּי יוֹחָנָן. יָרְדוּ לְסִימְפוֹן בְּשִׁיטַת רִבִּי מֵאִיר דְּקִידּוּשִׁין. רִבִּי יִרְמְיָה רִבִּי חִינָנָא חֲבֵרֵה דְּרַבָּנָן בָּעֵי. וְלָמָּה כְרִבִּי מֵאִיר. וַאֲפִילוּ כְרַבָּנָן. לֵית כֵּן. אָמַר רִבִּי אַבָּהוּ בְשֵׁם רִבִּי יוֹחָנָן. סֵדֶר סִימְפוֹן כָּךְ הוּא. אֲנָא פְלוֹנִי בַּר פְּלוֹנִי מְקַדֵּשׁ אוֹתָךְ. אַתְּ פְּלוֹנִית בַּת פְּלָן עַל מְנָת מִיתֵּן לִיךְ מִקָּמַת פְּלָן וּמִיכְנָסִינָיךְ בְּיוֹם פְּלוֹנִי. אִין אֲתָא יוֹם פְּלָן וְלָא כְנַסְתִּיךְ. לָא יְהֵוי לִי עָלַיִךְ כְּלוּם. וְיֵימַר. עַל מְנָת. שֶׁלֹּא יַכְפִּיל תְּנָייוּ. אִילּוּ לֹא כָפַל תְּנָייוּ מִי עָקַר קִידּוּשָׁיו. אָמַר רִבִּי יוֹסֵה כְּירְבִּי בּוּן. בְּכָל־אֲתַר אִית לֵיהּ לְרִבִּי מֵאִיר. מִמַּשְׁמַע לָאו אַתְּ שׁוֹמֵעַ הֵן. וְהָכָא לֵית לֵיהּ. אָמַר רִבִּי מַתַּנְיָה. עַל שֵׁם חוֹמֶר הוּא בַעֲרָיוֹת.

1 שלום G | טט.. | לסימפון G | לסיפון | 2 חברה דרבנן G | וחב]רהון דרבנין | 3 אבהו G | אבהוא | 4 אותך G | ליך את G | אנתי בת G | ברת | 5 יכפיל G | יכפול תנייו G | תניי | 6 תנייו G | תניי | 7 לאו | G לאוי הן G | היו והכא G | והכה ליה G | לה

[139]Rebbi Jehudah ben Shalom, Rebbi Jehudah bar Pazy in the name of Rebbi Johanan. They formulated the *symphon*[139A] according to Rebbi Meïr in *Qiddušin*. Rebbi Jeremiah: Rebbi Hananiah, the colleague of the rabbis, asked: Why does it have to follow Rebbi Meïr but not also the rabbis? Did not Rebbi Abbahu say in the name of Rebbi Johanan: The following is the contract text: "I, X son of Y, contract a preliminary marriage with you, Z, daughter of U, on condition that I shall give you property A and definitively marry you by day B. If that day should pass without me having taken you in, I shall have no claim on you." Why can he not say "on condition" but not double his stipulation? If he did not double his stipulation, could this eliminate the preliminary marriage? Rebbi Yose ben Rebbi Abun said, everywhere Rebbi Meïr holds that from "no" you infer "yes", except here? Rebbi Mattaniah said, one is more restrictive in matters of incest and adultery.

139 *Qiddušin* 3:3, Notes 133-136.
139A Greek συμφώνημα, -ατος, τό, "agreement"; cf. *Qiddušin* 3:2, Note 69 for details and legal standing of this marriage contract.

(21b line 26) לֹא הִתְנָה. נִשְׁמְעִינָהּ מִן הָדָא. הֲרֵי שֶׁעֵירֵב בֵּין שְׁנֵי תְחוּמִין. מְהַלֵּךְ בַּדָּרוֹם כְּעֵירוּבוֹ בַצָּפוֹן. בַּצָּפוֹן כְּעֵירוּבוֹ בַדָּרוֹם. מִיצַּע אֶת הַתְּחוּם אַל יָזוּז מִמְּקוֹמוֹ. בְּהֵמָה שֶׁלִּשְׁנֵי שׁוּתָּפִין. עֵירַב זֶה בַּצָּפוֹן וְזֶה בַדָּרוֹם. מְהַלֶּכֶת בַּדָּרוֹם כְּעֵירוּבוֹ שֶׁלָּזֶה בַּצָּפוֹן. בַּצָּפוֹן כְּעֵירוּבוֹ שֶׁלָּזֶה בַדָּרוֹם. מִיצַעַת אֶת הַתְּחוּם אַל תָּזוּז מִמְּקוֹמָהּ. שְׁחָטוּהָ. רַב אָמַר. אֵיבָרִים יוֹנְקִין זֶה מִזֶּה. עוּלָּא בַּר יִשְׁמָעֵאל אָמַר. אֵין אֵיבָרִים יוֹנְקִין זֶה מִזֶּה. מוֹדֶה רַב בְּחָבִית שֶׁהוּא חֶלְקוֹ מִשָּׁעָה רִאשׁוֹנָה.

1 התנה G | היתנה נישמעינה G | נשמעינה חדא G | הדא שעירב G | שערב בין שני G | בשני   2 כעירובו | כעירובי (2) G | מיצע G | מיצא 3 עירב G | ערב בצפון G | בדרום בדרום G | בצפון 4 מיצעת G | מיצאת איברים G | איברני   5 עולא G | עולה איברים G | איברין

כֵּינִי מַתְנִיתָהּ. בָּאוּ גוֹיִם מִיכָּן וּמִיכָּן. לֹא בָאוּ גוֹיִם לֹא מִיכָּן וְלֹא מִיכָּן. בָּאוּ גוֹיִם מִן הַמִּזְרָח עֵירוּבִי לַמַּעֲרָב. אִית תַּנָּיֵי תַנֵּי. בַּמִּזְרָח. מָאן דָּמַר. בַּמִּזְרָח. בְּאִילֵּין טַקְסִיווֹטֵי. מָאן דָּמַר. בַּמַּעֲרָב. בְּאִילֵּין רוֹמָאֵי.

1 כיני G | כני מיכן G | מיכאן   2 עירובי G | עירובו מאן G | מן באילין G | באלין 3 באילין G | בלין

If he did not stipulate? Let us hear from the following[140]: "If somebody made *eruvim* for two domains he can go to the South according to his *eruv* in the North, to the North according to his *eruv* in the South. If he split the domain[141] he may not move from his place." An animal belonging to two partners one of which made an *eruv* in the North and the other in the South. It may walk to the South according to the *eruv* of the one in the North and to the North according to the *eruv* of the one in the South. If they split the domain it may not move from its place. If they slaughtered it[142]. Rav said, limbs suck from one another. Ulla bar Ismael said, limbs do not suck from one another[143]. Rav agrees about an amphora that it was his part from before[144].

So is the Mishnah: If Gentiles come from both sides, if Gentiles do not come from either side[145]. "If Gentiles come from the East my *eruv* shall be in the West." Some Tannaim state, to the East[147]. He who says to the East, about these officers[148], he who says to the West, about these Romans[149].

140 Tosephta 3:4; Babli 50b; *Besah* 37b. Somebody made two different *eruvim* for the same Sabbath or holiday thinking that he would be able to use both of them.
141 If the two domains intersect only at one point he cannot move from that point.
142 On a holiday when slaughter is permitted. Babli *Besah* 37b.

143 According to Rav the partners can move the parts only in the common domain; according to Ulla bar Ismael each owner may move his part anywhere in his domain.
144 Since it was determined that *eruv* is a rabbinic institution one accepts that a later distribution retroactively determines

145 For אם לא באו one has to read לא באו.
146 If the Gentiles come to the East, his *eruv* shall be to the East. Why should he want to go to the East?

148 Greek ταξεώτης, -ου ὁ, "officer of a magistrate, member of *militia palatina*", whom it is important to humor.
149 Common soldiers, notoriously badly disciplined in the later Empire.

(21b line 36) פיס'. בָּא חָכָם מִן הַמִּזְרָח כול'. אִית תַּנָּיֵי תַנֵּי. בְּמַעֲרָב. מָאן דָּמַר. בַּמִּזְרָח. בְּאִילֵּין חֲכִימַיָּא. מָאן דָּמַר. בַּמַּעֲרָב. בְּרָגִיל.
1 פיס'. G | הלכ': כול' G | עירובו למזרח מאן G | מן באילין G | בלין 2 חכימיא G חכימייה מאן G | ומן במערב G - | ברגיל G | ברגול

Paragraph. "If a Sage comes from the East," etc. Some Tannaim state, to the West. He who says, in the East, about these Sages. He who says, in the West, about a fundraiser[150].

150   S. Liebermann, *Tarbiz* 4 (1933) pp. 378-379.

(21b line 38) פיס'. רִבִּי יְהוּדָה אוֹמֵר אִם הָיָה אֶחָד מֵהֶן כול'. רִבִּי יְהוּדָה אוֹמֵר.
1 פיס'. G | הלכ': ר' יהודה או' | G ר' יודה או' אם היה אחד מהם רגול ילך לו אצל [הר]גול שניהון רגילין למקום שירצה ילך

Paragraph. "Rebbi Jehudah says, if one of them was," etc. Rebbi Jehudah says [151][if one of them was a fundraiser, he should go to the fundraiser; if both of them were fundraisers he may go to the place of his choosing.]

151 Added from G; missing in L and the printed editions. It probably was omitted since it flatly contradicts the preceding statement from the discussion of Mishnah 6. But that describes what people do while in Mishnah 7 R. Jehudah prescribes what people should do.

(21b line 39) רִבִּי אֱלִיעֶזֶר אוֹמֵר כול'. וַחֲכָמִים אוֹמְרִים מְעָרֵב לְרוּחַ אַחַת. כֵּינִי מַתְנִיתָהּ. אוֹ מְעָרֵב לְרוּחַ אַחַת לִשְׁנֵי יָמִים. אוֹ אֵינוֹ מְעָרֵב כָּל־עִיקָר. מוֹדֶה רִבִּי אֱלִיעֶזֶר שֶׁאֵינוֹ מְעָרֵב חֲצִי יוֹם בַּדָּרוֹם וַחֲצִי יוֹם בַּצָּפוֹן. חֲצִי יוֹם בַּדָּרוֹם וַחֲצִי יוֹם בַּצָּפוֹן לִבְנֵי עִירוֹ. אָמְרוּ לוֹ. כְּשֵׁם שֶׁלֹּא חֲלֻקֶּת לָנוּ יוֹם אֶחָד כָּךְ לֹא תַחֲלוֹק לָנוּ שְׁנֵי יָמִים. וְשָׁוִוין שֶׁלֹּא יִתְּנֶנּוּ בַסַּל. אָמַר רִבִּי בָּא. שֶׁמָּא יִשְׁכַּח וְיֹאכְלֶנּוּ. נָתַן בַּסַּל. מוֹלִיךְ אֶת הַסַּל לְשָׁם. אָכַל אֶת אֶחָד מֵהֶן הֲרֵי זֶה חֲמָר גָּמָל.
1 ר' אליעזר... לרוח אחת G הלכ' כיני G כני 2 אליעזר G ליעזר 4 ושווין G ושוויים 5 חמר גמל G כחמר וגמל

"Rebbi Eliezer says," etc. "But the Sages say, either one makes an *eruv* to one side." So is the Mishnah: Either one makes an *eruv* to one side for two days or one does not make an *eruv* at all[152]. Rebbi Eliezer agrees that one cannot make an *eruv* for half a day in the South and one for half a day in the North, for half a day in the South and one for half a day (in the North)[153] for the people of his place. They told him, just as you did not split the day for us, so do not split two days for us[154]. They agree that he should not put them[155] in a basket. Rebbi Abba said, that he should not forget and eat it. If he did put it into a basket, he should bring the basket there. If he eats one of them he is a donkey driver-camel driver[156].

152 The words "in one direction" are missing in Mishnah 9.
153 The words in parentheses are clearly out of place but they are also found in G.
154 Cf. Note 22. Even though the sanctity of the Sabbath is different in kind from that of the holiday, for the *eruv* to become effective on the Sabbath one would have to invalidate the *eruv* for the holiday some time before sundown.
155 The *eruvim* for the two days.
156 If it cannot be determined which day's *eruv* was eaten both are potentially valid or invalid both days.

(21b line 43) תַּמָּן תַּנִּינָן. לָגִין שֶׁהוּא טְבוּל יוֹם מִן הֶחָבִית מַעֲשֵׂר טוֹבֵל. אִם אָמַר. הֲרֵי זֶה תְּרוּמַת מַעֲשֵׂר מִשֶּׁתֶּחְשַׁךְ. הֲרֵי זוּ תְּרוּמַת מַעֲשֵׂר. אִם אָמַר. הֲרֵי זֶה עֵרוּב. לֹא אָמַר כְּלוּם. רִבִּי יוֹנָה אָמַר. רִבִּי חָמָא כַּר עֲקִיבָה מַקְשֵׁי. מַתְנִיתָה דְּלֹא כְרִבִּי אֱלִיעֶזֶר. דְּרִבִּי אֱלִיעֶזֶר אָמַר. אֵין מְעָרְבִין לָאָדָם מִשֶּׁתֶּחְשַׁךְ. רִבִּי יִרְמְיָה בְּשֵׁם רִבִּי זְעִירָא. דִּבְרֵי הַכֹּל הִיא תַמָּן. בְּרַם הָכָא מִבַּחוֹל הוּא קָנָה לוֹ שְׁבִיתָה לִשְׁנֵי יָמִים. רִבִּי חַגַּיי בָּעֵי. הָיָה עוֹמֵד בַּחֲמִישִׁי בַּשַּׁבָּת וְאָמַר. תִּקָּנֶה לִי שְׁבִיתָתָה בַּשַּׁבָּת. עַל דַּעְתֵּיהּ דְּרִבִּי אֱלִיעֶזֶר קָנָה. עַל דַּעְתֵּיהּ דְּרַב לֹא קָנָה. אָמַר רִבִּי יוֹסֵה. וְלָמָה אֵין מְעָרְבִין לָאָדָם מִיּוֹם טוֹב לַשַּׁבָּת. שֶׁכֵּן מְעָרְבִין לָאָדָם מֵעֶרֶב שַׁבָּת לַשַּׁבָּת. בְּרַם הָכָא וְהוּא רָאוּי לְעָרֵב מֵעֶרֶב שַׁבָּת לַשַּׁבָּת. מְעָרֵב אֲפִילוּ בַּחֲמִישִׁי בַּשַּׁבָּת. אָמַר לְהֶן רִבִּי אֱלִיעֶזֶר. אִי אַתֶּם מוֹדִין לִי. שֶׁאִם עֵירֵב בַּכְּפָר בָּרִאשׁוֹן שֶׁהוּא מְעָרֵב בַּכְּרַךְ בַּשֵּׁינִי. שֶׁאִם אֲכָלוֹ בָּרִאשׁוֹן שֶׁהוּא עֵירוּב לָרִאשׁוֹן וְאֵינוֹ עֵירוּב לַשֵּׁינִי. הֲוֵי שְׁתֵּי קְדוּשּׁוֹת הֵן. וְאִינּוּן מְתִיבִין לֵיהּ. אֵין אַתָּה מוֹדֶה לָנוּ שֶׁאֵין מְעָרְבִין לְאָדָם כַּתְּחִילָּה בְּיוֹם טוֹב. הֲוֵי קְדוּשָּׁה אַחַת הִיא.

1 מן G | וּמלאוהו מן G | טובל G | טבל זה G | זו 3 חמא בר עקיבה G | חמה בר עוקבה אליעזר G | ליעזר 6 דרב G | דרבנן 7 לאדם G | לאדן G | הכא G | הכה 8 אליעזר G | ליעזר אי G | אין G | אתם G | אתן 9 מודין לי G | מודים לו עירב G | ערב בככר G | בכיכר (2) 10 לשיני G | לשני הוי G | הווי G | ואינון G | ואנין 11 לאדם G | לאדן הווי G | הוי

There we have stated[157]: "A flask[158] which had been immersed on the same day and [they filled it][159] from an amphora with *tevel* tithe, if he said that this shall be heave of the tithe after nightfall then it is heave of the tithe[160]. If he said this is *eruv*, he did not say anything.[161]" Rebbi Jonah said, Rebbi Hama bar (Aqiba) [Uqba][162] asked, is this Mishnah not following Rebbi Eliezer, since Rebbi Eliezer said, one does not make an *eruv* for a person after nightfall[163]? Rebbi Jeremiah in the name of Rebbi Ze`ira: There it is everybody's opinion. But here he acquires a place for Sabbath rest for two days while it still is a working day[164].

Rebbi Ḥaggai asked, if it was Thursday and he said, this should acquire for me a place for Sabbath rest, in Rebbi Eliezer's opinion he acquired, in (Rav's) [the rabbis'][162] opinion did he not acquire[165]? Rebbi Yose said, why can a person not make an *eruv* from holiday to Sabbath? Because a person makes an *eruv* from Sabbath eve to the Sabbath[166]. But here, since he can make an *eruv* from Sabbath eve to the Sabbath, he may make an *eruv* even from Thursday to the Sabbath[167].

[168]"Rebbi Eliezer said to them, do you not agree with me that if he used a loaf to make an *eruv* for the first day, that he may use a loaf to make an *eruv* for the second day, that if he ate it on the first day it is an *eruv* for the first day but is not an *eruv* for the second? Therefore these are two sanctities. They answered him, do you not agree with us that a person does not make a new *eruv* on a holiday? Therefore it is one sanctity."

157 Mishnah *Tevul Yom* 2:2.
158 Greek λάγυνος, ὁ.
159 Added from G and the Mishnah text.
160 Purification from impurity is in two steps. Immersion in a *miqweh* removes the impurity (*Lev.* 22:6) but only the following sundown creates purity for *sancta* (*Lev.* 22:7). Tithe given to the Levite is forbidden for everybody as *tevel* before heave of the tithe has been separated; the heave is a *sanctum* for the Cohen, the remainder becomes purely profane in the Levite's hand. The *tevel* filled into the flask is not a sanctum; since the flask is not impure it does not change the status of the fluid which it contains. After sundown it becomes pure for *sancta*; if at the same point in time the contents become heave, the heave is pure.
161 Since an *eruv* must be valid before sundown but at that time the contents of the flask still were *tevel* and forbidden as food even to the Cohen, the *eruv* is invalid.
162 The correct reading is from [G], the incorrect one from (L).
163 Since this is the reason while the *eruv* is invalid.
164 The rabbis also hold that on the day itself one cannot make an *eruv*; the Mishnah in *Tevul Yom* has no relevance for the disagreement here.
165 Since R. Eliezer permits to make on Thursday a separate *eruv* for the Sabbath if Friday is a holiday, he certainly must permit making on Thursday an *eruv* for a regular

Sabbath. But the rabbis' opinion in this matter cannot be determined from the Mishnah.

166 Rashba (col. 239) and Meïri (col. 133b) emend the text to read: Because a person *cannot make* an *eruv* from Sabbath eve (which is a holiday) to the Sabbath. If one refrains from emending the text one has to read the sentence as a rhetorical question: Because could a person make an *eruv* from Sabbath eve (which is a holiday) to the Sabbath?

167 If there is no holiday intervening.

168 A slightly different text Tosephta 4:1; still differently Babli 39a.

(21b line 60) פיס'. רִבִּי יְהוּדָה אוֹמֵר רֹאשׁ הַשָּׁנָה שֶׁהָיָה יָרֵא שֶׁמָּא תִתְעַבֵּר כול'. דְּאִיתְפַּלְגוּן. שְׁיָרֵי פְתִילָה שְׁיָרֵי מְדוּרָה שְׁיָרֵי שֶׁמֶן שֶׁכָּבוּ בַשַּׁבָּת מַהוּ לְהַדְלִיקָם בְּיוֹם טוֹב. רַב וְרִבִּי חֲנִינָה תְּרֵיהוֹן אָמְרִין. אָסוּר. רִבִּי יוֹחָנָן אָמַר. מוּתָּר. אָמַר רִבִּי מָנָא קוֹמֵי רִבִּי יוּדָן. מְכַפְּלָה פְּתִילָה גַּבֵּי בֵיצָה. אֲמַר לֵיהּ. מִן מַה דָּנָן חַמְיִין רַבָּנָן מְדַמֵּי לָהּ. הִיא הָדָא הִיא הָדָא. מְשׁוּם אַרְבָּעָה זְקֵינִים אָמְרוּ. הַנֶּאֱכַל עֵירוּבוֹ בָּרִאשׁוֹן הֲרֵי זֶה כִּבְנֵי עִירוֹ כַּשֵּׁינִי. רִבִּי חוּנָה בְשֵׁם רַב. הֲלָכָה כְּאַרְבָּעָה זְקֵינִים. רַב חִסְדַּאי בְּעָא. מַחְלְפָה שִׁיטָתֵיהּ דְּרַב. תַּמָּן אִיעֲבַד לָהּ שְׁתֵּי קְדוּשׁוֹת. וָכָא אִיעֲבַד לָהּ קְדוּשָׁה אַחַת. דְּאִיתְפַּלְגוּן. שְׁיָרֵי פְתִילָה שְׁיָרֵי מְדוּרָה שְׁיָרֵי שֶׁמֶן שֶׁכָּבוּ בַשַּׁבָּת. מַהוּ לְהַדְלִיקָם בְּיוֹם טוֹב. רַב וְרִבִּי חֲנִינָה תְּרֵיהוֹן אָמְרִין. אָסוּר. רִבִּי יוֹחָנָן אָמַר. מוּתָּר. אָמַר רִבִּי מָנָא קוֹמֵי רִבִּי יוּדָן. מְכַפְּלָה פְּתִילָה גַּבֵּי בֵיצָה. אֲמַר לֵיהּ. מִן מַה דָּנָן חַמְיֵי רַבָּנִין מְדַמֵּי לָהּ. הָדָא אָמְרָה. אִי אִידָא אִי אִידָא.

1 פיס'. ר' יהודה... כול'. - G | 2 מהו G מהוא 3 ר' | יור' מנא | 7 יודן יודן | 7 מנא מכפלה | 7 מפכא לה י מה אפכן פתילה | 7 - 4 ליה G | לה דן | 7י דאנן חמיין | 7G חמיי רבנן | 7G רבנין הדא | G הדה היא הדא G אי הדה היא הדא G אי אדא - 5 | 7 כל זה | 7G הוא כשיני | 7י בשיני - | G השם רב חונה ר' חונה | 7 רב הונא י רב חונה 6 חסדאי | 7G חסדא איעבד | 7G י עבד 7 וכא G | וכה י וחכא איעבד | 7י עבד ר' | יור' 8 מהו G מהוא להדליקם | 7 להדליקון 9 מכפלה | 7 מפכא לה י מה אפכן דן | 7י דאנן 10 אי אידא { 7G היא הדה (2)

Paragraph. "Rebbi Jehudah said, if a person was afraid that the New Year's Day might be complemented[25]," etc. [169]Because they disagreed: May the remainders of a wick, a fire, or oil that burned out on the Sabbath be lit on the holiday[170]? Rav and Rebbi Ḥanina both say it is forbidden, but Rebbi Joḥanan says, it is permitted. Rebbi Mana said before Rebbi Yudan, is it the reverse regarding an egg[171]? He said to him, since the rabbis compare it, it means that the two cases are identical[172].

They said in the name of four Elders[173]: If somebody's *eruv* was eaten on the first [day] he is like the people of his town on the second [day]. Rav Huna said in the name of Rav: Practice follows the four Elders[174]. Rav Ḥisda asked: the argument of Rav seems to be inverted. There, he makes it two sanctities, but here he makes it one sanctity. Because they disagreed: May the remainders of a wick, a fire, or oil that burned out on the Sabbath be lit on the holiday? Rav and Rebbi Ḥanina both say it is forbidden, but Rebbi Joḥanan says, it is permitted. Rebbi Mana said before Rebbi Yudan, is it the reverse regarding an egg? He said to him, since the rabbis compare it, it means that the two cases are identical[176].

169 This paragraph also is in *Ševi'it* 9:1 (Notes 24-30,7) and *Beṣah* 1:1 (60a l. 62,ʾ). The latter text is the original. The introductory sentence, "because they disagreed" makes no sense here but is intelligible in the two parallel sources.

While the starting quote is from Mishnah 10, the entire discussion refers to Mishnah 9, a Sabbath preceded or followed by a holiday which is not New Year's Day.

170 If the holiday falls on a Sunday, since it is forbidden to light fire on the Sabbath, the unburned oil or wood that was burning at the onset of the Sabbath, but later burned out or was extinguished by the wind are no longer usable on the Sabbath, they become *muqseh*. The rule that (*Ex.* 16:5) *they have to prepare what they are going to use* is given for the Sabbath but is transferred to holidays. Then since oil or wood were not usable a minute before the start of the holiday they cannot become usable on the holiday. If the rule is not transferred, the fuel becomes permitted at the end of the Sabbath.

171 Mishnah *Beṣah* 1:1: "An egg laid on the holiday, the House of Shammai say, may be eaten; the House of Hillel say, it may not be eaten." According to the Yerushalmi, in the opinion of the House of Shammai the egg is prepared since the hen itself is potential food and an egg inside a slaughtered hen is permitted food. According to the House of Hillel, the egg becomes something new by being laid. The new egg was not in existence before the holiday.

172 At least for the House of Hillel. Tosephta *Yom Tov* 1:3: "An egg laid on the Sabbath may be eaten on the holiday. R. Jehudah said in the name of R. Eliezer, the dispute is the same."

173 According to the Babli 38b the Elders are Rabban Simeon ben Gamliel, R. Ismael ben R. Joḥanan ben Beroqa, R. Eleazar ben R. Simeon, and R. Yose ben R. Jehudah. In Tosephta 4:2 the statement is R. Meïr's.

174 "There" is *Eruvin*, "here" is *Beṣah*, about the leftover fuel. If the status regarding the *eruv* can change from day to day, it is difficult to see why using the fuel should be forbidden. The Babli notes that Rav Ḥisda asked his question only after Rav Huna's death.

175 It is difficult to know why the Yerushalmi has no answer to Rav Ḥisda's question. The Babli gives several tentative explanations of Rav's position. The one consistent with the Yerushalmi is that only weekdays can prepare for holidays but the Sabbath cannot prepare for a holiday. Since the reason for Rav's ruling in the case of fuel is not based on the number of sanctities involved, his decisions are consistent.

(21b line 71) רִבִּי אֶחָא אָמַר לָהּ מִן אוּלְפָּן. רִבִּי יוֹסֵי אָמַר לָהּ מִן דִּיעָה. בְּאַרְבָּעָה זְקֵנִים כְּרִבִּי אֱלִיעֶזֶר. אָמַר רִבִּי מָנָא קוֹמֵי רִבִּי יוֹסֵה. רִבִּי מֵאִיר וְרִבִּי יוּדָה אֵין הֲלָכָה כְּרִבִּי יוּדָה. בְּאַרְבָּעָה זְקֵנִים כְּרִבִּי אֱלִיעֶזֶר. מָה אֵין תַּמָּן. שֶׁלֹּא זָכָה עֵירוּבוֹ. לֹא הָיִיתִי אוֹמֵר שֶׁיַּעֲקוֹר אֶת רַגְלָיו מִבְּנֵי עִירוֹ. כָּאן. שֶׁזָּכָה לוֹ עֵירוּבוֹ. לֹא כָל־שֶׁכֵּן. עֵירֵב בַּכִּכָּר בָּרִאשׁוֹן מְעָרֵב בַּכִּכָּר בַּשֵּׁנִי. וּבִלְבַד בְּאוֹתוֹ הַכִּכָּר. עֵירֵב בְּרַגְלָיו בָּרִאשׁוֹן מְעָרֵב בְּרַגְלָיו בַּשֵּׁנִי. עֵירֵב בְּרַגְלָיו מְעָרֵב בַּכִּכָּר. בַּכִּכָּר לֹא יְעָרֵב בְּרַגְלָיו. הֵיךְ מַה דְּאַתְּ אָמַר תַּמָּן. בְּרַגְלָיו לֹא יְעָרֵב בַּכִּכָּר. וְדִכְוָתָהּ. (בְּרַגְלָיו) בַּכִּכָּר לֹא יְעָרֵב בְּרַגְלָיו. לְהָקֵל לֶעָנִי שֶׁאֵין לוֹ כִּכָּר. הֵיךְ מַה דְּאַתְּ אָמַר תַּמָּן. בְּרַגְלָיו לֹא יְעָרֵב בַּכִּכָּר. וְדִכְוָתָהּ. בַּכִּכָּר לֹא יְעָרֵב בְּרַגְלָיו. לְהָקֵל לֶעָשִׁיר שֶׁלֹּא יֵצֵא וִיעָרֵב בְּרַגְלָיו. הֵיךְ מַה דְּאַתְּ אָמַר תַּמָּן. בְּרַגְלָיו לֹא יְעָרֵב בַּכִּכָּר. וְדִכְוָתָהּ. בַּכִּכָּר לֹא יְעָרֵב (בַּכִּכָּר). רִבִּי אָבוּן בְּשֵׁם רַבָּנִין דְּתַמָּן. עָשׂוּ אוֹתוֹ כְּהוֹלֵךְ לְעִירוֹ.

1 מן G | - גיעה G | דעה בארבעה G | ארבעה 2 אליעזר G | ליעזר 3 אליעזר G | ליעזר 4 כאן G | כן עירב G | ערב בשיני G | בשני 5 הככר G | הככר עירב G | ערב בשיני G | בשני עירו G | ערב בככר G | בככר 6 בככר G | בככר וככותה G | ודכוותה בככר G | ברגליו the remainder is not legible

Rebbi Aha said it from study, Rebbi Yose said it from reflection[176]; the four Elders concur with Rebbi Eliezer[177]. Rebbi Mana said before Rebbi Yose: between Rebbi Meïr and Rebbi Jehudah, does practice not follow Rebbi Jehudah[178]? The four Elders concur with Rebbi Eliezer! Since there where his *eruv* did not enter in force did I not say that he removed his feet from the inhabitants of his town, here where his *eruv* did enter in force not so much more[179]?

If he made an *eruv* with a loaf on the first [day], he makes the *eruv* with a loaf on the second, but it must be the same loaf. If he made an *eruv* with his feet on the first [day], he makes the *eruv* with his feet on the second[180]. If he made an *eruv* with his feet, may he make an *eruv* with a loaf, with a loaf may he not make an *eruv* with his feet? Since you are saying there, with his feet he may not make an *eruv* with a loaf, then with (his feet) [with a loaf][181] may he not make the *eruv* with his feet[182]? To make it easy for the poor person who has no loaf. Since you are saying there, with his feet he may not make an *eruv* with a loaf, then with with a loaf may he not make the *eruv* with his feet? To make it easy for the rich person that he does not have to go and make the *eruv* with his feet[183]. Since you are saying there, with his feet he may not make an *eruv* with a loaf, then with a loaf may he not make the *eruv* with a loaf? Rebbi Abun in the name of the rabbis there, they made him as if going to his town[184].

176 For R. Aha it is a tradition which he learned from his teacher, for R. Yose it is a logical inference.

177 R. Eliezer holds that on two consecutive days, one a Sabbath and one a holiday, a person may make two different *eruvim*. The Elders hold that if the *eruv* is nonexistent at the start of the second day, the person is no longer bound by it and therefore moves in a different domain on the second day.

178 A generally recognized principle, Babli 46b, Yerushalmi *Terumot* 3:1 (Note 26).

179 The argument here and in the following refers to the disagreements between R. Meïr and R. Jehudah in Mishnaiot 4:10-11. In Mishnah 10 R. Meïr permits only a poor person to make an *eruv* without anything, just by being at the Sabbath boundary at the start of the Sabbath, as if he were a traveller arriving at that spot which becomes his Sabbath center. R. Jehudah permits the same for everybody. Mishnah 11 is about a person sent to make an *eruv* for an entire village when on the way he was persuaded by somebody not to complete his errand where R. Jehudah, whom practice follows, holds consistently with his opinion in Mishnah 10 that he can walk as if he made the *eruv* since near sundown he was on his way.

In case of Mishnah 4:11 the fact that he started going away lets him move his Sabbath domain without an *eruv*, in the case of the four elders where there was a valid *eruv* for the first day it is difficult to understand why the *eruv* should have disappeared for the second day unless one follows R. Eliezer whom practice is not supposed to follow.

180 Babli 39a in the name of Samuel. As the Babli explains, one may not start a new *eruv* on a Sabbath or holiday; therefore either one uses the loaf which had been used for the first day or one makes the *eruv* by walking following Mishnah 4:10.

181 The scribe wrote "his feet", the corrector wrongly corrected to "a loaf".

182 If one may not start a new *eruv* on a Sabbath or holiday; then maybe one may not go to validate the *eruv* for the second day since it will look as if one made it new for that day.

183 Using the loaf first and then walking there also looks as if the *eruv* for the second day were different from that for the first and should be forbidden.

184 Using the loaf twice will not look like making two *eruvim* but since the loaf was at its place at sundown the first day he only goes home to where his Sabbath or holiday center was at the beginning of the first day.

(21c line 7) וְאוֹמֵר. אִם יוֹם טוֹב הַיּוֹם. יְבַטְּלוּ דְבָרַי וְיִקְרָא שֵׁם לְמַעְשְׂרוֹתָיו וְאֵינוֹ אוֹכְלָן. וּבַשֵּׁינִי קוֹרֵא שֵׁם לְמַעְשְׂרוֹתָיו וְאוֹכְלָן. מְחִלְפָה שִׁיטָתֵיהּ דְּרַב. תַּמָּן אִיעֲבַד לָהּ קְדוּשָׁה אַחַת. וָכָא אִיעֲבַד לָהּ שְׁתֵּי קְדוּשּׁוֹת. תַּמָּן קְדוּשָׁה אַחַת אֲרוּכָה הִיא. בְּרַם הָכָא אַחַת קוֹדֶשׁ וְאַחַת חוֹל. מְחִלְפָה שִׁיטָתֵיהּ דְּרַבָּנָן. תַּמָּן עָבְדִין לָהּ שְׁתֵּי קְדוּשּׁוֹת. וָכָא אִינּוּן עָבְדִין לָהּ קְדוּשָׁה אַחַת. תַּמָּן יוֹם טוֹב אֵצֶל שַׁבָּת כְּחוֹל אֵצֶל שַׁבָּת. בְּרַם הָכָא שְׁנֵיהֶן שָׁוִין. מוֹדִין חֲכָמִים לְרַבִּי יוּדָה בִּשְׁנֵי יָמִים טוֹבִים שֶׁלְרֹאשׁ הַשָּׁנָה שֶׁהֵן מִתַּקֶּנֶת נְבִיאִים הָרִאשׁוֹנִים.

2 ובשיני | G ובשני   למעשרותיו | G למעשרותיה   איעבד | G או עבד   3 וכא | G וכה   איעבד | G הוא עביד

הכא G | הכה   4 שיטתיה G | שיטתון דרבנן G | דרבניי - G | איגון וכא G | וכה - G | איגון   5 טוב G
- הכא G | הכה שניניה שוין G | שניהם שוים מודין G | מודים   6 יודה { G | יהודה מתקנת G | מיתקנת
נביאים { G | נבאיי הראשונים G | הראשניי

"And he says if today is holiday my words should be void but he gives a name to his tithes but does not eat from it. On the second [day] he gives a name to his tithes and eats from it.[185]" Rav's[186] argument seems inverted. There he treats it as one sanctity but here he treats it as two sanctities. There it is one long sanctity but here one is holy, the other profane[187]. The rabbis' argument seems inverted. There they treat it as two sanctities, but here they make it one sanctity. There a holiday next to a Sabbath is like weekday next to Sabbath but here both are equal[188]. The Sages agree with Rebbi Jehudah about the two days of the New Year which are an institution of the early prophets[189].

185 Tosephta 4:3, attributed to R. Jehudah. This refers to Mishnah 11, about a person who on the New Year wants to eat *tevel* produce. He cannot eat it on the first day, but if on both days he designates the same produce as heave and tithe, one of the designations will have been made on a non-holiday (presuming that none of the two is a Sabbath) and the remainder may be consumed on the second day.

186 This must read "R. Jehudah's" even though G agrees with L in reading "Rav's".

187 If either Friday or Sunday is a holiday it was established that R. Jehudah disagrees with the four Elders and holds that both Sabbath and holiday together form one sanctity and an *eruv* is either valid for both or not valid at all. But the two days of the New Year he treats as different sanctities.

188 Since practice follows the four Elders who permit two different domains for Sabbath and holiday but consider the two days of the New year as one long day.

189 That the two days of the New Year be kept as holidays even in the Land of Israel and treated as one sanctity.

(21c line 15) רִבִּי כָּא רִבִּי חִיָּיה בְשֵׁם רִבִּי יוֹחָנָן. בְּנֵי אִמֵּי נֶחֱרוּ־בִי וגו'. מִי גָרַם לִי לִהְיוֹת נוֹטֵר אֶת הַכְּרָמִים. עַל שֵׁם כַּרְמִי שֶׁלִּי לֹא נָטָרְתִּי¹ מִי גָרַם לִי לִהְיוֹת מְשַׁמֶּרֶת שְׁנֵי יָמִים בְּסוּרְיָא. עַל שֶׁלֹּא שָׁמַרְתִּי יוֹם אֶחָד בָּאָרֶץ. סְבוּרָה הָיִיתִי שֶׁאֲנִי מְקַבֶּלֶת שָׂכָר עַל שְׁנַיִם. וְאֵינִי מְקַבֶּלֶת שָׂכָר אֶלָּא עַל אַחַת.   מִי גָרַם לִי לְהַפְרִישׁ שְׁתֵּי חַלּוֹת בְּסוּרְיָא². עַל שֶׁלֹּא הִפְרַשְׁתִּי חַלָּה אַחַת בָּאָרֶץ. סְבוּרָה הָיִיתִי שֶׁאֲנִי מְקַבֶּלֶת שָׂכָר עַל שְׁתַּיִם. וְאֵינִי מְקַבֶּלֶת שָׂכָר אֶלָּא עַל אַחַת. רִבִּי יוֹחָנָן קָרֵי עֲלֵיהוֹן. גַּם אֲנִי נָתַתִּי לָהֶם חוּקִּים לֹא טוֹבִים. רִבִּי אַבָהוּ אֲזַל לַאֲלֶכְּסַנְדְּרִיאָה וְאַטְעִינוּן לוּלָבִין בְּשׁוּבְתָא. שָׁמַע רִבִּי מִי מַר. מָן מִי יָכוֹל לְהוֹן רִבִּי אַבָהוּ בְּכָל־שַׁתָּא. רִבִּי יוֹסֵי מִישְׁלַח כְּתִיב לְהוֹן. אַף עַל פִּי שֶׁכָּתַבְנוּ לָכֶם סִדְרֵי מוֹעֲדוֹת. עַל תְּשַׁנּוּ מִנְהַג אֲבוֹתֵיכֶם נוֹחֵי נָֽפֶשׁ.

1 וגו' G שמוני נוטרה את הכרמים כרמי שלי לא נטרתי נטר G | נוטרה   2 בסוריא G | בשורייה   3 שלא |

G שלו | G שמרתי | G שימרתי הייתי | G היתי 4 להפריש | G להיות מפרשת בסוריא | G בשו[רויה] שלא |
G שלו 5 שאני | G שני שתים | G שתים | 6 גם | G וגם טובים | G טובים ומשפטים לא יחיו בהן אבהו |
G אבהוא לאלכסנדריאה | G לכסנדרייה לולבין | G .. לבון 7 בשובתא | G בשובתה מי | G אמי מי יכול
להון | G מייבלון אבהו | G אבהוא שתא | G שתה יוסי | G יוסה מישלח כתיב | G שלח וכתב 8 להון | G
לון סדרי | G שדרי

[190]Rebbi Abba, Rebbi Hiyya in the name of Rebbi Johanan[191]: *My mother's sons bore ill-will against me,* (etc.) [*they made me a guard of the vineyards; my vineyard I did not guard.*][192] What caused me to guard the vineyards? Because *my vineyard I did not guard.* What caused me to keep two days in Syria[193]? Because I did not keep one day in the Land. I was thinking that I would be rewarded for both, but I am rewarded only for one. What caused me to separate two *hallot* in Syria[194]? Because I did not separate one *hallah* in the Land. I was thinking that I would be rewarded for both, but I am rewarded only for one. Rebbi Johanan read for them, *but I gave them prescriptions which are not good* [*and laws by which they cannot live*][195]. Rebbi Abbahu went to Alexandria and made them carry *lulavim* on the Sabbath[196]. Rebbi Immi heard it and said, who (feeds them) [brings them][197] Rebbi Abbahu every year[198]? Rebbi Yose sent and wrote to them: even though we wrote you the order of holidays, do not change the usage of your departed ancestors[199].

190 *Midrash Cant. rabba* 1(43), *Pesiqta dRav Cahana Šim`u* (ed. Buber p. 118a).
191 *Cant.* 1:6.
192 Addition from G.
193 Those parts of the kingdom of David and Salomon which were not part of the Second Commonwealth; its status was intermediary between that of the Land and the diaspora but holidays were kept there for two days as in the diaspora; cf. *Peah* 7:6 Note 119.
194 Biblical law prescribes *hallah* only for produce of the Land (*Num.* 15:18-19). Rabbinic practice extends the obligation to the rest of the world but, since the soil outside the Land is intrinsically impure, any *hallah* outside the Land is impure and must be burned. In Syria, some dough has to be given to the Cohen to be consumed in imitation of the obligation in the Land; cf. *Hallah* 4:7.
195 *Ez.* 20:25. He considers the second day of a holiday in the diaspora as a kind of punishment.
196 In a year in which the first day of *Sukkot* was a Sabbath he told the Jews of Alexandria to keep only one day of the holiday since he knew the (as yet unpublished) rules of calendar computation. Since the obligation to take the "four kinds" essentially is restricted to the first day (*Lev.* 23:40) he permitted the ceremony on a Sabbath against the rule that in the diaspora the "four kinds" may not be taken on the

Sabbath. (Cf. *Sukkah* 3:13).

197 The text of G [in brackets] is preferable over that of L (in parentheses).

198 In the absence of a published calendar, the exact computation of the date of the holiday depends on the presence of a competent scholar, which is rare outside the Land.

199 The action of R. Abbahu is officially disapproved of with the publication of the calendar rules. While today anybody who knows how to add and subtract can compute the Jewish calendar and there is no longer any ambiguity in fixing the holidays, the calendar rules were published by the Academy of R. Yose (the talmudic sources do not mention any participation of the Patriarch) with the explicit stipulation that they may be used only if the second day of holidays be observed outside the Land (Babli *Besah* 4b). {Quoted by R. Hananel *ad* 40b, *Roqeah* §198, *Ma`ase Roqeah* §93, *Or zarua`* §140 (vol. 2 p. 211a in the edition Jerusalem 2010).}

(21c line 26) פיס'. רִבִּי דוֹסָא בֶּן אַרְכִּינַס אוֹמֵר. הָעוֹבֵר לִפְנֵי הַתֵּיבָה כול'. מִפְּנֵי שֶׁאָמַר. אִם הַיּוֹם אִם אֶמֶשׁ. אוֹ יָבֹא כַּיֵי דָּמַר רִבִּי יַעֲקֹב בֶּרִבִּי אָחָא בְּשֵׁם רִבִּי יָסָא. הָעוֹבֵר לִפְנֵי הַתֵּיבָה בְּיוֹם טוֹב שֶׁלְרֹאשׁ הַשָּׁנָה אֵינוֹ צָרִיךְ לְהַזְכִּיר רֹאשׁ חוֹדֶשׁ. אוּף הָכָא כֵן.

1 פיס'. ר' דוסא...כול' | - G | 2 אם | G ואם | G התיבה | G התבה 3 חודש | G חדש הכא | G הכה

Paragraph: "Rebbi Dosa ben Hyrkanos said, the reader[29]", etc. Because[200] he says "whether it be today or tomorrow." Or it comes following what Rebbi Jacob the son of Rebbi Aḥa said, the reader[29] on New Year's Day does not have to mention the New Moon[201]. Also here it is so.

200 The Sages might disagree with R. Dosa because one does not formulate prayers intimating that the day might not be holy and holiday prayers inappropriate.

201 In the *musaf* prayer of the holiday the fact that it is a Day of New Moon is mentioned only indirectly in the quote of *Num.* 10:10 (Babli 40b; *Ševu`ot* 1:5 Note 156).

מי שהוציאוהו פרק רביעי

(fol.21c) **משנה א**: מִי שֶׁהוֹצִיאוּהוּ גּוֹיִם אוֹ רוּחַ רָעָה אֵין לוֹ אֶלָּא אַרְבַּע אַמּוֹת. הֶחֱזִירוּהוּ כְּאִילּוּ לֹא יָצָא. הוֹלִיכוּהוּ לְעִיר אַחֶרֶת נְתָנוּהוּ בַדִּיר אוֹ בַסַּהַר רַבָּן גַּמְלִיאֵל וְרִבִּי אֶלְעָזָר בֶּן עֲזַרְיָה אוֹמֵר מְהַלֵּךְ אֶת כּוּלָּהּ. רִבִּי יְהוֹשֻׁעַ וְרִבִּי עֲקִיבָה אוֹמֵר אֵין לוֹ אֶלָּא אַרְבַּע אַמּוֹת. מַעֲשֶׂה שֶׁבָּאוּ מִפְרַנְדִּין וְהִפְלִיגָה סְפִינָתָם בַּיָּם רַבָּן גַּמְלִיאֵל וְרִבִּי אֶלְעָזָר בֶּן עֲזַרְיָה הִלְּכוּ אֶת כֻּלָּהּ. רִבִּי יְהוֹשֻׁעַ וְרִבִּי עֲקִיבָה לֹא זָזוּ מֵאַרְבַּע אַמּוֹת שֶׁרָצוּ לְהַחֲמִיר עַל עַצְמָן:

Mishnah 1: If somebody was taken out by Gentiles or an evil spirit[1] he only has four cubits. If they brought him back[2] it is as if he had not left. If they conducted him to another town or put him into a sheep-pen, or a sheep corral[3], Rabban Gamliel and Rebbi Eleazar ben Azariah say he may walk its entirety; Rebbi Joshua and Rebbi Aqiba say, he only has four cubits. It happened that they came from Brundisium[4] when the ship went out to sea; Rabban Gamliel and Rebbi Eleazar ben Azariah walked its entirety[5]; Rebbi Joshua and Rebbi Aqiba did not stir out of their four cubits, for they wanted to be strict with themselves.

משנה ב: פַּעַם אַחַת לֹא נִכְנְסוּ לַנָּמֵל עַד שֶׁחָשֵׁיכָה אָמְרוּ לוֹ לְרַבָּן גַּמְלִיאֵל מָה אָנוּ לֵירֵד אָמַר לָהֶן מוּתָּר שֶׁכְּבָר הָיִיתִי מִסְתַּכֵּל וְהָיִינוּ בְתוֹךְ הַתְּחוּם עַד שֶׁלֹּא חָשֵׁיכָה:

Mishnah 2: Once they only entered the port[6] after nightfall. They asked Rabban Gamliel, may we descend? He told them it is permitted since I already was observing and we were inside the Sabbath domain before nightfall.

משנה ג: מִי שֶׁיָּצָא בִרְשׁוּת אָמְרוּ לוֹ כְּבָר נַעֲשָׂה מַעֲשֶׂה יֵשׁ לוֹ אַלְפַּיִם אַמָּה לְכָל רוּחַ. אִם הָיָה בְתוֹךְ הַתְּחוּם כְּאִילּוּ לֹא יָצָא שֶׁכָּל־הַיּוֹצְאִין לְהַצִּיל חוֹזְרִין לִמְקוֹמָן:

Mishnah 3: If somebody left with permission[7] when they told him that the deed already had been done he has 2'000 cubits in each direction. If this reached him inside the Sabbath domain[8] it is as if he never left, for all those who leave to save may return to their place.

משנה ד: מִי שֶׁיָּשַׁב בַּדֶּרֶךְ וְעָמַד וַהֲרֵי הוּא סָמוּךְ לָעִיר הוֹאִיל וְלֹא הָיְתָה כַוָּנָתוֹ לְכָךְ לֹא יִכָּנֵס דִּבְרֵי רַבִּי מֵאִיר. רַבִּי יוּדָה אוֹמֵר יִכָּנֵס. אָמַר רַבִּי יְהוּדָה מַעֲשֶׂה וְנִכְנַס רַבִּי טַרְפוֹן בְּלֹא מִתְכַּוֵּן:

Mishnah 4: Somebody who sat down on the road[9]; when he gets up, behold, he is close to a town[10]: since it was not his intention he may not enter, the words of Rebbi Meïr[11]. Rebbi Jehudah says, he may enter. Rebbi Jehudah said, it happened that Rebbi Tarphon entered without intention[12].

משנה ה: מִי שֶׁיָּשַׁן בַּדֶּרֶךְ וְלֹא יָדַע עַד שֶׁחֲשֵׁכָה יֵשׁ לוֹ אַלְפַּיִם אַמָּה לְכָל־רוּחַ דִּבְרֵי רַבִּי יוֹחָנָן בֶּן נוּרִי. וַחֲכָמִים אוֹמְרִים אֵין לוֹ אֶלָּא אַרְבַּע אַמּוֹת. רַבִּי אֶלְעָזָר אוֹמֵר הוּא בָאֶמְצָעַן. רַבִּי יְהוּדָה אוֹמֵר לְאֵי זֶה רוּחַ שֶׁיִּרְצֶה. וּמוֹדֶה רַבִּי יְהוּדָה שֶׁאִם בֵּרַר לוֹ בְּיָרֵד שֶׁאֵינוֹ יָכוֹל לַחֲזוֹר בּוֹ:

Mishnah 5: If somebody slept on the road and did not realize that night fell he has 2'000 cubits in every direction, the words of Rebbi Joḥanan ben Nuri, but the Sages say, he only has four cubits[13]. Rebbi Eleazar says, he is in the center; Rebbi Jehudah says, in any direction which he chooses. Rebbi Jehudah agrees that if he selected one he cannot retract it.

משנה ו: הָיוּ שְׁנַיִם מִקְצָת אַמּוֹתָיו שֶׁל זֶה לְתוֹךְ אַמּוֹתָיו שֶׁל זֶה מְבִיאִין וְאוֹכְלִין בָּאֶמְצַע וּבִלְבַד שֶׁלֹּא יוֹצִיא זֶה מִתּוֹךְ שֶׁלּוֹ מִתּוֹךְ שֶׁל חֲבֵירוֹ. הָיוּ שְׁלֹשָׁה וְהָאֶמְצָעִי מוּבְלָע בֵּינְתַיִם הוּא מוּתָּר עִמָּהֶן וְהֵן מוּתָּרִין עִמּוֹ. וּשְׁנַיִם הַחִיצוֹנִים אֲסוּרִין זֶה עִם זֶה.

Mishnah 6: If they were two[14] and some of the cubits of one were inside the cubits of the other they bring and eat in the middle on condition that one not transfer into the other's [domain]. If they were three and the middle one absorbed between them, he is permitted with them and they with him but the two outside ones are forbidden one with the other.

משנה ז: אָמַר רַבִּי שִׁמְעוֹן לְמָה הַדָּבָר דּוֹמֶה לְשָׁלֹשׁ חֲצֵירוֹת פְּתוּחוֹת זוֹ לָזוֹ וּפְתוּחוֹת לִרְשׁוּת הָרַבִּים. עֵירְבוּ שְׁתֵּיהֶן עִם הָאֶמְצָעִית הִיא מוּתֶּרֶת עִמָּהֶן וְהֵן מוּתָּרוֹת עִמָּהּ וּשְׁתַּיִם הַחִיצוֹנוֹת אֲסוּרוֹת זוֹ עִם זוֹ:

Mishnah 7: Rebbi Simeon says, to what is this similar? To three courtyards open to one another and open to the public domain[15]. If both [outer ones] made an *eruv* with the middle one, that one is permitted with them and they with it but the two outside ones are forbidden one with the other.

משנה ח: מִי שֶׁבָּא בַדֶּרֶךְ וְהָיָה יָרֵא שֶׁמָּא תֶחֱשַׁךְ וְהָיָה מַכִּיר אִילָן אוֹ גָדֵר אוֹמֵר שְׁבִיתָתִי תַחְתָּיו לֹא אָמַר כְּלוּם. שְׁבִיתָתִי בְעִיקָּרוֹ מְהַלֵּךְ מִמְּקוֹם רַגְלָיו וְעַד עִיקָּרוֹ אַלְפַּיִם אַמָּה וּמֵעִיקָּרוֹ וְעַד בֵּיתוֹ אַלְפַּיִם אַמָּה. נִמְצָא מְהַלֵּךְ מִשֶּׁחֲשֵׁכָה אַרְבַּעַת אֲלָפִים אַמָּה:

Mishnah 8: If somebody was on the road and afraid lest it get dark[16] but he knew of a tree or a wall and says, "my Sabbath rest shall be under it," he did not say anything[17]. "My Sabbath rest in its roots", he walks from the place of his feet to the roots 2'000 cubits and from the roots to his house 2'000 cubits; it turns out that he may walk 4'000 cubits after nightfall.

משנה ט: אִם אֵינוֹ מַכִּיר אוֹ אֵינוֹ בָקִי בַהֲלָכָה וְאָמַר שְׁבִיתָתִי בִמְקוֹמִי זָכָה לוֹ מְקוֹמוֹ אַלְפַּיִם אַמָּה לְכָל־רוּחַ. עֲגוּלּוֹת דִּבְרֵי רַבִּי חֲנַנְיָה בֶּן אַנְטִיגְנוֹס. וַחֲכָמִים אוֹמְרִים מְרוּבָּעוֹת כְּטַבְלָא מְרוּבַּעַת כְּדֵי שֶׁיְּהֵא נִשְׂכָּר אֶת הַזָּוִיּוֹת:

Mishnah 9: If he does not know or is not conversant with practice and said, my Sabbath rest shall be at my place, his place empowers him 2'000 cubits in every direction, circular according to Rebbi Ḥanania ben Antigonos. But the Sages say square like a square table, that he gain the corners[18].

משנה י: זֶהוּ שֶׁאָמְרוּ הֶעָנִי מְעָרֵב בְּרַגְלָיו. רַבִּי מֵאִיר אוֹמֵר אֵין לָנוּ אֶלָּא עָנִי. רַבִּי יְהוּדָה אוֹמֵר אֶחָד עָנִי וְאֶחָד עָשִׁיר. שֶׁלֹּא אָמְרוּ מְעָרְבִין בַּפַּת אֶלָּא לְהָקֵל עַל הֶעָשִׁיר שֶׁלֹּא יֵצֵא וִיעָרֵב בְּרַגְלָיו:

Mishnah 10: That is what they said, the poor person makes an *eruv* with his feet. Rebbi Meïr says, we only have the poor. Rebbi Jehudah says, both poor and rich; they said that one makes an *eruv* with bread, only to make it easy for the rich that he does not have to go out and make the *eruv* with his feet[19].

משנה יא: מִי שֶׁיָּצָא לֵילֵךְ לְעִיר שֶׁמְּעָרְבִין בָּהּ וְהֶחֱזִירוֹ חֲבֵירוֹ הוּא מוּתָּר לֵילֵךְ וְכָל־בְּנֵי הָעִיר אֲסוּרִין דִּבְרֵי רַבִּי יְהוּדָה. רַבִּי מֵאִיר אוֹמֵר כָּל־שֶׁהוּא יָכוֹל לְעָרֵב וְלֹא עֵירַב הֲרֵי זֶה חַמָּר גַּמָּל:

Mishnah 11: If somebody started to go to another town for which one makes an *eruv* but another person intercepted him, he is permitted to go but the remainder of the town is forbidden, the words of Rebbi Jehudah. Rebbi Meïr says, anybody who could have made an *eruv* but did not make the *eruv* is a donkey driver-camel driver[19].

משנה יב: מִי שֶׁיָּצָא חוּץ לַתְּחוּם אֲפִילוּ אַמָּה אַחַת לֹא יִכָּנֵס. רַבִּי שִׁמְעוֹן אוֹמֵר רַבִּי אֶלְעָזָר אוֹמֵר שְׁתַּיִם יִכָּנֵס שָׁלֹשׁ לֹא יִכָּנֵס. מִי שֶׁהֶחְשִׁיךְ חוּץ לַתְּחוּם אֲפִילוּ אַמָּה אַחַת לֹא יִכָּנֵס. רַבִּי שִׁמְעוֹן אוֹמֵר אֲפִילוּ חָמֵשׁ עֶשְׂרֵה אַמָּה יִכָּנֵס שֶׁאֵין הַמְשׁוּחוֹת מְמַצִּין אֶת הַמִּדּוֹת מִפְּנֵי הַטּוֹעִים:

Mishnah 12: If somebody left the Sabbath domain for even one cubit he may not reenter. Rebbi Simeon says, Rebbi Eleazar says, for two he may reenter, three he may not re-enter. If somebody was outside the Sabbath domain at nightfall for even one cubit he may not enter. Rebbi Simeon says, even fifteen cubits he may enter since the rope-spanners do not exhaust the measure because of errors[20].

1 He was insane and therefore not responsible when he left. He regained his senses outside and now must follow the rules of the Sabbath.

2 The Gentiles who had removed him without his cooperation brought him back without his initiative.

3 Cf. Mishnah 2:3. These places are not human dwellings but they are fenced in, which makes them similar to private domains.

4 With most Mishnah mss. read פרנדיסין, Brundisium, the usual harbor of departure for a trip from Italy to Palestine. The ship left on the Sabbath.

5 While they left the Sabbath domain of Brindisi on the Sabbath, this was a consequence of the Gentile mariner's action. Since on dry land one permits in such a case to walk the entire town in which they happen to find themselves, they may walk on the ship as their town.

6 This is Babli spelling. With the Halakhah one should read למן, Greek λιμήν, ή. They arrived at the harbor Friday evening after nightfall. If they entered the Sabbath domain after nightfall, RR. Joshua and Aqiba would have to stay within their 4 cubits. For the problem of Rabban Gamliel and R. Eleazar ben Azariah see the Halakhah (Notes 57-59).

7 If a border town is attacked by marauders, it may ask the nearby towns for armed help.

8 If at the moment when the help is no longer needed the person was no more than 1'999 cubits from the border of the Sabbath domain of his home town, he may reach this domain and, since he left with permission, walks all the way to his house. If the built-up area was within 2'000 cubits the statement is unnecessary since any built-up area is counted as 4 cubits.

9 Friday evening at twilight; he did not realize that he was close to a village but decided to spend the Sabbath on the road.

10 Within the town's Sabbath domain.

11 He may not go more than 2'000 cubits from the place where he started the Sabbath. Since he did not intend to be like a town dweller for this Sabbath, for him the entire built-up area is not counted as 4 cubits.

12 Since he started the Sabbath with the Sabbath domain, he may walk the entire

domain allowed to the town dwellers.

13   Everybody agrees that if he slept in a town during nightfall, his Sabbath domain is that of the town. But if he is outside of town, R. Johanan ben Nuri holds that he automatically has a Sabbath domain of 2'000 cubits in every direction but the Sages hold that a Sabbath domain can be acquired only by conscious selection. If he slept at sundown, he made no selection and has no domain. In the interpretation of the Yerushalmi, R. Jehudah agrees with R. Johanan ben Nuri but specifies that he may choose the center of his Sabbath domain at will and, therefore, walk 4'000 cubits in one direction (which must be chosen at the start and cannot be changed.)

14   Two people staying on the road over the Sabbath and both sleeping during twilight.

15   The three courtyards are in one row, and each one has a separate exit to the road. If one of the courtyards had no direct exit to the road it would be an appendix of an other courtyard and forced to have an *eruv* with the latter. But in the case here the *eruvim* are voluntary. Since the Yerushalmi does not comment on this Mishnah it must assume that this is practice, against the Babli which states that the majority disagrees with R. Simeon.

16   Before he can reach the next town.

17   The place must be defined to within 4 cubits to be valid.

18   In the first opinion the Sabbath domain is a circular disk of radius 2'000 cubits. In the second, authoritative, opinion it is a square of side length 4'000 cubits oriented strictly NS-EW. From the center along the diagonals in fact one may walk $2'000 \sqrt{2} = 2828$ cubits. Most importantly, this definition also applies to Sabbath domains of towns which always are rectangular domains oriented strictly NS-EW.

19   Chapter 3, Notes 179-184.

20   This introduces the first topic of the next Chapter, the determination of the Sabbath boundaries of a town. Since the exact determination of a linear distance would require multiple measurements, the officials charged with marking the borders will intentionally err on the side of caution. In case of need one may assume that the official measurement is 0.75% short of the true value.

(21d line 11) מִי שֶׁהוֹצִיאוּהוּ גּוֹיִם כול'. וְל'כֵּן מָה נָן אֳמְרִין. וְיֵעָשֶׂה כְּמִי שֶׁיָּצָא בִּרְשׁוּת וִיהֵא לוֹ אַלְפַּיִם אַמָּה לְכָל־רוּחַ. לְפוּם כֵּן מֵימַר. אֵין לוֹ אֶלָּא אַרְבַּע אַמּוֹת. וּמִנַּיִין לְאַרְבַּע אַמּוֹת. שֶׁבּוּ אִישׁ תַּחְתָּיו. וּמִנַּיִין לְאַלְפַּיִם אַמָּה. אַל־יֵצֵא אִישׁ מִמְּקוֹמוֹ בַּיּוֹם הַשְּׁבִיעִי: אוֹ חִלַף. אָמַר רִבִּי אליעזר. וְתַנִּינָן. אסא בֶּן עֲקִיבָה אוֹמֵר מָקוֹם מָקוֹם. נֶאֱמַר כָּאן מָקוֹם. וְנֶאֱמַר לְהַלָּן וְשַׂמְתִּי לְךָ מָקוֹם. מַה מָּקוֹם שֶׁנֶּאֱמַר לְהַלָּן אַלְפַּיִם אַמָּה. אַף מָקוֹם שֶׁנֶּאֱמַר כָּאן אַלְפַּיִם אַמָּה. אַרְבַּע אַמּוֹת שֶׁאָמְרוּ מְלֹא קוֹמָתוֹ וּפִישּׁוּט יָדָיִם. רִבִּי יְהוּדָה אוֹמֵר. הוּא וְשָׁלֹשׁ אַמּוֹת. כְּדֵי שֶׁיְּהֵא נוֹטֵל חָבִית מֵרַאֲשׁוֹתָיו וְנוֹתֵן אֶל מַרְגְּלוֹתָחו. כְּשֶׁהוּא נִפְנֶה נִפְנֶה מִן הַצַּד. וּבְשֶׁהוּא מִתְפַּלֵּל מִתְפַּלֵּל לוֹכְסוֹן.

1 ולכן | G דלכן   נן | G אנן   2 כן | G כן צריך   3 לאלפיים | G לאלפיין   4 אליעזר | G לעזר   ותנינן | G

ותני כן 6 ופישוט ידיים G | ופשוט ידייןG end of

"If somebody was taken out by Gentiles," etc. Otherwise[21] what would we say? He should be considered like someone who left with permission[22] and he should have 2'000 cubits in every direction. Therefore [it is necessary][23] to say that "he only has four cubits." From where the four cubits? *Stay everybody at his spot*[24]. And from where 2'000 cubits? *A person should not leave his place on the Seventh Day*[24]. Or switching, as (we have stated) [it was stated so:][25] "Issy ben Aqiba says "place, place"[26]. It is said here *place*, and it is said there, *I shall give you a place*[27]. Since the *place* mentioned there includes 2'000 cubits, so the *place* mentioned here includes 2'000 cubits." [28]"The four cubits which they mentioned are his full length and outstretched arms[29]. Rebbi Jehudah says, he and three cubits[30], so he can take an amphora from above his head and put it below his feet." If he relieves himself, he relieves himself at the side; if he prays, he prays in the diagonal[32].

21 Translating G; the text of L makes little sense.
22 Since he did not leave intentionally or even accidentally. Either he was taken by force or he left when insane and not obligated to keep any commandment.
23 Added from G.
24 *Ex.* 16:29.
25 The correct text is that of G in brackets since the quote is a *baraita*, not a Mishnah as implied by the text of L (in parentheses). *Mekhilta dR. Ismael*, ed. Horovitz-Rabin p. 262 (*Yalqut Shim`ony Qonteros Aharon*, ed. Ginzberg p. 318, *Siddur Rash*i #461.)
26 An argument by "equal cut"; the meaning of a word does not change from one use in the Pentateuch to another.
27 *Ex.* 21:13. The reference is to the cities of refuge which as levitic cities included a domain extending 2'000 cubits outside the built-up area.
28 Tosephta 3:11, Babli 48a, Tanḥuma Buber *Bemidbar* #9 (p. 8, Note 74)
29 When he lies down with arms outstretched behind his head. These justifications point more to a (Greek) cubit of 63cm than one of 55cm; cf. the Introduction.
30 The text of the Tosephta seems to make more sense: "3 cubits for his body and in addition 4 cubits so he can take . . .". This reading is required since the bottom of an amphora is at least one cubit in diameter; if he is permitted to move it from above his head to below his feet he already has at least 5 cubits.
31 Greek λοξός,-ή, -όν "oblique". Since he has to stay there for the Sabbath, he may relieve himself at one end of his domain and, since one may not pray within 4 cubits of excrement, he can move for prayers 5.6 cubits to the other end of the diagonal of his quadratic domain. The Babli 41b strongly disagrees and lets him leave the domain of 4 cubits to relieve himself.

(21d line 20) רִבִּי יודָה בֶּן פָּזִי בָעֵי. אַרְבַּע אַמּוֹת שֶׁאָמְרוּ תְּחוּם הֵן אוֹ אֵינָן תְּחוּם. אִין תֵּימַר. תְּחוּם הֵן. אֵין נוֹתְנִין לוֹ אַרְבַּע אַמּוֹת מִשְּׁנֵי מְקוֹמוֹת. אִין תֵּימַר. אֵינָן תְּחוּם. נוֹתְנִין לוֹ אַרְבַּע אַמּוֹת מִשְּׁנֵי מְקוֹמוֹת. אָמַר רִבִּי זְעִירָא. מַתְנִיתָהּ אָמְרָה כֵן. אַרְבַּע אַמּוֹת שֶׁאָמְרוּ תְּחוּם הֵן. וְהָתַנִּינָן. וּבִלְבַד שֶׁלֹּא יוֹצִיא זֶה מִתּוֹךְ שֶׁלּוֹ מִתּוֹךְ שֶׁל חֲבֵירוֹ כוּל׳.

Rebbi Jehudah ben Pazi asked, the four cubits which they mentioned: are they a domain or are they not a domain[32]? If you say that they are a domain, one does not give him four cubits from two places. If you say that they are not a domain, one gives him four cubits from two places. Rebbi Ze'ira said, the Mishnah says that the four cubits which they mentioned are a domain, as we have stated[33], "on condition that one not export into the other's [domain]."

32 The meaning of this sentence is not clear; every explanation must be tentative. Since a person may not stay in two different domains on one Sabbath, and since the person started the Sabbath in his domain, it would be logical to infer that once he leaves this domain he is without a domain and if his 4 cubits intersect with an established Sabbath domain he may walk through the entire domain. But if his 4 feet constitute his new domain then intersection with any other domain is irrelevant for him.

33 Mishnah 6, referring to people keeping the Sabbath on the road, who never had another Sabbath domain, and for whom there should be no question.

(21d line 25) לֹא אָמַר אֶלָּא הֶחֱזִירוּהוּ. הָא אִם חָזַר הוּא. אָסוּר. אָמַר רִבִּי אָחָא. דְּרִבִּי נְחֶמְיָה הִיא. דְּתַנֵּי. פֵּירוֹת שֶׁיָּצְאוּ לִרְשׁוּת הָרַבִּים וְחָזְרוּ. שׁוֹגֵג יֵאָכֵלוּ. מֵזִיד לֹא יֵאָכֵלוּ. רִבִּי נְחֶמְיָה אוֹמֵר. בֵּין שׁוֹגֵג בֵּין מֵזִיד לֹא יֵאָכֵלוּ. עַד שֶׁיַּחֲזִירָן לִמְקוֹמָן שׁוֹגֵג. וַאֲתִיָא דְּרִבִּי נְחֶמְיָה כְּרִבִּי מֵאִיר. דְּתַנֵּי. הַמְעַשֵּׂר וְהַמְבַשֵּׁל בַּשַּׁבָּת. שׁוֹגֵג יֵאָכֵל. מֵזִיד לֹא יֵאָכֵל. דִּבְרֵי רִבִּי מֵאִיר.

It only said, "if they brought him back." Therefore, if he returned by himself, he is forbidden[34]. Rebbi Aha said, this is Rebbi Nehemiah's. As it was stated[35]: "Produce which came into the public domain and returned, if in error it may be eaten, if intentional it may not be eaten. Rebbi Nehemiah says, whether in error or intentional it may not be eaten unless it was returned in error." Rebbi Nehemiah parallels Rebbi Meïr, as it was stated[36]: "If somebody tithed or cooked on the Sabbath, if in error it may be eaten, if intentional it may not be eaten, the words of Rebbi Meïr."

34 The same inference drawn in the Babli, 41b.
35 In the Babli, 41b/42a, the statement is about produce which was taken outside the Sabbath domain. The text here should not be amended since it is quoted in its original

form in *Roqeah* #184. and is implied by the quote in Tosaphot 42a *s.v.* מכלל. Since the food was moved illegally from its domain it becomes rabbinically prohibited for use on the Sabbath. The prohibition cannot be biblical since the produce itself was not changed (Maimonides *Hilkhot Šabbat* 6:24); it has the character of a fine.

36   Cf. *Šabbat* 3, Note 39, *Terumot* 2:3 Note 70; Tosephta *Šabbat* 2:15, Babli *Ketubot* 34a.

(21d line 30) קָנָה לוֹ שְׁבִיתָה וּבָאוּ גוֹיִם וְהִקִּיפוּהָ מְחִיצָה. רִבִּי חוּנָה אָמַר. לֹא הוֹעִילָה לוֹ מְחִיצָה כְלוּם. אֶלָּה מְהַלֵּךְ בָּאַלְפַּיִים וּמְטַלְטֵל בָּאַרְבַּע. חִייָה בְּרֵיהּ דְּרַב אָמַר. מְהַלֵּךְ וּמְטַלְטֵל בָּאַלְפַּיִים. רִבִּי יַעֲקֹב בַּר אֲחָא רִבִּי אֲבוּנָא בְשֵׁם חִייָה בְּרֵיהּ דְּרַב. מְהַלֵּךְ בָּאַלְפַּיִים וּמְטַלְטֵל בְּאַרְבָּעַת אֲלָפִים אַמָּה עַל יְדֵי זְרִיקָה. הָווֹן בְּעָיִין מֵימַר. מַה פְּלִיגִין כְּרִבִּי יְהוֹשֻׁעַ וּכְרִבִּי עֲקִיבָה. בְּרַם כְּרַבָּן גַּמְלִיאֵל וּכְרִבִּי אֶלְעָזָר בֶּן עֲזַרְיָה לֹא פְלִיגִין. וַאֲפִילוּ כְרַבָּן גַּמְלִיאֵל וּכְרִבִּי אֶלְעָזָר בֶּן עֲזַרְיָה פְלִיגִין. קַל הוּא מִי שֶׁקָּנָה לוֹ שְׁבִיתָה מִמִּי שֶׁלֹּא קָנָה לוֹ שְׁבִיתָה.

נְתָנוֹ עַל פֶּתַח הַדִּיר. עַל דַּעְתֵּיהּ דְּרִבִּי יְהוֹשֻׁעַ וְרִבִּי עֲקִיבָה נוֹתְנִין לוֹ שְׁתֵּי אַמּוֹת מִבִּפְנִים וּשְׁתֵּי אַמּוֹת מִבַּחוּץ. עַל דַּעְתֵּיהּ דְּרַבָּן גַּמְלִיאֵל וְרִבִּי אֶלְעָזָר בֶּן עֲזַרְיָה אֵין נוֹתְנִין לוֹ שְׁתֵּי אַמּוֹת מִבִּפְנִים וּשְׁתֵּי אַמּוֹת מִבַּחוּץ. שֶׁאִם אוֹמֵר אַתְּ לִיתֵּן לוֹ שְׁתֵּי אַמּוֹת מִבִּפְנִים וּשְׁתֵּי אַמּוֹת מִבַּחוּץ אוֹף הוּא מְטַלְטֵל בְּכָל־הַדִּיר כּוּלוֹ. נְתָנוֹ בְּאֶמְצַע הַדִּיר. הָיָה הַדִּיר חֶצְיוֹ בְּתוֹךְ הַתְּחוּם וְחֶצְיוֹ חוּץ לַתְּחוּם. רִבִּי אֲחָא אָמַר מִן אוּלְפָּן. רִבִּי יוּדָה אָמַר לַהּ מִן דֵּעָה. מַחֲלֹקֶת רַב חוּנָה וְחִייָה בְּרֵיהּ דְּרַב

If he acquired a place of Sabbath rest[37] when Gentiles came and surrounded him with a barrier. Rebbi[38] Huna said, the barrier is of no use for him[39] but he may walk 2'000 [cubits] and carry within four. Hiyya the son of Rav said, he walks and carries within 2'000[40]. Rebbi Jacob bar Aha, Rebbi Abuna in the name of Hiyya the son of Rav: He walks within 2'000 and carries within 4'000 cubits by throwing[41]. They wanted to say, their disagreement is following Rebbi Joshua and Rebbi Aqiba; but following Rabban Gamliel and Rebbi Eleazar ben Azariah they do not disagree. Even following Rabban Gamliel and Rebbi Eleazar ben Azariah they disagree[42]; one who had acquired a place of Sabbath rest is in better shape than one who had not acquired a place of Sabbath rest[43].

If they deposited him at the door of the sheep-pen[44]. In the opinion of Rebbi Joshua and Rebbi Aqiba one gives him two cubits inside and two cubits outside. In the opinion of Rabban Gamliel and Rebbi Eleazar ben Azariah one does not allow two cubits inside and two cubits outside, for if you would say that one allows him two cubits inside and two cubits outside then he could carry in the entire sheep-pen[45]. If they deposited him in the middle of the sheep-pen and the sheep-pen was partially inside the Sabbath domain and partially outside the Sabbath domain. Rebbi Aḥa said it from study, Rebbi Jehudah said it from reflection[46]: This is the disagreement of Rav Huna and of Ḥiyya the son of Rav[47].

37 A person staying on the road during the Sabbath, outside of town. Babli 42a.
38 Read: "Rav".
39 He denies the validity of any barrier made on the Sabbath.
40 He accepts the validity of a barrier erected for the Sabbath that it permits carrying. If the barrier had been made before the Sabbath and for human dwelling, the area enclosed by the barrier would be the dwelling and the Sabbath domain would extend outside for 2'000 cubits in every direction. But since the barrier was erected on the Sabbath, the domain where he may carry is extended but not the one where he can go (Rashi, 42a).
41 As long as the object thrown comes to rest within the barrier no Sabbath violation occurred, the restriction to 2'000 cubits being rabbinic in nature.
42 This sentence is documented in the writings of Spanish/Provençal Medieval authors (Rashba ad 42b col. 261, Ritba p. 74c, Meïri p. 159a), but it was missing in the Yerushalmi text available to Ashkenazi authors who assert that Rav Huna and Ḥiyya bar Rav must follow R. Joshua and R. Aqiba (Tosaphot 42a s.v. נכרים, *Or zarua* part 2 §144, p. 215b, Rosh Chapter 4 #2).
43 There is less reason to be lenient with a person forcibly abducted from his domain than with one who stays in his domain, only that the circumstances changed without his action.
44 This now refers directly to Mishnah 1, about a person abducted by Gentiles on the Sabbath.
45 Once one agrees that he can enter the sheep-pen, according to Rabban Gamliel he has the entire enclosed area (at least if this area is no more than 5'000 cubits^2).
46 Even though it was stated (Note 43) that the cases cannot be compared, the basic arguments of Rav Huna and Ḥiyya ben Rav can be applied here. Since for Ḥiyya the person may carry into the Sabbath domain, it is as if the Gentiles returned him and it is as if he had not left. For Rav Huna he must stay where he is (Note 33).

(21d line 44) רִבִּי זְעִירָא רַב חוּנָה בְשֵׁם רַב. מַה שֶּׁרָצוּ רִבִּי יְהוֹשֻׁעַ וְרִבִּי עֲקִיבָה לְהַחֲמִיר עַל עַצְמָן. זֹאת אוֹמֶרֶת שֶׁהֲלָכָה כְרַבָּן גַּמְלִיאֵל וּכְרִבִּי אֶלְעָזָר בֶּן עֲזַרְיָה. רִבִּי בָּא בְשֵׁם רִבִּי חִייָה בַּר אַשִּׁי. אַף בְּדִיר וּבְסַהַר הֲלָכָה כְרַבָּן גַּמְלִיאֵל וּכְרִבִּי אֶלְעָזָר בֶּן עֲזַרְיָה. חֲנַנְיָה בֶּן אֲחִי רִבִּי יְהוֹשֻׁעַ אוֹמֵר. כָּל־הַיּוֹם הָיוּ דָנִין אֵילוּ כְנֶגֶד אֵילוּ עַד שֶׁבָּא אֲחִי אַבָּא וְהִכְרִיעַ בֵּינֵיהֶן. וְהִתְקִין שֶׁתְּהֵא הֲלָכָה כְרַבָּן גַּמְלִיאֵל וּכְרִבִּי אֶלְעָזָר בֶּן עֲזַרְיָה בִּסְפִינָה. וּכְרִבִּי יְהוֹשֻׁעַ וּכְרִבִּי עֲקִיבָה בְּדִיר וְסַהַר.

מַה בֵּין סַהַר וּמַה בֵּין סְפִינָה. חֲבֵרַיָּא אָמְרֵי. סְפִינָה מִפְּנֵי שֶׁמְּחִיצוֹתֶיהָ עוֹלוֹת עִמָּהּ. אָמַר רִבִּי זְעִירָא. מִכֵּיוָן שֶׁעוֹקְרִין אוֹתָהּ מֵאַרְבַּע אַמּוֹת אֵילּוּ וְנוֹתְנִין אוֹתָהּ בְּאַרְבַּע אַמּוֹת אֵילּוּ. מַה נָּפֵק מִבֵּינֵיהוֹן. אִם הָיְתָה אַכְסַדְרָה. עַל דַּעְתְּהוֹן דַּחֲבֵרַיָּא מוּתָּר. עַל דַּעְתֵּיהּ דְּרִבִּי זְעִירָא אָסוּר. אִם הָיָה הַיָּם גַּלְנוּ. עַל דַּעְתְּהוֹן דַּחֲבֵרַיָּא אָסוּר. עַל דַּעְתֵּיהּ דְּרִבִּי זְעִירָא מוּתָּר. אָמַר רִבִּי זְעִירָא. מַתְנִיתָא אָמְרָה כֵן. אַרְבַּע אַמּוֹת שֶׁאָמְרוּ אֵינָן תְּחוּם.

Rebbi Ze'ira, Rav Huna in the name of Rav: Since Rebbi Joshua and Rebbi Aqiba wanted to be strict with themselves, this implies that practice follows Rabban Gamliel and Rebbi Eleazar ben Azariah[47]. Rebbi Abba in the name of Rebbi Hiyya bar Ashi: also for a sheep-pen, or a sheep corral, practice follows Rabban Gamliel and Rebbi Eleazar ben Azariah[48]. Hananiah the son of Rebbi Joshua's brother says, the entire day they were arguing one with the other until my father's brother came, decided between then, and instituted that practice follow Rabban Gamliel and Rebbi Eleazar ben Azariah for a ship and Rebbi Joshua and Rebbi Aqiba for a sheep-pen, or a sheep corral[49]. What is the difference between a sheep corral and a ship? The colleagues say, for a ship because its walls are part of itself[50]; Rebbi Ze'ira said, because one removes it from these four cubits and puts it into those four cubits[51]. What difference results between them? If it was a covered walkway[52], according to the colleagues it is permitted, according to Rebbi Ze'ira it is forbidden[53]. If the sea was calm, according to the colleagues it is forbidden, according to Rebbi Ze'ira it is permitted[54]. Rebbi Ze'ira said, the Mishnah says that the four cubits which they mentioned are not a domain[55].

47 Since the Mishnah states that they only stayed within their 4 cubits as personal restriction but not because they insisted that this was practice to be followed.
48 Babli 42b in the name of Rav.
49 Babli 43a.
50 Since the deck of the ship is enclosed by its railing the passenger does not necessarily notice the ship's motion; for him nothing changes during the day.
51 Babli 42b. Since the ship is permanently in motion, if one would define the Sabbath domain by the place on the surface of the earth where the person was at nightfall, he could not move at all, not even 4 cubits, since every moment he is at another place.
52 Greek ἐξέδρα, ἡ. The *exedra* has no walls. In analogy one considers a ship without railing, perhaps a raft.
53 One has to switch the statements. Since there is no railing, the argument of the colleagues does not apply; the person is restricted to his 4 cubits. For R. Ze'ira the absence of a railing does not make any difference.

54 Greek γαληνός, -ή, -όν "calm" (adj.). Assuming the ship being a sailboat which does not move in the absence of wind, it is difficult to see why walking the entire deck should be forbidden by anybody. It seems unlikely that here also one should switch the statements: for the colleagues there is no reason to forbid; for R. Ze'ira there might be an argument that he expected to be elsewhere on the Sabbath and now he is not there.

55 Earlier R. Ze'ira is quoted as stating the opposite (Note 33). But there the statement was about Sabbath domains on the ground, here the reference is to Mishnah 1 and the topic is domains on a ship. This makes good sense; there is no need to emend the text by switching the statements of R. Ze'ira and the colleagues as proposed by S. Liebermann.

(21d line 58) פיס׳. פַּעַם אַחַת לֹא נִכְנְסוּ לַלִּמֵן כּוּל״. מְצוּדוֹת הָיוּ לוֹ לְרַבָּן גַּמְלִיאֵל שֶׁהָיָה מְשַׁעֵר בָּהּ עֵינָיו בַּמֵּישָׁר. וְלָמָּה לִי עַד שֶׁלֹּא חֲשֵׁיכָה. וְלֹא רַבָּן גַּמְלִיאֵל הִיא. תִּיפְתָּר שֶׁהָיָה בַלִּמֵן יוֹתֵר מִבֵּית סָאתַיִם. וְלֹא יְהִיו מְחִיצוֹת גְּבוֹהוֹת עֲשָׂרָה. וְלֹא יְהִיו פְּרָצוֹת יוֹתֵר מֵעֶשֶׂר. וְלֹא יְהֵא עוֹמֵד כְּנֶגֶד עוֹמֵד וּפָרוּץ כְּנֶגֶד פָּרוּץ.

Paragraph. "Once they only entered the port," etc. Rabban Gamliel had a telescope[56] where he could estimate with his eyes in the plane. And why before nightfall? Even after nightfall; is this not Rabban Gamliel's[57]? Explain it if the port was larger than two *bet se'ah*[58], or the walls were not ten [hand-breadths] high[59] but were not open wider than ten [cubits] nor what was standing was opposite what was standing and what was breached opposite the breached[60].

56 Instead of the text's מצודות "citadels; traps" reading with R. Hananel (*ad* Babli 43b), *Sefer Ha'itim* (p. 54, Note 72), *Raviah* §386 (p. 417 Note 14), *Or zarua* II §6(2) (p. 12a; Note 51 there is incorrect), and a similar expression in Chapter 5 (Note 120): מְצוֹפִית "an instrument to see far". In the Babli 43b שפופרת "a tube".

57 Since the harbor is enclosed it should not be different from a sheep-pen where Rabban Gamliel permits to walk the entire domain.

58 Then the enclosure does not define a domain for the Sabbath unless it was for human dwelling, which a harbor may not be.

59 The minimum height for an enclosure, Mishnah 1:8.

60 Cf. Chapter 1, Note 241.

(21d line 62) פיס׳. מִי שֶׁיָּצָא בִרְשׁוּת כּוּל״. דְּלָכֵן מַה אֲנָן אֲמָרִין. יַעֲשֶׂה כְּמִי שֶׁיָּצָא בְאוֹנֶס וְלֹא יִהְיֶה לוֹ אֶלָּא אַרְבַּע אַמּוֹת. לְפוּם כָּךְ צָרִךְ מֵימַר. יֵשׁ לוֹ אַלְפַּיִים אַמָּה לְכָל רוּחַ. אָמַר רַב חוּנָה. וְהֵן שֶׁיִּהְיוּ אַרְבַּע אַמּוֹת אוֹכְלוֹת מִטְחוֹם טְבֶרְיָא וּמִטְחוֹם מַגְדָּלָה. רִבִּי חוּנָה בְּשֵׁם רַב אַדָּא בַּר אֲחֲוָה רִבִּי לָא בְּשֵׁם רִבִּי שִׁמְעוֹן בֶּן לָקִישׁ. וַאֲפִילוּ יָצָא לְמַגְדָּלָה וְחָזַר כְּאִילוּ לֹא יָצָא. רִבִּי

יְהוֹשֻׁעַ דְּרוֹמָיָה בָעֵי. עַד כְּדוֹן בְּשֶׁיָּצָא שׁוֹגֵג. וַאֲפִילוּ יָצָא מֵזִיד. אָמַר רִבִּי פִּינְחָס. מַתְנִיתָה אֶמְרָה כֵן. שֶׁכָּל־הַיּוֹצְאִין לְהַצִּיל חוֹזְרִין לִמְקוֹמָן. חוֹזְרִין אֲפִילוּ בַזַּיִּן.

תַּנֵּי. גּוֹיִים שֶׁבָּאוּ לָעֲיָירוֹת הַסְּמוּכוֹת לַסְפָר לִיטּוֹל מֵהֶן אֲפִילוּ תֶּבֶן אֲפִילוּ עֵצִים. יוֹצְאִין עֲלֵיהֶן בְּזַיִּן וּמַחֲזִירִין אֶת הַזַּיִּן לִמְקוֹמָן. בָּאוּ לָעֲיָירוֹת הַמּוּבְלָעוֹת. אֵין יוֹצְאִין עֲלֵיהֶן בְּזַיִּן אֶלָּא אִם כֵּן בָּאוּ לְעִיסְקֵי נְפָשׁוֹת. בָּרִאשׁוֹנָה הָיוּ מוֹלִיכִין אֶת הַזַּיִּן לַבַּיִת שֶׁהוּא סָמוּךְ לַחוֹמָה. פַּעַם אַחַת בָּאוּ עֲלֵיהֶן הַשּׂוֹנְאִין. הָיוּ מַדְחִיקִין לִיטּוֹל אֶת הַזַּיִּן וְהָרְגוּ אֵילּוּ מֵאֵילּוּ יוֹתֵר מִמַּה שֶׁהָרְגוּ מֵהֶן הַשּׂוֹנְאִין. הִתְקִינוּ שֶׁיְּהֵא כָּל־אֶחָד וְאֶחָד נוֹטֵל בְּבֵיתוֹ.

Paragraph. "If somebody left with permission," etc. For otherwise what would we say? That he should be treated like somebody who left by compulsion and he should have only four cubits. Therefore it was necessary to say, "he has 2'000 cubits in each direction." Rav Huna says, only if four cubits each intersect with the domain of Tiberias and with the domain of Magdala[61]. Rebbi Huna in the name of Rav Ada bar Ahawa, Rebbi La in the name of Rebbi Simeon ben Laqish. Even if he went to Magdala and returned he is as if he had not left[62]. Rebbi Joshua the Southerner asked: So far if he left in error[63]. Even if he left intentionally? Rebbi Phineas said, the Mishnah says so: "for all those who leave to save may return to their place.[64]"

[65]It was stated: "Gentiles who attack villages near the border to rob, even straw or even wood, one goes out against them armed and brings the weapon back to its place. If they attack interior villages one goes out only if it is a matter of life[66]. In earlier times they stored the weapons in a house close to the wall. Once they were attacked by enemies; they were in a crush to get their weapons and they killed one another more than what the enemies killed. They instituted that everybody should take from his house."

61 The distance from the Sabbath border of Tiberias to that of Magdala was less than 2'000 cubits. Therefore if somebody from Tiberias was informed just inside the border of the Sabbath domain of Magdala that he was no longer needed, he might return 2'000 cubits in the direction of Tiberias and end up 4 cubits inside the Sabbath domain of that city. Then he would be as if he had never left; cf. Note 8; Babli 44b.

62 Being at Magdala with permission lets him go back 2'000 cubits outside its Sabbath domain towards Tiberias. Since then he is inside the Sabbath domain of Tiberias it is as if he never left, even if he was informed only inside the town of Magdala itself.

63 Mishnah 3 only refers to the case that he genuinely believed that his services were urgently needed.

64 The inclusion of "all" means that the

| motives of those coming to help cannot be investigated. | 65 Babli 45a, Tosephta 3:5-6. |
| | 66 If they come to kill or kidnap. |

(22a line 1) פיס׳. מִי שֶׁיָּשַׁן בַּדֶּרֶךְ כול׳. אָמְרוּ. וַהֲלֹא בֵית מִדְרָשׁוּ שֶׁלְרִבִּי טַרְפוֹן הָיָה בְתוֹךְ אַלְפַּיִם אַמָּה. אוֹ שֶׁמָּא הִקְנָה עַצְמוֹ לִבְנֵי עִירוֹ מִבְּעוֹד יוֹם. אַשְׁכַּח תַּנֵּי. בְּשַׁחֲרִית זָרְחָה הַחַמָּה. אָמְרוּ לוֹ. רִבִּי. הֲרֵי הָעִיר לְפָנֶיךָ. הִיכָּנֵס.

Paragraph. "If somebody slept on the road,"[67] etc. They said, was not Rebbi Tarphon's house of study within 2'000 cubits[68]? Or maybe he made himself part[69] of his town when it was still daytime? It was found stated: In the morning the sun shone. They told him, rabbi, here the town is before you, please enter[70].

67 It is not clear whether this is a misquote of Mishnah 4 (to which the discussion is referring) or a correct quote of Mishnah 5.	to acquire his Sabbath resting place at . . ."
68 Then the reference to R. Tarphon would not support R. Jehudah.	70 He really was on a trip, slept outside and realized where he was in the morning. R. Jehudah might read שֶׁיָּשַׁן also in Mishnah 4. The objections stated before are raised in the Babli 45a about this *baraita*.
69 הקנה is short for הִקְנָה שְׁבִיתָתוֹ "intended	

(22a line 4) פיס׳. מִי שֶׁיָּשַׁן בַּדֶּרֶךְ וְלֹא יָדַע עַד שֶׁחֲשֵׁיכָה כול׳. רִבִּי זְעִירָא בְשֵׁם רִבִּי חִסְדָּיי. טַעֲמֵיהּ דְּרִבִּי יוֹחָנָן בֶּן נוּרִי. מֵאַחַר שֶׁאִילּוּ הָיָה עֵר הָיָה קוֹנֶה שְׁבִיתָה. יָשֵׁן לֹא קוֹנֶה לוֹ שְׁבִיתָה. אֵין לוֹ אֶלָּא אַלְפַּיִם אַמָּה לְכָל־רוּחַ. רִבִּי יוּדָה אוֹמֵר. וַאֲפִילוּ עֵר וְלֹא קָנָה לוֹ שְׁבִיתָה. אֵין לוֹ אֶלָּא אַלְפַּיִם אַמָּה לְכָל־רוּחַ. אַתְיָא דְּרִבִּי יוּדָה כְּרִבִּי יוֹחָנָן בֶּן נוּרִי. (וְדִרוּבָא כְּדְרִבִּי יוֹחָנָן בֶּן נוּרִי.) דְּרִבִּי יוֹחָנָן בֶּן נוּרִי אָמַר. מֵאַחַר שֶׁאִילּוּ הָיָה עֵר הָיָה קוֹנֶה לוֹ שְׁבִיתָה. הָיָה עֵר וְלֹא קָנָה לוֹ שְׁבִיתָה אֵין לוֹ אֶלָּא אַלְפַּיִם אַמָּה לְכָל־רוּחַ.

Paragraph. "If somebody slept on the road and did not realize until after night fell," etc. Rebbi Ze'ira in the name of Rebbi Ḥasdai. The reason of Rebbi Joḥanan ben Nuri: Since if he had been awake he would have acquired a Sabbath domain, when he was sleeping he did not acquire a Sabbath domain; he only has 2'000 cubits in every direction. Rebbi Jehudah says, even awake and he did not acquire a Sabbath domain; he only has 2'000 cubits in every direction[71]. Rebbi Jehudah's statement follows Rebbi Joḥanan ben Nuri's (and exceeds Rebbi Joḥanan ben Nuri's)[72]. For Rebbi Joḥanan ben Nuri said, since if he had been awake he would have acquired a Sabbath domain, if he was awake and did not acquire a Sabbath domain; he only has 2'000 cubits in every direction[73].

71 As explained in Mishnah 9, a Sabbath domain is a rectangular domain (for a single person a square) oriented exactly NS-EW. In a village or town, the geography of the place automatically defines the domain as explained in Mishnah 5:1. For a single person the domain can be determined only by a conscious choice. In the absence of such a choice the Sabbath region is a circle, for the Sages of diameter 8 cubits, for RR. Johanan ben Nuri and Jehudah (possibly also R. Eliezer) 2'000 cubits. For RR. Johanan ben Nuri and Eliezer the place of the person at sundown automatically is the center of the circle, for R. Jehudah the person may choose any point accessible to him when he awakes as center of his circle.

72 The text in parentheses was written by the scribe of L but (wrongly) deleted by the corrector who it seems understood רובא as name of a person whom he could not identify. Note by S. Liebermann.

73 The text is elliptic; missing is a statement that for R. Jehudah the person may choose to have his Sabbath circle so that he is at the border, not at the center, and therefore has 4'000 cubits in one direction, 0 cubits in the directions perpendicular and opposite to the chosen one.

(22a line 11) רִבִּי חוּנָה אָמַר. רַב נַחְמָן בַּר יַעֲקֹב בְּעָא. גֵּר שֶׁטָּבַל לְאַחַר שֶׁהֵאִיר הַמִּזְרָח. מֵאַחַר שֶׁאִילּוּ הָיָה עֵר הָיָה קוֹנֶה לוֹ שְׁבִיתָה. מָה אָמַר כָּא רִבִּי יוֹחָנָן בֶּן נוּרִי. נִישְׁמְעִינָהּ מִן הָדָא. דָּמַר רִבִּי יִצְחָק בַּר נַחְמָן בְּשֵׁם רִבִּי יְהוֹשֻׁעַ בֶּן לֵוִי. הֲלָכָה כְרִבִּי יוֹחָנָן בֶּן נוּרִי. בֵּירַר לוֹ מִבְּעוֹד יוֹם חוֹזֵר בּוֹ מִבְּעוֹד יוֹם. מִשֶּׁחֲשֵׁיכָה חוֹזֵר בּוֹ מִשֶּׁחֲשֵׁיכָה. בֵּרַר לוֹ מִבְּעוֹד יוֹם וְקָדַשׁ עָלָיו הַיּוֹם. נִישְׁמְעִינָהּ מִן הָדָא. לֹא יִכָּנֵס. דִּבְרֵי רִבִּי מֵאִיר. רִבִּי יוּדָה אוֹמֵר. יִכָּנֵס. לֹא עַל הָדָא אֲמָרַת אֶלָּא עַל רֵישֵׁיהּ דְּפִירְקָא. מִי שֶׁהוֹצִיאוּהוּ גוֹיִם אוֹ רוּחַ רָעָה. אִיתְאֲמָרַת עֲלֵיהּ. אָמַר רִבִּי בּוּן. מוֹדֶה רִבִּי יוּדָה שֶׁאִם בֵּרַר לוֹ שֶׁאֵינוֹ יָכוֹל לַחֲזוֹר בּוֹ:

Rebbi Huna said, Rav Nahman bar Jacob asked: if a proselyte immersed himself after sunrise. "Since if he had been awake he would have acquired a Sabbath domain," what does Rebbi Johanan ben Nuri say in this case? Let us hear from the following.[74] For Rebbi Isaac bar Nahman[75] said in the name of Rebbi Joshua ben Levi, practice follows Rebbi Johanan ben Nuri.

If he selected while it still was daytime, he may change his mind while it still is daytime; after nightfall he may change his mind after nightfall[76]. If he selected while it still was daytime, and the day became holy for him[77]? Let us hear from the following: "he may not enter, the words of Rebbi Meïr[11]; Rebbi Jehudah says, he may enter[78]" Not on this was it said, but on the start of the

Chapter; on "if somebody was taken out by Gentiles or an evil spirit," it was said . Rebbi Abun said, "Rebbi Jehudah agrees that if he selected one he cannot retract it.[79]"

74 Obviously there is a lacuna here, it is not said how to decide the question. A proselyte becomes Jewish by immersion in a *miqweh* for the purpose of conversion (for a male, after circumcision), attested to by a competent court. The latter condition excludes conversion on a Sabbath, a fact which Rav Nahman bar Jacob, chief judge of the Exilarch's court in Babylonia, must have known. The problem here is not about a proselyte but a general question about the Sabbath domain for a person who on Friday evening was unable or unqualified to choose a Sabbath domain; for example an insane person who became lucid overnight. Since R. Johanan ben Nuri restricts his argument to persons who on Friday evening were able to exercise judgment, it is unknown what his opinion would have been in this case.

75 Read: R. Nahman bar Isaac; Chapter 1, Note 62.

76 This question is possible only for R. Jehudah who permits the person to choose his Sabbath area on the Sabbath as long as it is a circle of radius 2'000 and contains the point at which he stands. For all others the area is uniquely determined at nightfall.

77 Cf. similar questions *Šabbat* 3, Note 55, Chapter 4, Note 70.

78 Since he went to sleep outside of town and R. Jehudah allows him to change his mind in the morning and to enter town, how can the Mishnah state that R. Jehudah agrees that if he chose once he cannot change his mind?

79 The question raised in the preceding Note is answered; R. Jehudah agrees that the person forcibly removed from his Sabbath domain has only one possibility of choice once he regains his freedom of choice. (R. Hananel *ad* 48a, *Sefer Ha'ittim* p. 68 Note 152.)

(22a line 20) פיס'. הָיוּ שְׁנַיִם. מִקְצָת אַמּוֹתָיו שֶׁלָּזֶה כול'. אַף עַל גַּב דְּרִבִּי חֲנַנְיָה בֶּן אַנְטִיגְנָס פְּלִיג עַל רַבָּנִין בָּאַמּוֹת. מוֹדֶה הוּא הָכָא בְּעִיבּוּרֵי עֲיָירוֹת.

הָיָה אֶחָד מַכִּיר אֶחָד שְׁאֵינוֹ מַכִּיר. זֶה שֶׁהוּא מַכִּיר מְהַלֵּךְ עִם זֶה שְׁאֵינוֹ מַכִּיר. וְזֶה שְׁאֵינוֹ מַכִּיר מְהַלֵּךְ עִם זֶה שֶׁהוּא מַכִּיר.

Paragraph. "If they were two, and some of the cubits of one," etc. Even though Rebbi Hananiah ben Antigonos disagrees with the rabbis about the cubits he agrees with them here about the environs of towns[80].

If one recognized and one did not recognize; the one who recognized may go with the one who did not recognize and the one who did not recognize may go with the one who recognized[81].

80 While the quote is from Mishnah 6, the reference is to Mishnah 9 but its original place must have been in the discussion of Mishnah 5:1, which is referred to as "here". Only for a single person does R. Hanina ben Antigonos define a Sabbath domain as circular; for villages and towns he agrees that it is rectangular.

81 This refers to Mishnah 8, where a traveller who remembers a landmark between his situation at sundown and the next village may declare this landmark as his Sabbath center. A stranger who walks with him may adopt the other's Sabbath center without knowing the geography. Babli 50b.

(22a line 24) פיס'. אָמַר רִבִּי שִׁמְעוֹן לְמָה הַדָּבָר דּוֹמֶה כול'. מִי שֶׁבָּא בַדֶּרֶךְ וְהָיָה יָרֵא שֶׁמָּא תֶחֱשַׁךְ כול'. אִם אֵינוֹ מַכִּיר אוֹ אֵינוֹ בַהֲלָכָה כול'. זוֹ הִיא שֶׁאָמְרוּ. הֶעָנִי מְעָרֵב בְּרַגְלָיו כול'. רִבִּי מֵאִיר סָבַר. עִיקַּר עֵירוּב בַּכִּכָּר. וְלָמָּה אָמְרוּ. בְּרַגְלָיו. לְהָקֵל עַל הֶעָנִי שֶׁאֵין לוֹ כִכָּר. וְרִבִּי יוּדָא אָמַר. עִיקַּר עֵירוּב בְּרַגְלָיו. וְלָמָּה אָמְרוּ. בַּכִּכָּר. לְהָקֵל עַל הֶעָשִׁיר שֶׁלֹּא יֵצֵא בְרַגְלָיו.

אַף עַל גַּב דְּרִבִּי יוּדָה אָמַר. עִיקַּר עֵירוּב בְּרַגְלָיו. וּבִלְבַד שֶׁלֹּא יֵשֵׁב לוֹ בְתוֹךְ בֵּיתוֹ וְיֹאמַר. תִּקָּנֶה לִי שְׁבִיתָתָה בְּמָקוֹם פְּלוֹנִי. אֶלָּא יֵצֵא לוֹ חוּץ (לְשָׂדֶה) [לַתְּחוּם] וְיֹאמַר. תִּקָּנֶה לִי שְׁבִיתָה בְּמָקוֹם הַזֶּה. וּמַמְתִּין שָׁם עַד חֲשֵׁיכָה. וְחוֹזֵר וּבָא לְעֵירוֹ. וְתַנֵּי כֵן. מַעֲשֶׂה בְּמִשְׁפַּחַת בֵּית מַמָּה וּמִשְׁפַּחַת בֵּית גּוּרְיוֹן מֵרוּמָה. שֶׁהָיוּ מְחַלְּקִין גְּרוֹגָרוֹת לַעֲנִיִּים בִּשְׁנֵי בַצּוֹרֶת. וְהָיוּ עֲנִיֵּי שִׁיחִין יוֹצְאִין וּמְעָרְבִין בְּרַגְלֵיהֶן. וּמַמְתִּינִים שָׁם עַד שֶׁתֶּחְשַׁךְ. וּלְמָחָר הָיוּ נִכְנָסִין וְאוֹכְלִין שָׁם וְחוֹזְרִין. וְכָל־מַה שֶׁהֵן עוֹשִׂין עַל פִּי חֲכָמִים הָיוּ עוֹשִׂין.

Paragraph. "Rebbi Simeon says, to what is this similar," etc. "If somebody was on the road and is afraid lest it get dark," etc. "If he does not know or is not conversant with practice," etc. "That is what they said, the poor person makes an *eruv* with his feet," etc.[82] Rebbi Meïr is of the opinion, the main point of an *eruv* is by a loaf[83]. Why did they say, by his feet? To make it easy for the poor who has no loaf. And Rebbi Jehudah said, the main point of an *eruv* is by his feet. Why did they say, by a loaf? To make it easy for the rich person that he does not have to go out by his feet[84].

Even though Rebbi Jehudah said, the main point of an *eruv* is by his feet, only that he should not sit in his house and say, my Sabbath rest should be acquired at place x. But he should go out to (the field) [the Sabbath boundary][85] and say, my Sabbath rest should be acquired at this place, and wait there until it gets dark; then return to his village. And it was stated thus[86]: "It happened that the family of Bet Mamma[87] and the family of Bet Gorion in Ruma were distributing dried figs in years of draught, that the poor of Shihin were going out, make *eruv* with their feet, waiting there until nightfall. The next day they were going there, ate there, and returned. And all their actions they were doing on the advice of the Sages."

82 The discussion is only about Mishnah 10.
83 *Eruv tehumim* can be made by depositing a meal at the Sabbath border, and this means bread with additions, or by staying at the place like a traveller.
84 But he may send his *eruv* by any member of his household. Babli 52a.
85 The text in parentheses is the scribe's, confirmed by Raviah (p. 457 Note 23); the text in brackets is the corrector's; it seems induced by the statement "my Sabbath rest should be acquired at *this place*", which in Raviah (*l. c.*, Note 24) reads ""my Sabbath rest should be acquired at *place x*", which means that R. Jehudah does *not* require the person to be at the Sabbath boundary but only to leave his house and go in the direction of his destination for the next day, when the rules of a traveller apply to him and he can determine his Sabbath center from a distance.
86 Babli 51b, Tosephta 3:17.
87 In the Babylonian sources "Mamal"; Raviah: "Dima."

(22a line 36) פִּיס׳. מִי שֶׁיָּצָא לֵילֵךְ לָעִיר. פָּתַר לָהּ תְּרֵין פִּתָרִין. אָמַר. אֲנִי מְעָרֵב עָלֶיךָ וְעַל בְּנֵי קַרְתָּךְ. וְעֵירֵב עַל בְּנֵי קַרְתֵּיהּ וְלֹא עִירֵב עָלוִי. הוּא אָסוּר לֵילֵךְ בְּאוֹתָהּ הָרוּחַ וּמוּתָּר בִּשְׁאָר כָּל־הָרוּחוֹת שֶׁבְּעִירוֹ. וְהֵן מוּתָּרִין בְּאוֹתָהּ הָרוּחַ וַאֲסוּרִין בִּשְׁאָר כָּל־הָרוּחוֹת שֶׁבְּעִירָן. פָּתַר לָהּ פִּתָר חוֹרָן. אָמַר. אֲנָא מְעָרֵב עָלֶיךָ וְעַל בְּנֵי קַרְתָּךְ. וְלֹא עִירֵב לֹא עָלוִי וְלֹא עַל בְּנֵי קַרְתֵּיהּ. הוּא מוּתָּר לֵילֵךְ בְּאוֹתָהּ הָרוּחַ. שֶׁכְּבָר קָנוּ לוֹ רַגְלָיו מֵאֶתְמוֹל. וְהֵן אֲסוּרִין לֵילֵךְ בְּאוֹתָהּ הָרוּחַ וּמוּתָּרִין בִּשְׁאָר כָּל־הָרוּחוֹת שֶׁבְּעִירוֹ.

Paragraph. "If somebody started to go to another town." One may give this two interpretations. If he said, I shall make an *eruv* for you and your townspeople, and made the *eruv* for his townspeople but not for him. He is forbidden to go in that direction[88] but permitted all other directions in his town; they are permitted to go in that direction but forbidden all other directions in their town[89].

One may give it another interpretation. If he said, I shall make an *eruv* for you and your townspeople and made the *eruv* neither for his townspeople nor for him. He is permitted to go in that direction for his feet already acquired for him the day before[90]; they are forbidden to go in that direction but permitted all other directions in his town.

88 More than 2'000 cubits.
89 Since the entire town is treated as if it were 4 cubits, they are forbidden all directions outside a circle of radius 2'000 centered at the place of the *eruv*. Making an *eruv tehumim* automatically shrinks the permitted space from a square of edge length 4'000 to a circle of diameter 4'000.
90 Following the rules of Mishnah 8.

(22a line 43) פיס׳. מִי שֶׁיָּצָא חוּץ לַתְּחוּם כול׳. רִבִּי אָחָא בְּשֵׁם רִבִּי חִינְנָא וְרַב חִסְדָּיי תְּרֵיהוֹן אָמְרִין. לֹא מַר אֶלָּא שְׁתַּיִם. הָא שְׁתַּיִם וְכָל־שֶׁהוּא יִכָּנֵס. דְּהוּא דְרִבִּי לְעָזָר. דְּרִבִּי לְעָזָר אָמַר. שְׁתַּיִם יִכָּנֵס. שָׁלֹשׁ לֹא יִכָּנֵס. אָמַר לוֹ רִבִּי יוֹסֵה. אָמְרִין דְּבַתְרֵהּ. שָׁלֹשׁ לֹא יִכָּנֵס. הָא שָׁלֹשׁ פָּחוּת כָּל־שֶׁהוּא יִכָּנֵס. הֲוֹון בָּעֲיי מֵימַר. מַה דָּמַר רִבִּי לְעָזָר בְּיוֹצֵא. הָא בְּמַחְשִׁיךְ לֹא. אַשְׁכַּח תַּנֵּי. הִיא אָדָא הִיא אָדָא. הֲוֹון בָּעֲיי מֵימַר. מַה דָּמַר רִבִּי שִׁמְעוֹן בְּמַחְשִׁיךְ. הָא בְּיוֹצֵא לֹא. אַשְׁכַּח תַּנֵּי. הִיא אָדָא הִיא אָדָא.

Paragraph. "If somebody left the Sabbath domain," etc. Rebbi Aḥa in the name of Rebbi Ḥinena and Rav Ḥasdai both are saying, he said only "two". Therefore could he enter with two and a little bit? Since this is Rebbi Eleazar's, as Rebbi Eleazar said, "for two he may re-enter, three he may not re-enter." Rebbi Yose told him, one says at the end, "three he may not re-enter," therefore three minus a little bit he may re-enter[91]. They wanted to say, what Rebbi Eleazar said is about one who left, therefore not about one who stayed overnight[92]. It was found stated, one is like the other. They wanted to say, what Rebbi Simeon said is about one who stayed overnight, therefore not about one who left. It was found stated, one is like the other.

91 The statement of R. Eleazar in Mishnah 12 does not permit to decide what happens if a person left the Sabbath domain for more than two but less than three cubits.
92 Since R. Eleazar speaks only about a person who left his Sabbath domain, not a traveller whose 2'000 (or 4'000) cubits end just two cubits short of the Sabbath domain of the next town. Since practice follows the Sages, these problems do not have to be resolved.

כיצד מעברין פרק חמישי

(fol.22a) **משנה א**: כֵּיצַד מְעַבְּרִין אֶת הֶעָרִים בַּיִת נִכְנָס בַּיִת יוֹצֵא פָּגוּם נִכְנָס פָּגוּם יוֹצֵא. הָיוּ שָׁם גְּדוּדִיּוֹת גְּבוֹהִין עֲשָׂרָה טְפָחִים וְכֵן גְּשָׁרִים וּנְפָשׁוֹת שֶׁיֵּשׁ בָּהֶן בֵּית דִּירָה מוֹצִיאִין אֶת הַמִּדָּה כְּנֶגְדָּהּ וְעוֹשִׂין אוֹתָהּ כְּמִין טַבְלָא מְרוּבַּעַת כְּדֵי שֶׁיְּהֵא נִשְׂכָּר אֶת הַזָּוִיּוֹת:

Mishnah 1: How does one complete towns? A house is recessed, a house is protruding, a superstructure[1] is recessed, a superstructure is protruding[2]. If there were walls of ruins ten hand-breadths high or bridges or mausoleums containing dwellings[3] they extend the measure correspondingly and one makes it like a rectangular table, in order to include the corners[4].

משנה ב: נוֹתְנִין קַרְפֵּף לָעִיר דִּבְרֵי רַבִּי מֵאִיר וַחֲכָמִים אוֹמְרִים לֹא אָמְרוּ בַקַּרְפֵּף אֶלָּא בְּבֵין שְׁתֵּי עֲיָירוֹת אִם יֵשׁ לָזוֹ שִׁבְעִים אַמָּה וְשִׁירַיִים וְלָזוֹ שִׁבְעִים אַמָּה וְשִׁירַיִים עוֹשֶׂה קַרְפּוּף לִשְׁתֵּיהֶן לִהְיוֹת כְּאַחַת. וְכֵן שְׁלֹשָׁה כְפָרִים הַמְשׁוּלָּשִׁים אִם יֵשׁ בֵּין שְׁנֵיהֶן הַחִיצוֹנִים מֵאָה וְאַרְבָּעִים וְאַחַת וּשְׁלִישׁ עָשָׂה הָאֶמְצָעִי אֶת שְׁלָשְׁתָּן לִהְיוֹת אֶחָד:

Mishnah 2: One gives a fore-court to the city[5], the words of Rebbi Meïr; but the Sages say that a fore-court was mentioned only between two villages, if each of them has seventy cubits and a remainder, the fore-courts of both make it one. Similarly three villages forming a triangle, if between the two outer ones there are 141⅓ [cubits], the middle one makes all three to be one[6].

משנה ג: אֵין מוֹדְדִין אֶלָּא בְחֶבֶל שֶׁל חֲמִשִּׁים אַמָּה לֹא פָחוֹת וְלֹא יָתֵר. וְלֹא יִמּוֹד אֶלָּא כְנֶגֶד לִבּוֹ. הָיָה מוֹדֵד הִגִּיעַ לְגַיְא אוֹ לְגָדֵר מַבְלִיעוֹ וְחוֹזֵר לְמִדָּתוֹ וּבִלְבַד שֶׁלֹּא יוֹצִיא חוּץ לַתְּחוּם. אִם אֵינוֹ יָכוֹל לְהַבְלִיעוֹ. בָּזוֹ אָמַר רַבִּי דּוֹסְתַּאי בֵּי רַבִּי יַנַּאי מִשּׁוּם רַבִּי מֵאִיר שָׁמַעְתִּי שֶׁמְּקַדְּרִין בֶּהָרִים:

Mishnah 3: One only measures with a rope of 50 cubits, neither less nor more. One should only measure holding up to his heart[7]. If he was measuring and came to a valley or a wall he circumvents it and returns to his measurement, on condition that he not exit the Sabbath domain[8]. If he cannot circumvent it, about this said Rebbi Dositheos ben Yannai in the name of Rebbi Meïr: I heard that one strip-measures[9] in the mountains[10].

משנה ד: אֵין מוֹדְדִין אֶלָּא מִן הַמּוּמְחֶה. רִבָּה לְמָקוֹם אֶחָד וּמִיעֵט לְמָקוֹם אַחֵר שׁוֹמְעִים לַמַּרְבֶּה. אֲפִלּוּ עֶבֶד אֲפִלּוּ שִׁפְחָה נֶאֱמָנִין לוֹמַר עַד כָּאן תְּחוּם שַׁבָּת שֶׁלֹּא אָמְרוּ חֲכָמִים בַּדָּבָר לְהַחְמִיר אֶלָּא לְהָקֵל:

Mishnah 4: Surveys may only be made by professionals. If one extended the place and restricted it at another, one listens to him who extends[11]. Even a slave or a slave woman are trustworthy to say up to here is the Sabbath domain since the Sages said in these matters not to restrict but to be lenient[12].

משנה ה: עִיר שֶׁל יָחִיד שֶׁנַּעֲשֵׂית שֶׁל רַבִּים מְעָרְבִים אֶת כּוּלָּהּ וְשֶׁל רַבִּים שֶׁנַּעֲשֵׂית שֶׁל יָחִיד אֵין מְעָרְבִין אֶת כּוּלָּהּ אֶלָּא אִם כֵּן עָשָׂה לָהּ כְּעִיר חֲדָשָׁה שֶׁבִּיהוּדָה שֶׁיֵּשׁ בָּהּ חֲמִשִּׁים דִּיּוּרִין דִּבְרֵי רַבִּי יְהוּדָה. רַבִּי שִׁמְעוֹן אוֹמֵר שָׁלֹשׁ חֲצֵרוֹת שֶׁל שְׁנֵי שְׁנֵי בָתִּים:

Mishnah 5: A village which is the property of one person[13] and becomes owned by many can have one *eruv* in its entirety; but for one of multiple ownership[14] which became one of single ownership one does not make an *eruv* in its entirety unless one leaves outside [a part] like the town Ḥadašah in Jehudah[15] which has 50 inhabitants[16], the words of Rebbi Jehudah. Rebbi Simeon says, three courtyards of two houses each.

משנה ו: מִי שֶׁהָיָה בַמִּזְרָח וְאָמַר לִבְנוֹ לְעָרֵב לוֹ בַמַּעֲרָב. בַּמַּעֲרָב וְאָמַר לִבְנוֹ לְעָרֵב לוֹ בַמִּזְרָח אִם יֵשׁ מִמֶּנּוּ וּלְבֵיתוֹ אַלְפַּיִם אַמָּה וּלְעֵירוּבוֹ יוֹתֵר מִכָּן מוּתָּר לְבֵיתוֹ וְאָסוּר לְעֵירוּבוֹ. לְעֵרוּבוֹ אַלְפַּיִם אַמָּה וּלְבֵיתוֹ יוֹתֵר מִכָּן מוּתָּר לְעֵירוּבוֹ וְאָסוּר לְבֵיתוֹ. הַנּוֹתֵן אֶת עֵירוּבוֹ בְּעִיבּוּרָהּ שֶׁל עִיר לֹא עָשָׂה כְלוּם. נְתָנוֹ חוּץ לַתְּחוּם מַה שֶּׁנִּשְׂכָּר הוּא מַפְסִיד:

Mishnah 6: If somebody was in the East and told his son to make him an *eruv* in the West, or in the West and told his son to make him an *eruv* in the East, if there are from his place to his house 2'000 cubits but to his *eruv* more than this, he is permitted up to his house but forbidden to his *eruv*[17]; if to his *eruv* 2'000 cubits but to his house more than that, he is permitted up to his *eruv* but forbidden to his house. If somebody puts his *eruv* in the complement of the town[1] he did not do anything[18]. If he puts it outside the domain[19] what he had gained he loses.

משנה ז: אַנְשֵׁי עִיר גְּדוֹלָה מְהַלְּכִין אֶת כָּל־עִיר קְטַנָּה. וְאַנְשֵׁי עִיר קְטַנָּה מְהַלְּכִין אֶת כָּל־עִיר גְּדוֹלָה. כֵּיצַד מִי שֶׁהָיָה בְעִיר גְּדוֹלָה וְנָתַן אֶת עֵירוּבוֹ בְעִיר קְטַנָּה. אוֹ בְעִיר קְטַנָּה וְנָתַן אֶת עֵירוּבוֹ בְעִיר גְּדוֹלָה מְהַלֵּךְ אֶת כּוּלָּהּ וְחוּצָה לָהּ אַלְפַּיִם אַמָּה. רַבִּי עֲקִיבָה אוֹמֵר אֵין לוֹ מִמְּקוֹם עֵרוּבוֹ אֶלָּא אַלְפַּיִם אַמָּה:

Mishnah 7: The people of a large town walk through all of a small town; the people of a small town walk through all of a large town[20]. How is that? If somebody lived in a large town and put his *eruv* in a small town, or in a small town and put his *eruv* in a large town, he walks through all of it[21] and outside of it 2'000 cubits. But Rebbi Aqiba says, he only has 2'000 cubits from the place of his *eruv*.

משנה ח: אָמַר לָהֶן רִבִּי עֲקִיבָה אִי אַתֶּם מוֹדִין לִי בְּנוֹתֵן אֶת עֵירוּבוֹ עַל פִּי הַמְּעָרָה שֶׁאֵין לוֹ מִמְּקוֹם עֵירוּבוֹ אֶלָּא אַלְפַּיִם אַמָּה. אָמְרוּ לוֹ אֵימָתַי בִּזְמָן שֶׁאֵין בָּהּ דִּיּוּרִין אֲבָל בִּזְמָן שֶׁיֵּשׁ בָּהּ דִּיּוּרִין מְהַלֵּךְ אֶת כּוּלָּהּ וְחוּצָה לָהּ אַלְפַּיִם אַמָּה. נִמְצָא קַל בְּתוֹכָהּ מֵעַל גַּבָּהּ. וְלַמּוֹדֵד שֶׁאָמְרוּ נוֹתְנִין לוֹ אַלְפַּיִם אַמָּה שֶׁאֲפִילוּ סוֹף מִדָּתוֹ כָּלָה בַּמְּעָרָה:

Mishnah 8: Rebbi Aqiba told them, do you not agree with me about one who puts his *eruv* at the mouth of a cave that he only has 2'000 cubits from the place of his *eruv*? They told him, when is this? If there are no dwellers in it, but if it is inhabited he walks through all of it[22] and outside 2'000 cubits. It turns out that the interior is easier than its top[23]. But for one who measures about whom they talked one gives 2'000 cubits even if his measure reaches its limit inside the cave[24].

1 Greek πῆγμα, τό. This expression is used for all structures that are not human dwellings. The *pegma* of a city wall is a watch tower. The example of the Babylonian Geonim (*Geonim Harkavi* p. 182) is a dove-cote.

2 Since the Sabbath domain of a built-up area is a rectangle oriented NS-EW one starts measuring from a line, oriented NS or EW, which touches the built-up area but leaves the area entirely to one side of the line. In mathematical terminology the completion of the town is the area enclosed on a map of the town by its support lines oriented NS and EW.

3 This also refers to bridges.

4 Cf. Chapter 4, Note 18.

5 One does not start to measure the 2'000 cubits outside the town from the wall of the (easternmost, northernmost, etc.) house but only at a distance of $\sqrt{5000} \sim 70^2/_3$ cubits (cf. Chapter 2, Note 82).

6 If the three towns form a triangle and the (necessarily parallel, either NS or EW) lines of support of two pairs of towns are no more than $2 \times 70^2/_3 = 141^1/_3$ cubits apart, the entire complex is considered one town and without an *eruv* each inhabitant may walk through all of them and outside 2'000 cubits measured from the outermost lines.

7 The measure should be made strictly horizontal. The two people holding the measuring tape hold it on their breasts, far from the ground, to hold it as exactly horizontal as possible.

8 If one measures, e. g., N to S, and

comes to an obstacle, one should go exactly E or W until the obstacle disappears, resume measuring due S, and then return on an exactly EW path to the original line and resume measuring.

9   One measures with a short rope of 4 cubits held horizontally.

10 As explained in the Halakhah, one measures with a rope of 4 cubits which can be held horizontal also on steep inclines. The 2'000 cubits which one determines are not actual distances but the length of the projection of a path onto the plane locally representing the surface of a flat Earth.

11 If the town has a traditional Sabbath boundary and a professional geometer tells them that at a certain place the actual boundary is farther away, one listens to the expert. The Yerushalmi does not express an opinion about what to do if the experts determine that the original border is too far away.

12 Since Sabbath boundaries are rabbinic institutions only.

13 And therefore is considered one dwelling where one may carry in the entire place without an *eruv*. If it turns into a place with multiple owners, an *eruv* is needed.

14 Where one needs an *eruv* to make it possible to carry in the alleys. If now an individual buys up all property in the village it should not be forgotten that the place originally needed an *eruv*; therefore some part should be left outside the main compound in which one may carry freely.

15 *Jos.* 15:37.

16 Including children and women.

17 This refers only to somebody who tells his son shortly before sundown on Friday to make an *eruv* for him, but he goes in the opposite direction and therefore could not reach the place of his *eruv* before sundown. Then the *eruv* is invalid for him, but since he ordered an *eruv* made he lost the rectangular domain of the town dwellers and now can only move in a circle of radius 2'000 cubits.

18 Since this is considered part of the town anyhow.

19 Not outside the Sabbath domain, since then he could not move outside of 4 cubits, but in the Sabbath domain outside the augmented town. Because he made an *eruv*, his Sabbath domain is a circle of radius 2'000 centered at the *eruv*; he loses not only the distances in the direction opposite to that of his *eruv* but also the rectangular shape of his domain.

20 The text of this Mishnah will be emended in the Halakhah.

21 Any built-up area in which from one house to the next there are less than $70^2/_3$ cubits, is considered as 4 cubits in this respect.

22 If the cave is inhabited it becomes a house and the entire cave is counted as 4 cubits.

23 If somebody puts his *eruv* on top of a cave where nobody dwells, he only has 2'000 cubits from the place of his *eruv*.

24 As noted before, by making an *eruv* one reduces his Sabbath domain to a circle of radius 2'000. If the *eruv* was deposited outside the cave he cannot walk inside the cave to a distance farther than 2'000 cubits from the *eruv* even though for the cave dwellers the entire cave is only counted as 4 cubits.

(22b line 28) כֵּיצַד מְעַבְּרִין אֶת הֶעָרִים כול'. בַּיִת נִכְנָס. מוֹצִיאִין אוֹתוֹ כְּנֶגֶד הָעִיר. פָּגוּם יוֹצֵא. מוֹצִיאִין אֶת הָעִיר כְּנֶגְדּוֹ.

"How does one complete towns," etc. "A house is recessed," one moves it out in line with the town; "a superstructure is protruding," one moves the town out in line with it².

רַב אָמַר. מְאַבְּרִין. וּשְׁמוּאֵל אָמַר. מְעַבְּרִין. מָאן דָּמַר. מְאַבְּרִין. מוֹסִיפִין לָהּ אֵבֶר. מָאן דָּמַר. מְעַבְּרִין. כְּאִשָּׁה עוֹבָרָה. תַּמָּן תַּנִּינָן. אֵין מְבָרְכִין עַל הַנֵּר עַד שֶׁיֵּיאוֹתוּ לְאוֹרוֹ׃ רַב אָמַר. יֵאוֹתוּ. וּשְׁמוּאֵל אָמַר. יֵעוֹתוּ. מָאן דָּמַר. יֵאוֹתוּ. אַךְ־בְּזֹאת נֵאוֹת לָכֶם. מָאן דָּמַר. יֵעוֹתוּ. לָדַעַת לָעוּת אֶת־יָעֵף דָּבָר. תַּמָּן תַּנִּינָן. לִפְנֵי אֵידֵיהֶן שֶׁלְּגוֹיִם. רַב תַּנֵּי. אִידֵיהֶן. וּשְׁמוּאֵל תַּנֵּי. עֵידֵיהֶן. מָאן דָּמַר. אִידֵיהֶן. כִּי קָרוֹב יוֹם אֵידָם. וּמָאן דָּמַר. עֵידֵיהֶן. וְעֵדֵיהֶם הֵמָּה וגו'. מַה מְקַיֵּים שְׁמוּאֵל טַעֲמֵיהּ דְּרַב. וְעֵדֵיהֶם הֵמָּה. שֶׁהֵן עֲתִידִין לְבַיֵּישׁ עוֹבְדֵיהֶן לְיוֹם הַדִּין.

²⁵Rav says *me'abberin*, and Samuel says *me'abberin*. He who says *me'abberin*, one adds a limb (אבר) to it. And he who says *me'abberin*, like a pregnant (עוברה) woman. There, we have stated²⁶: "One does not recite the benediction over a lamp unless one has profited from its light." Rav says *ye'utu*, and Samuel says *ye'utu*. He who says *ye'utu*, but with this we shall be agreeable to you²⁷. He who says *ye'utu*, to know, to inform the weary of wisdom²⁸. There we have stated²⁹: "Before the holidays of the Gentiles." Rav stated *'edehen* and Samuel stated *'edehen*. He who says *'edehen, for the day of their misfortune (אידם) is near*³⁰. He who says *'edehen, they are their witnesses* (עידיהם)²¹, etc. How does Samuel deal with Rav's reason, *they are their witnesses*? In the future they will bring to naught their worshippers on the Day of Judgment.

25 This is a re-arranged and slightly shortened paragraph from *Berakhot* 8:7, Notes 157-158. In the last example, from *Avodah zarah*, the text in *Berakhot* attributes the word with ע to Rav and with א to Samuel. This also is required by the text here.	26 Mishnah *Berakhot* 8:7. 27 *Gen.* 34:15. 28 *Is.* 50:4. 29 Mishnah *Avodah zarah* 1:1. 30 *Deut.* 32:35. 31 *Is.* 44:9.	

(22b line 37) רִבִּי יוֹחָנָן בְּשֵׁם רִבִּי הוֹשַׁעְיָה. מוֹסִיפִין לָהּ אֵבֶר. תָּלָה עֵינוֹי וְאִיסְתַּכֵּל בֵּיהּ. אֲמַר לֵיהּ. לָמָה אַתְּ מִסְתַּכֵּל בִּי. צָרְךְ לָךְ צְחַק לָךְ. לָא צְרָךְ לָךְ הִפְלִיג עָלָיךְ. תְּלַת עֲשַׂר שְׁנִין עֲבַר

עֲלֵיל קוֹמֵיהּ רַבֵּיהּ דְּלָא צָרִיךְ. רִבִּי שְׁמוּאֵל בְּשֵׁם רִבִּי זְעִירָא. אִילוּלֵא דַיּוֹ אֶלָּא שֶׁהָיָה מְקַבֵּל פְּנֵי רַבּוֹ. שֶׁכָּל־הַמְקַבֵּיל פְּנֵי רַבּוֹ כְּאִילּוּ מְקַבֵּל פְּנֵי שְׁכִינָה. רִבִּי בֶּרֶכְיָה רִבִּי יִרְמְיָה בְּשֵׁם רִבִּי חִייָה בַּר בָּא. כְּתִיב וּמשֶׁה֩ יִקַּ֨ח אֶת־הָאֹ֜הֶל וגו'. כַּמָּה הָיָה רָחִיק. רִבִּי יִצְחָק אָמַר. מִיל. וְהָיָה֙ כָּל־מְבַקֵּ֣שׁ משֶׁה אֵין כָּתוּב כָּאן. אֶלָּא וְהָיָה֙ כָּל־מְבַקֵּ֣שׁ יְיָ. מִיכָּן שֶׁכָּל־הַמְקַבֵּיל פְּנֵי רַבּוֹ כְּאִילּוּ מְקַבֵּל פְּנֵי שְׁכִינָה. רִבִּי חֶלְבּוֹ רִבִּי חוּנָה בְּשֵׁם רַב. כְּתִיב וַיֹּ֤אמֶר֙ אֵלִיָּ֣הוּ הַתִּשְׁבִּ֔י וגו'. וַהֲלֹא אֵלִיָּהוּ טִירוֹנִין לַנְּבִיאִים הָיָה. אֶלָּא מְלַמֵּד שֶׁכָּל־עֲמִידוֹת שֶׁעָמַד לִפְנֵי אֲחִיָּה הַשִּׁילוֹנִי רַבּוֹ כִּילּוּ עָמַד לִפְנֵי הַשְּׁכִינָה. רִבִּי חֶלְבּוֹ בָּשֵׁם אִילֵּין דְּבֵית שִׁילֹה. אֲפִילוּ אֵלִיָּהוּ מְבַקֵּשׁ מַיִם לְפָנָיו הָיָה אֱלִישָׁע נוֹתֵן עַל יָדָיו. מַה טַעֲמוֹ. פֹּה אֱלִישָׁ֣ע בֶּן־שָׁפָ֔ט אֲשֶׁר לָמַד תּוֹרָה אֵין כָּתוּב כָּאן. אֶלָּא אֲשֶׁר־יָצַ֥ק מַ֖יִם עַל־יְדֵ֥י אֵלִיָּֽהוּ כְּתִיב וְהַנַּ֗עַר שְׁמוּאֵ֛ל מְשָׁרֵ֥ת אֶת־יְיָ֖ לִפְנֵ֣י עֵלִ֑י. וַהֲלֹא לֹא מְשָׁרֵת אֶלָּא לִפְנֵי עֵלִי. אֶלָּא מְלַמֵּד שֶׁכָּל־שֵׁירוּת שֶׁשֵּׁרַת לִפְנֵי עֵלִי רַבּוֹ כִּילּוּ שָׁרַת לִפְנֵי שְׁכִינָה. תָּנֵי רִבִּי יִשְׁמָעֵאל. וַיָּבֹ֨א אַהֲרֹ֜ן וְכֹ֣ל | זִקְנֵ֣י יִשְׂרָאֵ֗ל לֶאֱכָל־לֶ֛חֶם עִם־חֹתֵ֥ן משֶׁ֖ה לִפְנֵ֣י הָאֱלֹהִֽים׃ וְכִי לִפְנֵי הָאֱלֹהִים אָכְלוּ. אֶלָּא מִיכָּן שֶׁכָּל־הַמְקַבֵּיל פְּנֵי חֲבֵירוֹ כִּילּוּ מְקַבֵּל פְּנֵי שְׁכִינָה.

[32]Rebbi Johanan in the name of Rebbi Hoshaia: one adds a limb to it. [33]He lifted his eyes and looked at him. He told him, why are you looking at me? Do I need you that you enjoy it? Thirteen years he went and came before his teacher even though he did not need him. Rebbi Samuel in the name of Rebbi Ze'ira: Was it not enough for him to have paid his respects to his teacher since anybody who pays his respects to his teacher is as if he paid his respects to the Divine Presence. Rebbi Berekhiah, Rebbi Jeremiah in the name of Rebbi Hiyya bar Abba. It is written[34] *and Moses would take the Tent*, etc. How far away was it? One *mil*[35]. It is not written "and it was that anybody asking Moses" but *and it was that anybody asking the Eternal*. From here that anybody visiting his teacher is as if he was visiting the Divine Presence. Rebbi Helbo, Rebbi[36] Huna in the name of Rav: It is written[37], *Eliahu from Tisbe said*, etc. Was not Eliahu the ruler[38] of the prophets? But it teaches that all the time he was standing before his teacher Ahiyya from Shilo it was as if he stood before the Divine Presence. Rebbi Helbo in the name of those of the House of Shilo: Even when Eliahu wanted water for his face Elisha would put it on his hands. What is the reason? *Here is Elisha ben Shafat*[39], it is not written here "who studied Torah", but *who poured water on Eliahu's hands*. It is written[40]: *The lad Samuel was serving the Eternal before Eli*. Did he not only serve Eli? But this teaches that all service which he rendered before his teacher Eli was as if he rendered if before the Divine

Presence. Rebbi Ismael stated[41]: *And Aaron and all the Elders of Israel came to eat bread with Moses's father-in-law before God.* Did they eat before God? But from here that anyone who receives a friend[42] is as if he received the Divine Presence.

32 Babli 53a. The entire Yerushalmi text is copied there by R. Hananel.
33 The text is parallel to *Sanhedrin* 11:6, Notes 68-69.
34 *Ex.* 33:7.
35 2'000 cubits. *Ex. rabba* 45(4).
36 Read: Rav.
37 *1K.* 17:1. The verse continues: *By the Living Eternal . . . before Whom I stood.*
38 Greek τύραννος, ὁ (*Arukh* טרן 3).
39 *2K.* 3:11.
40 *1S.* 3:1.
41 *Ex.* 18:12. *Mekhilta dR. Ismael Yitro Parašah* 1 (ed. Horovitz-Rabin p. 196).
42 In *editio princeps* of *Mekhilta*: Sages; similarly Babli *Berakhot* 64a.

(22b line 56) רִבִּי יַעֲקֹב בַּר אָחָא רִבִּי יָסָא בְשֵׁם רִבִּי יוֹחָנָן. כְּנֶגֶד הַשְׁקוֹף עַד אַלְפַּיִן אַמָּה. אָמַר רִבִּי יוֹסֵה לְרִבִּי יָסָא בַּר אָחָא. לֹא מִסְתַּבְּרָא אֶלָּא כְּנֶגֶד הַפָּגוּם. אֲבָל מִכְּנֶגֶד הָעִיר אֲפִילוּ כַּמָּה. אֲמַר לֵיהּ. אוֹף אֲנָא סָבַר כֵּן. אֲמַר לֵיהּ. וּמָה חֲמִית מֵימַר פָּגוּם. אוֹ נֹאמַר הָהֵן גַּו פָּגוּם. אָמַר רַב נַחְמָן. עַד רֹאשָׁהּ דִּמְדִינָתָא. מִילְתֵיהּ דְּרִבִּי שִׁמְעוֹן אָמְרָה כֵן. דָּמַר רִבִּי שִׁמְעוֹן בֶּן יוֹחַי. יָכוֹל אֲנִי לַעֲשׂוֹת שֶׁיְּהוּ מְהַלְּכִין מִצּוֹר לְצִידוֹן מִטִּיבֶּרְיָה לְצִיפּוֹרִין עַל יְדֵי מְעָרוֹת וְעַל יְדֵי בּוּרְגָּסִין.

מַהוּ לִיתֵּן פָּגוּם לְפָגוּם. מִילְתֵיהּ דְּרִבִּי שִׁמְעוֹן בֶּן לָקִישׁ אָמְרָה כֵן. נוֹתְנִין פָּגוּם לְפָגוּם. דָּמַר רִבִּי שִׁמְעוֹן בֶּן לָקִישׁ. יָכוֹל אֲנִי לַעֲשׂוֹת שֶׁתְּהֵא בֵּית מָעוֹן מִתְעַבֶּרֶת עִם טִיבֶּרְיָא וְאַתְּ רוֹאֶה אֶת הָאִיצְטַדְיוֹן כִּילּוּ הִיא מְלִיאָה בָּתִּים. וְהַקַּצְרִין נָתוּן בְּתוֹךְ שִׁבְעִים וּשְׁיָרַיִם לָאִצְטַדְיוֹן. וּבֵית מָעוֹן נָתוּן בְּתוֹךְ שִׁבְעִים וּשְׁיָרַיִם לַקַּצְרִים. וְאִין תִּמְשַׁח מִן פִּיגְמָא. לֵית נַפְשָׁא דְּסָרִיקִין בְּתוֹךְ שִׁבְעִים וּשְׁיָרַיִם. וְאִן תִּמְשַׁח מִן פְּחוּרְתָא. נַפְשָׁא דְּסָרִיקִין בְּתוֹךְ שִׁבְעִים וּשְׁיָרַיִם.

מַהוּ לִיתֵּן עִיבּוּר לְעִיבּוּר. מִילְתָא דְּרִבִּי שִׁמְעוֹן בֶּן יוֹחַי אָמְרָה כֵן. נוֹתְנִין עִיבּוּר לְעִיבּוּר. דָּמַר רִבִּי שִׁמְעוֹן בֶּן יוֹחַי. יָכוֹל אֲנִי לַעֲשׂוֹת שֶׁיְּהוּ מְהַלְּכִין מִצּוֹר לְצִידוֹן מִטִּיבֶּרְיָה לְצִיפּוֹרִין עַל כְּדֵי מְעָרוֹת וְעַל יְדֵי בּוּרְגָּנִין. כָּאן לְהִילּוּךְ וְכָאן לְעִיבּוּר.

Rebbi Jacob bar Aha, Rebbi Yasa in the name of Rebbi Johanan, from where do you augment? From the lintel[43] 2'000 cubits. Rebbi Yose said to Rebbi Yasa bar Aha: It seems reasonable only from the superstructure. But in front of the town it is unlimited[44]. He said, this also is my opinion. He said to him, what did you see to say "the superstructure"? Or should we say these in the back of the superstructure[45]? Rav Nahman said, at the end of the country[46]. The word of Rebbi Simeon implies this, since "Rebbi Simeon ben

Yoḥai said, I can cause that one may walk from Tyre to Sidon[47], from Tiberias to Sepphoris, by caves and by barns[48]."

May one add superstructure to superstructure[49]? The word of Rebbi Simeon ben Laqish implies that one adds superstructure to superstructure, since Rebbi Simeon ben Laqish said, I can cause that Bet Ma`on be in the completion of Tiberias. You consider the stadium as if it were full of houses, and the *castra*[50] are within 70 and remainder of the stadium, and Bet Ma`on is within 70 and remainder of the *castra*. If one considers the superstructure, the mausoleum of Siricon[51] is not within 70 and remainder, but if one considers the pottery[52], the mausoleum of Siricon is within 70 and remainder.

May one add completion to completion[53]? The word of Rebbi Simeon implies that one adds completion to completion, since "Rebbi Simeon ben Yoḥai said, I can cause that one may walk from Tyre to Sidon, from Tiberias to Sepphoris, by caves and by barns." Here for walking, there for completion[54].

43 The basic measurement is from the lintel of the city gate.

44 If the city walls form a rectangle and at the corners the towers extend over the walls, one does not extend the town beyond the towers. But if there are suburban dwellings in front of the walls one extends the definition of "city" to include all of suburbia on condition that between city wall and suburb the distance not be greater than $70^2/_3$ cubits.

45 It is difficult to make sense of this argument. In the opinion of S. Liebermann it means that one might consider the suburb as the real town and the original town as appendix ("superstructure") to this. Since the suburb has no walls, the entire problem of where to start measuring disappears; it is clear that one starts from the outermost wall of the outermost house.

46 He has no objection against extending the Sabbath domain of a city to contain all the country.

47 A full day's travel. Tosephta 4:11.

48 Greek πύργος, ὁ.

49 Are structures which are not dwellings counted as if they were dwellings so that they include an additional $70^2/_3$ cubits from which to count the town, possibly repeating the process many times.

50 *Castra, -orum, n.* a military camp; this is a dwelling.

51 It is not clear what was the additional structure appended to the stadium, which reduces the distance to the mausoleum to $70^2/_3$ cubits. The mausoleum itself was identified by an inscription, cf. S. Liebermann, Tarbiz 3, p.209.

52 Even if the mausoleum should have been inhabited, the potter's shop was not. Since together with the uninhabited appendix to the stadium it is needed to make

Bet Ma'on accessible from Tiberias, this proves that uninhabited structures are counted as if they were houses.

53 After the preceding argument it should be obvious that the answer is positive.

54 It could be that one finds a particular path that may be applied to one special situation. This does not mean that it can be applied to determine the Sabbath domain for everybody. Therefore the statement does not prove anything (but proof is not needed.)

(22b line 74) רִבִּי אָחָא אָמַר. אִיתְפַּלְגוּן רִבִּי חִייָה רוֹבָה וּבַר קַפָּרָא. חַד אָמַר הֲדָא דְאַתְּ מַר בְּעִיר גְּדוֹלָה. אֲבָל בְּעִיר קְטַנָּה לֹא תְהֵא הַתּוֹסֶפֶת יְתֵירָה עַל הָעִקָּר. וְחָרָנָה אָמַר. בֵּין גְּדוֹלָה בֵּין קְטַנָּה דַּיּוֹ אַלְפַּיִם.

אָמַר רִבִּי פִינְחָס. מַעֲשֶׂה בְתַלְמִיד וָתִיק לָמַד עִיבּוּרוֹ בְּשָׁלֹשׁ שָׁנִים וּמֶחֱצָה לִפְנֵי רַבּוֹ. וּבָא וְעִיבֵּר אֶת הַגָּלִיל. וְלֹא הִסְפִּיק לְעַבֵּר אֶת הַדָּרוֹם עַד שֶׁנִּטְרְפָה הַשָּׁעָה.

Rebbi Aḥa said, the Elder Rebbi Ḥiyya and Bar Qappara disagree. One said, this you are saying only about a large city. But for a small town the addition should not be more than the core[55]. But the other said, whether large or small, 2'000 is sufficient.

Rebbi Phineas said, it happened that a bright[56] student studied completions for three and a half years from his teacher; he went and completed Galilee[57]. He could not finish to complete the South before the time made it impossible[58].

55 This is a very restrictive condition. For example, if a town were a square of side lengths 1, the suburbs could extend only to a distance of .212 from the walls. The previous discussion always assumed that one has 2'000 cubits outside any augmentation.

56 Greek εὔθικτος, -ον.

57 He found enough barns and isolated farmhouses to make the entire Galilee into one Sabbath domain.

58 The South is the region around Lydda. "The time made it impossible" means that the political situation changed. Since the preceding paragraphs showed that in the time of R. Simeon ben Laqish the domain of Tiberias was not extended, the time of the student must be the 4th Century and the political situation which made the project impossible was that the Empire turned Christian.

(22c line 4) רִבִּי בָּא רַב יְהוּדָה בְּשֵׁם רַב. עִיר שֶׁהִיא בְנוּיָה כְּמִין קֶשֶׁת. אִם יֵשׁ בֵּין זוֹ לְזוֹ אַרְבַּעַת אֲלָפִים חָסֵר אַחַת. מְהַלֵּךְ אֶת כּוּלָּהּ וְחוּצָה לָהּ אַלְפַּיִם אַמָּה. אַרְבַּעַת אֲלָפִים. אֵין לוֹ מִמְּקוֹם עֵירוּבוֹ אֶלָּא אַלְפַּיִם אַמָּה. אָמַר רִבִּי אָחָא. סָבַר רִבִּי שְׁמוּאֵל. אֵין יִתֵּן סַנְדָּלוֹי הָכָא

הוּא אֲתֵי בְּרָא וְנַסֵּי לוֹן. וְאִין יִתֵּן סַנְדְּלוֹי הָכָא הוּא אֲתֵי בְּרָה וְנַסֵּי לוֹן. מִן כָּאן אֲתָא בְרָא וּמִן כָּאן אֲתָא בְרָא. מֵרוּחַ אַחַת אָסוּר מִשְׁתֵּי רוּחוֹת מוּתָּר.

רִבִּי בָּא בְשֵׁם רַב יְהוּדָה. הָיְתָה עִיר אַחַת גְּדוֹלָה וְיֵשׁ בָּהּ חָרִיץ עָמוֹק עֲשָׂרָה וְרָחָב אַרְבָּעָה. אַתְּ רוֹאֶה אוֹתוֹ כְּאִלּוּ מָלֵא עָפָר וּצְרוֹרוֹת. וְאִם לָאו. אַתְּ רוֹאֶה אוֹתוֹ כִּמְפוּלָּשׁ.

רִבִּי בָּא אַמִּי בַּר יְחֶזְקֵאל בְּשֵׁם רַב. עִיר שֶׁהִיא בְנוּיָה עַל שְׂפַת הַנַּחַל. אִם יֵשׁ בֵּינָהּ לַנַּחַל אַרְבָּעָה טְפָחִים. מוֹדֵד מִן הַחוֹמָה. שְׁלֹשָׁה? מוֹדֵד מִשְּׂפַת הַנַּחַל הַחִיצוֹנָה. וּבִלְבַד שֶׁלֹּא יְהֵא בַּנַּחַל יוֹתֵר מִשִּׁבְעִים וְשִׁירַיִים. מַה נָן קַיָּימִים. אִם מִתְלַקֶּטֶת עֲשָׂרָה טְפָחִים מִתּוֹךְ שָׁלֹשׁ. מוֹדֵד מִשְּׂפַת הַנַּחַל הַחִיצוֹנָה. אִם מִתּוֹךְ אַרְבַּע מוֹדֵד מִן הַחוֹמָה. אֶלָּא אִם כֵּאן אָנָן קַיָּימִים מִשָּׁלוֹשׁ וְעַד אַרְבַּע.

רַב אָמַר. עִיר שֶׁהִיא בְנוּיָה אוֹהָלִים. כָּל־אֶחָד וְאֶחָד מוֹדֵד מֵאָהֳלוֹ. הָיוּ שָׁם שְׁלֹשָׁה צְרִיפִין וּשְׁלֹשָׁה בּוּרְגָּנִין. מוֹדֵד מִן הַחִיצוֹן. הָתִיב אַסִּי. וְהָכְתִיב וְיָד תִּהְיֶה לְךָ מִחוּץ לַמַּחֲנֶה. הֵיאַךְ הָיוּ נִפְנִין לַחוּץ. רִבִּי חִייָה בְּרֵיהּ דְּרִבִּי שׁוּבְתַּי מַקְשֵׁי. הֵיאַךְ הָיוּ יוֹצְאִין לְבֵית מִדְרָשׁוֹ שֶׁלְּמֹשֶׁה מֹשֶׁה עָשָׂה לָהֶן שְׁלֹשָׁה צְרִיפִין וּשְׁלֹשָׁה בּוּרְגָּנִין. אָמַר רִבִּי יוֹסֵה. מִכֵּיוָן שֶׁהָיוּ חוֹנִין וְנוֹסְעִין עַל פִּי הַדִּיבֵּר כְּמִי שֶׁהָיוּ חוֹנִין לְשָׁעָה. אָמַר רִבִּי יוֹסֵי בֵּירִבִּי בּוּן. מִכֵּיוָן שֶׁהִבְטִיחָן הַקָּדוֹשׁ בָּרוּךְ הוּא שֶׁהוּא מַכְנִיסָן לָאָרֶץ. כְּמִי שֶׁהוּא לְעוֹלָם. עֲלָיהּ אָמַר רִבִּי אַבִּין. מֹשֶׁה עָשָׂה לָהֶן שְׁלֹשָׁה צְרִיפִין וּשְׁלֹשָׁה בּוּרְגָּנִין.

Rebbi Abba, Rav Jehudah in the name of Rav: If a town is built like a bow, if between the ends there is [a distance of] 3'999 [cubits] he walks its entirety and outside it 2'000; 4'000 he only has 2'000 cubits from the place of his *eruv*[59]. Rebbi Aha said, Rebbi Samuel explained it. If he would put his sandals at one place he could go outside and put them on; and if he would put his sandals at another place he could go outside and put them on. He could come from either side to the outside. From one side it is forbidden, from both sides it is permitted[60].

Rebbi Abba in the name of Rav Jehudah. If there was a large city and in it a ditch ten [hand-breadths] deep and four wide, one looks where it is full of earth and pebbles. Otherwise one considers it open[61].

Rebbi Abba, Ammi bar Ezechiel[62] in the name of Rav. If a city is built on the banks of a river, if between it and the river are four hand-breadths one measures from the wall, three one measures from the outer bank of the river[63] unless the river be [wide] more than 70 and remainder[64]. Where do we hold? If it descends ten hand-breadths in three [cubits] one measures from the outer bank of the river, if in four [cubits] one measures from the wall⁶⁵. So where we hold is between three and four.

Rav said, in a town built of tents, everybody measures from his tent. If there were three huts and three barns one measures from the outer one⁶⁶. Issy objected, is it not written⁶⁷, *a sign you should have outside the camp*? How could they relieve themselves outside⁶⁸? Rebbi Hiyya the son of Rebbi Sabbatai asked, how could they go to Moses's house of study? Moses built them three huts and three barns⁶⁹. ⁷⁰Rebbi Yose says, because they were travelling and camping by the Word, was it not temporary? Rebbi Yose ben Rebbi Abun said, since the Holy One, praise to Him, has promised them that he would bring them into the Land, it is as if it were permanent. Because of this⁷¹ Rebbi Abbin said, Moses built them three huts and three barns.

59 The town is built as a semi-circle. If the radius of the circle is < 2'000, every point in the semi-disk bounded by the circle and the chord (the diameter) joining its endpoints is accessible from the semi-circle. Therefore the chord is the border of the completed town and the Sabbath domain is a semi-disk of radius 4'000 plus a rectangular domain of 4'000×2'000 based on the chord plus two quarter disks of radius 2'000. This would imply that the statement of the Mishnah that a Sabbath domain always is a rectangular domain only applies to cities compactly built in the shape of a polygon, and this not in all cases; cf. Tosephta 4:4.

60 A line segment can be the border of the completion of a town only if all of its points are accessible from the town on the Sabbath. Therefore if the radius of the semi-circle is > 2'000, a point distant almost 2'000 from one side is not accessible from the other and the center is not accessible from anywhere. Therefore the chord cannot be the border of the completion; the Sabbath domain only is the set of all points of distance at most 2'000 from any point of the semi-circle. Babli 55a.

61 Translation and explanation are tentative. A ditch 10 deep and 4 wide is a domain by itself. If the ditch runs through the entire town, is nowhere filled or bridged, it splits the town into two separate towns; otherwise it is disregarded.

62 The brother of Rav Jehudah.

63 The bank far away from the city; the river being considered as part of the city wall.

64 Then the outer bank cannot be considered part of the city and one has to measure the Sabbath domain from the city wall.

65 If the slope from the wall to the river is steep, it is considered an extension of the wall; otherwise it simply is an empty stretch of land.

66 From the outermost tent. Babli 55b.

67 *Deut.* 23:13. The toilets had to be outside the camp. (Even though the verse is

written for a military expedition, the argument refers to the regular camp of the Israelites in the desert.) Since the camp was 12 *mil* wide (Chapter 3, Note 136), how could somebody on one side of the camp go and relieve himself on the other side if he could only go one *mil* from his tent?

69   One would have expected that the Tabernacle certainly would be the equivalent of 3 huts and 3 barns, turning the camp into a formal city.

70   Cf. *Šabbat* Chapter 7 Note 399, Chapter 12 Note 12. The quote of the present paragraph in *Qondros Aharon* edited by L. Ginzberg in his *Yerushalmi Fragments* p. 318 reads here the exact text of *Šabbat* Chapter 12. Cf. Babli 55b.

71   That the camp could be considered a permanent city. (*Qondros Aharon* reads "R. Abun").

(22c line25)   מְרַבְּעָהּ רְבוּעַ עוֹלָם. כְּדֵי שֶׁיְּהֵא מַעֲרָבָהּ לְמַעֲרָבוֹ שֶׁלְעוֹלָם וּדְרוֹמָהּ לִדְרוֹמוֹ שֶׁלְעוֹלָם. אָמַר רִבִּי יוֹסֵה. אִם אֵין יוֹדֵעַ לְכַוֵּין אֶת הָרוּחוֹת צֵא וְלַמֵּד מִן הַתְּקוּפָה. מִמָּקוֹם שֶׁהַחַמָּה זוֹרַחַת בְּאֶחָד בִּתְקוּפַת תַּמּוּז עַד מָקוֹם שֶׁהִיא זוֹרַחַת בְּאֶחָד בִּתְקוּפַת טֵבֵת אִילוּ פְּנֵי מִזְרָח. מִמָּקוֹם שֶׁהַחַמָּה שׁוֹקַעַת בְּאֶחָד בִּתְקוּפַת טֵבֵת עַד מָקוֹם שֶׁהִיא שׁוֹקַעַת בְּאֶחָד בִּתְקוּפַת תַּמּוּז אִילוּ פְּנֵי מַעֲרָב. וְהַשְׁאָר צָפוֹן וְדָרוֹם. הָדָא הוּא דִּכְתִיב הוֹלֵךְ אֶל־דָּרוֹם וְסוֹבֵב אֶל־צָפוֹן. הוֹלֵךְ אֶל־דָּרוֹם בַּיּוֹם. וְסוֹבֵב אֶל־צָפוֹן בַּלַּיְלָה. סוֹבֵב סוֹבֵב הוֹלֵךְ הָרוּחַ וְעַל־סְבִיבֹתָיו שָׁב הָרוּחַ: אִילוּ פְּנֵי הַמִּזְרָח וְהַמַּעֲרָב.

"One makes it rectangular in the four directions of the world[2,72], so that its Western direction be in the West of the world and its Southern direction be in the South of the world. Rebbi Yose said, if he does not know how to determine the directions let him go and learn from the solstices. From the place where the sun rises on the day of the summer solstice to the place where it rises on the day of the winter solstice is Eastern direction; from the place where the sun goes down on the day of the winter solstice to the place where it goes down on the day of the summer solstice is Western direction; the remainder are North and South. That is what is written[73], *it goes to the South and turns to the North. It goes to the South* during the day *and turns to the North* during the night; *all around in circles goes the wind, to its circuits returns the wind*, these are Eastern and Western directions[74]."

72   Babli 56a, Tosephta 4:6. R. Yose here is the Tanna, ben Ḥalaphta.

73   *Eccl.* 1:6.

74   The main directions of the wind.

(22c line 34) נִיחָא בְשִׁילֹה וּבְבֵית עוֹלָמִים. דָּמַר רִבִּי אָחָא בְשֵׁם שְׁמוּאֵל בַּר רַב יִצְחָק. כַּמָּה יָגְעוּ נְבִיאִים הָרִאשׁוֹנִים לַעֲשׂוֹת שַׁעַר הַמִּזְרָחִי שֶׁתְּהֵא הַחַמָּה מְצַמְצֶמֶת בּוֹ בְּאֶחָד בִּתְקוּפַת טֵבֵת וּבְאֶחָד בִּתְקוּפַת תַּמּוּז. שִׁבְעָה שֵׁמוֹת נִקְרְאוּ לוֹ. שַׁעַר סוּר. שַׁעַר הַיְסוֹד. שַׁעַר חֲרִיסִית. שַׁעַר אֵיתוֹן. שַׁעַר הַתָּוֶךְ. שַׁעַר חָדָשׁ. שַׁעַר הָעֶלְיוֹן. שַׁעַר סוּר. שֶׁשָּׁם הָיוּ טְמֵאִים פּוֹרְשִׁין. הָדָא הוּא דִכְתִיב סוּרוּ טָמֵא קָרְאוּ לָמוֹ. שַׁעַר הַיְסוֹד. שֶׁשָּׁם הָיוּ מְיַיסְּדִין אֶת הַהֲלָכָה. שַׁעַר חֲרִיסִית. שֶׁהוּא מְכוּוָּן כְּנֶגֶד זְרִיחַת הַחַמָּה. הֵיךְ מַה דְאַתְּ אָמַר הָאוֹמֵר לַחֶרֶס וְלֹא יִזְרָח. שַׁעַר הָאֵיתוֹן. שֶׁהוּא מְשַׁמֵּשׁ כְּנִיסָה וִיצִיאָה. שַׁעַר הַתָּוֶךְ. שֶׁהוּא מְיוּסָד בֵּין שְׁנֵי שְׁעָרִים. שַׁעַר חָדָשׁ. שֶׁשָּׁם חִידְּשׁוּ סוֹפְרִים אֶת הַהֲלָכָה. שַׁעַר הָעֶלְיוֹן. שֶׁהוּא לְמַעֲלָה מֵעֶזְרַת יִשְׂרָאֵל הַחֵיל וְעֶזְרַת נָשִׁים. וּמַעֲלָה יְתֵירָה הָיָה בְבֵית עוֹלָמִים.

One understands this for Shilo and the Temple[75], as Rebbi Aḥa said in the name of Samuel bar Rav Isaac, how much did the earlier prophets exercise themselves to make the Eastern gate so that the sun be exactly on it on the summer solstice and the winter solstice[76]. It was called by seven names: the gate "desist"[77], the foundation gate[78], the sun gate[79], the entrance gate[80], the middle gate[81] the new gate[82], the upper gate[83]. The gate "desist" since there the impure separate[84]; that is what is written[85], *desist, impure one calls them.* The foundation gate, for there practice was founded. The sun gate, since it was directed towards sunrise, as you are saying[86], *Who says to the sun not to shine.* The entrance gate, since it serves as entry and exit. The middle gate, since it is fixed between two gates[87]. The new gate, for there the Sopherim renewed practice. The upper gate, since it was higher than the courtyard of Israel and the courtyard of women[88]. The Temple had another distinction[89].

---

75 They could be exactly built EW-NS; this statement is the introduction to the next paragraph about the orientation of the Tabernacle in the desert.

76 It seems that one should read: the spring and autumn equinoxes, but there is no textual evidence for this.

77 *2K.* 11:6.

78 *2Chr.* 23:5.

79 *Jer.* 19:2.

80 *Ez.* 40:15.

81 *Jer.* 39:3.

82 *Jer.* 26:10.

83 *2Chr.* 24:20.

84 Anybody not pure was barred from the entire Temple Mount, but those who needed a Temple ceremony for purification, such as the healed sufferer from skin disease, did come to the entrance gate of the Temple proper.

85 *Lament.* 4:15.

86 *Job* 9:7.

87 The Temple door and the entrance gate to the Temple Mount.

88 R. Hananel (*ad Yoma* 26b, bottom) reads: since it was higher than the courtyard.

Probably it means that the Eastern gate was built higher than the wall and the other gates since it was crowned by a tower depicting the fortress of Susa (Mishnah *Middot* 1:3).

89 In quite a number of items was the Temple distinguished relative to the Tabernacle at Shilo.

(22c line 46) וּבַמִּדְבָּר מִי הָיָה מְכַוֵּין לָהֶם אֶת הָרוּחוֹת. אָמַר רִבִּי אָחָא. אֲרוֹן הָיָה מְכַוֵּין לָהֶם אֶת הָרוּחוֹת. הָדָא הוּא דִכְתִיב וְנָסְעוּ הַקְּהָתִים נוֹשְׂאֵי הַמִּקְדָּשׁ. זֶה הָאָרוֹן. וְהֵקִימוּ בְּנֵי מְרָרִי. אֶת־הַמִּשְׁכָּן עַד־בּוֹאָם: בְּנֵי קְהָת שֶׁעֲלֵיהֶן הָיָה הָאָרוֹן נָתוּן.

כֵּיצַד הָיוּ יִשְׂרָאֵל מְהַלְּכִין בַּמִּדְבָּר. רִבִּי חָמָא בַּר חֲנִינָא וְרִבִּי הוֹשַׁעְיָה. חַד אָמַר. כְּתֵיבָה. וְחָרְנָה אָמַר. קְקוֹרָה. מָאן דָּמַר כְּתֵיבָה. כַּאֲשֶׁר יַחֲנוּ כֵּן יִסָּעוּ. מָאן דָּמַר קְקוֹרָה. מְאַסֵּף לְכָל־הַמַּחֲנוֹת לְצִבְאוֹתָם. מָאן דָּמַר קְקוֹרָה. וּמָה מְקַיֵּים כְּתֵיבָה. כַּאֲשֶׁר יַחֲנוּ כֵּן יִסָּעוּ. מַה בַּחֲנִייָתָן עַל פִּי הַדִּיבֵּר אַף בִּנְסִיעָתָם עַל פִּי הַדִּיבֵּר. מָאן דָּמַר כְּתֵיבָה. מַה מְקַיֵּים קְקוֹרָה. מְאַסֵּף לְכָל־הַמַּחֲנוֹת לְצִבְאוֹתָם. לְפִי שֶׁהָיָה שִׁבְטוֹ שֶׁלְּדָן מְרוּבֶּה בְאוּכְלוֹסִין הָיָה נוֹסֵעַ בַּאַחֲרוֹנָה. וְכָל־מִי שֶׁהָיָה מְאַבֵּד דָּבָר הָיָה מַחֲזִירוֹ לוֹ. הָדָא הוּא דִכְתִיב מְאַסֵּף לְכָל־הַמַּחֲנוֹת לְצִבְאוֹתָם.

Who was determining them the directions in the desert[90]? Rebbi Aha said, the Ark did determine the directions for them. That is what is written[91], *then travelled the Kohatites, the carriers of the Sanctuary*, this is the Ark. *And* the Mererites *erected the dwelling before they came,* the Kohatites on whom the Ark was placed.

[92]How did Israel travel in the desert? Rebbi Hama bar Hanina and Rebbi Hoshaia[93]. One said, like a chest, but the other said, like a beam. He who said like a chest, *just as they camped so they travelled*[94]. He who said like a beam, *the collector of all camps with their armies*[95]. How does he who said like a beam explain him who said like a chest, *just as they camped so they travelled*? Just as they camped following the Word, so they travelled following the Word. How does he who said like a chest explain him who said like a beam, *the collector of all camps with their armies*? Since the tribe of Dan was so populous[95a] it travelled last and to anybody who had lost anything they would return it to him; that is what is written, *the collector of all camps with their armies.*

90 Since the Tabernacle had to be oriented strictly EW (*Num.* 2). *Tanhuma Bemidbar* (12).
91 *Num.*10:21.
92 Rashi *Num.* 10:25, 2:17.
93 In *Qondros aharon*: R. Joshua ben Levi.
94 *Num.*2:17.

95 Num. 10:25.   95a Greek ὄχλος, ὁ, "multitude".

(22c line 58) תַּנֵּי בְשֵׁם רִבִּי יוּדָה. אַף זִיזֶיהָ וְכָתְלֶיהָ הָיוּ נִמְדָּדִין עִמָּהּ. בָּעֵי רַב הוֹשַׁעְיָה. אֲוִיר חָצֵר מָהוּ שֶׁיִּמּוֹד עִמָּהּ. נִישְׁמְעִינָהּ מִן הָדָא. בַּיִת שֶׁנִּפְרַץ מֵרוּחַ אַחַת נִמְדָּד עִמָּהּ. מִשְּׁתֵּי רוּחוֹת אֵין נִמְדָּד עִמָּהּ. רִבִּי אָבִין בְּשֵׁם רַב יְהוּדָה. בְּשֶׁנִּיטְלָה קוֹרָתוֹ. אֲבָל אִם לֹא נִיטְלָה קוֹרָתוֹ נִמְדָּד עִמָּהּ. אִם בְּשֶׁנִּיטְלָה קוֹרָתוֹ לֹא כַאֲוִיר חָצֵר הוּא. תַּמָּן הוּקַף לְבֵית דִּירָה. בְּרַם הָכָא לֹא הוּקַף לְדִירָה. וּכְשֶׁהוּא מוֹדֵד לֹא יְהֵא מוֹדֵד מִן הָאֶמְצַעִי מִפְּנֵי שֶׁהוּא מַפְסִיד. אֶלָּא מִן הַקְּרָנוֹת.

It was stated in the name of Rebbi Jehudah: "Also its ledges and walls were measured with it.[96]" Rav Hoshaia asked: is the airspace of a courtyard measured with it[97]? Let us hear from the following: A house which was breached on one side is measured with it, from two sides it is not measured with it. Rebbi Abbin in the name of Rav Jehudah, if its beam[98] had been removed. But if its beam had not been removed it is measured with it. If the beam had been removed is it not like the airspace of a courtyard? There it was enclosed as a dwelling, here it was not enclosed as a dwelling.[99] "If he measures he should not be measuring from the center since he would lose, but from the corners.[100]"

96 Tosephta 4:7. One starts measuring not from the wall of the city or the last house but from the first place which is under the open sky.

97 If the town is completed by adding suburban buildings, are only houses added or any enclosed space?

98 The house is considered breached only if the ceiling beams also are missing.

99 Therefore only dwelling space is added as completion.

100 Tosephta 4:13, Babli 56b. Since one determines a Sabbath boundary as a straight line running either NS or EW it really does not matter where one starts measuring. The Tosephta states that one should not consider the starting point of the measuring as center of a circle but as a corner. The Sabbath domain always is a rectangular domain.

(22c line 65) פיס'. נוֹתְנִין קַרְפֵּף לָעִיר כול'. רַב חוּנָה בְשֵׁם. רִבִּי מֵאִיר וְרַבָּנִין מִקְרָא אֶחָד דּוֹרְשִׁין. רִבִּי מֵאִיר דָּרַשׁ. מֵקִיר הָעִיר. מַה תַּלְמוּד לוֹמַר וָחוּצָה. מִיכָּן שֶׁנּוֹתְנִין קַרְפֵּף לָעִיר. רַבָּנִין דּוֹרְשִׁין וָחוּצָה. מַה תַּלְמוּד לוֹמַר מֵקִיר הָעִיר. אֶלָּא מִיכָּן (שֶׁאֵין) [שֶׁ]נּוֹתְנִין קַרְפֵּף לָעִיר. הָדָא אֲמָרָה שֶׁנּוֹתְנִין קַרְפֵּף לָעִיר. רִבִּי יַעֲקֹב בַּר אָחָא רִבִּי אֲבוּנָה רִבִּי נָחוּם בְּשֵׁם שְׁמוּאֵל בַּר אַבָּא. סִלְקַת מַתְנִיתָא.

Paragraph. "One gives a fore-court to the city[5]," etc. Rav Huna in the name of [Rav][101]: Rebbi Meïr and the rabbis explain the same verse. Rebbi Meïr explained: *From the city wall*, why does the verse say, *outwards*[102]? From here that one gives a fore-court to the city. The rabbis explained, *outwards,* why does the verse say, *from the city wall*? From that one does (not)[103] give a fore-court to the city[104]. Does this not mean that one gives a fore-court to the city[105]? Rebbi Jacob bar Aha, Rebbi Abuna, Rebbi Nahum in the name of Rebbi Samuel bar Abba, the Mishnah is finished[105].

101 Missing in L, inserted from the quote of the text by Rashba, col. 334. Rav Huna is not known to have had any teacher but Rav.

102 *Num.* 35:4, Babli 57a. He reads the verse that one does not start measuring from the city wall but somewhere outside. The definition of "outside" is given over to the rabbinic authorities.

103 This was written by the scribe but (wrongly) deleted by the corrector who then (wrongly) inserted the relative pronoun in the following space.

104 They read the word as stating that one measures outward at a right angle to the wall, starting from the wall.

105 This refers to the second part of Mishnah 2, where it is stated that two villages less than $141^{1}/_{3}$ cubits apart are considered a single village for the rules of the Sabbath. This statement seems incompatible with the reading of the verse attributed to the rabbis.

106 Mishnah 2 should be split into two; the sentence "similarly three villages forming a triangle, if between the two outer ones are $141^{1}/_{3}$ [cubits], the middle one makes all three to be one" is Rebbi Meïr's only. Babli 57a in the name of Hiyya bar Rav.

(22c line 71) פיס'. וְכֵן שְׁלֹשָׁה כְפָרִים הַמְשׁוּלָשִׁים כול'. שְׁמוּאֵל אָמַר. בַּעֲשׂוּיִים שׁוּרָה. בַּר קַפָּרָא אָמַר. בַּעֲשׂוּיִים צוֹבָה. הַיְידֵנּוּ אֶמְצָעִי. נִיחָא מָאן דָּמַר. בַּעֲשׂוּיִים שׁוּרָה. מָאן דָּמַר. בַּעֲשׂוּיִים צוֹבָה. הַיְידֵנּוּ אֶמְצָעִי. אָמַר רִבִּי שְׁמוּאֵל אָחוֹי דְּרִבִּי בֶּרֶכְיָה. אֵין תִּמְשַׁח מִן הָהֵן. הַהֲנוּ אֶמְצָעִי. אֵין תִּמְשַׁח מִן הָהֵן. הַהֲנוּ אֶמְצָעִי. רִבִּי יַעֲקֹב בַּר אַחָא רִבִּי יָסָא בְּשֵׁם רִבִּי חֲנַנְיָה. וּבִלְבַד שֶׁלֹּא יְהֵא הָאֶמְצָעִי מוּפְלָג יוֹתֵר מֵאַלְפַּיִם אַמָּה. אָמַר רִבִּי יוֹסֵה. קַשְׁיָיתָהּ קוֹמֵי רִבִּי יַעֲקֹב בַּר אֲחָא. תַּנִּינָן. אִם יֵשׁ בֵּין שְׁנַיִהֶן הַחִיצוֹנִים מֵאָה וְאַרְבָּעִים וְאַחַת וּשְׁלִישׁ עָשָׂה הָאֶמְצָעִי שְׁלָשְׁתָּן. לְהַתִּיר שְׁנֵי הַחִיצוֹנִים. הָיוּ שְׁנַיִם. הָאֶמְצָעִי מָהוּ שֶׁיִּדּוֹן לְכָאן וּלְכָאן. מַה צְּרִיכָה לֵהּ. בְּשֶׁהָיוּ שְׁנַיִם מְהַלְּכִין. אֲבָל אִם הָיָה הָאֶחָד מְחַלֵּךְ נִידוֹן לְכָאן וּלְכָאן.

Paragraph[107]. "Similarly three villages forming a triangle," etc. Samuel said, if they are in a line[108]. Bar Qappara said, it they are like a tripod[109]. Which one is the middle one? It is understandable for him who said, they are in a line. For him who said, they are like a tripod, which one is the middle one? Rebbi Samuel, Rebbi Berekhiah's brother, said, if you are measuring from one, the other is the middle one; if you are measuring from one, the other is the middle one[110]. Rebbi Jacob bar Aha, Rebbi Yasa in the name of Rebbi Hanina, only if the middle one not be farther than 2'000 cubits[111]. Rebbi Yose said, I objected before Rebbi Jocob bar Aha, did we not state: "if between the two outer ones are $141^1/_3$ [cubits], the middle one makes all three [to be one][6]." To permit the two outer ones[112]. If there were two, could the middle one be counted for either side? His problem was if there were two people walking. But if one person is walking, it is counted for either side[113].

107 Continuation of the discussion of Mishnah 2.

108 The three villages are more or less in one line; meaning that if one walks from one of the outer ones to the other outer one by necessity one crosses the territory of the middle one.

109 An acute triangle.

110 In an acute triangle every edge can be chosen as basis; the remaining vertex then is between the other two.

111 The problem becomes acute only if one of the angles of the triangle is very small compared to the other two; then the vertex with the small angle is in between the other two. Babli 57b.

112 If the distance between villages A,B is < $141^1/_3$ and AC, BC are large but < 2'000 then since one may walk from A to C and from B to C one may make of A and B one village by *eruv* but not A and C nor B and C.

113 If there are 3 villages forming a triangle there is no problem. But if there are 5, A_1 A_2 B_1 B_2 C, and C is an acceptable third both for A_1B_1 and A_2B_2, there is a problem if two people are walking simultaneously from A_i to B_i (i=1,2) since it is not determined for which triangle C should be counted. But if only one person walks, since *eruvim* are rabbinic we may say that retroactively it became clear that C belongs to where it is needed.

(22d line 5) פיס' אֵין מוֹדְדִין אֶלָּא בְחֶבֶל שֶׁלַּחֲמִשִּׁים אַמָּה כול'. כַּמָּה הִיא מִידַת הַתְּחוּם. אַרְבָּעִים חֲבָלִים. לֹא פָחוֹת שֶׁהוּא נִמְתַּח וְנִשְׁבָּר. וְלֹא יָתֵר. שֶׁהוּא נִקְמָז וּמַפְסִיד. אִית תַּנָּיֵי תַנֵּי. מוֹדֵד בְּחֶבֶל שֶׁלְּפִשְׁתָּן. וְאִית תַּנָּיֵי תַנֵּי. בְּחֶבֶל שֶׁלְּשַׁלְשֶׁלֶת[114]. וְאִית תַּנָּיֵי תַנֵּי. בְּחֶבֶל שֶׁלְאַרְבַּע אַמּוֹת. אָמַר רִבִּי יוֹשֻׁעַ. אֵין לָךְ מִידָה שֶׁלְּאֶמֶת אֶלָּא שֶׁלְשַׁלְשֶׁלֶת. אֲבָל מַה אֶעֱשֶׂה וְכָתוּב בַּנְּבִיאִים חֲבָלִים וּפְתִיל־פִּשְׁתִּים בְּיָדוֹ וּקְנֵה הַמִּידָה.

הָיָה מִמֶּנּוּ לַנַּחַל שִׁבְעִים וְחָמֵשׁ אַמָּה. תְּרֵין אֲמוֹרִין. חַד אָמַר. מוֹדֵד בְּחֶבֶל שֶׁלַּחֲמִשִּׁים אַמָּה וְחוֹזֵר לַאֲחוֹרָיו עֶשְׂרִים וְחָמֵשׁ אַמָּה. וְחָרָנָה אָמַר. מוֹדֵד בְּחֶבֶל שֶׁלַּחֲמִשִּׁים אַמָּה וְהַשְׁאָר

מוֹדֵד בְּחֶבֶל שֶׁלְאַרְבַּע אַמּוֹת. הָיָה הַנַּחַל צַר מִלְּמַעְלָן וְרָחָב מִלְּמַטָּה. עַד חַמִּשִׁים אַמָּה אַתְּ רוֹאֶה אוֹתוֹ כִּילוּ מָלֵא עָפָר וּצְרוֹרוֹת. וְאִם לָאו אַתְּ רוֹאֶה אוֹתוֹ כִּי מִיתְרַפֵּס וְעוֹלֶה מִתְרַפֵּס וְיוֹרֵד. הָיָה הַנַּחַל מְעוּקָּם. רִבִּי חִסְדַּיי אָמַר. מְצוֹפוֹת וּמְשַׁעֵר בָּהּ בְּעֵינָיו בַּמִּישׁוֹר וְחוֹזֵר וְעוֹשֶׂה כֵן בָּהַר. רִבִּי אֲחָא רִבִּי חִינָּנָא רִבִּי יִרְמִיָּה רִבִּי שְׁמוּאֵל בַּר רַב יִצְחָק. וְהוּא שֶׁתְּהֵא מִידָּה יוֹצְאָה בָהַר אַרְבָּעָה טְפָחִים כְּדֵי מָקוֹם. רִבִּי יוֹסֵה רִבִּי אֲבוּנָה בְשֵׁם רַב יְהוּדָה רִבִּי יוּדָן מַטֵּי בָהּ בְּשֵׁם רַב. הָעֶלְיוֹן כְּנֶגֶד רֹאשׁוֹ וְהַתַּחְתּוֹן כְּנֶגֶד רַגְלָיו כָּל־עַמָּא מוֹדֵי שֶׁמְּקַדְּימִין¹¹⁵. הָעֶלְיוֹן כְּנֶגֶד רֹאשׁוֹ וְהַתַּחְתּוֹן כְּנֶגֶד מָתְנָיו כָּל־עַמָּא מוֹדֵי שֶׁמְּקַדְּדִין. מָה פְלִיגִין. כְּנֶגֶד לִבּוֹ. רִבִּי מֵאִיר אוֹמֵר. מְקַדְּדִין. וַחֲכָמִים אוֹמְרִים. אֵין מְקַדְּדִין.

Paragraph. "One only measures with a rope of 50 cubits," etc. How much is the measure of the Sabbath domain? 40 ropes. "Neither less" since it can be tightened and increases, "nor more" since it gets loose and loses[116]. Some Tannaim state, one measures with a linen rope, but some Tannaim state, with a chain rope[117], and some Tannaim state, with a rope of four cubits. [116]Rebbi Joshua said, there is no truer measure than with chains, but what can I do since in Prophets it is written ropes, *a linen twine was in his hand and a measuring rod*[118].

If from him to a river were 75 cubits. Two Amoraim, one said, he measures with a rope of 50 cubits and returns 25 cubits; but the other one said, he measures with a rope of 50 cubits and the remainder he measures with a rope of four cubits. If the river was narrow on top and wide below, up to 50 cubits one considers it as if full of dust and pebbles; otherwise one sees it inclining upwards and inclining downwards[119]. If the river was bent, Rebbi Hasdai says, with telescopes he estimates in the plain and does the same with a mountain[120]. Rebbi Aha, Rebbi Hinena, Rebbi Jeremiah in the name of Rebbi Samuel bar Rav Isaac: only if the measure results in the mountain four hand-breadths as a place[121]. Rebbi Yose, Rebbi Abuna in the name of Rav Jehudah, Rebbi Yudan has it in the name of Rav: If one holds it high above his head and the other by his feet, everybody agrees that one strip-measures[122]. The high one over his head and the low one on his hips, everybody agrees that one strip-measures[123]. Where do they disagree? On his heart; Rebbi Meïr says one strip-measures but the Sages say one does not strip-measure[124].

114 Read שְׁלְשֶׁלֶת.
115 Read מְקַדְּדִין.
116 Babli 58a.
117 A metal chain.

118 *Ez.* 40:3.

119 If a canyon is up to 50 cubits wide on top one simply measures on top and disregards what is below; otherwise one has to measure the slopes.

120 If one has a secure base of given length it is more accurate anyhow to determine lengths by measuring angles with a theodolite.

121 In mountainous terrain one measures with ropes of 4 cubits length. It is considered an incline which needs special treatment only if the difference in height for the length of the rope is 4 hand-breadths, $^2/_3$ of a cubit. Let α be the angle of inclination, this means $\sin α = .167$ or $α = 4.5°$. Since $\cos α = .958$, the error committed by measuring the slope instead of its horizontal projection is 1.42%.

122 While the Sages state in the Mishnah that one does not strip-measure at mountains, i. e., that one measures the distance on the ground, not the horizontal projection, they agree that if the slope is very steep the error would be too large and one must work with projections. To trans-late the rules given here into numbers would require exact data about the length of a cubit and the average height of a man; these are not available. For a rough estimate one may assume that the average height of a man be 3.5 cubits. Then if in a team of geometers one holds his end of the rope of 4 cubits on top of his head while the other, climbing up the mountain, has to hold his end at his feet in order to keep the rope horizontal, the slope is given by $\tan α = 3.5/4 = 0.875$ or $α = 41°11'$. In this case the distance measured on the slope would be $5^1/_3$ cubits; measuring on the slope instead of with an horizontal rope would decrease the Sabbath distance by more than a third. In this case the Sages have to agree with R. Meïr.

123 Probably that means $\tan α = .25$, $α \sim 14°$, the error in measurement is $\sim 5\%$.

124 If the difference is only half a cubit, $\tan α = .125$, $α \sim 7°$; the error in measurement is $\sim 1.2\%$, which is not worth the bother; the position of the Sages is justified.

(22d line 27) רִבִּי בָּא בְשֵׁם רַב יְהוּדָה רִבִּי זְעֵירָא בְשֵׁם מַר עוּקְבָן. אֵין מְקַדְּדִין אֶלָא בְחֶבֶל שֶׁלְחֲמִשִּׁים אַמָּה. רִבִּי זְעֵירָא בְשֵׁם רַב חִסְדָּאי. אֵין מְקַדְּדִין אֶלָא בֶהָרִים וְלֹא בְמָקוֹם עֲגֻלָּה עֲרוּפָה. נִיחָא כְמָאן דְּאָמַר. אֶלֶף מִגְרָשׁ וְאַלְפַּיִים תְּחוּם שַׁבָּת. בְּרַם כְּמָאן דָּמַר. אֶלֶף אַמָּה מִגְרָשׁ וְאַלְפַּיִים שָׂדוֹת וּכְרָמִים. כְּלוּם לֶמְדוּ לִתְחוּם שַׁבָּת לֹא מִתְּחוּם עָרֵי הַלְוִיִּים. לְעִיקָּר אֵין מְקַדְּדִין לַטְּפֵילָה מְקַדְּדִין.

וּמָנַיִין שֶׁלֹּא יְהוּ קוֹבְרִין בִּתְחוּם עָרֵי הַלְוִיִּים. רִבִּי אַבָּהוּ בְשֵׁם רִבִּי יוֹסֵה בֶּן חֲנִינָה. וּמִגְרְשֵׁיהֶם יִהְיוּ לִבְהֶמְתָּם וּלְכָל חַיָּתָם: לַחַיִּים נִיתְּנוּ. לֹא נִיתְּנוּ לִקְבוּרוֹת.

[125]Rebbi Abba in the name of Rebbi Jehudah, Rebbi Ze`ira in the name of Mar Uqba: One strip-measures only with a rope of 50 cubits. Rebbi Ze`ira in the name of Rav Ḥasdai: One strip-measures (only in mountains but)[126] not

for the place of breaking the calf's neck. This would be acceptable for him who says, 1000 cubits of open space and 2000 cubits of Sabbath domain. But for him who says, 1000 cubits of open space and 2000 cubits of fields and vineyards, did they not learn the Sabbath domain from the Levitic cities? For the main thing one does not strip-measure; does one strip-measure for the derivative?

[127]From where that one does not bury in Levitic cities? Rebbi Abbahu in the name of Rebbi Yose bar Ḥanina: *And their open spaces shall be for their animals . . . and all their lives*[128]. They were given for living; they were not given for burials.

125 This text is from *Sotah* 5:5, explained in detail in Notes 120-123 and *Makkot* 2:5 (Notes 141-142).

126 With the other two sources read: :Not for Levitic cities.

127 *Num.* 35:3.

128 This paragraph is copied here only as an appendix to the preceding; it does not belong here.

(22d line 34) פִּיס'. אֵין מוֹדְדִין אֶלָּא מִן הַמּוּמְחֶה כול'. הַהֶדְיוֹט שָׁרִיבָה אֵין שׁוֹמְעִין לוֹ.
אָמַר רִבִּי הוֹשַׁעְיָה. הַגִּיעוּךְ סוֹף תְּחוּמֵי שַׁבָּת שֶׁאֵינָן מְחוּוָרִין מִדְּבַר תּוֹרָה. רִבִּי מָנָא בָּעֵי.
נִיחָא אַלְפַּיִים אַמָּה אֵינוֹ מְחוּוָר. אַרְבָּעַת אֲלָפִים מְחוּוָר הוּא. רִבִּי שִׁמְעוֹן בַּר כַּרְסָנָא בְּשֵׁם רִבִּי
אֲחָא. אֵין לָךְ מְחוּוָר מְכוּלָּם אֶלָּא תְחוּם שְׁנֵים עָשָׂר מִיל כְּמַחֲנֵה יִשְׂרָאֵל.

Paragraph. "Surveys may only be made by professionals," etc. One does not listen to a non-professional who added[129].

[130]Rebbi Hoshaia said: You must conclude that the boundaries of Sabbath domains are not clear in the words of the Torah. Rebbi Mana asked, it is accepted that 2'000 cubits is not clear. Are 4'000 cubits not clear? Rebbi Simeon bar Carsana in the name of Rebbi Aḥa: The only clear case among all of them is the domain of twelve *mil* of the camp of Israel.

129 Greek ἰδιώτης, ὁ. A non-professional may testify to the limits of the traditional Sabbath domain (Tosephta 4:16, see below) but may not initiate any changes. Rashba col. 345.

130 Chapter 3, Notes 134-136.

(22d line 39) פיס'. עִיר שֶׁלְּיָחִיד שֶׁנַּעֲשֵׂית שֶׁל רַבִּים כול'. תַּנֵּי בְשֵׁם רִבִּי יוּדָה. אֵין מְעָרְבִין אוֹתָהּ חֲצִייָן. מִחְלְפָה שִׁיטָתֵיהּ דְּרִבִּי יוּדָה. דְּתַנֵּי רִבִּי חִייָה. כֵּיצַד מַתִּירִין רְשׁוּת הָרַבִּים. רִבִּי יוּדָה אוֹמֵר. לֶחִי מִיכָּן וְלֶחִי מִיכָּן. קוֹרָה מִיכָּן וְקוֹרָה מִיכָּן. וַחֲכָמִים אוֹמְרִים. לֶחִי וְקוֹרָה מִיכָּן וְעוֹשֶׂה צוּרַת פֶּתַח מִיכָּן. וְהָכָא אָמַר הָכֵין. לֹא עַל הָדָא אִיתְאֲמָרַת אֶלָּא עַל הָדָא. אֲפִילוּ עִיר גְּדוֹלָה כְּאַנְטוֹכִיָא וְאֵין בָּהּ אֶלָּא דֶּלֶת אַחַת בִּלְבַד מְעָרְבִין עָלֶיהָ. תַּנֵּי בְשֵׁם רִבִּי יוּדָה. אֵין מְעָרְבִין אוֹתָהּ חֲצִייָן. אָמַר רִבִּי יוֹסֵה. הָדָא אָמְרָה. בְּנֵי הַמָּבוֹי שֶׁנְּתָנוּ קוֹרָתָן עַל (גַּבֵּי) [פֶּתַח] הַמָּבוֹי אֵילוּ מוּתָּרִין וְאֵילוּ אֲסוּרִין. נָתְנוּ אֵילוּ וְאֵילוּ. אֵילוּ וְאֵילוּ אֲסוּרִין. כֵּיצַד הוּא עוֹשֶׂה. נוֹתֵן אֶת הַקּוֹרָה עַל פֶּתַח הַמָּבוֹי וּמַתִּיר אֶת הַמָּבוֹי. חֲמִשָּׁה מְבוֹאוֹת פְּתוּחוֹת לְמָבוֹי. נָתְנוּ קוֹרָתָן בְּאֶמְצַע הַמָּבוֹי. אֵילוּ מוּתָּרִין וְאֵילוּ אֲסוּרִין. נָתְנוּ אֵילוּ וְאֵילוּ אֵילוּ וְאֵילוּ אֲסוּרִין. אֵילוּ וְאֵילוּ אֲסוּרִין. כֵּיצַד הוּא עוֹשֶׂה. נוֹתֵן אֶת הַקּוֹרָה עַל פֶּתַח הַמָּבוֹי וּמַתִּיר אֶת הַמָּבוֹי. חַד רִבִּי פִּינְחָס סָלַק לְהָכָא. חָזָא בְּפֶתַח דְּשָׁקְתָא דְגִזּוֹרָאי. אָמַר לָהֶן. חִלַּקְתֶּם עֵירוּבְכֶם. אָמַר לֵיהּ רִבִּי יוּדָה בַּר שָׁלוֹם. לְחִיזּוּק בָּתִּים נַעֲשֵׂית.

Paragraph: "A village which is the property of one person[13] and becomes owned by many," etc. It was stated in the name of Rebbi Jehudah: One does not make an *eruv* in parts. Rebbi Jehudah's argument is inverted since Rebbi Hiyya stated:[131] How does one permit public domain? Rebbi Jehudah says, a lath on each side or a beam on each side, but the Sages say, a lath and a beam on one side and he makes a door frame on the other side. And here he says so? It was not said about this but about the following: Even a big city like Antioch, if it has a single gate one may make an *eruv*[132]. It was stated in the name of Rebbi Jehudah: One does not make an *eruv* in parts. Rebbi Yose said, this[133] implies that if people in an alley put a beam (in) [at the entrance][134] of the alley then these are permitted and those are prohibited. If both of them put it up, both are prohibited. What does he do? He puts the beam at the entrance of the alley and permits the alley[135]. If five alleys opened into one alley and they put their beam in the middle of the alley then these are permitted and those are prohibited[136]. If both of them put it up, both are prohibited. What does he do? He puts the beam at the entrance of the alley and permits the alley. Rebbi Phineas immigrated here. He looked at the entrance of the market of the shearers and said to them, did you split your *eruv*? Rebbi Jehudah bar Shalom told him, it was made to reinforce the houses[137].

131 Chapter 1, Note 147.

132 There is only one entrance; no traffic artery crossing the town. Then one *eruv* can be made for the entire city but no partial one. R. Jehudah states that either one makes no *eruv* at all or one makes one for the entire city. If one made two *eruvim* for two different parts of the city both would be invalid. Babli 59a/b.

133 Since the alley has only one exit it is similar to the city with only one gate. If one made two *eruvim* for two different parts of the alley both would be invalid.

134 The text in parentheses is the original text of the scribe, the one in brackets the corrector's. The corrector's text is impossible. Medieval quotes of the passage (Rashba col. 351, Ritba *ad* 59b p. 50d, Meïri *ad* 59a p. 227a, Rosh Chapter 5 No. 9) all read "in the middle", and this is the meaning of the scribe's text. The dwellers in the back part of the dead-end alley put their cross beam not at the entrance of the alley but in the middle. If the dwellers of the outer part do not make their own *eruv*, the back part *eruv* is valid. If both parts make their own *eruv*, neither of them is valid.

135 A single common *eruv*.

136 A beam at the entrance of a separate alley makes possible an *eruv* for that alley.

137 The beam was there for structural reasons; it was not intended for an *eruv*.

(22d line 55) אֶלָּא אִם כֵּן עָשָׂה חוּצָה לָהּ כְּעִיר חֲדָשָׁה שֶׁבִּיהוּדָה. כְּגוֹן צְנָן וַחֲדָשָׁה וּמִגְדַּל־גָּד: שֶׁיֵּשׁ בָּהּ חֲמִשָּׁה דִיּוּרִין. אֲפִילוּ אֲנָשִׁים נָשִׁים וָטָף. אַסִּי אָמַר. וּבִלְבַד יִשְׂרָאֵל. רִבִּי בָּא בַּר מָמָל שִׁמְעוֹן בַּר חִיָּיה בְשֵׁם רַב. בִּפְתוּחִין לְתוֹכָהּ. אָמַר רִבִּי מָנָא. מִכֵּיוָן שֶׁהֵן פְּתוּחִין לְתוֹכָהּ נַעֲשׂוּ כוּלָּן רְשׁוּת אַחַת.

"Unless one leaves outside like the town Ḥadašah in Jehudah." As *Senan, Ḥadašah, and Migdal-Gad*[138]. "Which has 5[139] inhabitants," even men, women, and children. Assi said, but only Israel. Rebbi Abba bar Mamal, Simeon bar Ḥiyya in the name of Rav: If they open into it[140]. Rebbi Mana said, since they open into it they all are made one domain[141].

138 *Jos.* 15:37.

139 With the Mishnah read: 50.

140 The houses which are left out of the *eruv* have to be accessible from the town, otherwise they could not be part of the *eruv* and leaving them out would not be reserving anything.

141 If houses belong naturally to the town there is no reason to leave them out of the *eruv*. Babli 60a.

(22d line 58) פִּיס׳. מִי שֶׁהָיָה בַּמִּזְרָח כול׳. מָן קוּשְׁיֵי מַקְשֵׁי לָהּ בַּר קַפָּרָא. לְמִזְרָח בָּנוֹ וּלְמַעֲרָב בָּנוֹ. נִיחָא אִם יֵשׁ מִמֶּנּוּ וּלְבֵיתוֹ אַלְפַּיִם אַמָּה וּלְעֵירוּבוֹ יוֹתֵר מִיכֵּן. מוּתָּר לְבֵיתוֹ וְאָסוּר לְעֵירוּבוֹ. לְעֵירוּבוֹ אַלְפַּיִם אַמָּה וּלְבֵיתוֹ יוֹתֵר מִכָּן. מוּתָּר לְעֵירוּבוֹ וּלְבֵיתוֹ אָסוּר.

Paragraph. "If somebody was in the East," etc. Because of the difficulty did Bar Qappara ask, the East of his son and the West of his son? One understands "if there are from his place to his house 2'000 cubits but to his *eruv* more than this, he is permitted up to his house but forbidden to his *eruv*[17]." "If to his *eruv* be 2'000 cubits but to his house more than that, he is permitted up to his *eruv* but forbidden to his house"[142]?

142 If one read the Mishnah as him being in one side of the town and his son in the other side it would be impossible for his house to be farther away than his *eruv*.

Therefore one has to read the Mishnah as "him to the East of his son and the West of his son". Babli 60b.

(22d line 62) פיס'. אַנְשֵׁי עִיר גְּדוֹלָה מְהַלְּכִין אֶת כָּל־עִיר קְטַנָּה כול'. כֵּינֵי מַתְנִיתָא. אַנְשֵׁי עִיר גְּדוֹלָה מְהַלְּכִין אֶת כָּל־עִיר קְטַנָּה. אַנְשֵׁי עִיר קְטַנָּה אֵינָן מְהַלְּכִין אֶת כָּל־עִיר גְּדוֹלָה. כֵּיצַד. לֵית כָּאן כֵּיצַד.

עִיר מָהוּ שֶׁתְּעָלֶה מִמִּדַּת אַלְפַּיִם. אָמַר רִבִּי חִזְקִיָּה רִבִּי סִימוֹן בְּשֵׁם רִבִּי יוֹחָנָן. אֵין עִיר עוֹלָה מִמִּדַּת אַלְפַּיִם. אָמַר רִבִּי אֶלְעָזָר. עִיר עוֹלָה מִמִּדַּת אַלְפַּיִם. בָּרִאשׁוֹנָה הָיוּ בְנֵי טִיבֶּרְיָא מְהַלְּכִין אֶת כָּל־חַמָּתָה. וּבְנֵי חַמָּתָה אֵינָן מַגִּיעִין אֶלָּא עַד הַכִּיפָּה. וְעַכְשָׁיו בְּנֵי חַמָּתָה וּבְנֵי טִיבֶּרְיָא עִיר אַחַת הִיא. אָמַר רִבִּי יִרְמְיָה. מַעֲשֶׂה בְרוֹעֶה אֶחָד זָקֵן שֶׁבָּא וְאָמַר לִפְנֵי רִבִּי. זָכוּר אֲנִי שֶׁהָיוּ בְנֵי מִגְדַּל עוֹלִין לְחַמָּתָה וּמְהַלְּכִין אֶת כָּל־חַמָּתָה וּמַגִּיעִין לֶחָצֵר הַחִיצוֹנָה הַסְמוּכָה לַגֶּשֶׁר. וְהִתִּיר רִבִּי שֶׁיִּהוּ בְנֵי מִגְדַּל עוֹלִין לְחַמָּתָה וּמְהַלְּכִין אֶת כָּל־חַמָּתָה וּמַגִּיעִין לֶחָצֵר הַחִיצוֹנָה עַד הַגֶּשֶׁר. וְעוֹד הִתִּיר רִבִּי שֶׁיִּהוּ בְנֵי גָדֵר יוֹרְדִין לְחַמָּתָה וְעוֹלִין לְגָדֵר. וּבְנֵי חַמָּתָהּ אֵינָן עוֹלִין לְגָדֵר. אָמַר רִבִּי מָנָא. מִפְּנֵי הָרְשׁוּיוֹת. אָמַר רִבִּי יוֹסֵי בֵּירִבִּיהּ בּוּן. לֹא מִן הַטַּעַם הַזֶּה אֶלָּא בְגִין דְּתַנִּינָן. אַנְשֵׁי עִיר גְּדוֹלָה מְהַלְּכִין אֶת כָּל־עִיר קְטַנָּה. וְאֵין אַנְשֵׁי עִיר קְטַנָּה מְהַלְּכִין אֶת כָּל־עִיר גְּדוֹלָה.

Paragraph. "The people of a large town walk through all of a small town," etc. So is the Mishnah: "The people of a large town walk through all of a small town, the people of a small town do not walk through all of a large town[143]. How is that?" There is no "how is that"[144].

Is a city counted in the measure of 2'000[145]? Rebbi Hizqiah said, Rebbi Simon in the name of Rebbi Johanan: A city is not counted in the measure of 2'000. Rebbi Eleazar said, a city is counted in the measure of 2'000[146]. In earlier times the people of Tiberias were walking through all its hot springs but the people of its hot springs came only to the cupola. But today for the people of Tiberias and the people of its hot springs it is one city[147]. Rebbi Jeremiah said, [148]"it happened that an old shepherd came and said before Rebbi, I remember the people of Magdala walking up to its[149] hot springs, walking through its hot springs and coming up to the outer courtyard close to the bridge; and Rebbi permitted that the people of Magdala walk up to its hot springs, walking through its hot springs and come up to the outer courtyard up to the bridge. [150]In addition, Rebbi permitted that the people of Gadara descend to their hot springs and return to Gadara but the people of the hot springs may not ascend to Gadara." Rebbi Mana said, because of the authorities[151]. Rebbi Yose ben Rebbi Abun said, it is not because of this but because we have stated "the people of a large town walk through all of a small town, the people of a small town do not walk through all of a large town[143]."

143 The Sabbath domain of the large city is measured from the completion; any village inside the domain is counted only as 4 cubits. If the Sabbath domain of the village reaches only the completion of the city but not the city itself, the city is not counted as 4 cubits for them.

144 The next part of the Mishnah is a new sentence, independent of the preceding text.

145 If that Sabbath domain of one town reaches another town, is the other town wholly incorporated in the Sabbath domain of the first or not?

146 For him a city is counted as 4 cubits only if he dwells there, not if it is in the Sabbath domain.

147 Enough houses have been built in between to make the hot springs part of the completion of Tiberias.

148 Tosephta 4:16. The Tosephta conflates the stories about Magdala and Gadara.

149 Since the hot springs of Tiberias are near the shores of Lake Genezareth, these must be different hot springs.

150 Babli 61a.

151 The citizens of Gadara are the masters of Hammat Gader and go there without permission; the people of Hammat Gader may go to Gadara only with permission.

(23a line 2) רִבִּי יִצְחָק בַּר נַחְמָן בְּשֵׁם רִבִּי חֲנָנָה. מַה פְּלִיגִין. בְּשֶׁנְּתָנוּ עֵירוּבָן בִּפְלַטְיָא. אֲבָל אִם נָתְנוּ עֵירוּבָן בְּבָתִּים אַף רִבִּי עֲקִיבָה מוֹדֶה. רִבִּי בָּא בְּרֵיהּ דְּרִבִּי פַּפֵּי בָעֵי. הָיְתָה עִיר שֶׁעֲירְבָה וְנָתְנוּ עֵירוּבָן בִּפְלַטְיָא לֹא כְמִי שֶׁנְּתָנוּ עֵירוּבָן בְּבָתִּים.

עִיר שֶׁחָרְבָה. רִבִּי לְעֶזֶר אוֹמֵר. מְהַלֵּךְ אֶת כּוּלָּהּ וְחוּצָה לָהּ אַלְפַּיִם אַמָּה. שְׁמוּאֵל אָמַר. אֵין לוֹ מָקוֹם עֵירוּבוֹ אֶלָּא אַלְפַּיִם אַמָּה. רִבִּי בָּא בַּר כַּהֲנָא רַב חִיָּיה בַּר אַשִּׁי בְּשֵׁם רַב. הַנּוֹתֵן עֵירוּבוֹ בְּדִיר אוֹ בְסַהַר מְהַלֵּךְ אֶת כּוּלָּהּ וְחוּצָה לָהּ אַלְפַּיִם אַמָּה. וְדִיר וְסַהַר לֹא כְמִי שֶׁחָרְבוּ נָתִּים וְדִיּוּרִין.

עִיר חֲדָשָׁה מוֹדֵד מִן הַבָּתִּים וִישָׁנָה מוֹדֵד מִן הַחוֹמָה. אֵי זוֹ הִיא חֲדָשָׁה וְאֵי זוֹ הִיא יְשָׁנָה. רִבִּי זְעִירָא בְשֵׁם רַב חִסְדָּאי. בָּנָה בָתִּים וְאַחַר בָּנָה חוֹמָה. זוֹ הִיא חֲדָשָׁה. בָּנָה חוֹמָה וְאַחַר בָּנָה בָתִּים. זוֹ הִיא יְשָׁנָה. רִבִּי זְעִירָא אָמַר. בֵּין זוֹ וּבֵין זוֹ חֲדָשָׁה. וְאֵי זוֹ הִיא יְשָׁנָה. כָּל־שֶׁהָיוּ בָהּ דִּיּוּרִין וְחָרְבוּ. רִבִּי זְעִירָא בְדַעְתֵּיהּ. דְּאִיתְפַּלְגוֹן. בָּנָה תִשְׁעָה לְשֵׁם קַרְפֵּף וְאֶחָד לְשֵׁם דַּייָר. אָמַר רִבִּי לָעְזָר. וַאֲפִילוּ בָּנָה אֶת הָעֲשִׂירִי לְשֵׁם דִּירָה. הֲרֵי הוּא כְדִירָה.

Rebbi Isaac bar Nahman in the name of Rebbi Ḥanina: Where do they disagree[152]? If they put their *eruv* in a public square. But if they put their *eruv* in houses even Rebbi Aqiba will agree[153]. Rebbi Abba the son of Rebbi Pappai asked: If it was a city which made an *eruv* and he put his *eruv* in a public square, is it not as if they gave their *eruv* in houses[154]?

A town which was destroyed[155]. Rebbi Eleazar says, he walks its entirety and outside 2'000 cubits. Samuel says, he only has 2'000 cubits [from] the place of his *eruv*. Rebbi Abba bar Cahana, Rav Ḥiyya bar Ashi in the name of Rab: If somebody deposits his *eruv* in a sheep-pen or a sheep-corral he walks its entirety and outside it 2'000 cubits. Are a sheep-pen or a sheep-corral not as if houses and apartments were destroyed[156]?

For a new city one measures from the houses; for an old one one measures from the wall[157]. What is new and what is old? Rebbi Ze'ira in the name of Rav Ḥasdai: If he built houses and afterwards built a wall, that is new; if he built a wall and then built the houses, that is old. Rebbi Ze'ira said, in both cases it is new, and what is old? Anything which had dwellings and they were destroyed. Rebbi Ze'ira follows his opinion, since they disagreed: If he built nine as fore-court and one for dwelling. Rebbi Eleazar said, even if he built the tenth as dwelling it is for dwelling[158].

152 R. Aqiba and the Sages in the second part of the Mishnah.

153 It is not very clear what this means. In the Babli 61b it is formulated: If somebody makes Sabbath in a ruined city (he lives there in one of the ruined houses) he walks through the entire city and outside 2'000 cubits, like a regular city dweller. But if he puts his *eruv* into a ruined city he only has 2'000 cubits from the place of his *eruv* (consistent with the thesis that he who makes an *eruv* loses all additions to the Sabbath domain. One has to assume that "depositing an *eruv* in a house" means making Sabbath in that house.)

154 If the inhabitants made an *eruv* to carry in the entire walled city, it is obvious that the entire city can be counted only as 4 cubits in the domain even for a person not domiciled there.

155 But the ruins and an outline of the wall are still standing.	158 The text clearly is elliptic. It seems that it should read: If an enclosure was built by several people, for R. Ze`ira it counts as built for a human dwelling if all builders intend it as such; for R. Eleazar it counts as such if at least one builder had this intention.
156 Sheep pens were never built for human dwelling, houses were even if now they are ruins. Since one makes Sabbath in a human dwelling, what holds for sheep pens certainly holds for ruined houses.	
157 Babli 26a.	

(23 line 17) פיס׳. אָמַר לְהֶן רִבִּי עֲקִיבָה אֵי אַתֶּם מוֹדִין לִי כוּל׳. רִבִּי יַעֲקֹב בַּר אָחָא בְּשֵׁם רִבִּי אֶלְעָזָר. קַל הוּא הַקּוֹנֶה שְׁבִיתָה בְּקַרְפֵּף מִן הַנּוֹתֵן עֵירוּבוֹ בַּקַּרְפֵּף. הַקּוֹנֶה שְׁבִיתָה בְּקַרְפֵּף מְהַלֵּךְ אֶת כּוּלּוֹ וְהוּצָה לוֹ אַלְפַּיִם אַמָּה. הַנּוֹתֵן עֵירוּבוֹ בַּקַּרְפֵּף אֵין לוֹ מְקוֹם עֵירוּבוֹ אֶלָא אַלְפַּיִם אַמָּה. רִבִּי זְעִירָא בָעֵי. אָמַר. תִּקָּנֶה לִי שְׁבִיתָה בְּקַרְפֵּף. אָמַר רִבִּי חֲנַנְיָה בְּרֵיהּ דְּרִבִּי הִלֵּל. מַחֲלוֹקֶת רִבִּי מֵאִיר וְרִבִּי יוּדָה. רִבִּי מֵאִיר אוֹמֵר. עִיקַּר עֵירוּב בַּכִּכָּר. בַּנּוֹתֵן עֵירוּבוֹ בַּקַּרְפֵּף אֵין לוֹ מְקוֹם עֵירוּבוֹ אֶלָא אַלְפַּיִם אַמָּה. רִבִּי יוּדָא אוֹמֵר. עִיקַּר עֵירוּב בְּרַגְלָיו. בְּאוֹמֵר. תִּקָּנֶה לִי שְׁבִיתָה בְּקַרְפֵּף. מְהַלֵּךְ אֶת כּוּלָּהּ וְהוּצָה לָהּ אַלְפַּיִם אַמָּה.

Paragraph. "Rebbi Aqiba told them, do you not agree with me," etc. Rebbi Jacob bar Aha in the name of Rebbi Eleazar. The one who acquires rest[159] in a fore-court has it easier than one who puts his *eruv* in a fore-court. He who acquires rest in a fore-court walks in its entirety and outside of it 2'000 cubits. He who puts his *eruv* in a fore-court only has 2'000 cubits from the place of his *eruv*[160]. Rebbi Ze`ira asked: If one said, rest should be acquired for me in the fore-court? Rebbi Hanania the son of Rebbi Hillel said, this is the disagreement of Rebbi Meïr and Rebbi Jehudah[161]. Rebbi Meïr is of the opinion, the main point of an *eruv* is by a loaf. If he puts his *eruv* in a fore-court he only has 2'000 cubits from the place of his *eruv*. Rebbi Jehudah said, the main point of an *eruv* is by his feet. If he said, rest should be acquired for me in the fore-court, he walks in its entirety and outside of it 2'000 cubits.

159 It is his place of residence for this Sabbath.	loses all additions to the circular domain of radius 2'000 cubits.
160 Since anybody who makes an *eruv*	161 Chapter 4, Note 83.

(23a line 26) גַּג הַמִּגְדָּל נִידּוֹן כָּעִיר. גַּג הַמְּעָרָה נִידּוֹן כְּשָׂדוֹת. מַה. דְּיוּרִין מַמָּשׁ. אוֹ אֲפִילוּ רְאוּיָה לְדִיּוּרִין. מִן מַה דָּמַר רִבִּי יִצְחָק בַּר נַחְמָן בְּשֵׁם רִבִּי חֲנִינָא. אַתְּ רוֹאֶה אוֹתָהּ כִּילוּ מְלֵיאָה מַיִם וָטִיט. הָדָא אָמְרָה אֲפִילוּ רְאוּיָה לְדִיּוּרִין. אָמַר רִבִּי יִצְחָק בֵּירִבִּי אֶלְעָזָר. הָדָא אָמְרָה עִיר שֶׁיֵּשׁ לָהּ שְׁנֵי פְתָחִים. אִם יֵשׁ בֵּין זֶה לָזֶה אַרְבַּעַת אֲלָפִים אַמָּה חָסֵר אַחַת. מְהַלֵּךְ אֶת כּוּלָּהּ וְחוּצָה לָהּ אַלְפַּיִם אַמָּה. אַרְבַּעַת אֲלָפִים אַמָּה. אֵין לוֹ מִמְּקוֹם עִירוּבוֹ אֶלָּא אַלְפַּיִם אַמָּה. אָמַר רִבִּי בָּא. אַסְבְּרֵי רִבִּי זְעִירָא. אִין יִתֵּן סַנְדָּלוֹי הָכָא הוּא אָתֵי בְרָא וְנָסֵי לוֹן. אִין יִתֵּן סַנְדָּלוֹי הָכָא הוּא אָתֵי בְרָא וְנָסֵי לוֹן. מַה בֵּין אָתֵי בְרָא וּמַה בֵּין אָתֵי בְרָא. מֵרוּחַ אַחַת אָסוּר מִשְׁתֵּי רוּחוֹת מוּתָּר.

רִבִּי אָחָא בְשֵׁם רַב חִינְנָא. אִם הָיְתָה נַגָּהּ שֶׁלַּמְּעָרָה אַרְבָּעָה אֲלָפִים אַמָּה. מְהַלֵּךְ אֶת כּוּלָּהּ וְחוּצָה לָהּ אַלְפַּיִם אַמָּה. עַל גַּבֵּי חוֹמָה אֲפִילוּ כַּמָּה מוּתָּר. אִם הָיְתָה נַגָּהּ שֶׁלַּמְּעָרָה שֵׁשֶׁת אֲלָפִים אַמָּה. מְהַלֵּךְ אֶת כּוּלָּהּ וְחוּצָה לָהּ עַל יְדֵי נִיבָּרִיּוֹת. אָחֲרֵי הַגַּגִּין מָהֶן. רִבִּי יוֹסֵה בְשֵׁם רִבִּי יַעֲקֹב בַּר אָחָא רִבִּי אֵינְיָיא בַּר פָּזִי בְשֵׁם רִבִּי יְהוּדָה רִבִּי אָחָא מַטֵּי בָהּ בְּשֵׁם שְׁמוּאֵל. אֲחוֹרֵי הַגַּגִּים מְטַלְטְלִין בָּהֶן אֲפִילוּ כּוֹר כּוֹרַיִים. רִבִּי מֵאִיר אָמַר. מְטַלְטְלִין בָּהֶן עַד בֵּית סָאתַיִים. אָמַר רִבִּי יוֹסֵי בֵּירִבִּי בּוּן. מִילְּתֵיהּ דְּרַב פְּלִיגָא עֲלוֹי. דְּתַנִּינָן תַּמָּן. כָּל גַּגּוֹת הָעִיר רְשׁוּת אַחַת. שְׁמוּאֵל אָמַר. עַד בֵּית סָאתַיִים. רַב אָמַר. מְטַלְטְלִין בָּהֶן אֲפִילוּ כּוֹר כּוֹרַיִים. הִיא אֲחוֹרֵי הַגַּגִּים הִיא אֲחוֹרֵי הַסְּפִינָה.

The roof of a tower is considered [part of] the town. The roof of a cave is considered as fields. What, really dwellers[162]? Or maybe just inhabitable? Since Rebbi Isaac bar Naḥman said in the name of Rebbi Ḥanina: one considers it as if filled by water and clay[163], this means even inhabitable. Rebbi Isaac ben Rebbi Eleazar said, this implies (a city)[164] which has two exits, if between one and the other there are 3'999 cubits one walks in its entirety and outside it 2'000 cubits, 4'000 cubits he only has 2'000 cubits from the place of his *eruv*. Rabbi Aḥa said; Rebbi Ze`ira explained it. If he would put his sandal anywhere he could go outside and put it on; and if he would put his sandal anywhere he could go outside and put it on. What is the difference from which side he comes? From one side it is forbidden, from both sides it is permitted[60].

Rebbi Aḥa in the name of Rav Hinena: If the roof of the cave was 4'000 cubits[165] he walks in its entirety and outside it 2'000 cubits, on top of a wall it is unlimited. If the roof of the cave was 6'000 cubits he walks in its entirety and outside it 2'000 cubits by the help of *nibariot*[166]. What about tops of roofs? Rebbi Yose in the name of Rebbi Jacob bar Aḥa, Rebbi Aeneas bar

Pazi in the name of Rebbi[167] Jehudah, Rebbi Aḥa brings it in the name of Samuel. On top of the roofs one carries even a *kor*, even two *kor*[168]. Rebbi Meïr said, one carries up to two *bet se'ah*. Rebbi Yose ben Rebbi Abun said, the word of Rav disagrees with him[169], as we have stated there[170]: "All roofs of a city form a single domain." Samuel said, up to two *bet se'ah*. Rav said, one carries there even a *kor*, even two *kor*. It is the same for tops of roofs and tops of ships[171].

162 This refers to Mishnah 10. Do we require that a cave be inhabited or only that it should be habitable?

163 His definition of "uninhabited" is "unhabitable"; therefore for him "inhabited" means " habitable".

164 It seems that for עיר "city" one should read מערה "cave".

165 Probably this again should read "4'000 - 1".

166 Possibly "protuberances", Arabic نبرة.

If the cave below is considered a human dwelling, the roof above it can be made similar to the roof of a house by subdividing it into several roofs by natural outcroppings.

167 Read: "Rav Jehudah".

168 Meaning *bet kor*, a surface area of 30 *bet seah* (Chapter 1, Note 288).

169 With both Samuel as quoted later, and R. Aha whose attribution is shown wrong.

170 Mishnah 9:1. Even though the houses below define different private domains, the roofs, although divided by walls, form a single domain on which one may carry from one house to the next

171 If ships are tied together in a harbor, one carries from ship to ship as one carries from roof to roof.

הדר פרק שישי

(fol.23a) **משנה א**: הַדָּר עִם הַנָּכְרִי בֶּחָצֵר אוֹ עִם מִי שֶׁאֵינוֹ מוֹדֶה בָּעֵירוּב הֲרֵי זֶה אוֹסֵר עָלָיו. רִבִּי לִיעֶזֶר בֶּן יַעֲקֹב אוֹמֵר לְעוֹלָם אֵינוֹ אוֹסֵר עַד שֶׁיִּהוּ שְׁנֵי יִשְׂרְאֵלִים אוֹסְרִין זֶה עַל זֶה:

Mishnah 1: If someone dwells with a Non-Jew in a courtyard or with one who rejects the notion of *eruv*[1], that one makes it forbidden for him[2]. Rebbi Eliezer ben Jacob says that he[3] never forbids unless there are two Jews who mutually forbid[4].

משנה ב: אָמַר רַבָּן גַּמְלִיאֵל מַעֲשֶׂה בִּצְדוּקִי אֶחָד שֶׁהָיָה דָר עִמָּנוּ בַּמָּבוֹי בִּירוּשָׁלַיִם אָמַר לָנוּ אַבָּא מַהֲרוּ וְהוֹצִיאוּ אֶת כָּל־הַכֵּלִים לַמָּבוֹי עַד שֶׁלֹּא יוֹצִיא וְיֶאֱסוֹר עֲלֵיכֶם. רִבִּי יְהוּדָה אוֹמֵר בְּלָשׁוֹן אַחֶרֶת מַהֲרוּ וַעֲשׂוּ צָרְכֵיכֶם בַּמָּבוֹי עַד שֶׁלֹּא יוֹצִיא וְיֶאֱסוֹר עֲלֵיכֶם:

Mishnah 2: Rabban Gamliel said, if happened that a Sadducee was dwelling with us in the alley in Jerusalem and my father told us be quick and bring all the vessels into the alley before he can bring out and forbid for you[5]. Rebbi Jehudah says it in another formulation, be quick and work in the alley before he can bring out and forbid for you[6].

משנה ג: אַנְשֵׁי הֶחָצֵר שֶׁשָּׁכַח אֶחָד מֵהֶן וְלֹא עֵירַב בֵּיתוֹ אָסוּר מִלְּהַכְנִיס וּלְהוֹצִיא לוֹ וְלָהֶם וְשֶׁלָּהֶם מוּתָּרִין לוֹ וְלָהֶן. נָתְנוּ לוֹ רְשׁוּתָן הוּא מוּתָּר וְהֵן אֲסוּרִין. הָיוּ שְׁנַיִם אוֹסְרִין זֶה עַל זֶה שֶׁאֶחָד נוֹתֵן רְשׁוּת וְנוֹטֵל רְשׁוּת וּשְׁנַיִם נוֹתְנִים רְשׁוּת וְאֵינָן נוֹטְלִין רְשׁוּת:

Mishnah 3: In a courtyard where one dweller forgot to make an *eruv*, his house is forbidden for him and them to bring anything in or take out[7], but theirs are permitted for them and him[8]. If they ceded their rights to him, he is permitted but they are forbidden[9]. If there were two they forbid one another since a single individual cedes rights and accepts rights but two may cede rights but cannot accept rights[10].

משנה ד: מֵאֵימָתַי נוֹתְנִין רְשׁוּת בֵּית שַׁמַּאי אוֹמְרִים מִבְּעוֹד יוֹם וּבֵית הִלֵּל אוֹמְרִים מִשֶּׁתֶּחְשַׁךְ. מִי שֶׁנָּתַן רְשׁוּתוֹ וְהוֹצִיא בֵּין שׁוֹגֵג בֵּין מֵזִיד הֲרֵי זֶה אוֹסֵר עָלָיו דִּבְרֵי רִבִּי מֵאִיר. רִבִּי יְהוּדָה אוֹמֵר מֵזִיד אוֹסֵר שׁוֹגֵג אֵינוֹ אוֹסֵר:

Mishnah 4: When may one start giving away rights? The House of Shammai say, as long as it is daylight[11], but the House of Hillel say, when it gets dark. If somebody gave away his rights and then brought out, whether in error or intentionally, he forbids, the words of Rebbi Meïr. Rebbi Jehudah says, intentionally he forbids, in error he does not forbid[12].

משנה ה בַּעַל הַבַּיִת שֶׁהָיָה שׁוּתָף לִשְׁכֵנִים לְזֶה בַיַּיִן וְלָזֶה בַיַּיִן אֵינָן צְרִיכִים לְעָרֵב. לָזֶה בַיַּיִן וְלָזֶה בַשֶּׁמֶן צְרִיכִין לְעָרֵב. רִבִּי שִׁמְעוֹן אוֹמֵר אֶחָד זֶה וְאֶחָד זֶה אֵינָן צְרִיכִין לְעָרֵב:

Mishnah 5: If the owner of a house participated with several neighbors with wine, they do not need to make an *eruv*. If with wine with one but oil with the other they need to make an *eruv*. Rebbi Simeon says neither of them has to make an *eruv*[13].

משנה ו חָמֵשׁ חֲבוּרוֹת שֶׁשָּׁבְתוּ בִטְרִיקְלִין אֶחָד בֵּית שַׁמַּאי אוֹמְרִים עֵירוּב לְכָל־חֲבוּרָה וַחֲבוּרָה. וּבֵית הִלֵּל אוֹמְרִים עֵירוּב אַחַת לְכוּלָּן. וּמוֹדִין שֶׁאִם מִקְצָתָן שְׁרוּיִין בַּחֲדָרִים אוֹ בַעֲלִיּוֹת שֶׁהֵן צְרִיכִין עֵירוּב לְכָל־חֲבוּרָה וַחֲבוּרָה:

Mishnah 6: Five groups who rested in one big hall[14] during the Sabbath, the House of Shammai say, a separate *eruv* for each of them, but the House of Hillel say, one *eruv* for all of them; however they agree that if some of them stayed for the Sabbath in separate rooms or on a second floor that each group needs a separate *eruv*[15].

משנה ז הָאַחִין הַשּׁוּתָּפִין שֶׁהָיוּ אוֹכְלִין עַל שׁוּלְחַן אֲבִיהֶן וִישֵׁנִין בְּבָתֵּיהֶן צְרִיכִין עֵירוּב לְכָל־(fol. 23b)אֶחָד וְאֶחָד. לְפִיכָךְ אִם שָׁכַח אֶחָד מֵהֶם וְלֹא עֵירֵב בִּיטֵּל רְשׁוּתוֹ. אֵימָתַי בִּזְמַן שֶׁמּוֹלִיכִין אֶת עֵירוּבָן לְמָקוֹם אֶחָד אֲבָל אִם הָיָה עֵירוּב בָּא אֶצְלָן אוֹ שֶׁאֵין עִמָּהָן דִּיּוּרִין בֶּחָצֵר אֵינָן צְרִיכִין לְעָרֵב:

Mishnah 7: Brothers sharing property who were eating at their father's table[16] but sleeping in their own houses[17] need an *eruv* for each of them. Therefore if one of them forgot and did not make an *eruv* he is deemed to have ceded his rights[18]. When? If they all bring their *eruvin* to one place[19] but if the *eruv* came to them, or there were no other dwellers with them[20], they do not need an *eruv*.

משנה ח חָמֵשׁ חֲצֵירוֹת פְּתוּחוֹת זוֹ לָזוֹ וּפְתוּחוֹת לַמָּבוֹי עֵירְבוּ בַּחֲצֵירוֹת וְלֹא נִשְׁתַּתְּפוּ בַּמָּבוֹי מוּתָּרִין בַּחֲצֵירוֹת וַאֲסוּרִין בַּמָּבוֹי וְאִם נִשְׁתַּתְּפוּ בַּמָּבוֹי מוּתָּרִין כָּאן וְכָאן. עֵירְבוּ בַחֲצֵירוֹת וְנִשְׁתַּתְּפוּ בַּמָּבוֹי שָׁכַח אֶחָד מִבְּנֵי הֶחָצֵר וְלֹא עֵירֵב מוּתָּרִין כָּאן וְכָאן. מִבְּנֵי הַמָּבוֹי וְלֹא נִשְׁתַּתֵּף מוּתָּרִין בַּחֲצֵירוֹת וַאֲסוּרִין בַּמָּבוֹי שֶׁהַמָּבוֹי לַחֲצֵרוֹת כֶּחָצֵר לַבָּתִּים:

Mishnah 8: Five courtyards were open to one another and open to an alley. If they made *eruvin* in the courtyards but did not participate in the alley, they are permitted in the courtyards and forbidden the alley, but if they participated in the alley the are permitted both here and there[21]. If they made *eruvin* for the courtyards and participated in the alley and one of the dwellers in a courtyard forgot and did not make an *eruv* all parties are permitted; if he dwelt in the alley and did not participate, they are permitted in the courtyards but forbidden in the alley since the relationship of alley to courtyards is like the one of courtyards to houses[22].

משנה ח שְׁתֵּי חֲצֵירוֹת זוֹ לִפְנִים מִזּוֹ עֵירְבָה הַפְּנִימִית וְלֹא עֵירְבָה הַחִיצוֹנָה הַפְּנִימִית מוּתֶּרֶת וְהַחִיצוֹנָה אֲסוּרָה. הַחִיצוֹנָה וְלֹא הַפְּנִימִית שְׁתֵּיהֶן אֲסוּרוֹת. עֵירְבָה זוֹ לְעַצְמָהּ וְזוֹ לְעַצְמָהּ זוֹ מוּתֶּרֶת בִּפְנֵי עַצְמָהּ וְזוֹ מוּתֶּרֶת בִּפְנֵי עַצְמָהּ. רִבִּי עֲקִיבָה אוֹסֵר אֶת הַחִיצוֹנָה שֶׁדְּרִיסַת הָרֶגֶל אוֹסַרְתָּהּ. וַחֲכָמִים אוֹמְרִים אֵין דְּרִיסַת הָרֶגֶל אוֹסֶרֶת:

Mishnah 9: Two courtyards, one inside the other[23]. If for the inner one they made an *eruv* but not the outer one, the inner one is permitted and the outer one forbidden. If the outer one but not the inner one, both are forbidden. If both made separate *eruvin*, both are permitted separately; Rebbi Aqiba forbids the outer one since the right of access makes it forbidden but the Sages say the right of access does not make it forbidden[24].

משנה י שָׁכַח אֶחָד מִן הַחִיצוֹנָה וְלֹא עֵירֵב הַפְּנִימִית מוּתֶּרֶת וְהַחִיצוֹנָה אֲסוּרָה. מִן הַפְּנִימִית וְלֹא עֵירֵב שְׁתֵּיהֶן אֲסוּרוֹת. נָתְנוּ אֶת עֵירוּבָן לְמָקוֹם אֶחָד שָׁכַח אֶחָד בֵּין מִן הַפְּנִימִית בֵּין מִן הַחִיצוֹנָה וְלֹא עֵירֵב. שְׁתֵּיהֶן אֲסוּרוֹת. וְאִם הָיוּ שֶׁל יְחִידִים אֵינָן צְרִיכִין לְעָרֵב:

Mishnah 10: If one of the outer courtyard forgot and did not make the *eruv*[25], the inner one is permitted and the outer one forbidden. If of the inner one, both are forbidden[26]. If they deposited they *eruvin* at one place[27] and one of them forgot, whether from the inner or the outer one, both are forbidden but if they belonged to single individuals they do not have to make an *eruv*[28].

1   A member of a Sadducee sect.
2   For the anonymous Tanna even a single Gentile prevents the Jew from using the courtyard on the Sabbath. For R. Eliezer ben Jacob the Gentile becomes a problem (to be discussed in connection with Mishnah 3) only if there are at least two Jewish dwellers in the courtyard.
3   A Gentile is nonexistent for the rules of the Sabbath; he can neither permit nor

prohibit.

4 If two Jews (including Sadducees) dwell in houses opening to the same courtyard they may not carry in the courtyard unless there be an *eruv*. The problem of the Sadducee is treated in the next Mishnah.

5 The argument behind the institution of *eruv haserot* is that a limited-access courtyard is not a public domain; it can be formally turned into a private domain by organizing a common meal of all dwellers in the courtyard. The *eruv*, a collection of food to which every family dwelling there has contributed, represents this common meal which does not have to be realized. If a rabbinic Jew does not want to be friendly with his neighbors, he can refrain from contributing to the *eruv* and instead cede his rights to carry in the courtyard to the members of the *eruv*. Then they will be able to carry there (as explained in the subsequent Mishnaiot) but he will be forbidden to do so.

We do know that Sadducees objected in principle to the institution of all kinds of *eruvin*, but the fragments of Sadducee *halakhah* available do not permit us to decide whether they considered a courtyard with a single exit to the street as private or public domain. It seems that different Sadducee sects had different opinions in this matter. All Sadducee sects did consider a dead-end alley as a street and public domain. If a Sadducee considers the courtyard as public domain he will not carry there; therefore he can be considered as ceding his rights to the rabbinic dwellers in the courtyard (Rashi on the Mishnah, 61b) and they can make the *eruv* among themselves; this argument certainly applies to alleys. If he considers the courtyard as private domain it will be impossible to make an *eruv*. If only one rabbinic family is living in the alley they can lay claim to the use of the alley by bringing a table and chairs from the house there before nightfall. If at sundown the alley was their dining space, anything the Sadducee will do later is irrelevant.

6 He does not require the set-up of pieces of furniture, only that the alley be working space at sundown.

7 If he does not participate in the *eruv*, the courtyard has the status of (rabbinic) public domain for his house. This status is of the house, not the person; it applies to everybody.

8 The *eruv* makes the courtyard the common domain of the remaining houses; this status also is of the houses, not the persons; it applies to everybody.

9 In this case there is no *eruv*.

10 While they may not accept ceded rights from a Jew they may buy the rights to carry in the courtyard from a Gentile dwelling there. Once the Gentile has accepted payment he cannot retract his cessation even if he should use courtyard or alley for which he received the money.

11 They hold that this cessation is a legal act and therefore prohibited on the Sabbath; the House of Hillel hold that it is an agreement among friends and a purely negative statement, a decision not to exercise one's rights, and as such permitted on the Sabbath.

12 Both R. Meïr and R. Jehudah consider the case that the person ceding his rights uses the courtyard before the others could

use it. If the use was intentional it proves that the cessation was retracted; if it was in error the cessation still is valid. R. Meïr agrees in principle but he treats unintentional infraction as an intentional one as a precaution, a "fence around the Law".

13   If all the people living around a courtyard or in an alley are in business together and own wine stored at one place in their courtyard or alley they do not need an *eruv* since some of the wine might be used as common food. R. Simeon extends this to several kinds of food belonging to several people as long as the foods are sometimes used together as food

14   Latin *triclinium*.

15   The people in question are all renters. If they have different units as bedrooms the relationship of the hall to the bedrooms is that of a courtyard to houses and the different groups must contribute to the *eruv*. A group is composed by people eating together; since an *eruv* is represented by a symbolic meal, an actual meal together obviates the need for an *eruv*.

16   And all food is provided by the father.

17   In the same courtyard.

18   Automatically.

19   In most Mishnah mss: למקום אחר "to another place" which is not their father's house.

20   If the *eruv* is at the father's house, the father's food counts for the entire family. Similarly a family compound does not need an *eruv*.

21   Participation in an alley makes separate *eruvin* in the courtyards unnecessary; defects in these *eruvin* become irrelevant. Participation in the alley is by courtyards, not by individual houses.

22   Also the *eruv* of a courtyard obviates the necessity for separate *eruvin* in multi-family buildings in that courtyard, but *eruvin* in multi-family buildings in a courtyard do not take the place of an *eruv* for the courtyard.

23   The inner courtyard has no direct exit to the street; its dwellers have the right to use the outer courtyard for exit and entry. An *eruv* in the inner courtyard has no influence on the outer one. An *eruv* for the outer one alone is incomplete since the inner courtyard has the same status as a multi-party dwelling opening into the courtyard.

25   A right of exit and entry is not necessarily a right of carrying things on the Sabbath.

25   And did not cede his rights.

26   As stated in Mishnah 9, there cannot be an *eruv* in the outer one if there is none in the inner one.

27   Their status is as if outer and inner courtyards made separate *eruvin*.

(23b line 24)   הַדָּר עִם הַנָּכְרִי בֶּחָצֵר כול'. חָצֵר שֶׁלְּנָכְרֵי כְּדִיר וְסַהַר שֶׁלְּבְהֵמָה. מְתִיבִין רַבָּנִין לְרִבִּי אֱלִיעֶזֶר בֶּן יַעֲקֹב. אִילוּ יִשְׂרָאֵל וּבְהֵמָה שֶׁהָיוּ דָרִים בְּחָצֵר שֶׁמָּא אֵין הַבְּהֵמָה אוֹסֶרֶת. כְּשֵׁם שֶׁהַבְּהֵמָה אוֹסֶרֶת כָּךְ הַגּוֹי אוֹסֵר. מֵתִיב רִבִּי אֱלִיעֶזֶר בֶּן יַעֲקֹב לְרַבָּנִין. אִילוּ יִשְׂרָאֵל וּבְהֵמָה שֶׁהָיוּ דָרִין בְּחָצֵר מָה הַבְּהֵמָה אוֹסֶרֶת. כְּשֵׁם שֶׁאֵין הַבְּהֵמָה אוֹסֶרֶת כָּךְ הַגּוֹי אֵינוֹ אוֹסֵר.

"If somebody dwells with a Non-Jew in a courtyard," etc. "A Non-Jew's courtyard is like a sheep-pen or a sheep-corral.[28]" The rabbis objected to Rebbi Eliezer ben Jacob: If a Jew and an animal[29] were living in a courtyard, would the animal not forbid? Just as an animal forbids so the Gentile forbids. Rebbi Eliezer ben Jacob objected to the rabbis: If a Jew and an animal were living in a courtyard, what would the animal forbid? Just as an animal does not forbid so the Gentile does not forbid.

28 Tosephta 5:19 (cf. Chapter 5, Note 156).
29 The animal belongs to another (Jewish) owner. Since the courtyard contains at least one dwelling, it is not subject to the 5'000 square cubits rule. The rabbis consider the barn as a dwelling if the owner is not the owner of the house. R. Eliezer ben Jacob denies that a barn is a dwelling.

(23b line 29) רִבִּי יַעֲקֹב בַּר אָחָא רִבִּי יָסָא בְּשֵׁם רִבִּי יוֹחָנָן. הֲלָכָה כְרִבִּי יוֹחָנָן בֶּן נוּרִי. רִבִּי הוֹשַׁעְיָה בָעֵי. מַה צְרִיכָה כְהָדָא דְתַנֵּי. רִבִּי לִיעֶזֶר בֶּן יַעֲקֹב. בְּרַם כְּרַבָּנִין. חֲלוּקִין עַל רִבִּי יוֹחָנָן בֶּן נוּרִי.

Rebbi Jacob bar Aha, Rebbi Yasa in the name of Rebbi Johanan: Practice follows Rebbi Johanan ben Nuri[30]. Rebbi Hoshaia asked, for what is this needed? For what we have stated, "Rebbi Eliezer ben Jacob[31]". But following the rabbis? The rabbis disagree with Rebbi Johanan ben Nuri[32].

30 Chapter 1, Note 62, Babli 46a. R. Johanan ben Nuri holds in contrast to the rabbis (representing R. Meïr) that a Sabbath domain can be acquired in sleep.
31 Tosephta 5:20: "Practice follows Rebbi Eliezer ben Jacob." Both in the case of R. Johanan ben Nuri and in that of R. Eliezer ben Jacob one follows the rule that "in matters of *Eruvin* one follows the lenient opinion." The concurrence of the cases of R. Johanan ben Nuri of R. Eliezer ben Jacob establishes this principle in general.
32 Therefore the rule that one follows the lenient opinion must be accepted.

(23b line 33) פיס׳. אָמַר רַבָּן גַּמְלִיאֵל מַעֲשֶׂה בִצְדוּקִי אֶחָד כול׳. רִבִּי אָחָא רִבִּי חִינְנָא בְשֵׁם כָּהֲנָא. אֵין הֲלָכָה כְרִבִּי יְהוּדָה. דְּלֹא כֵן מָה אֲנָן אֳמָרִין. רִבִּי יוּדָא וַחֲכָמִים. תְּהֵא הֲלָכָה כְרִבִּי יוּדָא. אֶלָּא בְגִין דָּמַר רִבִּי יַעֲקֹב בַּר אִידִי בְשֵׁם רִבִּי יְהוֹשֻׁעַ בֶּן לֵוִי. הֲלָכָה כְדִבְרֵי מִי שֶׁהוּא מֵיקַל בְּהִלְכוֹת עֵירוּבִין. וּמִדְּרִבִּי יִצְחָק בַּר נַחְמָן בְּשֵׁם רִבִּי יְהוֹשֻׁעַ בֶּן לֵוִי. הֲלָכָה כְרִבִּי יוֹחָנָן בֶּן נוּרִי. וְקַשְׁיָינָן עֲלָהּ. לֹא כֵן אָמַר רִבִּי יַעֲקֹב בַּר אִידִי בְשֵׁם רִבִּי יְהוֹשֻׁעַ בֶּן לֵוִי. הֲלָכָה כְדִבְרֵי מִי שֶׁמֵּיקַל בְּהִלְכוֹת עֵירוּבִין. וְלֹא כֵן אָמַר רִבִּי יִצְחָק בַּר נַחְמָן בְּשֵׁם רִבִּי יְהוֹשֻׁעַ בֶּן לֵוִי. הֲלָכָה כְרִבִּי יוֹחָנָן

בֶּן נוּרִי. וְקַשְׁיָינָן עֲלָהּ. סָבְרִין מֵימַר בְּיָחִיד אֵצֶל יָחִיד. אֲבָל יָחִיד אֵצֶל חֲכָמִים לֹא. אָתָא רִבִּי יַעֲקֹב בַּר אָחָא רִבִּי יַעֲקֹב בַּר אִידִי בְשֵׁם רִבִּי יְהוֹשֻעַ בֶּן לֵוִי. הֲלָכָה כְרִבִּי יוֹחָנָן בֶּן נוּרִי וַאֲפִילוּ חֲכָמִים חֲלוּקִין עָלָיו. וְכָא תָהֵא הֲלָכָה כְרִבִּי יוּדָה וַאֲפִילוּ חֲכָמִים חוֹלְקִין עָלָיו.

Paragraph. "Rabban Gamliel said, if happened that a Sadducee," etc. [33]Rebbi Aḥa, Rebbi Ḥinena in the name of Cahana: Practice does not follow Rebbi Jehudah. If it were not so what would we say? Rebbi Jehudah versus the Sages, practice should follow Rebbi Jehudah? But since Rebbi Jacob bar Idi said in the name of Rebbi Joshua ben Levi, practice follows the lenient opinion in *Eruvin*, and following Rebbi Naḥman bar Isaac in the name of Rebbi Joshua ben Levi, practice follows Rebbi Joḥanan ben Nuri, and we asked about it, did not Rebbi Jacob bar Idi say in the name of Rebbi Joshua ben Levi, practice follows the lenient opinion in *Eruvin*, and did not Rebbi Isaac bar Naḥman say in the name of Rebbi Joshua ben Levi, practice follows Rebbi Joḥanan ben Nuri? We asked about it, we would think to say that this refers to an individual versus an individual but not an individual versus the Sages. There came Rebbi Jacob bar Aḥa, Rebbi Jacob bar Idi in the name of Rebbi Joshua ben Levi, practice follows Rebbi Joḥanan ben Nuri even though the Sages disagree with him. Why should practice not follow Rebbi Jehudah even though the Sages disagree with him?

33 The scribe of the ms. wrote: או גרש בראשיה דפרקיה קדמייה דראשיה דמסכתא "One reads this at the start of the first Chapter at the start of the Tractate". This	was deleted by the corrector and replaced by the following text which is a slightly shortened copy from there, Chapter 1, Notes 58-65.

(23b line 45) רִבִּי יִרְמְיָה בְשֵׁם רַב. חָצֵר שֶׁיֵּשׁ לָהּ שְׁנֵי פְתָחִים וְיִשְׂרָאֵל וְגוֹי דָּרִין בְּתוֹכָהּ. בְּיִשְׂרָאֵל אַתְּ מְהַלֵּךְ אַחַר הָרָגִיל. וּבְגוֹי אַתְּ מְהַלֵּךְ אַחַר שֶׁאֵינוֹ רָגִיל. הָיָה יִשְׂרָאֵל מִיכָּן וְיִשְׂרָאֵל מִיכָּן וְגוֹי בָּאֶמְצַע. אֶחָד יִשְׂרָאֵל וְאֶחָד גּוֹי הוֹלְכִין אַחַר הָרָגִיל. בִּיטֵּל רְשׁוּתוֹ הָרָגִיל. נַעֲשָׂה שֶׁאֵינוֹ רָגִיל רָגִיל. הִשְׁכִּיר רְשׁוּתוֹ הָרָגִיל. נַעֲשָׂה שֶׁאֵינוֹ רָגִיל רָגִיל. עֵירַב שֶׁאֵינוֹ רָגִיל. לֹא הוּתַּר הָרָגִיל.

Rebbi Jeremiah in the name of Rav: If a courtyard has two gates[34] and an Israel and a Gentile live there; for the Israel one goes after the usual, for the Gentile one goes after the unusual[35]. If there were two Israel and the Gentile in between them, both for Israel and Gentile one goes after the usual[36]. If he[37] ceded the usual domain, the unusual becomes the usual. If he rented the usual domain, the unusual becomes the usual. If the unusual made an *eruv*, the usual one is not permitted.

34 The courtyard opens into two alleys; the question is whether it is required to participate in both alleys.

35 If the Israel participates in the alley which he most frequently uses, he does not prohibit the use of the second alley if he does not participate there (Babli 49a). But a Gentile interferes with the Sabbath use of any alley to which his courtyard opens and where at least two Jews are residing; both alleys must rent or accept a cession of his space from him.

36 If most of the dwellers of one part of the courtyard all use the same gate, one may assume that the minority in that part does the same.

37 If the Gentile either cedes or rents out his right to the use of the courtyard to the dwellers in one alley, he automatically becomes part of the dwellers in the other alley and they also must rent from him or ask for a cession.

(23b line 51) גֵּר תּוֹשָׁב וְעֶבֶד תּוֹשָׁב מְשׁוּמָּד בְּגִילּוּי פָּנִים הֲרֵי הוּא כְגוֹי לְכָל־דָּבָר. אִית תַּנָּיֵי תַנֵּי. הַקְּוֶוסְטוֹר אֹסֵר מִיַּד וְאַכְסַנְיָיא לְאַחַר שְׁלֹשִׁים. אִית תַּנָּיֵי תַנֵּי. הַקְּוֶוסְטוֹר אוֹסֵר לְאַחַר שְׁלֹשִׁים וְאַכְסַנְיָיא אֵינָהּ אוֹסֶרֶת לְעוֹלָם. מָאן דָּמַר. הַקְּוֶוסְטוֹר אֹסֵר מִיַּד. בְּרָגִיל. וְאַכְסַנְיָיא לְאַחַר שְׁלֹשִׁים יוֹם. בְּשֶׁאֵינוֹ רָגִיל. וּמָאן דָּמַר. הַקְּוֶוסְטוֹר אוֹסֵר לְאַחַר שְׁלֹשִׁים. בְּאִילֵּין דְּעַיְילִין בִּרְשׁוּת. וְאַכְסַנְיָיא אֵינָהּ אוֹסֶרֶת לְעוֹלָם. בְּאִילֵּין דְּעַיְילִין דְּלָא בִרְשׁוּת.

רִבִּי יַעֲקֹב בַּר אָחָא בְּשֵׁם רִבִּי לָעֲזָר. בִּיטּוּל רְשׁוּת בֵּינֵיהוֹן. רִבִּי מֵאִיר אוֹמֵר. יֵשׁ לוֹ בִיטּוּל רְשׁוּת. וְרַבָּנִין אָמְרִין. אֵין לוֹ בִיטּוּל רְשׁוּת. רִבִּי מֵאִיר אוֹמֵר. יֵשׁ לוֹ בִיטּוּל רְשׁוּת. וְאַתְּ אָמַר. מָהֲרוּ. אַף עַל גַּב דְּרִבִּי מֵאִיר אוֹמֵר. יֵשׁ לוֹ בִיטּוּל רְשׁוּת. מוֹדֶה הוּא שֶׁזָּכוּ בַּמָּבוֹי תְּחִילָּה. וְתַנֵּי כֵן. מִפְּנֵי שֶׁהוּא מְבַטֵּל רְשׁוּתוֹ כְיִשְׂרָאֵל. דִּבְרֵי רִבִּי מֵאִיר. בֵּין שׁוֹגֵג בֵּין מֵזִיד הֲרֵי זֶה אוֹסֵר. כֵּינִי מַתְנִיתָה. אֵינוֹ אוֹסֵר. רִבִּי אָחָא בְּשֵׁם רִבִּי חִינְּנָא. כָּל־עַמָּא מוֹדַיי שֶׁיֵּשׁ לוֹ בִּיטּוּל רְשׁוּת. מַה פְּלִיגִין. לַחֲזוֹר בּוֹ. רִבִּי מֵאִיר אוֹמֵר. מְבַטֵּל רְשׁוּתוֹ וְחוֹזֵר בּוֹ. וְרַבָּנִין אָמְרִין. מְבַטֵּל רְשׁוּתוֹ וְאֵינוֹ חוֹזֵר בּוֹ. רִבִּי מֵאִיר אוֹמֵר. מְבַטֵּל רְשׁוּתוֹ וְחוֹזֵר בּוֹ. וְאַתְּ אָמַר. מָהֲרוּ. אַף עַל גַּב דְּרִבִּי מֵאִיר אוֹמֵר. מְבַטֵּל רְשׁוּת וְחוֹזֵר בּוֹ. מוֹדֶה הוּא שֶׁזָּכוּ בַּמָּבוֹי תְּחִילָּה. וְתַנֵּי כֵן. מִפְּנֵי שֶׁהוּא מְבַטֵּל רְשׁוּתוֹ כְיִשְׂרָאֵל. דִּבְרֵי רִבִּי מֵאִיר. בֵּין שׁוֹגֵג בֵּין מֵזִיד הֲרֵי זֶה אוֹסֵר. כֵּינִי מַתְנִיתָה. אֵינוֹ אוֹסֵר.

A semi-convert[38] and a semi-converted slave[39] as well as an apostate acting in public[40] are like Gentiles in every respect[41]. There are Tannaïm who state[42]: "A quaestor[43] prohibits immediately and a troop of soldiers[44] after thirty days." There are Tannaïm who state: "A quaestor forbids after thirty days but a troop of soldiers never ever forbids." He who says, a quaestor prohibits immediately, if it is routine[45], and a troop of soldiers after thirty days, if it is not routine. But he who says a quaestor forbids after thirty days, if he enters by permission[46], but a troop of soldiers never ever forbids, if they enter without permission[47].

Rebbi Jacob bar Aha in the name of Rebbi Eleazar, they[48] disagree about ceding rights. Rebbi Meïr says, he may cede rights, but the rabbis[49] are saying, he may not cede rights. Rebbi Meïr says, he may cede rights, and you are saying, "be quick"[50]? Even though Rebbi Meïr says, he may cede rights, he agrees that they may lay claim to the alley beforehand[51]. It was stated thus: Because he may cede rights like a Jew, the words of Rebbi Meïr. "Whether in error or intentionally, he forbids." So is the *baraita*[52]: he does not forbid. Rebbi Aha in the name of Rebbi Hinena: Everybody agrees that he[53] may cede rights. Where do they disagree? To change his mind. Rebbi Meïr says he may cede his rights and retract it, but the rabbis say, he may cede his rights and cannot retract it. Rebbi Meïr says he may cede his rights and retract it, and you are saying, "be quick"? Even though Rebbi Meïr says, he may cede rights, he agrees that they may lay claim to the alley beforehand. It was stated thus: Because he may cede rights like a Jew, the words of Rebbi Meïr. "Whether in error or intentionally, he forbids." So is the *baraita*: he does not forbid.

38   A non-Jew who publicly has renounced idolatry. He has no obligation to keep the Sabbath.

39   A slave who refuses to be circumcised but has renounced idolatry. He has no obligation to keep the Sabbath.

40   He violates the Sabbath in public. Tosephta 5:18.

41   In all matters regarding the Sabbath. In other matters the apostate cannot escape being Jewish.

42   Tosephta 5:22, more or less the second version.

43   Latin *quaestor*, an official of the government's revenue service.

44   Greek ξενία, ἡ, from ξενός in the sense of mercenary soldier.

45   If he comes regularly to audit the local accounts he is a resident, not a passer-by, and one has to lease from him his right to use courtyard or alley on the Sabbath. But soldiers may be called to duty at any moment; they become residents according to one opinion if they stay for 30 days, in the other opinion never.

46   A government commission specifying his place of activity. This excludes an official charged to control the local tax office by making unannounced and unpredictable audits.

47   On the authority only of a local commander.

48 The first tradent in Mishnah 2 (who is R. Meïr), about the position of a Sadducee in matters of *eruv*.
49 R. Jehudah in the Mishnah.
50 Why should any action be needed when the Sadducee may cede his rights and resolve the problem by some words?
51 While the Sadducee may cede his rights, he is not obligated to do so and accommodate rabbinic Jews. Therefore preventive action may be preferable since R. Meïr asserts that the action of using the alley bars the Sadducee from claiming his rights to it.
52 While the text is identical with a sentence from Mishnah 4, one refers to a *baraita* whose subject is a Sadducee. Babli 69a.
53 The Sadducee. Babli 68b.

(23b line 71) פיס׳. אַנְשֵׁי חָצֵר שֶׁשָּׁכַח אֶחָד מֵהֶן וְלֹא עֵירֵב כול׳. שֶׁלָּהֶם מוּתָּרִין לוֹ וְלָהֶם. שֶׁבִּיטֵּל רְשׁוּתוֹ. מָהוּ שֶׁתַּחֲזוֹר חֲלִילָה. תַּלְמִידוֹי דְרַב בְּשֵׁם רַב. חוֹזֶרֶת חֲלִילָה. שְׁמוּאֵל אָמַר. אֵין חוֹזֶרֶת חֲלִילָה. מַתְנִיתָא פְּלִיגָא עַל שְׁמוּאֵל. שֶׁלָּהֶם מוּתָּרִין לוֹ וְלָהֶם. שֶׁבִּיטֵּל רְשׁוּתוֹ. וְהָתַנִּינָן נָתְנוּ לוֹ רְשׁוּתָן. הוּא מוּתָּר וְהֵן אֲסוּרִין. פָּתַר לָהּ. לִצְדָדִין הִיא מַתְנִיתָא.

Paragraph[54]. "In a courtyard where one dweller forgot to make an *eruv*," etc. "But theirs are permitted for them and him[8]." Because he ceded his rights. May this be repeated cyclically[55]? The students of Rav in the name of Rav: it may be repeated cyclically. Samuel said, it may not be repeated cyclically. The Mishnah disagrees with Samuel: "theirs are permitted for them and him[56]." Because he ceded his rights[57]. But did we not state: "If they ceded their rights to him, he is permitted but they are forbidden[58]"? He explains it that the Mishnah treats different cases[59].

54 Discussion of Mishnah 3.
55 If *n* people dwell in a courtyard and they made no *eruv*, may *n*-1 of them temporarily cede their rights to one to use the courtyard on the Sabbath, until each of them had his possibility of use, and then start the procedure anew? Babli 69b.
56 How could it be permitted to him if not that the others had ceded their rights to him?
57 The preceding argument is no good.
Since he ceded his rights he is like a visitor to the courtyard whose presence is irrelevant.
58 In the first sentence of the Mishnah, one ceded to the many. In the second sentence, the many ceded to one. This seems to prove that one may change the arrangements on the Sabbath.
59 The Mishnah describes different situations occurring on different Sabbaths.

(23b line 77) תַּנֵּי. אֶחָד שֶׁלֹּא עֵירֵב עֵירֵב נוֹתֵן רְשׁוּת לִשְׁנַיִם שֶׁעֵירְבוּ. וְאֵין שְׁנַיִם שֶׁעֵירְבוּ נוֹתְנִין רְשׁוּת לְאֶחָד שֶׁלֹּא עֵירֵב. וְלֹא שְׁנַיִם שֶׁעֵירְבוּ נוֹתְנִין רְשׁוּת לִשְׁנַיִם שֶׁלֹּא עֵירְבוּ. וְלֹא שְׁנַיִם שֶׁלֹּא

עֵירְבוּ נוֹתְנִין רְשׁוּת לשָׁנַיִם שֶׁעֵירְבוּ. וְאֵין שְׁנַיִם שֶׁלֹּא עֵירְבוּ נוֹתְנִין רְשׁוּת לשָׁנַיִם שֶׁלֹּא עֵירְיבוּ. הַכֹּל נוֹתְנִין רְשׁוּת וְנוֹטְלִין רְשׁוּת חוּץ מִשְּׁנַיִם שֶׁלֹּא עֵירְבוּ שֶׁהֵן נוֹתְנִין רְשׁוּת וְאֵינָן נוֹטְלִין רְשׁוּת.

רַב חִסְדַּאי אָמַר. עֲשָׂרָה יִשְׂרָאֵל שֶׁהָיוּ דָרִין בְּבַיִת אֶחָד. כָּל־אֶחָד וְאֶחָד צָרִיךְ לְבַטֵּל רְשׁוּתוֹ. אָמַר רִבִּי יָסָא. עֲשָׂרָה גוֹיִם שֶׁהָיוּ דָרִין בְּבַיִת אֶחָד. כָּל־אֶחָד וְאֶחָד צָרִיךְ לְהַשְׂכִּיר רְשׁוּתוֹ. אָמַר רִבִּי בָּא. מַעֲשֶׂה בְּאִשְׁתּוֹ שֶׁלְּפַרְסִי אֶחָד שֶׁהִשְׂכִּירָה חָצֵר שֶׁלָּהּ שֶׁלֹּא מִדַּעַת בַּעֲלָהּ. אֲתָא קוֹמֵי רִבִּי שְׁמוּאֵל וְשָׁרָא. סָבְרִין מֵימַר. אֲפִילוּ שַׁמָּשׁוֹ וּלְקִיטוֹ. הֲלָכָה. יִשְׂרָאֵל מְבַטֵּל וְהַגּוֹי מַשְׂכִּיר. וִיבַטֵּל הוּא הַגּוֹי. חָזַר הוּא בוֹ. מֵעַתָּה אֲפִילוּ מַשְׂכִּיר חָזַר הוּא בוֹ. מִיכָּן וָהֵילָךְ בְּגֵזֶל הוּא מִשְׁתַּמֵּשׁ.

עַד אֵיכָן. יָבֹא כַּיי דָּמַר רִבִּי יָסָא בְשֵׁם רִבִּי מָנָא בַּר תַּנְחוּם רִבִּי אַבָּהוּ בְשֵׁם רִבִּי יוֹחָנָן. אֵין קַרְקַע נִקְנֶה בְּפָחוּת מִשְׁוֵה פְרוּטָה. מִילְתֵיהּ דְּרִבִּי יַעֲקֹב בַּר אָחָא אָמַר. אֲפִילוּ בְאֱגוֹז. אֲפִילוּ בִתְמָרָה.

רִבִּי יַעֲקֹב בַּר אָחָא כַּד הֲוָה נְפִיק לְאַכְסַנְיָיא. אִין הֲוָה מַשְׁכַּח מֵיעֲבַד תַּקָּנָה הֲוָה עֲבַד. וְאִין לָא. מְבַדֵּר מָנוֹי. יְהַב חוּטְרָא הָכָא. סַנְדְּלָא הָכָא. דְּיִיסְקְיָא הָכָא. אָמַר רִבִּי מַתַּנְיָה. בִּשְׁהָיָה פּוּנְדְּקִי גּוֹי. אֲבָל אִם הָיָה פּוּנְדְּקִי יִשְׂרָאֵל אֵינוֹ חָשׁוּד לְטַלְטֵל.

It was stated[60]: "One who did not make an *eruv* cedes his rights to two who did make an *eruv* but two who made an *eruv* do not[61] cede to one who did not make an *eruv*. And two who made an *eruv* may not cede to two who made no *eruv*[62]. Also two who made no *eruv* may not cede to two who made no *eruv*. Everybody may cede his rights and accept rights except two who made no *eruv* who may cede rights but may not receive[62]."

Rav Ḥasdai[63] said, each single one of ten Israel who dwell in one house must cede his rights[64]. Rebbi Yasa said, each single one of ten Gentiles who dwell in one house must rent out his rights. Rebbi Abba said, it happened that a Persian's wife rented out her courtyard without informing her husband. The case came before Rebbi Samuel and he declared it legal[65]. They wanted to say, even his servant and farm-hand. Practice: An Israel cedes and the Gentile rents out[66]. Then why should the Gentile not cede? He might change his mind. Then even if he rented out he might change his mind! From then on he would use it in robbery[67].

How little? Should it come as what Rebbi Yasa said in the name of Rebbi Mana bar Tanḥum, Rebbi Abbahu in the name of Rebbi Joḥanan: real estate cannot be acquired with less than a *peruṭa*'s worth[68]? The word of Rebbi Jacob bar Aḥa implies even a walnut, even a date[69].

When Rebbi Jacob bar Aha went to a hostelry[70], when it was possible for him to put it in order, he did it[71]. Otherwise he would spread out his clothing. He would put his staff at one place, his sandals at another, his wallet at another[72]. Rabbi Mattaniah said, this you are saying if the hostel keeper[73] was a Gentile. But if the hostel keeper was an Israel, he is not suspected to carry[74].

60 Tosephta 5:17, Babli 70a.

61 In the Babylonian sources (Note 60) "do cede". This text seems to be required.

62 Since two who made no *eruv* prohibit the use of the courtyard to one another, cession of rights by other inhabitants is ineffective.

63 In Raviah (vol. 1, p. 462, n. 20) "Rav Hisda"; but in R. Hananel (*ad* 71a) as in our text "Rav Hasdai."

64 Or make an *eruv*. "Dwellers" are permanent residents. Similarly, to make an *eruv* in the staircase of a multi-family house one must rent the use of the space from all Gentile dwellers in the house.

65 Since the husband has the usufruct of his wife's property during marriage, a Jewish court could not accept the validity of a rental agreement of real estate concluded without the husband's knowledge. But since renting the use of the space for the Sabbath is a pure formality, it is accepted from wife, servant, or farm-hand. Cf. Babli 80a, bottom.

66 R. Hananel (*ad* 71a) has a more complete text: [R. Yasa in the name of R. Johanan: If an Israel and a Gentile live in one house,] practice is that . . . The same text is in *Šibbole Halleqet* (ed. Buber, p. 70)

and is quoted in Tosaphot 66a *s. v.* מערב, paraphrased by Ritba (ed. Warsaw, *ad* 66a, p. 109) "an Israel and a Gentile who live in a house of a courtyard, the Jew had to make an *eruv* and from the Gentile one has to rent"; similarly *Sefer Miswot Gadol* (ed. Venice p. 244a l.9).

67 From the moment he accepted money, what he does is irrelevant.

68 *Qiddušin* 1:3 Note 337, repeated there 1:5 p. 127, *Ma`aser šeni* 4:3 (Note 60). In *Qiddušin* the name tradition is: R. Yasa in the name of R. Mana, R. Tanhum, R. Abbahu in the name of R. Johanan.

69 Since the lease is a formality, not a reality, the qualifications of real estate law do not apply.

70 Greek ξενία, ἡ.

71 If there were other Jews, he tried to arrange an *eruv*.

72 Greek δισάκκιον, τό. He spread his things out in all rooms to that he could carry on the Sabbath in the entire building.

73 Greek adjective, πάνδοκος, -ον, "of a hostelry".

74 The hostel keeper is not suspected to carry in the rooms he prepared for the guests. If there are no other guests there is no need to disperse his things.

(23c line 19) פיס'. מֵאֵימָתַי נוֹתְנִין רְשׁוּת. בֵּית שַׁמַּי אוֹמְרִים כוֹל'. מֵאֵימָתַי נוֹתְנִין רְשׁוּת. כֵּן הִיא מַתְנִיתָא. מֵאֵימָתַי מְבַטְלִין רְשׁוּת. בֵּית שַׁמַּי אוֹמְרִים. מִבְּעוֹד יוֹם. וּבֵית הִלֵּל אוֹמְרִים.

מִשֶּׁתֶּחֱשָׁךְ. כֵּינֵי מַתְנִיתָא. בֵּית (שַׁמַּי) [הֵלֵּל] אוֹמְרִים. מִשֶּׁתֶּחֱשָׁךְ. דְּל כֵן הִיא מַתְנִיתָא מְקוּלֵּי בֵית שַׁמַּי וּמֵחוּמְרֵי בֵית הֵלֵּל.

Paragraph. "When may one start giving away rights? The House of Shammai say," etc. "When may one start giving away rights?" Is the Mishnah so: "When may one start ceding rights? The House of Shammai say as long as it is daylight[11], but the House of Hillel say, when it gets dark"? So is the Mishnah: The House of (Shammai) [Hillel][75] say, when it gets dark; because otherwise it would be of the leniencies of the House of Shammai and the strictures of the House of Hillel.

75   The text in parentheses is the scribe's, the one in brackets the corrector's correction.

The scribe's text is easily explained: If the Mishnah were permissive, it should be formulated as "until when may one cede." Since it says "when may one start" it is prescriptive, that cession of rights before this time is invalid. Since the Mishnah is not on the list of those where the House of Shammai is more lenient than the House of Hillel (*Idiut* 4), one has to emend the Mishnah and switch the places of "Shammai" and "Hillel". But the next paragraph shows that this emendation is impossible; one has to accept the corrector's emendation and read the Mishnah as: but the House of Hillel say, *even* when it gets dark.

(23c line 24) מִי שֶׁנָּתַן רְשׁוּתוֹ וְהוֹצִיא. כֵּינֵי מַתְנִיתָא. מִי שֶׁבִּיטֵּל רְשׁוּתוֹ וְהוֹצִיא. בֵּין שׁוֹגֵג בֵּין מֵזִיד הֲרֵי זֶה אוֹסֵר. כֵּינֵי מַתְנִיתָא. אֵינוֹ אוֹסֵר.
תַּנֵּי. שְׁנַיִם שֶׁהָיוּ שׁוּתָּפִין בֶּחָצֵר וּמֵת אֶחָד מֵהֶן. וְנָפַל הַבַּיִת יְרוּשָׁה לְאֶחָד מִן הַשּׁוּק. עַד שֶׁלֹּא חֲשֵׁיכָה הֲרֵי זֶה אוֹסֵר. מִשֶּׁחֲשֵׁיכָה אֵינוֹ אוֹסֵר. רַבִּי אָחָא בְשֵׁם רַבִּי חִינָּנָא. דְּבֵית שַׁמַּי הִיא. דְּבֵית שַׁמַּי אוֹמְרִים. אֵין מְבַטְּלִין רְשׁוּת מִשֶּׁתֶּחֱשָׁךְ. וּבֵית הֵלֵּל אוֹמְרִים. מְבַטְּלִין רְשׁוּת מִשֶּׁתֶּחֱשָׁךְ. אָמַר רִבִּי יוֹסֵה בֵּירִבִּי בּוּן. מִכֵּיוָן שֶׁמֵּת אֵין בִּיטּוּל רְשׁוּת גָּדוֹל מִזֶּה. הֲרֵי שֶׁהָיָה לְאֶחָד מִן הַשּׁוּק בַּיִת עִמָּהֶן בֶּחָצֵר וָמֵת. וְנָפַל הַבַּיִת יְרוּשָׁה לְאֶחָד מֵהֶן. עַד שֶׁלֹּא חֲשֵׁיכָה הֲרֵי זֶה אוֹסֵר. מִשֶּׁחֲשֵׁיכָה אֵינוֹ אוֹסֵר. עוֹד הִיא דְּבֵית שַׁמַּי. דְּבֵית שַׁמַּי אוֹמְרִים. אֵין מְבַטְּלִין רְשׁוּת מִשֶּׁתֶּחֱשָׁךְ. וּבֵית הֵלֵּל אוֹמְרִים. מְבַטְּלִין רְשׁוּת מִשֶּׁתֶּחֱשָׁךְ. מַהוּ לְבַטֵּל רְשׁוּת מִשֶּׁתֶּחֱשָׁךְ. רִבִּי חִייָה רִבִּי יָסָא רִבִּי אִימָּא סַלְקוֹן לַחֲמָתָהּ דְּגָדֵר. שְׁאָלוּן לְרִבִּי חָמָא בַּר יוֹסֵף. וְשָׁרָא. שְׁמָעִין רִבִּי יוֹחָנָן וָמַר. יָפֶה עֲשִׂיתָם. שָׁמַע רִבִּי שִׁמְעוֹן בֶּן לָקִישׁ וָמַר. לֹא עֲשִׂיתָם יָפֶה. מַה פְּלִיגִין. רִבִּי זְעִירָא אָמַר. לֹא פְּלִיגִין. מָאן דָּמַר. יָפֶה עֲשִׂיתָם. שֶׁשְּׁכַרְתֶּם. וּמָאן דָּמַר. לֹא עֲשִׂיתָם יָפֶה. שֶׁטִּילְטַלְתֶּם. רִבִּי בָּא אָמַר. פְּלִיגִי. מָאן דָּמַר. יָפֶה עֲשִׂיתָם. שֶׁשְּׁכַרְתֶּם וְשְׁטִילְטַלְתֶּם. מָאן דָּמַר. לֹא עֲשִׂיתָם יָפֶה. לֹא שֶׁשְּׁכַרְתֶּם וְלֹא שֶׁטִּילְטַלְתֶּם.

"If somebody gave away his rights and then brought out." So is the Mishnah: If somebody ceded his rights, "whether in error or intentionally, he forbids." So is the Mishnah: He does not forbid[76].

It was stated: "If two people were partners in a courtyard and one of them died, and the house fell as inheritance to an outside person. If before it became dark, this makes it forbidden; after dark it is not forbidden[77]." Rebbi Aha in the name of Rebbi Ḥinena: This is the House of Shammai's, for the House of Shammai say, one may not cede rights after dark, but the House of Hillel say, one may cede rights after dark[77]. Rebbi Yose ben Rebbi Abun said, since he dies there is no greater cession of rights than this[78]. "If an outside person owned a house in the courtyard with them when he died and the house fell as inheritance to a dweller in the courtyard. If before it became dark, this makes it forbidden; after dark it is not forbidden.[79]" Still this is the House of Shammai's, for the House of Shammai say, one may not cede rights after dark, but the House of Hillel say, one may cede rights after dark. May one cede rights[80] after dark? Rebbi Ḥiyya, Rebbi Yasa, Rebbi Immi went up to Hammat Gader[81]. They asked Rebbi Ḥama bar Joseph and he permitted. Rebbi Joḥanan heard them and said, you did the correct thing. Rebbi Simeon ben Laqish heard it and said, you acted incorrectly. Do they disagree? Rebbi Ze`ira said, they did not disagree. He who said, you did the correct thing, that you leased. But he who said, you acted incorrectly, that you moved[82]. Rebbi Abba said, they disagree. He who said, you did the correct thing, that you leased and moved. But he who said, you acted incorrectly, that you leased and that you moved[83].

---

76 R. Meïr is consistent that a Gentile living in a courtyard forbids the use of the courtyard on the Sabbath as long as one does not lease the use of the courtyard from him and he abides by the terms of the lease at least until sundown. But following R. Eliezer ben Jacob, who represents practice to be followed, one has to correct the Mishnah to: He does not forbid.

77 Tosephta 5:13, Babli 70b. The Tanna of the Mishnah holds that the heir as owner makes the courtyard forbidden without an *eruv* even if he does not live there, but if the courtyard was permitted at sunbdown it remains permitted for the entire Sabbath even if the situation changes.

78 Since he does no longer live there. The heir becomes a neighbor only by actually living there.

79 Tosephta 5:14, Babli 70b.

80 Since practice follows the House of Hillel it is obvious that one may cede rights after dark. The problem really is, "may one lease rights after sundown"? If the lease is a transaction, it is forbidden, if a formality, it is permitted.

81 In the Babli 65b the story is told of R. (Hanina) [Hama] bar Joseph, R. Hiyya, and R. Yasa (Assi) and it is clear that the owner of the hostelry was a Gentile; the question is about leasing, not ceding. The Gentile came only during the Sabbath.

82 They should not have moved their things in the hostelry before they leased the space since the appearance of the owner always was a potentiality.

83 He treats the lease as a transaction.

(23c line 42) רִבִּי בָּא בָּעֵי. אַף לְעִנְיָין מְחִיצוֹת כֵּן. הֵידְּ עֲבִידָא. הָיוּ שְׁנַיִם וְעֵירְבוּ עֵירוּב אֶחָד. וּבָא הַגּוֹי וְהוֹסִיף. כְּבָר נִכְנְסָה שַׁבָּת בְּאִיסּוּר. הָיוּ שְׁלֹשָׁה וְעֵירְבוּ שְׁנֵי עֵירוּבִין. וּבָא הַגּוֹי וּפָתַח. כְּבָר נִכְנְסָה שַׁבָּת בְּהֶיתֵּר. חֵיילֵיהּ דְּרִבִּי בָּא מִן הָדָא. כָּל־שַׁבָּת שֶׁנִּכְנְסָה בְּהֶיתֵּר מוּתָּר. בְּאִיסּוּר אָסוּר. חוּץ מִן הַמְבַטֵּל רְשׁוּת. וָמַר. חוּץ מִן הַמְבַטֵּל וּמִן הַמַּשְׂכִּיר. מַהוּ לִשְׂכּוֹר רְשׁוּת מִן הַפּוּנְדִּיק. רִבִּי חִינְנָא וְרִבִּי יוֹנָתָן סַלְקוֹן לַחֲמָתָה דְגָדֵר. אָמְרִין. נַמְתִּין עַד שֶׁיָּבוֹאוּ זִקְנֵי הַדָּרוֹם לְכָאן. אֲתָא רִבִּי (פרס) [נָתָן] דְּרוֹמָה וְשָׁאֲלוּן לֵיהּ וְשָׁרָא. שָׁמַע רִבִּי שִׁמְעוֹן בֶּן לָקִישׁ וְאָמַר. מֵאַחַר שֶׁהַגּוֹי בָּא וּמוֹצִיאָנִי לֹא עָשִׂינוּ כְּלוּם. שִׁמְעוֹן בַּר בָּא אָמַר. רִבִּי יוֹחָנָן בָּעֵי. מֵעַתָּה אֵין בָּתֵּינוּ שֶׁלָּנוּ. רִבִּי יוּסְטִי בֵּירִבִּי סִימוֹן בְּשֵׁם רִבִּי בַּייתוֹס. אֵין בָּתֵּינוּ שֶׁלָּנוּ לָדוּר עִמָּנוּ. הָא לָצֵאת אֵין מוֹצִיאִין אוֹתָנוּ. וּבְפוּנְדָּק מוֹצִיאִין אוֹתָנוּ.

Rebbi Abba asked, is it the same in the matter of partitions[84]? How is this? If there were two and they established one *eruv*, and a Gentile came and added; the Sabbath already had started in prohibition. If there were three but they established two *eruvim* and a Gentile came and opened; the Sabbath already had started in permission[85]. The strength of Rebbi Abba is from the following: Any Sabbath which started in permission is permitted, in prohibition is prohibited[86], except one who cedes rights; and he[87] would say, except one who cedes or leases. May one lease rights from the owner of a hostelry? Rebbi Hinena and Rebbi Jonathan went to Hammat Gader[88]. They said, we shall wait until the Elders of the South arrive here. There came Rebbi (Peres) {Nathan}[89] the Southerner; they asked him and he permitted. Rebbi Simeon ben Laqish heard it and said, since the Gentile may remove us[90], we did not do anything. Simeon bar Abba said, Rebbi Joḥanan asked, then our houses are not ours[91]? Rebbi Justus ben Rebbi Simon in the name of Rebbi Boethos: Our houses are not ours, to dwell with us[92]; but they cannot force us to leave; but in a hostelry they remove us.

84 Which make it possible to carry at the place of rest of a caravan, as explained in Chapter 1.
85 This text is from Chapter 1, Note 294.
86 Babli 70b.
87 R. Ze'ira and all authorities who permit leasing from a Gentile on the Sabbath.
88 The place chosen for proclamations about matters of the calendar.
89 In the quotes of this paragraph in the Responsa of Rashba (part 1 # 626; Responsa attributed to Nahmanides #218) he is quoted as R. Efes, who is known as Rebbi's scribe.
90 If he finds better paying hotel guests. He denies the validity of leasing rights in a Gentile hostelry as a matter of principle.
91 Since at any time the army may send soldiers to be quartered with us.
92 The army may cause inconvenience but the troops cannot remove us from our houses; one may accept R. Simeon ben Laqish's point of view and still practice leasing in courtyards or alleys.

(23c line 54) פיס׳. בַּעַל הַבַּיִת שֶׁהָיָה שׁוּתָּף לִשְׁכֵינִים כול׳. רִבִּי בָּא בְשֵׁם רִבִּי יְהוּדָה. בְּדֶרֶךְ הָאָרֶץ שָׁנוּ. לָזֶה בַיַיִן וְלָזֶה בַיַיִן. הוֹאִיל וְאֵינוֹ מַקְפִּיד עַל תַּעֲרוּבָתוֹ אֵין צָרִיךְ לְעָרֵב. לָזֶה בַיַיִן וְלָזֶה בַשֶּׁמֶן. הוֹאִיל וְהוּא מַקְפִּיד עַל תַּעֲרוּבָתוֹ צָרִיךְ לְעָרֵב. רִבִּי בָּא בַּר כַּהֲנָא רַב חִייָה בַּר אַשִׁי בְשֵׁם רַב. בִּנְתוּנִים בִּכְלִי אֶחָד הִיא מַתְנִיתָא. אָמַר רִבִּי זְרִיקָן. טַעֲמֵיהּ דְּרִבִּי שִׁמְעוֹן. שֶׁכֵּן דַּרְכָּן לִשְׁתּוֹתָן אֱנִיגָרוֹן. תַּנֵּי. רִבִּי אֶלְעָזָר בֶּן תַּדַּאי אוֹמֵר. בֵּין כָּךְ וּבֵין כָּךְ אֲסוּרִין עַד שֶׁיְעָרְבוּ. רִבִּי אָחָא בְשֵׁם רַב. הֲלָכָה כְרִבִּי אֶלְעָזָר בֶּן תַּדַּאי. רִבִּי יַעֲקֹב בַּר אָחָא בְשֵׁם רִבִּי זְעִירָא. אַתְיָא דְּרִבִּי אֶלְעָזָר בֶּן תַּדַּאי כְּרִבִּי מֵאִיר. הֵיידָן רִבִּי מֵאִיר. אָמַר רִבִּי מָנָא. רִבִּי מֵאִיר דּוּ אָמַר. עַל יְדֵי עֵירוּב עַל יְדֵי שִׁיתּוּף. אָמַר רִבִּי יוֹסֵה בֵירִבִּי בּוּן. רִבִּי מֵאִיר דּוּ אָמַר שֶׁאֵין מְעָרְבִין לְאָדָם אֶלָּא מִדַּעְתּוֹ. עַל דַּעְתֵּיהּ דְּרִבִּי מָנָא כְּרִבִּי זְעִירָא. עַל דַּעְתֵּיהּ דְּרַב כְּרִבִּי מֵאִיר. רִבִּי זְעִירָא בְשֵׁם רִבִּי יוֹחָנָן. בַּעֵירוּבִין וּבְתַעֲנִית צִיבּוּר נָהֲגוּ הַכֹּל כְּרִבִּי מֵאִיר. רִבִּי יַעֲקֹב בַּר אָחָא בְשֵׁם רִבִּי יוֹחָנָן. אַף בִּמְגִילַּת אֶסְתֵּר נָהֲגוּ הַכֹּל כְּרִבִּי מֵאִיר

Paragraph. "If the owner of a house participated with several neighbors," etc. Rebbi Abba in the name of Rebbi[93] Jehudah: They stated this in commercial practice[94]. Everybody with wine, since he does not care about mixing[95], it does not need an *eruv*. If with wine with one but oil with the other, since he cares about mixing, it needs an *eruv*. Rebbi Abba bar Cahana, Rav Ḥiyya bar Ashi in the name of Rav: The Mishnah refers to the case that all is in one vessel[96]. Rebbi Zeriqan said, the reason of Rebbi Simeon is that they are used to drink οἰνόγαρον[97]. It was stated[98]: Rebbi Eleazar ben Thaddeus says, in every case they are forbidden until they make an *eruv*. Rebbi Aḥa in the name of Rav: Practice follows Rebbi Eleazar ben Thaddeus. Rebbi Jacob bar Aḥa in the name Rebbi Ze'ira: Rebbi Eleazar ben Thaddeus follows Rebbi Meïr. Which [statement of] Rebbi Meïr? Rebbi Mana said, Rebbi Meïr who said, by an *eruv*, by participation[99]. Rebbi Yose ben Rebbi Abun said, Rebbi Meïr who said that one may not make an *eruv* for a person without his knowledge[100]. In the opinion of Rebbi Mana, following Rebbi Ze`ira, in the opinion of Rav following Rebbi Meïr[101]. Rebbi Ze`ira in the name of Rebbi Johanan: In matters of *eruvin* and public fast-days everybody follows Rebbi Meïr. Rebbi Jacob bar Aha in the name Rebbi Johanan: Even about the reading of the Esther scroll everybody follows Rebbi Meïr[102].

93   Read: Rav.
94   The language of the Mishnah is inconsistent. "Participation" refers to making an *eruv* in an alley, "neighbors" refer to dwellers in a courtyard. The Mishnah does not refer explicitly to either one; it uses the expression "participate" to describe partnership.
95   Since everything is in a large vessel and the relative shares of the partners have not been separated.
96   Babli 71a. Since it is not intentionally collected as *eruv* but is used as such because it happened to be available, it must be in one vessel.
97   "Wine-fish sauce".
98   Tosephta 5:9, Babli 71b.

99   Tosephta 6:6. He requires separate participation in an alley and *eruv* for courtyards in all cases.
100 Mishnah 7:11.
101 R. Mana interprets the statement of R. Ze`ira to imply that Rav accepts the position of R. Meïr.
102 In *eruvin* one follows R. Meïr that *eruv* for courtyards and participation for alleys must be separate acts, later in the Chapter, 23d l. 47; then *Ta`aniot* 67b 4:1 l. 57 (that on a public fast day the priestly blessing is given three times), *Megillah* 2:1 73b l. 26 (that the scroll has to be read from beginning to end). Babli 72a. These rules are popular usage, not rabbinic decrees.

(23c line 69) פיס'. חָמֵשׁ חֲבוּרוֹת שֶׁשָּׁבְתוּ בִּטְרִיקְלִין כול'. טְרִיקְלִין לִפְנֵיהֶם כְּחָצֵר שֶׁלְּבָתִּים. הָיוּ שָׁם פַּפִּילְיוֹנוֹת. כְּמִי שֶׁהֵן בָּתִּים. מָה נָן קַיָּימִין. אִם בְּשֶׁהָיוּ פַּפִּילְיוֹנוֹת מַגִּיעוֹת עַד הַקּוֹרוֹת. כָּל־עַמָּא מוֹדַיי שֶׁהֵן מְעָרְבִין עֵירוּב לְכָל־חֲבוּרָה וַחֲבוּרָה. אֵין שָׁם פַּפִּילְיוֹנוֹת מַגִּיעוֹת עַד הַקּוֹרוֹת. כָּל־עַמָּא מוֹדַיי שֶׁמְּעָרְבִין עֵירוּב אֶחָד לְכוּלָן. אֶלָּא כֵן אֲנַן קַיָּימִין בְּשֶׁהָיוּ פַּפִּילְיוֹנוֹת גְּבוֹהוֹת עֲשָׂרָה. שָׁוִין שֶׁאִם הָיוּ שׁוּתָּפִין בָּעִיסָה וּבַתַּבְשִׁיל שֶׁהֵן מְעָרְבִין עֵירוּב אֶחָד לְכוּלָן. רִבִּי שִׁיָין בָּעֵי. מֵעַתָּה אֲפִילוּ מִקְצָתָן שְׁרוּיִין בַּחֲדָרִים אוֹ בַעֲלִיּוֹת.

רִבִּי בָּא בְשֵׁם רַב יְהוּדָה. שְׁנֵי בָתִּים זֶה לִפְנִים מִזֶּה. עֵירֵב הַפְּנִימִי אֵין הַחִיצוֹן צָרִיךְ לְעָרֵב. עֵירֵב הַחִיצוֹן הַפְּנִימִי צָרִיךְ לְעָרֵב. אָמַר רִבִּי פִּינְחָס. אַף בְּמִצְרִים חֲלִיפִין. נָתַן עַל הַפְּנִימִי צָרִיךְ לִיתֵּן עַל הַחִיצוֹן. נָתַן עַל הַחִיצוֹן צָרִיךְ לִיתֵּן עַל הַפְּנִימִי. רִבִּי יַעֲקֹב בַּר אָחָא רִבִּי אַבָּהוּ בְשֵׁם

רִבִּי יְהוֹשֻׁעַ בֶּן לֵוִי. אֲפִילוּ לֹא עֵירְבוּ הַפְּנִימִי אֵין הַחִיצוֹן צָרִיךְ לְעָרֵב. לָמָּה. נַעֲשָׂה בֵית שַׁעַר. מִילְתֵיהּ אָמְרָה. אֵין בֵּית שַׁעַר לְיָחִיד. מִילְתֵיהּ דְּרַב אָמְרָה. יֵשׁ בֵּית שַׁעַר לְיָחִיד. דָּמַר רִבִּי בָּא בַּר יְהוּדָה בְּשֵׁם רַב. הָדָא דְתֵימַר בְּבֵית שַׁעַר שֶׁלְּיָחִיד. אֲבָל בְּבֵית שַׁעַר שֶׁלְּרַבִּים הֲרֵי זֶה עֵירוּב. וְהַדָּר שָׁם הֲרֵי זֶה אוֹסֵר עָלָיו. רִבִּי בָּא בְשֵׁם רַב יְהוּדָה. בִּשְׁנֵי בְנֵי אָדָם. אֶחָד שֶׁיֵּשׁ לוֹ רְשׁוּת וְאֶחָד שֶׁאֵין לוֹ רְשׁוּת. עֵירֵב זֶה שֶׁיֵּשׁ לוֹ רְשׁוּת הוּתָּר זֶה שֶׁאֵין לוֹ רְשׁוּת. עֵירֵב זֶה שֶׁאֵין לוֹ רְשׁוּת לֹא הוּתָּר זֶה שֶׁיֵּשׁ לוֹ רְשׁוּת.

Paragraph. "Five groups who rested in one big hall," etc. The big hall for them is like a courtyard for houses[103]. If there were tents[104] there, it is as if they were houses. Where do we hold? If the tents reach to the ceiling, everybody agrees that every group has to contribute to the *eruv*. If the tents do not reach to the ceiling, everybody agrees that one *eruv* is valid for all of them[105]. But we must hold that the tents were ten [hand-breadths] high[106]. They equally agree that if they join in dough and dishes that one *eruv* is valid for all of them[107]. Rebbi Ashian asked, then[108] even if part of them dwell in separate rooms or on upper floors?

Rebbi Abba in the name of Rav Jehudah: Two houses, one inside the other[109]. If the inner one made an *eruv*[110], the outer one does not have to make an *eruv*. If the outer one made an *eruv*, the inner one must contribute to the *eruv*[111]. Rebbi Phineas said, but in Egypt it was the other way. If he gave on the inner, the outer has to give. If he gave on the outer, the inner does not have to give[112]. Rebbi Jacob bar Aḥa, Rebbi Abbahu in the name of Rebbi Joshua ben Levi: Even if the inner one did not make an *eruv*, the outer one does not have to make an *eruv*. Why? It is treated as a porter's lodge[113]. His statement implies that there is no porter's lodge for a single dweller. Rav's statement implies that there is a porter's lodge for a single dweller, for Rebbi Abba bar[114] Jehudah said in the name of Rav: This refers to a porter's lodge of a single dweller. But for a porter's lodge of multiple dwellers it is an *eruv*, and one who dwells there forbids him[115]. Rebbi Abba in the name of Rav Jehudah: If there are two people, one is entitled, the other one is not entitled[116]. If the one entitled made an *eruv*, the one not entitled is permitted. If the one not entitled made an *eruv*, the one entitled is not permitted.

103 For the House of Shammai (Mishnah 6) even in one big hall an *eruv* is needed if people do not eat together.

104 Latin *papilio, -onis, m*. It seems that

the reference is to curtains providing privacy to the different groups.

105 If the hall is open to a courtyard, any contribution to the courtyard's *eruv* is to the benefit of all the dwellers there.

106 They are legal separations for the House of Shammai but do not provide privacy for the House of Hillel.

107 Since an *eruv* is a symbolic common meal, all participants in an actual meal are counted as one for the *eruv*.

108 If a common meal unites all dwellers in a house, the fact that they sleep in different rooms should not have any influence on the *eruv*. The Babli disagrees with the entire discussion, 72a.

109 "House" usually means "one-room apartment." The inner apartment has no direct exit to the courtyard; its dwellers must leave through the outher apartment.

110 For the courtyard reachable through the outer apartment.

111 Since the contribution of the dweller in the outer apartment does not say anything about the inner one whereas the outer apartment is necessary for the inner one as a porter's lodge.

112 Assuming that at the Exodus there was an inner apartment reacheable only through the outer one, smearing blood of the Passover sacrifice on the outer door-post (*Ex.* 12:7) also protected the inner one while blood on the inner door-posts did not protect the outer ones [S. Liebermann, *Tarbiz* 6 (1935) p. 235].

113 This is not treated as a separate house in the courtyard if nobody lives there; one does not need to include it in the *eruv* and one may not deposit the *eruv* in it. Babli 76a.

114 Read: Rav. Rebbi Abba, Rav Jehudah in the name of Rav.

115 Chapter 8, 25a l. 41; Babli 75b.

116 A squatter.

(23d line 13) פיס'. הָאַחִין הַשּׁוּתָּפִין שֶׁהָיוּ אוֹכְלִין עַל שׁוּלְחַן אֲבִיהֶן כול'. עִיקַּר דִּירָה אֵיכָן הִיא. רִבִּי יוֹנָה אָמַר. אִתְפַּלְגוּן רַב וּשְׁמוּאֵל. חַד אָמַר. בִּמְקוֹם פִּיתָּן. וְחַד אָמַר. בִּמְקוֹם שֵׁינָה. וְלָא יָדְעִין מָאן אָמַר דָּא וּמָאן אָמַר דָּא. מִן מַה דְּתַנֵּי שְׁמוּאֵל. לְמַעֲלָה מֵעֲשָׂרָה שְׁבוּת. הֲרֵי דוּ אָמַר. בִּמְקוֹם פִּיתָּן. מַתְנִיתָא פְלִיגָא עַל שְׁמוּאֵל. הָאַחִין שֶׁהָיוּ אוֹכְלִין כול'. רַב חִיָּיא בַּר אַשִׁי בְשֵׁם רַב. בִּמְקַבְּלֵי פְרָס מֵאֲבִיהֶן הִיא מַתְנִיתָא. מִכָּל־מָקוֹם אֵינָן שׁוּתָּפִין בָּמָה שֶׁהֵן אוֹכְלִין. אָמַר רִבִּי בָּא. אַסְבְּרֵי רִבִּי שְׁמוּאֵל אֲבִיהֶן זָכָה לָהֶן אֶלָּא בָמָה שֶׁהֵן אוֹכְלִין בִּלְבָד. מֵעַתָּה אֲפִילוּ אֵין הָעֵירוּב בָּא אֶצְלָן. עָשׂוּ אוֹתוֹ כְבַיִת שֶׁמַּנִּיחִין בּוֹ אֶת הָעֵירוּב. שְׁמוּאֵל אָמַר. הוּא וּבָנָיו וּבְנֵי בֵיתוֹ מְעָרְבִין בְּכִיכָּר אֶחָד. מַה וּפְלִיג. תַּמָּן הוּא אָמַר. בִּמְקוֹם פִּיתָּן. וְהָכָא אָמַר הָכֵין. פָּתַר לָהּ בְּשֶׁהָיוּ שְׁנַיִם שׁוּתָּפִין בּוֹ. וַתְיָא כַיי דָּמַר רִבִּי אַחָוָא בֶּרִבִּי זְעִירָא. מְעָרְבִין בַּחֲצִי כִיכָּר. וְתַנִּינָן. אֲפִילוּ מֵאָפֶה סְאָה וְהִיא פְרוּסָה אֵין מְעָרְבִין בָּהּ. וְתֵימַר הָכֵין. פָּתַר לָהּ בְּשֶׁהָיוּ שְׁנַיִם שׁוּתָּפִין בּוֹ.

Paragraph. "Brothers sharing property who were eating at their father's table," etc. Where is the main dwelling[117]? Rebbi Jonah said, Rav and Samuel disagreed. One said, at the place of their bread, but the other said, at the place of sleeping. We did not know who said what but since Samuel said, higher than ten [hand-breadths] is rabbinically forbidden, he must say, at the place of their bread[118]. The Mishnah disagrees with Samuel, "Brothers who were eating"[119]. Rav Hiyya bar Ashi in the name of Rav: The Mishnah is if they are sustained by their father[120]. In any case, are they not partners in what they are eating? Rebbi Abba said, Rebbi Samuel explained to me that their father gives them property rights only for what they are eating. Then even if the *eruv* does not come to them? They treated it as a house where they deposited the *eruv*[121]. Samuel said, he and his sons and the people of his house[122] make an *eruv* with one loaf. Does he disagree[123]? There he says, at the place of their bread, and here he says so[124]? He explains it if two persons were partners in it[125]. This is similar to what Rebbi Ahawa bar Rebbi Ze'ira said, one may make an *eruv* with half a loaf. But we have stated[126]: "Even if it was baked from a *se'ah* and was sliced one may not use it for *eruv*", and you are saying so? He explains it if two persons were partners in it[125].

117 Which determines the obligation for *eruv*.

118 S. Liebermann writes: I am at a loss to explain this.

As explained in *Šabbat* 1, Note 109, public domain extends only to 10 hand-breadths above the ground and any transport at this height is at most rabbinically forbidden on the Sabbath. This does not apply to private domain, such as a space 4 by 4 hand-breadths in a tree (Mishnah 3:3). One might conjecture that Samuel recognizes the possibility of placing his *eruv* in the tree so that he cannot stay there on the Sabbath but could eat the *eruv* standing up. The *eruv* is invalid for him who states that the main place is where one sleeps but valid for him who insists on the place of the food.

119 If they all eat at the same place, why should they have individually to contribute to the *eruv*?

120 If they do not pay for their food, the only person relevant at that place is the father. This is emphasized by R. Abba who insists that the sons have absolutely no say over the food. In the Babli 72b statement by Rav.

121 This refers to the next paragraph where it is discussed whether the dweller in the house in which the *eruv* is deposited has to contribute or not.

122 His wife.

123 Contradict himself?

124 The statement that the loaf contributed by the head of the household is valid for all members of the household seems to imply that this is true even if they are eating somewhere else. This contradicts the statement that the place of the meal is decisive.

125 It may be a loaf with multiple ownership so that everybody contributes

something.

126 Mishnah 7:10, where R. Joshua, whom practice follows, requires an undivided loaf for any *eruv*.

(23d line 27) בַּיִת שֶׁמַּנִּיחִין בּוֹ אֶת הָעֵירוּב. רִבִּי יַעֲקֹב בַּר אָחָא דָּמְכַת אִימֵּיהּ. אָמַר רִבִּי יָסָא לְרִבִּי אַבָּהוּ. תְּנִי לָהּ. וְתָנָא לָהּ. בֵּית שַׁמַּי אוֹסְרִין וּבֵית הִלֵּל מַתִּירִין. רִבִּי הַמְנוּנָא אָמַר. בַּיִת שֶׁמַּנִּיחִין בּוֹ אֶת הָעֵירוּב אֵינוֹ צָרִיךְ כְּלוּם. רִבִּי חַסְדַּאי אָמַר. נַעֲשָׂה כְשׁוּתָף. אָמַר לֵיהּ רִבִּי הַמְנוּנָא. מִלֵּיהוֹן דְּרַבָּנִין לָא שָׁבְקִין לָךְ. דְּאִיתְפַּלְגוֹן. מָבוֹי שֶׁצִּידוֹ אֶחָד גּוֹי וְצִידוֹ אֶחָד יִשְׂרָאֵל. רַב חוּנָה בְשֵׁם רַב אָמַר. עֵירְבוּ דֶּרֶךְ פְּתָחִים הַגּוֹי אוֹסֵר עֲלֵיהֶן. אַבָּא בַּר חוּנָה בְשֵׁם רִבִּי יוֹחָנָן. אֲפִילוּ עֵירְבוּ דֶּרֶךְ הַחֲלוֹנוֹת אֵין הַגּוֹי אוֹסֵר עֲלֵיהֶן. אִין תֵּימַר כְּשׁוּתָף הוּא. יֵיסָר. רִבִּי יַעֲקֹב בַּר אָחָא רִבִּי יָסָא בְשֵׁם רִבִּי יוֹחָנָן. בְּנֵי הַמָּבוֹי שֶׁנָּתְנוּ עֵירוּבָן בִּשְׁנֵי מְקוֹמוֹת. אִם מִבְּלִי מָקוֹם הֲרֵי זֶה מוּתָּר. אִם בִּשְׁבִיל לַחֲלוֹק עֵירוּבָן אָסוּר.

רִבִּי יוֹסֵה מֵיקַל לְהַהוּא דְאָמְרָהּ. עִיגוּל הוּא דְרַב. רִבִּי יוֹסֵי בֵּירִבִּי בּוּן מְבָרֵךְ עָלוֹי בְּלֵילֵי שׁוּבְתָּא. לוֹמַר שֶׁנַּעֲשָׂה בּוֹ מִצְוָה.

תַּמָּן תַּנֵּינָן. מְעָרְבִין בְּבַיִת יָשָׁן מִפְּנֵי דַרְכֵי שָׁלוֹם. אָמַר רִבִּי אַבּוּן בְּדִיּוּר יָשָׁן הוּא מַתְנִיתָא.

A house where they deposited the *eruv*. The mother of Rebbi Jacob bar Aha had died[127] when Rebbi Yasa said to Rebbi Abbahu, state it, and he stated: The House of Shammai forbid and the House of Hillel permit[128]. Rebbi Hamnuna said, the house in which the *eruv* is deposited does not need anything. Rebbi Hasdai said, he is made like a partner[129]. Rebbi Hamnuna told him, the words of the rabbis do not let you, as they disagreed[130]: An alley in which on one side dwelt a Gentile and on the other a Jew, Rav Huna in the name of Rav: even if they made an *eruv* through doors the Gentile prohibits it for them. Abba bar Huna[131] in the name of Rebbi Johanan, even if they made the *eruv* through windows the Gentile does not prohibit for them. If you are saying that he is like a partner, he should forbid[132]. Rebbi Jacob bar Aha, Rebbi Yasa in the name of Rebbi Johanan: If the people of the alley deposited the *eruv* in two places, if because the space was not enough, it is permitted, if in order to split the *eruv* it is forbidden.

Rebbi Yose made light of a person who said, this is a large ring[133]. Rebbi Yose ben Rebbi Abun recited the benediction of Sabbath nights over it because it was used for a commandment[134].

[135]There, we did state: "One puts an *eruv* in an old house, for communal peace". Rebbi Abun said, the Mishnah speaks of a prior dweller.

127 Since the mourner is forbidden to study Torah, he could not be asked about the status of the house. In *Tanhuma Noah* 16, R. Jacob bar Aha asked R. Abbahu who emphasized that practice follows the House of Hillel (*Tanhuma Buber Noah* 22).

128 If the dweller in the house does not contribute to the *eruv*, the House of Shammai declare the *eruv* invalid, the House of Hillel declare it valid (but maybe not desirable). The opinion of Rav Hamnuna is quoted as that of the House of Hillel in *Tanhuma Noah*. Tosephta 5:11, Babli 49b.

129 He joins with the other dwellers in the courtyard. Therefore if he has a loaf of bread in his house it is not required to be together with the *eruv* but if he has no bread he is a person who did not contribute to the *eruv*.

130 This is from Chapter 2, Notes 52,53.

131 In Chapter 2 correctly: Abba bar bar Hana.

132 If there are no exceptions to the duty to contribute the presence of a Gentile always should be an obstacle unless permission is bought from him.

133 He speaks of the *eruv* in vulgar terms.

134 Since the *eruv* is food it may (or should) be used after sundown, preferably for the bread used for *Qiddush*, the sanctification of the Sabbath, since already it is dedicated to religious purposes. Babli *Šabbat* 117b.

135 Mishnah *Gittin* 5:9, Halakhah 5:9 Note 231. If the *eruv* usually is deposited in one specific house in the courtyard it may be removed to another location if the old inhabitant is no longer there.

(23d line 41) פִּיס'. חָמֵשׁ חֲצֵירוֹת פְּתוּחוֹת זוֹ לָזוֹ כול'. וַאֲסוּרִין בַּמָּבוֹי שֶׁהַמָּבוֹי לַחֲצֵירוֹת כֶּחָצֵר לַבָּתִּים: מִפְּנֵי שֶׁהֵן פְּתוּחוֹת זוֹ לָזוֹ וּפְתוּחוֹת לַמָּבוֹי. אֲבָל אִם הָיוּ פְתוּחוֹת זוֹ לָזוֹ וְאֵינָן פְּתוּחוֹת לַמָּבוֹי אֲפִילוּ עֵירְבוּ אֲסוּרוֹת. אָמַר רִבִּי יָסָא. דְּרִבִּי עֲקִיבָה הִיא. דְּרִבִּי עֲקִיבָה אָמַר. דְּרִיסַת הָרֶגֶל אוֹסָרֶת.

עֵירְבוּ בַחֲצֵירוֹת וְלֹא נִשְׁתַּתְּפוּ בַמָּבוֹי. מַתְנִיתָא דְּרִבִּי מֵאִיר. דְּרִבִּי מֵאִיר אָמַר. עַל יְדֵי עֵירוּב וְעַל יְדֵי שִׁיתּוּף. נָהֲגוּ הַכֹּל כְּרִבִּי מֵאִיר. רִבִּי זְעִירָא בְשֵׁם רִבִּי יוֹחָנָן. אַף בִּמְגִילַּת אֶסְתֵּר נָהֲגוּ הַכֹּל כְּרִבִּי מֵאִיר. בָּעֵירוּבִין וּבְתַעֲנִית צִיבּוּר נָהֲגוּ הַכֹּל כְּרִבִּי מֵאִיר. רִבִּי יַעֲקֹב בַּר אֲחָא בְּשֵׁם רִבִּי יוֹחָנָן וּבְשֵׁם רִבִּי אֶלְעָזָר. אַף עַל גַּב דְּרִבִּי מֵאִיר אָמַר. יֵשׁ לוֹ בִּיטוּל רְשׁוּת. מוֹדֶה שֶׁאִם שָׁכַח אֶחָד מֵהֶן וְלֹא עֵירַב שֶׁהוּא נִסְמָךְ עַל שִׁיתּוּפוֹ. מָאן אִית לֵיהּ עַל יְדֵי עֵירוּב וְעַל יְדֵי שִׁיתּוּף. לֹא רִבִּי מֵאִיר. דְּרִבִּי מֵאִיר אָמַר. עַל יְדֵי עֵירוּב וְעַל יְדֵי שִׁיתּוּף. אָמַר לֵיהּ. מַה אַתְּ מַשְׁכַּח עֲלַייְהוּ הִילְכוֹת עֵירוּבִין. רִבִּי אֲחָא רִבִּי אִילָא. יָבֹא כָחָד מִינְּהוֹן. דְּחַד מִינְּהוֹן אָמַר. שָׁמָּא יֵלֵךְ לְחָצֵר שֶׁאֵינָהּ צְרִיכָה שִׁיתּוּף. אֵי זוֹ הִיא חָצֵר שֶׁאֵינָהּ צְרִיכָה שִׁיתּוּף. זוֹ חָצֵר רוֹגֶלֶת. וְהוּא רוֹאֶה אוֹתָן מְעָרְבִין וְלֹא מִשְׁתַּתְּפִין. אַף הוּא סָבוּר לוֹמַר. שֶׁמָּא עֵירוּב מוֹעִיל בְּלֹא שִׁיתּוּף. וְאֵין עֵירוּב מוֹעִיל בְּלֹא שִׁיתּוּף. וְחָרָנָה אָמַר. שֶׁמָּא יֵלֵךְ לְחָצֵר שֶׁכְּבָר שִׁיתֵּף. וְהוּא רוֹאֶה אוֹתָן מְעָרְבִין וְלֹא מִשְׁתַּתְּפִין. אַף הוּא לֹא מְעָרֵב וְלֹא מִשְׁתַּתֵּף.

Paragraph. "If five courtyards were open to one another," etc. "But forbidden in the alley since the relationship of alley to courtyards is like the one of courtyards to houses[22]". But if they were open to one another but not open to the alley they would be forbidden even if they made an *eruv*[136]. Rebbi Yasa said, this is Rebbi Aqiba's, since Rebbi Aqiba said, a right of access prohibits[137].

"If the courtyards made *eruvin* but did not participate in the alley." The Mishnah is Rebbi Meïr's since Rebbi Meïr said, by an *eruv* and by participation[99]. Everybody follows Rebbi Meïr. Rebbi Ze`ira in the name of Rebbi Johanan: Even about the reading of the Esther scroll everybody follows Rebbi Meïr[102]. In matters of *eruvin* and public fast-days everybody follows Rebbi Meïr. Rebbi Jacob bar Aha in the name Rebbi Johanan and in the name of Rebbi Eleazar: Even though Rebbi Meïr says that he may cede rights he agrees that if one of them forgot and did not contribute to the *eruv*, that he may rely on his participation[138]. Who holds "by an *eruv* and by participation," not Rebbi Meïr? Since Rebbi Meïr said, by an *eruv* and by participation. [139]He told him, why do you make us forget the practices of *eruvin*? Rebbi Aha, Rebbi Ila; it should be like one of them. For one of them said, maybe he comes to a courtyard which does not need participation. Which is a courtyard which does not need participation? That is the customary courtyard[140]. He sees them preparing an *eruv* but not participating. Then he will infer to say that maybe an *eruv* is valid without participation? But no *eruv* is valid without participation[141]. And the other one will say, maybe he comes to a courtyard which already participated. He sees them preparing an *eruv*[142] but not participating. Then he will neither make an *eruv* nor participate[143].

136 If the inner courtyards can reach the alley only through the outermost courtyard and each courtyard made an *eruv* for itself, those courtyards where others have a right of access remain prohibited as explained in Mishnah 9.

137 Mishnah 9. But for the rabbis a right of access is not a right of transport and separate *eruvin* are possible.

138 Even though R. Meïr requires separate *eruvin* for courtyards and participation for alleys in all situations, this is only a precautionary measure as explained later in the paragraph; in an emergency, such as a defective or incomplete *eruv*, he will agree that in principle the participation in the alley permits carrying in the courtyards.

139 It seems that the text here is corrupt.

The argument is that R. Meïr requires both *eruv* and participation because otherwise there would be the danger that people (in the formulation of the Babli 73b, the children) would forget the principles of *eruv* and participation as explained by RR. Ila and Aha.

140 The courtyard which always is used to deposit the participation. Since the house where the *eruv* is deposited in a courtyard does not have to contribute, so the courtyard where the participation is deposited does not have to contribute by the rule formulated at the end of Mishnah 8.

141 This is proposed as R. Meïr's argument which only is alluded to in the tannaitic sources here, Babli 71b, Tosephta 6:6. It is obvious that this applies only if there is no participation at all, not if one person forgot his contribution. This justifies the argument of Note 138.

142 Clearly this must read "neither making an *eruv* nor participating" since the Mishnah does not require *eruv* if there is participation in the alley.

143 In this situation there is no support for the argument of Note 138; therefore the text stated that this argument applies only "according to one of them".

(23d line 59) פְּשִׁיטָא מְעָרְבִין בַּחֲצֵירוֹת וּמִשְׁתַּתְּפִין בְּמָבוֹי. מְעָרְבִין בַּחֲצֵירוֹת אִם רָצוּ לְהִשְׁתַּתֵּף בְּמָבוֹי אֵינָן מִשְׁתַּתְּפִין. וְאִם נִשְׁתַּתְּפוּ בְּמָבוֹי אִם רָצוּ לְעָרֵב מְעָרְבִין. וְתַנֵּי. מְעָרְבִין וּמִשְׁתַּתְּפִין כְּאַחַת. דִּבְרֵי רִבִּי מֵאִיר. וַחֲכָמִים אוֹמְרִים. מְעָרְבִין בַּחֲצֵירוֹת אוֹ מִשְׁתַּתְּפִין בְּמָבוֹי. אִם מְעָרְבִין בַּחֲצֵירוֹת מוּתָּרִין בַּחֲצֵירוֹת וַאֲסוּרִין בְּמָבוֹי. וְאִם נִשְׁתַּתְּפוּ בְּמָבוֹי מוּתָּרִין כָּאן וְכָאן. אָמַר לָהֶן. אַף אַתֶּם מְשַׁכְּחִין עָלֵינוּ הִילְכוֹת עֵירוּבִין. שֶׁהַמָּבוֹי לַחֲצֵירוֹת כְּחָצֵר לַבָּתִּים:

כַּמָּה חֲצֵירוֹת יְהוּ בְמָבוֹי. רַב וּשְׁמוּאֵל תְּרֵיהוֹן אָמְרִין. אֵין פָּחוּת מִשְׁתַּיִם. רִבִּי יַעֲקֹב בַּר אָחָא בְּשֵׁם רִבִּי יוֹחָנָן. אֲפִילוּ חָצֵר מִיכָּן וּבֵית מִיכָּן. בַּיִת מִיכָּן וַחֲנוּת מִיכָּן. רַב נַחְמָן בַּר יַעֲקֹב בָּעֵי. מָבוֹי אֵין פָּחוּת מִשְּׁנַיִם חֲצֵירוֹת. חָצֵר אֵין פָּחוּת מִשְּׁנֵי בָתִּים. מָבוֹי שֶׁאָרְכּוֹ וְרָחְבּוֹ שָׁוֶה אֵינוֹ נִיתָּר בְּלֶחִי וְקוֹרָה אֶלָּא בְפַסִּים כְּחָצֵר. שְׁמוּאֵל שָׁאַל לְרַב. כַּמָּה יְהֵא אוֹרְכּוֹ יוֹתֵר עַל רָחְבּוֹ. וְהוּא אָמַר לֵיהּ. כָּל־שֶׁהוּא. הָכֵן דָּרַיָּיא דְּאַרְעָא דְיִשְׂרָאֵל מְרַבְּעָן.

אָמַר רִבִּי יָסָה. עַד דַּאֲנָא תַמָּן שְׁמָעִית קָל רַב יְהוּדָה שָׁאַל לִשְׁמוּאֵל. הִפְרִישׁ שְׁקָלוֹ וָמֵת. אָמַר לֵיהּ. יִפְּלוּ לִנְדָבָה. מוֹתָר עֲשִׂירִית הָאֵיפָה שֶׁלּוֹ. רִבִּי יוֹחָנָן אָמַר. יוֹלִיכֵם לְיָם הַמֶּלַח. רִבִּי לָעֶזֶר אָמַר. יִפְּלוּ לִנְדָבָה. בְּעוֹן קוֹמוֹי. מַהוּ לְבַטֵּל רְשׁוּת מֵחָצֵר לְחָצֵר. אֲמַר לוֹן. מְבַטְּלִין רְשׁוּת מֵחָצֵר לְחָצֵר.

It is obvious that "one makes *eruv* for courtyards and participates in alleys. If one makes *eruv* for courtyards, if they want to participate in the alley they may not participate[144]. But if they participated in an alley, if they want to make it *eruv* they may do so[145]." And it was stated:[146] "One makes *eruv* and participates simultaneously, the words of Rebbi Meïr. But the Sages say, one makes *eruv* for courtyards or participates in alleys." If they made *eruv* for the courtyards, they are permitted in the courtyards and forbidden in the alley.

But if they participated in the alley they are permitted here and there. He told them, also you will cause the rules of *eruv* to be forgotten among us[141], for the relationship of alley to courtyards is like the one of courtyards to houses[22].

How many courtyards must be in an alley? Rav and Samuel both say no less than two[147]. Rebbi Jacob bar Aha in the name of Rebbi Johanan: Even a courtyard on one side and a house on the other, a house on one side and a store on the other. Rav Nahman bar Jacob asked: An alley has no less than two courtyards, does a courtyard have no less than two houses? [148]An alley whose length and width are equal is not permitted by lath or beam but by planks like a courtyard. Samuel asked Rav, by how much must their length exceed their width? He told him, anything. The dwellers in the Land of Israel make them square.

Rebbi Yasa said, when I still was there I heard the voice of Rav Jehudah asking Samuel, if somebody put aside his *šeqel* and died? He told him, it should be used for voluntary gifts[149]. The excess of his tenth of an *epha*,[150] Rebbi Johanan said, he should bring it to the Dead Sea[151]; Rebbi Eleazar said, it should be used for voluntary gifts. They asked before him[152]: May one cede rights from courtyard to courtyard[153]? He told them, one may cede rights from courtyard to courtyard.

144 An *eruv* must be deposited in a house in the courtyard; participation can be deposited anywhere in the alley. An *eruv* must be made with a whole loaf of bread; the rules for participation are much more flexible. It is obvious that an *eruv* cannot simultaneously be used as participation since it cannot be at two places at the same time. On the other hand, participation makes an *eruv* unnecessary for everybody except R. Meïr. Babli 71b.

145 To treat the participation also as *eruv* if it is a valid *eruv* and deposited in that particular courtyard.

146 Tosephta 6:6, Babli 71b.

147 Chapter 1, Note 137. Differently Babli 74a.

148 Chapter 1, Notes 133, 135.

149 It is stated in Mishnah *Qiddušin* 1:6 that "a promise to Heaven is like delivery to an individual." Therefore if money was dedicated for the yearly Temple tax and the person died before it was delivered to the tax collectors, it can neither be given as tax nor revert to profane status. It is stated here that it should be given to the Temple for its special fund with which animals are bought for elevation offerings at times when no other offerings are on the altar. The Temple tax itself may be used only for obligatory offerings.

150 The daily flour offering of the High

Priest, to be paid from his own pocket (*Lev.* 6:13). If the High Priest designated money for his offering at a specified day and not all of it is used, the situation is similar to that of the Temple tax of a deceased person.

151 Where it would be dissolved by the chemicals in the water, i. e., it should be destroyed so that nobody could have usufruct from it.

152 It seems that this refers to R. Yasa, whose traditions in a different matter are quoted preceding the question.

153 This may refer either to the situation described in Mishnah 9, an inner courtyard which has right of egress through an outer one and did not make an *eruv* together with the outer yard, or two houses on both sides of a collapsed building where one cannot make an *eruv* for the space between the houses since *eruvin* are instituted only for courtyards (Rashi *ad* 66b). The answer given here is in the Babli attributed to R. Johanan.

(24a line 1) בְּעוֹן קוֹמֵי רִבִּי יָסָה. הֵיךְ מַה דְּאַתְּ מַר תַּמָּן בְּכֵלִים שֶׁשָּׁבְתוּ בֶחָצֵר מְטַלְטְלִין אוֹתָן בֶּחָצֵר. וְדִכְוָותָהּ. כֵּלִים שֶׁשָּׁבְתוּ בְמָבוֹי מְטַלְטְלִין אוֹתָן בַּמָּבוֹי. וּבְשַׁבָּת שׁוֹאֲלוֹן לֵיהּ. וְלֹא אֲגִיבוֹן. דְּלָא רִבִּי יָסָא אָמַר אֶלָּא כָל־מִלָּא וּמִלָּא בְאַתְרָהּ. כַּד דַּאֲתוֹן לְעֵירוּבִין אֲמַר לוֹן בְּשֵׁם רִבִּי יוֹחָנָן. כֵּלִים שֶׁשָּׁבְתוּ בְמָבוֹי מְטַלְטְלִין אוֹתָן בַּמָּבוֹי. רַב אָמַר. אֵין מְטַלְטְלִין אוֹתָן אֶלָּא בְאַרְבַּע אַמּוֹת. אָמַר רִבִּי יוֹסֵה בֵּירִבִּי בּוּן. רַב כְּדַעְתֵּיהּ וְרִבִּי יוֹחָנָן כְּדַעְתֵּיהּ. רִבִּי יוֹחָנָן דּוּ אָמַר. קוֹרָה מַתֶּרֶת בְּלֹא שִׁיתּוּף. הֲוֵי דוּ אָמַר. מְטַלְטְלִין בְּכָל־הַמָּבוֹי. רַב דּוּ אָמַר. אֵין קוֹרָה מַתֶּרֶת בְּלֹא שִׁיתּוּף. הֲוֵי דוּ אָמַר. אֵין מְטַלְטְלִין בּוֹ אֶלָּא בְאַרְבַּע אַמּוֹת. עַל דַּעְתֵּיהּ דְּרִבִּי יוֹחָנָן. לְאֵי זֶה דָבָר מִשְׁתַּתֵּף בְּכָל־הַמָּבוֹי. אָמַר רִבִּי יוֹסֵה בֵּירִבִּי בּוּן. כְּדֵי לַעֲשׂוֹת כָּל־הָרְשׁוּיוֹת כְּאַחַת.

[154]They asked before Rebbi Yasa: Since you say about implements which were resting anywhere in the courtyard, one may move them in the entire courtyard, similarly concerning implements which were resting anywhere in a dead-end street, may one move them in the entire dead-end street? They asked him in *Šabbat* and he did not answer since Rebbi Yasa said, each matter only at its place. When they came to *Eruvin* he told them in the name of Rebbi Johanan: one may move implements which were resting anywhere in a dead-end street in the entire dead-end street. Rav said, one may move them only four cubits. Rebbi Yose ben Rebbi Abun said, Rav is consistent and Rebbi Johanan is consistent. Since Rebbi Johanan says that a beam permits without participation, it is he who says that one may move in the entire dead-end street. Since Rav said that a beam does not permit without participation, it is he who says that one may move it only within four cubits.

In Rebbi Johanan's opinion, why does one participate in the entire dead-end street? Rebbi Yose ben Rebbi Abun said, to make all domains as one.

154 *Šabbat* Chapter 19, Notes 36-43.

(24 line 13) פְּשִׁיטָא. נִסְמָכִין עַל שִׁיתּוּפֵי הַמָּבוֹי. מָהוּ לִיסָּמֵךְ עַל שִׁיתּוּפֵי חֲצֵירוֹת. רִבִּי יַעֲקֹב בַּר אָחָא וְרִבִּי זְעִירָא תְּרֵיהוֹן. חַד בְּשֵׁם מַר עוּקְבָן וְחַד בְּשֵׁם רַב נַחְמָן בַּר יְהוּדָה. נִסְמָכִין עַל שִׁיתּוּפֵי חֲצֵירוֹת בְּשַׁבָּת הָרִאשׁוֹנָה מִדּוֹחַק. רִבִּי יוֹסֵה בֵּירִבִּי בּוּן בְּשֵׁם רַב יְהוּדָה. כְּגוֹן אַנְשֵׁי בַּר דְּלָיָה שֶׁאֵינָן מַקְפִּידִין עַל פרוטטָן. רִבִּי בָּא בְּשֵׁם רַב יְהוּדָה. וַאֲפִילוּ לֹא כְגוֹן אַנְשֵׁי בַּר דְּלָיָה שֶׁאֵין מַקְפִּידִין עַל פרוטטָן.

תַּנֵּי. מַעֲשֶׂה שֶׁהָיוּ מְסוּבִּין בַּאֲוִיר חָצֵר וְקָדְשָׁה עֲלֵיהֶן הַשַּׁבָּת. אֲתָא עוֹבְדָא קוֹמֵי שְׁמוּאֵל וְאָמַר. מִכֵּיוָן שֶׁהִתְחִילוּ בְתַבְשִׁיל מִבְּעוֹד יוֹם מוּתָּר. הָדָא אָמְרָה. וַאֲפִילוּ מְסוּבִּין בַּאֲוִיר חָצֵר. הָדָא אָמְרָה. אֲפִילוּ לֹא עֵירְבוּ. הָדָא אָמְרָה. וַאֲפִילוּ לֹא כִיוֵינוּ. הָדָא אָמְרָה. שְׁתֵּי רְשׁוּיוֹת מִשְׁתַּמְּשׁוֹת בִּרְשׁוּת אַחַת. הָדָא אָמְרָה. נִסְמָכִין עַל שִׁיתּוּפֵי חֲצֵירוֹת בְּשַׁבָּת הָרִאשׁוֹנָה מִדּוֹחַק.

It is obvious that one may rely on participation in alleys[155]. May one rely on participation in courtyards? Both Rebbi Jacob bar Aha and Rebbi Ze`ira, one in the name of Mar Uqban, the other in the name of Rav Nahman bar Jehudah[156]: One may rely on participation in courtyards in an emergency on the first Sabbath. Rebbi Yose ben Rebbi Abun in the name of Rav Jehudah: For example those of Bar Delaiah who do not insist on their small change[157]. Rebbi Abba in the name of Rav Jehudah: Even not like those of Bar Delaiah who do not insist on their small change.

It was stated[158]: It happened that they were assembled for a meal in the open courtyard when the Sabbath turned holy[159]. The case came before Samuel who said, since they started eating the dish when it still was daytime it is permitted[160]. This implies even assembled for a meal in the open courtyard. This implies, even if they did not make an *eruv*. This implies, even if they did not intend to[161]. This implies that two domains may not use one domain[162]. This implies, one may rely on participation in courtyards in an emergency[163].

155 Maimonides (*Eruvin* 5:14) reads the statement as referring to intentional participation for the alley. However, the example given in the next paragraph indicates that any partnership, even if not intended as formal participation, may be counted as one for the rules of the Sabbath.

156 A name not otherwise mentioned in the Talmudim; this name does not appear in the quote of this paragraph by Ravad in his

Note on Maimonides *Eruvin* 5:14

157 Both Maimonides and Ravad read פרוסתן "their piece of bread" instead of פרוטתן "their small change". Their reading seems preferable since an insistence on one's own piece of bread negates the idea of participation in a common meal. In the Babli 49a the people of ורדינא ("town of roses", which in the opinion of S. Liebermann is the same as ברדליה by a common change of letters א-ה, נ-ל, ו-ב) are characterized as misers; it must not read the word "not" in this sentence.

158 Since the story is Amoraic, probably the word תני should be deleted.

159 All the dwellers in the courtyard were at a (wedding?) feast held in the open courtyard on Friday afternoon.

160 Since they all ate from the same food at sundown, the common food may represent an *eruv* for this courtyard.

161 Nobody intended from the start that the food should be used as *eruv*; Samuel's ruling was forced by the fact that if it could not be counted as *eruv* they could not continue with their festivity. Babli 85b, in Rav's name 73b.

162 This sentence makes no sense here; it is copied from a similar chain of inferences in Chapter 7, discussion of Mishnah 5.

163 Since one refers to an emergency it is not necessary to state that permission is given only for a single Sabbath.

(24a line 24) פְּשִׁיטָא. עֵירוּב צָרִיךְ בָּיִת. שִׁיתּוּף מָהוּ שֶׁיְּהֵא צָרִיךְ בָּיִת. (רִבִּי אֲחָא בְשֵׁם רַב. נוֹתְנוֹ בֵּין בַּאֲוֵיר בֵּין בְּחָצֵר בֵּין בַּאֲוֵיר בֵּין בְּמָבוֹי.) מִילְתֵיהּ דְּרַב אָמְרָה. עֵירוּב צָרִיךְ בָּיִת. מִילְתֵיהּ דִּשְׁמוּאֵל אָמְרָה. שִׁיתּוּף צָרִיךְ בָּיִת. מַתְנִיתָא דִשְׁמוּאֵל פְּלִיגָא עֲלוֹי. שִׁיתּוּף נוֹתְנוֹ בְּבֵית שַׁעַר. רִבִּי בּוּן בַּר חִיָּיה רִבִּי אַבָּהוּ בְשֵׁם רִבִּי יוֹחָנָן. נוֹתְנוֹ בֵּין בַּאֲוֵיר חָצֵר בֵּין בַּאֲוֵיר מָבוֹי.

It is obvious that an *eruv* needs a house[164]. Should a participation need a house? [165](Rebbi Aha in the name of Rav: One may put it either in the airspace of a courtyard or the airspace of the alley.[166]) The word of Rav implies that an *eruv* needs a house[167]. The word of Samuel implies that participation needs a house. A *baraita* of Samuel disagrees with him: Participation may be put into the porter's lodge[168]. Rebbi Abun bar Ḥiyya, Rebbi Abbahu in the name of Rebbi Joḥanan: one may put it either in the airspace of a courtyard or the airspace of the alley.

164 Mishnah 8:4. The *eruv* is valid only if deposited in one of the houses of the courtyard for which it is intended, cf. Note 128.

165 This text was written by the scribe but deleted by the corrector. S. Liebermann points out that the correction is erroneous since it is needed to understand the text and is quoted by Rashba (col. 448) from his text of the Yerushalmi. The Babli 85b explicitly

disagrees with this ruling and excludes the airspace of the alley.
166 In each clause the second בֵּין is redundant and missing in Rashba's quote.
167 Since he authorizes airspace only for participation.
168 A *baraita* recited in Samuel's academy, explicitly disagreeing with Mishnah 8:4 (quoted by Tosaphot 72a, *s. v.* בפת).

(24a line 29) פיס'. שְׁתֵּי חֲצֵירוֹת זוֹ לְפָנִים מִזּוֹ כול'. אָמַר רִבִּי יוֹסָה. דְּרִבִּי עֲקִיבָה הִיא. דְּרִבִּי עֲקִיבָה אָמַר. דְּרִיסַת הָרֶגֶל אוֹסֶרֶת. אָמַר רִבִּי לָא בְשֵׁם רִבִּי יַנַּאי. דְּרִיסַת הָרֶגֶל אֲסוּרָה וְאוֹסֶרֶת.

Paragraph. "Two courtyards, one inside the other,[169]" etc. Rebbi Yose said, this is Rebbi Aqiba's since Rebbi Aqiba said, the right of access makes it forbidden [169]. Rebbi La said in the name of Rebbi Yannai, forbidden right of access makes it forbidden[170].

169 Mishnah 9. All of the Mishnah except the Sages' statement is R. Aqiba's.
170 Only if the people having right of access to the courtyard are forbidden to carry in the courtyard do they prohibit the people of the courtyard to carry there. Cf. Babli 59b, 65b, 75a.

(24a line 31) פיס'. שָׁכַח אֶחָד מִן הַחִיצוֹנָה כול'. שָׁכַח אֶחָד מִן הַחִיצוֹנָה וְלֹא עֵירַב. הַחִיצוֹנָה אֲסוּרָה שֶׁלֹּא עֵירְבָה. וְהַפְּנִימִית אֲסוּרָה שֶׁנָּתְנוּ עֵירוּבָן בְּמָקוֹם אָסוּר. שָׁכַח אֶחָד מִן הַפְּנִימִית וְלֹא עֵירַב. הַפְּנִימִית אֲסוּרָה שֶׁלֹּא עֵירְבָה. וְהַחִיצוֹנָה אֲסוּרָה שֶׁנָּתְנוּ עֵירוּבָן בְּמָקוֹם אָסוּר. שֶׁדְּרִיסַת הָרֶגֶל אוֹסֶרֶת. שָׁכַח אֶחָד מִן הַחִיצוֹנָה וְלֹא עֵירַב. נִיחָא הַחִיצוֹנָה אֲסוּרָה שֶׁלֹּא עֵירְבָה. הַפְּנִימִית לָמָּה. מִפְּנֵי שֶׁנָּתְנוּ עֵירוּבָן בְּמָקוֹם אָסוּר. הֲרֵי לֹא נָתְנוּ עֵירוּבָן בְּמָקוֹם אָסוּר. אֶלָּא שֶׁדְּרִיסַת הָרֶגֶל אוֹסֶרֶת. הֲרֵי אֵין כָּאן דְּרִיסַת הָרֶגֶל אוֹסֶרֶת. אָמַר רִבִּי יָסָא. מִכֵּיוָן שֶׁנָּתְנוּ כִּנְקוֹם אֶחָד נַעֲשׂוּ כוּלָּן רְשׁוּת אַחַת.

Paragraph. "If one of the outer courtyard forgot," etc. [171]If one of the outer courtyard forgot and did not make the *eruv*[25], the outer one is forbidden since they do not have an *eruv*; the inner one is forbidden because they put their *eruv* at a forbidden place. If one of the inner courtyard forgot and did not make the *eruv*, the inner one is forbidden since they do not have an *eruv*; the outer one is forbidden because they put their *eruv* at a forbidden place, since the right of access makes it forbidden. "If one of the outer courtyard forgot and did not make the *eruv*;" one understands that the outer one is forbidden because they have no *eruv*. Why the inner one? Because they put their *eruv* at a forbidden place. But if they did not put their *eruv* at a forbidden place? But because the right of access makes it forbidden. There is no right of access which makes it forbidden[172]! Rebbi Yasa said, because they put it at one place they all were made one domain.

171 This is a discussion of the third case in Mishnah 10, that the two courtyards deposited their *eruvin* at one and the same place and one dweller forgot to contribute. Then all dwellers are forbidden to carry in the courtyards but for different reasons. Babli 75b.

172 If the *eruv* is in the inner courtyard and one of the outer ones failed to contribute, there seems to be no reason to forbid the inner one since they can move in their place without any special right of access and the place is correct. R. Yasa points out that since an *eruv* is invalid if it is not deposited in a house of its own courtyard, the fact that the two *eruvin* are deposited together is enough to make the two domains one and if one is forbidden so is the other.

(24a line 2) רַב חוּנָה בְּשֵׁם רַב. אֵין תּוֹרַת חָצֵר לַגּוֹי. אֵין תּוֹרַת דַּקָּה לַגּוֹי. אֵין תּוֹרַת חָצֵר לַגּוֹי שֶׁאִם הָיָה שָׁרוּי בָּעֶלְיוֹנָה אַתְּ מוֹרִידוֹ לֶאֱסוֹר. אֵין תּוֹרַת דַּקָּה לַגּוֹי שֶׁאִם הָיָה שָׁרוּי בַּפְּנִימִית אַתְּ מוֹצִיאוֹ לֶאֱסוֹר. רִבִּי לָא בְשֵׁם רִבִּי אֶלְעָזָר. יֵשׁ תּוֹרַת חָצֵר לַגּוֹי. שֶׁאִם הָיוּ יִשְׂרָאֵל וְגוֹי דָּרִים בַּפְּנִימִית לְעוֹלָם אֵינוֹ אוֹסֵר עַד שֶׁיְּהוּ שְׁנֵיהֶן יִשְׂרָאֵל. רִבִּי בָּא בְשֵׁם רַב יְהוּדָה. מִי שֶׁיֵּשׁ לוֹ דָקָה לִפְנִים מִבֵּיתוֹ גָּבוֹהַּ עֲשָׂרָה טְפָחִים. בְּיִשְׂרָאֵל אֵינוֹ אוֹסֵר וּבְגוֹי אוֹסֵר. מַחְלְפָה שִׁיטָתֵיהּ דְּרִבִּי בָא. תַּמָּן אָמַר רִבִּי בָּא רַב יְהוּדָה בְשֵׁם שְׁמוּאֵל. כּוֹתֶל שֶׁהִקִּיפוּהוּ סוּלָּמוֹת מִיכָּן וּמִיכָּן מְעָרְבִין שְׁנַיִם וְאֵין מְעָרְבִין אֶחָד. אָמַר רִבִּי יוֹסֵי בְּיִרְבִּי בּוּן. תַּמָּן עַל יְדֵי סוּלָּמוֹת הֵן נִידּוֹנִין כִּפְתָחִים. בְּרַם הָכָא דֶּרֶךְ הָעֶלְיוֹנִים לֵירֵד לְמַטָּן. אֵין דֶּרֶךְ הַתַּתְתּוֹנִים לַעֲלוֹת לְמַעְלָן.

Rav Huna in the name of Rav: There is no rule of enclosure[173] for a Gentile; there is no rule of stone partitions[174] for a Gentile. There is no rule of enclosure for a Gentile; for if he dwelt on an upper floor you take him down to forbid[175]. There is no rule of stone partitions for a Gentile for if he dwelt in the inner [courtyard] you would take him out to forbid. Rebbi La in the name of Rebbi Eleazar: There is a rule of enclosure for a Gentile, for if an Israel and a Gentile were dwelling in the inner [courtyard] he never forbids unless there be two Israel[176]. Rebbi Abba in the name of Rav Jehudah: He who has a stone partition inside his house ten hand-breadths high, if an Israel he does not forbid, if a Gentile he forbids[177]. The argument of Rebbi Abba seems inverted. There Rebbi Abba said, Rav Jehudah in the name of Samuel: If a wall was surrounded by ladders on both sides one makes two *eruvin* but not one *eruv*[178]. Rebbi Yose ben Rebbi Abun said, there because of the ladders they have the status of doors, but here from the upper floors one is used to descend, from the lower one is not used to ascend[179].

173 It seems that this is not "courtyard" but from the same root حظار "wall, partition, screen."

174 An informal wall of دَكَة "cobblestone".

175 If the Gentile lives on the upper floor of a multi-family house or in the inner courtyard behind a separate partition he still is counted as dwelling in the courtyard and prohibits carrying by the Jewish inhabitants as long as his rights are not leased by his Jewish neighbors.

176 Following R. Eliezer ben Jacob in Mishnah 1.

177 A Jew who is aware of the rules of the Sabbath and erects a partition between his property and the courtyard shows that he is not to be counted as part of the courtyard. But a Gentile can be expected to change his mind at any time; therefore he cannot be considered separated until his rights have been leased from him; cf. Note 10.

178 The following sentence makes it clear that S. Liebermann is correct to read וְאִין "and if" and not וְאֵין "but not". In that case one must assume that a word רָצוּ "they so desire" is missing, probably because the scribe or his *Vorlage* misread וְאִין as וְאֵין; although one has to assume that the same error was made in Chapter 7 (24b line 70) and the text as in the ms. is quoted by R. Hananel *ad* 75a.. According to the text as it stands the two statements of R. Abba reinforce one another. If two courtyards which are connected by ladders, of difficult access, must have separate *eruvin*, then a Jew who barricades himself so that his access to the courtyard is difficult, should not be counted as dwelling there. But in the corrected reading the statements seem to contradict one another; the dwellers in the courtyard should not be able to disregard the one who barricaded himself in his house.

179 Similarly, a dweller in the inner yard must pass through the outer one, but a dweller in the outer one has no reason to enter the inner.

חלון פרק שביעי

(fol.24a) **משנה א**׃ הַחַלּוֹן שֶׁבֵּין שְׁתֵּי חֲצֵירוֹת אַרְבָּעָה עַל אַרְבָּעָה בְּתוֹךְ עֲשָׂרָה מְעָרְבִין שְׁנַיִם וְאִם רָצוּ מְעָרְבִין אֶחָד. פָּחוֹת מֵאַרְבָּעָה עַל אַרְבָּעָה אוֹ לְמַעְלָה מֵעֲשָׂרָה מְעָרְבִין שְׁנַיִם וְאֵין מְעָרְבִין אֶחָד׃

Mishnah 1: If a window between two courtyards is four-by-four [hand-breadths] within ten [hand-breadths], one makes two *eruvin* but if they wish they make one *eruv*[1]. If less than four-by-four [hand-breadths] or higher than ten [hand-breadths], one makes two *eruvin* and cannot make one *eruv*[2].

משנה ב׃ כּוֹתֶל שֶׁבֵּין שְׁתֵּי חֲצֵירוֹת גָּבוֹהַּ עֲשָׂרָה וְרָחָב אַרְבָּעָה מְעָרְבִין שְׁנַיִם וְאֵין מְעָרְבִין אֶחָד. הָיוּ בְרֹאשׁוֹ פֵּירוֹת אֵילּוּ עוֹלִין מִכָּן וְאוֹכְלִין וְאֵילּוּ עוֹלִין מִכָּן וְאוֹכְלִין וּבִלְבַד שֶׁלֹּא יוֹרִידוּ לְמַטָּן. נִפְרַץ הַכּוֹתֶל עַד עֶשֶׂר אַמּוֹת מְעָרְבִין שְׁנַיִם וְאִם רָצוּ מְעָרְבִין אֶחָד מִפְּנֵי שֶׁהוּא כְּפֶתַח. יוֹתֵר מִכָּן מְעָרְבִין אֶחָד וְאֵין מְעָרְבִין שְׁנַיִם׃

Mishnah 2: If a wall between two courtyards is ten [hand-breadths] high and four wide, one makes two *eruvin* and cannot make one *eruv*[2]. If produce was lying on top of it, both partiess may climb up and eat them; only they may not take them down[3]. If a wall was torn down up to ten cubits, one makes two *eruvin* but if they wish they make one *eruv*. More than this, one makes one *eruv* but may not make two[4].

משנה ג׃ חָרִיץ שֶׁבֵּין שְׁתֵּי חֲצֵירוֹת עָמוֹק עֲשָׂרָה וְרָחָב אַרְבָּעָה מְעָרְבִין שְׁנַיִם וְאֵין מְעָרְבִין אֶחָד אֲפִילּוּ מָלֵא קַשׁ אוֹ תֶבֶן. מָלֵא עָפָר אוֹ צְרוֹרוֹת מְעָרְבִין אֶחָד וְאֵין מְעָרְבִין שְׁנַיִם׃

Mishnah 3: If a ditch between two courtyards is ten [hand-breadths] deep and four wide, one makes two *eruvin* but cannot make one *eruv* even if it is full of straw or provender. If it is full of dust or pebbles, one makes one *eruv* but cannot make two *eruvin*[5].

משנה ד׃ נָתַן עָלָיו נֶסֶר כָּל־שֶׁהוּא רָחָב אַרְבָּעָה טְפָחִים וְכֵן שְׁתֵּי כְצוֹצְרָיֹּת זוֹ כְּנֶגֶד זוֹ מְעָרְבִין שְׁנַיִם וְאִם רָצוּ מְעָרְבִין אֶחָד. פָּחוֹת מִכָּן מְעָרְבִין שְׁנַיִם וְאֵין מְעָרְבִין אֶחָד׃

Mishnah 4: If one put a plank of any kind over it[6] which is four [hand-breadths] wide, or two balconies[7] one opposite the other, one makes two *eruvin* but if they wish they make one *eruv*. Less than this, one makes two *eruvin* but cannot make one *eruv*.

משנה ה: מַתְבֵּן שֶׁבֵּין שְׁתֵּי חֲצֵירוֹת גָּבוֹהַּ עֲשָׂרָה טְפָחִים מְעָרְבִין שְׁנַיִם וְאֵין מְעָרְבִין אֶחָד. אֵלּוּ מַאֲכִילִין מִכָּאן וְאֵלּוּ מַאֲכִילִין מִכָּאן. נִתְמַעֵט הַתֶּבֶן מֵעֲשָׂרָה טְפָחִים מְעָרְבִין אֶחָד וְאֵין מְעָרְבִין שְׁנַיִם:

Mishnah 5: If a straw-heap between two courtyards is ten [hand-breadths] high, one makes two *eruvin* but cannot make one *eruv*. Each feeds from his side. If the straw became less than ten [hand-breadths] high, one makes one *eruv* but cannot make two *eruvin*[8].

משנה ו: כֵּיצַד מִשְׁתַּתְּפִין בַּמָּבוֹי מַנִּיחַ אֶת הֶחָבִית וְאוֹמֵר הֲרֵי זוֹ לְכָל־בְּנֵי הַמָּבוֹי וּמְזַכֶּה לָהֶן עַל יְדֵי בְנוֹ וּבִתּוֹ הַגְּדוֹלִים וְעַל יְדֵי עַבְדּוֹ וְשִׁפְחָתוֹ הָעִבְרִים וְעַל יְדֵי אִשְׁתּוֹ. אֲבָל אֵינוֹ מְזַכֶּה לֹא עַל יְדֵי בְנוֹ וּבִתּוֹ הַקְּטַנִּים וְלֹא עַל יְדֵי עַבְדּוֹ וְשִׁפְחָתוֹ הַכְּנַעֲנִים מִפְּנֵי שֶׁיָּדָן כְּיָדוֹ:

Mishnah 6: How may one participate[9] in an alley? One puts down an amphora and says, this shall be for all dwellers in the alley, and transfers rights through his adult son or daughter or his male or female Hebrew slave[10] or through his wife[11]. But he cannot transfer rights through his minor son or daughter or his Canaanite[12] male or female slave because their hand is like his own.

משנה ז: נִתְמַעֵט הָאֹכֶל מוֹסִיף וּמְזַכֶּה וְאֵין צָרִיךְ לְהוֹדִיעַ. נִיתוֹסְפוּ עֲלֵיהֶן מוֹסִיף וּמְזַכֶּה וְצָרִיךְ לְהוֹדִיעַ:

Mishnah 7: If the food became less[13] he adds, transfers rights, but does not have to notify. If [dwellers] are added he adds, transfers rights, and has to notify[14].

משנה ח: כַּמָּה הוּא שִׁעוּרוֹ בִּזְמַן שֶׁהֵן מְרוּבִּין מְזוֹן שְׁתֵּי סְעוּדוֹת לְכוּלָּן. וּבִזְמַן שֶׁהֵן מוּעָטִין כַּגְּרוֹגֶרֶת לְכָל־אֶחָד וְאֶחָד:

Mishnah 8: What is the required amount? If they are many, food for two meals for all of them. If they are few, the volume of a dried fig for each person[15].

משנה ט: אָמַר רַבִּי יוֹסֵי בַּמֶּה דְבָרִים אֲמוּרִים בִּתְחִילַּת הָעֵירוּב אֲבָל בְּשְׁיָרֵי הָעֵירוּב כָּל־שֶׁהוּא. לֹא אָמְרוּ לְעָרֵב בַּחֲצֵירוֹת אֶלָּא שֶׁלֹּא לְשַׁכַּח אֶת הַתִּינוֹקוֹת:

Mishnah 9: Rebbi Yose said, when has this been said? When one starts an *eruv*. But remains of an *eruv*[16] [are valid] in any quantity. They said to make *eruv* for courtyards only lest the children forget[17].

משנה י: בַּכֹּל מְעָרְבִין וּמִשְׁתַּתְּפִין חוּץ מִן הַמַּיִם וּמִן הַמֶּלַח דִּבְרֵי רִבִּי אֱלִיעֶזֶר. רִבִּי יְהוֹשֻׁעַ אוֹמֵר כִּכָּר הוּא עֵירוּב. אֲפִילּוּ מָאֲפֵה סְאָה וְהִיא פְרוּסָה אֵין מְעָרְבִין בָּהּ. כִּכָּר בְּאִסָּר וְהוּא שָׁלֵם מְעָרְבִין בּוֹ:

Mishnah 10: Anything and participation except water and salt, the words of Rebbi Eliezer. Rebbi Joshua says, an *eruv* is a loaf of bread. Even if a *se'ah* was baked but is sliced one may not use it for *eruv*; a loaf the size of an *as*[18] which is complete may be used for *eruv*.

משנה יא: נוֹתֵן אָדָם מָעִיי לַחֶנְוָנִי אוֹ לַנַּחְתּוֹם כְּדֵי שֶׁיִּזְכֶּה לוֹ בָעֵירוּב דִּבְרֵי רִבִּי אֱלִיעֶזֶר. וַחֲכָמִים אוֹמְרִים לֹא זָכוּ לוֹ מְעוֹתָיו. וּמוֹדִין בִּשְׁאָר כָּל־אָדָם שֶׁזָּכוּ לוֹ מְעוֹתָיו שֶׁאֵין מְעָרְבִין לְאָדָם אֶלָּא מִדַּעְתּוֹ. אָמַר רִבִּי יְהוּדָה בַּמֶּה דְבָרִים אֲמוּרִים בְּעֵירוּבֵי הַתְּחוּמִין אֲבָל בְּעֵירוּבֵי חֲצֵירוֹת מְעָרְבִין לְדַעְתּוֹ וְשֶׁלֹּא לְדַעְתּוֹ לְפִי שֶׁזָּכִין לוֹ לְאָדָם שֶׁלֹּא בְּפָנָיו וְאֵין חָבִין לוֹ אֶלָּא בְּפָנָיו:

Mishnah 11: A person may give an *obolus*[19] to a grocer or a baker to acquire part in his *eruv*, the words of Rebbi Eliezer. But the Sages say, his money did not acquire for him[20]. They agree for anybody else that his money does acquire for him, because one makes an *eruv* for a person only with his agreement. Rebbi Jehudah explained, when has this been said? For *eruv* of domains, but *eruvin* of courtyards one makes with or without his agreement since one may give benefits to a person in his absence but impose obligations on him only in his presence[21].

1   The window is simply a rectangular opening in the wall between two courtyards, not closed with glass or anything else. If the opening is at least 4 hand-breadths wide and 4 high it is usable as a door. If the lower rim of the hole is no more than 10 hand-breadths from the ground, the wall at that place is not considered an obstacle. The status of the two courtyards is as if they were connected by a real door; it is up to the dwellers in the courtyards to decide whether to treat them as one or two.

2   A wall 10 hand-breadths high is a partition which separates the courtyards completely. In addition, an opening less than 4-by-4 in size is difficult to use; it cannot substitute for a door.

3   If on the top of the wall there is any food, it may be taken from either side on the Sabbath if it is accessible by ladders before the start of the Sabbath. If the top of the wall is 4 hand-breadths wide it defines a

domain by itself which cannot be included in the *eruv* of either side. In this case the food may not be taken down.

4 As mentioned in Note 1, any wall not higher than 10 hand-breadths may be (but need not be) disregarded.

5 A ditch 10 hand-breadths deep and 4 wide from wall to wall is treated as if it were a wall more than 10 hand-breadths high. If the ditch is used for storage but contents will be removed and used in the foreseeable future, it remains a separation for the rules of the Sabbath. But if it is filled with material which probably will not be removed, it does not divide from the moment that the actual ditch is no longer 10 hand-breadths deep.

6 Over the ditch. While there are no requirements for the thickness of the plank it must be strong enough to carry a person. If the plank is less than 4 hand-breadths wide, people are afraid to use it and therefore it cannot be counted as a connection between the two sides and two separate *eruvin* are required.

7 Cf. *Šabbat* 11:2, Note 3. The roadway between the two balconies represents a ditch. The statements of Note 6 apply here also.

8 It is assumed that the straw heap fills the entire space between the two courtyards from wall to wall. Then the straw acts as a temporary wall. If at the start of the Sabbath one cannot move from one side to the other one must make two *eruvin*. But if the temporary wall is no more than 10 hand-breadths high it *must* be disregarded and one *eruv* is obligatory.

9 How may one person arrange participation of all dwellers in an alley? This does not exclude that everyone may contribute his own share of food.

10 The institution of Hebrew slavery disappeared at the end of the First Commonwealth; cf. *Qiddušin* 1:2.

11 All these are legally persons in their own right; they may accept gifts from the owner in behalf of others.

12 All slaves that could be held during the Second Commonwealth and later, cf. *Qiddušin* 1:3. These and minor children have no independent legal standing and no property separate from that of their owner or father; therefore giving to them is like giving to oneself, without legal consequences.

13 If part of the food of a valid *eruv* was lost by evaporation or because it was eaten by mice.

14 This implies that the person who makes the *eruv* or arranges the participation from his own money (Note 9) has to inform all dwellers benefiting from his act. Therefore he also has to inform the newcomers that they are included.

15 The minimum amount of food which may not be carried without an *eruv* is the volume of a dried fig; Mishnah *Šabbat* 7:4.

16 The first week an *eruv* is used the correct amount is required. Once the *eruv* is valid, it remains so in future weeks as long as some of it is in existence.

17 The argument of R. Meïr in the preceding Chapter. Children may not be aware of participation in the alley and get the impression that carrying on the Sabbath is permitted everywhere.

18 In Imperial Rome a small copper coin.

19 The smallest silver coin, $1/_6$ of a *denar*.

20 Since movables are not acquired until

taken in possession (Mishnah *Qiddušin* 1:5) the person would have to tell the grocer to be his agent and deliver his part to a third person who then acquires it for him. The only thing he cannot do is give money to acquire part of the loaf which the baker will bake as *eruv* without any further action.

21 Since the person who makes an *eruv* of domains loses the right to go in the opposite direction, such an *eruv* cannot be made for him without his agreement. But *eruv* of courtyards or participation in alleys gives him the right to carry there without imposing any obligations and therefore can be made without him being asked.

(24b line 20) חַלּוֹן שֶׁבֵּין שְׁתֵּי חֲצֵרוֹת כול׳. הַסְּרִיגִים מְמַעֲטִין בָּהּ לְעִנְיָין שַׁבָּת. אֲבָל לְעִנְיָין חֲזָקוֹת אֵין מְמַעֲטִין בָּהּ. קַשׁ וְתֶבֶן אֵין מְמַעֲטִין בָּהּ. עָפָר וּצְרוֹרוֹת מְמַעֲטִין בָּהּ. אָמַר רִבִּי יוֹסֵה בֵּירִבִּי בּוּן. עָלוּ בָהּ עֲשָׂבִים אֵין מְמַעֲטִין בָּהּ.

"If a window between two courtyards," etc. Lattice work[22] diminishes it for the laws of Sabbath, but it does not diminish for the laws of presumed possession[23]. Straw and provender do not diminish in it; pebbles and provender do diminish in it[24]. Rebbi Yose ben Rebbi Abun said, if grasses grew in it, they do not diminish it.

22 If the window was closed by vertical and horizontal bars it cannot be used as door and two separate *eruvin* are required.

23 A person may prove ownership by a claim of lawful acquisition combined with proof of undisturbed possession during three years; for the laws of real estate properties connected by a window with bars may still be counted as one; Mishnah *Bava batra* 3:8.

24 Anything which is disregarded for the rules of ditches (Mishnah 3) is disregarded for windows.

(24b line 23) בְּעוֹן קוֹמֵי רִבִּי אַבָּא. הֵיךְ מַה דְּאַתְּ אָמַר בְּחַלּוֹן שֶׁבֵּין שְׁתֵּי חֲצֵירוֹת. וְדִכְוָותָהּ בְּחַלּוֹן שֶׁבֵּין שְׁנֵי בָתִּים. אָמַר לוֹן. אִין. וְדִכְוָותָהּ בְּחַלּוֹן שֶׁבֵּין שְׁנֵי גַגִּים. אָמַר לוֹן. אִין. מַהוּ לְעָרֵב דֶּרֶךְ לוּלִים. אָמַר רִבִּי אַבָּמָרִי. מַחֲלוֹקֶת רַב וּשְׁמוּאֵל. דְּתַנִּינָן תַּמָּן. כָּל גַּגּוֹת הָעִיר רְשׁוּת אַחַת, שְׁמוּאֵל אָמַר. עַד בֵּית סָאתַיִם. רַב אָמַר. אֲפִילוּ כּוֹר אֲפִילוּ כּוֹרַיִים.

They asked before Rebbi Abba: Concerning what you are saying about a window between two courtyards, is it the same for a window between two houses? He told them, yes. Is it the same for a window between two roofs? He told them, yes. May one make an *eruv* across skylights[25]? Rebbi Abba Mari said, it is a disagreement between Rav and Samuel, as we have stated there: "All roofs of a city are one domain.[26]" Samuel said, up to two *bet se'ah*; Rav said, even a *kor*, even two *kor*[27].

25 Between the living quarters and the flat roof.
26 Mishnah 9:1.
27 The Mishnah does not spell out what kind of domain is formed by the roofs. For Samuel, roofs are places which are not fenced in for dwellings; they follow the rule of corrals where carrying is only allowed if the surface area is at most 5'000 square cubits. If the total area of the roofs is larger, an *eruv* would be ineffective; the roof cannot be part of the *eruv* domain of the house. But for Rav one is permitted to carry on connected roofs without limitations (even if the total area be larger than 2 *bet kor*, 60 *bet se'ah*); the *eruv* may be extended to the roof. The Babli has a very different tradition, 89a-90b.

(24b line 29) לֹא סוֹף דָּבָר כָּל־אַרְבָּעָה עַל אַרְבָּעָה בְּתוֹךְ עֲשָׂרָה. אֶלָּא אֲפִילוּ מִקְצַת אַרְבָּעָה בְּתוֹךְ עֲשָׂרָה כְּמִי שֶׁכָּל־אַרְבָּעָה עַל אַרְבָּעָה בְּתוֹךְ עֲשָׂרָה... הָיָה בָהּ הֶיקֵּף תִּשְׁעִים וְשִׁשָּׁה טְפָחִים. אֲפִילוּ כָּל־שֶׁהוּא בְּתוֹךְ עֲשָׂרָה כְּמִי שֶׁכָּל־אַרְבָּעָה עַל אַרְבָּעָה בְּתוֹךְ עֲשָׂרָה. הָיְתָה עֲגוּלָה וְהָיָה בוֹ הֶיקֵּף תִּשְׁעִים וכו'.

Not only that the entire four-by-four [hand-breadths] must be within ten [hand-breadths] but even if part of four-by-four [hand-breadths] are within ten [hand-breadths]it is as if all four-by-four [hand-breadths] were within ten [hand-breadths][28]. If the circumference was 96 hand-breadths, if only the most minute amount was within ten [hand-breadths] it is as if all of four-by-four [hand-breadths] were within ten [hand-breadths][29]. If it was round of circumference 90, etc[30].

28 Babli 76a.
29 If the window is square, 4-by-4 *cubits*, each side is 24 hand-breadths, so that the total circumference is 96 hand-breadths. As S. Liebermann points out, the Yerushalmi implies that a window 4-by-4 hand-breadths must start visibly lower ("part of it") than 10 hand-breadths from the ground but if it is 4-by-4 cubits the most minute amount, not visible by the naked eye, is sufficient.
30 This sentence is a corrector's addition to the ms. and probably should be deleted. A circular hole is a qualifying window if it contains an inscribed square of side lengths 4. A circumference has to be about 11% larger than 16 hand-breadths to qualify as a 4 hand-breadth window or 96 hand-breadths for the 4 cubits rule.

(24b line 34) מָהוּ לְמָעֵט בְּכֵלִים. רִבִּי חִייָה בַּר אַשֵׁי אָמַר. מְמָעֲטִין בְּכֵלִים. רִבִּי יוֹנָה רִבִּי יִצְחָק בַּר טְבָלַיי אָמַר רִבִּי יוֹחָנָן. אֵין מְמָעֲטִין בְּכֵלִים. תַּמָּן אָמְרֵי. מַחֲלוֹקֶת רִבִּי חִייָה רַבָּה וְרִבִּי יִשְׁמָעֵאל בֵּירִבִּי יוֹסֵי. חַד אָמַר. אָסוּר. וְחַד אָמַר. מוּתָּר. מָאן דָּמַר. אָסוּר. שֶׁמָּא יִשְׁכַּח וִיטַלְטְלֶנּוּ. הוֹרֵי רִבִּי יוֹחָנָן בַּר מַרְיָיה לְמִיכְבּוֹשׁ עָלוֹי כּוֹף.

תַּנֵּי. בַּכֹּל מְמַעֲטִין. בָּאֲבָנִים וּבִלְבֵנִים וּבְסוּלָם צוֹרִי וּבְסוּלָם מִצְרִי. וְהוּא שֶׁקְּבָעוֹ. רִבִּי בָּא בְשֵׁם רַב יְהוּדָה. וַאֲפִילוּ לֹא קְבָעוֹ. וְהָא תַנֵּי. וְהוּא שֶׁקְּבָעוֹ. אָמַר רִבִּי בָּא. וְהוּא שֶׁיִּיחֲדוּ לָכֵן. הוֹרֵי רִבִּי לָא כְדֵין תַּנִּייָה. וְהוּא שֶׁקְּבָעוֹ. רִבִּי יוֹנָה רִבִּי יוֹסֵה תְּרֵיהוֹן. חַד בְּשֵׁם מַר עוּקְבָּן וְחַד בְּשֵׁם רַב נַחְמָן בַּר יַעֲקֹב. צָרִיךְ שֶׁיְּהֵא בֵּין שְׁלִיבָה לִשְׁלִיבָה פָּחוּת מִשְּׁלֹשָׁה. צָרִיךְ שֶׁיְּהֵא בּוֹ רוֹחַב אַרְבָּעָה טְפָחִים. וְהָעַמּוּדִין מַשְׁלִימִין לָאַרְבָּעָה. יָסָא אָמַר. כּוּפַת שֶׁהִדְרִיגוֹ מְמָעֵט. מִכָּל־מָקוֹם אֵין הָעוֹמְדִין מַשְׁלִימִין לַעֲשָׂרָה. נַעֲשִׂית כִּשְׁלִיבָה עָבָה. רִבִּי יָסָא בְשֵׁם רִבִּי בּוּן בַּר כַּהֲנָא. צָרִיךְ שֶׁיְּהֵא מָשׁוּךְ מִן הַכּוֹתֶל אַרְבָּעָה טְפָחִים כְּדֵי מָקוֹם. רִבִּי חִזְקִיָּה בְשֵׁם רִבִּי בּוּן בַּר כַּהֲנָא. אוֹתָהּ שְׁלִיבָה שֶׁהִיא מְמָעֶטֶת אֶת הָעֲשָׂרָה צְרִיכָה שֶׁתְּהֵא מְשׁוּכָה מִן הַכּוֹתֶל אַרְבָּעָה טְפָחִים כְּדֵי מָקוֹם. רִבִּי יַעֲקֹב דְּרוֹמַיָּא בָעֵי. הֵבִיא דוֹפֶן שֶׁלְּשִׁבְעָה טְפָחִים וּמֶחֱצָה וְהִגְבִּיהוֹ מִן הָאָרֶץ פָּחוּת מִשְּׁלֹשָׁה. מוּתָּר. תַּמָּן אַתְּ אָמַר. כָּל־הַפָּחוּת מִשְּׁלֹשָׁה כְּסָתוּם. וְכָא אַתְּ אָמַר. כָּל־הַפָּחוּת מֵאַרְבָּעָה כְּסָתוּם. אֵין אַתְּ בָּעֵי מַקְשִׁיָּא הָכֵין קָשֵׁי. הֵבִיא דוֹפֶן שֶׁלְּאַרְבָּעָה טְפָחִים וְכָל־שֶׁהוּא וְהִגְבִּיהוֹ מִן הָאָרֶץ שְׁנֵי טְפָחִים חָסֵר כָּל־שֶׁהוּא. יָבֹא כַּיי דָּמַר רִבִּי יוֹחָנָן. הָעוֹמֵד וְהֶחָלָל מִצְטָרְפִין לָאַרְבָּעָה. וְהוּא שֶׁיְּהֵא הָעוֹמֵד רָבָה עַל הֶחָלָל.

May one reduce using utensils[31]? Rebbi Ḥiyya bar Ashi said, one may reduce using utensils. Rebbi Jonah, Rebbi Isaac bar Tevlai: Rebbi Joḥanan said, one may not use utensils. There[32], they said, it is a disagreement between the Elder Rebbi Ḥiyya and Rebbi Ismael ben Rebbi Yose. One said, it is forbidden; but one said, it is permitted. He who said that it is forbidden, maybe he would forget and move it[33]. Rebbi Joḥanan bar[34] Marius instructed to cover it with a heap of sand[35].

It was stated[36]: "One may use anything to reduce, stones, bricks, a Tyrian or an Egyptian ladder if it was fastened[37]." Rebbi Abba in the name of Rav Jehudah: Even if it was not fastened. But was it not stated "if it was fastened"? Rebbi Abba said, if it was dedicated for this purpose[38]. Rebbi La instructed following this Tanna, only if it was fastened. Both Rebbi Jonah and Rebbi Yose, one in the name of Mar Uqban, and one in the name of Rav Naḥman bar Jacob: It is necessary that between two steps[39] there be less than three [hand-breadths] and each be four hand-breadths wide; the posts complement the four[40]. Yasa said, a block in which he carved steps reduces[41]. In any case, the posts do not complement ten; it is like a high step[42]. Rebbi Yasa in the name of Rebbi Abun bar Cahana: It must be stretched four hand-breadths from the wall as separate place. Rebbi Ḥizqiah in the name of Rebbi Abun bar Cahana: The step which reduces from ten must be stretched four hand-breadths from the wall as a separate place[43]. Rebbi Jacob the Southerner asked: [44]If one brought a board of seven hand-breadths and raised it less than three from the ground, is it permitted? There you are saying, everything less than three [handbreadths] is considered closed, and here you should be saying, everything less than four [handbreadths] is considered closed. If you want to object, object to the following: If one brought a wall of slightly more than four hand-breadths and raised it less than two hand-breadths from the ground, should it come following what Rebbi Johanan said, what is standing and empty space combine for four hand-breadths, on condition that what is standing be more than the empty space?

31 If the window in the wall is more than 10 hand-breadths from the ground, may one use utensils on the ground below the window to reduce the distance so that it would be permissible to make a common *eruv*? As the Babli 77a points out the problem is that utensils may be moved on the Sabbath and therefore are disqualified as building materials.

32 In Babylonia.

33 As noted before, utensils may be moved but utensils used as part of the building become *muqseh*; this may easily be overlooked.

34 This is the scribe's text, erroneously changed by the corrector into כד.

35 Arabic كوفة.

36 Tosephta 7:10. "Anything" seems to mean any building material.

37 A Tyrian ladder is very heavy and not intended to being moved. Therefore the use of such a ladder to facilitate crossing from one courtyard to the other is unproblematic. But an Egyptian ladder is light and built to being moved; its use presents all problems connected with the use of utensils. Egyptian ladders are not mentioned in the Tosephta. Rashba (*ad* 77a, col. 470) prefers to read in the text that only Egyptian ladders must be permanently fixed to the wall.

38 An Egyptian ladder is acceptable even unfastened if it is intended to be a permanent fixture at the wall.

39 Of any ladder used to climb up to the window.

40 The total width of the ladder, posts and steps, must be 4 hand-breadths.

41 A big stone or a block of wood into which steps are carved is an acceptable ladder for the rules of *eruv*.

42 These are two different statements. The length of the posts of a ladder is irrelevant for the rules of *eruv*; only the steps count and the uppermost step must be within ten hand-breadths of the lower rim of the window. A block of wood with carved steps is not under the 3 hand-breadths rule since the block itself is a high step.

43 The statement of R. Hizqiah explains of the one of R. Yasa. Only the step which is counted as being less than 10 hand-breadths from the window must be a domain in its own right.

44 This is from Chapter 1, Notes 253-255. In Mishnah 1:9 ropes represent a wall if they are less than 3 hand-breadths apart but in Mishnah 7:1 a hole is an opening only if it is at least 4 wide and high.

(24b line 57) פיס'. כּוֹתֶל שֶׁבֵּין שְׁתֵּי חֲצֵירוֹת כוּל'. וְלָמָה לִי רָחָב אַרְבָּעָה. וַאֲפִילוּ אֵינוֹ רָחָב אַרְבָּעָה. בְּגִין מַתְנֵי הָדָא דְבַתְרָהּ. אֵילּוּ עוֹלִין מִכָּן וְאוֹכְלִין וְאֵילּוּ עוֹלִין מִכָּן וְאוֹכְלִין. לֹא הָיָה רָחָב אַרְבָּעָה. רִבִּי בָּא בְשֵׁם רַב. אָסוּר לְכָאן וּלְכָאן. רִבִּי זְעִירָא בְשֵׁם רַב. מוּתָּר לְכָאן וּלְכָאן. מִחְלְפָא שִׁיטָתֵיהּ דְּרִבִּי בָּא. תַּמָּן אָמַר רִבִּי בָּא רַב יְהוּדָה בְשֵׁם שְׁמוּאֵל. זְרָקָהּ וְנָחָה עַל רָאשֵׁי מְחִיצוֹת חַיָּב. וְכָא אָמַר הָכֵין. תַּמָּן אַתְּ רוֹאֶה אוֹתָהּ כִּילוּ מְלִיאָה עָפָר וּצְרוֹרוֹת. וְהָכָא מָה אִית לָךְ. תֵּדַע לָךְ דָּמַר רִבִּי אָחָא רִבִּי חִינְנָא בְשֵׁם רִבִּי יוֹחָנָן. זִיזִין וּכְתָלִים שֶׁהֵן גְּבוֹהִין עֲשָׂרָה וּרְחָבִין אַרְבָּעָה מוּתָּר לְכָאן וּמוּתָּר לְכָאן וּבִלְבַד שֶׁלֹּא יַחֲלִיף. רִבִּי יוֹחָנָן בָּעֵי. מִחְלְפָא שִׁיטָתֵיהּ דְּרִבִּי בָּא. תַּמָּן אָמַר רִבִּי בָּא רַב יְהוּדָה בְשֵׁם שְׁמוּאֵל. זְרָקָהּ וְנָחָה עַל רָאשֵׁי מְחִיצוֹת חַיָּב. וְהָכָא הוּא אָמַר הָכֵין. הֵיךְ מָה דְּאַתְּ אָמַר תַּמָּן. אַתְּ רוֹאֶה אוֹתָהּ כִּילוּ מְלִיאָה עָפָר וּצְרוֹרוֹת. אוֹף הָכָא כֵן. שָׁמַעְנוּ מְחִיצוֹת בִּרְשׁוּת הַיָּחִיד. שָׁמַעְנוּ מְחִיצוֹת בִּרְשׁוּת הָרַבִּים. רִבִּי בָּא רַב יְהוּדָה בְשֵׁם שְׁמוּאֵל. כּוֹתֶל שֶׁהִקִּיפוּהוּ סוּלָּמוֹת מִיכָּן וּמִכָּן מְעָרְבִין שְׁנַיִם וְאֵין מְעָרְבִין אֶחָד. אָמַר רִבִּי יוֹסֵי בֶּרִבִּי בּוּן. מִכֵּיוָן שֶׁלֹּא כִּיוְונוֹ נַעֲשׂוּ כִפְּתָחִים.

Paragraph. [45]"If a wall between two courtyards," etc. Why does it have to be four [hand-breadths] wide? Even if it is not four [hand-breadths] wide? Because of what is stated later: "both sides may climb up and eat them.[3]" If it is not four [hand-breadths] wide, Rebbi Abba in the name of Rav: it is forbidden for both sides. Rebbi Ze'ira in the name of Rav: it is permitted for both sides. The argument of Rebbi Abba seems inverted[46]. There Rebbi Abba said, Rav Jehudah in the name of Samuel: If he threw it and it came to rest on top of a partition he is liable[47]. And here, he says so[48]? There one considers it as if filled with dust and pebbles. Here, what do you have? You should know this since Rebbi Aḥa, Rebbi Ḥinena said in the name of Rebbi Joḥanan: Ledges and walls high ten [hand-breadths] and wide four are permitted for both sides, on condition that he may not exchange[49]. Rebbi Joḥanan[50] asked. The argument of Rebbi Abba seems inverted. There Rebbi Abba said, Rav Jehudah in the name of Samuel: If he threw it and it came to rest on top of a partition he is liable. And here, he says so? You are saying there, one considers it as if filled with dust and pebbles; here it is the same.

We heard about partitions in a private domain, we heard about partitions in a public domain[51]. [52]Rebbi Abba, Rav Jehudah in the name of Samuel: If a wall is surrounded by ladders on both sides, one makes two *eruvin* and may not make one *eruv*. Rebbi Yose ben Rebbi Bun said, since they are not at the same place, are they like doors?

45 Mishnah 2.
46 Since there seems to be no reason to forbid taking the food in this case.
47 If somebody stands in the public domain and throws something for more than 4 cubits and it come to rest on the narrow top of a fence of a private domain it is considered as coming to rest inside the private domain; the thrower is liable for a biblical Sabbath violation.
48 Since he forbids access to the top of a narrow wall between private domains he must hold that this is a separate domain; then there is no difference whether the wall be four hand-breadths wide or not, against the statement of the Mishnah.

The answer is that if one considers the private domain as filled up with dust or pebbles to the height of the fence, the top of the fence clearly belongs to the private domain. But here one is speaking of a wall between two private domains where the argument is inappropriate.

49 *Šabbat* Chapter 1 Note 170, Babli *Šabbat* 8b, 99b.
50 For reasons of chronology it is difficult to accept the reading "R. Johanan". *Pene Moshe* emends to "R. Hanan".
51 The statement about partitions in private domains is Mishnah 2, about public domains is the one of Rav Jehudah quoted in the preceding paragraph.
52 Cf. Chapter 6 Note 178. Here one is forced to read אֵין. It is clear from the earlier discussion (Note 37) that two connecting ladders on a wall permit but do not require making a single *eruv* (Babli 60a).

(24b line 72) תַּנֵּי. כָּל־כּוֹבְשֵׁי כְבָשִׁים עוֹלָה אַמָּה וְכוֹנֵס שָׁלֹשׁ. חוּץ מִכִּיבּוּשׁוֹ שֶׁלְמִזְבֵּחַ שֶׁהוּא כְמִתְלַקֵּט עֲשָׂרָה טְפָחִים מִתּוֹךְ שָׁלֹשׁ וּשְׁלִישׁ אֶצְבַּע. שֶׁהַמִּזְבֵּחַ עֶשֶׂר אַמּוֹת וְכִיבּוּשׁוֹ שְׁלֹשִׁים וּשְׁתַּיִם.

עָשָׂה מִסְטְוָנָה עַל פְּנֵי כָל־הַכּוֹתֶל וְיֵשׁ בּוֹ רוֹחַב אַרְבָּעָה טְפָחִים. מְעָרְבִין שְׁנַיִם וְאֵין מְעָרְבִין אֶחָד. אַרְבַּע אַמּוֹת מְעָרְבִין אֶחָד וְאֵין מְעָרְבִין שְׁנַיִם.

הָדָא דְאַתְּ אָמַר בִּגְדוֹלָה. אֲבָל בִּקְטַנָּה בְּרוּבָּהּ. אֵי זוֹ הִיא גְדוֹלָה וְאֵי זוֹ הִיא קְטַנָּה. כָּל־שֶׁרוּבָּהּ יוֹתֵר מֵעֶשֶׂר בְּעָשֶׂר. הָא פָחוּת מֵעֶשֶׂר בְּרוּבָּהּ. הָדָא דְאַתְּ אָמַר בְּאֶמְצַע. אֲבָל מִן הַצַּד לֹא בְדָא. וְהֵי דֵינוֹ צָד וְהֵי דֵינוֹ אֶמְצַע. נֵימַר. אִם יֵשׁ שָׁם עוֹמֵד אַרְבָּעָה הַיְינוּ אֶמְצַע. אִם לָאו הַיְינוּ צָד.

It was stated: The raising of a ramp is one cubit when he progresses three except for the ramp of the altar which collects ten hand-breadths for three and one third fingers, since the altar was ten cubits [high] and its ramp thirty-two[53].

If one made a bench along the entire wall which is four hand-breadths wide one makes two *eruvin* and may not make one; with four cubits one makes one *eruv* and may not make two[54].

That is if it is large but if it is small by most of it. What is large and what is small? Any where most of it is at least ten, by ten; therefore less than ten by most of it. That is meant in the middle, but not from the side. What is on the side and what is in the middle? If what is standing is four [hand-breadths] it is in the middle, otherwise it is on the side[55].

53   Cf. Babli *Zevahim* 63a. The standard for building ramps was height : base = 1:3 except the altar where it was 10:32. The sentence "which collects ten hand-breadths for three and one third fingers" is corrupt. In *Arukh, s. v.* כבש the reading is וְכָל־תֵּל הַמִּתְלַקֵּט עֲשָׂרָה טְפָחִים מִתּוֹךְ חָמֵשׁ אַמּוֹת הוּא שְׁלִישׁ "any hill which rises 10 hand-breadths for 5 cubits (30 hand-breadths) is one third."

54   One might conjecture that for "and may not make one" one should read "and if they wish they may make one" since if the wall was not higher than 10 hand-breadths over the step which is 4 wide the Mishnah allows making one *eruv*. The new statement of the *baraita* is that if the step was easy to use, being 4 cubits wide, the wall less than 10 hand-breadths high becomes a permanently open door and one *eruv* is mandatory.

55   This is a direct commentary on the last statement of Mishnah 2 that if the wall is torn down up to 10 cubits one may make one *eruv*. If the entire wall is only 11 cubits and 10 are missing there is no wall and it should be impossible to make 2 *eruvin*. Therefore the statement of the Mishnah may apply directly only to walls more than 20 cubits long.

(24c line 6) פיס'. הָא תֶּבֶן לְבַטְּלוֹ לֹא בִיטֵל. מַתְנִיתָא דְלָא כְרִבִּי יוֹסֵי. דְּרִבִּי יוֹסֵי אָמַר. תֶּבֶן וּבִיטְּלוֹ מְבוּטָּל. רִבִּי יוֹסֵי בֵּירִבִּי בּוּן בְּשֵׁם רַב חִסְדָּא. דִּבְרֵי הַכֹּל הִיא. וּמָה דָמַר רִבִּי יוֹסֵי. בְּשֶׁבְּלָלוֹ בֶעָפָר. יֵשׁ תֶּבֶן שֶׁהוּא כֶעָפָר וְעָפָר שֶׁהוּא כְתֶּבֶן. תֶּבֶן שֶׁאֵין עָתִיד לְפַנּוֹתוֹ הֲרֵי הוּא כֶעָפָר. וְעָפָר שֶׁעָתִיד לְפַנּוֹתוֹ הֲרֵי הוּא כְתֶּבֶן. דְּבֵית רִבִּי יַנַּאי אָמְרֵי. חִיפָּהוּ מַחֲצָלִיּוֹת בִּיטֵל. אִיתָא חֲמֵי. מִילֵּהוּ מַחֲצָלִיּוֹת לֹא בִיטֵל. חִיפָּהוּ מַחֲצָלִיּוֹת בִּיטֵל. מִילֵּהוּ חָרִיּוֹת צְרִיכָה. רִבִּי זְרִיקָן רִבִּי אִמִּי בְּשֵׁם רִבִּי שִׁמְעוֹן בֶּן לָקִישׁ. וַאֲפִילוּ רוֹק.

Paragraph.   [56]Therefore straw to be disregarded cannot be disregarded. Does the Mishnah not follow Rebbi Yose, since Rebbi Yose said, straw said to be disregarded is disregarded[57]? Rebbi Yose ben Rebbi Abun in the name of Rav Ḥisda: It is everybody's opinion. What Rebbi Yose said, if he mixed it with dust[58]. "There is straw which is treated like dust and dust which is treated like straw. Straw not to be removed is like dust; dust to be removed is like straw.⁵⁹" In the House of Rebbi Yannai they said: If he covered it with mats it is disregarded. Come and see: If he filled it with mats it is not disregarded⁶⁰, if he covered it with mats it is disregarded⁶¹. If he filled it with branches of date palms it is problematic⁶². Rebbi Zeriqan, Rebbi Immi, in the name of Rebbi Simeon ben Laqish: Even thin sheets⁶³.

56 Commentary on Mishnah 3. The text is taken from a discussion of the impurity of the dead, *Nazir* 9:2 Notes 79-87, *Pesahim* 7:7 34d l. 27.

57 This refers to the rules of the tent-impurity caused by a corpse. A "tent" is any covered space in which there is at least one hand-breadth of space between the corpse and the roof. If the space is enclosed, the impurity is restricted to the "tent"; anything above the ceiling and below the floor of the "tent" is pure. But if the entire space between floor and ceiling is filled with matter, there is no tent and the impurity extends indefinitely above and below the tent space. This is known as "squeezed impurity" (Mishnah *Ahilut* 15:1,5,6). It is implied in Tosephta *Ahilut* 15:5 that R. Yose restricts "squeezed impurity" to material permanently deposited; but a storage of straw which is to be removed in the future is not counted as filler.

58 Not really "mixed with", but "treated like," as formulated in the Tosephta.

59 Statement of R. Yose in Tosephta *Ahilut* 15:5; quoted in *Eruvin* 79a. "Straw" stands here for "material to be removed," "dust" for "permanent filling."

60 Since the filling can easily be removed, the ditch still separates.

61 If a ditch is filled with any material, even straw, but this is covered with mats to create a floor from one side to the other, the courtyards become one and require one *eruv*. *Šabbat* 100a.

62 No ruling is available in this case.

63 This translation is tentative; it follows the *Pesahim* text, reading רָק. Neither the text here רוֹק "spittle" nor the one in *Nazir* רֵיק "emptiness" are appropriate.

(24c line 14) פיס'. אִית תַּנֵּי. מְעָרְבִין שְׁנַיִם וְאֵין מְעָרְבִין אֶחָד. אִית תַּנֵּי. מְעָרְבִין אֶחָד וְאֵין מְעָרְבִין שְׁנַיִם. מָאן דָּמַר. מְעָרְבִין שְׁנַיִם וְאֵין מְעָרְבִין אֶחָד. פָּחוֹת מִכָּאן בְּנֶסֶר. מָאן דָּמַר. מְעָרְבִין אֶחָד וְאֵין מְעָרְבִין שְׁנַיִם. פָּחוֹת מִכָּאן בְּחָלָל.

Paragraph⁶⁴. Some state "one makes two *eruvin* and cannot make one *eruv*." Some state, "one makes one *eruv* and cannot make two *eruvin*." For him who says "one makes two *eruvin* and cannot make one *eruv*", "less than this" refers to the plank. For him who says, "one makes one *eruv* and cannot make two *eruvin*," "less than this" refers to the space⁶⁵.

64 This refers to Mishnah 4.
65 If the ditch is not 10 hand-breadths deep or the balconies not 10 hand-breadths above the ground.

(24c line 18) פיס'. אָמַר רִבִּי אֶלְעָזָר. כֵּינֵי מַתְנִיתָא. אֵילּוּ מְמַלְאֵין קוּפָּתָן מִיכָּן וּמַאֲכִילִין. וְאֵילּוּ מְמַלְאֵין קוּפָּתָן מִיכָּאן וּמַאֲכִילִין. אָנַר רִבִּי חַגַּיי. כַּד הֲוֵינָן יָתְבִין קוּמֵי מְנַחֵם הֲוֵינָן אָמְרִין. שֶׁלֹּא תֹאמַר אֵינוֹ כְסוֹתֵר אוֹהָלִים אֶלָּא כְסוֹמֵךְ אוֹהָלִים. שֶׁאִם הָיָה הַתֶּבֶן מְרוּדָּד שֶׁהוּא סוֹמְכוֹ לְצִידֵי הַקּוּפָה. רַב הוֹשַׁעְיָה בָּעֵי. עֲשָׂאוֹ לְסָדִין וּסְמָכוֹ לַכִּסֵּא מָהוּ. נֶאֱמַר כָּאן לְשָׁעָה וְנֶאֱמַר כָּאן לִשְׁהוֹת.

תַּנֵּי. מַתְבֵּן שֶׁבֵּין שְׁתֵּי חֲצֵירוֹת. זֶה פוֹתֵחַ פִּתְחוֹ מִיכָּן וּמַאֲכִיל וְזֶה פוֹתֵחַ פִּתְחוֹ מִיכָּן וּמַאֲכִיל. נִתְמַעֵט הַתֶּבֶן מֵעֲשָׂרָה טְפָחִים. שְׁנֵיהֶן אֲסוּרִין עַד שֶׁיְּעָרְבוּ. לְפִיכָךְ אִם רָצָה אֶחָד מֵהֶן לִסְתּוֹם אֶת פִּתְחוֹ וּלְבַטֵּל רְשׁוּתוֹ. הוּא אָסוּר וַחֲבֵירוֹ מוּתָּר. (וְכֵן בְּבוֹר) [חָרִיץ] שֶׁבֵּין שְׁתֵּי חֲצֵירוֹת. הָדָא אָמְרָה. שֶׁאֵין מְבַטְּלִין מֵחָצֵר לְחָצֵר. הָדָא אָמְרָה. אֲפִילוּ לֹא עֵירְבוּ. הָדָא אָמְרָה. וַאֲפִילוּ לֹא כַיְיוּנוּ. הָדָא אָמְרָה. שֶׁאֵין שְׁתֵּי רְשׁוּיוֹת מִשְׁתַּמְּשׁוֹת בִּרְשׁוּת אַחַת. הָדָא אָמְרָה. לָזֶה בְּפֶתַח וְלָזֶה בְּפֶתַח שְׁנֵיהֶן אֲסוּרִין. וְכֵן הַבַּיִת שֶׁבֵּין שְׁתֵּי חֲצֵירוֹת. וּדְלָא כְרִבִּי מֵאִיר דְּאָמַר. בַּיִת הַנָּעוּל אָסוּר.

Paragraph. Rebbi Eleazar said, so is the Mishnah[66]: "Each fills his pail and feeds from his side." Rebbi Ḥaggai said, when we were sitting before Menaḥem we used to say, lest you say that he is not like one taking down tents but one who supports tents, for if the straw was flattened he supports it by his pail[67]. Rav Hoshaia asked: What if he used a sheet and supported it by a chair? It is meant here temporarily, but it is meant there for permanence.

It was stated:[68] "A straw heap between two courtyards. Each one opens his door and feeds. If the straw was less than ten hand-breadths, both are forbidden until they make an *eruv*. Therefore if one of them wants to block his door and cede his rights, he is forbidden but his neighbor is permitted." (And so it is with a cistern) [A ditch][69] between two courtyards. This implies that one may not cede from courtyard to courtyard[70]. This implies, even if they did not make an *eruv*. [71]This implies, even if they did not intend to. This implies that two domains may not use one domain. This implies, if each of them uses his door, both are forbidden. And so it is with a house between two courtyards, not following Rebbi Meïr, who said that a locked house is forbidden[72].

66 Mishnah 5. One should not read the Mishnah as requiring that the cattle be brought to feed from the straw; the straw may be taken in containers and carried to the animal barn. Rejected by the Babli 79a.

67 Since the heap of straw acts as a wall between the courtyards, forcing two *eruvin*, should taking straw from it not be classified as tearing down a wall, prohibited on the Sabbath? Even taking straw to smoothe the surface of the heap might be construed as prohibited activity. Therefore the statement of R. Eleazar is required; changing the shape of a straw heap is not a building activity since, as noted in the sequel, these are only temporary changes whereas building leaves long term results.

68 Tosephta 6:17.

69 The text in parentheses was originally written by the scribe; he himself then deleted it and replaced it by the text in brackets which makes the sentence a meaningless quote from Mishnah 3. The original statement seems to be that from a cistern between two houses, where in general one may not draw water on the Sabbath (Mishnah 8:7), if one of the owners locks his door and cedes his rights, the other party may use the cistern without problems.

70 Since cession alone is not enough without locking the door.

71 Chapter 6, Notes 161,162.

72 Mishnah 8:5.

(24c line 32) פִּיס'. תַּנֵּי. אֵין מְזַכֶּה לָהֶן בְּחָבִית שֶׁבְּמַרְתֵּף. אָמַר רַב הוֹשַׁעְיָה. שֶׁמָּא יִשְׁכַּח וְיִשְׁתֶּנָּה.

מָה נָן קַיָּימִין. אִם בִּגְדוֹלָה. זָכָה בְּסִימָנִין. אִם בִּקְטַנָּה. הַקָּטָן זָכָה. אָמַר רִבִּי יוּדָן בַּר שָׁלוֹם קוֹמֵי רִבִּי יוֹסֵי. תִּיפְתָּר כְּמָאן דָּמַר. הַקָּטָן תּוֹרֵם. אָמַר לֵיהּ. אֲפִילּוּ כְּמָאן דָּמַר. אֵין הַקָּטָן תּוֹרֵם. הַקָּטָן זָכָה. עַל דַּעְתְּהוֹן דְּרַבָּנִין דְּתַמָּן נִיחָא. תַּמָּן אֲמָרִין בְּשֵׁם רַב נַחְמָן בַּר יַעֲקֹב. כָּל־שֶׁנּוֹתְנִין לוֹ אֱגוֹז וּמַשְׁלִיכוֹ צְרוֹר וְנוֹטְלוֹ הַמּוֹצִיא בְּיָדוֹ כְּמוֹצִיא לְאַשְׁפָּה דָמֵי. אֱגוֹז וְנוֹטְלוֹ צְרוֹר וּמַשְׁלִיכוֹ גְּזֵילוֹ גֶּזֶל מִפְּנֵי דַרְכֵי שָׁלוֹם. אֱגוֹז וּצְרוֹר וְנוֹטְלוֹ וּמַצְנִיעוֹ וּמֵבִיאוֹ לְאַחַר זְמַן גְּזֵילוֹ גֶּזֶל גָּמוּר. זָכָה לְעַצְמוֹ אֲבָל לֹא לַאֲחֵרִים. רַב הוּנָא אָמַר. כְּשֵׁם שֶׁזָּכָה לְעַצְמוֹ כָּךְ זוֹכֶה לַאֲחֵרִים. הַכֹּל מוֹדִין שֶׁאֵין מַתְּנָתוֹ מַתָּנָה. דִּכְתִיב כִּי־יִתֵּן אִישׁ. מַתְּנַת אִישׁ מַתָּנָה. מַתְּנַת קָטָן אֵינָהּ מַתָּנָה. דִּבְרֵי חֲכָמִים. רִבִּי יוּדָה בֶּן פָּזִי בְּשֵׁם רִבִּי יוֹחָנָן רִבִּי יַעֲקֹב בְּשֵׁם רִבִּי יוֹחָנָן. לְעוֹלָם אֵין גְּזֵילוֹ מְחוּוָּר עַד שֶׁיָּבִיא שְׁתֵּי שְׂעָרוֹת. רִבִּי אַבָּהוּ בְּשֵׁם רִבִּי יוֹחָנָן. הָדָא דְאַתְּ אָמַר. לְהוֹצִיא מִמֶּנּוּ בְּדִין. אֲבָל לַקָּרְבָּן וְלִשְׁבוּעָה כָּל־עַמָּא מוֹדֵי עַד שֶׁיָּבִיא שְׁתֵּי שְׂעָרוֹת. בְּרַם כְּרַבָּנָן דְּהָכָא. רִבִּי יוֹסֵי בָּעֵי. מֵעַתָּה אַף לְעַצְמוֹ לֹא יִזְכֶּה. דִּכְתִיב אֶל־רֵעֵהוּ. עַד שֶׁיְּהֵא כִרְעֵהוּ. רִבִּי יוֹסֵי בֵּירִבִּי בּוּן בְּשֵׁם רִבִּי שְׁמוּאֵל בַּר רַב יִצְחָק. יָרְדוּ לָהּ בְּשִׁיטַת הַפַּיּוֹטוֹת. הַפַּיּוֹטוֹת מִקְחָן מֶקַח וּמִמְכָּרָן מִמְכָּר בַּמִּטַּלְטְלִין: וְהָא תַנֵּינָן. אֲבָל אֵין מְזַכֶּה לֹא עַל יְדֵי בְנוֹ וּבִתּוֹ הַקְּטַנִּים. וְלֹא עַל יְדֵי עַבְדּוֹ וְשִׁפְחָתוֹ הַכְּנַעֲנִים. מִפְּנֵי שֶׁיָּדָן כְּיָדוֹ. רַבָּנִין דְּקַיְסָרִין אֲמָרִין. כָּאן בְּשֶׁיֵּשׁ דַּעַת לְתִינוֹק. כָּאן בְּשֶׁאֵין דַּעַת לְתִינוֹק.

תַּמָּן תַּנִּינָן. הַשּׁוֹאֵל אֶת הַפָּרָה וְשִׁלְחָהּ לוֹ בְּיַד בְּנוֹ בְּיַד עַבְדּוֹ בְּיַד שְׁלוּחוֹ. . . וָמֵתָה פָּטוּר. לֵית הָדָא אָמְרָה שֶׁהָעֶבֶד מְזַכֶּה מֵרַבּוֹ לְאַחֵר. אָמַר רִבִּי לְעָזָר. תִּיפְתָּר בְּעֶבֶד עִבְרִי. אָמַר רִבִּי יוֹחָנָן. וַאֲפִילוּ תֵימַר בְּעֶבֶד כְּנַעֲנִי. תִּיפְתָּר בְּאוֹמֵר לוֹ. פְּתַח לָהּ וּבָאָה מֵאֵלֶיהָ. וְתַנֵּי כֵן. הִנְהִיגָהּ הַמְשִׁיכָהּ קָרָא לָהּ וּבָאת נִתְחַיֵּיב לְשַׁלֵּם כְּשׁוֹאֵל. רִבִּי זְעִירָה שְׁמַע לָהּ מִן אָבֵל אֵין מְזַכֶּה לֹא עַל יְדֵי בְנוֹ וּבִתּוֹ הַקְּטַנִּים וְלֹא עַל יְדֵי עַבְדּוֹ וְשִׁפְחָתוֹ הַכְּנַעֲנִים מִפְּנֵי שֶׁיָּדָן כְּיָדוֹ׃ לֵית הָדָא אָמְרָה שֶׁאֵין הָעֶבֶד זוֹכֶה מֵרַבּוֹ עַל אַחֵר. תִּיפְתָּר כְּרִבִּי מֵאִיר דְּאָמַר. יַד עֶבֶד כְּיַד רַבּוֹ דָּמֵי. וְהָא תַנֵּי. אִשְׁתּוֹ. אִית לָךְ מֵימַר דְּרִבִּי מֵאִיר עֶבֶד יַד אִשָּׁה כְיַד בַּעֲלָהּ. רִבִּי חֲנַנְיָה בְשֵׁם רִבִּי פִּינְחָס. תִּיפְתָּר כָּהֵן תַּנָּיָא. דְּתַנְיָא²²ᵃ. אִשְׁתּוֹ אֵינָהּ פּוֹדָה לוֹ מַעֲשֵׂר שֵׁינִי. רִבִּי שִׁמְעוֹן בֶּן אֶלְעָזָר בְּשֵׁם רִבִּי מֵאִיר. אִשְׁתּוֹ פּוֹדָה לוֹ מַעֲשֵׂר שֵׁינִי. דְּהֵן תַּנָּיָא עָבַד רִבִּי מֵאִיר יַד עֶבֶד כְּיַד רַבּוֹ וְלֹא עָבַד יַד אִשָּׁה כְיַד בַּעֲלָהּ.

Paragraph⁷³. It was stated: He cannot transfer rights to the amphora which he has in the cellar⁷⁴. Rav Hoshaia said, lest he forget and drink from it.

Where do we hold⁷⁵? If she is an adult, she becomes free by the signs [of puberty]. If she is underage, may an underage person transfer rights? Rebbi Yudan bar Shalom said before Rebbi Yose: Explain it following him who said that a minor may give heave⁷⁶. He answered him, but even according to him who says that a minor cannot give heave, the minor can acquire rights. ⁷⁷This is acceptable following the opinion of the rabbis there. There, they are saying in the name of Rav Nahman bar Jacob: One to whom one gives a nut and he throws it away, a pebble and he keeps it, what one finds in his hand is as if found on a garbage heap; a nut and he keeps it, a pebble and he throws it away, what one robs from him is robbery because of the ways of peace; a nut or a pebble and he takes, hides them, and produces them later, what is robbed from him is total robbery. He can acquire for himself but not for others. Rav Huna said, just as he can acquire for himself so he can acquire for others. Everybody agrees that his gift is not a gift, since it is written⁷⁸, *if a man give*, a man's gift is a gift, the gift of a minor is no gift, the words of the Sages. Rebbi Jehudah ben Pazi in the name of Rebbi Johanan, Rebbi Jacob [bar Aha]⁷⁹ in the name of Rebbi Johanan: Robbing from him is never clear robbery⁸⁰ unless he grew two pubic hairs. Rebbi Abbahu in the name of Rebbi Johanan: That which you say is to make one pay by a law suit; but to have to bring a sacrifice for a [false] oath everybody agrees only after he grew two pubic hairs⁸¹. But following to the rabbis here, Rebbi Yose asked that even for himself he should not be able to acquire since it is written⁷⁸ *to his neighbor*, only if he be like his neighbor. Rebbi Yose ben Rebbi Abun in the name of Rebbi Samuel ben Rav Isaac: They came to it by the rules of school children as we have stated⁸²: "School children's buying is buying and their selling is selling, for movables." But did we not state: "But he cannot transfer rights through his minor son or daughter or his Canaanite¹² male or female slave because their hand is like his hand." The rabbis of Caesarea say, here a minor with knowledge⁸³, there a minor without knowledge.

⁸⁴There, we have stated⁸⁵: "If somebody borrows a cow and [the lender] sent her to him through his son, his slave, or his agent, in case it died he is not liable." Does this not say that a slave is able to transfer rights from his master to another person? Rebbi Eleazar said, explain it about a Hebrew slave. Rebbi Johanan said, you can even explain it for a Canaanite slave, it he told him, open the gate for her and she will go by herself, as we have stated: If he led her, drew her, called her and she followed him, he is required to pay as a borrower. Rebbi Ze`ira understood it from here: "But he cannot make them acquire through his minor son or daughter or his Canaanite male or female slave, because their hand is not like his hand." Does this not imply that a slave is not able to transfer rights from his master to another person? Explain it following Rebbi Meïr since Rebbi Meïr makes the hand of the slave the hand of his master. But did we not state "his wife"? Rebbi Meïr holds that the hand of the wife is the hand of her husband! Rebbi Ḥananiah said in the name of Rebbi Phineas, explain it following the Tanna who stated⁸⁶: "His wife cannot redeem Second Tithe for him. Rebbi Simeon ben Eleazar says in the name of Rebbi Meïr, his wife can redeem Second Tithe for him." For that Tanna, Rebbi Meïr makes the hand of the slave the hand of his master but not the hand of the wife the hand of her husband!

72a Babylonian spelling.
73 Referring to Mishnah 7:6.
74 The amphora has to be kept separated lest it be accidentally used on weekdays. Babli 68a.

75 From here to the end of the discussion of Mishnah 6 the text is from *Ma`aser Šeni* 4:4, Notes 80-97.

The problem is that the Mishnah enables a Hebrew slave girl to act as an agent. But a Hebrew woman can only be sold into slavery by her father (*Ex.* 21:7-11) while she is in his power and only for as long as she would be in his power. This means that when she is legally an adult she either is the wife of the man who bought her or she is a free woman. The inclusion of the female Hebrew slave seems to be inappropriate since the Mishnah explicitly excludes the owner's own minor children.

76   The status of a minor in matters of heave and tithes is a matter of dispute, *Terumot* 1:1 Notes 56-59.

77   The remainder of this paragraph also is in *Gittin* 5:9 Notes 234-238.

78   *Ex.* 22:6.

79   Added from the parallels; missing here but necessary.

80   Robbing a minor may be prosecutable under police law, not under biblical criminal law.

81   A minor might be able to bring a suit to recover what was taken from him but since he is not subject to criminal law in case of perjury he may not atone by a sacrifice.

82   Mishnah *Gittin* 5:9.

83   A minor whose vows may be valid.

84   This paragraph also is in *Qiddušin* 1:3, Notes 383-390.

85   Mishnah *Bava mesia'* 8:4. The borrower of livestock is responsible if the animal is injured or dies while in his custody (*Ex.* 22:13). The responsibility of the borrower starts the moment he takes control of the animal. As long as the animal is driven by the owner's slave, it is in the owner's hand and the borrower is not responsible. But (as stated in the part of the Mishnah not quoted here) if the borrower said, send it to me through your slave, and something happens on the way, the borrower is responsible.

86   Tosephta *Ma'aser šeni* 4:7. The Babli *Qiddušin* 24a restricts the statement of R. Simeon ben Eleazar to the case where the wife inherited Second Tithe. Since R. Meïr holds that Second Tithe is Heaven's money, the Second Tithe does not become part of the estate. If the wife now redeems the tithe with household money, the money is the husband's but the tithe is not; therefore, no additional fifth is due. The Babli rejects the conclusion of the Yerushalmi here.

(24c line 66) פיס'. מָהוּ מוֹדִיעַ. הֲלָכָה. לֵית הָדָא אָמְרָה שֶׁאֵינוֹ מְזַכֶּה לָהֶם בְּגוּפוֹ שֶׁלְּאוֹכֵל. אָמַר רִבִּי חֲנִינָה. תֵּיפְתָּר שֶׁגְּרָרוּהוּ עַכְבָּרִים.

Paragraph[87]. Why does he notify? By practice. Does this not imply that he does not transfers rights to the food proper[88]? Rebbi Ḥanina said, explain it if rats dragged it away.

87   Referring to Mishnah 7. Why does he have to notify in the second case but not in the first? Not by logical necessity but by rabbinic decree.

88   If the food became less than the required quantity because he took from it, it would be theft if he did not retain full ownership of everything. But this contra-

dicts the nature of *eruv*. Therefore the case must be restricted to shrinkage by external causes and the first question also is moot.

(24c line 68) פיס'. רַב אָמַר. מְרוּבִּין שִׁבְעָה עָשָׂר. מוּעָטִין שִׁשָּׁה עָשָׂר. אָמַר רִבִּי יוֹחָנָן. כָּל־שֶׁאִילּוּ יֵחָלְקוּ וְיֵשׁ בּוֹ כִגְרוֹגֶרֶת לְכָל־אֶחָד וְאֶחָד מְרוּבִּין. וְאִם לָאו הֵן מוּעָטִין. פיס'. הֲווֹן בָּעֵי מֵימַר. וְלָא פְלִיגֵי. מַה דְּאָמַר רַב כְּרִבִּי מֵאִיר. מָאן דָּמַר רִבִּי יוֹחָנָן כְּ רִבִּי יוֹחָנָן בֶּן בְּרוֹקָה. כַּמָּה הֵן שְׁיָרֵי עֵירוּב. כַּיי דָמַר רִבִּי יוֹסֵי בְּשֵׁם רִבִּי הוֹשַׁעְיָה. אֵזוֹב שֶׁהִזָּה בוֹ פַּעַם אֶחָד כָּשֵׁר. מִיכָּן וָאֵילַךְ שְׁיָרַיִים. אוּף הָכָא כֵן.

Paragraph[89]. Rav said, many are seventeen, few are sixteen. Rebbi Joḥanan said, any if it were distributed there would be the volume of a dried fig for everybody are many, otherwise they are few[90]. (Paragraph.[91]) They wanted to say that they do not disagree; what Rav said follows Rebbi Meïr, and he who follows Rebbi Joḥanan follows Rebbi Joḥanan ben Beroqa[92].

What are remains of an *eruv*? Similar to what Rebbi Yose said in the name of Rebbi Hoshaia: A hyssop with which he sprinkled once is qualified; more that that are remains[93]. And here it is the same.

89 Referring to Mishnah 8.
90 It is clear that the places of "many" and "few" have to be switched.
91 This note is misplaced; it should refer to discussion of Mishnah 9 but this is the next paragraph.
92 The basis of this discussion is Mishnah 8:2 where for a multi-party *eruv teḥumim* R. Meïr requires food for two weekday meals irrespective of numbers but R. Johanan ben Beroqa requires a loaf that can be bought for a *dupondius* if 4 *se'ah* (24 *qab*) are a tetradrachma (4 *denarii* = 48 *dupondii*) (*Qiddušin* 1:1 Notes 100-107). Therefore his loaf has a volume of $^1/_2$ *qab* or of 12 standard eggs which are 24 standard dried figs. Rebbi Simeon requires only $^2/_3$ of this volume, 16 dried figs. Therefore one has to read "R. Simeon" instead of "R. Meïr" since the latter does not distinguish between the many and the few. In this interpretation "many" for R. Johanan are 25. The Babli disagrees, 80b.
93 If a hyssop was qualified and used once to sprinkle water with ashes of the Red Cow it remains qualified even if some leaves fall off (Mishnah *Parah* 11:8).

(24c line 74) פיס'. אָמַר רִבִּי יְהוֹשֻׁעַ בֶּן לֵוִי. מִפְּנֵי מַה מְעָרְבִין בַּחֲצֵירוֹת. מִפְּנֵי דַרְכֵי שָׁלוֹם. מַעֲשֶׂה בְּאִשָּׁה אַחַת שֶׁהָיְתָה דְבוּבָה לַחֲבֵירָתָהּ. וְשָׁלְחָת עֵירוּבָהּ בְּיַד בְּרָהּ. נַסְתֵּיהּ וְכַפְּתֵיהּ וּנְשַׁקְתֵּיהּ. אֲתָא אֲמַר לְאִימֵּיהּ. אֲמָרָה. הָכֵין רַחֲמָה לִי וְלָא הֲוַוֹת יָדְעָה. מִתּוֹךְ כָּךְ עָשׂוּ שָׁלוֹם. הָדָא הוּא דִכְתִיב דְּרָכֶיהָ דַרְכֵי־נוֹעַם וְכָל־נְתִיבוֹתֶיהָ שָׁלוֹם:

Paragraph[94]. Rebbi Joshua ben Levi said, why does one make *eruv* of courtyards? Because of peaceful relations. It happened that a woman was hostile to another and sent her her *eruv* through her son. She took him, embraced him, and kissed him. He went and told it before his mother. She said, obviously she loves me and I did not know it. As a consequence they made peace. That is what is written[95] *its ways are ways of pleasantness and all its paths peace.*

94 This paragraph is from Chapter 3, Notes 84-86.
95 Prov. 3:17.

(24d line 3) פיס'. רִבִּי אַבָּהוּ בְּשֵׁם רִבִּי יוֹחָנָן. זֹאת אוֹמֶרֶת שֶׁאֵין הַמָּעוֹת קוֹנוֹת דְּבַר תּוֹרָה. מֵעַתָּה אֲפִילוּ בָּא לוֹ אֵצֶל הַחֶנְוָנִי. שַׁנְיָא הִיא. שֶׁמָּא יִשְׁכַּח וְיוֹצִיאֶנָּה. רִבִּי אָחָא בְּשֵׁם רִבִּי חִינְּנָא. אַבָּא לֹא אָמַר כֵּן. אֶלָּא וַחֲכָמִים אוֹמְרִים לֹא זָכוּ לוֹ מְעוֹתָיו. זֹאת אוֹמֶרֶת שֶׁהַמָּעוֹת קוֹנוֹת דְּבַר תּוֹרָה. מוֹדִין בִּשְׁאָר כָּל־אָדָם שֶׁיִּכּוּ לוֹ מְעוֹתָיו. שֶׁכֵּן חֶנְוָנִי מְזַכֶּה לָהֶן עַל יְדֵי אַחֵר. שֶׁאֵין מְעָרְבִין לָאָדָם אֶלָּא מִדַּעְתּוֹ. מַתְנִיתָא דְּרִבִּי מֵאִיר. דְּרִבִּי מֵאִיר אָמַר. עַל יְדֵי עֵירוּב עַל יְדֵי שִׁיתּוּף. רִבִּי זְעִירָא בְּשֵׁם רִבִּי יוֹחָנָן. בָּעֵירוּבִין וּבְתַעֲנִית צִיבּוּר נָהֲגוּ הַכֹּל כְּרִבִּי מֵאִיר. רִבִּי יַעֲקֹב בְּשֵׁם רִבִּי יוֹחָנָן. אַף בִּמְגִילַת אֶסְתֵּר נָהֲגוּ הַכֹּל כְּרִבִּי מֵאִיר.

Paragraph[96]. Rebbi Abbahu in the name of Rebbi Johanan: This implies that money does not transfer title as word of the Torah. Then even if he comes to the grocer? There is a difference, maybe he would forget and sell it[97]. Rebbi Aha in the name of Rebbi Hinena[98]: My father did not say so but: "But the Sages say, his money did not acquire for him[20]." This implies that money does transfer title as word from the Torah[99]. "They agree for anybody else that his money does acquire for him," because the grocer will transfer title through a third person. "Because one makes an *eruv* for a person only with his agreement;" the Mishnah is Rebbi Meïr's[100] since Rebbi Meïr said, by an *eruv*, by participation. Rebbi Ze`ira in the name of Rebbi Johanan: In matters of *eruvin* and public fast-days everybody follows Rebbi Meïr. Rebbi Jacob [bar Aha][79] in the name of Rebbi Johanan: Even about the reading of the Esther scroll everybody follows Rebbi Meïr.

96 Discussion of Mishnah 11.
97 If money did transfer title by biblical standards, the Sages could not abolish a biblical law and decree that his money could not be effective. But then it should be possible to deposit the *eruv* with the grocer,

in which case the taking possession by the grocer should transfer property as required, which seems to be excluded by the Sages' opposition to R. Eliezer. The answer is that as a matter of biblical law this is permitted, only rabbinically it is prohibited since one is afraid that the grocer inadvertently might sell the loaf designated as *eruv*.

98 He is R. Hanina, son of R. Abbahu (S. Liebermann.)

99 Babli 81b, *Bava mesi`a* 47b, in the name of R. Johanan. Since the Mishnah states that in general money may be used to transfer title, this must be biblical law.

100 Chapter 6, Notes 99-102.

(24d line 12) רִבִּי יִצְחָק בֶּן חֲקוּלָה בְּשֵׁם רִבִּי יוּדָן נְסִייָא. מְעָרְבִין לְאָדָם עַל כּוֹרְחוֹ. וְתַנֵּי כֵן. כּוֹפִין בְּנֵי מָבוֹי זֶה אֶת זֶה לַעֲשׂוֹת לָהֶם לֶחִי וְקוֹרָה. וְהָתַנֵּי. הֲרֵי שֶׁאָמְרוּ לוֹ לְעָרֵב וְהוּא אֵינוֹ מְמָאֵן. הָיָה מְמָאֵן כּוֹפִין אוֹתוֹ. אָמַר רִבִּי מֵאִיר. מַתְנִיתָא דְּרִבִּי מֵאִיר. אָמַר רִבִּי יוֹסֵי בֵּירִבִּי בּוּן. תֵּיפְתָּר כְּדִבְרֵי הַכֹּל שֶׁהָיָה צְדוֹקִי. וְהָתַנֵּי. הַשּׁוֹכֵחַ וְלֹא עֵירֵב בֵּין שׁוֹגֵג בֵּין מֵזִיד הֲרֵי זֶה אוֹסֵר. דִּבְרֵי רִבִּי מֵאִיר. רִבִּי יוּדָן אוֹמֵר. מֵזִיד אוֹסֵר. שׁוֹגֵג אֵינוֹ אוֹסֵר. מֵזִיד אוֹסֵר. מְעָרְבִין לוֹ עַל כָּרְחוֹ. אֶלָּא מִשּׁוּם קְנָס. מֵעַתָּה הוּא אָסוּר וַחֲבֵירָיו מוּתָּר. מִכֵּיוָן שֶׁיְּכוֹלִין לְעָרֵב וְלֹא עֵירֵב קוֹנְסִין אוֹתוֹ. וְלֵית לֵיהּ לְרִבִּי מֵאִיר. זָכִין לְאָדָם שֶׁלֹּא בְּפָנָיו וְאֵין חָבִין לוֹ. סָבַר רִבִּי מֵאִיר. לֵית הֲדָא זְכוּ. לֹא בָעֵיי בַר נָשׁ יֵיעוּל חֲבֵרַיָּיא לְבֵיתֵיהּ בַּר מִדַּעְתֵּיהּ.

רִבִּי בָּא בְּרֵיהּ דְּרִבִּי פַּפֵּי בְּשֵׁם דְּרִבִּי חָמָא בַר חֲנִינָה. מַעֲשֶׂה בְּאִשָּׁה אַחַת שֶׁעִירְבָה לַחֲמוּתָהּ בְּלֹא דַעְתָּהּ. וְאָתָא עוֹבְדָא קוֹמֵי רִבִּי יִשְׁמָעֵאל וּבִיקֵּשׁ לֶאֱסוֹר. אָמַר לֵיהּ רִבִּי חִייָה. כָּךְ שָׁמַעְתִּי מֵאָבִיךְ. כָּל־מָה שֶׁאַתְּ יָכוֹל לְהָקֵל בְּעֵירוּבִין הָקֵל.

Rebbi Isaac Haqula[101] in the name of Rebbu Jehudah the Prince: One forcibly makes an *eruv* for a person[102]. It was stated thus[103]: "The dwellers in an alley force one another to install lath or beam," and it was stated: If they told him to make an *eruv* and he does not object[104]. If he objects does one force him? Rebbi Yudan said, the *baraita* is Rebbi Meïr's. Rebbi Yose ben Rebbi Abun said, one may explain it according to everybody if he is a Sadducee. But was it not stated[105]: "If one forgot and did not make an *eruv*, whether in error or intentionally he forbids, the words of Rebbi Meïr. Rebbi Jehudah says intentionally he forbids, in error he does not forbid." Intentionally he forbids; may one not make *eruv* for him forcibly? But it[106] must be a fine. Then he should be forbidden but everybody else permitted. Since they could make an *eruv* and did not make it one fines him[107]. But does Rebbi Meïr not hold that one may make something in favor of another person without his knowledge, only one may not impose a disadvantage on him[108]?

Rebbi Meïr holds that this is not a favor; a person does not want that a neighbor may come to his house except on his invitation.

Rebbi Abba the son of Rebbi Pappai in the name of Rebbi Ḥama bar Ḥanina: It happened that a woman made an *eruv* for her mother-in-law without her knowledge. The case came before Rebbi Ismael[109] who wanted to forbid. Rebbi Ḥiyya told him, I heard from your father that if you can be lenient in *eruvin* you should be lenient[110].

101 Meïri (*ad* 80a, p. 313) reads: R. Jacob bar Idi.
102 If the majority of the dwellers in a courtyard or alley decide to make an *eruv* they can appeal to the court to force the minority to participate.
103 Tosephta *Bava mesi`a* 11:18.
104 In that case they can make the *eruv* also for him without a problem. The question is whether R. Jehudah Nesia also allows to force a person who explicitly objects to making an *eruv*.
105 Tosephta 5:15.
106 Since the problem can be eliminated by making the *eruv* for everybody without asking, why should anybody be forbidden?
107 He is forbidden because he did not participate in the *eruv* and everybody else is forbidden since they did not make the *eruv* forcibly.
108 A general principle, Mishnah 11 here and *Gittin* 1:6.
109 R. Ismael ben R. Yose ben Halaphta.
110 Babli 80a; there the roles are switched.

חלון פרק שמיני

(fol.24d) **משנה א**: כֵּיצַד מִשְׁתַּתְּפִין בַּתְּחוּמִין מַנִּיחַ אֶת הֶחָבִית וְאוֹמֵר הֲרֵי זֶה לְכָל־בְּנֵי עִירִי לְכָל־מִי שֶׁיֵּלֵךְ לְבֵית הָאָבֵל אוֹ לְבֵית הַמִּשְׁתֶּה וְכָל־מִי שֶׁקִּיבֵּל עָלָיו מִבְּעוֹד יוֹם מוּתָּר מִשֶּׁחֲשֵׁיכָה אָסוּר שֶׁאֵין מְעָרְבִין מִשֶּׁתֶּחְשָׁךְ:

Mishnah 1: How does one participate for domains? One puts down[1] an amphora and says, this is for all people of my town who intend to go to a house of mourning or to a wedding feast[2]. Anybody who accepted when it still was daytime is permitted[3], after dark it is prohibited since one may not make an *eruv* after dark.

משנה ב: כַּמָּה הוּא שִׁיעוּרוֹ מָזוֹן שְׁתֵּי סְעוּדוֹת לְכָל־אֶחָד וְאֶחָד מְזוֹנוֹ לַחוֹל אֲבָל לֹא לַשַּׁבָּת דִּבְרֵי רַבִּי מֵאִיר. רִבִּי יְהוּדָה אוֹמֵר לַשַּׁבָּת אֲבָל לֹא לַחוֹל אֵילּוּ וְאֵילּוּ מִתְכַּוְּונִין לְהָקֵל. רִבִּי יוֹחָנָן בֶּן בְּרוֹקָה אוֹמֵר מִכִּכָּר בְּפוּנְדְיוֹן מֵאַרְבַּע סְאִין בְּסֶלַע. רִבִּי שִׁמְעוֹן אוֹמֵר מִשְּׁתֵּי יָדוֹת לַכִּכָּר מִשְּׁלֹשׁ לַקַּב. חֲצָיָיהּ לְבֵית הַמְנוּגָּע וַחֲצִי חֶצְיָיהּ לִפְסוֹל אֶת הַגְּוִיָּה:

Mishnah 2: What is its measure? Food for two meals for everybody, food for weekday but not the Sabbath, the words of Rebbi Meïr; Rebbi Jehudah says for Sabbath but not for weekday. Both of them intended to be lenient[4]. Rebbi Joḥanan ben Beroqa says, a loaf for a *dupondius* if four *seah* are a *tetradrachma*[5]. Rebbi Simeon says, two thirds of a loaf if three are made from a *qab*[6]; half of this for the leprous house,[7] and half of this half bring impurity to a body[8].

משנה ג: אַנְשֵׁי חָצֵר וְאַנְשֵׁי מִרְפֶּסֶת שֶׁשָּׁכְחוּ וְלֹא עֵירְבוּ כָּל־שֶׁגָּבוֹהַּ עֲשָׂרָה טְפָחִים לַמִּרְפֶּסֶת פָּחוּת מִכֵּן לֶחָצֵר. חוּלְיַת הַבּוֹר וְהַסֶּלַע גְּבוֹהִים עֲשָׂרָה טְפָחִים לַמִּרְפֶּסֶת פָּחוּת מִכֵּן לֶחָצֵר. בַּמֶּה דְבָרִים אֲמוּרִים בִּסְמוּכָה אֲבָל בְּמוּפְלֶגֶת אֲפִילּוּ הִיא גְבוֹהָה עֲשָׂרָה טְפָחִים לֶחָצֵר. אֵי זוֹ הִיא סְמוּכָה כָּל־שֶׁאֵינָהּ רְחוֹקָה אַרְבָּעָה טְפָחִים:

Mishnah 3: If people of a courtyard and those on a balcony forgot and did not make an *eruv*[9], anything higher than ten hand-breadths belongs to the balcony, less than this to the courtyard. The enclosure of a cistern or a rock[10] ten hand-breadths high belong to the balcony, less than this to the courtyard. When has this been said? If it is close. But if it is far away even if it is ten hand-breadths high it belongs to the courtyard. What is close? Any which is not four hand-breadths distant.

משנה ד: הַנּוֹתֵן אֶת עֵירוּבוֹ בְּבֵית שַׁעַר בְּאַכְסַדְרָה וּמִרְפֶּסֶת אֵינוֹ עֵירוּב וְהַדָּר שָׁם אֵינוֹ אוֹסֵר עָלָיו. בְּבֵית הַתֶּבֶן בְּבֵית הַבָּקָר בְּבֵית הָעֵצִים בְּבֵית הָאוֹצָרוֹת הֲרֵי זֶה עֵירוּב וְהַדָּר שָׁם אוֹסֵר עָלָיו. רִבִּי יְהוּדָה אוֹמֵר אִם יֵשׁ שָׁם תְּפוּסַת יָד שֶׁל בַּעַל הַבַּיִת אֵינוֹ אוֹסֵר עָלָיו:

Mishnah 4: If one deposits his *eruv* in a porter's lodge[11], a porch[12], or a balcony, it is no *eruv* and any person who might dwell there does not forbid him. In a storage room for straw, in a cowshed, in a storage room for wood, or a general storage area, it is an *eruv* and any person who might dwell there does forbid him[13]. Rebbi Jehusah says, if the householder retains rights of use he does not forbid him[14].

משנה ה: הַמַּנִּיחַ אֶת בֵּיתוֹ וְהָלַךְ לִשְׁבּוֹת בְּעִיר אַחֶרֶת אֶחָד נָכְרִי וְאֶחָד יִשְׂרָאֵל הֲרֵי זֶה אוֹסֵר דִּבְרֵי רִבִּי מֵאִיר. רִבִּי יְהוּדָה אוֹמֵר אֵינוֹ אוֹסֵר. רִבִּי יוֹסֵה אוֹמֵר נָכְרִי אוֹסֵר יִשְׂרָאֵל אֵינוֹ אוֹסֵר שֶׁאֵין דֶּרֶךְ יִשְׂרָאֵל לָבוֹא בַּשַּׁבָּת.

Mishnah 5: If somebody leaves his house to stay in an other town for the Sabbath, whether he be Gentile of Jewish, he forbids[15], the words of Rebbi Meïr. Rebbi Jehudah says, a Gentile forbids but a Jew does not forbid since it is not Jewish to come on the Sabbath.

משנה ו: רִבִּי שִׁמְעוֹן אוֹמֵר אֲפִילוּ הִנִּיחַ אֶת בֵּיתוֹ וְהָלַךְ לִשְׁבּוֹת אֵצֶל בִּתּוֹ בְּאוֹתוֹ הָעִיר אֵינוֹ אוֹסֵר שֶׁכְּבָר הִסִּיעַ מִלִּבּוֹ:

Mishnah 6: Rebbi Simeon says, even if he left his house and went to keep the Sabbath at his daughter's in the same town he does not forbid since already he does not think of it any more.

משנה ז: בּוֹר שֶׁבֵּין שְׁתֵּי חֲצֵרוֹת אֵין מְמַלְּאִין מִמֶּנּוּ בַּשַּׁבָּת אֶלָּא אִם כֵּן עָשׂוּ לוֹ מְחִיצָה גְּבוֹהָּ עֲשָׂרָה טְפָחִים בֵּין מִלְּמַטָּן בֵּין מִתּוֹךְ אוֹגְנוֹ. אָמַר רַבָּן שִׁמְעוֹן בֶּן גַּמְלִיאֵל בֵּית שַׁמַּאי אוֹמְרִים מִלְּמַטָּן וּבֵית הִלֵּל אוֹמְרִים מִלְמַעְלָן. אָמַר רִבִּי יְהוּדָה לֹא תְהֵא מְחִיצָה גְּדוֹלָה מִן הַכּוֹתֶל שֶׁבֵּינֵיהֶן:

Mishnah 7: From a cistern between two courtyards one may not draw water on the Sabbath[16] unless one made for it a partition ten hand-breadths high, either below or inside its rim[17]. Rabban Simeon ben Gamliel said, the House of Shammai say below but the House of Hillel say above[18]. Rebbi Jehudah says, a partition should not be more than the wall in between them[19].

משנה ח: אַמַּת הַמַּיִם שֶׁהִיא עוֹבֶרֶת בֶּחָצֵר אֵין מְמַלִּין מִמֶּנָּה בַּשַּׁבָּת אֶלָּא אִם כֵּן עָשׂוּ לָהּ מְחִיצָה גְבוֹהָה עֲשָׂרָה טְפָחִים בַּכְּנִיסָה וּבַיְצִיאָה. אָמַר רַבִּי יְהוּדָה מַעֲשֶׂה בְאַמָּה שֶׁל אָבֵל שֶׁהָיוּ מְמַלִּין מִמֶּנָּה עַל פִּי זְקֵנִים בַּשַּׁבָּת אָמְרוּ לוֹ מִפְּנֵי שֶׁלֹּא הָיָה בָהּ כַּשִּׁעוּר:

Mishnah 8: From a water canal[20] which crosses a courtyard one does not draw on the Sabbath unless one made a partition ten hand-breadths high at its entrance and exit. Rebbi Jehudah said, it happened that from the water canal of Abel one was drawing water[21] on the instruction of Elders on the Sabbath. They told him, because it did not have the measure[22].

משנה ט: כְּצוֹצְרָא שֶׁהִיא לְמַעְלָה מִן הַיָּם אֵין מְמַלִּין מִמֶּנָּה בַּשַּׁבָּת אֶלָּא אִם כֵּן עָשׂוּ לָהּ מְחִיצָה גְבוֹהָה עֲשָׂרָה טְפָחִים בֵּין מִלְמַעְלָן בֵּין מִלְמַטָּן. וְכֵן שְׁתֵּי כְצוֹצְרָיוֹת זוֹ לְמַעְלָה מִזּוֹ עָשׂוּ לָעֶלְיוֹנָה וְלֹא עָשׂוּ לַתַּחְתּוֹנָה שְׁתֵּיהֶן אֲסוּרוֹת עַד שֶׁיְּעָרִיבוּ:

Mishnah 9: From a balcony above the sea one may not draw water on the Sabbath unless one made a partition ten hand-breadths high either above or below[23]. Similarly, two balconies one on top of the other[24], if they made for the upper one but not for the lower one both are forbidden until they make an *eruv*.

משנה י: חָצֵר שֶׁהִיא פְחוּתָה מֵאַרְבַּע אַמּוֹת אֵין שׁוֹפְכִין לְתוֹכָהּ מַיִם בַּשַּׁבָּת אֶלָּא אִם כֵּן עָשׂוּ לָהּ עוּקָה מַחְזֶקֶת סָאתַיִם מִן הַנֶּקֶב וּלְמַטָּן בֵּין מִבִּפְנִים בֵּין מִבַּחוּץ אֶלָּא שֶׁמִּבַּחוּץ צָרִיךְ לִקְמוֹר וּמִבִּפְנִים אֵין צָרִיךְ לִקְמוֹר. רַבִּי אֱלִיעֶזֶר בֶּן יַעֲקֹב אוֹמֵר בִּיב שֶׁהוּא קָמוּר אַרְבַּע אַמּוֹת בִּרְשׁוּת הָרַבִּים שׁוֹפְכִין לְתוֹכוֹ מַיִם בַּשַּׁבָּת. וַחֲכָמִים אוֹמְרִים אֲפִלּוּ גַג אוֹ חָצֵר מֵאָה אַמָּה לֹא יִשְׁפּוֹךְ עַל פְּנֵי הַבִּיב אֲבָל שׁוֹפֵךְ הוּא עַל הַגַּג וְהֵן יוֹרְדִין לַבִּיב. הֶחָצֵר וְהָאַכְסַדְרָה מִצְטָרְפִין בְּאַרְבַּע אַמּוֹת:

Mishnah 10: If a courtyard be less that four [by four] cubits one may not pour water in it on the Sabbath unless one make for it a sump containing two *seah* below the hole[25], whether inside or outside; only that outside one has to cover but inside one does not have to cover[26]. Rebbi Eliezer ben Jacob says, one may pour water on the Sabbath into a sewer which is covered for four cubits in the public domain, but the Sages are saying, even from a roof or a courtyard 100 cubits [wide] one may not pour into the sewer[27] but one may pour onto the roof and it flows down into the sewer. Courtyard and porch combine for four cubits[28].

משנה יא: שְׁתֵּי דְיָטוֹת זוֹ כְּנֶגֶד זוֹ מִקְצָתָן עָשׂוּ עוּקָה וּמִקְצָתָן לֹא עָשׂוּ עוּקָה אֶת שֶׁעָשׂוּ עוּקָה מוּתָּרִין וְאֶת שֶׁלֹא עָשׂוּ עוּקָה אֲסוּרִין:

Mishnah 11: Two rows of apartments[29], one opposite the other, one side made a sump, the other did not make a sump. Those who made a sump are permitted, those who did not make a sump are forbidden.

1 At the place where he wants to extend the Sabbath domain.

2 Or any public meritorious act.

3 It still needs a deliberate act by anybody who wants to use this *eruv* even though it was given for potentially everybody.

4 In R. Meïr's practice, people eat more on the Sabbath because they have more time to eat and it is a festive occasion; in R. Jehudah's practice people eat more on weekdays since they need the energy for work whereas on the Sabbath there is no exertion and, therefore, less hunger.

5 A *dupondius* is half an *obolus* or one twelfth of a *denarius* (*drachma*). Therefore a *dupondius* is $1/_{48}$ of a *tetradrachma* (cf. *Qiddušin* 1:1, Note 100.) A *qab* is $1/_6$ of a *se'ah* (cf. *Berkhot* 3:4 Note 164) or $1/_{24}$ of 4 *se'ah*. The Halakhah states that the baker takes $1/_3$ from above (which is $1/_2$ from below) for his overhead and profit. Therefore R. Johanan ben Beroqa requires a loaf made from $2/_3$ of $1/_2$ (or $1/_3$) *qab* of flour.

6 $2/_9$ of a *qab*, $1/_9$ less than required by R. Johanan ben Beroqa.

7 It is stated in *Lev*. 14:46 that anybody who enters a locked-down leprous house becomes impure immediately; v. 14:47 states that if somebody eats in the house even his garments become impure. This is interpreted rabbinically to mean that garments become impure if the wearer stays in the house the time needed for eating half a loaf of bread (Mishnah *Nega'im* 13:9).

8 If anybody eats the volume of a quarter loaf of impure food, he may not eat sanctified food unless he purify himself in a *miqweh*.

9 In a two-story, multi-party building where the stairs are on the outside and a balcony is built along the entire length of the house by which one has access to the different apartments on the upper floor. If the dwellers on the upper floor made an *eruv* among themselves but not with the other dwellers in the same courtyard, they may carry on the common balcony but not in the courtyard.

10 Cf. Mishnah *Šabbat* 11:2, Note 8.

11 A small room for the guard at the entrance to the courtyard. This and the following are not places built as dwellings.

12 Greek ἐξέδρα, a covered walkway without walls.

13 Since these buildings are enclosed structures they may occasionally be rented out as apartments; therefore they are acceptable places for depositing an *eruv* of courtyards. People occupying these premises are required to contribute to the *eruv* which otherwise would be incomplete and invalid.

14 If the owner reserved for himself the right to occasionally use the building which he rented out as a dwelling, it remains his

space and is included in his contribution to the *eruv*; the renter is not obligated to contribute.

15 The Jew unless he contributes to the *eruv*; the Gentile unless permission was bought from him.

16 Unless the two courtyards made a common *eruv*.

17 Either in the water or at least inside the rim of the cistern even if it does not touch the water.

18 It even may be high above the rim of the cistern as long as its projection would split the water into two parts.

19 The walls are enough of a separation to let each party draw water on its side without additional partition.

20 Ten hand-breadths deep and four wide. In general this is a separate *karmelit* and not part of the courtyard.

21 Without separate partitions for every courtyard the canal is crossing.

22 Not 10 hand-breadths deep and 4 wide.

23 The house is on a lakeshore, the balcony is built over the lake, and there is a hole in the balcony through which a pail may be lowered to draw water. While obviously water is always moving and it cannot be asserted that water drops found under the balcony on the Sabbath were there at sundown, since the restriction is purely rabbinic it is enough that under the balcony one make a symbolic wall whose extension would enclose the water.

24 Over the same water, with the holes in the balconies one directly on top of the other.

25 Since the space is so small one has to assume that water poured into the courtyard will run off into the public domain. Then pouring the water may look as if one were pouring from a private into the public domain, which would look like a Sabbath violation. Therefore one requires that there be a sink absorbing 2 *se'ah* (about 25 l) of the run-off. If later there is an overflow from this sink it is not directly the result of pouring out water and therefore one may pour out water in unlimited amounts.

26 This makes the sink an extension of the courtyard; it no longer is counted as public domain.

27 Since it looks like pouring into the public domain.

28 If the sum of the areas is at least 16 square cubits nothing has to be excavated.

29 Greek δίαιτα, ἡ. The two rows of houses share a common courtyard but no *eruv*.

(25a line 3) כֵּיצַד מִשְׁתַּתְּפִין בַּתְּחוּמִין כול׳. וְלֹא תַנִיתָהּ. מְזַכּוּן. וְלָמָה לֹא תַנִינָן מְזַכּוּן. שְׁמוּאֵל אָמַר. תַּמָּן תַּנִינָן. מְזַכּוּן. צָרִיךְ לְזַכּוֹת. בְּרַם הָכָא דְּלָא תַּנִּינָן. מְזַכּוּן. אֵינוֹ צָרִיךְ לְזַכּוֹת. רִבִּי יוֹחָנָן אָמַר. קוּלֵּי חוּמְרִין בַּדָּבָר. מָה אִינּוּן תַּמָּן שֶׁעֵירוּבֵי חֲצֵירוֹת מִדִּבְרֵיהֶן אַתְּ אוֹמֵר. מְזַכִּין. עֵירוּבֵי תְחוּמִין מִדְּבַר תּוֹרָה לֹא כָל־שֶׁכֵּן. אַתְיָיא דְרַב כְּרִבִּי יוֹחָנָן. אָמַר רִבִּי יוֹסֵי בֵּירִבִּי בּוּן. כְּדֵי לַעֲשׂוֹת כָּל־הָרְשֻׁיּוֹת כְּאַחַת.

"How does one participate for domains," etc. One does not state "one transfers rights.[30]" Why does one not state "one transfers rights"? Samuel said, there[31] we stated that "one transfers rights," one has to transfer rights; but here, where we did not state "one transfers rights", one does not have to transfer rights. Rebbi Johanan said, it is a matter of a conclusion *de minore ad maius*. If there, where *eruvin* of courtyards are a rabbinic institution you are saying that one has to transfer rights, not so much more *eruvin* of domains which are words of the Torah[32]? Rav follows Rebbi Johanan[33], (and)[34] Rebbi Yose ben Rebbi Abun said, to treat all domains equally[34].

30 In Mishnah 7:6, about participation in an alley.

31 Mishnah 7:6. He holds that for *eruvin* of domains no transfer of rights is necessary (Babli 80a). Probably in his eyes such a transfer would be impossible. For participation in an alley the persons to whom the rights are transferred form a well defined group: all dwellers in the alley. But for *eruvin* of domains the Mishnah requires a conscious act of joining the *eruv*; it cannot be known beforehand who is going to join and who won't.

32 He holds that a transfer of rights "to whom it may concern" is required. This is not mentioned in the Mishnah since it is a logical consequence of Mishnah 7:6.

33 In the Yerushalmi since is indicated only here; in the Babli 80a it is stated that Rav and Samuel disagree about the matter.

34 The scribe wrote ומר "and said" which was corrected (probably wrongly) by the corrector into אמר "he said".

35 In the scribe's version of the text, R. Yose bar Rebbi Abun disagrees with R. Johanan and holds that Rav may require transfer of rights as a practical matter, to equalize the rules for all kinds of *eruvin* and not as a logical necessity.

(24a line 9) פיס'. רִבִּי מֵאִיר אוֹמֵר. בְּחוֹלָא דְּלֵית לֵיהּ מַה לוֹכַל הוּא אוֹכֵל פִּיתָּא צִבְחָר. בְּשַׁבָּתָא דְּאִית לֵיהּ מַה לוֹכַל הוּא אוֹכֵל פִּיתָּא סַגִּין. רִבִּי יוּדָן אוֹמֵר. בְּחוֹלָא דְּלֵית לֵיהּ מַה לוֹכַל אוֹכֵל פִּיתָּא סַגִּין. בְּשׁוּבְתָא דְּאִית לֵיהּ מַה לוֹכַל הוּא אוֹכֵל פִּיתָּא צִבְחָר. וְתַנֵּי כֵן. קְרוֹבִים דְּבָרֵיהֶן לִהְיוֹת שָׁוִין. אִיתָא חֲמֵי. אָהֵן עֲבַד עִיגוּלָא תְּרֵי עֲשָׂר בֵּעִין. וְאָהֵן עֲבַד עִיגוּלָא תְּמָנֵי. וְתֵימַר הָכֵין. רַב הוּנָא אָמַר. צֵא מֵהֶן שְׁלִישׁ לִיצִיאָה. רִבִּי יוֹסֵי בֵּירִבִּי בּוּן נְפַק לֵיהּ לְאִילֵּין נַחְתּוֹמַיָּא כְּהָדָא דְּרַב הוּנָא וּלְחוּד כָּהֵן שִׁיעוּרָא.

Paragraph[36]. Rebbi Meïr says, on a weekday, when he has nothing to eat, he eats little bread. On the Sabbath, when he has something to eat, he eats a lot of bread[37]. Rebbi Jehudah says, on a weekday, when he has nothing to eat, he eats a lot of bread. On the Sabbath, when he has something to eat, he eats little bread[38].

It was stated: Their words[39] are close one to another. Come and see: One makes a loaf [the volume of] twelve eggs[40], the other makes a loaf of eight, and you are saying so? Rav Huna said, deduct a third for expenses[41]. [42]Rebbi Yose ben Rebbi Abun gave to the bakers according to the statement of Rav Huna, but only for these measures[43].

36 Discussion of Mishnah 2.
37 R. Meïr states the rules for very poor people who have only a little bread for weekday meals and save all their money for a Sabbath meal.
38 R. Jehudah states his rule similarly for people who have no additions to the bread on weekdays and therefore eat only bread, but on the Sabbath they have meat and vegetables and therefore eat little bread.
39 Rebbi Johanan ben Beroqa and R. Simeon. Babli 82b.
40 The Yerushalmi defines the volume of a *qab* as that of 24 eggs; this makes the volume of a standard egg about 89cm³. The text of the Mishnah implies that a loaf of R. Johanan ben Beroqa is half a *qab* and that of R. Simeon one third of a *qab*. These measures are far apart.
   Since a *qab* is 16 *quartarii*, this makes the *quartarius*, the standard volume (*revi`it*) of a ritual cup, equal to the volume of 1½

eggs. This is not found in the Babli but is accepted by the Medieval authorities (Alfasi *Pesahim* §763). In the Babli (83a) a *modius* is estimated as volume of 217 eggs. Based on the data collected by F. Hultsch, *Griechische und römische Metrologie*², Berlin 1882, the *modius* in question is either the Egyptian provincial of 11.8 l or the Syrian large *modius* of 17.5 l. The Yerushalmi *quartarius* is the Roman measure (Mishnah *Kelim* 17:11) of 133.2 cm³, whereas 1½ Babli eggs, which according to Rav Nissim (*ad* 82b) define the Gaonic *quartarius*, are either 82 or 121 cm³.
41 As explained in Note 5, this makes the difference between the loaf sizes only ⅑ *qab*.
42 *Peah* 8:6, Notes 77-78.
43 For larger quantities, the price to be paid to miller and baker may be less and can be freely negotiated without being unfair to the baker.

(24a line 16) פיס'. וְלֹא שֶׁל תַּחְתּוֹנִים הִיא. אָמַר רִבִּי יוּדָן. זֹאת אוֹמֶרֶת. חוּרְבַת רְאוּבֵן בְּתוֹךְ חָצֵר שִׁמְעוֹן וְשִׁמְעוֹן מִשְׁתַּמֵּשׁ בָּהּ. כְּמִי שֶׁהִיא שֶׁלּוֹ.

פְּשִׁיטָא הָדָא מִילְתֵיהּ. לָזֶה בְּפֶתַח וְלָזֶה בְּפֶתַח שְׁנֵיהֶן אֲסוּרִין מִן הַבַּיִת שֶׁבּוֹ שְׁתֵּי חֲצֵירוֹת. לָזֶה בִזְרִיקָה וְלָזֶה בְשִׁלְשׁוּל. שְׁמוּאֵל אָמַר. שִׁלְשׁוּל מוּתָּר שֶׁהוּא כְדַרְכּוֹ. וּזְרִיקָה אֲסוּרָה שֶׁאֵינָהּ כְּדַרְכָּהּ. רַב אָמַר. לֹא עָשָׂה כְלוּם. מַתְנִיתִין פְּלִיגָא עַל רַב. כָּל־שֶׁגָּבוֹהַּ עֲשָׂרָה טְפָחִים לַמַּרְפֶּסֶת. פָּחוּת מִכָּן לֶחָצֵר. לֹא לָזֶה בִזְרִיקָה וְלֹא לָזֶה בְשִׁלְשׁוּל הִיא מַתְנִיתָא. בְּתוֹךְ שְׁלֹשָׁה טְפָחִים לָעֶלְיוֹנָה שֶׁהִיא לְמַעֲלָה מֵעֲשָׂרָה טְפָחִים לַתַּחְתּוֹנָה. מַה פְּלִיגִין רַב וּשְׁמוּאֵל. בְּשָׁוֶוה.

Paragraph[44]. Is it not of the lower ones[45]? Rebbi Yudan said, this implies that if Ruben's ruin stands in Simeon's domain and the latter uses it, it is as if it were his[46].

The following is obvious. If both of them are by a door[47], both of them are forbidden the house (in which are) [between][48] two courtyards. For one of them by throwing and for one by lowering[49]. Samuel says, lowering is permitted since it is ordinary but throwing is forbidden since it is not ordinary. Rav said, it did not do anything[50]. Our Mishnah disagrees with Rav: "anything higher than ten hand-breadths belongs to the balcony, less than this to the courtyard." The Mishnah refers to the case that neither one uses by throwing nor by lowering; within three hand-breadths of the upper one which is more than ten hand-breadths from the lower one[51]. Where do Rav and Samuel disagree? If it is equal[52].

44 Discussion of Mishnah 4.
45 Why should the top of a rock standing in the courtyard belong to the balcony's domain while being in the courtyard which is the ground floor's domain?
46 For the laws of the Sabbath, not property rights are essential but right of undisturbed use and easy accessibility. It is presumed that Ruben does not live in the courtyard and does not use the space on the Sabbath.
47 The entire paragraph has a parallel in the Babli, 83b. Between two courtyards where the inhabitants did not make a common *eruv* there is space easily accessible by doors from each side.
48 The text reads בּוֹ "in it"; one should read בֵּין "in between".
49 There are no doors, only solid walls. One side has access only by throwing things over the wall; the other side has easy access to the top of its wall and may lower things into the intermediate space without exertion.
50 Both sides are equally forbidden.
51 In the case of the Mishnah there is ease of use for the dwellers on the balcony but difficulty for the occupants of the courtyard. But if the top of the hill is more than 3 hand-breadths from the balcony the entire hill belongs to the courtyard even if access is easier from the top than from the bottom.
52 In the dispute between Samuel and Rav there is only difficult access; Rav follows the reasoning given in Note 46, Samuel considers difficult access as easy if it is of the kind frequently used on weekdays.

(24a line 25). הָיָה שָׁם חוּרְבָה. רִבִּי יוֹחָנָן אָמַר. נוֹתֵן חוּרְבָה לְבַעֲלֶיהָ. עַד כְּדוֹן בְּמִשְׁתַּמֵּשׁ בְּחוּרְבָה דֶּרֶךְ פִּתְחוֹ. הָיָה מִשְׁתַּמֵּשׁ בְּחוּרְבָה דֶּרֶךְ חַלּוֹן. רִבִּי אָחָא בְשֵׁם רִבִּי יוֹחָנָן. אֲפִילוּ כֵן נוֹתֵן חוּרְבָה לְבַעֲלֶיהָ.

רִבִּי אֶלְעָזָר בֵּירִבִּי שִׁמְעוֹן בְּשֵׁם רַב הוֹשַׁעְיָה. הָיוּ שָׁלֹשׁ. זֶה מִשְׁתַּמֵּשׁ בְּחוּרְבָה דֶּרֶךְ פִּתְחוֹ וְזֶה מִשְׁתַּמֵּשׁ בְּחוּרְבָה דֶּרֶךְ פִּתְחוֹ. וְהָאֶמְצָעִית אֲסוּרָה. אֵימָתַי. שֶׁהָאֶמְצָעִית שֶׁלִּשְׁנֵיהֶן. אֲבָל אִם הָיְתָה אֶמְצָעִית לְאֶחָד מִן הַשּׁוּק. זֶה מִשְׁתַּמֵּשׁ בְּאַחַת וְזֶה מִשְׁתַּמֵּשׁ בְּאַחַת וּבַשְּׁנִיּוֹת.

If there was a ruin there, Rebbi Johanan says, one gives the ruin to its owner[53]. That is in case he uses the ruin through his door. If he uses the ruin through a window? Rebbi Aha in the name of Rebbi Johanan, even in this case one gives the ruin to its owner[53].

Rebbi Eleazar (ben Rebbi Simeon)[54] in the name of Rebbi Hoshaia: If there were three; each one uses a ruin through his door and the middle [space] is forbidden[55]. When is this? If the middle [space] belonged to both of them. But if the middle [space] belonged to a person from the market, one uses one [property] and the other one uses one [property] and a second one[56].

52 If the ruin stands between two courtyards which do not have a common *eruv*.
53 Even if the owner's access is more difficult than that of the other side.
54 The text in parenthesis has to be deleted with the quote by Rashba (*Eruvin ad 84b*, col. 528). The tradent is R. Eleazar ben Pedat, one generation younger than Rav Hoshaia and three than R. Eleazar ben R. Simeon.

Babli 85a in the name of Rav.
55 Parallel to the situation described in Note 52 there are two ruins, one adjacent to each courtyard, and an empty space in between. Since each courtyard made an *eruv* by itself, the ruins belong to the corresponding courtyards.
56 If the middle space belongs to an absent landowner who does not use it, the space is allocated to the person who actually uses it during the week; cf. Note 46.

(24a line 32) אָמַר רִבִּי יוֹחָנָן. הָעוֹמֵד וְהֶחָלָל מִצְטָרְפִין לְאַרְבָּעָה. וְהוּא שֶׁיְּהֵא הָעוֹמֵד רָבָה עַל הֶחָלָל. רִבִּי זְעִירָא בָּעֵי. עַד שֶׁיְּהֵא עוֹמֵד שֶׁכָּאן וְעוֹמֵד שֶׁכָּאן רָבָה. אָמַר רִבִּי יוֹסֵה. פְּשִׁיטָא לְרִבִּי זְעִירָא שֶׁאֵין הָעוֹמֵד מִצַּד אֶחָד מִצְטָרֵף. פְּשִׁיטָא לֵיהּ שֶׁיְּהֵא הָעוֹמֵד מִצַּד אֶחָד רָבָה. לֹא צְרִיכָה דְּלֹא אֲפִילוּ עוֹמֵד הַשֵּׁינִי.

[57]Rebbi Johanan said, what is standing and the hollow combine together to four, but only if what is standing is more than the hollow[61]. Rebbi Ze`ira asked, only if what is standing on each side is more? Rebbi Yose said,

it is obvious for Rebbi Ze'ira that what is standing on one side only does not combine; it is obvious for him that one side must be more. He only questions even the second standing part.

57   This paragraph is from *Šabbat* 11, Notes 59-63.

(24a line 36) רִבִּי יִרְמְיָה בְּשֵׁם רִבִּי שְׁמוּאֵל בַּר רַב יִצְחָק. מִשְּׁלֹשָׁה וְעַד אַרְבָּעָה הִיא מַתְנִיתָה. פָּחוֹת מִשְּׁלֹשָׁה אֲפִילוּ יוֹתֵר מֵעֶשֶׂר מוּתָּר. אַרְבָּעָה אֲפִילוּ פָּחוֹת מֵעֶשֶׂר אָסוּר. אֶלָּא אֲנָן קַיָּימִין מִשְּׁלֹשָׁה עַד אַרְבָּעָה.

כְּשֶׁאֵין שָׁם תִּקְרָה. אֲבָל יֵשׁ שָׁם תִּקְרָה אֲפִילוּ גָבוֹהַּ כַּמָּה שֶׁלְתַחְתּוֹנִים הִיא. אָמַר רִבִּי. בְּשֶׁאֵין שָׁם נָקֶב. אֲבָל אִם יֵשׁ שָׁם נָקֶב מְשְׁתַּמֵּשׁ דֶּרֶךְ הַנָּקֶב.

[58]Rebbi Jeremiah in the name of Rebbi Samuel bar Rav Isaac: the Mishnah is from three to four [hand-breadths]. Less than three even more than ten [cubits] is permitted, four even less than ten [cubits] is prohibited. Where do we hold? From three to four[59].

If there is no cover; but if there is a cover it belongs to those on the ground floor. Rebbi [ ][60] said, is there is no hole there. But if there is a hole one uses it through the hole[61].

58   The same text is in Chapter 1, Note 224.
59   If the hill is within three hand-breadths of the balcony, it belongs to the balcony even if it is by ten hand-breadths higher than the balcony. If it is farther than 4 hand-breadths, it belongs to the courtyard irrespective of height since it can not be accessed directly from the balcony. The conditions of the Mishnah only apply if the distance from the balcony is between 3 and 4 hand-breadths.
60   The name of an Amora is missing.
61   There is no hill but a cistern built above ground. If the cistern is covered it belongs to the courtyard since the dwellers on the balcony have to descend to the ground to remove the cover. But if there is a hole through which a pail can be lowered to draw water it belongs to the balcony if the other conditions are satisfied.

(24a line 41) פיס'. רִבִּי יְהוּדָה בְּשֵׁם רַב. הָדָא דְאַתְּ מַר בְּבֵית שַׁעַר שֶׁלְיָחִיד. אֲבָל בְּבֵית שַׁעַר שֶׁלְרַבִּים הֲרֵי זֶה עֵירוּב וְהַדָּר שָׁם אוֹסֵר עָלָיו.

דְּבֵי רִבִּי יַנַּאי אָמְרִי. אֲפִילוּ יָתֵד לִתְלוֹת בּוֹ מִנְעָלוֹ. רִבִּי בָּא בַּר חִינָּנָא אָמַר. אֲפִילוּ נְשָׁתוֹת אֲפִילוּ טַבְּלָה. רַב אָמַר. וּבִלְבַד דָּבָר הַנִּיטָּל בַּשַּׁבָּת. אָמַר רִבִּי בָּא. מַעֲשֶׂה בְּאֶחָד שֶׁהָיָה לוֹ לוּל שֶׁלְתַרְנְגוֹלִין לִפְנִים מִבֵּיתוֹ שֶׁלְחַבֵירוֹ. נִכְנָס שֶׁלֹּא בִרְשׁוּתוֹ. אֲתָא עוֹבְדָא קוֹמֵי רַב. אָמַר. כֵּיוָן

שְׁזְקוּק לִיתֵּן לִפְנֵיהֶן מַיִם כְּמִי שֶׁהוּא דָבָר הַנִּיטָּל בַּשַּׁבָּת. רִבִּי יַעֲקֹב בְּשֵׁם שְׁמוּאֵל. תַּלְמִידוֹי דְרִבִּי יוֹחָנָן סַלְקוּן לְעַכְבָּרֵי וְסָמְכוּן עַל הָדָא דְרִבִּי יַנַּאי. חִזְקִיָה לֹא אָמַר כֵּן אֶלָּא רִבִּי חִיָּיה רִבִּי אַסִי וְרִבִּי אַמִי סַלְקוּן לְעַכְבָּרֵי וְשָׁמְעוּן מִן דְּבֵית רִבִּי יַנַּאי. הֲלָכָה כְּרִבִּי יוּדָה.

New paragraph[62]. Rebbi[63] Jehudah in the name of Rav: This you only say referring to a porter's lodge of a single family dwelling. But for the porter's lodge of the many it is an *eruv* and he who dwells there forbids for you[64].

The House of Rebbi Yannai are saying, even a peg to hang his shoes on[65]. Rebbi Abba bar Ḥinena said, even a metal plate[66], even a table. Rav said, but only what may be moved on the Sabbath. Rebbi Abba said, it happened that a person had a chicken coop inside another person's house, where he could enter without asking for permission. The case came before Rav who said, since he is obligated to give them water it is as if it could be moved on the Sabbath. Rebbi Jacob in the name of Samuel: The students of Rebbi Joḥanan ascended to Akhbara and relied on the statement of Rebbi Yannai. Ḥizqiah does not say so but: Rebbi Ḥiyya, Rebbi Assi, and Rebbi Ammi[67] ascended to Akhbara and heard from the House of Rebbi Yannai that practice follows Rebbi Jehudah.

62 Discussion of Mishnah 4.
63 Read: "Rav".
64 The moment that the porter's lodge has to be occupied at all times it is to be assumed that the porter lives there; this turns the porter's lodge into an apartment which has to participate in the *eruv*.
65 This paragraph discusses the statement of Rebbi Jehudah that the dweller in a rented apartment can be disregarded in matters of *eruv* if the landlord has the right to enter at all times. It is enough that a peg be reserved for the landlord's shoes.
66 With R. Hananel *ad* 85b read עֲשָׁשִׁית.
67 Babylonian spelling for the Babylonians R. Ḥiyya bar Abba, R. Yasa, and R. Immi, students of R. Joḥanan.

(24a line 51) פיס'. הָדָא הִיא דְרִבִּי מֵאִיר. דְּרִבִּי מֵאִיר אוֹמֵר. הַבַּיִת הַנָּעוּל אוֹסֵר. יָכוֹל לָבוֹא עַל יְדֵי עֵירוּב וְעָבַר וּבָא. מַר עוּקְבָּן בְּשֵׁם רַב. הֲלָכָה כְּרִבִּי (שִׁמְעוֹן) [מֵאִיר].

Paragraph[68]. This is Rebbi Meïr's, since Rebbi Meïr says, a locked house forbids[69]. Could he not come by an *eruv*, or transgress and come[70]? Mar Uqban in the name of Rav: Practice follows Rebbi (Simeon) [Meïr][71].

68 Discussion of Mishnaiot 5-6.
69 Any house in the courtyard must contribute (or at least receive its share by a transfer of ownership) even if it is

temporarily unoccupied.

70 This contradicts R. Yose's statement, that a Jew will not come to his house if he started the Sabbath at another place.

71 The scribe wrote "Simeon" (as stated in the Babli, 86a); the corrector changed it to "Meïr". The correction makes sense; if practice followed R. Simeon it would not have to be mentioned since it already was stated that practice about *eruvin* in general follows the most lenient opinion (Chapter 7, Note 110). S. Liebermann conjectures that the first sentence of the next paragraph still belongs to this Mishnah: "Mar Uqban in the name of Rav: Practice follows Rebbi Simeon; the words of the rabbis disagree" (i. e., practice follows R. Meïr.)

(24a line 53) פיס׳. מִילֵּיהוֹן דְּרַבָּנִין פְּלִיגִין. דָּמַר רִבִּי יַעֲקֹב בְּשֵׁם רִבִּי יְהוֹשֻׁעַ בֶּן לֵוִי. וְהוּא שֶׁתְּהֵא מְחִיצָה מְשׁוּקַּעַת בַּמַּיִם לְשַׁלְשֵׁל דְּלִי. וְלֹא נִמְצְאוּ שְׁתֵּי רְשׁוּיוֹת מִשְׁתַּמְּשׁוֹת בִּרְשׁוּת אֶחָד. שִׁיעֲרוּ לוֹמַר. אֵין הַדְּלִי הוֹלֵךְ יוֹתֵר מֵאַרְבָּעָה טְפָחִים. רִבִּי טְבַלאי בְּשֵׁם רַב. אֵין חוּרְבָה לַמָּיִם. הָיָה שָׁם תִּקְרָה. רוֹאֶה אַתָּה כִּילוּ יוֹרֶדֶת וְסוֹתָמֶת. הָיָה שָׁם אֲמֶלְתָרָה. אַתְּ רוֹאֶה אוֹתָהּ כִּילוּ יוֹרֶדֶת וְסוֹתָמֶת.

מִיחְלַף שִׁיטַת רִבִּי יְהוּדָה. תַּמָּן אָמַר. רִבִּי יוּדָן פּוֹטֵר בַּמָּיִם. שֶׁאֵין בָּהֶן מַמָּשׁ׃ וָכָא אָמַר הָכִין.

אָמַר רִבִּי הוּנָא. וְהוּא שֶׁתְּהֵא מְחִיצָה בּוֹלֶטֶת לְתוֹךְ חֲלַל שֶׁלַּבּוֹר.

Paragraph[72]. The words of the rabbis disagree[71], as Rebbi Jacob[73] said in the name of Rebbi Joshua ben Levi: Only if the partition is lowered into the water to lower a pail[74]. Do not two different domains use the same domain? They supposed to say that no pail moves more than four hand-breadths[75]. Rebbi Tevelai in the name of Rav: The rules of a ruin do not apply to water[76]. If there was a ceiling, one considers it as if it went down and locked[77]. If there was a cross-beam[78], one considers it as if it went down and locked.

The argument of Rebbi Jehudah is inverted. There[79] he said, "Rebbi Jehudah does not apply this to water since it has no consistency."

Rebbi Huna said, but the partition must extend into the hollow of the cistern[80].

72 Discussion of Mishnah 7.

73 Rashba (*ad* 86b, col. 533) reads: R. Jacob bar Idi. Instead of "to lower a pail" he reads: "the full size of a pail."

74 Since water is always moving, it is impossible to know which molecules will be where at a given time. The answer is that this is irrelevant; at the time the pail is lowered it will draw water only from the side of the cistern allocated to its part. Babli 86b.

76 The restrictions imposed in the earlier

Mishnaiot in this Chapter do not apply to water. Babli 86b.

77 If part of the roof of the houses of one courtyard extends above the cistern it defines the domain allotted to this courtyard.

78 Greek, cf. Chapter 1, Note 41.

79 Mishnah *Besah* 5:4. If a woman borrows baking ingredients on a holiday from another with a different *eruv tehumin*, the resulting cake may be moved only in the domain common to both women. R. Jehudah instructs to disregard this rule concerning water. Why here does he require the existence of a wall? No answer is given. In the quote by R. Hananel (*ad* 87a), this paragraph is missing and the statement of R. Huna refers directly to that of R. Tevelai.

80 Even the House of Hillel require that a hanging partition has to extend into the hollow of the cistern.

(24a line 61) פיס׳. מַתְנִיתִין בָּעֲמוּקָה עֲשָׂרָה וְרָחָב אַרְבָּעָה וּבְפָרוּצָה מִיכָּן וּמִיכָּן. נְפְרָצָה מֵרוּחַ אַחַת נוֹתֵן לֶחִי וְקוֹרָה מִיכָּן. נְפְרָצָה מִיכָּן וּמִיכָּן נוֹתֵן לֶחִי וְקוֹרָה מִיכָּן וְעוֹשֶׂה צוּרַת פֶּתַח מִיכָּן. לֹא נִמְצָאוּ שְׁתֵּי רְשֻׁיּוֹת מִשְׁתַּמְּשׁוֹת בִּרְשׁוּת אַחַת. רִבִּי יוֹסֵי בֵּירִבִּי בּוּן בְּשֵׁם רַבִּי שְׁמוּאֵל בַּר רַב יִצְחָק. תִּיפְתָּר שֶׁהָיוּ בָתִּים מִצַּד אֶחָד.

פְּשִׁיטָא הָדָא מִילְּתָא. עֲמוּקָה עֲשָׂרָה וְאֵינָהּ רְחָבָה אַרְבָּעָה מוּתָּר לְטַלְטֵל וּמוּתָּר לְמַלּאוֹת. רְחָבָה אַרְבָּעָה וְאֵינָהּ עֲמוּקָה עֲשָׂרָה פְּשִׁיטָא שֶׁמּוּתָּר לְטַלְטֵל. מַהוּ לְמַלּאוֹת. רִבִּי חִינְנָא אָמַר. מוּתָּר. רִבִּי מָנָא אָמַר. אָסוּר. מַתְנִיתִין פְּלִיגָא עַל רִבִּי מָנָא. אָמְרוּ לוֹ. מִפְּנֵי שֶׁלֹּא הָיָה בָהּ כַּשִּׁיעוּר: לֹא הָיְתָה לֹא עֲמוּקָה עֲשָׂרָה וְלֹא רְחָבָה אַרְבָּעָה. אֲבָל אִם הָיְתָה עֲמוּקָה עֲשָׂרָה וְאֵינָהּ רְחָבָה אַרְבָּעָה אָסוּר. וַאֲפִילוּ רְחָבָה אַרְבָּעָה וְאֵינָהּ עֲמוּקָה עֲשָׂרָה מוּתָּר. מַה דַּהֲוָה עוֹבְדָא הֲוָה עוֹבְדָא.

Paragraph[81]. The Mishnah if it is deep ten [hand-breadths] and wide four [hand-breadths][20] and open on both sides. If it is open on one side one puts a beam or a lathe on that side[82]. If it is open on both sides one puts a beam or a lathe on one side and makes the shape of a door at the other. Do not two different domains use the same domain[83]? Explain it if there were houses on one side[84].

The following is obvious: If it is ten deep but not four wide one may move and fill[85]. If it was four wide[86] but not ten deep it is obvious that one may move. May one fill? Rebbi Ḥinena said, it is permitted. Rebbi Mana said, it is forbidden. Our Mishnah disagrees with Rebbi Mana: "They told him, because it did not have the measure." It was neither ten deep nor four wide[87]. But if it had been ten deep but not four wide[88] it would have been forbidden. Even if it is four wide but not ten deep it is permitted. The case happened as it happened[89].

81 Discussion of Mishnah 8.

82 As S. Liebermann points out, this cannot describe the situation of the Mishnah that a water canal runs through a private domain since beam and lathe are appropriate only for alleys. Therefore one has to assume that the canal at Abel was running in the alleys and the problem is to let the dwellers in an alley draw water on the Sabbath.

83 If the canal is wide and deep enough to constitute a *karmelit* domain in itself it would be impossible to make a common *eruv* for both sides of the street. This in itself should prevent anybody from drawing water on the Sabbath.

84 The objection is well taken. One has to assume that there were houses only on one side; the other side was bounded either by a solid wall or by uninhabited areas.

85 From a canal running through an alley. Any ditch which is not 4 hand-breadths wide at the surface does not interfere with *eruv* (Mishnah 7:3).

86 This is implied by Mishnah 7:3.

87 Babli 87a.

88 It is obvious that one has to read: if it would *not* have been ten deep but four wide.

89 No logical derivations are possible for rules derived from actual happenings since there the conditions are not subject to adjustment.

(24a line 73) פיס'. רִבִּי זְעִירָא רַב יְהוּדָה בְשֵׁם רַב. וְהוּא שֶׁתְּהֵא מְחִיצָה מְשׁוּקַּעַת בַּמַּיִם כִּמְלוֹא הַדְּלִי. וְלֹא נִמְצְאוּ שְׁתֵּי רְשׁוּיוֹת מִשְׁתַּמְּשׁוֹת בִּרְשׁוּת אַחַת. אָמַר רַב הוּנָא. וְהוּא שֶׁתְּהֵא מְחִיצָה בְּתוֹךְ שְׁלֹשָׁה טְפָחִים לַכְּצוֹצְרָה.

תַּנֵּי. רִבִּי חֲנַנְיָה בֶּן עֲקַבְיָה אוֹמֵר. כְּצוֹצְרָה שֶׁהִיא לְמַעְלָה מִן הַיָּם פּוֹתֵחַ אֶת הַמַּעֲזִיבָה וּמְשַׁלְשֵׁל וּמְמַלֵּא. רִבִּי יַעֲקֹב בַּר אֲחָא בְשֵׁם רִבִּי יָסָא. וְהוּא שֶׁיֵּשׁ בַּנֶּקֶב אַרְבָּעָה טְפָחִים. וְהוּא שֶׁיֵּשׁ בּוֹ רוֹחַב אַרְבָּעָה. וְהוּא שֶׁיִּהְיוּ מְחִיצוֹת גְּבוֹהוֹת עֲשָׂרָה. תַּמָּן אָמְרֵי. אֲפִילוּ אֵין מְחִיצוֹת גְּבוֹהוֹת עֲשָׂרָה נַעֲשִׂית כְּמִשְׁמֶּרֶת חַד. רִבִּי אִידִי אָמַר קוֹמֵי רִבִּי חִייָה. מוּתָּר לְמַלּוֹת וְאָסוּר לִשְׁפּוֹךְ. אָמַר לֵיהּ. כַּד נִמְנֶה חֲכָמִים נִמְנֶה לָךְ עִמְּהוֹן. אָמַר רִבִּי מָנָא. מִגְּהַר הֲוָה עִימֵּיהּ. אָמַר רִבִּי יוֹסֵי בֵּירָבִּי בּוּן. מִי לֹא אָמַר לֵיהּ. מוּתָּר לְמַלּוֹת. שֶׁמְּמַלֵּא מִמְּחִיצָתוֹ. וְאָסוּר לִשְׁפּוֹךְ. שֶׁשּׁוֹפֵךְ חוּץ לִמְחִיצָתוֹ.

Paragraph[90]. Rebbi Ze`ira, Rav Jehudah in the name of Rav: Only if the partition is lowered into the water to lower a pail[74]. Do not two different domains use the same domain[91]? Rav Huna said, only if the partition be within three hand-breadths of the balcony[92].

It was stated: [93]Rebbi Hanania ben Aqabia says, if a balcony protrudes over the sea, one opens the floor covering, lowers down, and fills. Rebbi Jacob bar Aha in the name of Rebbi Yasa: Only if the hole is four hand-breadths long, and only if it is four hand-breadths wide, and if the walls are ten hand-breadths high[94]. There[95] they are saying, even if the partitions are not ten hand-breadths high it is made like a funnel[96]. Rebbi Idi said before Rebbi Ḥiyya: One is permitted to fill but forbidden to pour out[97]. He said to him, when we will ordain Sages, we shall ordain you with them[98]. Rebbi Mana said, he shouted[99] at him. Rebbi Yose ben Rebbi Bun said, did he not say to him that one is permitted to fill, since he fills inside his partition, but forbidden to pour out, for he pours outside of his partition[100]?

90 Discussion of Mishnah 9.

91 This refers to the second case of the Mishnah, that two balconies are built over the sea, one on top of the other (S. Liebermann). Since the Mishnah states that they did not make a common *eruv*, how can the upper floor draw water through the domain of the lower balcony?

92 The upper balcony can draw water only if it is wider than the lower one and the pail is lowered outside the lower balcony, more than 3 hand-breadths removed from it. Then the water is drawn in a domain unique to the upper balcony.

93 A different version is in Babli, 97b. One should not explain the Yerushalmi on the basis of the different Babli version.

94 If the enclosure of the balcony is 10 hand-breadths high it may serve as the required partition for the House of Hillel; then a hole up to 4-by-4 hand-breadths large can be made in the floor of the balcony to draw water.

95 In Babylonia.

96 The walls of the balcony together with the floor form an oversized funnel which is made to connect with the water below. This is enough of a distinction not to require walls ten cubits high. (The Babli 16a/b which requires the balcony to be a hammock is difficult to understand.)

97 With a different interpretation, as Babylonian rule, in Babli 88a.

98 This must be meant ironically since R. Idi already was ordained. The question is, is it ironic since the statement is obvious or is it a criticism because the statement is false?

99 Arabic مجهر "shouting". In a parallel expression *Yebamot* 8:6 (Note 230), R. Mana uses מְנַחֵךְ "made fun of". This may be the intended word here also.

100 It certainly is rabbinically forbidden to pour water from a private domain directly into a *karmelit*, such as the sea. As noted in the sequel, the sea intended is a lake.

(24b line 8) אָמַר רִבִּי חִייָה בַּר בָּא. לֹא אָמַר רִבִּי חֲנַנְיָה בֶּן עֲקַבְיָה אֶלָּא בְיָם שֶׁל טְבֶרְיָה. שֶׁהֶהָרִים מַקִּיפִין אוֹתָהּ. רִבִּי לָעָזָר שָׁאַל לְרִבִּי יוֹחָנָן. הָהֵן פְּיוֹסְרוֹס זָרַק מִתּוֹכָהּ לִרְשׁוּת הָרַבִּים אוֹ מֵרְשׁוּת הָרַבִּים לְתוֹכָהּ. אָמַר לֵיהּ. עַל דַּעְתָּךְ אֵין רְשׁוּת הָרַבִּים לְעוֹלָם. רֵישׁ לָקִישׁ אָמַר. לְעוֹלָם אֵין רְשׁוּת הָרַבִּים עַד שֶׁתְּהֵא מְפוּלֶּשֶׁת מִסּוֹף הָעוֹלָם וְעַד סוֹפוֹ. מוּחְלְפָה שִׁיטַת רֵישׁ לָקִישׁ. דְּאָמַר. אֵין רְשׁוּת הָרַבִּים בָּעוֹלָם הַזֶּה אֶלָּא לֶעָתִיד לָבֹא. שֶׁנֶּאֱמַר כָּל־גֶּיא יִנָּשֵׂא.

מַתְנִיתָא פְּלִינָא עַל רֵישׁ לָקִישׁ. אֵיזוֹ הִיא רְשׁוּת הַיָּחִיד. שְׁבִילֵי בֵית גִּלְגֵּל. וְכֵן כַּיּוֹצֵא בָהֶן. רְשׁוּת הַיָּחִיד לַשַּׁבָּת וּרְשׁוּת הָרַבִּים לַטּוּמְאָה.

אָמַר רִבִּי יוֹחָנָן. לֹא אָמַר רִבִּי יוֹסֵי אֶלָּא לְעִנְיַין סוּכָּה. אֲבָל לְעִנְיַין שַׁבָּת אַף רִבִּי יוֹסֵי מוֹדֶה. מִילְתֵיהּ דְּרִבִּי חֲנִינָא אָמְרָה אַף לְעִנְיַין שַׁבָּת. דָּמַר רִבִּי חֲנִינָה. שִׁלְטוֹן בָּא לְצִיפּוֹרִי וְתָלוּ לוֹ קָטִיּוֹת. וְהִתִּיר רִבִּי יִשְׁמָעֵאל בֵּירִבִּי יוֹסֵי לְטַלְטֵל תַּחְתֵּיהֶן. כְּשִׁיטַת אָבִיו. רִבִּי יוֹסֵי בֵּירִבִּי בּוּן בְּשֵׁם רִבִּי שְׁמוּאֵל בַּר רַב יִצְחָק. אַתְיָיא דְּרִבִּי יוֹסֵי בֵּירִבִּי חֲנִינָא כְּרִבִּי חֲנַנְיָה. וּתְרוַויְיהוֹן פְּלִיגֵי עַל שִׁיטַת רִבִּי יוֹחָנָן. דָּמַר רִבִּי יוֹחָנָן. רִבִּי יוּדָן וְרִבִּי יוֹסֵי וַחֲנַנְיָה בֶּן עֲקַבְיָה שְׁלָשְׁתָּן אָמְרוּ דָבָר אֶחָד. רִבִּי יְהוּדָה דְגְשָׁרִים מְפוּלָשִׁים. רִבִּי יוֹסֵי הָא דְסוּכָּה. רִבִּי חֲנַנְיָה בֶּן עֲקַבְיָה דְּתַנֵּי. רִבִּי חֲנַנְיָה הִתִּיר שְׁלֹשָׁה דְבָרִים. הִתִּיר כְּצוֹצְרָא. וְעִינָה שֶׁבַּיָּם. וַהֲבָאַת אֲלִינְטִית.

Rebbi Ḥiyya bar Abba said, Rebbi Ḥanania ben Aqabia said it only for Lake Genezareth since mountains surround it[101]. Rebbi Eleazar asked Rebbi Joḥanan, if one threw from a circular road[102] into public domain or from public domain into it[103]? He said to him, in your opinion a public domain does not exist. Rebbi Simeon ben Laqish said, there is no public domain unless it be open from one end of the world to the other. The argument of Rebbi Simeon ben Laqish seems inverted[104] since he said, there is no public domain in this world, only in the future as it is written[105], *every valley will be lifted*. A Mishnah[106] disagrees with Rebbi Simeon ben Laqish: "What is a private domain? The paths of Bet-Gilgul[107]. Private domain regarding the Sabbat[108] but public domain for impurity[109]."

[110]Rebbi Joḥanan said, Rebbi Yose said it only for Tabernacles[111], but in the matter of the Sabbath even Rebbi Yose agrees. The word of Rebbi Ḥanina implies that it is even for the Sabbath, as Rebbi Ḥanina said, a ruler came to Sepphoris and they suspended quilts[112]; Rebbi Ismael ben Rebbi Yose permitted carrying under them following his father's argument. Rebbi Yose ben Rebbi Abun in the name of Rebbi Samuel ben Rav Isaac: Rebbi Yose ben Rebbi Ḥanina comes like Rebbi Ḥanania and both disagree with Rebbi Joḥanan's argument, as Rebbi Joḥanan[113] said, Rebbi Jehudah, and Rebbi Yose, and Ḥanania bar Aqabia all three said the same. Rebbi Jehudah of the open bridges[114], Rebbi Yose that of tabernacles, Rebbi Ḥanania ben Aqabia as it was stated[115]: Rebbi Ḥanania permitted three things, he permitted a balcony, and seaweed[116], and bringing bathtowels[117].

101 A similar statement in the Babli 87b, but there the reason given is that the shore of the lake is everywhere private domain with no public access to the water except harbors which also are private installations for the rules of the Sabbath. The statement here, that a valley surrounded by mountains is never public domain, is not found elsewhere.

102 This word appears in many forms is the Yerushalmi: *Berakhot* 9:2 (Note 81) פווסרוס, פופסדס, *Terumot* 8:10 אפיפסרוס, אפיפסרון (but this may be another word), *Šeqalim* 7:2 פיוסרוס. S. Liebermann identifies the word as πρόσοδος, ἡ, "access road". This assumes that Roman roads in the East where built in the style of the great straight roads in Italy which passed by the walled cities, which had to be accessed by smaller roads branching off from the main road. But these access roads are not less frequented nor more difficult to use than the main road. E. Guggenheimer (*Berakhot loc. cit.*) reads περίοδος, ἡ, "way around, circuit, circular path".

103 The question of R. Eleazar is whether a circuitous road, of difficult use but public property and open for use by the public, nevertheless should be considered private property for the rules of the Sabbath.

104 His first statement seems to imply that somewhere in the world there exists public domain.

105 *Is.* 40:4.

106 *Taharot* 6:6.

107 In the definition of the Babli (22b), any road on which the carrier of a load cannot run; according to Rashi because of an incline, according to Maimonides because of obstacles in the road.

108 Not really private domain but *karmelit*.

109 A public domain for the rules of impurity, where cases of doubt may be disregarded, is any place accessible to the public, even if it is private property.

110 A parallel text is *Sukkah* 1:9. Since the reference to the rules of *Sukkah* is formulated there differently from here, the texts in their second parts are different versions, rather than straight copies.

111 Mishnah *Sukkah* 1:10. The essence of a tabernacle is a temporary thatched roof, but it also needs at least three walls. According to the majority opinion the walls must start no more than 3 hand-breadths from the ground; R. Yose admits walls 10 hand-breadths wide hanging from the top.

112 Sheets sewn together from rectangular pieces of cloth.

113 Obviously one has to read: R. Yose ben Ḥanina.

114 Mishnah 9:5, where R. Jehudah defines the space under a bridge as private domain if the underpinning of the bridge structure extends 10 hand-breadths below the roadway.

115 *Šabbat* 3, Notes 101-103; Babli 87b.

116 Reading עצה with the text in all parallel sources.

117 *Šabbat* 22:5, Note 21.

(25b line 26) רִבִּי אַבָּהוּ בְשֵׁם רִבִּי יוֹסֵי. הָדָא דְאַתְּ אָמַר בְּמִשְׁתַּמְּשׁוֹת דֶּרֶךְ הַנֶּקֶב. אֲבָל מִשְׁתַּמְּשׁוֹת לַחוּץ מוּתָּר. וְתַנֵּי כֵן. שָׁלֹשׁ כְּצוֹצְרִיּוֹת זוֹ עַל גַּבֵּי זוֹ אָסוּר לְהִשְׁתַּמֵּשׁ מִן הָעֶלְיוֹנָה לַתַּחְתּוֹנָה דֶּרֶךְ הָאֶמְצָעִית אֲבָל מִשְׁתַּמֵּשׁ מִן הֶחָצֵר לַגַּג וְאֵינוֹ חוֹשֵׁשׁ. אָמַר רִבִּי שְׁמוּאֵל בַּר רַב

יִצְחָק. הָדָא דְאַתְּ מַר מִבִּפְנִים. אֲבָל מֵחוּץ אָסוּר. רִבִּי זְעִירָא אָמַר. בֵּין מִבַּחוּץ בֵּין מִבִּפְנִים אָסוּר. מַתְנִיתָא פְלִינָא עַל רִבִּי זְעִירָא. מְשַׁלְשְׁלִין קְדֵירַת בָּשָׂר מֵעַל גַּבֵּי זִיז שֶׁגָּבוֹהַּ עֲשָׂרָה וְרָחָב אַרְבָּעָה. אִם הָיְתָה חַלּוֹן בֵּינְתַּיִים שֶׁלְאַרְבָּעָה טְפָחִים אָסוּר. שֶׁאֵין מְשַׁתְּמְשִׁין מֵרְשׁוּת לִרְשׁוּת דֶּרֶךְ רְשׁוּת. מָה עֲבַד לָהּ רִבִּי שְׁמוּאֵל בַּר רַב יִצְחָק. פָּתַר לָהּ (בשבויה) בְּשָׁוֶה.

Text of R. Hananel (ad 88a):

ר' אבא ור' יוסי הדא דאת אמרת במשתמשות דרך הנקב אבל משתמשות מחוץ מותר. ותני כן ג' גזוזטראות זו ע"ג זו אסור להשתמש מן העליונה לתחתונה דרך האמצעית. אבל משתמש מן החצר לגג ואינו חושש הדא דקאמר בפנים אבל מבחוץ אסור. ר' זעירא אמר בין מבחוץ בין מבפנים אסור. מתניתא פליגא על ר' זעירא משלשין קדרות בשר מעל גבי זיז שגבוה י"ט ורחב ד' אם היה חלון בינתים של ד"ט אסור. שאין מרשות לרשות דרך רשות. ר' שמואל בר רב יצחק פתר לה בשבויה.

[118]Rebbi Abbahu in the name of Rebbi Yose[119]: This[120] you are saying if they are using the hole. But if they are using the outside it is permitted[121]. It was stated thus: If three balconies are one above the other[122] it is forbidden to pass from the upper one to the lower one passing by the middle one, but one may pass from the courtyard to the roof without worry[123]. Rebbi Samuel ben Rav Isaac says, this[124] you mean from the inside but from the outside it is forbidden[125]. Rebbi Ze'ira said, both inside and outside are forbidden[126]. A *baraita* disagrees with Rebbi Ze'ira[127]: "One lowers a pot with meat from a ledge which is ten [hand-breadths] high and four wide[128]. If a window of four hand-breadths was in between[129] it is forbidden since one does not pass from one domain to another through a [third] domain." What does Rebbi Samuel bar Rav Isaac do with this? He explains it (if captive) [if equal][131].

118 There exists a complete text of this difficult passage in the commentary of R. Hananel of Kairawan to the Babli, 88a. While this text obviously was written from memory and is influenced by Babylonian spelling, and the reproduction of the text in the Wilna Babli may give rise to some questions, it is a testimony predating the Leiden ms. by more than 250 years and shows that the emendations proposed by the standard commentaries have to be rejected summarily.

119 The version of R. Hananel, "R. Abba and R. Yose", Amoraim of the last generation, is preferable to the Leiden text which quotes the third generation Amora R. Abbahu in the name of the fourth generation Tanna R. Yose (ben Ḥalafta), unless one wants to read "R. Yasa" in place of "R. Yose."

120 The statement of the Mishnah that if two balconies one above the other and both above the sea without *eruv* may not draw water.

121 He seems to disagree with Rav Huna (Note 92) that for the laws of the Sabbath the balcony extends 3 hand-breadths beyond its actual width but allows the upper balcony

to draw water through an appropriate hole if it extends in any way further than the lower balcony.

122 Without common *eruv*.

123 In a multi-story house with a high atrium and several occupants without an *eruv* one may not lower anything from the top to the bottom through the airspace belonging to third parties. But outside the house from roof to courtyard there is no problem even if the house has more than one floor and no *eruv* was made inside.

124 The statement of the Mishnah (Note 120).

125 Even with an *eruv*. If one refers the statement of R. Samuel bar Rav Isaac to R. Abbahu's statement, one would have to read "permitted". Since R. Hananel's testimony makes emendation impossible, the statement has to refer even to a single balcony.

126 In the case of two balconies, inside use is forbidden without an *eruv* and outside in all cases,

127 Tosephta 8:4.

128 This defines a domain by itself but since it is not inhabitable it does not require an *eruv*. Since the ledge is outside the house, it contradicts both R. Samuel bar Rav Isaac and R. Ze`ira.

129 A window 4-by-4 wide and 4 deep is a domain by itself; the dish cannot be lowered through such a window.

130 The text "as equal" in the Leiden ms. is an unjustified later correction of the scribe's and R. Hananel's incomprehensible בשבויה; it may be disregarded. Possibly R. Samuel bar Rav Isaac may explain the Tosephta suggesting that the ledge is not as usual outside but "captive" inside the house.

(25b line 35) פיס'. שִׁיעֲרוּ מְקוֹם תַּשְׁמִישׁ לְאָדָם סָאתַיִם. וְאַרְבַּע אַמּוֹת מַבְלִיעוֹת סָאתַיִם. נִיקָבָה הָעוּקָה. אִית תַּנֵּי. אֵין צָרִיךְ לִפּוּק. וְאִית תַּנֵּי. צָרִיךְ לִפּוּק. נִתְמַלְאֵת הָעוּקָה. אִית תַּנֵּי. צָרִיךְ לִשְׁפּוֹךְ. אִית תַּנֵּי. אֵין צָרִיךְ. אָמַר רִבִּי מָנָא. חַד תַּנָּא הוּא. מָאן דָּמַר. צָרִיךְ לִפּוּק. אוֹסֵר לִשְׁפּוֹךְ. מָאן דָּמַר. אֵין צָרִיךְ לִפּוּק. מוּתָּר לִשְׁפּוֹךְ. אָמַר לֵיהּ רִבִּי חִייָה בַּר מָרְיָיה. הָכִי אָמַר רִבִּי יוֹנָה אָבוּךְ הָוָה בַר. קָטִיפְּרַס. מִבִּפְנִים אֲפִילוּ יוֹתֵר מֵעֶשֶׂר מוּתָּר. מִבַּחוּץ אֲפִילוּ פָּחוּת מֵעֶשֶׂר מוּתָּר. אֶלָּא אֲנָן קַיָּימִין בְּשָׁוֶוה.

Paragraph[131]. They estimated (the place of)[132] what a person uses is two *se'ah* and four cubits absorb two *se'ah*[133]. If the sump sprung a hole[134], there are Tannaïm who state that one does not have to plug; there are Tannaïm who state that one has to plug. If the sump was full, there are Tannaïm who state that one has to empty, there are Tannaïm who state that one does not have to. Rebbi Mana said, it is one Tanna. He who says that one has to plug forbids to pour out[135], he who says that one does not have to plug permits to pour out. Rehbi Ḥiyya bar Marius said to Rebbi Mana: So said your father Rebbi Jonah, thinking about it[136]: If it is sloping[137] inside, even more than ten is permitted[138]; outside even less than ten is permitted. What we are dealing with if it is level.

131 Discussion of Mishnah 10.
132 Probably the word מקום should be deleted.
133 A person on one day uses no more than 2 *se'ah* of water and an unpaved area of 16 square cubits can absorb 2 *se'ah* per day. Babli 88a/b.
134 And then any additional water which is poured into the yard will immediately cause water to flow into the public domain.
135 He reads לשפוך as "to pour into the yard". If it is necessary to plug the hole so that no water may flow from it into the public domain, it will be forbidden to pour anything into the yard for the rest of the day.
136 Reading בָּהּ for בר "outside".
137 Greek καταφερής, -ές.
138 Obviously this has to read "forbidden". If the yard is on an incline, any water spilled there will immediately flow into the public domain. But if the outside is sloping into the courtyard, the water will remain in the yard.

(25b line 42) מַתְנִיתָא פְּלִיגָא עַל רִבִּי יוֹחָנָן. הֶחָצֵר וְהָאַכְסַדְרָה מִצְטָרְפִין בְּאַרְבַּע אַמּוֹת. פָּתַר לָהּ בְּשָׁוֶוה. מַתְנִיתָא פְּלִיגָא עַל רֵישׁ לָקִישׁ. הַמַּרְפֶּסֶת הַגַּג וְהֶחָצֵר מִצְטָרְפִין בְּאַרְבַּע אַמּוֹת. אָמַר רִבִּי חֲנַנְיָה. עוֹד הִיא בְשָׁוֶוה. דַּע לָךְ שֶׁהוּא כֵן. דְּתַנֵּי. הַבַּיִת וְהָעֲלִיָּה הֶחָצֵר וְהָאַכְסַדְרָה אֵינָן מִצְטָרְפִין. לֹא בְשֶׁאֵין שָׁוִין.

אָמַר רִבִּי יִרְמְיָה. רִבִּי מֵאִיר וְרִבִּי אֱלִיעֶזֶר בֶּן יַעֲקֹב שְׁנֵיהֶן אָמְרוּ דָבָר אֶחָד. רִבִּי אֱלִיעֶזֶר בֶּן יַעֲקֹב דְּתַנִּינָן. רִבִּי אֱלִיעֶזֶר בֶּן יַעֲקֹב אוֹמֵר. בִּיב שֶׁקָּמוּר אַרְבַּע אַמּוֹת בִּרְשׁוּת הָרַבִּים שׁוֹפְכִין בּוֹ מַיִם בַּשַּׁבָּת. וַחֲכָמִים אוֹמְרִים. אֲפִילוּ גַג אוֹ חָצֵר מֵאָה אַמָּה לֹא יִשְׁפּוֹךְ עַל פִּי הַבִּיב. רִבִּי מֵאִיר דְּתַנֵּי. סִילוֹנוֹת שֶׁבַּכְּרָכִין אַף עַל פִּי שֶׁנְּקוּבִין יִשָּׁפֵךְ בָּהֶן מַיִם בַּשַּׁבָּת. דִּבְרֵי רִבִּי מֵאִיר. וְתָנֵּי כֵן. אִם הָיְתָה מַזְחִילָה מוּתָּר. אִם עוֹנַת הַגְּשָׁמִים הִיא מוּתָּר. צִינּוֹרוֹת מְקַלְּחִין בּוֹ אָסוּר. וְהָתָנֵי בַּר קַפָּרָא. אִם הָיָה מָקוֹם צָנוּעַ מוּתָּר. הָדָא פְּלִיגָא עַל רַב וְלֵית לֵיהּ קַייָם. דְּרַב אָמַר. כָּל־שֶׁאָסוּר מִשּׁוּם מַרְאִית הָעַיִן אֲפִילוּ בְּחַדְרֵי חֲדָרִים אָסוּר.

The Mishnah disagrees with Rebbi Johanan: "Courtyard and porch combine for four cubits[28]." He explains it if they are level. A *baraita* disagrees with Rebbi Simeon ben Laqish: The terrace, the roof, and the courtyard combine for four cubits. Still it is if they are level. You should know that it is so since it was stated: The house, the upper floor, the courtyard, and the porch do not combine. Is that not because they are not level[139]?

Rebbi Jeremiah said, Rebbi Meïr and Rebbi Eliezer ben Jacob both said the same. Rebbi Eliezer ben Jacob as we have stated: "Rebbi Eliezer ben

Jacob says, on the Sabbath one may pour water into a sewer which is covered for four cubits in the public domain, but the Sages are saying, even from a roof or a courtyard 100 cubits [wide] one may not pour into the sewer." Rebbi Meïr as it was stated: In large cities one may pour water into flows even though they are perforated, the words of Rebbi Meïr[140]. [141]And it was stated thus, if it was a drainpipe it is permitted; in the rainy season it is permitted[142]; streaming spouts are forbidden and Bar Qappara stated, if it occurred at a hidden place it is permitted. This disagrees with Rav and he cannot explain it, since Rav said that everything forbidden because of a bad impression is forbidden even in the most private room.

139 Since the disagreement between R. Johanan and R. Simeon ben Laqish is not indicated, it is difficult to assess the meaning of the discussion. An educated guess (by *Qorban haEdah*) is that R. Johanan holds that domains can be added only if they are on equal heights; the questioner assumed that the porch was higher than the courtyard. In the *baraita* quoted as opposing R. Simeon ben Laqish it is clear that courtyard and rooftop cannot be of equal height. It is conjectured that he holds that the list of the Mishnah, yard and porch, is exhaustive; this would exclude terrace and rooftop. The answer is that he accepts yard and everything on the same level, porch and everything on the same level. In this interpretation the *baraita* does not allow one to add the surface areas of courtyard and rooftop.

140 If a river is diverted into many small currents which run in streets and through courtyards (as can be seen, e. g., in Freiburg i. B., Germany), one may pour water into them on the Sabbath since it will not be noticed.

141 The main discussion about prohibitions added because people may get a bad impression, which also includes the text here, is in *Kilaim* 9:2 (Notes 34-40, *Eruvin* problem Note 39). Rav's opinion is accepted in the Babli (*Šabbat* 64b, 164b, *Beṣah* 9a, `*Avodah zarah* 12a) but consistently rejected in the Yerushalmi.

142 Babli 88b. The Babli holds that during the rainy season there never was any rabbinic prohibition because everything is being wet anyhow.

כל גגות פרק תשיעי

(fol. 25b) **משנה א:** כָּל־גַּגּוֹת הָעִיר רְשׁוּת אַחַת וּבִלְבַד שֶׁלֹּא יְהֵא גַג גָּבוֹהַּ עֲשָׂרָה אוֹ נָמוֹךְ עֲשָׂרָה דִּבְרֵי רִבִּי מֵאִיר. וַחֲכָמִים אוֹמְרִים כָּל־אֶחָד וְאֶחָד רְשׁוּת בִּפְנֵי עַצְמוֹ. רִבִּי שִׁמְעוֹן אוֹמֵר אֶחָד גַּגּוֹת וְאֶחָד חֲצֵירוֹת וְאֶחָד קַרְפֵּיפוֹת רְשׁוּת אַחַת לְכֵלִים שֶׁשָּׁבְתוּ לְתוֹכָן וְלֹא לְכֵלִים שֶׁשָּׁבְתוּ בְּתוֹךְ הַבַּיִת:

Mishnah 1: All rooftops of a town form one domain on condition that no roof be ten [hand-breadths] higher or ten lower, the words of Rebbi Meïr[1], but the Sages say that each roof is a domain by itself. Rebbi Simeon says, not only rooftops but also courtyards and corrals[2] are single domains for vessels which started the Sabbath in them but not for vessels which started the Sabbath in the house[3].

משנה ב: גַּג גָּדוֹל סָמוּךְ לְקָטָן הַגָּדוֹל מוּתָּר וְהַקָּטָן אָסוּר. חָצֵר גְּדוֹלָה שֶׁנִּפְרְצָה לִקְטַנָּה הַגְּדוֹלָה מוּתֶּרֶת וְהַקְּטַנָּה אֲסוּרָה מִפְּנֵי שֶׁהִיא כְּפִתְחָהּ שֶׁל גְּדוֹלָה.

Mishnah 2: If a large roof is adjacent to a small one[4], the large one is permitted but the small forbidden. If a large courtyard is open to a small one, the large one is permitted but the small forbidden since it acts as a door to the large one.

משנה ג: חָצֵר שֶׁנִּפְרְצָה לִרְשׁוּת הָרַבִּים הַמַּכְנִיס מִתּוֹכָהּ לִרְשׁוּת הַיָּחִיד אוֹ מֵרְשׁוּת הַיָּחִיד לְתוֹכָהּ חַיָּיב דִּבְרֵי רִבִּי אֱלִיעֶזֶר. וַחֲכָמִים אוֹמְרִים מִתּוֹכָהּ לִרְשׁוּת הָרַבִּים אוֹ מֵרְשׁוּת הָרַבִּים לְתוֹכָהּ פָּטוּר מִפְּנֵי שֶׁהִיא כַּכַּרְמְלִית:

Mishnah 3: If a courtyard is open to the public domain[5], anybody who brings from it into a private domain or from a private domain into it is liable, the words of Rebbi Eliezer. But the Sages say from it into the public domain and from the public domain into it one is not liable since it is like *karmelit*.

משנה ד: חָצֵר שֶׁנִּפְרְצָה שְׁתֵּי רוּחוֹת וְכֵן בַּיִת שֶׁנִּפְרַץ מִשְּׁתֵּי רוּחוֹתָיו וְכֵן מָבוֹי שֶׁנִּיטְּלָה קוֹרָתוֹ אוֹ לְחָיָיו מוּתָּרִין בְּאוֹתָהּ שַׁבָּת וַאֲסוּרִין לֶעָתִיד לָבֹא דִּבְרֵי רִבִּי יְהוּדָה. רִבִּי יוֹסֵי אוֹמֵר אִם מוּתָּרִין בְּאוֹתָהּ שַׁבָּת מוּתָּרִין לֶעָתִיד לָבֹא. וְאִם אֲסוּרִין לֶעָתִיד לָבֹא אֲסוּרִין בְּאוֹתָהּ שַׁבָּת:

Mishnah 4: If a courtyard became open on both sides[6], or a house became open on both sides[6], or an alley whose beam or lathes were removed, they are permitted the same Sabbath but forbidden in the future, the words of Rebbi Jehudah. Rebbi Yose says, if they are permitted the same Sabbath they are permitted in the future, and if they are forbidden in the future they are forbidden this Sabbath[7].

משנה ח: הַבּוֹנֶה עֲלִיָּה עַל גַּבֵּי שְׁנֵי בָתִּים וְכֵן גְּשָׁרִים הַמְפוּלָּשִׁין מְטַלְטְלִין תַּחְתֵּיהֶן בְּשַׁבָּת דִּבְרֵי רִבִּי יְהוּדָה וַחֲכָמִים אוֹסְרִים. וְעוֹד אָמַר רִבִּי יְהוּדָה מְעָרְבִין בְּמָבוֹי הַמְפוּלָּשׁ וַחֲכָמִים אוֹסְרִין:

Mishnah 5: If somebody builds an upper floor connecting two houses[8], and similarly open bridges[9], one carries under them, the words of Rebbi Jehudah, but the Sages forbid it[10]. In addition, Rebbi Jehudah said that one may make an *eruv* for open alleys but the Sages forbid it[11].

1 All vessels which were on any rooftop at nightfall Friday evening may be transported from one roof to any other without an *eruv* and even if the inhabitants of the different houses made *eruvin* for themselves. But if the level of roofs differs by at least 10 hand-breadths, each level constitutes a domain by itself and one may not carry from one to the other without an appropriate *eruv*.

2 Cf. Chapter 2, Note 6.

3 Without an *eruv* one may carry any vessel of the courtyard from one place to any other in the yard; only moving vessels from a house to the yard or vice versa is forbidden.

4 This follows the Sages in Mishnah 1. The situation is supposed to be the same as described in the second part of the Mishnah for courtyards: the larger extends beyond the smaller roof on both sides; if a person fromf the smaller house uses his roof to go to the larger roof, the smaller roof plays the role of entrance gate to the larger one. Therefore the dweller in the smaller house may use his own roof only if he made an *eruv* with the larger house.

5 There is no entrance gate and anyone entering is not trespassing. For the opponents of R. Eliezer, the status of the yard is no different from shoulders of a public road (*Šabbat* 1, Note 73); transporting from the yard to either the public road or a private house is only rabbinically forbidden.

6 Before the Sabbath it was a private domain. On the Sabbath it became open and now can be used as a shortcut by the public.

7 Therefore it is forbidden immediately on the first Sabbath.

8 The houses are on two different sides of the public road; the construction creates a bridge between the sides. Since the outer walls of this bridge are at least 10 hand-breadths high, in R. Jehudah's opinion they constitute acceptable partitions which

turn the space between them into a private domain. In the opinion of the anonymous majority, no part of a public road may be made private.

9 A bridge open to the public as part of a public road. It is assumed that the railings at the sides of the bridge are 10 hand-breadths high and can act as partitions between the space under the bridge and the outside.

10 Since the formulation is "prohibited" but not "he is liable", the argument of R. Jehudah is accepted in principle but rejected rabbinically.

11 If an alley is not a dead end it is a thoroughfare even if it cannot be used for vehicular traffic.

(25c line 8) כָּל־גַּגּוֹת הָעִיר רְשׁוּת אַחַת כּוֹל׳. רִבִּי יוֹסֵי בֵּירִבִּי בּוּן אָמַר. אִתְפַּלְגוּן רַב וּשְׁמוּאֵל. שְׁמוּאֵל אָמַר. עַד בֵּית סָאתַיִם. וְרַב אָמַר. מְטַלְטְלִין בָּם אֲפִילוּ כּוֹר אֲפִילוּ כּוֹרַיִים. הֲווֹ בָעֵי מֵימַר. מַה פְּלִיגֵי רִבִּי מֵאִיר וְרַבָּנָן. בְּשֶׁעֵירְבוּ. אֲבָל בְּשֶׁלֹּא עֵירְבוּ. פָּתַר לָהּ כְּשֶׁהָיוּ כּוּלָּן לְאָדָם אֶחָד. מַתְנִיתִין שֶׁהָיוּ כּוּלָּן עוֹלִין אוֹ בְסוּלָּם צוּרִי אוֹ בְסוּלָּם מִצְרִי. אֲבָל אִם הָיוּ כּוּלָּן עוֹלִין בְּסוּלָּם מִצְרִי וְאֶחָד עוֹלֶה בְסוּלָּם צוּרִי. אוֹתוֹ שֶׁלְּצוּרִי נַעֲשָׂה כְפֶתַח וְהַשְּׁאָר נַעֲשָׂה כְמִטְרַפֵּס וְעוֹלֶה כְמִטְרַפֵּס וְיוֹרֵד.

"All rooftops of a town form one domain," etc. Rebbi Yose ben Rebbi Abun said, Rav and Samuel disagree[12]. Samuel said, up to two *bet se'ah*. Rav said, one carries there even a *kor*, even two *kor*. They wanted to say, where do Rebbi Meïr and the rabbis disagree? If they made an *eruv*[13]. But if they did not have to make an *eruv*, he explains it if all [houses] were the property of one person[14]. Our Mishnah if all of them were climbing up either on a Tyrian or an Egyptian ladder[15]. But if all were climbing up using an Egyptian ladder except for one using a Tyrian, the Tyrian becomes a door[16] and the remaining ones are as if climbing up and climbing down.

12 Since rooftops are not built as dwellings, their status is comparable to that of corrals, subject to the same restrictions; Chapter 5, Note 167; Babli 89a.

13 If the houses belonged to different owners and they made an *eruv* for the whole walled town, in the majority opinion the *eruv* does not extend to the rooftops which are not intended as dwellings.

14 Since in a corral one may carry only if it is not more than 2 *bet se'ah*, the same applies to rooftops. The rabbis may hold that roofs of different houses are different domains even if all belong to one and the same person.

15 An Egyptian ladder is small and movable; a Tyrian is large and fixed.

16 Using a Tyrian ladder really is using a staircase; using an Egyptian is inconvenient exercising. Since the owner of the Tyrian ladder has easy access, he is the legitimate user of all rooftops, to the exclusion of the others who may walk there but not carry (Chapter 8, Note 46).

(25c line 15) מַהוּ לְטַלְטֵל בְּכוּלוֹ. שְׁמוּאֵל אָמַר. מְטַלְטֵל בְּכוּלוֹ. רַב אָמַר. אֵין מְטַלְטְלִין בּוֹ אֶלָא בְּאַרְבַּע אַמּוֹת. מַתְנִיתִין פְּלִיגָא עַל רַב. גַּג גָּדוֹל סָמוּךְ לְקָטָן. הַגָּדוֹל מוּתָּר וְהַקָּטָן אָסוּר. נִיחָא הַגָּדוֹל מוּתָּר בְּאַרְבַּע אַמּוֹת. וְהַקָּטָן אָסוּר בְּאַרְבַּע אַמּוֹת. וְיֵשׁ אָסוּר בְּאַרְבַּע אַמּוֹת. רַב וּשְׁמוּאֵל אָמְרֵי. שֶׁנּוֹתְנִין לוֹ אַרְבַּע אַמּוֹת בִּפְנֵי פִתְחוֹ. רִבִּי יוֹסֵי בֵּירִבִּי בּוּן בְּשֵׁם שְׁמוּאֵל אָמַר. כְּשֶׁהָיָה שָׁם פֶּתַח פָּתוּחַ לַגַּג. אֲפִילוּ כֵן הַגָּדוֹל מוּתָּר. שֶׁלֹּא נִפְרַץ בִּמְלוֹאוֹ. וְהַקָּטָן אָסוּר. שֶׁנִּפְרַץ בִּמְלוֹאוֹ.

May one carry in all of it[17]? Samuel said, he carries in all of it. Rav said, he only carries within four cubits[18]. Our Mishnah disagrees with Rav: "If a large roof is adjacent to a small one, the large one is permitted but the small forbidden." One understands that of the large one four cubits are permitted. But of the small one is forbidden four cubits? Is anything forbidden in four cubits? Do not Rav and Samuel say that one allows him four cubits in front of his door[19]? Rebbi Yose ben Rebbi Abun said in Samuel's name: If there was a door open to the roof[20], even then the large one is permitted since it is not completely open, and the small one is forbidden because it is completely open.

17 This question is asked for the rabbis who oppose R. Meïr. Since each rooftop is a separate domain it is a question whether it has the status of a backyard of a single house where one may carry without restriction. A backyard, or a multiple dwelling courtyard, is bounded by walls but the borders between flat roofs of contiguous houses may not be easily seen. Does one say that the walls between houses may ideally be extended over the roofs?

18 The Babli, 90a, interchanges the names.

19 Not only may one carry distances less than 4 cubits in the public domain, one even may carry in a multi-family courtyard without *eruv* within 4 cubits of one's door. There is absolutely no situation where one is not permitted to carry up to a distance of 4 cubits.

20 In the opinion of S. Liebermann, if the house was built on a slope and the roof opened on a courtyard, the large roof forms one domain with the courtyard since on both sides where it is joined to the small one there is railing which counts as a wall, whereas the smaller roof is forbidden without an *eruv* since no wall indicates that it is separated from the large roof.

(25c line 22) רִבִּי מֵאִיר אוֹמֵר. אֵין אַתֶּם מוֹדִין לִי בְּכֵלִים שֶׁשָּׁבְתוּ בֶּחָצֵר שֶׁמְּטַלְטְלִין אוֹתָן בֶּחָצֵר. מַה נִּשְׁתַּנָּה גַּג מֵחָצֵר. אָמְרוּ לוֹ. לֹא. אִם אָמַרְתָּ בְּחָצֵר שֶׁאֵין לָהּ דִּיּוּרִין לְמַטָּה. תֹּאמַר בְּגַג שֶׁיֵּשׁ לוֹ דִּיּוּרִין לְמַטָּה. אָמַר לָהֶן. הֲרֵי שֶׁהָיְתָה הֶחָצֵר לְמַעֲלָה מִן הַגַּג מָהוּ. אָמְרוּ לוֹ. לֹא.

אִם אָמַרְתָּ בְּחָצֵר שֶׁאֵין כָּל־אֶחָד מַכִּיר אֶת מְקוֹמוֹ. תּאֹמַר בְּגַג שֶׁכָּל־אֶחָד מַכִּיר אֶת מְקוֹמוֹ. אָמַר לָהֶן. הֲרֵי שֶׁהָיְתָה הֶחָצֵר חֲלוּקָה בִּפְסִיסִיוֹת מָהוּ. עַד כָּאן הָיְתָה תְשׁוּבָה. אָמַר רִבִּי יוֹסֵי בֵּירִבִּי בּוּן. מִיכָּן וָהֵילָךְ הָיוּ מֵשִׁיבִין לְפָנָיו. אָמְרוּ לוֹ. לֹא. אִם אָמַרְתָּ בְּחָצֵר שֶׁמְּחִיצוֹתֶיהָ עוֹלוֹת עִמָּהּ. תּאֹמַר בְּגַג שֶׁאֵין מְחִיצוֹתֶיהָ עוֹלוֹת עִמָּהּ. וַהֲוָה מֵימַר לוֹן. אוֹף אֲנָא אִית לִי עָמוֹק כְּגוֹבַהּ.

"[21]Rebbi Meïr says, do you not agree with me that vessels which started the Sabbath in a courtyard may be moved in the courtyard[22]? What is the difference between a roof and a courtyard? They told him, no. If you say about a courtyard, which has no dwellers under it, what can you say about a roof, which has dwellers under it? He asked them, what if the courtyard was higher than the roof[23]? They told him, no. If you say about a courtyard where nobody knows his place, what can you say about a roof where everybody knows his place? He asked them, what if the courtyard was split by pebbles[24]? Up to this point there was an answer[25]." Rebbi Yose ben Rebbi Abun said, from here on they were answering him in person; they told him, no. If you say about a courtyard whose dividers rise about it, what can you say about a roof whose dividers do not rise about it? He was telling them, in fact I am equating depth and height.

21 Tosephta 7:14.
22 This is stated as commonly accepted rule in Tosephta 5:19,23.
23 The house was built into a hillside and the courtyard is the extrension of the roof.
24 With the Tosephta read פסיפס Greek ψῆφος, ὁ.
25 Cf. Mishnah *Makhširin* 8. One would have expected the name of a Tanna stating the objections of R. Meïr's students.

(25c line 32) תַּנֵּי. אָמַר רִבִּי יוּדָה. בִּשְׁעַת הַשְׁמָד הָיִינוּ נוֹטְלִין אֶת הַסֵּפֶר וְהָיִינוּ עוֹלִין מֵחָצֵר לְגַג וּמִגַּג לְגַג אַחֵר וְיוֹשְׁבִין וְקוֹרִין. וְלֹא אָמַר אָדָם דָּבָר. אָמְרוּ לוֹ. אֵין שְׁעַת הַשְׁמָד רְאָיָיה. אָמַר רִבִּי. שׁוּנִין הָיִינוּ אֵצֶל רִבִּי שִׁמְעוֹן (בְּבִקְעָה) [בִּתְקוֹעַ]. וְהָיִינוּ נוֹטְלִין שֶׁמֶן וַאֲלִינְטִית וְהָיִינוּ נִכְנָסִין מֵחָצֵר לְגַג וּמִגַּג לְקַרְפֵּף וּמִקַּרְפֵּף לְקַרְפֵּף. עַד שֶׁהָיִינוּ מַגִּיעִין לְקַרְפֵּף הַסָּמוּךְ לְמַעֲיָין וְיוֹרְדִין וְטוֹבְלִין בּוֹ.

אִשְׁכְּחַת אָמַר. אַרְבַּע פַּלְגְוָון. כָּל־גַּגּוֹת הָעִיר רְשׁוּת אַחַת הֵן. רִבִּי יוּדָן אוֹמֵר. חָצֵר וְגַגּוֹת רְשׁוּת אַחַת הֵן. רִבִּי שִׁמְעוֹן אוֹמֵר. חָצֵר וְגַג וְקַרְפֵּף אַחַת הֵן לַכֵּלִים שֶׁשָּׁבְתוּ בְתוֹכָן וְלֹא לַכֵּלִים שֶׁשָּׁבְתוּ בְתוֹךְ הַבָּיִת.

It was stated[26]: "Rebbi Jehudah said, in times of persecution[27] we were taking the scroll[28] and climbing from courtyard to roof, from a roof to another roof, and sitting down and reading. They told him, times of persecution are no proof[29]." "[30]Rebbi said, when we were studying with Rebbi Simeon (in a valley) [in Tekoa][31], we were taking oil and a bath towel[32] and going from a courtyard to a roof, and from the roof to a corral, and from one corral to another corral, until we came to the corral adjacent to the spring, and descending and immersing ourselves in it."

You may say that there are four disagreements. "All rooftops of a town form one domain.[33]" Rebbi Jehudah says, courtyard and rooftops form one domain. "Rebbi Simeon says, courtyards, rooftops, and corrals are single domains for vessels which started the Sabbath in them but not for vessels which started the Sabbath in the house"[34].

26 Tosephta 5:24; Babli 91a.
27 The Hadrianic persecutions when study of Torah was forbidden.
28 A Torah scroll.
29 Since the restrictions are rabbinic, not biblical, they may be overridden by biblical obligations; this does not diminish their validity.
30 Tosephta 5:24; Babli 91a, *Šabbat*

147b, *Menahot* 72a.
31 The text in parentheses is the scribe's; the text in brackets is the corrector's following the consensus of the Babli texts. It is difficult to locate R. Simeon in Judea.
32 Latin *linteum, -i, n.*.
33 R. Meïr's opinion in the Mishnah.
34 The fourth opinion is that of the rabbis for whom each rooftop is a separate domain.

(25c line 41) רִבִּי יוֹחָנָן אָמַר. בְּשֶׁלֹּא עֵירְבוּ. אֲבָל בְּשֶׁעֵירְבוּ נַעֲשִׂית חָצֵר כְּבָתִּים. וְהַגַּגּוֹת רְשׁוּת בִּפְנֵי עַצְמָן. אָמַר רִבִּי זְעִירָא. הִיא עֵירִיבוּ הִיא שֶׁלֹּא עֵירִיבוּ. מַתְנִיתִין פְּלִיגָא עַל רִבִּי זְעִירָא. לֹא לְכֵלִים שֶׁשָּׁבְתוּ בְתוֹךְ הַבַּיִת: אִם בְּשֶׁלֹּא עֵירִיבוּ. הָדָא צוֹרְכָא. לְהוֹצִיא מִן הַגַּג אָסוּר. לֹא כָל־שֶׁכֵּן לַגַּג. אָמַר רִבִּי בּוּן בַּר כַּהֲנָא קוֹמֵי רִבִּי לָא. בְּשֶׁעֵירְבָה זוֹ בִּפְנֵי עַצְמָהּ וְזוֹ בִּפְנֵי עַצְמָהּ. אֲפִילוּ כֵן לֹא לַכֵּלִים שֶׁשָּׁבְתוּ לְתוֹכוֹ.

Rebbi Johanan said, if they did not make an *eruv*. But if they made an *eruv* the courtyard becomes like the houses[35]. Rebbi Ze'ira said, it is the same whether they made an *eruv* or they did not make an *eruv*[36]. Our Mishnah disagrees with Rebbi Ze'ira: "not for vessels which started the Sabbath in the house." If they did not make an *eruv*, is this necessary? It is forbidden to remove from the roof, not so much to the roof[37]? Rebbi Abun bar Cahana said before Rebbi La: When each one made an *eruv* by itself; even then not for the vessels which started the Sabbath in the house[38].

35 R. Jehudah and R. Simeon cannot refer to the cases where each courtyard made an *eruv* for itself since they permit carrying from one to the other by way of the roofs. Since with an *eruv* one may bring vessels from the houses into the courtyard, they also would allow bringing vessels from one house to another in another courtyard via the roof. Cf. Babli 91a.

36 Since vessels from the house are explicitly excluded by R. Simeon, the situation considered by R. Johanan cannot occur.

37 Since the vessels cannot be removed from house to courtyard, for RR. Jehudah and Simeon certainly they cannot be brought to any roof.

38 Even with an *eruv* and it is possible to bring vessels into the courtyard and onto the roof, they cannot be moved to any other roof nor to another courtyard. R. Ze'ira is not contradicted by the Mishnah.

(25c line 47) פיס׳. רַבָּנָן דְּקַיְסָרִי בְשֵׁם רִבִּי יוֹסֵי בֵּירִבִּי בּוּן. אַתְיָיא דִשְׁמוּאֵל לְרַב וּתְרַוַויהוּ פְלִיגִין עַל שִׁיטָתֵיהּ דְּרִבִּי יוֹחָנָן. דְּתַנִּינָן. כָּל־גַּגּוֹת הָעִיר רְשׁוּת אַחַת׳. שְׁמוּאֵל אָמַר. עַד בֵּית סָאתַיִּים. וְרַב אָמַר. מְטַלְטְלִין בָּם אֲפִילוּ כּוֹר אֲפִילוּ כּוֹרַיִים.

Paragraph. [39]The rabbis of Caesarea in the name of Rebbi Yose ben Rebbi Abun: It follows that Samuel and Rav both disagree with the opinion of Rebbi Johanan, as we have stated: "All rooftops of a town form one domain." Samuel said, up to two *bet se'ah*. Rav said, one carries there even a *kor*, even two *kor*.

39 A slightly garbled restatement of the first paragraph in this Chapter. The spelling תרויהו is Babylonian Aramaic in place of Yerushalmi תריהון.

(25c line 51) גַּג גָּדוֹל סָמוּךְ לְקָטָן הַגָּדוֹל מוּתָּר וְהַקָּטָן אָסוּר. מַתְנִיתִין בְּאוֹתוֹ הַגָּג. אֲבָל בְּגַג אַחֵר אָסוּר. בְּשֶׁאֵינוֹ שָׁוֶה. אֲבָל אִם הָיָה שָׁוֶה מוּתָּר. מַתְנִיתִין פְּלִיגָא עַל שְׁמוּאֵל. חָצֵר גְּדוֹלָה שֶׁנִּפְרְצָה לִקְטַנָּה הַגְּדוֹלָה מוּתֶּרֶת וְהַקְּטַנָּה אֲסוּרָה. וִיטַלְטְלוּ בָהּ עַד מְקוֹם מְחִיצוֹת. חֲבֵרַיָיא אָמְרִין קוֹמֵי רִבִּי יוֹסֵי בְשֵׁם רִבִּי אֲחִייָה. מַה דָּמַר שְׁמוּאֵל. בְּשַׁבָּת זוֹ. מַה דְּהִיא מַתְנִיתִין. בְּשַׁבָּת הַבָּאָה. מָה נָן קַיְימִין. אִם בְּשֶׁעֵירְבוּ עֵירוּב אֶחָד. בֵּין בַּשַּׁבָּת זוֹ בֵּין בַּשַּׁבָּת הַבָּאָה יְהוּ מוּתָּרִין. אִם בְּשֶׁלֹא עֵירְבוּ כָּל־עִיקָּר. בֵּין בַּשַּׁבָּת זוֹ בֵּין בַּשַּׁבָּת הַבָּאָה יְהוּ אֲסוּרִין. מַה דַהֲוָה עוֹבְדָא הָכִי הֲוָה עוֹבְדָא. אָמַר רִבִּי בּוּן בַּר כַּהֲנָא קוֹמֵי רִבִּי לָא. בְּשֶׁעֵירְבָה זוֹ בִפְנֵי עַצְמָהּ וְזוֹ בִפְנֵי עַצְמָהּ. אֲפִילוּ כֵן הַגְּדוֹלָה מוּתֶּרֶת. שֶׁנִּפְרְצָה בִמְלוֹאָהּ. וְהַקְּטַנָּה אֲסוּרָה. שֶׁלֹא נִפְרְצָה בִמְלוֹאָהּ.

"If a large roof is adjacent to a small one[4], the large one is permitted but the small forbidden." Our Mishnah [refers to] one roof only, but on another roof it is forbidden[40]. If it is not level, but if it is level it is permitted[41]. Our Mishnah disagrees with Samuel: "If a large courtyard is open to a small one, the large one is permitted but the small forbidden." Should one not be able to move there up to the place of the partitions[42]? The colleagues said before Rebbi Yose in the name of Rebbi Aḥiyya: What Samuel said, on this Sabbath itself[43], what the Mishnah deals with the next Sabbath. Where do we hold? If they made one *eruv* together, they should be permitted both on this and on the next Sabbath. If they did not make any *eruv*, they should be forbidden both on this and on the next Sabbath. The case happened as it happened[44]. Rebbi Abun bar Cahana said before Rebbi La: When each of them made separate *eruvin*, nevertheless the large one is permitted since it is breached along its entire length and the small one is forbidden since it was not breached along its entire length[45].

40 Following the Sages in Mishnah 1, even if the two roofs belong to the same owner, it only is permitted to carry from the large onto the small but not from the small onto the large (Chapter 2, Notes 48,91).

41 The Mishnah may even be read as following R. Meïr, in case there is a step from the large roof down to the small.

42 Why is a person living in the smaller house not permitted to use his roof if he keeps his distance from the large roof?

43 It is not quite clear which of Samuel's statements the discussion refers to. It seems that one reads in the Mishnah the expression נפרצה as "was torn down" not as a prior state but that it was torn down on the Sabbath and Samuel holds (Chapter 6, Notes 158ff.) that what was permitted at the start of the Sabbath remains so for the entire Sabbath.

44 Chapter 8, Note 89.

45 It seems clear that one has to switch the places of "breached" and "not breached."

(25c line 62) פיס׳. רִבִּי זְרִיקָא רִבִּי יַעֲקֹב בַּר בּוּן בְּשֵׁם רִבִּי חֲנִינָה. לֹא אָמַר רִבִּי לָעֵזֵר אֶלָּא מִמְּקוֹם מְחִיצוֹת בְּשֶׁנִּיטְלוּ רָאשֵׁי זָוִיּוֹת מִיכָּן וּמִיכָּן. וּבִלְבַד בְּאַרְבָּעָה. רִבִּי זְעִירָא וְרִבִּי אִילָא תְּרֵיהוֹן אָמְרֵי. אָסוּר שֶׁלֹּא מִמְּקוֹם מְחִיצוֹת. אֲבָל מִמְּקוֹם מְחִיצוֹת אֲפִילוּ רַבָּנָן מוֹדוּ. אָמַר רִבִּי זְרִיקָן. זִימְנִין סַגִּין פְּשָׁטִית עִם רִבִּי יַעֲקֹב בַּר בּוּן וְלֹא שְׁמָעִית מִינֵּיהּ דָּא מִילְתָא. אָמְרִין לֵיהּ. וְלֵית בַּר נַשׁ הֲוֵי שְׁמַע מִילָּה דְּלֵית חַבְרֵיהּ שְׁמִיעַ לֵיהּ. רַב יִרְמְיָה בְּשֵׁם רַב. בְּשֶׁנִּיטְלוּ רָאשֵׁי זָוִיּוֹת מִיכָּן וּמִיכָּן. וּבִלְבַד בְּשָׁוֶה.

Paragraph[46]. Rebbi Zeriqa, Rebbi Jacob bar Abun in the name of Rebbi Ḥanina: Rebbi Eleazar said this only for the place of partitions if the main parts had been removed on both sides[47], and only four [handbreadths]. Rebbi Ze`ira and Rebbi Illa both are saying, it is forbidden not at the place of partitions, but at the place of partitions even the rabbis agree⁴⁸. Rebbi Zeriqan said, many times I explained [the Mishnah] with Rebbi Jacob bar Abun and never heard this from him⁴⁹. They said to him, does it not happen that one person hears something which another does not hear? Rav Jeremiah in the name of Rav: if the main partitions had been removed on both sides, and only if it is level⁵⁰.

46 Discussion of Mishnah 3.

47 In this opinion, R. Eleazar holds that a courtyard used as a passageway remains *karmelit* except for the two entrances where at the place of the missing walls a strip 4 hand-breadths wide each is added to the public domain.

48 In their opinion R. Eleazar declares the entire courtyard as public domain. The opinion attributed to R. Eleazar in Note 47 is attributed here to the rabbis who in addition permit the dwellers around the courtyard to make an *eruv*.

49 A similar expression of R. Zeriqan is in *Šabbat* 3, after Note 57.

50 The courtyard open on both sides becomes public domain only if it is level with the roads on both sides.

(25c line 70) פיס'. וְלָמָּה לִי מִשְׁתֵּי רוּחוֹתֶיהָ. אֲפִילוּ מֵרוּחַ אַחַת. וְלֹא רַב הוּא. דְּרַב אָמַר. חָצֵר נִיתֶּרֶת בִּשְׁנֵי פַסִּין. רִבִּי שְׁמוּאֵל בְּשֵׁם רִבִּי זֵירָא. בְּמַחֲלוֹקֶת. מָאן דָּמַר תַּמָּן בְּפַס אֶחָד וָכָא בְּפַס אֶחָד. מָאן דָּמַר תַּמָּן בִּשְׁנֵי פַסִּין וָכָא בִּשְׁנֵי פַסִּין. נִפְרָץ מִן הָאֶמְצָע מוּתָּר. שְׁמוּאֵל אָמַר. אָסוּר. אָמַר רִבִּי זְעִירָא. אִין לֵית הָדָא אוּלְפָן דִּשְׁמוּאֵל קַשְׁיָא. נִפְרָץ כָּל־אוֹתוֹ הָרוּחַ. אָמַר רִבִּי יוֹסֵי בֵּירִבִּי בּוּן. הָדָא הִיא אַכְסַדְרָה. אִילּוּ אַכְסַדְרָה. שָׁמָּה אֵינָהּ מוּתֶּרֶת.

אָמַר רִבִּי יוֹחָנָן. לֹא אָמַר רִבִּי לִיעֶזֶר אֶלָּא בְחָצֵר וּבְמָבוֹי. אֲבָל בַּבַּיִת כְּגֶשֶׁר הוּא.

רַב וְרִבִּי יוֹחָנָן אָמְרֵי. אָסוּר בֵּין בְּשַׁבָּת זוֹ בֵּין בְּשַׁבָּת הַבָּאָה.

Paragraph⁵¹. Why do I need "on both sides"⁶? Even on one side! Does this not follow Rav, as Rav said, a courtyard becomes permitted by two planks⁵²? Rebbi Samuel in the name of Rebbi Ze`ira: It is a disagreement. He who says there by one plank⁵³, here also by one plank; he who says there by two planks, here also by two planks. If it became breached in the middle it is permitted⁵⁴; Samuel said it is forbidden. Rebbi Ze`ira said, if that of Samuel is not what he learned, it is difficult⁵⁵. If one entire side was breached? Rebbi Yose ben Rebbi Abun said, that is [the case of] the porch; if it were a porch, would it not be permitted⁵⁶?

Rebbi Johanan said, Rebbi Eliezer⁵⁷ said this only for a courtyard and an alley; but is a house like a bridge⁵⁸?

Rav and Rebbi Johanan say, it is forbidden both on this Sabbath and the coming Sabbath[59].

51 Discussion of Mishnah 4.

52 Rav's statement is recorded only in the Babli, 12a: Rav Sheshet said in the name of Rav Jeremiah bar Abba who said in the name of Rav: The Sages agree with Rebbi Eliezer about planks of a courtyard (cf. Mishnah 1:2).

53 Rabbis opposing Rebbi, Babli 12a.

54 If walls are standing at both sides of the breach, the breach is a door. Even if the breach is wider than 10 cubits, if the standing walls are at least 4 hand-breadths wide they act as planks.

55 If Samuel's statement is an old Babylonian tradition, it has to be accepted as rabbinic decree. If it is presented as a new ruling, it seems to be illogical.

56 Since a porch has no walls, the rules of the courtyard cannot be more restrictive than those of a porch. This is R. Ze`ira's objection to Samuel's statement.

57 This refers to Mishnah 3 where in all other references the name of the Tanna is Eleazar.

58 A house, even if it is a public building open to all and a passage through it may serve as a shortcut, is never treated as public domain.

59 In Mishnah 4, practice is decided following R. Yose; since it is forbidden in the future it must be forbidden now.

(25d line 3) אָמַר רִבִּי יוֹחָנָן. כּוּשָׁתְּ וְקֵירוּיָה וּמָבוֹי וְגֵר וְעַם הָאָרֶץ. חֲמָרִים.

כּוּשָׁתְּ. דִּתְנָן. הַכּוּשָׁתְּ וְהַחֶכֶס וְרָאשֵׁי בְשָׂמִים נִלְקָחִים בְּכֶסֶף מַעֲשֵׂר וְאֵינוֹ מְטַמֵּא טוּמְאַת אוֹכְלִין דִּבְרֵי רִבִּי עֲקִיבָא. אָמַר רִבִּי יוֹחָנָן בֶּן נוּרִי. אִם נִלְקָחִים בְּכֶסֶף מַעֲשֵׂר. מְטַמְּאִין טוּמְאַת אוֹכְלִין. וְאִם אֵינָן מְטַמֵּא טוּמְאַת אוֹכְלִין. אַף הֵן לֹא יְלָקְחוּ בְּכֶסֶף מַעֲשֵׂר: רִבִּי יוֹחָנָן אָמַר. חֲמָרִים. מְטַמְּאִין טוּמְאַת אוֹכְלִין וְאֵינָן נִיקָחִין בְּכֶסֶף מַעֲשֵׂר.

קְרוּיָיה. דְּתַנִּינָן תַּמָּן קְרוּיָה שֶׁהִטְבִּילָהּ בְּמַיִם שֶׁהֵן רְאוּיִין לְקַדֵּשׁ וכו'. רִבִּי יוֹחָנָן אָמַר. חוֹמָרִין. אֵין מְקַדְּשִׁין בָּהּ לֹא בַתְּחִילָּה וְלֹא בַסּוֹף.

מָבוֹי. דְּתַנִּינָן תַּמָּן וְכֵן מָבוֹי שֶׁנִּיטְלָה קוֹרָתוֹ כו'. רִבִּי יוֹחָנָן אָמַר. חוֹמָרִין. אֲסוּרִין בֵּין בְּשַׁבָּת זוֹ בֵּין בְּשַׁבָּת הַבָּאָה.

גֵּר. דְּתַנֵּי. גֵּר שֶׁנִּתְגַּיֵּיר וְהָיוּ לוֹ יֵינוֹת. וְאָמַר. בָּרִי לִי שֶׁלֹּא נִתְנַסֵּךְ מֵהֶן. בִּזְמַן שֶׁנַּעֲשׂוּ עַל גַּב עַצְמָן. טְהוֹרִים לוֹ וּטְמֵאִים לָאֲחֵרִים. עַל גַּב אֲחֵרִים. טְמֵאִין בֵּין לוֹ וּבֵין לָאֲחֵרִים. רִבִּי עֲקִיבָה אוֹמֵר. אִם טְהוֹרִין לוֹ. יְהוּ טְהוֹרִין לָאֲחֵרִים. אִם טְמֵאִין לָאֲחֵרִים. טְמֵאִים לוֹ. רִבִּי יוֹחָנָן אָמַר. לְחוֹמָרִין. טְמֵאִים בֵּין לוֹ וּבֵין לָאֲחֵרִים.

עַם הָאָרֶץ. דְּתַנֵּי. עַם הָאָרֶץ שֶׁנִּתְמַנָּה לִהְיוֹת חָבֵר. וְהָיוּ לוֹ טְהוֹרוֹת וְאָמַר. בָּרִי לִי שֶׁנַּעֲשׂוּ בְטַהֲרָה. בִּזְמַן שֶׁנַּעֲשׂוּ עַל גַּב עַצְמוֹ. טְהוֹרוֹת לוֹ וּטְמֵאוֹת לָאֲחֵרִים. עַל גַּב אֲחֵרִים. טְמֵאוֹת בֵּין

לוֹ בֵּין לַאֲחֵרִים. רִבִּי עֲקִיבָה אוֹמֵר. אִם טְהוֹרוֹת לוֹ טְהוֹרוֹת לַאֲחֵרִים. אִם טְמֵיאוֹת לַאֲחֵרִים.
טְמֵאוֹת לוֹ. רִבִּי יוֹחָנָן אָמַר. חוֹמָרִין. טְמֵאוֹת בֵּין לוֹ וּבֵין לַאֲחֵרִים.

[60]Rebbi Johanan said, *costos*, and hollowed squash, and alley, and convert, and vulgar, are restrictive.

Costos as we have stated[61], "*costos*, and cardamon, and important spices[62] may be bought with tithe money[63] but do not become impure by impurity of foodstuff, the words of Rebbi Aqiba. Rebbi Johanan ben Nuri said, if they may be bought with tithe money they become impure by impurity of foodstuff, and if they do not become impure by impurity of foodstuff they may not be bought with tithe money." Rebbi Johanan said, restrictive[64]: they become impure by impurity of foodstuff and may not be bought with tithe money.

Hollowed squash as we have stated[65]: "A hollowed squash which one immersed is water suitable for sanctification, etc." Rebbi Johanan said, restrictive, one may not sanctify either at the beginning or at the end.

Alley, as we have stated there[66], "or an alley whose beam was removed, etc." Rebbi Johanan said, restrictive, it is forbidden both on this Sabbath and the coming Sabbath[59].

Proselyte, as it was stated: If a proselyte converted while he had wines, and said, it is clear to me that no libations were made from it, if he made it by himself it is pure for him but impure for others[67], by others it is impure both for him and for others. Rebbi Aqiba said, if they are pure for him they should be pure for others; if impure for others they should be impure for him. Rebbi Johanan said, restrictive, impure for him and for others.

Vulgar, as it was stated: If a vulgar person who was inducted as a fellow[68] has food made in purity and he said, it is clear to me that it was prepared in purity, if he made it by himself it is pure for him but impure for others, by others it is impure both for him and for others. Rebbi Aqiba said, if they are pure for him they should be pure for others; if impure for others they should be impure for him. Rebbi Johanan said, restrictive, impure for him and for others.

60 A shortened version of a text in *Hagigah* 3:4 (79c l.22).
61 Mishnah *Uqesin* 3:5. תנן is Babylonian Aramaic. *Costos,-i, f.*, Greek κόστος, an Oriental aromatic plant.
61 Spices used for incense. These spices are not food but may be used as additives in the preparation of food.
62 Money dedicated as Second Tithe which may be spent only on pure food or drink in Jerusalem.
63 The Mishnah is stated as an argument, not as a statement, to permit in practice to accept each argument even though this results in two mutually contradictory restrictions.
64 Mishnah *Parah* 5:3. "Sanctify" means to put some of the ashes of the Red Cow into the water to use it to purify from the impurity of the dead. This water has to be taken from flowing water (*Num.* 19:17).

Since the squash, used as a pot, will absorb of this water, immediately after it has been immersed in flowing water it might be used in the ceremony, but later the water retained in its walls will invalidate new water drawn by the hollowed squash. In the Mishnah, R. Joshua argues that if at the start the squash was acceptable it always should be acceptable, if later it is not acceptable neither should it be at the start (since the point in time when it becomes unacceptable is not well defined.)
65 This is here, Mishnah 4, proof that the *Hagigah* text is original.
66 As wine prepared by a Non-Jew, cf. *Avodah zarah,* Chapters 2-5.
67 A fellow is a person observing all rules of purity in the absence of a Temple, cf. Introduction to Tractate *Demay*, pp. 349-350.

(25d line 23) פיס'. רַב הוּנָא אָמַר. אֵין רְשׁוּת הָרַבִּים מְקוּרָה. אָמַר רִבִּי שִׁמְעוֹן בַּר כַּרְסָנָה. וְלֹא מִן הַמִּדְבָּר לָמַדְתָּ. וּמִדְבָּר מְקוּרָה הָיָה. מַתְנִיתִין לֹא אָמְרָה כֵן. אֶלָּא וְכֵן גְּשָׁרִים הַמְפוּלָּשִׁין מְטַלְטְלִין תַּחְתֵּיהֶן בַּשַּׁבָּת דִּבְרֵי רִבִּי יוּדָה. וַחֲכָמִים אוֹסְרִין. לֹא אָמַר אֶלָּא וַחֲכָמִים אוֹסְרִין. הָא חַיָּיב חַטָּאת אֵין כָּאן.

מָהוּ שֶׁיְּהֵא צָרִיךְ מְחִיצָה. רַבָּא אָמַר. צָרִיךְ מְחִיצָה. רִבִּי יוֹסֵי אָמַר. אֵין צָרִיךְ מְחִיצָה. אָמְרוּ חֲבֵרַיָּא קוֹמֵי רִבִּי יוֹסֵי. יָאוּת אָמַר רִבִּי בָּא. דְּתַנִּינָן. אָמַר רִבִּי יוּדָן. לֹא תְהֵא מְחִיצָה גְבוֹהָה מִכּוֹתֶל שֶׁבֵּינֵיהֶן. אָמַר לוֹן. תַּמָּן שֶׁיֵּשׁ שָׁם תִּקְרָה אֵין צָרִיךְ מְחִיצָה. בְּרַם הָכָא שֶׁאֵין שָׁם תִּקְרָה צָרִיךְ מְחִיצָה. דְּאָמַר רַב יְהוּדָה. הָדָא דְאַתְּ מַר. מְפוּלָּשִׁין לִבְקָעָה. אֲבָל אִם הָיוּ מְפוּלָּשִׁין לִרְשׁוּת הָרַבִּים אָסוּר. בְּשֶׁאֵין שָׁם מְחִיצָה. אֲבָל יֵשׁ שָׁם מְחִיצָה מוּתָּר.

Paragraph[68]. Rav Huna said, no public domain[69] is roofed. Rebbi Simeon bar Carsana said, did you not learn from the desert, and was the desert not roofed[70]? Our Mishnah does not say so, but "and similarly open bridges, one carries under them the words of Rebbi Jehudah, but the Sages forbid it." It only says "but the Sages forbid it;" therefore there is no liability of a purification offering[71].

Does it need a partition[72]? Rebbi Abba said, it needs a partition. Rebbi Yose said, it does not need a partition. The colleagues said before Rebbi Yose, does Rebbi Abba not say it correctly? As we have stated[73], "Rebbi Jehudah says, a partition should not be more than the wall between them." He said to them, there[74], where there is a roof, it does not need a partition. But here, where there is no roof, it needs a partition, as Rav Jehudah said, if it is open to an agricultural area[75], but if it is open to the public domain it is forbidden if there are no partitions, but if there is a partition it is permitted.

68 Discussion of Mishnah 5.

69 For the rules of the Sabbath, not in other respects. Babli *Šabbat* 98a.

70 As the Babli *loc. cit.* explains, all rules of the Sabbath are derived from the Tabernacle in the desert, and the space under the carts used by the Levites to transport the disassembled Tabernacle was roofed public domain.

71 Since "forbidden", in contrast to "liable", in talmudic terminology means "rabbinically, not biblically, forbidden."

72 Following R. Jehudah, is the space under a bridge automatically private domain? The roadway represents a roof; does one say that the borders of the roadway define imaginary walls (as stated in Chapter 1, Notes 40,42), or does the definition of private domain imply the existence of actual walls (which seems to be implied by *Šabbat* 16, Note 84)?

73 Mishnah 8:7.

74 In the case of the Mishnah here, where the roadway is a roof.

75 He notes that R. Jehudah considers the area under the bridge as automatic private domain only if that domain is bordered by *karmelit*; if it were bordered by public domain in the biblical sense, even R. Jehudah would require actual partitions (standing or hanging.)

המוציא תפילין פרק עשירי

(fol. 25d) **משנה א:** הַמּוֹצִיא תְפִילִּין מַכְנִיסָן זוּג זוּג. רַבָּן גַּמְלִיאֵל אוֹמֵר שְׁנַיִם שְׁנַיִם. בַּמֶּה דְבָרִים אֲמוּרִים בַּיְשָׁנוֹת אֲבָל בַּחֲדָשׁוֹת פָּטוּר. מְצָאָן צְבָתִים אוֹ כְרִיכוֹת מַחְשִׁיךְ עֲלֵיהֶן וּמְבִיאָן. וּבַסַּכָּנָה מְכַסָּן וְהוֹלֵךְ לוֹ:

Mishnah 1: He who finds *tefillin*[1] brings them in pair by pair; Rabban Gamliel says, two by two[2]. When has this been said? For used ones, but for new ones[3] he is not liable. If he found them in heaps or bundles[4] he stays there until it becomes dark and then brings them, but in times of danger[5] he covers them and goes away.

משנה ב: רִבִּי שִׁמְעוֹן אוֹמֵר נוֹתְנִין לַחֲבֵירוֹ וַחֲבֵירוֹ לַחֲבֵירוֹ עַד שֶׁהוּא מַגִּיעַ לֶחָצֵר הַחִיצוֹנָה. וְכֵן בְּנוֹ נוֹתְנוֹ לַחֲבֵירוֹ וַחֲבֵירוֹ לַחֲבֵירוֹ אֲפִילוּ הֵן מֵאָה. רִבִּי יְהוּדָה אוֹמֵר נוֹתֵן אָדָם חָבִית לַחֲבֵירוֹ וַחֲבֵירוֹ לַחֲבֵירוֹ אֲפִילוּ חוּץ לַתְּחוּם. אָמְרוּ לוֹ לֹא תְהַלֵּךְ זוֹ יוֹתֵר מֵרַגְלֵי בְעָלֶיהָ:

Mishnah 2: Rebbi Simeon says, he gives them to another person, and this one to another, until one reaches the outermost courtyard[6]. Similarly with his son[7], he gives him to another person, and this one to another, even if they are one hundred. Rebbi Jehudah says, a person may give an amphora to another person, and this one to another, even outside the Sabbath domain. They said to him, it should go no farther than its owner's feet[8].

משנה ג: הַקּוֹרֵא בַסֵּפֶר עַל הָאַסְקוּפָּה וְנִתְגַּלְגַּל הַסֵּפֶר מִיָּדוֹ גּוֹלְלוֹ אֶצְלוֹ. הָיָה קוֹרֵא בְרֹאשׁ הַגַּג וְנִתְגַּלְגַּל הַסֵּפֶר מִיָּדוֹ עַד שֶׁלֹּא הִגִּיעַ לַעֲשָׂרָה טְפָחִים גּוֹלְלוֹ אֶצְלוֹ וּמִשֶּׁהִגִּיעַ לַעֲשָׂרָה טְפָחִים הוֹפְכוֹ עַל הַכְּתָב. רִבִּי יְהוּדָה אוֹמֵר אֲפִילוּ אֵינוֹ מְסוּלָּק מִן הָאָרֶץ אֶלָּא כִמְלוֹא הַחוּט גּוֹלְלוֹ אֶצְלוֹ. רִבִּי שִׁמְעוֹן אוֹמֵר אֲפִילוּ בָאָרֶץ עַצְמָהּ גּוֹלְלוֹ אֶצְלוֹ שֶׁאֵין דָּבָר מִשּׁוּם שְׁבוּת עוֹמֵד בִּפְנֵי כִתְבֵי הַקּוֹדֶשׁ:

Mishnah 3: He who reads a scroll on the threshold[9] and the scroll rolls away from his hand, rolls it back to himself[10]. If he was reading on a rooftop and the scroll rolls away from his hand, if it did not reach ten hand-breadths[11] he rolls it back to himself; but after it reached ten hand-breadths he turns it upside down on the writing. Rebbi Jehudah says, even if it is removed from the ground only a thread's width he rolls it back to himself. Rebbi Simeon says, even from the ground itself he rolls it back to himself[10], since no rabbinic Sabbath prohibition stands before Holy Scripture.

משנה ד: זִיז שֶׁלִּפְנֵי הַחַלּוֹן נוֹתְנִין עָלָיו וְנוֹטְלִין מִמֶּנּוּ בַּשַּׁבָּת. עוֹמֵד אָדָם בִּרְשׁוּת הַיָּחִיד וּמְטַלְטֵל בִּרְשׁוּת הָרַבִּים בִּרְשׁוּת הָרַבִּים וּמְטַלְטֵל בִּרְשׁוּת הַיָּחִיד. וּבִלְבַד שֶׁלֹּא יוֹצִיא חוּץ לְאַרְבַּע אַמּוֹת: לֹא יַעֲמוֹד אָדָם בִּרְשׁוּת הַיָּחִיד וְיַשְׁתִּין בִּרְשׁוּת הָרַבִּים בִּרְשׁוּת הָרַבִּים וְיַשְׁתִּין בִּרְשׁוּת הַיָּחִיד. וְכֵן לֹא יָרוֹק. רַבִּי יְהוּדָה אוֹמֵר אַף מִי שֶׁנִּתְלַשׁ רוּקוֹ מִפִּיו לֹא יְהַלֵּךְ אַרְבַּע אַמּוֹת עַד שֶׁיָּרוֹק:

Mishnah 4: On a ledge in front of a window[12] one puts things on the Sabbath and removes from there. A person may stand in a private domain and move something in the public domain, in the public domain and move something in the private, on condition that he not move it more than four cubits. A person may not stand in a private domain and urinate in the public, or in the public and urinate in the private. Similarly, he may not spit. Rebbi Jehudah says, even somebody whose spittle was accumulating should not walk four cubits before spitting[13].

משנה ה: לֹא יַעֲמוֹד אָדָם בִּרְשׁוּת הַיָּחִיד וְיִשְׁתֶּה בִּרְשׁוּת הָרַבִּים. בִּרְשׁוּת הָרַבִּים וְיִשְׁתֶּה בִּרְשׁוּת הַיָּחִיד אֶלָּא אִם כֵּן הִכְנִיס רֹאשׁוֹ וְרוּבּוֹ לְמָקוֹם שֶׁהוּא שׁוֹתֶה וְכֵן בַּגַּת. קוֹלֵט אָדָם מִן הַמַּזְחִילָה לְמַטָּה מֵעֲשָׂרָה טְפָחִים וּמִן הַצִּנּוֹר וּמִכָּל־מָקוֹם שׁוֹתֶה:

Mishnah 5: A person may not stand in a private domain and drink[14] in the public domain, in the public domain and drink in a private domain, unless he put his head and most of his body there where he drinks; the same holds for a wine press. A person may collect[15] from a leader lower than ten hand-breadths, and drink[16] anywhere from a gutter.

משנה ו: בּוֹר בִּרְשׁוּת הָרַבִּים וְחֻלְיָתוֹ גְבוֹהַּ עֲשָׂרָה טְפָחִים חַלּוֹן שֶׁעַל גַּבָּיו מְמַלִּין מִמֶּנּוּ בַּשַּׁבָּת. אַשְׁפּוֹת בִּרְשׁוּת הָרַבִּים גְּבוֹהַּ עֲשָׂרָה טְפָחִים חַלּוֹן שֶׁעַל גַּבָּהּ שׁוֹפְכִין לְתוֹכָהּ מַיִם בַּשַּׁבָּת:

Mishnah 6 If the railing around a cistern in the public domain is ten hand-breadths high, one may fill from it through a window above it on the Sabbath[17]. If a dungheap in the public domain is ten hand-breadths high, one may pour waste water onto it through a window above it on the Sabbath.

משנה ז: אִילָן שֶׁהוּא מֵיסַךְ עַל הָאָרֶץ אִם אֵין נוֹפוֹ גָּבוֹהַּ מִן הָאָרֶץ שְׁלֹשָׁה טְפָחִים מְטַלְטְלִין תַּחְתָּיו שָׁרָשָׁיו גְּבוֹהִין מִן הָאָרֶץ שְׁלֹשָׁה טְפָחִים לֹא יֵשֵׁב עֲלֵיהֶן. הַדֶּלֶת שֶׁבַּמּוּקְצֶה וַחֲדָקִים שֶׁבַּפִּרְצָה וּמַחֲצָלֵת אֵין נוֹעֲלִין בָּהֶן אֶלָּא אִם כֵּן הָיוּ גְבוֹהִין מִן הָאָרֶץ:

Mishnah 7: A tree which gives a round shadow[18] on the ground, if its crown is less than three hand-breadths from the ground one may carry under it[19]. One may not put back the door of a shed[20], or the thorns in a breach, or a mat, unless they are higher than the ground.

משנה ח: לֹא יַעֲמוֹד אָדָם בִּרְשׁוּת הַיָּחִיד וְיִפְתַּח בִּרְשׁוּת הָרַבִּים בִּרְשׁוּת הָרַבִּים וְיִפְתַּח בִּרְשׁוּת הַיָּחִיד אֶלָּא אִם כֵּן עָשׂוּ לוֹ מְחִיצָה גְּבוֹהָה עֲשָׂרָה טְפָחִים דִּבְרֵי רִבִּי מֵאִיר. אָמְרוּ לוֹ מַעֲשֶׂה בְשׁוּק שֶׁל פַּטָּמִין שֶׁהָיָה בִירוּשָׁלַםִ שֶׁהָיוּ נוֹעֲלִין וּמַנִּיחִין אֶת הַמַּפְתֵּחַ בְּחַלּוֹן שֶׁעַל הַפֶּתַח. רִבִּי יוֹסֵי אוֹמֵר שׁוּק שֶׁל צַמָּרִין הָיָה:

Mishnah 8: A person may not stand in a private domain and unlock in the public domain, in the public domain and unlock in a private domain unless there was made for him a partition ten hand-breadths high, the words of Rebbi Meïr[21]. They told him, it happened at the market of the cattle feeders in Jerusalem that they locked up and put the key into the window above the door. Rebbi Yose says, it was the market of the wool vendors[22].

משנה ט: נֶגֶר שֶׁיֵּשׁ בְּרֹאשׁוֹ קְלוֹסְטְרָא רִבִּי לְעָזָר אוֹסֵר וְרִבִּי יוֹסֵה מַתִּיר. אָמַר רִבִּי לְעָזָר מַעֲשֶׂה שֶׁל בֵּית הַכְּנֶסֶת בִּטְבֶרְיָה שֶׁהָיוּ נוֹהֲגִין בּוֹ הֶיתֵּר עַד (fol. 26a) שֶׁבָּא רַבָּן גַּמְלִיאֵל וְהַזְּקֵנִים וְאָסְרוּ לָהֶן. רִבִּי יוֹסֵה אוֹמֵר אִיסּוּר הָיוּ נָהֲגִין בּוֹ בָּא רַבָּן גַּמְלִיאֵל וְהַזְּקֵנִים וְהִתִּירוּהוּ לָהֶן:

Mishnah 9: If a bolt is topped by a lock[23], Rebbi Eleazar forbids and Rebbi Yose permits. Rebbi Eleazar said, it happened at the synagogue of Tiberias that they used to permit it until Rabban Gamliel and the Elders came and forbade it to them. Rebbi Yose says, they used to consider it forbidden when Rabban Gamliel and the Elders came and permitted it to them.

משנה י: נֶגֶר הַנִּגְרָר נוֹעֲלִין בּוֹ בַּמִּקְדָּשׁ אֲבָל לֹא בַמְּדִינָה. וְהַמּוּנָּח כָּאן וְכָאן אָסוּר. רִבִּי יְהוּדָה אוֹמֵר הַמּוּנָּח בַּמִּקְדָּשׁ וְהַנִּגְרָר בַּמְּדִינָה: מַחֲזִירִין צִיר הַתַּחְתּוֹן בַּמִּקְדָּשׁ אֲבָל לֹא בַמְּדִינָה. הָעֶלְיוֹן כָּאן וְכָאן אָסוּר.

Mishnah 10: With a dragged bolt[24] one locks at the Temple but not in the countryside, but the one left alone is forbidden here and there. Rebbi Jehudah says, the one left alone in the Temple and the dragged one in the countryside. One may replace the lower hinge at the Temple but not in the countryside; the upper one is forbidden here and there[25].

משנה יא: מַחֲזִירִין רְטִיָּה בַּמִּקְדָּשׁ אֲבָל לֹא בַמְּדִינָה אִם בַּתְּחִלָּה כָּאן וְכָאן אָסוּר. קוֹשְׁרִין נִימִין בַּמִּקְדָּשׁ אֲבָל לֹא בַמְּדִינָה אִם בַּתְּחִלָּה כָּאן וְכָאן אָסוּר. חוֹתְכִין יַבֶּלֶת בַּמִּקְדָּשׁ אֲבָל לֹא בַמְּדִינָה אִם בִּכְלִי כָּאן וְכָאן אָסוּר:

Mishnah 11: One replaces a wound dressing in the Temple[26] but not in the countryside; a new one is forbidden here and there. One ties strings[27] in the Temple but not in the countryside; a new one is forbidden here and there. One cuts a wart in the Temple[28] but not in the countryside; using an implement is forbidden here and there.

משנה יב: כֹּהֵן שֶׁלָּקָה בְאֶצְבָּעוֹ כּוֹרֵךְ עָלֶיהָ גֶמִי בַּמִּקְדָּשׁ אֲבָל לֹא בַמְּדִינָה אִם לֹא הוֹצִיא דָם כָּאן וְכָאן אָסוּר. בּוֹזְקִין מֶלַח עַל גַּבֵּי הַכֶּבֶשׁ בִּשְׁבִיל שֶׁלֹּא יַחֲלִיק וּמְמַלִּין מִבּוֹר הַגּוֹלָה בַּגַּלְגַּל בַּשַּׁבָּת מִבּוֹר הַגָּדוֹל וּמִבְּאֵר הַקַּר בְּיוֹם טוֹב:

Mishnah 12: A Cohen who has a wound on his finger binds bast on it in the Temple but not in the countryside[29]; it there is no blood[30] it is forbidden here and there. One sprinkles salt on the ramp[31] so it should not be slippery and one fills from the cistern of the Diaspora with a wheel on the Sabbath[32], from the large cistern and from the cold well[33] on a holiday.

משנה יג: שֶׁרֶץ שֶׁנִּמְצָא בַמִּקְדָּשׁ כֹּהֵן מוֹצִיאוֹ בַּהֲמְיָנוֹ שֶׁלֹּא לְשַׁהוֹת אֶת הַטֻּמְאָה דִּבְרֵי רַבִּי יוֹחָנָן בֶּן בְּרוֹקָא. רַבִּי יְהוּדָה אוֹמֵר בִּצְבַת שֶׁל עֵץ שֶׁלֹּא לְהַרְבּוֹת אֶת הַטֻּמְאָה.

Mishnah 13: If a crawling animal[34] was found in the Temple, a Cohen carries it outside in his belt in order not to continue the impurity, the words of Rebbi Johanan ben Beroqa. Rebbi Jehudah says, with wooden tongs[35] in order not to increase impurity.

משנה יד: מֵאֵיכָן מוֹצִיאִין אוֹתוֹ מִן הַהֵיכָל וּמִן הָאוּלָם וּמִבֵּין הָאוּלָם וְלַמִּזְבֵּחַ דִּבְרֵי רַבִּי שִׁמְעוֹן בֶּן נַנָּס. רַבִּי עֲקִיבָא אוֹמֵר מָקוֹם שֶׁחַיָּיבִין עַל זְדוֹנוֹ כָּרֵת וְעַל שִׁגְגָתוֹ חַטָּאת מִשָּׁם מוֹצִיאִין אוֹתוֹ וּשְׁאָר כָּל־הַמְּקוֹמוֹת כּוֹפִין עָלָיו פְּסַכְתֵּר. רַבִּי שִׁמְעוֹן אוֹמֵר מָקוֹם שֶׁהִתִּירוּ לְךָ חֲכָמִים מִשֶּׁלְּךָ נָתְנוּ לְךָ שֶׁלֹּא הִתִּירוּ לְךָ אֶלָּא מִשּׁוּם שְׁבוּת:

Mishnah 14: From where does one remove it? From the Temple Hall, and the vestibule, and from between the vestibule and the altar, the words of Rebbi Simeon ben Nannas[36]. Rebbi Aqiba says, from a place where one is liable for extirpation in case of criminal intent and a purification offering if in error one removes it; at all other places one places a wine cooler[37] over it. Rebbi Simeon said, at a place where the Sages permitted it to you they gave it from your own since they only permitted because of rabbinic Sabbath restrictions[38].

1   Phylacteries, to be worn on weekdays, one on the arm and one on the head. Since they contain passages of Torah (*Ex.* 13:1-10, 11-16; *Deut.* 6:4-9, 11:13-21), they are holy and may not be left unprotected lying in the open on the road. Since the rule that phylacteries are *muqseh* and not to be worn on the Sabbath is rabbinic, in case of need the rabbinic restriction is waved; the *tefillin* may be worn as clothing; bringing them to a safe place in this way is a meritorious act, not a Sabbath desecration.

2   Even though on weekdays one never wears *tefillin* this way, since it is possible to wear two pairs simultaneously it is preferable to reduce the number of trips, i. e., the number of violations of rabbinic Sabbath restrictions.

3   They look like *tefillin* but in fact might be amulets for which no rules are waived.

4   Heaps are lightly tied together, bundles are tied pair by pair.

5   When the exercise of Jewish rites is prosecuted by the government.

6   Since nobody transports the *tefillin* more than 4 cubits, the entire heap may be brought to safety in one operation. The only rabbinic restriction which is violated in this case is that of *muqseh*.

7   A baby circumcised in the fields.

8   No vessel under the control of its owner may be transported into a domain inaccessible to its owner on the Sabbath.

9   *Šabbat* 1, Note 68.

10   Even though part of the scroll is now in the public domain, as long as he holds on to part of the scroll, rolling it back is not transporting from public to private domain.

11   Since the airspace over public domain above 10 hand-breadths from the ground is exempt space, taking the scroll back from the air over the public domain does not infringe any rabbinic rule.

12   If it is at least 4 hand-breadths wide and 10 hand-breadths above ground, it is a separate domain, and may be used by people in the house and on the street.

13   Since the spittle is to be spat out, carrying it in the mouth for more than 4 cubits would be a Sabbath violation.

14   Using a cup. If he would bring the cup to drink in the public domain it would be a biblical Sabbath violation; therefore drinking with his body in the public domain is a rabbinic violation.

15   Using a cup. Since the water is filled in the public domain, the entire transaction is in the public domain (on condition that the place of filling not be within 3 hand-breadths of the roof.)

16   Without a vessel, even within 3 hand-breadths of the roof.)

17   Since the space within the enclosure is private domain and the airspace above 10 hand-breadths from the ground is exempt space, it is possible to use one private domain while standing in another private domain if the connection is through exempt space.

18   The Babli and Maimonides read מיסך.

19   If the branches reach close to the ground for more than half the

circumference, they define the space under the tree as a private domain.

20   It is presumed that the door does not move on hinges but has to be taken off and put back on some hooks. Then it is impossible to move the door without creating an impression in the dirt floor. Since this is a necessary consequence of moving the door, it qualifies as intentional digging, a Sabbath violation. The same argument applies to the other examples in the Mishnah.

21   From the rules of the Sabbath it would be possible to take a key in the public domain either from a place not 4 cubits away or above 10 hand-breadths from the ground, open the door, and return the key. R. Meïr forbids, to avoid that the key inadvertently would be brought into the house (private domain) or be moved in the public domain lower than 10 hand-breadths from the ground. It is possible to use a key if the place of use is *karmelit* or private domain.

22   They disagree about the facts of the case, not the underlying practice.

23   Latin *claustrum*, *-i*, *n.*, Greek κλεῖστρον, τό. Since the bolt with a thick end could also be used as a bludgeon it should qualify as an implement which can be moved freely. Nevertheless R. Eleazar (in the Babli R. Eliezer, unlikely to be correct) forbids unless it be tied to the building since otherwise inserting the bolt would be classified as building.

24   It is loosely tied to the building, not noticed to be part of it. It is forbidden to replace a bolt separate from the building and not tied to anything since this would be building.

25   Hinges of doors of chests. The lower one does not carry a load and may be inserted without tools or force, at most a rabbinic violation; the upper one which carries the load must be fixed either by being hammered in or fixed with screws, both biblical Sabbath violations.

26   Since the garments of the priests are biblically prescribed, they cannot wear anything (e. g., shoes) which would be between them and the holy places, vessels, or sacrifices. Therefore the Cohen wearing a bandage must remove it during his period of service. He may replace it in the Temple, where rabbinic restrictions are suspended, but not outside.

27   Greek νῆμα, ἡ, "string" of musical instruments. Tying a new string would make an unusable instrument usable; this is biblically forbidden also in the Temple where biblically forbidden work on the Sabbath is only permitted for the explicitly required sacrifices. Making a permanent knot is also biblically forbidden (Mishnah *Šabbat* 7:2), only making a temporary loop is permitted. Since this leaves the violin unusable, the Mishnah is re-interpreted in the Halakhah.

28   A wart disqualifies an animal as sacrifice (*Lev.* 22:22); if it developed on the Sabbath and could not have been removed before that day it may be removed as long as no tools are used and therefore biblical desecration of the Sabbath is avoided..

29   The bast is no textile and is permitted. While curing illnesses is rabbinically forbidden on the Sabbath and dressing is part of the healing process, it is permitted in the Temple if needed for the service.

30   In the Babli and Maimonides: If in

order to extract blood.
31 The incline leading from the floor of the Temple court to the top of the altar.
32 Which otherwise is rabbinically forbidden since it could lead to agricultural use.
33 A certain water well, not every well.
34 One of the animals whose carcass is a source of original impurity (*Lev.* 11:29-30). It has to be removed to avoid spreading impurity. Even though the Cohen's belt is sanctified, its impurity may be removed by the sundown following its immersion in a *miqweh*.

35 Wooden implements which do not have a cavity are impervious to impurity.
36 But at all other places in the Temple court one places a metal pot over it and removes it after the end of the Sabbath.
37 Greek ψυατήρ, -ῆρος. It must be a metal pot whose impurity can be removed in a *miqweh*, not a clay pot which would have to be broken into pieces.
38 Rabbinic leniencies regarding rabbinic restrictions do not necessarily have to follow a logically consistent system.

(26a line 24) הַמּוֹצֵא תְפִילִּין כול'. הַמּוֹצֵא תְפִילִּין מַכְנִיסָן זוּג זוּג. דֶּרֶךְ מַלְבּוּשׁ. אַחַת בְּרֹאשׁוֹ וְאַחַת בִּזְרוֹעוֹ. רַבָּן גַּמְלִיאֵל אוֹמֵר שְׁנַיִם שְׁנַיִם. שְׁנַיִם בְּרֹאשׁ וּשְׁנַיִם בִּזְרוֹעַ.

"*"He who finds tefillin,*" etc. "He who finds *tefillin*[1] brings them in pair by pair;" as clothing, one on his head and one on his arm. "Rabban Gamliel says, two by two[2]," two on his head and two on his arm.

רִבִּי אַבָּהוּ רִבִּי אֶלְעָזָר. הַנּוֹתֵן תְּפִילִּין בַּלַּיְלָה עוֹבֵר בַּעֲשֵׂה. שֶׁנֶּאֱמַר וְשָׁמַרְתָּ אֶת־הַחוּקָּה הַזֹּאת מִיָּמִים יָמִימָה: יָמִים וְלֹא לֵילוֹת. וְהָא רִבִּי אַבָּהוּ יָתִיב וּמַתְנֵי בְּרַמְשָׁא וּתְפִילִּין עָלֽוֹי. מִצְדָדִין הָיוּ כְּמִין פִּיקְרִין הָיוּ בְּיָדוֹ. אִית דְּבָעֵי מֵימַר. לֹא מַר אֶלָּא. הַנּוֹתֵן. אֲבָל אִם הָיוּ עָלָיו מִבְּעוֹד יוֹם מוּתָּר. וְאִית דְּבָעֵי מֵימַר. מִצְוָתָן עַד שֶׁתְּכַלֶּה רֶגֶל מִן הַשּׁוּק. אִית דְּבָעֵי נִשְׁמְעִינָהּ מִן הָדָא. וְהָיוּ לְךָ לְאוֹת. מִי שֶׁצְּרִיכִין אוֹת. יָצְאוּ שַׁבָּתוֹת וְיָמִים טוֹבִים שֶׁהֵן גּוּפָן אוֹת. וְלֹא כְבָר כָּתוּב מִיָּמִים יָמִימָה. לֵית לָךְ אֶלָּא כַּיי דָּמַר רִבִּי יוֹחָנָן. כָּל־מִילָה דְלָא מְחוּוְּרָא מְסַמְּכִין לֵיהּ מִן אַתְרִין סַגִּין.

[39]Rebbi Abbahu in the name of Rebbi Eleazar[40]: He who puts on *tefillin* in the night transgresses a positive commandment. What is the reason? *You shall keep this law . . ., from day to day*[41]; "days" not nights. But Rebbi Abbahu sat studying at night with his *tefillin* on his head! He put them on the side; they were like a deposit[42] in his keeping. Some want to say, he only meant "not to put them on," but when they were on him during daytime it would be permitted. Some want to say that the obligation is until the foot is disappearing from public places[43]. Some want to say, let us hear it from the following: *It shall be for you a sign*[44], when you need it for a sign, but not

holiday or Sabbaths that are all sign. But is it not written *from day to day*? You have only what Rebbi Johanan said: Everything that is not clear one supports from many places.

נָשִׁים מְנַיִין. וְלִמַּדְתֶּם אֹתָם אֶת־בְּנֵיכֶם. וְלֹא בְנוֹתֵיכֶם. הַחַיָּיב בַּתּוֹרָה חַיָּיב בִּתְפִילִּין. נָשִׁים שֶׁאֵין חַיָּיבוֹת בַּתּוֹרָה אֵין חַיָּיבוֹת בִּתְפִילִין. הֲתִיבוּן. הֲרֵי מִיכַל בַּת שָׁאוּל הָיְתָה לוֹבֶשֶׁת תְּפִילִּין. אֵשֶׁת יוֹנָה הָיְתָה עוֹלָה לָרֶגֶל. וְלֹא מִיחוּ בְיָדָם חֲכָמִים. רִבִּי חִזְקִיָּה בְּשֵׁם רִבִּי אַבָּהוּ. אִשְׁתּוֹ שֶׁלְּיוֹנָה הֵיאשָׁבָה. מִיכַל בַּת שָׁאוּל מִיחוּ בָהּ חֲכָמִים.

Women from where? *And you should teach them to your sons*[45], but not to your daughters. Anyone who is obliged to study Torah is obliged for *tefillin*, women who are not obliged to study Torah are not obliged for *tefillin* They objected, but did not Michal, the daughter of Saul, wear *tefillin*, and did not the wife of Jonah make the pilgrimage to the Temple, and the Sages did not object?. Rebbi Ḥisqiah in the name of Rebbi Abbahu: Jonah's wife was turned back, the Sages objected[46] to Michal the daughter of Saul.

39 Most of this and the next paragraph are in *Berakhot* 2:3, Notes 104-115. A text closer to the formulation here is in *Pesiqta Rabbati* 22 (ed. Ish-Shalom p. 112b, Notes 47-54).

40 In *Pesiqta rabbati*: R. Johanan.

41 *Ex.* 13:10.

42 Reading with the two other sources פיקרין instead of פיקדון "wool flakes".

43 As long as there is traffic in the streets. This statement is missing in *Berakhot*.

44 *Ex.* 13:19.

45 *Deut.* 11:19.

46 In both parallel texts: מיחו בידיה "interfered with her", i. e., actually forbade it.

(26a line 40) הֲווֹן בָּעֵי מֵימַר. עַל דַּעְתּוֹן דְּרַבָּנָן אֵין מְחוּוָּר. עַל דַּעְתֵּיהּ דְּרַבָּן גַּמְלִיאֵל מְחוּוָּר. אָמַר רִבִּי יִרְמְיָה בְּשֵׁם רִבִּי שְׁמוּאֵל. שִׁיעֲרוּ לוֹמַר. עַד מָקוֹם שֶׁגָּבְהוֹ שֶׁל רֹאשׁ מַחֲזִיק. וְכַמָּה מַחֲזִיק. שְׁתַּיִם. מֵעַתָּה אֲפִילוּ בָחוֹל. אָמַר רִבִּי חַגַּיי. אִין בָּעֵי מֵיתַב. יְהַב. אָמַר רִבִּי זְרִיקָא. אַסְבְּרִי רַב הַמְנוּנָא. עַד מָקוֹם שֶׁמּוֹחוֹ שֶׁל תִּינוֹק רוֹפֵף. תַּמָּן תַּנִּינָן. עַל תַּרְנְגוֹל שֶׁנִּסְקַל בִּירוּשָׁלַיִם שֶׁהֲרַג אֶת הַנֶּפֶשׁ. רָאָה רֹאשׁוֹ שֶׁל תִּינוֹק רוֹפֵף. הָלַךְ וְנִיקְרוֹ.

They wanted to say, in the rabbi's opinion it is not clear; in Rabban Gamliel's opinion it is clear[47]. Rebbi Jeremiah said in the name of Rebbi Samuel: They estimated to say, up to the place where it can be placed on the top of the head[48]. For how many is there space? Two. Then even on weekdays? Rebbi Ḥaggai said, if he wants to put there, he puts[49]. Rebbi Zeriqa said, Rav Hamnuna explained to me, up to the place where the baby's brain is soft. There we have stated[50]: "About a chicken which was stoned in Jerusalem because it had killed a person." It saw that the skull of the baby was soft; it went and picked it.

47 The rabbis hold that the verse, *it shall be for you a sign,* does not necessarily imply that *tefillin* may not be worn on a Sabbath. Therefore they require that the *tefillin* be worn as if it were a weekday to avoid any Sabbath violation. Rabban Gamliel holds that the inference from the verse is absolutely valid; wearing the *tefillin* is a violation in itself, and therefore he prescribes, not simply permits, wearing two *tefillin* in order to demonstrate that they are not worn *qua tefillin.*

48 The head *tefillin* have to be placed at the top of the forehead, where it becomes horizontal. R. Jeremiah disputes the inference drawn in the first sentence and notes that Rabban Gamliel also may hold that not wearing *tefillin* on the Sabbath is general practice but not biblical commandment; only he biblically permits wearing two pairs of *tefillin* simultaneously.

49 In effect it would be permitted to wear two pairs simultaneously. [*Sefer HaTerumah, Tefillin,* §213 (ed. Warsaw 1897 p. 116c top, ed. Jerusalem 2010, col. 490) reads the passage as inviting people to change the placement of the head *tefillin* at will but permitting only one pair. This seems to be reading the Yerushalmi text on the basis of the Babli 95b.]

50 Mishnai *Idiut* 6:1.

(26a line 47) אָמַר רִבִּי יוֹסֵי. כֵּינִי מַתְנִיתָא. וּבִלְבַד עַל יְדֵי שְׁנַיִם. רִבִּי יוֹסֵי בֵּירִבִּי בּוּן בְּשֵׁם רִבִּי אָחָא. וַאֲפִילוּ שְׁנַיִם שְׁנָיִם. הֲווּ בָּעֵי מֵימַר. עַל דַּעְתּוֹן דְּרַבָּנָן אֵין מְחוּוָּר. עַל דַּעְתֵּיהּ דְּרִבִּי אָחָא מְחוּוָּר. וִיבִיאֵם בְּיָדוֹ. מוּטָב לַהֲבִיאָם דֶּרֶךְ מַלְבּוּשׁ וְלֹא דֶרֶךְ מַשּׂוֹי. מוּטָב לִדְחוֹת אֶת הַשַּׁבָּת פַּעַם אַחַת וְלֹא שְׁנֵי פְעָמִים.

תַּנֵּי. אֶחָד הָאִישׁ וְאֶחָד הָאִשָּׁה. הֲוֹון בָּעֵי מֵימַר. מָאן דָּמַר. מְחוּוָּר הוּא. נִיחָא. מָאן דָּמַר. אֵינוֹ מְחוּוָּר. לֹא יְהֵא מְחוּוָּר אֵצֶל הָאִישׁ וִיהֵא מְחוּוָּר אֵצֶל הָאִשָּׁה. אָמַר רִבִּי לָעְזָר. מָאן תַּנָּא. אִשָּׁה. רַבָּן גַּמְלִיאֵל. דְּתַנֵּי. טָבִי עֶבֶד רַבָּן גַּמְלִיאֵל הָיָה נוֹתֵן תְּפִילִין וְלֹא מִיחוּ בְיָדוֹ חֲכָמִים. וְכָא מִיחוּ בְיָדוֹ. הוּא עֶבֶד הִיא אִשָּׁה.

Rebbi Yose said, so is the Mishnah: Only by pairs[47]. Rebbi Yose ben Rebbi Abun in the name of Rebbi Aḥa: Even by pairs[51]. They wanted to say, in the rabbi's opinion it is not clear; in Rabban Aḥa's opinion it is clear[52]. Could he not bring them in his hand? It is better to bring them as garment[53] not as load. It is better to push the Sabbath away once not twice.

It was stated[54]: Whether he be a man or a woman. They wanted to say, he who said that it is clear, is understandable. He who said that it is not clear, should it not be clear for a man but clear for a woman[55]? Rebbi Eleazar said, who is he who stated "woman"? Rabban Gamliel[56]! As it was stated[57]: Tabi the slave of Rabban Gamliel was putting on *tefillin* and the Sages did not interfere with him. Did they here interfere with him[58]? It is the same for a slave or a woman[59].

51   This refers to the statement of Rabban Gamliel in Mishnah 1. R. Aha follows R. Jeremiah in holding that Rabban Gamliel might consider the Sabbath as biblically a time for *tefillin*.

52   A repetition of a sentence from the preceding paragraph , quoted as background for the question in the next sentence. If Rabban Gamliel holds that *tefillin* are biblically forbidden on the Sabbath, and transporting them on the Sabbath is a violation, why not simply carry them?

53   Then the Sabbath is violated only rabbinically.

54   Tosephta 8:15.

55   Since in the preceding it was stated that the Sages disapproved of (or interfered with) a woman putting on *tefillin*, then it should be clear that the Sabbath is not a time for *tefillin* for a woman and the rules for men and women should be different.

56   This is the reading of two of the ms. sources in the Tosephta. In R. Eleazar's opinion, the rabbis might oppose a woman putting on *tefillin* to preserve them on the Sabbath.

57   The same statement in *Sukkah* 2:1 (52d l.45).

58   If this refers to Michal the daughter of Saul it should be "her" not him". It may simply be a copy from the discussion in *Sukkah*, referring to Tabi.

59   Since both women and slaves are exempted from positive commandments tied to fixed times, and *tefillin* are not to be worn during nighttime.

(26a line 56) בַּמֶּה דְבָרִים אֲמוּרִים. בַּיְשָׁנוֹת. אֲבָל בַּחֲדָשׁוֹת מוּתָּר. לָמָּה. יְשָׁנוֹת בְּדוּקוֹת חֲדָשׁוֹת אֵין בְּדוּקוֹת. תַּנֵּי. תְּפִילִין צָרִיךְ לְבוֹדְקָן אַחַת לִשְׁנֵים עָשָׂר חוֹדֶשׁ. דִּבְרֵי רִבִּי. רַבָּן שִׁמְעוֹן בֶּן גַּמְלִיאֵל אוֹמֵר. אֵינָן צְרִיכוֹת בְּדִיקָה. הִלֵּל הַזָּקֵן אוֹמֵר. אֵילוּ מֵאַבֵּי אִמָּה הֵן. מָצָא שְׁנַיִם שְׁלֹשָׁה צְבָתִין בּוֹדֵק זוּג רִאשׁוֹן מִצְּבַת רִאשׁוֹן. וְכֵן בַּשֵּׁנִי וְכֵן בַּשְּׁלִישִׁי. יִצְחָק בֶּן אֶלְעָזָר שָׁאַל. אֶחָד חֲזָקָה לְכוּלָּם אוֹ כָּל־אֶחָד וְאֶחָד בִּפְנֵי עַצְמוֹ. אֵין תֵּימַר. אֶחָד חֲזָקָה לְכוּלָן. בּוֹדֵק זוּג רִאשׁוֹן מִצְּבַת רִאשׁוֹן. אֵין תֵּימַר. כָּל־אֶחָד וְאֶחָד חֲזָקָה בִּפְנֵי עַצְמוֹ. בּוֹדֵק שְׁלֹשָׁה זוּגוֹת מִכָּל־צְבָת וּצְבָת.

"When has this been said? For used ones, but for new ones[3] he is free." Why? Old ones are checked, new ones are not checked[60]. It was stated[61]: One has to check *tefillin* once every twelve months, the words of Rebbi. Rabban Simeon ben Gamliel says, they do not need checking. Hillel the Elder said, these are from my maternal grandfather. If he found two or three heaps, he checks the first pair of the first bundle; the same with the second or the third[62]. Isaac ben Eleazar[63] asked: Does one create a presumption for all of them or is each one of them for itself? If you are saying that one creates a presumption for all of them, he checks the first pair of the first heap[64]. If you are saying that each one creates a presumption for itself, he checks three pairs from each heap.

60   This is the practical definition of "new" and "old" in the Mishnah. The obligation to take care of them applies only if it is clear that the items are (rabbinic) *tefillin* and neither amulets nor non-standard *tefillin* (such as the *tefillin* from Qumran).

61   *Mekhilta dR.. Simeon ben Yohai Ba* 17 (ed. Horovitz-Rabin p. 69), cf. *Tanhuma Bo* 14 (end) (*Sefer Wehizhir* ed. I. M. Freimann p. 8), with Shammai in place of Hillel. Quoted by Tosaphot *Menahot* 43a.

62   The presumption is that of validity of the *tefillin*; in general *prima facie* evidence of validity is established by three checks. A similar rule regarding buying *tefillin* from a place not under rabbinic supervision is in Tosephta *Avodah zarah* 3:8.

63   There are at least two Amoraim of this name.

64   In this case one reads the Tosephta as meaning that one may freely choose the batch from which one examines one pair. In the second alternative one has to establish regular presumption of validity for every separate batch. Cf. Babli 97a.

(26a line 65) וּבַסָּכָּנָה מְכַסָּן וְהוֹלֵךְ לוֹ׃ אִם הָיָה עוֹנַת גְּשָׁמִים הֲרֵי זֶה מְעַטֵּף בְּעוֹר וּמְכַסָּן. רִבִּי אָחָא בְּשֵׁם רִבִּי בָּא. הָדָא דְתֵימַר בְּרַךְ. אֲבָל בְּקָשֶׁה כְּמַשּׂוּי הוּא. בְּשֶׁהָיָה הַמָּקוֹם מְנֻדְרָן. אֲבָל לֹא הָיָה הַמָּקוֹם מְנֻדְרָן לֹא בְדָא.

"But in times of danger[5] he covers them and goes away." "If it was in the rainy season he covers himself with leather and covers them.[65]" Rebbi Aḥa in the name of Rebbi Abba: This you are saying if it is soft. But if it is hard it is like a load[66]. If the place was at an incline, but if it was not an incline this does not apply[67].

65   Cf. Tosephta 8:16.

66   He goes home and takes a sheet of soft leather which he uses as a raincoat until he returns to the place of the *tefillin* (or in the case of the Tosephta, a Torah scroll) and covers them. But a hard sheet which cannot be used as a raincoat may not be taken out on the Sabbath since this would be a biblical violation.

67   If the *tefillin* were immersed in standing water and ruined by the time he returns from his house, trying to cover them in leather would be futile; he is not required to do anything.

(26a line 69) פִּיס'. רִבִּי אֱלִיעֶזֶר וְרִבִּי אֲבְדְּיָמֵי תְּרַוַּיְיהוּ בְּשֵׁם רִבִּי מָנָא. חַד אָמַר. בְּתִינוֹק שֶׁלְסַכָּנָה. מוֹתִיב לֵיהּ חַבְרַיָּיא. אִם בְּתִינוֹק שֶׁלְסַכָּנָה יְבִיאוֹ בַיָּד. אָמַר לֵיהּ. בְּיָכוֹל לַהֲבִיאוֹ דֶּרֶךְ הֶיתֵר.

רֵישׁ לָקִישׁ בְּשֵׁם לֵוִי סוֹכַיָא. בִּמְעָרָה מִכַּד לְכַד הִיא מַתְנִיתָא. דְּלָא כֵן רִבִּי יְהוּדָה כְּדַעְתֵּיהּ. דְּרִבִּי יְהוּדָה אוֹמֵר. מַשְׁקֶה טוֹפֵחַ.

Paragraph[68]. Rebbi Eliezer[69] and Rebbi Eudaimon in the name of Rebbi Mana: In the case of a baby in danger[70]. His colleague objected to him: If in the case of a baby in danger should he not carry him in his hand[71]? He answered him, if he can bring him in a permitted way[72].

Rebbi Simeion ben Laqish in the name of Levi from Sokho[73]: If he pours from vessel to vessel[74]. For if it were otherwise, would Rebbi Jehudah follow his own opinion, as Rebbi Jehudah said, fluid to wet[75]?

68 Discussion of Mishnah 2.
69 Read: R. Eleazar. R. Mana is R. Mana I.
70 If Jewish rites are forbidden and the baby is circumcised in the field and has to be carried back to his mother.
71 Since if performing the circumcision in the fields is a necessity it supersedes the prohibitions of the Sabbath (Šabbat 19) or if the actual state of the baby is that of critically ill, saving its life also supersedes the prohibitions of the Sabbath. In any case it seems unnecessary to form a human chain to carry the baby.
72 In the Babli (97b) Levi the old man (סבא).
73 But if no human chain can be formed, the baby is carried by one person.

74 This refers to R. Jehudah's statement that an amphora can be transported like a baby. This is corrected; the amphora cannot be carried more than 4 cubits, but its contents can transported an unlimited distance, since for him fluids are not bound to the place they were in at the start of the Sabbath (Chapter 8, Note 79; Mishnah Beṣah 5:4).
75 This statement is cryptic, since the expression "fluid to wet" is only used in questions regarding the transmission of prohibitions or impurity. R. Jehudah certainly does not hold that wet materials have the status of water. But R. Jehudah's statement in the Mishnah certainly is consistent with his statement in Beṣah 5:4. Cf. Šabbat 2, Note 140.

(26a line 72) פִּיס'. מַתְנִיתָא בְּאִיסְקוּפָּה מוּתֶּרֶת. אֲבָל חוּץ לָאִסְקוּפָּה אֲסוּרָה. תֵּיפְתַּר שֶׁהָיָה יוֹשֵׁב וְקוֹרֵא בּוֹ מִבְּעוֹד יוֹם וְשָׁכַח וְהוֹצִיאוֹ. עַד שֶׁלֹּא הִגִּיעַ לַעֲשָׂרָה טְפָחִים גּוֹלְלוֹ אֶצְלוֹ. מִשֶּׁ הִגִּיעַ לַעֲשָׂרָה טְפָחִים אָסוּר. רִבִּי יַעֲקֹב בַּר אָחָא בְּשֵׁם רִבִּי יָסָא. דְּרִבִּי יוּדָה הִיא דְּאָמַר. אָסוּר לְהִשְׁתַּמֵּשׁ בָּאֲוִיר עֲשָׂרָה טְפָחִים.

מִשֶּׁהִגִּיעַ לַעֲשָׂרָה טְפָחִים הוֹפְכוֹ עַל הַכְּתָב. לָמָּה. שֶׁלֹּא יִתְבַּזֶּה הַכְּתָב. וְאַתְיָיא כְדָמַר רִבִּי אָחָא בְּשֵׁם רִבִּי שְׁמוּאֵל בַּר נַחְמָן. סֵפֶר שֶׁאֵין עָלָיו מַפָּה הוֹפְכוֹ עַל הַכְּתָב שֶׁלֹּא יִתְבַּזֶּה הַכְּתָב. רִבִּי יוּדָה אוֹמֵר אֲפִילוּ אֵינוֹ מְסוּלָּק מִן הָאָרֶץ אֶלָּא מְלֹא הַחוּט גּוֹלְלוֹ אֶצְלוֹ. מִחְלְפָה שִׁיטָתֵיהּ דְּרִבִּי יוּדָה. תַּמָּן הוּא אָמַר. אָסוּר לְהִשְׁתַּמֵּשׁ בָּאֲוִיר עֲשָׂרָה. וָכָא אָמַר הָכֵין. אָמַר רִבִּי יוֹחָנָן. לֵית כָּאן רִבִּי יוּדָה אֶלָּא רִבִּי מֵאִיר. דִּבְרֵי חֲכָמִים. רִבִּי יוֹסֵי אוֹמֵר בְּשֵׁם רִבִּי יוֹחָנָן. לֹא סוֹף דָּבָר סֵפֶר אֶלָּא אֲפִילוּ פַּסוּקְיָא אָמַר.

Paragraph. The Mishnah: On the threshold it is permitted, but outside the threshold it is forbidden[76]. Explain it that he was sitting there reading when it still was daytime, or he forgot and took it out[77]. Before it reaches ten hand-breadths he rolls it back to himself. After it reaches ten hand-breadths it is forbidden. Rebbi Jacob bar Aḥa in the name of Rebbi Yasa: It is Rebbi Jehudah's who said that it is forbidden to use the airspace within ten hand-breadths[78].

"But after it reached ten hand-breadths he turns it upside down on the writing." Why? That the writing should not be debased. This parallels what Rebbi Aḥa said in the name of .Rebbi Samuel bar Naḥman: If a scroll is not covered by a cloth one turns it upside down on the writing so that the writing should not be debased[79].

"Rebbi Jehudah says, even if it is removed from the ground only a thread's width he rolls it back to himself.." The argument of Rebbi Jehudah is inverted. There[78] he says, it is forbidden to use the airspace within ten hand-breadths; and here he says so? Rebbi Joḥanan said, here there is no Rebbi Jehudah, only Rebbi Meïr, the words of the Sages. Rebbi Yose said in the name of Rebbi Joḥanan: Not only a scroll but even a belt[80].

76 In the public domain one may not move anything which is more than 4 cubits from the mover.

77 Since the threshold is *karmelit*, it should have been forbidden to bring the scroll to the threshold in the first place. It either must have been there before the start of the Sabbath or was brought there inadvertently.

78 *Šabbat* 11, Note 49.

79 Also *Megillah* 1:7, 71d l. 31; *Sopherim* 3:16.

80 Latin *fascia, -ae, f.* "band, girdle". The rule of the Mishnah is one of the rules of *karmelit*, not a special leniency for holy writings.

(26b line 9) לֹא אָמַר אֶלָּא אַחַת אֲבָל שְׁתַּיִם אָסוּר. שֶׁאֵין שְׁתֵּי רְשׁוּיוֹת מִשְׁתַּמְּשׁוֹת בִּרְשׁוּת אַחַת. בְּשֶׁאֵין בָּהֶן רוֹחַב אַרְבָּעָה. אֲבָל יֵשׁ בָּהֶן רוֹחַב אַרְבָּעָה הָדָא דָמַר רִבִּי אֲחָא בְשֵׁם רִבִּי יוֹחָנָן. זִיזִין וּכְתָלִין שֶׁגְּבוֹהִין עֲשָׂרָה וְרָחְבִּין אַרְבָּעָה מוּתָּר לְכָאן וּלְכָאן. וּבִלְבַד שֶׁלֹּא יַחֲלִיף.

פיס׳. לֹא סוֹף דָּבָר עוֹמֵד בִּרְשׁוּת הַיָּחִיד וּמְטַלְטֵל בִּרְשׁוּת הָרַבִּים. בִּרְשׁוּת הָרַבִּים וּמְטַלְטֵל בִּרְשׁוּת הַיָּחִיד. וּבִלְבַד שֶׁלֹּא יוֹצִיא חוּץ לְאַרְבַּע אַמּוֹת: אָמַר רַב. מַתְנִיתָא אָמְרָה כֵן. לֹא יַעֲמוֹד אָדָם בִּרְשׁוּת הַיָּחִיד וְיִפְתַּח בִּרְשׁוּת הָרַבִּים בִּרְשׁוּת הָרַבִּים וְיִפְתַּח בִּרְשׁוּת הַיָּחִיד אֶלָּא אִם כֵּן עָשׂוּ לוֹ מְחִיצָה גְבוֹהָה עֲשָׂרָה טְפָחִים. דִּבְרֵי רִבִּי מֵאִיר.

[81]It speaks only about one, but two are forbidden, for two domains cannot use one domain[82]. If it is not four wide. But if it is four wide, that is what Rebbi Aḥa said in the name of Rebbi Joḥanan: Ledges and walls high ten [hand-breadths] and wide four are permitted for both sides, on condition that he may not exchange[83].

Paragraph. Not only[84] "a person may stand in a private domain and move something in the public domain, in the public domain and move something in the private, on condition that he not move it more than four cubits." Rav said, a Mishnah says so, "A person may not stand in a private domain and unlock in the public domain, in the public domain and unlock in a private domain unless there was made for him a partition ten hand-breadths high, the words of Rebbi Meïr[85]."

81 Discussion of Mishnah 4.
82 The Mishnah is formulated in the singular; this implies that from a window of one house one is permitted to use a ledge below the window only if the ledge is not reachable from another house. Here it is assumed that the ledge is not within 10 hand-breadths from the ground; then it would be part of the public domain, but not 4 hand-breadths wide, which would make is a separate domain.

83 Chapter 7, Note 49.
84 The Mishnah is anonymous; it is presumed to follow R. Meïr. But R. Meïr in Mishnah 8 states that one may not stand in one domain and act in another; so either the Mishnah is somebody else's teaching and should not be formulated as anonymous, or one has to emend to "a person may *not* stand."
85 Mishnah 10:8.

(26b line 18) רַב אָמַר. בִּפְתִיחָה. רִבִּי יוֹחָנָן אָמַר. בִּפְתִיחָה. דְּל כֵּן רִבִּי יוּדָה כְדַעְתֵּיהּ דְּאָמַר. מַשְׁקֶה טוֹפַח חִיבּוּר.

לֹא סוֹף דָּבָר עוֹמֵד בִּרְשׁוּת הַיָּחִיד וּמַשְׁתִּין בִּרְשׁוּת הָרַבִּים. אֶלָּא אֲפִילוּ עוֹמֵד בִּרְשׁוּת הָרַבִּים וּמַשְׁתִּין בִּרְשׁוּת הָרַבִּים וְהֵן מִתְגַּלְגְּלִין וְיוֹרְדִין לִרְשׁוּת הַיָּחִיד אָסוּר. אָמַר רִבִּי יוֹסֵי בֵּירִבִּי בּוּן. לֹא סוֹף דָּבָר עוֹמֵד בִּרְשׁוּת הָרַבִּים וּמַשְׁתִּין בִּרְשׁוּת הַיָּחִיד. אֶלָּא אֲפִילוּ עוֹמֵד בִּרְשׁוּת הַיָּחִיד וּמַשְׁתִּין בִּרְשׁוּת הַיָּחִיד וְהֵן מִתְגַּלְגְּלִין וְיוֹרְדִין לִרְשׁוּת הָרַבִּים אָסוּר. אָמַר רִבִּי יָסָא. הָדָא אָמְרָה סִילוֹן הָעוֹמֵד בִּרְשׁוּת הָרַבִּים גָּבוֹהַּ עֲשָׂרָה וְרָחָב אַרְבָּעָה אֵין שׁוֹפְכִין לְתוֹכוֹ מַיִם שֶׁמִּתְגַּלְגְּלִין וְיוֹרְדִין.

Rav said, about soot. Rebbi Johanan said, about soot[86], since does not Rebbi Jehudah say, moist fluid creates a connection?

Not only if he stands in a private domain and urinates in the public domain, but even if he stands in the public domain and urinates in the public domain, but if it rolls down into a private domain it is forbidden. Rebbi Yose ben Rebbi Abun said, not only if he stands in the public domain and urinates in a private domain, but even if he stands in a private domain and urinates in a private domain, but if it rolls down into the public domain it is forbidden. Rebbi Yasa said, this implies in a spout standing in the public domain, ten [hand-breadths] high and four wide[87], one may not pour water which would roll down and exit.

86 For the unintelligible "soot" read כִּיחוֹ "his phlegm". This refers to the statement of R. Jehudah in the Mishnah that one may not walk with spittle in his mouth. There are two objections to the formulation of the Mishnah, first that spittle may be swallowed and therefore can be carried in one's mouth and second that for R. Jehudah the moisture remaining in the mouth still should be counted as spittle; if the Mishnah really meant spittle, R. Jehudah should forbid walking in the public domain to everybody.

87 Which therefore is a separate private domain. For "R. Yasa" read "R. Yose."

(26b line 27) פיס'. נִיחָא בִּרְשׁוּת הַיָּחִיד וְיִשְׁתֶּה בִּרְשׁוּת הָרַבִּים. בִּרְשׁוּת הָרַבִּים וְיִשְׁתֶּה בִּרְשׁוּת הַיָּחִיד אֵין פִּיו לְמַעֲלָה מֵעֲשָׂרָה טְפָחִים. שַׁנְיָיא הִיא שֶׁמִּתְגַּלְגְּלִין וְיוֹרְדִין. תַּנֵּי. גָּמָל שֶׁרֹאשׁוֹ וְרוּבּוֹ מִבִּפְנִים מַלְעִיטִין אוֹתוֹ מִבִּפְנִים. מִבַּחוּץ מַלְעִיטִין אוֹתוֹ מִבַּחוּץ. נִיחָא מִבִּפְנִים מַלְעִיטִין אוֹתוֹ מִבִּפְנִים. מִבַּחוּץ מַלְעִיטִין אוֹתוֹ מִבַּחוּץ אֵין פִּיו לְמַעֲלָה מֵעֲשָׂרָה טְפָחִים.

Paragraph[88]. One understands "in a private domain and drink[14] in the public domain.[89]" "In the public domain and drink in a private domain," is his mouth not higher than ten hand-breadths[90]? There is a difference since it is running off downwards. It was stated[91]: A camel whose head and most of its body is inside one force-feeds inside, outside one force-feeds outside. One understands "inside one force-feeds inside." But "outside one force-feeds outside," is its mouth not higher than ten hand-breadths[92]?

88 Discussion of Mishnah 5.
89 Then his body is an extension of the private domain and drinking is transporting the water from public to private domain (or at least looks like transporting and is rabbinically forbidden.)
90 His mouth is in exempt space and transporting from private to exempt space is not even rabbinically prohibited.
91 Babli 20b, bottom. Cf. Chapter 2, Notes 60ff.
92 Since the camel's belly probably also is more than 10 hand-breadths from the ground, the answer given for humans cannot apply. The second part of the *baraita* cannot be correct.

(26b line 33) רִבִּי יוֹסֵי בֵּירִבִּי בּוּן מְחִלְפָה שְׁמוּעֲתֵיהּ. לֹא כֵן אָמַר רִבִּי יַעֲקֹב בַּר אָחָא בְּשֵׁם רִבִּי חֲנִינָה. שֶׁכָּל־שְׁלֹשָׁה וּשְׁלֹשָׁה שֶׁהֵן סְמוּכִין לַמְחִיצָה כִּמְחִיצָה. תִּיפְתָּר בְּיוֹצֵא חוּץ לִשְׁלֹשָׁה שֶׁאֵין בּוֹ רוֹחַב אַרְבָּעָה.

Rebbi Yose ben Rebbi Abun has contradictory traditions. Did not Rebbi Jacob bar Aḥa say in the name of Rebbi Ḥanina that any three [hand-breadths] near a partition are like the partition? Explain it if it is outside of three hand-breadths but it is not four wide[93].

93 This refers to the second part of the Mishnah, drinking from gutters and leaders after a rainstorm. Why does the Mishnah state that from gutters one may drink while standing in the public domain. Even if the gutters are outside the roof, within three hand-breadths they still are considered part of the roof and are private domain. But if they are outside of three hand-breadths in exempt domain they are accessible as long as they do not form a domain by themselves, containing a square of edge length 4 hand-breadths. Cf. *Šabbat* 1, Note 107.

(26b line 36) נָעַץ קָנֶה וְהִקִּיפוֹ מְחִיצָה וְזָרַק מֵרְשׁוּת הָרַבִּים לְתוֹכוֹ. רִבִּי יִצְחָק בֶּן אֶלְעָזָר אוֹמֵר. כְּמַחֲלוֹקֶת. הָתִיב רִבִּי יוּדָן. וְהָתַנִּינָן. הָיְתָה עוֹמֶדֶת בְּרֹאשׁ הַגַּג וּזְרָקוֹ לָהּ. כֵּיוָן שֶׁהִגִּיעַ לַאֲוִיר הַגַּג הֲרֵי זוֹ מְגוֹרֶשֶׁת. אָמַר רִבִּי אֶלְעָזָר. מַתְנִיתָא אֲמָרָהּ בְּגַג שֶׁיֵּשׁ לוֹ מַעֲקֶה וְהוּא שֶׁיָּרַד לַאֲוִיר מַעֲקֶה. וְשֶׁאֵין לוֹ מַעֲקֶה שֶׁיָּרַד לַאֲוִיר שְׁלֹשָׁה שֶׁהֵן סְמוּכִין לַגַּג. שֶׁכָּל־ שְׁלֹשָׁה שֶׁהֵן סְמוּכִין לַגַּג כְּגַג הֵן.

If one inserted a stick, surrounded it by a partition, and threw into it from the public domain. Rebbi Isaac ben Eleazar says, a case in dispute[94]. Rebbi Yudan objected: But did we not state[95]: "If she was standing on the top of her roof and he threw it to her, as soon as it reached the roof's airspace she is divorced." Rebbi Eleazar said, the Mishnah speaks about a roof with a parapet, after it descended into the airspace of the parapet[96]. If there is no parapet, only if it descended into three [hand-breadths] close to the roof since any three [hand-breadths] close to the roof are like the roof.

94 In contrast to a similar *baraita* quoted in the Babli *Šabbat* 7a, it is assumed that the top of the stick does not qualify as a domain, it does not contain a square of 4-by-4 hand-breadths, but the partition encloses such an area. The dispute is centered on Rebbi's assertion that any domain is considered filled to the top (*Šabbat* Chapter 1, Note 138; also cf. Note 117). Therefore, for him the top of the stick defines a domain since it is extended to cover the entire area within the partition at the level of the stick's top. For Rebbi and his followers the thrower is liable; for his opponents the thrower is only rabbinically forbidden as throwing from a private domain to *karmelit*.

95 Mishnah *Gittin* 8:3. Cf. *Gittin* 8:3, Notes 48-58. A bill of divorce becomes effective only if it is delivered into the hands (i. e., the ownership) of the wife (*Deut.* 24:1). This rule is undisputed; why should the Sabbath rule be in dispute?

96 The moment the divorce document clears the parapet and would have come to rest if the airspace enclosed by the parapet would be solid matter. But the rules of divorce and of the Sabbath cannot be compared; *Gittin* 8:3, Note 96.

(26b line 41) אָמַר רִבִּי חִיָּיה. וְכֵן בְּגַת לְעִנְיָין מַעֲשֵׂר.
רִבִּי יְהוּדָה אוֹמֵר. דְּרִבִּי מֵאִיר הִיא. דְּאָמַר. אַתְּ רוֹאֶה אֶת הַכּוֹתֶל כְּגָמוּס. רִבִּי יַעֲקֹב בַּר אָחָא בְּשֵׁם רִבִּי לְעָזָר. דִּבְרֵי הַכֹּל בְּמִשְׁתַּפֵּעַ עֲשָׂרָה טְפָחִים מִתּוֹךְ שָׁלֹשׁ. רִבִּי יוֹסֵי בָּעֵי. אִם בְּמִשְׁתַּפֵּעַ עֲשָׂרָה טְפָחִים מִתּוֹךְ שָׁלֹשׁ. כְּגָג הֵן. מָה נַן תַּמָּן שֶׁאֵינוֹ צָרִיךְ נִיחָא אַתְּ אָמַר עַד שֶׁיָּנוּחַ. כָּאן שֶׁצָּרִיךְ נִיחָא לֹא כָל־שֶׁכֵּן. אֲמַר רִבִּי חֲנִינָא קוֹמֵי רִבִּי מָנָא. מִכָּל־מָקוֹם לֹא נָח. אֲמַר לֵיהּ. מִכֵּיוָן שֶׁאֵין בּוֹ רוֹחַב אַרְבָּעָה אֲפִילוּ נָח כְּאִילוּ לֹא נָח.

Rebbi Hiyya said, "the same holds for a wine press," refers to tithes[97].

[98]Rebbi Jehudah[99] says, it is Rebbi Meïr's who said, one considers the wall as if hollowed out[100]. Rebbi Jacob bar Aha in the name of Rebbi Eleazar: It is everybody's opinion if it is inclined ten hand-breadths for three [cubits][101]. Rebbi Yose asked, if it is inclined ten hand-breadths for three [cubits], is it not a roof[101]? Where are we? There[103], where it does not have to come to rest, you say only after it came to rest; here where it is necessary that it come to rest[104], not so much more? Rebbi Hanina said before Rebbi Mana, in any case

it did not come to rest! He told him, since it is not four[105] wide it is as if it did not come to rest.

97 The remark about a wine-press in Mishnah 5 refers to Mishnah *Ma'serot* 4:4 where it is stated that one may drink from freshly pressed untithed grape juice if one may return the unused part into the vat. This is now qualified that on the Sabbath one has to be mostly inside the building of the winepress. Babli 99b, *Šabbat* 11b.

98 S. Liebermann writes: This paragraph is one of the most incomprehensible in the entire Yerushalmi and I was not able to understand it.

99 The Amora usually referred to as R. Yudan.

100 Reading נָמוֹס for גמוס, cf. *Šabbat* Chapter 11 Note 77. The problem is the statement in the Mishnah that collecting water from the leader coming down from the roof is permitted only within 10 hand-breadths from the ground. It should be permitted at any height since above 10 hand-breadths it is exempt space. Therefore the Mishnah must be R. Meïr's who might consider the lower end of the leader as an imaginary 4--by-4 hole in the wall which counts as an ideal private domain.

101 The roof is not flat but inclined at an angle of arcsin(10/18) ~ 18.5°. Then the water does not come to rest on the roof, it still is rainwater, and the rules of *Šabbat* Chapter 1 Note 106 do apply. In that case he is able to collect the water anywhere. This fits the statement of the Mishnah for the gutters but not for the leaders.

102 A roof slanted not more than 18.5° still is usable as a roof. May one not imagine the raindrops to come to rest on the roof?

103 In the case of the divorce document quoted in the preceding paragraph, it must become the wife's property. The kinematics of the process are irrelevant. Nevertheless, the document thrown into the wife's property becomes hers only if it cannot escape from that property, i. e., if either it comes to rest on the property or it moves in a space bounded on all sides by fences higher than the future path of the document.

104 Since the action of transporting on the Sabbath is complete only if the object transported comes to rest.

105 On the slanted roof the raindrops come to rest only in the gutters which do not count as domains. Therefore following the argument of R. Johanan in *Šabbat* Chapter 1 Note 106; the Mishnah must follow R. Meïr; it cannot be everybody's opinion. The paragraph is incomprehensible since the argument is presen- ted as supporting the opposite conclusion.

(26b line 48) פִּיס'. אֵין אַתְּ רוֹאֶה עָמוֹק כְּגָבוֹהַּ. שֶׁאֵין בְּפִיו רוֹחַב אַרְבָּעָה. עַד כְּדוֹן בְּסָתוּם. הָיָה מוּפְלָג. רַב וּשְׁמוּאֵל. חַד אָמַר. נוֹתֵן נֶסֶר. וְחַד אָמַר. נוֹעֵץ קָנֶה. וְלֹא יָדְעִינָן מָאן מַר דָּא וּמָאן מַר דָּא. מִן מַה דְּתַנֵּי שְׁמוּאֵל. לְמַעֲלָה מֵעֲשָׂרָה שְׁבוּת הוּא דֵּין אָמַר. נוֹתֵן נֶסֶר.

הָיוּ שְׁנַיִם. תְּרֵין אֲמוֹרִין. חַד אָמַר. עֲשָׂרָה. וְחוֹרָן אָמַר. אַרְבָּעָה. מְתִיב מָאן דָּמַר עֲשָׂרָה לְמָאן דָּמַר אַרְבָּעָה. לֹא נִמְצְאוּ שְׁתֵּי רְשׁוּיוֹת מִשְׁתַּמְּשׁוֹת בִּרְשׁוּת אַחַת. אָמַר לֵיהּ. רְשׁוּת הָרַבִּים מְבַטֶּלֶת.

Paragraph[106]. Does one not consider depth equal to height[107]? If its mouth is not wide four [hand-breadths][108]. So far if it is blocked in. If it is far away[109]? Rav and Samuel; one said one puts in a plank; the other said, one plants a stick[110]. We did not know who said what. Since Samuel stated, higher than ten [hand-breadths] is rabbinically forbidden[111], he is the one who said that one puts in a plank.

If they were two[112]. Two Amoraim, one said ten [hand-breadths], the other one said four[113]. He who said ten objected to the one saying four: Does it not turn out that two domains use one domain? He told him, the public domain annuls[114].

106 Discussion of Mishnah 6.
107 Since a cistern usually is deeper than 10 hand-breadths (a premiss disputed by the Babli 99b), it defines a private domain whether or not it has a railing around. Why does the Mishnah insist on a railing?
108 If the opening does not contain a square of 4-by-4 hand-breadths it cannot define a domain by itself unless it is walled in by a wall at least 10 hand-breadths high.
109 The cistern is close to the house; even though it is in the public domain its status is *karmelit*. If it is farther away from the house to be genuine public domain, it needs some action to make it usable from a private domain (disputed by the Babli 99b).
110 The first opinion requires only a token separation, the second a genuine partition, even if hanging from the balcony, of 10 hand-breadths width.

111 He holds that biblically exempt space still is rabbinically forbidden. Therefore he must need a genuine partition to allow water to be drawn through what otherwise would be exempt space.
112 If a cistern was in the public domain and two houses on opposite sides could use its water on the Sabbath.
113 Following Rav, who in the case of a single house requires only a token partition, does one need a plank of fully 10 hand-breadths in the case of two houses or is a width of 4 hand-breadths sufficient? The numerals all are in the masculine.
114 Since the plank is hanging down, the water is drawn through exempt space, which for him is unquestionably permitted. It only is exempt space which uses the cistern below, and this is permitted.

(26b line 54)   וּבִלְבַד שֶׁלֹּא יְהֵא בּוֹ יוֹתֵר מִבֵּית סָאתַיִם. וְלֹא יְהוּ מְחִיצוֹת גְּבוֹהוֹת עֲשָׂרָה. וְלֹא יְהוּ פְּרָצוֹת יוֹתֵר מֵעֲשָׂר. וְלֹא יְהֵא עוֹמֵד כְּנֶגֶד עוֹמֵד וּפָרוּץ כְּנֶגֶד פָּרוּץ.

פיס׳. רִבִּי אֲחָא בְּשֵׁם רַב. אָסוּר לִתְלוֹשׁ שָׁרְשֵׁי זְמוֹרָה בַּשַּׁבָּת. הִיא שָׁרְשֵׁי אִילָן הִיא שָׁרְשֵׁי כְרוּב. בְּגָבוֹהִין שְׁלֹשָׁה. אֲבָל אִם אֵין גְּבוֹהִין שְׁלֹשָׁה כְּאֶרֶץ הֵם.

מַתְנִיתָא בְּשֶׁאֵין לָהֶן צִירִין. אֲבָל יֵשׁ לָהֶן צִירִין הֲדָא הִיא דְתַנֵּי. דֶּלֶת גּוֹדֶרֶת מַחֲצֶלֶת גּוֹדֶרֶת קַנְקִילּוֹן גּוֹדֵר. פּוֹתֵחַ וְנוֹעֵל בַּשַּׁבָּת וְאֵין צָרִיךְ לוֹמַר בְּיוֹם טוֹב. מַחֲצֶלֶת הַקְּשׁוּרָה וּתְלוּיָה בְּשַׁבָּת פּוֹתֵחַ וְנוֹעֵל בַּשַּׁבָּת וְאֵין צוֹרֶךְ לוֹמַר בְּיוֹם טוֹב.

[115]Only it should be no larger than two *bet se'ah*, or the walls ten [hand-breadths] high,[9] nor the opening wider than ten [cubits], nor what was standing was opposite what was standing and what was breached opposite the breached.

Paragraph[116]. Rebbi Aha in the name of Rav: It is forbidden to (tear off) [trample on][117] roots of a vine on the Sabbath. There is no difference between the roots of a [barren] tree or the roots of cabbage. If they are three [hand-breadths] high. But if they are not three [hand-breadths] high they are like the ground.

The Mishnah[118] refers to the case that there are no hinges. But if there are hinges that is what was stated[119]: "a hinged door, a hinged mat, hinged lattice gates[33], one may open and lock on the Sabbath, and it is not necessary to say on a holiday. If a mat was tied to and hanging from a pillar, one may open and lock on the Sabbath, and it is not necessary to say on a holiday."

115 Discussion of Mishnah 7. The domain under a tree becomes private only if the branches are low enough to count as partitions and the entire area under the tree is not more than 5'000 square cubits since it is not fenced in for human dwelling. Chapter 4, Notes 58-60; Babli 99b.

116 Discussion of the sentence regarding tree roots. The text also is in *Besah* 5:2 (63a l. 12). The Babli 100a reads the Mishnah differently.

117 With the text in *Besah* read לדוש instead of לתלוש. Tearing off branches is agricultural work and biblically forbidden as harvesting.

118 Discussion of the sentence about doors (cf. Note 20).

119 The text is from *Šabbat* Chapter 5, Notes 32-34. For גודר "fence in" one has to read גורר "drag" with the text in Tosephta 8:12, *Šabbat loc. cit.*, and the quotes by R. Hananel (last sentence in his Commentary to *Besah* Chapter 2) and *Or zarua` Šabbat* §55 (p. 67b) which refer to the last Chapter of *Eruvin* and read גורר.

(26b line 62) פיס'. רִבִּי אָחָא רִבִּי חִינְנָה בְשֵׁם כַּהֲנָא. אֵין הֲלָכָה כְּרִבִּי יוּדָה. רִבִּי אַבָּא בַּר פַּפֵּי בָעֵי. לָמָה עָבַד רִבִּי מֵאִיר אֶת הַכּוֹתֶל. כְּנָמוּם כְּנָקוּב. אִין תֵּימַר כְּנָמוּם. אֲפִילוּ לְמַעְלָה מֵעֲשָׂרָה מוּתָּר. אִין תֵּימַר כְּנָקוּב. אֲפִילוּ לְמַטָּה מֵעֲשָׂרָה אָסוּר. פֶּתַח גַּנּוֹת שֶׁיֵּשׁ לָהֶן בֵּית שַׁעַר. מִבִּפְנִים פּוֹתֵחַ וְנוֹעֵל מִבִּפְנִים. מִבַּחוּץ פּוֹתֵחַ וְנוֹעֵל מִבַּחוּץ. מִיכָּן וּמִיכָּן פּוֹתֵחַ וְנוֹעֵל מִיכָּן וּמִיכָּן. לֹא מִיכָּן וְלֹא מִיכָּן הֲרֵי זֶה נוֹטֵל אֶת הַמַּפְתֵּחַ וּפוֹתֵחַ וְנוֹעֵל וּמַנִּיחוֹ בִּמְקוֹמוֹ. בַּמֶּה דְבָרִים אֲמוּרִים. בִּזְמַן שֶׁהַמַּנְעוּל לְמַעְלָה מֵעֲשָׂרָה טְפָחִים. אֲבָל אִם הָיָה הַמַּנְעוּל לְמַטָּה מֵעֲשָׂרָה טְפָחִים. הֲרֵי זֶה נוֹטֵל אֶת הַמַּפְתֵּחַ מִתּוֹךְ הָאַסְקוּפָּה וּפוֹתֵחַ וְנוֹעֵל וּמַנִּיחוֹ בִּמְקוֹמוֹ. דִּבְרֵי רִבִּי מֵאִיר. וַחֲכָמִים אוֹמְרִים. אַף עַל פִּי שֶׁהַמַּנְעוּל לְמַעְלָה מֵעֲשָׂרָה טְפָחִים מֵבִיא הַמַּפְתֵּחַ מֵעֶרֶב שַׁבָּת וּפוֹתֵחַ וְנִכְנַס וּמְטַלְטְלוֹ בְּתוֹךְ הַבַּיִת וְנוֹעֵל וְנוֹתְנוֹ בַּחוֹר לְמַעְלָה מִן הַמַּשְׁקוֹף. אִם הָיָה הַחוֹר שֶׁלְאַרְבָּעָה טְפָחִים אָסוּר. שֶׁאֵין מִשְׁתַּמְּשִׁין מֵרְשׁוּת לִרְשׁוּת דֶּרֶךְ רְשׁוּת. הָדָא אֲמָרָה. כְּנָמוּם עָבַד לָהּ רִבִּי יוּדָה. נִיחָא מִבִּפְנִים צָרִיךְ בֵּית שַׁעַר. מִבַּחוּץ צָרִיךְ בֵּית שַׁעַר. לֹא נִמְצְאוּ שְׁתֵּי רְשָׁיוֹת מִשְׁתַּמְּשׁוֹת בִּרְשׁוּת אַחַת.

Paragraph[120]. Rebbi Aha, Rebbi Ḥinena in the name of Cahana: Practice does not follow Rebbi Jehudah[121]. Rebbi Abba bar Pappai asked: How did Rebbi Meïr treat the wall, as hollowed out or as pierced? If you say as hollowed out, even higher than ten [hand-breadths] it should be permitted. If you say as pierced, even below ten [hand-breadths] it should be prohibited[122]. "[123]The door of garden plots which have a gatekeeper's lodge[124], from the inside he opens and locks from the inside; from the outside he opens and locks from the outside; from both sides he opens and locks from both sides; from neither side he takes the key, opens and locks, and returns it to its place. When has this been said? If the lock is higher than ten hand-breadths. But if the lock is lower than ten hand-breadths he takes the key from the threshold, opens and locks, and returns it to its place, the words of Rebbi Meïr[125]. But the Sages are saying, even if the lock is higher than ten hand-breadths he brings the key on Friday, opens, enters, and moves it inside the house, locks, and puts it into a hole above the lintel[126]. If the hole was four hand-breadths wide it is forbidden, for one does not use one domain from another domain through a third domain[127]." This implies that Rebbi Jehudah treats it as hollowed out[125]. One understands that from the inside it needs a gatekeeper's lodge. Why does it need a gatekeeper's lodge from the outside? Does it not turn out that two domains use one domain[128]?

120 Discussion of Mishnah 8.

121 R. Jehudah is not mentioned in the Mishnah. Since the second mention of R. Jehudah at the end of the paragraph clearly should read "R. Meïr", one may assume that here also one should read "R. Meïr".

122 The discussion is not about the Mishnah, where R. Meïr requires that the door be entirely part of a private domain, but about the Tosephta quoted in the sequel. If R. Meïr considers any dent in the wall or in the door as a 4-by-4 cavity, this should make no difference if it is more than 10 handbreadths above the ground since one is permitted to move things from exempt space to *karmelit*. But if it is considered a hole open on both sides, i. e., connected to and being part of a private domain, then putting the key from the outside into the keyhole would be transporting from the public to a private domain and forbidden.

123 Related texts are Tosephta 8:12, Babli 101b.

124 Which is not built as a dwelling. In the first part of the Tosephta the door in question is assumed to be between the lodge and the gardens. "From the inside, from the outside" refers to the position of the doorhandle which allows to open or close the door from that direction.

125 Here is no gatekeeper's lodge. Since the threshold is *karmelit*, it follows that the keyhole also is considered *karmelit*; this proves that R. Meïr treats the keyhole not as part of the private domain.

126 Since they treat the hole as *karmelit* (below 10 hand-breadths) or exempt space (above 10 hand-breadths) as long as its real dimensions are less than 4-by-4 handbreadths.

127 From public domain through exempt space to private domain.

128 In the first part of the *baraita* one understands that a gatekeeper's lodge is needed so that in any case there is no carrying from a private domain to the public one. But from the outside, where the Sages of the Mishnah permit putting the key into a hole above the lintel, why should R. Meïr require an intermediate space? If one assumes that the door opens to the inside, the person standing at the outside has access to the inside through the *karmelit* represented by the threshold.

(26c line 3) פיס׳. אָמַר רִבִּי יוֹסֵי בֵּרִבִּי [ ] כִּדְבָרֵי מִי שֶׁמַּתִּיר עוֹשֶׂה הַנֶּגֶר טָפֵל לַקְּלוֹסְטְרָא. כְּדִבְרֵי הָאוֹסֵר עוֹשֶׂה הַקְּלוֹסְטְרָא טָפֵל לַנֶּגֶר.

Paragraph[129]: Rebbi Yose ben Rebbi [ ][130] said: He who permits makes the bolt an accessory to the lock; he who forbids makes the lock an accessory of the bolt.

129 Discussion of Mishnah 9.

130 Clearly there is a name missing here. R. Hananel (102a) quotes "Rav Yose" (probably a copyist's error), Ritba (*ad* 101a, p. 168a first line): R. Yose bar Abin. Probably the name should ben R. Abun.

(26c line) אֵי זֶהוּ נֶגֶר. אָמַר רִבִּי יוֹחָנָן. קָשׁוּר אַף עַל פִּי שֶׁאֵינוֹ תָלוּי. אָמַר רִבִּי יוֹחָנָן. מְשָׁכֵנִי חִילְפַּיי וְהִרְאֵנִי מִשַּׁלְבֵּית רִבִּי קָשׁוּר אַף עַל פִּי שֶׁאֵינוֹ תָלוּי. אָמַר רִבִּי יוֹחָנָן. אַתְיָא יְחִידָאָה דְּהָכָא כִּסְתָמָא דְתַמָּן. וִיחִידָאָה דְּתַמָּן כִּסְתָמָא דְהָכָא. רִבִּי יוֹסֵי בָּעֵי קוֹמֵי רִבִּי יִרְמְיָה. הֵיךְ עֲבָדִין עוּבְדָא. אֲמַר לֵיהּ. מִן מַה דְּאָמַר רִבִּי יוֹחָנָן. מְשָׁכֵנִי חִילְפַּיי וְהִרְאֵנִי שֶׁלְּבֵית רִבִּי קָשׁוּר אַף עַל פִּי שֶׁאֵינוֹ תָלוּי. הָדָא אָמְרָה. כְּרִבִּי יְהוּדָה עֲבָדִין. עַד שֶׁיְּהֵא קָשׁוּר בַּדֶּלֶת. רִבִּי יַנַּיי חָמוֹי דְּרִבִּי אַמִי. עַד שֶׁיְּהֵא קָשׁוּר בַּדֶּלֶת בְּדָבָר שֶׁהוּא יָכוֹל לְהַעֲמִידוֹ. נִגְרָא הֲדָא רִבִּי אֶלְעָזָר קָטַר בְּגָמִי. נִשְׁמַט אָסוּר. נִקְמַז. רִבִּי יַעֲקֹב בַּר אָחָא בְּשֵׁם רַבָּנָן. מְדַדֵּיהוּ בְרָאשֵׁי עֶצְבְּעוֹתָיו.

רִבִּי בָּא בַּר כַּהֲנָא רִבִּי חִייָה בַּר אַשִׁי בְּשֵׁם רַב. הֲלָכָה כְּרִבִּי יוֹסֵי.

[131]**What is a dragged bolt?** Rebbi Joḥanan said, tied but not hanging. Rebbi Joḥanan said, Ḥilfai pulled me and showed me one of the House of Rebbi tied but not hanging. Rebbi Joḥanan said, the single opinion here is parallel to the anonymous one there, and the anonymous there to the individual here. Rebbi Yose asked before Rebbi Jeremiah: how does one act in actuality? He said to him, since Rebbi Joḥanan said, Ḥilfai pulled me and showed me one of the House of Rebbi tied but not hanging, this implies that one acts following Rebbi Jehudah, except that it be tied to the door. Rebbi Yannai the father-in-law of Rebbi Immi said, only if it is tied to the door by something which can fasten it. Rebbi Eleazar's bolt was tied with bast. If it was detached it is forbidden; loose? Rebbi Jacob bar Aḥa in the name of the rabbis, he supports it with his finger tips.

Rebbi Abba bar Cahana, Rebbi Ḥiyya bar Ashi in the name of Rav, practice follows Rebbi Yose.

---

131 This paragraph is explained in *Šabbat* Chapter 17, Notes 70-83.

(26c line 15) פִּיס'. אָמַר רִבִּי יוֹסֵי בֵּירִבִּי בּוּן. לֹא כָל־שְׁבוּת הִתִּירוּ בַּמִּקְדָּשׁ.
תַּנֵּי. לֹא יְקַנֵּחַ אָדָם אֶת הָאַסְפְּלָנִית שֶׁלֹּא יָבוֹא לִידֵי מֵירוּחַ. וְהַמְמָרֵחַ בַּשַּׁבָּת חַייָב חַטָּאת. וְהָתַנֵּי. הֶחֱלִיקָה מִפַּטּוֹ מַחֲזִירָהּ מִלְמַעְלָן. הֶחֱלִיקָה מִלְמַעְלָה מַחֲזִירָהּ מִלְּמַטָּה. מְגַלֶּה מִקְצָת אַסְפְּלָנִית מִיכָּן וּמְקַנֵּחַ הַמַּכָּה מִיכָּן. וּמְגַלֶּה מִקְצָת אַסְפְּלָנִית מִיכָּן וּמְקַנֵּחַ הַמַּכָּה מִיכָּן. אֲבָל לֹא יְקַנֵּחַ אֶת הָאַסְפְּלָנִית שֶׁלֹּא יָבוֹא לִידֵי מֵירוּחַ. וְהַמְמָרֵחַ בַּשַּׁבָּת חַייָב חַטָּאת.

תַּנֵּי. רְטִייָה שֶׁשְּׁטָפְחָה מַחֲזִירִין אוֹתָהּ בַּשַּׁבָּת. רִבִּי יַעֲקֹב בַּר אָחָא בְּשֵׁם רִבִּי יָסָא. וְהִיא שֶׁשְּׁטוּפְחָה כְּנֶגֶד הַמַּכָּה. וְהָתַנֵּי. הֶחֱלִיקָה מִפַּטּוֹ מַחֲזִירָהּ מִלְמַעְלָן. הֶחֱלִיקָה מִלְמַעְלָן מַחֲזִירָהּ מִלְמַטָּן. וּבִלְבַד שֶׁלֹּא תֵצֵא רְשׁוּת כָּל־אוֹתָהּ הַמַּכָּה. רִבִּי יוֹסֵי בֵּירִבִּי בּוּן בָּשֵׁם רִבִּי יָסָא. מַכָּה

שֶׁנִּתְרַפְּאת נוֹתְנִין עָלֶיהָ רְטִיָּיה. שֶׁאֵינוֹ אֶלָּא כִּמְשַׁמְּרָהּ. רִבִּי בּוּן בְּשֵׁם רַבָּנָן דְּתַמָּן. נוֹתְנִין רְטִיָּיה עַל גַּבֵּי מַכָּה בַשַּׁבָּת שֶׁאֵינוֹ אֶלָּא כִּמְשַׁמְּרָהּ. אָמַר רִבִּי תַנְחוּמָא. חוּץ מֵעֲלֵי גְפָנִים שֶׁהֵן לִרְפוּאָה.
אָמַר רִבִּי הוּנָא. הֲדָא פוּאָה עִיקָּר טַב הִיא סַגִּין כָּד אִית בָּהּ חֲמִשָּׁה אוֹ שִׁבְעָה אוֹ תִּשְׁעָה קִיטְרִין וּבִלְבַד דְּלָא יִתֵּן מוֹי.
אֵין קוֹרִין פָּסוּק עַל גַּבֵּי מַכָּה בַשֵּׁם. וְהָדֵין דְּקָרָא עַל יַבְרוּחָה אָסוּר. בּוֹא וּקְרָא פָּסוּק זֶה עַל בְּנוֹ שֶׁהוּא מִתְבָּעֵת. תֵּן עָלָיו סֵפֶר אוֹ תְפִילִּין בִּשְׁבִיל שֶׁיִּישָׁן. אָסוּר. וְהָתַנֵּי. אוֹמְרִים הָיוּ שִׁיר שֶׁלִּפְגָעִים בִּירוּשָׁלַם. אָמַר רִבִּי יוּדָן. כָּאן עַד שֶׁלֹּא נִפְגַּע וְכָאן מִשֶּׁנִּפְגַּע. וְאֵי זֶהוּ שִׁיר פְּגָעִים. מָה־רַבּוּ צָרָי וְכָל־הַמִּזְמוֹר. יוֹשֵׁב בְּסֵתֶר עֶלְיוֹן עַד כִּי־אַתָּה יְיָ מַחְסִי.

Paragraph[132]. Rebbi Yose ben Rebbi Abun said, not every rabbinic Sabbath prohibition was permitted in the Temple[133].

It was stated: A person should not clean a wound dressing[134], to avoid spreading[135], since he who spreads on the Sabbath is liable for a purification sacrifice. And we have stated: If it[136] slipped below one puts it back from above, if it slipped above one puts it back from below. One may uncover part of the wound dressing and cleanse the wound from the other side, and uncover part of the wound dressing and cleanse the wound from the other side. But one may not cleanse the wound dressing to avoid spreading since he who spreads on the Sabbath is liable for a purification sacrifice.

It was stated: A plaster which was swollen one puts back on the Sabbath. Rebbi Jacob bar Aha in the name of Rebbi Yasa: Only if it was swollen over the wound, as it was stated: If it slipped below one puts it back from above, if it slipped above one puts it back from below on condition that it not leave the entire domain of the wound.

[137]Rebbi Yose ben Rebbi Abun in the name of Rebbi Yose: One may put a dressing on a healed wound since it is only protective. Rebbi Abun in the name of the rabbis there: One may put it on a wound on the Sabbath since it is only protective. Rebbi Tanhuma said, except vine leaves which only are for healing.

Rebbi Huna said, madder is a good root, the more the better. If it has five or seven or nine knots, only if it does not ooze fluid.

One does not recite a verse over a wound quoting the Name; the one which one recites about mandrakes is forbidden. Come and recite this verse for my son who is afraid, put on him a scroll, put on him phylacteries, so he will go to sleep, is forbidden. But did we not state, they used to recite the Song of the Afflicted in Jerusalem? Rebbi Yudan said, one means before he was hurt, the other after he was hurt. What is the Song of the Afflicted? *How many are my oppressors,* and the entire Psalm. *Sitting in the shelter of the Most High* up to: *Truly, You, Eternal, are my refuge.*

132 Discussion of Mishnah 11.

133 Since in Mishnah 10 it was stated that only a lower hinge but not an upper one may be replaced in the Temple, it follows that not all rabbinic restrictions are waved in the Temple; practically this means that only those acts which are mentioned in the remainder of the Chapter are authorized.

134 Latin *splenium*, Greek σπλήνιον, τό.

135 Smoothing a salve over the wound, which is a derivative of ממחק (Mishnah *Šabbat* 7:2).

136 The wound dressing.

137 The text from here on is explained in *Šabbat* Chapter 6, Notes 129-133.

(26c line 35) פיס'. קוֹשְׁרִין נִימָה בַּמִּקְדָּשׁ אֲבָל לֹא בַּמְּדִינָה. אֲמַר רִבִּי יוֹסֵי בֵּירִבִּי בּוּן. דְּרִבִּי שִׁמְעוֹן בֶּן אֶלְעָזָר הִיא. דְּתַנֵּי רִבִּי שִׁמְעוֹן בֶּן אֶלְעָזָר. נִימָא שֶׁבַּכִּינּוֹר שֶׁנִּפְסְקָה וּקְשָׁרָהּ הִיא אֵינָהּ מַשְׁמַעַת אֶת הַקּוֹל אֶלָּא מְשַׁלְשֵׁל מִלְּמַעֲלָן וְעוֹנֵב מִלְּמַטָּה. תַּנֵּי רִבִּי שִׁמְעוֹן בֶּן אֶלְעָזָר אוֹמֵר. הַכֹּהֲנִים וְהַלְוִיִּם וְיִשְׂרָאֵל וּכְלֵי שִׁיר מְעַכְּבִין אֶת הַקָּרְבָּן.

Paragraph[132]. "One ties strings[27] in the Temple but not in the countryside." Rebbi Yose ben Rebbi Abun said, this is Rebbi Simeon ben Eleazar's[138], as Rebbi Simeon ben Eleazar stated, if a broken violin string is tied it does not give a sound, but he strings from above and makes a loop below[139]. It was stated[140]: Rebbi Simeon ben Eleazar said, Cohanim, Levites, Israel, and musical instruments obstruct the sacrifice[141].

138 Differently Babli 102b.

139 Babli *Taanit* 27a, a statement of Samuel.

140 The Cohanim officiate, the Levites sing, the Israel are the *ma`amad*, representatives of the people for whom the daily sacrifices are offered. Since the Sabbath sacrifice is a biblical obligation, and musical accompaniment of the Levite's song is necessary, if there is no replacement violin (or guitar) available, R. Simeon ben Eleazar permits restringing the instrument on the Sabbath. The "one ties strings" in the Mishnah means tying with permanent knots; this contradicts the statement in the Mishnah that new strings are forbidden in the Temple. This latter statement cannot be R. Simeon ben Eleazar's.

(26c line 40) חוֹתְכִין יַבֶּלֶת בַּמִּקְדָּשׁ אֲבָל לֹא בַּמְּדִינָה. תַּמָּן תַּנִּינָן. חֲתִיכַת יַבַּלְתּוֹ אֵין דּוֹחִין. וְהָכָא אַתְּ אֲמַר הָכֵין. רִבִּי סִימוֹן בְּשֵׁם רִבִּי יְהוֹשֻׁעַ בֶּן לֵוִי בְּשֵׁם רִבִּי פְּדָת. מִפְּנֵי קִילְקוּל פַּייסוֹת. אָמַר רִבִּי . וְהֵן שֶׁהִפִּיסוּ. אָמַר רִבִּי שִׁמְעוֹן בֶּן לָקִישׁ בְּשֵׁם לֵוִי סוֹבַיָה. בֵּין בִּנְפְרֶכֶת בֵּין בְּשֶׁאֵינָהּ נִפְרֶכֶת. רִבִּי שִׁמְעוֹן בֶּן יָקִים אָמַר. כָּאן בְּלַחָה כָּאן בִּיבֵישָׁה. רִבִּי יוֹסֵי בֶּן חֲנִינָא אָמַר. כָּאן בְּיָד כָּאן בִּכְלִי. אַתְיָא דְּרִבִּי שִׁמְעוֹן בֶּן יָקִים כְּבַר קַפָּרָא. וּדְרִבִּי יוֹסֵי בֶּן חֲנִינָה כְּרִבִּי יוֹחָנָן. דְּתַנֵּי. כָּל־הַמְקַלְקְלִין פְּטוּרִין חוּץ מִן הַמַּבְעִיר וְהַעוֹשֶׂה חַבּוּרָה. בַּר קַפָּרָא אָמַר. אֲפִילוּ אֵינוֹ צָרִיךְ לְדָם אֵינוֹ צָרִיךְ לְאֵפֶר. אָמַר רִבִּי יוֹחָנָן. וְהוּא שֶׁיְּהֵא צָרִיךְ לְדָם אוֹ לְאֵפֶר. רִבִּי אָחָא רִבִּי חֲנִינָה בְּשֵׁם רִבִּי יוֹחָנָן. כָּאן וְכָאן בְּלַחָה אֲנַן קַיָּימִין. וְהוּא שֶׁיְּהֵא צָרִיךְ לְדָם.

2 בשם | פ - פדת | פ פדייה   3 ר' | פ ר' יוסה אמ' | פ -   לוי | פ ר' בין | פ ר' בין | פ כאן בין | פ וכאן   4 בן חנינא | פ ביר' חנינה   5 כאן | פ וכאן יקים | פ לקיש בן | פ בר   7 אינו | פ אפי' אינו או | פ והוא שיהא צריך

"One cuts a wart at the Temple[28] but not in the countryside." There[141] we have stated: "cutting his wart does not push aside;" and here you are saying so? Rebbi Simon in the name of Rebbi Joshua ben Levi in the name of Rebbi (Pedat) [Pedaya][142]: Because of vitiation of the lotteries[143]. Rebbi [Yose][144] said, but only if they drew lots. Rebbi Simeon ben Laqish said in the name of Levi Sobaya: Whether it can be scraped off or cannot be scraped off[145]. Rebbi Simeon ben Yaqim said, one if it is moist[146], the other if it is dry. Rebbi Yose ben Hanina said, here by hand, there by implement. It turns out that Rebbi Simeon ben (Yaqim) [Laqish][142] parallels Bar Qappara, and Rebbi Yose ben Ḥanina Rebbi Johanan, as it was stated[147]: All who destroy are not liable, except the incendiary and one causing an injury. Bar Qappara said, even if he did not need the blood, even if he did not need the ashes. Rebbi Johanan said, only if he needed the blood or the ashes. Rebbi Aḥa, Rebbi Ḥanina in the name of Rebbi Johanan: In both cases if it is moist, and only if he needs the blood[148].

141 Mishnah *Pesahim* 6:1. This does not refer to a Cohen but to the Passover sacrifice; if the 14ᵗʰ of Nisan falls on a Sabbath and the animal selected for the sacrifice unexpectedly develops a wart which makes it unfit as sacrifice, the wart cannot be cut on the Sabbath even if the animal already is in the Temple precinct.

The entire paragraph except for the introductory sentence is a slightly defective copy of a text in *Pesahim* 6:1, end (פ).

142 The correct text is the one in *Pesahim*, in brackets.

143 Every week another clan of Cohanim came to serve in the Temple, as described in *Yoma* Chapter 2. Every day the duties of the service were assigned among the eligible Cohanim by lotteries. One runs into trouble if after a lottery a Cohen turns out to be ineligible since he developed a wart (even

though warts are mentioned only for animals, *Lev.* 22:22).
144 The name is missing in *Eruvin*.
145 According to him scraping the wart off is forbidden even if it can be done without drawing blood. He must hold that this is a biblical prohibition.
146 If the wart cannot be removed without drawing blood. He holds that making a wound on the Sabbath is a biblical prohibition but if the wart can be removed without drawing blood the prohibition is only rabbinical and is waved in the Temple.
147 *Šabbat* Chapter 2, Note 153.
148 In *Pesahim* he needs the blood and therefore the prohibition is biblical and cannot be waved; in *Eruvin* he does not need the blood, the prohibition is rabbinic and is waved. Babli 103a.

(26d line 1) פיס׳. יְהוּדָה בְּרַבִּי אָמַר. לֹא שָׁנוּ אֶלָּא גָּמִי אֲבָל בְּיְנָגִיּוֹן אָסוּר מִפְּנֵי יִתּוּר בְּגָדִים. סָבְרִין מֵמַר. יִתּוּר בְּגָדִים כְּחִיסּוּר בְּגָדִים. רִבִּי יַעֲקֹב בַּר אָחָא בְּשֵׁם רִבִּי יָסָא. דְּרִבִּי חֲנִינָא. דְּאָמַר רִבִּי חֲנִינָא. בִּלְבַד שֶׁלֹּא יָחוּץ בֵּינוֹ לְבֵין בֶּגֶד וְלֹא בֵין בֶּגֶד לְבֶגֶד. עַל דַּעְתֵּיהּ דְּרִבִּי חֲנִינָה. אֵי זֶהוּ יִיתוּר בְּגָדִים. שְׁתֵּי כָתָנוֹת שְׁתֵּי מִצְנָפוֹת שְׁנֵי מִכְנָסַיִם שְׁנֵי אַבְנֵטִים. כֹּהֵן שֶׁלָּקָה בְּאֶצְבָּעוֹ וְכָרַךְ עָלֶיהָ אַבְנֵט. כָּל־שֵׁם אַבְנֵט פּוֹסֵל אוֹ אֵינוֹ פּוֹסֵל אֶלָּא מַלְבּוּשׁ.

תַּנֵּי. מַעֲלִים בְּדְיוֹבִיט וּמוֹטִיפִין בְּעֶדֶק לְחוֹלֶה בַּשַּׁבָּת. מַעֲלִין בְּדְיוֹבִיט. מִשְׁתַּמִּיחָה. מַטִּיפִין בְּעֶדֶק. אִית דְּבָעֵי מֵימַר. עִירְרָה. אִית דְּבָעֵי מֵימַר. קוּקְנֵיתָא. חָצֵר שֶׁיָּרְדוּ בָהּ גְּשָׁמִים וְהָיָה בָהּ בֵּית אָבֶל אוֹ בֵית מִשְׁתֶּה. הֲרֵי זֶה נוֹטֵל אֶת הַתֶּבֶן וּמְרַדֵּד. וּבִלְבַד שֶׁלֹּא יַעֲשֶׂה בַשַּׁבָּת כְּדֶרֶךְ שֶׁעוֹשֶׂה בַחוֹל. תַּנֵּי. אֵין מְמַלִּין בַּעֲדָשָׁה בַשַּׁבָּת. אִם כָּחַס עַל הַחֶבֶל אוֹ עַל הַמְּשִׁיחָה. מַתִּיר.

Paragraph[149]. Jehudah the important[150] said, they only stated "bast" but *bingion*[151] is prohibited because of excess clothing[152]. They wanted to say excess of clothing is like deficiency in clothing. Rebbi Jacob bar Aha in the name of Rebbi Yasa: Rebbi Ḥanina's, as Rebbi Ḥanina said, only it should not separate between him and a garment or between garment and garment[153]. In Rebbi Ḥanina's opinion, what is excess clothing? Two shirts, two turbans, two pants, two belts. If a Cohen was injured on his finger and wound a belt around it; is anything called "belt" inadmissible or only clothing?

It was stated:[154] "One lifts in a siphon and sprinkles with an ʿ*edeq* for a sick person on the Sabbath." One lifts in a siphon[155], משתמיחה[156]. And sprinkles with an ʿ*edeq*[157], some want to say [158]עיררה; some want to say, a small water pitcher[159]. [160]In a courtyard where it started to rain and there was a house of mourning or a wedding feast, one takes straw and beats it down[161] on condition that he should not do it on the Sabbath in the way he does it on a weekday. It was stated: One does not fill with a lentil[162] of the Sabbath. If he is afraid for the rope or the cord it is permitted[163].

149 Discussion of Mishnah 12.

150 In the Babli 103b he is called Rav Jehudah the son of Rebbi Hiyya.

151 This word has not been explained. Perhaps it is Egyptian, appearing in Greek as βύνιτος, ὁ "an Egyptian garment" (E.G.).

152 The priestly garments worn in the Temple are defined in *Ex.* 28:40. Priests are prohibited from wearing anything else while officiating.

153 Bandages are permitted only on body parts not covered by any priestly clothing.

154 Babli 104a with some variations in the spellings of the unexplained words. Tosephta *Šabbat* 2:8; cf. *Tosephta kiFshtutah Sabbath* p. 31-32.

155 Greek διαβήτης, τό. In the Babylonian sources the word appears as דיופי.

Producing sound mechanically is rabbinically forbidden on the Sabbath. An exception is made for medical purposes. It is permitted to make a contraption which can be put together without violating any Sabbath rule, which produces a monotonous sound which induces sleep in a sick person. For this one lifts water in a siphon which delivers water into an ʿedeq which according to the Gaonic Commentary to *Tahorot* (*Otzar Hagaonim* III, *Eruvin*, pp. 79,104) is a vessel with an opening on top and capillary holes at the bottom. If the vessel is kept filled steadily and a metal plate is put under it at some distance, the water coming though the capillary holes will create a faint monotonous sound which induces sleep.

156 The word is unexplained (and not listed in the Dictionaries, from Levy to Sokoloff). One may see its root in Arabic سمه "to run steadily" (said of horses).

157 In Babylonian sources ארק, אדק. The etymology is unknown.

158 Meaning and etymology unknown.

159 Diminutive of Syriac קוקא "water pitcher" (following Sokoloff.)

160 Babli 104a.

161 To make it possible for visitors to cross the yard.

162 The name of any ovaloid vessel (cf. *Avodah zarah* Chapter 5, Note 195).

163 If he needs much water and is afraid his old rope will break, he may draw water in a vessel not usually used for the purpose since then this is not done the way one usually does it during the week.

(26d line 13) מְמַלִּים מִבּוֹר הַגּוֹלָה בַּגַּלְגַּל בַּשַּׁבָּת. מִבּוֹר הַגָּדוֹל וּמִבּוֹר הַקַּר בְּיוֹם טוֹב: מִפְּנֵי מַה מְמַלִּים מִבּוֹר הַקַּר בַּגַּלְגַּל בְּיוֹם טוֹב: אֶלָּא בְּשָׁעָה שֶׁעָלוּ יִשְׂרָאֵל מִן הַגּוֹלָה חָנוּ עַל אוֹתָהּ הַבְּאֵר. וְהִתְנוּ עִמָּהֶן נְבִיאִים שֶׁיִּהְיוּ מְמַלִּים מִבּוֹר הַקַּר בַּגַּלְגַּל בְּיוֹם טוֹב: לֹא כָל־הַבְּאֵרוֹת הַקַּר הִתִּירוּ אֶלָּא אוֹתָהּ הַבְּאֵר שֶׁחָנוּ עָלֶיהָ בִלְבָד. הֵיךְ מָה דְאַתְּ אָמַר תַּמָּן. מַה שֶׁהוּתָּר הוּתָּר. וָכָא מַה שֶׁהוּתָּר הוּתָּר.

[164]"One fills from the cistern of the Diaspora with a wheel on the Sabbath, from the large cistern and from the cold well on a holiday." Why "may one

fill from the cold well with a wheel on the holiday"? But at the time when Israel came from the diaspora and camped at this well, the prophets among them stipulated that one could fill from the cold well with a wheel on the holiday. They did not permit all cold wells, only this well at which they camped. As you are saying there, what was permitted was permitted, and here what was permitted was permitted.

164 This paragraph is from Chapter 2, Notes 32, 33.

(26d line 19) פיס'. שֶׁרֶץ שֶׁנִּמְצָא בַּמִּקְדָּשׁ כוֹל'. אָמַר לוֹ רִבִּי יוֹחָנָן בֶּן בְּרוֹקָה. לֹא נִמְצֵאתָה מַשְׁהֵא אֶת הַטּוּמְאָה. אָמַר לוֹ. לֹא נִמְצֵאתָ מַרְבֶּה בְטוּמְאָה. אָמַר לוֹ. מוּטָב לַעֲבוֹר עַל מִצְוַת לֹא תַעֲשֶׂה שֶׁלֹּא בָאת לְיָדוֹ מִמִּצְוַת לֹא תַעֲשֶׂה שֶׁבָּאת לְפָנָיו. אָמַר רִבִּי יוֹסֵי בֵּירִבִּי בּוּן. אַתְיָיא אִילֵּין פְּלוּגָתָא כְּאִילֵּין פְּלוּגָתָא. דְּתַנִּינָן תַּמָּן. כֵּיצַד מַפְרִישִׁין חַלָּה בְטוּמְאָה בְּיוֹם טוֹב. רִבִּי אֱלִיעֶזֶר אוֹמֵר. לֹא תִקְרָא לָהּ שֵׁם עַד שֶׁתֵּאָפֶה. בֶּן בְּתֵירָה אוֹמֵר. תַּטִּיל לַצּוֹנֵין. אָמַר לוֹ רִבִּי יְהוֹשֻׁעַ. לֹא נִמְצֵאתָה כְשׂוֹרֵף קֳדָשִׁים בְּיוֹם טוֹב. אָמַר לוֹ רִבִּי אֱלִיעֶזֶר. מֵאֵילֵיהֶן הֵן נִשְׂרָפִין. אָמַר לוֹ רִבִּי יְהוֹשֻׁעַ. לֹא נִמְצֵאתָה עוֹבֵר עַל לֹא יֵרָאֶה וְלֹא יִמָּצֵא. אָמַר לוֹ. מוּטָב לַעֲבוֹר עַל מִצְוַת לֹא תַעֲשֶׂה שֶׁלֹּא בָאת לְיָדָךְ מִמִּצְוַת לֹא תַעֲשֶׂה שֶׁבָּאת לְפָנֶיךָ.

תַּמָּן תַּנִּינָן. הַנִּיתָּנִין בְּמַתָּן אַחַת שֶׁנִּתְעָרְבוּ בַּנִּיתָּנִין מַתָּנָה אַחַת. יִינָּתְנוּ מַתָּנָה אֶחָת. מַתָּן אַרְבַּע בְּמַתָּן אַרְבַּע. יִינָּתְנוּ מַתָּן אַרְבַּע. מַתָּן אַרְבַּע בְּמַתָּן אַחַת. רִבִּי אֱלִיעֶזֶר אוֹמֵר. יִינָּתְנוּ מַתָּן אַרְבַּע. רִבִּי יְהוֹשֻׁעַ אוֹמֵר. יִנָּתְנוּ מַתָּן אַחַת. אָמַר לוֹ רִבִּי אֱלִיעֶזֶר. לֹא נִמְצֵאתָ עוֹבֵר עַל בַּל תִּגְרַע. אָמַר לוֹ רִבִּי יְהוֹשֻׁעַ. לֹא נִמְצֵאתָ עוֹבֵר עַל בַּל תּוֹסִיף. אָמַר לוֹ. מוּטָב לַעֲבוֹר עַל מִצְוַת לֹא תַעֲשֶׂה שֶׁלֹּא בָאת לְיָדִי מִמִּצְוַת לֹא תַעֲשֶׂה שֶׁבָּאת לְיָדִי

. תַּמָּן תַּנִּינָן. הַכְנִיס רֹאשׁוֹ וְנָתַן עַל תְּנוּךְ אָזְנוֹ. יָדוֹ וְנָתַן עַל בֹּהֶן עַל יָדוֹ. וְרַגְלוֹ וגו'. מְחַלְפָה שִׁיטַת רִבִּי יְהוּדָה. תַּמָּן הוּא אוֹמֵר. אָסוּר לֶהֳעָרִים. וְכָא אוֹמֵר. מוּתָּר. תַּמָּן שֶׁמָּא יַכְנִיס רֹאשׁוֹ וְרוּבּוֹ וִיהֵא עָנוּשׁ כָּרֵת. בְּרַם הָכָא מִשּׁוּם מַכְנִיס כֵּלִים טְמֵאִים בַּשַּׁבָּת. מְחַלְפָה שִׁיטַת דְּרַבָּנִין. תַּמָּן אוֹמְרִין. מוּתָּר לֶהֳעָרִים. וְכָא אֲמָרִין. אָסוּר לֶהֳעָרִים. תַּמָּן דְּלָא יִסְאָב תִּיהּ תְּלָתָא זִמְנִין. בְּרַם הָכָא טוּמְאָה יְדוּעָה בִּפְנִים הִיא. אִיפְשַׁר לָהּ לָצֵאת בְּלֹא שָׁהוּת. בְּלֹא טוּמְאָה. אָמַר לוֹ. מוּטָב לַעֲבוֹר עַל מִצְוַת לֹא תַעֲשֶׂה שֶׁלֹּא בָאת לְיָדוֹ מִמִּצְוַת לֹא תַעֲשֶׂה שֶׁבָּאת לְפָנָיו.

Paragraph. "If a crawling animal[34] was found in the Temple," etc. Rebbi Johanan ben Beroqa said to him, did you not prolong the impurity? He answered him, did you not increase impurity? He told him, it is better to violate a prohibition that was not caused by him than a prohibition which will come before him[165]. Rebbi Yose ben Rebbi Abun said, this disagreement parallels another disagreement, as we have stated there[166], "how does one separate *hallah* in impurity on a holiday? Rebbi Eliezer says, one should not declare its name until after it was baked. Ben Bathyra says, he should put it into cold water." Rebbi Joshua said to him, are you not like one who burns *sancta* on a holiday? Rebbi Eliezer told him, it is burned automatically[167]. Rebbi Joshua said to him[168], are you not transgressing *it should not be seen, and it should not be found*? He told him, it is better to violate a prohibition that was not caused by you than a prohibition which will come before you[169].

There, we have stated[170]: "[Blood] to be given in one batch which was mixed with [blood] to be given in one batch should be given in one batch. That to be given in four batches with that to be given in four batches should be given in four batches. That to be given in four batches with that to be given in one batch, Rebbi Eliezer says, it should be given in four batches. Rebbi Joshua says, it should be given in one batch. Rebbi Eliezer said to him, would you not transgress *do not diminish*? Rebbi Joshua answered him, would you not transgress *do not add*?" He said to him, it is better to violate a prohibition that was not caused by me than a prohibition which will come before me.

There, we have stated[171]: "He enters his head and he puts on his ear's cartilage, his hand and he gives on his thumb, his foot," etc. Rebbi Jehudah's argument[172] is inverted. There he says, it is forbidden to act craftily[173], but here he says that it is permitted. There that he should not enter with his head and most of his body and be punishable by extirpation. But here it is because of bringing impure implements on the Sabbath[174]. The argument of the rabbis[172] is inverted. There they say, it is permitted to act craftily, but here they say, it is forbidden to act craftily. There that he should not defile himself three times, but here it is a known impurity inside; it is possible for it to be removed immediately. Without impurity[175]? He told him, it is better to violate a prohibition that was not caused by him than a prohibition which will come before him.

165 Since no human killed the animal which was found in the Temple, it is better to leave it there for some time than remove it while defiling a priestly garment.

166 Mishnah *Pesahim* 3:3. *Hallah* is the heave of bread dough to be given to a Cohen to eat in purity (cf. Introduction to Tractate *Hallah*.) Making food on a holiday is

permitted, but baking *mazzah* on Passover creates a problem if the flour is impure since the *hallah* must be given but may not be eaten; therefore it may not be baked, but then it will get sour and this is forbidden on Passover. R. Eliezer says that *hallah* should be declared not from the dough but from finished *mazzah*; R. Jehudah ben Bathyra says that it should be refrigerated and then burned in the evening (which is practical only in his mountain town of Nisibis). R. Joshua says that *hallah* should be given as usual and declared the Cohen's property; then it no longer is the baker's property and the prohibition (*Ex.* 13:6) *it should not be seen in your property and not be found in your property* does not apply.

167 Since R. Eliezer does not say that one should not separate *hallah* as dough, only that one may not call it *hallah*, this implies that he prescribes that the *hallah* dough be baked as separate *mazzah*. If the dough had been declared as *hallah* it would be an impure *sanctum* which could not be burned (or baked) on the holiday.

168 This should read: They said to R. Joshua.

169 R. Joshua to R. Eliezer. The dough will become sour by itself, but R. Eliezer requires one actively to bake the non-food *hallah*.

170 Mishnah *Zevahim* 8:10. Blood of all animal sacrifices has to be spilled at the walls of the altar. Blood of most holy sacrifices must be given to all 4 corners of the altar; that of simple sacrifices is given in one batch. If blood of different categories is mixed, one can satisfy only one requirement. R. Joshua is consistent in prescribing the minimal action.

171 Mishnah *Nega`im* 14:9. A sufferer from skin disease who was healed has to undergo a double process of purification (*Lev.* 14). A first ceremony outside of town followed by immersion in a *miqweh* purifies him for all purposes except for entry into the Temple. For complete purification he then has to bring sacrifices (depending on his financial situation); the blood of one of them has to be applied by a Cohen in the Temple precinct to ear, thumb, and great toe, of the healed person who still is forbidden to enter the Temple precinct. The Mishnah which is quoted only in parts reports that anonymous majority solves the puzzle by having the person to be purified present only a minimal surface to the priest inside while R. Jehudah requires him to present all three spots simultaneously. It is agreed that a biblical violation occurs only if head and most of the body of the unpurified person are inside the Temple precinct.

172 It seems that for "R. Jehudah" one has to read "the rabbis" and vice versa but there is no manuscript evidence to support this.

173 This translation of להעריב seems to be false but no other meaning is known. Probably S. Liebermann is correct that the sentence is copied here from *Pesahim* 3:3 where it is correctly applied to the positions of RR. Eliezer and Joshua.

174 It seems that for "on the Sabbath" one has to read "into the Temple".

In this comparison of the Mishnah in *Nega`im* to that in *Eruvin* it seems that the rabbis accept the position of R. Johanan ben Beroqa as practice to be followed. They prefer that the unpurified person enter the Temple precinct space three times to avoid the possibility of his inadvertently entering with most of his body; in *Eruvin* they prefer the speedy elimination of impurity since the presence of the belt, impure in derivative impurity, while prohibited, is not sanctionable (Maimonides, *Biat Miqdash* 3:17).

the risk of severe contamination to avoid repeted small contaminations, in *Eruvin* recommends waiting until the existing impurity can be eliminated without risk of increasing impurity.

175 R. Jehudah who in *Nega`im* accepts

(26d line 45) הוֹצִיא מִמָּקוֹם שֶׁחַיָּיבִין עָלָיו כָּרֵת וְנָפַל לְמָקוֹם שֶׁאֵין חַיָּיבִין עָלָיו כָּרֵת כְּבָר נְרְאֵית לָצֵאת. מָצָא אַחֵר בְּצִידוֹ מוֹצִיא אֶת שְׁנֵיהֶם אוֹ אֵינוֹ מוֹצִיא אֶלָּא אֶת שֶׁנִּרְאָה לָצֵאת.

If he removed it from a place where one is subject to extirpation for it and it fell into a place where one is not subject to extirpation for it, already it is subject to removal[176]. If he found another next to it, does he remove both of them or only the one subject to removal[177]?

176 If the dead crawling animal was removed from the Temple precinct but fell down on the Temple Mount where it remains a danger to people coming to the Temple in purity, it is to be removed to a place outside of the city.

177 If the second animal is not on the list of *Lev.* 11:29-30 and therefore does not cause original impurity. The question is not answered.

(26d line 48) הוּא הָיָה אוֹמֵר. צְבָת בִּצְבָת עֲבַד. צְבָתָא קַדְמִיתָא מָה הֲוַת. בִּירִיָּה הֲוַת. אָמַר רִבִּי חֲנִינָה קוֹמֵי רִבִּי מָנָא. וּמָה אַתְּ אָמַר לָהּ. מִצְבָתָא אַחַת לָמְדוּ כַּמָּה צְבִיתוֹת. וְכָא מִשְּׁבִיתָה אַחַת לָמְדוּ כַּמָּה שְׁבִיתוֹת.

"He used to say, a wrench is made by a wrench. How was the first wrench made? It was created.[178]" Rebbi Ḥanina said before Rebbi Mana: How do you explain this? From one wrench they learned many wrenches; from one Sabbath prohibition they learned many Sabbath prohibitions [179]."

179 Tosephta *Eruvin* 8:23 and *Hagigah* 1:9, quoted here as commentary to the statement of R. Simeon in Mishnah 14, that rabbinic Sabbath restrictions do not have biblical justification and do not necessarily follow a system.

The statement which denies technical invention to human intelligence is attributed to R. Jehudah in Mishnah *Avot* 5:6; the statement here also is in the name of R. Jehudah in *Sifry* §355 (ed. Finkelstein p. 418), *Mekhilta dR. Simeon ben Yoḥai ad Ex.* 16:32 (ed. Epstein-Melamed p. 115), Babli *Pesahim* 54a. However at other places both Talmudim characterize human invention as "knowledge of heavenly kind"; cf. Babli *loc. cit.*, Yerushalmi *Berakhot* 8:6, Note 128 (and the author's *The Scholar's Haggadah*,

pp. 220-221).
179 One rabbinic Sabbath prohibition will have prophetic roots; the others were introduced by successive generations.

Corrigendum

Unfortunately, there was an error in the title on the cover and on the title page of *Jerusalem Talmud, Fourth Order: Neziqin, Tractates Ševu'ot and 'Avodah Zarah*, edited by Heinrich W. Guggenheimer (Studia Judaica 61, Berlin/New York 2011, ISBN 978-3-11-025805-9) in part of the print run of this publication.

The correct title is *Tractates Ševu'ot and 'Avodah Zarah,* i.e. not *Tractates Ševi'it and 'Avodah Zarah.*

The tractate *Ševi'it* was previously published in 2001 in *Studia Judaica* volume 20.

We apologize for this error.

The publisher

Indices

Sigla

Parallel Texts from Yerushalmi Tractates

Yebamot	א	Pesahim	פ
Berakhot	ב,ב	Hagigah	צ
Genizah	ג	Peah	ק
Ma`aser Šeni	ד	Nedarim	ר
Ta`aniot	ח	Šeqalim	ש
Yoma	ו	Terumot	ת
Eruvin	ז	Terumot Chapter 2	ת
Hallah	ח	Ševi`it	7
Gittin	ט	Eruvin Chapter 6	6
Beṣah	י	Eruvin Chapter 7	7
Kilaim	כ	Šabbat Chapter 13	13
Demay	ל	Šabbat Chapter 16	16
Ma`aserot	מ	Šabbat Chapter 17	17
Sanhedrin	נ	Šabbat Chapter 18	18
Sukkah	ס	Šabbat Chapter 19	19
Avodah zarah	ע	Šabbat Chapter 20	20

Manuscript texts and early prints

Genizah Text edited by Abramson	A	Leiden Manuscript	L
Genizah Text edited by J.N. Epstein	E	Rome Manuscript of *Zera`im*	R
Genizah Text edited by Ginzberg	G		

Index of Biblical Quotations

Gen. 2:2	248	30:14	211	45:23	630	12:10	94
2:6	120	30:30	55	42:36	223	12:16	145,282
2:7	120	31:30	509	42:38	118	12:17	282
9:6	435	34:15	679	48:7	223	12:19	95
17:9	509	34:25	329,497			13:10	796
17:13	509	39:11	248	Ex. 4:26	509	13:16	77
27:47	214	40:15	509	12:9	85,285,630,643	13:19	796

Ex. 13:18	212	4:3	236	23:29	20	32:42	69
16:9	77	4:22	398	24:5	256	33:24	204
16:23	3	4:27	360,414	25:2	265	35:3	694
16:29	643	5:15	20	25:3	265	35:4	690
18:29	331	6:3	358	25:4	265		
18:12	681	6:21	149	25:7	309		
19:10	343	7:17	94	25:49	259	Jos. 2:6	89
19:15	55,328	7:10	20	27:34	411	6:3	81
20:4	252	11:16	69			6:4	81
20:8	252	11:18	93	Num. 3:32	358	7:2	333
20:9	72	11:24	313	4:16	358	14:15	457
20:10	443	11:29	313,417	10:33	33	15:37	678,696
20:20	370	11:32	337	16:30	16		
20:22	32	11:34	586	18:31	61	Jud. 7:3	599
22:6	750	11:37	365	23:22	228	7:19	598
22:19	252,254	11:38	313	31:50	214	8:21	215
23:12	72,184	12:3	95,96,497	35:29	254	8:27	335
23:17	513	12:4	462			8:33	322
23:18	95	13:34	97	Deut. 2:17	688	14:18	188
23:19	149	13:57	199	5:14	184	16:13	407
25:5	104,289	14:8	55	5:27	55		
25:6	32	14:46	331,758	5:26	55	1Sam. 1:24	186
25:10	32	15:16	328	7:1	69	3:1	681
26:1	103,370	15:19	97	7:3	69	8:4	222
26:2	292	15:20	328	6:1	306	25:9	596
26:14	289	15:32	343	6:7	10		
26:15	298	16:2	32	7:15	426	1K. 7:23	548,579
26:30	397	16:20	58	7:26	331,333	7:26	580
27:18	614	17:11	289	10:21	688	9:13	183
27:20	103	17:13	319	10:25	689		
30:33	261	18:5	436	11:19	10,796	2K. 2:12	122
31:12	33	18:6	261	12:13	265	3:11	681
32:4	215	18:12	260	12:14	265	11:6	687
33:7	681	18:16	260	13:18	329	19:3	118
34:14	252	18:19	239	14:2	331		
34:25	95	18:20	258	14:17	93	Is. 1:18	329
34:26	149	18:29	259	14:21	149	1:31	92
35:1	33,249	19:26	223	14:26	627	2:4	192
35:2	236	20:18	239	15:19	287	3:18	215
35:3	252,90,111	20:19	258	16:8	249,443	30:14	306
35:18	291	20:20	259	20:20	81	30:21	225
35:33	19	20:21	259,260	23:8	179	30:22	328,335
36:6	14	22:10	115	23:13	685	37:3	118
36:16	67	22:15	347	26:14	347	40:4	771
38:24	32	22:22	815	24:1	371,401	43:4	225
		23:3	236,443	28:48	426	43:16	119
Lev. 1:15	115	23:10	256	28:66	313	44:9	679
2:12	256	23:15	499	29:10	119	50:4	679
3:9	89	23:17	256	29:22	628	57:15	58
4:2	112,235,398	23:21	111	32:35	679	58:5	186

Is. 58:13	539	Ps. 3	210	7:10	183	10:5	457
61:11	328,339	10:3	410	10:28	427	10:8	436
		22:4	457	20:6	43	12:11	204
Jer. 2:30	116	32:10	454	20:13	120		
17:22	14	39:7	43,421	22:4	58	Dan. 1:8	67
19:2	687	45:4	214	23:31	309	3:25	228
26:10	687	49:1	420	30:19	328	3:27	109
39:3	687	55:16	119			3:28	228
		68:19	457	Job 9:7	687	5:7	209
Ez. 2:12	159	69:32	104,294	22;14	222	11:43	179
16:12	214	89:20	58	40:29	350		
37:14	58	91	219			Neh. 13:15	473
40:3	692	106:16	457	Cant. 4:9	319		
40:15	687	106:28	331	5:7	215	1Chr. 4:38	55
44:16	103	109:7	118	7:11	211	12:22	598
		111:10	58				
Am. 6:17	61	139:21	548	Thr. 4:11	687	2Chr. 4:5	580
8:14	222	150:1	457	4:20	454	23:5	687
Zech. 3:5	215					24:20	687
14:15	178	Prov. 2:5	58	Eccl. 1:6	686	35:13	630
Mal. 3:23	59	3:15	397	6:3	119		
		3:17	633,752	8:1	310		

Index of Talmudical Quotations

Babylonian Talmud

Berakhot 17a	48	7a	38,805	23b	94,272	38b	135,136
22a	69	7b	379	24a	102	39a	140
31b	120	8a	357	24b	94,608	40b	129,143,148,
32a	249	9a	40	25a	61		345
35b	630	9b	43,45	25b	90,102	41a	147
44a	630	11b	49,806	26a	101,102,103	41b	146
54b	643	12a	51,209	27b	103,430	42a	147
55a	310	12b	52,54	28a	107	42b	159,170
61a	363	13a	55	29a	105,107	43a	156,170
63b	506	14b	61	29b	105,108,138	44a	154,159
64a	681	17b	62,63,77	31a	120	45b	157
		18a	72,79	31b	270	46a	138,333
Šabbat 3a	27,34,57,	18b	78,134	32a	116,120	46b	370,391
	375,377	19a	78,80,81,82	32b	116	47b	162,166
3b	28,34	19b	82	34b	166	49a	168,169
4b	370,372	20a	85	35b	445	50a	169
5a	27,28,30	20b	88,89	36b	83	50b	212
5b	19,25,379	21a	89,100	37a	128,132	51a	175
6a	25,35,40,569	21b	93	37b	83	51b	178,187
6b	37	22a	138	38a	106,132,133	52a	178,187

Šabbat 53a	185	92b	54,355,360	122a	469	12b	565
54a	183,184,188	93a	360	123a	138	14a	571,574,
57a	194,195	93b	363	123b	473,476		575,576,578,579
57b	196,199	94a	362	124a	474,479,	14b	580
58a	196	94b	362,363		481	15a	577,581,668
59a	200	95a	123,282,	124b	107	15b	587
59b	200		290,294,296,363,365	125b	171,174	16a	370,571,
60a	202	95b	365	126a	480		587,588,768
60b	202,204	96a	14	127a	487	16b	595,596
61a	208,209	96b	374	128a	491	17a	596,598,599
64a	214	97a	372	129b	494	17b	599,643
64b	201,775	97b	249,373	131a	499	19b	606,608
65a	219	98a	396,788	133a	94	20a	609,610
65b	220	99b	357	134b	344,454	20b	604,804
66b	210,221	100a	379,380	135a	510,511	21a	610
67a	221222,223	100b	380,381,	137a	516,518,	21b	611
67b	315		384,557,745		520	22a	611,612
68a	232,315	101a	30	137b	521,527	22b	771
68b	316,386	101b	503	138a	200,283,	23a	613
69a	250	102a	484		527	26a	700
69b	237,238	102b	298	139b	529	27b	657,628
70a	112,249,252	103a	396	140a	529,530	29a	625
70b	244	103b	235	140b	531	30a	630
71a	245,246	104b	297,399,	141b	109,204	30b	631
73b	265		400	142b	459	31b	633,634
74a	278,280	105a	406,407	143a	107	33a	635,636
74b	284,291	105b	109	145a	270,276	33b	636
75a	290,294,314	106a	110,285	147a	278	34b	639
75b	289,296,297,	106b	413	147b	781	36a	639,644
	299,394	107a	419	149a	199	38b	651
76a	302	107b	51,109,419	153b	59	39a	650
76b	307,317	108a	421	154b	182,637	39b	653
77a	311	108b	277,431	156b	157,443	40b	656
78a	317	109a	427	157a	543	41b	663
78b	317	111a	427,428			42a	663,665
79b	319	112a	205	Eruvin 2a	551	42b	666
80a	21,319	112b	441	2b	569	43a	666
80b	17,320	113a	182,277,	3a	552,554	44b	668
81a	323		441,443,477	3b	556	45a	669
81b	323	114b	445	6a	569	46a	708
82a	323	115a	452	6b	562,569	46b	653
82b	331	116a	458	8b	571	49a	710,730
83b	173,337	117a	669	9a	531,571	50b	646,672
85a	219	117b	454,461,	9b	582	51b	673
86b	339,342,343		462,724	10a	556	52a	673
89b	348	118a	444	10b	559	53a	643,681
90a	348	120a	464,465	11a	569,592,	55a	291,685
90b	316,320	120b	158,159		596	55b	685
91a	354	121a	96,466	11b	572,593	56a	686
92a	358,371	121b	278	12a	565,573,785	56b	689

Eruvin 57a	690	101b	810	Megillah 52a	52	60a	278
57b	691	102a	477	32a	225	85a	111,252
58a	692	102b	813			92b	426
59a	696	103a	362,815	Taanit 27a	813	99a	410
59b	696,731	103b	815			Bava Mesi`a 47b	
60a	696,743	104a	816	Mo'ed Qatan 2b	272		753
60b	697	104b	604	3a	265	72b	38
61a	698			7a	55	107b	426
61b	699	Pesahim 6b	252			Bava Batra 19a	167
62a	562	25a	435	Hagigah 2a	513	26a	278
65b	717,731	27b	95				
67b	383	66a	505			Sanhedrin 4b	516
68a	749	69a	507	Yebamot 6b	112,	6b	410
68b	712	85a	85		254,285	62a	244
69b	712	90b	96	9a	386	62b	110
70a	714	101a	138	16b	110	68a	122
70b	716,717,718	108b	307,309	32a	115	74b	111
71a	719	109b	579	33b	112,116	75a	435
71b	719,726,727			34a	664	84b	112
72a	719,721,731	Yoma 6a	96	54b	260	85a	109
72b	722	66b	46,362	55a	259	101a	424,425
73b	726,730	67a	346	71a	520		
75a	731	75b	643	72a	95	Makkot 14b	261
75b	721,732	80b	429	72b	95,96		
76a	738	84b	414,466			Ševuot 19a	244
77a	138,741	87a	96	Ketubot 31a	19	27b	509
79a	745,747			31b	19	32b	386
80a	714,754,760	Sukkah 5a	32	34a	132		
80b	751	5b	32	35a	111	Avodah Zarah 7a	
81b	753	26a	48	38a	111		502
82b	761	38b	457	72a	116	12a	775
83a	311					20b	58
83b	762	Roš Haššanah 31b		Sotah 49b	199,200	27a	509,510
85a	763		346			27b	436
85b	730,731,765			Nedarim 49a	630	28a	430,431,432
86a	766	Besah 4b	656	49b	310	28b	430
87a	141,767,	9a	775			29a	199
	768,771	11b	393	Nazir 35b	627	30b	67
88a	769,772	12b	110,269			36b	61,69
88b	775	18a	123	Gittin 20a	402	72b	108
89a	739,778	18b	428	52b	134		
90a	779	24a	77,413	79a	370	Horaiot 3a	386
90b	739	24b	77				
91a	781,782	32a	107	Qiddušin 24a	750	Zevahim 12a	521
92a	616	33a	107	30a	43	63a	744
94b	556	36b	643			106a	265
97a	799	36a	170	Bava Qamma 2b	266	107b	261,265
97b	769,800	37b	646	16a	51		
99b	806,808			34b	110	Menahot 29b	451
100a	808			54b	627	37b	257

Menahot 41b	128	Keritut 3b	244	Meilah 15a	262	63a	93
43a	799	8b	55	20a	337	77b	222
46b	94	16a	243			79a	179
55b	252	17a	17,408,247	Arakhin 2b	513	103b	21
72a	781	20a	113				
98a	33	20b	109,112	Hulin 9a	350	Niddah 32a	347
103b	312			15a	132	33a	252
		Temurah 4b	94	16b	323	34a	69
Bekhorot 16a	71	18a	71	29a	555	67b	96
25a	288			31b	97		
				58a	51		

Jerusalem Talmud

Berakhot 1:2	427	6:1	643	Pesahim 2:1	95	3:2	76
1:5	48	8:8	204	2:4	137	4:2	577
2:3	796	9:1	651	4:1	81	4:4	275
2:9	46			5:8	38	5:1	170
3:4	69	Terumot 1:1	750	6:1	110,394,	5:4	800
3:5	45,102	2:1	54		505,814		
5:2	446	2:3	664	6:4	507	Megillah 1:7	801
6:8	424	3:1	653	6:7	516	1:11	398
8:1	820	3:3	132	7:7	745	2:1	719
8:7	679	5:3	311	10:1	306		
9:2	771	6:1	429			Ta`aniot 1:6	347
		7:1	111	Yoma 6:5	346	Taaniot 4:1	719
Peah 1:1	199	8:1	509	8:3	429		
2:6	142	8:5	67			Hagigah 1:1	513
7:4	274	8:10	771	Šeqalim 3:2	306	3:4	61,787
7:6	249	9:4	63	3:4	58		
8:5	628	10:2	136				
8:6	761	10:7	311	Sukkah 1:1	37,551,	Yebamot 2:3	612
		11:7	98,99,100		588,592	8:1	513,519,
Demay 2:2	121			1:9	141		520, 522
5:2	610	Ma`serot 1:6	147,	1:10	771	8:6	769
7:5	489		213	2:1	798	12:2	205
		2:1	634	2:4	585,635		
Kilaim 1:9	138	5:2	365	4:1	69	Sotah 1:2	37,353
2:2	54	Ma`aser Šeni 1:4				1:4	165
3:1	338		627	Besah 1:1	651	1:8	69
4:4	588,592	2:1	347,424	1:3	109,269	5:2	62
7:6	364	4:3	714	1:5	393,478	5:5	694
8:1	265,272	4:4	749	1:10	279	8:4	249
8:4	179	5:3	249	1:12	197	9:16	200
9:2	89,775			2:2	122		
9:7	293,406	Hallah 1:6	274	2:8	187	Ketubot 1:1	643
		1:9	410	2:5	145	8:11	69
Ševi`it 1:1	70			2:9	138		
4:2	98			3:1	417	Nedarim 4:9	466

6:1	630	1:7	43	7:11	235	2:1	246
		3:3	640,645	7:19	222		
Gittin 1:2	643			10:1	204	Avodah Zarah 1:1	
2:3	586,750	Bava Qamma 3:12		11:6	681		79
5:9	724		110			2:2	199,430
8:3	370			Makkot 2:7	694	2:9	67
		Bava Batra 2:1	166			3:4	143
Nazir 6:1	252			Horaiot 3:3	17,236	3:8	331
6:11	630	Sanhedrin 1:1	410	3:7	397,455		
9:2	745	7:3	54,272			Niddah 4:1	96
Qiddušin 1:3	714	7:5	257	Ševuot 1.5	656		

Mishnah

Berakhot 2:6	46	3:1	413	3:7	17	Ahilut 1:8	331
4:1	41	4:3	638			7:6	435
Peah 1:4	232	5:4	767	Zevahim 8:10	819	15:1	745
Kilaim 1:9	138	Megillah 1:5	479	11:7	149	18:1	62
3:1	328	1:8	269	Menahot 5:2	284	Nega`im 11:11	215
6:2	379	1:11	452	11:7	628	13:8	332
9:10	410	Hagigah 1:1	513	Keritut 3:4	25	14:2	55
Ševi`it 1:1	265	1:8	185	3:7	239	14:9	819
2:1	265			3:9	245	Parah 2:3	506
2:4	271	Yebamot 12:2	207	3:10	233,239,350	5:1	121
7:1	232	Sotah 9:16	199	4:5	359	5:3	787
Terumot 2:3	132	Nedarim 6:1	630	Temurah 3:1	71	5:5	324
5:2	488	Gittin 8:3	805	Bekhorot 3:3	287	5:7	336
10:2	136	Qiddušin 1:6	727	Me`ilah 4:1	262	11:8	751
Ma`serot 1:1	232			4:5	324	12:5	319
		Bava Qamma 1:1		Hulin 9:2	418	Zavim 1:1	343
Pesahim 3:3	818		266	Middot 4:1	14	8:12	61
5:9	475	2:10	113	2:5	33	Tahorot 4:5	62
5:10	85	7:4	161			6:4	37
6:1	814	Bava Mesia` 8:4	750	Kelim 1:1	266	6:6	771
6:9(6:5)	517	Bava Batra 3:8	738	9:5	168	Miqwaot 2:2	642
Šeqalim 3:2	307,487	Avodah Zarah 3:9		11:4	474	4:3	324,325
Sukkah 1:1	552		335	13:2	320	8:3	340,342
1:10	589	3:10	336	13:6	212	9:1	194
2:4	637	Ševuot 1:1	14	14:8	321	Makhširim 6:2	63
3:5	633	Avot 2:4	54	17:6	320	6:5	313
3:14	519	Idiut 1:5	67	17:7	231,267	Tevul Yom 2:2	649
Roš Haššanah 2:5		2:6	422	24:5	30	4:4	489
	494	2:7	200	27.12	105	Yadayim 4:4	179
Besah 1:1	651	4:1	313	28:1	107	4:5	452
1:2	269	6:1	797	28:2	105,106	Uqesin 2:10	365
1:9	282	8:1	313	28:8	103	3:5	787
1:11	199	Horaiot 2:8	236	28:10	215		

Tosephta[1]

Kilaim 2:6	617	4:13	220	13:14	469	4:16	694,698
Terumot 3:11	213	5:7	221	13:15	473	5:9	719
7:17	67	6:4	333	13:16	199	5:13	716
10:9	99	7:2	222	13:17	323,473	5:14	717
Ma'aser Šeni 4:7		7:3	222	14:1	475	5:15	754
	750	7:10	222	14:2	320	5:17	714
Šabbat 1:1	35	8:9	315,316	14:3	480	5:18	711
1:2	410	8:10	308,311,314	14:8	491	5:19	708,780
1:6	40	8:11	317	15:2	493	5:20	708
1:8	49	8:12	317	15:3	494	5:22	711
1:11	53	8:19	319	15:4	344	5:24	781
1:12	54	3:20	320	15:5	532	6:3	628
1:13	54	3:21	320	15:9	510,521	6:4	625
1:14	55	8:31	316	15:15	466	6:6	719,726,727
1:15	57	9:1	316	16:19	394	6:17	747
1:16	59	9:2	316	16:22	51	7:10	741
1:17	59	9:11	17,19,21			7:14	780
1:18	62	9:13	296	Eruvin 1:2	572	8:4	773
1:19	62	9:20	287	1:5	576	8:11	180
1:20	74	10:1	25	1:6	556	8:12	180,810
1:21	72,74	10:3	410	1:7	552	8:15	798
1:22	78	10:7	30	1:9	581	8:16	799
1:23	72	10:9	379	1:10	581	8:23	820
2:1	101	10:14	383	1:12	606		
2:3	102	11:1	298	1:13	611	Pesahim 5:1	507
2:4	103	11:3	394	1:15	609	5:7	409
2:6	108	11:7	408	2:3	595	10:1	487
2:8	816	11:8	399,400	2:5	599	Šeqalim 2:15	358
2:10	120	11:9	297	2:6	598,599	Sukkah 1:8	525
2:13	128	11:10	297	2:13	635	1:13	551
2:14	133	11:11	277	2:15	638	Yom Tov 1:3	651
2:15	132,664	11:15	400	3:4	646	1:11	481
2:16	132	12:1	407	3:5	669	2:18	138
2:21	135	12:4	419	3:6	669	2:19	180
2:22	140	12:5	419	3:7	81	3:1	413
3:1	134	12:12	427	3:11	662	Megillah 1:7	284
3:4	142	12:13	425	4:1	650	Hagigah 1:1	513
3:7	345	12:14	392,525	4:3	654	1:9	820
3:15	154	13:4	456	4:4	685		
4:2	185	13:5	458	4:6	686	Bava Mesia' 11:18	
4:5	185	13:6	462	4:7	689		754
4:7	199	13:7	462	4:11	682	Avodah Zarah 3:8	
4:9	209	13:13	80	4:13	689		799

---

1. For Tractates Šabbat and Eruvin the numbering of Chapters and Halakhot follows the edition of Liebermann (from the Vienna ms.) which differs from the numbering in Zuckermandel's edition based on the Erfurt ms.

Avodah Zarah 3:13		Idiut 1:9	422	Bava Meṣia' 3:13		Bava Batra 4:5	205
	510	Kelim Bava Qamma			212	4:14	364
8:5	435	7:17	324,325	8:14	391	Ahilut 15:5	745
						Nega'im 7:10	17

Midrashim

Mekhilta dR. Ismael 94, 95,213,252,461,662,681
Mekhilta dR. Simeon b. Yoḥai 72,94,252,254, 333,799,820
Sifra 27,38,48,55,96,97, 112,149,212,233,235, 241,252,256,257,331, 360,398,462,510,687
Sifry 10,81,265,347,627, 820
Gen. r. 179,333,343,509,

510
Ex. r. 681
Lev. r. 48,443,454
Eccl. r. 104,177
Cant. r. 58,419,655
Thr. r. 454
Tanḥuma 80,688,724, 799
Tanḥuma Buber 724
Midrash Samuel 598
Midrash Prov. 58
Pesiqta rabbati 795

Pesiqta dR. Cahana 655.
Semahot 5,8,79,599
Soferim 93,162,456,801
Avot dR. Natan 221
Targum Chr. 580
Yalqut Šimony 249,333, 662,686,688

Damascus Document 3,5,562,643

Rabbinic Literature

Adani S. 183,460
Alfasi 93,761
Amram Gaon 52
Arukh 195,200,205,215 273,744
Diqduqe Soferim 222, 291,361,391,542
Fraenckel D. 299,300, 477
Gaonic Commentary Tahorot 155,392,464, 477,491,816
Gaonim Harkavi 677
Hamkhria' 454
Hamanhig 80,443
Hananel 51,52,419,462, 464,571,598,656,667, 671,681,687,714,733, 765,767,772,808
Herschler M. 110,222
Ibn Migash 132
Kaliri 405
Leqah Tov 461
Ma'ase Roqeah 656
Maimonides 11,85,90,

293,306,316,353,368, 417,422,457,471,477, 452,497,543,599,631, 730,771,793,794,820
Meïri 275,277,443,477, 574,599,650,665,696, 754
Musaphia 333,423
Naḥmanides 93,110, 111,112,135,159,371, 384,398,442,477,553
Nissim Gerondi 132, 135,159
Nissim of Kairawan 41, 761
Noam Yerushalaim 324
Or Zarua 80,200,220, 238,268,270,286,290, 291,295,297,443,466, 555,656,665,667,808
Orhot Ḥayyim 227
Otzar Hegaonim 2,484, 816
Pene Moshe 477
Rashba 129,132,351,

384,399,410,407,432, 468,477,556,560,566, 574,577,578,598,599, 625,650,665,690,694, 696,706,718,731,741, 763,766
Rashi 89,199,212,323, 329,353,368,378,389, 392,399,419,464,484, 529,563,662,688,728, 771
Ratner B. 396
Ravad 212,730
Ravan 80,503
Raviah 58,383,466,484, 555,557,667,673,714
Ritba 14,132,399,407, 77,531,574,599,665 696,714,810
Roqeah 289,297,466, 664
Rosh 58,181,665,696
Seder Olam 228
Sefer Ha'ittim 383,667, 671

Sefer Ha`ittur 25,443	Šibbole Halleqet 443, 714	Wehizhir 461,799
Sefer Miswot Gadol 14, 566,714	Simson of Sens 338	Yefe Enayim 32,38
Sefer Hatterumah 797	Vidal of Tolosa 399	

Index of Greek, Latin, and Arabic Words

ἅλμη	417	διαβήτης	816	ἰάνθινος	104
ἀμίαντος	289	δίαιτα	135,368,759	Λιβυστικός	179
ἀμίς	333	δίκρανον	213,551	ἰδιώτης	45,694
ἀναβάτης ἀμβάτης	179	δισάκκιον	93,459,714	καθέδρα	138
ἀνάκλιτα	391	δίσχιστος	306	καῖρος	405,477
ἀνδρόγυνος	497	δόμος	573	καίρωμα	290
ἀποθήκη	169	ἐγκόλαψις	212	κάλαμος	287
ἀρουραῖος	378	ἕλικα	289	κᾶλον	171,391
ἀστρολόγος	226	ἐμβατή	147	καμάρα	33
βύνιτος	816	ἐμπίλια	464	καμῖνος	140
βῶλος	285	ἐξέδρα	557,666,758	καταφερής	774
γαληνός	667	ἐξώστρα	367	κατηγορέω	116
γάστρα	129	ἔπαρχος	466	καυκαλίς	628
γλαύκινος	104	ἐπὶ καταφυσᾶν	537	κερκίς	306
γύψος	108,284	ἐπιστύλιον	594	κιγκλίδες	180
δᾴδινος	91	εὔθικτος	683	Κιμωλία (γῆ)	329
δαμάσκηνος	77	εὔθυνος	225	κινάρα	280
δανειστής	118	ζωμήρυσις	475	κλεῖστρον	181,794
δεῖγμα	49,354	ζωνάριον	215	κνηστήρ	369
δελφική	479	ζυγόν, ζεῦγος	174	κολίας	537
δέννω [τὸν] δεῖνα	222	θέρμος	280,486	κολλύριον	72,284,479
δήλωμα	45	θρᾶνος	161	κολόβιον	215,464

κόλον	432	σίσαρον	134	lanicium	215		
κόμμι	389	σπληνίον	497	libellarius	49		
κοντός	623	σπόγγος	273,534	linteum	43,141,537,781		
κόπανον	275	σταλαγμία	215	margarita	195		
κοράλλιον	273	στέμμα	199	marsupium	363		
κόμη	198	στιβάδιον	35	matrona	310		
λάγυνος	490,649	στόμιον	215	miliarium	127		
λιμήν	660	συμφώνημα	645	misicus	467		
λοπάς	127,306,377	σχοῖνος	4	muria, muries	63		
λοξός	380,583,662	ταξεώτης	647	papilio	721		
λύγος	88	τετράπυλον	593	parum	610		
λύχνος	155	Τρεῖς Χάριτες	142	pileum	464		
μάλαγμα	284	τρώξιμος	273	pittacium	353		
μανιάκης	215	τύπος	213,299	quaestor	711		
μέλαθρον	551	τύραννος	681	scapus	20		
μελίτωμα	226	χάλκανθος	389	semita	38		
μηρία	507	χαλκίς	628	siser	134		
μηχανή	155	ψῆφος	78,284,391,780	solea	58		
μίσυ	285	ψυκτήρ	795	specula	53		
μολόχη	206	φάσηλος	280	splenium	813		
νάρθηξ	586	φορβειά	177	stibadium	35		
νῆμα	198,794			strata	35,207		
νίτρον	348	alica	274	subsellium	138,443,477		
ξενία	711,714	amiantus	289	sudarium	464,524		
ξένος	618	amictorium	464	tabula	30.534		
οἰνόμελι	422,524	antrum	275	thermae	142		
ὁλοσερικόν	215	braccae	464	tisana, ptisana	64		
ὄνος κατ' ὤμον	193,221	bucella (Ital.)	274	triclinium	707		
ὄρυζα	274	calamus	287	velamen	215		
ὄχλος	689	camara	33				
πάγκρεας	133	capillitium	195				
πανταρκής	435	castra	466,632				
παρασάγγης	4	cera	93	افسار .l (Persian)	178		
πατέλλα	293	claretum	423	اون	333		
περίοδος	771	claustrum	474,791	بنّ	477		
πῆγμα	677	coclear	192	حقّة	170		
πήλωμα	537	collare	192				
πίθος	413	conditus, -um	309,506	حندقوقا	628		
πίναξ	54,180,389	conditus	309	دَكَة	733		
πλατεῖα ὁδός	17	corius	478				
ποδοψέλλιον	213	corticeus	215	روستایی (Persian)	202		
πόλεμος	599	costos	787	زیز	419		
πολύτριχον	423	danista	119	سُدّه	155,631		
πρατήρ	313	delator	48	شرج	321		
πτισάνη	63	digma	354	شرط	290		
πύλη	206	domus	293	طلق	207		
πύργος	682	fascia	363,438,801	عص	134		
σάβανον	215	foliatum	49,193,306				
σαταρίς, σαταρνίς	215	frons	200				
σημεῖον	389	funda	353,464				

غفر	464	قمز	484	مجهر	769
فرفخ	628	قمقام	51	مدد	379
قبطرية	196	قوق	93	نبرة	702
قديس	215	كُس	333	نفش	407
ققل	628	كوفه	741	توبان ران (Persian)	464
قلب	212	لهلة	77	وسقه	302

Author Index

Abramson S. 356
Apicius 315
Azulay H.I.D. 166
Brelot J.B. 77,419
Brüll N. 274
Buber S. 461
Buxtorff Jr. 311
Cahana M. 252
De Lonzano M. 166
Epstein J.N. 37,38,102, 172,179,283,440,526
Fleischer H. L. 202
Freimann I.M. 461
Ginzberg, L. 1,14,16, 21,48,58,69,92,94,101, 106,115,141,212,226, 249,280,283,290,343, 478,505,581,631,662,

686
Hultsch, F. 3,761
Jastrow M. 91,289,478
Katan M. 464
Kohut A. 170,311
Krauss S. 311,460
Levi I. 455
Levy J. 290,816
Löw I. 91,207,460
Liebermann S. 4,17,19, 20,21,25,30,37,38,41 44,46,48,49,51,69,70, 81,91,93,100,109,115, 121,128,140,142,145, 152,155,161,166,170, 180,200,218,222,238, 261,270,275,277,280, 289,302,308,319,324,

375,379,383,392,398, 399,400,435,484,500, 503,516,518,537,552, 558,562,583,594,625, 647,667,670,682,721, 722,730,731,733,738, 753,766,768,779,806, 816,819
Mann J. 454
Milgram J. 149
Milham M.E. 315
Noth M. 333
Sokoloff M. 108,816
Sukenik A.L. 398
Sussman J. 290
Täubler E. 333
Wehr H. 77
Zuckermandel M. 128

Subject Index

Abolishing precedent 70
Absentee owner 716
Action for different purpose 90
Action, derivative 235
Action, incomplete 34
Action, primary 235
Advertising prostitution 289
Alley, between street and *karmelit* 567
Alley, L-shaped 562
Alley, wide 559
Alley, with multiple entrances 560
Alley, with side arms 566
Alley, X-shaped 562
Amulet, expert 185
Animals, Sabbath rest 542
Annulling one's rights 618
Aqueduct in street 775,768
Area of difficult access 546
As 737
Asherah 337
Auditor, resident 710

Baal berit 332
Baker's mark-up 758
Bath, medicinal 427
Ben Derosai's food 73
Bet Happeras 622
Bet kor 595,602
Bet qav 617
Bet rova 617
Bet seah 595
Binomial formula 614
Boethusian tradition 499
Braiding hair 290
Braids, bought 216
Breach in wall 785
Broken field 62
Brundisium 660
Building of/with vessels 299
Burka, Median women 192
Byssus 103

Calendar publication 656
Calendar, computed 506
Calendar, Mishnaic 506
Caravan camp 548
Caravan campimg 37
Carrying fluids 800
Categories of categories 263
Cave dwelling 678
Cereal offering 115
Cession, temporary 712
Childless 258
Circumcision on Sabbath 495
Circumcision on wrong day 516,518
Circumcision, preparation for 499
Cistern in *karmelit* 807
Cisterns on Temple Mount 604
Cohen disabled 115
Cohen's office in Temple 116
Comparison 331
Compounding lotions 479
Congregation, illiterate 309
Controlling animals 187
Cooked wine 309
Cooking on holiday 269
Corral 383,575,577
Courtyard as domain 474
Covered walkway 557
Covering blood 269
Creating new food 422
Cubit 4
Cubit, building 33
Cubit, vessel 33
Cutting of Head 270

Day of Atonement, preparing food 446
Day of Atonement, prohibitions 347
Days of Repentance 58
Dead-end alley 547
Dead-end street 502
De-circumcised 510

Dedication to Temple 631
Delivery of bills of divorce 370
Delivery on Sabbath 368
Dema`, lifting of 488
Demay 488,622,633
Denar weight 323
Deprivation 329
Disabilities of sacrifices 262
Disembodied voice 225
Ditch 737
Divine Names 456
Divorce document 805,806
Domain, animal 623,638
Domains, addition of 775
Donkey driver-camel driver 623
Door opener 480
Drawing lake water 141
Dried fig, volume of 231
Drinking as eating 347
Drinking in different domains 804
Dupondius 751,758
Durable actions 390,394
Dyeing of Friday 75
Dyeing on Sabbath 75

Edom 225
Egg freshly laid 170
Egg laid on holiday 651
Egg, easily cooked 320
Eggs, of impure birds 69
Egyptian Passover 721
Eighteen Prohibitions 11,61
Epiphany of Sinai, date 340
Equal part 332
Errors, multiple 244
Eruv haserot 622
643,706,707,724,727
Eruv of ships 381
Eruv tehumin 4,462,622,
643,653,673,699,760
Eruv tehumin, multiparty 717
Eruv, ad hoc 730

Eruv, by raw produce 627	*Het* for *He* 249	Indirect causation 162,450
Eruv, dissenter to 562	High Priest's offering 728	Injuries, internal 423
Eruv, Sadducee opposition 562	Hitting with hammer 387, 391,394	Intent to act 90,278
Eruv, without notice 738	Hole, imaginary 806,810	Intent, specific 287
Evidence of validity 799	Holiday on Sunday 651	Interpreting limits 554
Exempt space 28	Holiday, on Sabbath 507	Joint transgression 252
	Holy oil 261	
Fellow 41,787	Horns (musical) 392	Karaites 10
Fence, makeshift 616	Hot food, storing 165	*Karmelit* 22
Fence, minimal 597	House, leprous 331,758	*Kilaim*. rules of 338
Flower pot 364,365	House, multiparty 771	Killing lice 51
Food for holiday 77		Killing living beings 51
Food for Sabbath 77	Immersion, unintentional 97, 123	*Kirah* 83,126
Food overcooked 83		Knots, prohibited 438,440
Food preparation on holiday 524,527	Implements, using on Sabbath 470	Kochkiste 163
Four Cups 309	Impurity, by load 328,331	Ladder, Egyptian 741,778
Four Species 119,450,519, 633,655	Impurity, by motion 331	Ladder, Tyrian 741,778
	Impurity, by stepping on 193	Land of Gentiles 61
Fruit juice 536		Leavening 95
	Impurity, degrees of 61,108	Leaving ship on Sabbath 450
Gadara 698	Impurity, Gentile 61,69	Lettuce, preparation 52
Gaps disregarded 575	Impurity, of blood 313	Levites' song 813
Gematria 249	Impurity, of bodies 324	Liabilities, separate 247
Gentile contractor 79,81	Impurity, of carcass 313	Liability for sacrifice 359, 386
Gentile food 63	Impurity, of chain 177,180	
Gentile oil 71	Impurity, of chairs 161	Liability of borrower 750
Gentile, cession by 710	Impurity, of containers 337	Liability of professional 354
Gentile, leasing from 717, 733,759	Impurity, of food 61,121	Liability, for torts 113
	Impurity, of hands 62	Liability, multiple 111
Gentile, making light 468	Impurity, of hides 419	Lifting heave 534
Grace, text of 444	Impurity, of implements 476	Lighting on Sabbath Eve 90, 120
Greek, study of 63	Impurity, of pagan temple 336	*Log* 311
Hallah in Syria 655	Impurity, of sacrifices 261	
Hallah 818	Impurity, of semen 328,340	Mailing 80
Hallah, impure 819	Impurity, of skiff 173	Making brine 422
Hallel 456	Impurity, of skin disease 199	Making fire of Sabbath 111
hand-breadth 4		Malpractice, medical 425
Hanukkah 93	Impurity, of textiles 89,103, 302	Manufacturing 392
Havdalah 446		Marriage, not brokered 435
Healing on the Sabbath 210, 217,219	Impurity, of Torah scrolls 62,452	Measuring error 662
		Measuring rope 670
Heave 61,62	Impurity, of vessels 320	Medical procedures 424,430
Heave, impure 490	Impurity, preparation for 313	*Mem* privativum 235
Heave, rabbinical 63		Merit by sin 410
Hebrew slave 737	Impurity, terms of 342	Metamorphoses 51
Hermeneutical principles 252,253,256,257,258,265	Incest prohibitions 258,259, 261	Milk and meat 149
		Milling on Sabbath 73

Miqweh, disqualified	336	
Miqweh, water of	62	
Misuse of sancta	262	
Modius	311	
Modius, Egyptian	761	
Modius, Roman	761	
Modius, Syrian	761	
Moving among ships	381	
Moving from ship to sea		383
Moving in case of fire	449	
Moving thing prohibited for usufruct		348
Muqseh	3,152	
Nail studded shoes	204	
New Year's Day	624	
Obulus	737	
Offerings, most holy	256	
Oil to be burned	89,95	
Omer	499	
Participation	719,724,727	
Passover on Sabbath	12,84,85	
Passover, cooked	285	
Pathogens	323	
Peah	592	
Periods of oblivion	236	
Permanence of prior state		639,642
Pharisee	57	
Phylacteries	793	
Physician, qualified	432	
Place, inappropriate	143	
Portents	223	
Possession, presumed	738	
Potsherds	319	
Practice of Moses at Sinai		54
Prayers, conditional	624,656	
Prepared food	90,151	
Presumption of ownership		161
Priestly clans	814	
Priestly courses	204	
Produce stored in soil	441,472	
Producing sound	816	
Prohibition, biblical	643	
Prohibition, rabbinic	265	
Proselyte, Egyptian	179	
Prostheses	192,200	
Pruning in Sabbatical	272	
Psalms, number of	456	
Public building	785	
Purification of leper	819	
Purification sacrifice	17,27	
Purification, obstacle to	181	
Purifying water	787	
Purity at sundown	62,123	
Purity of animal gear	364	
Purity of libations	121	
Qiddush	46	
Qorban, qonam	630	
Quartarius	305,761	
Ramp of altar	256	
Raw materials	169	
Repairing equipment	106	
Resident, permanent	714	
Retroactive determinations		623,647
Revi'it, Babli	761	
Revi'it, Yerushalmi	761	
Riding on animals	182	
Right of access	725,728	
Rock as domain	381,383	
Rooftop domain	777	
Sabbath alert	445,475	
Sabbath domain of single person		670
Sabbath domain of Tiberias		668
Sabbath domain on ship	667	
Sabbath domain, acquisition		661,671,672
Sabbath domain, large city		698
Sabbath domain, odd shaped		685
Sabbath domain, size	661	
Sabbath, early start	97	
Sabbath, in Temple	12	
Sabbatical wine	309	
Sabbatical year, aftergrowth		140
Sabbatical year, extension		
		70
Sacrifice to Elohim	253	
Sacrifice, unusable	71	
Sadducee halakhah	706	
Sadducee tradition	499	
Saving a life	108	
Scalding food	149	
Seah	307	
Second Tithe	622,633	
Selecting on holiday	279,280,283	
Selecting on Sabbath	280	
Sex act, forbidden	236	
Shew-bread	475	
Ship docking on Sabbath		660
Shooter's remorse	385	
Sin, intentional	16	
sit	286,405	
Skilled labor	394	
Skin disease, purification		55
Smoothing a salve	813	
Solomon's Sea	579	
Sorcery	257	
Spelling, defective	339	
Square root approximation		614
Squeezing washcloth	142	
Standard tile	573	
Stadion	311	
Stones for hygiene	323	
Stringing musical instrument		794
Sukkah decorations	152	
Sukkah, making of	551	
Sukkah, roof of	103,552	
Surveying in mountains	693	
Syria	655	
Tahaš	104,295	
Talk, unnecessary	443,444	
Targum of Hagiographa	452	
Tefillin on Sabbath	797	
Tefillin, place of	797	
Telescope	667	
Temple tax of deceased	728	
Tent impurity	62,331,745	
Tevel	623,633,654	
Tevul Yom	342,649	

Threshold amounts 302,303, 315
Throwing in error 372
Throwing on Sabbath 26, 364,384
Throwing to wall 379
Tironian notes 389
Tithing on Sabbath 90
Tools of trade 472
Tools on Sabbath 54,155
Torah scroll with errors 451
Town, completed 675,689
Transfer of title 752
Transport, criminal 19
Treating toothache 428,429
Two Breads 256,489
Tying knot 291

Uncircumcised baby of Cohen 520,521
Uncle 259
Underage child 633
Underage girl 239

Unintended consequence 296
Using a key 794

Valley 22,37
Veil, Arabian women 192
Vermin, Eight Kinds 416, 795
Vertex of triangle 596
Vessel 324
Vessel, secondary 148
Vessels, combustible 107
Vessels, composite 391
Vulgar 41,57

Wall, human 204
Wall, virtual 551,612
Wart on sacrifice 508
Washing dishes on Sabbath 123
Water, daily use 774
Weaving 407
Well circled by animals 584

Well, breached 588
Well, enclosure of 602,612
Well-being sacrifice 20
Wicks, singeing 110
Wife acting for husband 714
Window 736
Window, size 739
Women wearing *tefillin* 796
Wooden carriage 155
Wooden implements, large 155
Work needed for purpose 109,113
Work, backhanded 23
Work, thinking 19
Work, unprofessional 297
Writing on Sabbath 246,396
Written prayer texts 455

Zav 11
Zuz 530

www.ingramcontent.com/pod-product-compliance
Lightning Source LLC
Chambersburg PA
CBHW020601300426

44113CB00007B/466